D1689382

The Social History of Crime and Punishment in America

The Social History of Crime and Punishment in America

AN ENCYCLOPEDIA

5

Wilbur R. Miller ■ EDITOR

State University of New York at Stony Brook

⑤SAGE reference

Los Angeles | London | New Delhi
Singapore | Washington DC

SAGE

Los Angeles | London | New Delhi
Singapore | Washington DC

FOR INFORMATION:

SAGE Publications, Inc.
2455 Teller Road
Thousand Oaks, California 91320
E-mail: order@sagepub.com

SAGE Publications India Pvt. Ltd.
B 1/I 1 Mohan Cooperative Industrial Area
Mathura Road, New Delhi 110 044
India

SAGE Publications Ltd.
1 Oliver's Yard
55 City Road
London EC1Y 1SP
United Kingdom

SAGE Publications Asia-Pacific Pte. Ltd.
3 Church Street
#10-04 Samsung Hub
Singapore 049483

Vice President and Publisher: Rolf A. Janke
Senior Editor: Jim Brace-Thompson
Project Editor: Tracy Buyan
Cover Designer: Bryan Fishman
Editorial Assistant: Michele Thompson
Reference Systems Manager: Leticia Gutierrez
Reference Systems Coordinators: Laura Notton,
    Anna Villasenor
Marketing Manager: Kristi Ward

Golson Media
President and Editor: J. Geoffrey Golson
Director, Author Management: Susan Moskowitz
Production Director: Mary Jo Scibetta
Layout Editors: Kenneth Heller, Stephanie Larson,
    Oona Patrick, Lois Rainwater
Copy Editors: Mary Le Rouge, Holli Fort
Proofreader: Barbara Paris
Indexer: J S Editorial

Copyright © 2012 by SAGE Publications, Inc.

All rights reserved. No part of this book may be reproduced or utilized in any form or by any means, electronic or mechanical, including photocopying, recording, or by any information storage and retrieval system, without permission in writing from the publisher.

Library of Congress Cataloging-in-Publication Data

The social history of crime and punishment in America : an encyclopedia /
Wilbur R. Miller, general editor.
    v. cm.
 Includes bibliographical references and index.
 ISBN 978-1-4129-8876-6 (cloth)
    1.   Crime--United   States--History--Encyclopedias.   2. Punishment--United
States--History--Encyclopedias. I. Miller, Wilbur R., 1944-
 HV6779.S63 2012
 364.97303--dc23
                            2012012418

SFI Certified Sourcing
www.sfiprogram.org
SFI-00453

12 13 14 15 16 10 9 8 7 6 5 4 3 2 1

Contents

Volume 5

1600 to 1776: Introduction — *1991*
PRIMARY DOCUMENTS
1609: Excerpt of Samuel de Champlain's Introduction of Firearms to the Indians — *2008*
1610 to 1611: Laws of the Colony of Virginia — *2009*
1637: Trial and Interrogation of Anne Hutchinson — *2010*
1641: Plymouth Colony Adultery Case — *2011*
1642: Capital Laws of New England — *2011*
1649: Maryland Act of Religion — *2012*
1662: Virginia Slave Laws — *2014*
1676: Bacon's Rebellion: The Declaration — *2015*
1689: Samuel Prince Describes the Boston Uprising — *2017*
1692: Accusations Against Elizabeth Proctor — *2019*
1706: Ann Putnam's Confession — *2020*
1741: Excerpt From the New York Negro Plot Trials Testimony — *2021*
1758: Mary Jemison's Account of Kidnapping by Indians — *2022*
1773: A First-Hand Account of the Boston Tea Party — *2025*

1777 to 1800: Introduction — *2029*
PRIMARY DOCUMENTS
1777: Slave Petition for Freedom to the Massachusetts Legislature — *2049*
1780: George Washington's Writings on Benedict Arnold's Treason — *2050*
1787: Thomas Jefferson on the Need for the Occasional Revolution — *2051*
1788: Excerpts From the Memoirs of Abigail Abbot Bailey — *2052*
1793: The Fugitive Slave Act of 1793 — *2053*
1794: Runaway Slave Notice — *2054*
1794: Washington Proclamation on the Whiskey Rebellion — *2055*
1795: *United States v. Mitchell* — *2057*
1799: John Adams: Proclamation on the Insurrection in Pennsylvania — *2059*
1799: The Shays Rebellion in Massachusetts — *2060*

1801 to 1850: Introduction — *2063*
PRIMARY DOCUMENTS
1807: Indictment of Aaron Burr — *2078*
1823: *Elkinson v. Deliesseline* — *2080*
1831: Nat Turner's Jailhouse Confession — *2080*
1835: President Jackson's Remarks to Congress on Indian Removal — *2083*
1838: William Lloyd Garrison's Declaration of Sentiments — *2085*
1844: *The Republic* Article on the Philadelphia Ethnic Riots — *2088*
1844: An Eyewitness Account of the Murders of Joseph and Hyrum Smith — *2090*

1851 to 1900: Introduction — 2097
PRIMARY DOCUMENTS
1851: The *Alabama Journal*'s Account of a Fatal Duel — 2113
1854: Excerpts From the Memoirs of Counterfeiter William Stuart — 2113
1861: Telegram From Major Robert Anderson to the Secretary of War — 2117
1861: Excerpt From the Memoir of Harriet Jacobs, a Slave Girl — 2117
1865: Excerpt From Thomas M. Harris's Documents on the Assassination Conspiracy — 2122
1865: A. G. Blair's Testimony on Inhumane Treatment at Andersonville Prison — 2124
1867: Edwin M. Hale's Treatise on Abortion — 2126
1869: Article on Jesse James's Bank Robbery — 2129
1871: Excerpt From Testimony in Congressional Hearings on the Ku Klux Klan — 2130
1874: Final Ransom Note in the Charley Ross Kidnapping — 2133
1875: *Chicago Daily Tribune* Story on the John C. Colt Murder Trial — 2134
1875: N. A. Jennings Tells of the Texas Rangers — 2137
1875: Cole Younger's Account of the 1875 Northfield, Minnesota, Bank Robbery — 2140
1878: Labor Leader Dennis Kearney's Anti-Chinese Address — 2145
1884: *New York Times* Article on the Greely Expedition — 2147
1885: Testimony of Chinese Laborer Survivors — 2148
1886: Anarchist Oscar Neebe's Commentary on the Haymarket Affair — 2149
1890s: Advertising by the Pinkerton Agency — 2150
1891: George Sontag's Account of His First Train Robbery — 2152
1892: Captain Richard H. Pratt on the Education of Native Americans — 2153
1896: Excerpt From the *Plessy v. Ferguson* Decision — 2156

1901 to 1920: Introduction — 2161
PRIMARY DOCUMENTS
1906: *New York Times* Article on the Murder of Stanford White — 2182
1909: The Department of Justice Creates the Bureau of Investigation — 2187
1909: "Lynching: A National Crime" Speech by Ida B. Wells-Barnett — 2188
1911: *New York Times* Article on the Triangle Shirtwaist Fire — 2189
1912: *New York Times* Article on Law Creating Shorter Factory Working Hours — 2191
1915: *Atlanta Constitution* Article on the Mob Abduction of Leo M. Frank — 2193
1918: John Deml's Account of Anti-German Sentiment — 2196
1919: Department of Justice Memorandum on Anarchists — 2197
1919: Emma Goldman's Account of Her Deportation — 2198
1919: W. M. Mink's Statement on the National Steel Strike — 2199

1921 to 1940: Introduction — 2201
PRIMARY DOCUMENTS
1921: *State of Illinois v. Edward Cicotte, et al.* — 2220
1924: An Act to Preserve Racial Integrity — 2221
1925: H. L. Mencken's Commentary on the Scopes Trial — 2223
1930: The Motion Picture Code of 1930 — 2224
1932: FBI Memorandum on Patent Infringement — 2226
1933: FBI Memorandum on the National Motor Vehicle Theft Act — 2229
1933: FBI Memorandum on the Leon Ulysses Mason Kidnapping and Extortion Case — 2230
1933: FBI Memorandum on Veteran Fraud — 2232
1933: *United States v. One Book Called "Ulysses"* — 2233
1933: Bonnie Parker's "The Ballad of Bonnie and Clyde" — 2237
1934: Excerpt From the Confession of Richard Albert Loeb — 2238

1934: Department of Justice Memorandum on the Extortion of Eli Lilly and Company *2240*
1934: Department of Justice Memorandum on the Extortion of the Ford Motor Company *2241*
1935: FBI Memorandum on August Luer Kidnapping and Vivian Chase *2242*
1935: "Why I Am a Dope Fiend" Pamphlet Against the Harrison Narcotic Law *2245*
1938: Department of Justice Memorandum on Federal Juvenile Offenders *2247*
1938: IRS Report on Huey Long's Louisiana Scandals *2249*
1940: FBI Memorandum on Mann Act Violations *2259*
1940: FBI Memorandum on Receiving the Twelve Millionth Fingerprint Card *2261*

1941 to 1960: Introduction *2263*
PRIMARY DOCUMENTS
1940s: Excerpt From the FBI Memorandum on the Jewish Hope Society Mail Fraud Scheme *2279*
1942: FBI Memorandum on the Extortions of Bing Crosby and Harold Lloyd *2279*
1942: FBI Memorandum on Henry Tatge's Failure to Report for Draft and Imprisonment *2281*
1942: FBI Memorandum on a Vagrant's Draft Trouble *2282*
1943: IRS Intelligence Unit Letter on the Thomas Pendergast Investigation *2282*
1943: FBI Memorandum on "King of the Gypsies" Draft Trouble *2283*
1943: FBI Memorandum on the Elmer Soller and Elmer Hartzel Sedition Case *2284*
1946: FBI Memorandum on a Military Prison Break and Crime Spree *2287*
1946: FBI Memorandum on Harboring Army Deserters *2288*
1947: FBI Memorandum on Draft Desertion *2289*
1948: FBI Memorandum on Clifford Carlyle Skaife's Crime Spree *2290*
1950: FBI Subject Files Used in the Kefauver Hearings on Organized Crime *2292*
1950: Statement of Bureau of Narcotics Commissioner Harry J. Anslinger *2294*
1951: FBI Memorandum on Hugh Rakes and the Whiskey Conspiracy *2297*
1951: Executive Order on the Interdepartmental Committee on Narcotics *2301*
1952: FBI Memorandum on a Case of Kidnapping, Involuntary Servitude, and Slavery *2302*
1954: Dr. J. Robert Oppenheimer Admits Lying During Investigation *2304*
1954: Communist Control Act *2305*
1954: The Comic Book Code of 1954 *2310*
1954: Senate Resolution 301: Censure of Senator Joseph McCarthy *2312*
1955: Congressional Report on Juvenile Delinquency *2313*
1955: Senate Subcommittee's Interim Report on Television and Juvenile Delinquency *2317*
1955: Trial Summary From *Mildred Juanita Adams v. United States of America* *2320*
1955: Concerned Citizen Letter About Drug Traffic *2322*
1955: Congressional Committee on Narcotics Interim Report *2323*
1959: FBI Memorandum on Narcotics Violator Ralph Ciccone *2325*
1959: FBI Report on Gaetano Lucchese *2326*
1960: Adolph Coors III Murder Report *2333*

1961 to 1980: Introduction *2337*
PRIMARY DOCUMENTS
1962: Treasury Department Memorandum on "Lucky" Luciano's Drug Ring *2359*
1962: Commission of Narcotics Report on Detroit Organized Crime and Racketeering *2360*
1962: Bureau of Narcotics Report on Kansas City Organized Crime and Racketeering *2362*
1963: Temporary Assignment of Narcotic Agents to Investigate Gambling *2366*
1963: Proposed John F. Kennedy Speech for the March on Washington *2366*
1963: Gerald R. Ford Interview on Working With John F. Kennedy *2367*
1964: President's Advisory Commission on Narcotic and Drug Abuse Press Release *2379*
1965: Customs Narcotics Report *2380*

1965: Presidential Assassination Law	2382
1966: Senator Robert F. Kennedy Communications on the New York Transit Strike	2383
1968: Robert F. Kennedy News Release on the Assassination of Martin Luther King Jr.	2386
1969: Department of Justice Statement on Miami Drug Smuggling	2387
1969: FBI Memorandum on Stolen Vehicle Case	2388
1969: HYMN Response to the Stonewall Riots	2390
1970: Testimony of Charles Manson in the Tate–LaBianca Murder Trial	2391
1974: Presidential Pardon Given to Richard M. Nixon	2394
1975: FBI Memorandum on Worldwide Church of God Allegations	2395
1977: FBI Internal Communications on Fugitive Ted Bundy	2398
1978: White House Memorandum on the 1868 Conviction of Dr. Samuel Mudd	2399
1980: Memorandum to President Jimmy Carter Regarding Love Canal	2404

1981 to 2000: Introduction 2407
PRIMARY DOCUMENTS

1981: White House Press Briefing on the Reagan Assassination Attempt	2427
1982: White House Directive on Managing Terrorist Incidents	2430
1985: National Security Decision Directive 179	2431
1990: Marla Hanson's Testimony to the Senate Judiciary Committee	2433
1991: Excerpt From *U.S. v. Exxon*	2435
1993: Parchman State Penitentiary Lonely Heart Scam	2436
1997: Excerpt From Monica Lewinsky and Linda Tripp's Telephone Conversations	2437
1998: President Clinton's Statement Following Grand Jury Testimony	2438
1999: FBI Report on Columbine High School Shooting	2439
2000: Amnesty International's Plea to President Clinton on Behalf of Juan Garza	2440

2001 to 2012: Introduction 2443
PRIMARY DOCUMENTS

2001: Excerpt From Department of Justice Report on Anthrax Attacks	2463
2002: Human Rights Watch Letter to President Bush Regarding Torture	2468
2004: Department of Justice Press Release on the Charges Against Kenneth Lay	2471
2005: Report From the National Institute of Justice on La Cosa Nostra	2474
2008: Official Charges Against Casey Anthony	2479
2010: *State of Utah v. Warren Steed Jeffs*	2480
2011: Excerpt From the BP Deepwater Horizon Natural Resource Damage Assessment	2484

Glossary	2487
Resource Guide	2499
Index	2507
Photo Credits	2606

1600 to 1776

INTRODUCTION

The policing, criminal law, procedure, and punishments that are associated with the criminal justice system have their roots in the American colonial experience. Some institutions, such as the jury trial, were brought from England, where they had existed since time immemorial; others were colonial innovations. Many of the defendant safeguards that are now considered commonplace were implemented slowly by colonial legislatures and courts as they sought to reform the existing English common law. These developments were uneven across the colonies based on local conditions and the different age of the colonies. Spanish and French colonies followed national variants of Roman or civil law; under Dutch rule New York followed Dutch law. Only Louisiana retained some elements of Roman law in its civil code.

The North American colonies that would one day form the United States operated as independent governments that owed their loyalty to the crown of England. All of the colonies functioned within the framework of the common law of England, but the degree to which they held to English law varied widely. In Massachusetts Bay, the colonists attempted to enact God's law on Earth by basing their legal code on the Bible, while in Virginia the common law remained as close to its original form as possible. The dominant view of legal scholars has been that common law was transferred to the new world by the colonists. However, a growing body of literature has suggested that the colonists did not simply import the common law with them, but sought to adapt it to local conditions and beliefs.

In the 17th and 18th centuries, the state of policing, substantive criminal law, criminal procedure, and punishment as it was established under English common law provided the basis of the common law that was implemented in the North American colonies.

Substantive criminal law refers to the prohibitions and duties that a person is expected to follow in a legal system. This is opposed to criminal procedure, which sets out the mechanism by which a person is tried for a breach of substantive criminal law.

Criminal Procedures and Policing in Seventeenth- and Eighteenth-Century England

In England, felonies—crimes that were punishable by death—included murder, arson, burglary, robbery, rape, and theft (if over 15 pounds sterling). These crimes were tried by judges from the central courts either in London at the Central Criminal Court (Old Bailey) or locally at an *assize* (periodic criminal court). Judges from the central courts would ride to several different assizes during their own court recesses, a practice that gave rise to the concept of riding circuit. The assizes were presided over by the central judge, who was assisted by the local justices of the peace. Assizes were used because it was too costly, inconvenient, and disruptive to transport all defendants, witnesses, and plaintiffs to London for trials. Crimes against the church, including blasphemy, witchcraft, and heresy, were governed by ecclesiastic courts until the reign of Henry VIII, when they were integrated as felonies into the common law. Treason cases were handled by the central courts, unless the crime was committed by a nobleman, in which case it was tried in the House of Lords.

The enforcement of criminal laws in England was extremely uneven until the 19th century. There was no professional police force anywhere in England until the formation of the Bow Street Runners in 1749, and then only in London. Until then, law enforcement consisted of village constables and local justices of the peace. County sheriffs were also employed in law enforcement, but they were more often involved in processing summons and other royal business. The common law required anyone who witnessed a crime or came across a dead body to raise the hue and cry, literally yelling about the crime and rousting their neighbors to look for the culprit. This system relied on the populace to serve as a law enforcement agency and provide information about any crime. The law also required local citizens to maintain weapons and horses in accordance with their stature in the community to aid in law enforcement, and made it a crime for any able-bodied male to refuse to assist in the apprehension of a criminal. In addition, the law required all unexplained deaths to be reported. All nonfelonies were handled locally by justices of the peace, who were also expected to bind over persons suspected of committing a felony for later trial and conduct the initial inquiry into felony cases. Justices of the peace did not deal exclusively with criminal matters; they were also expected to enforce numerous other regulations, from road maintenance to the licensing of taverns. The enforcement of criminal laws thus depended not only on the diligence of local officials, but also on the willingness of the populace to assist in prosecution and crime prevention at their own expense.

Once a suspect was apprehended, he or she would be brought before the local justice of the peace, who would hear the initial evidence against them and determine if they were to be bound over until the next assize. If a petty crime were committed, the justice could summarily try the case. This was an informal procedure and often occurred in the home of the justice of the peace. If the person were to be bound over, they would be turned over to the local jailer to be held or released on the bond of neighbors, friends, or family. At this point, the defendant was not formally charged. A grand jury, sometimes referred to as an indicting jury, would meet at the start of each assize and determine if there was enough evidence for charges to be brought. If the plaintiff failed to appear, the case was either dismissed or the plaintiff could be compelled to attend. Once all defendants were charged, the grand jury disbanded and individual trial juries would try the cases. The all-male juries often served on both grand and trial juries, especially in rural areas. In addition, one trial jury was often used to try several cases in quick succession.

Criminal trials under English common law in the 17th and 18th centuries were vastly different from modern criminal trials. The average felony trial lasted less than 30 minutes, and some were so quick that the defendant didn't know the result of their trial or even if they had been tried. The defendant was prohibited from having a defense lawyer until they were granted that right in 1839. Until the late 17th century, all prosecutions were brought by the victim, or in the case of murder, by the victim's heirs. The plaintiffs could have the assistance of lawyers, but they were expected to cover the costs themselves, without the aid of the crown. In cases involving crimes against the government, the king or his royal prosecutor would be employed to argue the case. The plaintiff was allowed to call witnesses and could compel them to attend the proceedings by the issuance of writs, and only prosecution witnesses could be sworn in before their testimony. In contrast, the defendant was not usually allowed to call any witnesses and had no means to compel anyone to attend the trial. Defendants and their witnesses, if any, were not allowed to be sworn before they gave testimony. This was initially seen as an advantage to defendants because they were not imperiling their souls if they did not reveal everything in their defense, but later became a liability because they were not obliged to tell the truth.

Although the jury trial was the last viable, and therefore primary, method of trial by the 17th century, it was not the official method. Older forms of trial continued to be practiced under certain circumstances, especially in rural areas. The most frequently used was compurgation, or trial by the swearing of oaths that the defendant was innocent. The number of persons required for swearing varied by the seriousness of the crime and the degree to which the court believed the defendant was guilty. This method of trial began to decline in the 16th century, and was limited to some petty property offenses and in civil trials by the 17th century. Trial by ordeal was supposed to have been abolished in the 13th century, but the ducking of suspected witches was essentially the continuation of the ordeal of cold water. Contrary to popular belief, the person being ducked was always supposed to be saved before they drowned.

Because the jury was not the official method of trial, a defendant had to select trial by jury. If a defendant refused to plead or put themselves before a jury, then there was no method to try them. In order to coerce defendants to agree to a jury trial, *peine forte et dure* (punishment by force and strength) was developed. *Peine forte et dure* developed into "pressing," which involved tying the silent defendants to the ground and placing rocks on them until they either agreed to a jury trial or died. Defendants were encouraged

This painting depicts Virginia planter Nathaniel Bacon confronting Governor William Berkeley in 1676, who refused to retaliate after Indians attacked the frontier. This first American rebellion involving frontiersmen included a mob of about 1,000 whites and blacks. Bacon obtained a militia commission at gunpoint in order to lead an attack on the Indians; then, his men burned and looted Jamestown.

to stand silent on the rule that the property of a convicted felon would be confiscated to the crown and the person's heirs would be disinherited. By standing mute, defendants could protect their estates, although they would suffer a terrible death.

There were no established rules governing the type of evidence that was permissible to submit to a court; hearsay, spectral evidence, uncorroborated accomplice testimony, and coerced confessions were all admissible to prove guilt or innocence. The standard of reasonable doubt was not firmly established as the required level of proof for a guilty verdict and a defendant could be convicted on the jury's persuasion of their guilt. Although an ill-defined level of proof, it was usually regarded as something more than mere presumption of guilt, but less than beyond reasonable doubt. One aspect working in favor of a defendant was that a jury's guilty verdict could be set aside if the defendant could show that a single juror had a reason to be biased against them. In contrast, an acquittal could never be set aside, even if it was subsequently shown that a jurors were biased toward the defendant.

This system appears very biased toward the prosecution, but acquittal rates were much higher in the 17th and 18th centuries than they are today. In general, the plaintiff or their attorney would present the evidence to the jury relating to the alleged crime and the defendant was expected to explain away the evidence presented against them. John Langbein has described this system as the "accused speaks" model of trial. This meant that there was no possibility of the defendant remaining silent, let alone having a right to remain so. The introduction of lawyers in the 18th century began the development of this right, as defendants were able to employ counsel to speak on their behalf.

The harshness of the system was initially mitigated by the fact that juries often knew the defendant personally and would therefore find them guilty of lesser offenses. Even after juries became more impersonal, there was an apparent continued impulse to mitigate the harshness of the common law, especially with first-time offenders and offenses against property. Plaintiffs were also prohibited from challenging any jurors, while the defendant could challenge 35 jurors without cause and an unlimited number for cause. Finally, benefit of the clergy allowed defendants to claim that they could not be punished because they were members of the clergy. This was established by requiring the defendant to read a passage from the Bible, but by the 17h century it was merely a proof of literacy, which could easily be circumvented by memorization of the passage, which was always the same. One could plead benefit of clergy only once, a brand on the thumb making that obvious

The Writ of Habeas Corpus was originally designed to ensure that a person was being held in custody, not to challenge unlawful detention. In the 16th century, the Court of King's Bench began to use the writ to challenge detention by magistrates, particularly the Privy Council. The regular use of the writ as a means of challenging unlawful detention was in place by the early 17th century. In 1679, the Habeas Corpus Act improved the force of the writ by requiring that the prisoner be presented before the issuing court within three days and that they be tried within two terms or be granted bail.

Until the 18th century, the primary forms of punishment in England were death, flogging, pillorying, the imposition of fines, and transportation. Although jails did exist, they were used almost exclusively to hold defendants until trial or before their sentence was carried out, or for special political prisoners. The punishment for all felonies was death, but this could be mitigated to transportation to the colonies for 7 to 15 years. Transportation was embraced because it mitigated the harshness of the system and provided a source of immigrants and cheap labor to new colonies. All death sentences were to be carried out by hanging, although nobles were usually granted the more dignified death of beheading. The exception to this was the crime of treason, which encompassed attempts to overthrow the monarchy or harm the king, the murder of a husband by his wife, or the murder of a master by a slave. A man who committed treason was to be hanged, drawn, and quartered, while a woman was to be burned. However, most women were strangled to death before they were set alight. Children over the age of 8 were subjected to all forms of punishment, including death, until the mid-19th century, although death was usually only imposed in murder cases when a child reached the age of 14. Fines were used for assaults and petty frauds, while pillorying was used for social disorder crimes such as adultery, selling defective goods, cheating at cards, sexual relations with a minor, homosexuality, and witchcraft that did not result in harm. Flogging was used as a punishment for petty larceny and eventually for grand larceny as juries began to mitigate grand larceny to avoid death sentences. Maiming, such as the mutilation of the nose or cutting off of one or both ears was a popular punishment before the English Civil War (1642–51) for bearing false witness, some property crimes against the church or government property, and repeat offenders. The linking of this punishment with the dreaded Court of Star Chamber, which was universally disliked before its abolition during the English Civil War, made these punishments less popular.

Substantive Criminal Law in the Colonies
All colonies diverged from the common law to some degree; some combined it with biblical or Mosaic law or new law reforms. During the 17th century, there was a widespread call for law reform in England to make the system more efficient and affordable. Some of these reforms were implemented by the American colonists before they were implemented in England. According to most charters, the laws of colonies were supposed to conform to the common law, but this provision was rarely enforced. In the late 17th century, when England began its attempt to force colonies to conform to the common law, the colonies retaliated by passing laws that were only in effect for three years and then reissued them after they lapsed. Therefore, if a law was struck down by the Privy Council, it would only remove the individual act under review. Three years was the average length of time it took the Privy Council to review and rule on a colonial act.

All substantive criminal laws indicate the type of behavior that is viewed by a particular culture as reprehensible and undermining of the established social order. There are numerous ways that substantive crimes can be subdivided, but can generally be categorized as traditional felonies, religious crimes, property crimes, state crimes, and social disorder crimes. Traditional felonies—murder, rape, arson, burglary, robbery, and theft of large sums of money—could be punished by death. In modern criminal law, felony is defined as a crime that carries imprisonment for more than a year. Religious crimes were those that undermined or challenged Christian beliefs, including heresy, witchcraft, blasphemy, and Sabbath breaking. Property crimes included the theft of property and its destruction, as well as trespassing onto another person's land. State crimes were technically the same as in England and included treason, sedition, counterfeiting, coin clipping, slave rebellion, and piracy. The final and largest category of social disorder usually included those that did not put the defendant's life at risk and included sex crimes, drunkenness, fighting, swearing, and family problems. The category of slave-related crimes is interesting because these laws prohibited both rebellions by slaves and excessive abuse of slaves, falling into the categories of social order, felonies, and state crimes.

The standard for traditional felonies was adopted in all colonies and, across the empire, included punishment by death. About half of all murders occurred within the family; there was a high number of infanticides and murders of servants or slaves. In North Carolina, infanticide was so common that all infant deaths not attributed to disease were investigated as potential homicides. Women were more likely to commit infanticide then men; however, both men and women were accused of killing servants. The

This mural by Rober Reid depicts the Boston Tea Party on December 16, 1773, one of the most famous uprisings by American colonists leading up to the country's independence. It was sparked by a dramatic increase in tea taxation by the British. Colonists costumed themselves as Indians, complete with war paint and hatchets for tomahawks.

murder of a servant or apprentice was usually caused by abuse or neglect and did not always result in the conviction of the defendant, because it was difficult to show intent to murder. The murder of a native by a settler often did not result in any charges being filed, let alone a conviction. In Plymouth colony, however, there were instances of settlers being convicted of robbing and murdering a native man. Omitting deaths occurring during war, the murder rate for colonial America was considerably lower than would be expected. There were fewer than 25 murder cases across all the American colonies before 1660. Almost all murders were committed by men.

There were few cases of rape tried in the 17th century, likely stemming from the problem of underreporting of rapes and the misclassification of the crime in some colonies. For example, in Massachusetts, consensual sex with a minor was not rape. In addition, many servants and few, if any, slaves would have reported rape when they were dependent on their masters for sustenance. The report of rapes increased in the 18th century, with around 200 cases per year by the eve of the American Revolutionary War (1775–83). Unsurprisingly, Virginia, Pennsylvania, and Massachusetts, the three most-populated colonies of the era, had the most rapes reported. Almost all rapes were committed by men, but there were instances of women being charged.

Arson was not unheard of, but was infrequent during the colonial era. Robberies and burglaries were more common in larger towns than in small villages. The number of thefts increased dramatically in the 18th century as the number of larger towns increased and the close-knit nature of communities disappeared. It has also been reported that during the 17th century, there was little of value to steal, which depressed the overall charges of theft. In fact, most cases of theft were of a petty nature, such as yarn or ribbon. The majority of arsons, burglaries, and robberies were committed by men.

The category of religious crimes is often misunderstood, especially in regard to the New England colonies, due to their implementation of biblical punishments for social disorder crimes. In a narrow sense, the common law category of religious crimes was limited to blasphemy, Sabbath breaking, witchcraft, and heresy. All of these acts were punishable in colonial courts in accordance with common-law procedures. In the New England colonies, the statutes often called for the death penalty to be inflicted for these crimes, but it was rarely, if ever, inflicted; the exception was witchcraft. The Body of Liberties of Massachusetts Bay stated that blasphemy was punishable by death, but this was never implemented. Many New England colonies made adultery, buggery (sodomy and/or bestiality), cursing of parents by children, and rebellion by children capital crimes in accordance with biblical precepts. This has led many to believe that these were religious offenses, but adultery and buggery were punishable under the common law as noncapital offenses. There seems to be no incidence of a rebellious child or curser of parents having been put to death, although several were flogged or removed from their homes. While there were instances of men being executed for buggery, it appears that these parts of the code were intended more as a guide to societal expectations than enforceable laws. However, the terminology regarding buggery had various meanings within early New England colonists: buggery usually referred to bestiality and sodomy to homosexuality, although on occasion, buggery referred to homosexuality and sodomy to bestiality.

The most unusual crime from a modern perspective was the criminalization of witchcraft. The act of witchcraft was not well defined in the statutes, covering everything from simple fortunetelling or necromancy to purported compacts with the devil and infliction of harm on individuals by supernatural methods. The most famous witchcraft cases occurred in Salem Village in 1692, which resulted in the execution of 19 persons. Contrary to popular belief, men were also convicted of practicing witchcraft, although the majority of those accused and convicted were women. Also in 1692, there was a series of witchcraft trials throughout Connecticut that resulted in several executions, but raised fewer problems. However, witchcraft cases occurred throughout New England and even in some southern colonies such as Virginia, Maryland, and North Carolina. In fact, the only case in which a suspected witch was ducked occurred in early 18th-century Virginia. As in England, witchcraft prosecutions declined rapidly in the early 18th century due to a growing perception that witchcraft could not be proven in a trial.

A closely related crime is heresy. However, what constituted heresy depended on the established religion of a given colony. For example, Massachusetts Bay famously expelled Anne Hutchinson for heresy during the antinomian controversy with her resettling in Providence. Therefore, what was heresy in Massachusetts Bay was permissible in Rhode Island. Similarly, Virginia established the Church of England, which would have made Puritan beliefs heretical. Although the substantive law remained the same, the definition of heresy varied among the colonies. Other religious infractions such as blasphemy or Sabbath breaking were more universally applied. Heresy typically resulted in banishment from a colony rather than death, but there were numerous instances of Quakers being executed in New England colonies for practicing their faith.

The opportunity to commit property crimes was limited during the first 80 years of settlement due to the isolated nature of settlements. As the colonies became more settled, roughly after 1740, the greater opportunity and increased impersonal nature of larger towns led to a dramatic increase in property crimes. Although men continued to commit a majority of serious property crimes, women began to commit an increasing percentage as the 18th century progressed. These crimes usually resulted in flogging or being forced to stand the pillory, as the thefts were often small amounts of linen, clothing, consumables, or other trifles. Most of these crimes were committed by apprentices, servants, or children, usually against their masters or neighbors. Trespasses were primarily civil matters by the 18th century. Although a few criminal cases of trespass did occur in North Carolina, the records are not sufficiently clear to determine if this correlated to the modern notion of trespassing.

Crimes against the state consisted primarily of sedition, piracy, the clipping of money, slave rebellions, and treason. Coin clipping was rarely punished in the colonies, likely due to the fact that coinage was scarce in all colonies and paper money was used beginning in the late 17th century to float colonial debt. Piracy was a major issue during the entire colonial era, but especially following the War of Spanish Succession (1701–14), when many privateers turned to outright piracy. In a few instances, such as the apprehension of Edward Teach in North Carolina, colonial magistrates worked with Royal Navy officials to pursue pirates. For the most part, piracy was a crime policed and punished by the navy in admiralty courts. The related crime of smuggling was often overlooked by colonial officials, especially with the rise in tensions with the crown leading up to the American Revolution and the fact that many legitimate merchants engaged in smuggling on the side; the increased view of the arbitrary nature of navigation laws also made smuggling a patriotic endeavor.

Treason was not a concern in the colonial era, with the notable exception of the execution of Jacob Liesler, a New York rebel against British authority in 1691. Of course, the British saw the American revolutionaries as traitors against Parliament and the crown. Petite treason encompassed the murder of husbands by wives or masters by slaves and was punishable as treason. However, there is no recorded instance of anyone being drawn and quartered or burned at the stake in any of the Atlantic colonies. Even during an incident in the West Indies, where a slave confessed to using witchcraft and poison to murder her master, she was not burned, but simply hung. The few instances of wives murdering their husbands also resulted in hanging, rather than burning. The one major state crime tried in the colonies was sedition. However, most sedition cases were in Maryland and Massachusetts Bay. The Rhode Island, Connecticut, and New Haven colonies did not have authorization to establish the charge of sedition. Although Virginia and Plymouth did have laws against sedition, they had relatively few cases. In Massachusetts Bay, all sedition cases were tied to heresy cases involving dissenting Puritans or Quakers and were resolved together. In Maryland, the key problem was a confrontation between the Catholic proprietors of the colony and the majority Protestant population that was exacerbated by Virginia's claim that Maryland had been illegally formed out if its territory. The political upheavals of 17th-century England were played out in Maryland and resulted in several cases of sedition and even a few treason cases. A few Virginians who had settled in the Chesapeake Bay area before the creation of Maryland attempted to use force to retain their land. In one instance, Virginia trader William Claiborne fought a naval battle against Maryland to defend a trading post he had established. After his defeat, the government of Maryland charged him with sedition in absentia, but he was never punished for the crime. Other than in these two colonies, sedition was a minor issue.

The largest group of criminal acts are lumped under the heading of social disorder crimes. These include sex crimes, simple assaults, slander, drunkenness, fighting, and spreading of false rumors. These crimes can be further divided between those that disturbed the public peace and those that did not. Often, the difference was simply where the crime took place; for example, a fight in public was an affray in North Carolina, while the same fighting in private was an assault. Breaches of public peace were often punished more severely than private actions, but the imposition of capital punishment usually depended more on the severity of the breach than where it occurred. Slander was usually considered a breach of the public peace because it was liable to lead to provocations and possible physical retaliation by the victim. Criminal slander actions were begun, but it appears that most of these cases were settled in civil court. Drunkenness, idleness, cursing, and excessive gambling were also punishable in most colonies, although idleness was a uniquely New England crime. Most of these crimes were punished with fines, although flogging and/or pillaring was also possible. In extreme cases, idleness could be punished by forcing the idler to be indentured or apprenticed to a master.

Samuel de Champlain was instrumental in the fur trade of New France. He advocated alliance of the colonies with the Indians and even introduced firearms to them.

Sexually related crimes other than rape were sometimes severely punished, especially in New England colonies. However, sexual acts were prosecuted just as often in the middle colonies as in New England, but rarely carried a capital punishment. Sex crimes included incest, sodomy or buggery, adultery, and fornication, as well as more unclear behaviors that were described as lewd. The penalties imposed for these crimes varied widely across the colonies, and some colonies did not apply them that often; Massachusetts Bay appeared to have severe penalties in its codes. Sexual relations between unmarried persons was a criminal act but could often be mitigated if the parties subsequently married, especially if the woman became pregnant. Fornication was usually punished by flogging or pillaring, even where harsher punishments were available. Adultery was a relatively minor crime in the southern and middle colonies, but was regarded as far more severe in New England. Only two persons were ever put to death for adultery, although technically it was a capital crime; most others were fined or whipped. The courts appear to have been equal in punishing the parties, regardless of gender or marital status.

Sodomy was a capital crime across the colonies, but there were relatively few cases of persons actually executed for it. More often, the person was banished or flogged for the offense. Bestiality, like sodomy, was a capital crime; the death penalty was regularly applied in the few cases that arose.

Criminal laws relating to slavery varied in their frequency and severity depending on how widespread the institution was in the given colony. The first laws relating directly to slavery were passed in Virginia in 1650; however, the first definition of a slave was not given until 1662. Most colonial-era slave codes were passed in the late 17th century or early 18th century and generally prohibited slaves from striking their master, running away, leaving their master's property without permission, owning weapons, or plotting to rebel. These early codes were relatively milder when compared to the draconian codes of the antebellum era. Nevertheless, these codes still provided for much harsher punishments than for free persons or indentured servants, which included branding, nose slitting, and other forms of maiming that had been generally abandoned. In addition, Virginia and other southern and middle colonies decriminalized assaults on slaves if perpetrated by their master or overseer. In New England, slaves were accorded more protection on paper, if not in practice. More importantly, it was established that non-Christians were entitled to fewer rights than Englishmen and that they were little more than property.

Policing in the Colonies

Especially in the 17th century, the colonies relied on the traditional English methods of crime prevention: the populace. Most areas continued to rely on the hue and cry established in medieval England. The majority of communities in the colonies relied on a combination of sheriffs and justices of the peace. As in England, victims were expected to report crimes to their local justices of the peace, but often, there was no threat of prosecution for failure to report, which led to underreporting. As there was no formal police force, the community at large was also expected to report suspected criminal activity. A person's reputation in a small village was often enough to either arouse suspicion or help exonerate them. The rural nature of the colonies seems to have made the antiquated

This 1853 lithograph by Junius Brutus Stearns shows George Washington, the farmer, overseeing his land while African American field workers harvest grain; Mt. Vernon is in the background. Early slave laws were passed in Virginia in 1650 but most were established from the late 17th to early 18th centuries. Slaves were prohibited from hitting their master, escaping, leaving their master's property without permission, owning weapons, or rebellion.

medieval institutions of the common law once more serviceable. A jury could be self-informing because neighbors usually knew each other's activities and the justices of the peace often knew the majority of people in their jurisdiction.

The first police force of any type established in the colonies was the Night Watch in Boston, but it was more of a citizen patrol than a formal organization. In most communities, constables, or citizens who held the office for a fixed term, served as the primary policing agent. In all colonies, they were usually not drawn from the elite due to the nature of their work, and thus helped to bring men of lower social rank into the justice system. Unlike modern police, the town constable was expected to be investigator, jailer (even keeping defendants in his own home at times), a general keeper of the peace, and court assistant. They were thereby called upon to do anything from breaking up fights to appearing at court sessions to provide evidence and ensure that paperwork was processed properly. The system seems to have worked well over the era, although there were instances of constables being fined for failure to appear at court or being negligent in carrying out their duties. The office of constable was an unpaid position that was accepted primarily for social prestige. Over time, the office became a paid post, but in rural areas it often remained unpaid. Dutch New Amsterdam had distinct officers: the Schout, a combination of sheriff and public prosecutor, and Schepens or elected constables. In 1658 the colony created a paid "rattle watch" for nightly patrol.

The office of sheriff, as in England, also served a law enforcement role. The sheriff was responsible for issuing writs and ensuring that witnesses appeared at court sessions. There was usually one sheriff per county with a few deputies. It was generally believed that the office of sheriff was more prestigious than that of constable; therefore, men of higher social status usually filled the post. As a sign of this prestige, the sheriff was usually required to post a bond in the event of any misconduct or damages that occurred during his tenure and as a way to limit the pool of suitable applicants. However, in southern colonies there were shortages of men who wanted to fill the post, evidenced by the facts that the North Carolina legislature passed a law fining anyone who turned down the post and that many eligible men paid the fine rather than take the position. Thus, the position often went to unscrupulous individuals who sought to use the office for profit. In the end, the most reliable source of law enforcement came from the people, as had been the case in England for centuries.

Criminal Procedure in the Colonies

One area in which the colonies introduced numerous improvements into the common law was the area of criminal procedure. The colonies witnessed a transformation of criminal trial procedure from the mid-17th century to the eve of the American Revolution. In the early years of most colonies, the "accused speaks" mode of trial was the only form available. As the colonies became more settled and established legal codes, alterations to the common law helped create the adversarial criminal trial that exists today. This process occurred at different times in the various colonies, and there is limited research on the degree to which the colonies transmitted legal innovations to each other and back to England.

As in England, all minor, noncapital offenses were handled locally by justices of the peace throughout the year. As in England, when a major crime arose, the justice would bind the defendant over to the next court of quarter sessions. The hierarchy of courts varied throughout the colonies, but all had a system of trial courts and usually had appeals to the governor's counsel in place by the 18th century. Although civil cases were appealable to the Privy Council, criminal cases were not. After the Boston Massacre in 1770, all criminal cases involving British officials or violations of the Navigation Acts were transferred to admiralty courts, which were then appealable in the common law system. In the early days of settlement, many colonies only had the central court in their primary city and would haul defendants and witnesses to that court. As in England, this system became impractical as settlements spread out. The colonies drew on their English heritage and established circuit courts to hear cases in the countryside. These courts were often given the same name as in England—quarter sessions—as they occurred four times a year. If a region became particularly backlogged with cases or if there was a series of interrelated cases, such as the Salem witchcraft trials, then a court of *oyer* and *terminer* (law French for "to hear" and "decide") could be established to hear just those cases.

One universally adopted innovation was the conducting of all legal matters, written and oral, in English. Previously, law French had been the language of the court, with the writs composed in Latin, although witnesses were questioned in English. This led many on both sides of the Atlantic to complain that the average defendant had no knowledge of the judicial process. The implementation of English-only proceedings briefly occurred in England under the Protectorate, but Latin and law French were restored with the monarchy in 1660. The colonies did not use Latin or law French for any of their procedures. Some colonists were educated as lawyers, but abandoned the other languages for practical and ideological reasons. Some Latin and law French terms continued to be used, but the bulk of legal work proceeded in English.

The primary mode of trial in the colonies was jury trial. Even in colonies that adopted the common law entirely, such as Virginia, New Jersey, and North Carolina, the other modes of trial were not used. There was only one instance of any trial by ordeal, indicating that the practice had been so out of use in England that it was not imported to the colonies. Compurgation, or oath swearing, was still used in England in the 17th century, but was not used in the North American colonies. The reason for this is not entirely clear. Colonies did not initially take the logical step of mandating trial by jury. The colonies became split on what to do with defendants who would not put themselves before a jury. Initially, most colonies simply entered a guilty verdict against the defendant and proceeded to sentencing. In the 18th century, this was changed so that a defendant who stood mute was understood to have pled not guilty and the court proceeded with a jury trial.

Although the procedure of peine forte et dure was technically available to deal with defendants who refused to submit to a trial by jury, there is only one confirmed case of its use. Giles Cory was pressed to death during the Salem witchcraft trials when he refused to submit to a jury trial. He proclaimed himself innocent and then stood mute when asked if he would be tried by a jury. His reasons for enduring such an excruciating death are not clear in the records and he left no memoir prior to the event. Other than one witch ducking, there is no evidence that any trials by ordeal were conducted in the North American colonies, nor is there any evidence that compurgation was regularly practiced. Although dueling was a fairly regular occurrence, particularly in the southern colonies, these were duels of honor and not judicial combat to adjudicate a criminal matter.

As in England, juries were composed of 12 men from the town or village in which the defendant resided. The division of indicting or grand jury and trial jury was continued in all colonies. The manner of selecting grand juries varied across the colonies, but they were usually selected either by the sheriff, court, town officials, or some combination. While this created the tendency for juries to be composed of large landholders or wealthy merchants, these grand juries continued to provide a degree of safety against local prejudice because the jurors were of sufficient prestige to refuse to indict people simply for being unpopular. Later, they were able to shield some colonists from royal overreaching by refusing to indict them for violating the unpopular Navigation Acts. The ability of defendants to challenge up to 35 jurors was also maintained, as was the requirement that guilty verdicts be unanimous and acquittals be ineligible for appeal. Initially, charges were brought by the victims of the accused, rather than by the state. The colonies generally followed the English lead and began to establish colonial prosecutors to handle the cases and thereby tie criminal adjudication closer to the state.

The colonists were particularly willing to expand the protections offered to defendants in criminal trials. In Massachusetts, the impetus for establishing a new code was actually the concern among colonists that the magistrates, Governor John Winthrop in particular, were too lenient in their application of the laws. The colonists insisted that the Court of Assistance pass a more rigorous set of laws based on biblical law. This resulted in numerous acts criminalized as capital offenses, as set forth in the Bible, but the lack of criminal procedure forced the colonists to rely on the common law. However, they did not feel bound by the literal word of the common law and implemented reforms to improve the law. One of the key reforms was the introduction of legal counsel for criminal defendants.

The Body of Liberties of Massachusetts Bay removed the prohibition of defendants having the assistance of counsel, but stated that a person could not practice law for profit. This stemmed from a conflict between the Puritan dislike of lawyers and the realization that legal counsel could benefit a criminal defendant. This was illustrated by the case against Anne Hutchinson, whom everyone believed was able to eloquently respond to her prosecutors because she was receiving legal counsel from her minister, Nathaniel

Men were also accused of practicing witchcraft in the colonies, as depicted by this 1892 lithograph by Joseph E. Baker titled "The Witch no. 2." The Capital Laws of New England provided that "If any man or woman be a Witch, that is, hath consulteth with a familiar spirit, they shall be put to death." The definition of "witchcraft" was broad and included fortunetelling, necromancy, pacts with the devil, and supernatural harm to others.

Ward. However, it is uncertain how often defendants utilized defense counsel. Massachusetts, Pennsylvania, and Rhode Island all allowed defendants to have the assistance of counsel by the end of the 17th century, a full 120 years before England would grant that right to defendants. The other colonies followed suit in the early 18th century, so it was in common practice by the time the U.S. Constitution was composed. There was no affirmative right for the state to provide a counsel to defendants, just the ability of defendants to employ one if so wished.

The introduction of lawyers into criminal proceedings enabled defendants to remain silent during their trials, leading to the right to not incriminate oneself. However, as the colonies were still transitioning from the "accused speaks" mode of trial to the adversary trial, this right was limited to defendants in their trial. The Fifth Amendment right against self-incrimination was far more sweeping in scope than any state law in effect at the time of the drafting, as it protected witnesses and theoretically all parties in any civil or criminal case. New Jersey, New York, Georgia, and South Carolina did not provide a right against self incrimination. The other states and Vermont, which was technically an independent republic, offered varying levels of the right to criminal defendants.

Another colonial innovation was the right to be secure against unlawful searches and seizures. However, this right was developed late in the colonial era and was tied to the growing disputes with England over the enforcement of imperial taxation. The repressive actions of the British in response to smuggling among colonial traders increased wariness regarding warrantless searches. There was a general common-law rule that required a warrant be issued before a person was arrested, a home searched, or items seized. However, customs officials used general warrants, which did not specify what was to be searched or seized, to search a home or business for smuggled goods. In addition, officials needed no additional authorization to seize any item they thought in violation of an act. In 1763, the Courts of England dealt with this issue in the case of John Wilkes, who successfully brought suit of criminal trespass against the officials involved in searching his home without a warrant. The case raised awareness in the colonies of the problem of general warrant searches, but the issue was not fully resolved until after the American Revolution.

The prohibition against double jeopardy in criminal cases stemmed from the prohibition against appeals of acquittals in the common law. Justice Coke was considered a driving force in affirming the rule that a defendant could not be tried twice for the same crime, although the burden to raise the issue was on the defendant. Given the speed of trials, it is likely that many defendants neglected to raise this objection. Colonial trials were no slower than their English contemporaries, which implies that the defense was not raised by them either.

By the eve of the American Revolution, many colonies had fully established criminal bars, and trials had begun to take the shape of the modern adversarial trial. A prime example was the trial of British soldiers following the Boston Massacre. John Adams offered to represent the defendants out of a belief that they could receive a fair trial only with legal representation, a staple of the modern criminal trial, but still rare in contemporary England. Although the trial would not have had the formal evidentiary or discovery rules of a modern trial, its basic form would have been familiar to a modern observer of criminal trials.

Punishment in the Colonies

As in England, most serious crimes were punishable by death, which was carried out by hanging. In most colonies, executions and the administration of all punishments were carried out by the county sheriff. However, many colonies hired executioners to conduct the hangings with the sheriff supervising. The desire to have the condemned person repent before their execution was in place in New England from the initial executions and became standard in the rest of the colonies by the late 17th century. The final confession, and sometimes a sermon based on the condemned's life and crimes, were also often preached and then published as a warning to future miscreants. In New England, these confessions and sermons also assisted in reestablishing order in society by having the wayward citizen request God's mercy and apologize for the crimes, thereby being reintegrated into society spiritually, even if executed physically. In England and the southern colonies, these statements lost their religious overtones in the early 18th century and became an early form of lurid, true-life crime stories, making heroes of such men as the notorious thief and jailbreaker Jack Sheppard.

The desire to have the accused confess and thereby rejoin society reflected New England society's focus on stability over retribution in meting out punishment. In the early colonial period, this led to a focus on noncapital punishments and shaming methods. The most popular forms of punishment were corporal punishments, usually flogging or birching, and the pillory. Men, women, and children were all subject to the same punishments, although the manner in which they were carried out differed according to gender, age, and social rank. Adults were usually punished in public, although there were instances of women of high social standing being chastised in private.

Children, male and female, were usually subjected to flogging, especially in New England colonies. These punishments would often occur privately in their homes or in the magistrate's home by their parents, although it would often take place in front of a town magistrate or appointee. If the crime was minor, or if the child confessed, then the child would be turned over to the parents for private correction in the home. If the child was an apprentice and of good character, he or she might be turned over for private correction to the master. Parents and masters were allowed to punish their wards to preserve the social hierarchy of the family, which was seen as the basis for colonial society. If a parent was thought unfit to chastise their child, then the issue of removing the child to a home that would instill discipline was raised. Servants or apprentices who were out of their own homes were the most likely to be punished in public, as there was less incentive to preserve a family unit. Children also could be removed from parents who were thought unfit. The goal was not only to punish the wayward child, but also to correct for future behavior and ensure that they became good members of the church and society.

Being made to stand the pillory or in stocks was used as a shaming practice throughout the colonies. As in England, the person was usually made to stand for one market day. In Massachusetts, the guilty person was sometimes made to stand the pillory after church services in order for the entire town to observe them. It is not clear if colonial perpetrators were subjected to the physical attacks endured by many English convicts as they stood the pillory or sat the stocks. In many instances, particularly sexual crimes or frauds, the convicted person was made to wear a sign describing their crime. A related punishment adopted in New England was the simple requirement that the convicted person had to stand up before the congregation or town meeting to describe their transgression and request forgiveness for it. This was usually used for minor infractions such as swearing, drunkenness, or Sabbath breaking. Later, the punishment could be combined with private correction for children or flogging for adults.

Flogging was the most common corporal punishment in the colonies and was usually limited to the biblical precept of 39 lashes, although there were cases of 60 being imposed in Virginia. Women of higher social status might also be flogged in front of few witnesses, usually their husbands or fathers and a few magistrates. Women of lower social status and almost all men were flogged in public. For reasons of modesty, women were usually flogged with their clothing on and men would be stripped to the waist. Some southern colonies, such as Maryland, prohibited the flogging of gentlemen as it was beneath their station. In that sense, the New England colonies were more egalitarian in their punishments. With the introduction of slavery, it became common practice for free men to be flogged with their shirts on, while slaves—male or female—were stripped to the waist. In New England colonies, flogging was the most common punishment inflicted, although it was often combined with a public apology before the town congregation. The flogging was typically carried out with a single stick or bundle of birch sticks, while in the southern colonies, a single stick or whip was more common.

There were a few instances of branding on the hand, which suggests that benefit of clergy may have been in practice in the colonies. However, no mention of the benefit was included in the records, so it is possible that, in a corruption of the technical English procedure, branding was the sentence. In Maryland, hog thieves were branded with an "H" on their shoulders after the second conviction. There were also a few instances of maiming as punishment in the middle and southern colonies. In Maryland, one of three burglars convicted before 1700 had his ear cut off as punishment for his crime, but this does not appear to have been a widespread practice. This is most likely due to the association of

"The Boston Massacre" in an engraving after the painting by Alonzo Chappel, 1868. On March 5, 1770, British soldiers, who were occupying Boston as a police force, fired into a crowd of Boston citizens after hostilities reached the boiling point. On March 27, the eight soldiers, Captain Preston, and four civilians who were alleged to have fired shots were all indicted for murder.

maiming penalties with the Star Chamber. Slaves were routinely subjected to maiming well after the practice was in decline in both England and the colonies.

The punishment of transportation did not exist in the colonies, as there was nowhere to transport the person. There were instances of a troublesome servant being sold to another owner, but this was not common. The courts could also reassign a servant due to neglect, abuse, or simply because they felt that the relationship was the root of the problem. However, having additional time added to their indenture was usually used as a punishment against servants who had committed a crime against their masters. Free men sometimes faced servitude if they could not afford to pay fines levied against them or if they were perceived as being idle.

Executions were carried out by hanging, regardless of the crime committed or social standing. As beheading was reserved for nobility in the common law, the lack of noblemen is the simple explanation for the absence of this form of punishment in the colonies. However, the lack of executions by burning may also point to the fact that the colonists were either attempting to create a universal criminal code or simplify the execution process. There were women convicted of petite treason who should have been burned under the common law, but this was never done. Similarly, no heretic was ever burned for their crime, although several were hanged. The atmosphere surrounding executions was far more somber in the colonies than in England, where salesmen, pickpockets, and conmen plied their trade before the scaffold and crowds jeered the condemned.

Primary Documents for Colonial Criminal Law

The archival sources available for colonial American law are extensive. A large portion of the archival material for colonies such as Massachusetts, Virginia, and New York have been microfilmed or printed in bound volumes. This has led to a proliferation of studies on the states that contain the most widely distributed materials. Many of the southern colonies have not had their records extensively published and have therefore generated far fewer case studies. There are numerous online sources that reproduce colonial charters and some of their legal codes. The Colonial Office papers have been printed for the entire era and contain the Privy Council's correspondence with colonial governors. As many colonial judges relied on justice of the peace manuals printed in England and shipped to the colonies, they are also a good source of information on the workings of colonial law in rural areas. In addition, copies of Edward Coke's commentaries were available in the larger colonial towns. English legal pamphlets, which also circulated to the colonies, would have been another source for contemporary lawyers and can shed some light onto the colonial legal system.

John Felipe Acevedo
University of Chicago

1609 PRIMARY DOCUMENT

Excerpt of Samuel de Champlain's Introduction of Firearms to the Indians

An explorer, diplomat, trader, and soldier, Samuel de Champlain established a trading post at Quebec in 1608 and became the central figure in the early history of New France and its fur trade. His multivolume memoirs about his life in New France helped draw interest to the colony while disseminating important information such as the need for the French to ally themselves with some of the local tribes. Here he chronicles the local Indians' first experience with firearms.

Our Indians all night long also kept their canoes close to one another and tied to poles in order not to get separated, but to fight all together in case of need. We were on the water within bowshot of their barricades. And when they were armed, and everything in order, they sent two canoes which they had separated from the rest, to learn from their enemies whether they wished to fight, and these replied that they had no other desire, but that for the moment nothing could be seen and that it was necessary to wait for daylight in order to distinguish one another. They said that as soon as the sun should rise, they would attack us, and to this our Indians agreed. Meanwhile the whole night was spent in dances and songs on both sides, with many insults and other remarks, such as the lack of courage of our side, how little we could resist or do against them, and that when daylight came our people would learn all this to their ruin. Our side too was not lacking in retort, telling the enemy that they would see such deeds of arms as they had never seen, and a great deal of other talk, such as is usual at the siege of a city. Having sung, danced, and flung words at one another for some time, when daylight came, my companions and I were still hidden, lest the enemy should see us, getting our firearms ready as best we could, being however still separated, each in a canoe of the Montagnais Indians. After we were armed with light weapons, we took, each of us, an arquebus and went ashore.

I saw the enemy come out of their barricade to the number of two hundred, in appearance strong, robust men. They came slowly to meet us with a gravity and calm which I admired; and at their head were three chiefs. Our Indians likewise advanced in similar order, and told me that those who had the three big plumes were the chiefs, and that there were only these three, whom you could recognize by these plumes, which were larger than those of their companions; and I was to do what I could to kill them. I promised them to do all in my power, and told them that I was very sorry they could not understand me, so that I might direct their method of attacking the enemy, all of whom undoubtedly we should thus defeat; but that there was no help for it, and that I was very glad to show them, as soon as the engagement began, the courage and readiness which were in me.

As soon as we landed, our Indians began to run some two hundred yards towards their enemies, who stood firm and had not yet noticed my white companions who went off into the woods with some Indians. Our Indians began to call to me with loud cries; and to make way for me they divided into two groups, and put me ahead some twenty yards, and I marched on until I was within some thirty yards of the enemy, who as soon as they caught sight of me halted and gazed at me and I at them. When I saw them make a move to draw their bows upon us, I took aim with my arquebus and shot straight at one of the three chiefs, and with this shot two fell to the ground and one of their companions was wounded who died thereof a little later. I had put four bullets into my arquebus. As soon as our people saw this shot so favourable for them, they began to shout so loudly that one could not have heard it thunder, and meanwhile the arrows flew thick on both sides. The Iroquois were much astonished that two men should have been killed so quickly, although they were provided with shields made of cotton thread woven together and wood, which were proof against their arrows. This frightened them greatly. As I was reloading my arquebus, one of my companions fired a shot from within the woods, which astonished them again so much that, seeing their chiefs dead, they lost courage and took to flight, abandoning the field and their fort, and fleeing into the depth of the forest, whither I pursued them and laid low still more of them. Our Indians also killed several and took ten or twelve prisoners. The remainder fled with the wounded. Of our Indians fifteen or sixteen were wounded with arrows, but these were quickly healed.

After we had gained the victory, our Indians wasted time in taking a large quantity of Indian corn and meal belonging to the enemy, as well as their shields, which they had left behind, the better to run. Having feasted, danced, and sung, we three hours later set off for home with the prisoners. The place where this attack took place is in 43° and some minutes of latitude, and was named Lake Champlain.

Source: de Champlain, Samuel. *The Works of Samuel de Champlain*. Vol. 2. Toronto: Champlain Society, 1925.
http://historymatters.gmu.edu/d/6594

See Articles: History of Crime and Punishment in America: Colonial; Native Americans; New York.

1610 to 1611
PRIMARY DOCUMENT

Laws of the Colony of Virginia

The permanent English settlement in the New World began with Jamestown, Virginia, in 1607, established by the Virginia Company of London, a joint-stock company chartered by King James I the previous year. These early laws, the first English laws in the Western Hemisphere, were neither created by legislators nor enforced by courts, but were adopted by orders of the governor and, notably, did not provide for trial by jury nor other elements of English common law.

Articles, Laws, and Orders, Divine, Politique, and Martiall for the Colony in Virginea: first established by Sir Thomas Gates Knight, Lieutenant General, the 24th of May 1610. exemplified and approved by the Right Honourable Sir Thomas West Knight, Lord Lawair, Lord Governour and Captaine General the 12th of June 1610. Againe exemplified and enlarged by Sir Thomas Dale Knight, Marshall, and Deputie Governour, the 22nd of June 1611.

2. That no man speake impiously or maliciously, against the holy and blessed Trinitie, or any of the three persons, that is to say, against God the Father, God the Son, and God the Holy Ghost, or against the knowne Articles of the Christian faith, upon paine of death.
3. That no man blaspheme God's holy name upon paine of death, or use unlawful oaths, taking the name of God in vaine, curse or banne, upon paine of severe punishment for the first offense so committed, and the second, to have a bodkin thrust through his tongue, and if he continue the blaspheming of God's holy name, for the third time so offending, he shall be brought to a martiall court, and there receive censure of death for his offense.
4. No man shall use any traitorous words against his Majesties Person, or royall authority upon paine of death. . . . .
14. No man shall give any disgracefull words, or commit any act to the disgrace of any person in this Colonie, or any part thereof, upon paine of being tied head and feete together, upon the guard everie night for the space of one moneth, besides to bee publikely disgraced himself, and be made uncapable ever after to possesse any place, or execute any office in this imployment.
15. No man of what condition soever shall barter, trucke, or trade with the Indians,

except he be thereunto appointed by lawful authority, upon paine of death. . . .

31. What man or woman soever, shall rob any garden, publike or private, being set to weed the same, or willfully pluck up therein any roote, herbe, or flower, to spoile and waste or steale the same, or robbe any vineyard, or gather up the grapes, or steale any eares of the corne growing, whether in the ground belonging to the same fort or towne where he dwelleth, or in any other, shall be punished with death.

The Marshall Lawes
1. No man shall willingly absent himself, when hee is summoned to take the oath of Supremacy, upon paine of death. . .
21. He that draweth his sword upon the Court of Guard, shall suffer death by the Armes which he weareth.
22. Hee that should draw his sword in a towne of Garrison, or in a Campe shall lose his right hand.
23. That souldier that shall goe out of the Fort, Towne or Campe other then by the ordinary guards, issues, waies, or ports, shall suffer death by the Armes which he carrieth. . . .
31. No man shall depart from his guard without leave of his officer, upon paine of punishment: and who so shall be set Centinell, shall not depart from it until he be relieved, nor sleepe thereof upon paine of death. . . .
38. No Souldier may speake or have any private conference with any of the salvages, without leave of his Captaine, nor his Captaine without leave of his chiefe Officer, upon paine of death.

Source: Waldrep, Christopher and Michael A. Bellesiles. *Documenting American Violence*. New York: Oxford University Press, 2006. Strachey, William, comp. *For the Colony in Virginea Britannia. Lawes Divine, Morall and Martiall, &c*. London for Walter Burre, 1612.

See Articles: History of Crime and Punishment in America: Colonial; Slavery; Virginia.

Trial and Interrogation of Anne Hutchinson

Anne Hutchinson (1591–1643) was an English Puritan who emigrated to Boston in 1634 after her local preacher was forced out of England. She began giving religious talks, commenting on (and sometimes criticizing) recent sermons for audiences, which included Governor Harry Vane. When Vane lost his reelection to one of Hutchinson's critics, John Winthrop, she stood trial for traducing (slandering) local ministers. The Mr. Wheelwright mentioned in the document is her ally and brother-in-law.

The Examination of Mrs. Ann Hutchinson at the Court at Newtown.
Mr. Winthrop, governor. Mrs. Hutchinson, you are called here as one of those that have troubled the peace of the commonwealth and the churches here; you are known to be a woman that hath had a great share in the promoting and divulging of those opinions that are causes of this trouble, and . . . you have spoken divers things as we have been informed very prejudicial to the honour of the churches and ministers thereof, and you have maintained a meeting and an assembly in your house that hath been condemned by the general assembly as a thing not tolerable nor comely in the sight of God nor fitting for your sex, and notwithstanding that was cried down you have continued the same, therefore we have thought good to send for you to understand how things are, that if you be in an erroneous way we may reduce you that so you may become a profitable member here among us, otherwise if you be obstinate in your course that then the court may take such course that you may trouble us no further, therefore I would intreat you to express whether you do not hold and assent in practice to those opinions and factions that have been handled in court already, that is to say,

whether you do not justify Mr. Wheelwright's sermon and the petition.

Mrs. Hutchinson. I am called here to answer before you but I hear no things laid to my charge.

Source: Hutchinson, Thomas. *History of the Colony and Province of Massachusetts.* Boston, 1767. Some spelling has been modernized.

See Articles: Boston, Massachusetts; Colonial Courts; Massachusetts; Puritans; Religion and Crime, History of.

1641
PRIMARY DOCUMENT

Plymouth Colony Adultery Case

Early New England laws of sexual conduct were derived from the biblical Old Testament, especially before the codification of laws provided explicit Plymouth laws from which to refer. Adultery was treated as a serious offense but was difficult to prove without a confession. As here, 17th-century sentences often involved corporal punishment or public humiliation in order to forestall the expense of building and maintaining a jail.

December 7, 1641 Governor Bradford (Plymouth Colony Record 2:28):

Forasmuch, as Thomas Bray, of Yarmouth, a single person, and Anne, the wyfe of Francis Linceford, haue committed the act of adultery and vncleanesse, and haue diuers tymes layne in one bed together in the absence of her husband, which hath beene confessed by both parties in the publike Court, the Court doth censure them as followeth: That they be both seuerely whipt immediately at the publik post, [and] that they shall weare (whilst they remayne in the gouernment) two letters, namely, an AD, for Adulterers, daily, vpon the outside of their vppermost garment, in a most emenent place thereof; and if they shalbe found at any tyme in any towne or place within the gouerment without them so worne vpon their vppermost garment as aforesaid, that then the constable of the towne or place shall take them, or wither of them, omitting so to weare the said two letters, and shall forthwith whip them for their negligence, and shall cause them to be immediately put on againe, and so worne by them and either of them; and also that they shalbe both whipt at Yarmouth, publikly, where the offence was committed, in such fitt season as shalbe thought meete by Mr. Edmond Freeman [and] such others as are authorized for the keepeing of the Courts in these partes.

Source: http://www.histarch.uiuc.edu/Plymouth/Lauria2.html#II

See Articles: Adultery; Colonial Courts; Fornication Laws; Massachusetts; Morality; Puritans.

1642
PRIMARY DOCUMENT

Capital Laws of New England

The codification of laws was necessary to ensure consistent court rulings. These Capital Laws appeared in a larger body of legal code called The Body of Liberties, which was comparable in scope to the Magna Carta. Its assembly was a collective effort spearheaded by the leaders of the colonial government and included the input of freemen and elders throughout the colony. Unlike the rest of the text, the Capital Laws specifically referenced biblical verses from which the laws were derived.

Capital Lawes of New-England, as they stand now in force in the Common-Wealth. By the Court, in the Years 1641, 1642.

Capital Lawes, Established within the Jurisdiction of Massachusetts.

1. If any man after legall conviction, shall have or worship any other God, but the Lord God, he shall be put to death. Deut. 13:6, &c and 17:2, &c. Exodus 22:30.
2. If any man or woman be a Witch, that is, hath consulteth with a familiar spirit, they shall be put to death.
3. If any persons shall blaspheme the Name of God the Father, Sonne, or Holy Ghost, with direct, expresse, presumptuous, or high-handed blasphemy, or shall curse God in the like manner, he shall be put to death.
4. [Murder by premeditated hatred]
5. [Murder by anger or passion]
6. [Murder by guile or poisoning]
7. If man or woman shall lye with any beast, or bruit creature, by carnall copulation, they shall surely be put to death; and the beast shall be slaine, and buried. Lev. 20:15, 16.
8. If a man lyeth with mankinde, as he lyeth with a woman, both of them have committed abomination, they both shall surely be put to death. Lev. 20:13.
9. If any person committeth adultery with a married, or espoused wife, the Adulterer and the Adulteresse, shall surely be put to death. Lev. 20:10, 18, 20; Deut. 22:23, 24.
10. If any man shall unlawfully have carnall copulation with any woman childe under ten years old, either with, or without consent, he shall be put to death.
11. If any man shall forcibly, and without consent, ravish any maid or woman that is lawfully married or contracted, he shall be put to death. Deut. 22:25, &c.
12. If any man shall ravish any maid or single woman (committing carnall copulation with her by force, against her will) that is above the age of ten yeares; he shall be either punished with death, or with some other grievous punishment, according to the circumstances, at the discretion of the Judges: . . .

Source: Broadside. Published in New England, 1643. http://www.swarthmore.edu/SocSci/bdorsey1/41docs/50-cou.html

See Articles: Adultery; *Book of the General Laws & Libertyes*; Colonial Courts; Massachusetts; Morality; Puritans.

1649 PRIMARY DOCUMENT

Maryland Act of Religion

Maryland was founded by Cecilius Calvert as a safe haven for Catholics such as himself who were persecuted in England. An early document in the development of religious freedom in the United States, this act guaranteed religious freedom for trinitarian Christians (including but not limited to Catholics), while criminalizing the denial of the divinity of Christ. Many Protestants opposed the law on the grounds that allegiance to Calvert would require allegiance to the pope.

Assembly Proceedings, April 2-21, 1649

Enacted and made at a General Sessions of the said Assembly held at St Marys on the one and twentieth day of April Anno Dom. 1649 as followeth viz:

An Act Concerning Religion

Forasmuch as in a well governed and Christian Commonwealth matters concerning Religion and the honor of God ought in the first place to bee taken, into serious consideration and endeavoured to bee settled. Be it therefore ordered and enacted by the Right Honorable Cecilius Lord Baron of Baltimore absolute Lord and Proprietary of this Province with the advise and consent of this Generall Assembly. That whatsoever person or persons within this Province and the Islands thereunto belonging shall from henceforth blaspheme God, that is Curse him, or deny our Saviour Jesus Christ to bee the sonne of God, or shall deny the holy Trinity the father sonne and holy Ghost, or the Godhead of any of the said Three persons of the Trinity or the unity of the Godhead, or shall use or utter any reproachfull Speeches, words or language concerning the said Holy Trinity, or any of the said three persons thereof, shall be punished with death and confiscation or forfeiture of all his or her lands and goods to the Lord Proprietary and his heires. And bee it also Enacted by the Authority and with the advise and assent aforesaid that whatsoever person or persons shall from henceforth use or utter any reproachfull words or Speeches concerning blessed Virgin Marv the Mother of Our Saviour or the holy Apostles or Evangelists or any of them shall in such case for the first offence forfeit to the said Lord Proprietary and his heirs Lords and Proprietaries of this Province the sume of five pound Sterling or the value thereof to be Levyed on the goods and chattells of every such person soe offending, but in case such Offender or Offenders, shall not then have goods and chattells sufficient for the satisfying of such forfeiture, or that the same bee not otherwise speedily satisfyed that then such Offender Or Offenders Shall be publiquely whipt and bee imprisoned during the pleasure, of the Lord Proprietary or the Lieut. or chief Governor of' this Province for the time being. And that every such Offender Or Offenders for every second offence shall forfeit tenne Pound or the value thereof to bee levyed as aforesaid, or in case Such offender or Offenders shall not then have goods and chattells within this Province sufficient for that purpose then to bee publiquely and severely whipt and imprisoned as before is expressed. And that every person or persons before mentioned offending herein the third time, shall for such third Offence forfeit all his lands and Goods and bee for ever banished and expelled out of this Province.

And be it also further Enacted by the same authority advise and assent that whatsoever person or persons shall from henceforth upon any occasion of Offence or otherwise in a reproachful manner or Way declare call or denominate any person or persons whatsoever inhabiting residing traffiqueing trading or commerceing within this Province or within any the Ports, Harbors, Creeks or Havens to the same belonging an heritick, Scismatick, Idolator, puritan, Independant, Prespiterian popish priest, Jesuite, Jesuited papist, Lutheran, Calvenist Anabaptist, Brownist. Antinomian, Barrowist, Roundhead, Separatist or any other name or terme in a reproachfull manner relating to matter of Religion shall for every such Offence forfeit and loose the some or tenne shillings sterling or the value thereof to bee levyed on the goods and chattells of every such Offender and Offenders, the one half thereof to be forfeited and paid unto the person and persons of whom such reproachfull words are or shall be spoken or uttered, and the other half thereof to the Lord Proprietary and his heires Lords and Proprietaries of this Province, But if Such person or persons who shall at any time utter or speake any such reproachfull words or Language shall not have Goods or Chattells sufficient and overt within this Province to bee taken to satisfie the penalty aforesaid or that the same bee not other speedily satisfyed, that then the person or persons soe offending shall be publickly whipt, and shall suffer imprisonment without bail or maineprise untill he she or they respectively shall satisfy the party soe offended or greived by such reproachfull Language by asking him or her respectively forgivenes publiquely for such his Offence before the Magistrate or chief Officer or Officers of the Towne or place where such Offence shall be given.

And be it further likewise Enacted by the Authority and consent aforesaid that every person and persons within this Province that shall at any time hereafter prophane the Sabbath or Lords day called Sunday by frequent swearing, drunkennes or by any uncivill or disorderly recreation or by working on that day when absolute necessity doth not require it shall for every such first offence forfeit 2s 6d sterling or the value thereof, and for the second offence 5s sterling or the value thereof, and for the third offence and soe for every time lie shall offend in like manner afterwards 10s sterling or the value thereof. And in case such offender and offenders shall not have sufficient goods or chattells within this Province to any of the said Penalties respectively hereby imposed for prophaning the Sabbath or Lords day called Sunday as aforesaid, That in Every such case the party see offending shall for the first and second offence in that kinde be imprisoned till he or she shall publickly in open Court before the cheife Commander

Judge or Magistrate, of that County Towne or precinct where such offence shall be committed acknowledg the Scandall and offence he hath in that respect given against God and the good and civill Government of this Province. And for the third offence and for every time after shall also bee publickly whipt.

And whereas the inforceing of the conscience in matters of Religion hath frequently fallen out to be of dangerous Consequence in those commonwealthes where it hath been practised, and for the more quiet and peaceable government of this Province, and the better to preserve mutuall Love and amity amongst the Inhabitants thereof. Be it Therefore also by the Lord Proprietary with the advise and consent of this Assembly Ordeyned & enacted (except as in this present Act is before Declared and sett forth) that no person or persons whatsoever within this Province, or the Islands, Ports, Harbors, Creeks, or havens thereunto belonging professing to believe in Jesus Christ, shall from henceforth bee any ways troubled, molested or discountenanced for or in respect of his or her religion nor in the free exercise thereof within this Province or the Islands thereunto belonging nor any way compelled to the belief or exercise of any other Religion against his or her consent, so as they be not unfaithfull to the Lord Proprietary, or molest or conspire against the civill Government, established or to bee established in this Province under him or his heires. And that all & every person and persons that shall presume Contrary to this Act and the true intent and meaning thereof directly or indirectly either in person or estate willfully to wrong disturbe trouble or molest any person whatsoever within this Province professing to believe in Jesus Christ for or ill respect of his or her religion or the free exercise thereof within this Province other than is provided for in this Act that such person or persons so offending, shall be compelled to pay trebble damages to the party so wronged or molested, and for every such offence shall also forfeit 20s sterling in money or the Value thereof, half thereof for the use of the Lord Proprietary, and his heires Lords and Proprietaries of this Province, and the other half for the use of the party so wronged or molested as a aforesaid. Or if the party so offending as aforesaid shall refuse or bee unable to recompense the party so_wronged, or to satisfy such fine or forfeiture, then such Offender shall be severely punished by publick whipping & imprisonment during pleasure of the Lord Proprietary, or his Lieutenant or cheife Governor of this Province for the time being without baile or maineprise . . .

Source: Browne, William Hand, Clayton Colman Hall, Bernard C. Steiner, and Maryland Historical Society. *Archives of Maryland*, Vol. 1. Baltimore: Maryland Historical Society, 1883. http://www.swarthmore.edu/SocSci/bdorsey1/41docs/56-mar.html

See Articles: Corporal Punishment; Maryland; Maryland Toleration Act of 1649; Morality; Religion and Crime, History of.

1662 PRIMARY DOCUMENT

Virginia Slave Laws

Virginia was one of the first colonies to pass laws explicitly approving the institution of slavery, which even in the 17th century was widespread enough to bring about the need for these laws. They defined the children of slave mothers as slaves and gave slave owners broad powers of discipline over their slaves. In 1691, this law was amended to make children of white mothers and black fathers indentured servants (as well as the mothers, if they could not pay a fee).

December 1662

Whereas some doubts have arisen whether children got by any Englishman upon a Negro woman should be slave or free, *be it therefore enacted and declared by this present Grand Assembly,* that all children born in this country shall be held bond or free only according to the condition of the mother; and that if any Christian shall commit fornication with a Negro man or woman, he or she so offending shall pay double the fines imposed by the former act.

September 1667
Whereas some doubts have risen whether children that are slaves by birth, and by the charity and piety of their owners made partakers of the blessed sacrament of baptism, should by virtue of their baptism be made free, *it is enacted and declared by this Grand Assembly, and the auhority thereof,* that the conferring of baptism does not alter the condition of the person as to his bondage or freedom; that diverse masters, freed from this doubt may more carefully endeavor the propagation of Christianity by permitting children, though slaves, or chose of greater growth if capable, to be admitted to that sacrament.

September 1668
Whereas it has been questioned whether servants running away may be punished with corporal punishment by their master or magistrate, since the act already made gives the master satisfaction by prolonging their time by service, *it is declared and enacted by this Assembly* that moderate corporal punishment inflicted by master or magistrate upon a runaway servant shall not deprive the master of the satisfaction allowed by the law, the one being as necessary to reclaim them from persisting in that idle course as the other is just to repair the damages sustained by the master.

October 1669
Whereas the only law in force for the punishment of refractory servants resisting their master, mistress, or overseer cannot be inflicted upon Negroes, nor the obstinacy of many of them be suppressed by other than violent means, *be it enacted and declared by this Grand Assembly* if any slave resists his master (or other by his master's order correcting him) and by the extremity of the correction should chance to die, that his death shall not be accounted a felony, but the master (or that other person appointed by the master to punish him) be acquitted from molestation, since it cannot be presumed that premeditated malice (which alone makes murder a felony) should induce any man to destroy his own estate.

Source: Hening, William Waller. *Statutes at Large; Being a Collection of all the Laws of Virginia,* Vol. 11. Richmond, VA: 1809–23.
http://www.swarthmore.edu/SocSci/bdorsey1/41docs/24-sla.html

See Articles: Corporal Punishment; Slavery; Slavery, Law of; Virginia.

1676
PRIMARY DOCUMENT

Bacon's Rebellion: The Declaration

In 1676, Virginian planter Nathaniel Bacon led a rebellion against Governor William Berkeley, who refused to retaliate after a series of Indian attacks on the frontier. It was the first American rebellion to involve frontiersmen, who formed part of the mob of about 1,000 whites and blacks. Bacon obtained a militia commission at gunpoint, empowering him to lead an attack on the Indians, and his men burned and looted Jamestown. Twenty-three rebels were hanged, and Berkeley was recalled to England.

1. For having, upon specious pretenses of public works, raised great unjust taxes upon the commonalty for the advancement of private favorites and other sinister ends, but no visible effects in any measure adequate; for not having, during this long time of his government, in any measure advanced this hopeful colony either by fortifications, towns, or trade.
2. For having abused and rendered contemptible the magistrates of justice by advancing to places of judicature scandalous and ignorant favorites.
3. For having wronged his Majesty's prerogative and interest by assuming monopoly of the beaver trade and for having in it

unjust gain betrayed and sold his Majesty's country and the lives of his loyal subjects to the barbarous heathen.
4. For having protected, favored, and emboldened the Indians against his Majesty's loyal subjects, never contriving, requiring, or appointing any due or proper means of satisfaction for their many invasions, robberies, and murders committed upon us.
5. For having, when the army of English was just upon the track of those Indians, who now in all places burn, spoil, murder and when we might with ease have destroyed them who then were in open hostility, for then having expressly countermanded and sent back our army by passing his word for the peaceable demeanor of the said Indians, who immediately prosecuted their evil intentions, committing horrid murders and robberies in all places, being protected by the said engagement and word past of him the said Sir William Berkeley, having ruined and laid desolate a great part of his Majesty's country, and have now drawn themselves into such obscure and remote places and are by their success so emboldened and confirmed by their confederacy so strengthened that the cries of blood are in all places, and the terror and consternation of the people so great, are now become not only difficult but a very formidable enemy who might at first with ease have been destroyed.
6. And lately, when, upon the loud outcries of blood, the assembly had, with all care, raised and framed an army for the preventing of further mischief and safeguard of this his Majesty's colony.
7. For having, with only the privacy of some few favorites without acquainting the people, only by the alteration of a figure, forged a commission, by we know not what hand, not only without but even against the consent of the people, for the raising and effecting civil war and destruction, which being happily and without bloodshed prevented; for having the second time attempted the same, thereby calling down our forces from the defense of the frontiers and most weakly exposed places.
8. For the prevention of civil mischief and ruin amongst ourselves while the barbarous enemy in all places did invade, murder, and spoil us, his Majesty's most faithful subjects.

Of this and the aforesaid articles we accuse Sir William Berkeley as guilty of each and every one of the same, and as one who has traitorously attempted, violated, and injured his Majesty's interest here by a loss of a great part of this his colony and many of his faithful loyal subjects by him betrayed and in a barbarous and shameful manner exposed to the incursions and murder of the heathen. And we do further declare these the ensuing persons in this list to have been his wicked and pernicious councilors, confederates, aiders, and assisters against the commonalty in these our civil commotions.

Sir Henry Chichley
William Claiburne Junior
Lieut. Coll. Christopher Wormeley
Thomas Hawkins
William Sherwood
Phillip Ludwell
John Page Clerke
Robert Beverley
John Cluffe Clerke
Richard Lee
John West
Thomas Ballard
Hubert Farrell
William Cole
Thomas Reade
Richard Whitacre
Matthew Kempe
Nicholas Spencer
Joseph Bridger
John West, Hubert Farrell, Thomas Reade, Math. Kempe

And we do further demand that the said Sir William Berkeley with all the persons in this list be forthwith delivered up or surrender themselves within four days after the notice hereof, or otherwise we declare as follows.

That in whatsoever place, house, or ship, any of the said persons shall reside, be hid, or protected, we declare the owners, masters, or inhabitants of the said places to be confederates and traitors to the people and the estates of them is also of all the aforesaid persons to be confiscated. And this we, the commons of Virginia, do declare, desiring a firm union amongst ourselves that we may jointly and with one accord defend ourselves against the common enemy. And let not the faults of the guilty be the reproach of the innocent, or the faults or crimes of the oppressors divide and separate us who have suffered by their oppressions.

These are, therefore, in his Majesty's name, to command you forthwith to seize the persons above mentioned as traitors to the King and country and them to bring to Middle Plantation and there to secure them until further order, and, in case of opposition, if you want any further assistance you are forthwith to demand it in the name of the people in all the counties of Virginia.

Nathaniel Bacon
General by Consent of the people.
William Sherwood

Source: "Declaration of Nathaniel Bacon in the Name of the People of Virginia, July 30, 1676." *Massachusetts Historical Society Collections*, v.9 (1871). http://historymatters.gmu.edu/d/5800

See Articles: Civil Disobedience; Political Dissidents; Riots.

1689 PRIMARY DOCUMENT

Samuel Prince Describes the Boston Uprising

From 1684 to 1686, English kings revoked the charter of the Massachusetts Bay Colony and assigned its territory to the Dominion of New England, appointing Edmund Andros the governor. Andros restricted town meetings and bolstered the Church of England. In 1689, the Boston militia and many citizens revolted, arresting dominion officials and Church of England members and reinstating colonial governments. The dominion was soon officially dissolved.

Boston, April 22, 1689.
Honored Sir,
I knew not any thing of what was intended, till it was begun; yet being at the north end of the town, where I saw boys run along the street with clubs in their hands, encouraging one another to fight, I began to mistrust what was intended; and, hasting towards the town-dock, I soon saw men running for their arms: but, ere I got to the Red Lion, I was told that Captain George and the master of the frigate was seized, and secured in Mr. Colman's house at the North End, and, when I came to the town-dock, I understood that Boolifant and some others with him were laid hold of; and then immediately the drums began to beat, and the people hasting and running, some with and some for arms, Young Dudley' and Colonel Lidgit with some difficulty attained to the Fort. And, as I am informed, the poor boy cried very much; whom the Governor sent immediately on an errand, to request the four ministers, Mr. Joylife, and one or two more, to come to him at the Fort, pretending that by them he might still the people, not thinking it safe for him at that time to come to them; and they returned him the like answer. Now, by this time, all the persons whom they concluded not to be for their side were seized and secured, except some few that had hid themselves; which afterwards were found, and dealt by as the rest. The Governor, with Palmer, Randolph, Lidgit, West, and one or two more, were in the Fort. All the companies were soon rallied together at the Town House, where assembled Captain Wintroup, Shrimpton, Page, and many other substantial men, to consult of matters; in which time the old Governor came among them, at whose appearance there was a great shout by the soldiers.

Soon after, the king's jack was set up at the Fort, and a pair of colors at Beacon Hill:

which gave notice to some thousands of soldiers on Charlestown side that the controversy was now to be ended; and multitudes would have been there, but that there was no need. The frigate, upon the tidings of the news, put out all her flags and pennants, and opened all her ports, and with all speed made ready for fight, under the command of the lieutenant-swearing that he would die before she should be taken; although the captain sent to him, that if he shot one shoot, or did any hurt, they would kill him, whom they had already seized. But he, not regarding that, continued under those resolutions all that day. Now, about four of clock in the afternoon, orders were given to go and demand the Fort; which hour the soldiers thought long for: and, had it not been just at that nick, the Governor and all the crew had made their escape on board the frigate—a barge being sent for them. But the soldiers, being so near, got the barge. The army divided, and part came up on the back side of the Fort, and part went underneath the hill to the lower battery, or sconce, where the red-coats were; who, immediately upon their approach, retired up the Fort to their master, who rebuked them for not firing at our soldiers, and, as I am informed, beat some of them. One of them, being a Dutchman, said to him, "What the Devil should I fight against a thousand men?" and so ran into the house.

When the soldiers came to the battery, or sconce, they presently turned the great guns about, and mounted them against the Fort, which did much daunt all those within; and were so void of fear, that I presume, had they within the Fort been resolute to have lost their lives in fight, they might have killed an hundred of us at once—being so thick together before the mouths of their cannons at the Fort, all loaden with small shot: but God prevented it. Then they demanded a surrender; which was denied them till Mr. West and another should first go to the Council, and, after their return, we should have an answer whether to fight or no.

And accordingly they did: and, upon their return, they came forth, and went disarmed to the Town House; and from thence, some to the close jail, and he under a guard in Mr. Usher's house. The next day, they sent the two colonels' to demand of him a surrender of the Castle, which he resolved not to give: but they told him, if he would not give it presently under hand and seal, that he must expect to be delivered up to the rage of the people, who doubtless would put him to death; so leaving him. But he sent and told them that he would, and did so; and so they went down, and it was surrendered to them with cursing. So they brought them away, and made Captain Fairwether commander in it. Now, by this time that the men came back from the Castle, all the guns, both in ships and batteries, were brought to bear against the frigate—which were enough to have shattered her to pieces at once—resolving to have her. But as it is incident to corrupt nature to lay the blame of our evil deeds anywhere rather than on ourselves, so Captain George casts all the blame now upon that devil Randolph; for, had it not been for him, he had never troubled this good people. So, earnestly soliciting that he might not be constrained to surrender the ship-for, by so doing, both himself and all his men should lose their wages, which otherwise would be recovered in Eng. land-giving leave to go on board, and strike the topmasts, close up the ports, and bring the sails ashore; and so they did. The country people came armed into the town in the afternoon, in such rage and heat, that it made us all tremble to think what would follow: for nothing would pacify them but he must be bound in chains or cords, and put in a more secure place;' and that they would see done ere they went away, or else they would tear down the house where he was to the ground. And so, to satisfy them, he was guarded by them to the Fort. And I fear whether or no the matter of settling things under a new Government may not prove far more difficult than the getting from under the power of the former, except the Lord eminently appear in calming and quieting the disturbed spirits of people, whose duty certainly now is to condescend, comply, and every way study for peace. So prays the assured well-willer to New England's happiness,

S. P.

Counsellor Clark' writ a very grateful letter to Mr. Bullifant, intimating what a faithful friend he had been to said Bullifant, and withal desiring said Bullifant, that if Lhere should news come out of England of a change, which he hoped in God it never would (as to Government), that said Bullifant would do him the favor as to send him word with expedition, that so he might make his escape, living so dangerously in the midst of his enemies, who were even ready to devour him; and the merchants have gotten this pamphlet, and resolve forthwith to print it. Farewell!

Source: Andrews, Charles M. *Narratives of the Insurrections, 1675–1690*. New York: Charles Scribner's Sons, 1915. http://www.swarthmore.edu/SocSci/bdorsey1/41docs/42-pri.html

See Articles: Boston, Massachusetts; Civil Disobedience; Political Dissidents; Riots.

1692
PRIMARY DOCUMENT

Accusations Against Elizabeth Proctor

John and Elizabeth Proctor were among the men and women tried for witchcraft during the Salem witchcraft trials of 1692 to 1693, one of several periods of mass hysteria and witchcraft paranoia in Anglo-American history. The Proctors were likely accused because of their criticism of witchcraft claims against others. Both were sentenced to death, but Elizabeth was spared due to her pregnancy. Only 10 years later, public opinion changed enough to force the courts to issue an apology.

Goody nurs: Samuel Nurs. Doth testifei to all above written

Rebcah Preson & Mary Tarbel for Rebecca Nurse.

We whos names are underwritten cane teftifie if cald to it that Goodde Nurs. Have been troubled with an infirmity of body for many years, which the juree of women seem to be afraid it should be something else.

Rebcah Preson   Mary Tarbel

Rebecca Nurse petition to the Court.

To ye Honoured Court of Oryer and Terminer now fitting in Salem this 28th of June An° 1692.

The humble petission of Rebeccah Nurse of Salem Village.

Humbly Sheweth

That whereas sum women did sarch your petissioner at Salem, as I did then conceive for sum Supernaturall Marke, And then one of the sd. women which is known to be, the Moaste Antiente skilfull, prudent person of them all as to any such concerne: Did express hirself to be: of a Contrary opinion from the Reft, and Did then Declare that shee saw nothing in or aboute yoer Honors poare pettissioner But what might Arife from a Naturall cause: And I then rendered the said persons a sufficient knowne reason as to myself of the moueing cause thereof which was by Exceeding weaknesses: decending partly from an overture of Nature and difficult Exigences that hath Befallen me In the times of my travels, And therefore yor yettissioner: Humbley prayes I that you Honours would be pleased to Admitt of some other women to Enquire into this Great: concerne, those that are Moast Grand wise and skillfull: namely: Ms. Higginson senr: Ms. Durkstone: Ms. Woodbery two of them being Midwives: Ms. Porter: together with such others, as may be choasen on that Account: before I am Brought to my trial: All which I hoape yor, Honours will take into yor. Prudent Consideration and find it requisite soe to doe: for my Life Lyes now in yor Hands, under God: And Being Conscious of my owne Innocency. I humbly begg that I may have liberty to manifest it to the wourld partly by the Meanes abovesaid: And yor

Poare pettissioner shall Evermore pray as in duty bound & c.

Rebecca Nurse:
hir Marke †

Complaint vs. Elizabeth Proctor

This 4th April 1692 Capt. Jonathan Walcott, and Leut Nathanill Ingersoll personally appeared before us and exhibited theire complaint in behalf of theire Majestyes sor yselves and severall of theire Neighbours against Sarah cloyes of Selem Village and Eliz. Procter ye wife of Jno Procter of Salem for high suspition of severall acts of witchcraft donne or committed by ym upon ye bodyes of Abigail Williams and John Indian of ye family of Mr. Sam: Parris and Mary Walcott daughter of one of ye complainants and Ann butnam and Mercy Lewis. Of ye family of Thomas Putnam. Whereby great hurt and damage hath bin donne to ye bodyes of sd persons, and therefore craved Justice.

Warrant v. Elizabeth Proctor.

Salem. April 4th 1692

There Being complaint this day made (before us) by Capt. Jonath Walcott, and Lt. Nathaniell Ingersull, both of Salem Village, in behalf of theire Majesties for themselves and also for severall of their neighbors against Sarah Cloyse the wife of Peter Cloyce of Salem Village and Elizabeth Proctor the wife of John Proctor of Salem sarmes for high suspition of Sundry acts of witchcraft donne or committed by them upon the bodyes of Abigaile Williams and John Indian both of Mr. Sam: Parris his family of Salem Village and Mary Walcott daughter of one of the above said complainants and Ann Putnam and Marcy Lewis, of the family of Thomas Putnam of Salem Village, whereby great hurt and damage hath beene donne to the bodyes of sd persons, aboue named therefore Craued Justice.

You are therefore in theire Majests names hereby required to apprehend and bring before us Sarah Cloyce the wife of Peter Cloyce of Salem Village and Elizabeth Procter the wife of John Proctor of Salem sarmes on Monday morning next, being the Eleventh day of this Instant Aprill aboute Eleven of the Clock, at the publike meeting house in the towne, in order to theire examination Relating to the premises abousd and here of you are not to faile.

Dated Salem. April 8th, 1692
John Hathorne
Jonathan Corwin

To George Herrick Marshall of the County of Essex.

You are likewise to warn and order Elis Hubert and Mary Warren not to faile of being present at ye aboue said tyme and place to give in wt evidence they know therein.

April 11th, 1692. I have taken the persons of Sarah Cloyce and Elizabeth Proctor and brought them before this honorable Courte to answer as above.

I have also warned ye above named Elizabeth Hubbart to answer as above.

Pr George Herrick Marshall of Essex.

Source: "Records of Salem Witchcraft." Vols. 1–2 (1969). Library of Congress, Call Number: BF1575.R3
Copied from the original documents

See Articles: Puritans; Religion and Crime, History of; Religion and Crime, Sociology of; Salem Witch Trials.

1706 PRIMARY DOCUMENT

Ann Putnam's Confession

The daughter of a powerful Salem family, Ann Putnam was a key witness in the Salem witchcraft trials when she was 12 years old. Among those she accused were Martha Corey, who was hanged to death, and her husband Giles, who chose to endure peine forte et dure (trial by ordeal, in this

case being slowly crushed with layers of stones) rather than submit to a jury trial. The latter seemed to be named principally for defending his wife, a pattern seen throughout the trials. Putnam's recanting came nine years after the death of her parents, who may have coached her testimony.

"I desire to be humbled before God for that sad and humbling providence that befell my father's family in the year about '92; that I, then being in my childhood, should, by such a providence of God, be made an instrument for the accusing of several persons of a grievous crime, whereby their lives were taken away from them, whom now I have just grounds and good reason to believe they were innocent persons; and that it was a great delusion of Satan that deceived me in that sad time, whereby I justly fear I have been instrumental, with others, though ignorantly and unwittingly, to bring upon myself and this land the guilt of innocent blood; though what was said or done by me against any person I can truly and uprightly say, before God and man, I did it not out of any anger, malice, or ill-will to any person, for I had no such thing against one of them; but what I did was ignorantly, being deluded by Satan. And particularly, as I was a chief instrument of accusing of Goodwife Nurse and her two sisters, I desire to lie in the dust, and to be humbled for it, in that I was a cause, with others, of so sad a calamity to them and their families; for which cause I desire to lie in the dust, and earnestly beg forgiveness of God, and from all those unto whom I have given just cause of sorrow and offence, whose relations were taken away or accused.

[Signed]

"This confession was read before the congregation, together with her relation, Aug. 25, 1706; and she acknowledged it."

"J. Green, Pastor."

Source: http://pages.uoregon.edu/mjdennis/courses/wk3_putnam.htm

See Articles: Puritans; Religion and Crime, History of; Religion and Crime, Sociology of; Salem Witch Trials.

1741
PRIMARY DOCUMENT

Excerpt From the New York Negro Plot Trials Testimony

The increased use of slaves in New York led to widespread fears of riots and revolts. In 1741, the winter had exacerbated an economic depression, and a 1739 slave revolt in South Carolina was a fresh memory. Fires were a common danger in the city, but when they broke out on April 6, they were taken as a sign of a slave revolt. Soon, half of the city's adult male slaves had been jailed, most soon freed. Numerous slaves and several whites were burned at the stake, hanged, or banished.

Saturday, May 9.
This afternoon orders were given for apprehending the several negroes mentioned by Peggy, to have been present at Romme's, at the time she said Romme and the negroes were talking of the conspiracy; those of them whom she knew by name, and were not before committed, were soon found and brought to jail.

In the evening the judges came to the city-hall, and sent for Peggy, and had the several negroes brought one by one, and passed in review before her, viz. Patrick (English's) Cato (col. Moore's) Curacoa Dick, Caesar, (alderman Pintard's) Brash (Mr. Jay's) and Jack (Breasted's) and she distinguished them every one, called them by their names, and declared, those were at the above mentioned meeting.

These negroes were each of them separately examined, and denied being at any such meeting, or that they knew any thing of the conspiracy.

At first, Cork (English's negro) was brought by mistake instead of Patrick, and Peggy declared, he was not English's negro which she meant; Cork was unfortunately of a countenance somewhat ill-favoured, naturally of a suspicious look, and reckoned withal to be unlucky too; his being sent for before the magistrates in such a perilous season, might be thought sufficient to alarm the most innocent of them, and occasion the appearance of their being under some terrible apprehensions; but it was much otherwise with Cork; and notwithstanding the disadvantage of his natural aspect, upon his being interrogated concerning the conspiracy, he shewed such a cheerful, open, honest smile upon his countenance (none of your fictitious hypocritical grins) that every one that was by, and observed it (and there were several in the room) jumped in the same observation and opinion, that they never saw the fellow look so handsome: Such an efficacy have truth and innocence, that they even reflect beauty upon deformity!

On the contrary, Patrick's visage betrayed his guilt: those who are used to negroes may have experienced, that some of them, when charged with any piece of villainy they have been detected in, have an odd knack or (it is hard what to call or how to describe it) way of turning their eyes inwards, as it were, as if shocked at the consciousness of their own perfidy; their looks, at the same time, discovering [revealing] all the symptoms of the most inveterate malice and resentment: this was Patrick's appearance, and such his behaviour upon examination, as served to induce one's credit to what Peggy had declared; so far at least, that he was present at a meeting when the conspiracy was talked of, and was one of the persons consenting to act a part in that infernal scheme; so that he was committed to jail, and the rest of them, whom Peggy declared, as they were produced, to be the persons she meant.

These negroes, impeached by Peggy, and committed upon her information, and which had passed in review before her, were likewise shewn to Mary Burton, who declared, that she did not remember, that ever she saw any of them at Hughson's, which seemed to add strength to what Peggy had declared in her examination, that this villainous scheme was carrying on at Romme's as well as Hughson's.

Deposition taken before one of the judges,— Abigail Earle, being sworn, deposeth, "that just before the going in of the afternoon church, on the same Sunday that coals were found in Mr. Murray's haystack, she saw three negro men coming up the Broadway; that she was then looking out of her window up one pair of stairs in the house where Mr. Williams now lives; and as they passed under the window, she heard one of them say, viz. *Fire, fire, scorch, scorch,* A LITTLE, *damn it,* BY AND BY! and then threw up his hands and laughed. That after the said negroes were gone by she went into Mrs. George's house and told her what she had heard: and about an hour after, when church was out, she saw the same negroes coming down the Broadway; and then shewed Mrs. George the negro that had spoke the aforesaid words: whereupon Mrs. George said, that is Mr. Walter's Quaco."

Lydia George being sworn, deposed, "that she heard the above written deposition of Abigail Earle read, and knows that all therein mentioned, which any ways relates to her the deponent, is true."

Upon these depositions Quaco was recommitted this evening.

Source: Horsmanden, Daniel. *The New-York Conspiracy, or a History of the Negro Plot, With the Journal of the Proceedings Against the Conspirators at New-York in the Years 1741–42.* New York: Southwick and Pelsue, 1810. http://historymatters.gmu.edu/d/6528

See Articles: African Americans; Civil Disobedience; Slavery.

1758 PRIMARY DOCUMENT

Mary Jemison's Account of Kidnapping by Indians

In 1824, James Seaver published a classic captivity narrative based on Mary Jemison's account to Seaver of her kidnapping at age 15, in 1758. Jemison was captured by a raiding party (which included Frenchmen as well as Shawnee Indians) during the French and Indian War. Though the raiders killed most of her family, in time she chose to remain with the Seneca Indians they traded her to, marrying an Indian and helping the Seneca negotiate the 1797 Treaty of Big Tree.

Having made fast to the shore, the squaws left me in the canoe while they went to their wigwam or house in the town, and returned with a suit of Indian clothing, all new, and very clean and nice. My clothes, though whole and good when I was taken, were now torn in pieces, so that I was almost naked. They first undressed me and threw my rags into the river; then washed me clean and dressed me in the new suit they had just brought, in complete Indian style; and then led me home and seated me in the center of their wigwam.

I had been in that situation hut a few minutes, before all the squaws in the town came in to see me. I was soon surrounded by them, and they immediately set up a most dismal howling, crying bitterly, and wringing their hands in all the agonies of grief for a deceased relative.

Their tears flowed freely, and they exhibited all the signs of real mourning. At the commencement of this scene, one of their number began, in a voice somewhat between speaking and singing, to recite some words to the following purport, and continued the recitation till the ceremony was ended; the company at the same time varying the appearance of their countenances, gestures and tune of voice, so as to correspond with the sentiments expressed by their leader:

"Oh our brother! Alas! He is dead—he has gone; he will never return! Friendless he died on the field of the slain, where his bones are yet lying un-buried! Oh, who will not mourn his sad fate? No tears dropped around him; oh, no! No tears of his sisters were there! He fell in his prune, when his arm was most needed to keep us from danger! Alas! he has gone! and left us in sorrow, his loss to bewail: Oh where is his spirit? His spirit went naked, and hungry it wanders, and thirsty and wounded it groans to return! Oh helpless and wretched, our brother has gone! No blanket nor food to nourish and warm him; nor candles to light him, nor weapons of war:—Oh, none of those comforts had he! But well we remember his deeds! —The deer he could take on the chase! The panther shrunk back at the sight of his strength! His enemies fell at his feet! He was brave and courageous in war! As the fawn he was harmless: his friendship was ardent: his temper was gentle: his pity was great! Oh! our friend, our companion is dead! Our brother, our brother, alas! he is gone! But why do we grieve for his loss? In the strength of a warrior, undaunted he left us, to fight by the side of the Chiefs! His war-whoop was shrill! His rifle well aimed laid his enemies low: his tomahawk drank of their blood: and his knife flayed their scalps while yet covered with gore! And why do we mourn? Though he fell on the field of the slain, with glory he fell, and his spirit went up to the land of his fathers in war! Then why do we mourn? With transports of joy they received him, and fed him, and clothed him, and welcomed him there! Oh friends, he is happy; then dry up your tears! His spirit has seen our distress, and sent us a helper whom with pleasure we greet. Dickewamis has come: then let us receive her with joy! She is handsome and pleasant! Oh! she is our sister, and gladly we welcome her here. In the place of our brother she stands in our tribe. With care we will guard her from trouble; and may she be happy till her spirit shall leave us."

In the course of that ceremony, from mourning they became serene—joy sparkled in their countenances, and they seemed to rejoice over me as over a long-lost child. I was made welcome amongst them as a sister to the two squaws before mentioned, and was called Dickewamis; which being interpreted, signifies a pretty girl, a handsome girl, or a pleasant, good thing. That is the name by which I have ever since been called by the Indians.

I afterwards learned that the ceremony I at that time passed through, was that of adoption. The two squaws had lost a brother in Washington's war, sometime in the year before, and in consequence of his death went up to Fort Pitt, on the day on which I arrived there, in order to receive a prisoner or oil enemy's scalp, to supply their loss. It is a custom of the

Indians, when one of their number is slain or taken prisoner in battle, to give to the nearest relative to the dead or absent, a prisoner, if they have chanced to take one, and if not, to give him the scalp of an enemy. On the return of the Indians from conquest, which is always announced by peculiar shoutings, demonstrations of joy, and the exhibition of some trophy of victory, the mourners come forward and make their claims. If they receive a prisoner, it is at their option either to satiate their vengeance by taking his life in the most cruel manner they can conceive of; or, to receive and adopt him into the family, in the place of him whom they have lost. All the prisoners that are taken in battle and carried to the encampment or town by the Indians, are given to the bereaved families, till their number is made good. And unless the mourners have but just received the news of their bereavement, and are under the operation of a paroxysm of grief, anger and revenge; or, unless the prisoner is very old, sickly, or homely, they generally save him, and treat him kindly. But if their mental wound is fresh, their loss so great that they deem it irreparable, or if their prisoner or prisoners do not meet their approbation, no torture, let it be ever so cruel, seems sufficient to make them satisfaction. It is family, and not national, sacrifices amongst the Indians, that has given them an indelible stamp as barbarians, and identified their character with the idea which is generally formed of unfeeling ferocity, and the most abandoned cruelty.

It was my happy lot to be accepted for adoption: and at the time of the ceremony I was received by the two squaws, to supply tile place of their mother in the family; and I was ever considered and treated by them as a real sister, the same as though I had been horn of their mother.

During my adoption, I sat motionless, nearly terrified to death at the appearance and actions of the company, expecting every moment to feel their vengeance, and suffer death on the spot. I was, however, happily disappointed, when at the close of the ceremony the company retired, and my sisters went about employing every means for my consolation and comfort.

Being now settled and provided with a home, I was employed in nursing the children, and doing light work about the house. Occasionally I was sent out with the Indian hunters, when they went but a short distance, to help them carry their game. My situation was easy; I had no particular hardships to endure. But still, the recollection of my parents, my brothers and sisters, my home, and my own captivity, destroyed my happiness, and made mc constantly solitary, lonesome and gloomy.

My sisters would not allow me to speak English in their hearing; but remembering the charge that my dear mother gave me at the time I left her, whenever I chanced to he alone I made a business of repeating my prayer, catechism, or something I had learned in order that I might not forget my own language. By practising in that way I retained it till t came to Genesee flats, where I soon became acquainted with English people with whom I have been almost daily in the habit of conversing.

My sisters were diligent in teaching me their language; and to their great satisfaction I soon learned so that I could understand it readily, and speak it fluently. I was very fortunate in falling into their hands; for they were kind good natured women; peaceable and mild in their dispositions; temperate and decent in their habits, and very tender and gentle toward me. I have great reason to respect them, though they have been dead a great number of years.

The town where they lived was pleasantly situated on the Ohio, at the mouth of the Shenanjee: the land produced good corn; the woods furnished plenty of game, and the waters abounded with fish. Another river emptied itself into the Ohio, directly opposite the mouth of the Shenanjee. We spent the summer at that place, where we planted, hoed, and harvested a large crop of corn, of an excellent quality.

About the time of corn harvest, Fort Pitt was taken from the French by the English.

The corn being harvested, the Indians took it on horses and in canoes, and proceeded down the Ohio, occasionally stopping to hunt a few days, till we arrived at the mouth of Sciota river; where they established their winter quarters, and continued hunting till the ensuing spring, in the adjacent wilderness. While at that place I went with the other children to assist the hunters to bring in their game. The forests on the Sciota were well stocked with elk, deer, and other large animals; and the marshes contained large numbers of beaver, muskrat, etc., which made excellent hunting for the Indians; who depended, for their meat, upon their success in taking elk and deer; and for ammunition and clothing, upon the beaver, muskrat, and other furs that they could take in addition to their peltry.

The season for hunting being passed, we all returned in the spring to the mouth of the river Shenanjee to the houses and fields we had left in the fall before. There we again planted our corn, squashes, and beans, on the fields that we occupied the preceding summer.

About planting time, our Indians all went up to Fort Pitt, to make peace with the British, and took me with them. We landed on the opposite side of the river from the fort, and encamped for the night. Early the next morning the Indians took me over to the fort to see the white people that were there. It was then that my heart bounded to be liberated from the Indians and to he restored to my friends and my country. The white people were surprised to see me with the Indians, enduring the hardships of a savage life, at so early an age, and with so delicate a constitution as t appeared to possess. They asked me my name; where and when I was taken—and appeared very much interested on my behalf. They were continuing their inquiries, when my sisters became alarmed, believing that I should be taken from them, hurried me into their canoe and recrossed the river—took their bread out of the fire and fled with me, without stopping, till they arrived at the river Shenanjee. So great was their fear of losing me, or of my being given up in the treaty, that they never once stopped rowing till they got home.

Shortly after we left the shore opposite the fort, as I was informed by one of my Indian brothers, the white people came over to take me back; but alter considerable inquiry, and having made diligent search to find where I was hid, they returned with heavy hearts.

Although I had then been with the Indians something over a year, and had become considerably habituated to their mode of living, and attached to my sisters, the sight of white people who could speak English inspired me with an unspeakable anxiety to go home with them, and share in the blessings of civilization. My sudden departure and escape from them, seemed like a second captivity, and for a long time I brooded the thoughts of my miserable situation with almost as much sorrow and dejection as had done those of my first sufferings. Time, the destroyer of every affection, wore away my unpleasant feelings, and I became as contented as before.

Source: Seaver, James E. *A Narrative of the Life of Mrs. Mary Jemison*. Canadaigua, NY: J. D. Bemis, 1824.
http://historymatters.gmu.edu/d/5794

See Articles: History of Crime and Punishment in America: Colonial; Kidnapping; Native Americans.

1773
PRIMARY DOCUMENT

A First-Hand Account of the Boston Tea Party

George Hewes was a shoemaker who later described his experiences of the Revolutionary era to historian James Hawkes. The Boston Tea Party is one of the most famous protests leading up to independence, precipitated by a severe increase in the tax on tea in order to raise money for the East India Company. It was the last straw in an ongoing dispute on British Parliamentary authority over the colonies. In other colonies, protests met little resistance; Boston was the exception.

Although the excitement which had been occasioned by the wanton massacre of our citizens, had in some measure abated, it was never extinguished until open hostilities commenced, and we had declared our independence. The citizens of Boston continued inflexible in their demand, that every British soldier should be withdrawn from the town, and within four days after the massacre, the whole army decamped. But the measures of the British parliament, which led the American colonies to a separation from that government, were not abandoned. And to carry into execution their favourite project of taxing their American colonies, they employed a number of ships to transport a large quantity of tea into the colonies, of which the American people were apprised, and while resolute measures were taking in all the capital towns to resist the project of British taxation, the ships arrived, which the people of Boston had long expected.

The particular object of sending this cargo of tea to Boston at that time, and the catastrophe which befell it, have been referred to in the preface. It has also been recorded, among the most important and interesting events in the history of the American revolution; but the rehersal of it at this time, by a witness, and an actor in that tragicomical scene, excites in the recollection of it a novel and extraordinary interest.

On my inquiring of Hewes if he knew who first proposed the project of destroying the tea, to prevent its being landed, he replied that he did not; neither did he know who or what number were to volunteer their services for that purpose. But from the significant allusion of some persons in whom I had confidence, together with the knowledge I had of the spirit of those times, I had no doubt but that a sufficient number of associates would accompany me in that enterprise.

The tea destroyed was contained in three ships, laying near each other, at what was called at that time Griffin's wharf, and were surrounded by armed ships of war; the commanders of which had publicly declared, that if the rebels, as they were pleased to style the Bostonians, should not withdraw their opposition to the landing of the tea before a certain day, the 17th day of December, 1773, they should on that day force it on shore, under the cover of their cannon's month. On the day preceding the seventeenth, there was a meeting of the citizens of the county of Suffolk, convened at one of the churches in Boston, for the purpose of consulting on what measures might be considered expedient to prevent the landing of the tea, or secure the people from the collection of the duty. At that meeting a committee was appointed to wait on Governor Hutchinson, and request him to inform them whether he would take any measures to satisfy the people on the object of the meeting. To the first application of this committee, the governor told them he would give them a definite answer by five o'clock in the afternoon. At the hour appointed, the committee again repaired to the governor's house, and on inquiry found he had gone to his country seat at Milton, a distance of about six miles. When the committee returned and informed the meeting of the absence of the governor, there was a confused murmur among the members, and the meeting was immediately dissolved, many of them crying out, Let every man do his duty, and be true to his country; and there was a general huzza for Griffins wharf. It was now evening, and I immediately dressed myself in the costume of an Indian, equipped with a small hatchet, which I and my associates denominated the tomahawk, with which, and a club, after having painted my face and hands with coal dust in the shop of a blacksmith, I repaired to Griffins wharf, where the ships lay that contained the tea.

When I first appeared in the street, after being thus disguised, I fell in with many who were dressed, equipped and painted as I was, and who fell in with me, and marched in order to the place of our destination. When we arrived at the wharf, there were three of our number who assumed an authority to direct our operations, to which we readily submitted. They divided us into three parties, for the purpose of boarding the three ships which contained the tea at the same time. The name of him who commanded the division to which I was assigned, was Leonard Pitt. The names of the other commanders I never knew. We were immediately ordered by the respective commanders to board all the ships at the same time, which we promptly obeyed. The commander of the division to which I belonged, as soon as we were on board the ship, appointed me boatswain, and ordered me to go to the captain and demand of him the keys to the hatches and a dozen candles. I made the demand accordingly, and the captain promptly replied, and delivered the articles; but requested me at the same time to do no damage to the ship or rigging. We then were ordered by our commander to open the hatches, and take out all the chests of tea and throw them overboard, and we immediately proceeded to execute his orders; first cutting and splitting the chests with our tomahawks, so as thoroughly to expose them to the effects of the water. In about three hours from the time we went on board, we had thus broken and thrown overboard every tea chest to be found in the ship; while those in the other ships were disposing of the tea in the same way, at the same time. We were surrounded by British armed ships, but no attempt was made to resist us. We then quietly retired to our several places of residence, without having any conversation with each other, or taking any measures to discover who were our associates; nor do I recollect of our having had the knowledge of the name of a single individual concerned in that affair, except that of Leonard Pitt, the commander of my division, who I have mentioned. There appeared to be an understanding that each individual should volunteer his services, keep his own secret, and risk the consequences for himself. No disorder took place during that transaction, and it was observed at that time, that the stillest night ensued that Boston had enjoyed for many months.

During the time we were throwing the tea overboard, there were several attempts made by some of the citizens of Boston and its vicinity, to carry off small quantities of it for their family use. To effect that object, they would watch their opportunity to snatch up a handful from the deck, where it became plentifully scattered, and put it into their pockets. One Captain O'Conner, whom I well knew, came on board for that purpose, and when he supposed he was not noticed, filled his pockets, and also the lining of his coat. But I had detected him, and gave information to the captain of what he was doing. We were ordered to take him into custody, and just as he was stepping from the vessel, I seized him by the skirt of his coat, and in attempting to pull him back, I tore it off; but springing forward, by a rapid effort, he made his escape. He had however to run a gauntlet through the crowd upon the wharf; each one, as he passed, giving him a kick or a stroke.

The next day we nailed the skirt of his coat, which I had pulled off, to the whipping post in Charlestown, the place of his residence, with a label upon it, commemorative of the occasion which had thus subjected the proprietor to the popular indignation.

Another attempt was made to save a little tea from the ruins of the cargo, by a tall aged man, who wore a large cocked hat and white wig, which was fashionable at that time. He had slightly slipped a little into his pocket, but being detected, they seized him, and taking his hat and wig from his head, threw them, together with the tea, of which they had emptied his pockets, into the water. In consideration of his advanced age, he was permitted to escape, with now and then a slight kick.

The next morning, after we had cleared the ships of the tea, it was discovered that very considerable quantities of it was floating upon the surface of the water; and to prevent the possibility of any of its being saved for use, a number of small boats were manned by sailors and citizens, who rowed them into those parts of the harbour wherever the tea was visible, and by beating it with oars and paddles, so thoroughly drenched it, as to render its entire destruction inevitable.

by George Robert Twelve Hewes

Source: Hawkes, James. *A Retrospect of the Boston Tea Party*. New York: S. S. Bliss, 1834. http://historymatters.gmu.edu/d/5799

See Articles: American Revolution and Criminal Justice; Civil Disobedience; Larceny; Magna Carta; Political Crimes, History of; Political Crimes, Sociology of; Political Dissidents; Proclamation for Suppressing Rebellion and Sedition of 1775; Tea Act of 1773; Townshend Acts of 1767; Tax Crimes.

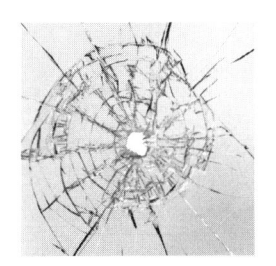

1777 to 1800

INTRODUCTION

Just as in most other aspects of society, the criminal justice system in the United States experienced significant changes, both philosophical and tangible, between 1777 and 1800. As the country grew from a group of individual colonies to a united new country, the system of crime and punishment also transformed from a vestige of English colonial law to a structure arranged to meet the republic's new and unique challenges. This era marked a shift in demography in the patterns of criminal activity, a transition in judicial priorities, and a change in the country's laws and institutions. It is also highlighted by an alteration in the forms and methods of punishment to not only meet the period's new liberal philosophies, but also to address the efficacy of old punishments on new criminals. The fulcrum levering this change was the American Revolution and the break that it brought with previous colonial policies, ties, and philosophies. In the years leading up to the Revolution, the colonists administered justice in much the same way as their English forebears, adapting their policies to the unique circumstances of close-knit, church-centered villages. As U.S. demographics evolved and the challenge of constructing a new, post-Revolution government began, the American system of crime and punishment experienced a centralization of the penal system and a fundamental renegotiation of national and state jurisdictions.

Pre-Revolutionary Criminal Justice Officials and Jurisdictions

Just as today, crimes in the 1770s were categorized and their jurisdictions were distributed among several different authorities. For the most part, minor crimes in the category of disorderly conduct—gambling, breaking the Sabbath, unruliness, public intoxication, and fighting—were handled by a local justice of the peace. Generally, the governor of the colony appointed these justices; after the American Revolution, however, they would be elected by the towns for seven-year terms. Minor humiliation and, in many cases, nominal fines were assessed by the local justice of the peace to handle nuisance crimes such as these.

Although these justices still chose to utilize public humiliation tactics in many instances, they also commonly chose the assessment of monetary fines as a reasonable punishment for smaller offenses. However, pre-Revolutionary America was not a particularly wealthy land, so in most cases fines simply proved unfeasible; offenders did not have the money to pay. Instead, justices exercised the option of sentencing offenders to servitude as an alternative to fining. Convicted criminals could then act as servants to the individual they had wronged until the court determined that their debt had been paid. In a small and intimate community, this served as a plausible alternative punishment. Although much of the criminal punishment code of the American colonies had been inherited directly from the English, uniquely American problems such as a lack of money made a difference in the way the courts handled crime and punishment. The American colonies' distance from England, their distinctive circumstances, and the individual colonies' isolation from one another meant that the local justices of the peace possessed a great deal of leeway and executive authority to interpret and adapt the old English common law practices that they had inherited to their own circumstances.

Most misdemeanors and minor felonies not handled immediately by the justice of the peace were handled by justices at the county level. County justices held court sessions four times a year. In these hearings, known as "quarter sessions," the officers of the county justice's court would process all those who stood accused or who awaited sentencing. These individuals were held most often in the county jail, or *gaol*, and would be tried, sentenced, or both during the quarter session. The removal and trial of the prisoners held in the county's gaol, known as "gaol delivery," was the key function of a county justice. In the gaol delivery process, the court or county judge ordered the county sheriff, via a document called a *mittimus*, to hand defendants over to the court's keeper (bailiff), who would be responsible for holding them until the end of trial. Crimes requiring these types of services by the county justice included most assaults, thefts, inciting riots, contempt of court or justice, the fathering of illegitimate children, and the running of unlicensed or disorderly taverns, inns, or other entertainments.

Crimes considered serious enough to warrant a death sentence, known as "capital felonies," fell under the jurisdiction of the court of oyer and terminer. These courts and their judges held appointments by the British monarch before 1776. Afterward, the courts' dockets became part of the duties of the U.S. Supreme Court. Courts of oyer and terminer met twice a year, delivering gaols by trying arson, armed burglary, treason, murder, and various sexual crimes. Those convicted of these offenses could still be given significant public punishments, and sentences of death were often carried out on the gallows in full view of the public in much the same manner.

Though the system of trying and punishing capital crime remained similar to England's methods even up to the eve of the American Revolution, cultural differences colored the justice system differently in the colonies. For example, even into the 1770s, American colonists still exhibited their Puritan backgrounds by focusing their police powers more intently on morality crimes such as sexual deviance, much more so than their English counterparts. Even for some years after the Revolution, sexual crimes such as sodomy were listed as capital felonies. Although the American system of correction and punishment remained for the most part a product of the English system, its occasional departure from the norm to address issues unique to the colonies, combined with a heavier emphasis on morality, made it distinctive.

Pre-Revolutionary Crimes of Sexuality and Immorality
The view of proper use of police powers as enforcing a morality that included raising sodomy and other sexual misdemeanors to capital status was the upshot of an American judicial philosophy inherited from the Puritans and religiously devout writers such as William Blackstone, who wrote extensively on the subject of criminal justice. The preoccupation with sexual morality was illustrated best by the cases of women in the

court system. Sexual offenses constituted by far the most common crime with which American women of the late 18th century were accused. Prosecutions and punishments of women for fornication and for adultery occurred at a much higher frequency in the American colonies than in Europe, with religiously devout colonies such as Pennsylvania and Massachusetts leading the others in the percentage of females accused and tried of these crimes. The strict prosecution of "immoral women" would continue well into the 1780s.

Although women in the colonies also appeared in court for theft and other common crimes, most accusations and prosecutions centered on immoral behavior or disruption of the "public order." Assault cases involving females usually involved domestic violence, rather than public instances of assault or battery.

American founding fathers relied heavily on the commentaries of William Blackstone (1723–80); the Ten Commandments and God's law were his guiding philosophies. A statue of Blackstone in his judicial robes stands in Washington, D.C.

Offenses against the public order generally consisted of lewd conduct, adultery, or operating "illegal ordinaries," a legal term for houses of prostitution, drunkenness, or gambling. For the authorities of the 1770s and 1780s, police powers were concerned as much with maintaining morality as with the prevention of property crime or other offenses not seen as acts of pure immorality. Common means of protecting society against all these threats were corporal or sanguinary punishments, with additional reliance on public humiliation and admonition.

Pre-Revolutionary Punishment: Public Humiliation and Admonition

In the years leading up to the American Revolution, punishment in the United States differed little from the correctional systems of its European counterparts. The biblical concept of *lex talionis*, "an eye for an eye," acted as the foundation for determining reasonable punishment. Mutilation was common; thieves would often lose fingers or have an ear "cropped," and adulterers or those convicted of manslaughter would usually receive brandings. Brandings increased in popularity due to their use in identifying criminals; for example, B stood for burglary, C for counterfeiting, and H for horse theft. These physical forms of punishment easily transferred to colonial systems.

Public humiliation, also a common category of punishment in Europe, became even more popular in pre-Revolutionary America because of the unique social construction of the American colonies. Inherited from the Puritans of the 17th century and used throughout the 18th century, the stocks, the pillory, and public whipping provided a dual function. For those still associated with the church, the public punishment system mirrored the custom of public confession. Since the Puritans associated sin and crime so

The massacre at Cherry Valley, New York, on November 11, 1778, led by a combined force of loyalists and Indians, killed 14 officers and 30 civilians. America responded with the Sullivan Expedition in 1779, driving Iroquois villagers in New York out of their homelands.

closely, public confession of crime and involvement of the town seemed sensible and appeared to fit with the confession of sin and engagement of the congregation. Throughout the colonial period, the town was seen as an extended congregation, so the sharing (confession) of the crime (sin) generally provided an effective tool for crime prevention and correction, at least in Puritan colonies.

This system changed little in the 18th century. Judges in colonies such as Massachusetts used public whippings, brandings, mutilations, and standing in the gallows, stocks, or pillory as default punishments for crimes of all sorts. The judges expected the public not only to witness the punishment but also to participate in the identification of criminal elements and prevention of future crimes in the event that those individuals remained unreformed. In order to ensure the participation of the community, judges usually scheduled the punishments on market days, important meeting days, or public holidays.

As the decades passed, the humiliation aspect of punishment increasingly came to be seen as the focus of the sentence rather than the corporal punishment. Thus, by the 1770s, public humiliation sentences usually lacked a lasting physical component such as branding or lashing, instead deferring to sentences of hours in the stocks or on the gallows with a rope around the neck. In either instance, it became increasingly common for the offender to wear a sign explaining his or her offense. Though relatively inane today, these punishments carried great weight and efficacy in the colonial period. The America of the late 18th century remained a group of small, closely knit towns separate enough to prevent much mobility of citizens. Most individuals lived and died within a few miles of their birthplaces. In a community where "everyone knew everyone," time spent in this state of public disgrace proved to be fairly effective in correcting and preventing crimes of all sorts. Though punishment methods across the colonies were relatively uniform, crimes were not; the governments of the colonies (and after the Revolution, the states) had to determine which offices would handle which types of crimes. Concern over what fell into federal jurisdiction, as opposed to state or local jurisdiction, became an issue as well. Despite the uniformity of humiliation punishment across the colonies, varying categories and degrees of crime nonetheless needed assignment to those most equipped to handle them.

Post-Revolutionary America
Following the U.S. victory over Britain, one of the major points of contact between the new republic and its citizens came from governmental enforcement of certain behaviors and protection of property, deriving from the state's police powers and strong property rights system. Police powers encompass legal policies directed toward the health, safety, welfare, and morality of a state's inhabitants, and by tradition (though not by codification in the U.S. Constitution), these have been largely the purview of the states, rather than the national government. Particularly in the earliest days of the United States, there was little national criminal law. This left much of the exercise of police powers, and thus the determination of what constituted unacceptable behaviors, to the 13 states to adopt and enforce upon their own residents.

The exceptions to this revolved around 18th-century concepts of property. Both the Articles of Confederation, ratified in 1781, and the U.S. Constitution, ratified in 1788, acknowledged and accepted the institution of slavery, the ownership of people as property, and the rights of the slave owner to control and to dispose of that property at will. Additionally, at the national level, there were strong protections of property rights more generally, built into the U.S. Constitution with lesser mention in the Articles of Confederation, which left such protections up to the 13 sovereign states. The protection of property (be it material or human) came to the forefront of American criminal justice policies. This shift of emphasis away from crimes of morality and toward more secular, financial crimes developed parallel to the country's urbanization, resulting in a loss of intimate village life in favor of the more anonymous and transient city lifestyle.

Although the 1770s resembled the American justice system of the preceding decades—close church ties, the litigation of morality, and punishments designed to use shame and humiliation to deter future crime—the years immediately preceding the American Revolution and the turbulent following decade resulted in alterations of criminal behavior, adjustments to the punishment structure, and shifts in the overall philosophy of crime and corrections.

Demographic Changes in Post-Revolutionary America
As the United States evolved from a collection of agrarian, rural colonies to a more centralized, rapidly urbanizing, and industrializing state, demographic trends associated with such changes began to produce a very different type of environment for both criminals and administrators of criminal justice. The country experienced rapid population growth during the last two decades of the 18th century, with the vast majority of the growth coming in the form of urban population. These individuals were newcomers, too; while earlier decades were highlighted by a population that rarely relocated, the post-Revolution period featured individuals who moved to bigger cities and had lived there for less than five years.

Besides independence and economic growth, another catalyst helped augment the sudden growth in urban population. A series of wars in the latter half of the century, from the War of Jenkins' Ear (1739–48) to the French and Indian War (1755–64) and, finally, the American Revolution (1776–83), produced a class of professional soldiers and a new segment in the American population. The existence of this occupational class and the challenges that these individuals experienced during the ebb and flow of war and peacetime created a new test for the American justice system.

The challenge is illustrated in the crime rates of the United States during war and peacetime. During the three wars, crime rates fell to all-time lows, with the largest decrease coming during the Revolution. Immediately after the end of each war, especially in the 1780s following the Revolution, crime rapidly increased. Most researchers point to the postwar economy and the return of professional soldiers to civilian life as the root cause. In some colonies, furloughed soldiers made up over half of those tried for capital and property crimes in the decade following the American Revolution. With a lack of available jobs and a skill set that lent itself well to a life of crime, the unemployed soldier posed a significant challenge to the American criminal justice system.

New classes of criminals and growing cities led to changes in the types of crime occurring most often in the new republic. A challenging postwar economy produced a scarcity of money, particularly for newly unemployed soldiers. In addition, as cities filled with people possessing no familial "roots" in the community, instances of property crime and fraud increased. Individuals who needed money or goods to survive and possessed no real attachment to the community in which they lived were far more likely to commit crimes of opportunity such as petty theft and burglary.

In the last 30 years of the 18th century, each decade reflected a lower rate of sexual and "moral" offenses while simultaneously undergoing marked increases in crimes such as fraud and property theft. Records across all the former colonies reflect this trend, with the clearest trend away from moral prosecution and toward property crime prevention evident in Massachusetts. Studies made by Linda Kealey and others have reflected significant trends in the Supreme Judicial Court of Massachusetts' dockets, painting a picture of a young republic wrestling with new types of crime and new types of criminals.

Changes in Post-Revolutionary Priorities: Property Crimes and Treason
Beyond just the demographic changes and the alteration in the types of crime being committed, the historical data from the courts of post-Revolutionary America reflect a fundamental shift in the priority of the judicial system. In the new, capitalist republic, crimes of morality moved behind crimes of economy in importance. In fact, property crimes not only dominated the crime rate, but also seemed to be the type of crime most doggedly pursued by the prosecutors of the 1780s and 1790s. Property crimes routinely exhibited the highest conviction rate, the lowest acquittal rate, and the lowest frequency of dropped cases in the two decades that closed the century.

The same held true for the prosecution of women during this period. Just as women were prosecuted for crimes of immorality in the decades preceding the Revolution, the decades immediately after the Revolution featured a markedly higher percentage of women prosecuted for property offenses. In all jurisdictions and with all types of offenders, both male and female, the need to address the safety and security of finances and personal property became the primary focus of governmental police powers and the criminal justice system. By the 1780s, they had ceased to be the enforcer of the church's code of morality and turned their focus to the more secular realm of business.

Property crimes did not represent the only issue the new republic found pressing, however. Although issues of morality found decreased interest in the American court system, crimes of sedition and treason increased in importance. Now leading a republic founded upon rebellious acts, the framers of the U.S. Constitution and the new state penal codes keenly felt the need to define and address the crimes of sedition and treason in their own courts. Because traitors to the British Crown now had the tricky task of defining treason, the state constitutions written in the late 1770s and early 1780s reflected hesitation to attack the problem directly. Laws were written limiting the ability of the executive branch to pardon spies or those inciting rebellion, requiring jury trial in the county where the treasonous act occurred and creating other "auxiliary" treasonous crimes like "traffic [or congress] with the enemy," "spreading disloyal utterances," and "confiscation of property of disaffected people."

A great deal of work took place on the treason laws, indicating a newfound interest in and squelching of this type of criminal offense, but it was a disjointed and scattered effort at best. In fact, the Committee on Spies, a creation of the Continental Congress designed specifically to assist the framers of the U.S. Constitution in bolstering internal security, recommended laws remarkably similar to those still on the books in England. While the rest of the country's statutes, laws, and philosophies in general were being reworked and totally overhauled for the service of a new, extraordinarily different country, the treason laws remained unchanged. The final recommendation of the committee, made on June 24, 1776, suggested laws almost identical to those passed under King Edward III. Even revolutionary, liberal thinker Thomas Jefferson, who participated in drafting the final version of the treason act, recommended to his home state of Virginia basically the same law a few months later.

Despite this deference to older English laws, the American legislators of the time soon had to face unique challenges to the treason laws. Fearing war with France and in reaction to the heightened tensions following the XYZ Affair, in which French agents sought to extort money from the U.S. government, Congress passed the Alien and Sedition

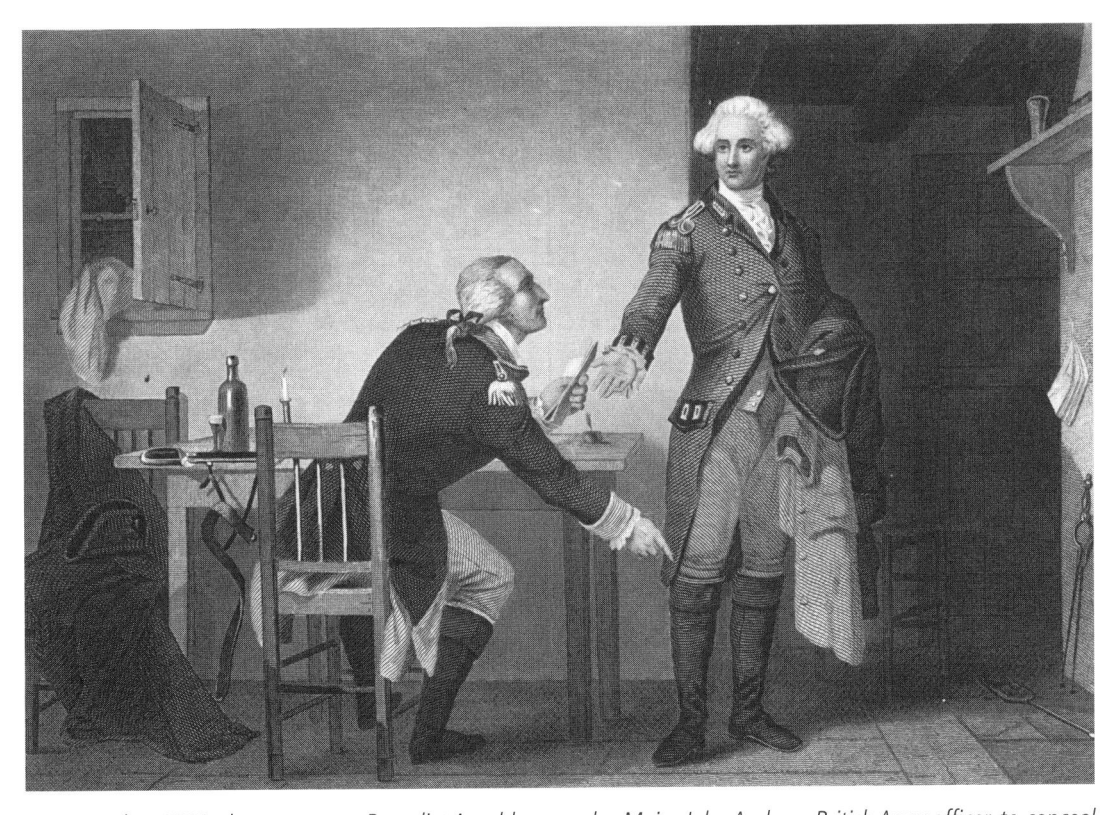

In September 1780, the treasonous Benedict Arnold persuades Major John Andre, a British Army officer, to conceal in his boot six papers written by Arnold that showed the British how to take the fort at West Point, New York, which Arnold commanded. Crimes of sedition and treason increased in importance, which presented a challenge for the leaders of the republic—who were considered rebellious and traitors to the British Crown.

Acts (1798). These four bills increased by nine years the residency requirement for U.S. citizenship to 14 years, authorized the president to detain or to deport aliens he found "dangerous to the peace and safety of the United States," and placed restrictions on free speech that was critical of the government. Both Jefferson and James Madison pushed the states to "interpose" themselves between these acts and their citizens, but neither, ultimately, was successful in finding support for the proposals. The rights of individuals, although identified in the Constitution, still required interpretation and dissemination by the framers of the new republic.

Criminal Law and the Articles of Confederation
In the post-Revolutionary United States, a move to codify "man's law" to make it knowable to all participants in the new republic was in order. This was something largely left up to the 13 states, however. Under the Articles of Confederation, there were no national courts, save for the national Congress when it sat in that capacity. Its jurisdiction covered maritime cases, including admiralty law and piracy, and cases of final appeal in disputes between states. Thus, state courts continued to adjudicate the vast majority of crime cases and to mete out punishments but without any overarching colonial authority seeking to create uniformity among them. At the same time, the Articles of Confederation and Congress did protect the institution of slavery nationally.

The Articles of Confederation acknowledged the convention of slavery but did so indirectly. According to Article IV, the articles applied only to free people. As well, Article IX prohibited Congress from restricting the import of "any species of goods or commodities whatsoever." Thus, while recognizing and allowing slavery, the articles left its regulation

This June 1798 British cartoon satires French–American relations after the XYZ Affair: America, represented by a woman in a headdress, is plundered by Frenchmen while Britain laughs. In May 1798, French agents attempted to extort money from the U.S. government, prompting Congress to pass the Alien and Sedition Acts of 1798. The bills increased the residency requirement for U.S. citizenship and authorized the president to deport "dangerous" aliens.

largely a matter for the individual states. One exception to this indirect support of slavery came with the British ceding of its lands in the United States up to the Mississippi River in settlement of the Revolutionary War. Congress passed the Northwest and Southwest Ordinances in 1787 to govern the vast territory. The Northwest Ordinance prohibited slavery north of the Ohio River but also included a Fugitive Slave Clause in Article 6, which provided that any escaped slave found in this territory could be "reclaimed and conveyed to the person claiming his or her labor or service as aforesaid."

The protection of property, human and material, strengthened with the Constitution, which the framers drafted to replace the Articles of Confederation and fortify the national government. The Constitution, together with its first 10 amendments, also codified criminal due process rights that guaranteed U.S. citizens certain protections meant to reinforce their position vis-à-vis the prosecuting government within an adversarial criminal justice system.

Criminal Law and the U.S. Constitution

The Constitution that the framers drafted in 1787 included several provisions that affected crime and punishment at the national and state levels. The Bill of Rights, the first 10 amendments to the Constitution agreed upon as part of the ratification bargaining over the Constitution itself, extended this federal influence over criminal prosecutions when ratified in 1791. Subsequent acts of Congress, including the Federal Judiciary Act of 1789, the Punishment of Crimes Act of 1790, and the Alien and Sedition Acts of 1798, led to limited federal involvement in the definition of crimes and the protection of those accused of them and provided some new tools for adjudication. Still, most prosecution and punishment of crime, as now, took place at the state level.

The U.S. Constitution tends to define the rights of those accused of crimes by the government negatively by outlining what the national and state governments cannot do—and therefore, what those accused are free to do. Consequently, Article I, Section 9 of the Constitution guarantees citizens the right of *habeas corpus*, or a procedural judicial challenge to their governmental imprisonment. As well, in Article I, Sections 9 and 10, the Constitution prohibits Congress and states' use of *ex post facto* laws, which would criminalize behavior after the fact, and bills of attainder, or trials by the legislatures, a violation of the "separation of powers" concept. Furthermore, under the Privileges and Immunities Clause in Article IV, Section 2, states may not criminalize behaviors for nonresidents that are legal for their own residents, nor may they deny nonresidents significant legal rights that they accord to their own residents. Under the Full Faith and Credit Clause, Article IV, Section 1, states also must respect the decisions of courts in other states, rather than retry lawsuits.

Additionally, the Constitution protects the rights of citizens to property via the Contracts Clause, Article I, Section 10. This clause prohibits states from passing any law that retroactively impairs contract rights, thus ending the practice under the Articles of Confederation of state legislatures granting private bills that relieved debtors of their obligations. Finally, the Constitution prevented even nonslave states from intervening in the slave–master relationship with the Rendition Clause, Article IV, Section 2, which prohibited application of free states' antislavery laws to fugitive slaves who had escaped there but instead required free states to return escapees to owners. These constitutional rights, prohibitions, and definitions shaped both criminal law and property rights through application at the national and state level.

Furthermore, the Bill of Rights crafted by the First Congress laid out a set of criminal due process rights. These familiar procedural protections include restrictions on the state's conduct toward anyone suspected of a crime, arrested for a crime, tried for a crime, and punished for a crime; thus, they encompass the entire spectrum of the criminal justice process. Among these mandates are the Fourth Amendment's right of an individual to be free from unreasonable searches and seizures (of person or evidence). As well, the Fifth Amendment, which applies largely to criminal proceedings, guarantees the accused the right to grand jury indictment, the right to be free from double jeopardy (being tried twice for the same crime), and the right to be free from self-incrimination. The Sixth Amendment deals with the rights of a criminal defendant as the trial takes place. Some of the pieces of this amendment include a speedy and public trial, an impartial jury, the right to compel favorable witnesses and to confront one's accusers, and the right to assistance of legal counsel.

Further, the Eighth Amendment prohibits excessive bails and fines and the state's use of cruel and unusual punishments. These amendments originally had an extremely limited application, concerning only those charged with federal crimes. Over time, however, two processes led to a broader adoption of this minimum standard of criminal due process. First, many states embraced all or some of the rights in the national Bill of Rights into their own bills of rights. Second, through various Supreme Court rulings, most of the rights found in the Bill of Rights now apply to the states as well as the national government.

The First Congress also acted to develop a court system to adjudicate crimes and define which crimes the federal government would pursue. Article III of the U.S. Constitution provided little structure for the national judicial system, beyond it consisting of "one Supreme Court, and ... such inferior courts as the Congress may from time to time ordain and establish." With the Federal Judiciary Act of 1789, Congress set up 13 district courts: One in each of the 11 states that had ratified the Constitution; courts for Kentucky and Maine, which then were parts of Virginia and Massachusetts; and three circuit courts—an eastern, a middle, and a southern court. The courts at both levels heard cases with original or trial jurisdiction, with the circuit courts trying the more serious cases. The circuit courts also heard district court appeals. Additionally, this act gave the Supreme Court the power of judicial review over state courts' decisions on federal questions, establishing a final federal say over federal laws and U.S. constitutional issues.

With the Punishment of Crimes Act of 1790, the First Congress also proceeded to define federal crimes. This Act defined 17 such offenses. Some were ordinary crimes federalized by the location where they occurred: U.S. forts, dockyards, arsenals, or other places under sole U.S. jurisdiction. Their unique national character—treason, piracy, counterfeiting of U.S. securities—federalized other crimes. This limited menu of crimes and places left most criminal prosecution and punishment in the hands of the states.

Congress also passed the Fugitive Slave Act in 1793, giving means to enforce the Constitution's Rendition Clause. This act allowed those hunting fugitives across the United States and its territories to capture runaways; upon simple oral confirmation of the person's slave status to a state or federal judge, the hunter won custody of the escaped slave, who had no legal recourse. Further, the act marked every escaped slave a lifelong fugitive, one who risked recapture at any time anywhere within the territory of the United States.

The Whiskey Rebellion (1794) highlighted the importance of the empowerment of federal courts in the prosecution of some criminal actions. When protestors in Pennsylvania and Kentucky reacted against higher excise taxes on distilled spirits, part of Treasury Secretary Alexander Hamilton's plan to pay off the national debt, President George Washington called on an overwhelming force made up of state militias to suppress them, labeling their acts as treason. Federal courts then prosecuted the protestors, reducing the possibility of juries reflecting local sympathies affecting the verdicts in these cases.

Post-Revolutionary Failure of Traditional Punishment Methods

Yet, no matter how clearly codified—whether liberal or traditional—the newly written U.S. Constitution and laws were, the country could not expect to keep crime at bay without an effective deterrent and corrections policy. Whether for property crime, violent capital felonies, or treason and sedition, by the 1780s, most officers of the American justice system saw that the old methods of punishment had ceased to make a serious impact. The American system had relied heavily upon humiliation and admonition as both deterrent and punishment in the previous century, to a good degree of success. However, changing demographics, the waning influence of the church and other religious institutions, a smaller interest in moral offenses and a stronger focus on money-related offenses all worked against traditional shaming punishments.

Crime, particularly the growing problem of theft, stopped being an issue contained neatly within a close-knit, intimate village. Instead, it had become more commonly the act of a stranger, newcomer, or transient. This caused humiliation punishments to lose their punch because it was unlikely that an offender could be shamed in front of people he or she had never even met. Remorse and shame experienced from stealing from extended family or longtime neighbors often sufficed to set the offender on the "straight and narrow," but facing total strangers during punishment did not hold the same weight, especially since the offender likely intended to move on to another town after the sentence anyway.

George Washington reviews his troops near Fort Cumberland, Maryland, in October 1794 before sending them off to suppress the Whiskey Rebellion in western Pennsylvania, where whiskey-grain farmers used violence to prohibit tax agents from collecting an excise tax intended to pay off the national debt. It was a test of the powers of the federal courts, which prosecuted for treason; the lack of local juries also diminished the effect of local sympathies.

Sentencing servitude upon an individual who was too poor to pay a fine also lacked real effect, for many of the same reasons. Townspeople proved far more willing to accept into their households people they had known their entire lives, than they were to take into service a transient with no family connections and no integration with the community. What would keep such an individual from using his sentence to steal again from inside the house he served, then move on to another unsuspecting community? This presented an issue rarely seen as a problem in the tightly constructed villages and hamlets of colonial America.

New trends in prosecution added to the changing criminal justice environment. An emphasis on retention and protection of personal wealth (now no longer being relocated to the British government, but instead being amassed within the country) and a more secular outlook on crime produced higher levels of property crime and fraud prosecution. Additionally, philosophical changes called for capital felonies to be defined more narrowly. Further, the option of "benefit of clergy" offered to many first-time offenders was drastically scaled back and, in some states, totally removed from the code of trial and punishment. The benefit of clergy had been a popular option in the more religiously oriented colonies of the 17th century. At times, it accorded those accused of serious crimes an opportunity for leniency based on a common acceptance of religious values. For the same reason, admonition and servitude were falling out of favor, and the use of the church to "shield" offenders lost ground in the years immediately following the Revolution.

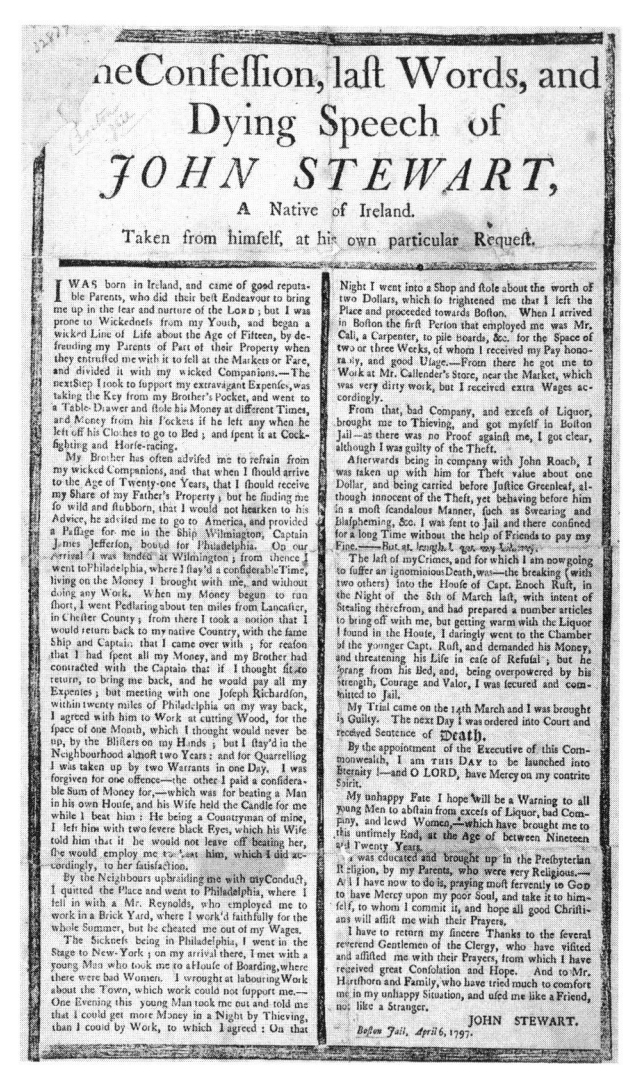

The April 6, 1797, confession of John Stewart from the Boston Jail warning "all young Men to abstain from excess of Liquor, bad Company, and lewd Women" details his early "wicked line of life" that culminated in attempted murder and a death sentence.

Up until the spike in urban population the United States experienced after the Revolution, reform in the penal code and punishment system hardly seemed necessary. Into the late 1760s and early 1770s, the vast majority of towns in Pennsylvania, Massachusetts, Connecticut, New York, and other relatively well-populated colonies contained fewer than 1,000 residents. The smaller, more agrarian colonies to the south enjoyed fewer still. Such low populations meant low tax bases and little in the way of human resources. Thus, the concept of jailing convicts made little sense; the small towns could not afford to maintain penitentiaries, and the self-policing residents used shaming and a rudimentary "neighborhood watch" to keep crime sufficiently under control. Adding the fact that nearly all citizens were members of the local church, and therefore even easier to monitor and keep "in the family," the old punishments had been doing the job.

After the Revolution, however, when populations began to concentrate in cities, the anonymous criminal confounded the old system. Increased industrialization provided more mobility, too, thus making cities even less like a family or congregation (and consequently less affected by familial or congregational punishments). Personal wealth, though, was on the increase, and the larger cities experienced a flood of new residents, many of them unemployed soldiers with the training to meet their economic needs through force, if necessary. Debates over what types of punishment to employ appeared throughout the states of the Union.

Development of New Punishment Alternatives in the New Republic

The county judges and justices of the peace, experiencing the changing crime problem on the front lines, developed into the proponents of new punishment solutions. Seeing that public chastisement or humiliation had lost all real effect, the judges used their flexibility in sentencing to explore new options. Selling convicts into servitude to pay off their criminal debts (either to society or a specific individual) had, in the past, provided a productive alternative, but townspeople rejected the idea when it meant taking in a total stranger. Moreover, the labor scarcity of the previous century turned into a labor surplus, so the need to find cheap labor (particularly in the bigger cities) was no longer an issue.

Gaols existed in every moderately sized city and in nearly every county. Although they had been used in the past only to hold individuals until their trial, some officials noted their possible use as a punishment instead. Local authorities, though, lacked the money to expand these buildings to accommodate the new usage. Judges and administrators at the state, rather than the county level increasingly took over the responsibility of criminal punishment out of necessity, especially in property crime cases.

With the renovation of county jails still lagging behind the problem and other punishments falling out of fashion, the state embarked on a new set of punishment options that included fines and hard labor. With more citizens gaining access to money and wealth, fining had developed into a more plausible option. As for those who lacked that monetary success, whom historian Michael Katz described as a "new dependent population," serving the city through hard labor in a workhouse or state-run factory seemed to fit both needs. First, it could replace humiliation and admonition with a threat unaffected by the criminal's connection to the community. Second, for a new cultural environment in which the factory and productivity were king, it made sure that the "undesirables" in society continued to be productive and useful.

By the close of the 18th century, the first state-run hard labor facility opened in the United States. Castle Island in Boston's harbor, home of one of the country's oldest forts, underwent reconstruction, resulting in a primitive type of penitentiary. Castle Island could be more accurately defined as a collection of state-run, hard-labor camps. The island camps were fully functional by 1785, with most of the labor camp construction completed by 1800. The island served as a bellwether for two important changes in American criminal justice. First, the camp complex signified a transition from older, community-based punishments designed to use the criminal's inclusion in the town to rehabilitate him. Now, the goal of the justice system was to remove the criminal from the town and separate him, either "fixing" his behavior, or at least getting some use from his labor. Second, because the Massachusetts state government built and administered the camp, it marked a movement toward centralization of criminal justice and a move from local, more intimate policing to organized, centralized methods. In short, punishment in the United States moved from being a public affair to a private one, marginalizing criminals out of the public eye and under the supervision of the state, not the community.

Sentencing convicts to Castle Island and later to other state-run facilities did not completely lack drawbacks. Debates began in the 1780s that still exist today, primarily about the standards applied when meting out punishment in such strict, harsh facilities. Those unable to pay fines were much more susceptible to hard labor sentencing, so places like Castle Island became not just a holding place for criminals but also one specifically geared to poor criminals. Slaves, minors, and unskilled workers received sentences of hard labor at double or triple the rate of farmers, landowners, or businessmen. Although the new types of punishment drew praise from proponents of industry and even the church, which routinely warned that "idle hands" led to crime, the fine/hard labor system in America also illustrated class discrimination at a new level.

Influences of the Enlightenment Philosophy on U.S. Criminal Justice
The conversion from an admonition-based, congregational system of punishment to a centralized scheme of workhouses and, eventually, penitentiaries, did not occur solely as a utilitarian response to changing demographics. The American Revolution and subsequently the French Revolution inspired significant movements in liberal philosophy. The thinkers and writers subscribing to the new "enlightenment philosophy" actively discussed crime and punishment, and their publications did much to encourage debate and experimentation. The United States was after all seen as a grand experiment in Enlightenment thought, as it was founded on principles including the inherent rights of man and the fair and equal treatment of citizens. There was no better place to establish experimental penitentiaries and workhouses and no better climate in which to debate their merits.

Reformation movements certainly were not unique to America, as the writings of philosophers like Montesquieu and Voltaire fueled the French Revolution and writers like Adam Smith, Thomas Paine, and Jeremy Bentham encouraged similar reforms in Britain. Each of these authors built on the ideas of the others, however, so American thought on criminal justice and reformation of punishment systems thrived. Of particular interest to the new country's earliest administrators were the writings of Baron Montesquieu. Beginning with his book *The Spirit of Laws*, published in 1748, Montesquieu argued against severe corporal punishments like branding and even some of the shaming techniques so popular at the time. He suggested that corporal punishment and humiliation violated the natural rights of citizens and existed as symptoms of unfit government. Not coincidentally, these ideals were echoed in the myriad of declarations on human rights coming out of the United States in the middle of the 1770s. The codification of treatises against cruel or unusual punishment commenced with the approval of a cruel and unusual punishment amendment to the Virginia Declaration of Rights, submitted by George Mason, a fervent student of the early Enlightenment works of Matthew Hale and William Blackstone, both stringent opponents of branding and humiliation. The urbanization of the country later in the century, during the 1780s and 1790s, augmented ideas of individuality and individual rights at the expense of the old communal lifestyles, so arguments like Montesquieu's achieved significant American support.

The development of individualist philosophies and the stress on natural, individual rights worked hand-in-hand with a country founded on and now emphasizing the importance of personal freedom. Ironically, though, this exceptional degree of freedom created unique problems for those fighting crime. An old adage manifested itself in Enlightenment America—where order thrives, so does oppression, but where freedom and liberty are the rule, crime inevitably follows. As a result, the president, governors, and county officials of the newborn country found themselves mired in a fight against exploding crime rates in excess of those in the more established European monarchies.

To reconcile policies designed to stem the tide of high crime with the religious ideals acting as the country's philosophical foundation, American Enlightenment thinkers addressed the legacy of Puritan theology and rationales concerning sin and law. The key to compromise rested in the Puritan theology of rehabilitation. Though the earliest Puritans strongly believed in innate human depravity and the inevitability of sin (which they equated with crime unequivocally), they believed just as strongly that the soul could be restored. Puritan thinkers such as Cotton Mather wrote extensively on "original sin" and "natural conscience," suggesting that sin clouded human conscience, but that proper instruction at the secular level, combined with heavenly grace, could clear it.

Consequently, although the early colonial forms of punishment involving humiliation tactics seemed antithetical to Enlightenment philosophy, they illustrated, at their simplest level, a belief in the ability of the criminal justice system to reform and rehabilitate criminals—an idea perfectly in line with writers such as Montesquieu. Further, the old Puritan notions about crime melded well with the new ideas when it came to the concept of separating the criminal from society. While the Puritans believed that criminal tendencies could be corrected through a practical approach, they also recognized that some criminals could become hardened and irreparable. The solution in the 17th and first half of the 18th century was banishment from the group. Now lacking community ties, the criminal could be banished instead to a state facility through hard labor or incarceration.

The concept of human perfectibility existed at the very root of the European Enlightenment, and it found a receptive audience in the new American republic, founded on similar ideas a century before. Activists then only needed to pose the optimistic idea that crime, and the human condition in general, could be repaired, restored, and rehabilitated. Work camps came to be seen as factories for rebuilding defective people; their evolution into the modern American penitentiary, defined as a house of corrections rather than punishment, existed as a logical next step.

Post-Revolutionary Role of Rationalism and Utilitarianism
Beyond ideologies on human rights and human rehabilitation, however, such writers as Montesquieu and Bentham prescribed a method of logical governance known as rationalism, or utilitarianism. The rationalists suggested rejection of scripture in favor of human logic and reason. To this end, rationalist writers suggested that government should be secular and, instead of basing policies on an interpretation of God's bidding, should attempt to maximize "secular utility" by providing the greatest possible level of happiness to the greatest possible number of citizens. For the rationalists, then, crime was no longer the same as "sin," because what made something a crime was not its biblical interpretation, but instead the harm it did to others. Beyond this, the only rational reason for punishment was to prevent future harm, not as retribution. Accordingly, the doling out of punishment was a necessary evil used only to prevent harm to the greater portion of society.

The most influential writings in America on the rationalist view of crime and punishment came from Cesare Beccaria. Though neither a lawyer nor a student of criminal justice, Beccaria wrote from the perspective of a logical outsider. His work on jurisprudence and punishment reached its apex with the 1764 publication of his *Essay on Crimes and Punishments*. In it, he recommended reforms and ideals still seen in the American justice system today. Besides proposing the utilitarian philosophy of "the greatest good for the greatest number," Beccaria suggested that crime should be defined as an injury to society and that punishment should be proportional to the measure of the injury the crime inflicted. He further stated that no punishment was justifiable unless it deterred future criminal conduct and that it should be speedy and humane. He made special note of the growing problem of property crime, suggesting that the only proportional punishment for stealing money or goods was paying a fine equitable to the financial injury. Barring that, only imprisonment could be a reasonable reaction. Beccaria's philosophies were studied extensively by Americans such as Jefferson, Madison, and Mason, and subsequently found their way into many aspects of American judicial and penal reform during their tenures in office.

This rationalist view of crime and punishment opened the way to the penitentiary system. If punishment could no longer be seen as retributive, then at best it must serve as rehabilitative. If rehabilitation could not be achieved, the most basic necessity to protect the greater good would be to remove the offender from society in order to prevent further harm. Through incarceration, the offender would sacrifice his personal freedom for the good of the larger portion of society around him. Furthermore, the rationalists began rejecting the notion that crime was inherent in men, but instead suggested that criminals were a product of a dysfunctional environment. Removal of the criminal from that family or other faulty environment not only protected the other members of society but also provided an opportunity for possible reform, since the individual was now located safely away from the bad influences around him.

The rationalists included Thomas Jefferson, appointed in 1777 as the chair of a committee to revise the legal codes in the states and at the federal level. The committee was asked to completely overhaul the laws of the British Parliament and rewrite them with a new slant toward the utilitarian Enlightenment philosophies. The results of the committee's work laid the foundation for the modern American criminal justice system. Among other changes, Jefferson's reformed code abolished the death penalty for all crimes but murder and treason, prescribed hard labor sentences in public works facilities for all other felonies, removed sentencing options deemed inhumane, and emphasized restrained, reasonable treatment of prisoners that emphasized their rehabilitation above all else. Although Jefferson and his colleagues built these statements firmly on European writings, the implementation of these ideas and the correlative construction of new federal and state workhouses and penitentiaries proved to be uniquely American.

Trends in the States: North Versus South

With the Declaration of Independence in 1776 and the end of British rule over the colonies, the harmonized approach to criminal law and prosecution receded. Differences developed with few restrictions. Generally, the advance of two broadly different state approaches to crime and punishment were observed from 1777 to 1800. Northern states moved to advance a new, rehabilitative model, while southern states continued with colonial traditions, buttressed by their continued attachment to plantation systems of justice.

The more liberal states such as Massachusetts and Pennsylvania led the adoption of the new policies, while more conservative states such as Georgia changed over more

The Walnut Street jail in Philadelphia, 1789, which was converted to a prison in 1790. As the first U.S. state-run prison, it modeled the northern practices of small, solitary rooms for hardened criminals, where they were to become penitent through silent contemplation. Women and children were separated from male and adult prisoners, respectively; combining ages was previously common practice, which resulted in exploitation.

slowly from the English common law system to the new American rationale, further reflecting just how radically different the new American approach had become.

Because of demographic pressures and changing criminal patterns, executives in the state governments, particularly in the north, had been considering the transition to a penitentiary system for years. As early as 1765, the state assembly in Massachusetts entertained funding construction of a new prison and public workhouse designed specifically for punitive incarceration.

Proponents of the construction included Peter Oliver, justice of the Massachusetts Superior Court; James Otis, the advocate general and influential Boston representative; Edward Trowbridge, attorney general of Massachusetts (a Superior Court justice by 1767); and Lieutenant-Governor Thomas Hutchinson. Although the implementation of the policy was well backed, funding was lacking. It would take the Enlightenment philosophy and the tangible, radical change of the American Revolution, together with the demographic requirements, changing criminal patterns, revolutionary ideology of reform, and a self-conscious willingness of Americans, to build a new utopian society to merge and allow the creation of a new experimental form of crime control.

Following the Revolution, northern states began to move to the new approach to crime as defined by an emphasis on redemption and rehabilitation. Their move away from public forms of punishment and corporal punishment to the use of rehabilitative prisons and the reclassifying of many previously capital crimes to less than capital evidenced this. In the north, reformers pushed for consistent, rather than severe punishment as the best means of deterrence and prevention. As these states moved from English common law to statutory or code law, the discretionary power of judges and juries waned. Pennsylvania, for instance, took the common law crime of murder and defined it statutorily into degrees, beginning in 1794, with descriptions of the circumstances and punishments that each degree of the crime could trigger. The use of set prison terms proportionate to the crimes committed and that included rehabilitative activity became the northern standard.

Pennsylvania's Walnut Street prison, converted from a jail in 1790, is illustrative of northern practices. The first state-run penitentiary in the United States, it included two housing models, common rooms, and small solitary rooms. Lesser criminals were allowed to interact with fellow convicts in the common rooms, but hardened offenders were closeted in extremely small cells and prohibited from most interactions to allow them to silently contemplate their failings and become penitent. Further, this prison separated women and debtors from male convicts as well as children from the adult population, reducing opportunities for exploitation. In another reform, Pennsylvania banned alcohol, which jailers would often bring and sell to prisoners. Additionally, the head warden of Walnut Street received a state salary, rather than "fees" paid by vulnerable prisoners. The prison employed convicts in useful industry, including nail making, shoe making, and weaving for outside contractors.

Southern states, on the other hand, did not typically respond to the opportunities offered in the post-Revolutionary period with a reform of criminal laws or punishments. In the south, slavery meant that the "adjudication" and punishment of much crime fell to private hands via the plantation system, which typically gave owners absolute power over slaves and "special courts," which enforced only slave codes, with unique and highly restrictive rules for the defendant slaves. Neither the plantation nor the state system focused on individual reform or rehabilitation, as did the north. Instead, slavery and its maintenance occupied much of the southern legal focus. Not only slave masters, but also any white had authority to summarily punish black-only crimes (such as owning hunting dogs) under southern slave codes, which usually applied to any black, regardless of status.

In the south, these systems provided a way for the dominant powers in local communities to ensure that their values were enforced, often violently, and sometimes outside of the legal system, although often with its tactic consent. For slaves, the transition from public punishment to private correctional punishment would continue to lag behind, with the plantation replacing the colonial village as the environment—the only one in which humiliation and admonition was still effective. For the rest of the country (and eventually the south as well), the general transition from community- and humiliation-based punishments to centralized, homogenized penitentiary systems administered at the state level proved to be the norm. This transition has been attributed to factors beyond demographic changes.

Transition to Penitentiaries: Other Factors Considered

Historians suggest a range of explanations as to why the penitentiary system finally took hold in the United States. David Rothman, in his *The Discovery of the Asylum: Social Order and Disorder in the New Republic*, suggests that reformers hoped the penitentiary would instill self-discipline in prisoners who had not received it from their dysfunctional environment. In his estimate, the penitentiary was seen more than just a disciplinary institution; it was a "total institution" that addressed rehabilitation, reduction of crime, treatment of insanity, and correction of poverty and idleness. In his writings, historian Michael Ignatieff stresses the capitalist aspects of the penitentiary and workhouse, which utilized factory-like schedules and rigid routines to help reform prisoners and, simultaneously, provided manufactured goods to the community. French philosopher Michel Foucault defines it as a new technology still designed to punish, but to punish "better" in a time when everything was being improved or modified to perform more efficiently. Finally, historian Michael Meranze uses the penitentiary's development in Philadelphia to illustrate how it was a response to the breakdown of traditional hierarchies. Rich artisans and businessmen of the city, with newfound political power, preferred institutions focusing on hard labor, since as a group they tended to link idleness with crime. For them, the productive citizen could be the redeemed citizen.

The rise of the penitentiary system in the United States likely involves aspects of all these explanations. Although incarceration was hardly a new idea, its function and definition changed. Citizens in Europe and even colonial America had been imprisoned for debt previously, but this was more as a form of coercion to pay than of deterrence or rehabilitation. County gaols held the accused until trial, and a lack of funding to build facilities for prisoners of war led to their use—particularly in Massachusetts—as holding facilities for military internment. Additionally, the gaols could be used to hold such political prisoners as Indians, Quakers, Jesuits, and loyalists. Despite the existence of jails (by 1776, most states mandated that each county maintain one), they had always been a second choice of penalty and were treated as an afterthought. Jail terms before the Revolution rarely ran beyond three months, and for most offenses, terms could be as little as 24 hours.

Adoption of the Penitentiary System in the New Republic

Relative to these figures, the adoption of the penitentiary as a method of corrections signified a sea change. Institutions deemed more appropriate for the larger, more anonymous cities they now served replaced older concepts of crime control favored by the intimate villages of the previous century. Just as the 17th-century criminal was seen as a family member who had gone astray and could be goaded back to the fold by his peers, the criminal of the late 18th century came to be seen first as a danger to productive society who must be removed for the community's protection, then as a subject of correction and rehabilitation through the repair of his faulty upbringing and the introduction of the habit of doing an honest day's work.

In accordance with the philosophical changes, the model of Pennsylvania's Walnut Street penitentiary was followed by every state in the Union, though again, the more "British" and conservative states seemed slower to embrace the American philosophy; South Carolina waited until 1868. Despite the slow adoption of the philosophy in some regions, once the penitentiary was embraced as the preferred method of a humane, humanist, and liberal society, a movement began that has yet to be replaced.

In keeping with the new logic that criminals were born of a dysfunctional subculture, the American citizens of the 1790s attempted to identify these individuals, seek them out, and incorporate them into the penitentiary system of rehabilitation as quickly as possible. As a result, the institution of professional police forces, trained to identify and apprehend these products of broken society, followed. The first such institution began as a reorganization of Boston's night watchmen. This group, which had served the city as watchmen since 1635, was reorganized into a salaried, professional force in 1796. Officers received badges, uniforms, and a special hooked weapon designed to grab runaway offenders.

Thus, the development of the penitentiary replaced community policing and tactics of humiliation and admonition because of a combination of new demographic pressures and changing philosophies about the nature of crime and corrections. The old public punishments, which were also crafted as examples to others, now carried on inside the walls of the new state prisons. Public whipping or standing in the prison's gallows in front of the other inmates were the punishments for prisoners found guilty of a prison's community rules. The instances of community discipline within the penitentiary walls illustrate an interesting irony of American jurisprudence. The

Puritan model of congregational policing had not left the American psyche completely; instead, the interpretation of crime, the understanding of criminals, and the definition of "congregation" and "community" altered to reconcile new Enlightenment philosophies with the challenges of a newly formed republic of free citizens.

Conclusion

The post-Revolutionary United States reflected high ideals and practical realities as it haltingly developed new legal, judicial, and penal systems to define, adjudicate, and punish crime in the federal republic. Its founding ideologies, economic priorities and structures, and federal division of power all contributed to the unique solutions that its citizens developed in their making of the new country.

Janet Adamski
University of Mary Hard-Baylor
Joshua Hyles
Baylor University

1777 PRIMARY DOCUMENT

Slave Petition for Freedom to the Massachusetts Legislature

On January 13, 1777, Prince Hall and seven other black men submitted a petition to the Massachusetts Revolutionary Council and the House of Representatives. It was the fifth petition submitted by slaves in Massachusetts since 1772. Petitioning the legislature for freedom was one of the few tactics available to slaves. In the colonial era, although it was attempted numerous times, these petitions were routinely denied or ignored as the colonial legislature lacked the authority to act. This 1777 petition, however, was unique: It came during the Revolutionary War, less then a year after the signing of the Declaration of Independence, when Massachusetts no longer acknowledged the British Parliament; even more importantly, it explicitly challenges the commonwealth by tying the ideals of the revolutionaries to the freedom craved by slaves.

To The Honorable Counsel & House of [Representa]tives for the State of Massachusitte [Massachusetts] Bay in General Court assembled, Jan. 13, 1777.

The petition of A Great Number of Blackes detained in a State of slavery in the Bowels of a free & Christian Country Humbly shuwith [showeth] that your Petitioners apprehend that thay [they] have in Common with all other men a Natural and Unaliable [inalienable] Right to that freedom which the Grat Parent of the Unavers hath Bestowed equalley on all menkind and which they have Never forfuted by any Compact or agreement whatever—but thay wher Unjustly Dragged by the hand of cruel Power from their Derest friends and sum of them Even torn from the Embraces of their tender Parents—from A popolous Pleasant and plentiful contry and in violation of Laws of Nature and off Nations and in defiance of all the tender feelings of humanity Brough hear Either to Be sold Like Beast of Burthen & Like them Condemnd to Slavery for Life—Among A People Profesing the mild Religion of Jesus A people Not Insensible of the Secrets of Rational Being Nor without spirit to Resent the unjust endeavours of others to Reduce them to a state of Bondage and Subjection your honouer Need not to be informed that A Life of Slavery Like that of your petioners Deprived of Every social privilege of Every thing Requisit to Render Life Tolable is far worse then Nonexistence.

[In Imitat]ion of the Lawdable Example of the Good People of these States your petitiononers have Long and Patiently waited the Evnt of petition after petition By them presented to the Legislative Body of this state and cannot but with Grief Reflect that their Success hath ben but too similar they Cannot but express their Astonishment that It has Never Bin Considred that Every Principle form which Amarica has Acted in the Cours of their unhappy Dificultes with Great Briton Pleads Stronger than A thousand arguments in favowrs of your petioners they therfor humble Beseech your honours to give this petion [petition] its due weight & consideration & cause an act of the Legislatur to be past Wherby they may be Restored to the Enjoyments of that which is the Naturel Right of all men—and their Children who wher Born in this Land of Liberty may not be heald as Slaves after they arrive at the age of twenty one years so may the Inhabitance of this Stats No longer chargeable with the inconstancey of acting themselves the part which they condem and oppose in others Be prospered in their present Glorious struggle for Liberty and have those Blessing to them, &c.

Source: Massachusetts Historical Society. *Collections of the Massachusetts Historical Society*. Vol. III, Fifth Series. Boston: Massachusetts Historical Society, 1877. http://historymatters.gmu.edu/d/6237

See Articles: African Americans; Massachusetts; Slavery; Slavery, Law of.

George Washington's Writings on Benedict Arnold's Treason

Benedict Arnold was a New Englander who became a general in the Continental Army after early victories in the Revolutionary War. Despite his successes, he made numerous enemies, some who were promoted in his stead, others who charged him with corruption. When Congress claimed (inaccurately) that he had mismanaged his funds, he began secret negotiations with the British, planning to turn over West Point. His betrayal was exposed, prompting his flight.

This, the best disposition you can of your force, so as to have a proportion of men in each work on the Westside of the River. You will see or hear from me further tomorrow. I am etc.

To Lieutenant Colonel John Jameson
Headquarters, Robinson's House, September 25, 1780, O'Clock P.M.
 Sir: I wish every precaution and attention to be paid to prevent Major Andre from, making his escape. He will without doubt effect it if possible and in order that he may not have it in his power. You will send him under the care of such a party and so many Officers as to preclude him from the least opportunity of doing it. That he may be less liable to be recaptured by the Enemy, who will make every effort to gain him. He had better be conducted to this place by some upper road rather than by the route thro Crompond. I would not wish Mr. Andre to be treated with insult, but he does not appear to stand upon the footing of a common prisoner of War and therefore he is not entitled to the usual indulgencies they receive, and is to be most closely and narrowly watched.
 General Arnold before I arrived here went off today to the Enemy, and is on board the Vulture Sloop of War. I am etc. Andre must not escape.

To Major General William Heath
Robinson's House, September 26, 1780
 Dr. Sir: In the present situation of things I think it necessary that You should join the Army, and request that You will do it. You will come to Headquarters: Yourself: the Route thro Litchfield will be the most eligible for You on account of security and You may direct your baggage to halt at Fish Kill for your further orders. I write to the Count de Rochambeau by this conveyance and I trust that your coming away now will not be attended with any material inconvenience to him.
 I cannot conclude without informing You of an event which has happened here which will strike You with astonishment and indignation. Major General Arnold has gone to the Enemy. He had had an interview with Major Andre, Adjutant Genl. of the British Army, and had put into his possession a state of our Army; of the Garrison at this post; of the number of Men considered as necessary for the defense of it; a Return of the Ordinance, and the disposition of the Artillery Corps in case of an Alarm. By a most providential interposition, Major Andre was taken in returning to New York with all these papers in General Arnold's handwriting, who hearing of the matter kept it secret, left his Quarters immediately under pretense of going over to West Point on Monday forenoon, about an hour before my arrival, then pushed down the river in the barge, which was not discovered till I had returned from West Point in the Afternoon and when I received the first information of Mr. Andre's captivity Measures were instantly taken to apprehend him, but before the Officers sent for the purpose could reach Verplank's point, he had passed it with a Flag and got on board the Vulture Ship of War, which lay a few miles below. He knew of my approach and that I was visiting with the Marquiss, the North and Middle Redoubts, and from this circumstance was so straitened in point of time that I believe, he carried with him but, very few if any material papers, tho he has a very precise knowledge of the Affairs of the post.
 The Gentlemen of General Arnold's family, I have the greatest reason to believe, were not

privy in the least degree to the measures he was carrying on, or to his escape. I am etc.

Source: Commins, S., ed. *Basic Writings of George Washington*. New York: Random House, 1948.

See Articles: American Revolution and Criminal Justice; Washington, George (Administration of).

1787 PRIMARY DOCUMENT

Thomas Jefferson on the Need for the Occasional Revolution

A Virginia lawyer, intellectual, and agitator for revolution, Thomas Jefferson was also the principal author of the Declaration of Independence and the wartime governor of Virginia, a job at which he fared poorly and was not reelected. At the time of this letter, the future president was minister to France, which was about to begin a bloody and ill-fated revolution inspired by America's war for independence. Busy in France during the Constitutional Convention held in Philadelphia, he wrote in praise of the recent Shays Rebellion.

To Colonel Smith.

Paris, November 13, 1787.

Dear Sir, I am now to acknowledge the receipt of your favors of October the 4th, 8th, and 26th. In the last, you apologize for your letters of introduction to Americans coming here. It is so far from needing apology on your part, that it calls for thanks on mine. I endeavor to show civilities to all the Americans who come here, and who will give me opportunities of doing it; and it is a matter of comfort to know, from a good quarter, what they are, and how far I may go in my attentions to them.

Can you send me Woodmason's bills for the two copying presses for the Marquis de La Fayette and the Marquis de Chastellux? The latter makes one article in a considerable account, of old standing, and which I cannot present for want of this article. I do not know whether it is to yourself or Mr. Adams, I am to give my thanks for the copy of the new constitution. I beg leave through you to place them where due. It will yet be three weeks before I shall receive them from America. There are very good articles in it, and very bad. I do not know which preponderate. What we have lately read, in the history of Holland, in the chapter on the Stadtholder, would have sufficed to set me against a chief magistrate, eligible for a long duration, if I had ever been disposed towards one; and what we have always read of the elections of Polish Kings should have forever excluded the idea of one continuable for life. Wonderful is the effect of impudent and persevering lying. The British ministry have so long hired their gazetteers to repeat, and model into every form, lies about our being in anarchy, that the world has at length believed them, the English nation has believed them, the ministers themselves have come to believe them, and what is more wonderful, we have believed them ourselves. Yet where does this anarchy exist? Where did it ever exist, except in the single instance of Massachusetts? And can history produce an instance of rebellion so honorably conducted? I say nothing of its motives. They were founded in ignorance, not wickedness. God forbid we should ever be twenty years without such a rebellion. The people cannot be all, and always, well informed. The part which is wrong will be discontented, in proportion to the importance of the facts they misconceive. If they remain quiet under such misconceptions, it is a lethargy, the forerunner of death to the public liberty. We have had thirteen States independent for eleven years. There has been one rebellion. That comes to one rebellion in a century and a half, for each State. What country before, ever existed a century and a half, for each State. What country before, ever existed a century and a half without a rebellion? And what country can preserve its liberties, if its rulers are not warned from time to time, that this people preserve the spirit of resistance? Let them take arms. The remedy is to set them right as to facts, pardon and pacify them. What signify a few lives lost in a century or two? The tree of liberty must be refreshed from time to time, with the blood of patriots and tyrants. It is its natural manure. Our convention has been too much impressed by the insurrection of Massachusetts; and on the spur of the moment, they are setting up a kite to keep the hen yard in order. I hope in God, this article will be rectified before the new constitution is accepted. You ask me if anything transpires here on the subject of South America? Not a word. I know that there are combustible materials there, and that they wait the torch only. But this country probably will join the extinguishers. The want of facts worth communicating to you, has occasioned me to give a little loose to dissertation. We must be contented to amuse, when we cannot inform.

Present my respects to Mrs. Smith, and be assured of the sincere esteem of, dear Sir, your friend and servant.

Source: Jefferson, Thomas, Andrew Adgate Lipscomb, Albert Ellery Bergh, and Richard Holland Johnston. *The Writings of Thomas Jefferson*. Washington, DC: Thomas Jefferson Memorial Association of the United States, 1903–04.

See Articles: Anarchists; Jefferson, Thomas; Jefferson, Thomas (Administration of); Massachusetts.

Excerpts From the Memoirs of Abigail Abbot Bailey

Abigail Bailey published her memoir in 1815, a shocking story in which her religious devotion contrasted with the violence and inhumanity of her husband, Town Selectman Asa Bailey, leading to Abigail's attempts to divorce him. Asa was physically and psychologically abusive in addition to raping the couple's teenage daughter, but Abigail was dependent on him and found it difficult to publicly defy him. The memoir has been compared to the captivity narratives of its era.

I Abigail Bailey do now undertake to record some of the dealings of the allwise God with me, in events, which I am sure I ought solemnly to remember, as long as I live.

April 15, 1767. I was married to Asa Bailey, just after having entered the 22nd year of my age. I now left my dear parent—hoping to find in my husband a true hearted and constant friend… But before one month, from my marriage day, had passed, I learned that I must expect hard and cruel treatment in my new habitation, and from my new friend.

Dec, 1788. He would spend his time with this daughter, in telling idle stories, and foolish riddles… had such conduct appeared toward any young woman besides his own young daughter, I should have no question what he intended. After a while Mr. B's conduct toward this daughter was strangely altered. Instead of idle songs, fawning and flattery, he grew very angry with her; and would wish her dead, and buried; and he would correct her very severely.

Among the many instances of his wickedly correcting her, I shall mention one. One morning Mr. B rose from bed, which it was yet dark. He immediately called this daughter and told her to get up. She obeyed. And as she knew her daily business, she made up her fire in her room, and sat down to her work. He sat by the fire in the kitchen. As my door was open, I carefully observed his motions… He sprang from his chair, and called his daughter. She left her work in her room and came immediately to him. In great rage, and with a voice of terror, he asked why she did not come to him, when he first called her? She respectfully told him that he called her to get up, which she immediately did, and went to her work. But she said she did not hear him call her to come to him. He seized his horse whip, and said, in a rage, he would make her know that when he called her, she should come to him. He then fell to whipping her without mercy. She cried and begged, and repeated her assertion, that she did not know he called her to come to him. She had done as he told her.

None can describe the anguish of my heart on the beholding of such scenes. How pitiful must be the case of a poor young female, to be subjected to such barbarous treatment by her own father; so that she knew of no way to redress!

Source: Bailey, Abigail Abbot and Ann Taves. *Religion and Domestic Violence in Early New England: The Memoirs of Abigail Abbot Bailey.* Bloomington: Indiana University Press, 1989.

See Articles: Child Abuse, History of; Child Abuse, Sociology of; Children's Rights; Domestic Violence, History of.

1793 PRIMARY DOCUMENT

The Fugitive Slave Act of 1793

Under the Articles of Confederation, there were provisions for dealing with fugitive criminals but none for fugitive slaves. This was one of the concerns brought before the Constitutional Convention by the South Carolina delegates, resulting in the provision in Article Four, Section 2, Clause 3 of the Constitution requiring that fugitive slaves from another state be returned to their owner. The Fugitive Slave Act created the legal mechanism for this to occur.

Statutes at Large, Chap. VII, p. 302,
February 12, 1793
Chapter VIIC

An Act respecting fugitives from justice, and persons escaping from the service of their masters.

Sec. 1. Be it enacted by the Senate and House of Representatives of the United States of America in Congress assembled, That whenever the executive authority of any state in the Union, or of either of the territories northwest or south of the river Ohio, shall demand any person as a fugitive from justice, of the executive authority of any such state or territory to which such person shall have fled, and shall moreover produce the copy of an indictment found, or an affidavit made before a magistrate of any state or territory as aforesaid, charging the person so demanded, with having committed treason, felony or other crime, certified as authentic by the governor or chief magistrate of the state or territory from whence the person so charged fled, it shall be the duty of the executive authority of the state or territory to which such person shall have fled, to cause him or her to be arrested and secured, and notice of the arrest to be given to the executive authority making such demand, or to the agent of such authority appointed to receive the fugitive, and to cause the fugitive to be delivered to such agent when he shall appear: But if no such agent shall appear within six months from the time of the arrest, the prisoner may be discharged. And all costs or expenses incurred in the apprehending, securing, and transmitting such fugitive to the state or territory making such demand, shall be paid by such state or territory.

Sec. 2. And be it further enacted, That any agent, appointed as aforesaid, who shall receive the fugitive into his custody, shall be empowered to transport him or her to the state or territory from which he or she shall have fled. And if any person or persons shall by force set at liberty, or rescue the fugitive from such agent while transporting, as aforesaid, the person or persons so offending shall, on conviction, be fined not exceeding five hundred dollars, and be imprisoned not exceeding one year.

Sec. 3. And it be also enacted, That when a person held to labour in any of the United

States, or in either of the territories on the northwest or south of the river Ohio, under the laws thereof, shall escape into any other of the said states or territory, the person to whom such labour or service may be due, his agent or attorney, is hereby empowered to seize or arrest such fugitive from labour, (b) and to take him or her before any judge of the circuit or district courts of the United States, residing or being within the state, or being any magistrate of a county, city or town corporate, wherein such seizure or arrest shall be made, and upon proof to the satisfaction of such judge or magistrate, either by oral testimony or affidavit taken before and certified by a magistrate of any such state or territory, that the person so seized or arrested, doth, under the laws of the state or territory from which he or she fled, owe service or labour to the person claiming him or her, it shall be the duty of such judge or magistrate to give a certificate thereof to such claimant, his agent or attorney, which shall be sufficient warrant for removing the said fugitive from labour, to the state or territory from which he or she fled.

Sec. 4. And it be further enacted, That any person who shall knowingly and willingly obstruct or hinder such claimant, his agent or attorney in so seizing or arresting such fugitive from labour, or shall rescue such fugitive from such claimant, his agent or attorney when so arrested pursuant to the authority herein given or declared; or shall harbor or conceal such person after notice that he or she was a fugitive from labour, as aforesaid, shall for either of the said offences, forfeit and pay the sum of five hundred dollars. Which penalty may be recovered by and for the benefit of such claimant, by the action of debt, in any court proper to try the same; saving moreover to the person claiming such labour or service, his right of action for or on account of the said injuries or either of them.

Approved, February 12, 1793

Source: http://academic.udayton.edu/race/02rights/slave02.htm

See Articles: Fugitive Slave Act of 1793; Slavery; Slavery, Law of.

1794 PRIMARY DOCUMENT

Runaway Slave Notice

While slavery is associated in hindsight with the southern states, this notice offering a reward for the return of a recently escaped slave comes from the Rising Sun *newspaper in Ulster County, New York. The $10 reward is comparable to other rewards offered in the period; in comparison, a slave would have sold for about $800. Colden suspects a neighbor of harboring his slave; until the Fugitive Slave Act in 1850, there were few legal repercussions for doing so.*

TWENTY DOLLARS REWARD.

Ran away from the subscriber on the 19th instant, a negro man named Peter, about 22 years of age, tall and of a yellowish complexion. He fled precipitately from his work in fear of a deserved correction. He only had on him a flannel shirt, a short jacket without sleeves, a pair of leather breeches, and woolen stockings. As this was the case, it is supposed that he must have been harboured by some ill-disposed neighbor, as not the least intelligence has been had of his being seen since. Any person taking up the said negro twenty miles from his master's house, and bringing him home, shall be entitled to the above reward of twenty dollars and all reasonable charges paid; but if in the neighbourhood, within twenty miles, then only ten dollars.

Alexander Colden
Coldenham, Ulster County,
May 21, 1794.

N. B. He speaks both English and Dutch, and has an impediment in his speech.

Source: http://www.hrvh.org/cdm4/item_viewer.php?CISOROOT=/hhs&CISOPTR=587)

See Articles: Fugitive Slave Act of 1793; Slavery; Slavery, Law of.

1794 PRIMARY DOCUMENT

Washington Proclamation on the Whiskey Rebellion

The constitutional federal government was empowered to levy taxes, and in 1791 taxed whiskey in order to pay off some of the national debt. Frontiersmen immediately complained that they were unfairly targeted, as many farmers turned surplus grain into whiskey, not only for sale but also to pay their workers. Tax resisters threatened violence from the start, and armed insurrection began in 1794, in western Pennsylvania. Washington did his best to suppress it with minimal casualties or acrimony.

BY AUTHORITY

By the president of the United States of America

A PROCLAMATION

Whereas, combinations to defeat the execution of the laws laying duties upon spirits distilled within the United States and upon stills have from the time of the commencement of those laws existed in some of the western parts of Pennsylvania.

And whereas, the said combinations, proceeding in a manner subversive equally of the just authority of government and of the rights of individuals, have hitherto effected their dangerous and criminal purpose by the influence of certain irregular meetings whose proceedings have tended to encourage and uphold the spirit of opposition by misrepresentations of the laws calculated to render them odious; by endeavors to deter those who might be so disposed from accepting offices under them through fear of public resentment and of injury to person and property, and to compel those who had accepted such offices by actual violence to surrender or forbear the execution of them; by circulation vindictive menaces against all those who should otherwise, directly or indirectly, aid in the execution of the said laws, or who, yielding to the dictates of conscience and to a sense of obligation, should themselves comply therewith; by actually injuring and destroying the property of persons who were understood to have so complied; by inflicting cruel and humiliating punishments upon private citizens for no other cause than that of appearing to be the friends of the laws; by intercepting the public officers on the highways, abusing, assaulting, and otherwise ill treating them; by going into their houses in the night, gaining admittance by force, taking away their papers, and committing other outrages, employing for these unwarrantable purposes the agency of armed banditti disguised in such manner as for the most part to escape discovery;

And whereas, the endeavors of the legislature to obviate objections to the said laws by lowering the duties and by other alterations conducive to the convenience of those whom they immediately affect (though they have given satisfaction in other quarters), and the endeavors of the executive officers to conciliate a compliance with the laws by explanations, by forbearance, and even by particular accommodations founded on the suggestion of local considerations, have been disappointed of their effect by the machinations of persons whose industry to excite resistance has increased with every appearance of a disposition among the people to relax in their opposition and to acquiesce in the laws, insomuch that many persons in the said western parts of Pennsylvania have at length been hardy enough to perpetrate acts, which I am advised amount to treason, being overt acts of levying war against the United States, the said persons having on the 16th and 17th of July last past proceeded in arms (on the second day amounting to several hundreds) to the house of John Neville, inspector of the revenue for the fourth survey of the district of Pennsylvania; having repeatedly attacked the said house with the persons therein, wounding some of them; having seized David Lenox, marshal of the district of Pennsylvania, who previous thereto had been fired upon while in the execution of his duty by a party of armed men, detaining him for some time prisoner, till, for the preservation of his life and the obtaining of his liberty, he found it necessary to enter into stipulations to forbear the execution of certain official duties touching processes issuing out of a court of the United States; and having finally obliged the said inspector of the revenue and the said marshal from considerations of personal safety to fly from that part of the country, in order, by a circuitous route, to proceed to the seat of government, avowing as the motives of these outrageous proceedings an intention to prevent by force of arms the execution of the said laws, to oblige the said inspector of the revenue to renounce his said office, to withstand by open violence the lawful authority of the government of the United States, and to compel thereby an alteration in the measures of the legislature and a repeal of the laws aforesaid;

And whereas, by a law of the United States entitled "An act to provide for calling forth the militia to execute the laws of the Union, suppress insurrections, and repel invasions," it is enacted that whenever the laws of the United States shall be opposed or the execution thereof obstructed in any state by combinations too powerful to be suppressed by the ordinary course of judicial proceedings or by the powers vested in the marshals by that act, the same being notified by an associate justice or the district judge, it shall be lawful for the President of the United States to call forth the militia of such state to suppress such combinations and to cause the laws to be duly executed. And if the militia of a state, when such combinations may happen, shall refuse or be insufficient to suppress the same, it shall be lawful for the President, if the legislature of the United States shall not be in session, to call forth and employ such numbers of the militia of any other state or states most convenient thereto as may be necessary; and the use of the militia so to be called forth may be continued, if necessary, until the expiration of thirty days after the commencement of the of the ensuing session; Provided always, that, whenever it may be necessary in the judgment of the President to use the military force hereby directed to be called forth, the President shall forthwith, and previous thereto, by proclamation, command such insurgents to disperse and retire peaceably to their respective abodes within a limited time;

And whereas, James Wilson, an associate justice, on the 4th instant, by writing under his hand, did from evidence which had been laid before him notify to me that "in the counties of Washington and Allegany, in Pennsylvania, laws of the United States are opposed and the execution thereof obstructed by combinations too powerful to be suppressed by the ordinary course of judicial proceedings or by the powers vested in the marshal of that district";

And whereas, it is in my judgment necessary under the circumstances of the case to take measures for calling forth the militia in order to suppress the combinations aforesaid, and to cause the laws to be duly executed; and I have accordingly determined so to do, feeling the deepest regret for the occasion, but withal the most solemn conviction that the essential interests of the Union demand it, that the very existence of government and the fundamental principles of social order are materially involved in the issue, and that the patriotism and firmness of all good citizens are seriously called upon, as occasions may require, to aid in the effectual suppression of so fatal a spirit;

Therefore, and in pursuance of the proviso above recited, I. George Washington, President of the United States, do hereby command all persons, being insurgents, as aforesaid, and all others whom it may concern, on or before the 1st day of September next to disperse and retire peaceably to their respective abodes. And I do moreover warn all persons whomsoever against aiding, abetting, or comforting the perpetrators of the aforesaid treasonable acts; and do require all officers and other citizens, according to their respective duties and the laws of the land, to exert their utmost endeavors to prevent and suppress such dangerous proceedings.

In testimony whereof I have caused the seal of the United States of America to be affixed to these presents, and signed the same with my hand. Done at the city of Philadelphia the seventh day of August, one thousand seven hundred and ninety-four, and of the independence of the United States of America the nineteenth.

G. Washington,
By the President,
Edm. Randolph

Sources: *Claypoole's Daily Advertiser* (August 11, 1794); and http://avalon.law.yale.edu/18th_century/gwproc03.asp

See Articles: American Revolution and Criminal Justice; Civil Disobedience; Presidential Proclamations; Tax Crimes; Washington, George (Administration of).

1795
PRIMARY DOCUMENT

United States v. Mitchell

John Mitchell was one of the insurrectionists in the Whiskey Rebellion, but the extent of his role isn't clear. He was talked into intercepting the U.S. mail—so that the rebels could ascertain local opinion on the whiskey tax—by one of the leaders, David Bradford, but he suffered from some degree of mental incapacity, and it's unknown how much he knew about the ramifications of his actions. He was one of only two insurrectionists convicted, but was pardoned by Washington.

The United States
v.
Mitchell

2 U.S. 348 (1795)

U.S. Supreme Court

Indictment for High Treason, by levying war against the United States. It was alledged, that the prisoner was one of the party that assembled at Couche's Fort, armed; that he proceeded thence to Gen. Neville's, and assisted at the burning of the general's house; that he attended with great zeal at the meeting at Bradock's field; and that on the day prescribed for signing a submission to the government he was intoxicated, refused to sign himself, and was active in dissuading others from signing. The circumstance of the prisoner's being at Couche's was proved by a number of witnesses; his being at Bradock's field, by one witness and his own confession; but there was only one positive witness to the fact of his having been at the burning of general Neville's house, tho' a second witness said 'it ran in his head that he had seen him there,' and a third declared that he had passed him on the march thither. The scope of the testimony as it respected the general object of the insurrection, and as it particularly applied to the prisoner, will be found sufficiently stated in the course of the arguments and charge.

The Attorney of the District (Rawle) having closed the evidence, proceeded to state the law, in support of the prosecution. So frequently and fully has the offence of levying war against the government been defined, that a doubt can hardly be raised upon the subject. Kings, it is true, have endeavoured to augment the number, and to perplex the descriptions, of treasons, as an instrument to enlarge their powers, and to oppress their subjects; but in Republics, and, particularly, in the American Republic, the crime of treason is naturally reduced to a single head, which divides itself into these Constitutional propositions: 1st. Levying war against the government, and 2ndly. Adhering to its enemies, giving them aid and comfort: In other words, exciting internal, or waging external, war, against the State. The second branch of the crime, thus designated, renders it unlawful and treasonable for any citizen to adhere to a foreign, public, enemy, whether assailing the frontiers, or penetrating into the heart, of our country. But while such a co-operation endangers the success and prosperity of the community, the effects of domestic insurrection, (which the first branch of the division contemplates) strike at the root of its existence; and, in free countries above all, must be prevented, or corrected, by the most vigilant and efficient sanctions of the law. What constitutes a levying of war, however, must be the same, in technical interpretation, whether committed under a republican, or a regal, form of government; since either institution may be assailed and subverted by the same means. Hence we are enabled, in the first stage of our own experience, to acquire precise and satisfactory ideas upon the subject, from the matured experience of another government, which has employed the same language to describe the offence, and is guided by the same rules of judicial exposition. By the English authorities, it is uniformly and clearly declared, that raising a body of men to obtain, by intimidation or violence, the repeal of a law, or to oppose and prevent by force and terror, the execution of a law, is an act of levying war. Doug. 570. Again; an insurrection with an avowed design to suppress public offices, is an act of levying war: And, although a bare conspiracy to levy war, may not amount to that species of treason; yet, if any of the conspirators actually levy war, it is treason in all the persons that conspired; and in Fost. 218, it is even laid down, that an assembly armed and arrayed in a warlike manner for a treasonable purpose is Bellum levatum, though not Bellum percussum. Those, likewise who join afterwards, though not concerned at first in the plot, are as guilty as the original conspirators; for in Treason all are principals; and whenever a lawless meeting is convened, whether it shall be treated as riot, or treason, will depend on the quo animo. 4 Bl. Com. 81. 1 H. H. P. C. 133. 4. Fost. 213. 210. 215. 218. 1 Hawk. P. C. 37. 4 Bl. Com. 35. 1 Hal. P. C. 440. 8 St. Tr. 247. 2 St. Tr. 586. 7. Keil. 19. 3 Inst. 9. The evidence, unfortunately, leaves no room for excuse, or extenuation, in the application of the law to the prisoner's case. The general and avowed object of the conspiracy at Couche's Fort, was to suppress the offices of excise in the Fourth Survey. As an important measure for that purpose, it was agreed to go to General Neville's house, and to compel him to surrender his office, and his official papers. Some of the persons who were at Couche's Fort, went, accordingly, to General Neville's, and terminated a course of lawless and outrageous proceedings by burning his house. The prisoner is proved by four witnesses to have been at Couche's Fort; and so far from opposing the expedition to General Neville's, he offered himself to reconnoitre. Being thus originally combined with the conspirators, in a treasonable purpose, to levy war, it was unnecessary that the purpose should be afterwards executed, in order to convict them all of treason, and much less is it necessary to his conviction, that he should have been present at the burning of General Neville's house, which was the consummation of their plot, or that the burning should be proved by two witnesses. But he is, likewise, discovered, by one of the witnesses at least, within a few rods of the General's, at the moment of the conflagration; and he is seen marching in the cavalcade, which escorted the dead body of their leader, in melancholy triumph, from the scene of action to Barclay's house. It is not necessary to consider the meeting at Bradock's field as an independent treason, though the avowed intention was to attack the garrison at Pittsburgh, and to expel certain public officers from the town; but the conduct of the prisoner on that occasion, concurring in every violent proposition that was made; and his refractory and seditious deportment on the day prescribed for signing the declaration of submission to the laws; are corroborat ve demonstrations of that mala mens, that dark and dreary turbulence of soul, which is regardless of every social, moral, and religious obligation.* The Counsel for the prisoner (E. Tilghman & Thomas) premised, that they did not conceive it to be their duty to shew, that the prisoner was guiltless of any description of crime against the United States, or the State of Pennsylvania; but they contended, that he had not committed the crime of High Treason; and ought, therefore, to be acquitted upon the present indictment. The adjudications in England upon the various descriptions of treason, have been worked, incautiously, into a system, by the destruction of which, at this day, the government itself would be seriously affected: but even there, the best judges and the ablest commentators, while they acquiesce in the decisions that have already taken place, furnish a strong caution against the too easy admission of future cases, which may seem to have a parity of reason. Constructive, or interpretative treasons, must be the dread and scourge of any nation that allows them. 1 Hal. P. C. 132. 259. 4 Bl. Com. 85. Take, then, the distinction of treason by levying war, as laid down by the Attorney of the District, and it is a constructive, or interpretative, weapon, which is calculated to annul all distinctions heretofore wisely established in the grades and punishments of crimes; and by whose magic power a mob may easily be converted into a conspiracy; and a riot aggravated into High Treason. Such, however, is not the sense which Congress has expressed upon this very subject; for, if a bare opposition to the execution of a law can be considered as constituting a traiterous offence, as levying war against the government, it must be equally so, in relation to every other law, as well as in relation to the excise law; and in relation to the Marshall of a Court, as much as in relation to the Supervisor of a District: And yet, in the Penal Code of the United States, the offence of wilfully obstructing, resisting, or opposing, any officer, in serving, or attempting to serve any process, is considered and punished merely as a misdemeanor. (1 Vol. Swift's Edit. p. 109. s. 22.) Let it be granted, that to compel Congress to repeal a law, by violence, or intimidation, is treason (and the English authorities rightly construed, claim no greater concession) it does not follow, that resisting the execution of a law, or attempting to coerce an officer into the resignation of his commission, will amount to the same offence. Let it be granted, also, that an insurrection, for the avowed purpose of suppressing all the excise offices in the United States, may be construed into an act of levying war against the government (and the English authorities speak expressly of the universality of the object, as an essential characteristic of this species of treason) it does not follow that an attempt to oblige one officer to resign, or to suppress all the offices in one district, will be a crime of the same denomination.

Source: http://supreme.justia.com/us/2/348/case.html

See Articles: Civil Disobedience; Political Dissidents; Riots; Supreme Court, U.S.

1799 PRIMARY DOCUMENT

John Adams: Proclamation on the Insurrection in Pennsylvania

Shortly after the Whiskey Rebellion, another insurrection arose in Pennsylvania: Fries's Rebellion, led by John Fries, a veteran of the Revolutionary War. Congress enacted new taxes to pay for the Quasi-War against France and was clumsy in handling their collection. Fries organized a movement to drive tax assessors out of Pennsylvania. While Adams pardoned Fries upon his treason conviction, his Federalists lost their support among the German-American communities.

Whereas, combinations to defeat the execution of the law for the valuation of lands and dwelling-houses within the United States, have existed in the counties of Northampton, Montgomery, and Bucks, in the State of Pennsylvania, and have proceeded in a manner subversive of the just authority of the government, by misrepresentations to render the laws odious, by deterring the officers of the United States to forbear the execution of their functions, and by openly threatening their lives: And whereas, the endeavors of the well-affected citizens, as well as of the executive officers, to conciliate a compliance with those laws, have failed of success, and certain persons in the county of Northampton, aforesaid, have been hardy enough to perpetrate certain acts, which I am advised, amount to treason, being overt acts of levying war against the United States, the said persons, exceeding one hundred in number, and, armed and arrayed in a warlike manner, having, on the seventh day of the present month of March, proceeded to the house of Abraham Lovering, in the town of Bethlehem, and there compelled William Nicholas, Marshal of the United States, and for the district of Pennsylvania, to desist from the execution of certain legal processes in his hands to be executed, and having compelled him to discharge and set at liberty certain persons whom he had arrested by virtue of a criminal process, duly issued for offenses against the United States, and having impeded and prevented the commissioners and assessors, in conformity with the laws aforesaid, in the county of Northampton aforesaid, by threats of personal injury, from executing the said laws, avowing as the motive of these illegal and treasonable proceedings an intention to prevent, by force of arms, the execution of the said laws, and to withstand by open violence the lawful authority of the government of the United States. And whereas, by the Constitution and laws of the United States, I am authorized, whenever the laws of the United States shall be opposed, or the execution thereof obstructed, in any State, by combinations too powerful to be suppressed by the ordinary course of judicial proceedings or by powers vested in the marshal, to call forth military force to suppress such combinations, and to cause the laws to be duly executed; and I have accordingly determined so to do, under the solemn conviction that the essential interests of the United States demand it. Wherefore I, John Adams, President of the United States, do hereby command all persons being insurgents as aforesaid, and all others whom it may concern, on or before Monday next, being the eighteenth day of this respective abodes. And I do, moreover, warn all persons whomsoever, against aiding, abetting, or comforting the perpetrators of the aforesaid treasonable acts, and I do require all officers and others, good and faithful citizens, according to their respective duties and the laws of the land, to exert their utmost endeavors to prevent and suppress such dangerous and unlawful proceedings.

In testimony whereof, &c.
John Adams
12 March, 1799

Source: Adams, John and Charles Francis Adams. *The Works [of] John Adams, Second President of the United States.* New York: AMS, 1971.

See Articles: Adams, John (Administration of); Civil Disobedience; Pennsylvania; Political Dissidents; Presidential Proclamations; Riots.

1799 PRIMARY DOCUMENT

The Shays Rebellion in Massachusetts

In 1799, farmer, soldier, and author William Manning published The Key of Liberty, *a political treatise on the dangers of the "few" (the elite) ruling over the "many" (most others). In the following selection, he writes of the Shays Rebellion, an armed uprising in the months before the Constitutional Convention in 1787. The rebellion was led by Daniel Shays, a Revolutionary War veteran who, like many others, faced difficulties collecting his back pay from the government.*

What most establishes me in the opinion that this plan will answer comes from my own observations of the operation of these causes in our own government, especially the causes, conduct, and final issue of the insurrection that happened in Massachusetts in 1785 and 1786. As I lived near the scene of action and received frowns from both sides for being opposed to their measures, it drew my closest attention and observation. And though I have been too lengthy already, yet I must here give a short history of it.

On The Shays Affair In Massachusetts

At the close of the British war, although our paper money died away and left the people greatly in debt by it, and a great public debt was on us by the war, yet there was a large quantity of hard money among us sufficient for a medium. But for want of the proper regulation of trade and with the prices of labor and produce being higher here than in other countries, our merchants shipped the hard money off, load after load, by the hundred thousand dollars together to Britain for trifling gewgaws and things that were of no service to us, until there was but little left. Taxes were extremely high. Some counties were two or three years behind. And with the prices of labor and produce falling very fast, creditors began calling for old debts and saying that they would not take payment in paper money. Those who had money demanded forty or fifty percent for it. And fee office officers demanded three or four times so much fees as the law allowed them, and were so crowded with business that sometimes it was hard to get any done. Property was selling almost every day by execution for less than half its value. The jails were crowded with debtors. And with the people being ignorant that all their help lay in being fully and fairly represented in the legislature, many small towns neglected to send representatives in order to save the cost—so that the Few only were represented at court [that is, the Massachusetts state legislature, known as the General Court], with an aristocratic Bowdoin as governor at their head.

Under all these circumstances, the people were driven to the greatest extremity. Many counties took to conventions remonstrances, and petitions to a court where they were not half represented. But not being heard, and in some instances charged with seditious meetings and intentions, under all these circumstances, some counties were so foolish as to stop the courts of justice by force of arms. This shook the government to its foundation. For instead of fatherly counsels and admonitions, the dog of war let loose upon them, and they were declared in a state of insurrection and rebellion.

In these circumstances, the Few were all alive for the support of the government, and all those who would not be continually crying, "Government, Government," or who dared to say a word against their measures, were called Shaysites and rebels threatened with prosecutions, etc. But with a large majority of the people thinking that there was blame on both sides, or viewing one side as knaves and the other as fools, it was with great difficulty and delay before a sufficient number could be raised and sent to suppress those who had closed the courts.

But the suppression was done with the loss of but few lives. This put the people in the most zealous searches after a remedy for their grievances. Thousands and thousands of miles were ridden to consult each other on the affair, and they happily effected it in a few months only by using their privileges as electors. Bowdoin was turned out from being governor and Hancock was almost unanimously elected in his place. Many of the old representatives shared the same fate, and a full representation was from every part of the state, which soon found out means redress the grievances of the people, though they were attended with the most difficult circumstances, so that everything appeared like the clear and pleasant sunshine after a most tremendous storm.

This is a striking demonstration of the advantages of an elective government and shows how a people may run themselves into the greatest difficulties by inattention in elections, and how they can retrieve their circumstances by attending to them again. This Shays affair never would have happened if there had then been such a society as I now propose. Many people then would have sacrificed half their interest to have been possessed of such means of knowledge.

This affair, too, is a striking demonstration of the madness and folly of rising up against a government of our own choice when we have constitutional means of redress in our own hands. For although it was supposed by many that if Hancock had been governor at that time—even after the courts were stopped—that the whole affair might have been settled with less than a thousand dollars cost; yet it was so managed that it cost the state (in time and money) near a million dollars, and it almost entirely ruined hundreds of honest, well-meaning men that only needed the means of knowledge I have described.

Thus, my friends, I have freely given you my opinion of the causes that destroy free governments and of a remedy against them, not in the language and style of the learned (for I am not able), but in as plain a manner as I am capable. And I have done it from a conviction that it was my duty, and for the happiness of mankind. If I have misrepresented anything or used any unbecoming language, it is for the want of knowledge and learning. For I am a true friend to all orders of men and individuals I are friends to true liberty and the rights of man. The remedy I have described is not a costly one, for confident I am that penny laid out in it would soon save pounds in other needless expenses. Therefore, unless you see more difficulty in applying it, or less need of it than I do, you will immediately put it on foot and never give over until such a society is established on such a lasting foundation that the gates of hell will not prevail against it—which may the Almighty grant is the sincere desire of a Laborer

Source: Manning, William. *The Key of Libberty, Shewing the Causes Why a Free Government Has Always Failed, And a Remidy Against It*. Billerica, MA: Manning Association, 1922. Written in 1798, with notes and a foreword by Samuel Eliot Morison.

See Articles: Civil Disobedience; Massachusetts; Riots; Tax Crimes.

1801 to 1850
INTRODUCTION

Americans encountered new challenges of independence from 1801 to 1850: an increasingly mobile population, and the realization that earlier methods to address crime and punishment were no longer adequate. In the first years of the 19th century, reformers attempted to meet these new challenges by developing and reforming institutions, including legal codes, police departments, and carceral facilities. Differences emerged between treatment of criminals in state or local facilities and depending on the location of such institutions, both in the north and the south. Crime and punishment in the antebellum period signaled the shift from colonial to American enforcement.

From 1801 to 1850, the new nation experienced significant change. Americans increasingly moved westward, transplanting or adopting their eastern institutions in new towns and cities. Immigrants also added to the growth and mobility of American society. Urban areas, especially New York, Boston, and Philadelphia, experienced new growth from population movement. City residents perceived increased criminal activity, including theft, public drunkenness, prostitution, and violent actions. Attitudes toward crime and punishment in the first decades of the 19th century demonstrate the nation's shift from the village and stronger local connections between people to a more mobile and transient society.

Enforcement of criminal activity also reflected a clear shift from earlier English colony governance to a republican form of government. Americans perceived that earlier mechanisms to control crime and shame criminals were no longer effective. More critically, they were no longer seen as compatible with democracy but instead represented tyranny reminiscent of monarchical rule. The reformation of law enforcement methods was intended to avoid endangering the liberties of American citizens.

Laws and Crime in the New Nation

After the American Revolution, leaders sought to create a system of laws and punishments that differed from that of the colonial era. England's legal code was a compilation of court cases, rather than a codified set of laws. Recognition of the limits of common law prompted the nation's first leaders to codify laws at both the national and state levels. During the Revolution, states drafted constitutions to stipulate the liberties of the people. Constitutions also presented the process for adding or amending laws in the future. Such written contracts were deemed critical to maintaining republican rule in the new nation. Laws could be amended as outlined by the constitutions, not changed as political leadership changed.

Nationally, this change was signified in the adoption of the U.S. Constitution and, more critically, the Bill of Rights. Americans wanted protections from the potential tyranny of their new national government. The new constitution and national laws meant that these protections should be available to all citizens in the nation. More importantly, Americans wanted to ensure that the law would be applied equally to all citizens. Under the English system, an individual could escape punishment (including death) if he or she was saved by the king's mercy. Such actions created a legal system based not on equity, but on patronage. As Americans wanted to create a more republican legal structure, crimes and punishments needed to be clearly articulated and equally applied to all.

Republican citizens and leaders were supposed to be educated, involved, and in pursuit of the good of the nation above individual desires. The definition of the term *citizen* was expanding to more individuals. As the antebellum period progressed, the nation increasingly emphasized the liberty of the white male population. States began to lift property restrictions on the franchise, meaning that more men than ever before could vote; therefore, participation in elections through voting and attending campaign events dramatically increased. Democracy replaced deference to political and social leaders, and politically, all white men were to be treated as equals. However, such changes were not beneficial to all.

New understandings of the role of the individual in society also influenced changes in defining and punishing criminals. Reformers sought to reform criminals, rather than use public humiliation, permanent alterations to criminals' bodies, or ostracization. In his 1996 book *Laboratories of Virtue*, history researcher Michael Meranze documents the shift from public punishment to the rise of the penitentiary and connects it to the rise of liberalism in the antebellum north, specifically in Philadelphia. He contends that imprisonment, through discipline, represented a different way of treating the body of the convicted. Public displays of corporal punishment were no longer generally accepted, and punishment moved out of the public eye. Reformers wanted to adopt more humane and equitable forms of law enforcement and punishment in the young nation.

A more mobile society also meant that previous communal connections between individuals were ineffective. Lower classes no longer deferred to the upper classes, residents no longer knew everyone within a village or small town, and encounters with strangers became more common. Worries about new types of crimes and criminals emerged in the first decades of the 19th century. "Confidence men," or men who presented themselves falsely for personal gain, were particularly dangerous in the new republic. Fears of gamblers and speculators who economically contributed nothing epitomized the potential dangers of a society that was more geographically mobile. Middle-class Americans feared criminals who would take advantage of them, often within the growing cities.

Urban areas especially saw a more visible underworld develop in the antebellum period. History researcher Timothy Gilfoyle examined the rise of prostitution in New York City during the 19th century in his book *City of Eros* (1992). Originally limited to specific streets near docks, brothels and streetwalkers expanded across the city. Madams enjoyed considerable power economically and legally before the professionalization of police enforcement. Rioters who targeted houses of prostitution had to repair the damage done to property, as protection of property was more critical than enforcement of sexual activity. An underworld of commercialized sex prospered in the antebellum city.

> MRS. BIRD, Female Physician, where can be obtained Dr. Vandenburgh's Female Renovating Pills, from Germany, an effectual remedy for suppression, irregularity, and all cases where nature has stopped from any cause whatever. Sold only at Mrs. Bird's, 83 Duane st, near Broadway.   n24 3m*
>
> TO THE LADIES—Madame Costello, Female Physician, still continues to treat, with astonishing success, all diseases peculiar to females. Suppression, irregularity, obstruction, &c., by whatever cause produced, can be removed by Madame C. in a very short time. Madame C's medical establishment having undergone thorough repairs and alterations for the better accommodation of her numerous patients, she is now prepared to receive ladies on the point of confinement, or those who wish to be treated for obstruction of their monthly periods. Madame C. can be consulted at her residence, 34 Lispenard st, at all times.— All communications and letters must be post paid.

An advertisement for Mrs. Bird and Madame Costello, "female physicians" to the "ladies," in the New York Sun *newspaper, February 24, 1842. "Restoration" of feminine "irregularity" was often code for abortion. Women offering such services had knowledge of herbs and other "restoratives": medical procedures were risky because transmission of infection was not well understood.*

The murder of Helen Jewett in April 1836 highlighted the visibility of prostitution. Jewett, a 23-year-old prostitute, was murdered in her room in New York City; a gash was on her head, her room was on fire, and there was a hatchet nearby. Earlier that evening, she had been visited by Richard Robinson, a frequent customer. Robinson was put on trial for Jewett's murder, but despite the overwhelming circumstantial evidence (including his cloak left at the scene), he was found "not guilty" by a jury in June. The case attracted national attention, not only because of the sensational nature of the murder, but also because it highlighted the increasingly visible underground world of prostitution in the city. Private citizens found that they could not compete with the financial power of the underground economy. Heightened visibility of crime further illustrated that new forms of enforcement were needed.

The media coverage of the Jewett Case highlighted the emerging "sporting culture" prevalent in New York City. Young men who worked as professionals during the day often spent their earnings on activities such as drink, gambling, and sex. Robinson symbolized the fluid nature of the early-19th-century city and the decreasing forms of earlier methods of supervision. Young men often headed to the city to make their fortunes. In this case, Robinson served as a clerk for the merchant Joseph Hoxie. During the colonial era, if young men were apprenticed out for a period of years to a master, they were under their constant supervision. They would work as an apprentice by day and live with the master at night, allowing them little freedom of movement. But by the 1820s and 1830s, this system was no longer practiced. Rather, young men came to the city and worked during the day, but lived on their own in boardinghouses. Time away from work was their own, and they lived a vibrant lifestyle emphasized by their economic and sexual independence that was unrestrained by parents, employers, or wives.

The existence of a visible urban sexual underworld would become less tolerated as the 19th century continued. Similarly, abortion was more accepted in the early years of the 19th century than later in the century. Helen Lefkowitz Horowitz, who surveyed sexual knowledge in 19th-century America, including abortion, found that early medical knowledge stressed the importance of maintaining a woman's health. Since it was often difficult to determine with accuracy if a woman was pregnant in the 18th and early 19th centuries, the lack of menstruation was seen as a problem that needed to be corrected. Midwives and other females often had knowledge of herbs or medicines to "restore" a woman's health. Abortions were legal under common law as long as the fetus had not "quickened," meaning that as long as a woman did not feel movement of the fetus, she had miscarried and had not committed a crime. After she had confirmation of pregnancy by feeling the fetus move, any abortive actions were defined as illegal.

As earlier communal networks became strained, women increasingly learned of medicines or abortificients from books, pamphlets, or male doctors. Urban areas provided women with opportunities to gain access to knowledge previously transmitted through female networks of married women, neighbors, and friends. Of the three New York City female abortionists who advertised their services, Madame Restell was the most famous. Restell, whose real name was Ann Trow Lohman, was an immigrant who supported herself and her daughter by working as a seamstress, and later as a practitioner of ways to "restore" a woman's menses. Her activities signify the shift of abortive medicines

"The Riot in Philadelphia" by H. Bucholzer shows how simmering ethnic tensions exploded on July 7, 1844. Nativist groups began a rumor that the Catholic Church was planning to remove the Bible from schools. When the Roman Catholic bishop persuaded school officials to use both the King James and Latin Vulgate bibles, Protestant mobs burned two Catholic churches on May 7 and rioted again in July, prompting intervention by the state militia.

from their private practice within female communities to a more public and commercial enterprise.

Medical procedures in the 19th century were dangerous, largely because germs and antiseptic procedures were unknown. Female abortionists were vulnerable to murder charges when women under their care died. In 1841, Lohman was arrested for the murder of Ann Maria Purdy and found guilty by a jury. Purdy had made a deathbed confession to her husband that she obtained an abortion from Madame Restell. However, Lohman's conviction was ultimately overturned by the New York Supreme Court, citing the inadmissibility of Mrs. Purdy's statements at the trial. Despite the reversal of her conviction, she continued to have legal troubles until her death in 1874.

New York strengthened its laws against abortions in 1845, making anyone found distributing or advising the use of abortificients liable to serving up to one year in jail. The law also ended the open advertisements of such services. Lohman was convicted again, this time under the 1845 law, and served a year in prison on Blackwell Island in 1847. Lohman's legal troubles foreshadowed the implementation of the use of obscenity laws (especially the Comstock Law) against such practices toward the turn of the century.

Police

Early American cities drew upon English models of watchmen and constables for law enforcement. Constables patrolled during the day, enforcing local ordinances and arresting disorderly individuals. Watchmen patrolled urban neighborhoods at night, suppressing rowdy and disorderly behaviors such as drinking, prostitution, and gambling. However, appointment as a watchman did not pay well and was often a second job. Many watchmen fell asleep, drank, or neglected their duties. The creation of police departments presented another challenge to early American republicanism. How could law enforcers protect the rights of property owners without overstepping their authority and endangering the liberty of everyday citizens?

Reformation of the watch and constabulary forces emerged slowly during the antebellum period. The early patrols were inexpensive to maintain, but critics complained that they were no longer effective in suppressing criminal activity. Organized police departments appeared first in the eastern cities, but leaders wanted to ensure that the public did not see them as threatening to the public's liberty. Philadelphia's first police force was a compilation of the watch, constables, and policemen. The force was small in comparison to the number of city residents. Additionally, in an effort to avoid a comparison to a standing army in the city, the first policemen did not wear uniforms.

Forces in cities such as Philadelphia and Chicago often implemented requirements limiting the pool of potential policemen to native-born Americans. Chicago men wanting to serve on the force had to demonstrate their ability to read, speak, and write in English. Nativists argued that immigrants, especially the Irish, would not be good candidates for the position. Policemen, although not yet professional or with codes of conduct to follow, depended on their standing in the community for the position. Reformers often criticized their effectiveness at targeting crime and vice districts, arguing that they were complicit in the continued existence of such activities. Large forces with detectives and patrolmen in uniforms only emerged during the second half of the century.

Political science professor Ann-Marie Szymanski, who examined the role of private protective societies in 19th-century New England, argues that local constabularies and courts, rather than a state police force, were the only crime controls in Massachusetts until the end of the century. To better combat theft, residents often formed private, voluntary associations. Perceived threats of trespassing and theft became more pronounced after the revolution, resulting in such groups such as the Worcester Association for the

Protection of Fruit and the Sheffield Association for the Detection of Horse Thieves. Although large cities began to develop police forces, more rural areas depended on other organizations to control crime in New England.

Carceral Institutions
A new institution to house criminals for longer periods of time was also born in the antebellum period. Punishment shifted from swift public action to longer terms of confinement. Much of the historical studies of punishment address national or state reforms. There were generally four types of detention institutions in the 19th century: state prisons, jails, juvenile reformatories, and workhouses. Administrators of each type of facility adhered to different philosophical principals, depending on those detained.

While the public punishments of the colonial era such as whipping, confinement to the stocks or pillory, or banishment were intended to elicit shame and future compliance with the law, Benjamin Rush and other reformers pressed for incarceration in Philadelphia prisons following the American Revolution. Rush argued that the public, physical punishments were problematic because they were too short to effect change, did not sufficiently deter crime, and elicited public sympathy for the criminal. Their efforts resulted in the construction of the Walnut Street Jail, which opened in 1784, and served as an example that later prisons followed.

Prisons, which were large facilities designed to hold those convicted of felonies for sentences longer than a year, had a clear philosophical basis: to separate criminals from society during their term. Inmates were detained long enough to be reformed so they would not engage in criminal activity upon release. Prisons were largely funded by the state, with money made from contracting out inmate labor helping to defray expenses. Wardens and administrators sought to maintain order with labor, discipline, and inmates' reflections of their previous actions. Generally, they were large institutions located outside of urban areas that held a large population. Inmates had little contact with those outside the prison walls.

Two different prison philosophies and structures emerged during this period: the Auburn and Pennsylvania systems. Under the Pennsylvania system, as exemplified at Eastern State Penitentiary in Philadelphia, inmates were segregated during their entire sentence. They worked, slept, ate, and remained in their cells, with no contact with any other inmate. The Auburn system, named for the New York state prison located there, also stressed the lack of communication with fellow detainees, but they were not physically separated during their entire term. Rather, Auburn inmates would sleep alone in their cells but work during the day with other prisoners in workshops. Silence was maintained in order to prevent the spread of corruption from criminal to criminal. Most state penitentiaries in the United States followed the Auburn system, and the Pennsylvania system was later abandoned throughout the nation. However, its philosophies still remained influential into the 20th century.

States slowly constructed institutions similar to the Walnut Street Jail in the early republic. As Adam J. Hirsch documents in *The Rise of the Penitentiary* (1992), Massachusetts formally shifted from "pillory to penitentiary" in 1813. Corporal punishment was not abolished until 1826. Pennsylvania, through Eastern State Penitentiary; and New York, through Auburn, led the other states from corporal punishment to incarceration as a preferred mode of punishment.

Prison administrators emphasized order, routine, and isolation in both systems to create a corruption-free environment. They also often stripped prisoners of their individuality by replacing their clothing with prison uniforms and cutting their hair upon entrance. Regimentation was deemed necessary to maintain order; prisoners ate the same food and moved in lockstep together, and some states included details in their laws that dictated the smallest details of an inmate's life, including what type of food would be served for meals, the specifications for uniforms, and the daily routine.

The ability of wardens and superintendents to achieve complete segregation, order, and discipline within the prisons was limited, however. Goals of complete isolation were unrealistic, because penitentiaries frequently housed more inmates than their capacity. Seeking to maintain order at all costs, wardens often resorted to punishments such as solitary confinement, along with physical measures, to maintain the silence deemed so critical to reformation.

Meranze details that prisoners at the Walnut Street Jail thwarted administrators' attempts to control and reform the inmate population, often working as slowly and poorly as possible. Rebecca McLennan relates in *The Crisis of Imprisonment* (2008) that prisoners held at Newgate, a New York prison, often rioted, slowed work, and sabotaged machinery and materials. They often used Sundays, set aside as a day of reflection, to gamble and sing bawdy songs. McLennan also asserts that in the 1810s and 1820s, reformers emphasized contract labor in hopes to counter shortcomings in the early prisons.

Smaller, local institutions, such as jails or lockups, held a variety of individuals, including those who were arrested, awaiting trial, and serving sentences for misdemeanors (less than a year). Local facilities had a diverse, ever-changing population of individuals who stayed for months, weeks, days, or even hours at a time. These institutions were often locally administered and funded, meaning that life inside largely depended on a variety of factors. Often, positions were filled by political appointees, based on an individual's connection to the party in power at the time. As a result, superintendents or jail officials may not have been well versed in penal philosophy or practices.

Facilities for juveniles also emerged during the era and sought to prevent young offenders from becoming adult criminals. Understandings of childhood as a separate period of time from adulthood did not fully develop

The arrest of abortionist Ann Lohman (Madame Restell) on the cover of The New York Illustrated Times, *February 1878. Suspected in the 1841 death of Mary Rogers and a purported client, Restell was arrested in 1878 and committed suicide shortly afterward.*

until much closer to the 20th century. The New York City House of Refuge became the first institution specifically opened to address the needs of juvenile offenders. The House of Refuge opened on January 1, 1825, in response to concern over the mingling of young and old criminals at Bellevue Prison. The institution was initially privately funded, but by 1829, public funds had replaced private monies. By 1850, five other cities followed New York's example: Boston, Philadelphia, New Orleans, Baltimore, and Cincinnati.

Administrators at houses of refuge attempted to relieve overcrowding and prevent recommitments by "placing out" inmates. Juveniles were indentured out, sometimes to farms in new states, including Illinois, Indiana, and Ohio. The indenture would last until their 21st birthday. Ideally, the youths would pick up the industrious habits and morals of an agrarian life that would keep them out of a future life of crime.

Initially, houses of refuge were privately or locally funded, but after the turn of the century, many states constructed and administered juvenile reformatories. The first state reformatory was established in Massachusetts in 1848. In Chicago, juvenile offenders were often held with adults in lockups, the jail, and the city prison. This changed during the Progressive Era, as city leaders built the John Worthy School at the House of Correction, eventually abandoned in favor of state institutions after 1915.

Workhouses, also known as houses of correction, were intermediate facilities between prisons and jails that shared the structural and administrative aspects of both. On one hand, they were often local institutions administered by city or county governments. Appointments were politically motivated, with little regard to previous experience in penal administration. Similarly, buildings and services for inmates were funded by city

"The Times," an engraving by H. R. Robinson, depicts the intoxication, violent mobs, and corruption rampant in the United States during the financial panic of 1837. In the background is a bridewell debtors' prison and an almshouse. In addition to overspeculation, the economic failure was blamed on President Andrew Jackson's economic policies, which were also responsible for the Cherokee relocation known as the Trail of Tears the following year.

budgets, dependent on revenues and popular will. However, because they only held those who had been convicted or fined for their offense, rather than those awaiting trial, they were more like prisons in structure, labor requirements, and discipline.

The Chicago Experience
Officials focused on detaining inmates, rather than reforming them. Additionally, since not all detainees were convicted of a crime or offense, the ability to punish or contract labor was significantly reduced. The Cook County Jail, along with the police lockups, served this function in Chicago. As a result, this population was the most fluid of the Chicago carceral institutions. Finally, lockups housed inmates within the city limits, allowing for more contact with outsiders, even during detainment.

Chicago illustrates the difficulties of the implementation of new penal philosophies, especially at the local level. An examination of Chicago's response to crime highlights the growing concern over criminal activity during the antebellum period. Early ordinances and laws in Chicago reflected its former status as a small frontier village. The first detention centers were small, temporary facilities, similar to those in colonial America. Community members self-policed and were wary of strangers. Most crimes were punished through fines, whipping, or the stocks. Americans began to emphasize detainment as a punishment as the 19th century progressed.

The first public law enforcers were nonprofessionals, selected for their standing in the community, not for previous experience. City officials relied upon watchmen and constables to maintain order in the frontier town. Men interested in patrolling as a member of the watch petitioned the city council for the post. For example, in 1843, Horace Scott submitted his petition as watchman along with the signatures of 30 neighbors who supported his request. City council members added more night watchmen as deemed necessary by citizens.

Watchmen or constables in Chicago who arrested ordinance violators took them to a justice of the peace for sentencing. If an arrest occurred overnight, the watchman detained the arrested individual in a watch house until the judge could be contacted the next morning. The construction of watch houses was sporadic and inexpensive. Often, the city council received requests for watch houses from citizens, then approved of the construction if it was deemed necessary. Council members would then accept bids for construction of the structures and select the cheapest one that met previously published specifications.

The appointment of watchmen and constables also reflected the informal procedure of early law enforcement in the burgeoning village. Much like the procedures for establishing watch houses, the process was informal. This did not mean that the post was without rules; the earliest watchmen in Chicago had to adhere to a limited code of conduct. Ordinances highlighted appropriate behavior while on duty. Watchmen could lose their position if they were not found on duty at night, if they did not report for duty at specified times, if they were found to be intoxicated while on patrol, or for other misconduct. For example, Alderman Levi Boone recommended the removal of Anthony Tierney as police constable in December 1846. Boone forwarded a petition to the council in which a complainant reported his experience in the watch house. The petitioner stated that although it was a cold night, Tierney made no accommodation for his comfort either in the form of a fire or blankets. The council concurred with Boone's proposal and removed Tierney.

Confinement in early Chicago was but one course of action available for punishment. Individuals convicted of petty crimes were also subject to public humiliation in the streets, such as performing work to benefit the city. During a two-month period, for example, 25 men worked the equivalent of 109.25 days of labor; five of those worked multiple times for a total of 40 hours. Early violators of city ordinances found themselves detained in small carceral buildings or laboring in view of the public. Many years passed before county and city officials implemented more permanent structures, professional administrators, and cohesive philosophies regarding detention and punishment in the growing city.

Chicago's city leaders slowly created ordinances allowing for the separation of those awaiting trial from those already convicted. Chicago's city charter, which was created and adopted in 1837, contained a provision for the city council to construct and administer a bridewell, or house of correction to confine individuals who violated city ordinances or misdemeanors. Those awaiting trial would continue to be held at the Cook County Jail or police lockups. The charter provided that the city council would be responsible for feeding, maintaining, and employing inmates at the city institution. City council members did not implement this law until they opened the bridewell 15 years later.

City leaders finally began to plan and construct the new facility to meet two goals: relieve overcrowding at the county jail and employ those detained. The proposed bridewell or workhouse could detain some held at the Cook County Jail, which had been overcrowded for years. The jail housed those found guilty of violating a city ordinance, awaiting trial, and convicted of misdemeanor crimes. In addition, inmates were idle, since no provision existed for work or prison labor. The proposed institution could employ inmates to offset potential expenses.

The bridewell finally opened December 15, 1851. The structure illustrated a shift to holding minor criminals in a more permanent facility, but without the later "professionalization" of other institutions such as its successor, the Bridewell House of Correction. Selection of the officers of the bridewell depended on political connections, rather than any previous carceral experience. Appointees administered the day-to-day management of the bridewell while under the control of the city council. None of the administrators of the bridewell had previous experience in detention.

Unlike the earlier Chicago carceral facilities, the bridewell only held those convicted of violating city ordinances or misdemeanors. The two-story wooden structure had 85 cells, each designed to hold one inmate. Those held at the bridewell experienced the realities of 19th-century incarceration: overcrowded conditions, poor food, and punishment within the structure to maintain order.

Andrew Jackson and the Native Americans
Native Americans also encountered the increasing strength of American laws designed to force their movement to the west. Early American settlers encountered Native Americans as they moved west in the early years of the republic. From the 1790s to the 1820s, the federal government negotiated treaties with tribes. Congress implicitly treated Indian tribes as foreign nations with sovereignty and rights to their lands by negotiating with them. However, it often proved difficult to negotiate treaties that proved workable to whole tribes who would accept money or goods for their land. In addition, treaties were often negotiated with native leaders who had no authority to speak for their tribes or to sell tribal lands, creating tensions on both sides.

Some leaders felt that assimilation of Indians into American society would benefit both sides. Missionary associations attempted to "civilize" Native Americans by converting them to Christianity and educating them about American culture. In 1819, Congress authorized $10,000 for missions to instruct Indians in reading, writing, religion, and agricultural practices. Missionaries also sought to explain American ideals of private property and gender roles, hoping to persuade Indian tribes to limit women to domestic activities, instead of farming. Additionally, they hoped to put men in the fields and refrain them from hunting. Such efforts were limited in success. For one thing, native women did not want to adopt a gender system in which they would be even more subordinate to men. Under the traditional system, women held power through growing crops and the freedom to leave a marriage when they wanted.

The Creek, Chickasaw, Choctaw, and Cherokee tribes each had tribal lands in Georgia, North Carolina, Tennessee, Mississippi, Florida, and Alabama. The land attracted white settlers wanting to grow cotton, and this attraction increased with rumors of gold in Georgia in 1829. The Cherokee had attempted to assimilate into American society, adopting written laws in 1808 and a constitution in 1827. Modeled after the U.S. Constitution, the Cherokee constitution set forth a bicameral legislature, an executive office, and a court system. Additionally, more than 200 of the wealthiest Cherokee had married with whites and adopted the white method of dress, cotton agriculture, and housing. Some even owned slaves. Finally, they declared their sovereignty from the state of Georgia.

However, President Andrew Jackson did not feel that native tribes should be seen as foreign. For Jackson, they were merely subjects of the U.S. government (not citizens who had the right to vote), who should be able to maintain villages and agricultural lands,

A restored cellblock in Eastern State Penitentiary, Philadelphia. The prison was abandoned in 1971 and is now a museum. Opened in 1829 and famous for its innovative, radial floor plan and segregated discipline, it was designed to inspire penitence in its inmates. The prison once held some of America's most notorious criminals, including bank robber "Slick Willie" Sutton and Al Capone. It became one of the most copied building designs in early America.

but not have their vast hunting grounds. In 1829, Jackson declared that Indians within U.S. borders could not remain independent and in sovereign control of tribal lands. One year later, Congress agreed and passed the Removal Act of 1830, appropriating $500,000 to move tribes west of the Mississippi.

The Cherokee's declaration of sovereignty from the state of Georgia was ultimately challenged by the state. President Jackson sided with Georgia, which argued that natives were subject to laws that the Cherokee had no voice in creating. The Cherokee sued the state of Georgia to prevent them from being subject to state laws. While the 1831 case was thrown out on a technicality, the 1832 case verdict (*Worcester v. Georgia*) favored the Cherokees. In its decision, the Supreme Court recognized the existence of the Cherokee nation as sovereign, relying on the nation's earlier treatment of Native American tribes. In the process, Chief Justice John Marshall emerged as Jackson's enemy, and despite the court's decision, Jackson proceeded to ensure the expansion of white settlers on Cherokee land.

A few representatives of the Cherokee nation signed the Treaty of New Echota on December 29, 1835. The treaty stipulated that the Cherokee people would be paid $4.5 million for compensation and granted equivalent land in the Indian Territory, and the federal government would cover the costs of relocation. In return, the Cherokee would

This 1850 lithograph condemns the Fugitive Slave Act, which Congress passed in September 1850. Federal commissioners could issue warrants for fugitive slaves and enlist posses and even civilians for apprehending slaves. The print shows two texts, one from Deuteronomy: "Thou shalt not deliver unto the master his servant which has escaped …" and the Declaration of Independence: "We hold that all men are created equal.…"

cede all their land east of the Mississippi. The treaty was ratified by the Senate, but several thousand Cherokee petitioned Congress to ignore the treaty, which was never signed by an official representative of the Cherokee Nation. As most Cherokee refused to leave by the voluntary deadline of May 1838, federal troops arrived to deport them. Most were removed at gunpoint from their homes over three weeks and gathered in camps. Moving in groups of 1,000 each, the Cherokee left for the 1,200-mile trip to Oklahoma known as the Trail of Tears.

Andrew Jackson's new policy of Indian removal highlighted the tensions of a new understanding of liberty in the 1820s. While Jacksonian democracy welcomed the "common man's" participation in politics, for Jackson and his Democratic supporters, this liberty only applied to white males. Women, African Americans, and Native Americans were excluded from attaining liberty because of their "dependent" status. No white man would be under another white man. The liberty of white men depended upon the exclusion of "inferior" others; white men could unite because they were socially "superior" to slaves and women. Even though elite men maintained political control over "common men," the idea of white male liberty served to gloss over class differences that could otherwise fracture white male unity.

The Antebellum Frontier

Violence in the form of criminal behavior is often associated with the frontier because of the perceived weak institutions of courts, police, and other modes of legal enforcement. In the antebellum period, Americans moved across the continent and new states entered the union. Researcher Nicole Etcheson argues that in the case of Massac County, Illinois, such violence was not extralegal, but rather reflected a battle over the function of the legitimate legal authority of the county. In a chapter in *Lethal Imagination: Violence and Brutality in American History* (1999), by Michael A. Bellesiles, she details violence that broke out between competing groups, the Flatheads and the Regulators, from 1846 to 1850.

The Regulators and Flatheads included respected members of the community, complicating traditional understandings of vigilantes seeking extralegal retribution for a lack of legal control. Regulators attacked an individual by the name of Mathis because they thought that he knew more about criminal activity in the area than he told authorities. The Flatheads, the local criminal gang, responded to the attack by countering that the Regulators threatened the civic order of the county.

Massac County was a sparsely populated, isolated frontier region. Etcheson contends that the outbreak of violence was not due to a lack of authority. Rather, she argues that the legal authorities did not have accepted legitimacy. Both the Regulators and Flatheads pointed to the violence of the other group as evidence of their threat to the county. Flatheads used the militia to thwart the Regulators' attack of the legal authority. Lacking a community consensus, the Regulators' efforts were unsuccessful. The violence largely ended by 1850, but continued to plague the region for part of the following decade.

The South and Slavery

Slavery shaped a distinct system of criminal laws and punishment in the antebellum American south. Although northern states abolished slavery after the Revolution, slavery became further entrenched in southern states. Slaves were limited by slave codes designed to further reinforce their status. Additionally, punishments deemed acceptable to use against a slave could not be used against white criminals. Masters violently enforced their will upon rebellious slaves. A master's power was codified through slave laws, which reinforced his complete ownership (and domination) of slaves. Whipping was the most common form of punishment meted out in the antebellum south. Violence could also take a number of other forms.

Masters wielded considerable power in southern society, but other whites could also punish slaves, even those they did not own. States used legal means to further ensure control over the slave population, and such laws served this purpose. Some of these punishments could be meted out after a trial for minor or severe offenses. A justice of the peace could try a slave and order physical punishment such as whippings, branding, or cropping.

Slaves could be convicted of any crime that a white could be punished for, as well as other crimes specific to their status as property. Slaves who ran away, engaged in business illegally, or incited a rebellion could be tried for such actions. Maintaining the legal culture of slavery was critical.

Southern legal codes were designed to maintain the power of masters over slaves, but this control was limited in some instances. Masters in South Carolina had to bring slaves to be tried for offenses that carried the death penalty, such as murder. Virginia executed 58 slaves from 1785 to 1865 for raping white women. Trials were meant to reinforce the racial and social hierarchy in the south, and executions were not meant to deprive an owner of his property. Therefore, statutes in the south often provided some compensation to owners of executed slaves.

Theoretically, slaves were protected from abuse or killing by their masters. Such cases, which were rarely brought to trial, were generally unsuccessful. African Americans, whether free or slave, had few rights in court. They could not testify against white men in a court, meaning that they or any African American witnesses could not appear in court. Restrictions meant that slaves treated cruelly on a plantation had virtually no recourse.

Nationally, federal protection of slavery created increasing conflict between the north and the south and defined new crimes. The Compromise of 1850 illustrates this. In 1850, California asked to be admitted to the Union as a free state. Many southerners opposed the measure, arguing that it would upset the equal balance of power in the Senate. While northern (those that excluded slavery) states had more representation than southern slave states in the House of Representatives, both had equal representation in the Senate. As a result, the south could always block northern legislation that threatened the protection of slavery.

In an effort to avoid sectional conflict, Henry Clay, a senator from Kentucky, offered a plan with four components that came to be known as the Compromise of 1850. First, California would come in the Union as a free state. Second, the slave trade, but not slavery, would be abolished in the nation's capital. Third, the status of slavery in the remaining territory from Mexico would be decided by the local white inhabitants. Fourth, a new and stronger Fugitive Slave Act would be enacted to reclaim escaped slaves, even those in the north. Southerners wanted slavery protected by the national government and allowed to extend into all new territories, but some northern politicians disliked the law because of the stronger fugitive slave law.

The new Fugitive Slave Act allowed special federal commissioners to determine the fate of alleged fugitive slaves, without benefit of a jury trial or even testimony from the accused. Local authorities would be prohibited from interfering with the capture of fugitives and the act required citizens to assist in a capture when federal agents called upon them. Southern leaders, who were normally strong defenders of local autonomy or states' rights, supported a measure that increased federal power to override local law enforcement and judicial procedures to secure the return of runaway slaves. Abolitionists and other private citizens faced new federal punishment for helping escaped slaves or refusing to assist with the capture of escaped slaves.

Conclusion
Slavery, immigration, and new understandings of governance in the young nation influenced the evolution of laws and carceral facilities. Americans created and reformed earlier methods of legal enforcement that would better meet the demands of a more mobile and democratic nation. Cities, states, and the national government implemented laws to ensure order.

Police forces and penitentiaries emerged in the antebellum period, and along with new institutions to address juvenile offenders, were reformed during the second half of the 19th century and into the 20th century.

Susan Garneau
Loyola University Chicago

1807 PRIMARY DOCUMENT

Indictment of Aaron Burr

Best remembered as the vice president who killed Alexander Hamilton in a duel, in his day, Burr was much more infamous as a conspirator who sought to reshape North America. At a time when the United States was a young democracy and European governments still threatened domination of the continent, Burr conspired to seize the Louisiana territory and form an American empire in the west. He was found not guilty because of a narrow definition of treason given the jury by Chief Justice John Marshall.

This is the indictment against Aaron Burr, as read in his trial on August 17, 1807.

Virginia District

In the Circuit Court of the United States of America in and for the Fifth Circuit and Virginia District:

The grand inquest of the United States of America, for the Virginia district, upon their oath, do present, that Aaron Burr, late of the city of New York, and state of New York, attorney at law, being an inhabitant of, and residing within the United States, and under the protection of the laws of the United States, and owing allegiance and fidelity to the same United States, not having the fear of God before his eyes, nor weighing the duty of his said allegiance, but being moved and seduced by the instigation of the devil, wickedly devising and intending the peace and tranquility of the same United States to disturb and to stir, move, and excite insurrection, rebellion and war against the said United States, on the tenth day of December, in the year of Christ, one thousand eight hundred and six, at a certain place called and known by the name of 'Blannerhassett's Island,' in the county of Wood, and district of Virginia aforesaid, and within the jurisdiction of this court, with force and arms, unlawfully, falsely, maliciously and traitorously did compass, imagine and intend to raise and levy war, insurrection and rebellion against the said United States, and in order to fulfil and bring to effect the said traitorous compassings, imaginations and intentions of him the said Aaron Burr, he, the said Aaron Burr, afterwards, to wit, on the said tenth day of December, in the year one thousand eight hundred and six, aforesaid, at the said island called 'Blennerhassett's Island' as aforesaid, in the county of Wood aforesaid, in the district of Virginia aforesaid, and within the jurisdiction of this court, with a great multitude of persons whose names at present are unknown to the grand inquest aforesaid, to a great number, to wit: to the number of thirty persons and upwards, armed and arrayed in a warlike manner, that is to say, with guns, swords and dirks, and other warlike weapons, as well offensive as defensive, being then and there unlawfully, maliciously and traitorously assembled and gathered together, did falsely and traitorously assemble and join themselves together against the said United States, and then and there with force and arms did falsely and traitorously, and in a warlike and hostile manner, array and dispose themselves against the said United States, and then and there, that is to say, on the day and in the year aforesaid, at the island aforesaid, commonly called 'Blannerhassett's Island,' in the county aforesaid of Wood, within the Virginia district and the jurisdiction of this court, in pursuance of such their traitorous intentions and purposes aforesaid, he, the said Aaron Burr, with the said persons so as aforesaid, traitorously assembled and armed and arrayed in manner aforesaid, most wickedly, maliciously and traitorously did ordain, prepare and levy was against the said United States, contrary to the duty of their said allegiance and fidelity, against the constitution, peace and dignity of the said United States, and against the form of the act of the congress of the said United States in such case made and provided And the grand inquest of the United States of America, for the Virginia district, upon their oaths aforesaid, do further present that the said Aaron Burr, late of the city of New York, and state of New York, attorney at law, being an inhabitant of, and residing within the United States, and under the protection of the laws of the United States, and owing allegiance and fidelity to the same United States, not having the fear of God before his eyes, nor weighting the duty of his said allegiance, but being moved and seduced by the instigation of the devil, wickedly devising and intending the peace and tranquility of the said United States to disturb, and to stir, move and excite insurrection, rebellion and war against the said United States, on the eleventh day of December, in the year of our Lord one thousand eight hundred and six, at a certain place called and known by the name of Blannerhassett's Island,' in the county of Wood and district of Virginia aforesaid, and within the jurisdiction of this court, with force and arms unlawfully, falsely, maliciously and traitorously did compass, imagine and intend to raise and levy war, insurrection and rebellion against the said United States; and in order to fulfil and bring to effect the said traitorous compassings, imaginations and intentions of him, the said Aaron Burr, he, the said Aaron Burr, afterwards, to wit: on the said last mentioned day of December, in the year one thousand eight hundred and six aforesaid, at a certain place commonly called and known by the name of 'Blannerhassett's Ialand,' in the said county of Wood, in the district of Virginia aforesaid, and within the jurisdiction of this court, with one other great multitude of persons whose names at present are unknown to the grand inquest aforesaid, to a great number, to wit: to the number of thirty persons and upwards, armed and arrayed in a warlike manner, that is to say, with guns, swords and dirks, and other warlike weapons, as well offensive as defensive, being then and there unlawfully, maliciously and traitorously assembled and gathered together, did falsely and traitorously assemble and join themselves together against the said United States, and then and there with force and arms did falsely and traitorously, and in a warlike and hostile manner, array and dispose themselves against the said United States, and then and there, that is to say, on the day and in the year last mentioned, at the island aforesaid, in the county of Wood aforesaid, in the Virginia district, and within the jurisdiction of this court, in pursuance of such their traitorous intentions and purposes aforesaid, he, the said Aaron Burr, with the said persons so as aforesaid traitorously assembled, and armed and arrayed in manner aforesaid, most wickedly, maliciously and traitorously did ordain, prepare and levy war against the said United States, and further to fulfil and carry into effect the said traitorous compassings, imaginations and intentions of him the said Aaron Burr, against the said United States, and to carry on the war thus levied as aforesaid against the said United States, the said Aaron Burr, with the multitude last mentioned, at the island aforesaid, in the said county of Wood, within the Virginia district aforesaid, and within the jurisdiction of this court, did array themselves in a warlike manner, with guns and other weapons, offensive and defensive, and did proceed from the said island down the river Ohio in the county aforesaid, within the Virginia district and within the jurisdiction of this court, on the said eleventh day of December, in the year one thousand eight hundred and six aforesaid, with the wicked and traitorous intention to descend the said river and the river Mississippi, and by force and arms traitorously to take possession of a city commonly called New Orleans, in the Territory of Orleans, belonging to the United States, contrary to the duty of their said allegiance and fidelity, against the constitution, peace and dignity of the said United States, and against the form of the act of the congress of the United States in such case made and provided.

Hay, Attorney of the United States, for the Virginia District

Indorsed: A true bill John Randolph

A copy Teste, William Marshall, Clerk

Source: http://law2.umkc.edu/faculty/projects/ftrials/burr/burrtrial.html

See Articles: Civil Disobedience; New Orleans, Louisiana; Political Dissidents; Riots; Virginia.

1823 PRIMARY DOCUMENT

Elkinson v. Deliesseline

In 1822, South Carolina passed the Negro Seaman Act, forcing free black sailors entering the state's waters into slavery if their captains did not pay an exorbitant fine. After Caribbean sailor Henry Elkison was accordingly jailed by Sheriff Francis Deliesseline, the law was found unconstitutional on the grounds that only Congress had such powers over interstate commerce; however, the federal government did not intervene when the state refused to acknowledge the ruling.

Ex parte HENRY ELKISON,
A Subject of his Britannic Majesty,
vs.
FRANCIS G. DELIESSELINE,
Sheriff of Charleston District.

On the unconstitutionality of the law under which this man is confined, it is not too much to say that it will not bear argument; and I feel myself sanctioned in using this strong language, from considering the course of reasoning by which it has been defended. Neither of the gentlemen has attempted to prove that the power therein assumed by the state, can be exercised without clashing with the general powers of the United States to regulate commerce: but they have both strenuously contended, that *ex necessitate* it was a power which the state must and would exercise, and indeed Mr. Holmes concluded his argument with the declaration that if a dissolution of the union must be the alternative he was ready to meet it. Nor did the argument of Col. Hunt deviate at all from the same course. Giving it in the language of his own summary, it was this: South-Carolina was a sovereign state when she adopted the constitution--a sovereign state cannot surrender a right of vital importance--South-Carolina therefore either did not surrender this right, or still possesses the power to resume it--and whether it is necessary, or when it is necessary to resume it, she is herself the sovereign judge.

Source: http://memory.loc.gov/cgi-bin/query/r?ammem/llst:@field(DOCID+@lit(llst054div0))

See Articles: Racism; Slavery; Slavery, Law of; South Carolina; State Slave Codes; Supreme Court, U.S.

1831 PRIMARY DOCUMENT

Nat Turner's Jailhouse Confession

31-year-old slave Nat Turner was sentenced to death and hanged three months after leading a slave rebellion in Virginia. For years, Turner had experienced visions he interpreted as messages from God, and he considered two solar eclipses to be signs of approval for his rebellion. After months of planning, over 70 blacks (including 30 free blacks) went house-to-house, freeing slaves and killing whites. Blaming Turner's intelligence, many states made it illegal to teach blacks to read and write.

SIR,—You have asked me to give a history of the motives which induced me to undertake the late insurrection, as you call it—To do so I must go back to the days of my infancy, and even before I was born. I was thirty-one years of age the 2d of October last, and born the property of Benj. Turner, of this county. In my childhood a circumstance occurred which made an indelible impression on my mind, and laid the ground work of that enthusiasm, which has terminated so fatally to many, both white and black, and for which I am about to atone at the gallows. It is here necessary to relate this circumstance—trifling as it may seem, it was the commencement of that belief which has grown with time, and even now, sir, in this dungeon, helpless and forsaken as I am, I cannot divest myself of. Being at play with other children, when three or four years old, I was telling them something, which my mother overhearing, said it had happened before I was I born—I stuck to my story, however, and related some things which went, in her opinion, to confirm it—others being called on were greatly astonished, knowing that these things had happened, and caused them to say in my hearing, I surely would be a prophet, as the Lord had shewn [shown] me things that had happened before my birth. And my father and mother strengthened me in this my first impression, saying in my presence, I was intended for some great purpose, which they had always thought from certain marks on my head and breast—[a parcel of excrescences which I believe are not at all uncommon, particularly among negroes, as I have seen several with the same. In this case he has either cut them off or they have nearly disappeared]—My grandmother, who was very religious, and to whom I was much attached—my master, who belonged to the church, and other religious persons who visited the house, and whom I often saw at prayers, noticing the singularity of my manners, I suppose, and my uncommon intelligence for a child, remarked I had too much sense to be raised, and if I was, I would never be of any service to any one as a slave—To a mind like mine, restless, inquisitive and observant of everything that was passing, it is easy to suppose that religion was the subject to which it would be directed, and although this subject principally occupied my thoughts—there was nothing that I saw or heard of to which my attention was not directed—The manner in which I learned to read and write, not only had great influence on my own mind, as I acquired it with the most perfect ease, so much so, that I have no recollection whatever of learning the alphabet—but to the astonishment of the family, one day, when a book was shewn me to keep me from crying, I began spelling the names of different objects—this was a source of wonder to all in the neighborhood, particularly the blacks—and this learning was constantly improved at all opportunities—when I got large enough to go to work, while employed, I was reflecting on many things that would present themselves to my imagination, and whenever an opportunity occurred of looking at a book, when the school children were getting their lessons, I would find many things that the fertility of my own imagination had depicted to me before; all my time, not devoted to my master's service, was spent either in prayer, or in making experiments in casting different things in moulds made of earth, in attempting to make paper, gunpowder, and many other experiments, that although I could not perfect, yet convinced me of its practicability if I had the means. I was not addicted to stealing in my youth, nor have ever been—Yet such was the confidence of the negroes in the neighborhood, even at this early period of my life, in my superior judgment, that they would often carry me with them when they were going on any roguery, to plan for them. Growing up among them, with this confidence in my superior judgment, and when this, in their opinions, was perfected by Divine inspiration, from the circumstances already alluded to in my infancy, and which belief was ever afterwards zealously inculcated by the austerity of my life and manners, which became the subject of remark by white and black.—Having soon discovered to be great, I must appear so, and therefore studiously avoided mixing in society, and wrapped myself in mystery, devoting my time to fasting and prayer—By this time, having arrived to man's estate, and hearing the scriptures commented on at meetings, I was struck with that particular passage which says : "Seek ye the kingdom of Heaven and all things shall be added unto you." I reflected much on this passage, and prayed daily for light on this subject—As I was praying one day at my plough, the spirit spoke to me, saying "Seek ye the kingdom of Heaven and all things shall be added unto you."

Question—what do you mean by the Spirit.

Ans. The Spirit that spoke to the prophets in former days—and I was greatly astonished, and for two years prayed continually, whenever my duty would permit—and then again I had the same revelation, which fully confirmed me in the impression that I was ordained for some great purpose in the hands of the Almighty. Several years rolled round, in which many events occurred to strengthen me in this my belief. At this time I reverted in my mind to the remarks made of me in my childhood, and the things that had been shewn me—and as it had been said of me in my childhood by those by whom I had been taught to pray, both white and black, and in whom I had the greatest confidence, that I had too much sense to be raised, and if I was, I would never be of any use to any one as a slave. Now finding I had arrived to man's estate, and was a slave, and these revelations being made known to me, I began to direct my attention to this great object, to fulfil the purpose for which, by this time, I felt assured I was intended. Knowing the influence I had obtained over the minds of my fellow servants, (not by the means of conjuring and such like tricks—for to them I always spoke of such things with contempt) but by the communion of the Spirit whose revelations I often communicated to them, and they believed and said my wisdom came from God. I now began to prepare them for my purpose, by telling them something was about to happen that would terminate in fulfilling the great promise that had been made to me—About this time I was placed under an overseer, from whom I ran away—and after remaining in the woods thirty days, I returned, to the astonishment of the negroes on the plantation, who thought I had made my escape to some other part of the country, as my father had done before. But the reason of my return was, that the Spirit appeared to me and said I had my wishes directed to the things of this world, and not to the kingdom of Heaven, and that I should return to the service of my earthly master—"For he who knoweth his Master's will, and doeth it not, shall be beaten with many stripes, and thus, have I chastened you." And the negroes found fault, and murmured against me, saying that if they had my sense they would not serve any master in the world. And about this time I had a vision—and I saw white spirits and black spirits engaged in battle, and the sun was darkened—the thunder rolled in the Heavens, and blood flowed in streams—and I heard a voice saying, "Such is your luck, such you are called to see, and let it come rough or smooth, you must surely bare it." I now withdrew myself as much as my situation would permit, from the intercourse of my fellow servants, for the avowed purpose of serving the Spirit more fully—and it appeared to me, and reminded me of the things it had already shown me, and that it would then reveal to me the knowledge of the elements, the revolution of the planets, the operation of tides, and changes of the seasons. After this revelation in the year 1825, and the knowledge of the elements being made known to me, I sought more than ever to obtain true holiness before the great day of judgment should appear, and then I began to receive the true knowledge of faith. And from the first steps of righteousness until the last, was I made perfect; and the Holy Ghost was with me, and said, "Behold me as I stand in the Heavens"—and I looked and saw the forms of men in different attitudes—and there were lights in the sky to which the children of darkness gave other names than what they really were—for they were the lights of the Saviour's hands, stretched forth from east to west, even as they were extended on the cross on Calvary for the redemption of sinners. And I wondered greatly at these miracles, and prayed to be informed of a certainty of the meaning thereof—and shortly afterwards, while laboring in the field, I discovered drops of blood on the corn as though it were dew from heaven—and I communicated it to many, both white and black, in the neighborhood—and I then found on the leaves in the woods hieroglyphic characters, and numbers, with the forms of men in different attitudes, portrayed in blood, and representing the figures I had seen before in the heavens. And now the Holy Ghost had revealed itself to me, and made plain the miracles it had shown me—For as the blood of Christ had been shed on this earth, and had ascended to heaven for the salvation of sinners, and was now returning to earth again in the form of dew—and as the leaves on the trees bore the impression of the figures I had seen in the heavens, it was plain to me that the Saviour was about to lay down the yoke he had borne for the sins of men, and the great day of judgment was at hand. About this time I told these things to a white man, (Etheldred T. Brantley) on whom it had a wonderful effect—and he ceased from his wickedness, and was attacked immediately with a cutaneous eruption, and blood ozed from the pores of his skin, and after praying and fasting nine days, he was healed, and the Spirit appeared to me again, and said, as the Saviour had been baptised so should we be also—and when the white people would not let us be baptised by the church, we went down into the water together, in the sight of many who reviled us, and were baptised by the Spirit—After this I rejoiced greatly, and gave thanks to God. And on the 12th of May, 1828, I heard a loud noise in the heavens, and the Spirit instantly appeared to me and said the Serpent was loosened, and Christ had laid down the yoke he had borne for the sins of men, and that I should take it on and fight against the Serpent, for the time was fast approaching when the first should be last and the last should be first.

Sources: Turner, Nat and Thomas R. Gray. *The Confessions of Nat Turner: The Leader of the Late Insurrection in Southampton, Va.* Richmond, VA: T. R. Gray, 1832; and http://historymatters.gmu.edu/d/6533

See Articles: African Americans; Civil Disobedience; Slavery; Riots; Virginia.

1835
PRIMARY DOCUMENT

President Jackson's Remarks to Congress on Indian Removal

Under Jefferson, the government's plan for Indians had been to encourage them to settle down in their own farming communities, and to leave them alone if they did so, but subsequent presidents rapidly shifted populations westwards by granting them new lands. Jackson formalized this in 1830, the second year of his presidency. Later in 1835, after this address, the Treaty of New Echota was signed, forcing the Cherokee Nation west on the Trail of Tears in 1938.

The plan of removing the aboriginal people who yet remain within the settled portions of the United States to the country west of the Mississippi River approaches its consummation. It was adopted on the most mature consideration of the condition of this race, and ought to be persisted in till the object is accomplished, and prosecuted with as much vigor as a just regard to their circumstances will permit, and as fast as their consent can be obtained. All preceding experiments for the improvement of the Indians have failed. It seems now to be an established fact that they cannot live in contact with a civilized community and prosper. Ages of fruitless endeavors have at length brought us to a knowledge of this principle of intercommunication with them. The past we cannot recall, but the future we can provide for. Independently of the treaty stipulations into which we have entered with the various tribes for the usufructury rights they have ceded to us, no one can doubt the moral duty of the Government of the United States to protect and if possible to preserve and perpetuate the scattered remnants of this race which are left within our borders. In the discharge of this duty an extensive region in the West has been assigned for their permanent residence. It has been divided into districts and allotted among them. Many have already removed and others are preparing to go, and with the exception of two small bands living in Ohio and Indiana, not exceeding 1,500 persons, and of the Cherokees, all the tribes on the east side of the Mississippi, and extending from Lake Michigan to Florida, have entered into engagements which will lead to their transplantation.

The plan for their removal and reestablishment is founded upon the knowledge we have gained of their character and habits, and has been dictated by a spirit of enlarged liberality. A territory exceeding in extent that relinquished has been granted to each tribe. Of its climate, fertility, and capacity to support an Indiana population the representations are highly favorable. To these districts the Indians are removed at the expense of the United States, and with certain supplies of clothing, arms, ammunition, and other indispensable articles; they are also furnished gratuitously with provisions for the period of a year after their arrival at their new homes. In that time, from the nature of the country and of the products raised by them, they can subsist themselves by agricultural labor, if they choose to resort to that mode of life; if they do not they are upon the skirts of the great prairies, where countless herds of buffalo roam, and a short time suffices to adapt their own habits to the changes which a change of the animals destined for their food may require. Ample arrangements have also been made for the support of schools; in some instances council houses and churches are to be erected, dwellings constructed for the chiefs, and mills for common use. Funds have been set apart for the maintenance of the poor; the most necessary mechanical arts have been introduced, and blacksmiths, gunsmiths, wheelwrights, millwrights, etc., are supported among them. Steel and iron, and sometimes salt, are purchased for them, and plows and other farming utensils, domestic animals, looms, spinning wheels, cards, etc., are presented to them. And besides these beneficial arrangements, annuities are in all cases paid, amounting in some instances to more than $30 for each individual of the tribe, and in all cases sufficiently great, if justly divided and prudently expended, to enable them, in addition to their own exertions, to live comfortably. And as a stimulus for exertion, it is now provided by law that "in all cases of the appointment of interpreters or other persons employed for the benefit of the Indians a preference shall be given to persons of Indian descent, if such can be found who are properly qualified for the discharge of the duties."

Such are the arrangements for the physical comfort and for the moral improvement of the Indians. The necessary measures for their political advancement and for their separation from our citizens have not been neglected. The pledge of the United States has been given by congress that the country destined for the residence of this people shall be forever "secured and guaranteed to them." A country west of Missouri and Arkansas has been assigned to them, into which the white settlements are not to be pushed. No political communities can be formed in that extensive region, except those which are established by the Indians themselves or by the United States for them and with the concurrence. A barrier has thus been raised for their protection against the encroachment of our citizens, and guarding the Indians as far as possible from those evils which have brought them to their present condition. Summary authority has been given by law to destroy all ardent spirits found in their country, without waiting the doubtful result and slow process of a legal seizure. I consider the absolute and unconditional interdiction of this article among these people as the first and great step in their melioration. Halfway measures will answer to purpose. These cannot successfully contend against the cupidity of the seller and the overpowering appetite of the buyer. And the destructive effects of the traffic are marked in every page of the history of our Indian intercourse.

Some general legislation seems necessary for the regulation of the relations which will exist in this new state of things between the Government and people of the United States and these transplanted Indian tribes, and for the establishment among the latter, and with their own consent, of some principles of intercommunication which their juxtaposition will call for; that moral may be substituted for physical force, the authority of a few and simple laws for the tomahawk, and that an end may be put to those bloody wars whose prosecution seems to have made part of their social system.

After the further details of this arrangement are completed, with a very general supervision over them, they ought to be left to the progress of events. These, I indulge the hope, will secure their prosperity and improvement, and a large portion of the moral debt we own them will then be paid.

Source: J. Richardson, ed. *A Compilation of the Messages and Papers of the Presidents*. New York: Bureau of National Literature, 1897.

See Articles: Indian Removal Act; Jackson, Andrew (Administration of); Native Americans.

1838 PRIMARY DOCUMENT

William Lloyd Garrison's Declaration of Sentiments

William Lloyd Garrison was the founder of the Liberator *(1831), a weekly abolitionist newspaper, and of the American Anti-Slavery Society (1833), for which Garrison wrote this declaration. Unlike some abolitionist groups, the AASS was uncompromising, demanding the immediate emancipation of all slaves. The AASS soon became uncomfortable with Garrison's nonviolent stance and inclusion of women, and he and his supporters founded the New England Non-Resistance Society.*

The Convention assembled in the city of Philadelphia, to organize a national Anti-Slavery Society, promptly seize the opportunity to promulgate the following Declaration of Sentiments, as cherished by them in relation to the enslavement of one-sixth portion of the American people.

More than fifty-seven years have elapsed since a band of patriots convened in this place to devise measures for the deliverance of this country from a foreign yoke. The corner-stone upon which they founded the Temple of Freedom was broadly this—"that all men are created equal; that they are endowed by their Creator with certain inalienable rights; that among these are life, LIBERTY, and the pursuit of happiness." At the sound of their trumpet-call, three millions of people rose up as from the sleep of death, and rushed to the strife of blood; deeming it more glorious to die instantly as free men, than desirable to live one hour as slaves. They were few in number—poor in resources; but the honest conviction that Truth, Justice, and Right were on their side, made them invincible.

We have met together for the achievement of an enterprise without which that of our fathers is incomplete; and which, for its magnitude, solemnity and probable results upon the destiny of the world, as far transcends theirs as moral truth does physical force.

In purity of motive, in earnestness of zeal, in decision of purpose, in intrepidity of action, in steadfastness of faith, in sincerity of spirit, we would not be inferior to them.

Their principles led them to wage war against their oppressors, and to spill human blood like water, in order to be free. Ours forbid the doing of evil that good may come, and lead us to reject, and to entreat the oppressed to reject, the use of all carnal weapons for deliverance from bondage; relying solely upon those which are spiritual, and might through God to the pulling down of strongholds.

Their measures were physical resistance—the marshalling in arms—the hostile array—the mortal encounter. Ours shall be such only as the opposition of moral purity to moral corruption—the destruction of error by the potency of truth—the overthrow of prejudice by the power of love—and the abolition of slavery by the spirit of repentance.

Their grievances, great as they were, were trifling in comparison with the wrongs and sufferings of those for whom we plead. Our fathers were never slaves—never bought and sold like cattle—never shut out from the light of knowledge and religion—never subjected to the lash of brutal taskmaster.

But those for whose emancipation we are striving—constituting at the present time at least one-sixth part of our countrymen—are recognized by law, and treated by their fellow-beings, as marketable commodities, as goods and chattels, as brute beasts; are plundered daily of the fruits of their tail without redress; really enjoy no constitutional nor legal protection from licentious and murderous outrages upon their persons; and are ruthlessly torn asunder—the tender babe from the arms of its frantic mother—the heart-broken wife from her weeping husband—at the caprice or pleasure of irresponsible tyrants. For the crime of having a dark complexion, they suffer the pangs of hunger, the infliction of stripes, the ignominy of brutal servitude. They are kept in heathenish darkness by laws expressly enacted to make their instruction a criminal offense.

These are prominent circumstances in the condition of more than two million of our people, the proof of which may be found in thousands of indisputable facts and in the laws of the slaveholding States.

Hence we maintain—that, in view of the civil and religious privileges of this nation, the guilt of its oppression is unequalled by any other on the face of the earth; and, therefore, that it is bound to repent instantly, to undo the heavy burdens, and to let the oppressed go free.

We further maintain—that no man has a right to enslave or imbrute his brother—to hold or acknowledge him, for one moment, as a piece of merchandise—to keep back his hire by fraud—or to brutalize his mind, by denying him the means of intellectual, social and moral improvement.

The right to enjoy liberty is inalienable. To invade it is to usurp the prerogative of Jehovah. Every man has a right to his own body—to the products of his own labor—to the protection of law—and to the common advantages of society. It is piracy to buy or steal a native African, and subject him to servitude. Surely, the sin is as great to enslave an American as an African.

Therefore we believe and affirm—that there is no difference, in principle, between the African slave trade and American slavery:

The every American citizen who retains a human being in involuntary bondage as his property, is, according to Scripture (Ex. Xxi 16), a man-stealer:

That the slaves ought instantly to be set free, and brought under the protection of law:

That if they had lived from the time of Pharaoh down to the present period, and had been entailed through successive generations, their right to be free could never have been alienated, but their claims would have constantly risen in solemnity:

That all those laws which are now in force, admitting the right of slavery, are therefore, before God, utterly null and void; being an audacious usurpation of the Divine prerogative, a daring infringement on the law of nature, a base overthrow of the very foundations of the social compact, a complete extinction of all the relations, endearments and obligations of mankind, and a presumptuous transgression of all the holy commandments; and that therefore they ought instantly to be abrogated.

We further believe and affirm—that all persons of color who possess the qualifications which are demanded of others, ought to be admitted forthwith to the enjoyment of the same privileges, and the exercise of the same prerogatives, as others; and that the paths of preferment, or wealth, and of intelligence, should be opened as widely to them as to persons of a white complexion.

We maintain that no compensation should be given to the planters emancipating their slaves:

Because it would be a surrender of the great fundamental principle, that man cannot hold property in man;

Because slavery is a crime, and therefore is not an article to be sold;

Because the holders of slaves are not the just proprietors of what they claim; freeing the slave is not depriving them of property, but restoring it to its rightful owner; it is not wronging the master, but righting the slave—restoring him to himself;

Because immediate and general emancipation would only destroy nominal, not real, property; it would not amputate a limb or break a bone of the slaves, but, by infusing motives into their breasts, would make them doubly valuable to the masters as free laborers; and Because, if compensation is to be given at all, it should be given to the outraged and guiltless slaves, and not to those who have plundered and abused them.

We regard as delusive, cruel and dangerous any scheme or expatriation which pretends to aid, either directly or indirectly, in the emancipation of the slaves, or to be a substitute for the immediate and total abolition of slavery.

We fully and unanimously recognize the sovereignty of each State, to legislate exclusively on the subject of the slavery which is tolerated within its limits; we concede that Congress, under the present national compact, has no right to interfere with any of the slave States in relation to this momentous subject:

But we maintain that Congress has a right, and is solemnly bound, to suppress the domestic slave trade between the several States, and to abolish slavery in those portions of our territory which the Constitution has placed under its exclusive jurisdiction.

We also maintain that there are, at the present time, the highest obligations resting upon the people of the free States to remove slavery by moral and political action, as prescribed in the Constitution of the United States. They are now living under a pledge of their tremendous physical force, to fasten the galling letters of tyranny upon the limbs of millions in the Southern States; they are liable to be called at any moment to suppress a general insurrection of the slaves; they authorize the slave owner to vote for three-fifths of his slaves as property, and thus enable him to perpetuate his oppression; they support a standing army at the South for its protection; and they seize the slave who has escaped into their territories, and send him back to be tortured by an enraged master or a brutal driver. This relation to slavery is criminal, and full of danger; IT MUST BE BROKEN UP.

These are our views and principles—these our designs and measures. With entire confidence in the overruling justice of God, we plant ourselves upon the Declaration of our Independence and the truths of Divine Revelation, as upon the Everlasting Rock.

We shall organize Anti-Slavery Societies, if possible, in every city, town and village in our land.

We shall send forth agents to lift up the voice of remonstrance, of warning, of entreaty, and of rebuke.

We shall enlist the pulpit and the press in the cause of the suffering and the dumb.

We shall aim at a purification of the churches from all participation in the guilt of slavery.

We shall spare no exortions nor means to bring the whole nation to speedy repentance.

Our trust for victory is solely in God. We may be personally defeated, but our principles never! Truth, Justice, Reason, Humanity, must and will gloriously triumph. Already a host is coming up to the help of the Lord against the mighty, and the prospect before us is full of encouragement.

Submitting this Declaration to the candid examination of the people of this country, and of the friends of liberty throughout the world, we hereby affix our signatures to it; pledging ourselves that, under the guidance and by the help of Almighty God, we will do all that in us lies, consistently with this Declaration of our principles, to overthrow the most execrable system of slavery that has ever been witnessed upon earth; to deliver our land from its deadliest curse; to wipe out the foulest stain which rests upon our national escutcheon; and to secure to the colored population of the United States all the rights and privileges which belong to them as men and as Americans—come what may to our persons, our interests, or our reputations—whether we live to witness the triumph of Liberty, Justice, and Humanity, or perish untimely as martyrs in this great, benevolent and holy cause.

Of the three-score signers of the Declaration not one was a woman. Such was the custom of the times, in regard to the public relation of the sexes, that Lucretia Mott and her Quaker sisters did not ask or expect to sign; the male delegates—even the members of their own sect—did not think to invite them. It was a significant mark of liberality that they had been permitted to participate in the proceedings of the Convention on an equal footing in other respects. Moreover, on Mr. Garrison's motion, seconded by Dr. Cox, it was resolved on this third day "that the cause of Abolition eminently deserves the countenance, and support of American women," after the British example. By other resolutions, "the ladies' anti-slavery societies" already in existence were hailed "as the harbinger of a brighter day," and more were called for. In still another, moved by Dr. Cox and seconded by William Goodell, the Convention presented "their thanks to their female friends for the deep interest they have manifested in the Anti-slavery cause" during the long and fatiguing sessions. And finally, Miss Crandall was assured of approval, sympathy and aid. Resolutions relating to free produce; the recreancy of a pro-slavery clergy; the guilt of withholding the Bible from slaves; colored conventions and societies for mutual improvement, and the like—concluded the business of the Convention. Beriah Green dismissed the assembly in words of thrilling solemnity, never to be forgotten by those who heard him, and ending "in a prayer to Almighty God, full of fervor and feeling, imploring his blessing and sanctification upon the Convention and its labors." So ended the successful attempt to give a national basis to the movement begun only three years before by the publication of the Liberator.

Source: Garrison, W. and F. Garrison. *William Lloyd Garrison, 1805–1879: The Story of His Life Told by His Children*. New York: Arno Press, 1969.

See Articles: African Americans; Quakers; Slavery.

1844
PRIMARY DOCUMENT

The Republic Article on the Philadelphia Ethnic Riots

The Philadelphia Ethnic Riots or Bible Riots took place from May 6–8 and July 6–7, 1844. Anti-Catholicism, which was persistent in the United States, had taken on new urgency with increases in immigration, and the nativism political movement condemned Catholics as antidemocratic and spread rumors that they tried to have the Bible removed from schools. The riots, which began with a fight between local Catholics and a nativist meeting, spiraled into the burning of churches and caused over a dozen deaths.

In conformity to the resolution adopted at the meeting of the preceding Friday evening, citizens favorable to the American Republican cause, assembled in Mass Meeting, on Monday afternoon, May 6th, at 4 o'clock, on an unoccupied lot, at the corner of Second and Master Streets. This lot is about 100 feet wide and 150 feet in length, and is bounded on the west by the Public School House, which fronts on Master Street. The staging for the officers and speakers was erected about the centre of the west side of the lot, against the school house fence. The whole extent of the lot was covered with persons who had assembled to participate in the proceedings. The meeting was organized in the usual way, and several gentlemen were called upon to address the assembled multitude. Mr. S. R. Kramer and General Smith successively took the stand; neither of them, however, occupying over ten minutes' time. Their addresses were remarkably mild in their character, and contained nothing against which the most scrupulous could have reasonably objected. While these gentlemen were speaking, several Irish carters came driving their carts into the lot, and forced their way through the crowd, nearly up to the speakers' stand, greatly annoying the people, and even exposing them to danger.

Each of these carts contained something more than an ordinary wheelbarrow load of yellow dirt which was brought there at that particular time, in that remarkably singular manner, and in such small quantities, for no good reason which has yet been assigned. Five or six of these diminutive loads were successfully brought in, and emptied in the midst of the crowd, as near to the staging as the drivers could conveniently force their carts. These loads of dirt still lie upon the spot where they were then thrown. They were not needed there at that particular time; neither has any use been made of them since. Neither of them was brought in until the meeting had assembled, nor was one sent there after the assembly had dismissed! And when it is understood, that at the very time when these carters were committing this inexcusable outrage upon the meeting, there was assembled in the market house, running parallel with Second street, on the north side of Master street, and a few yards west of the school house, a number of Irishmen opposed to the meeting, armed with firearms and other offensive weapons, none can for an instant doubt that these carters were sent there for the purpose of provoking an attack upon themselves, and of thus furnishing a plausible excuse for an assault in return upon the meeting, on the part of their friends in the market house and the surrounding buildings. There was evidently in all this a cunningly devised plan for the perpetration of a premeditated outrage, for the consummation of which the most fiendish preparation had been made.

But that Divine Providence which often takes the wicked in his own craftiness, and guards the innocent from harm, interposed most miraculously to avert the calamity which then pended over the American Republican cause. Had the carters to whom allusion has been made, been assailed with violence by the assembled people, a fearful and dreadful slaughter, far more extensive than that which really occurred, would doubtless have ensued. For in this spot, the citizens were almost entirely unprotected. They were surrounded by their enemies, as they fled in the only direction which could have promised security, toward the market house, they would have been met by the assassins who there remained concealed, awaiting a signal for the commencement of their work of death. Then, too, it would have been exceedingly difficult to have made it appear that the Native Americans were not the aggressors, and that their assailants were not only acting upon the defensive, of for the protection of their worthy friends, the carters. At the moment when the conduct of the carters was growing insufferable, and a slight demonstration of a disposition at interference was being manifested, Mr. Lewis C Levin was called to the stand. This circumstance restored tranquility for the space of a minute. But the moment that gentleman commenced his remarks,-before a solitary sentiment had been concluded by him, and before the subject of the carts had again drawn off the people's attention, the clouds suddenly discharged a torrent of rain upon the assembled multitude. For a second there was a pause, which was followed by a simultaneous rush for shelter in the market house.

So suddenly and entirely unexpected was this movement, that those of the Irish who were unquestionably awaiting some provocation for an attack upon the meeting, were confused and undetermined in regard to the nature of their further proceedings. The most of them, as the crowd rushed into the market, retreated to a row of buildings, consisting of a hose house and the dwellings of themselves and friends, situated in Cadwalader street, and facing the market house, at the distance perhaps of some 200 feet. Others, however, but their number was few, remained to contest the right of the citizens to the use of the market. This market house had previously been employed as a sort of rendezvous for the mob during the railroad and weavers' riots, which had previously disgraced that neighborhood, and they seemed to consider themselves solely entitled to its use. An attempt was here made to reorganize the meeting, but the few Irishmen who had now mingled with the native citizens, were determined that the organization should not take place. They produced the utmost noise and confusion, whenever any effort was made to speak, on the part of Mr. Levin, who had again arisen to continue his address; and so constant and violent was the uproar that it was impossible for that gentleman to be heard even by those who occupied places nearest to him. Among the most noisy of those who were now interrupting the proceedings of the meeting, was an athletic Irishman near the speaker, who brandished his naked arms above the heads of those around him, and swore terrible vengeance upon every one who should dare to come into contact with his clenched fists. So exceedingly violent was this man's conduct that some person at length attempted to eject him from the market house. A scuffle ensued between the two. The Irish rioter drew his antagonist to the outer side of the market, on that side which fronted the dwellings and the hose house of which mention has been made, when a stone was thrown from a party in the vicinity of the hose house, with tremendous violence, toward the market, which struck with great force against one of the stalls. This was instantly followed with the discharge of a musket from the same direction.

A scene of confusion and strife now took place which beggars all description. The first impulse of those in the market was to rush upon the party near the hose house who first assailed them, which they did driving them off in a great affright in every direction. But no sooner were they thus drawn out from the shelter of the market, upon the open space in front, and their open assailants dispersed, than a destructive fire was opened upon them with fowling pieces, rifles, and muskets, from roofs, windows, loopholes, yards and alleys of the houses in front, which was kept up without intermission, until the ground was vacated by the American Republican party. During this firing the utmost consternation prevailed, and men were shot down while endeavoring to escape from the scene of danger, without knowing from whence their injuries were received, so cautiously were their enemies concealed. One young man, about nineteen years of age, was engaged throughout the afternoon, in supporting the American flag, which hung over the speaker's stand.

This laudible employment rendered him an especial mark for the aim of the enemies of the cause he was maintaining. Two or three times had the flag fallen to the ground, and as often did George Schiffler, with the assistance of several others, again raise it, and cause its stripes and stars to float above their heads. But his efforts were unavailing; for a bullet at length pierced his heart, and he fell as senseless as the flag he supported, to the ground. He was carried to the store of an apothecary near by, where, in a few minutes, he ceased to exist on earth; and before the sun had gone down, the lifeless body of the noble patriotic boy was laid at the feet of a widowed and distracted mother. The flag which he had supported was torn, and leveled with the dust. The triumph however, was of short duration. For at half past six o'clock, a party of those who had been driven off amounting to about twenty in all, returned to the field of action, armed with rifles and muskets. This small party took a station immediately in front of the buildings occupied by the Irish assailants on the open space where their friends had been shot, and opened a brisk fire upon their enemies, over whom in a very short time, they obtained a complete victory. Soon after the fire was returned upon them, the Irish began to give way in evident alarm, the hose house was fired, and none of them dared to expose themselves sufficiently to attempt to extinguish the flames, which spread with astonishing rapidity until, within a very brief space of time, every house almost from which a gun was fired, was enveloped in the devouring element. The murderous creatures who occupied them, precipitately fled from the rear of their burning buildings, and were about falling into the hands of their conquerors, when the sound of the military was heard approaching, who, in a few moments, took possession of the entire ground, and arrested all further hostile proceedings.

Source: "The Kensington Massacre." *Republic, A Magazine for the Defence of Civil and Religious Liberty*, no. 1 (August 1845). Pennsylvania Historical Society.

See Articles: Irish Americans; Philadelphia, Pennsylvania; Religion and Crime, History of; Religion and Crime, Sociology of; Riots

1844 PRIMARY DOCUMENT

An Eyewitness Account of the Murders of Joseph and Hyrum Smith

The founder of the Latter-day Saint (LDS) movement, Joseph Smith led his followers to settle in Nauvoo, Illinois, after repeated troubles in Missouri. In Nauvoo, he was both mayor and militia commander and announced his candidacy for president in the upcoming 1844 election. When he declared martial law to deal with attacks from a competing LDS church, he and his brother were arrested for treason against Illinois and were killed by a lynch mob, leading to an LDS succession crisis.

The Afternoon of June 27, 1844.—I do not remember the names of all who were with us that night and the next morning in jail, for several went and came; among those that we considered stationary were Stephen Markham, John S. Fullmer, Captain Dan Jones, Dr. Willard Richards, and myself. Dr. Bernhisel says that he was there from Wednesday in the afternoon until eleven o'clock next day. We were, however, visited by numerous friends, among whom were Uncle John Smith, Hiram Kimball, Cyrus H. Wheelock, besides lawyers, as counsel. There was also a great variety of conversation, which was rather desultory than otherwise, and referred to circumstances that had transpired, our former and present grievances, the spirit of the troops around us, and the disposition of the governor; the devising for legal and other plans for deliverance, the nature of testimony required; the gathering of proper witnesses, and a variety of other topics, including our religious hopes, etc.

During one of these conversations Dr. Richards remarked: "Brother Joseph, if it is necessary that you die in this matter, and if they will take me in your stead, I will suffer for you." At another time, when conversing about deliverance, I said, "Brother Joseph, if you will permit it, and say the word, I will have you out of this prison in five hours, if the jail has to come down to do it." My idea was to go to Nauvoo, and collect, a force sufficient, as I considered the whole affair a legal farce, and a flagrant outrage upon our liberty and rights. Brother Joseph refused.

Elder Cyrus H. Wheelock came in to see us, and when he was about leaving, drew a small pistol, a six-shooter, from his pocket, remarking at the same time "Would any of you like to have this?" Brother Joseph immediately replied, "Yes, give it to me," whereupon he took the pistol, and put it in his pantaloons pocket. The pistol was a six-shooting revolver, of Allen's patent; it belonged to me, and was one that I furnished to Brother Wheelock when he talked of going with me to the east, previous to our coming to Carthage. I have it now in my possession. Brother Wheelock went out on some errand, and was not suffered to return. The report of the governor having gone to Nauvoo without taking the prisoners along with him caused very unpleasant feelings, as we were apprised that we were left to the tender mercies of the Carthage Greys, a company strictly mobocratic, and whom we knew to be our most deadly enemies; and their captain, Esquire (Robert F.) Smith, was a most unprincipled villain. Besides this, all the mob forces, comprising the governor's troops, were dismissed, with the exception of one or two companies, which the governor took with him to Nauvoo. The great part of the mob was liberated, the remainder was our guard.

We looked upon it not only as a breach of faith on the part of the governor, but also as an indication of a desire to insult us, if nothing more, by leaving us in the proximity of such men. The prevention of Wheelock's return was among the first of their hostile movements.

Colonel Markham went out, and he was also prevented from returning. He was very angry at this, but the mob paid no attention to him. They drove him out of town at the point of the bayonet, and threatened to shoot him if he returned. He went, I am informed, to Nauvoo for the purpose of raising a company of men for our protection. Brother Fullmer went to Nauvoo after witnesses. It is my opinion that Brother Wheelock did also. We all of us felt unusually dull and languid, with a remarkable depression of spirits. In consonance with those feelings, I sang a song, that had lately been introduced into Nauvoo, entitled, "A Poor Wayfaring Man of Grief," etc.

The song is pathetic, and the tune quite plaintive, and was very much in accordance with our feelings at the time, for our spirits were all depressed, dull, and gloomy, and surcharged with indefinite ominous forebodings. After a lapse of some time, Brother Hyrum requested me again to sing that song. I replied, "Brother Hyrum, I do not feel like singing;" when he remarked, "Oh, never mind; commence singing, and you will get the spirit of it." At his request I did so. Soon afterwards I was sitting at one of the front windows of the jail, when I saw a number of men, with painted faces, coming around the corner of the jail, and aiming towards the stairs. The other brethren had seen the same, for, as I went to the door, I found Brother Hyrum Smith and Dr. Richards already leaning against it. They both pressed against the door with their shoulders to prevent its being opened, as the lock and latch were comparatively useless. While in this position, the mob, who had come upstairs and tried to open the door, probably thought it was locked and fired a ball through the keyhole. At this Dr. Richards and Brother Hyrum leaped back from the door, with their faces towards it. Almost instantly another ball passed through the panel of the door, and struck Brother Hyrum on the left side of the nose, entering his face and head. At the same instant, another ball from outside entered his back, passing through his body and striking his watch. The ball came from the back, through the jail window, opposite the door, and must, from its range, have been fired from the Carthage Greys, who were placed there ostensibly for our protection, as the balls from the firearms, shot close by the jail, would have entered the ceiling, we being in the second story, and there never was a time after that when Hyrum could have received the latter wound. Immediately, when the ball struck him, he fell flat on his back, crying as he fell, "I am a dead man!" He never moved afterwards.

Brother Joseph as he drew nigh to Hyrum, and, leaning over him, exclaimed, "Oh! my poor, dear brother Hyrum!" He, however, instantly arose, and with a firm, quick step, and a determined expression of countenance, approached the door, and pulling the six-shooter left by Brother Wheelock from his pocket, opened the door slightly, and snapped the pistol six successive times. Only three of the barrels, however, were discharged. I afterwards understood that two or three were wounded by these discharges, two of whom, I am informed, died. I had in my hands a large, strong hickory stick, brought there by Brother Markham and left by him, which I had seized as soon as I saw the mob approach; and while Brother Joseph was firing the pistol, I stood close behind him. As soon as he had discharged it he stepped back, and I immediately took his place next to the door, while he occupied the one I had done while he was shooting. Brother Richards, at this time, had a knotty walking-stick in his hands belonging to me, and stood next to Brother Joseph a little farther from the door, in an oblique direction, apparently to avoid the rake of the fire from the door. The firing of Brother Joseph made our assailants pause for a moment. Very soon after, however, they pushed the door some distance open, and protruded and discharged their guns into the room, when I parried them off with my stick, giving another direction to the balls.

It certainly was a terrible scene. Streams of fire as thick as my arm passed by me as these men fired, and, unarmed as we were, it looked like certain death. I remember feeling as though my time had come, but I do not know when, in any critical position, I was more calm, unruffled, energetic, and acted with more promptness and decision. It certainly was far from pleasant to be so near the muzzles of those firearms as they belched forth their liquid flames and deadly balls. While I was engaged in parrying the guns, Brother Joseph said, "That's right, Brother Taylor, parry them off as well as you can." These were the last words I ever heard him speak on earth.

Every moment the crowd at the door became more dense, as they were unquestionably pressed on by those in the rear ascending the stairs, until the whole entrance at the door was literally crowded with muskets and rifles, which, with the swearing, shouting, and demoniacal expressions of those outside the door and on the stairs, and the firing of the guns, mingled with their horrid oaths and execrations, made it look like pandemonium let loose, and was, indeed, a fit representation of the horrid deed in which they were engaged.

After parrying the guns for some time, which now protruded farther and farther into the room, and seeing no hope of escape or protection there, as we were now unarmed, it occurred to me that we might have some friends outside, and that there might be some chance of escape in that direction, but here there seemed to be none. As I expected them every moment to rush into the room—

nothing but extreme cowardice having thus far kept them out—as the tumult and pressure increased, without any other hope, I made a spring for the window which was right in front of the jail door, where the mob was standing, and also exposed to the fire of the Carthage Greys, who were stationed some ten or twelve rods off. The weather was hot; we all of us had our coats off, and the window was raised to admit air. As I reached the window, and was on the point of leaping out, I was struck by a ball from the door about midway of my thigh, which struck the bone and flattened out almost to the size of a quarter of a dollar, and then passed on through the fleshy part to within about half an inch of the outside. I think some prominent nerve must have been severed or injured, for as soon as the ball struck me, I fell like a bird when shot, or an ox when struck by a butcher, and lost entirely and instantaneously all power of action or locomotion. I fell upon the window sill, and cried out, "I am shot!" Not possessing any power to move, I felt myself falling outside of the window, but immediately I fell inside, from some, at that time, unknown cause. When I struck the floor, my animation seemed restored, as I have seen it sometimes in squirrels and birds after being shot. As soon as I felt the power of motion I crawled under the bed, which was in a corner of the room, not far from the window where I received my wound. While on my way and under the bed, I was wounded in three other places; one ball entered a little below the left knee, and never was extracted; another entered the forepart of my left arm, a little above the wrist, and, passing down by the joint, lodged in the fleshy part of my hand, about midway, a little above the upper joint of my little finger. Another struck me on the fleshy part of my left hip and tore away the flesh as large as my hand, dashing the mangled fragments of flesh and blood against the wall.

My wounds were painful, and the sensation produced was as though a ball had passed through and down the whole length of my leg. I very well remember my reflections at the time. I had a very painful idea of becoming lame and decrepit, and being an object of pity, and I felt as though I would rather die than be placed in such circumstances.

It would seem that immediately after my attempt to leap out of the window, Joseph also did the same thing, of which circumstance I have no knowledge only from information. The first thing that I noticed was a cry that he had leaped out of the window. A cessation of firing followed, the mob rushed downstairs, and Dr. Richards went to the window. Immediately afterward I saw the doctor going towards the jail door, and as there was an iron door at the head of the stairs adjoining our door which led into the cells for criminals, it struck me that the doctor was going in there, and I said to him, "Stop, Doctor, and take me along." He proceeded to the door and opened it, and then returned and dragged me along to a small cell prepared for criminals.

Brother Richards was very much troubled, and exclaimed, "Oh! Brother Taylor, is it possible that they have killed both Brother Hyrum and Joseph? It cannot surely be, and yet I saw them shoot them;" and elevating his hands two or three times, he exclaimed, "Oh Lord, my God, spare Thy servants!" He then said, "Brother Taylor, this is a terrible event;" and he dragged me farther into the cell, saying, "I am sorry I can not do better for you;" and, taking an old, filthy mattress, he covered me with it, and said, "That may hide you, and you may yet live to tell the tale, but I expect they will kill me in a few moments!" While lying in this position, I suffered the most excruciating pain.

Soon afterwards Dr. Richards came to me, informed me that the mob had precipitately fled, and at the same time confirmed the worst fears that Joseph was assuredly dead. I felt a dull, lonely, sickening sensation at the news. When I reflected that our noble chieftain, the Prophet of the living God, had fallen, and that I had seen his brother in the cold embrace of death, it seemed as though there was a void or vacuum in the great field of human existence to me, and a dark gloomy chasm in the kingdom, and that we were left alone. Oh, how lonely was that feeling! How cold, barren, and desolate! In the midst of difficulties he was always the first in motion; in critical positions his counsel was always sought. As our prophet he approached our God, and obtained for us his will; but now our prophet, our counselor our general, our leader, was gone, and amid the fiery ordeal that we then had to pass through, we were left alone without his aid, and as our future guide for things spiritual or temporal, and for all things pertaining to this world, or the next, he had spoken for the last time on earth.

These reflections and a thousand others flashed upon my mind. I thought, why must God's nobility, the salt of the earth, the most exalted of the human family, and the most perfect types of all excellence, fall victims to the cruel, fiendish hate of incarnate devils?

The poignancy of my grief, I presume, however, was somewhat allayed by the extreme suffering that I endured from my wounds.

Soon afterwards I was taken to the head of the stairs and laid there, where I had a full view of our beloved and now murdered brother, Hyrum. There he lay as I had left him; he had not moved a limb; he lay placid and calm, a monument of greatness even in death; but his noble spirit had left its tenement, and was gone to dwell in regions more congenial to his exalted nature. Poor Hyrum! He was a great and good man, and my soul was cemented to his. If ever there was an exemplary, honest, and virtuous man, an embodiment of all that is noble in the human form, Hyrum Smith was its representative.

While I lay there, a number of persons came around, among whom was a physician. The doctor, on seeing a ball lodged in my left hand, took a penknife from his pocket and made an incision in it for the purpose of extracting the ball therefrom, and having obtained a pair of carpenters compasses, made use of them to draw or pry out the ball, alternately using the penknife and compasses. After sawing for some time with a dull penknife, and prying and pulling with the compasses, he ultimately succeeded in extracting the ball, which weighed about half an ounce. Some time afterwards he remarked to a friend of mine that I had "nerves like the devil" to stand what I did in its extraction. I really thought I had need of nerves to stand such surgical butchery, and

that, whatever my nerves may be, his practice was devilish.

This company wished to remove me to Mr. Hamilton's hotel, the place where we had stayed previous to our incarceration in jail. I told them, however, that I did not wish to go. I did not consider it safe. They protested that it was, and that I was safe with them; that it was a perfect outrage for men to be used as we had been; that they were my friends; that I could be better taken care of there than here.

I replied, "I don't know you. Whom am I among? I am surrounded by assassins and murderers; witness your deeds. Don't talk to me of kindness or comfort; look at your murdered victims. Look at me! I want none of your counsel nor comfort. There may be some safety here; I can be assured of none anywhere, etc."

They G-- d----- their souls to hell, made the most solemn asseverations, and swore by God and the devil, and everything else that they could think of, that they would stand by me to death and protect me. In half an hour every one of them fled from the town.

Soon after a coroner's jury were assembled in the room over the body of Hyrum. Among the jurors was Captain Smith of the "Carthage Greys" who had assisted in the murder, and the same justice before whom we had been tried. I learned of Francis Higbee as being in the neighborhood. On hearing his name mentioned, I immediately arose and said, "Captain Smith, you are a justice of the peace; I have heard his name mentioned; I want to swear my life against him." I was informed that word was immediately sent to him to leave the place, which he did.

Brother Richards was busy during this time attending to the coroner's inquest, and to the removal of the bodies, and making arrangements for their removal from Carthage to Nauvoo.

When he had a little leisure, he again came to me, and at his suggestion I was removed to Hamilton's tavern. I felt that he was the only friend, the only person, that I could rely upon in that town. It was with difficulty that sufficient persons could be found to carry me to the tavern, for immediately after the murder a great fear fell upon all the people, and men, women, and children fled with great precipitation, leaving nothing nor anybody in the town but two or three women and children and one or two sick persons.

by Elder John Taylor

Source: http://law2.umkc.edu/faculty/projects/ftrials/carthage/carthagehome.html

See Articles: Bigamy/Polygamy; Illinois; Religion and Crime, History of; Religion and Crime, Sociology of; Witness Testimony.

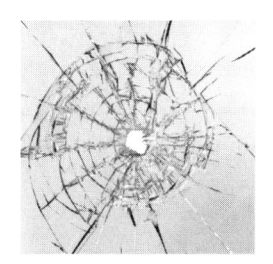

1851 to 1900

INTRODUCTION

The latter half of the 19th century was dominated by the U.S. Civil War, which brought new definitions to concepts of criminal justice. In the war's aftermath, the nation struggled to define criminal justice in its territories, and a series of moral crusades sought to rid the nation of vice and clean up corrupt criminal justice systems.

Antebellum Period
Concerns over slavery and its extension to new territories dominated criminal justice concerns in the period prior to the Civil War. Senator Henry Clay's Compromise of 1850 strengthened the Fugitive Slave Act of 1793 by criminalizing the conduct of those who assisted a runaway slave or refused to assist in the slave's return. One abolitionist, Sherman M. Booth, was arrested for arguing in his newspaper, the *Milwaukee Free Democrat*, against the capture of a fugitive Missouri slave named Joshua Glover. A mob stormed the jail and freed Glover, helping him escape to Canada. Booth was later rearrested and charged with violating the Fugitive Slave Act. The Wisconsin Supreme Court declared the act unconstitutional, resulting in the release of the state's fugitive slaves. The U.S. Supreme Court eventually chastised the Wisconsin court in *Ableman v. Booth* (1859), asserting that the federal courts and law were supreme in matters arising under the constitution and laws of the United States.

Dred Scott, a Virginia-born slave, had lived a significant period of his life in the free state of Illinois and the free territory of Wisconsin. After several years of suing for his freedom in state courts after his return to Missouri, in 1853, Scott sued for his freedom in federal court, which ruled against him. Scott then appealed to the U.S. Supreme Court, which ruled, in an opinion written by Chief Justice Roger B. Taney, that Scott's claim failed because he was not a citizen of the United States. In fact, Taney ruled that all African Americans, whether slave or free, were not citizens of the United States. The decision struck down the Missouri Compromise, since it deprived slave owners of their property under the Fifth Amendment to the U.S. Constitution. In effect, the decision denied blacks the most basic rights of citizenship and prohibited Congress from regulating slavery in the territories. However, for criminal justice purposes, *Dred Scott v. Stanford* was the first time the court invalidated congressional action through the due process provision of the Bill of Rights. Ultimately, *Dred Scott* exacerbated the tensions between slave and nonslave states and helped push the nation to war.

In 1856, John Brown, a radical abolitionist, was part of a group of men who hacked five proslavery men to death outside their cabins at Pottawatomie Creek, Kansas. Brown fled to New England, where he gathered forces and sought to force a slave uprising. On October 16, 1859, Brown and 21 conspirators, including five African Americans, attacked the U.S. military arsenal at Harpers Ferry, Virginia. Colonel Robert E. Lee led a military response, and after two days of fighting, Lee's forces killed 17 of the 21 conspirators, including two of Brown's sons. Brown was captured and was unable to rally slaves to his cause. He was quickly tried, convicted after 45 minutes of deliberation, and sentenced to death. He was hanged on December 2, 1859, surrounded by 2,000 soldiers.

Growing racial tensions eventually led to South Carolina's secession from the Union in December 1860, and the Civil War followed soon after.

The Civil War
In many ways, criminal justice fell to a standstill during the Civil War, as the nation became preoccupied with the conflict. However, Abraham Lincoln felt it paramount to preserve the Union at all costs. Consequently, in 1861, he suspended the writ of habeas corpus. The Great Writ, as the writ of habeas corpus has been called, allows citizens to appear before a judge and challenge the validity of their arrests. Some have asserted that the writ acts as a bulwark against secret arrests and imprisonments. Lincoln directed General Winfield Scott to suspend the writ on the Maryland border, given its large secessionist population and proximity to Washington, D.C. Several prominent officials were arbitrarily arrested, including a Baltimore secessionist named John Merryman, who was taken by Union military forces and held without charge. In *Ex Parte Merryman* (1861), the Supreme Court ruled that only Congress could suspend the writ and that the government had to allow Merryman to appear before a judge. Lincoln and other military officials simply refused to enforce the court's order. However, Merryman, like several others who were arrested on pretext, was released after a short period of incarceration when the threat had subsided.

During the suspension of the writ, over 14,000 people were arrested and held in jail, often without any sort of hearing. Others had their charges heard by military commissions, rather than courts. Only the war's end brought the release of many of these prisoners. The Supreme Court again reaffirmed the unconstitutionality of Lincoln's actions in *Ex Parte Milligan* (1866), when it held that Congress could not create military commissions nor suspend the Constitution in times of crisis. Lincoln expanded the scope of the writ after the war.

The Civil War also saw a series of riots across the nation, called the "draft riots," as many protested the government's efforts to draft citizens into wartime service. For $300, a rich white person could escape military service by hiring a replacement. Blacks, on the other hand, remained ineligible for the draft. The riots were motivated out of racial concerns, since many lower-class white people felt like they had to fight the war while blacks remained home and could take their jobs. Starting July 13, 1863, after the first names were drawn for the draft, hundreds of white men stormed the streets of New York City, beating, killing, and shooting people. They burned over 50 buildings to the ground, including two Protestant churches. It took the presence of thousands of state militia and federal military troops to restore order to the city. When the dust settled, over 100 people had been killed, including 11 black men who were lynched, and thousands had been injured.

Other riots occurred in Detroit, Charleston, Norfolk, Memphis, and New Orleans. Unseasoned local police forces had difficulty controlling riots and often turned to the

John Brown, the radical abolitionist, and a group of black and white conspirators hold officers captive at the Harpers Ferry military arsenal, Harpers Ferry, Virginia, on October 15, 1859, in the hopes of sparking a slave uprising. This scene from Frank Leslie's illustrated Newspaper *(1859) depicts the inside of the engine house just before the gate was broken down. Brown escaped but was soon captured, tried, and hung on the gallows on December 2.*

military or militia for protection. The rioters were able to take advantage of the instability of the period, as well as police forces that were drastically unprepared for large-scale urban rioting.

Rioting continued after the Civil War, reflecting racial and ethnic tensions. In 1871, white laborers killed 18 Chinese workers in Los Angeles over labor contentions and a desire for Chinese exclusion. In 1871 and 1872, in New York, Catholics and Protestants clashed during Protestant parades celebrating Protestant William of Orange's victory over Catholic King James. While six were killed in the first parade, over 60 were killed in 1872 when the state militia opened fire on the largely Catholic crowd.

During the war, the Confederacy sought to facilitate prisoner-of-war exchanges, given the large burden of feeding and caring for Union prisoners. While Lincoln did not want to formally recognize the Confederacy, in July of 1862, his administration negotiated a prisoner exchange system that became known as the Dix–Hill Cartel. Under the terms of the agreement, each side was to meet at announced locations and parole its prisoners to the other side. Prisoners were to be exchanged no later than 10 days after their capture. Paroled prisoners were prohibited from returning to battle. However, the Dix–Hill Cartel was short lived. The Confederacy refused to parole black prisoners and even threatened to treat them as slaves. Additionally, many prisoners, once exchanged, simply returned to the battlefield. For example, after the battles of Vicksburg and Port Hudson, the Union found that many of the 37,000 Confederate soldiers it had pardoned had simply returned and continued fighting.

Both sides had serious issues housing prisoners. Together, the north and south held more than 674,000 prisoners during the war, and historians estimate that more than

Andersonville Prison in Georgia, one of the most notorious prisons in the Confederacy. Over 32,000 prisoners were crammed into 26 acres that was supplied by a filthy, sewage-infested stream, which spread disease throughout the camp. The conditions in the camp were so poor that from 90 to 130 prisoners died per day. The prison's director, Major Henry Wirz, was convicted of war crimes and was hanged on the gallows.

56,000 people died in Civil War prisons. In fact, more people died in the camps than in any single battle in the war. Approximately 12 percent of Confederate captives died in Union prisons, while 15 percent of Union prisoners died in Confederate prisons. Some of these prisons gained infamy. Andersonville, a southern city-style prison, was perhaps the most notorious. At its peak, Andersonville held over 32,000 prisoners spread over 26 acres. The prison was surrounded by a 15-ft. pine log stockade. Guards were stationed in "pigeon roosts" every 30 yards along the top of the stockade. A small stream called Stockade Creek provided water and sanitation to the prisoners. However, because prisoners lacked the means to adequately dispose of waste, the stream soon turned into a maggot and sewage-infested latrine. The filthy stream spread disease all over the camp, prompting prison bureaucrats to note severe medical conditions among the inmates. The prison averaged 90 to 130 deaths a day. By the end of the war, over 13,000 prisoners died at the prison, representing about 29 percent of its inmates. After the war, the prison's director, Major Henry Wirz, was convicted of war crimes and was executed for his role in the governance of the prison.

Together, the north and the south created over 150 prison camps, but the south was not alone in having camps with serious problems. Northern officials took vacant barracks in Elmira, New York, surrounded them with a stockade, and housed Confederate prisoners. Originally built to accommodate 4,000–5,000 people, Elmira's prisoner population soon swelled to over 10,000. Like Andersonville, sanitation became a huge problem. All water drained into a small pond on the 32-acre encampment, resulting in the spread of serious disease. Prisoners were crowded into barracks and others had to suffer the winter packed into tents. Union doctors found thousands of cases of scurvy, since prisoners lacked adequate fruits and vegetables in their diets. In Elmira's 369 days of operation, 2,950 of the 12,122 prisoners died—a 24 percent death rate. The inmates called the prison "Hellmira," and it has been labeled the death camp of the north.

Civil War prison camps were constructed as temporary solutions during the conflict. Yet, they largely failed to provide for basic human needs. Prisoners captured rats for food. Diseases like smallpox, cholera, and malaria spread rapidly through the close and extremely unsanitary quarters. It took the war's end, rather than any sort of compelled desire to improve conditions, to close the prisons. In fact, the only person ever held responsible for actions in any of the prisons was Andersonville's director, largely as a result of a northern propaganda campaign that ignored the issues in its own prisons.

Reconstruction

Immediately after the Civil War, the Republican Congress enacted a series of measures designed to strengthen the federal government's power over southern rebels. In 1865, Congress passed the Thirteenth Amendment, abolishing slavery in the United States. Southerners responded to these attempts with more subtle measures aimed at keeping slavery intact. Black Codes, passed by southern legislatures, forbid African Americans to work (except for white employers), marry whites, or carry weapons. Unemployed blacks, or those unable to pay fines, could be arrested and then hired out to pay their fines. Most found that the codes were merely shrewd attempts to return to pre–Civil War slavery. Congress responded with the Fourteenth Amendment, providing that no person could be deprived of life, liberty, or property without due process of law and that all persons were entitled to equal protection under the law.

The constitutional amendments did not eradicate southern attempts to retain aspects of slavery. Convict leasing, a system where prisoners were hired out to local contractors, was criticized as yet another subtle attempt to retain slave status, since most of its subjects were African American. Southern prisons also experimented with chain gangs and other forms of convict leasing—practices that proved quite lucrative. Additionally, Confederate veterans, angry about the war's outcome, founded the Ku Klux Klan in Pulaski, Tennessee, in 1865. The Klan eventually grew to include hundreds of thousands of members and soon turned to acts of terror and violence in an attempt to prevent black voting. The Klan threatened and intimidated both blacks and the whites who supported them, but it also lynched and tortured blacks who sought to exercise their right to vote. Congress responded with the Fifteenth Amendment in 1870, prohibiting government from denying the vote based on race, color, or condition of prior servitude. The first attempt to enforce the amendments came in 1870, when Congress made it a federal offense for anyone to discriminate based on race in state elections. In 1870, Congress also gave federal officials control over federal elections. Congress also passed the Ku Klux Klan Act of 1871, which allowed the president to use military force to protect individual constitutional rights, suspend the writ of habeas corpus, and suppress insurrections. Under the act, individuals who denied others their constitutional rights would be guilty of a federal offense. The act also allowed blacks to sue for damages against those who had deprived them of voting rights.

Violence against blacks remained commonplace. In Vicksburg, Mississippi in 1873, a paramilitary white group demanded the resignation of African American Sheriff Peter Crosby. The mayor declared martial law and had Crosby arrested. An African American militia gathered and demanded the sheriff's release. A large white militia gathered in response, and when the black militia decided to retreat, the white company fired, killing dozens of blacks. On April 13, 1873, in Colfax, Louisiana, a group of men from the

White League, a white paramilitary group, attacked and killed nearly 100 black militiamen defending the local courthouse, and even attempted to take the Louisiana state capitol by force. Only the intervention of the U.S. military kept the "Colfax massacre," as it came to be called, from getting worse.

Citizen violence against African Americans remained common throughout the last half of the century. Ida B. Wells, a black newspaper owner, showed that as many as 188 lynchings occurred per year in the 1890s, nearly all of which were against southern blacks. In fact, historians estimate that between 1888 and 1903, over 2,000 blacks were lynched.

Federal intervention in state affairs, however, dropped dramatically in the latter half of the 19th century. In the *Slaughter-House Cases* (1873), the Supreme Court held that the privileges and immunities clause of the Fourteenth Amendment applied only to blacks who sought protection from discriminatory state laws, not to whites who alleged deprivations of their rights. The effect of the decision, however, was to ignore the importance of due process against discriminatory state laws. *Slaughter-House* prevented the due process clause from gaining importance in criminal cases. Additionally, in *Plessy v. Ferguson* (1896), the Supreme Court upheld southern laws establishing separate but equal public facilities, effectively excluding, for another half century, the equal protection clause as a constitutional remedy for the discriminatory treatment of minorities.

Southern prisons did not improve after the war; in fact, they were frequently used to imprison the black population. For example, between 1865 and 1890, the average number of white prisoners in southern prisons stayed fairly constant, at around 150. For blacks, however, the average of 150 in 1865 shot up dramatically to around 1,500 in the 1890s. In fact, many southern states opted to build or rebuild penitentiaries during this time. Many saw these actions as another attempt to enslave blacks.

Labor disputes were common in the era. In the 1870s, the Molly Maguires, Irish coal minors in eastern Pennsylvania, gained notoriety when they assassinated business executives, police officers, and mine administrative officials. A private detective from the Pinkerton National Detective Agency infiltrated the group and became the government's key witness in a series of high-profile trials. Forty Maguires were convicted and 20 were executed, including 10 on June 21, 1877, which became known as Black Thursday. The convictions remain somewhat controversial, given the fact that Irish Catholics were excluded from the jury and that most of the evidence came from either employees of the railroad and mining companies or former Maguires who became state's witnesses.

In 1865, the nation saw one of its most notable criminal trials when seven co-conspirators were tried for the assassination of Abraham Lincoln. John Wilkes Booth, a prominent actor and southern sympathizer, met in a boarding house owned by Mary Surratt with several other conspirators. Together, they decided to assassinate the president, Vice President Andrew Johnson, and Secretary of State William Seward. On April 15, 1865, Booth entered Ford's Theater in Washington, D.C., where Lincoln watched a play from a box seat. He entered Lincoln's box, shot him in the back of the head, then jumped from the balcony onto the stage, proclaiming, "sic semper tyrannus" ("thus always to tyrants!"). Booth fled the scene with the help of an accomplice. Seward's assassin, meanwhile, managed to gain access to the secretary's home and proceeded to stab him in bed. Seward survived the attempt. Johnson's assassin, however, failed to make an attempt on the vice president's life.

Booth fled mostly on land into Virginia, where he was eventually captured and killed by federal soldiers. Within days, the other conspirators were taken and charged. Attorney General James Speed, believing the crime to be an act of war, opted to try the case with a military tribunal, rather than a traditional civilian court. This had serious repercussions for the defendants, since the commission needed only find guilt, and a consequent death sentence, by a two-thirds majority. The defendants, charged with their parts in the conspiracy, were given a couple of days to prepare their defense. The military commission that tried the case operated in secret on its first day. It prevented the defendants from testifying and covered their heads with canvas hoods. The seven-week trial focused mostly on deeds of the Confederacy, and prosecutors presented little evidence to connect Mary Surratt with the conspiracy, except for her ownership of the boarding house where the scheme was entered into. The military judges ordered the execution of four of the co-conspirators, including Mary Surratt, a mere 12 weeks after Lincoln's assassination. Four other conspirators were sentenced to prison, three for life terms, and one for six years.

Another notable trial of the era was the impeachment of President Andrew Johnson. Early in 1868, Johnson made a series of moves to dismiss his secretary of war, Edwin M. Stanton, over disagreements about how Reconstruction should be handled. Congress supported Stanton's views, who in an attempt to stay, barricaded himself in his office for nearly 90 days. The House of Representatives moved to impeach Johnson on February 24, 1868, in 11 articles detailing crimes and misdemeanors, primarily his violation of the 1867 Tenure of Office Act, which prohibited presidents from removing officers while Congress was not in session. The three-month trial resulted in a verdict on May 26, which was one vote shy of convicting the president.

During this period, Congress also opted to adjust the number of members of the Supreme Court. In 1866, the Judiciary Act reduced the number of justices from 10 to seven. In 1869, Congress raised it to nine, its current number. Congress also eliminated the requirement that judges "ride circuit," having to travel frequently to hear cases.

The Old West
Tthe 19th-century west appears to have been a place of glamour, gunfights, and masculine men who conquered the rugged frontier. This exaggerated, dramatized version neglects the reality that criminal justice in the west was far-flung and often neglected. In reality, when westerners opted to punish criminals, their system more often tended toward vigilantism, rather than justice.

The hooded bodies of four of the Lincoln assassination conspirators —Mary Surratt, Lewis Payne, David Herold, and George Atzerodt— hang from the gallows on July 7, 1865, in front of a crowd. Surratt was the first woman executed by the U.S. government.

Towns sprang up where immediate needs arose, often the result of mining operations or cattle trains. Towns had few permanent residents and lacked the resources to provide stable, consistent law enforcement. Initially, some states and territories created anti-horse thief associations or other citizen-run vigilante groups or organizations, but they lacked the resources to support permanent police forces. Consequently, most law enforcement in the developing west was conducted by thinly spread military units. As towns grew, they often would gain a more consistent law enforcement presence, like a county sheriff or a U.S. marshal. However, local citizens also conducted much of their policing, if any policing existed at all. Communities also lacked the ability to create permanent jails or prisons, and until the advent of the railroad, many prisoners had to be transported by horseback to far-away territorial or state prisons. Western prisons tended toward the Auburn model—solitary confinement, silence, and labor. Most prisons were constructed by the territories, and later, when the territory became a state, became the local state penitentiary. These prisons placed little, if any focus on rehabilitation and tended, like most of their western counterparts, to focus on strict punishment.

Federal statutes dominated the law of the west. The Northwest Ordinance of 1787 gave lawmaking power to a federally appointed governor and three judges, who were charged with interpreting the common law until at least 5,000 adult males lived in the territory. When a territory became a state, it could adopt its own statutes and criminal procedure. However, states rarely innovated and created new laws. Usually, they would borrow the language and criminal code of a neighboring state, either in whole or in part, and adopt it as its own.

The west created its share of legends. After having been shot 11 times, James "Wild Bill" Hickok allegedly shot outlaw Dave McCanles and his gang of eight. In reality, Hickok shot McCanles in the back when he arrived to collect on a debt owed by Hickok's

According to an account in The Border Bandits *(1882) by J. W. Buel, on a cold February night in 1867, six men—each with a grievance—surrounded the home of Jesse James's stepfather Dr. Rueben Samuels, where James was holed up with a fever. As Dr. Samuels delayed the party, Jesse opened fire on the surprised group. Three were killed and two were wounded; Jesse fled for the wilderness and escaped, even eluding 50 horsemen who searched for a week.*

freighting company. Hickok fought in the Civil War (falsely claiming to have shot 50 Confederate soldiers with 50 consecutive bullets), and on the strength of his reputation he was able to win the election as sheriff of Ellis County, Texas, in 1869, and later as U.S. marshal. Hickok killed many outlaws but eventually was shot in the back during a poker game, holding the now famous "dead man's hand"—a pair of aces and a pair of eights.

Wyatt Earp was no less corrupt a lawman. Arrested for horse stealing in California and fired for corruption in Wichita, Kansas, where he served as city marshal, Earp moved to Tombstone, Arizona, in 1879. Earp and his brothers ultimately confronted the Clanton gang and, in a famous gun battle at the O.K. Corral, killed three of five members of the Clanton family. Many historians say that the Clantons were actually surprised by the Earps, who refused to negotiate. Townspeople chased the Earps out of Tombstone on murder charges.

Western judges often had no better standards than their law-enforcing counterparts. Most judges did not have legal training, since lawyers were few and far between. Judges would often travel from town-to-town and set up a makeshift courts, often in the company of a traveling cadre of lawyers. Judges frequently made somewhat unjust decisions. Judge Roy Bean fined people when he patronized the saloon, and once dismissed a murder charge because he felt it was not illegal to kill a Chinese person. Judge Isaac C. Parker sentenced 172 people to death in the Arkansas Territory and had 84 of those sentences overturned on appeal. Congress formally stripped him of his power in 1895. Judges and lawyers would carry guns, which were sometimes used in duels as a means to settle disputes. Legal codes were rarely used, and judges would sometimes meet in bars or taverns and decide cases on a commonsense, rather than legal, basis.

The west produced its share of famous outlaws. Brothers Jesse and Frank James, former Confederate soldiers, went on a campaign of bank robberies and murder. Officials from the Pinkerton National Detective Agency who were pursuing the brothers threw a bomb into their mother's house, killing their 9-year-old stepbrother and injuring their mother. Many saw the James, as Robin Hood figures. However, as the reward increased, the James's accomplice, Bob Ford, shot Jesse in the back of the head in 1882.

Billy the Kid swore to gain revenge for the killing of his adopted father figure, John Tunstall. Billy's gang, the Regulators, tracked down Tunstall's killer, William Morton, and executed him. Billy offered the New Mexico governor his cooperation against other outlaws, but the governor betrayed him and allowed Billy to go to prison. Billy escaped prison twice, killing two guards, but was later caught and killed in an ambush conducted by Sheriff Pat Garrett.

In 1874, the state of Texas created a special militia called the Texas Rangers. The Rangers were the most elite law enforcement group in the west in the late 19th century. They quelled riots and feuds and successfully captured over 3,000 outlaws between 1874 and 1882. Other than some allegations of racism against Hispanics and American Indians, the Rangers remained largely free from claims of corruption.

The rates of violence in both the south and the west during this period were quite high—as much as 10 times the national rate. Some historians attribute these rates to the relative lawless nature of these societies. Others claim that both societies had "cultures of honor" in which people felt obligated to respond to offensive statements with violence. Still others assert that the relative lack of stable law enforcement, coupled with ubiquitous poverty, contributed to high levels of violence.

Birth of Organized Crime
The 1850s and 1860s saw the birth of several forms of organized criminal activity. During the Civil War, Chicago's Michael McDonald found that he could collect commissions

on bounties that ranged from $100 to $1,000 from those wishing to avoid wartime service. He would then have his underlings enlist on these persons' behalf before deserting. Historians estimate that bounty jumping resulted in over 200,000 cases of army desertion during the war. Chicago particularly lacked a formal police force, prompting crime lords such as Roger Plant to operate gambling and prostitution rings with relative impunity.

This era saw the establishment of several political machines, or city bosses, most notably William M. Tweed, or "Boss Tweed," of New York City. Tweed rose to power when elected as a New York alderman and to a term in the U.S. Congress. When he returned to New York in 1857, he was elected to the New York Board of Supervisors, where he was able to manipulate city officials, control jobs and spending, and ultimately develop an army of supporters through political graft. At the peak of Tweed's power, he controlled the legislature, city government, police, and the courts. However, in 1871, Tweed was arrested and convicted for defrauding the city treasury of millions of dollars. His 12-year sentence was reduced to one year, after which he was rearrested but escaped to Spain. Tweed was eventually extradited to the United States and died in jail in 1878.

In 1872, a company known as Crédit Mobilier was created to assist in giving the appearance that the Union Pacific Railroad had chosen an independent contractor to build the railroad. The company sold stock in Union Pacific at huge discounts to congressmen to help them achieve political gain and financial profits. The *New York Sun* broke the scandal in 1872, resulting in a formal congressional investigation. Eventually, 30 members of Congress were implicated, including Vice President Schuyler Colfax and former Speaker of the House (and future president) James A. Garfield.

In 1899, America also became the home for a new group known as the Black Hand, a precursor to the Italian mafia. The Black Hand operated mostly from Sicily, its home, but soon exported its unique methods—kidnapping, extortion, and violence—to New Orleans. While gang members generally targeted Italians during this period, they would evolve into a national organized crime syndicate in the upcoming century.

Several crimes gathered significant public attention, given the increasing prominence of a media culture. In 1892, Lizzie Borden, the daughter of a high-society Massachusetts family, was charged with murdering her father and stepmother, Andrew Abbey Borden. The case captured wide notoriety, considering that Lizzie stood to inherit her family's fortune. Although the jury acquitted Lizzie, the case continues to remain controversial because the forensics and part of Lizzie's inquest testimony— which was barred from the trial and supposedly included a confession to her lawyer—were lost.

Another notable case involved Herman Mudgett, a con man who lived under the pseudonym of Dr. Henry Howard Jones. Holmes worked at a Chicago drug store, which he fraudulently purchased after murdering one of its owners. He built a three-story building across the street and opened it as a hotel during the 1893 Chicago World's Fair. The hotel contained a labyrinth of passages as well as a furnace for cremating bodies. Holmes lured mainly young females to the hotel where he tortured, killed, and burned their bodies. Others were locked in rooms while Holmes poisoned them with gas. He would then use acid to strip the bodies to skeletons and sell them to schools. Holmes was eventually captured and later confessed to having killed 27 people, though many claim his actual count is as high as 200. Holmes was hanged in 1896 and remains one of America's first documented serial killers.

Rise of Organized Police Forces

The latter half of the 19th century saw the increased development of organized police forces. Prior to the Civil War, local police forces either did not exist, or were poorly trained and lacked the resources to effectively do their jobs. Consequently, in the early 1850s, New York City—followed by New Orleans and Cincinnati (1852), Chicago and Philadelphia (1855), St. Louis (1856), Newark and Baltimore (1857), Detroit (1865), and Buffalo (1866)—developed formal, uniformed police forces similar to the London model. However, these cities did not fully adopt all of London's practices, like those that prevented officers from voting or living in certain parts of town. The London police, or "bobbies," also reported to Parliament; as opposed to the local authority, as in American jurisdictions.

These new police did not entirely replace local militias, which remained the predominant force in rural areas. Most communities required officers to live within the communities they policed. While this requirement was intended to keep officers close to their communities, it often resulted in a high proportion of Irish police officers, who often dominated urban political society. Furthermore, historians have been able to uncover the presence of black police officers in northern cities such as Chicago and Cincinnati beginning in the 1870s. Additionally, police departments did much more than provide traditional law enforcement during this time. Police departments in large cities housed hundreds of thousands of homeless people and held soup lines. In effect, the police department functioned as a general social service agency.

During the 1850s, urban police were accused of having overly strong ties to political machines, particularly in New York City. Many states decided that they could fix abuses by transferring police power from local authorities to states. Maryland, Massachusetts, Illinois, Ohio, Michigan, Indiana, Kansas, Louisiana, Nebraska, and Missouri all took

LEWD AND ABANDONED.

A caricature of notorious New Orleans prostitute Emma Johnson, from the Mascot, *May 21, 1892. Johnson is depicted with tentacles reaching out to entrap others, including men, an old man, an adolescent boy, and a young woman. While the 1850s and 1860s witnessed the beginnings of organized crime activity, which capitalized on vices such as gambling and prostitution, the latter half of the century saw the growth of organized police forces.*

steps to replace large urban police forces with state forces. In New York, the two resulting police forces competed for control of the city. In 1857, the two forces violently rioted, but a subsequent court decision legitimated the state force, leading New York City to disband its municipal police force. Americans, however, largely favored local policing, and state police forces lacked broad enforcement powers. As a result, most state police forces died out within a year or two, although some state police forces lasted a few decades. Additionally, the police, both private and public, were alleged to be overly close to corporations, and in the Haymarket bombing (1886) and Homestead strike (1892), the police allegedly use force to prevent laborers from rallying.

Labor strife became a subject of repeated concern in the latter half of the 19th century, often called the Gilded Age. Rallies against railroad and mining companies, in particular, often resulted in high levels of violence. The police forcibly and violently removed Coxey's Army, a group of labor protestors in Washington, D.C., from their protest camp. Military police called in to restore order from striking railroad workers in Martinsburg, West Virginia, eventually killed over 100 strikers. In 1894, these strikes culminated in the Pullman railroad strike in Chicago. President Grover Cleveland ordered the military to stop the strike, but the involvement of soldiers resulted in a massive riot that required the response of over 14,000 military and police officers before the violence was over.

The federal government expanded its law enforcement power during this period. During the Civil War, U.S. marshals mostly arrested southern sympathizers. After the war, however, the marshals helped maintain order during Reconstruction. They arrested nearly 7,000 southerners for civil rights violations, guarded polling places, and protected prominent African Americans. The marshals were also prominent figures in the west, many of whom achieved popular folk status. In reality, the marshals were often the only organized law enforcement presence in some territories, and they were few and far between. The marshals only arrested for violations of federal law, which included robbing the mail, desertion from the armed forces, or killing federal officials. Marshals could also swear in local citizens as deputies and form posses to pursue offenders. Posses were quite common in the west and often dispensed their own forms of vigilante justice, including the trial

In this Harper's Weekly *cover from July 16, 1892, armed Pinkerton men leave the barges of the Carnegie Steel Company at Homestead, Pennsylvania, after breaking the steel workers' strike. An armed battle killed and wounded several men.*

and execution of offenders on the spot. The marshals assisted all U.S. courts, served subpoenas, and transported federal prisoners. As territories achieved statehood (requiring at least 60,000 residents), the marshals eventually ceded most of their authority to state and local law enforcement. In 1865, President Lincoln created the Secret Service to investigate counterfeiting problems. It set up field offices and ultimately arrested several hundred counterfeiters. By 1867, the Secret Service was assigned to investigate any fraud against the United States and subsequently played a large part in investigating Ku Klux Klan actions in the south. Not until 1901, after the assassinations of James A. Garfield and William McKinley, did the Secret Service take up presidential protection.

The latter half of the 19th century also saw the emergence of a dominant private police force, the Pinkerton National Detective Agency, started by Scottish immigrant Allan Pinkerton. Initially, the Pinkertons performed railroad security, but they gained notoriety when Pinkerton convinced president-elect Abraham Lincoln to avoid stopping his train in Baltimore because of an assassination plot. The successful prevention of the attack helped the Pinkertons get involved in everything from personally protecting the president during the Civil War to pursuing outlaws like Butch Cassidy and Jesse James. However, they were also accused of corruptly supporting large corporations because of their role in breaking up striking laborers, particularly at the Carnegie Steel plant in 1892.

Gilded Age police officers worked long hours, often 12 hours a day, for five- or six-day shifts. They spent much of their time on foot, patrolling their district. Police departments had high turnover, often attributable to their ties to political machines. For example, Cincinnati's police force experienced over 80 percent turnover when its city government changed to a different political party.

Not only did organized police forces come to fruition, they were also able to utilize the development of new technologies designed to assist in the apprehension of criminals. Cesare Lombroso's *Criminal Man* (1876) theorized that criminals had certain degenerative physical characteristics, such as overly large hands, large body types, and asymmetrical faces. Richard Dugdale also theorized that criminality ran in families in his multigenerational study of the Juke family (1874). Dugdale's and Lombroso's works were wildly successful and shifted the focus more toward a scientific study of crime. Additionally, police departments began to collect photographs of offenders and disseminate them to the public at large. They also started using crime scene photography. Frenchman Alphone Bertillon created a system for measuring criminals in which officers would measure the person's head, arms, fingers, feet, and ears to help in subsequent identification. This system was quite popular until fingerprinting replaced it in the early 20th century. One other police technology to develop during this time was the callbox, first placed in New York City in 1867. An officer could turn a key in the box, which would send a signal to headquarters marking its location. Eventually, the boxes developed so that officers, by pulling levers and opening doors, could summon an ambulance or request emergency assistance.

Victorian Reformation Movement
Perhaps no other issue defines the latter half of 19th-century criminal justice more than national attempts to legislate morality through criminal statutes and to impose new Victorian images on components of the criminal justice system. These series of battles ultimately redefined American criminal justice and ushered in new 20th-century notions of fighting crime.

The first major battle involved drug addiction. The California gold rush brought Chinese immigrants, who popularized the smoking of opium, to America. Chinese immigrants soon became railroad employees. However, once the transcontinental railroad was complete, Chinese immigrants returned to California cities. San Francisco, whose residents were fearful and suspicious of the Chinese and their opium dens, became the first city to restrict drug use and outlaw drug possession when it criminalized the smoking of opium in 1875. Eleven other western states followed suit and outlawed opium in the last two decades of the 19th century.

In 1856, the Republicans adopted a platform designed to reign in the "twin relics of barbarism—polygamy and slavery." The Mormons of the Utah Territory practiced polygamy as part of their religious beliefs. While only a small subset of the population ever engaged in plural marriage, Mormon polygamists became the focus of a national criminal crusade. While Congress passed the Morrill Act in 1862, criminalizing polygamy and imposing five-year prison terms, prosecutors were unable to gain convictions without the cooperation of wives. After a Mormon polygamist challenged the act, the Supreme Court, in *Reynolds v. United States* (1879), ruled that the freedom of religion did not justify Mormons' attempts to commit crimes. Emboldened, Congress passed the Edmunds Act (1882) and the Edmunds–Tucker Act (1887). Together, these acts criminalized the newly created crime of cohabitation (which allowed Mormon polygamist convictions to be based on relatively scant evidence); disincorporated the church; seized church properties; and prevented Mormons from serving on juries, voting, or holding political office. Some 2,000 polygamist males were prosecuted and sentenced to terms in the territorial prison. The Supreme Court repeatedly upheld the convictions and taking of church property. In 1890, the church ultimately capitulated and officially renounced polygamy, formally ending the federal criminal prosecutions.

During this period, penny presses often contained abortion-related advertisements that many Victorians found highly objectionable. Congress, led by the U.S. postal agent Anthony Comstock, passed the Comstock Law in 1873, prohibiting the mailing of obscene material or the mailing of any material discussing abortion or contraception. Comstock also started Societies for the Suppression of Vice in many American cities. Obscenity became defined broadly to include pregnancy; many of the arts, such as Walt Whitman's *Leaves of Grass*; and books on birth control. Thousands of people were arrested for violations of the Comstock Laws, which many claimed was a result of Congress's overzealous censorship.

The crusaders also took on the problem of gambling. Members of Congress objected to Louisiana's state-run lottery on moral grounds, citing claims of alleged corruption. In 1868, Congress formally banned the lottery, using its power to criminalize the use of the U.S. mail to send lottery tickets. The Supreme Court ultimately upheld the ban under a massively expansive view of the Commerce Clause, reasoning that if an activity affected interstate commerce, then the federal government could step in, regulate, and criminalize it.

Victorian reformers turned their attention to police departments. Police officers in the Gilded Age were often hired not on their skill or merit, but on their loyalty to a particular political machine. Officers often had to bribe their superiors to advance or stay in the department and, as a result, regularly resorted to collecting protection money from local citizens and businesses. For example, in New York City, an officer who made $1,200 a year had to pay $1,600 to be a sergeant and over $12,000 to be a captain. Higher-ranking officers received cuts from the bribes and shakedowns. Police officers also had to pay a $250 annual fee to local politicians to keep their jobs. In Chicago, police officers were required to contribute to the local political party, as well as work in elections.

Allegations of severe police brutality were common. Police officers often resorted to beatings to extract confessions or to make public examples of those who disagreed with their methods. With the Pendleton Act of 1883, Congress made all federal appointments based on merit as opposed to open appointment. While the act did not apply to cities and states, it set the precedent that political spoils should not be the basis for governmental positions.

In 1895, future president Theodore Roosevelt led a crusade to expose corruption in New York City's police department and reformed the department's hiring and promotion processes to make them less dependent on graft and more on merit. New York City was not alone. Reformers throughout the nation sought to depoliticize their police departments, often with mixed results, as politicians often found ways to skirt the reform attempts.

Reformers also sought to fix the prisons of the period to make them more humane. In 1867, Enoch Wines and Theodore Dwight published the 70-volume *Report on the Prisons and Reformatories of the United States and Canada*, criticizing the deplorable conditions of most prisons. In particular, they advocated solitary confinement, followed with a period of labor in which a prisoner could earn an early release for good behavior. In 1870, Zebulon Brockway, head of the Rochester penitentiary, proposed reforming penitentiaries in the United States with his "Declaration of Principles" given at the National Prison Congress. In the declaration, he advocated classifying prisoners based on individual history, improving sanitation, rewarding well-behaved prisoners, depoliticizing the appointment of prison administrators, and a more judicious use of the pardoning power. To Brockway, indeterminate sentences would put the prisoner's destiny into his own hands and would ultimately help him return to society as a functional member.

The Comstock Law, headed by U.S. postal agent and Victorian reformer Anthony Comstock and passed in 1873 by Congress, prohibited any "obscene" materials in the mail, including material discussing abortion or contraception. This caricature of Comstock, printed in the August 22, 1906, edition of Puck, depicts Comstock as a prudish monk chastising any display of flesh, including shaved French poodles, mannequins, and horses.

Brockway took over the Elmira reformatory and was able to put his principles into action. Prisoners were classified and graded based on school, work, and general behavior. The Elmira system consisted of a regimented, six-days-per-week study and work program followed by mandatory Sunday religious services. Prisoners who did well received more comfortable beds, clothing, and food, while prisoners who did poorly received less comfortable items. In later stages, prisoners had to obtain a job in the community to be eligible for release. Successful prisoners could be pardoned as soon as a year later. Elmira's success inspired similar programs across the country, including Michigan (1877), Colorado (1890), and Wisconsin (1899). Brockway ultimately resigned in scandal since the Elmira reformatory was overcrowded and numerous incidents of prisoner abuse came to light. However, Brockway paved the path for prison systems of the 20th century and the more modern concept of parole.

Perhaps one of the most notable results of Gilded Age reform movements was the invention by Thomas Edison's employee Harold Brown of the electric chair, which was thought to usher in an era of more humane methods of execution. On August 6, 1890, in New York's Auburn prison, convicted murder William Kemmler became the first person executed with the chair. Despite claims for its humanity, it took several attempts for the electric charge to kill Kemmler. Martha Place became the first woman executed with the chair at Sing Sing prison in 1899. Once most of the problems were worked out, the electric chair became the dominant method of execution in the United States.

Indiana opened the first all-female prison in 1874, recognizing that women had needs that were different from men. Movements to humanize prison conditions were often led by female reformers, such as Ph.D.-educated penologist Katherine Bement Davis. Usually, the reformers saw female offenders as childlike in their capacity and in need of guidance and structure. Male prisons often built female prison wings, which generally were more homelike in appearance. Female prisoners never numbered more than a few hundred in the latter half of the 19th century, although many prisons began to add wings for female prisoners. Yet, following Indiana's lead, 20 all-female reformatories were built from 1870 to 1935.

Reformers also sought to improve the lives of juveniles. Juveniles would often be tried, convicted, and sentenced in the same courts and prisons as adults. Reformers felt that juveniles deserved different treatment. Juvenile reformatories—places where juveniles with criminal or vagrancy issues were housed and treated—took strong hold during this period. Reformers also moved to create separate trials for children, passed first in Massachusetts (1874) and Rhode Island (1892). Activists, composed mostly of upper- and middle-class women, focused their efforts on the particular needs of children. As a result of their efforts, Illinois created the first full-fledged juvenile court system in 1899.

Conclusion

The latter half of the 19th century can best be characterized as a period motivated largely by attempts to form new institutions of criminal justice, as well as to reform existing institutions. This reforming influence spread to an expanding federal influence over criminal justice, as polygamists, lotteries, and slaveholders found themselves the subjects of prosecution. The Civil War, and the period of instability to follow, resulted in sporadic and sometimes corrupt criminal justice systems that required a generation of reforming influence for real changes to take effect.

Samuel P. Newton
Weber State University

1851 PRIMARY DOCUMENT

The *Alabama Journal's* Account of a Fatal Duel

Dueling was always more strongly associated with the antebellum south and its concerns with honor and reputation, though by the 19th century, it was falling out of favor. The death of Alexander Hamilton accelerated the decline of dueling, as did advances in firearms, which made the practice fatal more frequently. In New Orleans, however, dueling remained a tradition until the end of the century; it was not outlawed in City Park until 1890, the traditional site.

FATAL DUEL.—We learn from the New Orleans papers that a duel was fought at U. N. Barracks, below that city, on the 10th inst., between Mr. J. W. Frost, of the "Crescent," and Dr. Thomas Hunt, which terminated in the death of the former. Double-barrelled guns were the weapons, and the distance forty paces. On the second fire Mr. F. was mortally wounded, the bullet passing through his left breast. He died within half an hour. Great excitement prevailed in relation to the matter, and efforts were being made to arrest those implicated, in accordance with a statute of that State prohibiting the practice of dueling. We clip the following from the N. O. correspondence of the Mobile Tribune:

"The immediate cause of offense was an altercation which took place at the Whig Meeting in Perdulo Street on Monday evening. It was, however, only the renewal of an ancient difficulty, arising out of the congressional election last fall, when Col. T. G. Hunt was a candidate before the Whig Convention, and Judge Hullard the law partner of Mr. Frost obtained the nomination. Another of the brothers of Col. Hunt became then involved in a personal difficulty with Mr. Frost, and the preliminary movements for a duel were made upon the part of Mr. Frost, but they failed. The whole correspondence was published at the time and is doubtless familiar to our readers. The ill feeling has rankled ever since, and the new canvass, in which Col. Hunt is again a candidate, revived it, produced the collision at "The Shades," and has ended in this lamentable manner. It has already been published that there was a meeting between the parties on Wednesday, which the police interrupted, and both challenger and challenged were bound over. They disregarded the bonds, went almost directly from the Recorder's office to the United States barracks, and finally closed up this most unhappy quarrel with the death of Mr. Frost by the hands of Dr. Hunt."

The Tribune learns, from a private source, that another duel, growing out of the above affair, is about to take place between Major Raney and Mr. Edwards.

Source: Daily Alabama Journal, v.5/136 (July 16, 1851).

See Articles: Murder, History of; Murder, Sociology of; New Orleans, Louisiana.

1854 PRIMARY DOCUMENT

Excerpts From the Memoirs of Counterfeiter William Stuart

William Stuart was born in 1788 to a Connecticut farming family; beyond that, knowledge of him comes from the memoir of his criminal career he published at age 66. Though claiming to warn the young against a life of vice, the memoir is written like an adventure tale, including daring escapes and double crosses. Though not a western gunslinger, Stuart's memoir was published at a time when the public was devouring tales of outlaws and bad men on the frontier.

I hired a black man to put me across the river, and I entered the forests, which in those days covered almost the whole country. The weather was warm, and I took a nap upon the leaves. When day-light appeared I bent my course to the N.E. and before night arrived at Coosahatchie, a village on the river of the same name. A widow woman kept tavern in the place, and I stopped for refreshments and rest. A neighbor of her's soon came into the barroom and wanted to borrow money of her, but she declined to lend him. This man became furious because of her denial, and abused the woman in the vilest terms. I saw that she was becoming afraid of him, so I told him that I should not take part in the quarrel, nevertheless I should not sit by any longer and permit him to revile her. He looked at me with disdain and contempt, and commenced his tirade upon me, and I took him by the collar and put him into the street, then went back and closed the door. The woman thanked me for the service I had rendered her, and offered to keep me as long as I would stay, without charge. Having had a hard time on board of our ship, I gratefully accepted her offer, and tarried with her, as Paul said, "for the space of many days."

She was blessed by nature with genius adequate to any emergency, and her features were unrivalled by the choicest specimens of statuary; her tresses, black as the raven's wing, descended gracefully from her head; her eyes were black and lustrous as an hour's; her face seemed wrought with exquisite beauty; and her form was chaste and finely modeled. Her age about thirty, with all the charms of eighteen years, while a little daughter, fatherless, looked to her for support and protection. When I became more acquainted with her, I found that she, like myself, was hardened by fraud, dishonesty and corruption.

She kept her house open during the greatest part of every night, and when the outer world was clothed in darkness, the slaves from the neighboring plantations brought her corn, fowls and pigs, and articles of merchandise, for which she scantily paid them in gewgaws and whisky. She was ripe for almost every enterprise, and was willing to engage in any object that promised a golden reward. As our acquaintance became more thorough, I often times recapitulated my pursuits, told her the stories of my life and escapes that fortune had cast in my way, and the stratagems to which I had had recourse in my eventful history. I gave her an outline of my counterfeiting process, and she entered into my plan with her whole heart. She gave me access to all her business, and reposed confidence in my ability to do all things well. She denied me nothing, but was eager to anticipate my wishes for the pleasure of obliging me. When the subject of counterfeit money was discussed, her anxiety to procure it banished almost every other thought from her mind, and she was willing to part with me for a season on no other terms than that I should obtain a large amount of funds, subject to her disposal. After staying at her house for three months, I agreed to go north, visit my friends, proceed to the Canadian mint, gather some thousands and return. She procured me genuine notes of the Savannah and Augusta banks as specimens for the engravers, and all things were in readiness for my absence during a month. I need not dwell on the parting scene though destined to be brief. It was accompanied with tearful eyes and throbbing heart.

I took my course for Charleston, and when in that city got a passage to New York on my way to Connecticut. At home I passed a few days, looked over my farm, called upon old associates, and laid plans for the future. I kept all my own special secrets. I never was guided by plans as advised in our conclaves, but adopted expedients as the time and circumstances indicated at the period of their occurrence.

Eliphalet Bennett and I started on foot for Canada together. He was a great genius in the way of wickedness, and the most heartless and graceless villain that I ever knew. His parents took great care in his having a thorough education. He passed through college and received its literary honors, engaged in the study of the law under the tuition of an able counselor and for a time promised to be an honor to his family and his profession. But he was a deeply wicked man, unmoved by affection or kindness, and though married early to an amiable lady, the connection was only productive of misery. He set fire to his house because his wife, contrary to his will, attended Methodist meetings, and was arrested and put in jail, but his wealth and friends saved him from punishment. He drank deeply, and seemed to delight in crimes of the greatest magnitude and of the most horrid depravity.

This man went with me after funds. When we got into the bounds of Vermont he frequently preached to the Methodist brethren, and usually closed his services in appeals to their liberality. He stated to his audiences that while away upon his circuit, his house and all that it contained was burnt, and that he was on his way to a rich brother in Canada for aid, and that the smallest sums that they could spare would avail him much. We collected money for him, and he borrowed an over-coat of one, and many garments of others, promising to return them when he came back. Thus we worked our way to Canada.

I left Bennett on the frontiers and went to my old friends, produced my specimen notes, and in a fortnight returned home with $40,000 in my belt. In latter days I had learned to take the by-paths, to save trouble and hindrance; said but little, and avoided respectable public houses. This purchase had exhausted all my means, and my family was poor, unless I made a saving in disposing of my counterfeit funds.

I now stowed my money in my favorite hiding places near home, and stayed a few weeks to prepare my household to live through the winter, while I was away in Georgia. My intentions were kept by me in perfect secrecy. No man was able to divine my purposes or even conjecture concerning them.

After a few weeks it was necessary that I should go to Cross River in Putnam County, NY, to transact some business, and on my way went through Ridgefield, and having lost my handkerchief, I stepped into the store of Abner Gilbert and bought one for one dollar, and by accident let his clerk have a bad five dollar note. I passed on eight or nine miles, stopped at a tavern at evening, and it was reported that a man dressed in short clothes had passed it. I tarried a little while, then left the house and went across the fields into a barn. This was empty and no place to rest. I now went out and gazed over the country, and spied a light in a house upon an eminence, and drew near to it, asked admittance and was received to their fireside. Soon I went to bed and was getting sleepy, when several men entered and inquired for me. As these men entered my room, I aroused from my slumbers and was about to jump through the window, but they seized me and I became quiet. While they were about the room, I slipped 2 five dollar notes under the bed-post, and have not learnt up to this day that they were ever found. They escorted me to Ridgefield the same night and put keepers over me, and I passed the night with my hands tied behind me. Next morning I offered Gilbert one hundred dollars to let me go, and his wife begged of him with tears in her eyes, but he was determined that my career should be checked.

Next day came on my trial, and I was sent to Danbury jail until the session of the court. I told the jailer that I had got home again, and he gave me some rum and I went into my room. My prospects were fair for Newgate but I cared very little about it. I was aware of the looseness of the watch that was held over me. Six or eight times a day Mr. Crofut, the jailer, with the still and stealthy step of a cat, would approach the grief-hole and peak at me. He did not intend that I should see him; but nothing escaped my vision, and though my face was frequently averted while he was casting suspicious glances at me, yet he never caught me unawares in any of my movements. I did not try to disturb his peace as I did that of his predecessor. I was pacific as a spaniel, and was thus throwing a mist before his eyes for future purposes.

It was in the last of November, 1817, if I rightly recollect, when I re-entered this den of sinners. I how had full leisure to take a retrospect of my previous life, and upon a rigid examination, after casting aside all my prejudices, was disposed to give a verdict against myself. Others had done wrong, violated the law, trampled upon justice, and outraged the good sense of the community, and were still abroad, verily leeches upon the country. In an evil hour I had been snatched up, and was compelled to look through grated windows and hear the rattling bolts of iron doors, while others were still bleeding the people at every pore. I comforted myself with the reflection that their turn, even if delayed, would eventually come.

But here I was, with irons about my ankles and wrists, that my keepers had unceremoniously brought into my presence unasked, introduced to them, and compelled me to accept them as my present associates. Though I scorned them, for the sake of politeness and courtesy, I informally received them to my embraces and shook hands with them, not cordially, but because there was a necessity in the case. I thought of my contract with the Georgia widow, but was in no condition now to return to her hospitable home and carry out our intentions. I did not so much as write her a letter, informing her of the disabilities under which I labored, nor to inform her that I had used due diligence to augment her interests in pecuniary matters. In all these things I was silent.

My stay in Danbury jail was about four weeks, and the evening before I was removed the jailor came in and searched me. I had all my implements for jail breaking about my person, and gave them all up to him and abandoned the project. Next day I was waited upon the sheriff to Fairfield. I was as cheerful as if I was going to a dance or a quilting frolic. They put me in the prison, infected as it had been in summer with bugs, fleas, and lice. It was now cold weather, and they did not annoy me. A short time thereafter my trial came on, and as the testimony against me was positive, the jury brought me in guilty. One of the witnesses swore falsely against me, but there was truth enough to convict a saint in the testimony of the others. I was sentenced to five years' hard labor in the state prison.

After the judge had sentenced me, I rose and asked his honor this question: "Suppose, sir" said I, "I die before my five years expire, shall I have to provide a substitute to serve out the remainder of my term? I hate to cheat the state; will you please inform me in these matters, for I am ignorant of the law?" The judge smiled, and told me that in case of death these things would not be required of me. I felt better after the sentence of the court, convinced that justice would be observed by my punishment.

While I lay in Danbury jail, the judges of the court, the lawyers the state's attorney, and many wealthy gentlemen engaged in mercantile pursuits, called on me and urged me to reveal to them the names of my associates, assuring me that I should leave the jail in a month and enjoy my liberty. My doctrine ever had been, and now is, if a person enters a secret society, no matter what its objects may be, and solemnly swears to keep secret all its operations and movements, none but those who are ready for perjury will be guilty of treachery. I told these men that I was my own counterfeiter, and that no man was acquainted with my operations. They knew I lied, and I knew it; but before I would entrap others to secure myself, I would be hanged on the nearest tree. I always inculcated a spirit of honor and integrity among our members, and if one of us should fall a victim to violated law, his mouth should be hermetically sealed in reference to his associates. I could keep a secret without effort, because it was pleasing to me to do so. The public are not benefitted by the confessions of a rascal, and his oath is worthless who accuses others to screen himself. Such men are obnoxious to the people, and whenever in after life they become witnesses in court, they are regarded by those who know them with scorn and contempt.

Source: Stuart, William. "Sketches of the Life of William Stuart." In *Bandits and Bibles: Convict Literature in 19th Century America*, edited by Larry E. Sullivan. New York: Akashic Books, 2003.

See Articles: Chain Gangs and Prison Labor; Connecticut; Counterfeiting; Prisoner's Rights.

Telegram From Major Robert Anderson to the Secretary of War

Southern slave states threatened secession from the United States even before Lincoln was elected, and by the time he took office in March 1861, the first seven of 11 Confederate states had made good on the promise. The Buchanan and Lincoln administrations refused to acknowledge the legitimacy of secession. Armed hostilities began in South Carolina, which had been the first state to secede. During Reconstruction, the state was home to the most prominent white paramilitary groups. This telegram, sent by Major Robert Anderson, commander of the Union garrison at Fort Sumter, notified Secretary of War Simon Cameron of the outcome of the battle that began the serious fighting of the war.

S.S.Baltic. Off Sandy Hook Apr. Eighteenth. Ten Thirty A.M. via New York. Hon. S. Cameron, Secy. War. Wash. Having defended Fort Sumter for thirty four hours, until the quarters were entirely burned, the main gates destroyed by fire, the gorge walls seriously injured, the magazine by flames and its door closed from the effects of heat. Four barrels and three cartridges of powder only being available and no provisions remaining but pork. I accepted terms of evacuation offered by General Beauregard being on same offered by him on the Elem. Enoch. Inst prior to the commencement of hostilities and marched out of the fort Sunday afternoon the fourteenth Inst with colors flying and drums beating bringing away company and private property and saluting my flag with fifty guns.

Source: Records of Adjutant General's Office, Archival Research Catalog, ARC ID: 594525.

See Articles: Lincoln, Abraham (Administration of); Slavery; South Carolina; State Slave Codes.

Excerpt From the Memoir of Harriet Jacobs, a Slave Girl

An escaped slave who became a prominent abolitionist, Jacobs published her memoir under the pseudonym Linda Brent in installments in the New York Tribune *before the collected edition was released in 1861. Its depictions of the humiliations and cruelties faced by female slaves helped to support the moral argument for the Union effort in the Civil War, and Jacobs continued to write during the war, informing readers about aspects of life in the wartime south.*

… I now entered on my fifteenth year—a sad epoch in the life of a slave girl. My master began to whisper foul words in my ear. Young as I was, I could not remain ignorant of their import. I tried to treat them with indifference or contempt. The master's age, my extreme youth, and the fear that his conduct would be reported to my grandmother, made him bear this treatment for many months. He was a crafty man, and resorted to many means to accomplish his purposes. Sometimes he had stormy, terrific ways, that made his victims tremble; sometimes he assumed a gentleness that he thought must surely subdue. Of the two, I preferred his stormy moods, although they left me trembling. He tried his utmost to corrupt the pure principles my grandmother had instilled. He peopled my young mind with unclean images, such as only a vile monster could think of. I turned from him with disgust and hatred.

But he was my master. I was compelled to live under the same roof with him—where I saw a man forty years my senior daily violating the most sacred commandments of nature. He told me I was his property; that I must be subject to his will in all things. My soul revolted against the mean tyranny. But where could I turn for protection? No matter whether the slave girl be as black as ebony or as fair as her mistress. In either case, there is no shadow of law to protect her from insult, from violence, or even from death; all these are inflicted by fiends who bear the shape of men. The mistress, who ought to protect the helpless victim, has no other feelings towards her but those of jealousy and rage. The degradation, the wrongs, the vices, that grow out of slavery, are more than I can describe. They are greater than you would willingly believe…

Every where the years bring to all enough of sin and sorrow; but in slavery the very dawn of life is darkened by these shadows. Even the little child, who is accustomed to wait on her mistress and her children, will learn, before she is twelve years old, why it is that her mistress hates such and such a one among the slaves. Perhaps the child's own mother is among those hated ones. She listens to violent outbreaks of jealous passion, and cannot help understanding what is the cause. She will become prematurely knowing in evil things. Soon she will learn to tremble when she hears her master's footfall. She will be compelled to realize that she is no longer a child. If God has bestowed beauty upon her, it will prove her greatest curse. That which commands admiration in the white woman only hastens the degradation of the female slave. I know that some are too much brutalized by slavery to feel the humiliation of their position; but many slaves feel it most acutely, and shrink from the memory of it. I cannot tell how much I suffered in the presence of these wrongs, nor how I am still pained by the retrospect.

My master met me at every turn, reminding me that I belonged to him, and swearing by heaven and earth that he would compel me to submit to him. If I went out for a breath of fresh air, after a day of unwearied toil, his footsteps dogged me. If I knelt by my mother's grave, his dark shadow fell on me even there. The light heart which nature had given me became heavy with sad forebodings. The other slaves in my master's house noticed the change. Many of them pitied me; but none dared to ask the cause. They had no need to inquire. They knew too well the guilty practices under that roof; and they were aware that to speak of them was an offense that never went unpunished.

I longed for someone to confide in. I would have given the world to have laid my head on my grandmother's faithful bosom, and told her all my troubles. But Dr. Flint swore he would kill me, if I was not as silent as the grave.

… I was very young, and felt shamefaced about telling her such impure things, especially as I knew her to be very strict on such subjects. Moreover, she was a woman of a high spirit. She was usually very quiet in her demeanor; but if her indignation was once roused, it was not very easily quelled. I had been told that she once chased a white gentleman with a loaded pistol, because he insulted one of her daughters. I dreaded the consequences of a violent outbreak; and both pride and fear kept me silent. But though I did not confide in my grandmother, and even evaded her vigilant watchfulness and inquiry, her presence in the neighborhood was some protection to me. Though she had been a slave, Dr. Flint was afraid of her. He dreaded her scorching rebukes. Moreover, she was known and patronized by many people; and he did not wish to have his villainy made public …

I would ten thousand times rather that my children should be the half-starved paupers of Ireland than to be the most pampered among the slaves of America. I would rather drudge out my life on a cotton plantation, till the grave opened to give me rest, than to live with an unprincipled master and a jealous mistress. The felon's home in a penitentiary is preferable. He may repent, and turn from the error of his ways, and so find peace; but it is not so with a favorite slave. She is not allowed to have any pride of character. It is deemed a crime in her to wish to be virtuous.

Mrs. Flint possessed the key to her husband's character before I was born. She might have used this knowledge to counsel and to screen the young and the innocent among her slaves; but for them she had no sympathy. They were the objects of her constant suspicion and malevolence. She watched her husband with unceasing vigilance; but he was well practiced in means to evade it …

… Sometimes he would complain of the heat of the tea room, and order his supper to be placed on a small table in the piazza. He would seat himself there with a well-satisfied smile, and tell me to stand by and brush away the flies. He would eat very slowly, pausing between the mouthfuls. These intervals were employed in describing the happiness I was so foolishly throwing away, and in threatening me with the penalty that finally awaited my stubborn disobedience. He boasted much of the forbearance he had exercised towards me, and reminded me that there was a limit to his patience. When I succeeded in avoiding opportunities for him to talk to me at home, I was ordered to come to his office, to do some errand. When there, I was obliged to stand and listen to such language as he saw fit to address to me. Sometimes I so openly expressed my contempt for him that he would become violently enraged, and I wondered why he did not strike me. Circumstanced as he was, he probably thought it was better policy to be forbearing. But the state of things grew worse and worse daily. In desperation I told him that I must and would apply to my grandmother for protection. He threatened me with death, and worse than death, if I made any complaint to her. Strange to say, I did not despair. I was naturally of a buoyant disposition, and always I had a hope of somehow getting out of his clutches. Like many a poor, simple slave before me, I trusted that some threads of joy would yet be woven into my dark destiny.

I had entered my sixteenth year, and every day it became more apparent that my presence was intolerable to Mrs. Flint. Angry words frequently passed between her and her husband….

After repeated quarrels between the doctor and his wife, he announced his intention to take his youngest daughter, then four years old, to sleep in his apartment. It was necessary that a servant should sleep in the same room, to be on hand if the child stirred. I was selected for that office, and informed for what purpose that arrangement had been made. By managing to keep within sight of people, as such as possible, during the day time, I had hitherto succeeded in eluding my master, though a razor was often held to me throat to force me to change this line of policy … [Now] I was ordered to take my station as nurse the following night. A kind Providence interposed in my favor. During the day Mrs. Flint heard of this new arrangement, and a storm followed I rejoiced to hear it rage.

After a while my mistress sent for me to come to her room. Her first question was, "Did you know you were to sleep in the doctor's room?"

"Yes, ma'am."

"Who told you?"

"My master."

"Will you answer truly all the questions I ask?"

"Yes, ma'am."

"Tell me, then, as you hope to be forgiven, are you innocent of what I have accused you?"

"I am."

She handed me a Bible, and said "Lay your hand on your heart, kiss this holy book, and swear before God that you tell me the truth."

I took the oath she required, and I did it with a clear conscience.

"You have taken God's hold word to testify your innocence," said she. "If you have deceived me, beware! Now take this stool, sit down, look me directly in the face, and tell me all that has passed between your master and you."

I did as she ordered. As I went on with my account her color changed frequently, she wept, and sometimes groaned. She spoke in tones so sad, that I was touched by her grief. The tears came to my eyes; but I was soon convinced that her emotions arose from anger and wounded pride. She felt that her marriage vows were desecrated, her dignity insulted; but she had no compassion for the poor victim of her husband's perfidy. She pitied herself as a martyr; but she was incapable of feeling for the condition of shame and misery in which her unfortunate, helpless slave was placed.

Yet perhaps she had some touch of feeling for me; for when the conference was ended, she spoke kindly, and promised to protect me. I should have been much comforted by this assurance if I could have had confidence in it; but my experiences in slavery had filled me with distrust. She was not a very refined woman, and had not much control over her passions. I was an object of her jealousy, and, consequently, of her hatred; and I knew I could not expect kindness or confidence from her under the circumstances in which I was placed. I could not blame her. Slaveholders' wives feel as other women would under similar circumstances. The fire of her temper kindled from small sparks, and now the flame became so intense that the doctor was obliged to give up his intended arrangement.

I knew I had ignited the torch, and I expected to suffer for it afterwards; but I felt too thankful to my mistress for the timely aid she rendered me to care much about that. She now took me to sleep in a room adjoining her own. There I was an object of her especial care, though not of her especial comfort, for she spent many a sleepless night to watch over me. Sometimes I woke up, and found her bending over me. At other times she whispered in my ear, as though it was her husband who was speaking to me, and listened to hear what I would answer. If she started me, on such occasions, she would glide stealthily away; and the next morning she would tell me I had been talking in my sleep, and ask who I was talking to. At last, I began to be fearful for my life. It had been often threatened; and you can imagine, better than I can describe, what an unpleasant sensation it must produce to wake up in the dead of night and find a jealous woman bending over you...

Why does the slave ever love? Why allow the tendrils of the heart to twine around objects which may at any moment be wrenched away by the hand of violence?... I did not reason thus when I was a young girl. Youth will be youth. I loved, and I indulged the hope that the dark clouds around me would turn out a bright lining. I forgot that in the land of my birth the shadows are too dense for light to penetrate....

There was in the neighborhood a young colored carpenter; a free born man. We had been well acquainted in childhood, and frequently met together afterwards. We became mutually attached, and he proposed to marry me. I loved him with all the ardor of a young girl's first love. But when I reflected that I was a slave, and that the laws gave no sanction to the marriage of such, my heart sank within me. My lover wanted to buy me; but I knew that Dr. Flint was too willful and arbitrary a man to consent to that arrangement. From him, I was sure of experiencing all sorts of opposition, and I had nothing to hope from my mistress. She would have been delighted to have got rid of me, but not in that way. It would have relieved her mind of a burden if she could have seen me sold to some distant state, but if I was married near home I should be just as much in her husband's power as I had previously been, for the husband of a slave has no power to protect her. Moveover, my mistress, like many others, seemed to think that slaves had no right to any family ties of their own; that they were created merely to wait upon the family of the mistress. I once heard her abuse a young slave girl, who told her that a colored man wanted to make her his wife. "I will have you peeled and pickled, my lady," said she, "if I ever hear you mention that subject again. Do you suppose that I will have you tending my children with the children of that nigger?" The girl to whom she said this had a mulatto child, of course not acknowledged by its father. The poor black man who loved her would have been proud to acknowledge his helpless offspring.

... How I dreaded my master now! Every minute I expected to be summoned to his presence; but the day passed, and I heard nothing from him. The next morning, a message was brought to me: "Master wants you in his study." I found the door ajar and I stood a moment gazing at the hateful man who claimed a right to rule me, body and soul. I entered and tried to appear calm. I did not want him to know how my heart was bleeding. He looked fixedly at me, with an expression which seemed to say, "I have half a mind to kill you on the spot." At last he broke the silence, and that was a relief to both of us.

"So you want to be married, do you?" said he, "and to a free nigger."

"Yes, sir."

"Well, I'll soon convince you whether I am your master, or the nigger fellow you honor so highly. If you must have a husband, you may take up with one of my slave."

What a situation I should be in , as the wife of one of his slaves, even if my heart had been interested!

I replied, "Don't you suppose, sir, that a slave can have some preference about marrying? Do you suppose that all men are alike to her?"

"Do you love this nigger?" said he, abruptly.

"Yes, sir."

"How dare you tell me so! he exclaimed, in great wrath. After a slight pause, he added, "I supposed you thought more of yourself; that you felt above the insults of such puppies."

I replied, "If he is a puppy I am a puppy for we are both of the negro race. It is right and honorable for us to love each other. The man you call a puppy never insulted me, sir; and he would not love me if he did not believe me to be a virtuous woman."

He sprang upon me like a tiger, and gave me a stunning blow. It was the first time he had ever struck me; and fear did not enable me to control my anger. When I had recovered a little from the effects, I exclaimed, "You have struck me for answering you honestly. How I despise you!"....

[He answered] "... I have wanted to make you happy, and I have been repaid with the basest ingratitude; but though you have proved yourself incapable of appreciating my kindness, I will be lenient towards you, Linda. I will give you one more chance to redeem your character. If you behave yourself and do as I require, I will forgive you and treat you as I always have done; but if you disobey me, I will punish you as I would the meanest slave on my plantation. Never let me hear that fellow's name mentioned again. If I ever know of your speaking to him, I will cowhide you both; and if I catch him lurking about my premises, I will shoot him as soon as I would a dog. Do you hear what I say? I'll teach you a lesson about marriage and free niggers! Now go, and let this be the last time I have occasion to speak to you on this subject."

Reader, did you ever hate? I hope not. I never did but once; and I trust I never shall again. Somebody has called it "the atmosphere of hell"; and I believe it is so.

... My lover was an intelligent and religious man. Even if he could have obtained permission to marry me while I was a slave, the marriage would give him no power to protect me from my master. It would have made him miserable to witness the insults I should have been subjected to. And then, if we had children, I knew they must "follow the condition of the mother." What a terrible blight that would be on the heart of a free, intelligent father! For his sake, I felt that I ought not to link his fate with my own unhappy destiny. He was going to Savannah to see about a little property left him by an uncle; and hard as it was to bring my feelings to it, I earnestly entreated him not to come back. I advised him to go to the Free States, where his tongue would not be tied, and where his intelligence would be of more avail to him. He left me, still hoping the day would come when I could be bought. With me the lamp of hope had gone out. The dream of my girlhood was over. I felt lonely and desolate.

... [Slaveholders] seem to satisfy their consciences with the doctrine that God created the Africans to be slaves. What a libel upon the heavenly Father, who "made of one blood all nations of men!" And then who are Africans? Who can measure the amount of Anglo-Saxon blood coursing in the veins of American slaves?...

No pen can give an adequate description of the all-pervading corruption produced by slavery. The slave girl is reared in an atmosphere of licentiousness and fear. The lash and the foul talk of her master and his sons are her teachers. When she is fourteen or fifteen, her owner, or his sons, or the overseer, or perhaps all of them, begin to bribe her with presents. If these fail to accomplish their purpose, she is whipped or starved into submission to their will. She may have had religious principles inculcated by some pious mother or grandmother, or some good mistress; she may have a lover, whose good opinion and peace of mind are dear to her heart; or the profligate men who have power over her may be exceedingly odious to her. But resistance is hopeless...

The slaveholder's sons are, of course, vitiated, even while boys, by the unclean influences everywhere around them. Nor do the master's daughters always escape. Severe retributions sometimes come upon him for the wrongs he does to the daughters of the slaves. The white daughters early hear their parents quarrelling about some female slave. Their curiosity is excited, and they soon learn the cause. They are attended by the young slave girls whom their father has corrupted; and they hear such talk as should never meet youthful ears, or any other ears. They know that the women slaves are subject to their father's authority in all things; and in some cases they exercise the same authority over the men slaves. I have myself seen the master of such a household whose head was bowed down in shame, for it was known in the neighborhood that his daughter had selected one of the meanest slaves on his plantation to be the father of his first grandchild. She did not make her advances to her equals, nor even to her father's more intelligent servants. She selected the most brutalized, over whom her authority could be exercised with less fear of exposure. Her father, half frantic with rage, sought to revenge himself on the offending black man; but his daughter, foreseeing the storm that would arise, had given him free papers, and sent him out of the state.

In such cases the infant is smothered, or sent where it is never seen by any who know its history. But if the white parent is the father, instead of the mother, the offspring are unblushingly reared for the market. If they are girls, I have indicated plainly enough what will be their inevitable destiny.

... I can testify, from my own experience and observation, that slavery is a curse to the whites as well as to the blacks. It makes the white fathers cry and sensual; the sons violent and licentious; it contaminates the daughters and makes the wives wretched. And as for the colored race, it needs an able than mine to describe the extremity of their sufferings, the depth of the degradation.

Yet few slaveholders seem to be aware of the widespread moral ruin occasioned by this wicked system. Their talk is of blighted cotton crops—not of the blight on their children's souls.

Sources: Jacobs, Harriet with L. Maria Child. *Incidents in the Life of a Slave Girl.* Boston, 1861;
and
Faust, Drew Gilpin. *James Henry Hammond and the Old South*. Baton Rouge: Louisiana State University Press, 1982.

See Articles: Rape, History of; Rape, Sociology of; Sexual Harassment; Slavery; Slavery, Law of.

1865
PRIMARY DOCUMENT

Excerpt From Thomas M. Harris's Documents on the Assassination Conspiracy

A physician and Union general, Harris served in the legislature of the new state of West Virginia after the war. He also served on the commission investigating the assassination of President Lincoln, which tried eight suspected conspirators: Samuel Arnold, George Atzerodt, David Herold, Samuel Mudd, Michael O'Laughlen, Lewis Powell, Edmund Spangler, and Mary Surratt. By that time, Booth had already been killed after a 10-day manhunt. The commission found all eight conspirators guilty in various degrees after 366 witnesses testified.

In lieu of General and Mrs. Grant, President Lincoln had taken Major Rathbone and Miss Harris, the step-son and daughter of Senator Harris, of New York, into the Presidential party. On reaching the theatre at a somewhat late hour, and after the play had commenced, as soon as the presence of the President became known, the actors stopped playing, the band struck up "Hail to the Chief," and the audience rose and received him with vociferous cheering.

The party proceeded along the rear of the dress circle, and entered the box that had been prepared for them, the President taking the rocking chair that had been placed there for him on the left of the box, and nearest to the audience, about four feet from the door of entrance to the box. Major Rathbone and the ladies found seats on the President's right. During this time the conspirators were on the alert, scanning the situation, passing about so as to keep up a communication with each other, in preparation for their work. Booth had arranged with Payne to assassinate Secretary Seward at the same time that he would assassinate the President; and no doubt had planned for Payne, after accomplishing his task, to join him and Herold in their flight, crossing the Eastern Branch at the Navy Yard bridge, and then to pass down through Maryland and cross the Potomac, at a selected point, into Virginia, where they might consider themselves as being safe amongst their friends. Secretary Seward was known to have received severe injuries from the upsetting of his carriage, and to be lying in a critical condition under the care of Dr. Verdi. Booth had planned to take advantage of this circumstance for gaining admittance for Payne into the sick chamber, where, by springing with the ferocity of a tiger upon the sick man, he might make quick work in dispatching him with his dagger. To this end he had prepared a package rolled up in paper, and had schooled Payne in the artifice, teaching him to represent himself as having been sent by Dr. Verdi with this package of medicine, which it was necessary he should deliver in person, as he had important verbal directions as to the manner of its use, which required him to see the Secretary. About ten o'clock Booth rode up the alley back of the theatre where he had been accustomed to keep his horse and having reached the rear entrance, called for Ned three times, each time a little louder than before. At the third call Ned Spangler answered to his summons by appearing at the door. Booth's first salutation was in the form of a question: "Ned, you will help me all you can, won't you?" To which Spangler replied,"Oh yes!" Booth then requested him to send "Peanuts" (a boy employed about the theatre), to hold his horse. Spangler gave the boy orders to do this, and upon the boy making the objection that he might be out of place at the time he had a duty to perform, Spangler bade him go, saying that he would stand responsible for him. The boy then took the reins, and held the horse for about half an hour, until Booth returned to reward him with a curse and a kick, as he jerked the rein from him preparatory to remounting for his flight. After entering the theatre, Booth passed rapidly across the stage, glancing at the box occupied by his intended victim, and looking up his accomplices, he passed out of the front door on to the walk where he was met by two of his fellow conspirators. One of these was a low, villainous-looking fellow, whilst the other was a very neatly-dressed man crossed the walk to the rear of the President's carriage and peeped into it. One of the witnesses, who was sitting on the platform in front of the theatre, had his attention arrested by the manner and conduct of these men, and so watched them very closely.

It was at the close of the second act that Booth and his two fellow conspirators appeared at the door. Booth said, "I think he will come down now"; and they aligned themselves to await his coming. Their communications with each other were in whispered tones. Finding that the President would remain until the close of the play, they then began to prepare to assassinate him in the theatre. The neatly-dressed man called the time three times in succession at short intervals, each time a little louder than before. Booth now entered the saloon, took a drink of whiskey, and then went at once into the theatre. He passed quickly along next to the wall behind the chairs, and having reached a point near the door that led to the passage behind the box, he stopped, took a small pack of visiting cards from his pocket, selected one and replaced the others;

stood a second with it in his hand, and then showed it to the President's messenger, who was sitting just below him, and then, without waiting, passed through the door from the lobby into the passage, closing and barring it after him. Taking a hasty, but careful, look through the hole which he had made in the door for the purpose of assuring himself of the President's position, and cocking his pistol and with his finger on the trigger, he pulled open the door, and stealthily entered the box, where he stood right behind and within three feet of the President. The play had advanced to the second scene of the third act, and whilst the audience was intensely interested Booth fired the fatal shot—the ball penetrating the skull on the back of the left side of the head, inflicting a wound in the brain (the ball passing entirely through the lodging behind the right eye), of which he died at about half-past seven o'clock on the morning of the fifteenth. He was unconscious from the moment he was struck until his spirit passed from earth. An unspeakable calm settled on that remarkable face, leaving the impress of a happy soul on the casket it had left behind.

Thus died the man who said, "Senator Douglass says he don't care whether slavery is voted up, or voted down; but God cares, and humanity cares, and I care."

As soon as Booth had fired his pistol, and was satisfied that his end was accomplished, he cried out, "Revenge for the South!" and throwing his pistol down, he took his dagger in his right hand, and placed his left hand on the balustrade preparatory to his leap of twelve feet to the stage. Just at this moment Major Rathbone sprang forward and tried to catch him. In this he failed, but received a severe cut in his arm from a back-handed thrust of Booth's dagger. Time was everything now to the assassin. He must make good his escape whilst the audience stood dazed, and before it had time to comprehend clearly what had happened. With his left hand on the railing, he boldly leaped from the box to the stage.

Source: Harris, T. M. *Assassination of Lincoln; A History of the Great Conspiracy: Trial of the Conspirators by a Military Commission and a Review of the Trial of John H. Surratt*. Boston: American Citizen Co., 1892.

See Articles: Booth, John Wilkes; History of Crime and Punishment in America: 1850–1900; Lincoln, Abraham (Administration of); Murder, History of; Political Crimes, History of; Political Dissidents.

1865
PRIMARY DOCUMENT

A. G. Blair's Testimony on Inhumane Treatment at Andersonville Prison

Andersonville prison opened in February 1864, consisting of about 16.5 acres enclosed by a 15 ft.-tall stockade to contain the Confederacy's prisoners of war. As Blair testifies, conditions were terrible: 12,913 of 45,000 prisoners died. It is a matter of debate how many died of negligence and how many died of deliberate war crimes. This testimony is taken from the trial of Henry Wirz, who had run the prison; he was hanged, the only convicted Confederate war criminal.

I was in the military service of the United States, in the 122d New York. I was taken prisoner on the 23d of May, 1864, at the battle of the Wilderness. I was taken to Libby Prison first, and from that to Andersonville, where I arrived about the first of June. Captain Wirz was in command of the prison when I arrived there.

I have heard a great many questions asked Captain Wirz about rations whenever he would come into camp. His reply was generally an oath, saying that we would get all the rations we deserved, and that was damned little.

Q: Did he ever say he would not give you rations if he could?

A: I never heard him make that exact remark.

Q: Did he make any similar remark?

A: Several days during the fore part of my imprisonment there we had no rations. The report came from good authority that he was the cause of it, he being in charge of the camp. [Interrupted by counsel for the accused.]

Question repeated.

A: I have not heard those words from his mouth.

Q: Did you hear any similar language used by Captain Wirz to that which I repeated to you? If so, state what the language was.

[Objected to by counsel for the accused on the ground that witness had already answered in the negative. After deliberation the objection was overruled.]

A: On one occasion when he was asked by several of the prisoners who had not had any rations for twenty-four hours, when they were to have any, he made remark that if the rations were in his hands we would not get any. That was in the beginning of July, 1864, just before or after the 4th.

I have seen him stand at the gate when sick men were carried out. The men were very anxious to get out of the sun into the shade, and they would rush out to a small passageway made in the large doors coming out, to suit him. I have seen him shove the well, and the sick who were being carried, over on their backs; or sometimes he would order the guards to do it. The condition of the men taken out of camp into the hospital was hopeless—all that I ever saw taken out.

I escaped from Andersonville in the latter part of July or the fore part of August. And got about thirty miles from the stockade when I was captured and brought back to the camp. I was kept over night, and then was put in the stocks. The first day that I was taken out of the stocks I was not put in the stockade that night. I was put in the stocks the next day, and then was returned to the prison with three other comrades. I do not recollect the exact number of hours I was kept in the stocks; I should think five or six hours.

Q: Did the prisoner give any orders in reference to your being put in the stocks?

A: Just before I was put in the stocks I saw him give some orders from his headquarters, and I supposed that those were the orders.

I saw prisoners shot on or near the dead-line, on several occasions. I was down, in the fore part of my imprisonment, to get water at the creek. That was the only resource for obtaining water, except you had a right in one of the wells. The crowd was very great there. It was absolutely necessary sometimes either to get over the dead-line or to thirst. I have seen men on five or six occasions either shot dead or mortally wounded for trying to get water under the dead-line. I have seen one or two instances where men were shot over the dead-line. Whether they went over it intentionally, or unconsciously from not knowing the rules, I cannot say. I think that the number of men shot during my imprisonment ranged from twenty-five to forty. I do not know that I can give any of their names. I did know them at the time, because they had tented right around me, or messed with me, but their names have slipped my mind. Two of them belonged to the 40th New York Regiment. Those two men were shot just after I got there, in the latter part of June, 1864.

Q: Did you see the person who shot them?

A: I saw the sentry raise his gun. I hallooed to the man. I and several of the rest gave the alarm, but it was to late. Both of these men did not die; one was shot through the arm; the other died; he was shot in the right breast. I did not see Captain Wirz present at the time. I did not hear any orders given to the sentinels, or any words from the sentinels when they fired; nothing more than they often said that it was done by orders from the commandant of the camp, and that they were to receive so many days furlough for every Yankee devil they killed. Those twenty-five or forty men were shot from the middle of June, 1864, until the 1st of September. There were men shot every month. I cannot say that I ever saw Captain Wirz present when any of these men were shot. I had no chance of seeing him unless he was in the stockade. The majority of those whom I saw shot were killed outright; expired in a few moments.

Q: Can you give a detailed description of those you saw killed and of the dates?

A: In regard to the dates I cannot give you any detail. I lost dates there, and did not know when Sunday came. I came very near being shot myself. A very large crowd had gathered at the stream of water, and I was reaching over the dead-line in order to get some water. I could not get it anywhere else, as I had no right to the wells. A bullet came, I should judge, within two or three inches of my right ear, striking one man through the arm, and mortally wounding another. These men were in their tents, unoffending.

Q: Were all these twenty-five or forty men shot by the sentries for crossing the dead-line or being near it?

A: Some were across it, and others not. I saw a man shot who was three feet inside the dead-line. I saw one shot on the 10th of July, just the day before the men whom we called the raiders were hung.

Q: Describe the circumstances that led to the men being shot.

A: I do not know, except from the great desire of sentries to get furloughs.

Q: Did you ever hear any order given by the prisoner in reference to firing grape and canister on the prisoners in the stockade?

A: He gave an order; I did not hear it; but there was an order given—

(Interrupted by counsel for the accused:)

Q: What order did you ever hear him give?

A: Captain Wirz planted a range of flags inside the stockade, and gave the order, just inside the gate, "that if a crowd of two hundred (that was the number) should gather in any one spot beyond those flags and near the gate, he would fire grape and canister into them."

Captain Wirz gave this order I was speaking of to the crowd of prisoners around the gate. He merely told them he would fire upon them if they gathered there. I did not hear him give the order to men outside. He warned us that if we gathered there in numbers he would fire upon us.

Q: Then it was not an order, but simply a warning.

A: Yes, sir.

Source: http://law2.umkc.edu/faculty/project/ftrials/Wirz/WIRZ.HTM

See Articles: Corporal Punishment; Georgia; Prisoner's Rights.

1867 PRIMARY DOCUMENT

Edwin M. Hale's Treatise on Abortion

Abortion has been practiced since ancient times, but advances in medicine in the 19th century made it safer (relatively speaking; one in six women died) and increased the number of skilled practitioners willing to perform a procedure or prepare a drug. Whether this led to an increase in abortions isn't clear, but abortion opponents believed that it did and supported increasingly stronger laws against it. Hale called for punishing the patient, not just the abortionist.

Great Crime of The Nineteenth Century.

Why Is It Committed?
Who Are the Criminals?
How Shall They Be Detected?
How Shall They Be Punished?

By Edwin M. Hale, M.D.
Chicago: C.S. Halsey, 147 S. Clare St.
—Buffalo, 238 Main Street.

SYMPATHY.—This emotion, so enabling and admirable in most cases, is often perverted from its proper channels, and made to be the cause of crime.

Even the best and purest of physicians cannot look upon the victim of a seduction, or a rape, without the keenest sympathy. That the best of medical men have been tempted to relieve the woman of the fruits of seduction and violence, is not surprising.

But the sympathies of the medical man, or any other person, should be under the dominion of religious principle. The injunction—"Thou shalt not kill," is as binding here as elsewhere.

Evidently the only consisted rule of action to adopt, is that laid down on a previous page when speaking of the victim of seduction or of violence.

SECTION II.

WHO ARE THE CRIMINALS?

We deem it our duty, as a medical man and a citizen, to point out fearlessly and perspicuously those who are in any way connected, criminally, with this great evil.

Generally they consist of four classes, viz:

The Principals.
Accessories Before the fact.
Accessories To the fact.
Accessories After the fact.

THE PRINCIPALS.

There are generally but two persons in a case of criminal abortion, who are to be considered as principals. In rare cases there may be more. Usually they stand, relatively, as follows:

1. The Mother. That the mother, who carries in her womb her unborn child, should be the chief criminal, is a startling proposition. Many persons will be inclined to disbelieve that such is the case. Those, however, who have investigated the subject, or who have had opportunities for observation, will not dispute the assertion.

    When it is known that the cases are very rare in which the crime is committed without the consent of the mother; when it is known that the cases are few in which the child is destroyed without her urgent desire; the proposition will not appear to improbable as at first sight.

    Examine all the inducements to the crime, mentioned heretofore, and it will be found that the cases are few in which the mother herself does not originate the plea, or act willingly from influences brought to bear on her from other sources.

In either case, she must be considered as one of the principals in the crime.

Even in cases where the husband or other person persuades the mother to its commission, or to allow another person to destroy the fetus, she is still a principal; for in no case need she succumb to influences not extending to actual physical force. The woman is individually responsible for all her acts of immorality.

In the married state, the wife has the moral and legal right to become a mother as often as possible. No law, human or Divine, can compel her to destroy, or permit the destroying of the fruits of conception.

Why then, in this view of the matter, should not the woman be considered the chief criminal, in nearly all cases, except when the abortion was induced on her person, by violence and against her will?

The law in this respect, has not been strict enough to meet the demands of justice. It has recognized, in most instances, only the person who destroys the child by drugs, instruments, or some physical force.

In a few instances, it has named the mother, who, by either of the above means, has destroyed the child in her own womb.

In but one instance, (the law of California,) does the law make a principal of the woman on whom the abortion is induced. This should be done in nearly all instances. If the woman is innocent, and the crime was committed against her will, and she was powerless to prevent it, there are many ways in which her innocence could be made to appear.

Physicians are often informed against by one of the guilty parents, causing thereby, a malicious prosecution. Such a law would prevent such persecution.

In fact, she is often more guilty than the person inducing the abortion, for she may, by various improper means, as bribes, threats, and other inducements, influence the physician or other person to commit the crime, when his better judgment and principle would revolt against it.

I do not hesitate to assert that if the woman be made a principal in most cases of abortion, it would diminish the crime two-thirds, and perhaps to a greater extent, especially in large towns and cities.

2. The Abortionist. Among the most prominent are a class of creatures, of both sexes, known to the law as Abortionists. These people have their corresponding analogies in the Thugs of India, and murderers everywhere, and make it their chief business to destroy, for money, or worse inducements, the innocent and unborn child.

Not only does their loathsome presence poison the moral atmosphere of great cities, but they infest the smaller towns. They even leave their slimy track in the quiet country, and pollute the green fields, the flowery prairies, and the pure forests, where the homes of good men and women should be found.

In the great cities, however, these vampyres most abound. Certain streets and localities, not always low and abandoned in their moral surroundings, are selected by these creatures as their habitat. Sometimes their presence is known only by the bad location they occupy, for the simple "Doctor ____," on the sign would indicate no nefarious calling. At other times, the word "Accoucher," is prostituted from its legitimate significance, and means to the abandoned, and sinful, only an "Abortionist." More frequently, they sail under the name of "Astrologist;" the possessor of an "Anatomical Museum;" one who treats "secret diseases," or attends to "private matters."

Female Abortionists, assume the name of "Midwives," "Nurses," "Fortune-tellers," "Madam____, Female Physician," et cetera, and under these apparently harmless avocations, ply their murderous trade. In the country, the business is managed differently. Hundreds of persons of both sexes, are constantly perambulating the country, stopping in the smaller towns and villages, who have for their chief means of subsistence, no other means of support than the induction of criminal abortion. Ostensibly they are "Professors," "Doctors," "Lecturers," etc., advertising to cure all the ills which flesh is heir to; perform wonderful surgical operations; lecture on anatomy, physiology, health, hygiene, phrenology, and various other topics of which they are perfectly ignorant.

In their advertisements, their harangues to the public, their conversations with private visitors, or in their lectures, they are sure to let drop some hint, by which the unprincipled may imply of what their secret business consists.

Follow these miscreants to their private consultation rooms, and you shall see where the most disgraceful scenes are enacted, and where hands and souls are stained by the blood of unborn babes.

Sometimes the vocation of "nurse," which should be a noble and holy calling, is prostituted to the sole purpose of criminal abortion. Such instances have come to the knowledge of medical men, as occurring in this, and other cities. In the instances alluded to, the monthly nurse has intimated to the lying woman, that there is no need of passing through the perils and pains of childbirth again; that in the early months of pregnancy the menses can be safely brought back; that they will instruct them how to accomplish it. By this means the mind of how many woman hitherto pure, may have been poisoned by such false and sinful temptations?

Among those who figure in the list of chief criminals, are the unnatural father, be he husband, seducer, or unlawful companion. Instances are on record, where the father has administered the potion, used an instrument, or resorted to physical force to destroy his unborn offspring.

We have even heard from undoubted evidence, that there have been instances where the mother of the pregnant woman—both belonging to those circles of society considered as "respectable,"—has, with her own hands, given the drug to cause abortion, and most revolting of all, used upon the person of her daughter, an instrument which caused the death of the fetus.

In the name of humanity, religion, and civilization, is it not time that some serious and determined effort was made by men of the medical, legal, and religious professionals, to extirpate these murderers?

Shall we allow the end of the Nineteenth Century to close upon a scene which will make the devils laugh, and the angels weep?

Can no law be framed, having for its object the prevention and punishment of the crime of abortion; a law so broad in its scope, so perfect in its details, that the principals above named, cannot escape detection, trial, and condign punishment?

It is a hopeful sign to see that the clergy are becoming aroused to a sense of their duty in this respect, and I cordially endorse the remarks of the author of a recent article on this subject, who says: "Quack doctors, irregular practitioners, and the whole race of vagrant female hyenas who will take fetal life for fifty dollars, and gratuitously kill or ruin the credulous wife or "unfortunate," should be treated as pests to be "purified by fire," if necessary. The odor of such a burnt offering would be more grateful than their offenses which smell to Heaven."

To recapitulate; The mother may be said to the chief criminal (a) when the desire for, and the accomplishment of the crime originates within herself, i.e. when she destroys of her own will, by means of drugs or violence, the unborn child, or procures its destruction by others. She may be said to be a chief criminal when she is influenced by others, to the commission of the crime, and allows them to cause by any means the destruction of the child in utero.

Besides the mother, the person who administers, or causes to be administered, any drug, to a pregnant woman, or uses any instrument for the purpose of the destruction of the child, without the consent of the mother, becomes the chief criminal; but if the person giving the drug, or using the instrument, is employed or influenced in any way, by the mother or others, to the commission of the crime, he or she, becomes a chief criminal.

Source: http://www.archive.org/details/greatcrimeofnine00hale

See Articles: Abortion; Religion and Crime, Sociology of; *Eisenstadt v. Baird*; *Griswold v. Connecticut*; *Roe v. Wade*.

1869 PRIMARY DOCUMENT

Article on Jesse James's Bank Robbery

A Confederate guerrilla during the Civil War, Jesse James began his career as a bank and train robber a year after the war ended. Much of the public sympathized with James and the James–Younger gang; the gang's activities transpired largely during Reconstruction, when the harsh treatment of the former Confederacy fueled the rapid romanticizing of the "lost cause" of the south. James's victims were the very wealthy, for whom the financially struggling common people had little affection.

The Bank Robbery At Gallentin, Mo.

The Cashier Shot and Killed.

We learned yesterday that John W. Streets, the cashier of the Davis county Savings Bank, at Gallentin, was shot and killed last Monday. The following are the particulars as told to us:

Two men rode up to the banking house and getting off their horses, one of them went in and asked Mr. Sheets to change a one hundred dollar bill. While doing so the other man went in and said:

"If you will write out a receipt, I will pay you that bill."

Mr. Sheets sat down to do so, and while he was writing, the man drew a revolver and shot him twice—once in the breast, and once through the head. The unfortunate banker fell from his chair dead.

The ruffians then turned upon Mr. McDonald, the clerk, and fired upon him twice, one of the shots taking effect in the fleshy part of one of his arms. At time of the shooting, one of them said with an oath, that "Sheets and Cox had been the cause of the death of his brother, Bill Anderson, and that he was bound to have revenge."

The two then robbed the bank of all the money in the outside drawer, and mounting their horses deliberately rode away.

As soon as they had left the bank the alarm was given, and a number of the citizens started in pursuit. The men were overtaken a short distance from town, shots were exchanged, and in the running fight, one of the rascals was hit. He fell from his horse, and the animal galloped off free. The man's companion came to his rescue, and assisting him to mount behind himself, the two made their escape.

There is a boldness and recklessness about this robbery and murder that is almost beyond belief…

Sources: *Kansas City Daily Journal of Commerce* (December 9, 1869); and
http://www.pbs.org/wgbh/americanexperience/features/primary-resources/james-newspapers

See Articles: Frontier Crime; James, Jesse; Missouri; Robbery, History of.

1871
PRIMARY DOCUMENT

Excerpt From Testimony in Congressional Hearings on the Ku Klux Klan

The first Klan was a white supremacist vigilante group that formed during Reconstruction to provide anonymity to its members while targeting freed blacks, Republicans (both black and white), and northerners. After five years of Klan activity, the federal government passed a series of laws from 1870 to 1871 to criminalize their activities, provide federal oversight of elections, turn many Klan tactics into federal crimes, and ban suspected Klan allies from juries in Klan trials.

Atlanta, Georgia, October 21.

MARIA CARTER (colored) sworn and examined.

By the Chairman:
Question. How old are you, where were you born, and where do you now live?
Answer. I will be twenty-eight years old on the 4th day of next March: I was born in South Carolina; and I live in Haralson County now.
Question. Are you married or single?
Answer. I am married.
Question. What is your husband's name?
Answer. Jasper Carter.
Question. Where were you on the night that John Walthall was shot?
Answer. In my house, next to his house; not more than one hundred yards from his house.
Question. Did any persons come to your house that night?
Answer. Yes, sir, lots of them; I expect about forty or fifty of them.
Question. What did they do at your house?
Answer. They just came there and called; we did not get up when they first called. We heard them talking as they got over the fence. They came hollering and knocking at the door, and they scared my husband so bad he could not speak when they first came. I answered them. They hollered, "Open the door." I said, "Yes, sir." They were at the other door, and they said, "Kindle a light." My husband went to kindle a light, and they busted both doors open and ran in—two in one door and two in the other. I heard the others coming on behind them, jumping over the fence in the yard. One put his gun down to him and said, "Is this John Walthall?" They had been hunting him a long time. They had gone to my brother-in-

law's hunting him, and had whipped one of my sisters-in-law powerfully and two more men on account of him. They said they were going to kill him when they got hold of him. They asked my husband if he was John Walthall. He was so scared he could not say anything. I said, "No." I never got up at all. They asked where he was, and we told them he was up to the next house, they jerked my husband up and said that he had to go up there. I heard them up there hollering "Open the door," and I heard them break the door down. While they were talking about our house, just before they broke open our door, I heard a chair fall over in John Walthall's house. He raised a plank then and tried to get under the house. A parcel of them ran ahead and broke the door down and jerked his wife out of the bed. I did not see them, for I was afraid to go out of doors. They knocked his wife about powerfully. I heard them cursing her. She commenced hollering, and I heard some of them say, "God damn her, shoot her." They struck her over the head with a pistol. The house looked next morning as if somebody had been killing hogs there. Some of them said "Fetch a light here, quick;" and some of them said to her, "Hold a light." They said she held it, and they put their guns down on him and shot him. I heard him holler, and some of them said, "Pull him out, pull him out." When they pulled him out the hole was too small, and I heard them jerk a plank part off the house and I heard it fly back. At that time four men came in my house and drew a gun on me; I was sitting in my bed and the baby was yelling. They asked, "Where is John Walthall?" I said, "Them folks have got him." They said, "What folks?" I said, "Them folks up there." They came in and out all the time. I heard John holler when they commenced whipping him. They said, "Don't holler, or we'll kill you in a minute." I undertook to try and count, but they scared me so bad that I stopped counting; but I think they hit him about three hundred licks after they shot him. I heard them clear down to our house ask him if he felt like sleeping with some more white women; and they said, "You steal, too, God damn you." John said, "No, sir," They said, "Hush your mouth, God damn your eyes, you do steal." I heard them talking, but that was all I heard plain. They beat him powerfully. She said they made her put her arms around his neck and then they whipped them both together. I saw where they struck her head with a pistol and bumped her head against the house, and the blood is there yet. They asked me where my husband's gun was; I said he had no gun, and they said I was a damned liar. One of them had a sort of gown on, and he put his gun in my face and I pushed it up. The other said, "Don't you shoot her. " He then went and looked in a trunk among the things. I allowed they were hunting for a pistol. My husband had had one, but he sold it. Another said, "Let's go away from here." They brought in old Uncle Charlie and sat him down there. They had a light at the time, and I got to see some of them good. I knew two of them, but the others I could not tell. There was a very large light in the house, and they went to the fire and I saw them. They came there at about 12 o'clock and staid there until 1. They went on back to old Uncle Charley's then, to whip his girls and his wife. They did not whip her any to hurt her at all. They jabbed me on the head with a gun, and I heard the trigger pop. It scared me and I throwed my hand up. He put it back again, and I pushed it away again.

Question. How old was your baby?
Answer. Not quite three weeks old.
Question. You were still in bed?
Answer. Yes, sir; I never got up at all.
Question. Did they interrupt, your husband in any way?
Answer. Yes, sir; they whipped him mightily; I do not know how much. They took him away up the road, over a quarter, I expect. I saw the blood running down when he came back. Old Uncle Charley was in there. They did not carry him back home. They said, "Old man, you don't steal." He said, "No." They sat him down and said to him, "You just stay here." Just as my husband got back to one door and stepped in, three men came in the other door. They left a man at John's house white they were ripping around. As they came, back by the house they said, "By God, goodbye, hallelujah!" I was scared nearly to

death, and my husband tried to keep it hid from me. I asked him if he had been whipped much. He said, "No." I saw his clothes were bloody, and the next morning they stuck to him, and his shoulder t almost like jelly.

Question. Did you know this man who drew his gun on you?

Answer. Yes, sir.

Question. Who was he?

Answer. Mr. Much.

Question. Where does he live?

Answer. I reckon about three miles off. I was satisfied I knew him and Mr. Hooker.

Question. Were they considered men of standing and property in that country?

Answer. Yes, sir; Mr. Finch is married into a pretty well-off family. He is a good liver, but he is not well off himself.

Question. How is it with Mr. Booker?

Answer. I do not know so much about him. He is not very well off.

Question. How with the Monroes?

Answer. They are pretty well-off folks, about as well off as there are in Haralson. They have a mill.

By Mr. Bayard:

Question. You said they had been looking a long time for John Walthall?

Answer. Yes, sir.

Question. Had they been charging John with sleeping with white women?

Answer. Yes, sir; and the people where he staid had charged him with it. He had been charged with it ever since the second year after I came to Haralson. I have been there four years this coming Christmas.

Question. That was the cause of their going after him and making this disturbance?

Answer. Yes, sir; that was it. We all knew he was warned to leave them long before he was married. His wife did not know anything about it. When he first came there he was staying among some white women down there.

Question. Do you mean living with them and sleeping with them?

Answer. He was staying in the house where they were.

Question. White women?

Answer. Yes, sir.

Question. Were they women of bad character?

Answer. Yes, sir; worst kind.

Question. What were their names?

Answer. They were named Keyes.

Question. How many were there?

Answer. There were four sisters of them, and one of them was old man Martin's wife.

Question. Were they low white people?

Answer. Yes, sir.

Question. Had John lived with them for a long while?

Answer. Yes, sir. They had threatened him and been there after him. They had got gone there several times to run them off. My house was not very far from them, and I heard them down there throwing rocks.

Question. Was it well known among you that John had been living with these low white women?

Answer. Yes, sir.

Question. Did he keep it up after he was married?

Answer. No, sir; he quit before he was married. I heard that a white woman said be came along there several times last year and said he could not get rid of them to save his life.

Question. Did John go with any other white women?

Answer: No, sir; not that I know of.

Question. Was he accused by the Ku-Klux of going with any of them?

Answer. They did not tell him right down their names. I heard them say, "Do you 'feel like sleeping with any more white women?" and I knew who they were.

By the Chairman:

Question. These women, you say, were a low-down class of persons?

Answer. Yes, sir; not counted at all.

Question. Did white men associate with them?

Answer. It was said they did.

Question. Did respectable white men go there?

Answer. Some of them did. Mr. Stokes did before he went to Texas, and several of the others around there. I do not know many men in Georgia any way; I have not been about much. I have heard a heap of names of those who used to go there. I came by there one night, and I saw three men there myself.

Question. You say John Walthall had been going there a good while?

Answer. Yes, sir; that is what they say.

Question. How long had he quit before they killed him?

Answer. A year before last, a while before Christmas. He was still staying at old man Martin's. I staid last year close to Carroll, and when I came back he had quit.

Question. Did he go with them any more after he married?

Answer. No, sir; be staid with his wife all the time. He lived next to me.

Question. How long had he been married before he was killed?

Answer. They married six weeks before Christmas, and he was killed on the 22d of April.

Source: U.S. Congress. *Testimony Taken by the Joint Select Committee to Inquire Into the Condition of Affairs in the Late Insurrectionary States*. Georgia, Vol. I. Washington, DC: Government Printing Office, 1872. and
http://historymatters.gmu.edu/d/6225

See Articles: Georgia; Ku Klux Klan; Race-Based Crimes; Racism.

1874 PRIMARY DOCUMENT

Final Ransom Note in the Charley Ross Kidnapping

In 1874, 4-year-old Charley Ross and his 6-year-old brother Walter were enticed into a horse-drawn carriage by the promise of candy and fireworks. Soon after Walter was dropped off unharmed, ransom notes for Charley were sent to his father Christian, including a demand of $20,000—roughly the equivalent of $400,000 today. Though the Ross's lived in a wealthy neighborhood, they had fallen into deep debt in the 1873 depression. The kidnapping and subsequent involvement of the Pinkertons became the first widely publicized ransom case in the United States, but Charley was never found.

On the 7th of November the following reply was received, dated Philadelphia:
[No. 23.]

PHILA., Nov 6.

Mr. Ros: we told you in the last positively we would not write you anymore. This dozing about puts us to no small amount of trouble we had left phila for New York thinking you were ready to close up the business. We told you positively procrastination is dangerous. Had we accomplished what we have been fishing for the last three months your child would now have been dead but we have not yet caught the fish we wanted. Yours is but a small item compared with something else. Walter said you owned the two new houses right opposite you or we should never troubled you. Mr. Ros you have asked to keep this negotiation a secret between ourselves it is a wise policy in your doings not that we fear being trapped in our own game. This is positively the last from us. If you are sincere you would be anxious to settle this business if you regard the life of your child. We mean to fulfill every promise we made you in good faith. The result depends entirely with yourself whom you appoint to transact this business for you we want at least two days notice before you come to New York for we may be 500 miles off and we ask for time to get there you can say Tuesday Nov. 10. Saul of Tarsus. (choose your own name say I will be stopping so and so all day. Do not leave the hotel wherever you may be stopping for one minute during the day). This thing must come and shall come to a close in a few days.

In this, the last letter received from the abductors, they hint that they have been trying for three months to steal another child, and had they succeeded my child would have been killed, and a ransom demanded for their new victim, compared with which the twenty thousand required from me would be an insignificant sum. They also state that Walter misled them regarding my circumstances by telling them I owned two new houses which had been built opposite to my residence. Tuesday, November 10th, is fixed as the day on which my representative is asked to be in New York to pay over the money, and the address of the personal is changed to "Saul of Tarsus."

More than four months had now passed since CHARLEY had been stolen. The police and detective agencies, with all their unremitted and almost superhuman efforts, had failed to find the thieves, or get a clue to the place where they had hidden their victim. Twenty three letters written and mailed in different places had been received from the abductors, bidding defiance to the best detective skill. Contrary to our expectation and hope, the abductors had not made a single error or the smallest slip, by which they could be traced; but with a shrewdness and cunning far above ordinary criminals, they had successfully evaded pursuit, and baffled every effort at discovery.

Four months were these of acute suffering to my family and friends; and now I was so ill that for a time my life was despaired of, and it was thought by my medical attendants that nothing but the speedy return of CHARLEY could restore my broken mind and body—that the load of trouble which was crushing me must be removed in order to a mental and physical restoration. The want of success in the past led to little hope of recovery of CHARLEY by the same appliances in the immediate present. Besides, Mrs. Ross was weighed down with the accumulation of trouble; and thus, in the double hope of saving my life and recovering CHARLEY, she consented to have the child restored by paying the ransom. This her brothers determined to do in the way pointed out by the abductors, paying them the money and taking the risk of getting the child afterwards. As the authorities both here and in New York knew of the change of address of the personals from "John" to "Saul of Tarsus," they were informed that it was the purpose of Mrs. Ross's brothers to redeem the child by paying the ransom which the abductors demanded, and on the 13th of November, Superintendent Walling wrote as follows to Captain Heins:

Dear Sir. — Please see Mr. Lewis and say to him that I think it dangerous for parties to meet relative to any negotiations for the child, with a large amouut of money, unless they have some officers within call, as the parties might be disguised, and in case the villains were to fail in making terms, they might take desperate chances to obtain the money.

Geo. W. Walling, Superintendent.

Source: Ross, Christian K. *The Father's Story of Charley Ross: A Full and Complete Account of His Abduction, With Incidents of the Search for His Recovery*. Philadelphia: Published for the Author, 1878.

See Articles: Kidnapping; Lindbergh Law; Philadelphia, Pennsylvania.

1875
PRIMARY DOCUMENT

Chicago Daily Tribune Story on the John C. Colt Murder Trial

The brother of firearm manufacturer Samuel, John Colt spent time as a bookkeeper, teacher, engineer, and riverboat gambler before finding success as a lecturer and author on the subject of double-entry bookkeeping. When a disagreement with printer Samuel Adams over the price of printing Colt's textbook turned violent, Colt struck Adams dead. He claimed self-defense, but was found guilty and died in a fire the day his execution was scheduled; conspiracy theories claimed that he escaped.

JOHN C. COLT: Did the Slayer of Adams Escape the Gallows? The Marvelous Story Put Forth by E B T

JOHN C. COLT.

Did the Slayer of Adams Escape the Gallows?

The Marvelous Story Recently Put Forth by the Paris "Figaro."

Statement by a Gentleman Connected with the New York Press at the Time.

There Can Be No Doubt that Colt Committed Suicide.

To the Editor of the *Chicago Tribune*:

CHICAGO, Dec. 1.—The strange "taking-off" of John C. Colt, who murdered Adams, a bookbinder, in a room corner of Broadway and Chambers street, New York, over thirty years ago, has excited the interest of the public at different periods ever since it occurred. In brief,

THE FACTS WERE THESE:

John C. Colt was the author of a system of bookkeeping, living in New York, and he gave his work into the hands of one Adams to bind in large quantities. One Saturday, Adams called at Colt's room, on Broadway, and urgently pressed the payment of his bill. Colt was living in rather a loose way, with a mistress, and had not the means to defray the amount presented. Colt disputed the bill, angry words ensued, and from this they came to blows. Colt, in his confession after his conviction, alleged that they fell on the floor together, and, as Adams had him in a tight place, gripping him in a tender part, he reached a hatchet, lying on the floor, near at hand, and dealt a blow WHICH DID THE BUSINESS for his assailant. Alarmed at what he had done, he cast about to see what he had better do to conceal what he now, in a cooler moment, deemed a crime of horrid magnitude. He conceived the idea of packing the body in a dry goods box, in his room; which he did. After spending the afternoon in wiping up the bloody floor, he went out at nightfall, and walked in the park, near the City Hall, meditating what his next course should be. He says, "At one time I resolved to go to my brother Sam and tell him all about it; but this I was afraid to do." His brother Samuel boarded at that time at the Astor House, and had not then secured a patent for the six-shooter pistol (of which, by the way, he was not the inventor, but only the one who utilized the discovery or another), but was engaged in partnership with a Mr. Robinson, in a ship-news enterprise and merchants' reading-room near Wall Street.

Adams was a married man and had a family. His absence from his business and home soon created an anxious search for his whereabouts; but no crew for a week was found, until the box in which Colt had placed his victim, packed in salt,

WAS TRACED TO THE SHIP KALAMAZOO,

lying at or near the foot of Wall street. The discovery was made by tracing the box through the carman who took it from Colt's rooms where he taught bookkeeping. The box was not "conveyed to New Orleans," as stated in the following narrative. The writer of this sketch was at that time on the editorial staff of the old *New York Times*, a Democratic paper then, and remembers very well the discovery, made on a Sunday evening, just eight days from the Saturday Adams was murdered. He was also engaged in assisting the reporters at the trial before Judge Kout.

No murder committed in New York in those days—not even the trial of Richard P. Robinson for the killing of Helen Hewett, in a house of ill-fame in Thompson street—created so great and wide-spread a sensation as that of Adams by Colt. Sheriff Gultek, after

Colt's conviction, received $1,000 from an anonymous source to aid in Colt's escape. This he handed over to the Mayor.

A plan was set on foot to enable Colt to
ESCAPE THE GALLOWS,
after Gov. Seward refused his pardon. It was to set fire to the Tombs, in which he was incarcerated, and, by disguising him as a fireman, he would easily escape. But this, ? most likely to the Sheriff's integrity, failed.

It was said, at the time, that a plan of legal acquittal was entertained, to be brought about in this wi?: It was to appeal from Gov. Seward's refusal to a Judge of the Supreme Court, and by bringing the matter before him, got an order to delay the execution ten hours, while it was being argued, and, if the result was not favorable, then to bribe the steamer to run on a bar in the Hudson, and thus let the time go by at which the execution was to take place. There was no telegraph in those days.

The Rev. Dr. Anthon, Rector of St. Mark's in the Bowery, was Colt's spiritual adviser, and he married Colt to his mistress in the cell the day before the execution was to take place. Colt professed repentance, and the clergyman called next morning to have a religious service with the doomed man. The Sheriff unlocked the door of Colt's cell, and the Doctor entered first. But he shrank back in horror at the scene which presented itself! There Colt lay, stiff and stark, with a
KNIFE STICKING IN HIS HEART.
The Doctor turned and came out and burst into tears.

The day appointed for the execution was dark and dreary in November. Crowds gathered at the street-corners in the lower part of the city, and it was not generally known that Colt had robbed the gallows of its victim. Soon the City Hall bell boomed out an alarm of fire, and, sure enough, it broke out in the Tombs Prison. From this circumstance arose the story which is repeated below, and probably nine out of ten of the old inhabitants known to the writer believed that Colt did escape in the guise of a fireman.

In a conversation with Mr. Robinson, Samuel Colt's partner, who died who or three years since, he informed me of all the circumstances which came under his own personal observation. He said, "There is
NOT A WORD OF TRUTH
about Colt's being alive. We, continued he, "had made an arrangement with Dr. —— and Dr. —— [leading physicians in the city] to be at the Shakespeare Hotel, on Duane street [a few blocks from the prison], with a galvanic battery, bath, etc., to resuscitate the body, which we were to secure immediately that the surgeon should pronounce him dead. But Colt killed himself, and there was an end of the matter. He was buried in St. Mark's ground, on Tenth street, near the Bowery, where he now lies."

This is written to explain the following letter from "Grace Greenwood" to the New York Times of Nov. 28, dated Paris, Nov. 7, 1875.

A STRANGE AND DISTORTED STORY.
Apropos of murder and Figaro, I am tempted to send you, for the benefit of your New York readers, a translation of a most astonishing and sensational story, which appeared here a few mornings since—of course, in the veracious journal of which I have spoken. Hartford papers will please copy:

"At Batiguolles, Rue le Mercier, a man who once had a criminal celebrity in New York, United States, died the other day. After many vicissitudes, he had come to our great city to hide and to be forgotten. This man was Charles Colt, father of the inventor of 'Colt's revolver.' In 1847 he lived in New York, on the route to Harlem, in a frame house surrounded by a garden, and separated from all other habitations. He had with him there a mistress, with whom he often quarreled; and one evening, in a moment of anger, he killed this woman, by striking her a blow on the temple with a carafe. In presence of the corpse, the unhappy man was forced to consider how most speedily to rid himself of it. An internal thought crossed his mind; he cut the body in pieces, and packed it in a case, salting it very strongly. Than he placed this case in a second, and shipped the dreadful package to New Orleans to a false address, giving himself also a fictitious name as the sender. He had, moreover, taken the precaution to keep the head, which he had interred in the garden of the house. Arrived at its destination, the case could not, of course, be claimed, as the address was invented, and after a little dulzy was sent back to New York, where it was opened, and the corpse discovered and identified by a peculiar mark on the neck. The buried head was found in the garden, and as suspicion pointed to Colt he was arrested, tried, and condemned to be hung. It is needless to say that the friends of the criminal took all the steps possible to clear him, but without success. On the evening before the day on which he was to be executed, a fire broke out in the interior of the Tombs, that celebrated prison of the Egyptian style in New York; the firemen penetrated into the jail, where one of them, killed by the family of Colt, carried to him a fireman's dress, by the aid of which he escaped in the tumult. When his flight was discovered it was too late; he had left New York and was lost in the American deserts. He went afterwards to Utah, to San Francisco, to Mexico, and from there to France, where he lived ignored in Paris, by the name of Kavannagh, which was that of his mother. Before his death, Colt, who was a Protestant, sent for a pastor, and, in his presence and before one of his neighbors, who has given us these details, revealed the truth concerning his life and his identity."

Mark the — touches, the mistress, the carafe, the birth-mark, the head buried in the garden. Set absurd as is this story, needlessly false and wildly improbable in most of its circumstances and details. It will remind many of the strange rumors which were afloat in New York after the suicide of young Colt, which occurred, I believe, on the eve of the execution to which he had been condemned for the murder of, not his mistress, but his creditor—rumors of the criminal having escaped through the connivance of certain under-officers of the Tombs, and of the body of another prisoner who had opportunely died in the Hospital, having been substituted for him. It also reminds me of a story which was told me in Hartford some fifteen years ago by a relative of mine, and a neighbor of the Colt family. It was suggested by our meeting on the streets old Mr. Colt bowed with years and sorrows. My relative startled me by expressing the belief that the unfortunate younger son of this vulnerable man was not dead, but then living in Europe, and told me that an old acquaintance of the homicide—who, by the way, had never believed him guilty of deliberate murder—had confided to him (my relative) a strange fact. Being in Paris a short time before, he had come suddenly upon his old friend. He recognized him instantly and perfectly and exclaimed, "My God, Colt, is this you?" He said the poor fellow, thrown off his guard did not for the moment attempt to deny his identity, and even smiled, then turned pale as death, stammered out "You are mistaken in the person, sir," and hurried away.

I certainly do not endorse this story, but it was told to me in perfect good faith. Certainly it is strange that the whirlpool of time, which has since swallowed so many horrible crimes and mysterious events, should cast up from its depths upon this distant shore this ghastly and fearfully distorted tragedy of the New World.

Source: "John C. Colt: Did the Slayer of Adams Escape the Gallows? The Marvelous Story Put Forth by E B T." *Chicago Daily Tribune* (December 1, 1875).

See Articles: Chicago, Illinois; Executions; Murder, History of.

1875 PRIMARY DOCUMENT

N. A. Jennings Tells of the Texas Rangers

The Texas Rangers were formally established in 1835, functioning as both a law enforcement agency and a paramilitary force as they developed over time. When 18-year-old Napoleon Augustus

Jennings joined the Rangers in 1874, they had just been reinstituted after Reconstruction forcibly disbanded them. The sparsely settled state was home to numerous outlaws, American and Mexican alike. In the popular imagination, the Rangers were the only ones able to impose law on the lawless.

While we were encamped at a place called Las Eucias, which we reached on June 5th, a Mexican brought the information to Captain McNelly that a party of raiders was crossing into Texas, below Brownsville, and going in the direction of La Para. Our camp was about twenty-five miles from Brownsville. Many Rangers were out on scouts at the time we received the information and but seventeen of the boys were in camp. This was on June 11th. McNelly at once ordered us to saddle up, and within fifteen minutes we were trotting after him and a Mexican guide over the prairie. Lieutenant Wright was in the party. So was Lieutenant Robinson.

We camped that night by a little, half-dried-up creek, and early the next morning a Mexican scout came in and said he had discovered the trail of the raiders. We ate a hurried breakfast and started out after the Mexican. In a short time we captured an advance scout of the raiders—one Rafael Salinas—and, by threatening him with instant death if he did not divulge what he knew of the robbers, we obtained much valuable information from him.

A little later we managed to catch another of the raiders and his story agreed with the one the first man had told us. This second scout said that the raiders had turned the cattle loose, as the men had become frightened when the first scout failed to return.

It was three days after that before we managed to head off the raiders. They had fourteen men and we had eighteen, including Captain McNelly. We found them with the cattle on a little bit of wooded rising ground surrounded by a swamp called Laguna Madre. The water was eighteen or twenty inches deep in it.

They were drawn up in line and were evidently expecting us. When they saw us, they drew off behind the rising ground and fired at a range of about one hundred and fifty yards with carbines.

"Boys," said Captain McNelly, " the only way we can get at those thieves is to cross through the mud of the swamp and ride them down. I don't think they can shoot well enough to hit any of us, but we'll have to risk that. Don't fire at them until you're sure of killing every time."

Following the Captain, we started across the swamp for the little hill, the Mexican marauders continually firing at us. When we got near the hill, the Captain put spurs to his horse and we followed him with a yell as we flew through the mud and up the hill. The Mexicans answered our yell with one of defiance and a volley. At first, we thought they had not done any execution, but we soon saw they had aimed only too well, for three of our horses went crashing to the ground, one after the other, throwing their riders over their heads. Lieutenant Robinson's horse was one of those shot, but Robinson continued to fight on foot.

Then came a single shot from the Mexicans, and one of the Rangers—L. S. Smith, popularly known in the troop as "Sonny"— threw his arms above his head, reeled in his saddle for a moment and fell headlong to the ground. We all saw him fall and the sight roused a fury in our hearts that boded ill for the men in front of us.

The Mexicans fired at us again, but this time did no harm. The next instant we were upon them, shooting and yelling like demons. They stood their ground for a moment only; then turned and fled. As they went they leaned forward on their horses' necks and fired back at us, but they were demoralized by the fury of our onslaught and could hit nothing.

Crack! bang! bang! went our revolvers, and at nearly every shot one of the raiders went tumbling from his saddle. We had ridden hard to get to that place and our horses were played out, but we never thought of giving up the chase on that account. The remembrance of poor young Smith's face, as he threw up his hands and reeled from his horse, was too fresh in our minds for us to think of anything but revenge.

Some of our enemies were well mounted, but even these we gradually overhauled. We flew over the prairie at a killing pace, intent only on avenging our comrade's death. When we finally did halt, our horses were ready to drop from exhaustion; but the work had been done—every man of the raiders but one was dead. Some of them fought so desperately that even when dismounted and wounded four or five times they continued to shoot at us. Lieutenant Wright, during the running fight, killed two men with one shot from his revolver. The men were riding on one horse when he killed them and both were shooting back at him.

The leader of the raiders, Espinoso, was thrown from his horse early in the fight. McNelly was after him and as soon as he saw Espinoso fall he, too, sprang to the ground. Espinoso jumped into a "hog wallow" in the prairie and McNelly took shelter in another one. Then they fought a duel. At last McNelly played a trick on the Mexican. The Captain had a carbine and a six-shooter. He aimed his carbine carefully at the top of Espinoso's hog wallow and then fired his pistol in the air. Espinoso raised his head, and the next instant a bullet from McNelly's carbine had passed through it and the Mexican bandit was dead.

Espinoso was the most famous of the raiders on the Eio Grande and one of the head men under the Mexican guerilla chief, Cortina. Cortina was a Mexican general, and at the head of all the cattle raiding. He had a contract to deliver in Cuba six hundred head of Texas cattle every week. About three thousand robbers were under him, and he was virtually the ruler of the Mexican border.

When we rode back to the hill where we first met the raiders, we discovered that we had killed only thirteen of them. The fourteenth was terribly wounded. His name was Mario Olguine, nicknamed "Aboja." He was known to the Mexicans as Aboja (the Needle) because he had such a quiet way of slipping into ranch houses, on raids, and murdering the inmates while they slept. Aboja was sent to jail, but died there, after lingering several weeks. We recovered 265 stolen cattle after the fight. We procured a wagon and took the body of young Smith to Brownsville. The next day the bodies of the thirteen dead Mexicans were brought to Brownsville and laid out in the plaza. Nearly the entire population of Matamoras, the Mexican town immediately across the Eio Grande from Brownsville, came over to see their dead countrymen. The Mexicans were very angry, and we heard many threats that Cortina would come across with his men and kill us all. McNelly sent back word to Cortina that he would wait for him and his men. Cortina's bandits outnumbered the Rangers and the United States forces at Fort Brown about ten to one at that time.

We gave Smith a fine military funeral. The Mexican raiders were all buried in one trench. The Mexican inhabitants of the town stood in their doorways and scowled at us whenever we passed, but they were afraid to express their hatred openly. They contented themselves with predicting that Cortina would come over and kill us. Had they but known it, one of our men, Sergeant George Hall, a cousin of McNelly's, was at that very time with Cortina, acting as a spy for us. Hall was on Cortina's boat, waiting with him for the cattle to ship to Havana. In the records of the United States Government at Washington there is doubtless a most interesting report which Hall made to the Federal authorities, for General Grant, who was President at the time, sent for Hall and personally received his report.

Grant was greatly interested in Cortina's movements, and it was said among those who knew how matters stood on the border and in Washington, that the President would have been glad to have a war break out between Mexico and the United States. Of that I will speak more fully in another place…

At the time of which I write, Matamoras was full of Mexican soldiers, and Cortina had put the place under martial rule. No person was allowed on the streets after sunset, except by special permit; that is, no Mexican was allowed on the streets. For some reason best known to Cortina, Americans were not included in the rule, and the Mexican sentries had orders to pass Americans. The Rangers were not slow to take advantage of this state of affairs, and we paid frequent visits to

Matamoras after nightfall. We went there for two reasons: to have fun, and to carry out a set policy of terrorizing the Mexicans at every opportunity. Captain McNelly assumed that the more we were feared, the easier would be our work of subduing the Mexican raiders; so it was tacitly understood that we were to gain a reputation as fire-eating, quarrelsome dare-devils as quickly as possible, and to let no opportunity go unimproved to assert ourselves and override the "Greasers." Perhaps everyone has more or less of the bully inherent in his make-up, for certain it is that we enjoyed this work hugely.

"Each Ranger was a little standing army in himself," was the way Lieutenant Wright put it to me, speaking, long afterward, of those experiences. The Mexicans were afraid of us, collectively and individually, and added to the fear was a bitter hatred.

Half a dozen of the boys would leave camp after dark and make their way over the river to Matamoras by way of the ferry. If we could find a fandango, or Mexican dance, going on, we would enter the dancing-hall and break up the festivities by shooting out the lights. This would naturally result in much confusion and, added to the reports of our revolvers, would be the shrill screaming of women and the cursing of angry Mexicans. Soldiers would come running from all directions. We would then fire a few more shots in the air and make off for the ferry, as fast as we could go.

Usually, at such times, we would be followed—at a safe distance—by a company or two of soldiers. Sometimes we would fire back, over their heads, and sometimes they would shoot at us; but we always got back safely to the Texas side. When we reached Brownsville, we would hunt up another *fandango* there were always some of these dances going on every night—and proceed, as in Matamoras, to break it up.

The news of our big fight with the raiders reached everyone's ears, and none was so bold as to attempt to resist our outrages upon the peace and dignity of the community, for such they undoubtedly were. But we accomplished our purpose. In a few weeks we were feared as men were never before feared on that border, and, had we given the opportunity, we should undoubtedly have been exterminated by the Mexicans, but there was "method in our madness," and we never gave them the chance to get the better of us.

Sources: Jennings, N. A. *A Texas Ranger.* New York: Scribners, 1899; and http://historymatters.gmu.edu/d/6534

See Articles: Texas; Texas Rangers.

1875
PRIMARY DOCUMENT

Cole Younger's Account of the 1875 Northfield, Minnesota, Bank Robbery

A Confederate guerilla soldier who served with Jesse James, Cole Younger was the eldest of the four Younger brothers. Shortly after the war, they began robbing banks, trains, and stagecoaches with Frank and Jesse James and others. The James–Younger Gang dissolved after 10 years due to the Younger brothers' capture after the attempted robbery of the First National Bank of Northfield, recounted here. The James brothers escaped, but the heyday of the gang was over.

"In telling the story of the Northfield bank robbery and its frightful results I have only to say that there is no heroism in outlawry, and that the man who sows is sure to reap. After Lee surrendered I tried my best to live at peace with the world and earn a livelihood. I'd been made a guerrilla by a provocation that few men could have resisted. My father had been cruelly murdered, my mother had been hounded to death, my entire family had been tormented and all my relatives plundered and imprisoned.

"From the mass of rubbish that has been written about the guerrilla there is little surprise that the popular conception of him should be a fiendish, bloodthirsty wretch.

"Yet he was in many cases, if not in most, a man who had been born to better things and who was made what he was by such outrages as Osceola, Palmyra and by a hundred raids in less famous but not less infamous, that were made by Kansas into Missouri during the war.

"When the war ceased those of the guerrillas who were not hung or shot or pursued by posses till they found the hand of man turned against them at every step, settled down to become good citizens in the peaceful walks of life, and the survivors of Quantrell's band may be pardoned, in view of the black paint that has been devoted to them, in calling attention to the fact that of the members of Quantrell's band who have since been entrusted with public place, not one has ever betrayed his trust.

"As for myself and brothers I wish to emphasize that we made an honest attempt to return to normal life at the close of the war, and had we been permitted to do so the name of Younger would never have been connected with the crimes that were committed in the period immediately following the war.

"That my life was good or clean I do not assert. But such as it was, it was forced upon me by conditions over which I had no control. Before final judgment is passed upon the men of my kind who were with me in those days I ask that the fact be considered that we were born in days when hatred was the rule and reared among scenes of violence.

"But I have been accused of many crimes of which I have not been guilty, and I am willing to take my oath that the crimes that were charged against me in Missouri were not mine. Never in all my life had I anything to do with any of the bank robberies in the state of Missouri which had been charged against myself and brothers.

"In the fall of 1868 my brothers, Jim and Bob, went with me to Texas. The next two or three years we spent in an honest life, my sister joining us and keeping house for us at Syene, Dallas County. He and Bob sang in the church choir. At that time Bob, who was only 17 fell in love with one of the young ladies in the village.

"I went down to Louisiana, and the story was told that I killed five men and shot five others because I had been robbed by a lot of crooked cattlemen. There is just this much truth about this incident: There was a crooked race, with me as the victim. After the race I fought a duel, but not over the race.

"The duel was forced upon me by a man named Captain James White. He circulated a scandalous tale about the young woman Bob was in love with. I sent word to him that he would have to apologize or fight. After the race I referred to White and I went to a neighboring plantation and fought it out. At the first shot his right arm was shattered at the shoulder. When he thought he was dying he apologized and admitted that he had circulated the story for the purpose of forcing a fight upon me.

"It was about this time that the Kansas City fair was robbed. This was charged against the Younger brothers, although not one of us had anything to do with it. Bob felt so keenly the notoriety that resulted from my duel and from the stories of the Kansas City robbery that he left Dallas, and later Jim and I followed him. About this time my brother John, who was only 14 years old when the war closed, was forced into a quarrel and murdered as wantonly as a man was ever murdered in the history of the west.

"When I was on the Pacific slope Missouri adopted the famous Drake constitution, which prohibited Confederate soldiers and sympathizers from practicing any profession, preaching the gospel or doing many other things under a penalty of a fine of not less than $500 or imprisonment for not less than six months. One section of this constitution gave amnesty to Union soldiers for all they had done after January 1, 1861, but held Confederates responsible for what they had done either as citizens or soldiers.

"The result of this was the persecution of all men who were not friendly with the carpet-bag administration following the war and there was no mercy shown to any of them. After a few days of seeing my friends and old comrades hounded and imprisoned I saw there was nothing left for me to do but gather together with those that were left and do the best we could.

"In passing swiftly over the scenes of violence in which we took part, I will take up the Northfield case by saying that we had decided to find a good bank, make a big haul, get away with the money, leave the country and start life anew in some foreign land.

"We were told that General Benjamin F. Butler had a big lot of money in the First National bank at Northfield, and that A.A. Ames, son-in-law of Butler, who had been a carpet-bag governor of Mississippi after the war, had a lot there also. We were not very friendly to Butler because of his treatment of Southerners during the war, and accordingly decided to make a raid on the Northfield bank.

"My brothers, Jim and Bob, Clell Miller, Bill Chadwell and three men named Pitts, Woods and Howard, were those who decided to take up the expedition. This was in the middle of August, and we spent a week in Minneapolis picking up what information we could about Northfield and the bank and playing poker. Then we passed another week in St. Paul, also looking for information as to the amount of money and the precautions taken in the bank to take care of it.

"Chadwell, Pitts, Bob and myself procured horses at St. Peter, where we stayed long enough to break them and to train them for the hard riding to which we knew they would be submitted later on. It was at St. Peter that I made the acquaintance of a little girl who afterwards was one of the most earnest workers for our parole.

"A little tot then, she said she could ride a horse, too, and reaching down, I lifted her up before me, and we rode up and down. I asked her her name and she said it was 'Horace Greeley Perry,' and I replied.

"No wonder you're such a little tot with such a great name.'

"'I won't always be little,' she replied. 'I'm going to be a great big girl and be a newspaper man like papa.'

"'Will you still be my sweetheart then, and be my friend?' I asked her, and she declared she would, a promise I was to remind her of years later under circumstances of which I did not dream then.

"Many years afterward with a party of visitors to the prison came a girl, perhaps 16, who registered in full, 'Horace Greeley Perry.'

"I knew there could not be two women with such a name in the world, and I reminded her of her promise, a promise which she did not remember, although she had been told how she had made friends with the bold, bad man who afterwards robbed the bank at Northfield.

"Very soon afterward, at the age of 18, I believe, she became, as she had dreamed, in childhood, 'a newspaper man,' editing the St. Peter Journal, and to the hour of my pardon she was one of the most indefatigable workers for us.

"A few years ago failing health compelled her removal from Minnesota to Idaho, and Minnesota lost one of the brightest newspaper writers and staunchest friends that a man ever knew. Jim and I had a host of advocates during the latter years of our imprisonment, but none exceeded in devotion the young woman, who as a little tot had ridden unknowingly with the bandit who was soon to be exiled for life from all his kin and friends.

"Preliminary work on the Northfield robbery was got down to during the last week of August 1876, and while Pitts and I were waiting for Bob and Chadwell, who had gone up there to look over the ground, we scouted all over the country thereabouts and around Madelia in order to get ourselves familiar with the lay of the land. When the two boys joined us we divided into two parties and started for Northfield along different routes.

"On Monday night, September 4, the party I was with reached Le Sueur Center, where we had trouble finding places to sleep, as court was in session. Tuesday night we put on at Cordova, and Wednesday we were in Millersburg. At the same time Bob and his crowd rounded up in Cannon City, which was south of Northfield.

"On Thursday morning, September 7, we all came together on the Cannon River, on the outskirts of Northfield. That afternoon I took a look at the bank, and in camp at dinner I told the gang that no matter what came off we mustn't shoot anybody. While I was making this point as strong as I could one of the crowd asked what we should do if they began shooting at us. Bob at once said that if I was so particular about not having any shooting the best thing for me to do was to stay outside and take my chances.

"Well, at last the time came. Bob, Pitts and Howard started for town ahead, the scheme being that they should round up in the town square and not go into the bank until the rest of the party joined them. It was fixed that Miller and I should go on guard right at the bank, while the rest of the gang was to wait at the bridge and listen for a pistol shot signal in case they were wanted for help. We had it schemed out that as there were no saddle horses around anywhere we could get off with a flying start and get away before they could stop us, wrecking the telegraph office if necessary to prevent any alarm being sent out by wire.

"Whiskey spoiled the whole plan. Between the time they left camp and reached the bridge the men who went ahead got away with a quart of whiskey—the first time I had ever known Bob to drink, and as a matter of fact, I didn't know he had done so then until the day and its terrible events were over. The blunder was that when these three men saw us coming, instead of waiting for us to get up with them they slammed right on into the bank regardless, leaving the door open in their excitement.

"I was out in the street, pretending I was having trouble with my saddle. Meantime I had told Miller to close up the bank door. A man named Allen, who kept a store nearby, was then trying to get into the bank, but Miller foolishly shouted at him and told him to get away. Allen at once became excited and saw that something was wrong, and ran off up the street shouting to everyone to get his gun, as the bank was being robbed.

"A Dr. Wheeler, who saw that something was happening out of the ordinary, began to yell 'Robbery!' Then I saw we were in for it, and would need all the help we could get. I first called to Miller to come inside and get out of harm's way and then I fired a signal to the three men at the bridge for them to come up and help us, as we had been trapped.

"Chadwell, Woods and Jim came galloping up, and at the same moment that they arrived I heard a shot fired inside the bank. The three boys were firing their guns as they rode along, shouting to everybody they saw to get out of the way and get indoors, but I am quite sure they never killed anybody. My theory always has been that the man Gustafson, who was shot down in the street, was struck by a glancing shot from some of the citizens' rifles, as they were out blazing away at this time.

"Miller was then shot by a man named Stacy and his face filled full of bird shot. A man named Manning killed Pitts' horse, and, as a matter of fact, the street was full of flying lead, coming from every direction. It wasn't long before I was wounded in the thigh by Manning, and the next instant he shot Chadwell through the heart.

"Dr. Wheeler, from an upper floor of a hotel, got a bead on Miller and brought him down, so that he soon lay dying in the middle of the street. Every time I saw a man pointing a gun at me I dropped off my horse and tried to drive the shooter under cover, but there were so many of them, and I couldn't see in every direction, so I soon found out that, wounded as I was, I was helpless. Meanwhile there was a tragedy going on inside the bank.

"Bob came out in a hurry and started down the street toward Manning, who ran into a store; hoping he would get a shot at Bob from under cover. Bob ran on, but didn't notice Dr. Wheeler, who was upstairs in the hotel, behind him, and Wheeler's third shot smashed Bob's right arm. Bob switched his gun to his left and got on Miller's horse, thinking that Miller was dead. By this Howard and Pitts had got out of the bank, and I told them that Miller was still alive and we'd have to save him. I told Pitts to put Miller on my horse, but when we lifted him I saw he was dead, so I told Pitts that I would hold off the crowd while he got away, as his horse had been killed. While Pitts ran, less than ten yards, I stood with my pistol pointed at anyone who showed his head, and then I galloped off and overtook him and took him up behind me.

"Pitts then confessed to me about the drinking, and said they had made an awful mess of it inside the bank. It had been arranged that they should hold up Joseph L. Heywood, the acting cashier, at his window, and after roping him get to the safe without any trouble. Instead of that, these three drink-crazed lunatics leaped over the rail and scared Heywood so badly that he immediately got on the defensive, and in a minute the alarm was out and it was all over.

"It seems that one of the robbers had waved his revolver at Heywood the minute he entered the bank and asked him if he was the cashier. Heywood had said he wasn't, and then the same question was put to the other two men who were in the bank. Each of the three said he was not the cashier, but the robber turned to Heywood, who was sitting at the cashier's desk, and said:

"'You're the cashier' open that safe d—n quick or I'll blow your head off.'

"Heywood jumped back and Pitts ran to the vault and got inside. Heywood then tried to shut him in, and was seized by the robbers, who told him to open the safe at once or he would not live another minute. Heywood told him there was a time lock on it that positively couldn't be opened, whereupon Howard pulled a knife and tried to cut Heywood's throat, the cashier having been thrown to the ground in the scuffle that had taken place. Incidentally, Pitts told me afterwards that Howard fired a pistol near Heywood's head, but only with the intention of frightening him.

"A. E. Bunker, the teller, by this time had tried to get hold of a pistol that was near where he was, but Pitts got the gun first, and it was found on him after he was killed, and consequently furnished just that much good evidence that we were the men at Northfield.

"The boys saw by this time that the safe could not be reached, so they asked Bunker about the money that was outside. Bunker pointed to a little tray full of small coins, and while Bob was putting them away in a sack Bunker made a dash through a rear window. Pitte fired at him twice, his second bullet going through his right shoulder.

"By this time the men in the bank had heard the commotion and firing outside and started to leave.

"Heywood, who had been on the floor, unfortunately rose at this instant, and Pitts, still under the influence of liquor, shot him through the head and killed him.

"Meantime we who had escaped slaughter in the terrible bombardment we had faced were trying to make out way to some safe place. Not far from Northfield we met a farmer, who lent us a horse for Pitts to ride, and we got past Dundas ahead of the news of the raid on the bank. We were also beating it at Millersburg, but at Shieldsville we ran into a squad of men who knew what had happened and were after us. These men had, foolishly for themselves, left their guns outside a house, and we didn't let them get hold of them until we had a good start, but they overtook us about four miles away and shots were exchanged without any trouble resulting.

"Soon there were a thousand men on our trail and about $5,000 in rewards for our capture. We tramped and camped and rode and watched in a strange country and among the lakes. We didn't know the trails and were afraid to try the fords and bridges, knowing that our hunters would be sure to keep their eyes on these places. Saturday morning we abandones our horses and decided to keep up the fight afoot. We tramped all night and put in Sunday near Marysburg. Bob's elbow by this time was in pretty bad shape and we had to go slow. Finally on Monday night and Tuesday we couldn't go anywhere, so we passed the time in a deserted house near Mankato. A man named Dunning found us there and we took him prisoner. On the theory that the dead are silent, some of the men wanted to kill him, but I wouldn't stand for that, so we made him swear by all that was holy that he wouldn't tell that he had seen us until we got away. Then we turned him loose. He lost no time in getting into Mankato and giving the alarm, and in a few minutes another posse was after us.

"That night Howard and Wood decided that they wouldn't hold back any longer and that we were losing valuable time because of Bob's wound, so they left us and went on west. They stole two horses very soon, and this helped us as well as them, for the posse followed the trail of the stolen horses, not knowing that we had divided.

"On Thursday morning, September 21, just two weeks after the raid, the end came. A party of forty men soon surrounded us and opened fire. We were cut off from our horses and our case was hopeless. We were on the open prairie and not ready for our last fight against such odds, we fell back into the Watonwan river bottom and hid in some bushes.

"When the iron doors shut behind us at the Stillwater prison we all submitted to the prison discipline with the same unquestioning obedience that I had exacted during the military service. The result was that we gained friends both in prison and outside. We had been in prison a little over seven years, when, on January 25, 1884, the main building was destroyed by fire at night. George F. Dodd was then connected with the prison, while his wife was matron. There was danger of a panic and a terrible disaster. Dodd released Jim and Bob and myself. To me he gave a revolver, Jim had an axe handle and Bob a small iron bar. We stood guard over the women prisoners, marched them from the danger of the fire, and the prison authorities were kind enough to say that had it not been for us there must have been a tremendous loss of life.

"I can say without fear of contradiction that had it been in our minds to do so we could have escaped from the prison that night, but we had determined to pay the penalty that had been exacted, and if we were ever to return to liberty it would be with the consent and approval of the authorities and public. A little later Jim was put in charge of the mail and library of the prison, while I was made head nurse in the hospital, where I remained until the day we were paroled.

"As the years went by the popular feeling against us not only subsided, but our absolute obedience to the minutest detail of the prison discipline won us the consideration, and I might even say, the esteem of the prison officials. In the meantime it had been a life sentence for Bob, he having died of consumption September 16, 1889.

"Jim and I went out into the world July 14, 1901, after serving a few months less than twenty-five years. Each of us immediately found work, and life again took on its normal hues. Poor Jim, however, was subject to periodical spells of deep depression. The bullet that shattered his upper jaw in our last fight in Madelia imbedded itself near the brain and was not removed until long after we were in the prison at Stillwater. That bullet was the cause of his occasional gloominess. After our release from prison Jim's health continued precarious. He finally gave up the fight, and on October 19, 1902, took his own life in a hotel in Minnesota.

"I am not exactly a dead man, but I have been shot twenty-eight times and am now carrying in my body fourteen bullets that physicians have been unable to extract. Twelve of these wounds I received while wearing the gray, and I have ever been proud of them, and it has been one of my keenest regrets that I did not receive the rest of them during the war with Spain."

Source: Sullivan, Larry E. *Bandits & Bibles: Convict Literature in Nineteenth-Century America*. New York: Akashic, 2003. Related By Thomas Coleman "Cole" Younger from: Wolfer, Henry. *Convict Life at the Minnesota State Prison, Stillwater, Minnesota*. St. Paul, MN: W. C. Heilbron, 1909.

See Articles: James, Jesse; Minnesota; Robbery, History of.

1878
PRIMARY DOCUMENT

Labor Leader Dennis Kearney's Anti-Chinese Address

An Irish immigrant to the United States, Kearney was the head of the Workingmen's Party of California, a nativist political party with the simple slogan, "The Chinese must go!" The Long Depression had begun in 1873 and would last most of the rest of the century. Working-class whites were frustrated by railroad companies and others hiring Chinese immigrants at low wages. While some responded with mob violence, Kearney successfully pursued anti-Chinese legislation.

Our moneyed men have ruled us for the past thirty years. Under the flag of the slaveholder they hoped to destroy our liberty. Failing in that, they have rallied under the banner of the millionaire, the banker and the land monopolist, the railroad king and the false politician, to effect their purpose.

We have permitted them to become immensely rich against all sound republican policy, and they have turned upon us to sting us to death. They have seized upon the government by bribery and corruption. They have made speculation and public robbery a science. The have loaded the nation, the state, the county, and the city with debt. They have stolen the public lands. They have grasped all to themselves, and by their unprincipled greed brought a crisis of unparalleled distress on forty millions of people, who have natural resources to feed, clothe and shelter the whole human race.

Such misgovernment, such mismanagement, may challenge the whole world for intense stupidity, and would put to shame the darkest tyranny of the barberous past.

We, here in California, feel it as well as you. We feel that the day and hour has come for the Workingmen of America to depose capital and put Labor in the Presidential chair, in the Senate and Congress, in the State House, and on the Judicial Bench. We are with you in this work. Workingmen must form a party of their own, take charge of the government, dispose gilded fraud, and put honest toil in power.

In our golden state all these evils have been intensified. Land monopoly has seized upon all the best soil in this fair land. A few men own from ten thousand to two hundred thousand acres each. The poor Laborer can find no resting place, save on the barren mountain, or in the trackless desert. Money monopoly has reached its grandest proportions. Here, in San Francisco, the palace of the millionaire looms up above the hovel of the starving poor with as wide a contrast as anywhere on earth.

To add to our misery and despair, a bloated aristocracy has sent to China—the greatest and oldest despotism in the world—for a cheap working slave. It rakes the slums of Asia to find the meanest slave on earth—the Chinese coolie—and imports him here to meet the free American in the Labor market, and still further widen the breach between the rich and the poor, still further to degrade white Labor.

These cheap slaves fill every place. Their dress is scant and cheap. Their food is rice from China. They hedge twenty in a room, ten by ten. They are whipped curs, abject in docility, mean, contemptible and obedient in all things. They have no wives, children or dependents.

They are imported by companies, controlled as serfs, worked like slaves, and at last go back to China with all their earnings. They are in every place, they seem to have no sex. Boys work, girls work; it is all alike to them.

The father of a family is met by them at every turn. Would he get work for himself? Ah! A stout Chinaman does it cheaper. Will he get a place for his oldest boy? He can not. His girl? Why, the Chinaman is in her place too! Every door is closed. He can only go to crime or suicide, his wife and daughter to prostitution, and his boys to hoodlumism and the penitentiary.

Do not believe those who call us savages, rioters, incendiaries, and outlaws. We seek our ends calmly, rationally, at the ballot box. So far good order has marked all our proceedings. But, we know how false, how inhuman, our adversaries are. We know that if gold, if fraud, if force can defeat us, they will all be used. And we have resolved that they shall not defeat us. We shall arm. We shall meet fraud and falsehood with defiance, and force with force, if need be.

We are men, and propose to live like men in this free land, without the contamination of slave labor, or die like men, if need be, in asserting the rights of our race, our country, and our families.

California must be all American or all Chinese. We are resolved that it shall be American, and are prepared to make it so. May we not rely upon your sympathy and assistance?

With great respect for the Workingman's Party of California.

Dennis Kearney, President
H. L Knight, Secretary

Sources: Kearney, Dennis and H. L. Knight. "Appeal From California: The Chinese Invasion. Workingmen's Address." *Indianapolis Times* (February 28, 1878); and

http://historymatters.gmu.edu/d/5046

See Articles: California; Chinese Americans; Racism; San Francisco, California.

1884 PRIMARY DOCUMENT

New York Times Article on the Greely Expedition

In 1881, the Proteus *embarked on its expedition to the "farthest north"—a northern latitude beyond the point of any previous expedition. First Lieutenant Adolphus Greely commanded the expedition, which had been commissioned by the U.S. government to collect scientific data. When two relief parties failed to reach the expedition, the government had no backup plan.* Proteus *was stranded with depleted supplies, and the men eventually found themselves eating their dead to survive.*

A Horrible Discovery

When the vessels of the Greely relief expedition reached St. John's the world was told that only six members of the Greely colony were living. One had been drowned, one had died on the way home, and seventeen, it was said, had perished miserably by starvation. This was a shocking story, but to-day there must be told a story still more appalling.

When their food gave out the unfortunate members of the colony, shivering and starving in their little tent on the bleak shore of Smith's Sound, were led by the horrible necessity to become cannibals. The complete history of their experience in that terrible Winter must be told, and the facts hitherto concealed will make the record of the Greely colony—already full of horrors—the most dreadful and repulsive chapter in the long annals of arctic exploration.

The discovery that Greely and his surviving companions were forced to choose between death and this way of preserving life, and made the choice of which we have spoken, multiplies a hundredfold the burden of responsibility that has rested upon the officer whose blunders brought so successful an expedition to such an end. Is it possible that, after this dreadful revelation, Gen. HAZEN will be able to retain his position? We do not think it is. There must be an inquiry by a military court, and we predict that neither social influence nor any influence will shield him this time from the punishment he deserves.

"From July, 1882, to August, 1883," said the Proteus court of inquiry in its report, "not less than 50,000 rations were taken in the steamers Neptune, Yantic and Proteus up to or beyond Littleton Island, and of that number only about 1,000 were left in the vicinity, the remainder being returned to the United States or sunk with the Proteus." Two costly expeditions had taken those provisions to Smith's Sound, but, owing to HAZEN'S instructions, poor Greely gained practically no benefit from them. So ignorant was this officer that he told GARLINGTON that the colonists' supplies would be exhausted in the Fall of 1883, when if fact they had been provisioned for twelve months longer. We have heretofore shown how GREELY'S instructions and the plain teachings of common sense were disregarded by this man. GREELY foresaw that he might be compelled to retreat down the west shore of Smith's Sound. He could establish provision depots along the upper part of the line, but those below must be established by the relief parties. In his letter of instructions he pointed out the spots on the west side where food should be placed, and then directed that a colony should be established on the other side. He even foresaw that he might reach Cape Sabine and then be unable to get across; therefore he directed that the relief colony should not only strive to find him by telescopes, but should also send sledge parties to the west side to rescue him. The instructions given to GARLINGTON were not in accordance with these.

The Proteus court make inquiry concerning the failure of the Garlington expedition. GREELY and his companions were absent, and could not testify. Therefore the court did not have all the facts before it. Now GREELY and five of his companions have returned and can testify. There is, moreover, additional subject matter to be investigated—the deaths of nineteen men and the horrible revelations concerning life in the tent. The inquiry should be completed, and Gen. HAZEN should be court-martialed without further delay.

Source: "A Horrible Discovery." *New York Times* (August 12, 1884).

See Articles: Military Courts; Military Police.

1885 PRIMARY DOCUMENT

Testimony of Chinese Laborer Survivors

The recounting of the massacre at Rock Springs, Wyoming Territory, that was sent to the Chinese Consol in New York highlighted one of many anti-Chinese crimes in the late 19th-century west. Many labor organizations were powerful voices stirring up white hatred against Chinese workers, and companies made it worse by relying on cheap Chinese labor to weaken white workers' bargaining position. The massacre, which resulted in 28 dead Chinese, was a response to the hiring of Chinese miners to replace striking workers; there were no convictions, and the grand jury refused to indict suspects.

We, the undersigned, have been in Rock Springs, Wyoming Territory, for periods ranging from one to fifteen years, for the purpose of working on the railroads and in the coal mines.

Up to the time of the recent troubles we had worked along with the white men, and had not had the least ill feeling against them. The officers of the companies employing us treated us and the white man kindly, placing both races on the same footing and paying the same wages.

Several times we had been approached by the white men and requested to join them in asking the companies for an increase in the wages of all, both Chinese and white men. We inquired of them what we should do if the companies refused to grant an increase. They answered that if the companies would not increase our wages we should all strike, then the companies would be obliged to increase our wages. To this we dissented, wherefore we excited their animosity against us.

During the past two years there has been in existence in "Whitemen's Town," Rock Springs, an organization composed of white miners, whose object was to bring about the expulsion of all Chinese from the Territory. To them or to their object we have paid no attention. About the month of August of this year notices were posted up, all the way from Evanston to Rock Springs, demanding the expulsion of the Chinese, &c. On the evening of September 1, 1885, the bell of the building in which said organization meets rang for a meeting. It was rumored on that night that threats had been made against the Chinese.

On the morning of September 2, a little past seven o'clock, more than ten white men, some in ordinary dress and others in mining suits, ran into Coal Pit No. 6, loudly declaring that the Chinese should not be permitted to work there. The Chinese present reasoned with them in a few words, but were attacked with murderous weapons, and three of their number wounded. The white foreman of the coal pit, hearing of the disturbance, ordered all to stop work for the time being.

About two o'clock in the afternoon a mob, divided into two gangs, came toward "Chinatown," one gang coming by way of the plank bridge, and the other by way of the railroad bridge. The gang coming by way of the railroad bridge was the larger, and was subdivided into many squads, some of which did not cross the bridge, but remained standing on the side opposite to "Chinatown"; others that had already crossed the bridge stood on the right and left at the end of it. Several squads marched up the hill behind Coal Pit No. 3.

One squad remained at Coal Shed No. 3 and another at the pump house. The squad that remained at the pump house fired the first shot, and the squad that stood at Coal Shed No. 3 immediately followed their example and fired. The Chinese by name of Lor Sun Kit was the first person shot, and fell to the ground. At that time the Chinese began to realize that the mob were bent on killing. The Chinese, though greatly alarmed, did not yet begin to flee.

The gang that were at the plank bridge also divided into several squads, pressing near and surrounding "Chinatown." One squad of them guarded the plank bridge in order to cut off the retreat of the Chinese.

Not long after, it was everywhere reported that a Chinese named Leo Dye Bah, who lived in the western part of "Chinatown," was killed by a bullet, and that another named Yip Ah Marn, resident in the eastern end of the town, was likewise killed. The Chinese now, to save their lives, fled in confusion in every direction, some going up the hill behind Coal Pit No. 3, others along the foot of the hill where Coal Pit No. 4 is; some from the eastern end of the town fled across Bitter Creek to the opposite hill, and others from the western end by the foot of the hill on the right of Coal Pit No. 5. The mob were now coming in the three directions, namely, the east and west sides of the town and from the wagon road.

Whenever the mob met a Chinese they stopped him and, pointing a weapon at him, asked him if he had any revolver, and then approaching him they searched his person, robbing him of his watch or any gold or silver that he might have about him, before letting him go. Some of the rioters would let a Chinese go after depriving him of all his gold and silver, while another Chinese would be beaten with the butt ends of the weapons before being let go. Some of the rioters, when they could not stop a Chinese, would shoot him dead on the spot, and then search and rob him. Some would-overtake a Chinese, throw him down and search and rob him before they would let him go. Some of the rioters would not fire their weapons, but would only use the butt ends to beat the Chinese with. Some would not beat a Chinese, but rob him of whatever he had and let him go, yelling to him to go quickly. Some, who took no part either in beating or robbing the Chinese, stood by, shouting loudly and laughing and clapping their hands.

Sources: "Memorial of Chinese Laborers, Resident at Rock Springs, Wyoming Territory, to the Chinese Consul at New York (1885)." In *Chink!* edited by Cheng-Tsu Wu. New York: World Publishing Company, 1972; and
http://historymatters.gmu.edu/d/5043

See Articles: Chinese Americans; Racism; Riots.

1886 PRIMARY DOCUMENT

Anarchist Oscar Neebe's Commentary on the Haymarket Affair

The Haymarket affair began as a workingman's rally in Chicago's Haymarket Square on May 4, 1886. When police moved to disperse the crowd, an unknown person threw dynamite at them. The explosion and subsequent gunfight killed seven police officers and at least four civilians. Labor activist and anarchist Oscar Neebe was one of several defendants accused of conspiracy, but there was virtually no evidence against anyone, and the police made no pretense of having identified the actual bomber.

I have been in the labor movement since 1875. I have seen how the police have trodden on the Constitution of this country, and crushed the labor organizations. I have seen from year to year how they were trodden down, where they were shot down, where they were "driven into their holes like rats," as Mr. Grinnell said to the jury. But they will come out! Remember that within three years before the beginning of the French Revolution, when laws had been stretched like rubber, that the rubber stretched too long, and broke—a result which cost a good many state's attorneys at that time their necks, and a good many honorable men their necks.

We socialists hope such times may never come again; we do everything in our power to prevent it by reducing the hours of labor and increasing wages. But you capitalists won't allow this to be done. You use your power to perpetuate a system by which you may make your money for yourselves and keep the wage-workers poor. You make them ignorant and miserable, and you are responsible for it. You won't let the toilers live a decent life.

Well, these are all the crimes I have committed. They found a revolver in my house, and a red flag there. I organized trade unions. I was for reduction of the hours of labor, and the education of laboring men, and the re-establishment of the *Arbeiter-Zeitung*—the workingmen's newspaper. There is no evidence to show that I was connected with the bomb-throwing, or that I was near it, or anything of that kind. So I am only sorry, your honor—that is, if you can stop it or help it—I will ask you to do it—that is, to hang me, too; for I think it is more honorable to die suddenly than to be killed by inches. I have a family and children; and if they know their father is dead, they will bury him. They can go to the grave, and kneel down by the side of it; but they can't go to the penitentiary and see their father, who was convicted for a crime that he hasn't had anything to do with. That is all I have got to say. Your honor, I am sorry I am not to be hung with the rest of the men.

Sources: Neebe, Oscar. "The Crimes I Have Committed." In *Anarchism: Its Philosophy and Scientific Basis, as Defined by Some of Its Apostles*, edited by Albert R. Parsons. Chicago: 1887. Reprinted in *Haymarket Scrapbook*, edited by Dave Roediger and Franklin Rosemont. Chicago: Charles H. Kerr, 1986; and http://historymatters.gmu.edu/d/47

See Articles: Civil Disobedience; Executions; Political Dissidents.

1890s PRIMARY DOCUMENT

Advertising by the Pinkerton Agency

The Pinkerton Agency was an important force in both crime and labor history in the 19th century. It had a widely varied history that included not only tracking outlaws such as Jesse James, Butch Cassidy, and the Sundance Kid, which immortalized the agency in dime novels and film, but also breaking strikes. For example, a private militia of 300 Pinkertons was hired to protect strikebreakers during the 1892 Homestead Strike. For a time, the agency was contracted by the Justice Department.

Sirs: We take this method of calling your attention to the advantages of private police patrol in case you are at any time in need of such services.

The Pinkerton Preventive Patrol was organized by the late Allan Pinkerton in 1850, it being the first uniformed police patrol in the city of Chicago, and from that time to date has had under its charge as watchmen all the banks and nearly all the wholesale and large retail business houses in Chicago. The members of this force are selected for their general aptitude for police duty, and are under strict discipline and in charge of experienced officers who have been trained to the business.

We are therefore prepared to furnish uniformed men whenever required, by the day, week, or month, for day or night duty, and we respectfully call the attention of those in charge of excursions, proprietors of public resorts, railroad and all other corporations who have to deal with large numbers of patrons or disaffected or striking employees, to the advantage of our patrol system.

A daily written report is furnished to our patrols, when required, of any irregularities or occurrences transpiring during the time our officers are on duty.

The Pinkerton Preventive Patrol has furnished the police for the Hocking Valley Coal and Iron Company of Ohio during their recent protracted strike; Chicago, Wilmington and Vermillion Coal Company of Illinois; Menominee Mining Company of Menominee, Mich.; Muskegon lumber merchants of Muskegon, Mich., lumber merchants of Saginaw City, Mich.; Rochester and Pittsburg Railroad and Coal and Iron Company of Pennsylvania; Burden Iron Company of Troy, N. Y.; and Troy Malleable Iron Works. Under its supervision was organized the first coal and iron police force in Schuylkill County, Pa., which was instrumental to a great extent by aiding our detectives in suppressing the Molly Maguires throughout the coalfields of Pennsylvania and preserving order there during the railroad riots of 1877.

The above list only comprises a few of the many corporations and individuals where the Pinkerton Patrol preserved order and protected property and employees who were willing to work while strikes were in progress.

Each season the Pinkerton Patrol furnishes the entire police protection for Manhattan Beach, Coney Island, N.Y.; Starins Glen Island (Long Island Sound), N.Y.; Coney Island Jockey Club, Sheepshead Bay, Long Island; the Rockaway Steeplechase Association, Cedarhurst, Long Island, N.Y.; the Washington Park Club and West Side Driving Park, Chicago; and the Illinois State Fair.

The Pinkerton Preventive Patrol is connected with Pinkerton's National Detective Agency, and is under the same management.

Corporations or individuals desirous of ascertaining the feeling of their employees, and whether they are likely to engage in strikes or are joining any secret labor organizations with a view of compelling terms from corporations or employers, can obtain on application to the superintendent of either of the offices, a detective suitable to associate with their employees and obtain this information.

At this time, when there is so much dissatisfaction among the laboring classes and secret labor societies are organizing throughout the United States. We suggest whether it would not be well for railroad companies and other corporations, as well as individuals who are extensive employers of labor, to keep a close watch for designing men among their own employees, who, in the interest of secret labor societies, are inducing their employees to join these organizations and eventually to cause a strike. It is frequently the case that by taking a matter of this kind in hand in time and discovering the ringleaders and dealing promptly with them serious trouble may be avoided in the future.

The reputation gained by the Agency and Patrol in the past will be a guarantee that any detective or officer furnished by us will be competent in every respect to discharge the duties required of him.

Watchmen for stores, docks, shipping, etc., etc., can be obtained at reasonable rates for permanent or special watching on application at either of the offices, which are connected by telephone.

Yours respectfully,
Robt. A. Pinkerton,
General Superintendent East Division,
New York.

Wm. A. Pinkerton,
General Superintendent West Division,
Chicago, Ill.

Sources: Senate Report 1280, 52nd Congress, 2nd Session: Investigation of Labor Trouble. Washington, DC: Government Printing Office, 1892; and http://historymatters.gmu.edu/d/5313

See Articles: Police, History of; Private Detectives; Private Police; Private Security Services

1891 PRIMARY DOCUMENT

George Sontag's Account of His First Train Robbery

The "he" and "me" of the first paragraph are John and George Sontag, respectively, brothers and train robbers from southern Minnesota. John had joined up with Chris Evans of California, and the Sontag Evans gang robbed trains for two years before petty thief George joined after a brief stint in the Nebraska State Prison. They were arrested in 1892; John was killed by a posse, and George served 15 years before dictating his memoir. He enjoyed a long career as a traveling lecturer.

This tale he recounted to me—the apparently free life he had led, the train robberies, the money he had secured from them, which appeared with but little effort, the easy manner in which he eluded capture; left a mighty deep left a mighty deep impression upon me. After he had gone, I spent many hours thinking of what he had told me.

Later, when he asked me to assist in holding up a train, he had to use no persuasion, for I had made up my mind that I would do so alone, if I could make arrangements.

John stayed at home only a short time, going back to California.

He had been back but a little while when he and Evans held up a train at Ceres. Their effort was not a success, as they were unable to get into the car.

Following this attempt John returned home. He had hardly been there a couple of days when he began to ask me about the trains in that section of the country. As I had spent many wears in braking, I was in a position to give him some valuable information.

I told him particularly of a train, No.3, thinking that he was gathering data for a robbery for himself and partner.

One day, however, he said: "George, let's take the folks up to Chicago, and leave them there, while we hold up that No. 3 train."

As I said, it did not take any coaxing to get me to go into a deal with him, so we took the folks up to the "Windy City," with the purpose of holding up that train.

Train No. 3 ran out of Chicago, leaving there at 11 p.m. After going over the ground, we found that we could not ride her out of the Union station, so I took a trip down the line one night, and discovered that we could stop the train at Western Union Junction. This being the only place we could intercept her, we decided to make Racine, Wisconsin, the base of operation, and accordingly we left for that city leaving the other members of the family in Chicago.

The night was in November, 1891, when we left Racine. It was dark and stormy, and as we made the trip afoot out of Racine our progress was slow. Indeed, we were about to give up the idea during a lull in the storm, fearing that we could not successfully bring the deal off. Finally we concluded to stick it out. The fact that it was the first snow of the winter, when we, with everyone else, was caught unawares, made the deed more hazardous, and we were more than ordinarily cautious.

The train came in at the Western Union, on time, and we boarded it. When out where we thought we had decided was the right place, we "stuck her up."

However, we ran one crossing too far, a fact that put the train in closer touch with the officials.

We were some time in getting into the car. We both had covered the engine crew and made them get out of the cab to assist us in getting into the car. The messengers would not open up, so we went to work to blow off the doors. After firing three charges of dynamite the messengers, two of them, came out and delivered up the keys.

I went into the car, and told one of the messengers whom I took with me, to open the safe. He said: "Sorry; no coin tonight."

I stepped back and, cocking both barrels of my gun, told him to dig up. He said: "For God's sake, boy, don't shoot; I'll get it." He dug between some boxes where the money had been hidden. I made a search of the car and found three small safes. The messenger told me they were time locks, and could not be opened. I told him to get them out, as we could open any kind of a safe. They were too heavy, so I threw in a stick of dynamite and blew the safes out of the car, badly damaging the latter.

John started with the bunch for the engine, I hollering to him to wait while I blew the safes open. He answered back: "Here comes a special from Racine." Racine was only seven miles away.

We took what money we had secured from the first "dig," $9,800, and left the scene.

The road was slushy, and we had a hard time getting to a cabin where we could break our guns and put them in their cases. We then proceeded to town. Arriving there we went home, our mother sleeping through the night and never dreaming that the sensation she saw in the papers next morning was caused by her two sons.

We learned that the safes that we blew out of the car contained $110,000, which, had we times our stop more correctly, we could have secured.

The crossing at which we stopped afforded an opportunity for the train crew to get word to Racine.

After we left the train and broke our guns, we kept to the track, as we knew that the posse would come on a train, and we could step aside if we saw the special. The train went on to Milwaukee, after we told the engineer to pull out.

Source: Sullivan, Larry E. *Bandits & Bibles: Convict Literature in Nineteenth-Century America*. New York: Akashic, 2003.

See Articles: Gangs, History of; Posses; Robbery, History of.

1892 PRIMARY DOCUMENT

Captain Richard H. Pratt on the Education of Native Americans

The "Indian problem" confronted the United States throughout the 19th century and beyond, as American territory expanded and filled out until there was no "frontier" left by the time of the 1890 census. The federal government shifted from relocating Indians in the west to forcibly absorbing them into America's melting pot. The 1883 Code of Indian Offenses criminalized "inappropriate" behavior by Indian adults, while Indian schools forcibly Americanized children.

A great general has said that the only good Indian is a dead one, and that high sanction of his destruction has been an enormous factor in promoting Indian massacres. In a sense, I agree with the sentiment, but only in this: that all the Indian there is in the race should be dead. Kill the Indian in him, and save the man.

We are just now making a great pretence of anxiety to civilize the Indians. I use the word "pretence" purposely, and mean it to have all the significance it can possibly carry. Washington believed that commerce freely entered into between us and the Indians would bring about their civilization, and Washington was right. He was followed by Jefferson, who inaugurated the reservation plan. Jefferson's reservation was to be the country west of the Mississippi; and he issued instructions to those controlling Indian matters to get the Indians there, and let the Great River be the line between them and the whites. Any method of securing removal—persuasion, purchase, or force—was authorized.

Jefferson's plan became the permanent policy. The removals have generally been accomplished by purchase, and the evils of this are greater than those of all the others combined....

It is a sad day for the Indians when they fall under the assaults of our troops, as in the Piegan massacre, the massacre of Old Black Kettle and his Cheyennes at what is termed "the battle of the Washita," and hundreds of other like places in the history of our dealings with them; but a far sadder day is it for them when they fall under the baneful influences of a treaty agreement with the United States whereby they are to receive large annuities, and to be protected on reservations, and held apart from all association with the best of our civilization. The destruction is not so speedy, but it is far more general. The history of the Miamis and Osages is only the true picture of all other tribes.

The Indians under our care remained savage, because forced back upon themselves and away from association with English-speaking and civilized people, and because of our savage example and treatment of them....

We have never made any attempt to civilize them with the idea of taking them into the nation, and all of our policies have been against citizenizing and absorbing them. Although some of the policies now prominent are advertised to carry them into citizenship and consequent association and competition with other masses of the nation, they are not, in reality, calculated to do this.

We are after the facts. Let us take the Land in Severalty Bill. Land in severalty, as administered, is in the way of the individualizing and civilization of the Indians, and is a means of holding the tribes together. Land in severalty is given to individuals adjoining each other on their present reservations. And experience shows that in some cases, after the allotments have been made, the Indians have entered into a compact among themselves to continue to hold their lands in common as a reservation. The inducement of the bill is in this direction. The Indians are not only invited to remain separate tribes and communities, but are practically compelled to remain so. The Indian must either cling to his tribe and its locality, or take great chances of losing his rights and property.

The five civilized tribes of the Indian Territory—Cherokees, Choctaws, Chickasaws, Creeks, and Seminoles—have had tribal schools until it is asserted that they are civilized; yet they have no notion of joining us and becoming a part of the United States. Their whole disposition is to prey upon and hatch up claims against the government, and have the same lands purchased and repurchased and purchased again, to meet the recurring wants growing out of their neglect and inability to make use of their large and rich estate ...

Under our principles we have established the public school system, where people of all races may become unified in every way, and loyal to the government; but we do not gather the people of one nation into schools by themselves, and the people of another nation into schools by themselves, but we invite the youth of all peoples into all schools. We shall not succeed in Americanizing the Indian unless we take him in in exactly the same way. I do not care if abundant schools on the plan of Carlisle are established. If the principle we have always had at Carlisle—of sending them out into families and into the public schools— were left out, the result would be the same, even though such schools were established, as Carlisle is, in the centre of an intelligent and industrious population, and though such schools were, as Carlisle always has been, filled with students from many tribes. Purely Indian schools say to the Indians: "You are Indians, and must remain Indians. You are not of the nation, and cannot become of the nation. We do not want you to become of the nation."

We make our greatest mistake in feeding our civilization to the Indians instead of feeding the Indians to our civilization. America has different customs and civilizations from Germany. What would be the result of an attempt to plant American customs and civilization among the Germans in Germany, demanding that they shall become thoroughly American before we admit them to the country? Now, what we have all along attempted to do for and with the Indians is just exactly that, and nothing else. We invite the Germans to come into our country and communities, and share our customs, our civilization, to be of it; and the result is immediate success. Why not try it on the Indians? Why not invite them into experiences in our communities? Why always invite and compel them to remain a people unto themselves?

It is a great mistake to think that the Indian is born an inevitable savage. He is born a blank, like all the rest of us. Left in the surroundings of savagery, he grows to possess a savage language, superstition, and life. We, left in the surroundings of civilization, grow to possess a civilized language, life, and purpose. Transfer the infant white to the savage surroundings, he will grow to possess a savage language, superstition, and habit. Transfer the savage-born infant to the surroundings of civilization, and he will grow to possess a civilized language and habit. These results have been established over and over again beyond all question; and it is also well established that those advanced in life, even to maturity, of either class, lose already acquired qualities belonging to the side of their birth, and gradually take on those of the side to which they have been transferred.

As we have taken into our national family seven millions of Negroes, and as we receive foreigners at the rate of more than five hundred thousand a year, and assimilate them, it would seem that the time may have arrived when we can very properly make at least the attempt to assimilate our two hundred and fifty thousand Indians, using this proven potent line, and see if that will not end this vexed question and remove them from public attention, where they occupy so much more space than they are entitled to either by numbers or worth.

The school at Carlisle is an attempt on the part of the government to do this. Carlisle has always planted treason to the tribe and loyalty to the nation at large. It has preached against colonizing Indians, and in favor of individualizing them. It has demanded for them the same multiplicity of chances which all others in the country enjoy. Carlisle fills young Indians with the spirit of loyalty to the stars and stripes, and then moves them out into our communities to show by their conduct and ability that the Indian is no different from the white or the colored, that he has the inalienable right to liberty and opportunity that the white and the negro have. Carlisle does not dictate to him what line of life he should fill, so it is an honest one. It says to him that, if he gets his living by the sweat of his brow, and demonstrates to the nation that he is a man, he does more good for his race than hundreds of his fellows who cling to their tribal communistic surroundings ...

No evidence is wanting to show that, in our industries, the Indian can become a capable and willing factor if he has the chance. What we need is an Administration which will give him the chance. The Land in Severalty Bill can be made far more useful than it is, but it can be made so only by assigning the land so as to intersperse good, civilized people among them. If, in the distribution, it is so arranged that two or three white families come between two Indian families, then there would necessarily grow up a community of fellowship along all the lines of our American civilization that would help the Indian at once to his feet. Indian schools must, of necessity, be for a time, because the Indian cannot speak the language, and he knows nothing of the habits and forces he has to contend with; but the highest purpose of all Indian schools ought to be only to prepare the young Indian to enter the public and other schools of the country. And immediately he is so prepared, for his own good and the good of the country, he should be forwarded into these other schools, there to temper, test, and stimulate his brain and muscle into the capacity he needs for his struggle for life, in competition with us. The missionary can, if he will, do far greater service in helping the Indians than he has done; but it will only be by practising the doctrine he preaches. As his work is to lift into higher life the people whom he serves, he must not, under any pretence whatsoever, give the lie to what he preaches by discountenancing the right of any individual Indian to go into higher and better surroundings, but, on the contrary, he should help the Indian to do that. If he fails in thus helping and encouraging the Indian, he is false to his own teaching. An examination shows that no Indians within the limits of the United States have acquired any sort of capacity to meet and cope with the whites in civilized pursuits who did not gain that ability by going among the whites and out from the reservations, and that many have gained this ability by so going out.

Theorizing citizenship into people is a slow operation. What a farce it would be to attempt teaching American citizenship to the negroes in Africa. They could not understand it; and, if they did, in the midst of such contrary influences, they could never use it. Neither can the Indians understand or use American citizenship theoretically taught to them on Indian reservations. They must get into the swim of American citizenship. They must feel the touch of it day after day, until they become saturated with the spirit of it, and thus become equal to it.

When we cease to teach the Indian that he is less than a man; when we recognize fully that he is capable in all respects as we are, and that he only needs the opportunities and privileges which we possess to enable him to assert his humanity and manhood; when we act consistently towards him in accordance with that recognition; when we cease to fetter him to conditions which keep him in bondage, surrounded by retrogressive influences; when we allow him the freedom of association and the developing influences of social contact—then the Indian will quickly demonstrate that he can be truly civilized, and he himself will solve the question of what to do with the Indian.

Sources: "Official Report of the Nineteenth Annual Conference of Charities and Correction" (1892). In *The Advantages of Mingling Indians With Whites, Americanizing the American Indians: Writings by the 'Friends of the Indian' 1880–1900*, edited by Richard H. Pratt. Cambridge, MA: Harvard University Press, 1973; and http://historymatters.gmu.edu/d/4929

See Articles: Indian Removal Act; Jefferson, Thomas (Administration of); Native Americans.

1896
PRIMARY DOCUMENT

Excerpt From the *Plessy v. Ferguson* Decision

In Plessy v. Ferguson *(1896), the Supreme Court upheld state laws instituting racial segregation, and the "separate but equal" doctrine remained a part of American law until 1954. Segregation was adopted throughout the south after the Civil War to preserve the physical and social separation of blacks from whites. Segregation had already been acknowledged by the 1890 Morrill Act, which provided separate black colleges in states where blacks were barred from attending land-grant colleges.*

Mr. Justice Brown:
This case turns upon the constitutionality of an act of the General Assembly of the state of Louisiana, passed in 1890, providing for separate railway carriages for the white and colored races ... The 1st Section of the statute enacts:

That all railway companies carrying passengers in their coaches in this state shall provide equal but separate accommodations for the white and colored races, by providing two or more passenger coaches for each passenger train, or by dividing the passenger coaches by a partition so as to secure separate accommodations: Provided, that this section shall not be construed to apply to street railroads No person or persons, shall be admitted to occupy seats in coaches, other than, the ones, assigned, to them on account of the race they belong to ...

By the 2nd Section it was enacted:
That the officers of such passenger trains shall have power and are hereby required to assign

each passenger to the coach or compartment used for the race to which such passenger belongs; any passenger insisting on going into a coach or compartment to which by race he does not belong shall be liable to a fine of $25, or in lieu of thereof, to imprisonment for a period of not more than twenty days in the parish prison; and should any passenger refuse to occupy the coach or compartment to which he or she is assigned by the officer of such railway, said officer shall have power to refuse to carry such passenger on his train, and for such refusal neither he nor the railway company which he represents shall be liable for damages in any of the courts of this state ...

The constitutionality of this act is attacked upon the ground that it conflicts both with the Thirteenth Amendment of the Constitution, abolishing slavery, and the Fourteenth Amendment, which prohibits certain restrictive legislation on the part of the states.

1. That it does not conflict with the Thirteenth Amendment, which abolished slavery and involuntary servitude except as a punishment for crime, is too clear for argument ... A statute which implies merely a legal distinction between the white and colored races—a distinction which is founded in the color of the two races, and which must always exist so long as white men are distinguished from the other race by color—has no tendency to destroy the legal equality of the two races or reestablish a state of involuntary servitude. Indeed, we do not understand that the Thirteenth Amendment is strenuously relied upon by the plaintiff in error in this connection.
2. By the Fourteenth Amendment, all persons born or naturalized in the United States and subject to the jurisdiction thereof are made citizens of the United States and of the state wherein they reside; and the states are forbidden from making or enforcing any law which shall abridge the privileges or immunities of citizens of the United States, or shall deprive any person of life, liberty, or property without due process of law, or deny to any person within their jurisdiction the equal protection of the laws.

The proper construction of this amendment was first called to the attention of this court in the *Slaughter-House Cases* ... which involved, however, not a question of race but one of exclusive privileges. The case did not call for any expression of opinion as to the exact rights it was intended to secure to the colored race, but it was said generally that its main purpose was to establish the citizenship of the Negro; to give definitions of citizenship of the United States and of the states, and to protect from the hostile legislation of the states the privileges and immunities of citizens of the United States as distinguished from those of citizens of the states.

The object of the amendment was undoubtedly to enforce the absolute equality of the two races before the law, but in the nature of things it could not have been intended to abolish distinctions based upon color, or to enforce social as distinguished from political equality, or a commingling of the two races upon terms unsatisfactory to either. Laws permitting, and even requiring, their separation in places where they are liable to be brought into contact do not necessarily imply the inferiority of either race to the other, and have been generally, if not universally, recognized as within the competency of the state legislatures in the exercise of their police power. The most common instance of this is connected with the establishment of separate schools for white and colored children, which has been held to be a valid exercise of the legislative power even by courts of states where the political rights of the colored race have been longest and most earnestly enforced....

While we think the enforced separation of the races, as applied to the internal commerce of the state, neither abridges the privileges or immunities of the colored man, deprives him of his property without due process of law, nor denies him the equal protection of the laws, within the meaning of the Fourteenth Amendment, we are not prepared to say that the conductor, in assigning passengers to the coaches according to their race, does not act at his peril, or that the provision of the 2nd Section of the act, that denies to the passenger compensation in damages for a refusal to receive him into the coach in which he properly belongs. is a valid exercise of the legislative power. Indeed, we understand it to be conceded by the state's attorney, that such part of the act as exempts from liability the railway company and its officers is unconstitutional.

The power to assign to a particular coach obviously implies the power to determine to which race the passenger belongs, as well as the power to determine who, under the laws of the particular state, is to be deemed a white and who a colored person. This question, though indicated in the brief of the plaintiff in error, does not properly arise upon the record in this case. since the only issue made is as to the unconstitutionality of the act, so far as it requires the railway to provide separate accommodations and the conductor to assign passengers according to their race.

It is claimed by the plaintiff in error that, in any mixed community, the reputation of belonging to the dominant race, in this instance the white race, is *property*, in the same sense that a right of action, or of inheritance, is property. Conceding this to be so for the purposes of this case, we are unable to see how this statute deprives him of, or in any way affects, his right to such property. If he be a white man and assigned to a colored coach, he may have his action for damages against the company for being deprived of his so-called property. Upon the other hand, if he be a colored man and be so assigned, he has been deprived of no property since he is not lawfully entitled to the reputation of being a white man.

In this connection, it is also suggested by the learned counsel for the plaintiff in error that the same argument that will justify the state legislature in requiring railways to provide separate accommodations for the two races will also authorize them to require separate cars to be provided for people whose hair is of a certain color, or who are aliens, or who belong to certain nationalities, or to enact laws requiring colored people to walk upon one side of the street and white people upon the other, or requiring white men's houses to be painted white and colored men's black, or their vehicles or business signs to be of different colors, upon the theory that one side of the street is as good as the other, or that a house or vehicle of one color is as good as one of another color. The reply to all this is that every exercise of the police power must be reasonable and extend only to such laws as are enacted in good faith for the promotion for the public good and not for the annoyance or oppression of a particular class....

So far, then, as a conflict with the Fourteenth Amendment is concerned, the case reduces itself to the question whether the statute of Louisiana is a reasonable regulation, and with respect to this there must necessarily be a large discretion on the part of the legislature. In determining the question of reasonableness, it is at liberty to act with reference to the established usages, customs, and traditions of the people, and with a view to the promotion of their comfort, and the preservation of the public peace and good order. Gauged by this standard, we cannot say that a law which authorizes or even requires the separation of the two races in public conveyances is unreasonable or more obnoxious to the Fourteenth Amendment than the acts of Congress requiring separate schools for colored children in the District of Columbia, the constitutionality of which does not seem to have been questioned, or the corresponding acts of state legislatures.

We consider the underlying fallacy of the plaintiff's argument to consist in the assumption that the enforced separation of the two races stamps the colored race with a badge of inferiority. If this be so, it is not by reason of anything found in the act, but solely because the colored race chooses to put that construction upon it. The argument necessarily assumes that if, as has been more than once the case, and is not unlikely to be so again, the colored race should become the dominant power in the state legislature and should enact a law in precisely similar terms, it would thereby relegate the white race to an inferior position. We imagine that the white race, at least, would not acquiesce in this assumption.

The argument also assumes that social prejudices may be overcome by legislation and that equal rights cannot be secured to the Negro except by an enforced commingling of the two races. We cannot accept this proposition. If the two races are to meet upon terms of social equality, it must be the result of natural affinities, a mutual appreciation of each other's merits, and a voluntary consent of individuals. As was said by the Court of Appeals of New York in *People v. Gallagher*,

This end can neither be accomplished nor promoted by laws which conflict with the general sentiment of the community, upon whom they are designed to operate. When the government, therefore, has secured to each of its citizens equal rights before the law and equal opportunities for improvement and progress, it has accomplished the end for which it was organized and performed all of the functions respecting social advantages with which it is endowed.

Legislation is powerless to eradicate racial instincts or to abolish distinctions based upon physical differences, and the attempt to do so can only result in accentuating the difficulties of the present situation. If the civil and political rights of both races be equal, one cannot be inferior to the other civilly or politically. If one race be inferior to the other socially, the Constitution of the United States cannot put them upon the same plane.

It is true that the question of the proportion of colored blood necessary to constitute a colored person as distinguished from a white person is one upon which there is a difference of opinion in the different states, some holding that any visible admixture of black blood stamps the person as belonging to the colored race (*State v. Chavers,* 5 Jones, [N.C.]1, p. 11); others that it depends upon the preponderance of blood (*Gray v. State*, 4 Ohio, 354; *Monroe v. Collins,* 17 Ohio St. 665); and still others that the predominance of white blood must only be in the proportion of three-fourths (*People v. Dean*, 14 Michigan, 406; *Jones v. Commonwealth*, 80 Virginia, 538). But these are questions to be determined under the laws of each state and are not properly put in issue in this case. Under the allegations of his petition it may undoubtedly become a question of importance whether, under the laws of Louisiana, the petitioner belongs to the white or colored race.

The judgment of the court below is, therefore, *affirmed.*

Sources: Plessy v. Ferguson, 163, U.S. 537 (1896); and http://historymatters.gmu.edu/d/5485

See Articles: Equality, Concept of; *Plessy v. Ferguson*; Segregation Laws; Supreme Court, U.S.

1901 to 1920
INTRODUCTION

The first two decades of the 20th century served as the midpoint in a series of significant social and economic changes that had a profound impact on crime and punishment in America. These years made up the bulk of what historians call the Progressive Era, a period that marked America's shift from a rural country of island communities to an interconnected, transcontinental nation with international reach and an increasingly strong and important national government. It was also a time of change, during which a national state and its attendant regulation and legislation overlapped and superseded community rule and informal justice.

Organizations from the private or social sphere did not relinquish their role in protecting the safety and security of individuals, remaining important throughout this period. They encouraged an outpouring of collective efforts at moral suasion, communal organization, and crime reform. In the cooperation and coordination of public and private—previously a realm of the churches—more secular approaches to crime and criminal justice reform took hold. Furthermore, even as national approaches grew in scope and importance, progressive reformists encouraged the placement of greater police powers in the hands of the local, state, and federal governments. This in turn encouraged the overlapping, and sometimes conflicting, spheres of a federalized criminal justice system in America.

The period from 1901 to 1920, therefore, was the turning point in America's shift from local and informal law enforcement and community standards to organized, professional, and federal law enforcement and national standards of crime and punishment. These effects were seen in the change that occurred in the crimes committed, the development of American law enforcement, changes in the criminal law and court procedure, and the growth of the American prison system.

Crime and Criminal Behavior in the Progressive Era
Progressive thought on crime and other social issues was a hybrid of secular thought and religious sentiment, which was reflected in the treatment of crime—especially concerning imprisonment—from 1901 to 1920. During this period, the popular explanation of criminal behavior remained a mix of belief in human sinfulness, rational choice, and

human atavism; alternate names for these approaches were the religious, classical, and positivist theories of crime. Much of this came to be reified in later decades into other criminological theories, such as the Chicago School.

Social Darwinism played an important role in Progressive Era criminological arguments. It was a support for much of the positivist arguments promulgated by the nascent group's experts, a growing class of social scientists that included sociologists, political scientists, economists, and psychologists. They began positing environmental and other structural causes of crime. Socialist economic criticisms played a role, especially Karl Marx's theory of alienation, as did more race-oriented theories emerging from the Social Darwin camp. The psychological theories of the day, also deeply tinged by Social Darwinism, had an impact. The administration of intelligence tests to thousands of people who entered the criminal justice system lent support to the theory that criminals, delinquents, and other antisocial persons were feebleminded. These people were often institutionalized or even sterilized to prevent them from harming themselves, others, and even future generations. Other elements of the Progressive Era eugenics movement encouraged setting limits on the propagation of the racial, ethnic, and economic groups that were seen as the source of criminal behavior.

This new understanding of human behavior, especially the antisocial element, was also grounded in religiously inspired sentiments. Ideals of reforming the sinful individual, forgiveness, and human charity marked much of the reformers' zeal for a "social gospel." There was an almost eschatological quality to many of the progressive dreams of creating a secular version of the heavenly kingdom. This approach culminated in the great political and legislative effort of 1919 to amend the U.S. Constitution and enact a prohibition regime, which commanded the attention of the criminal justice system through the next 15 years. Groups such as the Women's Christian Temperance Movement led this movement and many others that similarly sought to encourage the reform of wayward people, including criminals, and the brutality of systems in which they were found. Softer forms of social control were melded to harder forms of political control.

The industrial city, given its size, novelty, and profusion of immigrant classes, was the focus of these theories, and it would be the breeding ground for many private and public solutions to crime. Such explanations showed in the work of early muckraking journalists such as Jacob Riis. In his 1902 book, titled *The Battle with the Slum*, Riis adopted the observation of a New York inspector on whose work he had reported that slums were "the nurseries of crime." One such area, a slum on the East Side of New York at the southern end of Mulberry Street called the Bend, he recalled as "redolent of crime and murder." In the city, the older criminal justice system floundered and was rapidly replaced by new forms and approaches as America's urban population exploded between the end of the Civil War and the start of World War I. These changes eventually emerged in law enforcement, the courts, and the prisons.

This mix of new theories and old sentiments in progressive thought also had an impact on identifying criminals. The remnant means of logging criminal identities was the Bertillonage system, named after Frenchman Alphonse Bertillon, whereby elaborate measurements of physical characteristics were recorded to create what was thought to be a unique (or unique enough) set of numbers to indicate specific persons. The theory behind such measurements was that wicked acts correlated to physical abnormalities and atavistic traits. The failure of Bertillonage to predict or even uniquely identify criminals led to the system's disappearance, and fingerprinting soon supplanted it. Social Darwinism, though, continued to have an impact on the understanding of human behavior and led to more sociological understandings of crime.

Mulberry Street slum, New York City, ca. 1900. Author Jacob Riis, studying city slums with the eye of a New York inspector, observed that slums were rampant with crime. In particular, the southern end of Mulberry street was "redolent of crime and murder." New forms of law enforcement, including reformative and progressive thought, were explored to handle the population and crime surge in the era between the Civil War and World War I.

Progressive social scientists, lawyers, judges, and politicians all wanted a more scientific understanding of crime and criminals, but the crime statistics of the day were problematic. Their call for more and better crime statistics would have a lasting impact. The U.S. Census Bureau collected data that was useful for understanding the scope of American criminality, but critics argued that this paled in comparison to the range of data collected by European nations. To remedy this, a National Prison Association created a Committee on Criminal Statistics in 1904. Other groups, from various prison associations, bar associations, and more academic groups such as the American Institute of Criminal Law and Criminology, published study upon study of the crime problem, drawing on a variety of research. It would take two decades for the International Association of Chiefs of Police (IACP), and then the Federal Bureau of Investigation (FBI), to make a formal, national effort to collect crime data, but the call for such data had been heard.

Of the crimes that can be documented in this period, murder has received the most attention. It is estimated that the murder rate was less than 1.5 per 100,000 in 1900, but rose precipitously from approximately 1906 to 1907 and continued to climb to more than 6.5 per 100,000 by 1920, according to the Justice Research Statistics Association. In comparison to other Western nations, however, this rate was significantly higher; for example, the murder rate in New York was six times higher than that of England and Wales between 1914 and 1918. Other crimes were harder to mark, but

The funeral of "Dago Frank" Cirofici, one of four New York City criminals convicted of murdering Herman Rosenthal, takes place in lavish style in April 1914. He and his associates Harry Horowitz "Gyp the Blood," Louis Rosenberg (Rosenweig) "Lefty Louis," and "Whitey" Lewis (Frank Seidenshner) were executed at Sing Sing prison. Murder rates climbed from 1.5 per 100,000 in 1900 to more than 6.5 per 100,000 by 1920.

some observations were made. Burglary, robbery, and automobile thefts in American cities were similarly more prevalent than in European cities.

The growth of federal crime may also be tracked, and generally quite accurately, but only because there were so few federal crimes committed. The annual reports of the U.S. Secret Service suggested a leveling off of counterfeiting investigations, and the Bureau of Investigation (BOI), the FBI's predecessor, reported a significant increase in general, federal investigations, as Congress gave the new agency money and personnel to investigate interstate prostitution. This latter category of cases exploded between 1910 and 1913, but quickly declined after changes in bureau policy and priorities such as gun running and cross-border (Mexican border) revolutionary activity took precedent. On the subject of other crimes, conclusions are murkier. Some researchers have found that references to corruption and fraud peaked around 1840 and steadily declined from the 1870s, with much smaller spikes in 1910. Incidents of kidnapping remained few, but other violent crimes tracked the murder rate. In all, the period from 1901 to 1920 did not experience a great increase in criminal activity, at least on a per-capita basis; but as for absolute numbers, crime was on the rise.

The aftermath of the collapse of Reconstruction in 1877 and the long, slow decline of the promised freedom for African Americans in the southern states led to many significant criminal issues. The institution of various Jim Crow laws across the southern states did not always create criminal violations, but the increasing legal segregation opened many opportunities to charge southern blacks with various breaches of the peace as they were effectively disenfranchised. One such insidious development was the creation of a peonage system, whereby indebted status, whether from legitimate or manufactured debt, placed both southern whites and blacks (disproportionately blacks) into forced labor to pay off the debts. At times, the U.S. Department of Justice forcibly investigated such re-enslavement because the interstate impression of labor involved as civil rights law did not encompass such violations. Prosecution following investigation was a different matter; local legal culture and social pressure generally negated the government's ability to prosecute successfully against peonage under federal law, no matter how strong the evidence. Still, the Justice Department maintained positions dedicated to such investigations and continued to press them through the 1908 reorganization that created the BOI.

The threat of lynching remained in many places due to racial and ethnic animosity. The number of victims each year was a small percentage of overall murders and had been declining from its peak at the end of Reconstruction. As a tool of social control, though, its impact was disproportionate. Prominent cases of lynch mob "justice," such as the lynching of Leo Frank in Marietta, Georgia, in 1915 for the murder of Mary Phagen or the 1919 lynching of African American Willy Brown in southern Omaha, Nebraska, suggested an undercurrent of anti-Jewish and antiblack racism. For many decades, federal civil rights law could not touch the criminality of such acts and local forces tended to turn a blind eye. Often, however, there were also deeper issues involved. In the Brown case, for example, the background included violent labor clashes between black and eastern European workers and the economic dislocation that followed the rapid demobilization from World War I.

Racial conflict played a significant factor in another significant area of criminal activity: rioting. Over the first two decades of the 20th century, Americans engaged in at least 10 racially motivated riots. Some were fairly small, but several were quite large, including one that lasted several days in Washington, D.C. Riots were typically catalyzed by a single incident of violence, often committed by or against a law enforcement officer, and many exhibited the fault line between Caucasians and African Americans. Such clashes occurred across the country: riots in Atlanta and Brownsville, Texas, in 1906; a riot in Springfield, Illinois, in 1908, which partially led to the creation of the National Association for the Advancement of Colored People in Springfield in 1909; nationwide riots following the fight between boxer Jack Johnson and Jim Jeffries in 1910; riots in east St. Louis, Illinois, Philadelphia, and Houston all in 1917; and a riot in Washington, D.C., in 1919. Other ethnic conflicts, however, could also spark riots. The 1902 New York City riot, for example, was a conflict between Irish immigrants and New York police against local Jewish immigrants. Economic unrest, albeit tinged by racial conflict, was a catalyst in Nebraska in 1909, where a community of Greek immigrants, known as Greek Town, was attacked and driven out of the area by other groups. The fact that the Greek immigrants were strikebreakers added a deeper level of conflict to the cultural differences.

Criminal acts related to political ideas—that is, revolutionary ideologies—were also becoming a serious problem. On September 5, 1901, President William McKinley was assassinated by an anarchist named Leon Czolgosz. The same threat of violent anarchism had been roiling Europe for two decades prior to the murder, and would continue to be a worldwide issue and catalyst for many years. With the murder of the president, the threat of political violence became ensconced on the radical left of the political spectrum and was associated with eastern European immigrants.

In response, American immigration laws were changed to forbid the emigration of anarchists, and the U.S. Secret Service was assigned protective duties. The Secret Service and other federal agencies began to pay closer attention to developing domestic intelligence on radical threats; their activities were a mélange of law enforcement and domestic espionage that became increasingly controversial over time. From its beginning, the BOI investigated national security matters, including neutrality law violations that forbade supporting foreign revolution from U.S. soil to anarchist statute violations. The New York Police Department created a bomb squad to investigate anarchist threats in the city. Even private detective forces such as the William Burns Detective Agency (shortly thereafter known as the William Burns International Detective Agency) got involved, investigating the bombing of the offices of the *Los Angeles Times* and gathering evidence for local prosecutors against union members accused of the act. The threat of political violence continued through the decade, culminating in the 1919 mail bomb campaign, most likely committed by a small group of Italian anarchists. The federal government's sweeping overreaction, known as the Palmer Red Raids, was an effort to detain and deport all anarchist and communist aliens, regardless of their roles in illegal activity.

Along with the organization of urban societies, a correlating change in the organization of crime began to develop. The corrupt political and economic practices of the political machines were under attack and on the wane, but new organizations based on criminal violence and other acts began to be noticed. Chief among these was the nascent Italian immigrant-based Black Hand gang and their associated crimes. New York City was becoming a center of organized gang activity, and groups claiming to be Black Hand appeared in many U.S. cities by the early 1900s. The historiography on the movement's origins, whether transplanted or indigenous, is developing, but it is clear that the movement did not migrate in whole from Sicily, even if persons and practices were connected to the Italian Mafioso. Not yet as organized as the Mafia would be in later decades, Mafia techniques and immigrants from Sicily were developed in America and became known in major urban centers in the United States. Threats of violent extortion and retribution and notes left in such threats came to be attributed to the Black Hand, thereby making the reach of the group appear nationwide, whereas it was primarily a phenomena in New York, Chicago, and a handful of other cities.

Whatever its origins, the threat of organized crime was a reality in New York and other cities. Several large gangs operated within the wider New York community, including Italian ethnic gangs known as the Five Points Gang, out of which emerged notorious gangsters Johnnie Torrio and Alphonse Capone; the Black Hand gang under Giuseppe Morello; Irish ethnic gangs such as the White Hand Gang; Monk Eastman's Jewish ethnic gang; and a diverse collection of smaller criminal groups. Similar groups, though less well known, appeared in many major urban areas, including Boston, Chicago, and several west coast cities, but New York was the most significant.

In New York, elements of its police force became dedicated investigators of specific gang problems. The most well-known investigator at the time was New York police detective Joseph Petrosino, who came to be known as a chief investigator of Black Hand operations in the city. Despite the difficulty of acquiring willing witnesses and the code of silence adopted by gang members, Petrosino and other New York police officers were able to make advances against the gang. U.S. Secret Service agents, under the leadership of its New York agent in charge, William Flynn, also pursued gang members, especially their leader and known counterfeiter, Giuseppe Morello. In May 1909, in order to continue his investigations, Petrosino traveled to Palermo, Sicily, where he was murdered by elements of the Sicilian Mafia. Italian authorities launched major investigations, offering 10,000 lira for information. New York City held a large public funeral and awarded Mrs. Petrosino a lifetime pension in recognition of her husband's sacrifice.

Although such international connections were not usually pursued at that time, crime on the national level was rising in prominence. Theodore Roosevelt, as president and candidate for reelection, touted his experience in seeking criminal justice reform in New York City. In the following presidential election, both Democrat and Republican parties had platform planks on criminal justice issues, specifically fraud in the awarding of mineral rights and other concessions on federal lands.

President Roosevelt had embarked on a massive campaign to bring western lands under federal control in order to conserve their natural state and control their exploitation for mining, drilling, and other commercial concerns. However, because federal bureaucrats and legislators gained control over vast areas of natural wealth for which there was great demand, significant fraud followed. Using Secret Service personnel, the Department of Justice began to investigate these matters in 1904, and one senator was indicted for bribery in connection with land issues. In a separate matter, another congressman was also indicted on a criminal charge related to misuse of his office. Soon afterward, the Subcommittee of the House Appropriations Committee began holding hearings on the use of Secret Service personnel to investigate federal criminal violations. Some people contended that these hearings were retribution for earlier investigations into congressional members. The hearing transcripts suggest that the members' concerns were aimed at the abuse of power under Secret Service Chief John Wilkie, but baser motives have not been ruled out.

Congress then used an appropriations bill to curtail the role of the Secret Service in providing investigative personnel for the executive branch. In reaction to this change in federal practice, the attorney general created a small detective force in his department.

Nineteen members of the Black Hand Society are arrested at Fairmont, West Virginia, on March 27, 1909. Attracted to the area's mines and factories, Italians were a large ethnic group in the state; their businessmen were frequent targets. Organized crime was on the rise in the early 1900s, and the Black Hand was notorious in many cities across the United States for threats of blackmail and extortion. During prohibition, however, bootlegging became more profitable.

The heated issues of abuse of power rose again, not because of the attorney general's actions, but because a "lame duck" President Roosevelt suggested to Congress in a public message that it had limited the Secret Service's role solely because its members did not like being investigated for criminal activity. The back-and-forth debate enlivened a dull Washington winter, but accomplished little else. When Roosevelt left office two months later, the issue faded.

Crime was also becoming more visible with the rise of intercontinental communications by telephone, telegraph, and radio. Heinous acts in New York could be news in Chicago and Los Angeles the same day and vice versa. The crusading stories of the muckrakers exposed acts of violence and depravity from the peonage system in the south to the practices of butchers in Chicago to the unsafe practices that fed the tragic fire of the Triangle Shirtwaist Factory Fire in New York City in 1911. The national attention a journalist could bring to such issues, though not always crimes or concerns for law enforcement, often led to state and national attention. Journalist Ida Tarbell's articles on the machinations of the Standard Oil Trust fueled federal efforts to rein in monopolistic practices. Richard Barry's article on how the peonage system effectively enslaved people encouraged public outcries against the system and its connection to prison labor. Ray Stannard Baker turned public attention toward lynching. Upton Sinclair's book *The Jungle* turned stomachs with its descriptions of Chicago meat-processing abuses and fed a national outcry that led to the 1906 Pure Food and Drug Act, one of a growing number of national regulatory acts with potential criminal sanctions. And the death of more than 140 women at the Triangle Shirtwaist Factory led to the promulgation and enforcement of new workplace safety laws in New York City and the indictments of several factory owners for manslaughter; they were acquitted.

The ability for crime news to travel quickly and universally did not mean that it exactly resembled today's sensationalistic coverage. The murder case of Belle Gunness, a Norwegian immigrant who was thought to have lured dozens of people to their deaths—mostly men, but even some of her own children—is one example. Gunness's long trail of death began to unravel in May 1908 when the family of one of her victims began searching. Gunness disappeared, however, and authorities eventually discovered the remains of numerous homicide victims on her farm in La Porte, Indiana; her farmhand, Ray Lamphere, was arrested and charged with murder and arson. A headless corpse in a nightgown found in Gunness' burning house was thought to be Gunness; medical examination of the corpse, however,

Belle Gunness and her three children. The story of Gunness, who died a mysterious death and was suspected of luring and murdering dozens of others, including her own children, was covered by the nascent sensationalist press—a practice that was to grow over the decades.

cast some doubt, and the mystery remained. The newspapers of the day covered the events, but despite the sensationalist aspects of it—a "black widow" mass murderer, the mystery surrounding her disappearance, the grisly discovery of multiple bodies—the story did not achieve the attention that later cases, such as the Lindbergh Kidnapping (1932) or the hunt for Andrew Cunanan (1997), achieved as media sensationalism grew.

International communication contributed to both the advancement of criminological science and public interest in crime and its detection in other ways. In 1905, the International Police Exposition in St. Louis, Missouri, brought John Ferrier, a Scotland Yard officer, to the United States to expound on the utility of fingerprint identification. International concern over the trafficking of immigrant women led to conferences, debates, and legislative action throughout the Western world. In 1910, the U.S. Congress passed the Mann Act, also known as the White Slave Traffic Act, to combat this perceived threat. American law enforcement officers and researchers looked to Europe for the latest developments in police science and administration, and the exchange of ideas across the Atlantic was fruitful.

Another feature of the public's awareness of crime led to efforts at crime prevention. In an August 1913 issue of a popular magazine, the *Outlook*, New York Police Department (NYPD) Second Deputy Commissioner George S. Dougherty presented an extensive article discussing "The Public: The Criminal's Partner," complete with pictures illustrating how careless citizens were ripe for the efforts of pickpockets. Dougherty argued that, "If the public would cease to cooperate with the criminal, crime could be reduced to a minimum within a single year. Approaching crime prevention in another way, the Anti-Profanity League—a group whose aim was to end public cursing—used a religious anticrime message as part of its wider effort, calling profanity "Satan's hook" and suggesting that such moral failings could lead to greater ones such as crime. Many calls for greater social safety nets in the form of settlement houses and other charitable efforts used similar arguments.

Law Enforcement
American cities and towns were steadily building dedicated police forces from the end of the Civil War. Larger cities required changes in police management as the old watch and ward system gave way to a more military form of organization in larger cities. Typically, these police officers were politically appointed patrolmen, often making a decent wage but tied completely to the electoral spoils system of machine politics. They were prone to graft and an unbalanced administration of justice. They were also assigned to handle a variety of constituent services, from taking in boarders to reuniting lost children with their families, and they had a few investigative responsibilities. The very term *detective* often carried negative connotations, as investigative techniques—disguise, surveillance, and other subterfuge—were suspect and associated with criminal activity by the police.

The problem of law enforcement at the start of the 20th century was that the rapid growth of population and the proliferation of roads and communication lines made the local character of 19th-century enforcement untenable. Unlike European police, American police forces followed the style of local and municipal governments, meaning that smaller departments were often ad hoc, untrained, and underfunded, while the larger departments were creatures of the machine politics of America's growing urban centers. Even these larger departments tended to be decentralized, much like the city governments that created them; the power of the machines lay in the electoral districts, city wards, and neighborhoods. Although the officers who came out of this system could be well compensated, that compensation too often came from protection money and other small-scale but widespread corruption.

In response to the machine influence on law enforcement, progressives sought to "professionalize" police work, a strategy that would persist throughout the 20th century. It is clear that such moves had a significant influence on American police forces during the first decades of the 20th century. Urban historian Eric Monkkonen found a clear change in police work between 1890 and 1920, when forces changed their mission from providing a variety of services that fell under the rubric of "police power," such as returning lost children and housing the transient, to chasing robbers, thieves, and murderers. Arrests, or more accurately, temporary detentions for "victimless crimes" such as public drunkenness declined, while arrests for violent crimes increased. This change, which came from both internal and external forces, emerged from a narrowing of the purpose of police as other governmental and private structures like settlement houses took on the social aspects of police power and left the narrower enforcement role to police officers.

One significant progressive goal was to remove law enforcement from the reach of machine politics by bringing police forces under civil service rules. The establishment of police commissions and administrative boards had some influence as these reforms removed police administration, especially officer selection, from patronage politics. Even more significant was the use of civil service procedures, including the use of exam criteria to select candidate officers. By 1915, there were 204 police departments in the United States that hired personnel under civil service rules; although two-thirds of the federal government jobs fell under civil service requirements, it is not known how many of those were law enforcement related. Along with this move to "bureaucratize" law enforcement came a clear differentiation of various roles in the criminal justice system as the governing bodies of U.S. cities and states found that they needed police, detectives, prison officials, medical examiners, forensic scientists and, in general, a growing army of criminal justice workers, according to historian Thomas Friedman. This was followed by calls for professional standards and controls in order for law enforcement to be effective and to implement the latest organizational, scientific, and legal developments available. The institution of such standards and controls marked the first decades of the new century. This move toward professionalization during the first 20 years of the 1900s had a significant effect on the public image of the police officer and, eventually, their plain-clothes colleagues, the detectives; however, many hurdles remained.

The early 20th century, though, was not a period of vastly expanding law enforcement roles, at least on a per-capita basis. The large, mid-19th century increase in police forces had tapered off dramatically through the end of the 19th century. During the first decades of the 20th century, the number of police rose at much the same pace as the population as a whole. In Chicago, for instance, the number of residents per officer ranged from 478 officers per 100,000 to 512 per 100,000 in 1920, according to the Chicago Police Department.

The remuneration for police also varied. Those forces most in line with the progressive push for police professionalization offered reasonable salaries and advancement, as well as the job security of civil service positions. In other jurisdictions, police pay and benefits lagged and job requirements could be heavy. One answer to such problems was to organize. In 1915, two Pittsburgh, Pennsylvania, patrol officers formed "Fort Pitt Lodge #1" of a new organization called the Fraternal Order of Police (FOP). Its purpose was to offer a common voice to city officials on issues concerning police. Within two years, a national organization was formed and rapidly grew. However, the FOP was less of a union and more of a lobbying group and benevolent association; its name was deliberately selected to provide that impression because of the problematic relationship between law enforcement, unions, and politicians.

Other police jurisdictions, though, looked to the organized power of the union as a possible solution to labor unrest and job dissatisfaction with police work. The flash point of this movement occurred in Boston. In 1919, America faced a wave of labor unrest as more than 3,000 strikes took place throughout the country and terrorist violence threatened the peace. Seeing this unrest, many Boston police, unsatisfied with their pay and hours of work, made a petition to Edwin U. Curtis, the police commissioner, for permission to form a union and engage in collective bargaining. Curtis refused and suspended the leaders of the grassroots effort. Not long afterward, on September 9, a significant majority of the Boston Police Department, approximately 1,100 officers, went on strike. Rioting and unrest followed, and the mayor called in local militia units and petitioned the governor for additional aid. Massachusetts Governor Calvin Coolidge immediately called out the state National Guard units to restore the peace in Boston. Returning servicemen were offered the jobs of the striking officers, along with much of what the strikers had been requesting. The strike was broken and the process of unionizing American police was significantly delayed.

National law enforcement forces were even less developed and also experienced little growth; however, they underwent a significant change in focus and organization that would set their direction in the following decades. Prior to 1900, federal police

Rising standards of professionalism during the first two decades of the 1900s led to an improved public image of the police. A downtown Washington, D.C., officer uses a direct-to-station call box with an illuminated red globe to alert officers to the scene (left, ca. 1912). A policewoman directs traffic near the Carnegie Library in Washington, D.C. (right, ca. 1919). The first police matrons were relegated to clerical, juvenile, guard duty, and vice work.

personnel consisted of a variety of small investigative groups, some with law enforcement powers, and some without. The largest groups were the U.S. Secret Service in the Treasury Department, the U.S. Marshals in the Justice Department, and the U.S. Postal Inspectors. The term *secret service* was regularly used to describe all federal investigators. It was fraught with ambivalent, if not negative, connotations, much like the term *detective*. The connotations of "secret service" suggested spying, primarily in a domestic environment, which could lead to governmental abuses. The terminology for state and local police, although sometimes associated with strike-breaking activity, was not as shrouded.

The Secret Service, following federal laws that forbade the use of private detective services such as the Pinkerton Agency, provided investigations on an ad hoc, per diem basis to many agencies that required investigative assistance. The U.S. attorneys of the Department of Justice not only prosecuted criminals but also filled the role of detective and village constable, albeit with much hired help. Given the paucity of federal criminal law, this system was neither efficient nor optimal, but it was generally adequate to deal with the priorities and policies of the presidents and their attorneys general.

Under President Theodore Roosevelt, small changes with long-term consequences in this structure and approach began. He advocated the vigorous use of executive power and authorized his attorneys general to act against some trust combinations under the Sherman Antitrust Act of 1890, begin to enforce land fraud laws, and enact a more general expansion in the enforcement of federal criminal law. Federal legislation also

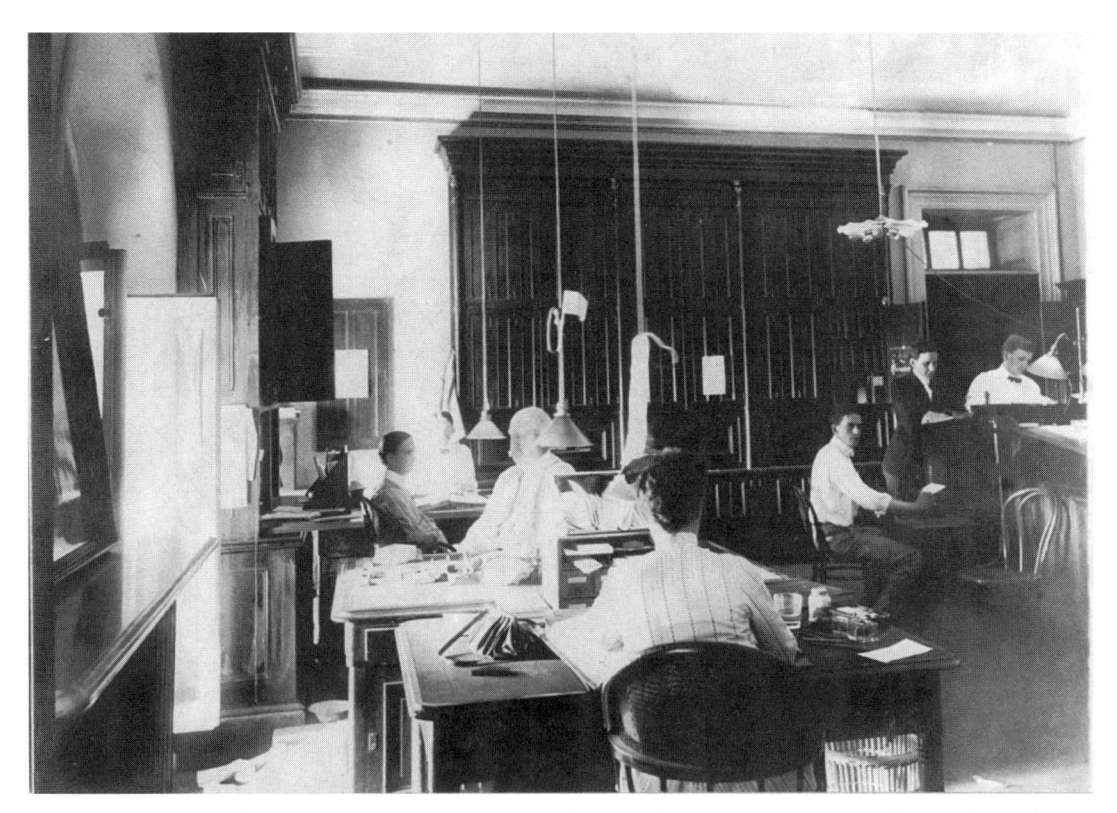

U.S. Secret Service employees at work, circa 1906. During that year, the U.S. Congress passed the Sundry Civil Expenses Act of 1907 to provide funds for the Secret Service to protect the president. The department had assumed the responsibility of protecting the president in 1902, with two operatives on the White House detail full-time.

continued to expand the scope of federal law. Anti-anarchist laws and neutrality laws began to form the basis for criminal subversion investigations and national security law. Even more important were laws aimed at political and economic corruption as people of the era feared the corruption between these entwined spheres of power. Roosevelt's vigorous application of older laws and the increase in newer ones began to tax the limits of this disorganized collection of agents and investigators.

August Vollmer represented and proselytized this new vision of professionalism in law enforcement. In 1905, he was elected town marshal and soon developed the Marshal Corps into a full-blown police department, of which he was appointed head in 1909. Other than a brief stint as chief of police in Los Angeles, Vollmer served in Berkeley, California, until 1932. During his tenure, he developed a police school, created a motorcycle and then automobile patrol, created the first unit to deal with juvenile crime and antisocial behavior, advocated the establishment of a criminology school, and experimented with the use of a newly developed lie detector. He brought radios into police work, created a system of police records, and insisted on using intelligence tests and educational qualifications to select new officers. In 1919, he was elected head of the IACP.

Professional organizations aimed at supporting and reforming enforcement continued to grow during the course of the Progressive Era. These organizations ranged in purpose from groups advocating the increased or decreased criminalization of various vices, from prostitution to alcohol and drug use. In 1902, an International Prison Association began meeting yearly to consider issues in prison reform. In 1909, the American Institute of Criminal Law and Criminology was organized in Chicago to consider and advance the development of the criminal justice system and its study. In 1915, the International Association for Identification was formed in Oakland, California, by Inspector Harry Caldwell of the Oakland Police Department and 21 other law enforcement officers; its purpose was to share information on criminal identification and to develop standards by which all law enforcement could regularize their identification work.

Citizen organizations also proliferated in the early 20th century. Chicago was a center for several key examples of these groups. In 1907, a group of leading Italian citizens, prominent businessmen, several ethnic organizations, and the Italian Chamber of Commerce in Chicago formed a group called the White Hand Society. Its aim was to combat Black Hand activities in the area. Several years later, in 1919, the Chicago Association of Commerce created the Chicago Crime Commission. The catalyst was a brazen payroll robbery in 1917, the murder of two security guards during the robbery, and an armed standoff between a handful of criminals and several hundred police officers. The association created a large committee to consider the problem of crime in Chicago and possible remedies to its perceived growth. The commission is still in existence today, working to improve the criminal justice system in Chicago by creating and supporting solutions to crime by educating the public.

Religious institutions also displayed keen interest in the problem of crime and enforcement. For many years during this period, the State Baptist Convention of Georgia had a standing committee on criminal law reform. It focused on the problem of the increase of crime in the country, its causes, and potential remedies. Business groups also became involved, sometimes significantly so. During the country's involvement in the World War II, an American Protective League—a force that numbered in the hundreds of thousands—was formed by three Chicago businessmen and allied itself to the Department of Justice. It provided the national government with a domestic security force that helped to identify political undesirables and draft dodgers, as well as a host of war-related crimes; laws passed soon after American entry in the war had made many aspects of subversive speech and action illegal for a period of time. The group often went beyond its role as an "eyes and ears" for the government and assumed law enforcement–like powers. Strong criticism and the quick end of the war led to the immediate dissolution of the group and the destruction of most of its domestic intelligence files.

Between 1901 and 1910, the use of fingerprints in criminal identification began to be used alongside and to rapidly supplant Bertillonage—the idea that a unique personal description could be created if enough standard physical descriptors and measurements were taken. The Henry system of classifying fingerprints, promulgated in 1900, was rapidly adopted in law enforcement because it was much simpler and less prone to error than the Bertillon measurements. Its adoption in the early 20th century led to a revolution in criminal history and identification recordkeeping and would spur the development of worldwide law enforcement communication networks for the sharing of criminal identification information.

American fascination with fingerprints was foreshadowed in Mark Twain's novel *Pudd'nhead Wilson: The Extraordinary Twins* in 1894, and individual law enforcement agencies began experimenting with fingerprints as evidence soon thereafter. As early as 1904, in the Sing Sing and Leavenworth federal prisons, the regular collection and collation of criminal prints began. The IACP also began to amass a collection, drawing on contributions from its membership to start the rudiments of a national criminal identification collection.

In 1910, following IACP discussion of the importance of fingerprints at its 1909 annual meeting, Frederick Augustus Brayley authored the first American textbook on taking, categorizing, and using fingerprints in criminal investigations. His book *Brayley's Arrangement of Finger Prints Identification and Their Uses* became an important first step in the advancement of fingerprint identification in the United States. The following year, fingerprint evidence was first cited in a murder trial in Chicago. The murderer left a series of prints in some fresh paint at the scene of the crime, and Chicago police captured the images through photography. Prosecution witnesses matched these prints to the fingers of Thomas Jennings, who was arrested near the crime scene with blood on his shirt and a gun of similar caliber and ammunition to that used to kill Clarence Hiller. Jennings was convicted and executed, tied to the scene of the crime by the prints left in the paint.

Other advances in forensic science also helped to advance the professionalism of American law enforcement investigations. In the 1902 case of *The Commonwealth v. John C. Best*, Massachusetts Supreme Court Chief Judge Oliver Wendell Holmes allowed the first use of ballistic comparison in a U.S. court case when he wrote in favor of the Commonwealth's case against the Best's appeal. In the lower court, the government argued that the rifling on bullets taken from the victim's body matched a test bullet fired from the accused's rifle. Holmes noted that this was the best evidence available. In February 1913, the U.S. Congress passed a law admitting that "where the genuineness of the handwriting of any person may be involved, any admitted or proved handwriting of such person shall be competent evidence as a basis for comparison by witnesses, or by the jury, court, or officer conducting such proceeding, to prove or disprove such genuineness." Many other examples of the courts and legislatures dealing with the admissibility of physical forensic evidence abound, as law enforcement officers and detectives secured positive and latent fingerprints, blood samples, handwriting samples, document exemplars, trace evidence, and a diversity of other evidence. The promise of progressive forensics seemed unbounded, and judges were open to considering the edges of science in the courts.

In a 1904 case in Colorado Springs, Colorado, police tried but failed to identify a body by its teeth; a few years later, a California dentist succeeded in identifying the remains of a murder victim by comparing the victim's teeth to the dental record of possible matches. The appointment of publically funded, medically trained personnel to provide forensic support developed steadily after Boston appointed a certified doctor as medical examiner in 1907. Chicago began to rely on people with growing expertise in aspects of forensic science such as T. Dickerson Cooke, a pioneer in criminal identification. The New York criminal justice system looked to medical professionals such as Alexander Gettler, a famous toxicologist, to supplement their investigative work, developing a small force of professional medical examiners and appointing Dr. Charles Norris as the first chief medical examiner in 1918.

In this political cartoon (ca.1906), President Roosevelt scares up the "octopi" of the trusts: hard coal, beef, and Standard Oil. His administration used the Sherman Antitrust Act of 1890 against monopolies that were deemed dishonest or harmful to public interests.

The forensic fields that grew the most quickly were based on observation and comparison of evidence to collected standards. Questioned document examination grew rapidly and played a role at various stages of the criminal justice system. In the 1900 Rice–Jones case, a key piece of prosecutive evidence, the identification of forgery of a will by a professional document examiner, led to the conviction of New York attorney James Baker and valet Charles Jones in the murder of Jones's boss, William Marsh Rice, a wealthy New Yorker. Advances in the application of discoveries in chemistry and biology, especially related to identifying and understanding physical evidence, awaited further developments in those scientific fields. For example, blood could be identified as animal or human, but typing that blood awaited more research in medical science before it was of use to forensic investigation. Still, the criminal justice system eagerly awaited such advances and soon began investigations to further the field. In 1919, Edward Oscar Heinrich (1881–1953), a Wisconsin-born chemical engineer, set up the first forensic science laboratory at the University of California, Berkeley, where he advanced research into the application of scientific practices into criminal investigations.

Private detective forces also continued to play a serious role in law enforcement investigations. Although their employment in federal law enforcement was prescribed and they were usually unwelcome in state or municipal investigations, private companies often brought them on as a supplement to, or a correction of, other law enforcement forces. Often, this was in the role as security guard, such as the more than 10,000 railroad police who were employed through much of this period, or on a more ad hoc basis as strike breakers or labor spies. In other instances, however, they provided the investigative muscle needed to break cases, such as William Burns's role in solving the bombing of the *Los Angeles Times* building that killed 21 people and wounded hundreds more. With much controversy and allegations of illegal tactics, Burns obtained evidence of the role of several labor radicals in the bombing, who were later convicted on their own admissions of guilt. Burns's example also indicated the revolving door that existed between public and private investigative work as he started his career in the U.S. Secret Service, ventured out to form the William J. Burns Detective Agency in 1909 (which in 2001 merged with Pinkerton to become part of Securitas Security Services USA Inc., the largest security services provider in the world), and returned to lead the BOI later in life. He spent his last years writing detective stories based on his experiences.

Some historians have argued that, ultimately, the progressive attempt to reform law enforcement failed. Econometric historian Robert Fogelson suggested that the political machines were too difficult to break and that officers resented the progressives' interventions. Reformers were viewed by the police as individuals who knew little about police work and whose proposals for change were ill conceived. Finally, the reforms failed because the idea of policing could not be divorced from politics—that is, the character of big-city police was interconnected with policymaking agencies that helped to decide which laws were enforced, which public was served, and whose peace was kept. Separating the police completely from politics could not take place in this environment. Against this backdrop, there were changing standards for law enforcement officers, from selection to training and assignment. Further, the growing application of more scientific-based detection techniques and the public fascination with these methods suggest positive change.

Criminal Law and Legislation
From 1901 to 1920, significant changes in the U.S. legal system developed in several areas. Progressives sought to strengthen national laws in several areas, from antitrust regulation to the creation of new federal criminal jurisdictions under Congress's authority to regulate interstate commerce. Efforts to regulate public safety through laws that regulated food production or those that controlled the use of narcotics were also characteristic of the times. This approach culminated in the institution of Prohibition between 1919 and 1920, an event that would have serious consequences in the following decade. Finally, as police forces began to adopt new, scientific procedures for identifying and gathering evidence, the courts had to consider these new sources of evidence and their applicability to determining guilt or innocence in criminal trials.

Nor was the legal system without its critics. In September 1909, President William Howard Taft commented to a Chicago audience, "It is not too much to say that the administration of criminal law in this country is a disgrace to our civilization." Perennial criticisms of the U.S. criminal justice system were all made during the Progressive Era, such as the length of time it took to bring a criminal to trial and conviction; the overturning of convictions due to technicalities; problematic personnel in law enforcement, courts, and prisons; and the sentimentality Americans bore toward certain crimes and criminal types.

Sumptuary regulation also introduced or continued to imbue certain "victimless" crimes with criminal elements. Antidrug measures using criminal violations also featured prominently during this period. In 1906, Congress moved to strengthen poisoning laws regarding narcotics in the District of Columbia under "An act to regulate the practice of pharmacy and the sale of poisons in the District of Columbia, and for other purposes." The Pure Food and Drug Act of 1906 also strengthened the regulatory regime over a wide variety of foods and drugs by Congress in 1906, and required that nationwide, all nonprescription sales of cannabis be properly labeled. Various state laws followed, some aimed at food production and others at the sale and use of various narcotics and cannabinoids. In 1914, the Harrison Narcotics Act (38 Stat. 785) limited the ability of doctors to prescribe certain narcotics and led to some criminal charges against those who prescribed such drugs contrary to the law. The argument over this later regulation sometimes took on a racial overtone, as proponents argued that drugs were having a disparate impact on various ethnic groups.

The regulation of other vices through civil and criminal means was also tied to progressive political goals. The national antiprostitution law known as the White Slave Traffic Act outlawed the transportation of women across state lines for immoral purposes. Aimed at progressive fears that pimps and traffickers from cities were luring immigrant and rural women into lives of prostitution in American cities, Congress provided the newly created BOI with significant resources to enforce the new act. In practice, though, few examples of serious trafficking were detected, and the law came to be criticized for its political and racial enforcement. The use of the act to target black boxer Jack Johnson for dating white women (some of whom had engaged in prostitution) and Farley Caminetti, the son of Democratic politician Anthony Caminetti and his friend Maury Diggs (married men caught in a prostitution sting) suggested a political component to its enforcement. In the latter case, an appeal to the Supreme Court in *Caminetti et al. v. United States* (242 US 470) upheld the Mann Act. It remains, albeit in amended form, a part of federal criminal law.

Laws regulating revolutionary speech and action were also significant in the early 20th century. Spurred by the assassination of President William McKinley in 1901, municipalities and the federal government looked to security legislation. The state of New York passed a criminal anarchy statute in 1902, not long after McKinley's assassination in Buffalo. The NYPD took special interest in the issue. Earlier in 1914, it created the Bomb Squad under Inspector Thomas Tunney to investigate certain Black Hand crimes. Soon after the start of World War I in 1914, New York, the centerpoint of U.S. commerce with Europe, became the target of German sabotage operations. The purpose of Tunney's Bomb Squad was to conduct investigations to protect the neutrality of the United States and the safety and property of New York's businesses. Although this was clearly federal work, the U.S. government was conflicted on how to deal with German intrigue. There were few federal laws that addressed the issue, and as far as criminal law was concerned, the sabotage was a local matter. Tunney and his squad filled a significant gap until the United States entered the war and Congress crafted serious national security legislation. After the war, the squad turned its focus to the real and feared threats of anarchist violence.

In 1903, Congress passed an immigration law known as the Anarchist Exclusion Act. Although not a criminal statute, as it held alien anarchists excluded from emigration to the United States, its enforcement was executed by federal police forces. The following year, the Secret Service was legislatively tasked with protecting the president. The entry of the United States into World War I in 1917 led to the passage of a more broadly worded, antisubversive measure in the Espionage Act of 1917, and one of the most significant clashes over the scope of federal authority to police and punish revolutionary action versus the First Amendment guarantees of the U.S. Constitution. The context for these battles was stark: a nation rapidly mobilized for a war that quickly ended, leaving a wake of international revolution, worldwide economic dislocation, and a series of politically inspired terrorist attacks.

Leading radicals such as perennial Socialist Party presidential candidate Eugene Debs, socialist Charles Schenck, well-known anarchists Alexander Berkman (previously convicted for the attempted murder of a financial magnate) and Emma Goldman, and many others fell under legal jeopardy of such laws. Debs was convicted of his antiwar rhetoric and his appeals were denied. Goldman and Berkman were deported under the Anarchist Exclusion Act; other anarchists, such as Jacob Abrams, Mollie Steimer, and Hyman Lachowsky were similarly convicted, culminating in the forced deportation of hundreds of alien anarchists to Soviet Russia in 1919. The cases of each of these groups or individuals led to significant Supreme Court hearings that eventually upheld their convictions. The victory was pyrrhic, however, as the dissents laid the rhetorical and philosophical groundwork for the overturning of several precedents: *Abrams v. United States*, 250 US 616 (1919); *Schenck v. United States*, 249 US 47 (1919); *Debs v. United States*, 249 US 211 (1919); and *Goldman v. United States*, 245 US 474 (1918).

Although the general legal, political, and cultural forces of the day were against the anarchists and more radical (or at least vocal) of the socialists—the exception was the widespread nature of union-oriented economic protest that roiled the nation between 1919 and 1920—a number of prominent individuals and groups emerged to challenge the application of the Espionage Act and similar laws. A number of well-known, left-

Anarchist Selig Cohen (aka Selig Silverstein) lies in a pool of blood in New York City's Union Square moments after the bomb he was carrying exploded prematurely in his hand, killing a bystander on March 28, 1908, during a demonstration of unemployed people. Cohen later died. When questioned, Emma Goldman denied knowing Silverstein, but blamed it on a police plot. March 1908 was an active day for anarchist violence across the country.

leaning lawyers came together in early 1920 to form the National Popular Government League to challenge the validity of the Palmer Red Raids. Later that year, the American Civil Liberties Union was created to combat actions of the government that it thought tread on the civil liberties of Americans.

In 1919, the most significant change in U.S. criminal law was enacted: The Eighteenth Amendment to the Constitution was ratified and then actuated by the Volstead Act. Together, these laws created Prohibition, the failed, 14-year attempt to outlaw the manufacture and sale of alcohol.

Trial and Punishment
American approaches to punishment changed significantly over the first decades of the 20th century. Although the number of federal prisoners grew—three federal prisons were created a few years before the new century—it remained an insignificant part of the overall total. A second trend, the slow rise in the overall number of prisoners nationwide, was more important. The Justice Policy Institute noted that the number of U.S. prisoners increased by 11,665 between 1900 and 1910 and by 13,224 over the next decade. However, with increases in the general population upward of 40 percent over the same period, these absolute increases in prison population represent a decline in the per capita incarceration rate. Given the sharp rise in the U.S. population, this trend gives further credence to a steady or slightly declining crime rate overall, or at least the number of arrests made. This would significantly change with the onset of Prohibition following the Volstead Act.

New philosophies of crime were a significant contributor to these changes. To some extent, progressive thought looked to the perfectibility of human nature, and reforms in criminal justice mirrored this. Prison reformers began to seek a rehabilitation model in many places, even as older models continued in others. These reformers looked away from punishment and pressed for innovative approaches to imprisonment such as parole, probation, and indeterminate sentencing—efforts that considered each potential prisoner as an individual who could be changed. Prison reform was such a popular approach that it explicitly entered the 1916 platform of the Democrat Party and was implicitly accepted in the Republican platform as the party argued that pursuing regulatory crimes of business was important, but should not be used to generally punish business. These prison reforms and even political stances set the tone for prison theory for much of the 20th century.

Progressive reformers also sought to challenge the treatment of juveniles as adults, the practice of leasing convict labor, and the abuses associated with chain gangs and work farms. Such practices were most closely associated with the criminal justice systems of the southern states. At the turn of the century, for example, Florida incarcerated 778 state convicts in 13 camps. These convicts were then leased out on contract for the hazardous job of harvesting materials used to make turpentine or phosphate. Several of these operations were investigated by the Department of Justice under federal anti-peonage laws, but few successful cases developed, despite serious investigative work by federal agents. Still, over the next several years, public pressure over the issue led to a significant reduction in chain gang practices, the ending of private hiring of convict labor, and the institution of prison-based and operated labor. The state of Mississippi found a way to deal with the end of the convict leasing system by opening Parchman Farm in 1901, a large-scale, plantation-style prison labor farm that by 1917 was divided into 12 camps (one for women).

Although the practice of considering probation and parole for convicts varied widely from state to state, the general adoption of both was a trend throughout the first decades of the 20th century. In some states, the bureaucratic apparatus for probation and parole matters were combined; in others, they were monitored separately, with courts considering issues of probation and another institution weighing the justification for parole. Massachusetts developed the first state system of probation in the 1880s and remained a pioneer in corrections reform through the early decades of the 20th century. California followed in 1903, and in New York, the State Probation Commission was created in 1907 to coordinate probation. In 1917, a State Division of Probation was established within the New York State Department of Corrections. Parole was equally important; for example, the 1910 biennial report of the Kansas State Penitentiary noted that the institution of parole in Kansas law two years earlier "is one of the greatest forward steps in prison law." By 1920, almost half of the states had adopted a statewide system of probation. The federal government adopted a similar practice of authorizing judges to consider probation and parole matters in the late 1920s.

Another significant change in prison matters was the beginning of efforts to remove juveniles from the regular criminal justice system, another social justice effort heavily supported by women's groups. Prior to the 20th century, children as young as 7 years of age could be treated within the adult criminal justice system. Although the first juvenile court systems were set up in 1899, the idea of separating errant youth from hardened criminals emerged from changing ideas of childhood, education, and punishment. The juvenile judge was to look on the child not as a criminal, but as a delinquent needing fostering care by the state. Reform schools and juvenile detention facilities were set up to institute these new theories aimed at rehabilitation of the offender and protection of the delinquent.

Although this progress generally held true for juvenile males in the criminal justice system, there were some differences in the treatment of young women. The majority of criminals and delinquents were men, who were much more likely to commit property or violent crimes, usually against a spouse, family member, or other close social connection. Women more often came into the criminal justice system on suspicion of moral charges, prostitution, drunkenness, disorderly conduct and, in some cases, "female precociousness," a euphemism for a woman perceived to be sexually advanced for her age. Incarceration could occur in either a state prison facility, usually reserved for more serious felonies; a municipal organization such as a city workhouse; or a privately run organization such as New York's Magdalen House or a halfway house run by a religious or other charitable organization. The latter was typically for those convicted of misdemeanors. Over time, prostitution offenses increased in reaction to the effort to halt "white slave traffic," and fines gave way to periods of confinement in some type of arrangement. In all, the system tended to be more paternalistic to young women (in some cases to the age of 35) than similarly aged men and boys.

Conclusion
By the end of the decade, criminal justice reformers looked back on their work and considered their successes and failures. Political scientist Raymond Fosdick wrote in his 1921 book *American Police Systems* that "American police do not favorably compare to European ones—in re local pride and public confidence in police, detailed training given to police, and care in shielding police from politics … but if one looks at how far things have come in 20, 40 years, there is substantial basis for encouragement." This, however, is a view from the front lines. Looking back at the changes over the first 20 years of the new century, there is evidence of significant changes in police structure, training, practices, and scope of work. Efforts to humanely deal with prisoners achieved national attention, and such pressure ensured an impact. Advances in

communication, transportation, and significant population growth meant newer and larger challenges, which the American criminal justice system met with innovation and change. Problems remained, especially concerning the extension of reasonable protections of constitutional liberties, the blight of racial segregation and injustice in the system, and other smaller problems, but the terms of debate had been set for much of the rest of the century.

John F. Fox, Jr.
Federal Bureau of Investigation

New York Times Article on the Murder of Stanford White

Manhattan architect Stanford White was murdered on June 25 by Harry Thaw, the millionaire husband of Evelyn Nesbit. White and Nesbit had a brief relationship five years earlier, in which she lost her virginity. Nesbit later married Thaw, but only after turning down his proposal repeatedly and telling him all about White. Thaw's mother offered Nesbit $1 million if she would testify that White had raped her. The resulting "trial of the century" was the basis for the 1955 movie The Girl in the Red Velvet Swing.

Thaw Murders Stanford White

Shoots Him on the Madison Square Garden Roof

ABOUT EVELYN NESBIT

"He Ruined My Wife,"
Witness Says He Said,

AUDIENCE IN A PANIC

Chairs and Tables Are Overturned in a Wild Scramble for the Exits

June 26—Harry Kendall Thaw of Pittsburg, husband of Florence Evelyn Nesbit, former actress and artist's model, shot and killed Stanford White, the architect, on the roof of Madison Square Garden at 11:05 o'clock last night, just as the first performance of the musical comedy "Mamzelle Champagne" was drawing to a close. Thaw, who is a brother of the Countess of Yarmouth and a member of a well known and wealthy family, left his seat near the stage, passed between a number of tables, and, in full view of the players and of scores of persons, shot White through the head. Mr. White was the designer of the building on the roof of which he was killed. He it was who put Miss Nesbit, Mrs. Thaw, on the stage.

Thaw, who was in evening clothes, had evidently been waiting for Mr. Whit's appearance. The latter entered the Garden at 10:55 and took a sear at a table five rows from the stage. He rested his chin in his right hand and seemed lost in contemplation.

Thaw had a pistol concealed under his coat. His face was deathly white. According to A. L. Belstone, who sat near, White must have seen Thaw approaching. But he made no move. Thaw placed the pistol almost against the head of the sitting man and fired three shots in quick succession.

Body Fell to the Floor

White's elbow slid from the table, the table crashed over, sending a glass clinking along with the heavier sound. The body then tumbled from the chair.

On the stage one of the characters was singing a song entitled "I Could Love a Million Girls." The refrain seemed to freeze upon his lips. There was dead silence for a second, and then Thaw lifted his pistol over his head, the barrel hanging downward, as if to show the audience that he was not going to harm any one else.

With a firm stride, Thaw started for the exit, holding his pistol as if anxious to have some one take it from his hand. Then came the realization on the part of the audience that the farce had closed with a tragedy. A woman jumped to her feet and screamed. Many persons followed her example, and there was wild excitement.

L. Lawrence, the manager of the show, jumped on a table and above the uproar commanded the show to go on.

"Go on playing!" he shouted. "Bring on that chorus!"

Girls Too Terrified to Sing

The musicians made a feeble effort at gathering their wits and playing the chorus music, but the girls who romped on the stage were paralyzed with horror, and it was impossible to bring the performance to an orderly close.

Then the manager shouted for quiet, and he informed the audience that a serious accident had happened, and begged the people to move out of the place quietly.

In the meanwhile Thaw had reached the entrance to the elevators. On duty there was Fireman Paul Broodin. He took the pistol from Thaw's hand, but did not attempt to arrest him. Policeman Debes of the Tenderloin Station appeared and seized his arm.

"He deserved it," Thaw said to the policeman. "I can prove it. He ruined my life and then deserted the girl." Another witness said the word was "wife" instead of "life."

A Woman Kissed Thaw

Just as the policeman started into the elevator with Thaw a woman described as dark-haired and short of stature reached up to him and kissed him on the cheek. This woman some witnesses declare was Mrs. Thaw.

The crowd was then scrambling wildly for the elevators and stairs. The employees of the Garden who knew Thaw, and nearly all of them did, as he visited the place often, did not seem greatly surprised at the tragedy. When Thaw entered the Garden in the early part of the show he seemed greatly agitated. He strolled from one part of the place to another, and finally took a seat in a little niche near the stage.

He was half hidden from the audience, but could see any one who might enter. It is believed that he knew just where White would sit, and had picked out this place in order to get at him without interference.

Henry Rogers of 222 Henry Street was seated at the table next to the one at which White was sitting when he was killed. He says that Thaw fired when the muzzle of his pistol was only a few inches from White's temple.

Another witness said that after firing three shots and looking at White as if to be sure that he was stone dead, Thaw uttered a curse and added:

"You'll never go out with that woman again."

A Woman Sat Near White

At another table adjoining that at which White was killed sat a woman dressed in white. It was believed for a time that she was a companion of White's and it was reported that she leaned over and kissed the face of the dead man, but this could not be verified, and it is positive that White was alone when he entered the Garden.

Some one in the audience hurried to the fallen man to see if assistance was needed. A great pool of blood had quickly formed on the floor. The tables had been pulled back and in the bright glare of thousands of electric lights it was quickly seen that White was beyond any earthly help.

A number of the actors and actresses left the stage, and away from the calcium and the footlights their painted faces showed strangely in the group of employees and friends of Thaw and the dead man which formed as the last of the audience left.

Thought it a Stage Trick

Two of them said that the reason the fright of the audience was not worse when the shots rang out was that just before the tragedy a dialogue concerning a burlesque duel had been carried on by two of the characters, and many people thought that the old trick of playing in the audience had been tried again.

As the lights of the Garden were dimmed, the body of White was straightened out, the arms brought to the sides, and the lets placed together. A sheet was obtained in one of the dressing rooms, and this was stretched over it.

While all of this was going on, Policeman Debes and his prisoner had reached the street entrance. Thaw never once lost his composure. His linen and his evening suit showed no signs of ruffling. Only the paleness of his face showed that anything had happened to excite him.

Wanted Mr. Carnegie to Know

"Here's a bill, officer," he said to the policeman before he started for the station. "Get Carnegie on the telephone and ell him that I'm in trouble."

The policeman and prisoner then walked through the crowd to Fifth Avenue, up the avenue to Thirtieth Street. As they turned the corner at the Holland House a number of cabmen who knew Thaw tipped their hats to him and he recognized their salute in return.

The trip up Thirtieth Street, across Broadway and Sixth Avenue, was without any excitement, and the prisoner reached the station without the usual crowd of curious people following.

Thaw did not seem to be intoxicated, but walked in a sort of daze. He made few comments on the way to the Tenderloin Station. Sergt. McCarthy asked him what his name was, and he answered:

"John Smith, 18 Lafayette Square, Philadelphia."

"What's your business?" he was asked.

"I am a student."

No charge was made on the books against this "John Smith." The detectives were sent out to investigate fully before a charge was made. Sergt. McCarthy asked him:

"Why did you do this?"

"I can't say," he replied apathetically.

Cards found on the prisoner read "Harry Kendall Thaw, Pittsburg." He made no comment when they were pulled out of his pocketbook.

Thaw Sent for Two Friends
Young Thaw walked dazedly to the back room. He waited a while, and then sent for Frederick W. Lowenfellow and Frederick Delafield. The reporters asked him to make a statement. He refused to do it.

Young Thaw had lighted a cigarette while he stood in front of the Sergeant's desk. In the back room he sat on a long bench that is used by reserves between two big policemen. He pushed his hat back on his head, stretched out his feet, and lit another cigarette. His eyes had a far-away look.

A number of his friends hurried over to the station to talk with the prisoner, but they were not allowed to see him. William Thaw, a brother of his who is stopping at the Holland House, had not been to see him up to nearly 3 o'clock.

When the detectives put on the case had brought in the witnesses and they had been examined in Capt. Hodgins's room, Thaw was charged with homicide and was locked in a cell.

The following witnesses were detained until the arrival of Coroner Dooley: Paul Brodin, a fireman, 698 Prospect Avenue, the Bronx; Lionel Lawrence, manager of the company playing at the Madison Square Roof Garden, 325 West Forty-second Street; Harry Silverstein, Marvin Pincher, 84 West Thirteenth Street; Warren Paxsen, 146 East Twentieth Street; Edward Carney, 467 Second Avenue.

Thaw Not Ready to Talk

Coroner Dooley reached the Tenderloin Station at 1:30 this morning and asked to see the prisoner. Thaw had sent the doorman out to buy him some cigars. He was smoking and seemed calm when the Coroner entered.

"Have you any statement to make to me?" the Coroner asked after he had made himself known.

"I don't care to make any statement now," Thaw replied. "I would appreciate it if you would tell Burr McIntosh or ex-judge Hornblower or Joseph H. Choate of what has happened."

"Mr. McIntosh is upstairs," he was told. "Do you want to see him?"

"No," he replied, "just tell him to call up Mr. Hornblower or Mr. Choate. Tell him not to call up Mr. Choate until morning. I would not like to get him out of bed."

Mr. Choate is at Stockbridge, Mass.

Mr. McIntosh took the message and left the station.

Coroner Dooley said that he found Thaw in good mental condition. He added that he believed the murder was done through jealousy.

When Thaw was searched in the station, $125 in paper money, $2.36 in coin, two silk handkerchiefs, two gold pencils, a gold watch, and a little pocket combination mirror case were found. These were taken by the Sergeant.

Mrs. White at St. James, L. I.
Mrs. Lizzie Hanlon, housekeeper for Mr. White at his residence, 121 East Twenty-first

Street, had not heard of the shooting when a reporter from The Times called shortly before midnight. She expressed the utmost horror, and could suggest no explanation.

The house is one of the most magnificently decorated in the city. Standing amid elaborate Italian decorations with carved marble and graceful fountains on every hand, Mrs. Hanlon gave what information she could. She said:

"Mr. White has been alone in the house for some time. Mrs. White has been away in the West for about three weeks or a month, but is now at her country residence at St. James, L. I.

"Lawrence White, Mr. White's son, came down from Harvard the other day. Both he and his father came in and dressed for dinner to-night, but they did not go out together, Mr. White leaving alone a few minutes before his son. I do not know where either of them went."

"Has Mr. Thaw been to the house to see Mr. White recently?" Mrs. Hanlon was asked.

"Mr. Thaw? I never heard of him. As far as I know Mr. White did not have any visitors here to-day."

Young White, with a friend, Leroy King, dined with his father last night at the Café Martin. Mr. White, his son says, was in the best of spirits and said nothing about any trouble.

After the dinner the party entered an electric automobile and went up to the New Amsterdam roof garden. There the two boys asked the elder White to stay and see the performance.

He said: "No, I thank you," adding that he was going elsewhere.

That was the last they saw of him.

Meant to Go to Philadelphia
Lawrence White says his father was thinking of going to Philadelphia last evening on a matter of business, and intended to up to the last possible moment, and only changed his plans in order to dine with the boys, who had just come down from Harvard.

"If he had only gone!" exclaimed the son in his grief.

Lawrence White said he had never seen Harry Thaw in his life and had never heard his father speak of him, and that he knew of absolutely nothing that could lead to such a tragedy. He was then informed that his father was dead and that the body was still...Garden. He departed for that ....ce at one.

Only One Bullet in Head
After the body was taken to the undertaker's a hasty examination was made. Three wounds were found. The fatal bullet entered the left eye. The other two bullets grazed the shoulders, leaving a flesh wound on each. The top of the head showed a mark, this having been caused by striking the edge of the table as the body fell to the floor.

By a strange coincidence White and Thaw and his wife dined at the Café Martin last night. With White was his son, Lawrence, and Leroy King, a friend. This party had a table on the porch.

Inside the café Thaw dined with his wife and his father-in-law. At no time of the evening did the two parties meet. Both White and Thaw were well known by the employees, and when the news of the tragedy was being told over the tables by the after-theatre patrons this coincidence was recalled.

Detectives Look for Mrs. Thaw
Mr. and Mrs. Thaw have been stopping at the Lorraine, Fifth Avenue and Fourth-fifth Street. Detectives were sent there to get a her as a witness, but she had not returned by 3 o'clock this morning.

At that hour Policeman Debes, who arrested Thaw gave this account of what happened:

I was on post at Twenty-sixth Street and Madison Avenue last night, and asked the manager of the Garden if there would be any shooting in the show. I did this because the use of firearms at Hammerstein's last week made me hurry and scurry for awhile, thinking the shooting was done on the street. he told me there was not.

"I heard three pistol shots and started for the Garden. I met the electrician of the place, who was on the run. He said that a man and a woman had been shot in the audience. I hurried upstairs and the first I saw was a woman who had fainted. Then I found Thaw with the firearm. I asked him if he had shot the man whose body I could see by the table?

""Yes," Thaw replied.

"Then he added that the man had ruined his life—or wife—I could not distinctly make out.

"Is he dead?'" he asked.

"I told him he was.

"'Well, I made a good job of it and I'm glad.' he added. Then a woman, who Manager Lawrence told me was Mrs. Thaw, ran up and embraced him and kissed him.

"'I didn't think you would do it in this way, she said. He whispered to her, patted her on the shoulder, and said that it would all come out all right.

"When we go to the street a number of women shook hands with the prisoner and sympathized with him. Some wanted to know why he had killed White but he did not answer."

A dispatch from Pittsburg last night said that Thaw and his wife were to have sailed for Europe to-morrow.

Mrs. William Than, mother of Mr. Thaw, sailed for London on the Atlantic Transport liner Minneapolis last Saturday. She is on her way to visit her daughter, the Countess of Yarmouth, who was Miss Alice Thaw.

WHAT WITNESSES SAY.

One Man Is Sure That Thaw's
Wife Was There

An eye witness thus described the shooting of Stanford White by Harry Thaw:

"Mr. Thaw had seats of the Twenty-sixth Street side of the theatre, down near the stage. A woman was near him. Thaw got up several times in the evening and walked around in the space in front of the stage.

"Mr. White entered about 11 o'clock. He had a little talk with Manager Stephens of the roof garden, and I heard him say to Mr. Stephens that he had just left the Manhattan Club. Mr. White took a seat just a few tables from Thaw. I saw Thaw walk up to Mr. White, say a word or two to him, and then pull a small pistol for his pocket and shoot him three times.

"The wounded man dropped off this chair, tilting the table as he fell. The audience did not go into hysterics right away. One reason for that, I take it, was that Fuller Spice and Gustavus K. Hicks, two of the characters in the play, had just been having a dueling dialogue, and at the time of the shooting Spice was on stage with six chorus girls. The audience seemed to think that the shooting was in the play.

"After a moment or two several women near Mr. White's table began to get hysterical. The orchestra seemed to have known what had taken place because of their proximity, but that tried desperately to keep the lively tune going. Now and then it would bread, and the audience would shout, 'Go on, go on! What's the matter there?'

"The orchestra braced up several times, but the tune kept hitching more and more until finally it trailed off pitifully. By that time the audience seemed to know what had happened."

Still another man who was at the show said he was sure that the woman who rushed up to Thaw after the shooting was Mrs. Thaw. He added:

"As Mrs. Thaw passed the body of White, she turned to me and said:

"'Is he dead?'

"I answered, 'Yes.'

"She cried: 'My God, Harry, you've killed him.'

"Thaw said, 'Kiss me, dear, before I go down stairs.

"That again said, 'Kiss me, dear.'

"Once more his wife threw her arms about him and kissed him.

"I never saw a face more full of agony as she turned around.

"Then a policeman came and Thaw went down in the elevator."

"The show as going along nicely, it was 'Mamzelle Champagne,' and my attention was on the stage until I noticed a strange-looking fellow who walked about in a nervous sort of way. His throat was muffled up, and it appeared to me that he was a man who seemed on the verge of delirium tremens. I said to the man friend who was with me that the fellow who was muffled up was either a prizefighter or an athlete in training, but when he came near us I saw that he was wildly excited.

"He muttered to himself several times and paced up and down the floor, turning now and then to see who was near him, as if he thought he was being followed. As he passed toward the rear of the place a woman near the man who was shot later leaned forward and whispered something. I t seemed to me that she was afraid of somebody or something.

"A waiter came along and I called his attention to the muffled man, remarking that he seemed foolish. The waiter said he had noticed the fellow around all evening and that something was wrong with him.

"Just then the fellow walked over to the side of the building where the tables were and craned his neck forward as if he suddenly spied the person he was looking for, and quickened his pace.

"'That fellow's going to grab somebody,' I said, turning to my companion, and when I again looked in the direction of the fellow I saw him with pistol in hand and pointing it downward at the man the table near by. Then he fired.

"Immediately after the shooting leaned forward and said something to the woman. It sounded like 'It's all right, don't worry. I'm not sorry I did it.'

"That settled the show. All about women were frantically pleading with their escorts to take them out of the place and into the street, but the escorts couldn't find a way out so easily.

"The woman who was sitting near the man who was shot evidently had lots of friends near at hand, for they got her away quickly. I think they took her behind the stage, for I saw a man leading her back.

"As that man who did the shooting had his neck muffled up, it seemed to me that he was trying to disguise himself while preparing to kill the other man.

Source: *New York Times* (June 26, 1906)

See Also: History of Crime and Punishment in America, 1900–1950; Murder, History of; New York City; Witness Testimony.

1909 PRIMARY DOCUMENT

The Department of Justice Creates the Bureau of Investigation

The Department of Justice's Bureau of Investigation was created to fill the need for federal criminal investigators. The 1887 Interstate Commerce Act had made the federal government responsible for interstate law enforcement, but Congress forbade the Department of Justice to use Treasury Department agents as investigators, resulting in the Bureau of Investigation. Its first project was investigating prostitution to enforce the Mann Act passed in 1910. In 1935, the FBI was made an independent bureau within the Department of Justice and acquired its modern name.

ORDER ESTABLISHING BUREAU OF INVESTIGATION OF THE DEPARTMENT OF JUSTICE

For the purpose of facilitating the investigation work under this Department, the office of the Chief Examiner shall hereafter be called the Bureau of Investigation, and the Chief Examiner is hereby authorized and designated to act as the Chief of the said Bureau, and as such shall have supervision over the work of all persons whose compensation or expenses are paid from the appropriation "Miscellaneous Expenses, United States Courts," or the appropriation "Detection and Prosecution of Crimes, "and who are employed for the purpose of collecting evidence or of making investigations or examinations of any kind for this Department or the officers thereof.

George W. Wickersham,
Attorney General
Department of Justice
Washington 25, D.C.
March 16, 1909

Source: FBI FOIA, March 16, 1909

See Articles: Federal Bureau of Investigation; Justice, Department of.

1909 PRIMARY DOCUMENT

"Lynching: A National Crime" Speech by Ida B. Wells-Barnett

African American journalist Ida Wells-Barnett (1862–1931) was active both in the women's suffrage movement and the early civil rights movement. Her campaign against lynching, a practice that had become rampant in the 1890s and would soon be glorified in the 1915 film Birth of a Nation, *brought her on a speaking tour of the United States and Europe. During a European tour, she clashed with suffragist Frances Willard, who had made numerous racist comments in her lectures on suffrage and temperance.*

The lynching record for a quarter of a century merits the thoughtful study of the American people. It presents three salient facts: First, lynching is a colorline murder. Second, crimes against women is the excuse, not the cause. Third, it is a national crime and requires a national remedy.

Proof that lynching follows the color line is to be found in the statistics which have been kept for the past twenty-five years. During the few years preceding this period and while frontier law existed, the executions showed a majority of white victims. Later, however, as law courts and authorized judiciary extended into the far West, lynch law rapidly abated, and its white victims became few and far between.

Just as the lynch law regime came to a close in the West, a new mob movement started in the South. This was wholly political, its purpose being to suppress the colored vote by intimidation and murder. Thousands of assassins, banded together under the name of Ku Klux Klans, "Midnight Raiders," etc., spread a reign of terror by beating, shooting and killing colored people by the thousands. In a few years, the purpose was accomplished and the black vote was suppressed. But mob murder continued.

From 1882, when 52 were lynched, down to the present, lynching has been along the color line. Statistics show that 3,284 men, women and children have been put to death in this quarter of a century….

During the last ten years, from 1899 to 1908 inclusive, the number lynched was 959. Of this number, 102 were white, while the colored victims numbered 857. No other nation, civilized or savage, burns its criminals; only under that Stars and Stripes is the human holocaust possible. Twenty-eight human beings burned at the stake, one of them a woman and two of them children, is the awful indictment against American civilization-the gruesome tribute which the nation pays to the color line.

Why is mob murder permitted by a Christian nation? What is the cause of this awful slaughter? This question is answered almost daily: always the same shameless falsehood that "Negroes are lynched to protect womanhood." Standing before a Chautauqua assemblage, John Temple Graves, al once champion of lynching and apologist for lynchers, said, "The mob stand! today as the most potential bulwark between the women of the South and such a carnival of crime as would infuriate the world and precipitate the annihilation of the Negro race." This is the never-varying answer of lyncher! and their apologists. All know that it is untrue. The cowardly lyncher revels it murder, then seeks to shield himself from public execration by claiming devotion to woman. But truth is mighty and the lynching record discloses the hypocrisy of the lyncher as well as his crime. …

Is there a remedy, or will the nation confess that it cannot protect its protectors at home as well as abroad? Various remedies have been suggested to abolish the lynching infamy, but year after year, the butchery of men, women, and children continues in spite of plea and protest. Education is suggested as a preventive, but it is as grave a crime to murder an ignorant man as it is a scholar. True, few educated men have been lynched, but the hue and cry once started stops at no bounds, as was clearly shown by the lynchings in Atlanta, and in Springfield, Illinois.

Agitation, though helpful, will not alone stop the crime. Year after year statistics are published, meetings are held, resolutions are adopted. And yet lynchings go on...

The only certain remedy is an appeal to law. Lawbreakers must be made to know that human life is sacred and that every citizen of this country is first a citizen of the United States and secondly a citizen of the state in which he belongs. This nation must assert itself and protect its federal citizenship at home as well as abroad. The strong men of the government must reach across state lines whenever unbridled lawlessness defies state laws, and must give to the individual under the Stars and Stripes the same measure of protection it gives to him when he travels in foreign lands. Federal protection of American citizenship is the remedy for lynching. ...

In a multitude of counsel there is wisdom. Upon the grave question presented by the slaughter of innocent men, women, and children there should be an honest, courageous conference of patriotic, law-abiding citizens anxious to punish crime promptly, impartially, and by due process of law, also to make life, liberty, and property secure against mob rule.

Time was when lynching appeared to be sectional, but now it is national-a blight upon our nation, mocking our laws and disgracing our Christianity. "With malice toward none but with charity for all," let us undertake the work of making the "law of the land" effective and supreme upon every foot of American soil-a shield to the innocent; and to the guilty, punishment swift and sure.

Source: http://patriotpost.us/document/lynching-a-national-crime

See Articles: Hanging, Lynchings; Race-Based Crimes; Racism.

1911 PRIMARY DOCUMENT

New York Times Article on the Triangle Shirtwaist Fire

The 1911 fire at the Triangle Shirtwaist Factory is the third-deadliest disaster in New York history, after the 9/11 attacks and the 1904 steamboat fire. During the blaze, 146 workers died, most of them young, recent immigrants. Many of those who died were trapped on the highest floors because the doors to the stairwells had been locked—not because of the fire, but instead to prevent unauthorized breaks from work. The owners were acquitted of manslaughter but lost a civil suit for a small amount of damages.

DEATH LIST IS 141; ONLY 86 IDENTIFIED

But Several More of the Injured in the Hospital are Expected to Succumb.

22 BEYOND RECOGNITION

Thirteen of the Dead Were Men—All the Rest Women—the Coroner's Summary.

March 27—When all the bodies of the victims of Saturday's fire had been counted, recounted, and checked by officials of the Coroner's office Coroner Holtzhauser made official announcement last night that the total number of the dead was 141.

Of this number 133 were found at the scene of the fire, either out on the sidewalk or huddled on the ninth floor of the factory building. Three died of their injuries in Bellevue Hospital, there in St. Vincent's Hospital, and two in New York Hospital. The total number identified at midnight was seventy-eight at the Morgue; eight dead in hospitals.

The unidentified still number 33. Of these 28 are women and 5 men. The other bodies are hopelessly charred and probably never will be identified. The total number of women who lost their lives in the fire, according to the Coroner's figures, is 128; the number of men is 13.

FIVE DYING IN HOSPITALS

Seven Others Who Are Less Badly Injured Being Cared For.

At the hospitals to which the victims of the Triangle waist fire were taken, it was stated last night that at least five more will probably die. The total number of survivors at the hospitals last night was twelve.

Three women who are in St. Vincent's Hospital are believed to be hopelessly injured. They are Sarah Kupla, 18, of 1,503 Webster Avenue, Bronx; Esther Harris, 21, of 131 Chester Street, Brooklyn, whose back is broken, and Annie Miller, 17, of 154 Attorney Street, who has a fractured leg and internal injuries. Five others at this hospital are expected to recover.

In the New York Hospital are Freda Valakowsky, 20 years old, of 639 East Twelfth Street, with a fractured leg and internal injuries, and Mrs. Daisy Fitze, of 11 Charlton Street, who has a compound fracture of the pelvic bone. Neither of these is likely to recover.

To these hospitals, as well as to Bellevue, where there were two survivors last night, crowds of relatives and friends of the injured and others who had been searching for hours without success for some one known to be in the building when the fire occurred and not accounted for, steadily streamed yesterday. If the physicians decided that the injured were strong enough to be seen the rules of the institutions were suspended for these visitors. Most of those in the hospitals received their injuries by jumping from the windows.

Freda Valakowsky graphically described to the attendants at the hospital her struggle to escape from the building. She remembered being pushed toward the window ledge by the frenzied girls and finally jumped from the window sill. The story told by Mrs. Fitze varied little.

One of the most pathetic scenes was the identification by her brother Louis of the body of Becky Nerberer of 19 Clinton street, at the New York hospital. Nerberer had inquired at the hospital Saturday night about his sister's condition and was told that she had a chance to live.

He returned at 3 o'clock yesterday morning and found her dead. He was so crazed with grief that attendants had to hold him. He said that his parents were expected to arrive in this country from Russia within a few weeks, and that passage money had been sent to them from his savings.

Prof. Sommer Tells of the Heroic Work They Did at the Fire.

Refusing to admit that he had played the role of a hero at the fire disaster of Saturday, as was reported in the press, Prof. Frank H. Sommer of the New York University Law School, which adjoins the ill-fated loft building, said yesterday at his home, 156 Heller Parkway, Newark, that the lion's share of credit belonged to the students of his class.

"All I can say is that I have been through it," Prof. Sommer continued. "It is too horrible to recount. Even if I should try, words would fail me."

At the time the fire started, Prof. Sommer was delivering a lecture to his class. When he saw the seriousness of the situation, he directed them in the work of rescuing fifty girls from the burning structure. He said that the Law School Building caught fire, but its occupants were in no danger except that to which they exposed themselves to save those begging to be taken from the building that was fast becoming a roaring furnace.

"After such an experience the mind is dazed," continued Prof. Sommer. "The recollection of it comes back in flashes and piecemeal. I remember it was about 5 o'clock. I was lecturing to a class of about fifty boys. All was quiet and serene, when suddenly we heard the toot of whistles and the sound of gongs and fire engines. I threw open the door of the lecture room, and then the door of the Law School Faculty room, which opens on an areaway separating our building from the burning one.

"Some of the boys followed me, and we saw the ten-story building across the areaway was on fire. The open space between us and that building was filled with smoke. There were ear-piercing shrieks, and girls appeared at the windows of the lofts in which was the waist factory.

"We hurried to the roof of our building, where two ladders had been left by painters, and the boys used these in the work of rescue. They worked like beavers, apparently never giving a thought to the possibility that their own building might catch fire from the flames that were leaping out into the open space.

"How it was done I don't know, but in surprisingly short time about fifty girls were brought across the ladders to safety. The boys paid no attention to the thick smoke and risked life and limb to steady the terror-stricken girls on the ladders. Some of the rescued were pitiable sights. In some cases it was necessary to beat out the flames that had caught their clothing, and many of them had blackened faces and singed hair and eyebrows.

"But our heroes were not ready to desert even after they had all of the girls in places of safety. They manned the standpipe and hose in our building and did efficient work, and other ran out to get the firemen to come in and save our property. As it was, the flames swept across the areaway, cracked the plate glass in our windows, and set fire to several of the rooms. Many books, papers, and documents were lugged out of the building by the volunteer workers."

SAVED HER FRIEND'S LIFE.

Survivor Tells of a Heroic Deed in the Mad Rush to Escape.

Annie Sprinsock of 501 Pennsylvania Avenue, East New York, told yesterday at her home a thrilling story of her escape. She was employed on the eighth floor, and as soon as the alarm was given ran to the dressing-room and snatched up her street clothes. When she got to the elevator shaft she remembered that she had left on the table of the dressing room her bag containing her week's wages, $8. She ran for it but could not find it.

As she reached the elevator shaft again the car was about to make its last trip. She just managed to squeeze aboard, the last of those that could find room. As the door was being jammed-to a friend called wildly to her not to desert her. She took the girl in her arms and by main force raised her above the heads of the others in the car. There she held her till the car reached the ground floor in safety.

Esther Harris of 131 Hester Street, East New York, was less fortunate, but managed to make her escape. As she reached the elevator the last trip of the car was over. In her despair she caught hold of the elevator cables and slid down those to safety. She was injured in the descent and is now in a hospital.

Abraham Robinowitz was one of those who jumped from the eighth floor only to be crushed to pieces in the street. He was to have been married next week to Miss Minnie Greenberg of 369 Watkins Street, and it was she who identified his body. Mary Leventhal was a bookkeeper in the factory, and nothing has been seen of her since the fire. Her father and mother and two little sisters, who live at 604 Sutter Avenue, East New York, are nearly beside themselves with grief.

Source: http://www.pbs.org/wgbh/american experience/features/primary-resources/triangle-death-list

See Articles: Children's Rights; New York City; Witness Testimony.

1912
PRIMARY DOCUMENT

New York Times Article on Law Creating Shorter Factory Working Hours

Labor organizations had been advocating shorter work weeks for decades (and had made some

progress from the mid-19th century extremes), and progressives had been attempting to reform child labor laws. In 1904, the National Child Labor Committee formed with the goal of eliminating child labor altogether. The Triangle Shirtwaist Factory fire helped bring public attention to these causes, especially since so many of the dead were women and teenagers, the only beneficiaries of the law reported on in this article.

SHORTER FACTORY HOURS

Law Forbids Working Women and Boys
More Than 54 Hours a Week

The law limiting the hours of employment in factories for women and boys under 18 years to fifty-four hours a week went into effect at 12 o'clock last night. This will affect more than 300,000 women, nearly two-thirds of whom are employed in New York City.

This amendment to the State labor laws was a result of the agitation that followed the Triangle shirtwaist factory fire. It permits women and boys to be employed overtime for one hour a day, provided that the total hours a week do not exceed fifty-four. A factory may employ women ten hours a day for five days, provided it does not keep them at work longer than four hours on the sixth day. Work by women and children on the seventh day is absolutely prohibited.

Canning factories are exempt from the operation of this law between June 15 and Oct. 15. Between those dates the present law, which permits the employment of women sixty hours a week, is allowed to remain in force in canneries.

The only protest which the State Labor Department has received from the manufacturers has come from candymakers. They have engaged Alfred J. Tolley as counsel and intend to attack the constitutionality of the law. They will make the plea that the exemption of canneries for a period of the year is an unjust discrimination and invalidates the entire law.

The new act further provides that women and children shall not be employed before 6 o'clock in the morning or after 9 o'clock at night. As there is a question whether the Legislature has the constitutional right to restrict the hours of labor for a woman more than 21, the law is so worded that it will apply to women under 21 even if the regulation is not upheld by the courts in regard to older women. This provision reads as follows:

No female minor under the age of 21 years, and no woman shall be employed or permitted to work in any factory in this State before 6 o'clock in the morning or after 9 o'clock in the evening.

The act of the Legislature prohibits the employment in factories of children under 14 years of age. No children between 14 and 16 years can be employed unless they have certificates showing they have had an eight-year public school course and that their health is first rate after a physical examination by two physicians. Further than that, no child under 16 years is allowed to work except between 8 o'clock in the morning and 5 o'clock in the evening.

Before it was amended, the State labor law limited the hours of employment of women in factories to sixty a week and not more than eleven in any one day. Most factories in New York City have been running on this basis. First Deputy Labor Commissioner John S. Whalen said yesterday that a good many manufacturing establishments had cut down the hours for women to fifty-four a week before the amendment was passed.

It has been demonstrated that long hours do not pay. More than $366,000,000 was reported lost last year to New York City and State factory workers by reason of 13,400,00 causes of illness. There are 31,000 factories in the State, with a total of 1,250,000 workers, by the last census. In a year these factories use $2,409,000,000 in raw materials and produce finished products to the value of $11,000,000 a day. Another reform which went into effect last night at 12 o'clock was an amendment forbidding smoking in factories, requiring fireproof receptacles for all waste and inflammable materials, directing that every factory shall be registered, with full particulars, at the State Labor Department, and prohibiting the employment of women within a month after they have given birth to children.

Yesterday the State Labor Department distributed printed notices to factories required them to give the hours during which the women in the different departments are to work. These notices are to be posted conspicuously, to aid State Labor Inspectors in learning how the law is being obeyed. The enforcement of the law against smoking and other safety regulations is left to the Fire Prevention Bureau.

Sources: *New York Times* (October 1, 1912); and
http://www.pbs.org/wgbh/americanexperience/features/primary-resources/triangle-legislation

See Articles: Children's Rights; New York City.

1915
PRIMARY DOCUMENT

Atlanta Constitution Article on the Mob Abduction of Leo M. Frank

The lynching of Leo Frank was a watershed moment in American antisemitism. He had been convicted of the death of Mary Phagan, one of his workers, but the case against him depended heavily on class and ethnic biases. The governor, unconvinced, commuted his sentence to life imprisonment, and a lynch mob stormed the prison two months later. None in the mob were prosecuted, and several became the founders of the second Ku Klux Klan that November. Thousands of Jews fled the south.

POSSES CHASE FRANK MOB

Prisoner Rushed From State Farm In An Automobile

Mob of Twenty-Five Men Invades Dormitory, Overpowers the Warden and Takes Charge of Prisoner. "Will Place Frank's Body on the Grave of Mary Phagan in Marietta" Declared Member of Mob. Frank made Desperate Resistance.

At 6 o'clock this morning posses of state officers and citizens from Baldwin and a number of other counties were still vainly seeking the mob which shortly before midnight last night abducted Leo M. Frank from the state prison farm, at Milledgeville, where he has been confined since his sentence was commuted to life imprisonment.

One posse from Milledgeville is headed by Captain J. H. Ennis, member of the legislature. He was one of the first to learn of the action of the mob at the state prison farm. Officials in practically every county in the state have been notified to be on the lookout, and the governor has announced that he will extend the Baldwin county authorities every aid in his power.

Milledgeville, GA, August 16.—A mob variously estimated at between twenty-five and seventy-five in number, overpowered warden, superintendent and guards at the Georgia state prison farm, near here, at 11 o'clock tonight and quickly got Leo M. Frank and rushed him away in an automobile.

First reports that it might be friends of Frank were dispelled when a prisoner said he had heard a member of the mob say that Frank's body would be placed tomorrow on the grave of Mary Phagan, at Marietta. Frank was serving a life term for the murder of the girl.

The mob was orderly, but worked with quick precision. Eight automobiles took the men to within a short distance of the prison. First all wires from the prison, and all except one from Milledgeville, were cut.

Five men went to the house of J. T. Smith, warden covered him with pistols and stood guard over him. Other men went to the house of J. M. Burke, superintendent of the prison, and held him under cover of their guns.

Practically every other member of the mob then rushed to the stockade gate the dormitory where Frank was being housed. Only yesterday the physicians discharged him from the hospital, where he had been since being murderously assaulted in the dormitory by William Creen.

TWO GUARDS ON DUTY.

As on the night Frank was attacked only two guards were on duty. The mob quickly overpowered chief Night Guard Hester and the other man on duty. Proceeded to the dormitory and within a few minutes seized Frank and rushed him back to the automobiles.

Those who had been holding Smith and Burke left as soon as Frank was brought out and joined their fellows. The automobiles—reported to number eight—then were started in the direction of Eatonton. Nothing more had been heard of them hours after they left.

Only one member of that part of the mob that went to the dormitory talked. He gave the commands to the guards which were backed up by the arms of the other members of the mob.

FIVE MEN MASKED.

Five were masked out of the thirty-five. They said they were from Marietta. Warden Smith's gasoline was emptied out from his auto.

The five men brought Frank out, holding him by hands and feet and hair. Frank resisted but to no avail. He mumbled but the excitement was so nothing can be remembered. The mob left Warden Smith and Superintendent Burke handcuffed, and they tied Frank's legs. Everything was done quietly, members of the mob saying they didn't want anyone's head, only wanted Frank.

GOVERNOR SHOCKED.

When notified by The Constitution early this morning of the affair, Governor Harris declared: "I am both shocked and aggrieved, and in common with all good people of Georgia who stand for law and order. I feel that a great wrong has been done, that our state will not look with approval on such an act."

The governor stated that he would put forth every effort in his official power to apprehend the members of the mob, should he be called on to furnish aid to the authorities at the state farm and in Baldwin county.

ENNIS HEADS POSSE.

Headed by Captain J. H. Ennis, representative in the legislature from Baldwin county, and the first in Milledgeville to learn of the smuggling of Frank from the prison farm, a posse of several automobiles filled with local officers started in pursuit of the mob of twenty-five shortly before 1 o'clock.

According to the story told to Captain Ennis by several negro convicts who were not locked up, a mob of twenty-five men in seven or eight automobiles arrives at the farm at 11:45 o'clock, overpowered and ties Warden Smith and two guards who were sleeping on the front porch, and went directly to the room where Frank was asleep.

The negroes rushed to the home of J. H. Satterfield, bookkeeper at the farm, and who lives on the state property, and told him that the mob had left with Frank, taking the road toward Eatonton, due north of here. Mr. Satterfield took one of the automobiles kept at the farm and went direct to Milledgeville, notifying Captain Ennis.

Captain Ennis sought to get in communication with the state farm, but found all telephone wires cut. The wires he found had also been cut on the Macon and Atlanta lines.

Notifying local officials a possee was formed that started in pursuit of the mob. At 2:30 this morning nothing had been heard from the searching party.

Prison Commissioners Davison and Rainey were at the farm and had retired to their rooms just before the mob came. They did not leave their room until the crowd had captured Frank and had left the farm. They will leave Milledgeville this morning for Atlanta. Mrs. Leo Frank was also in Milledgeville last night.

PLANNED WORK WELL.

Macon, GA, August 16—A long distance telephone message from Milledgeville via Augusta confirmed the rumor that a party of 25 men in automobiles had taken Leo M. Frank from the state farm there at 11:45 p.m. and had left with him in the direction of Eatonton. A message from Eatonton stated the automobiles had not passed through that city at 1 o'clock this morning.

When the mob first reached the state farm they separated into three groups. One went to the home of Captain Burke, the farm superintendent, and after calling him from the house they covered him with their guns and slipped the handcuffs on him. This group took Captain Burke to the prison farm dormitory and forced him to open the door.

Another group secured and handcuffed Warden Smith in the same manner as the other had done Captain Burke. Two guards sleeping on the front porch were overpowered and handcuffed.

Warden Smith and Captain Burke both declared they failed to recognize any of the members of the mob, but one of the convicts overheard a remark dropped by one member of the mob that they intended to take Frank to Marietta.

When the party reached the farm they overpowered Warden Smith and the guards who have been sleeping on the front porch of the prison dormitory since Frank has been confined there. All of them, including the warden, were handcuffed, and with the loss of little time, Frank was secured and placed in one of the automobiles. The cars then hurried away at full speed in the direction of Eatonton.

SATTERFIELD NOTIFIED.

J. H. Satterfield, bookkeeper at the farm, was awakened by some of the negro convicts after the men had left with Frank. As soon as he learned what had happened he hastened to Milledgeville and notified Representative Ennis.

The mob apparently planned their work well, for they carried it through without a hitch. Between Milledgeville and the State Farm and between Milledgeville and Macon, they cut telephone wires and it was fully an hour or more after they had secured their man and hastened on their way before the news came out.

As far as could be learned at an early hour this morning, none of the members of the mob were recognized. Some of them are said to have worn masks and all were heavily armed.

Not a shot was fired and no one was injured as far as known.

ALL QUIET IN MARIETTA.

Marietta, GA, August 17—If any residents of this town were in the mob that took Leo M. Frank from the state prison farm last night, or if it was intended to bring him to Marietta it was not generally known here at 3:15 o'clock this morning. Nothing had occurred at that hour to disturb the usual calm of the town.

Leo M. Frank was found guilty of the murder of Mary Phagan on August 25, 1913. He was the superintendent of the National Pencil company in Atlanta, in the basement of which the girl's body was found by a night watchman on the morning of April 27, previous.

Repeated attempts were made in the state courts to obtain a new trial for Frank, but without avail. Attempts to obtain a writ of habeas corpus in the federal district court of Atlanta and finally in the supreme court of the United States were futile.

On the night of June 21, this year, two days before the date set for the prisoner's execution, he was removed from the county jail in Atlanta and rushed to the state prison farm upon orders from Governor Slaton, now retired. The next day the governor announced that he had granted the petition made in Frank's behalf asking that his death sentence be commuted to life imprisonment.

The taking of Leo M. Frank from the prison last night was the culmination of numerous rumors of threats of mob violence against his life.

But one attack, however, had previously actually been made upon Frank. This was about a month ago, when William Creen, also serving a life term for murder, cut Frank's throat so severely that his life for days hung in the balance. Creen stole out of his bunk about 11 o'clock one night and managed to slip across the large sleeping room to Frank's bunk unobserved. He then drew across Frank's throat a large knife which he had smuggled from the kitchen.

Although Frank's head was cut practically half off by the stroke, his life was saved, largely through the efforts of Dr. McNaughton, also serving a term for killing.

The governor and the prison commissioners, a few weeks later, made an investigation at the state prison and, upon the confession of Creen, who assumed all responsibility for the set, exonerated all prison officials from responsibility.

Creen, in his confession to Governor Harris, swore that he committed the act without aid or suggestion from any one either inside or outside of the prison.

Frank, after he was wounded, was placed in a private room adjoining the warden's office, where he remained while he was convalescing. It is presumed that he was still in this room when he was taken by last night's mob.

For weeks all the guards of the prison, including Warden Smith, were required to sleep armed upon the front porch of the prison, which is just outside the room in which the wounded, convict was placed. It is not known whether this guard was still being maintained last night.

Source: http://www.leofrank.org/newspapers

See Articles: Posses; Prisoner's Rights; Vigilantism.

1918
PRIMARY DOCUMENT

John Deml's Account of Anti-German Sentiment

In addition to African Americans, Chinese, Jews, and Catholics, Germans faced periods of deep resentment from other Americans. The largest immigrant group in the early 20th century, they were hailed in a backward compliment as the most successful assimilators, but not all of them assimilated enough to escape persecution. Violent attacks on Germans increased as World War I began; others simply severed their social ties to German families, and sauerkraut was rebranded as "liberty cabbage."

A Statement made by John Deml of Outagamie County, Wisconsin, at Madison, Wisconsin, Tuesday, October 22, 1918.

About half-past twelve (continuing for more than an hour) Sunday morning October 20th, my wife awaked me, saying, that there were a large number of men on the front porch, pounding and rapping on the door, besides talking in a loud tone of voice. I was upstairs; then I came downstairs and went to the front door, where they were, and I asked them, who was there! Several answered at once, "The Council of Defense." I then asked them, "What do you want?" and they replied, "We want you to sign up." I replied, "I have done my share." And they asked me when, and I replied, "I did my share in the spring."(That is, I meant to say I had done my share in the third loan, when I subscribed for $450 in bonds.) To make it plain, on the 28th of September, at the opening of the fourth drive, I was notified by letter that my bond assessment would be $800. When Henry Baumann came to see me, I told him I could not possibly take $500 now but would take some, meaning a substantial amount, that is all I could afford; and he replied, "My orders are you must take $500 or nothing."

After I had replied that I had done my share in the spring, they demanded that I open the door and let them in. I told them I didn't have to open the door; then they undertook to force the door open, and went so far as to tear the screen door open; then they threatened to break down the door, and I said, "Come on then, boys." Then they appeared to be planning, and while they were doing that, I took the time to put my shoes on. By that time they were at the kitchen door, and they made a demand that I let them in through that door; then I went to the kitchen door and opened it and found a crowd of men (much larger than I expected) around the door, and then reaching out two by two around towards the front of the house. I left the door and walked to the front porch to see if they had done any painting (as they had previously painted a neighbor's mail-box); I walked to the road to see if they had painted my mail-box. And then I turned around to return to the house when they all at one time closed in on me like a vise; some grabbing my fingers or wrist, others my legs, and several of them were shouting, holding a paper before me, "Sign up." I said, "I will not sign up at this time of night." Then a man shouted, "Get the rope!" The first I knew was when the rope was about my neck and around my body under my arms. Someone then gave a sharp jerk at the rope and forced me to my knees and hands; at the same time some of them jumped on my back, and while bent over someone struck me in the face, making me bleed; then a man (whom I recognized) said, "Boys, you are going to far"; and then, as they got me away from them a little, I heard a man say, "You can't scare him." I answered,"I am not afraid of the entire city of Appleton." Then a man (whom I knew) got me to one side, and he said, "Let's go into the house and talk between ourselves." Then two men (whom I knew) went with me into the house, and we sat or stood around the table, and they still demanded that I sign up. I said, "I will not sign up for any man after being abused like this." Then a man (whom I knew) told me I would have to go with them, or, if I didn't go with them, would have to come to town that Sunday morning at 10 o'clock to see Mr. Keller. I told them that I would be there; they left; as they left, I noticed, and so did my family and neighbors, that they rode away in seven automobiles. I did not go to see Mr. Keller.

Signed, JOHN DEML.

Sources: "Prussianizing Wisconsin." *Atlantic Monthly*, v.11/1 (1919); and http://historymatters.gmu.edu/d/1

See Articles: German Americans; Race-Based Crimes; Racism; Wisconsin.

1919 PRIMARY DOCUMENT

Department of Justice Memorandum on Anarchists

This memo is notable not only for its subjects but also for the antisocialist viewpoint of its author, J. Edgar Hoover, which would tinge his direction of the FBI beginning in 1925. Alexander Berkman and Emma Goldman, friends and lovers, were in prison at the time for conspiracy to induce eligible men not to register for the draft; when released, they were deported to Russia, where they became disillusioned with Lenin's restrictions on the press and other disappointments.

Memorandum for Mr. Creighton.

I am attaching hereto a copy of a report received from the New York office relative to the cases of Alexander Berkman and Emma Goldman who are at present sojourning in the custody of the federal authorities but who will shortly be released, their sentences about to expire. Berkman by his own admission is an alien, while Emma Goldman has claimed at various times to be an American citizen through the naturalization of her father and again through the naturalization of her husband, but it appears that the immigration authorities who personally examined her claim reached the conclusion that she was not a citizen of the United States. Upon communicating with the Department of Labor this morning, I was informally advised that Emma Goldman's case had on several occasions been before the Department of Labor for consideration but that the Assistant Secretary, Mr. Post, had refused to sustain the recommendation of the immigration inspector, stating that there was not sufficient facts to warrant the issuance of the warrant for deportation. I have requested Mr. McClellan of the Bureau of Immigration to have a search made of their files and to submit the same to me for consideration relative to these two cases.

Emma Goldman and Alexander Berkman are, beyond doubt, two of the most dangerous anarchists in this country and if permitted to return to the community will result in undue harm.

Respectfully,

J. E. Hoover
Department of Justice
Washington, D.C.
August 23, 1919

Source: U.C. Berkeley/Dept. of Justice

See Articles: Anarchists; Hoover, J. Edgar; Political Dissidents.

1919 PRIMARY DOCUMENT

Emma Goldman's Account of Her Deportation

Goldman and Berkman's deportation came during the Red Scare that followed the Bolshevik Revolution (and subsequent fears that Russian communism would spread elsewhere) and the devastation of World War I. In some cities, socialist political parties were too popular to be dismissed as fringe elements; the growing power of labor organizations made a labor/socialist alliance seem inevitable and fearsome to some. For them, deporting "reds" and removing their influence was paramount.

The steps halted at our room. There came the rattling of keys; the door was unlocked and noisily thrown open. Two guards and a matron entered. "Get up now," they commanded, "get your things ready!" The girls grew nervous, Ethel was shaking as in fever and helplessly rummaging among her bags. Then the guards became impatient. "Hurry there! Hurry! " they ordered roughly. I could not restrain my indignation. "Leave us so we can get dressed," I demanded. They walked out, the door remaining ajar. I was anxious about my letters. I did not want them to fall into the hands of the authorities nor did I care to destroy them. Maybe I should find someone to entrust them to, I thought. I stuck them into the bosom of my dress and wrapped myself a large shawl.

In a long corridor dimly lit and unheated, we found the men deportees assembled little Morris Becker among them. He had been delivered to the island only that afternoon with a number of other Russian boys. One of them was on crutches; another, suffering from an ulcerated stomach, had been carried from his bed in the island hospital. Sasha was busy helping the sick men pack their parcels and bundles. They had been hurried out of their cells without being allowed even time to gather up all their things. Routed from sleep at midnight they were driven bag and baggage into the corridor. Some were still half-asleep—unable to realize what was happening.

I felt tired and cold. No chairs or benches were about, and we stood shivering in the barn-like place. The suddenness of the attack took the men by surprise and they filled the corridor with a hubbub of exclamations and questions and excited expostulations. Some had been promised a review of their cases, others were waiting to be bailed out pending final decision. They had received no notice of the nearness of their deportation and they were overwhelmed by the midnight assault. They stood helplessly about, at a loss what to do. Sasha gathered them in groups and suggested that an attempt be made to reach their relatives in the city. The men grasped desperately at that last hope and appointed him their representative and spokesman. He succeeded in prevailing upon the island commissioner to permit the men to telegraph, at their own expense, to their friends in New York for money and necessaries [sic].

Messenger boys hurried back and forth, collecting special-delivery letters and wires hastily scribbled. The chance of reaching their people cheered the forlorn men. The island officials encouraged them and gathered in their messages, themselves collecting pay for delivery and assuring them that there was plenty of time to receive replies. Hardly had the last wire been sent when the corridor filled with State and Federal detectives, officers of the Immigration Bureau and Coast Guards. I recognized Caminetti, Commissioner General of Immigration, at their head. The uniformed men stationed themselves along the walls, and then came the command, "Line up!" A sudden hush fell upon the room. " March!" It echoed through the corridor. Deep snow lay on the ground; the air was cut by a biting wind. A row of armed civilians and soldiers stood along the road to the bank. Dimly the outlines of a barge were visible through the morning mist. One by one the deportees marched, flanked on each side by the uniformed men, curses and threats accompanying the thud of their feet on the frozen ground. When the last man had crossed the gangplank, the girls and I were ordered to follow, officers in front and in back of us.

We were led to a cabin. A large fire roared in the iron stove filling the air with heat and fumes. We felt suffocating [sic]. There was no air nor water. Them came a violent lurch; we were on our way. I looked at my watch. It was 4:20 A.M. on the day of our Lord, December 21, 1919. On the deck above us I could hear the men tramping up and down in the wintry blast. I felt dizzy, visioning a transport of politicals doomed to Siberia, the tape of former Russian days. Russia of the past rose before me and I saw the revolutionary martyrs being driven into exile. But no, it was New York, it was America, the land of liberty! Through the port-hole I could see the great city receding into the distance, its skyline of buildings traceable by their rearing heads. It was my beloved city, the metropolis of the New World. It was America, indeed America repeating the terrible scenes of tsarist Russia! I glanced up—the Statue of Liberty!

Sources: Goldman, Emma. *Living My Life*. Vol. 2. New York: Dover Publications, 1970 (as an unabridged republication of the work originally published in 1931 by Alfred Knopf, New York; and http://historymatters.gmu.edu/d/15

See Articles: Hoover, J. Edgar; Political Dissidents.

1919 PRIMARY DOCUMENT

W. M. Mink's Statement on the National Steel Strike

Red Scare fears are amply demonstrated in this testimony given by W. M. Mink, mill superintendant of the Homestead Steelworks, to the Senate Committee on Education and Labor. The committee was investigating the cause and character of the nationwide steel strike, which had all but halted the American steel industry as 350,000 workers left their jobs. The Senate was not persuaded of foreign influence, and the strike fell apart in January 1920 as a result of infighting among union organizations.

STATEMENT OF MR. W. M. MINK

Senator STERLING: What is your name?
Mr. MINK: W. M. Mink.
Senator MCKELLAR: And what is your position?
Mr. MINK: I have charge of these mills here....
The CHAIRMAN: Well, will you give us your view of what this strike is about?
Mr. MINK: We think it is entirely the Bolshevik spirit.
The CHAIRMAN: Why do you think that?
Mr. MINK: Well, because they was gathering up the aliens; they have been practically alien, in my opinion, very few American citizens.

The CHAIRMAN: They worked among the foreigners, do you say?

Mr. MINK: They worked among the foreigners entirely.

The CHAIRMAN: And most of the foreigners are out?

Mr. MINK: Most of the foreigners are out; 99 per cent of the foreigners that are striking here—that is, the strikers that are out are foreigners.

The CHAIRMAN: Now, does this Bolshevik tendency that you speak of, do they get any literature from any sources?

Mr. MINK: Well, we have not seen any literature, but only stuff like this, they say that if the mills are not running - we do not see this ourselves, but we get it from other sources - that they are going to get a dollar an hour and are going to get the best jobs.

The CHAIRMAN: Are they going to man the mills themselves?

Mr. MINK: Yes, they are going to man the mills themselves.

The CHAIRMAN: And you really believe that there is a great deal of that Bolshevism about, do you?

Mr. MINK: Yes, I think there is. It is not a question of wages. They have never been getting more money than they have got, and the conditions are good.

The CHAIRMAN: How about their living conditions? How are they?

Mr. MINK: The living conditions are just what the men want. A lot of them have good jobs and they make good money, and they could live a whole lot better.

Sources: Investigation of Strike in Steel Industries, Hearings before the Committee on Education and Labor, U.S. Senate, 66th Congress, 1st Session;
and
http://historymatters.gmu.edu/d/8

See Articles: Civil Disobedience; Political Dissidents.

1921 to 1940
INTRODUCTION

The economic windfall that pervaded much of the Western world after World War I ensured a dramatically changing social, political, and geographic landscape in America. The Roaring Twenties also inspired not only unbridled enthusiasm but also a sea change with respect to trends in crime. The hastening shift from pastoral nation to industrial giant, which had begun in earnest over a generation earlier, further accelerated the movement and disbursement of both existing Americans and newly arrived immigrants toward expanding cities. The image of prosperity that came to typify the decade also served to deepen existing and entrenched divisions of wealth and labor. It ultimately served as the catalyst for new trends in crime and a new breed of criminal that was drawn en masse to burgeoning urban centers. As the demographic shifts of the 1920s resulted in changing values with respect to work and family life, so too was the rubric of crime and punishment in America required to undergo significant modernization. Both law makers and law enforcers struggled to keep pace with new and emerging threats to public safety, as well as the order and rule of government.

As the 1920s inspired decadence and indulgence alongside the cultural and economic infrastructure that appeared primed for criminal infiltration and the emergence of illegal markets, the Wall Street collapse and ensuing Great Depression of the interwar years brought new insights into the environmental causes of crime. As everyday people found themselves resorting to crime, or at least empathizing with the plight of criminals, maintaining and serving the public trust became an increasingly delicate job for law enforcement. In many cases, they were conflicted in their duties: gatekeepers of social order on one hand, and on the other, strikebreakers and underwriters of an unbalanced capitalist system that protected the few remaining wealthy citizens.

Exacerbating public skepticism regarding the traditional rule of law during this period was the expanded role of the commercial press. A quantum leap in the technical standards of film allowed the American media to steward popular debates on the place of crime while contouring public opinion on criminals and moderating the collective fear of crime. Through advances in motion picture sound production, Hollywood of the 1920s and 1930s inspired newfound public ambivalence about the role of the police, the credibility and accountability of the judicial system, and the romance and intrigue that accompanied the criminal outlaw as a sympathetic antihero of an economically and culturally changeable age.

Additionally mirroring the divisive, boom-or-bust nature of American life that epitomized this era was the polarization of ideological positions on crime by political stripe as well as region. In the northeast, the 1919 Volstead Act ensured that the 1920s and a good part of the 1930s would be defined by struggles with the enforcement of unpopular prohibition laws. The deep south—more agrarian and isolated than the cities of the midwest and seaboards—saw a host of challenges to its reductive definitions of criminality: laws and systems of punishment that often proved incongruous with the more secular values adopted by the rest of America.

Further complicating the maintenance of law and order across a diversifying and dynamic American landscape was the fact that industrial progress had enabled a new degree of mobility for criminals, ensuring a hastened means of escape, as well as allowing crime to routinely undertake a multijurisdictional and itinerant nature. This complicated the task of locating and tracking offenders, and caused additional logistical and procedural constraints in terms of arresting and returning criminals and fugitives across state lines and international borders.

The mass production and ensuing affordability of automobiles proved the most significant determinant of trends in crime during the interwar years. Henry Ford's adoption of the moving assembly line in lieu of individual handcrafting from a decade earlier allowed standardized interchangeable parts to be used in his automobiles, which were marketed to the American middle class for the first time. As one of one the great beneficiaries of the spendthrift 1920s, Ford's innovations had transformed the automobile from a luxury item to a staple commodity—and eventually a necessity of American life. Through the reduction of overall production costs, by 1925, nearly 10,000 Ford Model T automobiles were produced on a daily basis, all of them in signature Henry Ford black, offering criminals relative anonymity in their flight from the law. Further complicating law enforcement efforts was the lack of standardized license plates, which were not required in most states until the end of the decade. By 1927, when production began on the Ford Model A, over 15 million Model Ts had been sold or otherwise remained in existence—one car for roughly every eight Americans—subsequently reinventing how people traveled, socialized, and sought out their fortunes, whether legally or illegally. The new gypsying and motoring culture that made the nation smaller and more traversable also ensured a brand of rugged individualism and freedom to roam that favored criminal exploits. By the 1930s, the addition of surplus firearms, which had similar decreases in manufacturing costs, were both widely available and affordable to the criminal element—especially organized crime groups—affording them the logistical and tactical supremacy required to lay siege to American cities.

Of the many retrospectives offered by this explosively changing period, the most enduring cultural legacy for modern crime and punishment is the precipitous surge in state-sanctioned executions. As America seemed somewhat amorphous in its design and conscience during these transitional years, punishment was consistently harsh and was meted out expeditiously. The execution of convicts during this era therefore served not only as an expression of moral and political authority, but also, it was thought, as the ultimate deterrent. As now, death penalty advocates insisted that it deterred other would-be criminals and heeled an American public increasingly captivated by stories of criminal exploits. The drastically increased use of capital punishment is perhaps the enduring image of American justice with respect to this interwar period, with the United States putting to death a record 199 convicts in 1935 alone. It was a low point in the economic and social health of America that seemed light years from the optimism of decade earlier; and it provides a better understanding of the place of crime and punishment in America today.

Urbanization and Organized Crime

American urban centers from 1921 onward were sites of exceptional cultural upheaval, particularly in port cities where dockyards became the progenitors of globalization and foreshowed the increasingly terrestrial importance of the American economy and mercantile system. The result was the rise of what might now be described as a megacity, with New York City eclipsing the metropoles of Europe and Asia to become the most densely populated and multicultural place on Earth by the turn of the decade. During this same period, the city of Chicago, which two generations earlier had the distinction of being one of the fastest-growing cities in the world, saw its African American population more than double as its expanding industrial sector made it a destination for displaced rural workers from the south during the Great Migration. It was also becoming a labor center for an international constituency of tradespeople from Europe and Central America. In the west, Los Angeles in the 1920s was the site of massive urban—and ultimately suburban—expansion into the desert of the Old West, with commercial and residential construction turning a once-barren landscape into the home of over 80 percent of the world's motion picture production. In the south in the 1920s, Miami experienced a southern land boom unparalleled elsewhere in America, while the eastern cities of

A pair of bootleggers are apprehended by police after a frantic chase and crash in the busy streets of Washington, D.C., on January 21, 1922. Bootlegging was the mainstay of traditional organized crime during Prohibition and supported numerous other criminal enterprises such as smuggling, transport hijacking, illegal gaming, loan sharking, extortion, protection rackets, and prostitution.

Pittsburgh and Philadelphia became industrial powerhouses and sites of unprecedented population diversification, as well as sites of social and political conflict.

A natural consequence of this expedited rural-to-urban transition at the national level during this period was the disproportionate representation of crime, specifically organized crime, in these same cities. While historians continue to proffer a host of theories as to prevailing causal factors, the reality of the era is reducible to basic macroeconomics, as organized crime has always been about making money. American cities in the 1920s, and to a lesser extent the 1930s, were subsumed in a population boom that drew settlers and workers who compensated with disposable income for what they lacked in familial and community connections. These variables, coupled with an unprecedented economic surge and trends in consumerism, pushed against temperance laws during the Prohibition Era of 1919 to 1933. The aggregate result of these factors was the emergence of the ultimate seller's market in illicit goods peddled in an underground economy, one that required infrastructure and, most importantly, organization.

While organized crime is distinct from professional crime, which is a phenomenon that seized public imagination and became a priority for federal law enforcement during the 1930s, criminal organizations of the 1920s tended to function as cultural microcosms of their occupying cities. Mirroring the same racial and social divides in burgeoning American industrial cities of the time, organized crime groups endemic in this era also tended to focus on crimes deemed profitable according to the existing, or at least prevailing, local industries. The geographic and logistical advantages of America's industrialized cities for corporations and their workers made them equally coveted by organized crime. Port cities offered opportunities for smuggling and control of the docks, while land-locked cities offered a host of other opportunities based on factors such as population, climate, and proximity to interstate routes. In terms of immigration and ethnic distribution, cities were favored destination points for settlers from Ireland, Italy, and eastern Europe, while Scandinavians and Germans tended to opt for rural resettlement. In one sense, immigrant gravitation toward organized crime as delineated by creed and country of origin might be construed as a gesture of rejecting urban assimilation and an attempt to retain ethnic heritage. More significantly, these trends in seeking out cultural coherence are of key importance when examining the composition, hierarchies, and ideologies of these early, or traditional, organized crime groups—American gangs of Italian, Irish, and Jewish ancestry.

As bootlegging became the mainstay of traditional, organized crime during the Prohibition Era, it also spawned a number of ancillary illegal enterprises that continue to define the operations of many of these syndicates in their contemporary forms: smuggling, cargo hijacking and highway robbery, illegal gaming and bookmaking, loan sharking, extortion, "black hand" protection rackets, and prostitution. Forays into narcotics trafficking by traditional, organized crime groups have been a much more recent phenomenon; the practice was largely unheard of in the 1920s and 1930s. As these groups in their nascent forms began to diversify their revenue-generating activities, some things remained unchanged, including the violence and terror tactics used to protect and acquire capital. While otherwise conducting business by the same methods and corporate structure as many other American companies occupying the same urban spaces—with the exception of the illegal goods and services provided—increasingly bloody struggles for dominance defined the rise of the gangster in America. As the United States became prime real estate for traditional organized crime from the 1920s onward, the activities of this period allowed America to become the most active hub of organized crime in the world—a nation where petty gangs could thrive and evolve into global criminal empires.

Alphonse "Scarface" Capone

While no American city during this period was immune to the public violence associated with organized crime rivalries, no single urban area seemed able to challenge the infamous spectacles that were seen in Chicago, which by the late 1920s boasted over 1,000 identified gangs. The gangsters who emerged out of Chicago in the 1920s endure as some of the most mythologized and storied criminals in American history. Alphonse "Scarface" Capone, the gangster offering the greatest name recognition in the annals of American crime and enduring as the archetype of traditional organized crime, was first drawn to Chicago at the outset of the Prohibition Era in 1919 to pursue a fortune in bootlegging and reinvent himself after drawing considerable police attention in his native New York City. By 1930, he was the undisputed crime king of Chicago and much of the Midwest, controlling the shipment of liquor, as well as all gambling operations and brothels, while amassing a sizeable fortune even by today's standards. The move that secured Capone's place at the apex of the criminal underworld and as an icon of the organized crime culture, however, would also be his ultimate undoing.

On February 14, 1929, seeking to dispatch his lone remaining serious rival George "Bugs" Moran, Capone arranged for four members of his gang to attend the SMC Cartage Company warehouse and garage located in Chicago's North End, an area historically controlled by Moran's Irish gang. Acting on information that Moran would be present, Capone's thugs were dressed as Chicago police officers, with two in replica uniforms and two posing as plainclothes detectives. Moran arrived at the warehouse later than expected, happening upon the scene just in time to witness what appeared to be a police raid as the seven occupants were lined up against the wall in the usual fashion, but were then summarily machine-gunned to death. While Moran by pure happenstance survived Capone's professional hit that was cunningly veiled as a police shakedown, his organization did not, and he ceded control of the coveted North End to the Capone gang from that day.

The St. Valentine's Day Massacre, as it quickly became known, was a veritable game changer for organized crime in America—the tipping point where law enforcement tactics, public opinion, and the composition of gangs were forever altered. As the international media had a field day with the story of the massacre, complete with gory photographs of seven men lying in communal blood on a garage floor, Capone's notoriety and criminal celebrity now earned him the full attention the entire U.S. government—including President Herbert Hoover. Capone's once salutary public image also took a beating among city dwellers, who had until that time been largely unaffected by, and even ignorant of, the seemingly backstage nature of his criminal exploits. Collective moral outrage about the public barbarity of the massacre brought the stark realities of organized crime into people's homes for the first time, allowing them to see the gangs for what they really were. As organized crime very quickly became a pressing public issue, the pressure on law enforcement to curtail the activities of gangs mounted, with popular opinion shifting in line with dominant law-and-order ideologies. Citizens finally came to terms with the idea of Capone as little more than a criminal psychopath rather than urban folk hero and iconoclast, as some had previously preferred to believe. Having been unable to build a substantive criminal case against Capone for years, federal investigators, with the assistance of the Internal Revenue Service, soon opted for documentary evidence of income tax evasion in lieu of the elusive eyewitness evidence needed to support more serious felony charges such as murder. Following the St. Valentine's Day Massacre, Capone's time at the top was short-lived; he was in federal custody on tax charges by 1931. He was eventually transferred to Alcatraz in 1934, where he remained until 1939, when he was paroled to live out his

Dr. H. W. Evans, imperial wizard of the Ku Klux Klan, leads a Klan parade in Washington, D.C., in September 1926. Many U.S. minority groups were targeted by the Klan, especially in the South, where the Klan had a membership of over 4 million by 1924. The Klan migrated toward northeastern urban centers and became embedded in labor and government, and later in the midwest, where they capitalized on social, economic, and cultural tension.

remaining years in a largely vegetative state, his mind and body destroyed by syphilis, which eventually took his life in 1947.

The toppling of the Capone gang proved a small victory for law enforcement as a pantheon of other crime lords and gangsters stood waiting to assume his place—all of them prepared to escalate the level of violence normalized by Capone, if it proved necessary to secure his newly available territories. More importantly, urban organized crime in the wake of Capone continued to present some unique challenges for law enforcement during the 1930s and onward as criminal syndicates became more entrenched and began to grow organically and insidiously, evolving from myriad gangs of varying complexity into regional, national, and even international crime families. This evolution represented more than just a shift in the semantics used to describe criminal organizations. As crime families quickly annexed what were once manageable local gangs across a number of major cities, criminal conglomerates operating under the umbrella title of "the Mafia" (transliterated from the original *mafioso*) rose up as an amorphous entity with its particular brand of traditional organized crime.

The Mafia
As early as 1908, the New York Police Department (NYPD), recognizing the emerging threat of the Mafia during the city's massive waves of immigration, industrialization,

and densification, created an elite detective unit known as the Italian Squad. This unit, conducted under the direction of Italian American officers versed in the culture and language, was arguably America's first recognition of the increasing threat posed by the venerable Sicilian crime families that had effectively maintained unofficial control of the island through extortion and racketeering since the mid-19th century. While Mafia activities in Sicily and Italy as a whole began to wane under Benito Mussolini's fascist control from 1922 onward, the foundations laid in America by organized crime figures like Capone provided ripe territory for their pending trans-Atlantic expansion. While Capone certainly elevated the status of Chicago as an organized crime landmark, his arrest in 1931 coincided with the rise of a New York City franchise of the newly displaced Sicilian Mafia that had earlier been forecast by one-time NYPD commissioner and later U.S. President Theodore Roosevelt. As federal agents removed Capone from power and a hodgepodge of Chicago-based gangsters and rivals competed for his monopoly on the prohibited market, New York City emerged as the new capital of organized crime in America. The contemporaneous emergence of the so-called Five Families (Genovese, Gambino, Lucchese, Colombo, and Bonanno) that would go on to dominate New York City and become the crucible of the American Mafia—or Cosa Nostra—as the largest secret criminal organization in the world eventually spread to consume cities like Las Vegas, Miami, and Atlantic City. They even began to rival established syndicates in Boston, where traditional organized crime of Irish descent had previously operated with relative impunity.

Coupled with the criminal vacuum created in Chicago by the collapse of the Moran gang and fragmenting of the Capone gang following his arrest in 1931 was the dismantling of the Detroit-based Purple Gang—or Sugar House Gang—following the arrest of the group's upper echelon in 1932. Just as the hubris of the St. Valentine's Day Massacre in Chicago proved the death knell for the Capone Gang, the equally sensational and publicly vilified Collingwood Manor Massacre in a tenement in the west end of Detroit on September 16, 1931, proved to be a careless exercise of power that cost the Jewish American crime syndicate control of their bootlegging monopoly. While the Purple Gang was bankrupted and slowly asphyxiated during their murder trial in 1932, the remainder of the traditional organized crime gangs in America, generally of Irish American constitution, were disappearing across most cities outside of their Boston stronghold—Providence, St. Louis, St. Paul, and even Omaha—as assassinations, disappearances, and eventual absorption by emerging Mafia affiliates changed the power structure and tactics of organized crime in America.

Xenophobia and the Public Enemy Era

As organized crime syndicates operating in American cities during the 1920s and on into the early 1930s tended to be representative of the prevailing urban ethnic groups of the period—Italian, Irish, and Jewish—these same identifiable groups bore the brunt of cresting racial and cultural intolerance across the United States in response to unwelcome linguistic, ethnic, and religious pluralism. Nowhere was this more evident than in the south, where by 1924, the Ku Klux Klan had amassed a membership totaling over four million. The Klan eventually moved toward northeastern urban centers, where it could establish a foothold in both labor and government. Emboldened by the socioeconomic and cultural tension occurring in cities, the Klan quickly infiltrated municipalities such as Detroit, Chicago, and other areas across the midwest that seemed incongruous with the rural roots of the First Klan (1865–74), which was formed by disillusioned Confederate army veterans. But by the 1920s, the Second Klan had received a decisively welcome response from urban Americans increasingly radicalized in their view of both nonwhites and non-Americans, allowing the Klan to evolve from a cabal of thugs into what became known as the Invisible Empire that encompassed all walks of life. It became a secret society reaching the highest levels of government and legal influence on a national level.

Like organized crime, this second and more insidious incarnation of the Ku Klux Klan was spawned in part by the divisive social effects of Prohibition. The difference was that the Klan actually advocated the temperance movement as a larger symbol of American purity and virtue. As support for Prohibition laws became the ideological rallying point and propagandist linchpin that united millions of Americans under the banner of the Klan, their criminal and frequently murderous and terrorist methods amounted to more extraordinary examples of a pervasive trend in often militant nationalism brewing across the nation, even among moderates. Eventually, the Klan's Grand Dragon D. C. Stephenson—who at one time oversaw the Klan activities of 23 state chapters—was convicted for the 1925 rape and murder of a schoolteacher on an Indiana night train, which ensured that the Klan's influence began to recede sharply among northerners for the balance of the decade. Synonymous with the Second Klan's decline, however, was the emergence of a hardened criminal justice system that took over as the new barometer for public suspicion and derision for those deemed outsiders. It would seem as though this institutionalized fear of otherness was absorbed by the American courtroom as early as 1920, with reforms to the California Alien Land Law that same year further tightening restrictions on land ownership by noncitizens. Across the balance of America, the first Red Scare had also reached its height as both communists and anarchists were believed responsible for the bombing of Wall Street on September 1, 1920, in which 38 New Yorkers were killed. While never attributable to any single group or cause, it was a massacre that was contemporaneous with prevailing anti-European and anti-immigrant sentiments, regardless of race, color, or creed, and only served to deepen American angst and anger throughout the balance of the 1920s.

Sacco, Vanzetti, and the Slater–Morrill Murders
One possible flashpoint began with the events of the afternoon of April 15, 1920, when two employees of the Slater–Morrill Shoe Company factory located in Braintree, Massachusetts, were ambushed and shot to death while making a payroll deposit of nearly $16,000 in cash. The robbery-murder bore remarkable similarities to the failed robbery of the L. Q. White Shoe Company in Bridgewater, Massachusetts, on the previous Christmas Eve, in which shots were also fired but no one was injured. The investigation of the Slater–Morrill murders quickly focused on Italian anarchist groups, specifically the Galleanist group—also consisting of mostly Italian immigrants—which was later implicated in the September 16 Wall Street bombing, as well as a much larger and coordinated dynamite plot to murder political leaders, U.S. ambassadors overseas, and captains of industry throughout America for much of the decade to come. Along with the emerging gangs of traditional organized crime, the Galleanist group was thought the most dangerous threat to American society for most of the 1920s; it was later considered a forerunner to politically motivated domestic terrorism in America. By 1921, the U.S. Justice Department had several years' worth of mass arrests and roundups of known or suspected anarchists and communists on the books. While the Slater–Morrill murders escalated public fear of anarchist attacks and the ostracizing of Italian Americans, they also sparked public demands for swift justice and stricter sanctions against current and pending immigrants.

The May 5, 1920, arrest of Galleanist members and Italian nationals Nicola Sacco and Bartolomeo Vanzetti for the shoe company murders put faces to the much larger problem of xenophobia and ostracism of the foreign born that was subsuming an

Roscoe "Fatty" Arbuckle in an undated photograph from the Bain News Service. Famous for his 1912–15 Keystone Cops *series, he was implicated in the rape and manslaughter of Virginia Rappe, an actress who attended Arbuckle's hotel party in 1921. Although ultimately acquitted, Arbuckle's career was undone by the news media, an enraged public, and Will H. Hays, Hollywood's director of censorship and author of the later Hays Code of 1930.*

increasingly—and at times reluctantly—diverse America. Sacco and Vanzetti, having been in the United States since 1908, had already been identified as militant leftists and communist sympathizers following a 1918 raid on the Massachusetts office of a subversive, anarchist newspaper, where they had served as authors and contributors. The arrest and subsequent prosecution of both men initially seemed to be a matter of good timing and was met with prompt public relief, but was soon followed by the emergence of convoluted evidence issues and problems with eyewitness accounts. These revelations ultimately complicated the timeline and investigative narrative of what was predicted to be a straightforward prosecution, but that turned out to be a ponderous, two-part trial beginning in the summer of 1921—a spectacle that distilled Sacco and Vanzetti into archetypes of a new and virulent threat to America.

The court of public opinion rendered decisively guilty verdicts before the actual trial even began, but due process ensured an equally swift finding of guilt and sentences of death, with violent backlashes orchestrated by their supporters only serving to embolden the collective public anger and paranoia. By November 1925, when convicted murderer Celestino Madeiros admitted to being the trigger man at the shoe company robbery and the real killer of both Slater–Morrill employees, the crime had become the backstory. By

1925, Sacco and Vanzetti were no longer the subject of debate over guilt or innocence, but had been relegated to a larger discourse involving contempt of foreign nationals and all things generally deemed unpatriotic. They had devolved into little more than surrogate enemies of the American legal and social systems as prejudice toward outsiders permeated the courts and the public sphere. It seemed the public was satisfied that if the two weren't guilty of committing the Slater–Morrill robbery murders, they must be guilty of something else, including their participation in seditious, treasonous activities that ultimately threatened the very fabric of American freedom, and that the punishment still fit. The state's decision to deny the request for a new trial based on new evidence and pleas for clemency on the capital sentences seemed to corroborate the sentiments on a higher plane. Just after midnight on August 22, 1927, both men died in the electric chair.

The Murder of the Century

While Sacco and Vanzetti were languishing on death row in Massachusetts, by May 1924, their notoriety was eclipsed by University of Chicago law student Nathan Leopold

An effort to avoid press photographers stymied Charles A. Lindbergh (center) as he emerged from the White House using a side door after a meeting with President Roosevelt in 1939. The years of media frenzy and public hysteria over the 1932 kidnapping, ransom, and murder of his infant son, Charles Jr., drove the Lindbergh family into "voluntary exile" in Europe under assumed names in December 1935.

Jr. and his partner Richard Loeb, two high-functioning sociopaths who were wealthy, entitled, and Jewish. Moreover, they were openly homosexual. This combination of social blights was set against the backdrop of a period of intolerance of outsiders, who were treated with considerable suspicion and derision—especially when they were accused of what was considered an extraordinarily heinous crime, even amid the urban violence of the 1920s. Known at the time as "the murder of the century," the case was mulled over by criminologists and psychologists for decades, if for no other reason than its utter senselessness.

Based on their gross misinterpretation of the writings of German philosopher Frederich Nietzsche, Leopold and Loeb conceived of themselves as *übermenchen* (supermen) whose calling was to realize the full potential of their intellectual and spiritual superiority and commit the perfect crime. Immortalized in popular culture and crime history as the first publicized "thrill kill," Leopold and Loeb—aged 18 and 19, respectively—took months to plan a murder for the sole purpose of getting away with it, thereby validating their perceived superiority and immunity to the laws of man and nature. After abducting 14-year-old Robert Franks—a second cousin of Loeb—from the front of his private school on May 21, 1924, both men stabbed the boy to death with a chisel before using acid to chemically mutilate the corpse that they concealed in a rural area outside the city. A contrived ransom scheme to extort money from Franks's millionaire father was quickly abandoned after Leopold's bifocals were recovered from the body dump site by police, their custom hinging mechanism immediately narrowing the suspect pool to the three Chicago men who owned them. A swift guilty plea entered on behalf of the killers by their lawyer Clarence Darrow—whose role in the Scopes Monkey Trial in Tennessee the following year would complement the Franks murder as perhaps the defining cases of the decade—saved Leopold and Loeb from what would have been an almost certain death penalty if found guilty at trial. Darrow, who traditionally defended the downtrodden and working classes, not trust-fund children from moneyed families, quickly saw the futility in Leopold and Loeb's plan to mount an insanity defense. Mental illness would be seen as an aggravating rather than a mitigating factor, once paired with their existing ethnic and sexual incongruity with mainstream America.

Leopold, consenting to being used as a human medical research test subject while in state prison, was later paroled after serving 33 years, and he self-exiled to Puerto Rico in 1958. Loeb's life term, however, proved a circuitous death sentence after he was stabbed to death in a prison shower in 1936 by a fellow inmate. The responsible convict was ultimately exonerated on the grounds that he had acted in self-defense following an attempted rape by Loeb, although this motive has been contested as one of either notoriety or a simple disagreement over money or contraband.

The Scottsboro Boys and Mishandled Justice
Additional cases that defined this xenophobic epoch tended to reflect not so much emerging social prejudices but rather the influence that religious fundamentalism and entrenched racism had on the criminal justice system. Few cases are more emblematic of the jurisdictional inconsistencies of the American justice system of the period than the 1931 case of the Scottsboro Boys. Eight African American youths were illegally riding a rail line across the south when the train was detained in Alabama; all eight boys were arrested and charged with the rape of two young—and white—female passengers riding with them. The perfunctory and hurried trial in Scottsboro, Alabama, that followed, with lynch mobs descending on the jail holding the group, resulted in swift guilty verdicts for all boys ranging in age from 12 to 20. This was in spite of no real legal representation and what was later revealed to be a stacked, all-white jury. While

the Scottsboro case marked the end of all-white juries in felony trials in the south, two subsequent juries of varying racial composition upheld the original guilty verdict. They also upheld the penalty of death for all defendants, except the 12-year-old, because the sexual assault of a white woman by a black man was a capital offence in Alabama.

The case was never decisively resolved, even after being brought before the U.S. Supreme Court as well as the National Association for the Advancement of Colored People (NAACP). Nor was there any prospect of closure, even after the victims admitted to fabricating the details of the event. In the end, four of the eight were convicted of some crime, with one defendant, Clarence Norris, sentenced to life in prison in 1937. The case exposed the contradiction between expedited trials and death sentences suborned by institutionalized racism in the south, versus the glacial pace of the appeals process across the rest of America. Paradoxically, the Scottsboro Boys spent much of the intervening six years under armed guard, including by state militia troops, to ensure their protection from the same public to whom they were thought to pose a danger. The miscarriage of justice that is generally now accepted as having defined the Scottsboro case and its protracted aftermath through the courts is for the most part exceptional; the mishandling of the investigation and ensuing trials did not diminish, however, the seriousness of the crime problems elsewhere in America at the time.

The Public Enemy Era
Back in Chicago, the 1930s saw a mild tempering of its traditional organized crime problem with the incarceration of Capone, the oligopoly on illegal markets by the Five Families, and the end of Prohibition, which stifled the underground economy of bootlegging in most northern states by 1933. While the widespread—or at least popularized—resentment of immigrants and outsiders had to some extent also subsided by the 1930s, a new taxonomy of public menaces was identified by law enforcement during the volatile period that became known as the public enemy era (1931–34). Like the previous decade, this era was defined by egregious public violence in industrialized cities, but one where threats to American life could not be so readily scapegoated to identifiable minorities and ethnic groups.

The roots of the phrase *public enemy* is under debate, but its origins are generally attributed to either a 1930 edition of the *Chicago Tribune* or a speech by Chicago Crime Commission Chair Frank Loesch the same year. While originally used in the context of the Capone gang, the label of "public enemy" was ascribed to homegrown outlaws who, unlike the traditional organized crime syndicates before them, were definitively disorganized and thus all the more unpredictable and dangerous. The criminal element in Chicago, which had once managed to feign civility and relegate its activities to the city's underground, took on a new and more brutal conspicuousness during the 1930s, a shift in tactics that proved that the Chicago Police Department (CPD) was entirely unprepared and ill-equipped. The CPD fallen officer tally became something of a barometer for the scale of violent crime in the city during the public enemy era: 81 CPD officers were killed in the line of duty between 1930 and 1939, including an astounding 14 officers killed in 1931 alone.

Some of the most infamous mainstays of the era wreaked havoc in and around Chicago, including John Dillinger, Lester "Baby Face Nelson" Gillis, George "Machine Gun Kelly" Barnes, and Clyde Barrow and Bonnie Parker, since mythologized as Bonnie and Clyde. While committing brazen armed robberies, often coupled with murder, and suspected of the slayings of dozens of law enforcement officials across the American midwest, they exploited a buyer's market of stockpiled automobiles and firearms in a depressed economy. The nomadic, sporadic nature of their crimes reprised the traveling spirit that defined early America before industrialization, but also underscored that the automobile was a game changer in terms of the sanctity of rural communities. Motor vehicles enabled the violent crime that defined the social disorganization of the industrial city to very easily spread to small-town America. It was in fact the multijurisdictional and mobile nature of the crimes during the public enemy era as much as their indiscriminate brutality that drew the ire of the federal government and necessitated a standardized reporting and investigation system, as well as more modern and progressive methods of attacking a dynamic crime problem that had consumed the resources of all local law enforcement.

Federal Bureau of Investigation
Having appropriated the epithet "public enemy" as his own publicity tool, J. Edgar Hoover, the longest standing director of the Bureau of Investigation (BOI), used the epic crime sprees of the early 1930s to propel his agency to the forefront of law enforcement on an international level. Hoover had been a key player for the Department of Justice in locating and deporting leftist and suspect communists, including Galleano group members, in the years prior to the Sacco and Vanzetti arrests. By 1924, he was appointed by Attorney General Harlan Fiske Stone, at the direction of President Calvin Coolidge, as the sixth director head of the BOI. The BOI was founded as a counterintelligence agency in the aftermath of World War I and was later renamed the Federal Bureau of Investigation (FBI) in response to the carnage of the public enemy era in 1935. Under Hoover's watch, the BOI and later the FBI undertook increasingly complex investigations and diversified its mandate significantly over a considerably compressed timeline. By the close of the 1930s, the bureau oversaw all matters that were even vaguely or theoretically related to domestic security, including but not limited to kidnapping, commercial fraud and forgery, gaming and money laundering, racketeering and political corruption, narcotics, armed robbery, murders and assaults committed against law enforcement and other public officials, and all matters of subversion, including communism.

Hoover remains a controversial figure, simultaneously mythologized and vilified in popular culture. His often

FBI Director J. Edgar Hoover (left) escorts Louis "Lepke" Buchalter (center) in handcuffs to court in 1939. Buchalter, head of the Mafia hit squad Murder Inc., had been in hiding since 1937 and was tricked into surrender by Hoover and Walter Winchell.

underhanded and unscrupulous methods aside, the reality is that the bureau used its notoriety obtained during the public enemy era to catapult American law enforcement into a world leader in innovative and continuously evolving investigative methods as well as new policing technologies and training methods.

Since the 1930, the bureau has also been the repository for all crime data collected by local and state police departments across America using the Uniform Crime Report (UCR) system. Ostensibly reflecting crimes known or reported to the police as coded by offence type, entity type, and location (known colloquially as crime codes and role codes), the UCR data transference system was developed piecemeal in the late 1920s as the principle law enforcement legacy of the Progressive Era—along with the invention of the dictograph as the progenitor of modern wiretapping and telephonic surveillance. The UCR model was designed to allow, as it continues today, the analysis, warehousing, tabulation, and interpretation of all national crime statistics provided by accredited agencies across the United States.

While the statistical validity of these crime statistics, as well as the accuracy of on-source information collected, has been subject to debate, the UCR indices were taken at face value for many years and became the means by which the fledgling bureau identified and defined its mandate. The UCR system also allowed Hoover, responding to the uni-directional—but often unintentionally inaccurate or corrupted information—provided by thousands of police agencies across the country, to justify the bureau's expansion into new areas of criminal investigation and expenditures related to attacking the criminal infrastructure.

The qualification and education requirements for police officers varied greatly across the United States, and police department communication infrastructures were relatively polarized between urban and rural areas. Therefore, the reductive and shorthand nature of the UCR system assured that the same crime would be catalogued by the police much differently depending on where it was reported. An incident reported as a street mugging in Culver City (classified by the UCR index as a violent crime) might just as easily be coded, with precisely the same circumstances, as a larceny (a property crime) in Sioux City, depending on a number of variables. These include the means by which the incident is first reported (in person versus by telephone), as well as the experience of the investigating officer and the perceived credibility of the complainant. On a national scale, such minor discrepancies over the course of a calendar year have the ability to grossly and cumulatively misrepresent wider trends in crime, and it has been argued that the bureau capitalized on this interpretative nature of the UCR design in order to justify experimental forays during and after the public enemy era. While the reported crime rate across the United States was relatively stable between 1935 and 1940, the national murder rate reached its highest point of the 20th century in 1933, at 9.7 murders per 100,000 people. The data spread in this context points to fundamental discrepancies in terms of actual crimes committed versus only reported crimes, a schism that would allow the UCR system to effectively, though often spuriously, dictate public perceptions of and vulnerability to crime. It also contoured the operational policies and public image of the bureau as the exclusive custodian of this information.

Amid the lawlessness of the 1930s and the bureau's new instruments for measuring crime and translating it into tangible figures, the bureau became the gold standard for law enforcement recordkeeping around the world. It also established itself as the national authority on standardized professional training for law enforcement, developing its first forensic and technical laboratory in 1932. Later, in 1935, the FBI National Academy was founded to provide expert training for not only its own agents, but also law enforcement officers from across the United States, Canada, and eventually the world as the bureau developed increasingly methodical and scientific approaches to criminal investigation. Hoover centralized and professionalized training for bureau agents and expanded the focus on scientific approaches to crime. This led to a newfound focus on recruiting agents from interdisciplinary backgrounds that could be retooled to advance the interests and reputation of the bureau among international experts. By recruiting physicists, chemists, and linguists directly out of the universities, the bureau soon became a viable civil service alternative to traditional laboratory work for scholars and scientists, and Hoover quickly become a visionary with respect to the emerging role of experts in law enforcement and ensuring successful prosecutions.

Hoover's professionalization and diversification of the bureau and, ultimately, the nature of criminal investigation in the Western world, was made possible in part by seed money and statutory reforms that made the bureau one of the most significant beneficiaries of President Roosevelt's New Deal in 1933. By that time, Roosevelt had enacted legislation that significantly federalized crime suppression and provided the bureau with broad, sweeping powers to address the increased mobility of crime. By 1935, bureau agents were also fully armed in all circumstances, a procedural overhaul that followed the death of two agents in the Kansas City Massacre in June 1933. By 1940, there were field offices located in 42 U.S. cities as Hoover began to place renewed importance on the bureau's historical mandate of domestic surveillance of persons of interest, up to and including White House officials and even First Lady Eleanor Roosevelt by the time of the outbreak of World War II.

Hoover's "G-Men"
The dramatic expansion and professionalization of the bureau during the interwar years was partially a response to the multijurisdictional, violent crime that accompanied the public enemy era and balance of the 1930s, and the corresponding need for a national police agency with both administrative and street-level operational components. The bureau's growth as a bureaucracy and ideological instrument during this period was significant. The ability of the bureau to very quickly marshal public respect and attain iconic status, both domestically and internationally, was in part due to Hoover's efforts to brand the bureau as mythic institution that appealed to the American imagination, particularly American youth. The popularization of the term *G-Men* (for Government Men) to describe bureau agents from the mid-1930s is rumored to have originated with a plea for mercy by George "Machine Gun" Kelly during his September 1933 arrest, and Hoover perpetuated this folklore image as a public relations device, particularly as a contrast to the public enemy label. The radio serial *G-Men*, later renamed *Gang Busters*, was produced under Hoover's supervision when it debuted on NBC radio in July 1935. The series was later adapted by DC Comics, as well as film and television production studios. In 1936, a children's version for radio titled *The True Adventures of Junior G-Men* was hosted by famed bureau agent Melvin Purvis—instrumental in the manhunt for John Dillinger in 1934—and went on to inspire a global cultural phenomenon. By the end of the decade, Junior G-Men clubs had been formed in the United States and internationally, serving as a type of youth brigade in the bureau's war on crime and largely mimicking the established structure and reward system of the Boy Scouts, but with a clearly defined law-enforcement purview.

By the start of World War II in 1939, Hoover had become a household name and, along with Los Angeles Police Chief William H. Parker, endures as perhaps the most famous, or infamous, law enforcement leader in American history. By 1940, Hoover transformed the bureau into a federal law enforcement, domestic security, and internal spy agency, as well as an unrivaled propagandist and publicity machine. It evolved into a prominent brand name that would become the prototype for the public-image strategies of American police departments in the media and popular culture for the balance of the 20th century, including Parker's LAPD. Hoover's new FBI also mirrored the evolving methods of news media and Hollywood in regard to American crime and criminal celebrity. Hoover's G-Men phenomenon was not only a vehicle for advancing his own notoriety and the prestige of the bureau in a financially depressed America in need of heroes. It was also an antidote against the glorification of the criminal underworld and the sensationalizing of crime that the bureau, and all of American law enforcement, faced in their attempts to restore and maintain some semblance of order.

Changing Forms of Crime News
The commercial press of the interwar years, devoid of good news stories for most of the financially challenged 1930s, and yet remaining a highly competitive and profitable market, defined itself by increasingly sensational crime reporting. There was no lack of material during this quarrelsome era, and the media responded in kind by devoting considerable print space to indulging readers' fascination with the criminal element. Stories of kidnappings were especially lurid and seized the public imagination, as the 1920s and 1930s yielded some of the most historically significant kidnap–ransom–murder schemes on record, engendering a specific trade known as the "snatch racket" among a specific

On their first tour of duty, July 1, 1940, five of the 20 new members of the Capitol police force, some of whom were recruited from the FBI, Secret Service, and Metropolitan police, gather at the Capitol. War conditions in Europe prompted a 1939 presidential directive to strengthen the FBI's authority to investigate subversives in the United States; it was reinforced by the 1940 Smith Act outlawing advocacy of violent government overthrow.

breed of criminal who, along with the bootlegging gangster and public enemy, generally defined the era.

The Copycat Case of Marion Parker
As kidnapping crimes grew increasingly brazen and heinous, media reports became increasingly fixated on gory details, ultimately shaping not only the public fear of crime but also public outrage and collective demands for justice. The 1927 case of Marion Parker is especially notable for its elevation of public interest in kidnappings, in part because her abductor and killer became the first person of the decade to be executed for his role in a ransom-motivated abduction and murder. Her admitted killer, William Edward Hickman, was already a convicted felon, as well as a former employee of prominent Los Angeles investment bank manager Perry Parker. On December 15, 1927, he abducted Parker's 12-year-old daughter Marion from her junior high school. Following a volley of ransom letters in which Hickman typically called himself "the Fox," an agreement was eventually made for a ransom–captive exchange on December 17. When Hickman was handed $1,500 in cash while waiting in an idling vehicle, and with Marion Parker ostensibly seated beside him, Hickman pushed what turned out to be the dismembered and disemboweled corpse of his victim out the door as he sped away. It was horrifically revealed that Hickman had stuffed the eviscerated corpse of Marion Parker—killed within hours of her abduction—with rags and discarded clothes in order to use it as a prop, with the eyes and mouth wired open to mislead her family and authorities into believing that she was still alive in order to secure the ransom payment.

The breadth of the manhunt for Hickman that followed reflected the degree to which the crime horrified America, with over 50,000 police officers representing not only the BOI, but also various local and state law enforcement agencies and American Legion volunteers. Hickman was eventually located hiding in Oregon and returned back to Los Angeles to face trial. After his insanity plea was rejected by jurors, Hickman was swiftly convicted and, in 1928, was hanged at San Quentin. Prior to his execution, he confessed that the savage crime was motivated in part to seek revenge against Perry Parker, who had previously had him fired and charged with forgery offenses during his brief employment at the bank. The main motive, however, was Hickman's desire for the same media attention and public interest that had been bestowed on Leopold and Loeb and their similar modus operandi in 1924. This admission, if accurate, would make the Parker murder a significant case study in the role of the commercial press in inspiring copycat crimes.

The Lindbergh Kidnapping
The media furor and public spectacle that surrounded the kidnapping and murder of the Parker child, however, would soon be overshadowed by the events of March 1, 1932, when a nighttime intruder snatched the 20-month-old son of famed transatlantic aviator Charles Lindbergh from the second-story bedroom of his rural New Jersey home. The abduction of Charles Lindbergh Jr., not from a school or public place but out of his nursery while he slept, upped the ante in terms of the risks that ransom kidnappers of the wealthy and influential were prepared to assume as economic times worsened. The bold methodology of the crime, combined with the existing international celebrity of "Lucky Lindy," led to a nationwide manhunt that eclipsed the search for Marion Parker four years prior and endured for over 10 weeks as ransom demands of $50,000 in cash and gold certificates were levied in exchange for information on the child's whereabouts. After the ransom was paid and the information proved bogus, the remains of Charles Jr. were discovered by a passing motorist on a roadside just a few miles from the Lindbergh home on May 12. The Lindbergh Law, which made kidnapping a federal offense—and

thus the bailiwick of the BOI and FBI—was passed in Congress within a month of the recovery of the infant's body, although tracing the redemption of the gold certificates paid as ransom took significantly longer than expected.

By September 1934, the BOI and NYPD officers had a sufficient paper trail to place a Bronx tenement leased by German immigrant and freelance carpenter Bruno Hauptmann under discreet surveillance, and eventually the grounds to take him into federal custody on September 19. A search of Hauptmann's residence by authorities turned up a cache of nearly $14,000 of the outstanding ransom money hidden in his garage. Hauptmann was immediately extradited back to New Jersey to face charges of kidnapping, extortion, and first-degree murder.

Superlatives such as "the crime of the century" and "the trial of the century" were reprised from the Leopold and Loeb case nearly a decade prior, and were used liberally by the press as Hauptmann became an international curiosity, vilified even further when it was revealed that he was an illegal alien and former Imperial Army machine gunner during World War I. As a carnival-like atmosphere descended on the courtroom for the next six weeks, the American public attentively followed the progress of the trial, complete with photographs snapped by news cameras that were permitted in the courtroom. A jury eventually found Hauptmann guilty on all charges on February 13, 1935, and he was expeditiously sentenced to death by trial judge Thomas Trenchard. Professing his innocence until the end and refusing a gubernatorial offer to exchange a detailed confession for a stay of execution, Hauptmann was executed in the electric chair on April 3, 1936.

The "trial of the century" did not come to an end with Hauptmann's execution. As the media circus was protracted beyond the case, Charles Lindbergh, along with wife Anne Morrow Lindbergh and their new son, self-exiled to Europe to avoid begin dragged into the ceaseless, sensational, tabloid-like followups by the media. A reflection on the role of the media in not merely reporting on criminal trials, but also disrupting and even influencing the proceedings, led for calls to reconsider the value of permitting news cameras in the courtroom. Judge Trenchard had allowed the use of still photography during the proceedings of the Hauptmann trial, but had not considered the ongoing distractions caused by incessant mechanical noises, let alone the popping of flashbulbs. It also quickly became evident that some reporters had smuggled motion picture cameras into the court as bootlegged newsreel footage of the testimony began to surface. Lindbergh's reclusive behavior following the trial, fearful that the media's ongoing attention to the case would imperil the safety of his subsequent children, ensured that the divorce between the camera and the courtroom would endure as one of the defining legacies of the trial. By 1937, the American Bar Association had banned the use of audio-video recordings and still photography in all courtrooms, and Congress followed suit with respect to banning cameras from all federal proceedings. There was compliance in all states, except Colorado and Texas. The issue was not revisited until 40 years later, when advances in technology made camera operations and the presence of equipment more discreet and enabled their return to the courtroom on a provisional basis.

News and Entertainment Censures
By censuring the news industry in 1937, the American Bar Association followed to some extent the proscriptive trends in the censorship of crime stories earlier undertaken by Hollywood. The American news media, while not directly rebuked for their solicitous treatment of crime stories following Hickman's admission of celebrity envy, nor the proverbial circus of the Hauptmann trial, eventually inspired government censorship of representations of all criminal content in commercial productions for public audiences. While official "news" media emerged relatively unscathed, the Hollywood film

industry as the emerging cultural authority on crime and public opinion bore the brunt of demands to reign in the collective glorification of crime in America. From the debut of Warner Brothers' *The Jazz Singer* in 1927 as the first "talkie" film to the full-length feature with a synchronized soundtrack, the role of motion pictures as increasingly influential social commentaries and multimedia texts was reflected with crime films emerging as the industry staple. The public enemy era as romantically depicted in American film proved the final push that social conservatives and government regulators needed to enact the Motion Picture Production Code in 1930. Popularly known as the Hays Code after Hollywood's director of censorship at the time, Will H. Hays, the regulation was not consistently enforced until 1934, following the uproar surrounding director Howard Hawks's Capone biopic *Scarface: The Shame of a Nation*. While not relegated exclusively to crime films per se, the code still represented demands for moral reform in an age of social and financial uncertainty, when core values and respect for the law was tenuous at best.

Remaining in effect until 1968, when it was replaced by the Motion Picture Association of America film rating system that remains on the books today, the Hays Code was principally concerned with restricting the glorification and implied financial benefits of crime in film, as well as the idea that sexually liberal conduct was permissible or attractive. The code also required that films depict authority figures such as the police and elected officials with respect so as to not bring the administration of justice into disrepute. This distinction is significant in that one of the earlier silent era's stars, Roscoe "Fatty" Arbuckle, boasted a filmography defined by the mockery of the American police in the *Keystone Cops* franchise. Although not actively producing films by the time the Hays Code was consistently enforced in 1934, Arbuckle had already been targeted for censorship following his September 1921 arrest for manslaughter in the death of small-time actress Virginia Rappe. It was suggested on largely dubious evidence, including an alleged deathbed utterance, that Rappe's fatal bladder rupture was not the result of a pre-existing illness or botched abortion, but the consequence of the rotund Arbuckle's body weight bearing down on her frame during forced intercourse at a Labor Day party at a San Francisco hotel a few weeks earlier.

Following three consecutive and well-publicized trials, the reputation of the once acclaimed and innocuous comedian took a thrashing at the hands of tabloid opportunists such as William Randolph Hearst. Although ultimately acquitted following two consecutive mistrials, by the start of his third trial in March 1922, Hays had already banned Arbuckle's films, not for their content, but for their association with a man painted in the media—without evidence—as a sex-crazed, adulterous drunkard who partook in Hollywood orgies and indulged in illicit drugs.

All evidence points to Arbuckle as having been railroaded, and for reasons that never became clear; but his public humiliation and the dismissal of his contributions to American film and culture were undertaken as a personal crusade by Hays a full decade before his code came into effect. The Arbuckle scandal foreshadowed forthcoming trends in using the media to ensure circuitous justice through destroyed celebrity careers. It also ensured that the Hays Code, as the forerunner to McCarthyism, became the model by which Hollywood figures would become key players in debates over crime and punishment in America, and thus increasingly vulnerable to allegations of being unethical and un-American.

Michael Arntfield
University of Western Ontario
Vivien Miller
University of Nottingham

1921 PRIMARY DOCUMENT

State of Illinois v. Edward Cicotte, et al.

White Sox first baseman Chick Gandil was a friend of professional gambler Sport Sullivan, and the two of them conspired to fix the 1919 World Series. Team owner Charles Comiskey was not well liked and underpaid his players. Gandil used this to enlist several of his teammates to throw the series for a share of the gambling winnings. The "Black Sox" were banned from baseball for life, and owners hired federal judge Kenesaw Mountain Landis to oversee the sport as its first commissioner.

Bill of Particulars in the Case of
State of Illinois
v. Edward Cicotte, et al.
(February 1921)

STATE OF ILLINOIS
SS:
COUNTY OF COOK

IN THE CRIMINAL COURT
OF COOK COUNTY:

THE PEOPLE OF THE STATE OF ILLINOIS
vs.
EDWARD V. CICOTTE, et al.

Indictment No. 23912

Bill of Particulars as to Count 1, Count 2, and Count 3, of Indictment No. 23912, filled in conformity to rule entered July 5th, 1921, by his Honor Judge Hugo Friend, one of the Judges of the Criminal Court of Cook County.

The defendants in the above entitled cause, and each of them, are hereby notified that the State will offer evidence tending to show that the defendants, Edward V. Cicotte, Claude Williams, Joe Jackson, Fred McMullin, Arnold Gandill, George Weaver, Oscar Felsch and Charles Risberg, in September and October of 1919 were engaged as base ball players and were members of a base ball club known as the American League Base Ball Club of Chicago, a corporation;

That said American League Base Ball Club of Chicago was engaged to play in competition with a certain other base ball club known as the National League Base Ball Club of Cincinnati, Ohio, a certain series of games of base ball; some of the games of said series to be played in Chicago and other games of said series to be played in Cincinnati, Ohio;

That the defendants, William Burns and Hal Chase were at various times connected with base ball as professional base ball players but were not participants in any of the games of the above mentioned series;

That the defendants, Joseph J. Sullivan, Rachael Brown Abe Attell, Carl Zork, Ben Franklin, Ben Levi, Louis Levi, and David Zelzer were not connected with base ball as players, but were reputed to be gamblers or prized fighters and interested in the promotion of gambling enterprises and sporting events of questionable character;

That considerable public interest was manifested in the outcome of said series of games and each game of said series;

That each of said games was publicly regarded as an important sporting event and that the spectators of said games and each to them was required to pay an admission fee to the field where said games were played;

That the defendants participating in said games as players conspired, confederated and agreed together with the defendants not participating therein to so conduct themselves throughout the said games and each of said games and so manipulate their playing in each of said games as to make certain in advance of the playing in each of said games as to make certain in advance of the playing of said games the outcome thereof and the winner thereof, and so as to make certain in advance of the playing of all of the games of said series the outcome of the majority of the games of said series and the winner of the majority of said series of games;

And the defendants not participating in said games, as base ball players, conspired, confederated and agree together and with the defendants participating in said games to operate among the spectators of said games and others and the general public to procure divers large sums of money by means of and by use of the confidence game.

That one Charles C. Nims, a resident of Chicago, Illinois, was unlawfully, fraudulently and feloniously swindled out of the sum of $250.00 by the defendant, Joseph J. Sullivan, who was then and there engaged in carrying out the conspiracy aforesaid and who did then and there obtain from the said Charles C. Nims the sum of $250.00 by means and by use of the confidence fame contrary to the Statute in such cases made and provided.

And further particulars, the defendants are respectfully referred to the first, second, and third counts of said indictment.

Signed: Robert E. Crowe
State's Attorney of Cook County, Illinois

Signed: Geo E. Gorman
Assistant State's Attorney

Source: http://law2.umkc.edu/faculty/projects/ftrials/blacksox/particulars.html

See Articles: Gambling; Organized Crime, History of; Rothstein, Arnold

1924 PRIMARY DOCUMENT

An Act to Preserve Racial Integrity

The Act to Preserve Racial Integrity was one of two eugenics laws passed by the Virginia legislature in 1924. The accompanying Sterilization Act compelled sterilization for the "feebleminded," while the Racial Integrity Act defined every person as either "white" or "colored." Colored persons were those with any amount of nonwhite ancestry, who were prohibited from marrying whites. The state registrar even ordered the exhumation of suspected nonwhites buried in white cemeteries and reinterred them in colored cemeteries.

1. Be it enacted by the General Assembly of Virginia, That the State Registrar of Vital Statistics may as soon as practicable after the taking effect of this act, prepare a form whereon the racial composition of any individual, as Caucasian, negro, Mongolian, American Indian, Asiatic Indian, Malay, or any mixture thereof, or any other non-Caucasic strains, and if there be any mixture, then the racial composition of the parents and other ancestors, in so far as ascertainable, so as to show in what generation such mixture occurred, may be certified by such individual, which form shall be known as a registration certificate. The State Registrar may supply to each local registrar a sufficient number of such forms for the purpose of this act; each local registrar may personally or by deputy, as soon as possible after receiving said forms, have made thereon in duplicate a certificate of the racial composition as aforesaid, of each person resident in his district, who so desires, born before June fourteenth, nineteen hundred and twelve, which certificate shall be made over the signature of said person, or in the case of children under fourteen years of age, over the signature of a parent, guardian, or other person standing in *loco parentis*. One of said certificates for each person thus registering in every district shall be forwarded to the State Registrar for his files; the other shall be kept on file by the local registrar.

    Every local registrar may, as soon as practicable, have such registration certificate made by or for each person in his district who so desires, born before June fourteen, nineteen hundred and twelve, for whom he has not on file a registration certificate, or a birth certificate.

2. It shall be a felony for any person wilfully or knowingly to make a registration certificate false as to color or race. The wilful

making of a false registration or birth certificate shall be punished by confinement in the penitentiary for one year.
3. For each registration certificate properly made and returned to the State Registrar, the local registrar returning the same shall be entitled to a fee of twenty-five cents....
4. No marriage license shall be granted until the clerk or deputy clerk has reasonable assurance that the statements as to color of both man and woman are correct.
   If there is reasonable cause to disbelieve that applicants are of pure white race, when that fact is stated, the clerk or deputy clerk shall withhold the granting of the license until satisfactory proof is produced that both applicants are "white persons" as provided for in this act. The clerk or deputy clerk shall use the same care to assure himself that both applicants are colored, when that fact is claimed.
5. It shall hereafter be unlawful for any white person in this State to marry any save a white person, or a person with no other admixture of blood than white and American Indian. For the purpose of this act, the term "white person" shall apply only to the person who has no trace whatsoever of any blood other than Caucasian; but persons who have one-sixteenth or less of the blood of the American Indian and have no other non-Caucasic blood shall be deemed to be white persons. All laws heretofore passed and now in effect regarding the intermarriage of white and colored persons shall apply to marriages prohibited by this act.
6. For carrying out the purposes of this act and to provide the necessary clerical assistance, postage and other expenses of the State Registrar of Vital Statistics, twenty per cent of the fees received by local registrars under this act shall be paid to the State Bureau of Vital Statistics, which may be expended by the said bureau for the purposes of this act.
7. All acts or parts of acts inconsistent with this act are, to the extent of such inconsistency, hereby repealed.

Source: http://www2.vcdh.virginia.edu/encounter/projects/monacans/Contemporary_Monacans/racial.html

See Articles: African Americans; Native Americans; Racism; Virginia.

1925 PRIMARY DOCUMENT

H. L. Mencken's Commentary on the Scopes Trial

The trial of John Scopes for violating a Tennessee law against teaching evolution in state-funded schools brought together two of the most famous figures in the legal world: Clarence Darrow, who had defended Leopold and Loeb, defended Scopes; William Jennings Bryan, repeat presidential candidate and masterful orator prosecuted Scopes. It was the first major legal showcase for fundamentalism, a new, powerful, and increasingly political strain of Christianity. Scopes paid a $100 fine.

The Scopes Trial: Darrow's Eloquent Appeal Wasted on Ears That Heed Only Bryan, Says Mencken

Dayton, Tenn.—The net effect of Clarence Darrow's great speech yesterday seems to be precisely the same as if he had bawled it up a rainspout in the interior of Afghanistan. That is, locally, upon the process against the infidel Scopes, upon the so-called minds of these fundamentalists of upland Tennessee. You have but a dim notion of it who have only read it. It was not designed for reading, but for hearing. The clanging of it was as important as the logic. It rose like a wind and ended like a flourish of bugles. The very judge on the bench, toward the end of it, began to look uneasy. But the morons in the audience, when it was over, simply hissed it.

During the whole time of its delivery the old mountebank, Bryan, sat tight-lipped and unmoved. There is, of course, no reason why it should have shaken him. He has those hill billies locked up in his pen and he knows it. His brand is on them. He is at home among them. Since his earliest days, indeed, his chief strength has been among the folk of remote hills and forlorn and lonely farms. Now with his political aspirations all gone to pot, he turns to them for religious consolations. They understand his peculiar imbecilities. His nonsense is their ideal of sense. When he deluges them with his theological bilge they rejoice like pilgrims disporting in the river Jordan.

The town whisper is that the local attorney-general, Stewart, is not a fundamentalist, and hence has no stomach for his job. It seems not improbable. He is a man of evident education, and his argument yesterday was confined very strictly to the constitutional points -- the argument of a competent and conscientious lawyer, and to me, at least very persuasive.

But Stewart, after all, is a foreigner here, almost as much so as Darrow or Hays or Malone. He is doing his job and that is all. The real animus of the prosecution centers in Bryan. He is the plaintiff and prosecutor. The local lawyers are simply bottle-holders for him. He will win the case, not by academic appeals to law and precedent, but by direct and powerful appeals to the immemorial fears and superstitions of man. It is no wonder that he is hot against Scopes. Five years of Scopes and even these mountaineers would begin to laugh at Bryan. Ten years and they would ride him out of town on a rail, with one Baptist parson in front of him and another behind.

But there will be no ten years of Scopes, nor five years, nor even one year.

Such brash young fellows, debauched by the enlightenment, must be disposed of before they become dangerous, and Bryan is here, with his tight lips and hard eyes, to see that this one is disposed of. The talk of the lawyers, even the magnificent talk of Darrow, is so much idle wind music. The case will not be decided by logic, nor even by eloquence. It will be decided by counting noses -- and for every nose in these hills that has ever thrust itself into any book save the Bible there are a hundred adorned with the brass ring of Bryan. These are his people. They understand him when he speaks in tongues. The same dark face that is in his own eyes is in theirs, too. They feel with him, and they relish him.

I sincerely hope that the nobility and gentry of the lowlands will not make the colossal mistake of viewing this trial of Scopes as a trivial farce. Full of rustic japes and in bad taste, it is, to be sure, somewhat comic on the surface. One laughs to see lawyers sweat. The jury, marched down Broadway, would set New York by the ears. But all of that is only skin deep.

Deeper down there are the beginnings of a struggle that may go on to melodrama of the first caliber, and when the curtain falls at least all the laughter may be coming from the yokels. You probably laughed at the prohibitionists, say, back in 1914. Well, don't make the same error twice.

As I have said, Bryan understands these peasants, and they understand him. He is a bit mangey and flea-bitten, but no means ready for his harp. He may last five years, ten years or even longer. What he may accomplish in that time, seen here at close range, looms up immensely larger than it appears to a city man five hundred miles away. The fellow is full of such bitter, implacable hatreds that they radiate from him like heat from a stove. He hates the learning that he cannot grasp. He hates those who sneer at him. He hates, in general, all who stand apart from his own pathetic commonness. And the yokels hate with him, some of them almost as bitterly as he does himself. They are willing and eager to follow him—and he has already given them a taste of blood.

Darrow's peroration yesterday was interrupted by Judge Raulston, but the force of it got into the air nevertheless. This year it is a misdemeanor for a country school teacher to flout the archaic nonsense of Genesis. Next year it will be a felony. The year after the net will be spread wider. Pedagogues, after all, are small game; there are larger birds to snare—larger and juicier. Bryan has his fishy eye on them. He will fetch them if his mind lasts, and the lamp holds out to burn. No man with a mouth like that ever lets go. Nor ever lacks followers.

Tennessee is bearing the brunt of the first attack simply because the civilized minority, down here, is extraordinarily pusillanimous.

I have met no educated man who is not ashamed of the ridicule that has fallen upon the State, and I have met none, save only judge Neal, who had the courage to speak out while it was yet time. No Tennessee counsel of any importance came into the case until yesterday and then they came in stepping very softly as if taking a brief for sense were a dangerous matter. When Bryan did his first rampaging here all these men were silent.

They had known for years what was going on in the hills. They knew what the country preachers were preaching—what degraded nonsense was being rammed and hammered into yokel skulls. But they were afraid to go out against the imposture while it was in the making, and when any outsider denounced it they fell upon him violently as an enemy of Tennessee. Now Tennessee is paying for that poltroonery. The State is smiling and beautiful, and of late it has begun to be rich. I know of no American city that is set in more lovely scenery than Chattanooga, or that has more charming homes. The civilized minority is as large here, I believe, as anywhere else.

It has made a city of splendid material comforts and kept it in order. But it has neglected in the past the unpleasant business of following what was going on in the cross roads Little Bethels.

The Baptist preachers ranted unchallenged. Their buffooneries were mistaken for humor. Now the clowns turn out to be armed, and have begun to shoot.

In his argument yesterday judge Neal had to admit pathetically that it was hopeless to fight for a repeal of the anti-evolution law. The Legislature of Tennessee, like the Legislature of every other American state, is made up of cheap job-seekers and ignoramuses.

The Governor of the State is a politician ten times cheaper and trashier. It is vain to look for relief from such men. If the State is to be saved at all, it must be saved by the courts.

For one, I have little hope of relief in that direction, despite Hays' logic and Darrow's eloquence. Constitutions, in America, no longer mean what they say. To mention the Bill of Rights is to be damned as a Red.

The rabble is in the saddle, and down here it makes its first campaign under a general beside whom Wat Tylor seems like a wart beside the Matterhorn.

H. L. Mencken
Baltimore Evening Sun
July 14, 1925

Source: *Baltimore Evening Sun* (July 14, 1925). http://www.etsu.edu/cas/history/documents/menckendarrow.htm

See Articles: Darrow, Clarence; Famous Trials; Legal Counsel; News Media, Crime in; Scopes Monkey Trial.

1930
PRIMARY DOCUMENT

The Motion Picture Production Code of 1930

In 1915, the U.S. Supreme Court decided in Mutual Film Corporation v. Industrial Commission of Ohio *that free speech did not extend to motion pictures, which were "a business, pure and simple, originated and conducted for profit." By 1922, several states had instituted censorship boards, and the industry hired Will Hays to act as its own censor. With input from the Catholic community, Hays eventually released this official code, which bound studio movies until the rating system replaced it in 1968.*

Motion picture producers recognize the high trust and confidence which have been placed in them by the people of the world and which have made motion pictures a universal form of entertainment.

They recognize their responsibility to the public because of this trust and because entertainment and art are important influences in the life of a nation.

Hence, though regarding motion pictures primarily as entertainment without any explicit purpose of teaching or propaganda, they know that the motion picture within its own field of entertainment may be directly responsible for spiritual or moral progress, for higher types of social life, and for much correct thinking.

During the rapid transition from silent to talking pictures they have realized the necessity and the opportunity of subscribing to a Code to govern the production of talking pictures and of reacknowledging this responsibility.

On their part, they ask from the public and from public leaders a sympathetic understanding of their purposes and problems and a spirit of cooperation that will allow them the freedom and opportunity necessary to bring the motion picture to a still higher level of wholesome entertainment for all the people.

General Principles
1. No picture shall be produced which will lower the moral standards of those who see it. Hence the sympathy of the audience should never be thrown to the side of crime, wrongdoing, evil or sin.
2. Correct standards of life, subject only to the requirements of drama and entertainment, shall be presented.
3. Law, natural or human, shall not be ridiculed, nor shall sympathy be created for its violation.

Particular Applications I—Crimes Against the Law
These shall never be presented in such a way as to throw sympathy with the crime as against law and justice or to inspire others with a desire for imitation.
1. *Murder*
   a. The technique of murder must be presented in a way that will not inspire imitation.
   b. Brutal killings are not to be presented in detail.
   c. Revenge in modern times shall not be justified.
2. Methods of Crime should not be explicitly presented.
   a. Theft, robbery, safe-cracking, and dynamiting of trains, mines, buildings, etc., should not be detailed in method.
   b. Arson must be subject to the same safeguards.
   c. The use of firearms should be restricted to essentials.
   d. Methods of smuggling should not be presented.
3. *Illegal drug traffic* must never be presented.
4. *The use of liquor* in American life, when not required by the plot or for proper characterization will not be shown.

II—Sex
The sanctity of the institution of marriage and the home shall be upheld. Pictures shall not infer that low forms of sex relationship are the accepted or common thing.
1. *Adultery,* sometimes necessary plot material, must not be explicitly treated, or justified, or presented attractively.
2. *Scenes of Passion*
   a. They should not be introduced when not essential to the plot.
   b. Excessive and lustful kissing, lustful embraces, suggestive postures and gestures, are not to be shown.
   c. In general passion should so be treated that these scenes do not stimulate the lower and baser element.
3. *Seduction or Rape*
   a. They should never be more than suggested, and only when essential for the plot, and even then never shown by explicit method.
   b. They are never the proper subject for comedy.
4. *Sex perversion* or any inference to it is forbidden.
5. *White-slavery* shall not be treated.
6. *Miscegenation* (sex relationships between the white and black races) is forbidden.
7. *Sex hygiene* and venereal diseases are not subjects for motion pictures.

8. Scenes of *actual child birth*, in fact or in silhouette, are never to be presented.
9. *Children's sex organs* are never to be exposed.

III—Vulgarity
The treatment of low, disgusting, unpleasant, though not necessarily evil, subjects should be subject always to the dictates of good taste and a regard for the sensibilities of the audience.

IV—Obscenity
Obscenity in word, gesture, reference, song, joke, or by suggestion (even when likely to be understood only by part of the audience) is forbidden.

V—Profanity
Pointed profanity (this includes the words, God, Lord, Jesus, Christ—unless used reverently—Hell, S.O.B. damn, Gawd), or every other profane or vulgar expression, however used, is forbidden.

VI—Costume
1. *Complete nudity* is never permitted. This includes nudity in fact or in silhouette, or any lecherous or licentious notice thereof by other characters in the picture.
2. *Undressing scenes* should be avoided, and never used save where essential to the plot.
3. *Indecent or undue exposure* is forbidden.
4. *Dancing costumes* intended to permit undue exposure or indecent movements in the dance are forbidden.

VII—Dances
1. Dances suggesting or representing sexual actions or indecent passion are forbidden.
2. Dances which emphasize indecent movements are to be regarded as obscene.

VIII—Religion
1. No film or episode may throw ridicule on any religious faith.
2. *Ministers of religion* in their character as ministers of religion should not be used as comic characters or as villains.
3. *Ceremonies* of any definite religion should be carefully and respectfully handled.

IX—Locations
The treatment of bedrooms must be governed by good taste and delicacy.

X—National Feelings
1. *The use of the Flag* shall be consistently respectful.
2. *The history,* institutions, prominent people and citizenry of other nations shall be represented fairly.

XI—Titles
Salacious, indecent, or obscene titles shall not be used.

XII—Repellent Subjects
The following subjects must be treated within the careful limits of good taste:
1. *Actual hangings* or electrocutions as legal punishments for crime.
2. *Third Degree* methods.
3. *Brutality* and possible gruesomeness.
4. *Branding* of people or animals.
5. *Apparent cruelty* to children or animals.
6. *The sale of women* or a woman selling her virtue.
7. *Surgical operations.*

Source: "The Motion Picture Production Code of 1930." In *The Dame in the Kimono: Hollywood, Censorship, and the Production Code From the 1920s to the 1960s*, edited by Leonard J. Jeff and Jerold Simmons. New York: Grove Wiedenfeld, 1990.

See Articles: Adultery; Indecent Exposure.

1932
PRIMARY DOCUMENT

FBI Memorandum on Patent Infringement

Beginning in 1924, the Bureau of Investigation added Classification 27, Patent Matters, to its file system (Classification 28 is used for copyright matters.) The Bureau of Investigation doesn't investigate civil disputes, but does investigate possible patent law violations that could bear on criminal prosecutions. As explained in this memo, in this case, the fraudulent sale of patented automobile parts was so widespread that a civil suit wouldn't remedy the situation.

George Le Roy Curtis; John S. Holden; Walter Wulf; Carl Bierack; William Curtis; Bertram Puckett; Carl B. Coombs; Garland Retherford; Henry W. Greenberg; Benjamin Jacobs.

A lucrative, illicit trade in patented lubricator fittings for automobiles throughout the Mid-West was brought to light at St. Louis, Missouri, by the arrest of George LeRoy Curtis and five other individuals on a charge of conspiring to violate that section of the United States Code which prohibits the use of the word "patent" or "patentee" with intent to imitate or counterfeit the mark or device of the proper patentee.

As a general rule, the person holding the original patent in a case of this kind seeks his remedy by means of a civil suit, in which he charges infringement of patent rights and seeks to collect damages. In this particular case, however, the fraudulent sale of the product was so widespread that the owner of the patent could only hope to obtain relief through criminal prosecution, and complaint was accordingly made to the United States Attorney at St. Louis, who, in turn, referred the matter to the St. Louis office of the United States Bureau of Investigation.

George LeRoy Curtis was arrested as a result of an attempted sale of so-called "gyp" fittings, which infringed the patent, to an automobile dealer in St. Louis at an unusually low price. This dealer noted the number of the automobile license and reported it. At the time of this attempted sale, Curtis was using the name of C. H. Howard. His true identity, however, was established by Bureau Agents, who also ascertained that he was operating in St. Louis under the name of J. W. Gray, and had thousands of the spurious fittings in stock. Curtis, upon being apprehended, gave a signed statement to Special Agents of the United States Bureau of Investigation and, as a result, five other individuals, including four distributors and one manufacturer of the illicit product, were charged in an indictment returned on September 11, 1930, with violation of the section of the United States Code mentioned above. Further investigation revealed that the spurious fittings were marketed throughout the entire country and that their sales ran into hundreds of thousands. In order to fully ascertain the scope of the operations of these individuals and to establish the identity of the parties involved, the United States Bureau of Investigation carried its inquiry into New England, the West Coast, and all of the large cities of the Central West and the East.

Special Agents of the Bureau located and carefully examined correspondence which had passed between these individuals and their various associates. Several shipments of the illegally made product were found in transit, having been shipped to distant points. These shipments were impounded to be used as evidence. Special Agents, in their further investigation, encountered such obstacles as concealed identities, fly-by-night organizations, and bankrupt concerns. The focal point for the manufacture of these unlicensed fittings proved, upon investigation, to be Detroit, Michigan.

All of the above individuals engaged in this illicit commerce admitted knowledge of the fact that they were violating the Federal law in manufacturing and selling these fittings. Further investigation developed that some of the distributors and defendants who actually sold the fittings to the retail trade had no knowledge that the actual manufacture of the fittings was in violation of the Patent Laws. It developed further that in some instances the manufacturers themselves had no knowledge of the fact that they were manufacturing a patented article, in view of the fact that they manufactured the fittings according to specifications, the stamp containing the name of the holder of the original patent and the word "patent" being placed on the article by still a third party or corporation. It was revealed that two of the arrested individuals had been enjoined by the Court on an infringement suit for manufacturing and distributing similar articles more than a year previous, but that in spite of this injunction they had continued their surreptitious manufacture and sale of such articles. The comparative simplicity of the patented device, the fact that it sold for a nominal sum, and the further fact that it was much in demand in the automobile trade, all contributed to the success of this gigantic fraud.

As investigation was continued by Special Agents of the United States Bureau of Investigation, additional indictments were secured on November 19, 1930, charging conspiracy to violate the Patent Laws, against the following individuals: George LeRoy Curtis, William Curtis, Walter Wulf, Carl Bierack, Bertram Puckett, Henry W. Greenberg, Benjamin Jacobs and John S. Holden.

On the same date, a Federal Grand Jury at East St. Louis, Illinois, returned a separate conspiracy indictment against Carl B. Coombs and Garland Retherford.

The majority of the individuals against whom indictments were obtained became fugitives from justice and the United States Bureau of Investigation conducted an extensive search for many of them throughout the United States, which ultimately led to their apprehension and return to the jurisdiction in which they were to be tried.

Greenberg and Jacobs, who had sold the patent infringing products, were discharged by the United States Commissioner at Providence, Rhode Island, on January 23, 1931, and no further prosecutive action was taken against them. They were, however, restrained by a Federal injunction from dealing further in these articles.

The cases of the remaining conspirators were called for trial in February and March, 1931, at which time all of them entered pleas of guilty or nolo contendere. As a result of these pleas, the following sentences were imposed in Federal Court at East St. Louis and Danville, Illinois, respectively:

George LeRoy Curtis, on a plea of guilty, was sentenced to serve one year in jail. His sentence was suspended and he was placed on probation for a like period.

William Curtis, on a plea of guilty, was sentenced to serve ten months in the Vermilion County Jail.

Walter Wulf, on a plea of guilty, was sentenced to serve ten months in the Vermilion County Jail.

Carl Bierack, on a plea of guilty, was sentenced to serve one year in the Vermilion County Jail.

Bertram Puckett, on a plea of nolo contendere, was sentenced to serve thirty days in the Vermilion County Jail and was fined $400.00.

John S. Holden, on a plea of guilty, was sentenced to serve one year in jail. His sentence was suspended and he was placed on probation for a like period.

Carl B. Coombs, on a plea of nolo contendere, was sentenced to serve ninety days in the Vermilion County Jail and was fined $300.00.

Garland Retherford, on a plea of guilty, was sentenced to serve thirty days in jail. This sentence was suspended and he was placed on probation for one year and one day, and was fined $100.00.

John Edgar Hoover
Director

U.S. Bureau of Investigation
Department of Justice
Washington, D.C.
I.C. No. 27-59
December 21, 1932

Source: NARA-II, RG 65 FBI, Interesting Case Write-ups, Box 12

See Articles: Counterfeiting; Detroit, Michigan; Fraud; Hoover, J. Edgar; Justice, Department of; Rhode Island; White-Collar Crime, History of; White-Collar Crime, Sociology of.

1933 PRIMARY DOCUMENT

FBI Memorandum on the National Motor Vehicle Theft Act

In 1924, the Bureau of Investigation established Classification 26 for the Interstate Transportation of Stolen Motor Vehicles and Stolen Aircraft. The National Motor Vehicle Theft Act in 1919 had established that transportation of a stolen vehicle across state lines was a federal crime, and it was one of the increasingly common types of crime for which the Bureau of Investigation was formed. In 1970, the Department of Justice changed its prosecution guidelines, with most cases referred to state and local agencies. Multiple escape attempts are described in this report.

Patrick O'Hare alias Pat Smith alias J. Smith alias Patrick Collins alias James B. Collins Alias Pat O'Hare alias Pat O'Hara alias Pat Patrick.

The Pittsburgh Office of the Federal Bureau investigation began an investigation of Patrick O'Hare, with innumerable aliases, for violation of the National Motor Vehicle Theft Act, in the late summer and early fall of 1928. In October, 1928, at Wheeling, West Virginia, O'Hare was indicted for violation of the National Motor Vehicle Theft Act, and charged with interstate transportation of a Ford truck automobile from Pittsburgh, Pennsylvania to Parkersburg, West Virginia, on or about August 26, 1927, and the transportation of a Ford sedan from Barberton, Ohio to Williamstown, West Virginia, in addition to being charged with selling and disposing of the two above automobiles, knowing them to have been stolen.

While being removed by a Deputy United States Marshal from Wheeling, West Virginia to Parkersburg, West Virginia, on January 7, 1929, for trial on the above charges, he succeeded in effecting his escape. He became a Federal fugitive from justice, and the Bureau began an intensive search, which lasted more than four years, to effect his re-apprehension.

This escape, however, was not the first one effected by O'Hare. He had been arrested on November 31, 1922 by the police authorities of Akron, Ohio, charged with grand larceny of ten automobiles, at which time he made his escape, only to be re-arrested on May 5, 1925, upon which occasion he was sentenced to two years in the Ohio State Penitentiary, this sentence being suspended. He was later arrested by the Youngstown, Ohio Police Department, and was again successful in effecting his escape. On April 6, 1932, while in custody of the Detroit, Michigan police, by whom he had been arrested on a charge of driving while drunk, he made his escape by running through a plate glass window, but was soon apprehended and given a fine of $25 and a year's probation by the Michigan courts, under the name of James Collins.

The Detroit, Michigan police arrested O'Hare under the name of James B. Collins, on February 22, 1933. True to form, he again escaped by leaping from a second story window. However, he broke his leg upon this occasion and two days later was re-arrested and taken into Federal custody upon the old National Motor Vehicle Theft Act charges pending against him in West Virginia. Upon the occasion of this last arrest at Detroit, two stolen automobiles were found in his possession, in addition to a number of fictitious certificates of title. Investigation by Special Agents of the Bureau revealed that he was an expert at changing automobile numbers, and that he usually worked alone in his illegal activities.

The record of O'Hare reflects that his criminal activities began as early as September 15, 1908, upon which date he was sentenced, in the State Court at Pittsburgh, Pennsylvania, on a charge of felonious assault, to serve three years in the Western Penitentiary, at Pittsburgh, Pennsylvania, from which institution he was discharged on March 15, 1911. His record also reflects that he was indicted for murder at Marietta, Ohio, but was acquitted on this charge.

O'Hare was removed from Detroit to Wheeling, West Virginia, where on May 9, 1933 he was tried in Federal Court upon the National Motor Vehicle Theft Act charges pending against him there. The jury was out only twenty-five minutes and returned a verdict of guilty, whereupon Federal Judge W. E. Baker sentenced him to serve four years on one count of the indictment against him, three years on another count, and three years on still a third count, the sentences to run consecutively, making a total of ten years, to be served at the Northeastern Penitentiary, Lewisburg, Pennsylvania. Investigation by Special Agents of the Bureau revealed that O'Hare was an alien and had never become a citizen of this country. This fact was reported to the immigration authorities, together with the fact of his conviction, for whatever action they might deem appropriate to take in his case.

In addition to his conviction in the instant case, O'Hare has the following criminal court:

"As Patrick O'Hare, sentenced, Pittsburgh, Pennsylvania, September 15, 1908, Charge—felonious assault and battery; three years Western Penitentiary, Pittsburgh, Pa.; discharged March 15, 1911.

"As Patrick O'Hare, arrested Akron, Ohio Police Department on 10/31/22, charge grand larceny, ten automobiles: escaped. Apprehended and sentenced 5/5/25 to two years Ohio State Penitentiary; sentence suspended.

"As James Collins, arrested 4/6/32, Detroit, Michigan, charge - driving while drunk, sentence—fine $25 and 1 year probation.

John Edgar Hoover
Director

Federal Bureau of Investigation
U.S. Department of Justice
Washington, D. C.
I.C. #26-13874
(undated)

Source: NARA II, RG 65 FBI, Interesting Case Write-ups, Box 10, Folder IC 26 13874

See Articles: Federal Bureau of Investigation; Fraud; Identity Theft; Pennsylvania; West Virginia.

1933 PRIMARY DOCUMENT

FBI Memorandum on the Leon Ulysses Mason Kidnapping and Extortion Case

Most areas of FBI authority are assigned because a local or state authority lacks sufficient jurisdiction, as in interstate crimes. After the widely publicized kidnapping of the son of famed aviator Charles Lindbergh ended in the boy's death in 1932, the Federal Kidnapping Act was passed to give the Bureau of Investigation primary jurisdiction over kidnapping cases, with the proviso that an interstate case was assumed after seven days (reduced to one day in 1957). Kidnapping cases are Classification 7.

On the morning of April 22, 1933, Mrs. Bessie Collier, proprietress of the Collier Inn, 1807 Columbia Road, Northwest, Washington, D.C., received through the United States Mails the following anonymous letter:

"Listen now—don't try any rough stuff by getting the cops or anything just do as I say. We need $5000.00 'bucks' and we'll get it or your little grandchild, see. Put the money in 5 & 10 bills at the corner of the alley in a newspaper. Put money there at 12 o'clock April 27. If police get hold of this it'll be just too bad. Do you get this fatty? Just do as we ask and everything will be all right. Remember we need the money and we must get it, see."

Mrs. Collier immediately reported the matter to the Director of the Federal Bureau of Investigation, who in turn instructed the local Field Office of the Bureau to conduct a prompt and thorough investigation in view of the possibility that the grandchild, if kidnapped as threatened in the letter, would be carried interstate from the District of Columbia in violation of the Federal Kidnapping Act of July 8, 1932, Chapter 464, U. S. Statutes.

Special Agents interviewed and obtained from Mrs. Collier the names of all probable suspects known to her, including present and former employees of the several restaurants which she owned and operated. One by one these suspects were eliminated as a result of appropriate investigation concerning each. The chances of solving the case narrowed down to a plan whereby the guilty person would be taken into custody in the event he should call for the ransom at the appointed time and place. The letter, however, was not specific in regard to these, in that it did not indicate whether the money should be placed at Noon or Midnight of April 27th nor did it indicate the particular "corner", there being several corners in the alleys to the rear of Collier Inn. Nevertheless, a very careful survey was made of the entire neighborhood and plans were worked out whereby agents were to be placed at strategic points to cover all avenues of escape; nothing was left undone.

As the noon hour approached and the agents had taken up their respective positions, a truck came into the alley and dumped two tons of coal on the exact spot where arrangements had been made to place the decoy package of ransom money. Notwithstanding this unforeseen circumstance, the package was placed a short distance from the coal pile promptly at Noon. A colored man, who had already begun carrying in the coal, spied the package, opened it and seeing the one dollar bill on top of what appeared to be a stack of money quickly wrapped the package up again and carried it into the basement of the apartment where he had been taking the coal. Up to this time only a small portion of the coal had been removed in the basement but the balance was carried away in double quick time, the suspect constantly looking in all directions and in a suspicious manner. After completing his job, he left the scene with the package under his arm, shadowed by the agents who were accompanied by a detective member of the Metropolitan Police Department. In order that there be no excitement caused by arresting the suspect on the scene, he was permitted to walk several blocks away before he was taken into custody and questioned closely concerning his identity and activities. He established beyond a doubt that he was innocent of any participation in the extortion plot and was, therefore, released but not until after his statements had been carefully checked by the agents assigned to the case. In anticipation that the real extortionist might appear at Midnight, the same arrangements were again put into effect but without result.

Pursuing the investigation further and with the handwriting on the letter as the only clue on which to work, the agents obtained handwriting specimens of some seventy present and former employees of the Collier Inn. Those specimens were scientifically examined by experts who unhesitatingly selected the specimen procured from Leon U. Mason as being identical with the handwriting appearing on the original letter. Investigation was thereupon concentrated upon this individual and revealed that he had worked for Mrs. Collier as a waiter for the past five years; that he was twenty-one years of age and in attendance at a local colored teachers' college; that his movements prior to 5:00 P.M., Friday, April 21st, when the extortion letter was posted in the Mails, were of a suspicious nature and not in accordance with his usual routine. When Mason was confronted with these facts on the morning of May 6, 1933, fifteen days after he had mailed the letter, he quickly confessed his guilt and on June 30, 1933, in the Supreme Court of the District of Columbia, received a sentence of from three to six years in the penitentiary for the dastardly crime he had committed. The sentence was imposed on Mason in spite of his explanation that he had not intended to kidnap the attractive little two and one-half year old June Collier, grandchild of the recipient of the letter, but had written it to cause Mrs. Collier and members of her family misery and mental suffering in order that he might observe their reactions.

John Edgar Hoover
Director

Federal Bureau of Investigation
U.S. Department of Justice
Washington, D.C.

I.C. No. 7-62
August 21, 1933

Source: NARA-II, RG 65 FBI, Interesting Case Write-ups, Box 1

See Articles: Federal Bureau of Investigation; Kidnapping; Lindbergh Law.

1933 PRIMARY DOCUMENT

FBI Memorandum on Veteran Fraud

FBI Classification 17, Fraud Against the Government (Veterans Administration), was opened in 1921. Jurisdictional disputes have often arisen between the Veterans Administration (now the Department of Veterans Affairs), the Department of Labor, the Secret Service, and the FBI, which have hampered some investigations. While charged with investigating fraud by veterans as well as against them, the FBI is instructed by the attorney general to treat the latter more seriously.

Marian B. Rutherford, With Aliases
Veterans Bureau Matter
Defrauding The Government By Impersonating A Veteran

On November 10, 1932, the United States Attorney at Indianapolis, Indiana, notified the Cincinnati Office of the Bureau that a case had been brought to this attention wherein one Marian B. Rutherford., assuming the alias of Raymond Berry, had defrauded the Government by impersonating the veteran, Raymond Berry, and receiving Berry's compensation checks over a period of approximately ten months, from December, 1931, to August, 1932. Investigation conducted in this matter revealed that Marian B. Rutherford became acquainted with Raymond Berry, a World War Veteran, at North Platte, Nebraska, during the month of March, 1931. Berry and Rutherford traveled together for some time. During the month of March 1931, these two men took a trip together from Lincoln to Omaha and then to Brady, Nebraska. They parted company in Brady, Nebraska. After Rutherford left Berry, he discovered that certain articles of his wearing apparel and his Army discharge were missing. Berry has not seen his Army discharge or the clothing in question since that time.

Under date of October 29, 1931, Marian B. Rutherford, posing as Raymond Berry, made application for disability allowance under the provisions of the World War Veterans Act, at Bonham, Texas, giving in this application information concerning Berry's military and personal history. He swore to this application as Raymond Berry on the same date before J. C. Denton, Notary Public, Bonham, Texas. J. C. Denton, upon being interviewed, stated that he was the Adjutant for the local American Legion Post at Bonham, Texas, and in such capacity he notarized the affidavit of Rutherford under the alias of Berry. Under date of December 8, 1931, Rutherford changed his address to General Delivery, Honey Grove, Texas, in care of Lillian Rutherford, and this change of address was forwarded to the United States Veterans Bureau, 1505 Federal Street, Dallas, Texas, with the request that compensation checks for Berry be forwarded to that address. On December 16, 1931, his address was again changed to Greenville, Texas, in care of Mrs. Lillian Rutherford. On March 16, 1932, the address was again changed to Monrovia, Indiana, in care of James Eggers.

During this entire period monthly compensation checks were forwarded to Rutherford at the rate of $18.00 per month. These checks were forwarded to him until August 31, 1932, he having received on that date a total amount of $178.80. No disability allowance checks were forwarded to Rutherford after the August check had been received by him. The reason for the discontinuance of these checks was that the real Raymond Berry, under date of May 18, 1932, at North Platte, Nebraska, filed an application for disability allowance, and subsequent investigation revealed that he was the real veteran, and that Rutherford, under the alias of Berry, has been receiving compensation checks meant for Berry and had thereby defrauded the Government of the amount of $178.80.

Rutherford was located serving a sentence in the State Penitentiary, McAlester, Oklahoma. He was questioned relative to receiving the compensation checks and denied that he had ever filed application for disability allowance under the name of Raymond Berry. He stated that it might be possible that his brother, Robert Rutherford, had been the one who filed the application for disability allowance. Photographs of Marian Rutherford were secured and exhibited to various persons in Texas and Indiana to whom the fictitious Raymond Berry was known. In all cases the persons indentified Marian Rutherford as the individual who masqueraded as Raymond Berry.

On May 8, 1933, Rutherford was removed from Muskogee, Oklahoma, and he was delivered to the United States Marshal at Indianapolis, Indiana, on June 22, 1933. An indictment was returned against him at Indianapolis on April 26, 1933.

Upon being returned to Indiana, Rutherford was again questioned by agents of this Bureau. He stated at that time that his brother, Bob Rutherford, impersonated Raymond Berry, making the application for disability compensation, and that Bob Rutherford endorsed all checks. He stated that he, Marian, cashed all checks and assisted in spending the money.

On July 1, 1933, in the United States District Court at Indianapolis, Indiana, Rutherford entered a plea of guilty in this case and was immediately sentenced to serve three years in a United States Penitentiary.

Investigation is being continued for the purpose of definitely ascertaining whether Bob Rutherford did, in fact, sign the application for disability allowance.

During this investigation it was found that Marian Rutherford, under numerous aliases, had served time in various penal institutions throughout the Midwest and Southwest, and he has a long criminal record.

John Edgar Hoover
Director

Federal Bureau of Investigation
U. S. Department of Justice
Washington, D. C.
I.C. No. 17-4136
August 31, 1933

Source: NARA II, RG 65 FBI, Interesting Case Write-ups, Box 7, Folder IC 17-4136

See Articles: Federal Bureau of Investigation; Fraud; Identity Theft.

1933
PRIMARY DOCUMENT

United States v. One Book Called "Ulysses"

Irish author James Joyce serialized his novel Ulysses *from 1918 to 1920 in Chicago's* Little Review. *A stream-of-consciousness spin on the* Odyssey, *it became a cornerstone of modernist literature even before the American collected edition was brought out by Random House in 1933. Random House arranged a test case to see if the book would be acceptable under obscenity laws; in* United States v. One Book Called Ulysses, *Judge John Woolsey rules that serious literature may occupy itself with any subject matter.*

'5 F.Supp. 182 (1933)

United States
v.
One Book Called "Ulysses."

District Court, S. D. New York
December 6, 1933

The United States Attorney (Samuel C. Coleman and Nicholas Atlas, both of New York City, of counsel), for the United States.

Greenbaum, Wolff & Ernst, of New York City (Morris L. Ernst and Alexander Lindey, both of New York City, of counsel), for Random House, Inc.

Woolsey, District Judge.

The motion for a decree dismissing the libel herein is granted, and, consequently, of course, the government's motion for a decree of forfeiture and destruction is denied.

Accordingly a decree dismissing the libel without costs may be entered herein.

I. The practice followed in this case is in accordance with the suggestion made by me in the case of *United States v. One Book, Entitled "Contraception"* (D. C.) 51 F.(2d) 525, and is as follows:
After issue was joined by the filing of the claimant's answer to the libel for forfeiture against "Ulysses," a stipulation was made between the United States Attorney's office and the attorneys for the claimant providing:
1. That the book "Ulysses" should be deemed to have been annexed to and to have become part of the libel just as if it had been incorporated in its entirety therein.
2. That the parties waived their right to a trial by jury.
3. That each party agreed to move for decree in its favor.
4. That on such cross-motions the court might decide all the questions of law and fact involved and render a general finding thereon.
5. That on the decision of such motions the decree of the court might be entered as if it were a decree after trial.
It seems to me that a procedure of this kind is highly appropriate in libels such as this for the confiscation of books. It is an especially advantageous procedure in the instant case because, on account of the length of "Ulysses" and the difficulty of reading it, a jury trial would have been an extremely unsatisfactory, if not an almost impossible method of dealing with it.

II. I have read "Ulysses" once in its entirety and I have read those passages of which the government particularly complains several times. In fact, for many weeks, my spare time has been devoted to the consideration of the decision which my duty would require me to make in this matter. "Ulysses" is not an easy book to read or to understand. But there has been much written about it, and in order properly to approach the consideration of it it is advisable to read a number of other books which have now become its satellites. The study of "Ulysses" is, therefore, a heavy task.

III. The reputation of "Ulysses" in the literary world, however, warranted my taking such time as was necessary to enable me to satisfy myself as to the intent with which the book was written, for, of course, in any case where a book is claimed to be obscene it must first be determined, whether the intent with which it was written was what is called, according to the usual phrase, pornographic, that is, written for the purpose of exploiting obscenity.
If the conclusion is that the book is pornographic, that is the end of the inquiry and forfeiture must follow.
But in "Ulysses," in spite of its unusual frankness, I do not detect anywhere the leer of the sensualist. I hold, therefore, that it is not pornographic.

IV. In writing "Ulysses," Joyce sought to make a serious experiment in a new, if not wholly novel, literary genre. He takes persons of the lower middle class living in Dublin in 1904 and seeks, not only to describe what they did on a certain day early in June of that year as they went about the city bent on their usual occupations, but also to tell what many of them thought about the while.
Joyce has attempted—it seems to me, with astonishing success—to show how the screen of consciousness with its ever-

shifting kaleidoscopic impressions carries, as it were on a plastic palimpsest, not only what is in the focus of each man's observation of the actual things about him, but also in a penumbral zone residua of past impressions, some recent and some drawn up by association from the domain of the subconscious. He shows how each of these impressions affects the life and behavior of the character which he is describing.

What he seeks to get is not unlike the result of a double or, if that is possible, a multiple exposure on a cinema film, which would give a clear foreground with a background visible but somewhat blurred and out of focus in varying degrees.

To convey by words an effect which obviously lends itself more appropriately to a graphic technique, accounts, it seems to me, for much of the obscurity which meets a reader of "Ulysses." And it also explains another aspect of the book, which I have further to consider, namely, Joyce's sincerity and his honest effort to show exactly how the minds of his characters operate.

If Joyce did not attempt to be honest in developing the technique which he has adopted in "Ulysses," the result would be psychologically misleading and thus unfaithful to his chosen technique. Such an attitude would be artistically inexcusable.

It is because Joyce has been loyal to his technique and has not funked its necessary implications, but has honestly attempted to tell fully what his characters think about, that he has been the subject of so many attacks and that his purpose has been so often misunderstood and misrepresented. For his attempt sincerely and honestly to realize his objective has required him incidentally to use certain words which are generally considered dirty words and has led at times to what many think is a too poignant preoccupation with sex in the thoughts of his characters.

The words which are criticized as dirty are old Saxon words known to almost all men and, I venture, to many women, and are such words as would be naturally and habitually used, I believe, by the types of folk whose life, physical and mental, Joyce is seeking to describe. In respect of the recurrent emergence of the theme of sex in the minds of his characters, it must always be remembered that his locale was Celtic and his season spring.

Whether or not one enjoys such a technique as Joyce uses is a matter of taste on which disagreement or argument is futile, but to subject that technique to the standards of some other technique seems to me to be little short of absurd.

Accordingly, I hold that "Ulysses" is a sincere and honest book, and I think that the criticisms of it are entirely disposed of by its rationale.

V. Furthermore, "Ulysses" is an amazing tour de force when one considers the success which has been in the main achieved with such a difficult objective as Joyce set for himself. As I have stated, "Ulysses" is not an easy book to read. It is brilliant and dull, intelligible and obscure, by turns. In many places it seems to me to be disgusting, but although it contains, as I have mentioned above, many words usually considered dirty, I have not found anything that I consider to be dirt for dirt's sake. Each word of the book contributes like a bit of mosaic to the detail of the picture which Joyce is seeking to construct for his readers.

If one does not wish to associate with such folk as Joyce describes, that is one's own choice. In order to avoid indirect contact with them one may not wish to read "Ulysses"; that is quite understandable. But when such a great artist in words, as Joyce undoubtedly is, seeks to draw a true picture of the lower middle class in a European city, ought it to be impossible for the American public legally to see that picture?

To answer this question it is not sufficient merely to find, as I have found above, that Joyce did not write "Ulysses" with what is commonly called pornographic intent, I must endeavor to apply a more objective standard to his book in order to determine its effect in the result, irrespective of the intent with which it was written.

VI. The statute under which the libel is filed only denounces, in so far as we are here concerned, the importation into the United States from any foreign country of "any obscene book." Section 305 of the Tariff Act of 1930, title 19 United States Code, § 1305 (19 USCA § 1305). It does not marshal against books the spectrum of condemnatory adjectives found, commonly, in laws dealing with matters of this kind. I am, therefore, only required to determine whether "Ulysses" is obscene within the legal definition of that word.

The meaning of the word "obscene" as legally defined by the courts is: Tending to stir the sex impulses or to lead to sexually impure and lustful thoughts. Dunlop v. United States, 165 U. S. 486, 501, 17 S. Ct. 375, 41 L. Ed. 799; United States v. One Obscene Book Entitled "Married Love" (D. C.) 48 F.(2d) 821, 824; United States v. One Book, Entitled "Contraception" (D. C.) 51 F.(2d) 525, 528; and compare Dysart v. United States, 272 U. S. 655, 657, 47 S. Ct. 234, 71 L. Ed. 461; Swearingen v. United States, 161 U. S. 446, 450, 16 S. Ct. 562, 40 L. Ed. 765; United States v. Dennett, 39 F. (2d) 564, 568, 76 A. L. R. 1092 (C. C. A. 2); People v. Wendling, 258 N. Y. 451, 453, 180 N. E. 169, 81 A. L. R. 799.

Whether a particular book would tend to excite such impulses and thoughts must be tested by the court's opinion as to its effect on a person with average sex instincts—what the French would call *l'homme moyen sensuel*—who plays, in this branch of legal inquiry, the same role of hypothetical reagent as does the "reasonable man" in the law of torts and "the man learned in the art" on questions of invention in patent law.

The risk involved in the use of such a reagent arises from the inherent tendency of the trier of facts, however fair he may intend to be, to make his reagent too much subservient to his own idiosyncrasies. Here, I have attempted to avoid this, if possible, and to make my reagent herein more objective than he might otherwise be, by adopting the following course:

After I had made my decision in regard to the aspect of "Ulysses," now under consideration, I checked my impressions with two friends of mine who in my opinion answered to the above-stated requirement for my reagent.

These literary assessors—as I might properly describe them—were called on separately, and neither knew that I was consulting the other. They are men whose opinion on literature and on life I value most highly. They had both read "Ulysses," and, of course, were wholly unconnected with this cause.

Without letting either of my assessors know what my decision was, I gave to each of them the legal definition of obscene and asked each whether in his opinion "Ulysses" was obscene within that definition.

I was interested to find that they both agreed with my opinion: That reading "Ulysses" in its entirety, as a book must be read on such a test as this, did not tend to excite sexual impulses or lustful thoughts, but that its net effect on them was only that of a somewhat tragic and very powerful commentary on the inner lives of men and women.

It is only with the normal person that the law is concerned. Such a test as I have described, therefore, is the only proper test of obscenity in the case of a book like "Ulysses" which is a sincere and serious attempt to devise a new literary method for the observation and description of mankind.

I am quite aware that owing to some of its scenes "Ulysses" is a rather strong draught to ask some sensitive, though normal, persons to take. But my considered opinion, after long reflection, is that, whilst in many places the effect of "Ulysses" on the reader undoubtedly is somewhat emetic, nowhere does it tend to be an aphrodisiac.

"Ulysses" may, therefore, be admitted into the United States.

Moscato, Michael, and Leslie LeBlanc. *The United States of America v. One Book Entitled Ulysses by James Joyce: Documents and Commentary: A 50-Year Retrospective*. Frederick, MD: University Publications of America, 1984.

See Articles: Obscenity; Obscenity Laws; Supreme Court, U.S.; *United States v. One Book Called "Ulysses."*

1933
PRIMARY DOCUMENT

Bonnie Parker's "The Ballad of Bonnie and Clyde"

Like the outlaws of the Wild West, the bank robbers of the Depression era were romantic figures in the public eye, adventurers and antiheroes preying on corrupt elites. No one played up this romance more than Bonnie Parker, who peppered the media with snapshots of herself with her lover and partner Clyde Barrow, along with poems like "The Ballad of Bonnie and Clyde." Their career was somewhat minor, consisting of more gas station than bank robberies, but their sex appeal and dramatic deaths in a 1934 shootout became legend.

We, each of us, have a good alibi
For being down here in the joint;
But few of them are really justified,
If you get right down to the point.
You have heard of a woman's glory
Being spent on a downright cur.
Still you can't always judge the story
As true being told by her.
As long as I stayed on the island
And heard confidence tales from the gals,
There was only one interesting and truthful,
It was the story of Suicide Sal.
Now Sal was a girl of rare beauty,
Though her features were somewhat tough,
She never once faltered from duty,
To play on the up and up.

Sal told me this tale on the evening
Before she was turned out free,
And I'll do my best to relate it,
Just as she told it to me.
I was born on a ranch in Wyoming,
Not treated like Helen of Troy,
Was taught that rods were rulers,
And ranked with greasy cowboys. . . .
You've read the story of Jesse James
Of how he lived and died
If you're still in need of something to read
Here's the story of Bonnie and Clyde.
Now Bonnie and Clyde are the Barrow Gang,
I'm sure you all have read
how they rob and steal and those who squeal
are usually found dying or dead.
There's lots of untruths to these write-ups
They're not so ruthless as that
Their nature is raw, they hate all law
Stool pigeons, spotters, and rats.
They call them cold-blooded killers
They say they are heartless and mean
But I say this with pride, I once knew Clyde
When he was honest and upright and clean.
But the laws fooled around and taking him down
and locking him up in a cell
'Til he said to me, "I'll never be free,
So I'll meet a few of them in hell."
The road was so dimly lighted
There were no highway signs to guide
But they made up their minds if all roads were blind
They wouldn't give up 'til they died.
The road gets dimmer and dimmer
Sometimes you can hardly see
But it's fight man to man, and do all you can
For they know they can never be free.
From heartbreak some people have suffered
From weariness some people have died
But all in all, our troubles are small
'Til we get like Bonnie and Clyde.
If a policeman is killed in Dallas
And they have no clue or guide
If they can't find a fiend, just wipe the slate clean
And hang it on Bonnie and Clyde.
There's two crimes committed in America
Not accredited to the Barrow Mob
They had no hand in the kidnap demand

Nor the Kansas City Depot job.
A newsboy once said to his buddy
"I wish old Clyde would get jumped
In these hard times we's get a few dimes
If five or six cops would get bumped."
The police haven't got the report yet
But Clyde called me up today
He said, "Don't start any fights, we aren't working nights, we're joining the NRA."
From Irving to West Dallas viaduct
Is known as the Great Divide
Where the women are kin, and men are men
And they won't stool on Bonnie and Clyde.
If they try to act like citizens
And rent a nice flat
About the third night they're invited to fight
By a sub-gun's rat-tat-tat.
They don't think they're tough or desperate
They know the law always wins
They've been shot at before, but they do not ignore
That death is the wages of sin.
Some day they'll go down together
And they'll bury them side by side
To few it'll be grief, to the law a relief
But it's death for Bonnie and Clyde.

Source: http://historymatters.gmu.edu/d/5061

See Articles: Bonnie and Clyde; Film, Crime in; Great Depression; Robbery, History of.

1934
PRIMARY DOCUMENT

Excerpt From the Confession of Richard Albert Loeb

The Leopold and Loeb trial was one of many dubbed "the trial of the century." The two teenagers (19 and 18 years of age), inspired by Nietzsche's philosophy, decided to commit "the perfect crime" and kidnapped and murdered 14-year-old Bobby Franks, who was actually Loeb's distant cousin. At the advice of their lawyer Clarence Darrow, they pled guilty to avoid a jury trial, and Darrow convinced the judge to sentence them to life imprisonment, rather than execution in light of their youth. Even so, Leopold's father, dissatisfied with Darrow's results, later reneged on his contract to pay him. In January 1936, a fellow inmate killed Loeb in a razor fight in the prison shower.

Made in the office of the State's Attorney of Cook County, Criminal Court Building, Chicago, Illinois, on Saturday, May 31, 1934, at 4:00 o'clock A.M.
Present: John Sbarbaro, Assistant State's Attorney; Captain William Shoemaker; F.A. Sheeder, Shorthand Reporter.

Mr. Sbarbaro:

Q: State your full name.

A: Richard Albert Loeb

Q: What is your occupation?

A: Student

Q: Where are you a student?

A: University of Chicago

Q: How old are you?

A: Eighteen.

Q: Calling your attention to the 21st day of May just tell us in your own words if you know anything unusual relative to the disappearance of Robert Franks.

A: On the 21st of May Leopold and myself intended to kidnap one of the younger boys from the Harvard School.

Q: Well, approximately, how long before the 21st day of May had you discussed it?

A: Oh, a month and a half, I should say, or two months… It was broached—the plan was broached by Nathan Leopold, who suggested that as a means of having a great deal of excitement, together with getting quite a sum of money.

Q: Now, on the 21st day of May, 1924 just tell where you met Leopold and what happened. State it in your own words.

A: ...perhaps I better start with the 20th of May. On the 20th of May Leopold and I purchased at two hardware stores on Cottage Grove avenue, some rope... I purchased, myself, alone, both the chisel and rope. We then proceeded down the street to a drug store, where Leopold.... succeeded in purchasing a bottle of hydrochrolic acid.

Q: Where did you get the gags?

A: The gags were at Leopold's house.

Q: Did you see him write any notes on the typewriter?

A: Yes, I saw him write all of them.

Q: What notes do you have reference to?

A: I have reference to the note demanding the $10,000 in ransom.

Q: And what was the essence of that note?

A: The essence of that note demanded $10,000, and told Mr. Franks that his son was safe; specified a certain way in which that money should be wrapped, in a cigar box, told Mr. Franks that everything would be all right, the son would be returned to him within six hours, if he obeyed our instructions; but that if he disobeyed any of the instructions, that his son would be killed.

Q: And where did you go from there?

A: We went out to Jackson Park, where we parked for, I should judge, between three quarters of an hour and an hour, because we wanted to wait until the Harvard School let out before starting any operations... We didn't stay there long; turned, and went down Hyde Park Boulevard, turned and went north on Ellis avenue. We proceeded north on Ellis avenue until we caught a glimpse of Robert Franks, coming south on the west side of Ellis avenue. As we passed him, he was just coming across or past 48th street. We turned the car around, Leopold getting into the back seat. I drove the car, then, south of Ellis avenue, parallel to where young Francks was, stopped the car, and while remaining in my seat, opened the front door and called to Franks that I would give him a ride home. He said no, he would just as soon walk; but I told him I would like to talk to him about a tennis racket; so he got in the car... just after we turned off Ellis avenue, Leopold reached his arm around young Franks, grabbing his mouth and hit him over the head with the chisel. I believe he hit him several times, I do not know the exact number. He began to bleed and was entirely conscious, he was moaning... At this time Leopold grabbed Franks and carried him over back of the front seat and threw rags and gagged him by sticking it down his throat, I believe. We then drove further south on the main highway until we turned at a road which I believe leads to Gary. We went down this road a ways, and then turned off the road on another deserted road, this deserted road leading west. We stopped the car, got out, removed young Franks' shoes, hid them in some bushes and removed his pants and stockings, placing them in the car. We did this in order that we might be save the trouble of too much undressing him later on...We dragged the body out of the car, put the body in the robe and carried it over to the culvert. Our original scheme had been to etherize the boy to death. This, however, we found unnecessary, because the boy was quite dead when we took him there. We knew he was dead, by the fact that rigor mortis had set in, and also by his eyes; and then when at that same time we poured this hydrochloric acid over him, we noticed no tremor, not a single tremor in his body; therefore we were sure he was dead.

Q: And then what did you do?

A: Then I went to the opposite side of the culvert, where the water runs out, and where you can get at the water very easily, where I washed my hands which had become bloody through carrying the body.

Source: Statements of Nathan F. Leopold and Richard Albert Loeb, made in the Office of the State's Attorney of Cook County, Folder 3, Box 2, Harold S. Hulbert Papers, Series 55/23, University Archives, Northwestern University. and
http://www.library.northwestern.edu/libraries-collections/evanston-campus/university-archives/digital-collections-and-exhibits/leopold

See Articles: Darrow, Clarence; Famous Trials; Kidnapping; Leopold and Loeb.

Department of Justice Memorandum on the Extortion of Eli Lilly and Company

Classification 9 in the FBI's system, extortion is the use of coercion—such as the threat of violence rather than the actual violence of robbery—to obtain money, goods, or services, and is especially associated with blackmail and with organized crime's "protection" rackets. Techniques described in this memorandum, such as the determination of the model of typewriter, are typical of the methodologies and resources available to the FBI that local and state agencies lacked.

Mr. Eli Lilly, President of Eli Lilly and Company, manufacturers of Pharmaceuticals and Biologicals, Indianapolis, Indiana, received through the United States Mails on April 27, 1934 a letter demanding the sum of $25,000.00 with a threat to kidnap Mr. Lilly in the event the sum specified was not paid. This letter was typewritten, well worded, and apparently written by someone possessing more than an average education. It directed Mr. Lilly to ride a train on the Pennsylvania Railroad from Vincennes to Indianapolis, Indiana on the afternoon of May 1, 1934 and that somewhere en route he would notice a signal consisting of a white flag, at which time he was to throw from the train the package containing the $25,000.00.

Mr. Lilly first turned this letter over to the Indianapolis Police Department who conducted an investigation and followed the directions contained in the letter. Two detectives riding the train as specified in the letter between Vincennes and Indianapolis, noticed a white flag as the train passed a point in Morgan County, Indiana between Whitaker, Indiana and Paragon, however, no package was thrown from the train. Subsequent to this investigation the Division of Investigation was notified of the receipt of the letter by Mr. Lilly and together with the Indianapolis Police Department, conducted an investigation which finally resulted in the apprehension of the two persons responsible for the writing of the letter.

It was learned that on May 1, 1934 James Carlos McNeill and James Byron Woods were seen loitering near the place where the signal had been erected. It also developed that McNeill was a graduate of the Paragon High School and had also attended the Indiana University for approximately five years, at which latter institution he was well regarded and quite active in campus activities. Woods was found to be a graduate of the Paragon High School and had also attended the Normal School at Danville, Indiana. In view of the fact that the extortion letter appeared to have been written by someone possessing a good education, and in further view of the fact that McNeill and Woods were seen loitering about the location where the signal had been placed, they were considered as logical suspects in the sending of the extortion letter.

Department of Justice Memorandum on the Extortion of the Ford Motor Company

This case of extortion of the Ford Motor Company was a fairly simple one, which authorities in a city as large as Detroit probably could have handled by themselves without undue difficulty. The immediate involvement of the FBI, despite the lack of any evident interstate dimension to the crime, was probably due to the prominence of the Ford family and the possibility, therefore, of a conspiracy or the involvement of organized crime. Note that Edward Lickwala was sentenced only five days after the crime.

On October 15, 1934, the Detroit, Michigan Office of the Division of Investigation, U. S. Department of Justice, was informed that an extortion by Mr. Edsel B. Ford, President of the Ford Motor Company. The anonymous letter demanded that Mr. Ford place the sum of $5,000 in five-dollar and ten dollar bills in a candy box, and leave it on the first rear porch of the house located at 3341 Medbury Street, Detroit, Michigan, at eleven o'clock p.m., October 12, 1934, threatening that upon noncompliance Mr. Ford would be killed.

Subsequent to the receipt of this extortion letter, a decoy package was placed on the designated porch and kept under surveillance by several employees of the Ford Motor Company and local law enforcement officials who shortly thereafter took into custody an individual who had picked up the decoy package at eleven thirty p.m., October 12, 1934, which had been observed on the porch by his wife, but who had replaced it after he had apparently noted its contents.

An intensive investigation which was immediately initiated by Special Agents of

Prior to questioning McNeill and Woods an examination of the extortion letter reflected that the same had been written with a Royal typewriter. Numerous inquiries were made at Paragon concerning possessors of Royal typewriters, and the search finally narrowed down to one Gail Guy who possessed a Royal typewriter of the type used in writing the extortion note. Guy was questioned as to whom he had loaned his typewriter in the past several months and finally admitted that he had loaned the same to Woods. A further examination of the typing contained in the extortion letter with that of the type on Guy's machine resulted in the discovery that the same were identical.

Woods and McNeill were questioned by Special Agents of this Division which resulted in both of these individuals signing statements in which they admitted joint authorship of the letter written to Mr. Lilly and eliminated Guy from any participation or knowledge of the letter. Both claimed that they had written the letter to Mr. Lilly merely as a joke and had conceived the idea from reading kidnapping and detective stories.

On June 27, 1934 McNeill and Woods entered pleas of guilty to an indictment charging them with violation of Title 18, Section 338-A, U.S.C.A. which pertains to the sending of extortion letters through the United States Mails, and on their pleas were sentenced each to serve five years in the Atlanta Penitentiary.

John Edgar Hoover
Director

Division of Investigation
U. S. Department of Justice
Washington, D.C.
I.C. No. 7-849
July 10, 1934

Source: NARA-II, RG 65 FBI, Interesting Case Write-ups, Box 2

See Articles: Forensic Science; Indiana; Justice, Department of; Kidnapping; Robbery, Sociology of.

the Division of Investigation on October 15, 1934 reflected that the first floor apartment located at 3341 Medbury Street had been vacated by a Polish family during the early morning of October 8, 1934 and that another family had moved into the same apartment during the afternoon of October 9, 1934. Specimens of the handwriting of the individual who had picked up the decoy package and of the handwriting of his wife were obtained, but there was no similarity with the extortion note, and it was apparent that he had inadvertently picked up the decoy package concerning which he knew nothing.

About nine o'clock p.m., October 16, 1934, two employees of the Ford Motor Company, who had previously assisted in the surveillance of the decoy package, were seated in an automobile when one Edward Lickwala approached them and stated that he had some information which he desired to furnish. He was immediately taken to the Detroit Office of the Division of Investigation where upon thorough interrogation he admitted that he alone was responsible for the writing and mailing of the extortion letter to Mr. Ford. His handwriting was found to be identical with the writing appearing in the extortion note.

Edward Lickwala, who is twenty years of age and of Polish descent, stated in his confession that he specified the money should be placed on the night of October 12, 1934, four days after he had written the letter because he felt this arrangement would give Mr. Ford ample time to comply with the demand. He further stated he had observed that the family residing in the lower apartment of the house located at 3341 Medbury Street was moving on October 8, 1934 and, therefore, it would be an ideal place for the money.

The criminal record of Lickwala reflects that on July 22, 1931 he was arrested by the Detroit Police Department on the charge of investigation for tampering with an automobile, but was discharged. On September 27, 1931 he was again arrested by the Detroit Police Department on the charge of investigation for robbery, but was discharged. In connection with the latter arrest, Lickwala admitted to Special Agents of the Division of Investigation that he and a friend obtained a revolver and intended to hold up the clerk in a store of the Kroger Grocery and Baking Company, but that while they were waiting at the street intersection for the clerk to close the store, a police officer took them into custody after he had become suspicious of their actions.

On October 17, 1934, the Federal Grand Jury, then in session at Detroit, Michigan, returned a true bill of indictment, charging Lickwala with the violation of Title 18, Section 338-A, United Stated Code Annotated, pertaining to the sending of extortion letters through the United States Mails, and on the same date after Lickwala had entered a plea of guilty, he was sentenced by the United Stated District Judge, Edward J. Moinet, to a term of ten years in the United States Penitentiary at Leavenworth, Kansas.

John Edgar Hoover
Director

Division of Investigation
U.S. Department of Justice
Washington, D. C.
I.C. No. 7-281
November 7, 1934

Source: NARA-II, RG 65 FBI, Interesting Case Write-ups, Box 1

See Articles: Detroit, Michigan; Justice, Department of; Kidnapping.

1935 PRIMARY DOCUMENT

FBI Memorandum on August Luer Kidnapping and Vivian Chase

One of the better-known gangsters of the 1930s, Vivian Chase was a studied contrast from Bonnie

Parker: while Parker dictated her legend to the press, Chase threatened to kill associates who even revealed her parents or birthplace. She refused to talk to reporters after arrests, and even after her criminal career was in full swing, there are several long periods in which there is no record of her activities. Her killer was never identified.

During the past few years numerous desperate individuals have contributed in a criminal way to the unenviable notoriety which the Middle West has received. Not the least important of these contributors was Vivian Chase. Mystery surrounds her beginning. She is alleged on the one hand to have been born in Kansas City, Missouri, while on the other to have been born in Colorado. Those who at times were believed to have been her relatives disclaimed the relationship. As for her parentage, she never disclosed their identity to law enforcement officers. Society can only allege that this woman began, flourished and faded. Her career centered itself in the Middle West and Southwest.

She was an associate and paramour of criminals of the dangerous type during the entire course of her adult life. She was the companion of Charles Mays, now deceased, a notorious police character of Kansas City and St. Louis, Missouri. Vivian Chase also participated in crimes of major importance. She first gained notoriety by virtue of her participation in the robbery of the Montgomery County National Bank at Cherryvale, Kansas. In this robbery she allied herself with Lee Flourney and Charles Mays, both of whom were later killed by officers at Picher, Oklahoma. She then married George Chase, who later met his death under questionable circumstances.

After a career in Kansas City, Missouri, Vivian Chase proceeded to St. Louis, Missouri, with several of her gangster companions. In St. Louis she continued her association with the underworld element, and became acquainted with the desperado later to be notoriously known as Walter "Irish" O'Malley. Vivian Chase will always be most widely remembered for her participation in the August Luer kidnapping. In preparing for the perpetration of this offense, she and O'Malley augmented their ranks by enlisting the aid of Percy Michael Fitzgerald, Randol Eugene Norvell, Christ Nicola Gitcho and Lloyd "Blackie" Doyle. O'Malley, Norvell and Vivian Chase formed the nucleus of this group and for several months made plans for this major kidnapping. Meanwhile several other notorious criminals were brought into this group but many of them were killed or captured in an attempted bank robbery before the Luer abduction could be effected. It is often felt by the underworld that a crime can be more successfully completed and the possibilities of detection reducted if the cloak of respectability can in some manner be injected into the offense. Norvell, O'Malley and Chase therefore allied themselves with certain individuals who presumable bore good reputations in their communities. These persons were to be used to "finger" the proposed victim of their sinister designs.

At about nine o'clock on the evening of July 10, 1933, August Luer, age seventy-seven, a wealthy, retired meal packer and banker, was forcibly kidnapped from his home at 759 Washington Avenue, Alton, Illinois, by three men and a woman, members of a gang of nine, who had conspired to effect his abduction. The kidnapping was witnessed by his wife, an elderly lady of seventy-five, who made desperate efforts to prevent the kidnapping and who was brutally assaulted as a result of her attempts to frustrate the abduction.

On the evening mentioned, Vivian Chase and Walter O'Malley made inquiries at the Luer home in Alton, Illinois, as to the address of a neighbor, Henry Busse. After receiving the desired information, Vivian Chase and O'Malley requested permission to use the telephone, which was granted. Vivian Chase and O'Malley entered the house closely following by Percy Michael Fitzgerald. Vivian Chase proceeded down the hall to where the telephone was located and immediately cut the wires. Fitzgerald forced Mrs. Luer into the front room adjoining the hallway. O'Malley rushed into the living room and seized Mr. Luer, dragging the aged banker through the living room and hall and down the front steps to the waiting automobile driven by Randol Eugene Norvell.

Victim Luer was transferred in and out of three different cars and was transported first to Madison, Illinois, were he was taken to the basement of a store building owned by Christ Nicola Gitcho. After remaining here for a few hours, Mr. Luer was removed to the farm of Mike Musiala, located approximately three miles distant from East St. Louis, Illinois, where he was confined in a prearranged cell which consisted of a crudely improvised cave. Numerous telephone calls and ransom notes were transmitted to the Luer family, demanding a ransom of $100.000.00 for the release of Victim Luer, but due to the complicated nature of the instructions, the Luer family was unable to comply with the instructions, in consequence of which no ransom was ever paid. In despair, O'Malley and Fitzgerald, after holding Mr. Luer a kidnapped victim for five days, released Mr. Luer, without the knowledge or consent of the remainder of the gang.

Within a short time after Mr. Luer's release, Vivian Chase was positively identified as one of the participants in the kidnapping. On July 27, 1933, she became the subject of an Identification Order issued by the Federal Bureau of Investigation. Diligent and relentless efforts were made to cause her apprehension but only occasionally was any information secured to indicate the location of her many hideouts and gangster associates. Not long after Mr. Luer's release, six of the participants in the abduction were apprehended, convicted and sentenced to long terms in the penitentiary. As soon as her immediate associates became too "hot" and in imminent danger of apprehension, she abandoned them for the company of the less notorious but equally desperate gansters. She clung to her good friend and fellow gangster, Walter "Irish" O'Malley, but on May 27, 1935, he was apprehended by a Special Agent of the Federal Bureau of Investigation, in Kansas City, Missouri, and fortune again favored Vivian Chase in being absent from his company on that day. O'Malley was speedily removed to Edwardsville, Illinois, where on June 27, 1935, he was sentenced to serve the remainder of his natural life in the penitentiary.

Now, only "Blackie" Doyle and Vivian Chase remained of the goup which had so callously invaded the home and kidnapped August Luer. But Vivian Chase had been the mistress of many men, and she found little difficulty in once more winning a place in the heart and confidence of another group of Middle West bad men. Appealing to their vanity and emotions she played her role with her now companions amid old surroundings. Her daring was comparable to that of her male associates, but her audacity made her both respected and feared. She was not the usual passive and respectful moll who clings to her gangster companions, but was active in the execution of well planned offenses.

The boldness and careless disregard for the safety which sometimes characterize the activities of the underworld often give rise to fears and doubts on the part of associates. The unexpected demise of a gangster at the hands of his companions cannot always be completely understood, and oftentimes the explanation is left largely to speculation. After the apprehension of O'Malley in Kansas City, Missouri, Vivian Chase doubled her efforts to avoid apprehension. No information of value was obtained as to her location.

On the morning of November 3, 1935, a Ford Sedan was abandoned in the rear of St. Luke's Hospital in Kansas City, Missouri. At eleven o'clock on Sunday morning, November 3, 1935, a passerby observed blood dripping from the running board of the abandoned automobile. Peering inside, he observed the body of a woman "stuffed" in a jack-knife position on the floorboards between the front and rear seats. The woman was dead.

Examination of the body disclosed that the woman had been murdered by being shot with a .45 caliber bullet, the projectile puncturing the right collar bone, passing through the right lung, emerging from the body and falling on the floor. A fingerprint examination was immediately conducted, resulting in a positive identification. The body was that of Vivian Chase.

The following is the criminal record of Vivian Chase as disposed by the files of the Identification Division of the Federal Bureau of Investigation, United States Department of Justice: As Mrs. George M. Chase, No. 12697, arrested Police Department, Kansas City, Missouri, December 23, 1923; charge, investigation; dismissed for want of prosecution. As Vivian Davis, No. 3144, arrested Police Department, Wichita, Kansas, February 14, 1926; charge, drunk, investigation, vagrancy.

John Edgar Hoover
Director

Federal Bureau of Investigation
U. S. Department of Justice
Washington, D. C.
I.C. No. 7-88
November 20, 1935

Source: NARA-II, RG 65 FBI, Interesting Case Write-ups, Box 1

See Articles: Justice, Department of; Kidnapping; Women Criminals, History of Women Criminals, Sociology of

1935
PRIMARY DOCUMENT

"Why I Am a Dope Fiend" Pamphlet Against the Harrison Narcotic Law

The 1914 Harrison Narcotics Tax Act was an early drug-control law regulating cocaine and opiates, which had only recently become associated with crime. Drug-control laws principally worked to generate revenue through fines, not to impose criminal punishments. Even the Uniform State Narcotic Drug Act that was drafted in 1934 to bring about a stricter drug code, which this pamphlet supports but which was only adopted by nine states, was concerned with fines instead of felonies.

At thirty three years of age, in the prime of life when most men's lives begin, mine is ended. Dope? No, the Harrison Law has broken me, and made me the tramp I am today, but I am carrying on, and will fight unto the end for a Better Law than the Harrison Law; one that will protect the future generations from that dreadful curse—DOPE. Here is a brief sketch of my life—(there are many, many more like mine):

In 1918 I heard the call of the Minute Men—and answered, I spent several months in training before I went overseas. We had not been across the 'pond' long before the war was ended, but our company was short of men and we worked hard, sometimes going two and three days, without rest. It was in the wintertime and often I would find a nice soft mud-hole, roll up in my blanket and go to sleep. Awakening in the morning, we often found our blankets frozen to our bodies.

Soon I took down the arthritis and laying in the hospital several months, where I was given Morphine for relief.

Of course, we hardly blame anyone for giving 'medicine' to relieve pain, and I was suffering a great deal. Then too, there were so many sick and wounded at that time, and the doctors all so overworked, that about all they had time for was to inject morphine, apply Iodine, and give C. C. Pills. I was finally shipped to America, several months ahead of my company and was soon discharged—(with a habit), at Camp Funston, Kansas. I presume I could have gotten a medical discharge if I had not been so anxious to get home, but like most of the boys, I was ready to sign anything for my release. Since then, my life has been one of misery.

I spent three years in a Chiropractic College and graduated in 1922. I was considered one of the best adjusters that ever left that school. I practiced a while in Denver, but it was hard for me to get my "Medicine" so it kept me moving around a lot to connect.

By 1930 the high price of Narcotics (caused by the Harrison Law) broke me, and made a tramp out of me.

I then became what is known as the "Boot & Shoe Dope Fiend, one who travels here & there, "catch as catch can."

In 1934, the same government I had offered my all in 1918, sent me to Leavenworth for thirteen months, because I forged a prescription for one shot of morphine, the same affliction they discharged me with in 1919.

While in Leavenworth I saw so many 'repeaters' coming back, that I swore I would never again use illegal narcotics in this country, but let the racketeers get their prison fodder elsewhere, rather than for me to keep the old mill grinding.

One hears these so called Narcotics Educational Societies broadcasting over the radio and about all they knew is what the politicians tell them. I have lived the life of the unseen dread and I know whereof I speak. The only cured dope fiend is the dead dope fiend. I have fought this losing fight for seventeen years, have taken all kinds of cures, been to private hospitals, state hospitals, veterans hospitals, jails, has reduction cures, etc. Yet I broke off once for four years, then weakened, Morphine calls and back you come. You never feel normal without it. Your food doesn't taste right. During the whole of the period I abstained from it, there seemed ALWAYS to be something missing.

If the average addict could get his "medicine" at a reasonable price, and did not have to duck and dodge the law continually, he would settle down and become a useful citizen. A dope fiend wants no one's life, nor their money, all he wants is his "medicine".

After traveling extensively in these United States, and conversing with thousands of small town doctors, I would say there are close to one million people in America, using drugs in some form or other.

So you can readily see that the Harrison Law has done nothing to decrease this number, for before this law was enacted, there were not nearly this number of addicts.

Will I return to drugs? Just as surely as history repeats, so does an addict if he lives. I would not return to drugs here, but before I exile myself to become a beach comber in some foreign country where I will be free from the chains of this unjust law, I am making this effort to pave the way for a Repeal, in the years to come.

I feel that as an American citizen, I owe it to my people and my country to sacrifice my pride and bare my life as it is, and as are thousands of others who have fallen beneath this curse of curses.

I say, my friends, that it is time for a new beginning of a New Deal for addicts and above all, protection for future generations.

If my idea is adopted, a ten year old school boy could readily see that in fifty years there need not be a single addict in America. How?

First, repeal the Harrison Narcotic Law, so that all addicts may buy their 'medicine' at drug stores, at reasonable prices, as they did before this law was enacted. That removes all peddlers, just as the repeal of the 18th Amendment is removing the bootleggers, in the wet states. Because, just as long as there is a huge profit in selling dope, so long will we have men pedaling dope. For it is not a fact that one of the weaknesses of the human race is lust for gold?

Then, pass a law, making it a capital punishment for anyone to give anyone else, who is NOT an addict, narcotics in any form. That will stop it, and stop it quickly. That will be the only way they will ever end this curse.

Your taxpayers spend millions of dollars in trying to enforce the Harrison Narcotic Law. Your business men, also lose millions through shoplifting, and other petty larceny, by addicts, who are trying to support their habit which costs them $50.00 to $75.00 weekly. While if they could buy it legally at drug stores, it would run 75 cents weekly. Quite a contrast, Isn't it!

You, the public, are becoming more enlightened concerning the dope fiend, year by year.

You can probably remember when all dope fiends were considered desperate criminals, morons, etc. but history has proved all of this to be a grave mistake.

Dillinger; Capone; Darrow; Floyd; Hamilton; Leopold; Leob; Hickman; and so on: None of them were addicts.

I hate to leave America, the land I love. You know I will miss the grand old Rockies and its countless beautiful fishing spots, where I have spent so many pleasant vacations.

Yet I can never be satisfied to live here without my "medicine."

I used to feel ashamed to think of myself, a strong, healthy looking man, allowing anything to conquer me so completely, but after losing a seventeen year fight, I have accepted my fate as inevitable.

But I shall not leave without putting up a stiff fight to protect our future Americans. I shall travel from state to state, putting out these little booklets in order to expose the Harrison law as it really is.

Now, if you wish to help me to get those laws passed, so the future generations will not be jeopardized by this curse, then you may mail me any amount of money you care to donate to this cause, and, I promise, I shall carry this fight to the White House itself.

Best Wishes And Good Luck
J.J. Crabtree
Mailing Address:
C/O Western Hotel
Oklahoma City, Okla.

Source: Records of the Drug Enforcement Agency, Subject Files of the Bureau of Narcotics and Dangerous Drugs, 1916–1970.

See Articles: Drug Abuse and Addiction, History of; Drug Abuse and Addiction, Sociology of; Narcotics Laws.

1938
PRIMARY DOCUMENT

Department of Justice Memorandum on Federal Juvenile Offenders

The 1938 Federal Juvenile Delinquency Act (JDA) was the first federal legislation to provide special treatment for juveniles. Common law and state statutes defined an "age of accountability," before which a child could not be tried as a criminal. Specifics varied, but common law held that a child under 8 years of age was incapable of a crime. The JDA defined juveniles as a category separate from adults and was later amended and supplanted by the 1974 Juvenile Justice and Delinquency Prevention Act.

To All United States Attorneys,
United States Probation Officers,
United States Marshals,
And Other Arresting Officers:
Re: Federal Juvenile Offenders Under 18 Years of Age

You have heretofore received a copy of the "Federal Juvenile Delinquency Act," approved June 16, 1938. This statute, which was sponsored by Attorney General Cummings, gives recognition to the principle, long established in state juvenile court legislation, that juvenile offenders need specialized care and treatment. Among other things, the Act provides for the prompt initiation, hearing, and disposition of juvenile cases through prosecution by information and trial without jury before a district judge, who may hold court for that purpose at any time and place within the district, in chambers or otherwise.

In order that the provisions of this Act may be carried out effectively and in the spirit in which they were intended, the following instructions are given for the guidance of the various officials concerned:

All Arresting Officers
1. Upon the arrest of a juvenile, the arresting officer shall immediately notify, by telephone or telegram, the United States Probation Officer of the District in which the arrest is made, and shall also immediately notify the Director of the Bureau of Prisons on Probation Form No. 18, "Notice of Arrest of Juvenile" (copy attached) and send a duplicate copy of this notification to the probation officer. (The marshal need not notify the probation officer of such arrest by means of a jail card. Jail cards should, however, still be sent to the Bureau of Prisons).
2. The provision in the Act that a juvenile is not to be detained in a jail or similar

place, unless it is necessary to assure the safe custody of such juvenile or to insure his safety, or that of others, should have strict compliance. Whenever feasible, the juvenile, pending action by the court, should be left by the arresting officer in the custody of his parents, relatives, or other responsible persons.

3. If such juvenile must be detained in a jail or similar institution, he is to be held in custody in a room or other place apart from adults, if such facilities are available. Juvenile detention homes, jails and other institutions used for juveniles awaiting trial must be approved by the Attorney General. Instructions concerning such approved facilities will be issued in the near future.

4. Whenever a court disposes of a juvenile case by ordering the delinquent committed to the custody of the Attorney General, the marshal shall wire the Attorney General for designation of an agency before carrying out the commitment. This is the same procedure as has been followed with juveniles sentenced to types of institutions other than jails.

Probation Officers

1. Immediately upon receipt from the arresting officer of notice of the arrest of a juvenile, the probation officer shall proceed to make careful investigation of the case and assist the arresting officer and the committing magistrate, by furnishing information as to the advisability of releasing the juvenile on bail or recognizance, or, if detention is necessary, as to the availability of suitable detention facilities.

2. A report, including substantially the same information as the pre-sentence investigation report required by Circular No. 3072 shall be furnished promptly to the Court and to the United States Attorney in order that both may have all the information needed to deal properly with the case. The report should make recommendation regarding the advisability of diverting the case to state authorities as required by Section 662a, Title 18. Duplicate copies of this report should be forwarded promptly to the Department.

3. Whenever a court places upon probation a juvenile whose home or residence is in another judicial district, and the court order either implies or directs that he shall return to such other district, the probation officer should immediately communicate the facts to the Bureau of Prisons and await appropriate instructions.

United States Attorneys

1. The Procedure authorized by this Act shall be applied in the cases of all persons who have not reached their 18th birthday at the time of the offense, and who have violated any Federal statute, not punishable by death or life imprisonment, except in the cases of those:
(a) Whose cases can properly by diverted to state authorities under the United States Code, Title 18, Section 662a;
(b) Who do not consent in writing;
(c) Whose cases, in the opinion of the United States Attorney, should be dealt with under regular criminal procedure in the public interest. In every case falling within this exception the United States Attorney shall promptly submit a statement of the facts and his reasons to the Department.

2. The Department regards the Act as applicable to all juveniles, even where offenses were committed prior to its passage. The provisions of the Act are procedural and remedial, making the Act an exception to the general rule that statutes are not to be construed retroactively.

3. No set form is required either for the "information" filed against the juvenile, or for the written "consent" of the juvenile as a prerequisite to the procedure authorized by the Act. The United States Attorney is charged with the duty of assuring himself that the juvenile has been fully apprised of his rights and of the consequences of such consent, if given, and understands the same, before the consent is executed. An appropriate statement to that effect should be included either in the

consent, or the minutes of the court. The consent should be signed in the presence of the judge and no persuasion should be used on the juvenile to give the consent.

In order that the purpose of this Act may be fully realized, the closest cooperation will be necessary among all Federal officials dealing with juvenile offenders.

Please acknowledge receipt of this circular.

Joseph B. Keenan
Assistant to the Attorney General

Department of Justice
Washington, D. C.
Circular No. 3154
August 26, 1938

Source: NARA-II, RG 170, Subject Files of Bureau of Narcotics 1916-1970, Box 54, F: 0370-3, legal info circular

See Articles: Juvenile Corrections, History of; Juvenile Corrections, Sociology of; Juvenile Courts, History of; Juvenile Delinquency, History of; Juvenile Delinquency, Sociology of; Juvenile Justice, History of.

1938
PRIMARY DOCUMENT

IRS Report on Huey Long's Louisiana Scandals

The entertaining Internatl Revenue Service (IRS) account of Huey Long details one of the enduring characters of 20th century politics: "The Kingfish," governor and senator of Louisiana. Long inspired not only Robert Penn Warren's Pulitzer-winning novel All The King's Men *(1946), but also John Dos Passos's* Number One *(1943), and Sinclair Lewis's 1936* It Can't Happen Here *about a populist president who introduces an American fascist regime. The latter was written with the goal of hurting Long's presidential campaign.*

Introduction

The history of a modern absolute despotism within the boundaries of the theoretically free and sovereign commonwealth of 48 states found its birth in the rise to political power of Huey Pierce Long. Born in a log cabin in Winn Parish, in north-central Louisiana, of humble parentage, Huey Long received his early education in Winnfield, Louisiana. Winn Parish is located in perhaps the poorest section of Louisiana, where during Huey's boyhood the people eked out a bare existence from the soil. Before the civil War the people of Winn Parish had no slaves and a great number of them could not even afford the luxury of a mule. Their inheritance was the earth the richer owners would not touch. This was a fitting environment for the rise of a man who was to lead millions of rural people in protest against their lot.

Much of the story of Huey Long's early life is legendary, and misinformation has been spread as to the economic status of his family. According to his own account (branded as a vote-hunting lie by his brothers and sisters) his early life was one of Lincolnesque hardships and endeavors. In his political orations, he occasionally referred to his own childhood, illustrating his argument with incidents which were purely imaginary. He told a very touching story about a non-existent pony with a red saddle, which had been taken from him by the cruel taxgatherers. He told of various business enterprises in which he was engaged as a boy and as a youth, and how he sold soap, vegetable oil, and patent medicine from door to door in his struggle for success.

His political life started early. While still a schoolboy, he managed an older friend's campaign for tick inspector. In his last year of high school, Huey formed a political organization among the students which prescribed rules for the students to follow. The faculty protested the club and, after Huey's refusal to disband the club, he was expelled from school. In retaliation, he drew up a petition, persuaded a majority of the patrons to sign, and the principal was discharged.

Huey crammed an exacting three year law course into eight months. He passed the state bar examination at the age of twenty-one and returned to Winnfield to begin practice.

He often remarked that he studied law with the sole idea of being a politician, and "came from the bar examination running for office." The law, for most public offices in Louisiana, required the holder to be thirty, some required the holder to be thirty-five. Huey found that for office of Railroad Commissioner the law provided no minimum age requirement. At the age of twenty-four he announced for the position as one of four contestants against a highly popular incumbent.

Huey's first bid for public office was something new in Louisiana political campaigns. He penetrated remote sections about which candidates had never before bothered. He discussed all farm problems with the farmers and flattered them by soliciting their advice on economic affairs. He avoided all the parish centers and cities to which candidates usually gave their particular attention, and concentrated on the scattered people of the hills and hollows.

Huey poured everything he had into his campaign. Toward the close of the campaign, his finances began to run low and he borrowed $500 from an elder Winnfield friend, O. K. Allen, whom he later rewarded by making him his personal governor of Louisiana. Although he lost practically every courthouse town, his country vote was enough to elect him by a narrow margin.

The Railroad Commission was of very minor importance at the time Long became a commissioner. Almost overnight under his leadership it became all important. He rained circulars on the populace on every subject and traveled to all parts of the state in connection with his official duties.

He blasted at the big companies and the "corporation lawyers." He publicly insulted them at every opportunity, branding them as double dyed thieves, scalawags, and looters. He was particularly bitter against the Standard Oil Company of Louisiana. His maneuvers resulted in a ruling by the Railroad Commission which held that the oil pipe lines were common carriers, subject to state regulation for the first time in Louisiana.

Huey's political opponents claimed that his election to the Railroad Commission destroyed whatever sense of proportion or rationality he may once have possessed. He was alleged to have developed a habit of swaggering about in railroad trains, whenever he had occasion to travel, boasting to whomever would listen that he ran the railroads, that railroad officials had to do whatever he ordered and that they trembled at the sound of his voice. It has further been said of him that if he failed to receive from railroad employees such treatment as would be accorded an emperor in his own dominion, he became enraged, blustered, and threatened to have the employee, summarily discharged.

On his thirtieth birthday in 1923, Huey announced his candidacy for governor. The law provides that the minimum age for governor in Louisiana is thirty. He conducted his campaign for governor along the same lines as his previous campaign for Railroad Commissioner. He was able to carry north Louisiana practically unanimously, but the strong vote in New Orleans was sufficient to defeat him in one of the closest political races in years.

The effectiveness of his unsuccessful campaign was a great surprise to many people who had never considered him seriously as a political factor. Despite his defeat, his election four years later was considered a certainty.

In the second campaign for governor in 1928, Huey was prepared. His platform was based on share the wealth, although his organized "Share the Wealth" movement had not yet been conceived. He launched his campaign at a rally with hundreds of banners bearing the slogan "Every Man a King but No Man Wears a Crown." His platform was free bridges, paved roads throughout the state, and free textbooks for school children—all without a penny's cost to the poor people. He promised to make "all those corporation high muckety-mucks bear the taxes" to pay for these.

He was elected in this second campaign for governor and his inauguration was something the like of which the people of Baton Rouge had never seen before. Fifteen thousand people from all parts of Louisiana's poorest sections came by horse, by car, by bus, and by pirogues, at Huey's invitation, to see "their governor" inaugurated. Huey entertained them on the lawn of the capitol with hillbilly music and pink lemonade.

After Huey took office he immediately instituted the doctrine that "anybody that ain't with us, is against us" and fired every office holder, every department head, every clerk, lawyer or janitor over whom he had control, and replaced them with his men. He engaged the services of "Battling Bozeman", an ex-pugilist, as his bodyguard, who was carried on the payroll of the State Highway Department. Bozeman was carefully instructed to deny any suggestion that his duties with Long were those of a bodyguard.

The customary procedure in regard to appointive officers was for the governor to send the names of the appointees to the legislature for confirmation, after which the office-holders could not be removed without good cause. Instead of following this procedure, Huey demanded undated resignations of his appointees before they took office, so that he might remove anyone who displeased him by merely filling in the date, and writing his acceptance of the resignation. A number of such resignations were accepted and persons removed from office thereby, although the procedure was entirely illegal.

Although Huey's first legislative session did not run along smoothly, by trading patronage and making concessions he was able to carry through bills, or constitutional amendments to be submitted to the voters, for a $30,000,000 bond issue to give the farmers their roads, for free school books and for increased appropriations for hospitals and other institutions.

Huey's first few months as governor were probably the stormiest of his political career. Although he was able to control the legislature, his opponents gave him plenty of trouble. He did not sit in his office like other governors, he believed in direct action. He walked up and down the legislative halls during the sessions, buttonholing members to give orders on how to vote. In one speech he bragged that he dealt with the legislature "like a deck of cards." Of one of the legislators he remarked, "We bought him like a sack of potatoes."

Huey's method of dealing with political issues and officials caused much dissension in his own ranks during the early months of his governship. Robert Ewing, his strongest newspaper backer, and John Sullivan, political leader in New Orleans, soon broke with him, branding him as a would-be Napoleon. His control of the legislature, if it ever existed, was broken by his efforts to pass an occupational tax which was bitterly opposed by his friends as well as his opponents. Rumors were prevalent that several legislators were considering the propriety of a move to impeach, and it was reported that a committee of several opposition members of the House of Representatives were engaged in drawing up impeachment charges.

Huey became thoroughly frightened when these rumors continued and appeared to be authentic, and on March 25, 1929, known in Louisiana History as "Bloody Monday," he had his forces prepare for an attempt to put through a motion to adjourn sine die. His opponents, however, were in a fighting mood and were equally well prepared to resist such an attempt. At the next meeting both sides attempted to get recognition and the session immediately turned into a free-for-all fist fight. Men slugged each other with ink wells, brass knucks, and anything else that happened to be in sight. In the midst of the turmoil, Huey's Speaker of the House, John B. Fournet, recognized a Long man's motion to adjourn sine die and, although the representatives could not have heard Fournet's request for a vote, he announced that the voting machine showed that 68 members had voted for adjournment. (It was later proved that no voting on the adjournment had been recorded.) The legislators refused to adjourn, however, and appointed another representative temporarily to succeed Fournet as Speaker of the House. Huey's opponents gained control of the session and proceeded with the impeachment charges.

This was the first time in the history of Louisiana that a governor had been impeached. In the bill for impeachment there were nineteen articles which were as follows:

First, it was charged that Long had used the appointive power of the Governor with the hopes of influencing and in the attempt to influence the judiciary of the State and that he had publicly boasted that he controlled the State.

Second, that he had bribed or attempted to bribe a member or members of the State Legislature.

Third, that he habitually required undated resignations of his appointees as a condition of their appointment, so as to provide himself with the power of removing them at any time, although the terms of their offices were fixed by the Constitution.

Fourth, that he had personally and through board controlled, wasted, misused, misapplied, and misappropriated funds and property of the State.

Fifth, that he had contracted illegal loans contrary to the provisions of the State Constitution.

Sixth, that he had removed officials for political purposes and used his power over educational institutions as a political weapon.

Seventh, that he had, in time of peace and without the request of the civil authorities, used his power as Commander-in-Chief of the militia to override the courts and civil authorities.

Eighth, that he had attempted to force official bodies in the parishes to follow his dictation as the price of permitting the passage of certain legislation affecting those parishes.

Ninth, that he constantly carried concealed weapons.

Tenth, that he had repeatedly been guilty of violent abuse of the officials of the State, of members of public boards, and of private individuals.

Eleventh, that he had been guilty of gross personal misconduct in various places.

Twelfth, that he had usurped the prerogatives of the Legislature and its committees, and had caused the breaking of quorums of such committees, his purpose being to prevent the consideration of certain legislation.

Thirteenth, that he had illegally and by a trick awarded the contract for the penitentiary's refrigerating plant to W. K. Henderson.

Fourteenth, that he had attempted to blackmail one of the legislators.

Fifteenth, that he had caused the Executive Mansion to be destroyed without legal authorization to do so.

Sixteenth, that he had illegally disposed of or destroyed the furniture and fixtures from the Executive Mansion.

Seventeenth, that he issued a parole for Elmer Dunnington without the slightest legal authorization to do so.

Eighteenth, that he intruded upon the sessions of the House of Representatives and the Senate without legal authorization for doing so.

Nineteenth, that he attempted to bribe Battling Bozeman (his bodyguard) to kill J. Y. Sanders, Jr. (one of the legislators).

The legislature began hearing testimony and Huey took to the road in a sound truck to tell the people of Louisiana that he was a victim of "octopuses (corporations) and lying newspaper."

The House of Representatives voted impeachment and sent the charges to the Senate for trial. Everything looked black to the Long supporters. At the beginning of the session, however, the Long forces pulled their big surprise. One of the Long legislators brought forward a document, bearing the signatures of fifteen Senators, containing the agreement that they would vote for acquittal regardless of any evidence. This number was enough to prevent the two-thirds majority necessary to remove Long from office. The other legislators protested vigorously but they were obviously defeated by the document which immediately became famous as the "Round Robin."

Huey showed the world what it meant to serve him well. The "Famous Fifteen" who had signed the "Round Robin" document became judges, high-paid attorneys, and departmental heads of various state offices. Some of them went into private business and raked in enormous profits from state contracts.

After the failure of the impeachment trial, Huey Long grew expansive and began to find new uses for his despotism. Nothing could stop him now. He boasted of his title of "Kingfish" and frequently disregarded all routine procedure in transacting state business. He gave contracts to whatever companies he chose without going through the formalities of securing bids. If a cement company suggested that perhaps the contract should be taken up with the Highway Department he would roar, "Hell, I am the Highway Department!" He succeeded in increasing the bond issues for road improvements to $100,000,000, and secured an appropriation of $5,000,000 to build the "tallest capitol in the world."

Huey's particular pet was Louisiana State University. There can be no doubt that the reason for his interest in L. S. U. was vindictive. He was getting even with his Alma Mater, Tulane University, which had refused him an honorary degree after he became governor. He set out to make Tulane look like a "little red school house," and to do this no expense was to be spared. He appointed a relatively obscure educator, James Monroe-Smith, who was dean of small Southwestern College at Lafayette, as head of the University. Smith was a pliable man who would not interfere with Huey's expansion program and who (as will later be shown) was without moral scruples. Huey, himself, remarked on several occasions that he chose Smith because "He has a hide as thick as an elephant's," and on one occasion he added, "There ain't a straight bone in Jim's body. But he does what I want him to, and he's a good president."

Huey spent $9,000,000 on construction at the University and operating expenses rose from $1,500,000 to $3,500,000 per annum. Enrollment was so heavy that thousands were forced to live a considerable distance from the school, and Huey advertised that everyone could have a college education for the asking. He gave orders to build up a football that could beat Tulane and scouts were sent to preparatory schools all over the country to offer probably the most liberal scholarships ever offered to college athletes. He found out the number of pieces in the largest college band and ordered one ten pieces larger. Professional musicians were attracted by the "music scholarships," which were surpassed only by the "athletic scholarships," and L. S. U. built up the only college band that could go into formations—no matter how intricate—with only "blackboard rehearsals."

The millions spent at L. S. U. opened another avenue of graft for Louisiana politicians in the form of "commissions" of "kickbacks" on contracts. Huey made it possible for Smith to have practically dictatorial powers at L. S. U. and through Smith, he was able to award contracts without the formality of bids, or, if bids were let, he could still choose the contractors by advising certain ones to bid low and they could add "extras" to the contract price after the contract had been awarded. Some of these so-called "extras," on which bids were not required, amounted to more than the original contract, and it was principally on these contracts that the favored contractors were finally convicted as a result of the Intelligence Unit's "scandals investigations."

Another source of graft was the state operated Levee Board of Orleans Parish. The Levee Board issued bonds in 1931, 1932, and 1933 in the sum of $5,628,000, the proceeds of which were to be used for improvements and development of the lakefront on Lake Pontchartrain and the construction of the Shushan Airport (name later changed to New Orleans Airport at a cost of $30,000 after Shushan's conviction in 1939.)

The Louisiana Conservation Department, which was to play such an important part in the later "Scandals investigations" came into prominence under the Huey Long regime. Long chose one of his strongest financial backers, R. S. Maestri, to head it after accepting the undated resignation of the former head. (It was necessary in this case to mobilize the national guard to oust this official.) Huey saw possibilities in the Conservation Department, which he once termed as a "coon-chasing and possum-watching brigade," when the state oil lands came into prominence because of newly discovered oil pools.

Huey set up his own newspaper for spreading the virtues of his administration and to carry on his vituperative attacks against any that dared to oppose him. He employed some of the best newspapermen in New Orleans and set up offices in Mississippi. He claimed that it was impossible for him to find a press in Louisiana, but he also was able to escape the libel laws. Everyone on the state payroll has to "volunteer" to subscribe to the paper and the state police and highway trucks were the circulation department.

In November 1930, Huey was elected to the United States Senate, although he refused to take his seat and let the lieutenant-governor, with whom he had broken in the early days of the impeachment proceedings, become governor. In 1931, however, the lieutenant-governor, Dr. Cyr, declared that since Huey had been elected to the United States Senate, he was no longer governor, and proceeded to have himself sworn in as governor. This gave Huey the opportunity he was looking for. He reasoned that since the lieutenant-governor; and since there was no vacancy in the governor's position, he could not be governor. Dr. Cyr was, therefore, left suspended in mid-air and Huey took his seat in the Senate and let the president pro tempore of the Senate succeed to the governorship.

In Washington, Huey attempted to deal with national politics in the same manner as he had dealt with Louisiana politics. He made unprecedented attacks on his fellow senators, especially the ones that represented some wealthier states, and began his "Share the Wealth" movement in earnest. He kept control of Louisiana's affairs and O. K. Allen, elected governor a short time after Huey went to Washington, was merely the mouthpiece of Long. Long invaded Arkansas in a speaking tour for Hattie Caraway and was successful in getting her elected to the Senate. After this, Huey threatened other senators with: "Watch out I'll be in your state next."

During the first week in September 1935 Huey Long returned from Washington to Louisiana for the purpose of jamming through in a special session of the legislature certain laws, among which was the re-districting of certain judicial districts in order to eliminate an unfriendly District Judge. The special session had been called to convene beginning Sunday night, September 8, at 9:00 PM. A meeting was held in "Huey's capitol" between Huey and his chief lieutenants in the late afternoon of September 8, and as Huey and his bodyguard and followers left the building, Huey was accosted by Dr. Carl Weiss, whose father-in-law was the District Judge to be the victim of the gerry-mandering legislation to be enacted that night.

What actually happened at this moment will probably never be known. However, within seconds Dr. Carl Weiss lay on the floor of the corridor in the capitol building his body riddled by more than 50 bullets, and Huey Long has received one shot in the abdomen. Eye witnesses claimed in official statements, although no inquest was ever held, that Dr. Weiss fired the shot into Senator Long's body. The weapon used by Dr. Weiss (at least the one picked up beside his bullet riddled body), so far as has ever been ascertained, was a .22 caliber pistol. The bullet removed from Long's body was from a .45 caliber pistol.

Huey Long was rushed to the Lady of the Lake Hospital at Baton Rouge where he was attended by Dr. Arthur Vidrine. Dr. Vidrine was a small town country doctor chosen by Huey Long sometime before as head of the New Orleans charity hospital, the largest of its kind in the South. Dr. Vidrine happened to be at Baton Rouge at the time as one of Huey Long's chief followers. Specialists were hurriedly summoned from New Orleans to operate on the Senator, however, due to an automobile accident the specialists did not reach Baton Rouge promptly and Dr. Vidrine proceeded to remove the bullet from Senator Long's body. Huey Long died on September 10 and his body was interred on the capitol grounds beneath eight feet of concrete reinforced with steel. A powerful searchlight is focused on his grave at night to this date, and fresh flowers are placed daily at his tomb, to which reference will be made later.

Huey's Lieutenants

At the same time that Huey was making his phenomenal rise to power, his "chosen few" were making equally sensational rises to wealth. Huey chose lieutenants who were interested in money only, and who, as long as their desires were satisfied, were satisfied to let Huey be the "Kingfish." Probably his most trusted lieutenant was Seymour Weiss, who was manager of the Roosevelt Hotel barber shop at the time Huey found him. Under Huey's tutelage, Weiss became a multimillionaire and one of the strongest political factors in the state. After Huey's death, Weiss became richer and more powerful.

Weiss was born on Friday, the thirteenth of September, 1896, at Bunkie, Louisiana. His father was a native of Austria, and his mother a native of Berlin. He received a grade school education in Bunkie and Abbeville, Louisiana, and after leaving school went to Alexandria, Louisiana, where he was employed as a clerk in a department store. In 1916 he moved to New Orleans where he was employed as a clerk in a shoe store until the outset of the war in 1917. He was in the infantry during the war and returned to New Orleans after the armistice to resume his position in the shoe store.

His connections with the Roosevelt Hotel began as manager of its barber shop. In succession he became business production manager, assistant manager, manager, vice-president, and in 1931 became president and managing director. Soon after that he became president of the Louisiana Hotel Men's Association and vice-president of the American Hotel Men's Association.

The First Series of Investigations: 1932 to 1934

Because of the political corruption which existed while Huey Long was building his kingdom, and the rough-shod tactics used by his political machine in crushing all opposition, it was little wonder that the Intelligence Unit was finally called upon to determine if some of the ill-gotten gains had not been overlooked in income tax returns.

Early in 1932 numerous complaints, both verbal and written from anonymous sources, from ordinary citizens and from responsible and highly respected persons throughout the state of Louisiana, were made to the Bureau of Internal Revenue, alleging that the expenditure of the $100,000,000 state road and public building program during the years 1928 to 1931 had yielded huge secret profits to certain state officials and to their close associates.

Many of the reports charged that the grafting officials had not properly reported their ill-gotten gains for tax purposes. The reports were so persistent and the allegations so specific in some instances that an investigation was commenced in July 1932 to determine their truth or falsity. Mr. Elmer L. Irey, Chief of the Intelligence Unit, was mindful of the fact that there had been intense factional political strife in Louisiana for several years, and took into consideration the possibility that these charges and allegations might have been made solely from motives of political animosity, with which matters the Intelligence Unit was not and could not be concerned. Special Agent in Charge A. D. Burford of the Intelligence Unit, was designated by Chief Irey to supervise the preliminary investigations and thereafter, when it appeared that the complaints had at least some foundation in fact, approximately 32 special agents and revenue agents from all parts of the United States were assigned to Louisiana to make the investigations. No stone was left unturned by the agents under Mr. Burford in attempting to trace the funds to those who received the huge profits on the state contracts. Although every conceivable obstacle was thrown in their way by the Louisiana politicians, the agents pressed doggedly forward.

Certain Louisiana banks and other business establishments at first refused to allow the special agents to examine their records on those closely connected with the Huey Long regime. It therefore became necessary to go through the formality of securing court orders before records were made available to the agents. Subsequent examination of the records in question in some instances revealed why such a concerted effort had been made to keep them from being examined by Chief Irey's agents. Deposits in currency, cancelled checks without endorsements, and other clues gave the agents a starting point from which to work. During the ensuing months the special agents began fitting the jigsaw puzzle together piece by piece, which, when completed, would show who actually received the many thousands of dollars in "kickbacks" paid by contractors on state projects.

Meanwhile the country was in the throes of the depression, and the particularly bitter national election of November 1932 was in the offing. Soon after the ballots in that election had been counted, resulting in the approaching change in the national administration, Secretary Ogden Mills called the Intelligence Unit's Chief, Mr. Irey, to the Treasury for a conference on the progress of the Louisiana investigations. He inquired if the cases could be completed and the evidence placed before a grand jury for action prior to March 4, 1933. Mr. Irey informed the Secretary briefly as to the difficulties which his agents had encountered in investigating the various cases, and explained that the cases could not be completed prior to that date. The Secretary then instructed Mr. Irey to have the agents suspend their investigations. He also directed that comprehensive preliminary reports be prepared in each case and that the overall developments be included in one report for consideration by his successor in office after March 4, 1933.

Chief Irey thereupon called Special Agent in Charge Burford to Washington to advise him of the Secretary's instructions, and it was arranged for the 32 agents who had been on the assignment to be returned to their respective posts of duty.

During the next few weeks, under Mr. Burford's direction, detailed reports of developments up to the date the investigations were suspended were prepared in compliance with the Secretary's instructions. There was assembled, to be included with the reports, all the evidence which had been secured. A memorandum was then prepared by Chief Irey to be placed on top of the case files, briefly outlining the more important developments of the investigation and setting forth what it was believed could be uncovered by further inquiry. The files were retained in Mr. Irey's office to be delivered to the new Secretary when he came into office. In the interim, however, statutory notices were sent to all taxpayers in cases where waivers providing for the extension of the statutory period for the collection of deficiencies could not be secured.

For the next few weeks immediately following the inauguration on March 4, 1933, the acute banking situation required the entire time night and day of the new incumbent, Secretary Woodin. Also the Commissioner holding office under the previous administration continued in his position until his successor was appointed, and it was not until November 1933, when Mr. Morgenthau became Under Secretary of the Treasury, and Acting Secretary, that Mr. Irey had an opportunity of carrying out the former Secretary's instructions with respect to delivery of the files in the Louisiana investigations to the new Secretary's office for further consideration.

Within the matter of a very few days after the files containing Mr. Irey's memorandum came to Secretary Morgenthau's attention, he called Mr. Irey to his office for consultation regarding what further steps should be undertaken. That conference resulted in instructions by Mr. Morgenthau that the investigations be immediately resumed and that they proceed with all vigor "letting the chips fall where they may." Mr. Morgenthau also announced that he wanted this same policy followed in all cases throughout the time he continued as head of the Treasury Department.

In compliance with Secretary Morgenthau's instructions, Mr. Irey recalled Special Agent in Charge Burford to Washington, where plans were formulated for resuming the Louisiana investigations. Arrangements were made for the reassignment of the special agents and revenue agents, and the Intelligence Unit's investigations were resumed immediately thereafter.

In the following months the agents were successful in obtaining evidence which disclosed that graft had been paid on practically every contract let by the state after Huey Long became governor. Involved in the cases under inquiry by the special agents were 232 individuals, 42 partnerships and 122 corporations, covering 1,007 tax years. The investigations covered those who were in any way connected with the persons receiving graft payments, contractors on state projects, and companies that sold cement, sand and shells to the Highway Commission. Likewise, the income tax returns of the dealers who sold steel, guard rails, asphalt, trucks and tractors to the state of Louisiana during the same period of time were checked by the agents to determine what "commissions" had been paid, and to identify the persons who ultimately received them.

It was found that some of these companies and contractors had claimed the graft commissions as business expenses on their returns. In a great number of instances those who received these funds failed to report them in their income tax returns.

The investigations also extended to the operators of the larger gambling establishments in Louisiana. Gambling on a big scale was openly permitted in New Orleans, and this city boasted of some of the largest gambling places in the south. The agents found that the operators in some instances had withdrawn substantial funds from their businesses which the circumstances showed were neither business expenses nor losses. In addition these operators had accumulated substantial wealth which could not be accounted for by an examination of their returns over a period of years. There seemed to be no difference of opinion in the public's mind as to the fact that a large payoff by the gamblers had been made, and there was little difference of opinion as to who received the protection money.

The investigations continued through 1934 and approximately two million dollars in additional taxes and penalties were recommended for assessment. As a result of the Intelligence Unit's work, 24 indictments were returned by a grand jury at New Orleans, charging evasion and conspiracy to evade income taxes by 24 individual defendants and 3 corporations.

In the course of the investigations, Senator Long broke with the national administration and exerted every effort to have the investigations dropped. He used his newspaper and radio facilities to charge persecution—shouting loudly that the "New Deal" investigators were swarming in Louisiana like bees in an effort to "get something on me." Huey had a good reason for being alarmed—his most trusted lieutenants were under indictment. A final report on his case, in which it was recommended that criminal proceedings be instituted, was submitted by the agents on September 4, 1935. Mr. Irey, Chief of the Treasury's Intelligence Unit, and Special Agent in Charge Burford immediately conferred with former Governor Dan Moody of Texas, who had been appointed Special Assistant to the Attorney General to handle the prosecution. On September 7th they agreed that the evidence warranted prosecution of Senator Long and decided to place the facts before the grand jury which was to meet on October 3rd. On the day following the conference Huey was fatally shot.

The first defendant to be brought to trial was State Representative Joseph Fisher who was interested in several contracts let by the Louisiana Highway Commission on which he received "commissions" in connection with the purchase and hauling of shell for highway construction. He was found guilty on April 26, 1935, and sentenced to serve a term of eighteen months in Atlanta.

The second case to be tried was that of A. L. Shushan—one of the largest and, considered by the attorneys, the best case of the series. The trial began on October 8, 1935, before United States District Judge William H. Barrett of Augusta, Georgia, who was assigned as special judge for the case. The Government counsel was headed by Amos W. M. Woodcock, Special Assistant to the Attorney General. On October 25, 1935, much to the surprise of the Government (and the judge, who had congratulated Woodcock on winning the case), the jury returned a verdict of "not guilty." A most unusual outbreak by the friends of the Long regime, who had packed the courtroom, followed the returning of the verdict. The press of New Orleans described it as follows:

"Cheers swept over the Federal court as soon as the jury's verdict was read."

"Violence broke out when the judge left the stand. Long's former bodyguards wielded fists and night sticks to punch and club photographers."

The next cases were set for trial on the calendar beginning May 29, 1936. On that day, United States Attorney Rene A. Viosca appeared in court and made a motion to dismiss the remaining cases (some fifteen of the gamblers and business contractors had theretofore entered pleas of guilty or nolo contendere), stating as follows:

"With respect to the remaining cases, the Government wishes to file motions to dismiss them. I have given the most careful consideration to these cases and am firmly of the opinion that the Government has no reasonable hope to secure convictions in any of them. For that reason, I am filing the motions to dismiss them."

Mr. Viosca also stated that the "Cases are weak" and the "Changed atmosphere" in Louisiana since Long's death, made convictions very improbable.

The public's reaction to the dismissals was national in scope. Papers in all parts of the country devoted editorials in scoring the dismissals. Next to the Treasury Department's Intelligence Unit, the grand jurors who had devoted nine months of their time and had met in fifty-one sessions during the investigations were perhaps the most chagrined as a result of United States Attorney Viosca's action. Nine of the members addressed a letter to the Attorney General in sharp criticism of the Department of Justice for dropping prosecution of the cases. They stated in the letter, which appeared in all the New Orleans newspapers, as follows:

"As to whether the cases were 'weak' this same United States Attorney . . . presented these 'weak' cases to us for investigation. As to there being a 'changed atmosphere' in New Orleans, if this is meant a change in the wish of the law-loving people of the United States to see that crime is punished, we challenge the statement. It is not true; there is not and cannot be in New Orleans, or elsewhere, a 'changed atmosphere' with regard to the punishment of crime. If that statement as to the 'changed atmosphere' were limited to official circles, we would readily agree."

The letter concluded with a request that former State Representative Joe Fisher, "possibly one of the least of the offenders," be released from prison since he was now the victim of "gross and unwarranted official discrimination."

The Treasury Department, particularly the Intelligence Unit, was disappointed in the outcome of the cases, especially in view of the fact that the special agents had worked many hours overtime in assembling the evidence in each case. Mr. Irey stated before a congressional committee that if there had been a "deal" the Treasury had no part of it; that "We made careful investigations and accumulated a mass of evidence which we felt, and which we still feel, provided the basis for successful prosecutions."

In order to show that the Treasury had no part in the dismissals, the Secretary ordered that no conference be held on the pending civil cases unless attended by a special agent of the Intelligence Unit and that "not one penny of the taxes or penalties be compromised." A special calendar was set by the Board of Tax Appeals to hear the cases in the latter part of 1937 and the early part of 1938. Special representatives of the Bureau's Chief Counsel were sent to New Orleans to handle the prosecution of the cases and the Treasury spared no expense to bring the necessary witnesses from all parts of the country to New Orleans. One by one the taxpayers, whose indictments had been dismissed, admitted that the contentions of the Government were right and settled their cases by payment of all taxes and fraud penalties before their cases were called for trial. Robert S. Maestri, Seymour Weiss, Estate of O. K. Allen, Estate of Huey Long, and many others, including A. L. Shushan, did not consider their chances of winning before the Board of Tax Appeals worth the cost of going to trial. A few of the gamblers and smaller politicians chose to go to trial but the Government won every case. Thus cases which were considered "too weak" for criminal prosecution were won 100 percent before the Board of Tax Appeals on exactly the same evidence as was presented to the grand jury in 1934 and 1935. Approximately $2,000,000 in additional taxes and penalties was paid into the Treasury by the individuals and corporations involved in the investigations. The successful civil prosecution of the Louisiana cases caused national comment regarding the dismissal of the criminal cases.

Political Set-Up In Louisiana After Huey's Death

The death of Long created a political turmoil in Louisiana that perhaps has never been equaled in any of the other 47 states. A dictator had built up an empire within a sovereign state—and had taken steps to include the other 47 states in it—but he had never included the possibility of his death in his plans. He had powerful leaders, but he had never shared power with them; had never favored one over the other in a political way. Obviously, the millionaires, such as Maestri, Shushan, and Weiss were not the type to carry on Huey's "Share the Wealth" program, which was the basis of his power. There were other leaders, however, that aspired to be the successor to the "Kingfish"—O. K. Allen, the old friend whose loan of $500 was repaid by Huey by making him an "OK" governor; James A. Noe, whose manipulations with state oil and gas leases had made Huey a fortune; Gerald L. K. Smith, a Shreveport preacher who had been dismissed by his congregation for devoting too much time to Huey's "Share the Wealth" movement; Allen Ellender, Speaker of the House; and John B. Fournet, who had tried so hard to prevent Huey's impeachment. Even Earl Long, brother of Huey, who had fought Huey for years but who had made a reconciliation shortly before Huey's death, also claimed recognition.

Source: U.S. Internal Revenue Service. *Story of the Work of the Intelligence Unit.* Washington, DC: Library of Congress, 1943. Call Number: HV6783.A47

See Articles: Internal Revenue Service; Louisiana; Political Crimes, History of; Political Crimes, Sociology of.

1940
PRIMARY DOCUMENT

FBI Memorandum on Mann Act Violations

"White slavery" is an old euphemism for prostitution. A moral panic over an unconfirmed report of a crime ring kidnapping European girls and forcing them to work in Chicago brothels led to the 1910 White Slave Traffic Act, or Mann Act, which criminalized the interstate transport of women for "immoral purposes." Originally intended to refer to prostitution, as in this memo, the language was later interpreted to penalize statutory rape, polygamy, and (in its first prosecution) interracial sex.

Rinaldo De Butch, With Aliases: Rinaldo Debuch, "Butch;"
Richard Hill, With Aliases: "Woody," "Witty;"
John Edward Foster;
Harold Elwood Custer.

On August 20, 1939, a telephone call was received at the Huntington, West Virginia, Field Division of the Federal Bureau of Investigation, United States Department of Justice, from the Chief of Police at Parkersburg, West Virginia. The Chief advised that he had received information that at 12:15 a.m. on the same day, four men had forcibly taken a female inmate from a house of prostitution at Parkersburg, West Virginia, and transported her to Steubenville, Ohio, in an automobile. Inasmuch as this indicated a violation of the Federal Kidnapping Statute, an immediate investigation was initiated by Special Agents of the FBI.

Through the cooperation of the Police Department at Steubenville, Ohio, DeButch and his three accomplices, Richard Hill, John Edward Foster and Harold Elwood Custer, were taken into custody along with the victim of their abduction, who for the purposes of this narrative will be described as Jean Davis.

Upon being interviewed by Special Agents, Jean Davis related that she was then twenty-nine years of age and had been practicing prostitution since she was fifteen years of age. Her education extended only as far as the sixth grade of the elementary schools. During 1938 she made the acquaintance of DeButch and they began to live together at Steubenville, Ohio, as man and wife. While living with DeButch, she practiced prostitution at his behest and furnished him with all of her earnings from this source. In May of 1939, she decided to leave DeButch due to his abusive treatment of her, and hitchhiked her way to Parkersburg, West Virginia, where she obtained work in a house of prostitution. DeButch later visited her on several occasions demanding money and endeavoring to persuade her to return to Steubenville to practice prostitution for his personal gain. On one occasion he threatened to inform her mother that she was leading a life of shame. She refused his requests and declined either to give him money or to return with him to Steubenville, Ohio.

Miss Davis went on to relate that shortly after midnight on August 20, 1939, DeButch and his three companions appeared at the house of prostitution where she was employed and insisted that she return with them to Steubenville. She again refused and DeButch, taking from his pocket what appeared to be a gun and making the statement that he was also armed with a knife, forcibly abducted her with the assistance of his friends and transported her back to Steubenville in his personal car. She informed that she struggled to avoid being kidnapped but was overcome by the strength of her abductors, who prevented her from screaming and held her by the arms until she was placed in the car. She was scantily clad at this time and was not allowed an opportunity to secure her clothes. Her version of the kidnapping was confirmed by other inmates of this house of prostitution and several passersby on the street. The car was driven by DeButch and the party arrived back in Steubenville at about 3:30 in the morning. DeButch openly informed her that he was returning her in order that she might practice prostitution for him. DeButch let his friends out and paid them each one dollar for their assistance, and then took Jean Davis to his residence where they were shortly thereafter arrested by local officers.

Rinaldo DeButch advised Special Agents investigating this case that after Jean Davis left him he attempted to locate her in several nearby Ohio towns without success and finally contacted her mother, who resided in Pennsylvania. DeButch claimed that her mother made the request of him that he locate her daughter and bring her to her mother's home. Subsequent investigation revealed that DeButch had actually visited Miss Davis' mother seeking her whereabouts, but that Mrs. Davis had made no request to have her daughter returned home. DeButch at first denied the kidnapping, but after further questioning admitted that he and his friends had forcibly transported Miss Davis back to Ohio against her will.

He insisted that he was not armed with a gun or knife, but had used a small flashlight to give the impression that he was carrying a gun. However, Harold Elwood Custer advised the Special Agents that DeButch actually did have a gun at the time of the kidnapping, which Custer himself had furnished to him. Custer had borrowed this gun from one of his friends and thereafter DeButch and he together purchased cartridges for it at a second hand shop in Steubenville. He also insisted that his only purpose in effecting the abduction was to try to take her out of a life of shame, and he professed that he had a deep love for her. He admitted, however, that he had previously lived with Miss Davis as man and wife and accepted her earnings while she practiced prostitution in the City of Steubenville, Ohio.

DeButch's associates, upon questioning by Special Agents, all admitted their participation in this offense and the fact that they accepted money from DeButch for their assistance in carrying out the abduction. Harold Elwood Custer advised that DeButch, while the quartetts was being held in the Steubenville jail, threatened to get even with them if they testified against him in the Federal Court.

As a result of this investigation, a Federal Grand Jury sitting at Wheeling, West Virginia, returned indictments against DeButch and his co-defendants on October 18, 1939, charging them with violation of both the Federal Kidnapping Statute and the White Slave Traffic Act, the latter charge being based upon the interstate transportation of Miss Davis for an immoral purpose. On arraignment DeButch's accomplices all entered pleas of guilty to the kidnapping charge and each was sentenced to serve one year and one day in a Federal penitentiary. DeButch entered a plea of not guilty to the kidnapping charge. After a jury trial he was found guilty and on December 4, 1939, was sentenced to serve twenty years in a Federal institution. DeButch thereafter pleaded guilty to the White Slave Traffic Act charge and received an additional five-year sentence for this offense, making a total sentence of twenty-five years which he must serve.

The records of the Identification Division of the FBI reflect that DeButch was first arrested in 1934 for assaulting a Federal officer and was sentenced to pay a fine of $200 and serve a term of three years in a Federal institution, from which sentence he was conditionally released on March 15, 1937. He was next arrested on November 12, 1938, by the Police Department at Steubenville, Ohio, on a charge of grand larceny and was bound over to the State Grand Jury under $2,000 bond. This charge is yet pending against him. His last arrest was on August 20, 1939, in connection with instant case. DeButch at the time of his arrest in this case was thirty-seven years of age; married and separated from his lawful wife. According to his own statements he had resided in Steubenville, Ohio, for some thirty years, being employed at odd jobs during that time. During 1937, he was engaged in the numbers racket and worked for a time in a local gambling house. It was reported that during prohibition days he was engaged in distilling and transporting bootleg liquor.

The files of the FBI contain no criminal record for Richard Hill. At the time of his arrest in this case, Hill was twenty years of age, single and had completed the 9th grade in elementary schools.

The Criminal record of John Edward Foster reflects that he was first arrested on April 23, 1933, by the Police Department at Steubenville, Ohio, as a suspicious person and discharged. His next arrest was for his participation in this case. At the time of this arrest he was twenty-two years of age, single and had completed the 8th grade.

The records of the identification Division of the FBI reflect that Harold Elwood Custer was arrested by the Steubenville, Ohio, Police Department on October 18, 1938, for investigation, which charge was later dismissed. His next arrest occurred in connection with this case, and at that time he was twenty-one years of age, single and had completed his high school education.

Federal Bureau of Investigation
United States Department of Justice
Washington, D. C.
I.C. No. 7-2872
September 26, 1940

Source: NARA-II, RG 65 FBI, Interesting Case Write-ups, Box 3

See Articles: Kidnapping; Mann Act; Slavery.

1940
PRIMARY DOCUMENT

FBI Memorandum on Receiving the Twelve Millionth Fingerprint Card

Classification 32 is Fingerprint Matters in the FBI's file classification system, consisting of administrative information on fingerprints. Bureau of Investigation administrator D. M. Ladd—best known for authoring the FBI memo warning that the film It's a Wonderful Life *was communist propaganda—details the depth and usefulness of the FBI's fingerprint files in anticipation of the Bureau of Investigation's 1940s campaign to convince local law enforcement agencies to fingerprint all suspects.*

On January 19, 1940, the Identification Division received its twelve millionth fingerprint card. This care reflected the fingerprints of one E. J. Raybak arrested by the Police Department of Shelbyville, Tennessee, on January 14, 1940, on a charge of grand larceny. It is interesting to note that the fingerprint card contained the notation that Raybak refused to tell any criminal record and refused to answer when questioned with reference to his residence. Upon receipt of this card in the Identification Division of the Federal Bureau of Investigation, it was classified and searched through our records. It was identified as being the record of an individual whose FBI number is 263419 and who, according to the files of this division, was first arrested as George Babe Malarkey on July 16, 1923, by the Police Department at Berkeley, California, for attempted burglary. No disposition is shown as to this arrest and he was marked to be held for the Alameda Police Department.

He was next heard from as Harry Stevens when he was arrested by the Police Department at Louisville, Kentucky, on June 9, 1924, for housebreaking, and no disposition is shown for this arrest.

On March 24, 1925, fingerprints were received from the State penitentiary at Nashville, Tennessee, for this individual as Harry Stevens, where he had been received to serve a term of from three to five years and one day for housebreaking and larceny.

On July 30, 1930, he was arrested by the Police Department at Cincinnati, Ohio, at Patrick Kelley, for burglary at Glendale, Ohio and was returned to Glendale, Ohio.

The next that was heard of him was the receipt of his fingerprints as Pat Kelley from the State Penitentiary at Columbus, Ohio where he was received to serve a term of from one and a half to fifteen years for burglary and larceny.

Two years later, or February 28, 1932, he was received at the State Penitentiary at Nashville, Tennessee, as Harry B. Stephens for housebreaking and larceny to serve a term of one to three years.

On October 1, 1933, he was arrested, according to the files of this Bureau, by the Police Department at Shaker Heights, Ohio, as John Mallory as a suspicious person, and he was turned over by that department to the Cleveland, Ohio Police Department, on October 3, 1933.

September 19, 1939, he was arrested by the Police Department at Nashville, Tennessee, as Harry B. Stevens for housebreaking and larceny, and there is contained in the files a wanted notice for this individual indicating that he escaped from the Police Station at Nashville on September 20, 1939.

Since his escape from the Police Department, he has been involved in other files, as is reflected by the fact that the Federal Bureau of Investigation was conducting an investigation relative to the theft and interstate transportation of an automobile and this individual as Henry Slevenski was identified as having been the person responsible for the theft and transportation of this car and, accordingly a wanted notice was placed in the files of the Bureau for this individual on October 9, 1939.

Respectfully,
D. M. Ladd

Federal Bureau of Investigation
United States Department of Justice
Washington, D. C.
January 19, 1940

Source: NARA II, RG 65, Class 32

See Articles: Federal Bureau of Investigation; Fingerprinting; Justice, Department of.

1941 to 1960

INTRODUCTION

During America's involvement in World War II from 1941 to 1945, millions of young men fought Nazi fascism and Japanese imperialism abroad. Americans at home continued to grapple with old forms of crime, while encountering new ones that grew out of wartime disruption of civilian life. With fathers at war or working long hours in war industries, and mothers often also working, many people worried that children left alone at home would become juvenile delinquents. At the same time that women were urged to contribute to the war effort, mothers who left latch-key children to fend for themselves were often condemned. Many police officers enlisted in the military, leading to manpower shortages that hampered efforts to cope with crime. In some cities, civilians volunteered as auxiliary police for the duration of the war. They combined support of the regular force, and sometimes civil defense functions. Police work remained a man's realm; women were hired by the police force, but mostly as dispatchers or clerks. Women also conducted social work with children and young women.

An old concern about the morality of unsupervised young women resurfaced in the form of "V-girls," amateur prostitutes who patriotically serviced men on leave or in the military camps. The military was mostly concerned about venereal disease and conducted aggressive campaigns against it. Organized crime participated in the black market for scarce consumer goods and counterfeiting of ration stamps. Mafiosi were bitter enemies of Benito Mussolini, who provided valuable intelligence to the U.S. Army when it was preparing to invade Italy in 1943. Homicide rates dropped during the war, but people continued to kill for personal motives. Capital punishment prevailed, as in the 1930s. About half of those executed were black, a pattern that continued into the 1950s.

Zoot Suit Riots and Racial Tensions

Development of wartime industry caused massive migration to cities with shipyards, converted automobile plants, and aircraft factories. This influx strained urban infrastructure and heightened racial tensions. Major race riots erupted in 1943. In Los Angeles, conflict between Anglos and Chicanos (native-born Mexicans) began with the apparent murder of Jose Diaz in Sleepy Lagoon, a reservoir in southeast Los Angeles. The area was the scene of *pachuco* gang fights, and newspapers began a hysterical campaign against

President Harry Truman is flanked by members of the National Conference on Prevention and Control of Juvenile Delinquency, January 27, 1948. Juvenile arrests and detentions increased from 1941 to 1942 and continued after the war; arrests approximately doubled in the late 1940s and 1950s. Possible explanations include a white, middle-class youth subculture focused on consumerism, while minority unemployment rates doubled that of young whites.

"zoot suiters." The zoot suit—featuring baggy pleated trousers, a double-breasted suit jacket reaching almost to the knees, and a conspicuous watch chain, often topped by a fedora hat—was the badge of tough Chicano kids, the pachucos. Even though some evidence suggested that Diaz was hit by a car, the police rounded up over 20 young Chicanos, charging them with murder or attempted murder. After a very irregular trial, the all-white jury voted to convict 12 defendants, reduce charges, or acquit the remainder. Local people rallied around the young men, forming a defense league.

The Zoot Suit Riots broke out as a series of clashes between white servicemen and pachucos in their zoot suits. The zoot suits, because of its generous use of cloth, actually violated wartime clothing rationing and was only manufactured by bootleg tailors. To soldiers and sailors, it was a symbol of unpatriotic evasion of military duty. After a series of conflicts, in June 1943, swarms of sailors and marines invaded East Los Angeles in a fleet of 20 taxicabs. They beat and stripped the zoots off any Chicanos they encountered. The police, including off-duty officers, joined in the attacks and arrested scores of people, none of them white. Finally, the U.S. Navy had to make Los Angeles off limits to its personnel, but most residents of the city thought they had committed a patriotic act against a criminal element. San Jose, Oakland, San Diego, Detroit, Chicago, and New York also witnessed attacks on zoot suiters, who were African American, Filipino, or Chicano.

Detroit had seen explosive population growth when its auto plants converted to military production, creating pressures on housing and competition for jobs. Tensions were exacerbated because the migrants included whites from Appalachia and blacks from the south. As in Los Angeles, June was a month of attacks between whites and blacks, apparently started by an individual fight and fed by rumors of people being murdered or raped. The riots lasted three days: Stores were burned or looted, cars were overturned, and passing motorists or streetcar passengers were beaten. The great majority of people injured and arrested were black. Order was finally restored with the arrival of the military. Whites accused black "hoodlums" of initiating and carrying on the violence; blacks pointed to discrimination in hiring and housing, police brutality, and racism.

Harlem had been mostly left behind in the 1920s prosperity, suffered deeply during the depression, and missed out on the wartime industrial boom. The August 1943 riot repeated the pattern of a riot in 1935, in that it began with a black–white confrontation. A black soldier tried to protect a woman from being beaten by a police officer, who then shot and wounded him. A rumor that the soldier had been killed set off a wave of rioting that foreshadowed the 1960s riots—people burned and looted white-owned stores in their neighborhoods. Police and troops saturated the neighborhood to restore order, and Mayor Fiorello La Guardia helped calm things down by providing food for Harlem residents.

Japanese Internment Camps and Criminal Espionage
The largest racial issue during the war was the "relocation," or internment of Japanese residents from western states in camps. Whites on the Pacific Coast had long agitated against Japanese land ownership, and early in the 20th century, California passed a law forbidding alien landholding. There were not many American-born Japanese at the time, but by 1942, there were many who prospered, especially in truck farming. After Pearl Harbor, there were rumors of Japanese spies and demands that the Japanese be moved from the coast. President Franklin D. Roosevelt, supported by California Attorney General Earl Warren, supported the U.S. Army's plan of forcing Japanese people to sell their property on short notice, usually for low prices, and shipping them to internment camps. There was little evidence of Japanese spying; a military officer said that the lack of evidence only proved how wily they were. The FBI was given the job of organizing the round-up. Life in the camps was bleak and alienating, and family relations suffered. Young, interred men were given a way out—they could enlist in the U.S. Army to fight in Europe. Many served bravely; in fact, the Japanese American unit received the most decorations during the war. The Supreme Court upheld internment in *Korematsu v. United States* (1944).

The FBI not only rounded up innocent Japanese, it also pursued real spies. Before the Japanese attack on Pearl Harbor, the U.S. government began to pay attention to Axis espionage activities. The Nazis were active among the German American Bund. The Japanese and other countries were active among their nationalist groups. These groups would be the subject of a small number of criminal espionage cases in the years ahead. As early as 1940, President Roosevelt set up the Special Intelligence Service (SIS), staffed by Federal Bureau of Intelligence (FBI) men and supported by lawyers from the bureau. The service's mission was to counter or undermine Axis propaganda and aid in Latin America, where numerous Germans and Japanese lived. By 1944, the SIS was successful in eliminating the threat. The FBI investigated the Duquesne Spy Ring in 1941, which was the largest espionage operation to date. A total of 33 Nazi spies were convicted and given long prison sentences. The 19 who pled "not guilty" were unlucky; they were convicted by a Brooklyn federal jury two days after Hitler declared war on the United States on December 11, 1941. During the war, the FBI investigated sabotage in June 1942 when German U-boats landed trained saboteurs on Long Island, New York; and Ponte Vedra Beach, Florida. A coast guardsman first discovered the New York contingent, but allowed them to pass. One agent, fearing capture, turned himself in and aided the FBI in finding and arresting his former comrades. They were caught, and those who refused to cooperate with the government were condemned to death by a secret military tribunal convened by President Roosevelt. On July 31, the court issued a ruling in *Ex parte Quirin*, 317 U.S. 1 (1942), that allowed the secret military tribunal and the death sentence. Six of the eight were subsequently executed, and two were given prison sentences.

Even though the Soviet Union was officially an ally during the war, mistrust of communism persisted. In 1940, Congress passed the Alien Registration Act, which punished individuals who advocated "the duty, necessity, desirability, or propriety of overthrowing or destroying any government in the United States by force or violence, or attempts to do so." Smith was a southern Democrat who opposed labor unions, so he intended his measure to apply to left-wing groups. The first prosecution and trial was against the left—the Socialist Workers Party. However, by 1944, a group of 30 people charged with Nazi sympathies was put on trial under the law. Most of the leftists were convicted, but the government could not make a case against the diverse collection of isolationists and pro-Germans it had charged. After the war, the Smith Act was used again to attack the left, with more than 120 communists indicted between 1949 and 1956. During 1940–42, New York State's Rapp-Coudert legislative committee investigated "Communist influence" in the New York City public education system. As a result, left-wing professors in the City College and schoolteachers were fired.

Wartime Films and War Crimes Trials

Hollywood joined the war effort with films about enemy agents. *Saboteur* was a 1942 film directed by Alfred Hitchcock about saboteurs who seek to damage the American aircraft industry. Crime fighting was the subject of popular culture as characters such as Dick Tracy, the Tarantula (anticipating Spider Man), and Captain America brought fictional criminals to the halls of justice. During the war, movies were not subject to rationing and Hollywood continued to produce crime movies. Among those released in 1941 were *Ellery Queen and the Perfect Crime*, *High Sierra*, *The Maltese Falcon*, *Dressed to Kill*, *Under Age*, *Shadow of the Thin Man*, and *Dick Tracy vs. Crime, Inc.* Prison was also the subject in movies such as *Convicted* and *Sullivan's Travels* as directors presented audiences with explorations of criminal behavior. Crime films continued to be of interest with *This Gun for Hire*, *Larceny, Inc.*, and *Bowery at Midnight* serving as the top crime movies of 1942. Prison movies included *Men of San Quentin*, *Lady Gangster*, and *Three Smart Saps*. Detective novels also continued their popularity. In 1943, Crime movies continued to attract audiences to *Laura*, *Double Indemnity*, *The Mask of Dimitrios*, and *Murder My Sweet*. Prison movies such as *Lady in the Death House* and *Delinquent Daughters* made enough money for Hollywood to continue the formula. In 1944, Americans were still watching prison and crime movies such as *Prison Mutiny* and the *Crime Doctor's Strangest Case*. In the interest of wartime morale, it was good for audiences to see crime fighters like Sherlock Holmes triumph in films like *Sherlock Holmes and the Secret Weapon* and *Sherlock Holmes in Washington*. Crime fighting served as an analogy for the fighting abroad.

After the war's close, a new type of crime riveted people's attention. War crimes trials of German and Japanese leaders revealed the depths of enemy cruelty. The idea of war crimes was not new, but this was the first time that accused people were actually put on trial and executed. Since then, war crimes have become a pillar of international law. On August 8, 1945, the Allies adopted the London Charter of the International Military Tribunal, usually called the London Charter. It set the standard for the war crimes trials that would try defeated Nazis at Nuremberg. The charter defined the laws, crimes, and procedures to be used for trying war criminals. The crimes involved were war crimes, crimes against the peace, and crimes against humanity. In general, obeying orders would not be accepted as a mitigating factor in prescribing punishment.

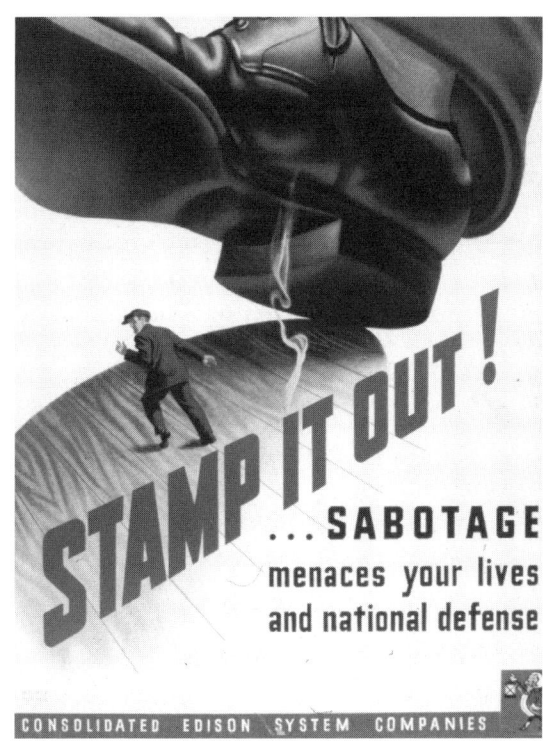

Sabotage was a very real fear during wartime, as exemplified by the July 1942 military trial of the eight German nationals who landed by submarine of the U.S. coast intent on destroying strategic targets. The poster (left) was printed by the Office for Emergency Management War Production Board between 1942 and 1943. A sentinel (right) keeps vigil against saboteurs at a large defense plant in December 1941.

Crimes against the peace were acts that violated the Kellogg-Briand Pact (1929). It outlawed preparing and coming wars of aggression, especially if they violated treaty obligations. War crimes included deliberate killing of civilians or prisoners. At the time, crimes against humanity were focused on the Nazi genocide. The Nuremberg Tribunal was organized following the criminal law procedures practiced by the civil law systems of Europe, rather than English common law. Consequently, the trials were conducted before a panel of judges, rather than before a jury, as the determiner of fact. The system allowed for wider use of hearsay evidence.

Defendants could cross-examine witnesses, as well as present evidence in their defense. If convicted, a defendant could make an appeal to the Allied Control Council. The main Nazi leaders were hanged on October 16, 1946, at Nuremberg for war crimes; others were imprisoned for various terms. In later years, trials for crimes against humanity committed by those responsible for the concentration camps would continue to take place.

In Tokyo, the International Military Tribunal for the Far East (IMTFE) was convened on April 29, 1946. Also known as the Tokyo Trials, the Tokyo War Crimes Tribunal, or the Tribunal, it was convened to try 28 top leaders of the Empire of Japan for war crimes. Over 5,000 others would be charged with lesser war crimes. Emperor Hirohito and a few others were excluded for political reasons. Six received death sentences and were hanged December 23, 1948, at Sugamo Prison in Ikebukuro. On June 18, 1947, Japanese Admiral Shigematsu Sakaibara was hanged for war crimes. During the Japanese occupation of Wake Island, he had ordered the massacre of all civilians. He was later convicted by a military tribunal. Elsewhere, other Japanese military officers and personnel were executed for war crimes.

The Supreme Court dealt with important business in 1946. On February 4, it decided *In re Yamashita,* in which General Tomoyuki Yamashita's attorneys argued technical issues involving the military trial of Yamashita—the commanding general of the Japanese Army in the Philippines. He was charged with failing in his duty as an army commander to control his troops, and it was found that he had in fact permitted them to commit atrocities against civilians and prisoners of war. Yamashita was convicted and sentenced to death. The case was controversial because it sought to establish command responsibility for war crimes. The court announced the Yamashita Standard for hierarchical responsibility for war crimes. Yamashita was hanged on February 23, 1946.

Two days after Yamashita's execution, the court decided *Ashcraft v. Tennessee*, 327 U.S. 274 (1946), in which it expressed a dim view of coerced confessions. This would move police work more in the direction of using forensic evidence for convictions, rather than confessions. It was nearly the last case heard by Chief Justice Harlan Fisk Stone, who died April 22, 1946. The court's work did not stop with the loss of the chief justice. On June 10, it decided *Pinkerton v. United States,* 328 U.S. 640 (1946), in which it enunciated the principle of "Pinkerton liability," extending the concept of conspiracy in criminal conduct to include both substantive offenses committed pursuant to the conspiracy, and the conspiracy itself.

Organized Crime After the War
In the immediate postwar years, murder rates began to rise, and organized crime continued to make the headlines. In the 1940s, Benjamin "Bugsy" Siegel persuaded his crime boss to invest in the Flamingo Hotel in Las Vegas, Nevada, where gambling was legal. In 1946, several major crime figures met in Havana, Cuba, where they discussed the amount of money they were investing in the Flamingo Hotel, which was not yet open. Some wanted to kill Siegel, but his friend, Myer Lansky, was able to persuade them to relent. By the time of the second investor meeting, the hotel had turned a small profit. Later, it began to lose money, largely through Siegel's poor business skills. At a third meeting, the bosses decided to "hit" Siegel. He was shot to death in Beverly Hills, California, on June 20, 1947. A few minutes later, criminal associates of Lansky took control of the Flamingo. The takeover was a sign of organized crime's adaptability and ability to infiltrate new enterprises. The mob ran most of the gambling business in Las Vegas undisturbed until Nevada passed the Corporate Gaming Act in 1969. This measure, through a revised system of licensing, allowed publicly traded corporations to own casinos. The mob found ways to continue operating around the law, but suffered after state and federal prosecutions in the 1970s and 1980s.

However, organized crime still posed a threat to the American way of life after the war, and the government began to seriously investigate and prosecute mobsters. In 1949, newspaper articles in a number of cities reported on the problem of organized crime exposed by a number of state and local crime commissions. Not only was corruption of political and law enforcement officials by gangsters revealed, but also the threat they posed to the integrity of the American economy through their infiltration of interstate commerce and labor racketeering. The murders of mobsters in different cities added to the interest of the U.S. Senate in racketeering.

In 1950, Senator Estes Kefauver introduced legislation to allow the Senate to investigate organized crime and its involvement in interstate commerce. The Senate Select Committee to Investigate Organized Crime in Interstate Commerce (the Kefauver Committee) held hearings in across the United States through August 17, 1951. The hearings led to revenge killings of those who had testified against the mob. In Chicago, William Drury, a former police captain, and Marvin Bass, an attorney for the Cook County Republicans, testified before the Kefauver Committee. On September 25, 1950, both men were shot to death at separate locations. Chicago mobsters Paul Ricca and Louis Campagna were investigated, but were not prosecuted due to insufficient evidence.

In November 1957, the American Mafia was fully exposed. On November 14, a summit meeting of the American Mafia bosses was held at the rural home of Joseph "Joe the Barber" Barbara in Apalachin, New York. About 100 Mafiosi attended the meeting—some flew in from Italy and Canada. Local law enforcement called in state police reinforcement and the FBI when a multitude of expensive automobiles from across the country suddenly appeared in their town. The home was eventually raided, and over 60 crime bosses were detained after many were rounded up after fleeing into the woods. Many threw away their guns and large cash rolls before their apprehension. The news of such a large assembly of underworld figures brought credibility to the existence of a national crime syndicate, which J. Edgar Hoover had long refused to exist. After this, Hoover created the Top Hoodlum Program and sought out organized crime figures. In 1958, the Sicilian Mafia and their American counterparts took steps to reorganize following their exposure at Apalachin.

Vincent "Chin" Gigante of the Genovese Family crime ring, in custody in New York City in 1957 regarding the attempted murder of Genovese family Boss Frank Costello. During the trial, Gigante's defense team challenged the credibility of the eyewitness, leading to his acquittal in 1958.

McCarthyism, the Red Scare, and Puerto Rican Nationalism

Typically seen as an era of conformity and middle-class comfort, the 1950s were also a period of fear. The advent of the cold war by 1947 sparked a second Red Scare in America. Anti-communism, which had persisted through the 1930s and wartime, was strongly promoted at first by private red hunters, and then by official government policy. Many police departments organized red squads that sent agents to infiltrate suspected political groups, and FBI director J. Edgar Hoover returned to his original mission of crushing the left with great enthusiasm. As a result, publicly recognized members of the Communist Party were prosecuted in the 1950s. The fear was heightened when Americans learned that the Soviet Union had detonated an atomic bomb. Investigations revealed extensive Soviet espionage during and after World War II in the United States and elsewhere.

Stolen American atomic science had aided the successful development of the Soviets' atomic weapons. Convicted for giving the Soviets secret information, Julius and Ethel Rosenberg were sentenced to death and electrocuted on June 19, 1953, at New York's Sing Sing Prison. Although they denied their guilt, the opening of secret Soviet files after the fall of the Soviet Union in the 1990s revealed that they had engaged in espionage. The American VERONA cable intercepts also pointed to their role as spies. This notorious case and other threats—real or imagined—promoted the anti-Communist crusade of Senator Joseph McCarthy and the subsequent era of McCarthyism.

McCarthyism existed both before and after the Wisconsin senator's crusade. By the late 1940s, the Smith Act was used against communists, and President Harry S. Truman's administration had begun removing government employees who refused to sign loyalty oaths. Under the program, the FBI ran background checks on civil servants and conducted further investigation of people with past or present left-wing affiliations. McCarthy concentrated mainly on government employees, and state legislatures launched campaigns against civil servants suspected of communist or socialist sympathies. It was believed that McCarthy went too far when he targeted the U.S. Army in 1954, but after his demise, the House Committee on Un-American Activities (HUAC) continued the crusade against the left well into the 1960s. Anti-communism was at the foundation of American conservative ideology, active even before the Russian revolution in the form of attacks on non-communist leftists. Fears of the cold war turning into a nuclear holocaust and revelations of spying gave the ideology focus and power during the 1950s.

A mostly forgotten political scare or threat of the early 1950s was radical Puerto Rican nationalism. In October 1950, political unrest in Puerto Rico led to an attempted revolt in the name of Puerto Rican independence. In the fighting that followed, revolutionaries tried to kill the island's first democratically elected governor, Luis Muñoz Marín. The fighting killed 28 people, of whom seven were police officers and one was a national guardsman. Some of the surviving nationalists were prosecuted on various charges. Nearly 100 others were wounded. Marin harshly suppressed the followers of the independence movement.

On November 1, 1950, Puerto Rican nationalists tried to kill President Harry Truman. He was staying at the Blair House while the White House was being renovated. The assassins, Oscar Collazo and Grisello Torresola, tried to force their way into the Blair House. During the heated gun battle between the Secret Service and the assassins, White House policeman Leslie Coffelt was mortally wounded, but was able to shoot and kill Torresola before dying. The attempt put President Truman in direct danger, but he was not harmed. Collazo was

American communists Julius and Ethel Rosenberg leave the courthouse in 1951 after being found guilty by jury that year for conspiracy to commit espionage during a time of war. They were executed in Sing Sing prison on June 19, 1953.

heavily injured and captured. He was convicted and sentenced to death. The sentence was commuted to life by Truman, and later to time served by President Jimmy Carter in 1979. On March 1, 1954, four Puerto Rican Nationalists attacked the U.S. Congress in the House of Representatives. They unfurled a Puerto Rican flag and then began firing from the Ladies' Gallery. Lolita Lebrón, Rafael Cancel Miranda, Andres Figueroa Cordero, and Irving Flores Rodríguez fired 30 rounds into the House, wounding five members of Congress as the House was debating an immigration bill. Captured immediately, their death sentences were commuted to long prison terms by President Eisenhower.

Street Gangs and Motorcycle Gangs

An old problem, street gangs, began to take new forms in the 1950s. The decade was a time of significant Puerto Rican immigration to New York City. Once there, Puerto Rican street gangs developed. Prominent among them were the Mau Maus, who took their name from the Mau Mau Uprising in Kenya. Among the leaders were Nicky and Israel Navarez.

The gangs of the 1950s were ethnically diverse, and included members of the thousands of Puerto Ricans and African Americans that had immigrated to New York City after World War II. Older gangs were Irish, Italian, Jewish, or other ethnic groups. Unemployed and confined to slum areas, pride of turf was a major factor in their defense. The gangs developed distinctive clothing styles or "colors," gang rules, and other social forms. They were especially sensitive to disrespect: Even simple disagreements were a form of aggression met with fighting. These arranged battles were called "rumbles," in which weapons such as baseball bats, studded belt buckles, knives, machetes, pipes, and even guns were used. In Brooklyn, rumble season began on Memorial Day in Prospect Park. It ended with the onset of inclement weather in the fall.

The gangs in New York City symbolized by Nicky Cruz were new. The older gangs had involved immigrant adults. The new gangs were comprised of teenagers who were often products of their local environments. They became ruthless and amoral. Besides the Mau Maus in Brooklyn, there were the Jokers, Bishops, and the Barons. East Harlem had the Dragons, Red Wings, and Egyptian Kings; the Jesters and Amsterdams controlled Washington Heights; and the Fordham Baldies and Golden Guineas controlled the Bronx.

New York street gangs were romanticized in the 1957 Broadway musical *West Side Story*. With music by Leonard Bernstein and using the novel by Arthur Laurents, William Shakespeare's tale of *Romeo and Juliet* was told in New York City's Upper West Side neighborhood. The antagonists are two rival street gangs—the Puerto Rican Sharks and the mostly Italian Jets. However, Tony of the Jets falls in love with Maria, sister of the leader of the Sharks, Bernardo. The tragedy was also told in the film *West Side Story* in 1961.

In Chicago, as well as Los Angeles, African American gangs emerged from clubs. The clubs were formed as protective associations in the face of racial discrimination and to protect their members from violence committed by white clubs. Some black clubs tried to make political connections, and others were merely social. Some began to engage in criminal activities such as theft, robbery, and assaults. Some emerged from car clubs in the Los Angeles area, including the Low Riders, Coasters, Highwaymen, and Road Devils. Chicano gangs date back at least to the 1940s. They were early users of marijuana and began the practice of communicating through painted graffiti. Murders were uncommon, although gang violence was frequent.

In the 1950s, the opiate heroin was used widely for medicinal purposes; however, growing concern about its addictiveness led to its criminalization. Because the drug was illegal, supplying it was very profitable. By the mid-1950s, heroin was linked to many violent crimes and was spreading in use. By 1960, the French Connection became a link to raw opium from the Middle East or southeast Asia. Opium was shipped to Marseille, France, where it was converted into heroin. In France, the raw opium was manufactured into heroin, and then smuggled into the United States for street sales to narcotics users or "junkies." People "nodding off" became a familiar sight in poor, urban neighborhoods. Some of the older Mafia gangs at first declined to be involved in drug trafficking, but newer groups, including African Americans, had no qualms about dealing in such a profitable commodity. Drug dealing became a route to upward mobility, though a dangerous one, for young, unemployed youths. Some street gangs were active in the trade.

Another type of gang that became conspicuous in the 1950s was the motorcycle or outlaw biker gang. One of the earliest appeared in Chicago in 1936—the McCook Outlaws. The group began with the legitimate motives of motorcycle touring and racing, but rowdy parties and drinking were part of their activities. They began as noisy, but not criminal, outfits, but exist today as the Outlaws Motorcycle Club. Biker gangs can be violent and disorderly, but are not professional criminal associations, though they often have their share of drug dealers and thieves among their members. Many World War II veterans returned home disoriented and restless, looking to replicate the excitement of combat. Motorcycles helped many to fulfill that need and often provided the camaraderie of other veterans. Many clubs were sponsored by the American Motorcycle Association (AMA), but some bikers left the organization, blaming it for what they thought was exaggerated criticism of the violence that had erupted 1947 in Hollister, California.

The AMA had sponsored motorcycle racing in towns across the United States since the 1930s. The 1947 event in Hollister was the first since the war began, so enormous numbers of bikers flooded the town. Biker groups in attendance included the Pissedoff Bastards of Bloomington and the Boozefighters. Hollister at first welcomed the bikers, but they began to drink too much and roar through the small town's streets. The small police force could not cope with thousands of rowdy drunks. Popular media, including *Life* magazine, sensationalized the "riot" and aroused the fears of respectable Americans. Some people responded to the media

Bernard Spindel whispers in the ear of James R. Hoffa after the October 15, 1957, court session during which they pleaded innocent to five counts of perjury in illegal wiretap charges that threatened to loosen his powerful grip on the Teamsters Union.

hype by saying that only about 1 percent of bikers engaged in drunken rows, and the term was used by marginal groups who called themselves the "one-percenters" or "outlaws." Outlaw motorcycle clubs started emerging all over the United States and included clubs like the Bandidos Motorcycle Club, Pagans Motorcycle Club, and Hell's Angels Motorcycle Club. With the arrival of the Vietnam War, the clubs experienced sharp increases in membership as veterans found acceptance and solace there. Ironically, Hollister recovered so quickly after 1947 that it invited the bikers back and celebrated the riot's 50th anniversary in 1997.

The style of motorcycle and street gangs influenced urban teenagers, whose offenses may have been only a bit of shoplifting or speeding. Leather jackets, tight blue jeans, hair slicked back into the D.A. (which stood for duck's ass, later softened into ducktail) style, and a certain swagger marked the "hood" ethos of the 1950s. Girls wore very tight sweaters and skirts. Some of these youths smoked marijuana (pot), but most mimicked adults in smoking cigarettes. As with Hip Hop music today, some middle-class white suburban teenagers, as well as working-class urbanites, adopted the "gang" image. Rock and Roll music, "dangerously" influenced by blacks, was part of the image. Elvis Presley was the model for young people who cultivated the hoodlum look.

Less threatening, older counterparts of the hoods were the Beatniks, whose only crime was smoking marijuana. Sometimes, they followed the example of black jazz musicians and started using heroin, but usually they drank wine, had no means of earning a living, and engaged in art and literature. They were also sensationalized in the media, but many made genuine contributions to American culture. The owner and manager of the City Lights bookstore in San Francisco, who sold Allen Ginsberg's poem "Howl," were tried in California for obscenity, but literary experts successfully convinced the judge that the poem was genuine literature, not obscene.

Both the reality of gangs and the hood style aroused fears of juvenile delinquency that had surfaced during the war. Hollywood contributed to the image with movies like *Blackboard Jungle*. More serious youth behavioral problems were explored in street gang violence with movies such as *Crime in the Streets* and *Young and Dangerous* (1957). Juvenile delinquency (JD) movies became a new subgenre of the gangster and *film noir* movies. Ever since the 19th century heyday of dime novels, critics have accused popular media of encouraging crime. In 1954, psychologist Frederic Wertham published *Seduction of the Innocent*. He claimed that violent imagery in the mass media and in comic books was harmful to children, leading them to delinquency. All of his evidence was anecdotal. He included superhero comic crime fighters with other comics. He claimed that sex, drugs, and other "adult matters" were in "crime comics." The book sparked a campaign for censorship of comics. Wertham was called upon to testify on crime comics before the U.S. Senate Subcommittee on Juvenile Delinquency, which was formed in 1953. As the film studios had done in the 1930s, comic book publishers voluntarily established the Comics Code Authority and modified some images to pacify Congress and the public.

Professionalization of the Police Force
An example of old-fashioned corruption surfaced in June 1954. Albert Patterson won the Alabama Democratic Party nomination for attorney general. He was an attorney from Phenix City, Alabama, who campaigned on the promise to clean up corruption after the Phenix City political machine had turned the town into a center for prostitution. Between 1945 and 1954, the number of prostitutes living and working there had grown to over 1,000. The corruption included much of the local government. Prostitutes were at times

Mounted police clashing with Philadelphia, Pennsylvania, electrical plant strikers in 1946. During that year alone, there were 4,985 strikes involving 4,600,000 workers lasting 116 million days, and mounted police were employed in cities across the United States to clear workers from the streets and to attempt to maintain order.

trucked across the river into Georgia to service their clients. On the night of June 18, Patterson was returning to his car when he was shot three times by an unknown gunman. The national news reported the sordid story. The governor of Alabama declared martial law in Phenix City. The entire civilian government was reconstituted as 743 indictments were issued. The principal suspect sent to prison for the assassination was Deputy Sheriff Albert Fuller. Cases such as this required a more professional police force than what had existed during the war.

The postwar migration of millions of people to the suburbs had an impact on policing, encouraged by a Government Issue (G.I.) bill offering low mortgage rates for veterans, the building of an interstate highway network, redlining of urban neighborhoods, "white flight," and income tax deductions for mortgage and auto loan interest charges. The foot patrolman on the beat could not be as effective in spread-out suburban neighborhoods. The Ford Motor Company manufactured large numbers of police cars as officers were moved into automobiles. Radios in patrol cars became standard with improved radio technology between 1941 and 1960. The technology allowed for rapid response to criminal activity and for coordinating units in the field. Patrol cars took over city policing as well, but they became a disadvantage similar to suburbia: Police were isolated from local residents in their vehicles and the visibility of officers as a means of crime prevention gave way to an emphasis on effective response to crime.

The outbreak of the Korean conflict again caused manpower shortages for many police departments. Auxiliary groups that had been dormant since the end of World War II were reactivated to supplement police officers. The low rate of pay for police was a factor in some of these shortages in the postwar era. It also promoted a movement toward unionization. Fraternal Orders of Police had begun early in the century; however, unions asserted the power to bargain for improved pay and conditions. In some cities like New York, they became powerful not only within the police, but also a political force that supported tough approaches to crime. Nevertheless, pay and working conditions for police remained uneven across the country.

Police professionalism grew during the 1950s. Orlando Wilson of Berkeley, California, used his extensive police work experience to advocate that departments should require new recruits to have a college education and emphasized the use of police using patrol cars, mobile radios, and mobile crime laboratories. He believed that two-way radios enabled supervision of patrol officers and therefore led to more efficient policing. Wilson was dean of Berkeley's school of criminology during the 1950s and was a major force for legitimating the field in academia. His most influential work, *Police Administration* (1943), remained a powerful influence in the 1950s. He advised Dallas, Texas; Nashville, Tennessee; Birmingham, Alabama; and Louisville, Kentucky on the reorganization of their police departments.

Another leader in California was William Parker, who became police chief of Los Angeles on August 9, 1950. Parker was a "professionalizer" who transformed a corrupt and inefficient police department into one of the best in the nation. He, like J. Edgar Hoover, was a great self-promoter, who advised the popular TV show *Dragnet*, featuring Los Angeles Police Department (LAPD) detectives matter-of-factly investigating cases. Parker and the series star, Jack Webb, were good friends. Parker, seeking to reduce the influence of politicians, did not care about community relations. He thought that he could create a better police force through oversight by administrators and a military-like organization. Parker initiated a police academy and emphasized proactive policing that would exercise more force, but less uncontrolled violence. Parker actually reduced the size of the force, believing that fewer, more professional officers would make it more efficient and less corrupt. He called the LAPD a "thin blue line" between order and chaos. Like many professionalizers, his efforts to avoid corruption distanced the police from the local community, especially since he favored the use of patrol cars. Nevertheless, Parker's LAPD was accused of racism and brutality toward Los Angeles' African American and Latino residents. Many people saw Parker as a lackey of the city's mostly white power structure, but Parker actually desegregated the LAPD. Resentment of police attitudes and treatment were an important factor behind the Watts Riots of 1965.

Serial Killers and Prison Riots

Americans of the 1950s were introduced to the concept of the serial killer. It was not that serial killers had not existed earlier, but the end of the decade saw a period of numerous serial murders. One of the most sensational cases was teenager Charles Starkweather. After murdering a gas station attendant, he and his 14-year-old girlfriend murdered 11 people as they drove through Nevada and Wyoming in 1958. After a high-speed car chase, they were finally captured on January 29, 1958. Starkweather was executed, while his mentally deficient girlfriend served 18 years in prison.

While the public did not sympathize with Starkweather, some people felt sympathy for Caryl Chessman. Chessman was not a serial killer, but a serial kidnapper and rapist. He was accused of being the "red light bandit," tricking victims into stopping by using a flashing red light on his car to make them think he was a police officer. He had a long criminal record. Chessman was tried and convicted for kidnapping and rape in 1948. At that time, California prescribed the death penalty for the crime of kidnapping with bodily harm. Chessman came under that provision because he was charged with dragging some of his victims from their cars before raping them. Chessman insisted on his innocence, sometimes saying that he was mistaken for another person, that he knew who the real killer was, that he was victim of a frame-up, and that any information regarding his involvement in the "red light" crimes had been extracted though torture. He spent the 1950s on death row acting as his own attorney, filing numerous appeals that eventually reached the Supreme Court, which held that California had to review the original trial for the procedural irregularities that Chessman claimed.

The state's review concluded that the trial was proper and Chessman was scheduled for execution in 1960. He had previously escaped several execution deadlines. Chessman pled his case through letters and no less than four books: *Cell 2455, Death Row* (1954), *Trial by Ordeal* (1955), *The Face of Justice* (1957), and *The Kid Was a Killer* (1960). His first book became a movie in 1955, starring William Campbell as Chessman. He became a celebrity, receiving support from people around the world, including Norman Mailer, Robert Frost, Eleanor Roosevelt, and Billy Graham. He came to represent the evils of the death penalty in the United States at a time when most European nations had done away with it. Chessman's luck ran out on May 2, 1960. While in the gas chamber, which was filling with gas, a judge's clerk called the warden to announce a new stay of execution for Chessman. The warden said that it was not possible to stop the proceedings, because opening the gas chamber door would release fumes that would kill the other people at the execution. The clerk had at first dialed the wrong number, and the delay cost Chessman his life.

Advances in psychology allowed for improved study of criminal behavior. In the case of serial killers, researchers found that they commit multiple murders during a period

Japanese Americans standing in front of internment posters with "Instructions to all persons of Japanese ancestry." President Franklin D. Roosevelt signed the executive order authorizing the evacuation of more than 127,000 Japanese Americans in February 1942. They were sent to internment camps in the interior of the country and were held for the duration of World War II.

of time with a cooling off period between killings. Their pattern of killing in a series becomes part of their criminal modus operandi (MO). Some use a particular kind of weapon, or focus on a specific type of victim. The psychological examination of serial killers has found that their behaviors were formed in early childhood.

Prison riots greatly increased during the 1950s. During World War II, prisons had emptied, as many prisoners were paroled to allow them to join the military service. However, conditions returned their normal status after the war. In the 1950s, with rising prison populations, overcrowding became common, as did a rash of prison riots. On May 20, 1951, Utah State Prison experienced a major riot. Between 1950 and 1953, there were many riots in federal and state penitentiaries around the country, with 20 occurring in 1952 alone. In 1959, a major prison riot broke out at the Montana State Prison, led by two inmates—Jerry Myles and Lee Smart. The riot lasted 36 hours and was finally suppressed by the Montana National Guard. The riot was sparked by chronic overcrowding and deteriorating conditions in the prison.

The reasons for widespread riots were unclear because overall, American prisons were more humane than they had ever been. Still, such widespread rioting implied that something was very wrong with the penal system. Were prisons intended to reform convicts, punish them, or simply to separate them from society? Part of the problem was that prison staff morale had declined because of low pay, corruption, and mismanagement. The prison industry had also changed from free-market enterprises into prison shops that produced goods that could not be sold to the public, but only to other state institutions. Since advocating more money for prisons was not politically popular, it often took riots by the inmates to spur improvements and increased funding. What became clear was that correction science was not exact. Rehabilitation efforts were not effective because there were very high recidivism rates. In addition, society at large was not well protected from some of the most dangerous people it produced. Overall, though, most of America's commitment to rehabilitation remained.

Civil Rights Movement
Perhaps the most significant long-term impact of the 1950s was the beginning of the civil rights movement. The south's white supremacist order had been successfully challenged earlier in the courts, and President Truman desegregated the U.S. Army in 1948. Parts of its structure had been chipped away, but segregation still stood firm in the early 1950s. On May 17, 1954, the U.S. Supreme Court issued its ruling in *Brown v. Board of Education* that racial segregation in public schools was unconstitutional. The decision gave the nation plenty of time to implement the ruling. Lynching still occurred in the United States as late as 1955, when Emmett Louis Till was murdered on August 28. He was a teenage African American who was visiting relatives in the Mississippi Delta town of Money from his home in Chicago. He was brutally murdered, and his weighted body was dropped into the Tallahatchie River. The men responsible for the killing were acquitted by a local jury. Because J. Edgar Hoover was concerned about communists, he focused more on the communist connections to anti-lynching groups than on this type of crime. The civil rights movement would soon follow.

On December 1, 1955, Rosa Parks was arrested in Montgomery, Alabama, for refusing to obey racial segregation seating laws on a public bus. The arrest sparked the civil rights movement and Martin Luther King, Jr., began his career of activism. Civil rights activists were arrested, but their convictions (for civil disobedience) would be overturned. Eventually, the Supreme Court did not legalize civil disobedience, but declared the laws that had been violated unconstitutional, meaning that no law had been broken. Congress passed a modest Civil Rights Act in 1957, and President Dwight D.

Eisenhower reluctantly began the first serious enforcement of the *Brown* decision by ordering federal troops to protect the integration of the Little Rock, Arkansas, high school. In 1960, Greensboro, North Carolina, experienced sit-in demonstrations that intensified the civil rights movement. One result was the Civil Rights Act of 1960, which put voting rights in southern states under close federal inspection for decades to come.

Conclusion
During the 1940s and 1950s, Americans united to fight a "good war" and create a vast expansion of the American dream of consumption, but they had their share of crime and disorder. Wartime America had its unique problems and issues, along with ordinary murder and larceny. In the 1950s, fears of juvenile delinquency and gangs, organized crime, and political subversion underlay what has often been seen as an era of complacency and conformity.

Andrew J. Waskey
Dalton State College

1940s PRIMARY DOCUMENT

Excerpt From the FBI Memorandum on the Jewish Hope Society Mail Fraud Scheme

Classification 36 in the FBI's file classification system is mail fraud (including wire, radio, and television fraud, as well as the fraudulent use of credit cards). The U.S. Postal Service has primary responsibility for mail fraud cases, but the FBI is often used in investigating them and may initiate investigations. Mail fraud, a federal crime since 1872, has long been relied on by swindlers for its relatively low risk and low expense. The scheme of operating a fake charity is common.

SCHEME TO DEFRAUD

The society, the subject ARTHUR MICHELSON as its president and executive head, has used three major methods to obtain funds: radio broadcasts by subject ARTHUR MICHELSON, distribution through the mail of the Jewish Hope and circular letters, and evangelistic trips by subject ARTHUR MICHELSON.

The society, by its articles of incorporation and all statements in connection with the above methods of obtaining funds, claims to be a benevolent organization, with the primary purpose of converting Jews to Christianity. Since it is a benevolent association, the expenses of its work are paid by donations. The success of the work naturally depends on the amount of money received. In order to show donors that the organization is a worthy cause, is successful, needs the money and is sound financially, subject ARTHUR MICHELSON, as head of the society, has made several false representations. These representations are summarized in the next section of this report entitled "False Representations."

Subject ARTHUR MICHELSON has made or approved these misrepresentations in order to increase the volume of the donations. Although he claims to receive a salary like any other employee, either he or his relatives has received directly from the corporation $9,023.00, in addition to his salary from 1940 to 1943 inclusive. He also received personally during this period at least $7,830.49, which he kept for his own use. He claims that this latter amount was from gifts given him personally. This amount was not recorded on the books of the society.

This makes a total of $17,418.49, which is 3% of the total amount of donations received during the same period. In the year 1942 subject ARTHUR MICHELSON or his family received, in addition to his salary, $9,355.37, which was 7.38% of the total revenue of the society for that year.

Source: NARA II, RG 65, Class 36 Mail Fraud, Box 4, F 36 Sub 2523

See Articles: Embezzlement; Fraud; Jewish Americans.

1942 PRIMARY DOCUMENT

FBI Memorandum on the Extortions of Bing Crosby and Harold Lloyd

In most cases, an extortionist has little to no ability to make good on his threat. Celebrities are frequent targets of extortion, in part because of their wealth, visibility, and accessibility (making it easy for an extortionist to be aware of them and communicate a threat), and in part because of organized crime's long involvement in the entertainment industry. Outside of this incident, Crosby had been extorted on at least one other occasion, by the Mafia.

Samuel Rubin, With Aliases; Bing Crosby; Harold Lloyd—Victims
Extortion

Bing Crosby, the motion picture actor and radio star, received the following letter on June 22, 1942, which was postmarked June 18, 1942, at Los Angeles, California: "IF—MONEY—NOT—TOMORROW—YOU—WILL—NOT—BE—ALIVE—TO—SPEND—ANY—OF—IT—WHEN—YOU—ARE—DEAD—TODAY—THANKS—GEO BAKER."

The reverse side of the above communication carried the return address of George Baker, General Delivery, Los Angeles, California. Another portion of a car found in the same envelope carried this message, "DEAR BING—SEND—$1000 DOLLARS—TO—ME—OR—I—WILL—COMMIT—SUICIDE—I—WILL—KILL—YOU OR—YOUR KIDS - $1000—GEO BAKER—SEND TODAY OR ELSE."

Since the mailing of this type of letter comes within the purview of the Federal Extortion Statute, the matter was reported to the Los Angeles Field Division of the Federal Bureau of Investigation and an investigation was initiated. It might be noted that the above referred to letter had been re-routed in the mails and a delay of several days therefore existed before the Federal authorities were notified of the violation. The significance of this delay will be explained later.

Special Agents subsequently ascertained that Harold Lloyd, who was formerly quite prominent in motion pictures, received a similar threatening letter on June 24, 1942, which also bore the signature of George Baker.

Arrangements were made by the Federal Bureau of Investigation to cover the General Delivery window in Low Angeles by a surveillance in order that the extortionists might be apprehended. Thereafter, on July 2, through the cooperation of Lieutenant Lowell Lyons of the Los Angeles Police Department, as individual who called for mail addressed to George Baker was arrested. When questioned by Special Agents, he readily admitted writing the extortion letter and explained that he had read an article in the newspapers which dealt with a similar occurrence, wherein a letter had been addressed to a prominent movie actor and that the Government, after taking the extortionist into custody, placed him in a trade school. Baker went on to say that he had no money, was hungry and was without a home. The implication was strong during the questioning that in reality Baker didn't expect his extortion scheme to produce results, but merely wished to procure a place to stay and at the same time, possibly learn a trade. He pointed out that he had obtained the addresses of Bing Crosby and Harold Lloyd from penny post cards which he had seen in a local drug store.

A complaint was filed by Special Agents before the United States Commissioner in Los Angeles on July 3, 1942, and Baker was held to await the action of a Federal Grand Jury. On the same day that the complaint was filed, Harold Lloyd received another threatening letter signed—George Baker. The writer in this case reiterated his demand for one thousand dollars and instructed that the money be sent to General Delivery, Los Angeles, California. At the bottom of the note, Baker indicated that he would call for the money at the Post Office in person. This letter was postmarked June 29, 1942, showing it was mailed by the subject before his arrest. It was learned that Bing Crosby had also received another letter from Baker which had been mailed on June 29, 1942.

Since it had been learned from the subject at the time he was questioned that he had made one call at the Post Office prior to his arrest and had not been taken into custody due to the delay in routing the original extortion letter, it was apparent that Baker had been disappointed, and in his second letter to Harold Lloyd therefore, he was careful to point out that he would call in person at the General Delivery window. He wanted to make certain that his second appointment with the authorities did not fail.

After it was learned that Harold Lloyd had received the letter mentioned above Baker was re-interviewed at which time he admitted that his name was Samuel Rubin, and that he was born on February 25, 1912, in Providence,

Rhode Island. Inquiry in Providence resulted in determining that Rubin, alias Baker, had never been inclined to work steadily and had spent most of his life, after graduation from high school, on the road as a hobo.

He was examined by a psychiatrist and found to be normal. After his indictment by a Federal Grand Jury on August 7, 1942, he pleaded guilty and received a sentence of five years in the penitentiary. The sentence also provided that he was to be placed on probation for a period of five years after the expiration of his actual sentence. No prior criminal record was reported

John Edgar Hoover
Director
Federal Bureau of Investigation
United States Department of Justice
Washington, D.C.
I.C. #5-9370

Source: NARA-II, RG 65 FBI, Interesting Case Write-ups, Box 4

See Articles: Federal Bureau of Investigation; Insanity Defense; Justice, Department of.

1942 PRIMARY DOCUMENT

FBI Memorandum on Henry Tatge's Failure to Report for Draft and Imprisonment

The FBI file system's Classification 25 is reserved for files related to the Selective Service Act, including failure to register for the draft, furnishing false information to the draft board, refusal to serve, encouraging draft evasion or resistance, the corruption of local draft boards, and applications for conscientious objector status. After World War II, the FBI began investigating the violation of reemployment rights of veterans. Henry Tatge's case is simply one of draft evasion.

Melvin Henry Tatge
Selective Service

Melvin Henry Tatge was sentenced to serve five years in a Federal penitentiary on June 9, 1942, for his failure to report for a physical examination as ordered by his local draft board. Tatge, at the time of his arrest by members of the Minneapolis Police Department, stated that he would not serve in the Army and would run away from any place that they put him. On being arrested Tatge threatened the arresting officers with, "You guys will be sorry when Hitler comes over here and breaks your d--- necks."

Tatge was ordered to report for a physical examination by his local draft board at Supervisor, Wisconsin, and in an endeavor to avoid taking the examination he went to Minneapolis, Minnesota where he secured employment in the Salvation Army. When he was requested to show his registration card, he did so and likewise furnished the order to report for a physical examination. Upon being questioned regarding his failure to comply with the order, he became violent and it was necessary to call out additional members of the police department in order to take him into custody. On subsequent questioning he reiterated that he was opposed to military service and exhibited a very belligerent attitude during the trial. He was sentenced to serve five years in a Federal penitentiary.

John Edgar Hoover
Director
Federal Bureau of Investigation
United States Department of Justice
Washington, D. C.
I.C. #25-94415
December 5, 1942

Source: NARA II, RG 65 FBI, Interesting Case Write-ups, Box 8, Folder IC 25 94415

See Articles: Federal Bureau of Investigation; Federal Prisons; Justice, Department of.

1942 PRIMARY DOCUMENT

FBI Memorandum on a Vagrant's Draft Trouble

This FBI memo is a good example of the breadth of detail sometimes contained in FBI records of minor matters (in this case involving no crime). Civilian Defense Work refers to the Office of Civilian Defense, a massive civil defense effort overseen by New York Mayor Fiorello LaGuardia and First Lady Eleanor Roosevelt and consisting of 11 million volunteers. Most of the civil defense efforts were spent preparing for attacks on American soil that never occurred.

A 34 year vagrant negro, arrested on September 4, 1942, by the San Francisco Police Department, did not have a Selective Service registration certificate. When interviewed by a Special Agent of the FBI, he said that he knew he was supposed to have registered and thought he had; that on registration day he went to the fire station near his home and told the fireman that he wished to "register for the war." He said he was asked many questions, that he signed a paper, and that he was then fingerprinted. The fireman who registered the vagrant was interviewed and said he remembered him as having been one of the persons who registered for Civilian Defense Work. The United States Attorney saw that the delinquent had committed an unintentional violation and permitted him to be inducted into the Army in lieu of prosecution.

> John Edgar Hoover
> Director
> Federal Bureau of Investigation
> United States Department of Justice
> Washington, D. C.
> I.C. #25-121695
> December 5, 1942

Source: NARA-II, RG 65, Interesting Case Write-ups, Box 8 F: IC 25 1211695

See Articles: Federal Bureau of Investigation; Justice, Department of; Vagrancy.

1943 PRIMARY DOCUMENT

IRS Intelligence Unit Letter on the Thomas Pendergast Investigation

The IRS's Intelligence Unit was created in 1919 to investigate tax fraud. Its value in the war on crime became apparent in 1931, when the government decided that the IRS's evidence of Al Capone's tax evasion was the most compelling weapon they had against him and obtained a conviction for 11 years in prison. The Intelligence Unit continued to investigate suspected criminals, whose illegal earnings went unreported, but were easier to prove than the means by which they were earned.

This is a story of the work of the Intelligence Unit, with the cooperation of Internal Revenue Agents, Narcotic Agents and other Federal officers, in bringing to justice leaders of the lawless element which for many years ruled Kansas City, Missouri. It begins with the conviction of John Lazia, a gangster overlord of the Capone type, and continues through to the conviction of Thomas J. Pendergast and his principal lieutenants, Robert E. O'Malley, Charles V. Carrollo, Otto P. Higgins, John J. Pryor and Matthew S. Murray. The investigation was conducted in various years through the decade from 1931 to 1941 and resulted in the elimination of the so-called Pendergast machine.

Special Agent Rudolph H. Hartmann was in charge of the principal investigations, including that involving Pendergast. The story was written by him. The other agents who were active in this assignment are named in the story. Charles O'B. Berry, as agent in charge of the Kansas City Division, was in general charge of the entire investigation.

Elmer L. Irey
Chief, Intelligence Unit
I.C. #V6783: A47
April 1, 1943

Source: U.S. Internal Revenue Service. *Story of the Work of the Intelligence Unit*. Washington, DC: IRS, 1943.

See Articles: Internal Revenue Service; Narcotics Laws; Organized Crime, History of; Organized Crime, Sociology of.

1943
PRIMARY DOCUMENT

FBI Memorandum on "King of the Gypsies" Draft Trouble

The Romani people (Gypsies) were prevalent enough in mid-century New York City for the city's Welfare Council to create a Committee on Gypsy Problems. One member was Carl de Wendler-Funaro, a non-Romani who worked as the secretary of Steve Kaslov, the "king" of some or all of the local Gypsy community. This meant that he served as a liaison between them and other communities and attempted to solve problems that arose, such as helping one man evade the draft.

Steve Kaslov, with aliases
Steve Kasloe, Tom Demetro
King Of The Gypsies;
Selective Service

Steve Kaslov, 55 King of the Red Bandanna Russian Gypsies in New York City is traditionally responsible for aiding his fellow gypsies with their daily problems. In accordance with this tradition, he knowingly corroborated the false information of Tom DeMetro to the effect that DeMetro had a wife and a son who were entirely dependent upon him, and thereby attempted to prevent his induction into the Army. In fact, DeMetro's alleged wife is his sister and the child is his nephew. The King was sentenced to a year and a day in a Federal Penitentiary on June 1, 1942.

Kaslov claimed to be a coppersmith by trade, but had been unemployed for quite some time and received relief from the New York City Relief Department. He was also receiving $99.00 each month from Home Relief for the support of his wife and five children ranging from 18 to 31 years of age. Tom DeMetro claimed a 3-A classification from his Local Board for the reason that he had a wife and a small son who were solely dependent upon him for support. He claimed that he had married his wife July 5, 1939 and that the child was born June 2, 1940. King Kaslov vouched for the truth of DeMetro's statement and stated that he recalled marrying the couple in July 1939, but stated that, in accordance with Gypsy custom, no record was kept of the marriage.

It was disclosed by FBI investigation that DeMetro's alleged wife was his sister and the child was his nephew. The King finally admitted that he had knowingly made false statements regarding his friend's liability for military service and was given a sentence of a year and a day in a Federal Penitentiary and severely reprimanded by the court. Prosecution of DeMetro was declined pending his future compliance with the Selective Service regulations.

John Edgar Hoover
Director
Federal Bureau of Investigation
United States Department of Justice
Washington, D.C.
I.C. #25-94603
April 7, 1943

Source: NARA II, RG 65 FBI, Interesting Case Write-ups, Box 8, Folder IC 25 94415

See Articles: Civil Disobedience; Federal Prisons; Justice, Department of.

FBI Memorandum on the Elmer Soller and Elmer Hartzel Sedition Case

Hoover's pride in the investigative innovations of the FBI is clear in this memorandum, which Hoover himself describes as an unremarkable case except for the investigative resources brought to bear. Determining the type of paper used in a leaflet, building a database of individuals who would have access to it, and coming up with the leaflet's mailing list was exactly the kind of labor-intensive but drab work that solved many cases.

Elmer Soller
Elmer Hartzel
Sedition

The personalities involved as defendants in this case were drab, ordinary types of individuals with no spectacular or particularly interesting qualities. Likewise, the subject matter, the anonymous distribution of literature directed against the country's war effort and morale, although imminently dangerous had it been allowed to continue unrestricted, was not of such a nature as to elicit special, unusual or human appeal. However, considered from the viewpoint of investigative processes and technique, the case is one of engrossing interest and parallels almost any which fiction has been able to offer.

During the latter part of June and the early part of July, 1942, a large number of individuals and organizations throughout the country, all prominent in military, political, educational, industrial, or civic pursuits, received, in the United States mails, copies of mimeographed leaflets captioned, "The British: An Inferior Breed," and "The Jew Makes a Sacrifice: The Forthcoming Collapse of America." These leaflets, one copy of each, were received in envelopes postmarked at Chicago, Illinois, and were unaccompanied by any indication as to their source.

As suggested by their titles, the leaflets were extremely anti-Semitic and anti-British. In addition to heaping the most vicious and scurrilous opprobrium on the Jews and the British, the messages set forth in the leaflets were also devoted to an attack on America's participation in the war, the motives of the American Government, and America's foreign policy. In language both abusive and filthy, the British and the Jews were pictured as predatory and unprincipled individuals who, through their connivance with a "disloyal" American Government had been able to involve the American people in a war, neither justified nor righteous, against Germany. Americans were portrayed as mere chattels carrying out assignments given them by internationalists of Jewish and British domination and forced on them by an incompetent and puppet Government.

Hardly before the shock and particularly inflammatory nature of these leaflets could be forgotten by the persons who received them, other anonymous mimeographed leaflets similar in form and content made their appearance during August 1942 under similar circumstances. These leaflets, like those received in June and July, 1942, were mailed anonymously at Chicago, Illinois, and for the most part were directed to the same individuals who had received the leaflets previously issued. Quite obviously they had emanated from the source responsible for the leaflets previously received. This literature did not differ significantly from the leaflets first distributed and merely continued and expanded on the theme that America's participation in the war is uncalled for, unjustified, and the result of foreign pressure, described as "Jewish" and "British," exerted on a weak but willing and obsequious American Government. The phraseology used in the leaflets appearing during August was by comparison even more uncouth and villainous, indicating that the writer felt more confident that his identity could not be detected and that his nefarious activities could not be halted.

Persons who received these various leaflets were, almost without exception, highly incensed that their names should have been used in connection with the distribution of such inflammatory and seditious material and accordingly a great many individuals forwarded the leaflets, together with the envelopes in which they were enclosed, to the FBI. As time went on, almost 200 leaflets made their way in this manner to the FBI and, accordingly, it was possible to a substantial extent to reconstruct the mailing list utilized by the distributor of the literature. This line of endeavor was to later prove particularly helpful inasmuch as it was apparent that the unknown subject's mailing list was replete with numerous errors. It was observed that the names of individuals, organizations, and addresses appearing on the envelopes in which the literature was enclosed were frequently set forth at slight variance with the correct name of the individual, organization, or address for which the literature was intended. These variations were, of course, subsequently of great assistance in definitely proving the source of the literature when the defendants were identified and access was gained to the sources from whence their mailing list had been compiled.

The fact that so many of the leaflets were referred to the FBI was of itself of great assistance in connection with the technical examinations performed in this case. So many copies of the leaflets as well as their accompanying envelopes were available for examination that it was possible for the Laboratory technicians to reconstruct the typing, mimeographing, sealing and mailing of the leaflets. These examinations reflected that all of the literature had emanated from a single source and, of course, from an examination of the leaflets complete data was available as to the general type of mimeographing machine, typewriter, paper, and other materials used by the unknown subject.

With regard to the paper used by the unknown subject, the Laboratory examinations were particularly helpful. It was determined that two types of paper, one bearing the watermark "Expedite" and the other "Speed-O-Print," had been used. "Expedite" paper is a rather common type and has a large use and distribution. However, "Speed-O-Print" paper is not so common and comparatively speaking has a rather limited distribution. Although the purchasers of paper of these types in the Chicago area during the period of several months prior to the appearance of the instant leaflets were, of course, myriad, definite investigative leads were revealed by the Laboratory examinations.

Subsequently, the Chicago office in following out these leads and, of course, giving particular consideration to the purchasers of "Speed-O-Print" and "Expedite" paper and the individuals having access to the type of mailing list suggested by the list of the names of the recipients of the literature know to the Bureau began a long and laborious investigation in an effort to separate the "wheat from the chaff." This inquire was carried out methodically and painstakingly with almost mathematical certainty.

Attention was eventually directed to the Reliable Letter and Addressing Service at 800 West North Avenue, Chicago, Illinois. This concern, operated by one Elmer Soller, was engaged in the business of commercial printing and addressing. Additional inquiry established that Soller, in keeping with his trade, possessed a typewriter and mimeographing machine, and that he had, during the pertinent periods, purchased various and sundry writing materials, including "Expedite" and "Speed-O-Print" paper. Subsequently, examinations of the typewriter and mimeographing machine belonging to the Reliable Letter and Addressing Service were performed by the Bureau's Technical Laboratory, and in this manner it was established that all of the leaflets involved in this case were prepared on these machines. Later, further investigation revealed that the leaflets had been written by one Elmer Hartzel of Chicago, and that this individual had taken them in their rough draft form to Soller in order that they might be mimeographed on a large scale, Soller was aware of the seditious content of the leaflets, but abided by Hartzel's request that the whole affair be maintained on a confidential basis. After the leaflets had been run off on the mimeographing machine, he returned them to Hartzel who then distributed them through the mails.

During the course of subsequent interviews, both Hartzel and Soller fully admitted their participation in the writing, mimeographing and distribution of the leaflets and revealed that approximately 600 copies of the various leaflets had been distributed. Laboratory examinations, as well as their own admissions, further identified them as the distributors of several other similar leaflets, such as "Revolution Will Come to America" and "The Blood Sacrifice," distributed several months prior to America's involvement in the war.

The background and previous activities of Hartzel and Soller were those which might be expected of the authors and distributors of anonymous literature. Hartzel was born during 1891 at New Castle, Pennsylvania, and at the time of writing the leaflets involved in this case, was employed as an inspector at the Pullman Standard Car Company at Chicago. He has previously held similar positions with other industrial concerns. Despite the good pay and satisfactory livelihood which he had been able to earn, he had apparently never fully appreciated the advantages and opportunities offered him by this country. Among his fellow workmen he bore the reputation of being extremely critical of the American Government and favorably disposed toward Germany and Hitler. However, despite his apparently impelling belief in Hitler and the Germans, Hartzel had not chosen to openly declare the full extent of his true beliefs. Although he had, in the course of his conversation with fellow employees, several times signified his attitude toward the German race and German cause, he was not possessed with sufficient fortitude to expound in public on his ideas. Hartzel chose to convey his opprobrious and filthy ideas through the medium of anonymous literature.

Soller was an appropriate confidant and collaborator for a man of Hartzel's type. Small in stature and fawning and servile in manner, he was the type of person usually and characteristically identified with anonymous, stealthy and underhanded methods. He was born in 1903 at Chicago, and lived most of his life in that city where he was engaged principally in the printing business. He was the type of individual, mediocre in mental processes and subservient to easy guidance, who may be best used as a pawn in almost any sort of undertaking.

After the identification of the source of the leaflets involved in this case, the United States Attorney at Chicago, with the permission of the Department of Justice, authorized prosecution of Soller and Hartzel under Wartime Sedition Statute. Specifically, the violation charged that the defendants had conspired with one another in an endeavor to undermine the loyalty and morale of the armed forces of the United States.

The trial of this matter commenced in Federal Court at Chicago on January 4, 1943, and extended until January 14, 1943, when the Jury returned a verdict finding the defendants guilty of the offense charged. Attorneys for the defense immediately advanced motions for new trials, but the court, on hearing the motions on February 8, 1943, overruled them and imposed sentences of five years and one year and one day on Hartzel and Soller, respectively.

This case presents a very clear and graphic example of the contributions which can be made to modern law enforcement through the utilization of technical processes. The convicted defendants elected to carry out their seditious and morale endangering efforts under the cover of anonymity. Accordingly, the basic problem involved was that of identifying the responsible parties. This was accomplished not according to the characteristic trappings of fiction by following out hunches or acting on conjectures, but rather through methodical and painstaking investigation supplemented and assisted by leads furnished through technical examination of typewriter specimens, paper, watermarks, et cetera.

It is quite obvious, of course, that the general public, specifically the many recipients of these leaflets who had the foresight to forward the literature to the FBI, was of great assistance in the solution of this case. As pointed out previously, the laboratory's examinations and the exhaustive investigation carried out identified the guilty parties and brought them to justice. However, much was contributed to the solution of the case by the fact that the FBI, and particularly its laboratory technicians, had available so many specimens on which to base their examinations. Quite clearly this case constitutes a classic example of the fruitful results that may be achieved through the cooperation of alert members of the public with law enforcement organizations.

The dangerous and demoralizing propaganda of the convicted defendants who, according to their own admissions, intended to prepare and distribute in the future other leaflets of a similar type, has been silenced. These men, who in a very practical way were interfering with the public morale and successful prosecution of the war effort, have now learned the meaning of the laws safeguarding our national security, as well as the effectiveness of the processes and instrumentalities of the agency charged with the responsibility of enforcing our wartime national security laws.

John Edgar Hoover
Director
Federal Bureau of Investigation
United States Department of Justice
Washington, D. C.
I.C. #14-362
July 3, 1943

Source: NARA-II, RG 65 FBI, Interesting Case Write-ups, Box 6

See Articles: Civil Disobedience; Federal Bureau of Investigation; Racism; Sedition Act of 1918.

1946 PRIMARY DOCUMENT

FBI Memorandum on a Military Prison Break and Crime Spree

Crimes committed on military bases are frequently prosecuted as federal crimes, although the jurisdictional overlap between federal agencies like the FBI and military authorities can be complicated. However, especially in the 1940s, the FBI had greater investigative resources and manpower for a case like this, which begins with inmates in a military jail overpowering their guards and proceeds to armed robbery and auto theft. This FBI memo provides specific details, despite the FBI's limited involvement.

Charles Henry Wright, with alias;
Silas Henry Burgess, with aliases;
William Martin Hagan,
George Dauge Ledger, with alias;
Theodore Ernest Hall;
Justice Richard Harrington, with alias;
Reagan Ellsworth Thompson, with aliases;
Edward Oland Byus.

Federal Firearms Act;
Theft Of Government Property;
National Motor Vehicle Theft Act;
Illegal Wearing Of The Uniform;
Crime Of Government Reservation.

The above eight subjects were inmates of the United States Disciplinary Barracks at Camp Peary, Virginia. On November 9, 1945 they overpowered two United States Marine Corps work detail guards, taking two Reising submachine guns escaped from custody.

The entire group proceeded to Virginia Highway #60 where they commandeered a 1936 Chevrolet operated by a salesman whom they held up with machine guns. On the same evening they also held up a woman at Menchville, Virginia, ordering her to give them the keys to her 1940 Ford parked in front of her home. It was then believed the group headed for Newport News, Virginia.

On the following day the men held up a man at the point of machine guns at South Hill, Virginia and took from him his 1940 Plymouth Sedan. They then proceeded in their stolen automobiles to the vicinity of Corbin, Kentucky where they accosted another man and a woman companion, forced them out of their car and stole it.

The group then committed an armed robbery of a service station near Berea, Kentucky, obtaining gasoline and oil and between $79 and $80 in cash. They continued their cross-country flight in the 1941 Plymouth and a 1940 Buick to Harrison, Ohio where Wright and Burgess were 1st out of the Plymouth driven by Thompson. These two escapees then stole a 1940 Ford Coach in which they were later apprehended in Cincinnati by local police.

Thompson, in the 1941 Plymouth, drove on alone to Iowa where he sold one of the machine guns to an Ida Grove, Iowa man. Later Thompson was apprehended in Grinnell, Iowa where the stolen Plymouth was recovered.

The main group composed of Hall, Hagan, Harrington, Ledger, and Byus continued in the Buick to Walled Lake, Michigan, where they were apprehended by the Michigan State Police. They were subsequently removed to Cincinnati, Ohio for trial.

In Cincinnati, Ohio all seven subjects with the exception of Thompson were indicted on two counts for violation of the National Motor Vehicle Theft Act. Upon pleas of guilty each was sentenced to five years on the first count and two years on the second count, the sentences to run concurrently.

Thompson entered pleas of guilty to both counts of an indictment returned against him in Cedar Rapids, Iowa, charging him with a violation of the National Motor Vehicle Theft Act and with the sale of Government property. He was sentenced to serve four years on each count, the sentences to run concurrently, and was charged with costs of $25.

These subjects received total actual sentences of 39 years with 14 suspended and 4 years actual concurrent.

United States Department of Justice
Federal Bureau of Investigation
Washington 25, D.C.
I.C. #4-157
August 9, 1946

Source: NARA-II, RG 65 FBI, Interesting Case Write-ups, Box 1

See Articles: Automobile and the Police; Military Courts; Military Police.

1946 PRIMARY DOCUMENT

FBI Memorandum on Harboring Army Deserters

The author of this FBI memorandum even includes the headline of a newspaper story covering the fairly minor event. Short-term desertions from army bases were common, and in many cases, absent without leave (AWOL) soldiers were just blowing off steam before returning to base like truant students. Technically, the maximum penalty for desertion during wartime is the death penalty, but it is rare for deserters to be punished with more than a short prison sentence.

Laura Ellen Jones: Isobel Ada Roggins: Virginia Mary Ploof
Deserter (Harboring):
Conspiracy

Typical of deserter harboring cases is that involving Laura Ellen Jones, Isobel Ada Roggins, and Virginia Mary Ploof, who concealed Privates Joseph Lee Meyers and Houser Becker after their escape from the Military Police guardhouse at Albany, New York, on the night of January 8, 1944.

The three girls resided on Eagle Street in Albany, New York, and Meyers, who had gone Absent Without Leave from Camp Patrick Henry, Virginia, on December 23, 1942, had hidden out in the girls' apartment before he was caught and was placed in the guardhouse at Albany. Private Becker had gone Absent Without Leave from Camp Stewart, Georgia, on December 24, 1945.

Both missing soldiers were apprehended by Albany police officers at approximately 9 p.m. on January 9, 1944, although the three young women had previously denied that the men were in their apartment and had stated that they had not seen Meyers or Becker.

Misses Jones, Roggins, and Ploof were indicted by a Federal Grand Jury at Albany,

New York, on January 19, 1964 on charges of conspiracy to harbor deserters and for the actual harboring of deserters. On March 1, 1944, the three entered pleas of guilty. Miss Jones was sentenced to serve 8 months but this sentence was suspended and she was placed on probation for one year. Misses Roggins and Ploof were sentenced to serve 6 months each, but their sentences were suspended and they were placed on probation for one year each.

In reporting on the arrest of the three young women, a New York newspaper headlined its account as follows: "The Girls Were Hospitable, the Boys AWOL—So the Eagle Street Roost was Raided, the Doves were Caged."

At the time of the incident, Miss Roggins was 21 and Misses Jones and Ploof were both 20 years of age.

Federal Bureau of Investigation
United States Department of Justice
Washington, D. C.
I.C. #42-4029
February 7, 1946

Source: NARA II, RG 65, Class 42, Box 1, F: 424029

See Articles: Military Courts; Military Police.

1947 PRIMARY DOCUMENT

FBI Memorandum on Draft Desertion

This cut-and-dried Classification 25 case again demonstrates that even by 1945, the FBI's resources had grown considerably, and that Hoover's campaign to have law enforcement agencies fingerprint their suspects and share their data was bearing fruit. Without fingerprint information, there would have been little hope of identifying and apprehending the draft evader described in this memo. Prosecution was likely declined because by the time of the indictment, the war had been over for six months.

Joseph William Cormier, with alias, Joseph William Rafferty
Deserter; Selective Service.

An individual using the name, Joseph William Rafferty, registered at a Local Draft Board in Buffalo, New York, in November, 1945. Investigation disclosed that the information supplied by Rafferty was fictitious and he was indicted on March 15, 1946, by the Federal Grand Jury for the Western District of New York for failure to report for induction.

FBI Agents forwarded Rafferty's original registration card to the FBI Laboratory with the request that a handwriting examination he made against any fingerprint cards, among the more than 100 million on file, bearing the signatures of persons with the same name as Rafferty.

A search was made of the alphabetical files of the Identification Division on the name, Joseph W. Rafferty. A comparison of signatures with the subject's signature as it appeared on his registration card identified him as Joseph William Gormier.

This man's criminal record disclosed that he was last fingerprinted by the Palm Beach, Florida, Police Department when he applied for a job as a waiter at a local hotel. He was apprehended at once and in a signed statement to Agent Cormier stated he was a Navy deserter. He readily admitted, also, his violation of the Selective Training and Service Act.

Prosecution on the Selective Service violation was declined by the United States Attorney at Buffalo and the subject was released to Naval authorities.

United States Department of Justice
Federal Bureau of Investigation
Washington 25, D. C.
I.C. #25-5768
May 20, 1947

Source: NARA II, RG 65 FBI, Interesting Case Write-ups, Box 8, Folder IC 25 5768

See Articles: Fingerprinting; Military Courts; Military Police.

1948 PRIMARY DOCUMENT

FBI Memorandum on Clifford Carlyle Skaife's Crime Spree

Dick Skaife was a throwback to the outlaws of earlier generations, at least for a few months. His case is unusual not just for his character—he boasted of his shootouts, committed burglaries, stole automobiles, forged checks, and robbed a post office—but also for his lack of apparent connections to organized crime, a gang, or even a partner. Criminals usually begin their career gradually enough to develop criminal contacts and associations, often in prison.

Clifford Carlyle Skaife, with aliases, Dick Skaife, John E. Cox, Clifford Carlyle Skaife, Richard Skaife, Clifford C. Skaife, Dick Hail, R. J. Williams, R. E. Williams, R. E. Griffiths, Jack Mallory.

Theft From Interstate Shipment
National Motor Vehicle Theft Act
National Stolen Property Act.

The brief and spectacular one-man crime wave of Clifford Carlyle Skaife in western Wisconsin, eastern Iowa, and eastern Minnesota, came to an abrupt but equally spectacular end with his apprehension at a hideout cabin near Sparta, Wisconsin, on May 19, 1945, after an intensive search by FNI Agents and local law enforcement agencies.

Upon apprehension Skaife readily admitted that he had committed two violations of the National Motor Vehicle Theft Act, burglarized the United States Post Office at Potosi, Wisconsin, forged endorsements on many United States Government checks and on Grant County, Wisconsin, checks stolen from a number of interstate shipments, passed a large quantity of worthless checks, and committed many local burglaries—in the course of a four-month, single-handed reign of lawlessness in west-central Wisconsin.

This investigation necessitated the utmost care because of Skaife's known boasts to shoot it out with arresting officers. FBI Agents found it necessary to enter many lonely regions looking for Skaife and to masquerade as farmers and hunters in rural taverns in their attempts to locate Skaife.

Recoveries made during the course of the investigation consisted of two stolen automobiles valued at $1,650.00, ten checks of Grant County, Wisconsin, in the amount of $4,603.24, nineteen United States Government checks totaling $570.00 and various miscellaneous stolen articles valued at $162.00.

Clifford Carlyle Skaife, more commonly known as Dick Skaife, was a two time loser in the Wisconsin State Courts and served time in the Green Bay Reformatory and at the Waupun State Prison prior to 1942. His original sentences were for breaking and entering and for forgery. He was the thirty-year-old father of two small children residing in Dodgeville, Wisconsin, and had been a driver for the Yellow Truck Lines of Madison, Wisconsin, for several months when he embarked upon his new career of crime. He began by pilfering from various interstate shipments that were entrusted to his care as a driver for the Yellow Truck Lines. The first theft from interstate shipment that came to the attention of the authorities as having been perpetrated by Skaife was on January 29, 1945, when the Montgomery Ward Branch in Platteville, Wisconsin, attempted to return some defective kitchen cabinets to the Chicago Warehouse of Montgomery Ward for repairs. Skaife, the Yellow Truck Lines driver to whom this shipment was entrusted, preferred to deliver these kitchen cabinets to his own home in Dodgeville.

On February 1, 1945, shipments of miscellaneous material from St. Louis, Missouri, to

Belmont, Darlington, Mineral Point, Platteville, and Dodgeville, Wisconsin, were given to Skaife in Madison, Wisconsin, for final delivery. He took one carton to his home and delivered the rest of the shipment. This carton contained miscellaneous notions.

On February 17, 1945, Skaife took one carton of general mill supplies, including bolts, nuts, screws and six hog waterers, from a shipment originating in Dubuque, Iowa, intended for a distributor in Belmont, Wisconsin. This carton was likewise taken to Skaife's home and was recovered during the investigation of the case.

On February 24, 1945, Skaife, who had a key for all the freight depots on his Yellow Truck Lines route, entered the Chicago and Northwestern Depot at Dodgeville, Wisconsin, at 8:30 p.m., using his key, and looked for any interesting items that he might steal. He noticed a shipment of Marvel cigarettes which had been consigned from Proviso, Illinois, on February 22, 1945, to a Dodgeville, Wisconsin, distributor. Skaife took two cases of these cigarettes. A short time before reaching Madison he concealed them alongside the road and continued his trip, taking the truck to the company garage in Madison. He then rented an automobile and went out to retrieve the cigarettes. After loading them in the back of the car he picked up two girl hitchhikers. Before leaving the girls, he gave each several cartons of cigarettes.

During the early part of March, Skaife continued with his petty thefts from interstate shipments and also burglarized several homes. On March 16, 1945, he stole a Packard sedan which was parked in front of a Dodgeville mine, and after burglarizing a filling station, a produce house, and a scale house in the vicinity, drove to Minnesota. At St. Paul he tried to secure a job driving a truck but was unable to do so and on March 21, 1945, he returned to Wisconsin, where as a result of a flat tire he was forced to abandon the Packard automobile near Hillsboro.

Because of the inconvenience of being without an automobile, Skaife on March 22, 1945, stole a black Studebaker Commander sedan at Spring Green, Wisconsin. This automobile served him for approximately a month, during which time he made many trips to Iowa and Minnesota for the purpose of cashing checks and visiting taverns with various women.

On March 29, 1945, Skaife entered the Chicago, Milwaukee, St. Paul and Pacific Railroad Station at Platteville, Wisconsin, using an old pass key, to see what was available. He stole one pair of shoes and a case of catsup from an interstate shipment. Shortly thereafter he again picked up two girl hitchhikers with whom he had several drinks. He then passed a fifty dollar check in order to take them for an airplane ride. After the ride he took them to dinner at the airport restaurant and, finding that the restaurant had no catsup, he went out to his car and brought in three bottles from the stolen case and gave them to the proprietor. Before parting from the girls he gave them another fifty dollar fraudulent check.

At April 5, 1945, at 1:00 a.m., Skaife's spending money having run a bit low, he parked the Studebaker in front of the Post Office at Potosi, Wisconsin, went to the back of the building and with the use of a screwdriver removed a window and entered. He gathered up from two hundred to three hundred pieces of mail which were lying on a sorting table. He then re-entered the automobile and drove to a point about two miles from town, where he parked, opened the letters, took out all the checks and burned the remaining correspondence. He immediately set out for Iowa and commenced cashing the checks which he had stolen, including twenty-seven United States Treasury Checks in the total amount of $750.00 and fourteen County of Grant checks amounting to $5,531.46. He cashed some of these checks at Pottsville, Monona, and Guttenberg, Iowa, using various aliases.

The Studebaker automobile was abandoned by Skaife on April 21, 1945 at LaCrosse, Wisconsin, and he obtained a second-hand Ford by cashing another Grant County check. He received $111.00 in change from the automobile dealer.

On April 30, 1945, when the pursuit of Skaife became a bit too warm, he drove this automobile into the Wisconsin River and pinned a suicide note to it written to his small son as a hoax to distract his pursuers. Skaife then started to hitch-hike west and reached as far as the Dakotas when he decided to return to Sparta, Wisconsin, believing that some of the heat was off. He lived in a cabin just outside the city limits of Sparta.

On April 23, 1945, the Milwaukee Office of the Federal Bureau of Investigation was informed of the various activities of Skaife and FBI Agents took up the search after filing a complaint on April 27, 1945, at Madison, Wisconsin, charging Skaife with violation of a Federal statute in connection with his theft of two cases of Marvel cigarettes from the shipment moving in interstate commerce between Proviso, Illinois, and Dodgeville, Wisconsin, and his theft of five pieces of merchandise moving in interstate commerce from Galeswood, Illinois, to Darlington, Wisconsin.

The utmost care was necessary in searching for Skaife inasmuch as he had openly boasted that he would resist arrest by any law enforcement officer, and it was known that he was an excellent shot with the revolver, rifle and shotgun.

On May 19, 1945, Skaife was captured by local law enforcement officials near Sparta. On May 23, 1945, he was taken by FBI Agents to Madison, Wisconsin, where he pleaded guilty to two charges of automobile theft and one charge of theft from interstate shipment. He received a five year sentence on each of the three counts, these sentences to run concurrently.

United States Department of Justice
Federal Bureau of Investigation
Washington 25, D.C.
I.C. #15-13838
March 20, 1948

Source: NARA-II, RG 65 FBI, Interesting Case Write-ups, Box 6

See Articles: Federal Bureau of Investigation; Robbery, Contemporary; Robbery, History of; Wisconsin.

1950 PRIMARY DOCUMENT

FBI Subject Files Used in the Kefauver Hearings on Organized Crime

Senator Estes Kefauver was the chair of the Senate Special Committee to Investigate Crime in Interstate Commerce, which held hearings from 1950 to 1951 to examine the increased reports of organized crime activity since the end of World War II. Prohibition had ended in 1933, but the power of the Mafia didn't wane; Lucky Luciano established the Commission, a ruling committee consisting of the boss of the Chicago Outfit and the heads of New York's Five Families, to reduce infighting and vulnerability. The Mafia expanded its activities into various areas of crime and was reputed to have infiltrated the major labor unions, which was one of the main objects of concern for the Committee. The Committee's aim was to prove the existence of a Sicilian American crime conspiracy operating throughout the country, but it failed to do so. The Society of the Banana refers to an Ohio-based Black Hand group.

There are references in the 1909 report of the International Association of Chiefs of Police to Post Office Department prosecution of Mafia members. I asked Chief Post Office Inspector Garner if they had any reports and he kindly made available such files as are here.

In the Annual Report of the Post Office Department for 1909, there is a general statement under "Black Hand Cases." This is to the effect that early in June, 1909, inspectors had secured evidence to indicate the existence of a secret society among Italians, the sole purpose of which was to secure money by blackmail. In this connection, the inspectors had arrested 14 Italians.

In the Post Office Inspector's file is a clipping of a *Washington Star-News* editorial dated June 9, 1909. This refers to vigorous prosecutions in Ohio and West Virginia of the Black Hand as contrasted to no action in New York where the Black Hand and Tammany go hand-in-hand.

Other newspaper clippings refer to some Columbus, Ohio cases. There a Black Hand ring, with headquarters at Marion, Ohio, is alleged to have extorted $230,000 from victims. One clipping is from the Columbus, Ohio Dispatch dated December 5, 1909 and refers to the "absolute silence of the Italians" when the Black Hand subject is raised.

There is a specimen of an extortion letter, in Italian of course, warning against notifying the police signed La Terrible Mano Mera. It is decorated with the skull and crossbones and with a dagger through a heart. This file also contained a handwritten document presumed to be the bylaws and regulations of the Mafia in which they alluded to themselves at Society of Banannas. Mr. Gayner supplied me with a translation of this from the Italian and it is appended.

A 1930 report signed by four Post Office inspectors refers to Black Hand gangs operating in Chicago, Illinois, through 1918-1920. It refers to 12 arrests and the sentencing on May 26, 1920, at Chicago, Illinois, of one MARTELLO and two others to 10 years in Leavenworth. There are the usual references to intimidation of witnesses, fear of reprisal, secrecy and the like.

There are no detailed reports of evidence in the Post Office files here. Such as are available are merely concerned with the progress of court action. Apparently any detailed reports of evidence that were made are retained in the field files.

Chief Garner said their files did not indicate that they had been concerned with the Black Hand since 1920.

(Of course prohibition gave another outlet to the peculiar genius of the Mafia at that time.)

By-Laws and Regulations of the Society of Banannas

Art. 1. The person who tries to reveal the secrets of this society will be punished with death.

Art. 2. A member who offends one of his companions, staining his honor, will be punished according to Art. 1;

Art. 3. The member who tries to do harm to another branch of the society, or to the family of other companions, if this harm shall have been grave, will be undressed and marked on his body with the mark of infamy and called with word of contempt, "Swindler," and if the offense is more grave, he will be stabbed.

Art. 4. The person who is a coward and does not sustain the punishment assigned to him by the society, he will be punished in accordance with Art. 3.;

Art. 5. The member who profits by the opportunity of the plan of another member, is punished as prescribed in Art. 3; if the misdemeanor is less grave he must make restitution within 24 hours of that which he caused to be lost, and he will be cut off from his share of the profits for two months;

Art. 6. The member who offends another companion with offensive titles, if the offense is considered grave, will not only lose his right of membership but will also be stabbed. If the offense is less grave, he will be cut off from his share of the profits for 3 months and at the same time must do his duty;

Art. 7. The member who has received the insult and resents it himself, without notifying the society, is punished according to Art. 3;

Art. 8. The member who abandons one of his companions in the time of need will be held to be a traitor, and then punished according to Art. 3;

Art. 9. The person appointed to inspect must always go around and maintain good order as it is prescribed, passing all the news around. Failing in this for the first time, he will be cut off from his share of the profits for 3 months, the second time he will be stabbed.

Art. 10. A reunion of the society cannot be called for a visiting member if he is not known.

Art. 11. The person who goes away must pass the news and tell the "local" in the place where he goes how long he will be there, and if he carries a message he must leave his pledge. Failing to do this, he will be punished according to Art 6.;

Art. 12. The person who shall have been called to use the knife and does not go through fear, will be punished according to Art. 3.;

Art. 13. The person who deals sparingly, (does not do his duty) will be punished according to Art. 3 at a convenient place by the society with a brand on his face.;

Art. 14. The person who refutes the call of command, will, for the first time be deprived of his share for 3 months; for the second time, from one to two cuts with the knife, for the third time, from two to five cuts, as the society thinks best, and to follow his work as prescribed; if it be grave, he will be punished according to Art 3 without having any benefits from the society.

Art. 15. The person who is sent somewhere by the society will be paid by the day and for the journey;

Art. 16. There can be no excuse for failures or penalties in conformity with the articles. However there may be extenuating circumstances in case of drunkenness.

M. L. Harney
June 23, 1950

Source: NARA-II, RG 170 Records of the DEA, Subject files of Bureau of Narcotics, Box 50, F: Kefauver's Crime and Conference Senate Crime Commission.

See Articles: Chicago, Illinois; Organized Crime, History of; Organized Crime, Sociology of; Prohibition.

1950 PRIMARY DOCUMENT

Statement of Bureau of Narcotics Commissioner Harry J. Anslinger

The Federal Bureau of Narcotics was an agency in the Treasury Department, established in 1930 to replace older narcotics agencies and assume some of the enforcement responsibilities of federal narcotics laws. Harry Anslinger, who had previously worked in the Bureau of Prohibition, was its first commissioner and served until 1962. He campaigned diligently for stricter drug control laws, harsher sentencing, and the treatment of marijuana usage as a serious drug problem.

Enforcement of narcotics laws in this country for a generation has not only stopped the spread of narcotic addiction but has reduced its incidence by more than half. This reduction has been steady and unspectacular. But over the years, it has represented a great gain against the traffic. The downward trend in the traffic and in addiction, which was continued and was even accelerated through the war years, recently has shown a reversion. Some retrogression was to be expected. However, the recent increase in addiction, mainly among young hoodlums, and the more ready availability of heroin in many parts of the country has been marked.

Since it is a truism that addicts make addicts and because a majority of the persons who become addicted cannot be cured by any means presently known, there is a tremendous responsibility on law enforcement to prevent addiction by shutting off sources of narcotic supply. Our present situation suggests that our agent force is numerically inadequate. We are carrying on with about the same appropriation as we had 20 years ago. The fact that we have practically the same funds as in the immediate prewar days means that our agent force has been reduced about one-fourth from that period. This is a severe attrition in an organization which must be spread so thinly.

The Bureau of Narcotics is daily concerned with interstate criminal organizations. This is obviously the case since most of the narcotics in the illicit traffic are not produced within the United States but flow here from abroad. On being landed here, they are distributed throughout the country. This distribution is accomplished sometimes by individuals, but more generally by organizations of greater or less complexity. Sometimes a relationship between individuals in these organizations will be merely on the order of buyer and seller. More often it will consist of a number of persons in a common conspiracy to distribute drugs. Persons may shift from one organization to another and intermittently in and out of the traffic.

However, our experience has taught us that once a man has had a taste of the business, he is a logical suspect to repeat. Before the war, some of the most important gangsters in the country were in the illicit narcotic traffic at one time or another.

Such hoodlums as "Waxey" Gordon, "Legs" Diamond, "Lucky" Luciano and their organizations have from time to time dipped into narcotics traffic. Perhaps the most notorious gang was the so-called Murder, Inc., headed by Louis "Lepke" Buchalter. This was not only an interstate but actually an intercountry and intercontinent organization obtaining its supplies in China and distributing them from New York throughout the country, particularly to the southwest. At the time, we estimated this organization smuggled into this country and distributed enough narcotics to supply one-fifth of the entire addict population.

Sometimes big shot racketeers get into the narcotic traffic by merely financing ventures of others. Sometimes they "muscle in" on a lucrative business built up by lesser criminals. Buchalter was a good example. We proved that circumstance in the case where we convicted him and he got a 12 year sentence on narcotics charges. On the other hand, Emanual "Mendy" Weiss, often considered Buchalter's first lieutenant, actually participated directly in the narcotics business for several years. We arrested Weiss when he became a fugitive on narcotics and murder charges and he was successfully prosecuted with Buchalter for murder by the New York authorities. Naturally the interest of major racketeers in the narcotic traffic is as far removed as possible from overt participation. It may be only a small item of their manifold operations. Assembling of competent evidence against them is a tremendously difficult undertaking.

Interstate crime operations may take some specialized forms. Before the war we had to deal with a situation where the facilities of a Chinese Tong were being used in the interstate distribution of drugs. In the war years, we had to cope with the depredations of bands of accomplished robbers and burglars who, from centralized points, ranged all over the map robbing and burglarizing legitimate wholesale narcotics stocks. Incidentally, in meeting this problem, we found the interstate flight from justice law to be of great help in those cases where it appeared the prosecution should be locally on robbery or burglary charges rather than for a Federal narcotic offense.

Organizations of interstate racketeers are the underground railway over which passes crime of all sorts in this country.

In 1947, through breakdown in controls in that country, a tremendous quantity of cocaine, the output of 17 clandestine factories, became available in Peru. Many seamen on ships plying between our east coast and Peru engaged in smuggling this drug, and the aggregate result was that a very substantial amount of cocaine was brought in. Within several months, cocaine appeared in the illicit narcotic traffic in almost every section of the country. Prior to that time, the cocaine traffic had been practically non-existent for more than 15 years. Tremendous efforts by this Government and the Peruvians have materially reduced the influx of cocaine. The suppression of this traffic has averted a serious crime wave.

Anyone who reads the daily papers must realize that interstate criminals in commercial rackets (of which narcotics is one) number among their ranks some of the most dangerous and deadly thugs in the country.

Joseph Sica and Alfred Sica of California are hoodlums with important underworld connections in the east and in California to which state they came some years ago. In 1949, a narcotics case was developed against the Sicas principally on the testimony of one Abraham Davidian. Early this year while the case was pending for trial, Davidian was shot to death while sleeping in his mother's home in Fresno, Calif.

Another West Coast case of great importance was developed in 1944. This concerned a New York-California-Mexico smuggling ring in which Salvatore Maugeri and others were convicted. During the course of the investigation, a narcotic agent working undercover learned that one of the ring with whom he was negotiating, Charles "Big Nose" LaGaipa, of Santa Cruz, Calif., was in bad odor with some of his criminal associates. LaGaipa disappeared. He never has been found. His car was recovered with blood on the seat and brain tissue on the dashboard.

One Ignazio Antinori of Tampa, Florida, went to Havana, Cuba, frequently to obtain narcotics for middle western associates. Their leader was Joseph DeLuca. Allegedly because he delivered some drugs of poor quality and did not promptly make restitution, Antinori was killed in Tampa by shotgun fire in 1940. In 1942, we arrested DeLuca, Antinori's two sons, Paul and Joseph, and several others. They were convicted in a trial in which Carl Carramusa, a codefendant appeared as a witness for the Government. Carramusa moved to Chicago to escape possible vengeance by the combine. In 1945, as he was repairing a tire in front of his home, he was killed by a shotgun blast before the eyes of his 15 year old daughter. The murder is unsolved. Neighbors who could have furnished information remain silent because of fear.

Many other such incidents could be cited.

With the help of our sister services in the Treasure and with the fine support of law enforcement officers throughout the country, we have employed all our resources to reduce the internal narcotic traffic. With about 2% of the Federal criminal law enforcement personnel, we account for more than 10% of the persons committed to Federal penal institutions.

Through the United Nations, where I am the United States Representative on the Commission on Narcotic Drugs, and through other channels of international cooperation, this Government has been exerting every effort to see that the external sources of narcotic drugs are eliminated. Right now, we are trying to bring about agreement among producing countries, particularly in the Near East, to reduce their production to medical needs. The present main source of supply for heroin in this country is now Turkey; for opium, it is Iran. Drugs may come direct or by way of Europeans way-stations. Mexico, an important source of supply in war years, has happily been reduced in prominence, except for marijuana, due to the efforts of its Government to suppress the traffic and because alternative supplies are now available from the Near East.

Where requested, we have assisted foreign police in apprehending some of their international traffickers supplying this country with drugs. We maintain, in booklet form, a watch list of major international narcotic suspects. We distribute this in strategic points in this country and abroad. We believe this has served to restrict the movements of many of these racketeers and it regularly results in the apprehension of some of them. On one occasion, the assistance of this list served to break up an international smuggling ring in a matter of a few days.

What I have said probably forecasts the recommendations I would make. The narcotic traffic is a vicious, commercial racket which lives on the slow murder of its customers.

1. The average prison sentence meted out in the Federal Courts is 18 months. Short sentences do not deter. In districts where we get good sentences the traffic does not flourish. Both the League of Nations and the United Nations have recommended

more severe sentences as one of the best methods to suppress the traffic.

2. There should be a substantial increase in the authorized strength of the Bureau of Narcotics.
3. Federal law enforcement agencies dealing with racketeers should be provided with the means of protecting Government witnesses and persons furnishing information under all circumstances. This might mean changes in the appropriation act language of some services. Also, the criminal laws dealing with the protection of witnesses might be strengthened.
4. I submit as worthy of study a proposal that some centralized agency maintain a gallery of major interstate racketeers and systematically collect, correlate and disseminate information respecting them, a procedure along the lines of the Treasury Department lists of major narcotic suspects. Often the operations of modern big-times racketeers are so diverse and so extensive geographically that few individual local officers can comprehend their magnitude or realize the significance of the small segment which is within their ken. A device of this sort which would spotlight the operations of a major criminal would prove most helpful.
5. I would like to see more of the states set up special state narcotic law enforcement squads as is the case in Pennsylvania and California. Also, I would like to see more cities organize special police narcotics squads similar to those of Los Angeles and New York.

June 28, 1950

Source: NARA-II, RG 170 Records of the DEA, Subj Files of Bureau of Narcotics 1916–1970, Box 50, Kefauver's Crime Conference, Senate Crime Comm.

See Articles: Bureau of Alcohol, Tobacco, Firearms and Explosives; Drug Enforcement Administration; Luciano, "Lucky;" Murder, History of; Narcotics Laws.

1951 PRIMARY DOCUMENT

FBI Memorandum on Hugh Rakes and the Whiskey Conspiracy

The Franklin County Liquor Conspiracy in which Hugh Rakes played a role is also known as the Great Moonshine Conspiracy or the Whiskey Conspiracy. FBI memoranda like this one are some of the only records of the conspiracy; the official trial transcript and court records disappeared in the 1950s. The sheriff and his deputies enlisted people to make moonshine and then collected protection money from them; at least one witness was killed by unknown shooters days before the trial.

This is primarily the story of Hugh Rakes, an uneducated man, hardly able to read or write, born and raised in southwest Virginia, who built a vast dairy empire through the successful three year operation of a gigantic check kiting scheme.

The story begins and ends with an attempt to bribe a juror and embraces the two longest trials in the history of the Commonwealth of Virginia since Aaron Burr was tried for treason in 1807.

In 1936 in southwest Virginia, twenty-four conspirators were tried in the now notorious Franklin County Liquor Conspiracy case which lasted eleven weeks. Hugh Rakes, then thirty-six years of age, was not a defendant in this case but several of his friends were defendants, so Rakes obligingly attempted to bribe one of the jurors. He was convicted of this offense of May 23, 1936, and sentenced to two years and $1,000 fine.

In 1941 Rakes began to buy dairy farms in Virginia and to remodel and modernize these farms. For his own estate he bought Court Manor at New Market, Virginia, one of Virginia's most famous estates. Rakes reputedly was worth over $500,000. He apparently started with $40,000 capital which was borrowed from Farmers and Merchants State Bank of Fredericksburg, Virginia, Inc. Rakes' available cash and credit limits at banks were quickly exhausted and as his expenses continued to mount he began to kite checks. He did this principally through three banks in Virginia, the Planters Branch of the Farmers and Merchants State Bank of Fredericksburg, Virginia, Inc., the Floyd County Bank of Floyd, Virginia, and the Purcellville National Bank of Purcellville, Virginia. The kite from time to time was passed through other banks in Virginia and West Virginia.

A check kite is a scheme in which one tenders a check on his bank account at some place other than where the bank is located and against insufficient funds in the bank. Before the check arrives at that bank several days later the drawer "covers" it by making a sufficient deposit in the account with another bad check drawn on a second bank at another location. After going through normal banking channels this second check arrives at the second bank days later and is again covered by a third check which may be drawn on the first bank or still another bank and is likewise drawn against insufficient funds. This cycle continues, and usually enlarges, enabling the person operating the kite to obtain money without having any substantial balance to his credit at any bank or ever depositing any real money or assets to meet the checks, which are kept in a constant flow by the banks involved. Once a kite is started it, of course, must eventually break—either by the perpetrator taking up all the outstanding bad checks with good money or by the discovery of the kite and "grounding" it at one of the banks, resulting in a loss to that bank.

The kite that Rakes operated, being so large, so constant, and so widespread, necessarily involved the assistance and cooperation of officials of the banks involved and also of other persons who exchanged checks with Rakes, forged notes for him, and otherwise aided him in maintenance of this kite.

Rakes' principal partner in this scheme was William Reeves Gardner, Vice-President of the Planters Branch of the Farmers and Merchants State Bank of Fredericksburg, Virginia, Inc. The kite required so much running around by Rakes to cover his checks that he left with Gardner blanks with his signature on them, drawn on other banks, and Gardner would fill in the necessary amounts as they were needed. Paul Karsten, Jr., Assistant Vice-President at the Fredericksburg Bank, on several occasions during Gardner's absence from the bank would see that Rakes' checks were covered when they came in. Joseph A. Sowers, Cashier of the Floyd County Bank, Floyd, Virginia, gave similar aid at his bank, and Kyle N. Weeks, a lawyer with offices in the Floyd Bank, when Rakes was not available to cover checks arriving there, would issue checks or drafts with Rakes' signature, or get other friends of Rakes to issue them. D. E. Nelson, a realtor in Roanoke, Virginia, and Harry Lamson, a Washington, D. C., businessman, both aided in the scheme by permitting their own bank accounts to be used to take up kited checks and by using their personal checks to keep the kite operating. D. E. Nelson also allegedly forged a note for $75,000 at the Planters Branch of the Farmers and Merchants State Bank of Fredericksburg, Virginia, Inc., to take up a group of the kited checks. Nelson denied the forgery, but at the trial in which Nelson was convicted an FBI handwriting expert testified that the signature on this note was written by D. E. Nelson.

From September, 1942 to April, 1944, Rakes negotiated over seven and three-quarter million dollars of kited checks. For all thirty days of this one and one-half year period Rakes did not have sufficient balance in all of his bank accounts to pay for the checks outstanding each day against those bank accounts. During this period Rakes acquired sixteen dairy farms worth approximately one and one-half million dollars against which, however, were first deeds of trust or a loan of one million dollars which Rakes obtained from an insurance company. The amount of money floating between the banks in this kite from time to time would grow so that it was too unwieldy to handle. Each time this happened, Rakes and Gardner would permit all the kited checks outstanding to flow into the Planters

Branch at Fredericksburg, Virginia (Gardner's bank) and take up all these kited checks with a note. These notes, of course, would be as worthless as the checks which they replaced. The kite could then start up again at zero. The Virginia banking laws prohibit the loaning of money to any one customer of a bank in an amount in excess of 15 per cent of the bank's capital. It was, therefore, necessary to have a person other than Rakes as maker on these notes. In some cases persons assisting Rakes in his scheme would sign the notes. In other cases Rakes would get other friends, not participating in the scheme, to sign the notes as accommodation, guaranteeing payment of the note himself. In still other instances Rakes would allegedly forge a person's name to the note without the knowledge of the person whose name he had signed. Rakes denied these forgeries, but at his trial an FBI handwriting expert testified that Rakes wrote the signatures of the makers on five of these notes which totaled $153,000.

In April, 1944, the kite broke. Bank examiners at the Floyd County Bank noticed the large transactions in Rakes' account and a similarity of deposits and withdrawals. They checked transactions at the Planters Branch next and found some of the unsecured notes issued to take up the kited checks. The Federal Bureau of Investigation was called in.

The FBI Agents then began a painstaking analysis and tracing of the bank transactions of Hugh Rakes. In an investigation which was pursued for two years the kite was traced step by step back to 1941. The participation in the scheme by other persons gradually unfolded. The notes, together with handwriting specimens of persons involved in the scheme, were submitted to the FBI Laboratory and the forgeries were discovered.

It was found that Gardner received at least $35,000 as gratuity from Rakes for Gardner's part in concealing and assisting the kite. Other commissions paid to other bankers involved in the kite were also found. One of these bankers cleared over $70,000 in commissions from Rakes for his service in placing loans for Rakes' benefit and giving financial advice. During the course of the investigation by the FBI, William R. Gardner was indicted by the Commonwealth of Virginia on a charge of embezzlement. He was convicted and on June 22, 1945, was sentenced to seven years.

When the kite broke in April, 1944, it was found that there was over $650,000 in notes at the Planters Branch of the Farmers and Merchants State Bank of Fredericksburg, Virginia, from which Hugh Rakes received benefit. It was necessary for the Federal Deposit Insurance Corporation to take over that bank and liquidate it to insure that individual depositors would not lose their savings. The Federal Deposit Insurance Corporation realized $225,000 from Rakes' properties after paying off mortgages and estimated a net loss of $425,000 as a result of Rakes' transactions.

The facts developed by FBI Agents were presented to a Federal Grand Jury at Richmond, Virginia, and on October 17, 1945, an indictment was returned, charging ten defendants with violation of the Federal Reserve Act. All of the persons who have been mentioned above were indicted, and, in addition, three others, two of whom were bank presidents.

On March 3, 1947, the trial of nine of the ten defendants was begun in United States District Court, Richmond, Virginia. William R. Gardner had been excused from this trial due to illness and was to be tried later. This trial lasted almost eight weeks, and on April 25, 1947, the jury returned a verdict of guilty against all nine defendants.

On Sunday, April 20, 1947, just before the case was to go to the jury, one of the jurors was approached with an offer of "easy money" if he would hang the jury. The juror properly refused the offer and immediately reported it to the District Judge trying the case. After the trial was over several of the defendants joined in a motion to declare a mistrial due to the prejudice against all defendants which might have been engendered in the jurors' minds as a result of this attempt to bribe one of them. The motion was granted and a mistrial declared.

A new trial of eight of the defendants, including Gardner, was begun in Richmond, Virginia, January 5, 1948. Two of the defendants convicted in the first trial had not joined in the motion for a mistrial, electing to accept the verdict and the sentence imposed at the first trial. These were Paul Karsten, Jr., who was placed on probation for one year, and D. E. Nelson, who was fined $1,000.

At the second trial William R. Gardner pleaded guilty and defendants Harry Lamson, Kyle Menefee Weeks, and Joseph A. Sowers, pleaded nolo contendere. The remaining defendants pleaded not guilty. The jury on January 27, 1948, returned a verdict of guilty against Hugh Namon Rakes. The three defendants who have not been named were acquitted. The court imposed the following sentences:

> William R. Gardner, sentenced to five years' imprisonment, to run concurrently with the seven years sentence imposed by the Commonwealth of Virginia;
>
> Hugh Namon Rakes, sentenced to three years' imprisonment, a $10,000 fine and five additional years suspended, with probation to begin after service of the three year sentence;
>
> Kyle Menefee Weeks, sentenced to a $5,000 fine;
>
> Joseph A. Sowers, sentenced to a $3,000 fine; and
>
> Harry Lamson, sentenced to a $3,000 fine.

In the meantime, FBI Agents had been busy gathering evidence on the attempt to bribe a juror. The man who made this improper approach to a juror was found to be Leslie Earl Martin, a gasoline station employee. Martin readily admitted his crime, giving a full confession and naming Robert Lee Hicks, an attorney in Richmond, Virginia, as the person who procured him to attempt to bribe. According to Martin, Hicks had indicated that he would supply the money to bribe the juror. Hicks had indicated that he would supply the money to bribe the juror. Hicks, when interviewed, categorically denied any knowledge of the bribery attempt or any contact with Martin for this purpose. FBI Agents began surveilling Hicks and at the same time utilizing Martin as an informant. Martin did not tell Hicks that he had confessed and Hicks arranged meetings with Martin to make him offers of money if he would continue his silence. These were observed by FBI Agents. Hicks, in subsequent interviews, denied having these meetings with Martin.

Martin was indicted by the Federal Grand Jury, Richmond, Virginia, October 6, 1947. The court appointed at attorney to represent Martin but Hicks prevailed upon Martin to dismiss this attorney and retain another attorney, named by Hicks. Martin agreed to this and was tried November 25, 1947, on a plea of not guilty. No evidence was presented by the defense attorney except a showing by the Clerk of the Court that Robert Lee Hicks had not yet been indicted. Martin was convicted and sentenced to three years' imprisonment.

Hicks then continued contact with Martin's family, repaying them the cost of Martin's trial and appealing and meeting with them to make offers of money for them to hold for Earl Martin and asking the family to prevail upon Martin not to testify against Hicks. These meetings were also observed by FBI Agents.

On April 5, 1948, Hicks was indicted by a Federal Grand Jury at Richmond, Virginia, on the charge of corruptly endeavoring to influence a juror. He was tried and convicted on a not guilty plea October 14, 1948, and was sentenced to serve four years' imprisonment.

Federal Bureau of Investigation
United States Department of Justice
Washington 25, D. C.

I.C. #29-11101, #51-331
February 28, 1951

Source: NARA-II, RG 65 FBI, Interesting Case Write-ups, Box 12

See Articles: Confidence Games and Frauds; Moonshine; Prohibition; Virginia.

1951 PRIMARY DOCUMENT

Executive Order on the Interdepartmental Committee on Narcotics

This executive order was an early movement in shifting federal narcotics policy toward the modern "war on drugs" mentality. Most drug control laws were still based on fines; the idea of the drug dealer as a dangerous criminal element who should be imprisoned, while present in popular culture and the rhetoric of some agency officials, was not yet reflected in law. After President Truman's order, the Boggs Act followed in 1952, instituting the first mandatory sentences for drug crimes.

Immediate Release
Executive Order 10302
Interdepartmental Committee on Narcotics

By virtue of the authority vested in me as President of the United States, and subject to the provisions of section 214 of the Independent Offices Appropriation Act, 1946 (59 Stat. 134; 31 U.S.C. 691), it is ordered as follows:

Section 1. There is hereby established the Interdepartmental Committee on Narcotics, which shall have as members one representative of each of the Departments of the Treasury, State, Defense, Justice, and Agriculture, and of the Federal Security Agency. The head of each such department and agency shall designate the representative thereof, and shall also designate an alternate representative. The Chairman of the Committee shall be designated by the President, from among its representative members or as an additional member.

Section 2. It shall be the duty of the said Committee:

(a) To maintain information regarding Federal, State, and local law-enforcement action taken in connection with the illegal sale and use of narcotic drugs and marijuana, and to disseminate such information to Federal, State, and local law enforcement agencies and crime commissions.

(b) To maintain information regarding the character and effects of narcotic drugs and marijuana and the nature and results of drug addiction.

(c) To examine and study problems and developments arising in the administration and enforcement, national and international, of the laws and conventions relating to narcotic drugs and marijuana.

(d) To examine and study the problems of prevention and control of drug addiction and habituation and of the treatment and rehabilitation of addicts and other habituated persons.

(e) To advise the President as to such problems and developments, and to recommend such international, national, State, and local measures, as, in the opinion of the Committee, should be taken with respect to such problems.

(f) To perform such other functions, authorized or permitted by law, with respect to the enforcement of the laws relating to narcotic drugs and marijuana or with respect to other matters within the scope of this section as the President may direct.

Section 3. All executive departments and agencies of the Government are requested to cooperate with the said Committee and to furnish it such available information as it may require for the performance of its duties; but this order shall not be construed as otherwise modifying the functions or responsibilities of any such department or agency.

Harry S. Truman
The White House
November 2, 1951

Source: NARA II, RG 65 DOT Narcotics Files, Box 1, F

See Articles: Drug Abuse and Addiction, Contemporary; Drug Abuse and Addiction, History of; Drug Abuse and Addiction, Sociology of; Narcotics Laws; Truman, Harry S. (Administration of).

1952 PRIMARY DOCUMENT

FBI Memorandum on a Case of Kidnapping, Involuntary Servitude, and Slavery

While rarely used in official records now (though retained in many newspapers), the use of dashes with a first and sometimes last letter to avoid printing a profane word, but leaving no doubt about the word, was common practice for most of the 20th century. The FBI in particular was considered one of the more strait-laced and moralistic federal bodies under Hoover's leadership. The "nolle prosequi" order mentioned is an order to not prosecute.

Cecil Allen Kennedy
John William Davis

Kidnapping; Involuntary Servitude
And Slavery; Obstruction Of Justice;
Conspiracy

In June, 1950, Jesse and Irene Smith*, a negro man and his wife, moved from Tifton, Georgia, to the turpentine farm of Cecil Kennedy at Jasper, Florida, where Jesse had contracted to work as a turpentine chipper. The couple soon became dissatisfied and decided to leave since Jesse did not feel he was making as much money as he should.

They then moved to the turpentine farm of S. P. Johnson at Sycamore, Georgia, on August 3, 1950, without notifying Kennedy that they were leaving and without paying him the approximate sum of $136.50 which they owed him. This sum represented a small grocery account at the turpentine commissary and a state fine which Kennedy had paid for Jesse in order to get him out of jail at Tifton, Georgia, so he could move to the farm.

After the Smiths' departure, Kennedy made efforts personally and through his employees to locate them. Among other things, he telephoned John Blake*, a turpentine farmer at Sycamore, Georgia, to determine whether they were employed by him. Blade advised him that they were not working for him but they were working for S. P. Johnson, another turpentine farmer in Sycamore.

On August 21, 1950, Kennedy and John Davis, one of his turpentine foremen, went to Sycamore in Kennedy's car. They contacted Blake to enlist his aid in locating Johnson's turpentine quarters. Blake agreed to help them and borrowed a pick-up truck from a friend at Ashburn, Georgia, three miles from Sycamore, since Kennedy felt the Smiths might recognize his car and hide.

The three men arrived at the quarters about midnight on August 21. They were then faced with the problem of locating the Smiths, since Blake did not know which house they occupied. They inquired at two houses before learning the correct location. In making these inquiries, either Kennedy or Davis would go to the front of the house, while the other went to the rear. Blake remained in the truck. Residents of the quarters observed pistols in their possession, became alarmed, and scattered to the woods as a rumor spread that the quarters were being "raided."

After locating the exact house which the Smiths occupied, Davis knocked at the front while Kennedy guarded the rear. Jesse Smith heard the knock and called out "Who is there?" Davis replied "Open up and see." Jesse then opened the door and observed Davis standing on the ground with a pistol in his hand. He also saw Kennedy come around from the side of the house with an axe handle in his hand and a pistol protruding from his pocket. Both men cursed and told Jesse to get his clothes ready to go. Jesse asked Kennedy if he would not be satisfied if he paid him the money he owed him. Kennedy answered, "H--- no, I'd rather have you than the d--- money." Kennedy then told Jesse that he would "bust his brains out if he did not get ready to go." Jesse and Irene Smith then loaded their clothing on the back of the pick-up truck. Kennedy told them to get in the back and instructed Davis to stay in the back with them and to shoot Jesse's "brains out" if he tried to run.

Jesse Smith's father was in the kitchen of the house when Kennedy and Davis arrived. Upon determining what was happening, he slipped out of the back door and ran to the residence of a turpentine foreman for Johnson and reported what was happening. This foreman dressed immediately but was unable to get to the quarters before the pick-up truck departed. He called the Sheriff of Ashburn, Georgia, and the Georgia State Patrol at Tifton, Georgia, giving them a description of the truck in order that efforts might be made to intercept it.

However, Kennedy and his party had proceeded to Ashburn, Georgia, where they transferred from the truck to Kennedy's car. Kennedy and Davis then left Blake at his house and proceeded south to Jasper, Florida, stopping en route at Valdosta, Georgia, where Kennedy got something to eat while Davis remained in the car with the Smiths. Just before arrival at the Kennedy farm, they stopped the car on a dirt road and instructed Jesse and Irene to lean over the back of the car. Kennedy then beat them in turn with an axe handle while Davis stood by with his pistol in his hand. Kennedy told them that the beating was to "teach them a lesson."

The Smiths were then taken to the home of a relative in Kennedy's quarters where they were told to spend the remainder of the night. Kennedy instructed Jesse to report to work the following morning under the threat of death. Jesse reported as instructed and was taken to the turpentine woods to commence work. However, instead of working, he slipped out of the woods and hitchhiked back to Georgia.

He arrived in Ashburn, Georgia, in several days and was placed in the county jail by the Sheriff for protective custody. While in jail he was examined by a local physician who reported that the bones of both of his buttocks were completely bruised in an area of five by eight inches on each buttock.

Upon determining that Jesse was in jail at Ashburn and that people in that area were aroused about the matter, Kennedy, accompanied by the Sheriff from Jasper, Florida, returned Irene Smith to Georgia so she could join Jesse. The Smiths then moved back into Johnson's quarters.

Before a Federal Grand Jury at Macon, Georgia, on February 5, 1951, Jesse and Irene Smith both reneged on their signed statements and informed the grand jury that they had freely and voluntarily returned with Kennedy and Davis to Jasper, Florida. As a result of their testimony, the grand jury returned a "no true bill."

Subsequent investigation was conducted to determine whether the Smiths had actually exaggerated the matter at the outset or whether something had occurred which influenced them to testify falsely. Interviews with the smiths failed to satisfactorily resolve the matter. However, it was ascertained that they were living on a farm near Valdosta, Georgia, at the time they were subpoenaed by the grand jury. They called on the owner of this farm for assistance in obtaining transportation to Mason, Georgia. The latter, in turn, called Kennedy at Jasper, Florida, to discuss the matter with him. Kennedy told him that he was going to Macon and would take the Smiths with him.

Accordingly, Kennedy picked up the Smiths at this farm on Sunday, February 4, 1951, and took them to Macon, Georgia. En route he asked Jesse what he intended to tell the grand jury. Jesse replied that he was going to tell the truth. Kennedy then asked him if he saw him with a gun and Jesse told him that he did.

Kennedy then told Jesse that he should not mention that since he would do him a favor a lot quicker than the Federal Government would. He stated that he would cause both of them trouble by mentioning the gun. Jesse understood that this meant that if he caused Kennedy trouble that Kennedy would then cause him trouble.

Upon arrival in Macon, Kennedy gave the three witnesses money for their hotel rooms and arranged to meet them the next day at the bus station after the grand jury hearing. Jesse and Irene discussed the matter that night in their hotel room and decided that in view of Kennedy's conversation they would be safer if they reneged on their original statements. Jesse remarked that it occurred to him that he had to work in the woods alone all day and that it would be easy for someone to kill him and hide his body.

After the hearing before the grand jury, Kennedy returned Jesse and Irene to their home. In addition, he took Jesse's father, who was also a Government witness, to his home at Alapaha, Georgia. He inquired of these witnesses as to what had occurred at the grand jury and was assured that everything appeared to be all right. He asked Jesse what he told the jury and Jesse replied that he did not tell about the guns and did not say that he and Irene were forced to return to Florida. When Kennedy put the Smiths out at their residence, he thanked them for helping him.

Both said that Kennedy told them not to tell anyone that he took them and to say that they had gone by bus or train.

The case was presented to a Federal Grand Jury at Macon, Georgia, a second time on April 13, 1951, at which time three indictments were returned. One charged Kennedy with obstructing justice and intimidating witnesses in the Macon Division of the Middle District of Georgia. The second charged the same violation in the Valdosta Division of the Middle District of Georgia. The third charged Kennedy and Davis in the first count with kidnapping the Smiths, and in the second count charged them with conspiracy to hold the Smiths in a condition of peonage.

Davis was arrested at Jacksonville, Florida, on April 19, 1951, and posted bond in the sum of $3,500 on the same date. Kennedy was arrested at Jacksonville on April 20, 1951, and posted bonds on the same date totally $7,500.

All three indictments were transferred to the Albany Division of the Middle District of Georgia for trial. On October 2, 1951, both Kennedy and Davis entered pleas of nolo contendere at Albany regarding the conspiracy violation. Kennedy was fined $3000 and placed on probation for two years while Davis was fined $500 and placed on probation for two years. An order of nolle prosequi was entered on all other counts and indictments by the Government.

*Fictitious

United States Department Of Justice
Federal Bureau Of Investigation
Washington 25, D. C.
I. C. #7-5829
November 24, 1952

Source: NARA-II, RG 65 FBI, Interesting Case Write-ups, Box 3

See Articles: Kidnapping; Race-Based Crimes; Racism.

1954 PRIMARY DOCUMENT

Dr. J. Robert Oppenheimer Admits Lying During Investigation

In the 1940s, Oppenheimer was one of the key physicists in the Manhattan Project to develop the first nuclear weapons, and has since been called "the father of the atomic bomb." After the war, he became an adviser to the Atomic Energy Commission. Though he had freely disclosed his casual association with communist groups and was closely watched by the FBI during the war, after this letter, he was essentially excommunicated from government work because of the ongoing Red Scare.

Dear Mr. President:
You may be interested in an interim report on the hearing of Dr. Oppenheimer before the Board of which Gordon Gray is the chairman. The case continues to occupy the attention of commentators and columnists and cartoonists, mostly sympathetic to Oppenheimer thus far. The testimony developed in the hearings

has been sensational. It is, of course, being held in strict confidence here.

On Wednesday, Oppenheimer broke and admitted, under oath, that he had lied (the word itself being used a number of times) to security officers of the Army on various occasions; that he had many continuing relations with persons known to him to be Communists while he was engaged on the atomic bomb project and subsequently; and that, as recently as during last December while abroad, he spent two evenings in company with a former academic associate, the same individual who had acted as intermediary between certain Soviet agents and him in 1942 or 1943 in what he characterized as an unsuccessful approach for the delivery of technical information to the Russians.

The hearings are continuing with the presentation of a number of character witnesses. The Counsel who have been in attendance feel that an extremely bad impression toward Oppenheimer has already developed in the minds of the board.

Daily copies of the transcripts are being furnished to the Department of Justice.

Respectfully,
The President
Augusta, Georgia
April 16, 1954

Western Union Telegram, April 19, 1954
ADMIRAL LEWIS STRAUSS
ATOMIC ENERGY COMMISSION

PLEASE FORWARD IF ADMIRAL STRAUSS IS NOT IN WASHINGTON
THANK YOU FOR YOUR INTERIM REPORT THE COPY YOU SENT TO ME HAS BEEN BURNED

DWIGHT D. EISENHOWER

Source: Collection HH-STRAU:
Lewis L. Strauss Papers
Archival Research Catalog (ARC) ID: 187134

See Articles: Eisenhower, Dwight D. (Administration of); Espionage.

1954 PRIMARY DOCUMENT

Communist Control Act

The Red Scare after World War II was a response to very real cold war tensions between the United States and the Soviets. The Communist Control Act, which criminalized the Communist Party of the United States, had considerable support from liberals, who hoped it would clarify the sharp separation between communists and the mainstream left wing. The FBI opposed it out of fear that it would make communists more difficult to monitor. The U.S. Supreme Court did not rule on the constitutionality of the act, which went unenforced.

U.S. Statutes at Large, Public Law 637,
Chp. 886, p. 775-780

AN ACT

To outlaw the Communist Party, to prohibit members of Communist organizations from serving in certain representative capacities, and for other purposes.

Be it enacted by the Senate and House of Representatives of the United States of America in Congress assembled, That this Act may be cited as the "Communist Control Act of 1954."

Findings of Fact
Sec. 2. The Congress hereby finds and declares that the Communist Party of the United States, although purportedly a political party, is in fact an instrumentality of a conspiracy to overthrow the Government of the United States. It constitutes an authoritarian dictatorship within a republic, demanding for itself the rights and privileges accorded to political parties, but denying to all others the liberties guaranteed by the Constitution. Unlike political parties, which evolve their policies and programs through public means, by the reconciliation of a wide variety of individual views, and submit those policies and programs to the electorate at large for approval or disapproval, the policies and

programs of the Communist Party are secretly prescribed for it by the foreign leaders of the world Communist movement. Its members have no part in determining its goals, and are not permitted to voice dissent to party objectives. Unlike members of political parties, members of the Communist Party are recruited for indoctrination with respect to its objectives and methods, and are organized, instructed, and disciplined to carry into action slavishly the assignments given them by their hierarchical chieftains. Unlike political parties, the Communist Party acknowledges no constitutional or statutory limitations upon its conduct or upon that of its members. The Communist Party is relatively small numerically, and gives scant indication of capacity ever to attain its ends by lawful political means. The peril inherent in its operation arises not from its numbers, but from its failure to acknowledge any limitation as to the nature of its activities, and its dedication to the proposition that the present constitutional Government of the United States ultimately must be brought to ruin by any available means, including resort to force and violence. Holding that doctrine, its role as the agency of a hostile foreign power renders its existence a clear present and continuing danger to the security of the United States. It is the means whereby individuals are seduced into the service of the world Communist movement, trained to do its bidding, and directed and controlled in the conspiratorial performance of their revolutionary services. Therefore, the Communist Party should be outlawed.

Proscribed Organizations
Sec. 3. The Communist Party of the United States, or any successors of such party regardless of the assumed name, whose object or purpose is to overthrow the Government of the United States, or the government of any State, Territory, District, or possession thereof, or the government of any political subdivision therein by force and violence, are not entitled to any of the rights, privileges, and immunities attendant upon legal bodies created under the jurisdiction of the laws of the United States or any political subdivision thereof; and whatever rights, privileges, and immunities which have heretofore been granted to said party or any subsidiary organization by reason of the laws of the United States or any political subdivision thereof, are hereby terminated: Provided, however, That nothing in this section shall be construed as amending the Internal Security Act of 1950, as amended.

Sec. 4. Whoever knowingly and willfully becomes or remains a member of (1) the Communist Party, or (2) any other organization having for one of its purposes or objectives the establishment, control conduct, seizure, or overthrow of the Government of the United States, or the government of any State or political subdivision thereof, by the use of force or violence, with knowledge of the purpose or objective of such organization shall be subject to all the provisions and penalties of the Internal Security Act of 1950, as amended, as a member of a "Communist-action" organization.

(b) For the purposes of this section, the term "Communist Party" means the organization now known as the Communist Party of the United States of America, the Communist Party of any State or subdivision thereof, and any unit or subdivision of any such organization, whether or not any change is hereafter made in the name thereof.

Sec. 5. In determining membership or participation in the Communist Party or any other organization defined in this Act, or knowledge of the purpose or objective of such party or organization, the jury, under instructions from the court, shall consider evidence, if presented, as to whether the accused person:

(1) Has been listed to his knowledge as a member in any book or any of the lists, records, correspondence, or any other document of the organization;

(2) Has made financial contribution to the organization in dues, assessments, loans, or in any other form;

(3) Has made himself subject to the discipline of the organization in any form whatsoever;

(4) Has executed orders, plans, or directives of any kind of the organization;

(5) Has acted as an agent, courier, messenger, correspondent, organizer, or in any other capacity in behalf of the organization;

(6) Has conferred with officers or other members of the organization in behalf of any plan or enterprise of the organization;

(7) Has been accepted to his knowledge as an officer or member of the organization or as one to be called upon for services by other officers or members of the organization;

(8) Has written, spoken or in any other way communicated by signal, semaphore, sign, or in any other form of communication orders, directives, or plans of the organization;

(9) Has prepared documents, pamphlets, leaflets, books, or any other type of publication in behalf of the objectives and purposes of the organization;

(10) Has mailed, shipped, circulated, distributed, delivered, or in any other way sent or delivered to others material or propaganda of any kind in behalf of the organization;

(11) Has advised, counseled or in any other way imparted information, suggestions, recommendations to officers or members of the organization or to anyone else in behalf of the objectives of the organization;

(12) Has indicated by word, action, conduct, writing or in any other way a willingness to carry out in any manner and to any degree the plans, designs, objectives, or purposes of the organization;

(13) Has in any other way participated in the activities, planning, actions, objectives, or purposes of the organization;

(14) The enumeration of the above subjects of evidence on membership or participation in the Communist Party or any other organization as above defined, shall not limit the inquiry into and consideration of any other subject of evidence on membership and participation as herein stated.

Subversive Activities Control Act Amendment

Sec. 6. Subsection 5 (a) (1) of the Subversive Activities Control Act of 1950 (50 U.S.C. 784) is amended by striking out the period at the end thereof and inserting lieu thereof a semicolon and the following: "or

"(E) to hold office or employment with any labor organization, as that term is defined in section 2 (5) of the National Labor Relations Act, as amended (29 U. S. C. 152), or to represent any employer in any matter or proceeding arising or pending under that Act."

Communist-Infiltrated Organizations

Sec. 7. (a) Section 3 of the Subversive Activities Control Act of 1950 (50 U. S. C. 782) is amended by inserting, immediately after paragraph (4) thereof, the following new paragraph:

"(4A) The term 'Communist-infiltrated organization' means any organization in the United States (other than a Communist-action organization or a Communist-front organization) which (A) is substantially directed, dominated, or controlled by an individual or individuals who are, or who within three years have been actively engaged in, giving aid or support to a Communist-action organization, a Communist foreign government, or the world Communist movement referred to in section 2 of this title, and (B) is serving, or within three years has served, as a means for (i) the giving of aid or support to any such organization, government, or movement, or (ii) the impairment of the military strength of the United States or its industrial capacity to furnish logistical or other material support required by its Armed Forces: Provided, however, That any labor organization which is an affiliate in good standing of a national federation or other labor organization whose policies and activities have been directed to opposing Communist organizations, any Communist foreign government, or the world Communist movement, shall be presumed prima facie not to be a 'Communist-infiltrated organization.'"

(b) Paragraph (5) of such section is amended to read as follows:

"(5) The term 'Communist organization' means any Communist-action organization, Communist-front organization, or Communist-infiltrated organization."

(c) Subsections 5 (c) and 6 (c) of such Act are repealed.

Sec. 8. (a) Section 10 of such Act (50 U. S. C. 789) is amended by inserting, immediately after the words "final order of the Board requiring it to register under section 7," the words "or determining that it is a Communist-infiltrated organization."

(b) Subsections (a) and (b) of section 11 of such Act (50 U. S. C. 790) are amended by inserting immediately preceding the period at the end of each such subsection, the following: "or determining that it is a Communist-infiltrated organization."

Sec. 9. (a) Subsection 12 (e) of such Act (50 U. S. C. 791) is amended by:

(1) striking out the period at the end thereof and inserting in lieu thereof a semicolon and the word "and"; and

(2) inserting at the end thereof the following new paragraph:

"(3) upon any application made under subsection (a) or subsection (b) of section 13A of this title, to determine whether any organization is a Communist-infiltrated organization."

(b) The section caption to section 13 of such Act (50 U. S. C. 792) is amended to read as follows: "Registration Proceedings before the Board."

Sec. 10. Such Act is amended by inserting, immediately after section 13 thereof, the following new section:

Proceedings with Respect to Communist-Infiltrated Organizations

"Sec. 13A. (a) Whenever the Attorney General has reason to believe that any organization is a Communist-infiltrated organization, he may file with the Board and serve upon such organization a petition for a determination that such organization is a Communist-infiltrated organization. In any proceeding so instituted, two or more affiliated organizations may be named as joint respondents. Whenever any such petition is accompanied by a certificate of the Attorney General to the effect that the proceeding so instituted is one of exceptional public importance, such proceeding shall be set for hearing at the earliest possible time and all proceedings therein before the Board or any court shall be expedited to the greatest practicable extent.

"(b) Any organization which has been determined under this section to be a Communist-infiltrated organization may, within six months after such determination, file with the Board and serve upon the Attorney General a petition for a determination that such organization no longer is a Communist-infiltrated organization. "(c) Each such petition shall be verified under oath, and shall contain a statement of the facts relied upon in support thereof. Upon the filing of any such petition, the Board shall serve upon each party to such proceeding a notice specifying the time and place for hearing upon such petition. No such hearing shall be conducted within twenty days after the service of such notice.

"(d) The provisions of subsections (c) and (d) of section 13 shall apply to hearings conducted under this section, except that upon the failure of any organization named as a party in any petition filed by or duly served upon it pursuant to this section to appear at any hearing upon such petition, the Board may conduct such hearing in the absence of such organization and may enter such order under this section as the Board shall determine to be warranted by evidence presented at such hearing. "(e) In determining whether any organization is a Communist-infiltrated organization, the Board shall consider: "(1) to what extent, if any, the effective management of the affairs of such organization is conducted by one or more individuals who are, or within two years have been, (A) members, agents, or representatives of any Communist organization, and Communist foreign government, or the world Communist movement referred to in section 2 of this title, with knowledge of the nature and purpose thereof, or (B) engaged in giving aid or support to any such organization, government, or movement with knowledge of the nature and purpose thereof; "(2) to what extent, if any, the policies of such organization are, or within three years have been, formulated and carried out pursuant to the direction or advice of any member, agent or representative of any such organization, government, or movement;

"(3) to what extent, if any, the personnel and resources of such organization are, or within three years have been, used to further or promote the objectives of any such Communist organization, government, or movement;

"(4) to what extent, if any, such organization within three years has received from, or furnished to or for the use of, any such Communist organization, government, or movement any funds or other material assistance;

"(5) to what extent, if any, such organization is, or within three years has been, affiliated in any way with any such Communist organization, government, or movement;

"(6) to what extent, if any, the affiliation of such organization, or of any individual or individuals who are members thereof or who manage its affairs, with any such Communist organization, government, or movement is concealed from or is not disclosed to the membership of such organization; and

"(7) to what extent, if any, such organization or any of its members or managers are, or within three years have been, knowingly engaged:

"(A) in any conduct punishable under section 4 or 15 of this Act or under chapter 37, 105, or 115 of title 18 of the United States Code; or

"(B) with intent to impair the military strength of the United States or its industrial capacity to furnish logistical or other support required by its armed forces, in any activity resulting in or contributing to any such impairment.

"(f) After hearing upon any petition filed under this section, the Board shall (1) make a support in writing in which it shall state its findings as to the facts and its conclusions with respect to the issues presented by such petition, (2) enter its order granting or denying the determination sought by such petition, and (3) serve upon each party to the proceeding a copy of such order. Any order granting any determination on the question whether any organization is a Communist-infiltrated organization shall become final as provided in section 14 (b) of this Act.

"(g) When any order has been entered by the Board under this section with respect to any labor organization or employer (as these terms are defined by section 2 of the National Labor Relations Act, as amended, and which are organizations within the meaning of section 3 of the Subversive Activities Control Act of 1950), the Board shall serve a true and correct copy of such order upon the National Labor Relations Board and shall publish in the Federal Register a statement of the substance of such order and its effective date.

"(h) When there is in effect a final order of the Board determining that any such labor organization is a Communist-action organization, a Communist-front organization, or a Communist-infiltrated organization, such labor organization shall be ineligible to:

"(1) act as representative of any employee within the meaning or for the purposes of section 7 of the National Labor Relations Act, as amended (29 U.S.C. 157);

"(2) serve as an exclusive representative of employees of any bargaining unit under section 9 of such Act, as amended (29 U.S.C. 159);

"(3) make, or obtain any hearing upon, any charge under section 10 of such Act (29 U.S.C. 160); or

"(4) exercise any other right or privilege, or receive any other benefit, substantive or procedural, provided by such Act for labor organizations.

"(i) When an order of the Board determining that any such labor organization is a Communist-infiltrated organization has become final, and such labor organization theretofore has been certified under the National Labor Relations Act, as amended, as a representative of employees in any bargaining unit:

"(1) a question of representation affecting commerce, within the meaning of section 9 (c) of such Act, shall be deemed to exist with respect to such bargaining unit; and

"(2) the National Labor Relations Board, upon petition of not less than 20 per centum of the employees in such bargaining unit or any person or persons acting in their behalf, shall under section 9 of such Act (notwithstanding any limitation of time contained therein) direct elections in such bargaining unit or any subdivision thereof (A) for the selection of a representative thereof for collective bargaining purposes, and (B) to determine whether the employees thereof desire to rescind any authority previously granted to such labor organization to enter into any agreement with their employer pursuant to section 8 (a) (3) (ii) of such Act.

"(j) When there is in effect a final order of the Board determining that any such employer is a Communist-infiltrated organization, such employer shall be ineligible to:

"(1) file any petition for an election under section 9 of the National Labor Relations Act, as amended (29 U.S.C. 157), or participate in any proceeding under such section; or

"(2) make or obtain any hearing upon any charge under section 10 of such Act (29 U.S.C. 160); or

"(3) exercise any other right or privilege or receive any other benefit, substantive or procedural, provided by such Act for employers."

Sec. 11. Subsections (a) and (b) of section 14 of such Act (50 U.S.C. 793) are amended by inserting in each such subsection, immediately after the words "section 13," a comma and the following: "or subsection (f) of section 13A."

Sec. 12. If any provision of this title or the application thereof to any person or circumstances is held invalid, the remainder of the title, and the application of such provisions to other persons or circumstances, shall not be affected thereby.

Approved August 24, 1954, 9:40 a.m., M.S.T.

Source: U.S. Statutes at Large, Public Law 637

See Articles: Espionage; Internal Security Act of 1950; Political Crimes, History of; Political Dissidents.

1954 PRIMARY DOCUMENT

The Comic Book Code of 1954

Other than the most popular titles, superhero comics declined after World War II, and horror, crime, and romance comics eclipsed them, mirroring the genres found in pulp magazines. Psychologist Fredric Wertham published Seduction of the Innocent *in 1948, and it became the* Reefer Madness *of comics, alleging that comics would warp the emotional well-being and sexuality of children and young people. Just as television had self-regulated, so did comic book publishers.*

Code Of The Comics Magazine Association Of America, Inc.

Adopted October 26, 1954

Preamble

The comic-book medium, having come of age on the American cultural scene, must measure up to its responsibilities.

Constantly improving techniques and higher standards go hand in hand with these responsibilities.

To make a positive contribution to contemporary life, the industry must seek new areas for developing sound, wholesome entertainment. The people responsible for writing, drawing, printing, publishing, and selling comic books have done a commendable job in the past, and have been striving toward this goal.

Their record of progress and continuing improvement compares favorably with other media in the communications industry. An outstanding example is the development of comic books as a unique and effective tool for instruction and education. Comic books have also made their contribution in the field of letters and criticism of contemporary life.

In keeping with the American tradition, the members of this industry will and must continue to work together in the future.

In the same tradition, members of the industry must see to it that gains made in this medium are not lost and that violations of standards of good taste, which might tend toward corruption of the comic book as an instructive and wholesome form of entertainment, will be eliminated.

Therefore, the Comics Magazine Association of America, Inc. has adopted this code, and placed strong powers of enforcement in the hands of an independent code authority.

Further, members of the association have endorsed the purpose and spirit of this code as a vital instrument to the growth of the industry.

To this end, they have pledged themselves to conscientiously adhere to its principles and to abide by all decisions based on the code made by the administrator.

They are confident that this positive and forthright statement will provide an effective bulwark for the protection and enhancement of the American reading public, and that it will become a landmark in the history of self-regulation for the entire communications industry.

Code For Editorial Matter

General standards—Part A

(1) Crimes shall never be presented in such a way as to create sympathy for the criminal, to promote distrust of the forces of law and justice, or to inspire others with a desire to imitate criminals.

(2) No comics shall explicitly present the unique details and methods of a crime.

(3) Policemen, judges, Government officials and respected institutions shall never be presented in such a way as to create disrespect for established authority.

(4) If crime is depicted it shall be as a sordid and unpleasant activity.

(5) Criminals shall not be presented so as to be rendered glamorous or to occupy a position which creates a desire for emulation.

(6) In every instance good shall triumph over evil and the criminal punished for his misdeeds.

(7) Scenes of excessive violence shall be prohibited. Scenes of brutal torture, excessive and unnecessary knife and gunplay, physical agony, gory and gruesome crime shall be eliminated.

(8) No unique or unusual methods of concealing weapons shall be shown.

(9) Instances of law-enforcement officers dying as a result of a criminal's activities should be discouraged.

(10) The crime of kidnapping shall never be portrayed in any detail, nor shall any profit accrue to the abductor or kidnaper. The criminal or the kidnaper must be punished in every case.

(11) The letters of the word "crime" on a comics-magazine cover shall never be appreciably greater in dimension than the other words contained in the title. The word "crime" shall never appear alone on a cover.

(12) Restraint in the use of the word "crime" in titles or subtitles shall be exercised.

General standards—Part B

(1) No comic magazine shall use the word horror or terror in its title.

(2) All scenes of horror, excessive bloodshed, gory or gruesome crimes, depravity, lust, sadism, masochism shall not be permitted.

(3) All lurid, unsavory, gruesome illustrations shall be eliminated.

(4) Inclusion of stories dealing with evil shall be used or shall be published only where the intent is to illustrate a moral issue and in no case shall evil be presented alluringly, nor so as to injure the sensibilities of the reader.

(5) Scenes dealing with, or instruments associated with walking dead, torture, vampires and vampirism, ghouls, cannibalism, and werewolfism are prohibited.

General standards—Part C

All elements or techniques not specifically mentioned herein, but which are contrary to the spirit and intent of the code, and are considered violations of good taste or decency, shall be prohibited.

Dialogue

(1) Profanity, obscenity, smut, vulgarity, or words or symbols which have acquired undesirable meanings are forbidden.

(2) Special precautions to avoid references to physical afflictions or deformities shall be taken.

(3) Although slang and colloquialisms are acceptable, excessive use should be discouraged and, wherever possible, good grammar shall be employed.

Religion

(1) Ridicule or attack on any religious or racial group is never permissible.

Costume

(1) Nudity in any form is prohibited, as is indecent or undue exposure.

(2) Suggestive and salacious illustration or suggestive posture is unacceptable.

(3) All characters shall be depicted in dress reasonably acceptable to society.

(4) Females shall be drawn realistically without exaggeration of any physical qualities.

NOTE.—It should be recognized that all prohibitions dealing with costume, dialog, or artwork applies as specifically to the cover of a comic magazine as they do to the contents.

Marriage and sex

(1) Divorce shall not be treated humorously nor represented as desirable.

(2) Illicit sex relations are neither to be hinted at nor portrayed. Violent love scenes as well as sexual abnormalities are unacceptable.

(3) Respect for parents, the moral code, and for honorable behavior shall be fostered. A sympathetic understanding of the problems of love is not a license for morbid distortion.

(4) The treatment of live-romance stories shall emphasize the value of the home and the sanctity of marriage.

(5) Passion or romantic interest shall never be treated in such a way as to stimulate the lower and baser emotions.

(6) Seduction and rape shall never be shown or suggested.

(7) Sex perversion or any inference to same is strictly forbidden.

Code For Advertising Matter

These regulations are applicable to all magazines published by members of the Comics Magazine Association of America, Inc. Good taste shall be the guiding principle in the acceptance of advertising.

(1) Liquor and tobacco advertising is not acceptable.

(2) Advertisement of sex or sex instruction books are unacceptable.

(3) The sale of picture postcards, "pinups," "art studies," or any other reproduction of nude or seminude figures is prohibited.

(4) Advertising for the sale of knives or realistic gun facsimiles is prohibited.

(5) Advertising for the sale of fireworks is prohibited.

(6) Advertising dealing with the sale of gambling equipment or printed matter dealing with gambling shall not be accepted.

(7) Nudity with meretricious purpose and salacious postures shall not be permitted in the advertising of any product; clothed figures shall never be presented in such a way as to be offensive or contrary to good taste or morals.

(8) To the best of his ability, each publisher shall ascertain that all statements made in advertisements conform to fact and avoid misrepresentation.

(9) Advertisement of medical, health, or toiletry products of questionable nature are to be rejected. Advertisements for medical, health, or toiletry products endorsed by the American Medical Association, or the American Dental Association, shall be deemed acceptable if they conform with all other conditions of the Advertising Code.

Sources: Senate Committee on the Judiciary. *Comic Books and Juvenile Delinquency, Interim Report, 1955*. Washington, DC: United States Government Printing Office, 1955; and http://historymatters.gmu.edu/d/6543

See Articles: Morality; Obscenity; Obscenity Laws.

1954 PRIMARY DOCUMENT

Senate Resolution 301: Censure of Senator Joseph McCarthy

McCarthy is emblematic for the Red Scare of the 1950s. As it had many inciters, it would have occurred without him, but McCarthy became the public face of accusing fellow Americans of communist subversion. As early as 1950, he produced what he claimed was a list of known communists in the State Department, and this fear of communist infiltration became known as McCarthyism. When he was finally censured, it was for only two of the 46 charges listed by a special committee.

United States Senate Resolution

Resolved, That the Senator from Wisconsin, Mr. McCarthy, failed to cooperate with the Subcommittee on Privileges and Elections of the Senate Committee on Rules and Administration in clearing up matters referred to that subcommittee which concerned his conduct as a Senator and affected the honor of the Senate and, instead, repeatedly abused the subcommittee and its members who were trying to carry out assigned duties, thereby obstructing the constitutional processes of the Senate, and that this conduct of the Senator from Wisconsin, Mr. McCarthy, is contrary to senatorial traditions and is hereby condemned.

Sec 2. The Senator from Wisconsin, Mr. McCarthy, in writing to the chairman of the Select Committee to Study Censure Charges (Mr. Watkins) after the Select Committee had issued its report and before the report was presented to the Senate charging three members of the Select Committee with "deliberate deception" and "fraud" for failure to disqualify themselves; in stating to the press on November 4, 1954, that the special Senate session that was to begin November 8, 1954, was a "lynch-party"; in repeatedly describing this special Senate session as a "lynch bee" in a nationwide television and radio show on November 7, 1954; in stating to the public press on November 13, 1954, that the chairman of the Select Committee (Mr. Watkins) was guilty of "the most unusual, most cowardly things I've ever heard of" and stating further: "I expected he would be afraid to answer the questions, but didn't think he'd be stupid enough to make a public statement"; and in characterizing the said committee as the "unwitting handmaiden," "involuntary agent" and "attorneys-in-fact" of the Communist Party and in charging that the said committee in writing its report "imitated Communist methods — that it distorted, misrepresented, and omitted in its effort to manufacture a plausible rationalization" in support of its recommendations to the Senate, which characterizations and charges were contained in a statement released to the press and inserted in the Congressional Record of November 10, 1954, acted contrary to senatorial ethics and tended to bring the Senate into dishonor and disrepute, to obstruct the constitutional processes of the Senate, and to impair its dignity; and such conduct is hereby condemned.

Source: http://patriotpost.us/document/
senate-resolution-301-censure-of-
senator-joseph-mccarthy

See Articles: Eisenhower, Dwight D. (Administration of); McCarthy, Joseph.

1955
PRIMARY DOCUMENT

Congressional Report on Juvenile Delinquency

The only overt effect of the Senate Subcommittee on Juvenile Delinquency's investigation was on comic book publishers, which by the end of the decade had returned their focus to superheroes and resisted producing comic books aimed at adults until the 1980s. Nevertheless, the threat not only of government censorship, but also (more realistically) of negative publicity, kept a tight leash on entertainment for a long time.

84TH CONGRESS
1st Session Senate

Juvenile Delinquency

Interim Report of the Subcommittee of the
Committee On The Judiciary to Study
Juvenile Delinquency in the United States
United States Senate
Eighty-Third Congress

Second Session
Pursuant To
S. Res. 89 and S. Res. 190
(83rd Congress, 1st and 2nd Session)

I. Objectives Of The Subcommittee

Immediately after its organization, and pursuant to the directive of Senate Resolution 89, the subcommittee set for its objectives the following:

(a) Factfinding, to determine the extent, causes, character and contributing factors with respect to juvenile delinquency; the adequacy of existing treatment and preventive measures; the efficacy of existing Federal laws relating to juvenile delinquents and youthful offenders, including those laws relating to narcotic addiction; and the manner and effects of Federal sentencing procedures;

(b) Focusing public attention, through the factfinding process, upon existing problems, including the use of narcotics, relating to juvenile delinquency and the commission of offenses by youths throughout the country; and

(c) Recommending, on the basis of the facts found, such measures and action as the subcommittee may determine to be needed to prevent juvenile delinquency and the commission of criminal offenses by youths, and to rehabilitate those children and youths who have already embarked upon delinquent or criminal careers or who have become narcotic addicts.

The subcommittee made investigations on the community level in every major geographical section to determine the total implications of the nationwide scope of the problem. At these community hearings, the subcommittee attempted to develop information within the community relative to the following:

(a) The extent and character of juvenile delinquency within the community.

(b) The existence, if any, of organized juvenile gangs; the extent to which these gangs operate, and the activities in which they are engaged.

(c) The extent of the use of narcotics and synthetic drugs among juveniles in the community.

(d) The existence in the community of living conditions which contribute to delinquency with particular attention to such conditions in relation to children of migratory workers and other socially disadvantaged groups of children.

(e) The use of alcoholic beverages by juveniles contrary to law, and the effect it may have upon their delinquency.

(f) The existence in the community of adult exploitation of juveniles by recruiting them into crime, by encouraging them to gamble, by directing their criminal activities, or by profiting from their criminal exploits, i.e. fencing stolen goods by juveniles, and white slavery.

(g) The extent to which communities have developed successful programs for the prevention of juvenile delinquency and for the rehabilitation of delinquent children and youths, including juvenile courts and probation procedures, detention facilities, etc.

Methods of investigation utilized have varied according to subject matter. In broad terms, the subcommittee has conducted three types of investigations—community investigations, investigations of special problems, and investigations into relevant Federal programs.

In advance of each community hearing an investigating or factfinding team was sent into the community. The aim of the team was to determine the extent, causes, character, and contributing factors with respect to juvenile delinquency and to arrange for the presentation of these data in a logical and forceful manner at the hearing. Team members contacted and worked with community officials and agencies. They also made firsthand observations in the community.

It should be emphasized that the subcommittee staff did not conduct surveys of community programs in the fields of mental health, recreation, social welfare, and education. They did, however, through the aid of local persons secure a general picture of the adequacy of existing treatment and preventive measures relating to juvenile delinquency. These materials were then organized for presentation at subcommittee hearings.

Investigations of both special problems and the various Federal programs concerned with juvenile delinquency involved the collection and analysis of materials from throughout the United States. These were collected by use of questionnaires and through field investigations and observations conducted by various members of the subcommittee staff.

II. The National Problem

Size, Seriousness, And Other Characteristics
During its 17 months' work, the subcommittee has tried to assemble a complete picture of juvenile delinquency—its extent, nature, and causes—on a nationwide basis. To this end, some 3,000 letters of inquiry were directed to law-enforcement officials, judges, educators, crime commissions, and welfare and mental-health agencies throughout the country. Thousands of replies, including hundreds of unsolicited letters, many accompanied by copies of detailed studies, were received from persons and organizations interested in the problems and located in communities of every size. The subcommittee also scheduled hearings designed to secure a broad, national view of the problem. Persons invited to testify at these hearings represented a variety of backgrounds and points of view, and included a large number who had made outstanding contributions to the advancement of knowledge regarding the causes of juvenile delinquency and methods through which it may be prevented. Also included were individuals who had given noteworthy leadership in the development of programs designed to rehabilitate juvenile delinquents and youthful offenders.

Increase In Number
Following the end of World War II, the number of juvenile delinquents decreased until, in 1948, there were less than 300,000 appearing annually before the juvenile courts. Then, in 1949, with the stresses and strains of the cold war and the Korean hostilities, juvenile delinquency again began to rise. Since 1948, a steadily increasing number of American boys and girls have become involved in delinquency each year. The best available figures on the subject on a national basis, are those compiled by the Children's Bureau, based on cases handled by juvenile courts. The stream of children through the Nation's juvenile courts grew from 300,000 in 1948 to 435,000 in 1953, and only 10 percent of this increase can possibly be attributed to the enlarged juvenile population. (The actual number of children who have broken the law, including those whose cases were disposed of without court action, probably exceeds one million and a quarter. This figure assumes that there are at least three juvenile offenders brought to the attention of the police for every child actually brought before the juvenile courts.) By 1960, this country will have a further enlarged population, age 10 through 17 years. If the rate of juvenile delinquency continues to mount at the rate experienced during the past 5 years, the number of boys and girls going through the juvenile courts annually may well total 785,000 by that date.

Present Efforts To Prevent Delinquency
In testimony before the subcommittee it was estimated that unless the disgraceful spiraling increase in juvenile crime can be stopped, instead of 1,250,000 between the ages of 10 and 17 now getting into trouble with the police, we shall have 1,700,000 such youngsters in the year 1960. The stakes in the fight to prevent delinquency are therefore great. But even if we should somehow succeed in arresting the increase in rate of juvenile delinquency, we cannot afford to become complacent. A million and a quarter youngsters a year getting into trouble with the police is many, many more than this Nation can afford. The challenge is to prevent as many as possible of these children from taking the first wrong turn on the road to waywardness and to somehow turn those who do back onto the right road.

The fight against juvenile delinquency must be a two-pronged fight. We must devote sufficient energy and resources not just to rehabilitate boys and girls after they get into trouble but also to prevent their getting into trouble in the first place.

It must be emphasized that just as juvenile delinquency has many and varied causes, so its prevention must encompass a myriad of different types of programs and attacks. But of one thing we can be quite certain. If this Nation continues its present feeble attempts to prevent juvenile delinquency, we can be certain that the harvest we will reap in later years will be a bigger and tougher crop of juvenile delinquents and youthful and adult criminals, ultimately requiring more and more prisons.

Forms Of The Problem
The National Auto Theft Association in Chicago told the subcommittee that, from 1948 on, the number of automobiles stolen by persons under 17 years of age has steadily risen. In 1952, 70 percent of all automobiles stolen were stolen by boys or girls under 17 years of age. Such thefts involve a loss of millions of dollars to the automobile owners of the Nation.

During 1952, 37 percent of all persons arrested for robberies were under 21 years of age. This young age group accounted for 47 percent of all arrests made for larceny, 68 percent of those for auto theft, and even 35 percent of all arrests for rape.

One of the most sinister of all delinquency problems is that of narcotic addiction among children. The subcommittee was told that there are today an estimated 7,500 juvenile addicts in New York City alone; in Los Angeles County, 8 percent of the children brought before juvenile courts have had contact with narcotics; in Denver it was found that 80 to 90 percent of all Spanish American boys brought into juvenile courts have had such contact; in Oklahoma City, approximately 250 children between 13 and 18 years of age were regularly addicted to drugs, and in Iowa, investigations revealed that 25 percent of the girls admitted to the State training school for girls habitually used marijuana.

The problem of the use of narcotics and dangerous drugs by juveniles is discussed in detail in a later section of this report. Here it will suffice to note that although some of the experts appearing before the subcommittee disagreed about the seriousness of the problem, the total evidence available indicates that there has been a large increase in drug violations by juveniles during the past 5 years in most of our urban centers.

Increase In Seriousness Of Acts In Lower Age Groups
The growing seriousness of the problem of juvenile delinquency is also underscored by the fact that an increasing number of younger boys and girls are committing serious offenses. During each successive year since 1948, for example, a larger number of persons under 18 years of age have been involved in such offenses as burglaries, robberies, and automobile thefts.

Delinquency Increased In Nonurban Areas
Heretofore, juvenile delinquency has been thought of as a big-city problem, and indeed it does achieve its most acute form in large metropolitan areas. It should be noted, however, that whereas juvenile delinquency increased 29 percent nationwide between 1948 and 1952, the number of juvenile offenders appearing in court serving populations of less than 100,000 increased 41 percent.

An increase both in the number of boys and girls committing offenses and in the severity of these offenses has been noted in every region of the United States. Although many individual communities seem excepted, communities reporting such increases range in character from rural and semirural to large urban centers.

Neither are particular forms of delinquent conduct peculiar to one type of community or to any one geographical region. Juvenile drug addiction would seem to represent the only exception to this rule, in that it is limited to communities where there is substantial traffic in illicit drugs. Gangs, commonly considered a big city phenomenon, for example, also appear in communities relatively small in size. While the pattern of juvenile delinquency varies from community to community, these differences do not appear to be directly related to size, wealth, or other obvious differentials.

Delinquency Exists In All Economic Groups
Although physically deteriorated and socially disorganized neighborhoods, usually termed "slum areas," contribute disproportionately

to the delinquency caseloads of police and juvenile courts, economical well-to-do communities also produce many juvenile delinquents. As a matter of fact, certain forms of delinquent conduct appear more prevalent in the latter type of neighborhoods. An investigation into the widespread use of synthetic drugs by juveniles in Oklahoma City revealed that not one of the juveniles involved came from the so-called wrong side of the tracks.

It is also reasonable to believe, and it was so testified, that in many instances delinquents from better neighborhoods are less likely to come to the attention of the police and courts. School authorities may be more inclined to permit parents of means and status to work out the problems of their children, for example, than parents with no financial ability and standing. The children of parents with available funds may be sent quietly to private psychiatrists or to boarding schools and consequently, the transgressions of those children are not likely to be presented to the juvenile court.

III. Special Problems

Juvenile Delinquency Among Indian Children
The subcommittee, over a period of many months, received numerous communications from Indian leaders, public officials and the general public expressing concern over juvenile delinquency problems on Indian reservations. As a result, the subcommittee decided to probe the problem of juvenile delinquency among Indians, and the procedures for handling such delinquents, including the adequacy of existing statutes and facilities.

Time did not permit a full investigation of juvenile delinquency among all Indian children. This report, therefore, relates only to those reservations from which substantial data were received. Scattered and inconclusive data received by the subcommittee from reservations not fully explored suggest that the situation on certain reservations may be far different from that revealed in this report as to living conditions, income levels, law and order, education, health, welfare, assimilation, and other factors related to juvenile delinquency.

Neither is it possible in this brief summary to report fully on some of the differences among those reservations from which substantial data were secured and which, therefore, are included in the report. This report describes the general prevailing situation as the record reveals it and includes a few illustrations of some marked differences prevailing among the reservations included. For example, in the field of education, the report points out that the average daily attendance of Indian children has improved greatly. This was testified to in the North Dakota hearing. However, it is a well-known fact that many of the Navaho children in Arizona are not provided any school at the present time and even fewer attended school as little as 6 years ago. Further investigations should be made and hearings held in additional geographical areas to complete the picture.

Source: NARA-II, RG 65, DOT, Narcotics Files, Box 2 F: Senate Comm. Juvenile Delinquency

See Articles: Gangs, Contemporary; Gangs, History of; Gangs, Sociology of; Juvenile Delinquency, History of; Juvenile Delinquency, Sociology of.

1955 PRIMARY DOCUMENT

Senate Subcommittee's Interim Report on Television and Juvenile Delinquency

This account of the Code of Practices for Television Broadcasters, a self-regulatory standards code used until the 1990s, comes from the 1954 to 1955 hearings of the Senate Subcommittee to Investigate Juvenile Delinquency. During

the 1950s, covalent bonds began to be created between the public dialogue about wayward youth and the public concern for the entertainment that young people were exposed to, whether that entertainment was television, comic books or, eventually, video games.

The National Association of Radio and Television Broadcasters

The National Association of Radio and Television Broadcasters (formerly known as the National Association of Broadcasters) is a trade association of the radio and television industry, organized in 1923. The NARTB provides industry services relating to labor, public and government relations, engineering, research and legal developments. On May 1, 1955, membership included 1,234 AM (amplitude modulation) stations, 327 FM (frequency modulation) stations and 3 national radio networks, Columbia Broadcasting System, Mutual Broadcasting System, and National Broadcasting Co., Inc. On the television side, the National Association of Radio and Television Broadcasters had 267 television stations as members and all 4 national television networks, American Broadcasting Co., Columbia Broadcasting System, DuMont Television Network and the National Broadcasting Co., Inc....

Activities leading to the adoption of a code for television were begun simultaneously with the licensing of stations. The experience of many years of operation in radio broadcasting pointed to the desirability of early agreement upon standards of programs. The NARTB Television Code became effective March 1, 1952. Subscribers are entitled to display a seal of good practice signifying compliance with code standards.

The code is printed in booklet form and includes a preamble, section on advancement of education and culture, community responsibility, treatment of news and public events, controversial public issues, political telecasts, religious programs, presentation of advertising. Several pages are devoted to regulations dealing with acceptability of program material, including such items as:

(o) The presentation of cruelty, greed and selfishness as worthy motivations is to be avoided.

(q) Criminality shall be presented as undesirable and unsympathetic. The condoning of crime and the treatment of the commission of crime in a frivolous, cynical, or callous manner is unacceptable.

(r) The presentation of techniques of crime in such detail as to invite imitation shall be avoided.

(s) The use of horror for its own sake will be eliminated; the use of visual or aural effects which would shock or alarm the viewer, and the detailed presentation of brutality or physical agony by sight or by sound are not permissible.

(t) Law enforcement shall be upheld, and the officers of the law are to be portrayed with respect and dignity.

(u) The presentation of murder or revenge as a motive for murder shall not be presented as justifiable.

(x) The appearance or dramatization of such persons featured in actual crime news will be permitted only in such light as to aid law enforcement or to report the news event.

Responsibility toward children is accorded separate attention in the code. This section is quoted in its entirety as follows:

1. The education of children involves giving them a sense of the world at large. Crime, violence, and sex are a part of the world they will be called upon to meet, and a certain amount of proper presentation of such is helpful in orienting the child to his surroundings. However, violence and illicit sex shall not be presented in an attractive manner, nor to an extent such as will lead a child to believe that they play a greater part in life than they do. They should not be presented, without indications of the resultant retribution and punishment.
2. It is not enough that only those programs which are intended for viewing by children shall be suitable to the young and immature. Television is responsible for insuring that programs of all sorts which

occur during the times of day when children may normally be expected to have the opportunity of viewing television shall exercise care in the following regards:

(a) In affording opportunities for cultural growth as well as for wholesome entertainment.

(b) In developing programs to foster and promote the commonly accepted moral, social, and ethical ideals characteristic of American life.

(c) In reflecting respect for parents, for honorable behavior, and for the constituted authorities of the American community.

(d) In eliminating reference to kidnapping of children or threats of kidnapping.

(e) In avoiding material which is excessively violent or would create morbid suspense, or other undesirable reactions in children.

(f) In exercising particular restraint and care in crime or mystery episodes involving children or minors.

Thad H. Brown, Jr., director of television, NARTB, testified as a witness before a subcommittee of the Committee on Interstate and Foreign Commerce of the House of Representatives on September 16, 1952, regarding the television code which had then been in operation for 6 months. He said:

Why was this action taken? Because, for one thing, there was a sense of watchful waiting on behalf of Congress and on behalf of accountable and responsible organizations. Quite frankly, the shadow of incipient censorship by Government regulation was evident * * * In the formative days of the movies, six States apparently found it necessary and desirable to establish motion picture censorship boards. In 1926, the motion picture industry initiated its first code. Since that time, not one additional State has established a board to censor movies. On the other hand, and this is interesting, the six boards established prior to the initiation of the movie code are still in existence * * * Both by the program standards committee and by the entire television membership of the association, there was clearly apparent to an observer a voluntary sense of responsibility shown by the pioneer telecasters (and there were only 108 at this time) to develop and continue insofar as was comparatively possible, a wholesome stature for the commercial television broadcast industry in the years to come. . . .

Ralph Hardy, then vice president in charge of Government relations of the NARTB, testified in June 1954, before the Subcommittee To Investigate Juvenile Delinquency with regard to the method devised "for assuring reasonable observance of the code provisions." A television code review board (consisting of 5 members who are appointed by the president of the NARTB to serve 2-year terms without compensation) is responsible for the administration, interpretation, and enforcement of the code. He pointed out that this code review board meets at least four times a year for considering complaints received by the NARTB concerning specific programs, series of programs, or advertising practices on the television stations or networks.

Harold E. Fellows, president and chairman of the board of directors of the NARTB, testified on October 20, 1954, that the television code review board may file charges against a station before the television board of directors. Upon an affirmative two-thirds vote, the board of directors may void, remove, or temporarily suspend a subscription and the authority to further identify itself as a code station through the seal of good practice.

Since subscribers have responded immediately to code review board suggestions, no such charges have been filed before the board of directors . . .

Appendix

The Television Code Of The National Association Of Radio And Television Broadcasters

(Effective March 1, 1952; second edition March 1954)

(By the National Association of Radio and Television Broadcasters, Washington, D.C.)

Preamble

Television is seen and heard in every type of American home. These homes include children and adults of all ages, embrace all races and all varieties of religious faith, and reach those of every educational background. It is the responsibility of television to bear constantly in mind that the audience is primarily a home audience, and consequently that television's relationship to the viewers is that between guest and host.

The revenues from advertising support the free, competitive American system of telecasting, and make available to the eyes and ears of the American people the finest programs of information, education, culture and entertainment. By law the television broadcaster is responsible for the programming of his station. He, however, is obligated to bring his positive responsibility for excellence and good taste in programming to bear upon all who have a hand in the production of programs, including networks, sponsors, producers of film and of live programs, advertising agencies, and talent agencies.

The American businesses which utilize television for conveying their advertising messages to the home by pictures with sound, seen free-of-charge on the home screen, are reminded that their responsibilities are not limited to the sale of goods and the creation of a favorable attitude toward the sponsor by the presentation of entertainment. They include, as well, responsibility for utilizing television to bring the best programs, regardless of kind, into American homes.

Television, and all who participate in it are jointly accountable to the American public for respect for the special needs of children, for community responsibility, for the advancement of education and culture, for the acceptability of the program materials chosen, for decency and decorum in production, and for propriety in advertising. This responsibility cannot be discharged by any given group of programs, but can be discharged only through the highest standards of respect for the American home, applied to every moment of every program presented by television.

In order that television programming may best serve the public interest, viewers should be encouraged to make their criticisms and positive suggestions known to the television broadcasters. Parents in particular should be urged to see to it that out of the richness of television fare, the best programs are brought to the attention of their children. . . .

Sources: Senate Committee on the Judiciary, Subcommittee to Investigate Juvenile Delinquency, Television and Juvenile Delinquency, interim report, 1955, Committee Print; and
http://historymatters.gmu.edu/d/6558

See Articles: Indecent Exposure; Morality; Obscenity; Obscenity Laws; State Blue Laws; Violent Crimes.

1955 PRIMARY DOCUMENT

Trial Summary From *Mildred Juanita Adams v. United States of America*

The circumstances of Mildred Juanita Adams's acquittal evince an ongoing problem in the use of undercover agents and informants in law enforcement—not only the line between apprehension and entrapment, but also the question of whether it is fair, ethical, or useful to enable a suspect to commit a crime that they might be willing to commit but would not commit without the intervention of the undercover informant.

No. 15001.
United Stated Court of Appeals,
Fifth Circuit,
March 25, 1955

Defendant was convicted of selling heroin. The United States District Court for the Northern District of Texas, T Whitfield Davidson, C. J., entered judgment of conviction and defendant appealed. The Court of Appeals, Tuttle, Circuit Judge, held that where defendant obtained narcotics at request of government informer who was under surveillance of narcotics officers and acting at their direction, and where defendant made no profit on transfer of narcotics to such informer, defendant was merely purchasing agent or messenger for seller and could not be convicted of selling narcotics.

Reversed with directions to enter verdict of acquittal.

Poisons

Where defendant obtained narcotics at request of government informer who was under surveillance of narcotics officers and acting at their direction, and where defendant made no narcotics to such informer, defendant, was merely purchasing agent or messenger for seller and could not be convicted of selling narcotics. Narcotic Drugs Import and Export Act, 2, as amended 21 U.S.C.A. 174, 18 U.S.C.A. 2421 et. Seq.

Charles W. Tessmer, Dallas, Tex., for appellant.

William O. Braecklein, Asst. U. S. Atty., Fort Worth, Tex., for apellee.

Before BORAH, RIVES and TUTTLE, Circuit Judges.

TUTTLE, Circuit Judge.

Appellant was convicted on two counts of selling heroin in violation of 21 U. S. C.A. 174, on evidence which may be summarized as follows: McKinney, a Government informer, drug addict, and confidence man with a record of several convictions, testified that he met appellant about October 1, 1953, at Dallas, Texas, through a mutual friend and fellow addict whom he had met at Forth Worth U.S. Public Health Hospital. On the occasion of his meeting with appellant, they and several others took some heroin in McKinney's apartment, according to his testimony. He saw her again on October 15, at her apartment, at which time she said she would try to see her "connection" that evening to obtain heroin. McKinney said he conveyed this information to Federal Narcotics Agent Taylor, who searched him and gave him $50, and watched appellant pick him up in her car. McKinney said she delivered ten capsules to him later that evening in exchange for the $50. The following day McKinney saw her again and gave her some opium; that evening she lent him two capsules of heroin and said she was going back for more heroin the next night. A meeting was arranged between the two. Taylor advanced McKinney $40 after searching him. Appellant picked up McKinney, drove to the same street corner as before, left the car, and returned with eight capsules of heroin, six of which she gave him for the $40. McKinney testified that appellant never took more than $5 a capsule, which he knew to be the standard price in Dallas; that he did not know whether she made a profit; but that she had stated that "the more she buys from this connection the stronger the percentage is."

Narcotics Agents Taylor and Finley testified that they had advanced money to McKinney to buy the heroin and kept both McKinney and the appellant under surveillance on the occasion of the second transaction. A Government chemist identified the substance in the capsules as containing heroin.

The appellant herself took the stand and testified that she had a record of numerous arrests for vagrancy, one conviction for possession of narcotics, and a conviction of violating the Mann Act, 18 U.S.C.A. 2421 et seq. She said she met McKinney on September 7, 1953, at her apartment; that he told her he could not get along on opium and asked her to buy some heroin for him; that he said he was broke but had two addict friends who would give him part of the narcotics he obtained if he could arrange for their supply; that she bought heroin for him on October 14 for $70 and more on October 16 for $40. She explained that she purchased the narcotics for McKinney because the doctor's office where he obtained opium was closed and he had no place to buy narcotics in Dallas. She had tried to arrange with her "connection" for McKinney to buy directly, but the connection refused to allow this for fear of detection. McKinney did not want to go over to Fort Worth where he did have a source, and was sick with the addict's withdrawal symptoms; having been sick herself, appellant felt sorry for him and for this reason purchased the narcotics for him at no profit to herself. She also said she lent him to capsules on the 15th. According to her testimony, one could get a discount only at $500 purchases of heroin in Dallas.

We find it unnecessary to consider all of the specifications of error, since we believe that the appellant's motion for acquittal should have been granted. We think that no reasonable jury could fail on this evidence to entertain a reasonable doubt that the appellant sold the heroin as alleged. In United States v. Sawyer, 8 Cir., 210 F 2d 169, the evidence as to the part played by the defendant in the transaction was conflicting, but the trial court refused to include charge an explanation as to the difference between dealing with a purchaser as seller and acting for him as a procuring agent. The Court held that this was error, and in reversing for a new trial the court said, 210 F.2d 170:

"In these circumstances, we think the court should at least have pointed out to the jury that if they believed that the federal agent asked the defendant to get some heroin for him and thereupon the defendant undertook to act in the prospective purchaser's behalf rather than his own and in so doing purchased the drug from a third person with whom he was not associated in selling, and thereafter delivered it to the buyer, the defendant would not be a seller and could not be convicted under this indictment. This may be obvious to a lawyer, but we are not sure that in the circumstances of this case the distinction between a seller and a procuring agent was equally clear to laymen. The government having elected to charge the defendant with the crime of sale rather than illegal possession, the jury should have been alerted to the legal limitations of the sale concept in relation to the circumstances of this case."

We agree with this statement of the applicable legal principle; in the present case, however, there was no materially conflicting evidence. All of the evidence was quite consistent with the appellant's acting only as a purchasing agent or messenger instead of a seller. There was no evidence from which a sale from her to McKinney could be spelled out beyond a reasonable doubt; nor was there any evidence that she profited in any way from the transactions or was associated with her "connection" in selling narcotics (except for the quite equivocal fact of the two purchases themselves).

Therefore, the verdict of guilty of the offense of selling heroin must have been based upon speculation, and the court should have directed a verdict of acquittal.

The judgment is reversed with directions to enter a verdict of acquittal.

Source: NARA-II, RG 170 Records of the DEA, Subj Files of Bureau of Narcotics 1916-1970, Box 54, F: 0370-3 Legal information circular

See Articles: Appeals; Appellate Court; Entrapment; Narcotics Laws; Police Abuse.

1955 PRIMARY DOCUMENT

Concerned Citizen Letter About Drug Traffic

Because Prohibition was so profitable for organized crime groups that smuggled alcohol and operated speakeasies, and because this connection between Prohibition and the rise of the Mob has always been well known to the public, the argument in this letter to the U.S. assistant attorney general is one that has been put forth many times. It is also true that drug trafficking has become more profitable and more violent as drug laws have shifted from fines to imprisonment, although correlation does not prove causation.

Honorable Warren Olney, III
Assistant Attorney General
Washington, D. C.

Dear Sir:

A short time ago a magazine, the name of which I cannot now remember, published an article about you. Among other things it said that you head the Federal Narcotics Bureau.

Recently our legal newspaper reported the breaking up of a "dope ring" and the taking of narcotics valued at two to three million dollars. Similar reports appear in the newspapers with considerable regularity.

I am sure you are aware that the primary object of the slimy crews that carry on this nefarious business is money—very, very big money, and not, as reported by some publications, an attempt by Red China to make a nation of drug degenerates out of us. I am also sure that you would be interested in any method that would eliminate this fabulous money-getting, horrible youth destroying, illicit occupation.

It is my belief that the narcotic traffic could be stopped within 90 days simply by taking the profit out of it, and to me that seems quite simple. For example, let us take morphine. Purchases through legitimate channels, the daily requirements of the average addict could be sold to him at 10,000 percent profit for much less than a single dose purchased superstitiously. At such a profit, the addict would carry the administrative load and without great financial strain. Other types of addiction could be similarly handled.

In his broadcast of June 2, Paul Harvey reported 69,000 addicts in these United States exclusive of marijuana. In another 10 years it will be 140,000. Don't you think something constructive should be done?

If you are interested, I should like to discuss the situation further with you.

Respectfully,
Geo. A. Stevens, M.D.
Sioux Falls, South Dakota
June 9, 1955

Source: NARA-II, RG 65, DOT, Narcotics Files, Box 3 F: Justice Dept

See Articles: Criminalization and Decriminalization; Drug Abuse and Addiction, Contemporary; Drug Abuse and Addiction, History of; Drug Abuse and Addiction, Sociology of; Narcotics Laws

1955 PRIMARY DOCUMENT

Congressional Committee on Narcotics Interim Report

Shortly after this report, Congress passed the Daniel Act, significantly increasing the penalties for drug crimes, both possession and trafficking. In some cases, penalties increased by a factor of almost 10 compared to those established only five years earlier in the Boggs Act. While the committee report was a factor, the televised Kefauver hearings on organized crime also stirred public interest in cracking down on drug cartels.

The Committee has given extended consideration to the matter of fixing penalties of appropriate severity for violators of the narcotics laws. It has been impressed with the importance of assuring not only deterrents to this category of crimes, but also of facilitating social as well as medical rehabilitation of those offenders who are users of the drugs. It has considered the special problems of three distinct but closely related groups of persons.

(a) Violators of the narcotics laws whose involvement is of an exclusively criminal character, and who are not themselves addicts or habitual users of the drugs. It has been noted that this group includes the highest proportion of major criminals, with respect to other forms of crime as well as the narcotics offenses committed by them.

(b) Peddlers who are themselves addicted. This group is composed largely of persons with records of delinquency or criminality preceding as well as following their addiction. Criminal activity of persons in this category is usually, but not exclusively, restricted to relatively petty crime, except for their involvement in the drug traffic; in this field they are commonly found in the lowest retail brackets. They are however much the more numerous, their aggregate contribution to the traffic is very large, and their control presents peculiarly difficult problems of enforcement and rehabilitation. This results in part from the fact that their personal involvement with the drugs is associated with some degree of incapacity for normal social adjustments, diminished response to corrective and rehabilitative efforts and the impetus of a habit which can be supported only at an expense beyond the legitimate earning capacity of the average citizen.

(c) Addicted persons with either no records of criminal activity, or records of delinquency not involving violations of the narcotics laws other than possession of the drugs. Anti-social activity among this group is commonly found to be of a petty character, but must, in combination with such legitimate activities as occupy the addict, be sufficiently be product to support the high costs of addition. This is the least homogenous of the three groups; its members range from unemployables with serious psychiatric problems, to highly skilled professional people. It is the class from which a majority of peddlers are recruited, and it provides the essential market of consumers for the illicit traffic. It includes also the most hopeful subjects of the curative and rehabilitative programs, and those undergoing voluntary treatment in the public and private hospitals.

The Committee has found itself in immediate agreement with respect to the first and the third of these groups. For the commercial type of trafficker, motivated solely by hope of gain from his handling of the drugs, it was agreed that penalties of a severe type are indicated. With respect to the third group, not involved in importation, manufacture, or sale of drugs, it is felt that the problem is principally one of appropriate treatment and rehabilitation, with subsequent guidance by interested social agencies within the individual's community. However, note has been made of the fact that in certain instances tangible evidence involving known major traffickers may depend solely upon possession of drugs. It is felt therefore that any scale of penalties applicable to possession should be broad enough in range to cover both the relatively innocuous and the serious offenders.

With respect to the second group, those involved in both trafficking and personal use of the drugs, the question has been raised as to whether the levels of punishment most likely to serve as effective deterrents may not obstruct the reform and ultimate rehabilitation of the individuals concerned. While recognizing the probable validity of such arguments, the Committee believes that first consideration must be given to the protection of society from the trafficker, without respect to his status as an addict.

It is to be hoped that the extension of treatment and rehabilitative services into communities importantly affected, as recommend elsewhere in this report, will not only aid in reducing the problem of addiction, but also compensate in some degree the effects of longer prison terms on convicted addict drug peddlers. The Committee has noted the fact that the addict-trafficker has in the past shown a high rate of recidivism, both as addict and as peddler. Where he retains or returns to psychological independence on the drug, he is often less responsive to the deterrents than the more hardened, ordinary criminal. The growing experience of the States and local committees with enforcement and treatment programs will produce additional valuable and much needed on the peculiarly difficult problem of the addict in crime. Such information should receive close and continued study at all levels of government.

The Committee has arrived at the conclusion that there is need for a continuation of the policy of summary punishment, or a more severe character, as a deterrent to narcotic law violations. It therefore recommends the increase of both maximum and minimum sentences, for first as well as subsequent offenses. With respect to the mandatory features of such penalties, and prohibition of suspended sentences or probation, the Committee fully recognizes objections in principle. It feels, however, that for this class of crimes, these features must be accepted as essential elements of the desired deterrents, in defining the gravity of the offense and the assured penalty to follow.

December 21, 1955

Source: NARA-II, RG 65, DOT, Narcotics Files, Box 4 F: Penalties

See Articles: Drug Abuse and Addiction, Contemporary; Drug Abuse and Addiction, History of; Drug Abuse and Addiction, Sociology of; Narcotics Laws.

1959 PRIMARY DOCUMENT

FBI Memorandum on Narcotics Violator Ralph Ciccone

The FBI wasn't the only agency maintaining thorough files. Harry Anslinger wasn't as prominent as J. Edgar Hoover, but he guided the Federal Bureau of Narcotics from its founding in 1930 until 1962. Although most resources were devoted to heroin and opium trafficking investigations, the Federal Bureau of Narcotics kept tabs on as many forms of drug violations as they could. The Federal Bureau of Narcotics was merged into the Bureau of Narcotics and Dangerous Drugs in 1968, and the Drug Enforcement Administration in 1973.

Bureau Of Narcotics
District #2
General File Title: GF: National List Violators
Report Made At: New York City, New York
Date: May 25, 1959
By: Albert Garofalo, Narcotic Agent
Related Files: May 28, 1959

Subject of this Memorandum: Recommendation for inclusion of Ralph John Ciccone in National List Book of Narcotic Violators.

Details:
1. NAME: RALPH JOHN CICCONE
2. ALIASES: RUFUS BROWN, RALPH DE MARCO, LOUIS CARBONETTE, SLIP LIP.
3. DESCRIPTION: Italian descent, 5'7" tall, 150 lbs., born in New York City on September 15, 1910, grayish-black hair, hazel eyes, medium build and scars on the left side of his nose and his upper lip.
4. LOCALITIES FREQUENTED: Residence, 19 West 69th Street, New York City. Frequents Saylor's Bar, 2153 2nd Avenue, New York City, Moulin Rouge Club, 47 W. 52nd Street, New York City., and 500 Club, Atlantis City, New Jersey.
5. CRIMINAL ASSOCIATES: Anthony PORCELLI, Guido PENOSI, Nicholas MARTELLO and Paul CORREALE.
6. FACSIMILE OF SIGNATURE:
7. CRIMINAL HISTORY: Dates from January 1935 to May 1959 and includes arrests from Grand Larceny of checks to violations of Federal Narcotic Laws. He was last convicted and sentenced on May 8, 1959 to 7 and ½ years for violation of Federal Narcotic Laws.
8. MODUS OPERANDI: One of the largest wholesale narcotic interstate traffickers. CICCONE knows every important narcotic violator in the United States and was in partnership with Anthony PORCELLI, receiving their supply through Guido PENOSI from sources in New Orleans, Louisiana.
Subject: Recommendation for inclusion of Ralph CICCONE in National List Book of Violators.
9. AGENCIES WITH INFORMATION: United States Bureau of Narcotics, Federal Bureau of Investigation, United States Coast Guard, New York City Police Department.
10. IDENTIFICATION: F.B.I. #881 562 N.Y.C.F.D. # 131 332

11. Attached hereto are two photographs of Ralph CICCONE dated October 15, 1958.

Copy of this memo furnished to:
Albert Garofalo
Narcotic Agent
George H. Gaffney
District Supervisor

Source: Records of the Drug Enforcement Agency, Subj Files of the Bureau of Narcotics and Dangerous Drugs 1916-1970.

See Articles: Italian Americans; Narcotics Laws; Organized Crime, History of.

1959 PRIMARY DOCUMENT

FBI Report on Gaetano Lucchese

"Tommy" Lucchese was the boss of the Lucchese crime family, one of New York's Five Families. Lucchese endured moves by the federal authorities to denaturalize him and investigations into his business by the attorney general and the FBI, as well as the Banana War waged by Joe Bonnano, only to die of a brain tumor in 1967. His chosen successor was in prison, and the Lucchese family came under the control of Carmine Tramunti.

SUBJECT:
Gaetano Lucchese (Under Active Investigation By U.S. Immigration & Naturalization Service)

ALIASES:
Tom Lucchese, Tom Brown, Tom Arra, "Three Finger Brown," Tom Branda.

DESCRIPTION:
Born on December 1, 1899, at Palermo, Sicily. 5'5," 150 lbs., brown eyes, grey hair, wears glasses.

LOCALITIES:
Resides at 74 Royale Street, Lido Beach, Long Island, New York. Frequents garment districts of New York City, Miami Beach, Florida, various locations on Long Island and New Jersey.

FAMILY BACKGROUND:
Wife: Catherine
Son: Baldassari
Daughter: Frances (married to Carlo Gambino's son Tom)
Brothers: Anthony, Joseph
Sisters: Pietra, Concetta, Rosalie (wife of Joe Rosato)
Father: Baldassari
Mother: Francesca

CRIMINAL RECORD:
F.B.I. # 168 275
New York City P.D. # B-68 834
Immigration & Naturalization Service File # 2207-51652.

SUMMARY AND BACKGROUND:
THOMAS LUCCHESE, alias "THREE FINGER BROWN," as he is commonly known, is reputed to be one of the leading figures in syndicated crime in the United States today. In this respect, it appears that he has replaced in underworld prominence, VITO GENOVESE, now incarcerated in a Federal penitentiary (fifteen years) after being convicted in a Federal narcotics conspiracy case. LUCCHESE has long been closely associated with the most notorious racket elements in this country. In addition, he has succeeded in befriending some of the most important political and judicial personages in the New York City area.

LUCCHESE migrated to the United States from Palermo, Sicily, in 1911, and was admitted to citizenship in 1943, at Newark, New Jersey. He has been a subject of investigation by the Immigration and Naturalization Service since the time he was Naturalized. Although he admitted to a prior felony conviction (grand larceny-auto theft), he neglected to mention several subsequent arrests (including two arrests for homicide).

LUCCHESE, slowly but methodically, rose in criminal stature since about the end of the prohibition era (late twenties). He commenced his career as a common gunman and steadily gained prominence among his underworld brethren—now achieving his coveted position. It was in 1928 when his name first became known to the New York City Police Department. At that time JOSEPH ROSATO (his brother-in-law), one JOHN GUIDO (Now deceased) and he were identified as the perpetrators of a homicide with a gun on one LOUIS CERASULO. The police investigative reports indicate that the victim was implicated, along with his assailants, in an extortion (protection) racket of the chicken markets in the Harlem area. The identifying witnesses (victim's wife and mother) recanted their earlier positive identification before the institution of any criminal proceedings. The three men were subsequently released and each had his records of arrest removed from the files of the New York City Police Department pursuant to the provisions of the New York State Code of Criminal Procedure.

By 1940, LUCCHESE had already reached a prominent position in the local crime syndicate by becoming chieftain of the infamous 107th Street Mob (East Harlem area of New York City). His stature here can be fully appreciated when note is taken of the criminal caliber of his subordinates in this powerful closely knit underworld organization. His immediate subordinates were DOMINICK PETRELLI, alias "THE GAP" with an extensive criminal record and the notorious MICHAEL COPPOLA , alias "TRIGGER MIKE." Some of LUCCHESE's lower echelon subordinates included JOSEPH GAGLIANO, PHILIP LOMBARDI, alias "BEN TURPIN," JOHN SCHILLACI, FRANK LIVORSI, alias "CHEECH" and JOSEPH STRACCI, alias "JOE STRETCH." In this same organization, headed by LUCCHESE, were also such import and narcotic traffickers as ALFREDO FELICI, JOHN ORMENTO, JOSEPH VENTO, PASQUALE GENESE and SALVATORE SANTORA.

LUCCHESE's present position and influence in the crime syndicate is best borne out by the fact that in APRIL, 1960, an emissary of his, THOMAS EBOLI, alias TOMMY RYAN (present reputed head of the "Thompson Street—Greenwich Village Mob") visited SALVATORE LUCANIA, alias "LUCKY" LUCIANO in Italy seeking counsel and guidance on the problems of maintaining a peaceful coexistence among the various underworld factions and contingents.

CHRONOLOGY:

The New York City Police Department has the following record of THOMAS LUCCHESE under their number B-68 334:

October 2, 1921: As THOMAS LUCCHESE, N.Y.C., Grand Larceny—Auto. January 19, 1922, 3 years, 8 months to 19 years, State Prison.

August 30, 1927: As THOMAS ARRA, N.Y.C., Receiver. On August 31, 1927, discharged.

July 18, 1928: As THOMAS LUCCHESE, N.Y.C., Homicide. On July 24, 1928, discharged.

September 8, 1930-As THOMAS LUCCHESE, Homicide. On February 26, 1931, dismissed.

November 18, 1935: As THOMAS LUCCHESE, Manhattan, Vagrancy. On November 18, 1935, discharged.

On July 4, 1931, at Cleveland, Ohio, JOSEPH BIONDO, SALVATORE LUCANIA, alias "LUCKY" LUCIANO and LUCCHESE were arrested together as suspected racketeers and released on the same day.

Records in the office of New York County District Attorney FRANK HOGAN indicate that LUCCHESE left Harlem in 1930 and went to Jackson Heights, Queens. He returned to Manhattan in 1933, 88th Street between Madison and Park Avenues. In 1936 he moved to Fort Lee, New Jersey, where he stayed until 1944. (Ref. 1)

In 1937, during the investigation of a narcotic conspiracy case resulting in the indictment of nearly 100 violators in New York

City, it was repeatedly asserted by witnesses that an individual named "THREE FINGER BROWN" (alias of LUCCHESE) was the leader of the narcotics trafficking mobs in New York. All of the statements were inadmissible at the trial, and the suspect could thus not be implicated in the conspiracy case of SAM MACEO, et al. (Ref. 2)

In 1939, in developing investigative leads as to many important narcotic distribution groups operating out of the notorious 107th Street, East Harlem area of New York City, underworld informants repeatedly asserted that LUCCHESE was an underworld leader concerned with various criminal undertakings. However, these informants also stated that LUCCHESE managed to avoid arrest because he stayed sufficiently in the background from the overt acts—committed by others. (Ref. 2)

In March, 1941, District Supervisor GEORGE WHITE, then Narcotic agent, raided Dukes Clam Bar, 783 Palisades Avenue, Grantwood, New Jersey, headquarters for the notorious WILLIE MORRETTI gang, and found LUCCHESE in conference with MORRETTI and other known underworld characters. (Ref. 3)

In 1942, DOMINICK LAVIANO, a known narcotic trafficker of importance, was under investigation and the name of LUCCHESE appeared numerous times in interviews and records of telephone calls. (Ref 4)

In 1943, in the SAM BERNSTEIN case, involving a large narcotic conspiracy, the name of WILLIE MORETTI and THOMAS LUCCHESE appeared, and records showed their association. A telephone call was made from MORETTI's home on April 4, 1943 to FL ushing 3-9225. This was a telephone in the residence of LUCCHESE in Malba, Long Island. (Ref. 4)

Sponsors on LUCCHESE's petition for naturalization (he was admitted to citizenship, 1943, at Newark, New Jersey) were: THOMAS VALENTI, manufacturer, 2637-12th Street, Astoria, Long Island, and ANTHONY VADALA, 3919 103rd Street, Corona, Long Island. VADALA is the real name of TONY GRIO, and is the uncle of LUCCHESE's wife. He is the operator of the Grio Press, believed by the Kings County District Attorney in 1947 to be printing sheets and Italian lottery tickets. (Ref. 5)

In 1944, LUCCHESE and his entire family registered in a New York City election giving their Parsons Blvd., Malba, Long Island address. LUCCHESE stated that he lived continuously in New York State for the past 33 years. (he entered the United States from Italy in 1911) LUCCHESE, however, had just previously been naturalized a United States Citizen in New Jersey. As of this time, he had not been given his "partial restoration of civil rights." This is a significant factor in that LUCCHESE stated under oath to the Immigration and Naturalization Service, in his application for citizenship, that he lived in Palisades, New Jersey, between 1933 and 1934 (up to the time he became naturalized). It then became obvious that he committed perjury, either to the New York City Board of Elections or to the Immigration and Naturalization Service. During this period it was rumored that he sought to be naturalized in New York, but without success because of his criminal record. However, he made a "connection" in New Jersey with the Immigration and Naturalization Service and therefore pretended to domicile in that state. (Ref. 6)

It becomes apparent that LUCCHESE committed a crime when he voted in Queens, New York, in 1944. First, he was not eligible to vote, even if properly domiciled, because he had not yet received partial restoration of his "civil rights." Second, he either committed perjury to the New York City Board of Elections or to the Immigration and Naturalization Service as to his domicile. (Ref. 6)

LUCCHESE has befriended and became closely associated with several well known and influential political figures in the New York City area. At the ALFRED E. SMITH Memorial Dinner, at the Waldorf Astoria Hotel in New York City on October 18, 1946, the following persons were seated at table #62:

THOMAS LUCCHESE, LOU KAUFMAN, JAMES BRUNO, MARIO G. DIPINO,

CHARLES RAMSGATE, SAMUEL REISS, ALFRED SANTANGELO, AND VINCENT R. IMPELLITTERI. (Ref. 7)

At the ALFRED E. SMITH Memorial Dinner at the Waldorf Astoria Hotel in New York City on August 28, 1948, the following persons were seated at table #32:

THOMAS LUCCHESE, JAMES BRUNO, LOUIS J, CAPOZZOLI, MYLES LANE, AMEDEO LAURITANO, JAMES MERLI, ROCCO A. PARELLA, ARTHUR H. SCHWARTZ, and FRANCIS VALENTE. (Ref. 7)

In January, 1949, ARMAND CHANKALIAN, city Councilman JOHN MERLI and LUCCHESE drove to Miami Beach, Florida. They stayed at the Hotel Martinique until February 6, 1949. MERLI was Tammany Hall elections chairman. (Ref. 7)

The printed program for the St. Patrick's Day Dinner in New York City in 1949, lists the following persons as seated at table # 208:

THOMAS F. MURPHY, JACK AARON, ARMAND CHANKALIAN, LOUIS J. COBLENTZ, LESLIE KIRSCH, THOMAS LUCCHESE, EDWARD W. McDONALD, JAMES M. McINERNEY, EDWARD E. RIGNEY, and SOL WOOD. (Ref 7)

The printed program for the St. Patrick's Day Dinner in New York City the following year lists the following persons seated at table #16:

THOMAS F. MURPHY, JACK AARON, PETER ARNO, LOUIS J. COBLENTZ, THOMAS LUCCHESE, EDWARD W. McDONALD, JAMES M. McINERNEY, DENNIS J. McMABON, EDWARD E. RIGNEY, and SOL WOOD. (Ref. 7)

In March, 1949, a check of LUCCHESE's toll calls, showed 45 calls to AMADEO LAURITANO, then Assistant to Chief of the Criminal Division of the United States Attorney's Office, Southern District of New York, Myles Lane. LAURITANO was later appointed a New York City magistrate by Mayor Vincent B. Impellitteri. (Ref. 8)

LUCCHESE is godfather to Magistrate LAURITANO's son. Magistrate LAURITANO was discharged as an Assistant United States Attorney by then United States Attorney Saypol, after admitting the LUCCHESE relationship; a few months thereafter is when Mayor Impellitteri appointed LAURITANO a City Magistrate. LUCCHESE has publicly appeared at political dinners and functions with Mayor Impellitteri, Myles Lane, AMADEO LAURITANO, ARMAND CHANKALIAN and Thomas Murphy. (Ref. 9)

Edward Reid, New York Daily News Columnist, obtained a copy of a lengthy letter written by the then New York City Police Commissioner (now Federal Judge) Thomas F. Murphy to United States Senator Alexander Wiley. Wiley was in possession of much information concerning the relationship between Murphy and LUCCHESE and thus, as a member of the Senate Judiciary Committee, refused his confirmation. Murphy in an attempt to purge himself with Senator Wiley, made some astonishing admissions and disclosures in his letter to the Senator. Murphy said in the letter that he was a guest at the LUCCHESE home and that he and LUCCHESE had attended several social-political functions together. He said that his friendship with LUCCHESE was based of his "knowledge" that LUCCHESE was a reputable and important "businessman." That he contemplated returning to the private practice of law and considered LUCCHESE a potential "client" and for that reason cultivated his friendship. Later Judge Murphy said, he became aware of LUCCHESE's criminal record but passed it off as insignificant. (Ref. 6)

From Edward Reid it was also developed that LUCCHESE and Armand Chankalian, Administrative Assistant to United States Attorney Myles Lane, once went to United States District Court Judge Thomas Meany (Neward, New Jersey) in an attempt to influence his judgment in a case involving a close friend of LUCCHESE. It is believed that this close friend of LUCCHESE is SETTIMO

ACCARDO, alias "BIG SAM" ACCARDO, who is at the present time a fugitive in a Federal narcotic case, having jumped $92,000 bail. Mr. Reid stated that Judge Meany would testify to this attempted influence on him. (Ref. 5)

In an appearance before the New York Parole Board in March, 1949, LUCCHESE in his application for a certificate of "good conduct" stated that he was financially interested in the following concerns:

Grand View Construction Co., 740 Fulton Avenue, Mount Vernon, N.Y. This company built a project at Horseheads, New York, and received a $250,000 F.H.A. loan. The company also participated in the construction of the Catskill Thruway.

International Window Cleaning Co., 211 West 36th Street, N.Y., N. Y.

Empire Metal Bath Co. and Fordham Hoisting Co., both of 2373 Washington Avenue, Bronx, N. Y.

L & J Realty Co., 48-15 108th Street, Corona, Long Island.

Wingdale Country Club, Wingdale, New York.

Braunell, Ltd., 262 West 38th Street, New York, N.Y.

Balfran Blouse Co. and Bobfran Blouse Contractors, both of 140 West Street, New York, N.Y.

One of LUCCHESE's principal legitimate business interests is in Braunell, Ltd., of which he is vice-president. The subsidiaries of this company are: Pleasant Coat Co., Pleasant, New Jersey, and Bob France Coat Co., 48-15 108th Street, Corona, Long Island, manufacturers of women's coats and suits. In connection with the Braunell Company (holding company), it was as a result of LUCCHESE being friendly with CHARLES SILVERS of the American Woolen Company, that Braunell was able to obtain material during the war period, when there was a critical shortage of wool. There were indications of a black market operation, shared in by SILVERS. SILVERS has served as President of the Board of Education of the City of New York since 1952 to the present time. (Ref. 11)

In April, 1950, LUCCHESE was granted a certificate of "good conduct" from the New York State Parole Board, thus permitting the right to vote. This was the only civil right asked for by LUCCHESE. He also applied for naturalization, establishing legal residence in New Jersey, believing this would enhance his chances of being naturalized. LUCCHESE, in submitting his petition to the Immigration and Naturalization Service. Admitted his felony conviction of 1922 but neglected to include four subsequent arrests (all discharged). (Ref. 12)

In the 1950 investigation of the narcotic activities of the notorious JACK DRAGNA (now deceased) and his associates in California, a written notation was found in DRAGNA's house, "Melba, 106 Parsons Blvd., Long Island, N.Y." In the investigation of the February 14, 1950, murder of NICK DeJOHN in Los Angeles, California, (DeJOHN was a lieutenant of JACK DRAGNA), GIORLAMO ADAMO, alias "MOMO" was searched. In the course of searching ADAMO, the following note was found: "TOMMY BROWN, FLushing 3-9225, 106 Parsons Blvd., Malba, Long Island." Closely associated with this underworld group were the notorious SICA BROTHERS (ALFRED AND JOSEPH), formerly members of the WILLIAM MORRETTI Mob in New Jersey. JACK DRAGNA was regarded by the California Police authorities to be the No. 1 crime chieftain in that area. (Ref. 5)

On February 3, 1951, in an interview with Edward Corsi, a former New York State Commissioner of Labor (also Republican candidate for Mayor of New York City in 1949), he stated that he, like LUCCHESE, was a former East Harlem resident and knew the political situation there. He stated that Mayor Impellitteri (now Queens County Judge) and

LUCCHESE frequently met in Bentivegna's Restaurant, 55 East Houston Street, New York, New York. He further stated that the Mayor was a guest at the LUCCHESE home on a number of occasions. Mr. Corsi also stated that LUCCHESE was a very strong supporter of the late Congressman Vito Marcantonio—who appointed LUCCHESE's son a cadet at West Point in 1947. (Ref. 13)

Narcotic Agent Joseph Amato, in a memorandum report 184, dated June 23, 1952, stated that he was reliably informed that LUCCHESE and Mayor Impellitteri dined together at an average of three times a week at Lanza's Restaurant, 1st Avenue between 10th and 11th Streets, New York City, as well as occasional meetings at Bentivegna's Restaurant, 55 East Houston Street, New York, New York. (Ref. 14)

The address of Bentivegna's Restaurant, 55 East Houston Street, New York, N.Y. was found in the possession of SALVATORE LUCANIA, alias "LUCKY" LUCIANO, following the arrest of VINCENT TRUPIA in Italy. TRUPIA was arrested in possession of a large quantity of narcotic drugs. He was the American emissary of the DiPALERMO BROTHERS of the Lower East Side of New York City. It was concluded at that time that the Bentivegna Restaurant address was a mail drop between LUCANIA and LUCCHESE. (Ref. 5)

Early in 1952, a reliable informant gave Narcotic Agent George White (Now District Supervisor, San Francisco, California) considerable factual information concerning LUCCHESE's relationship with ABE CHAIT—garment center trucker, long under investigation by the Internal Revenue Service. Names of various underworld characters were given who were supposed to be on CHAIT's payroll as "Ghosts," i.e., they received weekly checks for about $100 and after cashing the checks, they would return the proceeds to CHAIT. This was a tax evasion scheme used by CHAIT with LUCCHESE. In return, the "Ghosts" received coveted bookmaking concessions in the garment area. Although Agent White passed this information on to the Internal Revenue Service no action was ever taken. (Ref. 6)

Former Narcotic Agent Price Spivy in a memorandum report 184, dated August 13, 1952, stated that he had very reliable information to the effect that LUCCHESE handles any type of criminal activity. This source stated that LUCCHESE is the "boss" and that his underlings carry out his instructions, all with his knowledge and consent. The same informant stated that LUCCHESE does not get orders from anyone; he acts in agreement and harmony with other mob heads, with VITO GENOVESE as coordinator. Inter-mob questions are received at a meeting of the minds, or general agreement by LUCCHESE, et al. (Ref. 2)

Another example of LUCCHESE's name and address being possessed by numerous underworld characters is found in the Orsini—SHILLITANI narcotic smuggling case in 1952. The entry "TOMMY BROWN, FLushing 3-9225" was found in the address book of FLORENCE SHILLITANI when she was arrested in this case.

In a confidential memorandum by George White to Commissioner Harry J. Anslinger, dated February 3, 1953, White discusses his being summoned before a "Special Rackets" Grand Jury to testify as to all available information known to him about LUCCHESE. United States Attorney Lane, a close associate of LUCCHESE appeared, however, more interested in White's activities and informers than about any possible criminality on the part of his friend LUCCHESE. The informant, Eugene Giannini, who supplied much of his information on his return from Italy on April 14, 1952, was murdered in gangland style at about the time of the Grand Jury inquiry. Mr. Lane demanded that White divulge the names of all of his informants who had supplied information against LUCCHESE. Having refused to so comply, WHITE was cited for contempt of Court, and in fact incarcerated. Mr. Lane also brought before the Grand Jury other narcotic agents who had some knowledge of WHITE's informants and belabored them with questions about WHITE, shutting off the witnesses when they attempted to volunteer factual information about LUCCHESE's background and reputation. (Ref. 15)

In a memorandum report 184 by Narcotic Agent Armando Muglia, dated July 8, 1955, it is reported that according to U.S. Customs Agent James A. Flynn, LUCCHESE, ANTHONY ANASTASIA, alias "TOUGH TONY," and other underworld characters use Andrea (Andrew) Torregrossa's Funeral Chapel at 345 Avenue U, Brooklyn, New York, as a meeting place. Torregrossa owns another funeral parlor at 1305 79th Street, Brooklyn, N. Y. It was alleged that there is a great deal of "racket money" invested in these two mortuaries. (Ref. 16)

Narcotic Agent Howard Chappell, stated in a letter to District Supervisor George White, dated November 27, 1956, that he interviewed the well-known singer and actor Mario Lanza and that the latter was very cooperative. Lanza stated to Agent Chappell that in April or May, 1955, while at home and in the company of prizefighter Rocky Marciano, he was visited by LUCCHESE, one IRVING BERMAN and an unidentified third person. Lanza, who was in financial straits, was visited by these three men who were obviously aware of his plight, to discuss financial matters. LUCCHESE informed Lanza that if he wanted to work for him, all financial problems would be resolved. Lanza then reported to Agent Chappell that the three men pointed out to him that they similarly assisted Frank Sinatra out of his financial plights, a few years previously, and that he prospered ever since. Lanza told his visitors that he was not interested in their proposition. Lanza's close personal friend and business manager, Al Teitelbaum, stated to Agent Chappell that the offer made by the three men, through BERMAN, $150,000 in return for a 10% interest in Lanza. This offer was flatly rejected by Lanza. Teitelbaum stated that he was led to believe that the money was to be furnished by LUCCHESE through BERMAN. BERMAN, with no known criminal record, was obviously a sychophant for LUCCHESE as well as for other underworld characters. Lanza also stated that Marciano confided in him that he was required to turn over 50% of all his earnings to the same syndicate, through his manager, Al Weil, in order to extricate himself from their clutches. (Ref. 17)

LUCCHESE's brother-in-law JOSEPH ROSATO, alias "JOE PALISADES," attended the 1957 criminal conclave at Apalachian, New York. It is believed that he represented the interests of LUCCHESE at this meeting. LUCCHESE's power in the garment center is in part reflected by the fact that ROSATO operates the only non-unionized trucking company in the garment center, the S & R Trucking Company, 460 West 35th Street, New York, N.Y. (Ref. 18)

LUCCHESE's daughter FRANCES is married to TOM GAMBINO whose father, CARLO GAMBINO, was another attendee at the 1957 Apalachian Conference. CARLO GAMBINO and his brother PAUL are notorious Brooklyn racketeers engaged for many years in manifold underworld endeavors.

In December, 1958, it was reported that one LAWRENCE KNOHL was handling real estate transactions for LUCCHESE and other "East Harlem" underworld characters in the Southeastern section of the United States. These transactions included the purchasing of hotels, motels and apartment buildings. In Savannah, Georgia, this group is reported to own the General Oglethorpe Hotel, the Dratton Arms Apartment Building and the Savannah Motor Lodge. Little is known about KNOHL other than the fact that he was sued by the Federal Government for a half million dollars in 1958 in the Eastern District of New York in connection with a "housing fraud." An income tax evasion case involving $281,860.69 was also pending against him in New York the same year. KNOHL is reputed to have also associated with the late ALBERT ANASTESIA and FRANK COSTELLO (now incarcerated in a Federal Penitentiary). (Ref. 20)

District Supervisor John Cusack of the Bureau of Narcotics, Rome, Italy, reported on February 1, 1961, that a reliable and knowledgeable source in Italy recently stated that in view of the recent incarceration of VITO GENOVESE, leadership of the crime syndicate was assumed by LUCCHESE. LUCCHESE has always been extremely close to LUCANIA and has steadfastly protected LUCANIA's "rights" in his absence, and made a particularly vigorous effort to insure that LUCANIA was well taken care of. This course believes that since GENOVESE and later LUCCHESE wrestled control away from FRANK COSTELLO, LUCANIA fared better. Prior to their take-over, LUCANIA received between $2,000 and $3,000 per month. Source is informed that LUCANIA now receives between $10,000 and $12,000 per month and, in addition, source is impressed that LUCANIA is living more affluently under the new regime than at any time since his arrival in Italy. (Ref. 19)

This same source has determined that THOMAS EBOLI, alias TOMMY RYAN, visited LUCANIA during January, 1961, as well as in April, 1960. The reported purpose of EBOLI's visit with LUCANIA was to confer with him on behalf of LUCCHESE. The source stated that there are indications that EBOLI plans to be a regular visitor with LUCANIA to discuss policy and planning with him as an emissary of LUCCHESE. LUCANIA's advice and support is being sought by LUCCHESE, through EBOLI, to enable the former to maintain his position in the syndicate and at the same time preserve gangland peace. Source stated that there exists a general apprehension in the underworld that a gang war in the syndicate is more apt to erupt now or in the near future than at any time since the end of the prohibition era. (Ref. 19)

LEADS:
1. At the present time LUCCHESE is under very active investigation by the Immigration and Naturalization Service.
2. The following persons because of their apparent knowledge of the methods and manipulations of LUCCHESE and their previous display of candor, if interviewed may prove fruitful: EDWARD CORSI, AL TEITELBAUM, Federal Judge THOMAS MEANY, EDWARD REID, and NEWBOLD MORRIS. In addition, the old files of the now defunct New York City and the New York State Crime Commissions may be very revealing.
3. An extensive audit of the books and activities of the numerous "legitimate" enterprises, alluded to in this report as being owned or dominated by LUCCHESE, may give rise to an income tax evasion case.
4. Mail coverage of the several restaurants and other known meeting places of LUCCHESE and his associates, referred to in this report as likely mail drops, may prove revealing. An astute and experienced racketeer as LUCCHESE would not use his own home for the receipt of mail or telephone calls.
5. Efforts to cultivate the informative services of certain persons in the entertainment and prize-fighting business, i.e., Al Teitelbaum and Rocky Marciano, may develop the close ties and controls of LUCCHESE in these fields of endeavor. Ostensibly, the glitter of performing "artists" has attracted much of LUCCHESE's attention and interest over the years.
6. Discreet conferences with certain political personages New York City, such as former Judge Ferdinand Pecora, who lost the New York City mayoral race to Impelliterri in 1949, may prove worthwhile. Judge Pecora may have much repressed feelings about LUCCHESE, who supported Impelliterri, which may be uncovered during such conferences.

Source: NARA-II, RG 65, DOT, Narcotics Enforcement, Box 1 F: Narcotics Investigation

See Articles: Italian Americans; Organized Crime, History of; Organized Crime, Sociology of.

1960 PRIMARY DOCUMENT

1960 Adolph Coors III Murder Report

Adolph Coors III, the heir to the Coors beer empire, was murdered in February 1960, but his

body was not found until September. A massive manhunt throughout the United States and Canada finally apprehended his kidnapper and murderer, Joseph Corbett Jr., in October. Corbett had been sentenced to prison in 1951 for another murder, but after a transfer to a minimum security prison, he had escaped and encountered Coors. He was sentenced to life imprisonment, was paroled after serving a total of just over 20 years, and committed suicide in 2009 at age 80.

Federal Bureau Of Investigation
Narrative Of Crime

ADOLPH COORS, III, Executive of Adolph Coors Company, Golden, Colorado, left his home located in a rural area near Morrison, Colorado, about 8:00 a.m., February 9, 1960, en route to his business office in Golden, Colorado. He was driving an International Travelall.

This Travelall was observed by a neighbor at approximately 8:15 a.m. and 10:00 a.m., February 8, 1960, parked on a single car width bridge crossing Turkey Creek. This bridge was on the route traveled by Mr. COORS from his residence to Golden. At about 10:20 a.m., February 9, 1960, a route driver for a milk company moved the International Travelall off the bridge as he had to cross it. At that time he noted the motor and radio were on. The milkman examined the area and noticed a red spot which he thought might be blood in the dirt on this bridge. He examined the area around the bridge and in the creek noticed a tan baseball type cat and a brown hat. The milkman reported this incident to the Colorado State Highway Patrol.

Subsequent investigation on February 9, 1960, by the Jefferson County Sheriff's Office, Golden, Colorado, resulted in the location of a pair of eyeglasses. One lens in these glasses was broken. The glasses were found in the water of the creek near the bridge. The glasses were subsequently identified as having been prescribed and made for ADOLPH COORS III.

On February 10, 1960, a letter was received addressed to Mrs. ADOLPH COORS III, Morrison, Colorado. The letter which was postmarked 3:00 p.m., February 9, Denver, Colorado, set forth that Mrs. COORS' husband had been kidnapped and his car was by Turkey Creek. The letter demanded $500,000 for the return of her husband and requested when the money was ready that a tractor be advertised for sale in the *Denver Post*.

On September 11, 1960, information was received that a key chain with a small pen knife and keys attached had been found below a dump near Shamballah Ashrama, Colorado. The pen knife on this chain bore the initials A.C. III.

Articles of clothing including a jacket, shirt, trousers, and shoes were subsequently found and identified as having been those worn by ADOLPH COORS III. Also found was a tie clasp bearing the initials A.C. III. The pen knife appearing on the key chain and the tie clasp were also identified as having been worn by ADOLPH COORS III.

Bones were found in the general vicinity of the location of the clothing which were subsequently identified by a pathologist as being those of a human male, approximately the same age and size as ADOLPH COORS III.

A skull was also found in this area and an examination of the teeth by the dentist of ADOLPH COORS III resulted in positive identification of the skull as being that of ADOLPH COORS III.

Two irregular shaped holes were found in the right scapula bone found in this area. These holes were so positioned with respect to holes which were also found in the right shoulder area of the jacket, shirt, and undershirt, to indicate they were probably made by the same missiles which made the holes in the garments. It was indicated that the holes in the right shoulder area of the jacket appeared to be bullet entrance holes made by a contact or near contact shot. The holes were of such size to suggest they could have been made by a caliber .38 weapon although another caliber weapon could have been used.

Attached are photographic copes of a map showing the general area and showing main roads from the Denver Civic Center to the ADOLPH COORS III home, and an aerial photograph of the area including the home of

ADOLPH COORS III and the bridge at Turkey Creek.

Source: NARA II, RG 65, Class 7 Kidnapping, Box 353, F: 7 371

See Articles: Colorado; Kidnapping; Murder, Contemporary; Murder, History of.

1961 to 1980

INTRODUCTION

Between 1960 and 1980, the nation's approach to crime and punishment underwent revolutionary changes in terms of federal coordination, funding, and practical enforcement. The typical local police officer in 1960 paid scant attention to federal rules and viewed federal agencies like the Federal Bureau of Investigation (FBI) primarily as a source for technical expertise in forensic evidence, academy training, and statistics. Funding for local police came mostly from the local community, and the vast majority of rules and procedures for daily operations were determined at the local and state levels. By 1980, the situation had changed dramatically. In every stage of police interaction with the public—stopping a suspect, making arrest, presenting evidence at trial, sentencing and punishment, and parole and release—the local law enforcement officer was guided by federal rules. A host of new federal agencies actively participated in joint enforcement operations in local precincts, and a variety of community programs were paid for, at least partially, with federal dollars. Even in the most remote corners of the country, the local police officer no longer operated in the isolation of the neighborhood community, but instead acted within the broader guidelines of national policies of crime and punishment.

Within universities, criminologists continued to disagree over the fundamental causes of crime and the best way of sentencing offenders and deterring would-be criminals. Since the early 1800s, scholars debated whether it was better to protect society by deterring criminals through harsh penalties, or to improve society by correcting criminals through more therapeutic sentences. Both sides of this long-standing debate have enjoyed periodic moments of dominant influence, but the discussions were usually limited to local venues like town councils, state prison boards, and state legislatures. The resulting policy changes derived from these debates were limited to local jurisdictions, and different regions of the country pursued diametrically different approaches.

During the 1930s, Attorney General Homer Cummings of the Roosevelt administration briefly engaged in a national debate on a new federal plan for law enforcement during the onset of the New Deal program, but the discussion was limited mostly to professional training and centralized crime statistics. At the start of the 1960s, Attorney General Robert Kennedy revived the national debate on crime control, which included a host of ambitious legislative proposals—most of which failed to pass. In 1965, President Lyndon Johnson included crime control as a secondary objective in his War on Poverty, resulting in several legislative changes. By the end of the decade, Richard Nixon became the first president-elect to prepare a strategy for national crime control, which included sections on how to improve presidential leadership, state and local law enforcement communication and cooperation, federal law enforcement, organized crime control, narcotics and dangerous drug control, obscenity laws, prison reforms, bail reform, and the rampant crime problem in the nation's capital. There were strong differences between President Johnson and President Nixon in their approaches to crime and punishment, which reflected the same age-old debates between deterrence and correction, but both presidents generally provided room for both models in their administrations. The 1960s political debates over crime and punishment were unique because they were held on a national stage, and the resulting policy changes impacted all jurisdictions throughout the federal, state, and local levels.

By the 1970s, both the deterrence and correction approaches to crime and punishment received significant federal support, and advocates of each priority gained opportunities to advance their policy preferences. In areas such as drug enforcement and organized crime control, advocates of deterrence gained dominance through harsher federal penalties and more rigidly enforced sentencing guidelines. In other areas, such as drug addiction and urban police enforcement, advocates for rehabilitation and correction gained dominance through the introduction of a wide variety of therapeutic sentencing options, increased use of probation, and public education programs. An uneasy coexistence between opposing theories of crime and punishment persisted throughout the 1970s, until it was shattered by a poor economy combined with a growing public perception that "nothing works" to reduce recidivism and aggregate crime rates. By 1980, federal authorities shared responsibility for a host of areas of enforcement and sentencing previously reserved for state and local authorities, and lawmakers on both sides began calling for greater consistency in federal priorities.

Criminal Correction Versus Criminal Deterrence
The debate among criminologists and law enforcement officials over the most effective way to reduce crime and deal with offenders can be traced back to the 19th century, and is strongly associated with other weighty questions of democratic freedom and individual rights. By the start of the 20th century, two different models had emerged at opposite ends of a spectrum of theories on the subject. On one end, a model of rehabilitation through therapeutic corrections emerged primarily from the research of sociologists at leading universities, especially the University of Chicago, which had by the 1920s gained a national reputation for expertise in criminology. On the other end, a cadre of reform-minded law enforcement officials led by Berkeley, California, Police Chief August Vollmer began developing standards of professionalism in an effort to improve public safety through a model of criminal deterrence, which emphasized methodological efficiency to increase the certainty of punishment and deter future criminals. Although supporters of both views often shared the stage in public debates, the premises that underlie each model often led to conflicting policy choices.

The criminal corrections model assumes that most crimes are not the result of freely chosen decisions, but instead reflect the limited choices available in a dysfunctional social environment. Social scientists search for those experiences that most contribute to criminal behaviors and use the information to proscribe treatment plans to neutralize criminality. In contrast, the criminal deterrence model presumes that individuals freely choose to live within or outside the law. Those choices are often colored by a corrupted

Idle youths in the Second Ward, or Chicano Area, in El Paso, Texas, during the summer of 1972. Juvenile delinquency was one of the foremost concerns in crime control by 1960 and continued to be a major focus through the following decade; standards for trial proceedings for juveniles, which were less formal than those for adults, were debated.

sense of moral standards, or an incomplete understanding of the consequences of criminal behavior. Crime is deterred when public examples of corruption are minimized, positive role models are maximized, and the threat of punishment for criminal behaviors is made certain.

Both of these models strive to improve the local environment of would-be criminals, but for different ends. The corrections model places the greatest blame for crime on social conditions, and therefore places much more emphasis on correcting conditions and rehabilitating offenders, who are seen more as victims than as perpetrators. The deterrence model places the greatest blame for crime on individuals, where the positive examples of a nurturing environment must be equally balanced by the negative threat of punishment in order for individuals to make fully informed decisions.

By 1960, one of the primary topics of crime control at the local and national level focused on the problem of juvenile delinquency. In part, this was due to the unprecedented growth in the number of children age 11 to 18 following World War II, which is referred to as the "baby boom generation." Over a third of the 170 million people living in the United States in 1960 were in their teens or were young adults. As that generation of youth reached adulthood, crime rates increased proportionally. The FBI's uniform crime reports indicated a slow, but steady increase in crime rates throughout the 1950s before jumping in all categories in 1960. Twice as many crimes were committed in 1960 than in 1950, with a 14 percent increase from 1959 to 1960 alone. Minors under 18 years of age accounted for two-thirds of the arrests for car theft, half of the arrests for burglary, and a quarter of the arrests for robbery and forcible rape.

Urban districts saw the greatest increase in juvenile crime, with 14 percent of all arrests made against youth under 18 years of age. Most of the violence was attributed to an increase in the number of urban gangs, which FBI Director J. Edgar Hoover described as a prime source of "vicious acts of vandalism, wanton brutality, and mounting savagery." This strong reaction is in part because of the contrast to the relatively peaceful conditions of the 1950s, as well as the fact that Hoover and others were most disturbed by the nature of these crimes, which appeared to represent a generational attack on authority. In 1960, 9,621 police officers were assaulted, including 48 who were killed in the line of duty. In New York City, there was an average of five attacks on police officers made by youth offenders per day, including throwing bricks, stones, beer bottles, and other garbage on police from rooftops.

Policymakers reacted to the rising baby boom generation in one of two ways. Those adhering to the corrections model cited the squalid conditions of many urban districts, particularly in black neighborhoods and among the new immigrants who had yet to fully assimilate. The combination of poverty, mixed with tense racial and ethnic diversity caused urban youth to band together in a form of brotherhood against what they

New York Police Department Police officers standing on the street with guns drawn and pointed upward during the July 1964 Harlem race riots. Officer Thomas Gilligan fatally shot 15-year-old James Powell of Harlem on July 16, 1964, sparking rioting and unrest. Urban America saw the greatest increase in crime in the early 1960s; in 1960 alone, nearly 10,000 police were assaulted and 48 were killed in the line of duty.

perceived as a hostile culture. As a symbol of that culture, police officers received the most hostility from minority groups. Suggested solutions to juvenile delinquency included some form of sensitivity training for both urban residents and police officers, matched by community action programs to reestablish the image of policemen as protectors rather than threat to local communities. In addition, advocates argued that the penalties for criminal behavior should take into account the complex social conditions and that judges should be given greater flexibility in sentencing, including more therapeutic options to better help offenders adjust to the norms of American society. In the long term, advocates of the corrections model believed that any successful solution to juvenile delinquency required at least an equal public commitment to ending urban poverty, reversing poor education rates, and opening more economic and social opportunities for urban youth.

In contrast, the advocates of the criminal deterrence model placed primary blame on the lack of resources available to the police. Urban populations declined while suburban populations increased by a 4:1 ratio, leaving police officers responsible for greater areas without an equivalent increase in police resources. Most police departments suffered from low budgets and low salaries ($175 per month for a 48-hour week, which was about half the national salary average), with large responsibilities (two officers per 1,000 residents). Proposed solutions included requests for more resources to support local law enforcement, including money for public education programs to teach adults to better respect the role of police and instill in their children a greater respect for the law. Finally, the courts were accused of being too lenient. As Hoover explained in an interview to the *Congressional Quarterly* in 1961, "undeserved paroles, probationary terms ... politically expedient pardons" resulted in soft sentencing for youth who committed violent crimes. He added, "officers risk their lives to bring hardened offenders to justice only to have them unleashed on society again," and as a result, "society pays a terrible price in the toll of innocent citizens ravished or murdered." For advocates of the criminal deterrence model, the guarantee of swift punishment was essential for crime control.

In 1960, the vast majority of law enforcement was conducted by local police and paid for by local governments, with punishments handed out by local and state agencies. As long as the primary operations of law enforcement and prison management remained under local and state jurisdiction, these two models of crime control were unevenly applied throughout the country. Debates between two views took place within the halls of local county council meetings or within state agencies, often with very different results, depending on the personality of the officials in charge. Consequently, the conditions of police stations, courtrooms, and jailhouses in the south were significantly different from conditions in the urban north or rural west. By the mid-1960s, the issues of crime and punishment assumed national proportions, and the intensity of the debates increased significantly as the resulting decisions meant the difference of millions of dollars in federal aid.

Communists, Mobsters, and Klansmen
In the midst of the rising debate over juvenile delinquency, there were three other movements in federal law enforcement originating from the late 1940s and 1950s that converged by 1960 to push federal lawmakers toward a more comprehensive approach to crime and punishment. These movements included efforts that began in the late 1940s to limit espionage and subversion from communist operatives, efforts in the early 1950s to break organized crime operations, and efforts in the mid 1950s to end legalized racial discrimination in the southern states. By the time President John F. Kennedy took office in 1961, all three efforts captured the attention of federal lawmakers, including the new attorney general, Robert F. Kennedy. He built upon the momentum of the previous

decade to launch a new proactive approach to crime, which relied much more heavily on federal leadership.

Both the president and his brother had direct experience with anticommunism, organized crime control, and civil rights. In 1950, John Kennedy joined 126 Republicans and 160 Democrats in voting for the Internal Security Act, which President Truman had vetoed the day before. The 1950 law required all subversive organizations to register with the attorney general's office and created an independent Subversive Activities Control Board (SACB) to examine suspected organizations to determine if they should be identified as subversive. Membership in a subversive organization and support for its principles was never illegal; for example, it was never illegal to be a member of the communist party or to believe in communism. The primary concern of lawmakers like Kennedy was that a foreign entity (namely the Soviet Union) might exploit America's First Amendment guarantees to unduly influence American culture through the use of "front organizations." These groups appeared to reflect grassroots American politics by appealing to common cultural ideals such as civil rights, international peace, and work equity. In practice, however, communist fronts used their organizations to advance the party line directed from Moscow.

Lawmakers like Kennedy were less concerned by the specific ideology than they were of the foreign influence over the American electorate. For this reason, the Internal Security Act of 1950 and its later revision, the Communist Control Act of 1954, received broad support from both parties. Lawmakers responded to the public demand to expose the dangers of foreign-based subversion, which lawmakers often described as "the enemy within."

Anticommunists of Kennedy's generation mostly reacted to the experiences of World War II and the memory of both Adolf Hitler's atrocities in Europe and Joseph Stalin's brutal dictatorship in the Soviet Union. By the end of the 1950s, those memories became less dominant and anticommunism became less pronounced as a priority of internal security. The threat, however, of a national conspiracy to undermine domestic law and order remained just as strong under a different guise of organized crime. As early as the 1930s, the popular images of Al Capone, "Lucky" Luciano, and Frank Costello dominated popular culture as movies like *Scarface*, *Little Caesar*, and *Public Enemy* helped to paint a picture of a growing underworld menace. In the early 1950s, Tennessee Senator Estes Kefauver competed with Joseph McCarthy for the nation's attention as he toured the country, exposing real-life underworld syndicates in New York, Chicago, Detroit, St. Louis, Kansas City, and nine other cities. These early televised hearings excited the public imagination but had little impact on federal crime policy. It was not until 1957 that federal agencies paid more serious attention to the reality of nationally organized crime. A small-town police sergeant stumbled across an old farmhouse in Apalachin, New York, where he saw a dozen limousines inconspicuously parked in the woods. A raid later that day led to the arrest of 66 reputed mobsters, including the heads of the New York crime families Joe Adonis, Albert Anastasia, Joe Bonanno, Frank Costello, Tommy Lucchese, and Joe Profaci, as well as Steve Magaddino from Buffalo, New York, Tony Accardo from Chicago, Carlos Marcello from New Orleans, Santo Trafficante from Florida, and Johnny Scalish from Cleveland, Ohio. After this event, the national attention easily shifted from the "communist menace" to the "organized crime menace."

There were many similarities between communist and organized crime conspiracies. They both relied on secret organizations to violate national laws, evade police enforcement, and escape effective prosecution through corruption of public officials. More importantly, they both took advantage of America's freedom of speech and association to marshal resources to deceive innocent citizens, exploit human weakness, and undermine neighborhood cultures to create antagonistic relationships between those "inside" and those "outside the group," including the law enforcement agents trying to capture them. From the perspective of criminal deterrence, communists and mobsters both represented an attack on public standards of law and order and threatened to corrupt youth by demonizing authority while also glorifying lawlessness. From the corrections perspective, communists and mobsters represented different attempts to escape from the overly harsh conditions of a dysfunctional social environment. For many lawmakers, organized crime was much easier to deal with than communism because it did not include the complicated ideological associations that follow free speech and political dissent. The emergence of organized crime as a national threat appealed to both older anticommunist lawmakers and the younger generation preoccupied by rising rates in juvenile delinquency and other common street crimes.

Both John Kennedy and his brother Robert worked directly on a Senate committee that targeted the infiltration of organized criminals in labor organizations. John Kennedy served as senator on the committee, and his brother Robert served as lead council for the committee chair, John L. McClellan. Their committee was largely responsible for compiling the evidence of organized corruption in several national unions, including the Teamsters. In 1960, Robert Kennedy published a book called *The Enemy Within*, which detailed his role on the committee and contributed to his brother's campaign success later that year. As president, John Kennedy appointed his brother to serve as attorney general, and Robert Kennedy's main legislative agenda for crime control included most of the recommendations made by the McClellan committee for which he had previously

President Kennedy (left) and Attorney General Robert F. Kennedy (right) meet with J. Edgar Hoover, director of the FBI, in the White House Oval Office on February 23, 1961. Both Kennedys worked on a Senate committee that targeted the infiltration of organized criminals in labor organizations. Robert Kennedy reopened the national debate on crime control and introduced ambitious legislation, but most of these efforts failed to pass.

worked. For the first time since the 1930s, the full weight of the Department of Justice (DOJ) stood behind a national program to combat organized crime.

Concurrent with these two movements, another even more popular movement to use federal resources to compel racial equality had grown steadily since the late 1940s. The Fourteenth and Fifteenth Amendments explicitly forbade discrimination based on race, but since the Civil War, the federal government had largely turned a blind eye to the racial injustices that were occurring in practice (legally or not) in the south. After the egregious atrocities of Hitler's race-based regime during World War II, Americans throughout the country, especially in the urban north and west, became equally intolerant of racial inequalities at home. The Supreme Court decision of *Brown v. Board of Education* in 1954 represented only one of hundreds of similar lawsuits filed by the NAACP during the late 1940s. By the mid-1950s, public attention was drawn to media images of southern segregation and apparent misuse of local police to perpetuate a system of segregation that most Americans outside the south found disturbing. In 1957, President Dwight D. Eisenhower sent in the National Guard to enforce the desegregation of public schools in Little Rock, Arkansas. By 1961, college students from across the country organized "freedom rides" to demonstrate the inequity of segregation on public transportation in the south, and President John F. Kennedy ordered federal marshals to ride along to guarantee their protection.

The Democratic Party had traditionally been tied to a bloc of southern voters who supported segregation and resisted federal efforts to impose desegregation. For this reason, Democrat President John F. Kennedy was limited in his ability to actively campaign for new federal civil rights legislation. Republican President Eisenhower had pushed for the civil rights acts of 1957 and 1960, which Kennedy had been forced to oppose. During the first two years of his administration (1961 and 1962), Kennedy did not initiate any civil rights legislation, even though Republicans worked on a bill to defund any recipient of federal aid that engaged in segregation. Kennedy's silence, however, did not mean he was not personally in favor of racial equality and desegregation. As the leader of his party, Kennedy balanced its regional wings and avoided civil rights issues; but as chief executive, Kennedy and his brother Robert used the resources of the DOJ to strictly enforce the civil rights bills that were already legally enforced. By June 1963, two months before Martin Luther King Jr. led the 100,000-strong march on Washington to deliver his "I Have a Dream" speech, Robert Kennedy had already instructed his assistant attorneys general across the country "to render significant service as a catalyst, coordinator, and supporter of local community action to desegregate public facilities and upgrade Negro employment." By the end of 1963, John F. Kennedy was able to harness strong public support to carefully initiate a push for a new, more comprehensive civil rights bill for 1964. Kennedy was assassinated before the bill was formally introduced and passed, but the new President Lyndon Johnson—a southerner with a weak civil rights record—was able to claim ownership of the bill and push it to final passage in February 1964.

These three unrelated movements in federal crime policy tied to anticommunism, organized crime control, and civil rights dominated the DOJ and relevant congressional committees during the first years of the 1960s. Though unrelated in nature, all three movements emphasized the need for increased vigilance on the part of the federal government to more proactively guide a national crime control policy that would ensure public safety. Perhaps most critical in the confluence were the technical issues that each movement added to the discussion of crime and punishment, which policymakers were forced to grapple with over the next 15 years. The anticommunism movement raised the specter of subversive ideology undermining law and order. It also raised issues related to the First Amendment right of public dissent and Fifth Amendment rights of witnesses giving testimony and the proper use of immunity in compelling testimony. Likewise, the effort to control organized crime raised the alarm of wayward youth and of technology used to facilitate criminal operations. It also raised questions of First Amendment protections against guilt by association; Fourth Amendment protections against improper search and seizures, especially related to electronic eavesdropping devices; and Eighth Amendment protections against unusually harsh penalties for "professional criminals." The effort to enforce civil rights alerted lawmakers to the corruption that could occur when local authorities failed to uphold Fourteenth Amendment protections guaranteeing national standards of due process, or failed to provide Sixth Amendment guarantees of adequate access to legal counsel at all levels of police custody. At the same time, the call for civil rights could be so broadly interpreted as to justify violence, radical subversion, and lawlessness. The elevation of all these issues in the relatively short decade of the 1960s resulted in deeper polarity on issues of crime and punishment. Until the mid-1970s, these polarized debates resulted in greater federal support in a variety of measures that promoted both the corrections model and the deterrence model of crime control.

Corrections and the "War on Poverty"

The assassination of President John F. Kennedy in November 1963 sent shockwaves through the nation. The young Kennedy was a symbol of the burgeoning baby boom generation, and his promises of a "new frontier" seemed to resonate with the hope of futuristic change. Despite his advancing years, President Johnson capitalized on that youthful symbolism to introduce his Great Society program, which promised a new war on poverty, racism, and injustice. The Civil Rights Act of 1964 and the Voting Rights Act of 1965 served only as a prelude for a host of federal programs designed to alleviate the social conditions that led to local unrest. By directly linking poverty with racism and, indirectly, to social disorders such as crime and juvenile delinquency, Johnson was promoting a broad social policy that reinforced the corrections model of crime and punishment.

Johnson's announcement of his Great Society agenda was not without specific cause. During the summer of 1964, Johnson's reelection campaign was interrupted by news of race riots in the northern towns of Harlem, Rochester, New York, Paterson, New Jersey, and Philadelphia, resulting in five deaths and more than 500 wounded. Urban rioting was not new to the north, and clashes had occurred periodically in New York, Detroit, Cleveland, and Cincinnati since 1960, but most observers associated the conflicts with increased juvenile delinquency combined with sympathetic protests following the more dramatic civil rights demonstrations held in the south. The 1964 riots, however, were much larger and seemed to be more coordinated, which suggested a growing trend. Though Johnson remained far ahead in the polls, he nevertheless felt increasing pressure to act.

In 1964, crime and punishment had not yet become partisan issues, and most Republicans and Democrats viewed the riots independently from election rhetoric. Early in the summer, President Johnson and Republican challenger Barry Goldwater made a secret agreement not to bring up urban rioting or America's presence in Vietnam during the campaign. They both believed that the issues were too important for national unity to be trampled on through campaign expedience, and both sides kept their word. Nevertheless, Johnson's advisor warned the president that he should call together a national conference on the problem of crime, which would include a discussion of juvenile delinquency, organized crime, and urban riots. The president agreed, and shortly after his election, Johnson issued Executive Order 11236, calling for the

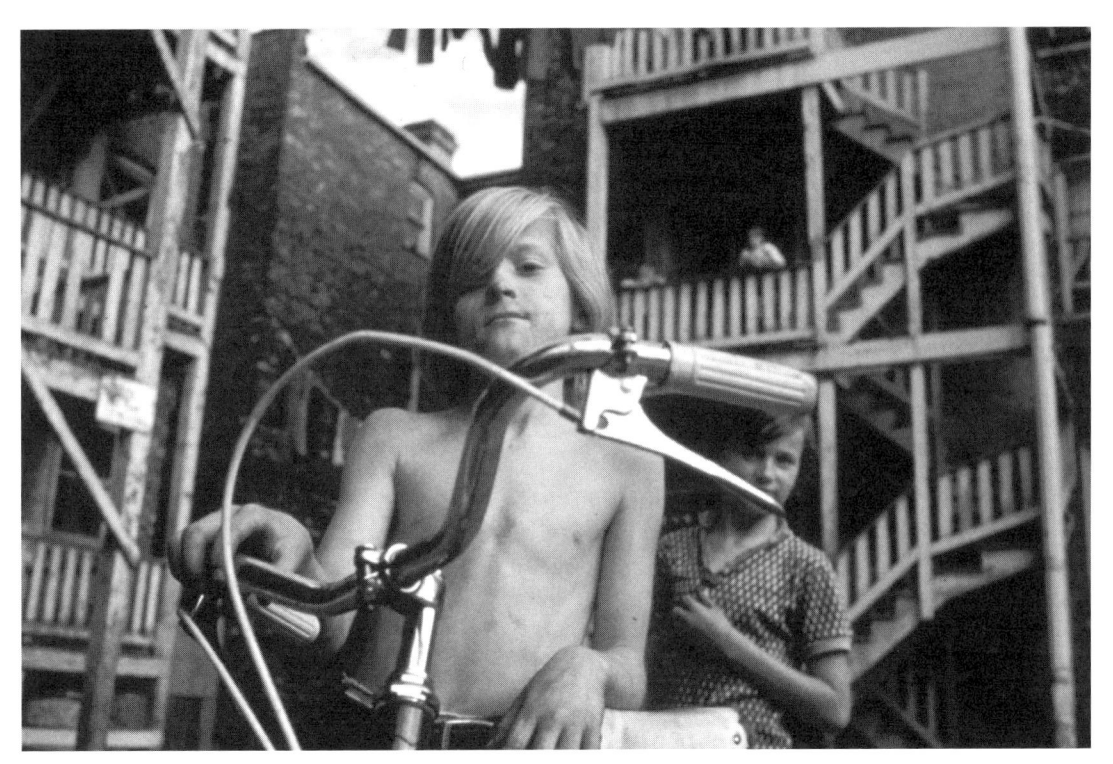

Children in Uptown, Chicago, a poor, inner-city neighborhood, in August 1974. Soon after taking office in 1963, President Lyndon Johnson launched his Great Society program to fight poverty, racism, and injustice, and indirectly, social disorders such as crime and juvenile delinquency. In this manner, Johnson reinforced the corrections model of crime and punishment, an approach that was criticized by proponents of the deterrence model.

president's commission on Law Enforcement and Administration of Justice. The President's Commission included representatives from distinguished academics in the fields of psychiatry, sociology, law, and prison reform, including practicing law enforcement leaders, and focused on several different aspects of crime in America.

In the first eight months of 1965, President Johnson submitted 65 requests for congressional action on specific bills. The Great Society agenda included a host of bills authorizing 40 new community development programs intended to eliminate poverty in urban areas, new housing and employment incentives, and 60 new programs providing funding for urban classrooms, interest-free student loans, and minority development. In the midst of this flurry of activity, Johnson's administration also introduced numerous crime prevention bills, which included funding requests to provide training for local police and grant money for local personnel management, research dollars for statewide surveys, and seed money for experimental "demonstration" projects, which included broad public education components. Also included were requests for prison alternatives, such as halfway houses, work release programs, rehabilitation clinics, and other therapeutic sentencing solutions. These bills became the Bail Reform Act, the Prisoner Rehabilitation Act, Criminal Justice Reform Act, and first Law Enforcement Assistance Act of 1965.

Throughout most of 1965, Johnson's Great Society program received broad support from both Republicans and Democrats, which included a relatively even distribution of advocates for both the corrections and deterrence models of crime control. Johnson's agenda did not appear to disturb either side, because crime and punishment were not yet politicized at the federal level. Instead, the object of conflict between the deterrence and corrections models was directed primarily toward the Supreme Court. Chief Justice Earl Warren was the center of an emerging national debate over a series of controversial decisions that seemed to disrupt the delicate balance between the rights of the criminal and the prerogatives of law enforcement. In his support were primarily advocates for the corrections model of crime control, joined by a strong contingent of civil libertarians. Warren's supporters praised the court's defense of individual liberties, including protections against unlawful searches and seizures and self incrimination. Not surprisingly, there were an equal number of opponents, which included advocates for the corrections model as well as a host of law enforcement officials who condemned the court for unfairly handicapping police in their ability to perform their duties. In 1965, there were petitions circulated around Washington, D.C., calling for Warren's impeachment, but none were successful.

The court decisions that created the most controversy were *Mallory v. United States* (1957), *Mapp v. Ohio* (1961), *Gideon v. Wainwright* (1963), *Escobedo v. Illinois* (1964), and *Miranda v. Arizona* (1966). These cases dealt with voluntary confessions, admissibility of evidence, and wiretapping. To some, these rulings seemed to change the primary focus of courtroom adjudication away from determining "guilt" or "innocence" to a new standard of whether or not "due process" was followed. Confessions were most troubling in this regard, because a confession seems to be irrefutable proof of a person's guilt. Since the 1930s, confessions had been judged according to whether they were voluntary or involuntary admissions—a confession obtained through coercion was deemed at the very least unreliable, while a voluntary confession virtually guaranteed conviction. The *Mallory* decision held that confessions contrived during illegal detentions, regardless of whether they were voluntary or not, were inadmissible as evidence. This decision was followed quickly by the *Mapp* case, which held that any evidence obtained through improper means would be excluded from evidence. This "exclusionary rule" had already been practiced in federal courts since the 1880s, but the *Mapp* decision applied the same rule to state courts through the Fourteenth Amendment. Since the vast majority of cases were handled at the state level, this decision had a dramatic impact on the way police handled evidence. Opponents of the decision argued that the ruling would let guilty people go free, even those who actually confessed their crime, because of a technical error when an officer mistakenly failed to follow proper procedures. Supporters of the *Mallory/Mapp* rules argued that exclusion was the only effective way to force police officers to follow due process.

The new emphasis on guaranteeing due process through court-defined guidelines further illustrated the need for lawyers to be present at all stages of incarceration, including interrogation after arrest, indictment, and all preliminary hearings before trial. The *Gideon* case in 1963 held that all people had a right to attorney, even if they did not have the funds to pay for one. The following year, in 1964, the court ruled in *Escobedo* that any testimony obtained from a defendant outside the presence of an attorney could be excluded. Two years later, the court followed with *Miranda*, holding that any statements obtained while under police custody, without full warning of the prisoner's rights to counsel, were inadmissible. These rights were applied to juvenile offenders the following year in *In Re Gault* (1967). Taken together, these decisions dramatically changed the way in which police questioned, searched, and obtained evidence to convict accused suspects. As a result, almost everyone who watches a police crime show now knows by heart the famous line given at the time of arrest: "You have the right to remain silent. Anything you say can and will be used against you in a court of law. You have the right to be speak to an attorney, and to have an attorney present during any questioning. If you cannot afford a lawyer, one will be provided for you at government expense."

Today, the Miranda rights are largely taken for granted, but in the mid-1960s, these rulings were very controversial. Lawmakers in both houses submitted multiple resolutions attempting to overturn these decisions. In a hypothetical case, a guilty man could confess his crime, only to find it later excluded from evidence due to police error, resulting in the guilty party going free. Prior to the *Miranda* decision, about 60 percent of all cases relied on voluntary confession to obtain a conviction. After *Miranda*, that rate fell to 44 percent. More dramatically, the number of cases involving violent crimes "cleared"—in which an officer identifies a guilty party—fell from 60 percent in 1965 to 45 percent by 1968. The decline in clearance rates for property crimes showed a similar pattern, with a drop from 24 percent down to 18 percent. Law enforcement officials argued that their ability to convict was hampered by an overly cautious set of rules that favored the criminal over the victim.

On the other side of the debate, civil libertarians argued that the decline in confessions and convictions reflects a positive trend of a more equitable justice system. In a hypothetical case, an overly zealous law enforcement officer jumps to a conclusion about an innocent man's guilt based on race, economic status, or some other characteristic from a presumed criminal profile. The officer takes the easy route by forcing the suspect into confessing to a crime by exploiting their ignorance or resorting to psychological intimidation. The "third degree" (or physical abuse) may have faded away in the 1930s, but there were many ways in which an officer could use isolation and emotional appeals to influence a suspect into making incriminating statements. In this case, the officer may clear the case through confession because it is easier than tracking down more objective evidence through proper scientific methods, but the civil libertarian would argue that the conviction was false and that true guilt or innocence was not determined without proper processes.

These perspectives involve differing presumptions about the nature of crime—whether the individual or their environment are most responsible, and whether the police serve to apprehend criminals or reenforce the majority conditions of the social environment. These perspectives were difficult to reconcile, and as these issues found their way into congressional hearings during the 1967–69 session, the issue of crime and punishment became increasingly polarized.

For the first two years of his administration, President Johnson seemed detached from these debates over civil liberties and criminal enforcement. By 1967, the various Task Force Reports of the President's Crime Commission started to appear. The collective report, titled *The Challenge of Crime in a Civil Society*, was comprised of a dozen separate Task Force Reports on police, causes of crime, sentencing and prisons, organized crime, and a half-dozen other areas. Though the collective report mostly emphasized a corrections model of crime and punishment, the separate task force reports often made contrary recommendations. The introduction to the *Challenge of Crime* linked rising crime rates to limited social and economic opportunities for the urban poor, many of whom belonged to frustrated racial and ethnic minority groups. It also recommended increased federal funding for more urban development programs to improve economic opportunities, more correction programs for rehabilitation, more diversity programs to enhance legitimacy of police within their communities, and more academic research into crime and punishment. At the same time, the Task Force on Organized Crime included recommendations calling for greater funding for state and local law enforcement, specific legislation for increased federal authority to use electronic eavesdropping, and increased authorities to compel testimony in organized crime investigations. Taken as a whole, advocates of both the corrections and the deterrence models could handpick the provisions, with which they most agreed to justify a competing legislative agenda.

President Johnson followed the release of the commission report with the announcement of a new crime-control package called the Safe Streets and Law Enforcement Act. The bill expanded federal funding of the Law Enforcement Administration Agency (LEAA), providing grants to local community and law enforcement agencies with the aim of finding innovative alternatives to traditional incarceration. The bill also included an expansive gun control provision, which was the special project of Ted Kennedy who, after the assassination of his brother John, wanted to outlaw the purchase of weapons through the mail. Fellow Democrat Senator John L. McCellan held much different views of crime and punishment than President Johnson, but he publicly supported the President's Commission and embraced the new Safe Streets Act. McClellan's Senate Committee held hearings on the bill, which eventually forced Johnson into taking a side in the debate over which policies were most effective in controlling crime.

The president's relationship with advocates of the deterrence model of crime control soured dramatically in 1967. In late 1966, Johnson had already sent signals that he supported corrections over deterrence when he vetoed the District of Columbia Crime Bill, which contained a variety of measures opposed by civil libertarians, including an antiobscenity provision, mandatory minimum sentences, and detention procedures for suspects short of arrest. During the summer of 1967, Johnson publicly supported Senator Edward Long's hearings into the federal government's use of wiretaps and eavesdropping devices against civil rights leaders. For some civil libertarians, the fact that the federal government used wiretaps and bugs for any purpose seemed to prove an underlying assertion that the police were more interested in "controlling" neighborhoods than they were in "protecting" them. The fact that these tools were used against civil rights leaders further reinforced a growing belief that the spike in juvenile crime and urban

In August 1963, a crowd of African Americans gather behind a fenced-off area during a civil rights march on Washington, D.C., where an estimated 200,000–300,000 people gathered. On the other side of the fence, police remove a protesting woman.

rioting reflected an act of political resistance to authoritarian police practices. Johnson announced that he would support any bill formally outlawing the use of all electronic surveillance technologies in criminal cases, which upset many law enforcement officials who argued that they were necessary for apprehending and deterring crime.

At the same time, Johnson formed a National Advisory Commission on Civil Disorders to investigate the number of urban riots that seemed to escalate each summer. Riots in the Watts section of Los Angeles during the summer of 1965 caused $175 million in damages, and left 35 dead and more than 1,000 injured. The summer of 1966 brought a similar outbreak, though on a smaller scale. Overall crime rates continued to skyrocket, even in less volatile areas—in a year that experienced only a 1 percent population growth, violent crime increased 11 percent and property crimes grew by 10 percent, nearly twice and three times the previous year's rates. Also, crime in the nation's capital was worse than it had been in a decade. Johnson's National Advisory Commission published the *Kerner Report* (named after Otto Kerner who chaired the commission), which pointed to poor housing conditions, high unemployment, and overaggressive use of police force as the main causes of the rioting. It placed special importance on the frustrations of racial and ethnic minorities, who felt incapable of escaping the impoverished ghettos. The famous quote from the report warned that, "our nation is moving toward two societies, one black, one white—separate and unequal." The report placed that blame for most of these conditions on white America for creating a culture hostile to minorities, and on the law enforcement system, which abused its authority while policing urban communities. Johnson's support for these conclusions alienated many of those who sympathized with law enforcement.

By 1968, the vocal opposition that advocates of the crime deterrence model had reserved mostly for the Warren Court was equally directed toward President Johnson. Senator McClellan used his Senate hearings to introduce several amendments to the Safe Streets Bill that were entirely contrary to Johnson's original intent. Following recommendations made by the president's Task Force on Organized Crime, McClellan inserted provisions to circumvent parts of the *Mallory* and *Mapp* decisions by stipulating that voluntary confessions would be admissible if made concurrent with arrest; he also included other provisions providing federal agents with stronger authority to issue search and seizure warrants. Other additions prohibited federal employment of anyone convicted in state courts for participating in or organizing riots. Johnson's LEAA provision was modified to allow states to directly administer the money outside of federal oversight and, most significantly, McClellan called for explicit authorization for court-enforced wiretapping and electronic surveillance powers.

Johnson opposed all of the new additions and tried to initiate parliamentary maneuvers in Congress to remove them for the final bill, but he was unsuccessful. By April 1968, Johnson signed the Civil Rights Act of 1968, which included the Fair Housing Act that explicitly forbade discrimination in the sale or rental of housing. This was a direct response to the *Kerner Report,* and Johnson hoped it would lessen some of the support for the Safe Streets Bill that was still stuck in Congress. The Housing Act seemed an insufficient solution for the problem of urban riots, and public pressure for some direct action on crime control was too intense.

That week, Martin Luther King Jr. was murdered in public by a sniper's bullet, and three months later, on June 5, Robert Kennedy was murdered during a public rally in Los Angeles after winning the California and South Dakota primaries. Gallop polls named "crime and law enforcement" as the number one problem facing America, and further indicated that 63 percent of the public believed that the courts were too "soft" on crime and 45 percent wanted tougher laws and stronger police. The specter of uncontrolled crime in America forced Johnson's hand, and he was compelled to support the Safe Streets Bill, even though he opposed at least half of its provisions. Congress passed McClellan's version of the bill by an overwhelming majority in the week following Robert Kennedy's assassination, and the president reluctantly signed it four hours before the deadline. In an example of political compromise, the Safe Streets and Crime Control Act of 1968 provided almost equal support for both the corrections and deterrence models of crime and punishment.

Law and Order and Deterrence
Despite his landslide victory in 1964, President Johnson was unable to secure enough support to guarantee his nomination in 1968. Historians debate the reasons why Johnson lost so much support in the short period between 1966 and 1968, but it is clear that issues of crime and punishment played some role in the process. The Republican nominee, Richard Nixon, staged a campaign that promised to more proactively address the problems of urban rioting, combat rising crime rates, and instill greater respect for "law and order" within all classes of society, especially among the young. The assassination of Robert Kennedy, who was emerging as the Democratic Party's frontrunner after Johnson quietly withdrew, seemed to help Republicans more than Democrats, and Nixon defeated the new Democratic nominee, Hubert Humphrey, by a respectable margin.

From first appearances, President Nixon's election in 1968 might be seen as a triumph of the criminal deterrence model of crime and punishment. For the first time in history, an American president developed a detailed guidebook for a federally led crime-control policy, even before entering office. Prior administrations never took such a step because policies for crime control and punishment were almost exclusively reserved for state authorities to administer. Yet, one of the lasting legacies of Johnson's administration was his promotion of both of these issues into the national spotlight. Nixon's administration made "law and order" a top priority. Within his first year in office, Nixon successfully guided several federal crime control bills through Congress, including the Organized Crime Control Act and the Comprehensive Drug Abuse Prevention and Control Act of 1970. Both laws provided tools for greater coordination among law enforcement agencies, stiffer penalties for certain crimes, and less flexibility in sentencing. Nixon's law-and-order agenda empowered law enforcement with a host of new tools to investigate, apprehend, and prosecute offenders, which strongly favored a deterrence model on crime. At the same time, none of these new laws overturned the programs initiated by Johnson. In fact, in most cases, especially in drug enforcement, Nixon's policy continued to incorporate many elements from both the corrections and deterrence models. This dual approach defined the approach to crime and punishment throughout most of the 1970s.

The Organized Crime Control Act of 1970 was a crime package nearly 40 years in the making. It contained nine separate provisions, many of which were first conceived in the 1930s and 1950s. The long delay was mostly due to the fact that criminal prosecutions, with few exceptions, were usually conducted at the local level using state laws. For decades, federal lawmakers resisted passing specific legislation to empower federal law enforcement officers, who might intrude on the jurisdiction and autonomy of local police. The fear of organized crime forced lawmakers to reconsider. News of corruption among local officers, local prosecutors, members of city councils, and some police chiefs compelled Congress to add new tools at the federal level to fight criminal organization that might span several cities or even multiple states. In 1963, supposed mafia enforcer Joseph Valachi testified before McClellan's Senate committee, exposing the secret society

A 1970s anti-drug poster from the U.S. Customs Service warns of narcotics infiltration. President Nixon placed heavy blame on neighborhood crime for the rampant use of illegal drugs and pursued the problem as strenuously as he pushed for federal organized crime control. By 1970, federal statistics indicated that 200,000 people were addicted to heroin and 1 million had used marijuana. Death rates from drug abuse tripled between 1960 and 1970.

of organized crime. In 1968, his memoirs were published, and the image of a nationally organized crime syndicate captured the imaginations of both the public and Congress. The Organized Crime Control Act was, in part, a final response to the threat.

Many of the provisions for the 1970 crime package followed the recommendations made by President Johnson's Task Force on Organized Crime, which had also borrowed ideas from earlier recommendations made by smaller commissions from the 1930s and 1950s. Some of these included the authority to create special grand juries with broad powers to investigate any criminal violation, even beyond the initial mandate. These juries could sit for months at a time, appeal directly to the attorney general in case local prosecutors or investigators were reluctant to act, and present detailed reports of their findings. Other provisions included enhanced penalties for certain categories of criminals, including habitual offenders who repeatedly committed the same crimes, professional criminals who earned their living from criminal activities, and organized criminals who cooperated with others to avoid apprehension. Advocates for the criminal deterrence model of crime control strongly supported these measures because they seemed to counteract "soft" parole boards or "weak" judges at the local level who failed to adequately punish hardened criminals. Other critics, including advocates for the corrections model, complained that the new laws did not take into account the variety of other explanations for repeat offenders. It was possible that a "hard" judge might impose a sentence of 30 years in prison to a young offender who engaged in a crime spree.

Other provisions of the Organized Crime Control Act included special protections guaranteeing the safety of cooperating witnesses. Law enforcement agents routinely complained about the unwillingness of witnesses to testify out of fear for their lives from mob retaliation, and these new powers seemed to address that problem. Civil libertarians sympathized about needing to protect witnesses, but they were concerned by related provisions that gave prosecutors the authority to compel testimony by granting limited immunity for specific crimes. The Fifth Amendment prohibits involuntary self-incrimination, but granting immunity to a suspect forced them to testify because they faced no risk of punishment. The new law authorized judges to hold witnesses for contempt if they failed to testify under immunity. Civil libertarians argued that these powers were too reminiscent of 1950s hearings on anticommunism, when communist informants were jailed for failing to testify against their associates. Though the law was explicitly written to prosecute organized criminals, critics argued that the same laws could also be used to prosecute other political dissenters, protestors, or rioters. Moreover, since these were federal laws, they could be applied in any of the 50 states through the Fourteenth Amendment.

The most enduring measure of the Organized Crime Control Act was a provision called the Racketeer Influenced Corrupt Organizations (RICO) Act. The law provided special penalties for criminals who used electronic communication tools in the regular course of business to commit several crimes over an extended period of time. In theory, the law was intended to target mobsters who used legitimate businesses as fronts for their criminal operations. In addition, the law also provided civil provisions, which meant that, even if the police failed to prosecute the corrupt business, competing businesses could sue on the basis that they were deceived through criminal organization. At the time it was passed, RICO received little attention and was ignored for almost seven years. Late in the decade, federal prosecutors noticed its value and began holding workshops on how to use the law to launch federal investigations. The RICO statute eventually became one of the federal government's most powerful tools for prosecuting mob bosses, resulting in the conviction of all five heads of the New York crime families by the mid-1980s. At the same time, the fear of some civil libertarians that the law could be used for alternate purposes also proved accurate. The civil component of the RICO law was reinterpreted as a new breach of contract penalty, and by the mid-1980s, the law was routinely used by companies to sue their competitors for infractions that had little to do with organized crime. By the 1990s, the number of civil RICO cases skyrocketed to more than a 1,000 per year, including several famous lawsuits against large tobacco companies, small-arms manufacturers, the Major Baseball League, the Los Angeles Police Department, and even the Catholic Church.

One of the most significant results of Nixon's organized crime push was that it initiated a new program of federal strike forces, which coordinated the resources of federal agents directly with state and local law police. The idea of creating ongoing bodies of federal–local coordination to solve complex crime problems first arose from the American Bar Association during the 1950s, and Robert Kennedy resurrected the idea during his tenure as attorney general, but it was not implemented in either instance. The Nixon administration gave full support behind the model and piloted it for large eastern cities known for heavy mob infiltration, including Brooklyn, Detroit, Philadelphia, Newark, and Miami. By the end of the 1970s, the Strike Force Program quickly expanded to include a variety of targets, from illegal drug operations to youth street gangs. These strike forces brought federal law enforcement officers into the daily routines of local police precincts in almost all large urban areas.

President Nixon offset his push for more comprehensive federal organized crime control with an equally stronger federal response to local neighborhood crime, which he blamed largely on the wide use of illegal drugs. While not dismissing the problems of poverty and racism, Nixon argued that a majority of property crimes were committed by drug addicts who found it necessary to steal and commit other crimes to support their habits. Federal statistics in 1970 reported 200,000 people addicted to heroin, mostly among people in their late 20s. More than 1 million people used marijuana, 10 percent of whom were considered chronic users, most of them in their late teens. Of greatest concern was the death rate due to drug abuse that tripled between 1960 and 1970 and increased five times for people under age 24. Nixon's new drug enforcement agenda sought to distinguish between the severities of different drugs to counteract the long-term effects of youthful experimentation.

The Comprehensive Drug Abuse Prevention and Control Act of 1970 consolidated the various drug enforcement departments spread across the government into a single new Drug Enforcement Agency, which was given more funding and more agents to operate. In the new system, all drugs were reclassified according to their usefulness and potential for abuse. Five categories were created, with Category V including drugs that required some medical supervision but were not likely to be abused, and Category I reserved for drugs that were highly addictive with no legitimate medical use. This ranked schedule system allowed police the freedom to prioritize their enforcement strategies—less emphasis was placed on marijuana, while more emphasis was placed on heroin. Nixon followed up with an executive order creating the Special Action Office for Drug Abuse Prevention, which created a national network of federally funded treatment centers to help those addicted to drugs. The new drug classification system also empowered state legislatures to tailor their criminal codes to match the severity of the drug and the severity of the offense. In 1973, New York Governor Nelson Rockefeller pushed for new legislation that provided lesser punishments for drug possession when the amounts were limited to personal use and much harsher punishments for possession of amounts needed for distribution. These laws were intended to distinguish between the drug user and the drug dealer. Advocates of the deterrence model applauded Rockefeller's more severe punishments, including imprisonment for drug dealing, which had usually been reserved for more violent crimes. Advocates of the corrections model supported the new federal funding for treatment centers as part of the solution to crime, but they were less supportive of the overall impact of the new war on drugs and its impact on the overall prison population. Between 1970 and 1980, the rate of prison growth at state and federal levels doubled from 4 percent to 8 percent per year. Actual prisoner counts in 1970 were twice that of the decade before, and the rates in 1980 were three times that of 1960.

The larger prison populations resurrected long-standing concerns about youth incarceration. Since 1899, youth had been treated differently than adult offenders. The first juvenile court in Chicago was started with the goal of rehabilitating youth before they grew into adult criminals. These courts operated with much less formal procedures so that the judge could act as a "parent of the country" to deal with the individual circumstances of each child with greater flexibility. Punishment usually meant mandatory attendance to a reform school, even if the property crime or other crime of violence would otherwise have resulted in a prison sentence for adults. Very few records were kept, and the youthful crimes were supposed to be forgotten to allow offenders the opportunity to grow into responsible and law-abiding adults. Youth courts were one of many programs to come from the corrections model of crime and punishment.

Yet by the 1960s, disagreement arose, even among corrections advocates, about the usefulness of such informal proceedings. There was a concern that the same informality that allowed judges to waive normal punishments for youthful crimes might also be used to pass harsher sentences with few opportunities for appeal. In 1966, the Supreme Court held in *Kent v. United States* that juveniles were entitled to some formal preliminary hearings if they chose them. The following year, the court held in *In re Gault* that juveniles were entitled to the same rights of due process as adults, which included a list of *Miranda*-like warnings. Critics of these rulings argued that the formalization of juvenile courts would undermine its original purpose, which was not to hear adversarial cases between competing attorneys, but to serve as a sort of social agency to rehabilitate wayward youth. Nevertheless, in 1970, the court ruled again in *In re Winship* that judges in juvenile courts were required to use the same standards of evidence used in adult courts when handing down their decisions. Several justices on the Supreme Court dissented in these cases, and the trend was eventually slowed the following year, when the *McKeiver v. Pennsylvania* decision ruled that juveniles were not entitled to a trial by jury.

At the other extreme among prison populations, the Supreme Court also reconsidered the constitutionality of the most extreme punishment that could be handed out by a judge—the death penalty. The basic rationale behind the death penalty is that some crimes are so egregious that they require the stiffest punishment possible to deter would-be offenders. At the time of the American Revolution, all of the thirteen colonies listed numerous crimes punishable by death, and the new federal government listed its own capital crimes in 1790. Debates over the value of the penalty as a tool of deterrence began as early as the 1840s. Three states abolished it before the Civil War, but after public executions were ended in favor of private venues, the issue faded. Calls for abolition reemerged prior to World War I, when eight more states, mostly in the west, abolished the penalty, but after 1917 the issue faded.

The question of abolition remerged in the late 1950s during the civil rights movement in the south. The gruesome murder of Emmett Till in 1955 highlighted the potential for local inequities after the two white men who were indicted for the murder were quickly acquitted by the local jury. They later admitted in an interview with a national magazine that they actually had committed the crime. Lawmakers on both sides of the segregation issue were outraged by Emmett Till's murder and the lack of conviction, and civil rights leaders effectively argued that justice in the south was enforced along racial lines—whites were less likely to be convicted for crimes against blacks, while blacks were routinely convicted and much more likely to be punished with more severe sentences. The misuse of justice was especially tragic when the punishment involved death. Rape was listed as a capital crime in most southern states, and critics argued that the law was reserved mostly for blacks who dared to resist the segregated system—some went so far as to call it "legal lynching."

By the 1960s, national attention was focused on a host of racial inequalities rising from the segregated society. This national conversation moved beyond race, however, when several non-southern states began re-examining the inconsistency with which the death penalty was applied. Some judges resorted to it frequently, while others—sometimes in the next courtroom—never used it. Between 1957 and 1969, the fear that the personal whim of a single judge might determine if a culprit received a prison sentence or a death sentence led eight more states to abolish capital sentences in favor of long prison terms. The Supreme Court became directly involved in these issues in 1968, when it ruled in *Witherspoon v. Illinois* (1968) that prospective jurors could not be excluded from capital cases based on their opposition to the death penalty. Four years later, the court ruled in *Furman v. Georgia* that capital punishment in many states was arbitrarily administered, and as such was a violation of Eighth Amendment protection against cruel and unusual punishment and the Fourteenth Amendment due process guarantee.

The court specifically identified racial bias as the primary reason for the arbitrary use of the death penalty, and declared that the penalty should not be administered anywhere unless it could be done in a clear and consistent manner, with frequent opportunities for appeal to eliminate the possibility that nonlegal factors, such as race, might influence the decision.

The immediate effect of *Furman* was that more than 600 death-row inmates across the country had their sentences automatically commuted to life in prison, and all future death sentences were placed on hold until each state established consistent procedures guaranteeing equal implementation. Opponents such as Georgia Lieutenant Governor Lester Maddax reacted to the *Furman* decision by calling it a "license for anarchy, rape, murder." Supporters, including members of the American Civil Liberties Union and the Legal Defense Fund, described the ruling as one more step toward a "more civilized" America. President Nixon, nevertheless, vowed to restore the penalty. Over the next four years, 35 states passed revised rules for the implementation of the death penalty, and in 1976, the court ruled in *Gregg v. Georgia* that the modifications were sufficient to guarantee equal implementation. The following year, Gary Gilmore became the first prisoner to be executed after the court lifted the ban on capital punishment.

From Watergate to "Nothing Works"
In 1972, President Richard Nixon won the presidential election by the largest electoral landslide in history. The "law and order" campaign played a major role in his success, in part because the new federal initiatives against organized crime and drug enforcement reflected a general expansion in federal leadership over crime control. The campaign also seemed an explicit antidote to the growing counterculture radicalism that was emerging on college campuses and from within the civil rights movement. The antiwar movement sparked a number of organizations that were committed to Marxist principles, opposed to American capitalism, and vocally encouraging open opposition to the existing social system as a racist, sexist, oppressive tool of wealth and privilege. Groups like the Students for a Democratic Society (SDS), Weatherman Underground, the Black Panthers, and Black Muslim groups opposed the war in Vietnam, not because they rejected violence, but because they believed that the war represented capitalist imperialism. The war, capitalism, and any expression of governmental oppression—racial or otherwise—were to be confronted and opposed by "any means necessary." At times, that resulted in the bombing of public buildings, orchestrated robberies, and violent unrest. The FBI reported more than 2,500 bombings in 1969 alone. While these organizations represented a tiny fraction of the larger civil rights movement, they often captured a much larger portion of the media attention.

Some of the campus radicalism spilled into the prison system, as increasingly crowded prisons began devolving into race-based gangs. The Black Muslim organization attracted black separatism within the prison yards, which was matched by white separatist gangs in the same institutions. These race-based tensions were magnified by the fact that many of the prison facilities were more than 30 years old and had not been built to hold so many inmates. Reforms in prison conditions had not kept pace with reforms in the criminal system. Race riots erupted in prisons periodically in the 1960s, including one in San Quinten in 1967 that involved 2,000 inmates. In all, there were 39 prison riots in 1969 and 59 in 1970. The bloodiest prison riot in American history occurred in 1971, when prisoners at the Attica Correctional Facility in New York killed a guard and ended up taking 39 prison workers hostage. The incident began in reaction to the death of a black militant leader at San Quentin, who was shot trying to escape. The 1,200 inmates of Attica described their insurrection as a political protest and demanded better conditions.

Hostage negotiations broke down after four days, and Governor Rockefeller ordered the prison be taken back by force. Police dropped tear gas into the yard before storming, resulting in the death of 10 hostages and 29 inmates and the wounding of 80 others. Both the inmates and the police were criticized for their handling of the Attica riot. Prisons across the country adopted more aggressive policies to prevent future uprisings, while at the same time lawmakers pushed for the construction of new prisons and the renovation of old sites to address some of the issues of overcrowding.

At the national level, the association with radical rhetoric and rioting in the streets, on campus, and behind prison walls helped shape the public's perception of a growing lawlessness among American youth that was arising from the new radical ideology. Nixon's law-and-order campaign provided some balance to the perception, which resulted in his 1972 landslide victory. Yet, just two years later, Nixon was forced to step down from office due to his association with what appeared to be a series of criminal activities led by high-ranking officials of his administration involved in the Watergate scandal. The apparent contradiction between the law-and-order agenda and Watergate contributed to a considerable disenchantment on both sides of the political spectrum. Democrat lawmakers launched an assault on the political power of certain federal law enforcement agencies, particularly the FBI and the Central Intelligence Agency (CIA). Republican lawmakers were cautious of voicing the pitch words of "law and order" because of their association with Nixon. Advocates of both the deterrence and corrections models were unsatisfied. Aggregate crime rates continued to climb, growth rates of prison populations continue to rise, and overall expansion of federal jurisdiction over crime and punishment continued to grow, despite the disgraced leadership.

One area that benefitted from the discord following Watergate was the LEAA program left over from President's Johnson Great Society. Funding increased steadily in the

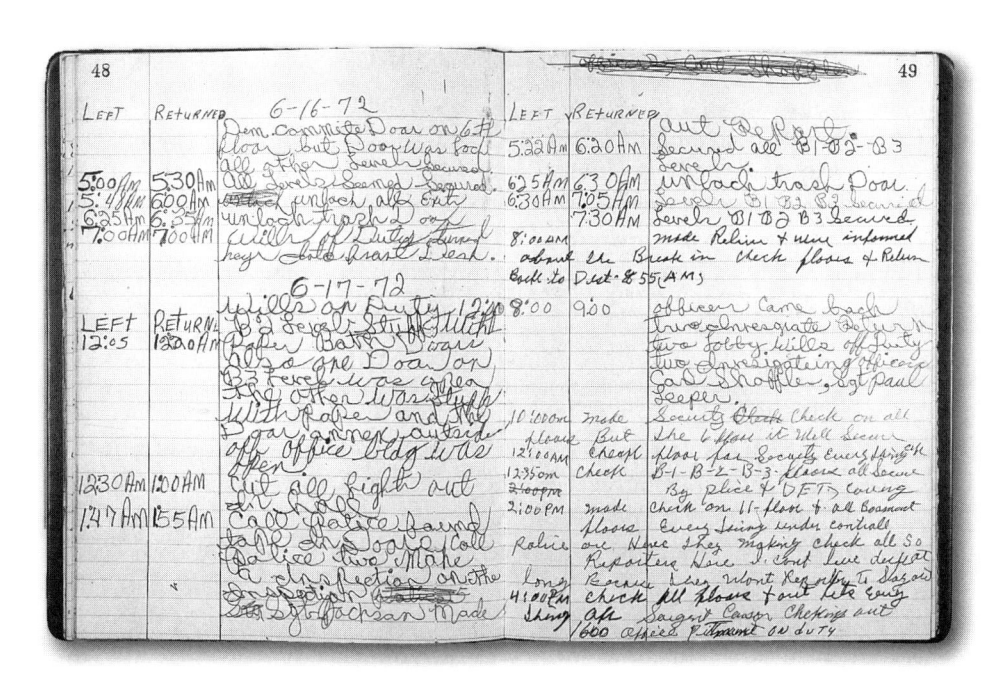

The first of two pages of the security officer's log of the Watergate Office Building showing the entries for June 17, 1972, the night of the break-in by five burglars connected to the Committee for the Re-Election of the President, a Nixon campaign fundraising group. Nixon resigned over the scandal, throwing the legitimacy of the political power wielded by certain law enforcement agencies into temporary disarray.

1970s, growing from $268 million in 1970 to more than a $1 billion during the mid-1970s. Part of the appeal was that advocates for both deterrence and corrections could use the federal grant program to support their pet projects. Some grants were used to create therapeutic outpatient clinics as alternatives to imprisonment. The number of adult prisoners who were granted early parole in order to participate in a therapeutic treatment option increased from 62,000 in 1965 to more than 156,000 in 1975. At the same time, other grants could be used by police departments to stock up on riot gear or fund experimental, interagency strike-force programs to reinforce local law enforcement efforts. Federal lawmakers responded to pressure from both sides of the political aisle. When the LEAA budgets continued to grow to the point that it competed with other social service programs, constituents from other departments began demanding some evidence of accountability during a time when the general economy was stagnating. This task proved quite difficult. Despite the large outflow of federal money, there was no appreciable decline either in aggregate crime rates or recidivism rates.

In 1974, a criminologist named Robert Martinson published a study of 231 different prison rehabilitation programs titled, "What Works? Questions and Answers About Prison Reform," which concluded that "with few and isolated exceptions, the rehabilitative efforts that have been reported so far have had no appreciable effect on recidivism." The corrections model of crime control was largely created and supported by criminologists who continually searched for the ultimate cause of criminal behaviors and routinely suggested possible therapeutic strategies for neutralizing those causes. Martinson's study seemed to completely contradict some of those basic principles. Policymakers who had always favored the more aggressive deterrence model immediately jumped on the study as proof of their position. To the question of "what works?" they inserted their answer: "nothing works!" Within the academic community, the "nothing works" controversy stirred up immediate reactions both in favor and in opposition. This debate affected policymakers during a time when the political environment was indecisive on policies related to crime and punishment. In 1975, another criminologist, James Q. Wilson, published *Thinking About Crime*, which essentially concluded that the most effective way to lower overall crime rates was to impose mandatory sentences. Wilson's argument provided an academic basis for lawmakers who wanted to dramatically change crime control policies to emphasize stronger deterrence and less corrective rehabilitation. Some of these policy changes began during President James Carter's administration, when he seriously reshuffled the LEAA program and dramatically cut back its funding in 1979. The most obvious policy shifts would wait until the 1980s, when President Ronald Reagan took office.

Conclusion
The history of crime and punishment between 1960 and 1980 is one of dynamic tension between rival priorities of rehabilitative corrections and crime deterrence. Though the advocates of each model disagreed—sometime significantly—over particular policy priorities, both models enjoyed considerable support through a wide variety of legislative and judicial changes. The most significant result of this ongoing dichotomy was a general increase in the role of federal involvement in law enforcement and sentencing. In this way, the most significant difference between 1960 and 1980 was the overarching presence of federal rules, agents, and money in the routine operations of state and local law enforcement agencies and corrections facilities.

Aharon W. Zorea
University of Wisconsin, Richland

1962 PRIMARY DOCUMENT

Treasury Department Memorandum on "Lucky" Luciano's Drug Ring

"Lucky" Luciano is considered the father of American organized crime. He not only established the Commission, which encouraged consolidating power instead of fighting over territory, but he also divided New York City into the Five Families. If a national organized crime conspiracy existed in midcentury America, it was due to the work of Luciano, Meyer Lansky, and Bugsy Siegel. Imprisoned from 1936 to 1946, he was then deported. Unable to oversee the Commission from afar, he began operating in Italy. Luciano was being shadowed by Italian narcotics agents when he died suddenly in Naples, Italy, on January 26. There were rumors of poison to silence him, but medical examiners determined that a heart attack was the cause.

Treasury Narcotics Agents to Return Fugitives to U. S. Saturday

A three-month international man-hunt led by U. S. Treasury narcotics agents for three fugitives from a New York conspiracy trial is scheduled to end with the return of the trio to the United States Saturday night, Henry L. Giordano, Acting Commissioner of Narcotics, announced today.

Scheduled to arrive at New York International Airport from Madrid, Spain, at 7:15 p.m. tomorrow, are Vincent Mauro, Frank Caruso, and Salvatore Maneri, escorted by four Spanish police officers and a U. S. Treasury narcotics agent. The fugitives will be arrested on the basis of outstanding fugitive warrants previously issued by the U. S. District Court at New York City.

Their arrest will climax a chase by Treasury narcotics agents who traced the movements of the trio from Nassau, Bahamas, to Kingston, Jamaica, to Caracas, Venezuela; to Nice on the French Riviera, to London, and finally to Spain.

Mr. Giordano said that when the fugitives were in Spain, their activities were connected with Charles "Lucky" Luciano who was then living in Naples. Italian Treasury policy, he said, had been questioning Luciano as to his role in assisting the three fugitives, and Luciano's arrest was imminent when he died on January 26.

On October 21, 1960, U. S. Treasury narcotics agents, working with the police of Westchester County, New York, arrested four men for possession of 23-1/2 pounds of pure heroin—worth an estimated $3 million on the illegal market. Subsequent investigation resulted in a narcotics conspiracy case involving 16 American and Canadian defendants.

Vincent Mauro, Frank Caruso and Salvatore Maneri were considered by the Narcotics Bureau to be principal members of this conspiracy. The United States Commissioner at New York City set bonds of $250,000 on Mauro and Caruso at the time of their arrest. The bonds were later reduced to $50,000 each. This was furnished and the two were set at liberty. Maneri, who was at liberty on a $5,000 immigration bond was released on an additional $10,000 bail bond.

On September 19, 1961, the date set for their appearance in Federal Court at New York City to plead to the indictment, all three defendants failed to appear. Their bonds were forfeited and warrants were issued for their arrest. Two other defendants in this case disappeared and were later found murdered

The remaining 11 defendants in the conspiracy were tried and found guilty on all charges on December 27, 1961. They are scheduled for sentencing later this month.

During this same period, Italian Treasury police, who were investigating narcotics trafficking in their country, were able to implicate all of the American and Canadian conspirators in the New York narcotics case, from leads furnished them by U. S. narcotics agents.

Mr. Giordano said that Italian authorities had long had Luciano under surveillance. A few months ago, while keeping him under surveillance, Italian police were led to an American, Henry Rubino, who held joint business interests with Vincent Mauro. It was discovered that Rubino was in contact with fugitives Mauro, Caruso and Maneri. This led to the discovery of the fugitives in Barcelona and Majorca, where they were arrested on January 22-23 of this year.

Following the arrests in Spain, the Italian Treasury Police implicated Rubino and Luciano in their narcotics conspiracy. Rubino was arrested at Naples on January 25, 1962. Luciano was questioned the morning of January 26, and was instructed to return the following day for more detailed interrogation, but on the afternoon of that day Luciano died at the Naples airport.

James A. Reed, Assistant Secretary of the Treasury, under whose supervision the Bureau of Narcotics operates, said he was impressed with the cooperation and coordination of the police forces involved.

He expressed thanks particular to the Spanish police and the Spanish authorities, and the Italian police for their work with U. S. Treasury agents against persons suspected of smuggling narcotics into the United States.

"Illicit trafficking in narcotic drugs is one of the most heinous crimes against humanity and this case illustrates the kind of international cooperation which benefits the peoples of all countries. The help of the Spanish and Italian police officials is greatly appreciated and has contributed materially to U.S. law enforcement," Assistant Secretary Reed said. Mr. Reed expressed his appreciation to the Justice and State Departments for the assistance rendered by them.

Treasury Department
Washington, D.C.
February 2, 1962

Source: NARA-II, RG 65, DOT, Narcotics Enforcement, Box 1 F: Narcotics Investigation

See Articles: Italian Americans; Luciano, "Lucky;" Narcotics Laws; Organized Crime, History of; Organized Crime, Sociology of.

1962 PRIMARY DOCUMENT

Commission of Narcotics Report on Detroit Organized Crime and Racketeering

The Detroit Outfit was the most powerful crime family outside of New York and Chicago, and at the time of this report was led by Joe Zerilli, who was succeeded by "Papa John" Priziola in 1977. The report also mentions the increase in African American organized crime, which had roots in 1920s Harlem and grew after World War II. One of the first black drug cartels operating on street corners, Young Boys Incorporated, formed in the Detroit Outfit in 1978 and soon controlled most of its heroin trade.

DATE: September 25, 1962
TO: Mr. H.L. Giordano, Commissioner of Narcotics, Washington, D.C.
FROM: Ross B. Ellis, District Supervisor, Detroit, Michigan
SUBJECT: Organized Crime and Racketeering

Reference is made to Bureau memorandum dated September 10, 1962, from Assistant to the commissioner Charles Siragusa, requesting a brief and up-to-date report relative to the organized crime and racketeering situation at Detroit, Michigan.

At Detroit, Michigan, organized crime and racketeering among the upper echelon Italians appears to be primarily concentrated on various gambling enterprises, labor racketeering and, in some instances, large scale theft rings. In recent years, it has also been the modus operandi of the Italian element to invest in several quasi-legitimate enterprises such as real estate, bars, restaurants, car washes, dry cleaning chains, and bakeries, as well as various other forms of legitimate business.

During the past several months, this office has conducted an investigation into the activities of major targets Raffaele QUASARANO and John PRIZIOLA. This investigation has been extremely extensive in view of the fact that information, even though of a nebulous nature, was received in this office to the effect that QUASARANO and John PRIZIOLA might possibly be considering a return to the illicit narcotic traffic. Our investigation to date has failed to reveal any information which would lend credence to the above.

The most significant developments in this investigation have established some positive and some suspected connections between PRIZIOLA, QUASARANO and certain apparently legitimate businesses, in current operation at Detroit. Our efforts in this matter have been closely coordinated with a special unit of the Detroit Police Department, the Criminal Information Bureau, which is headed by Inspector Vincent Piersante, one of the foremost opponents of organized crime and racketeering in Detroit. In the event our present investigation continues to fail to reveal any worthwhile information relative to the current activities of PRIZIOLA and QUASARANO, we anticipate shifting our investigation to other major racketeers at Detroit, Michigan.

Through all of our efforts in the fight against organized crime, we maintain a continual exchange of information with other enforcement agencies at the federal level. This is particularly true of the Intelligence Division of the Internal Revenue Service.

It is interesting to note that during recent months there appears to be a trend toward organization among the colored segment of narcotic violators. This has been particularly evidenced during the past year or two. In conducting investigations relative to most of our major peddlers at Detroit, we have been uncovering evidence of conspiracy to organize trafficking on a large scale level between factions in Detroit, New York and Chicago. It would appear that our most important colored violators at Detroit are joining together in groups consisting of three to five persons.

This group will then obtain large supplies of narcotics via mutual sources of supply at either New York or Chicago. The distribution at Detroit is then delegated to a handful of less important peddlers who handle practically all actual phases of the operation except the negotiations. As result of the above trend, we have found it more difficult to involve this type of peddler in an actual sale or possession case. In most instances today, our most successful approach to these people has been via the conspiracy route.

In all of our investigations of the aforementioned operations, there again has been no information uncovered which would reveal any association between our major colored violators and the prominent Italian racketeers at Detroit. In each instance where we culminated an investigation of this nature, we have determined the source of supply for the Detroit violators to be located in either New York or Chicago, and in one instance, Ontario, Canada.

Exemplary cases following in the above categories would be: Mich-4527, Ollie DUFF, Edith WILLIAMS, John Robert AUSTIN, William Bud JOHNSON and Richard BOYD. Each of these violators was, at one time, considered major in their own right. In the instant case, they conspired and organized for the purpose of large scale distribution of narcotics at Detroit, Michigan. Each of the above persons was known to have important sources of supply at both New York City and Chicago, Illinois, Mich-4542, Maceo THOMAS, Gus SAUNDERS, Hattie Mae THOMAS, Eloise SAUNDERS, Robert Lee HARRIS, Lillian BOYKIN. In this instance Gus SAUNDERS was considered the most important violator at Detroit, Michigan, during 1960 and 1961. Although this matter is presently pending trial, we feel confident that we will be able to prove that SAUNDERS and the others not only conspired, but did obtain on several occasions large quantities of narcotics from Maceo and Hattie Mae THOMAS, major violators at Chicago, Illinois.

In this instance, the overall operation involved the distribution of approximately one half-kilogram of heroin every two weeks at Detroit. It has been estimated that the overall operation of Maceo THOMAS at Chicago involved distribution of approximately one and one half-kilogram of heroin every week.

Mich-4543, Ralph MIXON, et al. This case is still in the process of investigation and grand jury proceedings. Here again, MIXON, who has been an important violator at Detroit for several years, conspired with other important violators to organize the distribution of narcotics at Detroit, Michigan. In this instance, this conspiracy has been traced to sources at Windsor, Ontario, Canada, whom we anticipate will be indicted along with the Detroit conspirators.

Ross B. Ellis
District Supervisor

Source: NARA-II, RG 170 Records of the DEA, Subj files of Bureau of Narcotics, Box 51, F: Organized Crime and Racketeering

See Articles: Detroit, Michigan; Narcotics Laws; Organized Crime, History of; Organized Crime, Sociology of.

1962 PRIMARY DOCUMENT

Bureau of Narcotics Report on Kansas City Organized Crime and Racketeering

Organized crime in Kansas City began around World War I, and it was a "wide-open" city during Prohibition, when Mafia ally Boss Pendergast controlled the government; no alcohol-related arrests were made during the time, a golden age for the Kansas City outfit. In the years after this report, the FBI began Operation Strawman, using wiretaps to investigate connections between the Kansas City outfit and the Tropicana casino, leading to several 1983 convictions.

RE: Organized Crime and Racketeering, Kansas City, Missouri

Mr. Phillips R. Smith
District Supervisor
Bureau of Narcotics
Kansas City, Missouri

Dear Sir:

1. Reference is made to Bureau memorandum directed to this office under date of September 14, 1962, by Mr. George H. Gaffney, Assistant to the Commissioner of Narcotics, requesting brief and current information concerning organized crime and racketeering in the State of Missouri and a resume of our enforcement activity against violators in this category.

2. Organized Crime in the Greater Kansas City Area has undergone considerable change in the past decade. In recent years, Kansas City has often been referred to by underworld characters as "the only cemetery in the United States with neon lights". This description is given by individuals who have not forgotten the "old days" and would like to operate their dice games in display windows on main thoroughfares of the downtown district as was the practice during the '30's or just outside the gates of defense plants as they did during World War II. At the present time organized crime in this area consists of gambling, handbook and policy wheel operations, football and basketball parlay tickets, wire service, prostitution and the fencing of stolen property. All of the gambling and betting enterprises are now "sneak" operations due to the fact that the underworld is no longer able to obtain the sanction of local authorities. As a result of this curtailment, many of the more prominent members have branched out to other sections of the country and now either own or have interest in gambling establishments at Lake Tahoe and Las Vegas, Nevada, Cape Canaveral, Florida.

3. Having obtained pre-legal advice in the matter, members of the local organization

have had knowledge for a number of years that in order to overcome their greatest law enforcement hazard—an indictment for Federal income tax evasion—it is necessary that they report income in sufficient amount to offset their visable expenditures. In an effort to overcome this peril, the majority of all hoodlums in the Kansas City organization have required interest in legitimate enterprises. Among the businesses in which they are interested are the wholesale distribution of produce, meat, tobacco and liquor; automobile franchise dealerships, truck and automobile leasing companies, money orders, insurance, and various types of the usual retail establishments. Whether such a business is a success or nonprofitable, it's actual operation is not always too important. The primary purpose of the investment is to furnish a medium through which a member and possibly some of his associates can "funnel" into legitimate channels for income tax purposes, large sums of money that have been derived from illegitimate sources. A recent example of such an operation was an audit made by the Alcohol and Tobacco Tax Unit of a small retail drugstore owned by Carl Civella, a well known Kansas City hoodlum, which reflected that during a 12-month period the store deposited $102,000.00 in addition to what appeared to be the regular receipts of the business.

4. There has been no indication that the members of the local organization or their associates have been involved in the herein traffic in Kansas City since the dissolution of the Carrella-Clayton-Dichiarinte combine in 1958. Their apparent reluctance to engage in the drug traffic is obviously due to the mandatory penalties and the heavy sentences that have been assessed narcotic law violators in this area. In addition, the organization feels that the narcotic traffic creates a stigma and an enforcement pressure that is detrimental to their more lucrative enterprises such as gambling.

5. In June 1961, Mr. James J. Featherstone of the Organized Crime and Racketeering Section of the Attorney General's Office arrived in Kansas City, Missouri, for the purpose of coordinating the investigative efforts of the Treasury Enforcement Agencies and the Department of Justice in their inquiries concerning organized crime. At that time, the District Headquarters Office of our Bureau at Kansas City, Missouri, had in protective custody a Government witness who had assisted in the making of a narcotic case against Anthony J. Biase, a widely known hoodlum of Omaha, Nebraska, who was closely associated with the organization in Kansas City, Missouri. As a result of the assistance rendered the Government, an unsuccessful attempt was made to assassinate the witness but he survived to identify his assailants. This witness, Kenneth B. Sheetz, had previously been associated with a number of prominent Kansas City hoodlums and organization members. During the intensive investigation that followed Mr. Featherstone's arrival in Kansas City, Sheetz was made available to all of the agencies concerned and in the months that followed this witness was interviewed by more than thirty groups of enforcement officers assigned to the organized crime investigation. In addition, all information contained in the files of the District Headquarters Office concerning the subjects under investigation was furnished the respective agencies and the agents conducting the inquiries were afforded the full cooperation of the entire personnel of the Kansas City Office.

6. Among the 23 hoodlum members of the local underworld organization who are under investigation by Mr. Featherstone's office in connection with Internal Revenue matters are fourteen who were originally proposed by the District Headquarters Office. The majority of the latter group are former drug traffickers and several have had prior convictions for violation of the Federal Narcotic Laws.

Some of the more important members of this group are as follows:

Nicholas Civella, Mafia Book No. 250. Although an intensive effort has been made by the Internal Revenue Service to develop sufficient evidence to warrant an income tax prosecution of Civella, it does not appear that the endeavor will be successful. This subject was one of the two Kansas City representatives who attended the Appalachian Meeting in November 1957 and has been on notice since that time that the Bureau of Internal Revenue was interested in him. Like the individuals mentioned in Paragraph 3 of this report, Civella makes it a point to report sufficient income to offset normal and visible expenditures.

Carl Civella. This subject is not so fortunate as his brother, Nicholas. An investigation of Carl's income tax return for a three year period revealed unreported income in excess of $50,000.00. A report of their investigation is now being prepared by the Internal Revenue Service and prosecution will be recommended, Carl Civella was formerly an active drug trafficker and was convicted for violation of the narcotic laws in Kansas City, Missouri, on December 27, 1939, our case file No-7511.

Sam Carrella. This important interstate narcotic trafficker was actively engaged in the whole distribution of heroin as recently as September 1958. Since the arrest and conviction of his associate, Jack Clayton, and the efforts that were made by our Bureau to implicate his source, Anthony J. Dichiarinte, and himself, Carrolla has remained dormant insofar as the drug traffic is concerned and has contented himself with his fencing activities. An intensive investigation is now being conducted by the Internal Revenue Service of financial items listed in Carrolla's returns and the prospects for the making of an income tax case against this subject appear to be excellent.

Feliz Ferina and Anthony J. Cardarella. These subjects are the hoodlums who attempted to assassinate Government witness, Kenneth B. Sheetz, on June 20, 1960, at Kansas City, Missouri. Ferina and Cardarella were indicted in this matter by the Jackson County Grand Jury at Kansas City, Missouri, for assault with intent to kill. Ferina was tried twice in State Court on this indictment. The first of these actions resulted in a mistrial and he was acquitted in the second proceeding. Ferina and Cardarella were convicted in the U. S. District Court at Kansas City, Missouri, on an indictment charging obstruction of justice in connection with the attempted assassination of Sheetz and were each sentence to ten years' imprisonment. Both Ferina and Cardarella were under investigation by the Internal Revenue Service for several months and although that agency has reported Ferina for failure to file returns for the years 1958 and 1959, and is now reporting Cardarella for approximately $9,000.00 in unreported income during the years 1958, 1959, and 1960, it is anticipated by Mr. Featherstone's office that the Tax Division will recommend against prosecution. This anticipated recommendation is based upon the fact that both of these defendants are presently under ten year sentence in the obstruction of justice case. It is the writer's opinion that the sentences received by Ferina and Cardarella were very meager in comparison with the seriousness of the offense which they committed against the Government and the permanent physical injuries which they inflicted upon Government witness Kenneth B. Sheetz. In view of these circumstances, it would appear that some effort should be made to remedy the decision of the Tax Division in these matters.

Charles A. Cacioppo. This is the individual who arranged with the local underworld organization for an attempt to assassinate Kenneth B. Sheetz, Government witness in the narcotic case against

Anthony J. Biase of Omaha, Nebraska, case Neb-766. During the period from 1939 to 1943, Cacioppo was actively engaged in the herein traffic in Kansas City, Missouri, but successfully evaded apprehension for this offense. An investigation of Cacioppo's income tax returns has been conducted by the Internal Revenue Service and a report is now being prepared by that agency in which prosecution will be recommended as to Cacioppo and two associates, Joseph and Sam LeGrotte on a charge of conspiracy to conceal Cacioppo's interest in a business, the owner of record being Joseph LeGrotte.

Joseph LaScoula and Michael LaScoula, National List No's 228 and 231 and Mafia Book 259 and 260 respectively. During the period from 1928 to 1943, the LaScoula Brothers were outstanding figures in the narcotic traffic at Kansas City, Missouri. Since that time, these subjects have operated gambling establishments in various locations in this area and are also well known for their fencing activities particularly diamonds and better quality jewelry. The LaScoula brothers are presently under investigation by the Internal Revenue Service and sufficient evidence has been obtained to warrant a recommendation of prosecution as to Michael LaScoula. It is also anticipated by that agency that adequate evidence can be developed to sustain a prosecution case against Joseph LaScoula.

7. A matter of particular interest to this office which is being coordinated by Mr. Featherstone through the joint efforts of the Alcohol and Tobacco Tax Unit and the Federal Bureau of Investigation in the perjury case against Frank LaRocca, a prominent member of the Mafia at Kansas City, Missouri. The offense in this case had as it's beginning an investigation conducted by our Bureau relative to the origin of a revolver discarded by one of the assailants who attempted to assassinate Government witness Kenneth B. Sheetz on June 20, 1960. This investigation revealed that the gun in question was one of twelve revolvers of similar caliber and type that were purchased by an unidentified individual at Elmer's Sporting Goods Store, Gunnison, Colorado, on October 30, 1957. Subsequent inquiry by the Alcohol and Tobacco Tax Unit positively identified the purchaser of these revolvers as Frank LaRocca of Kansas City, Missouri. Following this revelation, LaRocca was subpoenaed before a Federal Grand Jury at Kansas City, Missouri, and he emphatically denied that he had ever purchased a gun of any type in the State of Colorado. While it appears that justice has experienced some delay in this matter, it is anticipated that an indictment charging LaRocca with perjury will be returned in the very near future.

8. The District Headquarters Office at Kansas City, Missouri, has actively assisted Mr. Featherstone, his associates and all agencies who are taking part in the drive against organized crime and racketeering in this area and will continue this cooperation in an effort to successfully conclude this worthy endeavor by the Attorney General's Office.

9. As previously stated, the criminal organization at Kansas City, Missouri, and their associates are apparently not engaged in the illicit narcotic traffic; however, there are a number of hoodlums in this area who are excellent potentials and may at any time start, or resume, their activities in the drug traffic. The entire personnel of the District Headquarters Office is constantly on the alert for this type of violator.

Very truly yours,

C. A. Follmer
Narcotic Agent
Treasury Department
Bureau of Narcotics
Kansas City, 6, Mo.
October 4, 1962

Source: RG 170 Records of the DEA, Subj files of Bureau of Narcotics, Box 52, F: Organized Crime Conference

See Articles: Gambling; Internal Revenue Service; Kansas City, Missouri; Organized Crime, History of.

1963 PRIMARY DOCUMENT

Temporary Assignment of Narcotic Agents to Investigate Gambling

Criminal organizations do not divide their labor in the same way as law enforcement. The same organization may be involved in drug trafficking, gambling, smuggling, the corruption of state and local government, and tax evasion, without ill effects to its focus. In so doing, their crimes transpire across the jurisdictions of as many as a dozen different U.S. agencies. Interagency cooperation is vital, and the temporary assignment of agents—sometimes for years—is common.

In response to a request from the Attorney General, and with your approval, the Bureau of Narcotics is assigning, on a temporary basis, a group of narcotic agents in New York to investigate the relationship between narcotics traffic and illicit gambling. In order to coordinate this investigation with those conducted by the Internal Revenue Service, these narcotic agents are being temporarily assigned to work under the supervision of the Intelligence Division of Internal Revenue Service insofar as their activities relate to wagering, excise or income taxes. The information gathered and activities conducted will be coordinated with the U. S. Attorney for the Southern District of New York.

The U. S. Attorney, Mr. Morgenthau, believes that some question may be raised as to the authority of the selected narcotic agents to investigate matters coming under the wagering tax laws. In order to avoid any such question, it is recommended that the Federal Narcotic Agents in question be authorized, in addition to their regular duties, to engage in the detection, investigation and apprehension of violators of the wagering occupational and excise tax laws to the same extent as special agents of the Internal Revenue Service.

If you approve will you please sign the attached authorization.

Under Secretary Fowler
Assistant Secretary Reed
January 28, 1963

Source: Organized Crime (Gambling) folder in RG 170 Records of the DEA, Subj files of the Bureau of Narcotics 1916-1970, Box 52

See Articles: Gambling; Internal Revenue Service; Jurisdiction; Tax Crimes.

1963 PRIMARY DOCUMENT

Proposed John F. Kennedy Speech for the March on Washington

The Great March on Washington was a 1963 political rally in Washington, D.C. One of the largest rallies in history, it included a quarter of a million people gathering in support of the civil rights movement. The demonstration of popular support and raising of awareness—especially effective in the age before the 24-hour news cycle, when fewer news stories could be serviced in the few minutes allotted to the evening news—helped pass the Civil Rights Act and Voting Rights Act.

We have witnessed today in Washington tons of thousands of Americans—both Negro and white—exercising their right to assemble peaceably and direct the widest possible attention to a great national issue. Efforts to secure equal treatment and equal opportunity for all without regard to race, color, creed or nationality are neither novel or difficult to understand. What is different today is the intensified and widespread public awareness of the need to move forward in achieving these objectives—objectives which are older than this nation.

Although this summer has seen remarkable progress in translating civil rights from principles into practices, we have a very long way yet to travel. One cannot help but be impressed with the deep fervor and the quiet dignity that characterizes the thousands who have gathered in the Nation's Capital from across the country to demonstrate their faith and confidence in our democratic form of government. History has seen many demonstrations—of widely varying character and for a whole host of reasons. As our thoughts travel to other demonstrations that have occurred in different parts of the world, this Nation can properly be proud of the demonstration that has occurred here today. The leaders of the organizations sponsoring the March and all who have participated in it deserve our appreciation for the detailed preparations that made it possible and for the orderly manner in which it has been conducted.

The Executive Branch of the Federal Government will continue its efforts to obtain increased employment and to eliminate discrimination in employment practices, two of the prime goals of the March. In addition, our efforts to secure enactment of the legislative proposals made to the Congress will be maintained, including not only the Civil Rights Bill, but also proposals to broaden and strengthen the Manpower Development and Training Program, the Youth Employment Bill, amendments to the vocational education program, the establishment of a work-study program for high school age youth, strengthening of the adult basic education provisions in the Administration's education program and the amendments proposed to the public welfare work-relief and training program.

This nation can afford to achieve the goals of a full employment policy—it cannot afford to permit the potential skills and educational capacity of its citizens to be unrealized.

The cause of 20 million Negroes has been advanced by the program conducted so appropriately before the Nation's shrine in the Great Emancipator, but even more significant is the contribution to all mankind.

Source: Collection JFK-POF: Papers of John F. Kennedy: President's Office Files Archival Research Catalog (ARC) ID: 193810

See Articles: African Americans; Civil Disobedience; Civil Rights Laws; Kennedy, John F. (Administration of).

1963 PRIMARY DOCUMENT

Gerald R. Ford Interview on Working With John F. Kennedy

The Kennedy assassination is one of the most enduring subjects for conspiracy theories; even Americans otherwise skeptical of conspiracy theories often express doubt in the official account of Lee Harvey Oswald as the only participant, or even the only shooter. This is understandable; at best, the Oswald account lacks dramatic satisfaction, and as pointed out in this interview, no motivation was shared with the public. But as Ford says, there is no evidence of conspiracy.

Creator: Gerald R. Ford
Interviewer: Vicki Daitch
Date of Interview: July 8, 2003
Place of Interview: Avon, Colorado

DAITCH: This is Vicki Daitch. Today is July 8, 2003, and I'm interviewing President Gerald Ford at his home in Avon, Colorado. First of all, I just wanted to.... As you know, this is for the Kennedy library.

FORD: Right.

DAITCH: First of all, I just wanted to sort of.... I know you served in the House with John Kennedy for a brief while before he went into the Senate. Do you have any particular recollections about that time?

FORD: Well, I got to know Jack Kennedy when I first went to the House in January of 1949. He was elected two years ahead of me, and I was elected in 1948. By pure happenstance, they assigned newcomers suites in the Old House Office Building. And by pure happenstance, I was in one suite, and right across the hall, on the same corridor, he was in the other suite. So we became well acquainted over the two or four years that he served while I was there. We would walk back and forth from the Office Building to the floor of the House. Our staffs mingled. So it was a good relationship based on just more or less coincidence.

DAITCH: Now, you were close to the same age, though, too, right? You were young men first going into politics.

FORD: We were within a year or two of each other.

DAITCH: So did that sort of create any kind of camaraderie that might have not been so much if you were further apart?

FORD: Oh, I think so. And we were both relatively the same age. I was 35 or 36; he was roughly the same age. We had both served in the military, in the Navy. Ideologically, we had many differences. But on a personal basis, we had a good friendship.

DAITCH: Now you were both ideologically fairly moderate for your parties, is that fair to say?

FORD: Well, I was an internationalist as a Republican. I was against the isolationists, I was against the hard-line right wing. And if my recollection is correct, Jack Kennedy's views within the Democratic party were of the middle of the road.

DAITCH: Mmmm hmmm. Right. Now, how did you maintain your friendship after you moved to the Senate?

FORD: Well, we were separated with a different relationship. He was in the Senate; I was in the House. But we would run into each other at social events or other gatherings. It wasn't as frequent or as warm a friendship, but it was still a good relationship.

DAITCH: Right. Now, you were friendly— at that time were you also friendly with Nixon [Richard M. Nixon]?

FORD: Oh, yes. From my first day that I was in the House, after I was sworn in, Nixon came up to me, and he said, "I'm Dick Nixon from California. I'm glad to see you." Well, he and Kennedy had come in two years ahead of me. Right from the beginning, I had a very warm personal relationship with Dick Nixon. He went from the House to the Senate and to the vice presidency.

DAITCH: Right. Now, when he was vice president running against Kennedy, how was that? I mean obviously you would have supported Vice President Nixon. What was your sense of the election and their...?

FORD: Obviously I supported Nixon, but it wasn't a personal difference. It was ideological. I supported Nixon, and I did what I could to defeat Kennedy. But when Kennedy won in '60, very close race, I was reelected in the House. And on international matters, I supported the Kennedy administration. I had differences with them, ideologically, domestically.

DAITCH: Now, I know that the Kennedys felt, in particular by 1963, I guess people were gearing up for the '64 election, they were feeling pretty frustrated. We have some evidence in the library, you know, of conversations where they felt that partisan politics were preventing them from getting any domestic legislation, the progressive things that they were interested in in terms of health care and civil rights and that sort of thing. Do you remember, sort of, maybe having a little more friction around that time with the administration?

FORD: There is no doubt that on domestic issues I strongly differed with the Kennedy administration. I don't recall the particulars. That's a long time ago. But ideologically we just had different views. Now, on international matters, NATO [North Atlantic Treaty Organization], economic aid, military assistance for European nations, I was strongly in favor.

DAITCH: Were you surprised that Kennedy turned out to be so much of an internationalist, knowing that his father [Joseph P. Kennedy, Sr.] had been such an isolationist?

FORD: I understood it because Jack Kennedy came from a different era. His father was anti-British, anti-internationalism because he came from one generation. Jack came from a totally different era, different generation. So I understood it.

DAITCH: It probably seemed to be common sense to you at the time.

FORD: Well, I believed in it myself, and I was pleased to see that Kennedy, as a

Democrat, had similar views.

DAITCH: Right, right. I know that they were very frustrated about the civil rights. Obviously at the time there was so much conflict, in fact some really violent things that were going on. The Kennedys were criticized for not moving fast enough, and they were criticized for doing some of the things that they did. What was your take at the time [on] what they should have been doing?

FORD: Well, it's interesting. Johnson [Lyndon B. Johnson], who came later, was very much more aggressive on civil rights than Kennedy was. Johnson really moved forward vigorously on civil rights. And I think it was a contrast with the sort of hesitancy on the part of the Kennedys that upset the civil rights movement, etc.

DAITCH: The Kennedys claim that they couldn't get anything through Congress, and that's why they were hesitant: because Congress was so antithetical to the things that they were trying to do. Do you think that's a...?

FORD: There's no doubt that the Kennedy administration was not as skillful in dealing with the Congress as they should have been. It was even more evident when Johnson took over. He was a master of dealing with the Congress and that just reflected adversely on the inability of the Kennedys to work and get results with the Congress.

DAITCH: Right. I've heard people say, historians have said and other people, that they should have maybe used Vice President Johnson more in that capacity because he was such a master at it. Asked him to help more on things.

FORD: I always felt the Kennedy administration per se was hesitant, reluctant to deal with the Johnson wing of the Democratic party. There was a jealousy or whatever you want to call it. The Kennedys weren't going to do something to get Johnson to help them because then it would be a Johnson action rather than a Kennedy action. Human nature being what it is, the Kennedy people were reluctant.

DAITCH: Right. That's maybe understandable, as you say, from a human nature perspective.

FORD: I understood it. It was too bad. Human jealousy shouldn't interfere with desirable action, but that being what it is....

DAITCH: I wanted to go back to.... You were part of sort of a progressive group in the House in the early sixties, and I think about that—for me the context was instantly—I think about Kennedy being a young person who's doing and maybe saying the same kinds of things about let's get the country moving again, let's be vigorous. Was that sort of...? Were those similar impulses in both parties?

FORD: There were elements in both parties. The Democratic party had a heritage, particularly with the dominance of the Southern Democrats, to be very aggressive, to move out of the old mold. The Republicans, because of their defeat in '60, realized they had to do something to change their image. But the Southern Democrats were a roadblock to any real affirmative action on the part of the Democratic administration. It's interesting. When I went to Congress, there wasn't a single Republican below the Mason-Dixon Line.

DAITCH: Is that right?!

FORD: Not one. And now look at how the political geography has changed.

DAITCH: Yes, absolutely. It's really fascinating, and it's all about civil rights, isn't it?

FORD: That's right.

DAITCH: Absolutely. To me the sixties are such an interesting period because of the way the politics completely flip-flopped. It must have been difficult to—especially right at that moment when Kennedy was president and Johnson, too, I think. I mean what a difficult time to try to move forward on anything domestically.

FORD: It was difficult because the Democratic party was not unified, and the Republican party had its own splits: from the hard right to the moderates like myself. So it was a transitional period in American politics.

DAITCH: Right. I know you supported President Kennedy's internationalist policies. How about the.... I mean the things that now you look back and you say what a terrible mistake the Bay of Pigs and some other things. But on the other hand, you know, the Cuban Missile Crisis, especially with the papers and the tapes that have been made available now, it appears as if Kennedy really handled it masterfully in terms of avoiding nuclear war. It was a very scary moment. Do you, I mean looking back on it now and at the time, comparing, did you believe that he was handling it well?

FORD: I was somewhat in the center of what was happening. I had no control or jurisdiction. But I was a senior Republican on the Defense Appropriations Committee.

DAITCH: Oh, so you would have been kept aware.

FORD: So I was kept fully informed as to what was taking place. I had no jurisdiction over action. But I was informed on a daily basis by the top people in the Pentagon because I was on the committee that provided all the money for the Army, Navy, Air Force, and Marines. So I saw firsthand how skillfully the administration under Kennedy handled the matter.

DAITCH: You were impressed with it at the time? FORD: Very much so.

DAITCH: Did you have any sense of.... I mean if you look at, listen to, or read the transcriptions of some of the tapes, the discussions that took place in the ExComm, it's amazing how strongly and skillfully mostly Kennedy alone and a handful of other people, but there was a lot of pressure to act more aggressively. And I can't help but be struck by, for a young man who has considerable experience and is a man of some sophistication, but nevertheless how strongly he resisted doing anything too forceful or too likely to force Khrushchev [Nikita S. Khrushchev] into reacting himself.

FORD: That's a tribute, I think, to his good judgment. But I'll add this as a postscript: I firmly believe that a president is a better president if he's served in the military. There's something about serving in the military that gives you a broader perspective, regardless of what your role is. But having served in the military.... I spent four years in the Navy, Kennedy spent a long time, I don't remember how much. But your judgment is tempered by your exposure to the military. And I think it makes you a better president.

DAITCH: That's interesting. I would tend to agree with that. On the other hand—in terms of having a broader view maybe or being even resistant to going to war—on the other hand some of the people who were pressuring him to go to war were military people.

FORD: Well, it's a matter of individual exposure, what you think is right or wrong. I think the Kennedy final decisions were very sound in the Cuban Missile Crisis.

DAITCH: What about their other—and this will sort of lead us into the Warren Commission, which is very important for the library to understand. But what about the administration's policies were sort of, I don't know what the right word is, you know, the secrecy, the sort of aggressive pursuit of trying to undermine Castro's [Fidel Castro] regime, and, ultimately, we found out later, the assassination attempts. Were you aware of any of that at the time?

FORD: My recollection.... It's a good many years ago. I'm not accurate on that, so I don't really recall. I will say that this: Although we as Republicans thought Kennedy's popularity following the election of '60 would make him automatically reelected in '64, by '63 there was a growing anti-Kennedy political view. By '63, before he was assassinated, there was a feeling among Republicans we had a chance to beat him '64. Now maybe we were overly optimistic. But it was a different environment from '62 and '61.

DAITCH: Do you think because people.... There were a lot of areas in.... People look back now and sort of idealize the period, but there were a lot of areas in which he was struggling.

FORD: Vulnerable.

DAITCH: Yes, and not making a lot of progress. So by that time it was evident that there weren't any big things to show for the....

FORD: Right. So maybe we were overly optimistic. But at least the atmosphere was different.

DAITCH: Well, that's interesting because that goes back to what I had seen in some of the documents at the library, where they felt that they were sort of under attack. And probably the Republicans felt that they could be a little more aggressive. Let's talk about the assassination for a moment. I mean everybody.... The question is always, where were you, etc.? But what was that for you?

FORD: You know, I'm the sole, surviving member of that seven-member board.

DAITCH: Yes.

FORD: Well, the day of the assassination Mrs. Ford [Elizabeth Anne "Betty" Bloomer Ford] and I had gone into the District of Columbia to talk to an education counselor for one of our sons. As we came out of the meeting with the counselor, we turned the radio on. And that's how I heard about the assassination. I was shocked because of my personal friendship. I was shocked because I couldn't believe somebody would assassinate an American president. And Mrs. Ford and I went to the funeral, etc. I think it was Sunday night. The assassination had occurred on Friday, as I recall. Sunday night Mrs. Ford and I were sitting in our home in Alexandria, and I got a telephone call from President Johnson saying he was setting up this blue-ribbon group to investigate the assassination and wanted me to serve on it. I said, "Mr. President, I have major responsibilities in the House. I don't have time." And a typical Johnson technique, he twisted your arm, and I agreed. And that's how I got on the board with Hale Boggs [Thomas Hale Boggs], the chief justice [Earl Warren], Allen Dulles [Allen W. Dulles], John McCloy [John J. McCloy], two senators: from Kentucky [John Sherman Cooper] and Georgia [Richard B. Russell].

DAITCH: It was, in fact, a blue-ribbon panel.

FORD: Well, it was a very able panel, I'll say that.

DAITCH: So how did you work together, the panel? I mean I remember seeing some criticism or another that while the panel members weren't always there.... But you all had other responsibilities that you had to continue to....

FORD: I was probably one of the most conscientious in attending. Some of the others missed quite a bit. But they always had a top staff person present who could fill in for the absent member. But over all, I think our participation was good.

DAITCH: In terms of gathering the information, I assume there were staff people to gather the information and take depositions and that sort of thing?

FORD: Well, we hired as a group of I think six or seven top lawyers from all over the country. Arlen Specter was one of them.

DAITCH: Is that right!

FORD: He was a highly-thought-of lawyer of the Philadelphia area. He was one of the top lawyers we hired. They did a lot of the preliminary investigation. They as a group came up with a proposed draft of the Commission report. In that report they said, the staff in what they drafted, that there was no conspiracy, foreign or domestic. The Commission independently changed it. We said, as a Commission, we found *no evidence of a conspiracy*, foreign or domestic. Which is quite different.

DAITCH: Absolutely.

FORD: Now, the truth is there's been no evidence to change it. But we had to be a little more cautious.

DAITCH: Sure. Absolutely. Now did the Commission itself, did you get together, did you discuss the evidence and the papers that the staff people had drafted and that sort of thing?

FORD: Oh, yes. That's why we made the change about evidence of a conspiracy. We made two basic decisions: Lee Harvey Oswald committed the assassination. We were convinced of that. And we as a Commission stated that we found no evidence of a conspiracy, foreign or domestic.

DAITCH: Now, I have heard this sort of as, maybe it's intended a little bit as a criticism of the Commission, but more just as context for what the Commission was working with. But I have read in a couple of different places now that President Johnson wanted, and so did Bob Kennedy [Robert F. Kennedy] and some other people, wanted the Commission to be able to say this is not a conspiracy, this is not a KGB [Komitet gosudarstvennoi bezopasnosti] plot, this is not a Castro plot. Was there pressure to sort of come up with that conclusion?

FORD: No pressure on me. So I'm not a good witness on that. There may have been pressure on the chief justice or other members. But from my point of view, it was not pressure to come to any conclusion one way or another.

DAITCH: Right. It's, apparently they feared that there would be a movement in the country to do something if people thought it was a KGB plot or something like that. But, in fact, there really was no evidence to that effect.

FORD: None that I saw. But we had a very able staff who did a good job interrogating witnesses, Marina [Marina N. Prusakova Oswald], the wife and the mother [Marguerite Oswald]. They were very odd.

DAITCH: Yes. Which sort of explains a little bit about Oswald, I suppose.

FORD: Right, right.

DAITCH: Did you actually talk to any of these people? Or were you present?

FORD: Oh, I was present and interrogated all of the lead witnesses: Marina, the mother, and so forth.

DAITCH: Right. And what was your impression of Marina, for example?

FORD: Well, the mother was kookie.

DAITCH: Really?

FORD: You can understand why the son was odd. The wife, who was a Russian—Oswald married her in the Soviet Union. She was surprisingly able. I have a feeling, and I think others shared it, that he, Oswald, assassinated Kennedy because he was being prodded by his wife...

DAITCH: Really!?

FORD: ...on his impotence and so forth, and he had to do something to display his bravado. Now, that's a theory.

DAITCH: That's interesting. Did you think that she was prodding him specifically toward that kind of act or that was just his way of...?

FORD: That was his action. I don't think she suggested that particular action.

DAITCH: One of the criticisms of the Warren Commission.... I think in recent years historians have sort of tried to take a more serious look at the Commission rather than the usual conspiracy, the kookie thing. But one of the criticisms has been that the Commission didn't do enough. In fact, I think one of the staff members said that he felt that one of the weaknesses of the report, I can't remember which one, was that Oswald's motive was never really clarified enough for the American people to really get their mind around it and feel comfortable about why he did it.

FORD: I don't recall a staff member raising that question. What I told you a few minutes ago, that's my own judgment. Now, I think it may well have been shared by others on the Commission. But we never wrote it in the report, to my knowledge.

DAITCH: Yes, the person's name was Burt Griffin [Burt W. Griffin]. I don't know if that rings a bell.

FORD: Oh, he was one of the top lawyers we hired, along with Arlen Specter. Yes, I've forgotten where he came from, but he was one of the top lawyers that we drafted to come and help us.

DAITCH: I wonder if a little bit of this.... It's very easy to say those things in retrospect in terms of at the time it seemed like the motivation was fairly complete, and part of it is in fact that the man was unstable and that sort of thing. But to put it in the political context of our government's pursuit of Castro and attempted assassinations, which some of these people—apparently Castro knew about them, and he made mention of them so the pro-Castro community in the United States was aware of them.

FORD: Well, I just don't have that recollection 40-some years later. I had my own views that I recollect. Some of the others I wouldn't be able to testify.

DAITCH: Right. Now you knew at the time, though, that Oswald had been sort of hanging around with these pro-Castro organizations, and he had gone to Mexico to try to...

FORD: New Orleans. He had been to the Castro embassy in Mexico. We were all familiar with that, yes.

DAITCH: But you didn't find any real connection with...

FORD: I didn't see it, no.

DAITCH: Right. I don't think anyone still has come up with that, but at the time. Now obviously you were one of the main people who was the driving force behind some of the groups in the 1970's, in Congress—the committees and the commissions—to bring some of these secretive CIA activities more to light and to make the government more accountable for those things.

FORD: Right.

DAITCH: And that's one of the moments in history when people started to, again, aside from the conspiracy kooks, when people started to say, well, why didn't the Warren Commission uncover this? Because people.... I mean certainly Allen Dulles would have been aware probably.

FORD: He certainly should have because of his previous responsibilities.

DAITCH: Right. And maybe John McCloy.

FORD: Possibly.

DAITCH: Possibly. Who else? I think Dick Russell maybe might have known.

FORD: He could have.

DAITCH: But in any case, that some of the members of the Warren Commission probably would have known that there were these secret attacks against, and a fairly aggressive program of attack, against Castro, and that the Commission didn't try to put Oswald's acts in the context of that. Do you think that's a valid criticism?

FORD: It probably is as a Monday morning quarterback. At the time we thought we did a thorough job. Whether we slipped up on this particular aspect, history can only come up to its own conclusion. But, I think at the time a majority of the members of the Commission thought we had done a thorough job.

DAITCH: Right. Now what we also know is that the CIA and the FBI did not release to the Commission certain....

FORD: Correct. Which was unconscionable.

DAITCH: Right. I guess Richard Helms testified, he was the person who was...

FORD: In charge of the CIA.

DAITCH: Right. And he's testified that, well, even if we had released that material, it wouldn't have changed the conclusions. Which is probably true.

FORD: I think that's a fair assessment.

DAITCH: Given that, do you think that that was a decision that the CIA [Central Intelligence Agency] and the FBI [Federal Bureau of Investigation] had the authority to make in terms of not releasing that information to the Commission?

FORD: I think they made a mistake in not giving us all of the data they had available. And their judgment was not good in not giving us the full story.

DAITCH: Right, right. But you don't think that it would have changed anything?

FORD: From what I know about the additional evidence, I don't think it would have changed our basic decisions.

DAITCH: I have to tell you that the things that are available now are wonderful as a result of those commissions and as a result of the more recent...

FORD: I'm sure there's data now that we wish we had but never got. Not that they would have changed the two conclusions. But it would have been a more interesting scenario.

DAITCH: Mmmm hmmm. I think the context is one of the things that, you know, historians now are—in particular Max Holland has said, and I think there's something to be said for this, he puts the whole thing in the context of the Cold War. And that's very important from a historical perspective to understand the seriousness with which all of that was taken and the importance of I guess what you would call espionage and intelligence activities. And the fact that our government was withholding secrets from other branches of our government was maybe....

FORD: Well, history of government is that departments are not always forthright with their competitors in their government. That's human nature. Whether it's right or wrong, that's the way it works.

DAITCH: And if you can get by with it....

FORD: Right.

DAITCH: It's, I think, a very important point historically to understand at that time the context.

FORD: Let me ask you this: You are much more knowledgeable in certain areas than we as a commission were because of new evidence. My impression, without getting into the details, is that none of the new evidence would basically change our two conclusions.

DAITCH: No, I don't think it does at all. And I think serious historians don't find that it does either. The biggest thing I think that historians want to add is the context of the.... There's a historian who has written—a journalist, I think, who's written a historical book. His name is Gus Russo. It's called *Live by the Sword*. His thesis, it seemed a little harsh to me, but basically his thesis is that, look, the Kennedy brothers, especially Bob Kennedy, were pursuing Castro very aggressively, and that that was common knowledge in the pro-Castro community...

FORD: Right.

DAITCH: And that that is the political context in which Lee Harvey Oswald acted. He figured, hey, if the American government is pursuing Castro, trying to assassinate him, then it's perfectly legitimate for me to turn around and try to assassinate the American president.

FORD: That's a theory. There's no concrete evidence that that would have transpired any differently. Now, whenever I'm asked what are my current conclusions, I have a one-page statement that I have typed up, made available. People send me a copy of the Warren Commission. On my views I have this one-page statement that says: "As the sole surviving member of the Warren Commission, I agree with the basic decisions that Lee Harvey Oswald committed the assassination, and we found no evidence of a conspiracy." I sign it, date it, and send it back. I won't get into an argument with people who have a different viewpoint.

DAITCH: Right. And again, I think that legitimate historians tend to agree with that perspective. I think this fellow Gus Russo has done a tremendous amount of research. And again, there's no question that there was this secret aggression toward the Castro regime.

FORD: Right.

DAITCH: That's a matter of historical fact. But he suggests that one of the reasons why Bob Kennedy also didn't want to pursue it much further, he wasn't aggressive.... Actually, let me ask you that: Did you find that Bob Kennedy wasn't terribly—[he] didn't want to spend a lot of time talking about it?

FORD: Hi, dear.

[BREAK]

FORD: ...as a zealot on a number of things than Jack was. His handling of the McCarthy [Joseph R. McCarthy] hearings. He was a tiger. Jack was more of a diplomat. So I would say that Bobby would have maybe even different.... Wendy [the dog], you go away and leave us.

DAITCH: Oh, I can't help petting a dog if there's one around.

FORD: Well, I've kind of lost the question.

DAITCH: The question was you knew both Bob and Jack Kennedy. And this fellow Russo has argued that one of the reasons that Bob Kennedy didn't pursue it more, the assassination investigation, was that he felt guilty for pushing the assassination attempts....

FORD: On Castro. That's possible. In comparing Jack and Bobby, as I said a moment ago, Jack was a diplomat, Bobby was a tiger. And Teddy [Edward M. Kennedy] is sort of in between.

DAITCH: I think of him more of the sort of master congressperson moving things through Congress.

FORD: Right. He's more of a legislator.

DAITCH: Legislator, yes. I think that it's an interesting proposition, and I don't know whether—you were there, and you knew Bob Kennedy, if you sort of had the sense that he wasn't pushing the investigation, or any sense of....

FORD: I didn't have the feeling that in the Commission there was any Bobby Kennedy influence. Maybe I didn't.... I know he never contacted me, to my knowledge or recollection. That's just a difference in the family.

DAITCH: Yes. It's an amazing family. I've also heard about Bob Kennedy that he, after the assassination, and I'm sure it wasn't an overnight thing, but that he.... I mean you spoke about him being such a tiger and he was a very aggressive person in a lot of ways during that period. But then afterward there's sort of a softer side, if you will, that came out. Do you remember seeing that or feeling that?

FORD: Not particularly, no. I never was close to Bobby. I was much closer to Jack. And I would be even more close to Ted because of our long friendship. I've got real admiration for Ted. He and Caroline [Caroline Lee Kennedy Schlossberg] gave me the award up in Boston just a year or so ago which I was deeply grateful for, considering the previous attitude in reference to the pardon of Nixon. Profile in Courage from the two Kennedys was a wonderful admission that I was right and, in retrospect, they were wrong.

DAITCH: Sure. Absolutely.

FORD: And I appreciated it.

DAITCH: Oh, yes. I think it was one of those things.... I don't know them personally. But from the perspective of being around the Library, I think that people, you know, uniformly there believe that it was the right thing to do, you know, and that it was an act of courage to do it at the time.

FORD: Not wise politically.

DAITCH: No, not so much. But very much in the spirit of what the award is about, I think. Just for the tape we'll say we're talking about the Profiles in Courage Award by Caroline Kennedy and Senator Kennedy.

FORD: You haven't asked me anything about Jack Ruby.

DAITCH: Yes. Tell me about what you knew about Jack Ruby at the time.

FORD: I never knew anything about him prior to being on the Commission. But on the Sunday, the chief justice and I, with two or three staff people, flew to Dallas to spend about five hours interrogating Jack Ruby.

DAITCH: You did! I didn't know that.

FORD: We went to.... He was in the custody of the sheriff or whoever was controlling him. Our group with the chief justice interrogated him. He was unstable, to put it mildly. The critical question was: Why did you assassinate Oswald? And his consistent answer—he was asked many times—his consistent answer was: He didn't want to force Mrs. Kennedy to testify in a criminal trial against Oswald.

DAITCH: Really!

FORD: Strange point of view. But he demanded that he be given a lie detector test, which we finally agreed to. [CHANGE TO SIDE B OF TAPE] ...how he happened to be at the right time to do what he did. For example, the postal service had an inspector who was one of those who interrogated Ruby. You say, well, why was a postal inspector involved? Well, the Post Office Department had some jurisdiction that got him involved. This postal inspector on that Sunday that Ruby shot Oswald was at church. He called and said to the people holding Ruby, would they hold up until he got there to further interrogate him. And that delay made it possible that Oswald and Ruby happened to be there at the right time. So it wasn't a planned assassination of Oswald. It was pure happenstance.

DAITCH: Is that right! See, I'm not an assassination expert. I don't know that much about the assassination itself, as you can probably tell. But I'm fascinated with this response of that he didn't want Mrs. Kennedy to have to testify against Oswald. And if it's not a planned thing, at least he showed up with a gun. So he had some idea of....

FORD: What he was going to do.

DAITCH: Yes.

FORD: Well, he had a reputation of being involved with the Mafia and bad elements in the Dallas area.

DAITCH: Right. So he might have carried a gun all the time, you're thinking?

FORD: Right.

DAITCH: Yes. So he did elaborate on this concept of not wanting Mrs. Kennedy to testify?

FORD: I don't recall. But there was no question. That was his justification.

DAITCH: That is weird. Now, is there any evidence that he knew Mrs. Kennedy at all?

FORD: Not that I recall.

DAITCH: That is very weird.

FORD: He was a very odd character in the Dallas community.

DAITCH: Yes, yes, I knew that about him. His connections with the Mafia and all that, obviously that's one of the big theories. Did the Warren Commission actually investigate? Do you think that there was much time spent investigating the theory of having some Mafia, of Oswald also having Mafia connections?

FORD: I don't recall that as a member. But I'm sure our staff looked into that area.

DAITCH: Right. And really found nothing.

FORD: Not that we thought was a direct connection.

DAITCH: Right. Now what about the Clay [Clay L. Shaw] Trial and all that that occurred a little bit later? You must have been following that with some interest.

FORD: Well, that was in New Orleans, as I recall. He was a publicity hound, local district attorney [Jim C. Garrison], who made very serious charges but couldn't substantiate any of them. I don't recall the details, but he was a self-seeking, self-promoter.

DAITCH: As a Commission member, you didn't see anything about any of that that you thought, oh, my, we should have looked into this?

FORD: Again, I'm sure the staff did. But I don't recall we as a Commission spending a lot of time on it.

DAITCH: Right. Are there things that, you know, in subsequent years, over time, different things come out and this and that. But from today's perspective, are there things that you look back and you say, well, I wish we had pushed harder on this aspect of the investigation?

FORD: I think anytime you're in a capacity as a commission, you do a nine-month job under some pressure to get a conclusion. In retrospect, you can always say, well, I wish we had looked a little deeper into this. But then you evaluate, did we come up with the right answer? And again, I repeat, I think our conclusions were basically right. And I've seen no subsequent evidence, contrary to Oliver Stone and his movie, which was not a documentary. It was far from it. But he raised a lot of questions that the public wants some new answers to.

DAITCH: Right, right. I think those answers are going to be forthcoming in terms of the review board has released....

FORD: The Congressional board really hasn't come up with any new evidence.

DAITCH: Oh, no, no, not at all. But just new answers to the same old questions: The documents are there. You know, they answer some more questions. It still doesn't change anything.

FORD: Right.

DAITCH: But, you know, for people who want to dig.... And that's a good thing.

FORD: I always say there are still people who raise questions about Lincoln's [Abraham Lincoln] assassination. So from now until eternity we'll have questions raised about the Kennedy assassination.

DAITCH: Sure. Well, I do think it's such a shocking thing, it's such a horrifying moment in time, and such a frightening thing for the nation. And even in particular at that moment in national history. There was a very real threat of nuclear war.

FORD: Of course when I was president, I had two assassination attempts. Squeaky Fromme [Lynette Fromme], who was part of the Manson [Charles M. Manson] Gang in Sacramento, and Sara Jane Moore in San Francisco. I never understood why they wanted to assassinate me, but they sure tried.

DAITCH: Yes, yes. But again, that sort of suggests.... I'm thinking back to the question about motive in terms of the people who have said that, well, maybe the Commission should have come up with a more clear-cut motive for Oswald. Maybe there isn't always.

FORD: Well, all we could go by was what he told us. And he consistently took that point of view as murdering Oswald. I don't think there was ever any definitive motive that the Commission could land on about Oswald assassinating Kennedy. I have my feeling; I've expressed it. And others may have agreed or differed. But I don't think the

Commission ever came up with a conclusion as to the motive.

DAITCH: I have a question for you that's a little different. But from the perspective of a former president, there have been various biographers and other types of historians have had these two views of Kennedy: On the one hand he certainly knew that his brother and the CIA were aggressively pursuing Castro up to the point of assassination. On the other hand, probably the most recent biographer of Kennedy has said that Kennedy knew that the idea had been kicked around, but that he was not really in favor of it, and that he had said that he thought it was a bad idea. From the point of view of having been president, do you think that it's possible that he didn't know that they were really aggressively pursuing Castro?

FORD: Because of his relationship with his brother, who was his attorney general, and because a president ought to know those things, I have to assume he did. I have no categorical evidence. But as president and particularly with his brother as attorney general, I have to assume he knew.

DAITCH: I mean I understand that once in a while there are and have been these occasional sort of rogue people in the CIA or FBI or whatever. But this seems to have been a pretty formalized program.

FORD: I wouldn't doubt that a bit, although I don't know for sure.

DAITCH: The newer evidence is suggesting that it was at that time being established that it was pretty heavily pursued. I know that that's just your opinion, but I wanted to ask you that because I think it is a historical question. And to the extent that some people want to say that it was sort of John Kennedy's own fault that he was assassinated because he was trying to assassinate Castro.

FORD: Castro. Well, you can't guarantee that sequence. You can't help but believe it's a possibility. But I don't have any concrete evidence. There are a number of books that support the Commission. In my office back in California I must have three or four books by respectable authors supporting the Commission. I've forgotten the titles and the names.

But we have some support in the editorial area.

DAITCH: Well, I'm a historian myself, and I think that by far the view among real historians is that the Commission did a good job and came to the right conclusions.

FORD: Mark Lane was a self-seeker. Oliver Stone came up with a good movie, but a lousy documentary.

DAITCH: No history really.

FORD: Right.

DAITCH: But do you think that some of this comes from, I don't know how to put it, other than sort of a psychic desire among the American people for some kind of closure or some explanation for such a seemingly random or inexplicable act? You know, why did he do that, and how could that happen?

FORD: I'm not sure I understand the question.

DAITCH: I guess what I'm asking is why do you think that people do continue to pursue this and continue to want more explanations? FORD: Well, there's a human nature fascination with conspiracies. This is an ideal area for the reasons you know very well: That the public just, as I said a 20 moment ago, people are still talking about the Lincoln assassination. Did Booth [John Wilkes Booth] do it? And if so, why? And so forth. So I don't think the public question is going to go away. It's probably going to continue and fester and fester forever.

DAITCH: Yes, because even if you accept that Oswald did it, the question of why is....

FORD: Another issue.

DAITCH: Yes, it is sort of inexplicable. I have another.... This is unrelated and kind of an oddball question.

FORD: Go ahead.

DAITCH: I read this in, again, one of the biographies. A biographer of Kennedy has said that Kennedy.... As you know, all the news about Kennedy's physical ailments, which were kind of suspected at the time maybe, but people didn't realize how extensive his medical problems were; but that apparently one of his physician's offices, there was an attempt to break into it. So this biographer has suggested, sort of slyly, I thought, that perhaps—and this was during the 1960 presidential campaign—that maybe Vice President Nixon had something to do with the attempted break-in on Kennedy's physician's office because he was looking for dirt.

FORD: I've never heard that before.

DAITCH: Have you not?

FORD: Never heard that. I can't imagine Nixon authorizing that. But I've never felt very friendly to Ehrlichman [John D. Ehrlichman] and Haldeman [H. R. Haldeman], and their operations in the Nixon administration were somewhat questionable. So it's possible. But I don't know that as a fact.

DAITCH: Right. I wondered whether.... I mean I knew that you had been friendly with Nixon from way back. But I wondered if you had thought that he had changed or if that would have been something that he might have considered at the time.

FORD: Well, I knew Nixon very well. My wife and I knew Pat [Thelma Catherine "Pat" Ryan Nixon] and Dick over many years. Nixon always in my presence acted responsibly. Now, some of the things I've learned from tapes, I don't like. But I think that's a reflection of Haldeman and Ehrlichman, to be honest with you.

DAITCH: Sort of an influence.

FORD: As chiefs of staff, etc.

DAITCH: Here's another, and again, this is unrelated. I'm sorry to sort of...

FORD: No, that's all right. Go ahead.

DAITCH: ...dash around, but some of these things I.... I'm asking you for opinions because obviously you have so much experience in these issues yourself and in these events. This is a what-if question about Kennedy that people have been wondering about ever since the assassination. It's the Vietnam question. You know, so many people have argued, well, Kennedy, would have never gotten us mired into that. And other people have said, look, he's the one who had sent more advisors over there to begin with. You knew him, and you knew his policies, and you knew his international policies in particular.

FORD: Well, from my recollection, it was the Kennedy administration that sent our first combat forces to Vietnam. As I recollect, they sent 5,000 combat troops, 1962. Of course, Johnson accelerated that commitment many times. [BREAK] Johnson certainly added to our commitment in Vietnam. Whether Kennedy would have done the same, I can't tell you because all he did was make our initial combat commitment. You can argue one way or another. But the only evidence I know is that the first 5,000 were a commitment by the Kennedy administration.

DAITCH: Right. People have argued, again, both ways. One of the arguments is that Kennedy didn't have anything to prove. He had already sort of backed down Khrushchev in the Cuban Missile Crisis, and that he wouldn't have wanted to escalate. Again, maybe suggesting sort of the same thing you were talking about of having had military experience that he might not want to get too involved. FORD: That's all speculation, and I wouldn't pass judgment on that.

DAITCH: It's a difficult question. It's just something that so many people have been trying to work out for so many years.

FORD: Well, the pro-Kennedy people would argue he would not have gotten mired in Vietnam. The truth is he made the first military combat commitment.

DAITCH: That's right.

FORD: Now whether that indicates anything to a major expansion or not is a question; you just don't know.

DAITCH: Exactly. Well, I should let you go here because obviously your time is valuable.

FORD: Well, I've enjoyed it. Can we have a transcript of this for my library?

DAITCH: Oh, absolutely. Yes.

FORD: I mean we won't use it. We'll just have it for the archives.

DAITCH: Oh, sure. What will happen is.... Well, I can turn these off now. But we can....

Source: John F. Kennedy Library Oral History Program. Gerald R. Ford recorded interview by Vicki Daitch, July 8, 2003.

See Articles: Civil Rights Laws; Kennedy, John F. (Administration of); Oswald, Lee Harvey; Organized Crime, History of.

1964 PRIMARY DOCUMENT

President's Advisory Commission on Narcotic and Drug Abuse Press Release

Many efforts to criminalize or regulate "pep pills" (most of which contained benzylpiperazine) failed, including this legislation and a later attempt to impose maximum quotas on the manufacture of the pills. The 1970 Comprehensive Drug Abuse Prevention and Control Act, though, included Title II of the Controlled Substances Act, which established five categories ("schedules") of controlled substances; in 2002, benzylpiperazine was finally added as a controlled substance.

From the offices of:

Senator Thomas J. Dodd (D-Conn.)
Room 241, Senate Office Building,
Washington, D.C.
Capitol 4-3121, Ext. 2951

Cong. James J. Delaney (D-N.Y.)
Room 455, House Office Building
Washington, D.C.
Capitol 4-3121, Ext. 3965

For Release—January 25, 1964, Saturday a.m.

WASHINGTON, D. C., January 25, 1964—The President's Advisory Commission on Narcotic and Drug Abuse was lauded today in a joint statement issued by Senator Thomas J. Dodd (D-Conn.) and Congressman James J. Delaney (D-N.Y.).

President Johnson is releasing today the commission's report supporting pioneering legislation introduced last year by Dodd and Delaney which would place strong controls over the distribution of pep pills and sleeping pills millions of which are presently diverted into illicit channels. This traffic has resulted in a staggering increase in addition among juveniles.

The Advisory Commission is an outgrowth of the first White House Conference on Narcotics held here two years ago. The White House group pointed out the growing abuse of "psychotoxic" drugs and made a strong plea for stronger legislation to cope with it. The Commission praised a plan introduced by Dodd and Delaney last year which would regulate the sale of many of these drugs, but urged expansion of the plan to keep up with the new products rapidly coming into the market.

The two legislators plan to introduce new legislation which will augment this recommendation. It will crack down not only on the illicit sale of barbiturates and "pep pills," but will also affect the manufacturers and distributors of non-narcotic drugs which are "capable of producing psychotoxic effects or anti-social behavior." The Dodd-Delaney plan would not restrict the medical or research use of these drugs but would eliminate non-medical sales and require sales and shipment records that could be traced from manufacturer to consumer.

The emphasis of the new bill, like that in the 1963 plan, will be on the sale of drugs to juveniles. A "pusher clause " will make the unauthorized sale of the drugs to minors a criminal offense and doubles the present jail sentence for such a crime.

In their statement, Senator Dodd and Congressman Delaney said, "While we must recognize the value of these drugs to the practice of medicine, their abuse, especially by youngsters, has tragic consequences. Law enforcement officers across the country are unanimous in their recognition of the direct relationship between these drugs and robberies, sex offenses, beatings and even murder. The major tragedy, however, is not the one that shows clearly on the police blotter. It is the physical and psychological deterioration of the drug user, particularly the youth. Some of these drugs are as physically addicting as heroin and the addict will go just as far to feed his or her habit.

The Commission also urged Congressional action on a resolution introduced by Senator Dodd calling for the establishment of a Joint American-Mexican Commission on Narcotics. Investigations by Senator Dodd have shown that Mexico is one of the chief sources of supply of opium, heroin and marijuana for the Southwestern part of the United States.

Source: NARA-II, RG 65, DOT, Narcotics Enforcement, Box 7 F: White House Conf.

See Articles: Drug Abuse and Addiction, History of; Drug Enforcement Administration; Narcotics Laws.

1965
PRIMARY DOCUMENT

Customs Narcotics Report

The U.S. Customs Service was formed in 1789 to supervise the collection of tariffs on imported goods. It became the agency principally responsible for monitoring the passage of goods into the United States, including smuggling, drug trafficking, and human trafficking. In 2003, the Customs Service was absorbed by the Department of Homeland Security; its functions are now carried out by Immigration and Customs Enforcement and the Bureau of Customs and Border Protection.

Date: July 28, 1965

From: Lester D. Johnson—Commissioner of Customs
Subject: Quarterly Narcotic Report

Report For Second Quarter 1965
Pursuant To Assistant Secretary's Memo of July 23, 1964

Total customs seizures for the quarter were as follows:

	Number of seizures	*Weight— Grams*
Heroin	62	1,456
Opium, raw	—	—
Opium, smoking	1	1,809
Other narcotics	65	1,290
Marijuana	187	1,548,434

The largest of the few heroin seizures made during the quarter was only 5 ounces, but one of the cases included the arrest on April 9 of Onesimo BOTELLO Garza, a major distributor in the part of Mexico across from Roma, Texas, who delivered 105 grams to undercover officers.

Another happening of interest was the forcible medical search of Barbara Jean HENDERSON on June 10, with the recovery of 3-1/2 ounces of heroin from within her body. This search had been sanctioned by the U.S. attorney when customs agents questioning the traveler on her arrival at San Ysidro had found she was connected with a notorious trafficker in Los Angeles who customarily used women to smuggle in the manner described.

Students who boarded an Indian vessel at Longview, Washington, on May 6 in search of foreign coins were approached by a quartermaster offering 4 pounds of opium. They introduced to him a potential buyer in the form of an undercover CPI, who was able to seize the drug and arrest the violator.

On June 24 customs agents at Miami supplied Federal narcotic agents with funds and personnel used in the completion of two purchases of cocaine from Peru. The first buy was 600 grams, with the arrest of a Peruvian and a Puerto Rican, and the second lot was 1 kilo, with 3 American violators taken into custody.

While the center of activity involving marijuana remains in California, four substantial cases were developed in Texas. Two of these were made by undercover operations at Brownsville. The first brought seizure of 57 pounds on April 6, with the arrest of 3 violators from Matamoros, and on April 29 the officers seized 38 pounds, arresting 2 more residents of Mexico. State narcotic agents cooperated in both instances.

The third case involved a convoy operation of the sort common a few years ago. Officers followed a suspect car from Laredo to Refugio, where they searched it, finding 103 pounds of marijuana and 2 grams of heroin. The two occupants agreed to proceed with the intended delivery in Chicago. There on May 27 customs agents arrested the consignee, Juan ESCOBEDO, who had figured in 2 previous convoy cases that did not develop sufficient evidence to support his apprehension. Following the Chicago delivery, agents in Laredo arrested the shipper and seized another 18 pounds of marijuana.

The last of the Texas cases mentioned arose on June 13 when a public health officer at El Paso found 60 pounds of marijuana in the car driven by an Italian living in Chicago. The smuggler said he was working for a trafficker there, and agreed to carry out delivery; however, when the load arrived in Chicago, nobody came to claim it.

What turned out to be the biggest of the California cases originated when a customs inspector at Tecate found 317 pounds of marijuana in a car driven by 2 young Mexicans. With a customs agent "riding shotgun" one of them went on to deliver in Los Angeles to Francisco Martinez LIANTAUD, a Cuban who had only by chance missed arrest in another convoy case last Thanksgiving. Extension of the current investigation brought the total arrests to 8 and incidental searches raised total seizures of marijuana to 757 pounds.

Another large California case culminated a night-time surveillance at Jacumba, in the mountains about 80 miles east of San Diego. Customs agents saw 510 pounds of marijuana transferred across the boundary fence into a station wagon driven by Lloyal D. HUGHES, of Long Beach. They followed him for some distance with the object of apprehending his customer, but were forced to close in when he began to traverse resort areas where there was a chance he might evade the pursuit.

Thirteen other cases involving 42 to 150 pounds each, with a total of 1,351 pounds, originated in San Ysidro. Ten of these were the result of information developed by customs agents and CPIs; one originated in the suspicion of a CPI watching border traffic; while a customs inspector and an immigrant inspector, searching without information, made one each. In 4 instances suspect cars were followed to Los Angeles. One case brought no arrests, but the other 12 yielded 23 defendants. These included 5 Cubans in 5 different cases, 1 Puerto Rican, 1 Briton, and 6 presumed Mexicans.

A long-distance operation grew out of a surveillance performed by customs agents at San Diego on two New Yorkers in a suburban motel. When one of these shipped to New York 2 large suitcases smelling of marijuana, agents in the latter city were informed, and monitored the delivery on June 8. The recipients turned out to be the shippers themselves, who had returned from the Coast, and marijuana weighing 84 pounds was found in the suitcases.

While small personal supplies of marijuana can be found in the crew quarters of nearly every vessel reaching our ports, shipments of commercial size arriving by sea are rare. One such was a lot of 50 pounds found concealed in 12 green engine room cushions on a Colombian ship at Baltimore on May 14. It was traced to an oiler who said it had been entrusted to him in Santa Marta, Colombia.

While technically amphetamines are not narcotics, they present enough of the same problems that it is deemed worthwhile to report the seizure at Laredo on June 23 of 25,000 pills, the largest lot ever encountered in Texas and one of the largest lots ever found anywhere in the United States. Antioco Orlando GONZALEZ, owner of 3 drug stores in Nuevo Laredo, had smuggled them into the country and delivered them to a Food & Drug inspector acting under cover. On developing the information which originated the case, the Food & Drug officers had followed previous practice by inviting customs agents to participate, in order to take advantage of our wider powers where smuggled merchandise is involved.

Twenty-year sentences are not seen every day or every week, but 4 were handed down in the San Diego district during May. Two of these involved first offenders—Fred Douglas

DAVIS, a Las Vegas peddler arrested at the San Diego airport last December 7 while waiting for the delivery of 93 grams of smuggled heroin, and Ulysses Grant LEEKS, arrested at San Ysidro on March 14 in an attempt to smuggle 140 pounds of marijuana and 3 ounces of heroin for an undisclosed principal.

The other two recipients of 20-year terms were John E. LEWIS, an important New York trafficker, and Charles E. WHITE, another New Yorker who on November 8 attempted to smuggle through San Ysidro 27 ounces of heroin and ½ ounce of cocaine intended for Lewis. In addition to the imprisonment, these violators were fined $60,000 and $20,000, respectively.

June 18 saw the extradition from Canada of three conspirators in the RIVARD heroin case. On that date customs agents armed with a Presidential warrant took custody of Julien GAGNON, Charles Emile GROLEAU, and Joseph Raymond JONES. The defendants were flown in a Coast Guard plane directly to Laredo, Texas, where they are in jail awaiting trial next September. At that time they will be joined by the head of the gang, Lucien RIVARD himself, who was apprehended on July 16 at a hideout near Montreal, and is presently in jail in Houston.

Source: NARA-II, RG 65, DOT, Narcotics Enforcement, Box 5 F: Narcotic Reports

See Articles: Drug Abuse and Addiction, Contemporary; Drug Abuse and Addiction, History of; Drug Abuse and Addiction, Sociology of; Drug Enforcement Administration; Smuggling.

1965
PRIMARY DOCUMENT

Presidential Assassination Law

Following the Kennedy assassination, the Presidential Assassination law was passed to define as a federal offense the murder, assault, or kidnapping of the president, president-elect, or vice president of the United States. The law not only increased the penalties beyond what would be incurred for the murder, assault, or kidnapping of some other individual, but also ensured that the matter would be investigated and prosecuted by federal authorities, which would be provided with special powers.

Chapter 84—Presidential and Presidential Staff Assassination, Kidnapping, and Assault

(a) Whoever kills
  (1) any individual who is the President of the United States, the President-elect, the Vice President, or, if there is no Vice President, the officer next in the order of succession to the Office of the President of the United States, the Vice President-elect, or any person who is acting as President under the Constitution and laws of the United States, or
  (2) any person appointed under section 105(a)(2)(A) of title 3 employed in the Executive Office of the President or appointed under section 106(a)(1)(A) of title 3 employed in the Office of the Vice President, shall be punished as provided by sections 1111 and 1112 of this title.
(b) Whoever kidnaps any individual designated in subsection (a) of this section shall be punished
  (1) by imprisonment for any term of years or for life, or
  (2) by death or imprisonment for any term of years or for life, if death results to such individual.
(c) Whoever attempts to kill or kidnap any individual designated in subsection (a) of this section shall be punished by imprisonment for any term of years or for life.
(d) If two or more persons conspire to kill or kidnap any individual designated in subsection (a) of this section and one or more of such persons do any act to effect

the object of the conspiracy, each shall be punished
(1) by imprisonment for any term of years or for life, or
(2) by death or imprisonment for any term of years or for life, if death results to such individual.

(e) Whoever assaults any person designated in subsection (a)(1) shall be fined under this title, or imprisoned not more than ten years, or both. Whoever assaults any person designated in subsection (a)(2) shall be fined under this title, or imprisoned not more than one year, or both; and if the assault involved the use of a dangerous weapon, or personal injury results, shall be fined under this title, or imprisoned not more than ten years, or both.

(f) The terms "President-elect" and "Vice-President-elect" as used in this section shall mean such persons as are the apparent successful candidates for the offices of President and Vice President, respectively, as ascertained from the results of the general elections held to determine the electors of President and Vice President in accordance with title 3, United States Code, sections 1 and 2.

(g) The Attorney General of the United States, in his discretion is authorized to pay an amount not to exceed $100,000 for information and services concerning a violation of subsection (a)(1). Any officer or employee of the United States or of any State or local government who furnishes information or renders service in the performance of his official duties shall not be eligible for payment under this subsection.

(h) If Federal investigative or prosecutive jurisdiction is asserted for a violation of this section, such assertion shall suspend the exercise of jurisdiction by a State or local authority, under any applicable State or local law, until Federal action is terminated.

(i) Violations of this section shall be investigated by the Federal Bureau of Investigation. Assistance may be requested from any Federal, State, or local agency, including the Army, Navy, and Air Force, any statute, rule, or regulation to the contrary notwithstanding.

(j) In a prosecution for an offense under this section the Government need not prove that the defendant knew that the victim of the offense was an official protected by this section.

(k) There is extraterritorial jurisdiction over the conduct prohibited by this section.

Source: http://codes.lp.findlaw.com/uscode/18/I/84

See Articles: Death Row; Executions; Federal Bureau of Investigation; Federal Prisons; Kennedy, John F. (Administration of); Kidnapping; Murder, Sociology of.

1966 PRIMARY DOCUMENT

Senator Robert F. Kennedy Communications on the New York Transit Strike

Bobby Kennedy didn't announce his candidacy for president until 1968, when it became clear that many Democrats were dissatisfied with President Johnson's Vietnam policies. But his detractors accused him of treating his entire political life as a campaign for an eventual presidency, and his role in the New York City transit strike was no exception: Conservative papers pointed out that Kennedy was publicly silent for much of the strike (which lasted for 12 days), until it was clear it was ending.

January 4 Telegram To Mayor John V. Lindsay
Dear Mr. Mayor:
I just want you to know I am prepared to assist you in any way appropriate to reach an

early and fair settlement of the transit strike. Please call on me if I can be of any assistance.

Robert F. Kennedy

Response From Mayor Lindsay
Dear Senator Kennedy:
Thank you for your telegram. This is an extraordinary time for New York and I thank you for your offer to help. I would appreciate having any suggestions you may have.

Mayor John V. Lindsay

January 10 Statement of Senator Robert F. Kennedy
It is clear that the transit strike has become a catastrophe to the city and to the people of New York. The loss to individual wage-earners, to businesses, and to the city itself requires the extended effort of all parties to the negotiations to reach an early and equitable conclusion. I urge that the negotiations go on a 24-hour basis and that they not recess until they have reached a fair and responsible settlement. It is imperative that the strike end by this weekend.

On January 4 I informed Mayor Lindsay that I was prepared to assist in any appropriate way in the efforts to reach an early and fair settlement of the strike. I have discussed this matter with the Mayor again today and have repeated to him my offer of assistance.

January 10 Telegram to Dr. Nathan P. Feinsenger, Chairman of Transit Strike Mediation Panel
Senator Robert F. Kennedy today sent the following telegram to transit strike mediation panel chairman, Dr. Nathan P. Feinsenger, with copies to other public officials and persons as indicated in the text below:

The transit strike has now gone on for ten days. Allowing it to continue any longer in the face of the staggering losses which it is causing is intolerable. The devastating losses which are filling up each day far exceed the differences between the parties. Its continuance through this week will cause wide-spread personal tragedy throughout the city. People are unable to get to their jobs. Thousands are having to spend hard-earned savings for food and rent. The city government is losing millions of dollars a day in revenue, wage earners and small businesses are suffering tremendously. Many will soon be driven into bankruptcy.

Despite your earnest efforts, the ordinary processes of collective bargaining have failed to produce agreement, even though they have had ample time in which to operate. Weeks of negotiations preceded the strike and ten days of bargaining have gone on during the tie-up. Ten days which have been catastrophic for the citizens of the city. A new initiative is needed to create a basis for settlement. I therefore respectfully suggest that you, the mediating panel, based on your intimate knowledge of the comparatively small differences between the parties, make public the exact differences now separating them and make a public proposal for resolution of those differences.

Your undertaking to make a public proposal can help to bring a fair and responsible settlement. I am sending copies of this telegram to the parties, to the Mayor, to the Governor, and to the Secretary of Labor.

Report on New York City Transit Strike January 10, 1966—3:04 P. M.
Senators Robert F. Kennedy and Jacob K. Javitz announced today a federal grant of $221,453.02 by the Office of Economic Opportunity to speed up the processing of applications for small business loans during the transportation crisis in New York City.

"Under today's grant," the Senators stated: "Your small Business Development Centers will be established immediately in temporary locations around the city. For the period of the strike emergency, the centers will be used for the processing of both regular Small Business Loan applications and lease under the Anti-Poverty program. The federal Small Business Administration is being invited to staff the temporary centers until the emergency is over. The four centers will be moved to permanent locations when the strike is over."

"The four temporary centers," the Senators went on, "will be in the offices of the borough presidents of Manhattan, Brooklyn, Bronx, and Queens. In addition, the Office of Economic Opportunity will make available for the processing of emergency loan applications the facilities of the two permanent Small Business Development Centers already in operation. These centers are located at 361 West 125th Street and 35 Fifth Avenue.

The separate remarks of Senator Kennedy follows:

"The strike is having disastrous effects on thousands of individuals and small businesses in New York City, and I have been in constant contact with agencies in the Executive Branch of the Federal Government to insure that all possible aid is given during the period of the strike to prevent wide-spread financial ruin. I am, therefore, gratified that the Office of Economic Opportunity had made this grant. I expect that other steps will be taken by CEO and other agencies within the next few days.

"I am especially pleased that the Office of Economic Opportunity was able to process the grants for the temporary centers so quickly. This grant and other measures which the Federal Government has taken and will take within the next few days will make a great difference in helping small businessmen in New York City meet the current crisis. Office of Economic Opportunity Administrator Sargent Shriver has assured me that his agency will continue to do everything in its power to assist the people in New York City during this emergency

Report on New York City Transit Strike January 19, 1956—3:00 PM

Senators Robert F. Kennedy and Jacob K. Javitz announced today a federal grant of $221,453.02 by the Office of Economic Opportunity to speed up the processing of applications for small business loans during the transportation crisis in New York City.

"Under today's grant," the Senators stated: "Your small Business Development Centers will be established immediately in temporary locations around the city. For the period of the strike emergency, the centers will be used for the processing of both regular Small Business Loan applications and lease under the Anti-Poverty program. The federal Small Business Administration is being invited to staff the temporary centers until the emergency is over. The four centers will be moved to permanent locations when the strike is over."

"The four temporary centers," the Senators went on, "will be in the offices of the borough presidents of Manhattan, Brooklyn, Bronx, and Queens. In addition, the Office of Economic Opportunity will make available for the processing of emergency loan applications the facilities of the two permanent Small Business Development Centers already in operation. These centers are located at 361 West 125th Street and 35 Fifth Avenue.

The separate remarks of Senator Kennedy follows:

> The strike is having disastrous effects on thousands of individuals and small businesses in New York City, and I have been in constant contact with agencies in the Executive Branch of the Federal Government to insure that all possible aid is given during the period of the strike to prevent wide-spread financial ruin. I am, therefore, gratified that the Office of Economic Opportunity had made this grant. I expect that other steps will be taken by CEO and other agencies within the next few days.
>
> I am especially pleased that the Office of Economic Opportunity was able to process the grants for the temporary centers so quickly. This grant and other measures which the Federal Government has taken and will take within the next few days will make a great difference in helping small businessmen in New York City meet the current crisis. Office of Economic Opportunity Administrator Sargent Shriver has assured me that his agency will continue to do everything in its power to assist the people in New York City during this emergency.

Source: Collection JFK-RFK:
Robert F. Kennedy Papers
Archival Research Catalog (ARC) ID: 194021

See Articles: Civil Disobedience; Kennedy, Robert F.; New York City.

1968 PRIMARY DOCUMENT

Robert F. Kennedy News Release on the Assassination of Martin Luther King Jr.

One of the most significant civil rights leaders in history, Martin Luther King Jr. was only 39 years old when he was killed in 1968. Kennedy's speech was impromptu; he had learned of King's shooting shortly before a scheduled stop on his three-week-old presidential campaign. Few present had yet heard the news. King's killer, segregationist and repeat felon James Earl Ray, was soon apprehended, but was convinced that George Wallace would soon be elected president and pardon him.

Senator Robert F. Kennedy
Indianapolis, Indiana
April 4, 1968

I have bad news for you, for all of our fellow citizens, and people who love peace all over the world, and that is that Martin Luther King was shot and killed tonight.

Martin Luther King dedicated his life to love and to justice for his fellow human beings, and he died because of that effort.

In this difficult day, in this difficult time for the United States, it is perhaps well to ask what kind of a nation we are and what direction we want to move in. For those of you who are black—considering the evidence there evidently is that there were white people who were responsible—you can be filled with bitterness, with hatred, and a desire for revenge. We can move in that direction as a country, in great polarization—black people amongst black, white people amongst white, filled with hatred toward one another.

Or we can make an effort, as Martin Luther King did, to understand and to comprehend, and to replace that violence, that stain of bloodshed that has spread across our land, with an effort to understand with compassion and love.

For those of you who are black and are tempted to be filled with hatred and distrust at the injustice of such an act, against all white people, I can only say that I feel in my own heart the same kind of feeling. I had a member of my family killed, but he was killed by a white man. But we have to make an effort in the United States, we have to make an effort to understand, to go beyond these rather difficult times.

My favorite poet was Aeschylus. He wrote: "In our sleep, pain which cannot forget falls drop by drop upon the heart until, in our own despair, against our will, comes wisdom through the awful grace of God."

What we need in the United States is not division; what we need in the United States is not hatred; what we need in the United States is not violence or lawlessness; but love and wisdom, and compassion toward one another, and a feeling of justice toward those who still suffer within our country, whether they be white or they be black.

So I shall ask you tonight to return home, to say a prayer for the family of Martin Luther King, that's true, but more importantly to say a prayer for our own country, which all of us love—a prayer for understanding and that compassion of which I spoke.

We can do well in this country. We will have difficult times; we've had difficult times in the past; we will have difficult times in the future. It is not the end of violence; it is not the end of lawlessness; it is not the end of disorder.

But the vast majority of white people and the vast majority of black people in this country want to live together, want to improve the quality of our life, and want justice for all human beings who abide in our land.

Let us dedicate ourselves to what the Greeks wrote so many years ago: to tame the savageness of man and make gentle the life of this world.

Let us dedicate ourselves to that, and say a prayer for our country and for our people.

Source: http://www.jfklibrary.org/Research/Ready-Reference/RFK-Speeches/Statement-on-the-Assassination-of-Martin-Luther-King.aspx

See Articles: Civil Rights Laws; Kennedy, Robert F.; King, Martin Luther, Jr.; Ray, James Earl.

1969 PRIMARY DOCUMENT

Department of Justice Statement on Miami Drug Smuggling

Drug smuggling is the traditional backbone of the illegal narcotics industry. While marijuana can be grown domestically and methamphetamine can be manufactured cheaply, drugs like opium, heroin, and cocaine come from beyond U.S. borders, processed from crops that can't be grown in the American climate or without attracting the attention of law enforcement. Much of the efforts of narcotics agents has been spent trying to stop the inflow.

United States Department of Justice
Washington, D.C.
AIRMAIL
Miami, Florida
January 10, 1969

Commission of Customs
Office of Investigations
Bureau of Customs
Washington, D.C. 20226
Attention: Andrew Agathangelou

Dear Sir:
At your request there is outlined below the circumstances surrounding the proposal that Pat Johnstone, 21 year old female, proceed to Managua, Nicaragua to bring into the United States to Miami, Florida a quantity of cocaine for delivery to members of a Cuban narcotic trafficking ring based in Miami.

On about September 10, 1968 I received information that Gloria Richard, young white Miami female was in Nicaragua with her five year old son, Shane, to bring back cocaine to the United States at Miami. This lookout was not productive.

On or about September 19, 1968 the same informant reported that Carlos Inchaustegui and Mario Marrero, Cuban refugees in Miami, were, with others, connected with a cocaine laboratory in Managua, Nicaragua which is operated by Cuban refugees under the protection of the Chief of Immigration of Nicaragua. This ring was reported to use young women as couriers and body carriers as the means of concealment.

The informant produced Pat Johnstone who related to Agent Romano and me that she had made two trips to Nicaragua and on one of these occasions had brought three kilos of cocaine through the Miami International Airport Customs posing as a pregnant woman and delivered it to Inchaustegui and Marrero who were waiting outside the Customs enclosure.

She related many other facts and names not here pertinent. Agent Romano verified the trips by Johnstone and through his investigation has implicated about nine traffickers and ten couriers.

Agent Romano placed lookouts and personally led CPI's working the Customs enclosure to intensify efforts on all Nicaragua flights which effort resulted in the apprehension of Denise Betancourt with a body carry of three kilos of cocaine. Her case is pending. With the United States Attorney at Miami, negotiations are underway with her lawyer to possibly secure her testimony as a witness in the case against the Cuban traffickers.

Shortly after this ring was revealed to Customs, I became aware that the Miami Bureau of Narcotics was conducting a parallel investigation of the same principals concerning their domestic traffic. I met with them and we jointly compared information to our mutual benefit and reached an agreement that we would closely coordinate our investigation and neither Service would take unilateral action.

We further agreed that we should attempt to apprehend a courier and jointly hold a surveillance of her as she made a delivery to the principals.

During our initial interview with Johnstone, she was queried as to any offers of the principals to send her back to Nicaragua. She stated that she had not yet been approached but likely would be. She was asked that if she was approached would she consider making the delivery under our direction. She stated that she would and asked that if she was successful she get consideration in her pending State case. She has now been approached to make another trip.

Negotiations are underway between the United States Attorney and Johnstone's lawyer concerning any consideration she might receive for her services. Investigators will make no decisions in this field.

It is proposed that Johnstone will return to Nicaragua for these traffickers and be allowed to complete the delivery of cocaine to these traffickers under the joint supervision of Customs and Narcotics.

To reply specifically to the questions posed by the Bureau, they are answered as follows:

1. Seizure
   It is agreed that Customs will take actual physical custody of the narcotics and both Services will jointly participate in the prosecution and all other facets of the case.

2. Approach
   The informer approached Customs and told her story without promise of coercion.

3. That she acts on her own and not as an agent of the Government.
   I agree with the United States Attorney that this is largely a question of semantics. She and her lawyer have been carefully admonished that her trip is voluntary and that she must not consider herself as an "agent" of the Government and cannot say she is acting for Customs.
   The legal facts are, however, at any time her trip is approved by the Government she is acting for the Government and any other view is unrealistic.

4. Does the United States Attorney authorize the trip and subsequent apprehension as outlined?

The United States Attorney will approve this facet of the proposal if all other questions are resolved to his satisfaction. These questions concern his discussions with the defense lawyer.

This Strike Force is interested in the successful conclusion of this case and has assigned me to coordinate Customs' action with the Bureau of Narcotics and Dangerous Drugs. I have encountered no problems in this field and have had complete cooperation from both Services.

Yours truly,
G. L. Latimer

Source: United States Department of Justice. NARA-II, RG 170 Subj files Bureau of Narcotics, Box 53, F: Miami project

See Articles: Customs Service as Police; Miami, Florida; Narcotics Laws; Smuggling.

1969 PRIMARY DOCUMENT

FBI Memorandum on Stolen Vehicle Case

The FBI Laboratory, which assisted in this case, began as the Criminological Laboratory in 1932 and evolved as resources and technology permitted. Beginning in 1942, it was designated a separate division within the Bureau of Investigation, headed by an assistant director. By that point, it had initiated files on typewriter standards, fraudulent checks, fingerprints, anonymous letters, automotive paint, firearms, blood types, and cryptanalysis. Today, most of its records are computerized.

Interstate Transportation of Stolen Motor Vehicle

Shortly after midnight on April 14, 1967, a deputy sheriff from Delaware County, Oklahoma, was awakened by a phone call and told that a 1967 red Mustang had run off the road near Flint Hill, Oklahoma, and was badly wrecked. The deputy hurried to the scene located a few miles west of the Oklahoma-Arkansas State Line and observed the wreckage. He could find no one in or near the vehicle. After processing the car, he began a search of bars and clubs in the area looking for a witness to the accident. He soon located a young man at a lodge near the scene of the wreck who admitted owning the car and being in the accident. This person identified himself as Chester F. Griffith of Hartford, Connecticut, and displayed a Connecticut driver's license as proof of identification. Griffith exhibited no nervousness and ultimately convinced the deputy there was no need for concern, and as the owner of the vehicle, he would take care of things in the morning.

Early the next day an automobile dealer in Siloam Springs, Arkansas, towed the wrecked vehicle into his shop. He then called the motel where Griffith was staying to inquire what repair work should be done on the car. The car dealer learned that Griffith had hurriedly departed the motel that morning, leaving no forwarding address. The dealer also was told that Griffith tried to sell the wrecked Mustang for $200 just prior to leaving the motel.

I.C. #26-380830

The car bore a North Carolina license, and the Oklahoma Highway Patrol checked it through North Carolina authorities. The North Carolina Highway Patrol advised they had no record of the car ever being registered in North Carolina, and, further, that the license tag on the vehicle checked to a 1965 Ford owned by an individual in Asheville, North Carolina. Once this information was obtained, the FBI Resident Agency in Miami, Oklahoma, was notified, and an investigation was conducted to determine if a possible interstate transportation of stolen motor vehicle violation existed.

Immediate inquiries by the FBI in North Carolina and Tennessee disclosed that the North Carolina license on the Mustang had been stolen on or about April 1, 1967. Further, a Tennessee license plate found in the trunk of the car had been reported stolen on March 10, 1967, in Briceville, Tennessee. A trace of the serial number for the Mustang revealed that the car was registered to an automobile company in Brandon, Mississippi. The car had been stolen from the new car lot on or before April 11, 1967, when an inventory determined it to be gone.

Now that it had been established the vehicle was stolen and had been transported interstate, the FBI investigation centered on the person identifying himself as Chester F. Griffith.

Through a check of records in Connecticut, the FBI determined that Chester F. Griffith was probably identical with Chester Ferris Griffith, Jr., a 29-year-old native of Upton, Massachusetts. Griffith presently a parole violator from Connecticut and had a lengthy criminal record, including several car thefts in the states of Massachusetts, Connecticut and Tennessee. He was described as being heavily tattooed on both arms, hands, and fingers, and reportedly had a habit of chewing his fingernails. His whereabouts were unknown to Connecticut authorities. A photograph was obtained and immediately forwarded to the FBI in Oklahoma. This photograph was exhibited to available witnesses, including a barmaid at a club in Delaware County who had dated Griffith. Chester Ferris Griffith, Jr., was positively identified as being identical with the person driving the 1967 red Mustang.

While photographs of Griffith were being shown to other witnesses, the Document Section of the FBI Laboratory in Washington, D.C., was comparing the signature of Chester F. Griffith found on a registration card at the Siloam Springs motel against known handwriting on fingerprint cards of Chester Ferris

Griffith, Jr. The FBI Laboratory concluded that the signatures were identical.

After an FBI Agent discussed the facts in this case, United States Attorney in Tulsa, Oklahoma, authorized the filing of a complaint charging Griffith with violating the Interstate Transportation of Stolen Motor Vehicle Statute. The United States Commissioner in Miami, Oklahoma, issued a warrant for his arrest and set bond at $5,000. Griffith was now a Federal fugitive, and a vigorous investigation began to locate and arrest him.

No less than 17 FBI Offices through the country participated in the search for Griffith. Every relative and past employer of Griffith were interviewed. Police department and sheriff's office records at the numerous locations Griffith had been arrested were checked for any clue leading to his whereabouts. All of Griffith's criminal associates were contacted for information as to his location.

Griffith's flight as an FBI fugitive came to an abrupt end on March 19, 1968. On that date, a supervisor at FBI Headquarters in Washington, D.C., telephoned the Oklahoma City FBI Office and indicated the Identification Division had made a positive identification of Griffith based on fingerprints submitted by the Provo, Utah, Police Department, showing the arrest of Johnny Griffith on March 11, 1968, on a charge of grand larceny-auto theft. The FBI Office at Salt Lake City quickly verified Griffith's arrest and the fact that he was still in custody. Griffith had been charged with stealing a Ford from Provo on February 20, 1968. He had transported this car to Vail, Colorado, and was arrested there and extradited to Utah. An FBI Agent in Denver, Colorado, later consulted the United States Attorney concerning the interstate transportation of this vehicle; however, prosecution by the Government was declined in favor of prosecution by the Provo authorities.

The FBI's interest in Griffith did not end at this point, for on March 27, 1968, Griffith successfully escaped from the Utah County Jail in Provo by pushing a jailer against the door. The jailer suffered a deep gash in his head which required a number of stitches. When Griffith escaped, he had a knife on his person which he had fashioned. He stole $75 from the jail treasury. An immediate search was ordered, and Griffith was apprehended the next morning in Provo. He was charged with escape, assault and battery, and larceny, in addition to the previous charges. On April 2, 1968, Griffith was found guilty of all local charges in Provo and was sentenced to serve one to ten years in the Utah State Penitentiary.

On November 4, 1968, Griffith appeared United States District court, Salt Lake City, Utah, and was sentenced to serve two years' imprisonment for violating the Interstate Transportation of Stolen Motor Vehicle Statute, concerning the transportation of the 1967 Mustang from Brandon, Mississippi, to Delaware County, Oklahoma, in April 1967. The sentence was to run concurrently with Griffith's imprisonment in the Utah prison.

United States Department of Justice
Federal Bureau of Investigation
Washington, D.C. 20535
February 5, 1969

Source: NARA-II, RG 65 FBI, Interesting Case Write-ups, Box 11

See Articles: Federal Bureau of Investigation; Robbery, Contemporary; Witness Testimony.

1969
PRIMARY DOCUMENT

HYMN Response to the Stonewall Riots

The word homophile, *as a love-focused alternative to* homosexual, *has fallen out of use, but was associated with the early gay-rights movement of the 1950s and 1960s. The Homophile Youth Movement in Neighborhoods (HYMN) was run by Craig Rodwell, the most significant gay-rights activist of the era, and this leaflet is a response to the riots at the Stonewall Inn, a Mafia-owned gay* bar in Greenwich Village. The riots galvanized the movement, and the first gay pride marches took place throughout the country a year later.

Get the Mafia and the Cops Out of Gay Bars
The nights of Friday, June 27, 1969 and Saturday, June 28, 1969 will go down in history as the first time that thousands of Homosexual men and women went out into the streets to protest the intolerable situation which has existed in New York City for many years — namely, the Mafia (or syndicate) control of this city's Gay bars in collusion with certain elements in the Police Dept. of the City of New York. The demonstrations were triggered by a Police raid on the Stonewall Inn late Friday night, June 27th. The purported reason for the raid was the Stonewall's lack of a liquor license. Who's kidding whom? Can anybody really believe that an operation as big as the Stonewall could continue for almost 3 years just a few blocks from the 6th Precinct house without having a liquor license? No! The Police have known about the Stonewall operation all along. What has happened is the presence of new "brass" in 6th Precinct which has vowed to "drive the fags out of the Village."

Many of you have noticed one of the signs which the "management" of the Stonewall has placed outside stating "Legalize Gay bars and lick the problem." This is untrue and they know it. Judge Kenneth Keating (a former US Senator) ruled in January, 1968 that even close dancing between Homosexuals is legal. Since that date there has been nothing illegal, per se, about a gay bar. What is illegal about New York City's Gay bars today is the Mafia (or syndicate) stranglehold on them. Legitimate Gay businessmen are afraid to open decent Gay bars with a healthy social atmosphere (as opposed to the hell-hole atmosphere of places typified by the Stonewall) because of fear of pressure from the unholy alliance of the Mafia and the elements in the Police Dept. who accept payoffs and protect the Mafia monopoly.

We at the Homophile Youth Movement (HYMN) believe that the only way this monopoly can be broken is through the action of Homosexual men and women themselves. We obviously cannot rely on the various agencies of government who for years have known about this situation but who have refused to do anything about it.

Therefore we urge the following:

1. That Gay businessmen step forward and open Gay bars that will be run legally with competitive pricing and a healthy social atmosphere.
2. That Homosexual men and women boycott places like the Stonewall. The only way, it seems, that we can get criminal elements out of the Gay bars is simply to make it unprofitable for them.
3. That the Homosexual citizens of New York City, and concerned Heterosexuals, write to Mayor Lindsay demanding a thorough investigation and effective action to correct this intolerable situation.

Homophile Youth Movement—HYMN
201 Mercer Street
New York, N.Y. 10003
June 28, 1969

Source: http://www.pbs.org/wgbh/american experience/features/primary-resources/ stonewall-leaflet

See Articles: Corruption, Contemporary; Corruption, History of; Organized Crime, Contemporary; Organized Crime, Sociology of.

1970 PRIMARY DOCUMENT

Testimony of Charles Manson in the Tate–LaBianca Murder Trial

The leader of the commune-cult Manson Family, Charles Manson had led a life of brutality on both the giving and receiving ends since childhood. In

1960s San Francisco, his off-kilter blend of philosophies he'd picked up in prison made him a convincing guru, and the Manson Family developed around him. He soon became obsessed with the Beatles' White Album *and his belief in its coded messages; acting on them, the Manson Family went on a killing spree. He remains in prison.*

Direct Testimony:
There has been a lot of charges and a lot of things said about me and brought against the co-defendants in this case, of which a lot could be cleared up and clarified....

I never went to school, so I never growed up to read and write too good, so I have stayed in jail and I have stayed stupid, and I have stayed a child while I have watched your world grow up, and then I look at the things that you do and I don't understand....

You eat meat and you kill things that are better than you are, and then you say how bad, and even killers, your children are. You made your children what they are....

These children that come at you with knives. they are your children. You taught them. I didn't teach them. I just tried to help them stand up....

Most of the people at the ranch that you call the Family were just people that you did not want, people that were alongside the road, that their parents had kicked out, that did not want to go to Juvenile Hall. So I did the best I could and I took them up on my garbage dump and I told them this: that in love there is no wrong....

I told them that anything they do for their brothers and sisters is good if they do it with a good thought....

I was working at cleaning up my house, something that Nixon should have been doing. He should have been on the side of the road, picking up his children, but he wasn't. He was in the White House, sending them off to war....

I don't understand you, but I don't try. I don't try to judge nobody. I know that the only person I can judge is me ... But I know this: that in your hearts and your own souls, you are as much responsible for the Vietnam war as I am for killing these people....

I can't judge any of you. I have no malice against you and no ribbons for you. But I think that it is high time that you all start looking at yourselves, and judging the lie that you live in.

I can't dislike you, but I will say this to you: you haven't got long before you are all going to kill yourselves, because you are all crazy. And you can project it back at me ... but I am only what lives inside each and everyone of you.

My father is the jailhouse. My father is your system.... I am only what you made me. I am only a reflection of you.

I have ate out of your garbage cans to stay out of jail. I have wore your second-hand clothes... I have done my best to get along in your world and now you want to kill me, and I look at you, and then I say to myself, You want to kill me? Ha! I'm already dead, have been all my life. I've spent twenty-three years in tombs that you built.

Sometimes I think about giving it back to you; sometimes I think about just jumping on you and letting you shoot me ... If I could, I would jerk this microphone off and beat your brains out with it, because that is what you deserve, that is what you deserve....

If I could get angry at you, I would try to kill everyone of you. If that's guilt, I accept it ... These children, everything they done, they done for the love of their brother....

If I showed them that I would do anything for my brother—including giving my life for my brother on the battlefield—and then they pick up their banner, and they go off and do what they do, that is not my responsibility. I don't tell people what to do....

These children [indicating the female defendants] were finding themselves. What they did, if they did whatever they did, is up to them. They will have to explain that to you....

It's all your fear. You look for something to project it on, and you pick out a little old scroungy nobody that eats out of a garbage can, and that nobody wants, that was kicked out of the penitentiary, that has been dragged through every hellhole that you can think of, and you drag him and put him in a courtroom.

You expect to break me? Impossible! You broke me years ago. You killed me years ago....

[Judge Older asked Manson if he had anything further to say.]

I have killed no one and I have ordered no one to be killed. I may have implied on several different occasions to several different people that I may have been Jesus Christ, but I haven't decided yet what I am or who I am. Some called him Christ, Manson said. In prison his name was a number. Some now want a sadistic fiend, and so they see him as that. So be it. Guilty. Not guilty. They are only words. You can do anything you want with me, but you cannot touch me because I am only my love... If you put me in the penitentiary, that means nothing because you kicked me out of the last one. I didn't ask to get released. I liked it in there because I like myself.

[Judge Older told Manson, "You seem to be getting far afield." He told Manson to stick to the issue raised in the trial.]

The issues? ... Mr. Bugliosi is a hard-driving prosecutor, polished education, a master of words, semantics. He is a genius. He has got everything that every lawyer would want to have except one thing: a case. He doesn't have a case. Were I allowed to defend myself, I could have proven this to you... The evidence in this case is a gun. There was a gun that laid around the ranch. It belonged to everybody. Anybody could have picked that gun up and done anything they wanted to do with it. I don't deny having that gun. That gun has been in my possession many times. Like the rope was there because you need rope on a ranch.... It is really convenient that Mr. Baggot found those clothes. I imagine he got a little taste of money for that....They put the hideous bodies on [photographic] display and they imply: If he gets out, see what will happen to you....[Helter Skelter] means confusion, literally. It doesn't mean any war with anyone. It doesn't mean that some people are going to kill other people... Helter Skelter is confusion. Confusion is coming down around you fast. If you can't see the confusion coming down around you fast, you can call it what you wish. . Is it a conspiracy that the music is telling the youth to rise up against the establishment because the establishment is rapidly destroying things? Is that a conspiracy? The music speaks to you every day, but you are too deaf, dumb, and blind to even listen to the music... It is not my conspiracy. It is not my music. I hear what it relates. It says "Rise," it says "Kill." Why blame it on me? I didn't write the music....

Danny DeCarlo... said that I hate black men, and he said that we thought alike... But actually all I ever did with Danny DeCarlo or any other human being was reflect him back at himself. If he said he did not like the black man, I would say "O.K." So consequently he would drink another beer and walk off and say 'Charlie thinks like I do.' But actually he does not know how Charlie thinks because Charlie has never projected himself. I don't think like you people. You people put importance on your lives. Well, my life has never been important to anyone....

[Linda Kasabian] gets on the stand and she says when she looked in that man's eyes that was dying, she knew that it was my fault. She knew it was my fault because she couldn't face death. And if she can't face death, that is not my fault. I can face death. I have all the time. In the penitentiary you live with it, with constant fear of death, because it is a violent world in there, and you have to be on your toes constantly....

[I taught the Family] not to be weak and not to lean on me....I told [Paul Watkins],"To be a man, boy, you have to stand up and be your own father." So he goes off to the desert and finds a father image in Paul Crockett....

I do feel some responsibility. I feel a responsibility for the pollution. I feel a responsibility for the whole thing....To be honest with you, I don't recall ever saying "Get a knife and a change of clothes and go do what Tex says." Or I don't recall saying "Get a knife and go kill the sheriff." In fact, it makes me mad when someone kills snakes or dogs or cats or horses. I don't even like to eat meat-that is how much I am against killing....

I haven't got any guilt about anything because I have never been able to see any wrong... I have always said: Do what your love tells you, and I do what my love tells me ... Is it my fault that your children do what you do? What about your children? You say there are just a few? There are many, many more, coming in the same direction. They are running in the streets-and they are coming right at you!

Cross-Examination by Vincent Bugliosi:

Q: You say you are already dead, is that right, Charlie?

A: Dead in your mind or dead in my mind?

Q: Define it any way you want to.

A: As any child will tell you, dead is when you are no more. It is just when you are not there. If you weren't there, you would be dead.

Q: How long have you been dead? . . To be precise about it, you think you have been dead for close to 2,000 years, don't you?

A: Mr. Bugliosi, 2,000 years is relative to the second we live in.

Q: Suffice it to say, Department 104 is a long way from Calvary, isn't that true?...

Q: The jury in this case never heard a single, solitary word you said... Mr. Manson, are you willing to testify in front of the jury and tell them the same things that you have testified to here in open court today?

[Kanarek objected and Judge Older sustained the objection. Older asked Manson if he now wished to testify before the jury. He replied, "I have already relieved all the pressure I had." Manson left the stand. As he walked by the counsel table, he told his three co-defendants, "You don't have to testify now."]

Source: http://law2.umkc.edu/faculty/projects/ftrials/manson/mansontestimony-m.html

See Articles: Insanity Defense; Los Angeles, California; Manson, Charles; Parker, William; Religion and Crime, Sociology of; Serial and Mass Killers; Terrorism.

1974 PRIMARY DOCUMENT

Presidential Pardon Given to Richard M. Nixon

Despite the involvement of President Richard Nixon and his administration in a number of illegal activities, including bugging opponents' offices, using federal agencies to harass political groups, and breaking into Democratic headquarters in the Watergate hotel, Nixon was never charged with a crime. He claimed neither prior knowledge of nor involvement with lawbreaking. He resigned, rather than face impeachment, and his successor's pardon was preemptive to avoid a trial. In doing so, Ford strained other connections—including that of his press secretary and longtime friend, Jerald terHorst, who resigned moments before the pardon, calling it "a blunder."

GRANTING PARDON TO
RICHARD NIXON

BY THE PRESIDENT OF THE
UNITED STATES OF AMERICA

A PROCLAMATION

Richard Nixon became the thirty-seventh President of the United States on January 10, 1972 for a second term by the electors of forty-nine of the fifty states. His term in office continued until his resignation on August 9, 1974.

Pursuant to resolutions of the House of Representatives, its Committee on the Judiciary conducted as inquiry and investigation on the impeachment of the President extending over more than eight months. The hearings of the Committee and its deliberations, which received wide national publicity over television, radio, and in printed media, resulted in votes adverse to Richard Nixon on recommended Articles of Impeachment.

As a result of certain acts or omissions occurring before his resignation from the

Office of President, Richard Nixon has become liable to possible indictment and trial for offenses against the United States. Whether or not he shall be so prosecuted depends on findings of the appropriate grand jury and at the discretion of the authorized prosecutor. Should an indictment ensue, the accused shall then be entitled to a fair trial by an impartial jury, as guaranteed to every individual by the Constitution.

It is believed that a trial of Richard Nixon, if it become necessary, could not fairly begin until a year or more has elapsed. In the meantime, the tranquility to which this session has been restored by the events of recent weeks could be irreparably lost by the prospects of bringing to trial a former President of the United States. The prospects of each trial will cause prolonged and divisive debate over the propriety of exposing to further punishment and degradation a man who had already paid the unprecedented penalty of relinquishing the highest elective offices of the United States.

NOW, THEREFORE, I, Gerald R. Ford, President of the United States, pursuant to the pardon power conferred upon me by Article II, Section 2, of the Constitution, have granted and by those presents do grant a full, free, and absolute pardon unto Richard Nixon for all offenses against the United States which he, Richard Nixon, has committed or may have committed or taken part in during the period from January 10, 1969 through August 9, 1974.

IN WITNESS THEREOF, I have hereonto set my hand this eighth day of September, in the year of our Lord nineteen hundred and seventy-four, and of the Independence of the United States of America the one hundred and ninety-ninth.

Source: General Records of the United States Government Archival Research Catalog (ARC) ID: 299996

See Articles: Ford, Gerald (Administration of); Nixon, Richard (Administration of); Political Crimes, Contemporary; Presidential Proclamations; *United States v. Nixon*; Watergate.

1975 PRIMARY DOCUMENT

FBI Memorandum on Worldwide Church of God Allegations

The Worldwide Church of God (there are many unrelated groups also called "Church of God") was founded in 1934 by Herbert Armstrong as a radio ministry. In addition to these recorded allegations, the group has been beset by financial and sex scandals, infighting, Armstrong's ousting of his own son, a failed attempt to sue the makers of Raiders of the Lost Ark *for plagiarism, and the embarrassment of Armstrong's predictions about the end of the world proving false in 1972.*

Herbert W. Armstrong;
Garner Ted Armstrong;
Worldwide Church of God
Eric Ralph Williams—Victim
Kidnapping Matter_____

Date of Transcription: April 23, 1975
Mr. RALPH (EVELYN) WILLIAMS furnished the following information to a representative of the Federal Bureau of Investigation.

Mrs. EVELYN WILLIAMS, 1312 East University Avenue, Oxford, Mississippi, telephonically furnished the following additional information:

WILLIAMS stated that she desired to furnish the name of BARRY CHASE, 2419 Monticello Drive, Mesquite, Texas, telephone number 214-285-6567, as an individual who was a defecting minister from the Worldwide Church of God who knows the inner workings of this "cult." WILLIAMS stated that CHASE would be able to furnish valuable information on this group.

WILLIAMS also stated that in the pamphlets published by this Worldwide Church of God the Legal Department furnishes instructions to older members on how to leave their money and property to the Worldwide Church of God without any legal fees.

WILLIAMS also stated that ANDERSON has the hierarchy at Pasadena, California, set up like a corporation and that the hierarchy live like kings, stating that both ARMSTRONGs have three houses each and at least one of them reportedly has $70,000 in paintings displayed in one of these homes.

Date of Transcription: 4/17/1975
Mrs. RALPH (EVELYN) WILLIAMS, Highway Six West, Oxford, Mississippi, contacted at her place of business, Williams Antiques, 1312 University Avenue, Oxford, Mississippi, furnished the following information:

WILLIAMS stated that after she and her husband, RALPH WILLIAMS, had a child, which later developed leukemia and going through this tragic situation, she began to listen to the World Tomorrow radio program and HERBERT W. ARMSTRONG. She estimated that she first began listening to these radio programs during 1960. She added that HERBERT W. ARMSTRONG's son, TED ARMSTRONG, later took over this program.

WILLIAMS stated that she did write to the World Tomorrow Radio Program and in turn was contacted by a KELLY BARFIELD, who was the field representative of this organization.

WILLIAMS added that this World Tomorrow Radio Program is now known as World-Wide Church of God and has its headquarters at Ambassador College in Pasadena, California.

WILLIAMS stated that after being initially contacted by KELLY BARFIELD, they were next contacted by a CARL MC NAIR and CURTIS COWAN.

COWAN was formerly a tire buffer at the Firestone Tire Company in Memphis, Tennessee.

WILLIAMS stated that her son, ERIC RALPH WILLIAMS, who was born on September 28, 1943, at Greenwood, Mississippi, was in his last year at Memphis State University, Memphis, Tennessee.

WILLIAMS stated that CARL MC NAIR contacted her son, ERIC, and she later learned that her son was becoming a convert to the World-Wide Church of God. WILLIAMS added that MC NAIR talked her son into leaving Memphis State University before he graduated and with less than one semester left to obtain his degree and that their son, ERIC, went to Pasadena, California, to attend Ambassador College.

WILLIAMS stated that the Ambassador College is nothing more than a front for the World–Wide Church of God.

WILLIAMS stated that she has learned that one of the first things that this World-Wide Church of God does is to wipe out the past of any converts. She also stated that 20 percent is taken from the head of the household income as a tithe and that every third year the members are assessed another ten percent of the head of the household's income.

WILLIAMS also stated that this cult does not want its members to vote in any election in the United States and did not want its members to serve the country in any fashion.

WILLIAMS also stated that this cult teaches that there is nothing wrong with drinking wine and that wine and alcoholic beverages are consumed even by the children of the members of this cult.

WILLIAMS also stated that the publication of this cult "The Plain Truth" teaches that if anyone disagrees with them they are disagreeing with God.

WILLIAMS stated that her son, ERIC, is still with this cult stating that he originally taught in their school system and then ran a camp that this cult had in Orr, Minnesota. WILLIAMS stated that this camp and land were apparently obtained from a wealthy family by the name of ERICSON (Phonetic) after the son of one of the many wealthy ERICSON individuals got "hooked" by this same cult.

WILLIAMS advised that her son is currently located at Big Sandy, Texas, where this cult has opened another school which is known as Ambassador College. WILLIAMS explained that this cult owns the land, buildings, and the houses of the faculty members stating that many of these houses are $75,000 to $100,000 homes.

WILLIAMS stated that her son is going to be "elevated" and is to become the head basketball coach of Ambassador College at Big Sandy, Texas.

WILLIAMS advised that her son is married to the former BILLIE JEAN SHIELDS, who was originally from Dallas, Texas, and they currently have two children.

WILLIAMS explained that the hierarchy of this "cult" decided that her son, ERIC, and BILLIE JEAN SHIELDS were to be married and according to her daughter-in-law this marriage was announced at an assembly without their knowledge. WILLIAMS explained that the hierarchy of this cult decides who will get married and who the marriage partners will be. WILLIAMS also stated that as a result of this marriage, her son and daughter-in-law were given $500 from this organization.

WILLIAMS also explained that this cult does not allow its members to receive any medical care and that there have been several instances where children have died or have been brutally mistreated.

WILLIAMS stated that members of the "cult" claim conscientious objector status while attending these Ambassador Colleges while their magazines tell their members to watch for the building of the temple which was to be followed by a war, the coming of Christ to Earth, to set up a kingdom and that their cult would force all nations to obey them even if it meant that millions of people would have to be killed.

WILLIAMS stated that her son, when he joined this "cult," was a gullible individual and has now been completely brainwashed.

WILLIAMS also stated that she and her husband were never really considered members of this "cult" as they are extremely suspicious of any individuals with any type of education, stating that they prey on the illiterate and poorly educated people. WILLIAMS stated that she is now in the process of trying to contact and contacting former members of this organization to expose the organization for what it really is. In this regard, WILLIAMS stated that in 1970, an attorney, STANLEY RADER, associated with this cult, although he is not a member and RADER is now the attorney and chief legal counsel to HERBERT W. ARMSTRONG. As such, he flies all over the world with ARMSTRONG in one of their large private jets and brings gifts to the various heads of state in an effort to meet them and carry on unknown transactions.

WILLIAMS stated that this organization pays no taxes and relies on "religious freedom" as a defense to any allegations brought against them.

WILLIAMS stated that she, in October, 1971, in Squaw Valley, heard HERBERT W. ARMSTRONG state that he had taken in eighty million dollars and after expenses had sixty million left. WILLIAMS recalled that they were advised not to write these figures down as this information could be used by their "enemies."

WILLIAMS stated that she has learned that this "cult" now has associated with them a Dr. JOHN HUBBARD OVERTON, to offset the claim that they deny medical treatment to their members and children, that he reportedly is from the State of Louisiana and in checking with the authorities in Louisiana, she found out that he is not licensed to practice medicine. She also stated that a Dr. ROBERT KUHN, who reportedly is a brain surgeon from the eastern part of the country is also associated with this organization in some manner.

WILLIAMS furnished the name of DON E. KIRSOPP, 475 Wylie Drive, Baton Rouge, Louisiana, as a former member, stating that KIRSOPP's wife, while a member, was denied medical treatment and surgery and almost died before he realized what was happening.

WILLIAMS also stated that GEORGE SCHWARTZ, 6730 Royal Palm Avenue, Perrine, Florida, spent approximately $19,000 in legal fees to regain custody of his child after this "cult," in his absence, persuaded his wife to divorce him and took his child in this process.

WILLIAMS identified PAUL HAECKER, 419 Pecan Drive, South Houston, Texas, as an individual who has a copy of the directory furnished by this "cult" on how to avoid prosecution by law enforcement officials in the event that a child dies.

WILLIAMS also stated that this "cult" is now attempting to get their Ambassador

Colleges accredited and to obtain foreign students solely for the purpose of getting the funds that these students will have. She stated that she is attempting to show the appropriate authorities that these schools do not have the proper faculty and that the Ambassador Colleges are nothing but fronts to obtain money for HERBERT W. ARMSTRONG and his organization.

WILLIAMS identified MILO WILCOX of Windsor, Colorado, as an individual who was connected with this "cult" for thirteen years.

WILLIAMS stated that WILCOX has now left this organization and he reportedly has nine hours of tapes with the confrontation between TED ARMSTRONG, son of HERBERT W. ARMSTRONG, and the approximately thirty-five ministers of this "cult" which broke away from the organization. WILLIAMS also stated that Dr. JOSEPH HOPKINS is another individual who has studied the ARMSTRONG organization and that HOPKINS is on the faculty at West Minister College, New Wilmington, Pennsylvania.

WILLIAMS also identified Mrs. JEAN BURCHAM from West Memphis, Arkansas, as another individual, who as a result of membership in the "cult" was separated from her husband and lost three of her children, the children being taken by her husband to Tucson, Arizona, and subsequently to Eugene, Oregon, where they reportedly are presently located.

WILLIAMS also stated that cards are kept on all of the members of this organization and that members who leave are denounced as "demon possessed apostates" and are labeled as enemies.

WILLIAMS also stated that although this organization does not want its members to vote or in any way serve this country in Big Sandy, Texas, this organization ran a man as Mayor of this community and then turned out en masse and voted him in. WILLIAMS stated that this was formerly a dry area but within several weeks, at least eight whiskey stores opened in this community.

WILLIAMS concluded by stating that Mrs. HENRY W. PETERSON, 6410 North East, 181st Street, Seattle, Washington, the mother of CONRAD COMMEAU, who was a pilot on one of HERBERT W. ARMSTRONG's jets and who formerly worked herself in this "cult" had much more information concerning the operation and tactics of this organization.

On April 15, 1975, Mrs. RALPH (EVELYN) WILLIAMS telephonically contacted the Oxford, Mississippi, Resident Agency and advised that she and her husband have tried and begged their son, ERIC RALPH WILLIAMS to return to Oxford and the WILLIAMS family.

WILLIAMS advised that their son, ERIC, has told them, Mr. and Mrs. RALPH WILLIAMS to stay out of his life, stating that his, ERIC's, purpose in life was to protect H. W. ARMSTRONG.

United States Department of Justice
Federal Bureau of Investigation
Jackson, Mississippi 39205
April 28, 1975

Source: NARA II, RG 65, Class 7 Kidnapping, Box 352, F: 7-HQ 16112

See Articles: Corruption, Contemporary; Corruption, History of; Corruption, Sociology of; Kidnapping; Religion and Crime, Contemporary; Religion and Crime, History of; Religion and Crime, Sociology of.

1977
PRIMARY DOCUMENT

FBI Internal Communications on Fugitive Ted Bundy

Charismatic serial killer Ted Bundy was first arrested in 1975 after failing to pull over for a routine traffic stop; a subsequent investigation led to his conviction on kidnapping charges. Investigations continued while he was in prison, and he was charged with homicide for the first time. In

1977, he twice escaped during courtroom appearances. More homicide charges were filed, and while on death row, Bundy confessed numerous murders before his 1989 execution.

Subject: Ted Bundy (Part 1 of 2)

Fm Salt Lake City (88-6895) (P)
To Denver   Routine
Seattle   Routine

Theodore Robert Bundy, Aka Ted Bundy—Fugitive. Upac—Escape.
00: Salt Lake City.

On June 9, 1977, Salt Lake County attorney's office issued escape warrant for subject, requested unlawful flight warrant be issued. same date Ausa James W. Mc Conkle II, Salt Lake City, authorized filing of complaint charging subject with violation title 18, U. S. Code, Section 1073. Complaint filed before U. S. Magistrate Daniel A. Alsup by SA ——— warrant is issued. Bond recommended $100,000 cash.

Subject described as: WMA, DOB November 24, 1946 at Burlington, Vermont, 6' 175 lbs., blue eyes, brown hair, SSAN 533-44-4655.

SU—88-6895 PAGE TWO
Denver at Aspen, Colorado. Conduct appropriate investigation to locate subject.
   Seattle ———
   Salt Lake City at Salt Lake City, Utah. Obtain address for ——— and set out leads to ——— also maintain contact with Salt Lake County so for additional background and set out additional leads.
   "In view of type of crime subject has been convicted of he should be considered armed and dangerous—escape risk."

   BT

   Source: http://vault.fbi.gov/Ted%20Bundy%20/Ted%20Bundy%20Part%201%20of%202/view

See Articles: Bundy, Ted; Murder, Contemporary; Murder, History of; Murder, Sociology of; Serial and Mass Killers.

1978 PRIMARY DOCUMENT

White House Memorandum on the 1868 Conviction of Dr. Samuel Mudd

Mudd was one of eight people charged with and convicted of conspiracy to murder President Lincoln. He had treated Booth for an injury sustained while fleeing and waited more than a full day before notifying authorities, drawing suspicion. He was spared the death penalty and imprisoned at Fort Jefferson, Florida, where he took over the position of prison doctor during a yellow fever outbreak, leading to his pardon in 1869. Repeated attempts to clear Mudd's name failed.

The White House
Washington
May 24, 1978

Memorandum for: Bob Lipshutz
From: Patrick Apodaca
Subject: Conviction of Dr. Samuel Mudd

We have discussed whether a legal theory might be developed to challenge Dr. Mudd's conviction of conspiracy in the Lincoln assassination and thereby justify some form of action by the President in this case.

Three lines of argument could serve this purpose. By relying on the Supreme Court's decision in Ex Parte Milligan, 4 U.S.2 (1865), a case involving analogous facts, it can be argued that Dr. Mudd's conviction by a Military Commission was illegal because (1) he was deprived of his constitutional right to trial by jury in a civil court and indictment by a grand jury, and (2) President Andrew Johnson was without authority to appoint a military commission to try him. Thirdly, an argument can be made that the trial was procedurally defective to the extent of depriving Dr. Mudd of due process of law.

(1) Denial of Constitutional Guarantees Under Article 3. Section 2, Clause 3 of the Constitution, and the Fifth and Sixth Amendments.

Article 3, Section 2, Clause 3 of the Constitution provides that "the trial of all crimes, except in cases of impeachment, shall be by jury..." The Sixth Amendment guarantees that "in all criminal prosecutions, the accused shall enjoy the right to a ....trial by an impartial jury..."

The Fifth Amendment provides that "no person shall be held to answer for a capital, or otherwise infamous crime, unless on a presentment or indictment of a grand jury, except in cases arising in the land or naval forces, or in the militia, when in actual service in time of war or public danger..."

The question is whether Dr. Mudd's case is within the scope of these provisions or whether it falls within an exception to their application.

Arguably, since Dr. Mudd was charged with an offense against the Commander-in-Chief of the Army, his prosecution was expressly excepted from the protection of the Fifth Amendment (and by implication the Sixth) as a case "arising in the land or naval forces." However, this language has been interpreted to extend court martial jurisdiction for service related crimes only to members of the armed forces. O'Callahan v. Parker, 395 U.S. 258(1968). Attempts by the government to bring nonmembers within the exception have failed. See e.g., Toth v. Quarles, 350 U.S.11(1955) (discharged soldier): Kinsella v. Singleton, 361 U.S. 234(1958) (civilian dependents accompanying military personnel overseas). The case law would seem to foreclosure any significant argument that Dr. Mudd, a civilian, was excluded from the prosecution of a jury trial because of this exception.

Section 2 of Article 3 is generally understood to preserve the right to trial by jury only in those cases in which it had been recognized at common law at the time of its adoption. District of Columbia v. Colts, 282 U.S. 63(1930).[1] Therefore, a second exception having possible application in the Mudd is the common law exception for trials of enemy belligerents for offenses against the law and usages of war. Cf. Ex parte Quirim, supra 45. It has been asserted that under this exception, military jurisdiction over Dr. Mudd was properly established because he was charged as an enemy of the Union for offenses against the law of war. See 11 Op. A.G. 297, 316(1965). But such were not the formal charges against his and, had they been, it is doubtful that a clear case could have been made for invoking jurisdiction on this basis.

The Supreme Court has applied this exception narrowly in the case of United States citizens. I have found only one Supreme Court case, Ex parte Quirin, supra, upholding a military trial within the United States of a U.S. citizen charged with belligerent acts against the government. That case is distinguishable since it involved a U.S. citizen who during World War II established a substantial presence in Germany—a foreign country against which the United States had declared war—and who subsequently surreptitiously reentered the United States under orders of the German high command for the purpose of sabotaging strategic defense plants. By contrast, the instant case involved a civil insurrection, rather than an international conflict or a foreign enemy against which war had been declared. In addition there was no evidence that during the Civil War Dr. Mudd established a presence in any Confederate state or entered into any relationship with Confederate officers that could bind him to act on their orders. To the extent that any substance can be attached to the charges against Dr. Mudd, his acts should have been characterized as political rather than as acts of war which would provide a basis for military jurisdiction. CP Ex parte Milligan, supra.

While it is doubtful that Dr. Mudd's case could be construed to fall within either of the above exceptions, there remains the further question of whether the constitutional safeguards under discussion could be abrogated by the government under the circumstances of civil insurrection then prevailing.

In a landmark case involving similar facts, the Supreme Court held that the government cannot in pursuance of its powers to conduct war [2] establish martial law jurisdiction to try citizens in states which, during the Civil War, upheld the authority of the government and where courts were open and their process unobstructed. Ex parte Milligan, supra.

Milligan represents an historic expostulation of the supremacy of a citizen's right to trial by jury over any express or implied powers granted to the government by the Constitution. The majority opinion[3] makes clear that the suspension of the right could occur only in the event of practical unavailability of a trial in the civil courts because they had been obstructed in a manner impairing their effective operation. The court distinguished this and other guarantees in the Constitution "which time had proved were essential to its preservation" from the writ of habeas corpus, the only safeguard that the government in its discretion can suspend when the safety of the country so requires. Id. at 127. The court summarized its view that actual unavailability of a trial in a civil court is a condition to the lawfulness of a substitute military trial of a civilian as follows:

"(T)here are occasions when martial rule can be properly applied. If, in foreign invasion or civil war, the courts are actually (emphasis added) closed, and it is impossible to administer criminal justice according to law, then on the theatre of active military operations, where war really prevails, there is a necessity to furnish a substitute for the civil authority, thus overthrown , to preserve the safety of the army and society; and as no power is left but the military, it is allowed to govern by martial rule until the laws can have their free course. As necessity creates the rule, so it limits its duration; for, if this government is continued after the courts are reinstated, it is a gross usurpation of power. Martial rule can never exist where the courts are open, and in the proper and unobstructed exercise of their jurisdiction. It is also confined to the locality of actual war." Id. at 127.

In denying Dr. Mudd's petition on a writ of habeas corpus in 1868, The District Court of Florida held the Milligan case inapposite,[4] On careful consideration of the Supreme Court's decision, however, the factual distinctions which the court made are unpersuasive.

In addition, the District Court chose to ignore crucial similiarities between the two cases.

Apparently attempting to characterize Dr. Mudd's offense as against the military, the District Court pointed out that Dr. Mudd was convicted of conspiracy to assassinate the Commander-in-Chief of the Army. But this was no greater a "military" offense than the acts for which Lambdin Milligan was convicted including holding communication with the enemy, conspiracy to seize munitions of war stored in arsenals, and liberating prisoners of war. Id. at 6-7. The District Court also noted that the charged crime was committed in a fortified city (Washington, D.C.) which had been invaded during the war and it gave importance to the fact that military orders were transmitted therein. The Court failed to note, however, that though not actually invaded, the jurisdiction involved in Milligan (Indiana) was within the military lines of the Army of the United States, and the theatre of military operations and had been constantly threatened to be invaded by the enemy. Id. Finally, and more importantly, the District Court failed to discuss the crux of the Milligan decision, i.e., whether the civil courts in Washington were operational at the time of Dr. Mudd's trial in June of 1865. I have found no evidence that they were not available and ready to try the Lincoln conspirators and, presumably, the District Court opinion would have pointed this fact out to buttress its conclusion had such been the case. Moreover, Dr. Mudd's trial was held after the end of the Civil War,[5] a time which, under the Milligan doctrine, should have demarcated the secular boundary of any possible military jurisdiction over civilians within Union territory.

(2) The President's Appointment of a Military Commission to Try Persons Charged With the Assassination of President Lincoln Was Unauthorized and Therefore Unlawful. By Executive Order and on the basis of an opinion of the Attorney General (II Op. A.G. 297(1865) President Andrew Johnson appointed a Military Commission to try the alleged conspirators in the Lincoln assassination. The Milligan case also represents

authority for the proposition that the President was without power to do so.

A point of difference between the majority and minority opinions in the case was whether the Congress had the power to authorize the Military Commission held in that case. As already noted, the majority concluded that the government was without power to apply military law to citizens of states that upheld its authority and in which the administration of the laws in the Federal courts remained unimpaired. While agreeing that the Military Commission in Milligan was illegal, the minority believed that the government possessed such power, but it had not been properly exercised in this instance.

With the exception of certain emergency situations in which the President may act pursuant to his powers as Commander-in-Chief,[6] the minority in Milligan viewed the power of extending martial law jurisdiction over civilians to rest within Congress.

By the Habeas Corpus Act of 1863, Congress authorized the President to suspend the writ of habeas corpus, with certain exceptions, and pursuant to this authority, on September 15, 1863, the President did in fact suspend the privilege. The Act authorized the President to arrest suspected persons, without giving cause for their detention on return to a writ of habeas corpus, but it neither expressly or impliedly authorized the President to establish procedures to try suspects by military jurisdiction or other authority. No other statute in force during this period would appear to have done so.

It cannot be argued that in June of 1865, after the cessation of hostilities and the surrender of the Confederate flag, that such an emergency existed as to empower the President to establish martial law in the District of Columbia without Congressional approval. Absent a clear expression of authority from Congress, therefore, the President was without authority to appoint the Military Commission in question.

(3) Denial of Due Process of Law Under the Fifth Amendment. The Justice Department's opinion on the Mudd case states "that there is little doubt that (Dr. Mudd's trial was not a fair trial by today's standards of due process. It probably was less fair a trial than Dr. Mudd would have received in a civil court in 1865."

The trial of the Lincoln conspirators was flawed by many serious procedural irregularities. Representative of these were the refusal to allow the accused to testify on their own behalf, the introduction of irrelevant testimony, the intimidation of witnesses, and the deliberate suppression of exonerative evidence in the possession of the government. e.g., Booth's diary, which might have overthrown the theory of a general plot to assassinate. See The Assassination of Abraham Lincoln, 1909, by David Miller Dewitt.

In addition, the sufficiency of the evidence against Dr. Mudd was questionable. The Military Commission convicted Dr. Mudd of participating in the assassination plot against Lincoln and of knowingly aiding and abetting the escape of Booth and Merold. On the basis of their review of evidence, the Justice Department concludes that the testimony on the behalf of Dr. Mudd was far stronger than that of the prosecution and that the Military Commission "seemed clearly determined to find guilt." The declarations in the Warrant of Pardon granted by President Andrew Johnson are further authority that the case against Dr. Mudd was highly questionable.

The procedure irregularities at trial and the insufficiency of evidence on which Dr. Mudd's conviction was based lent strong support to an argument that Dr. Mudd was denied due process of law under the Fifth Amendment.

The foregoing arguments would support the view that the Mudd case is deserving of favorable action by the President. But the extent and form of such action should be governed by other questions concerning the President's authority to act in this case, the precedent setting effect of any action and the separation of powers doctrine.

Generally, I see four options open to the President:

(1) A public proclamation declaring the conviction of Dr. Samuel Mudd null and void.
(2) A letter to Congress and the Mudd family expressing the President's personal

opinion that Dr. Mudd was innocent. The statement would not purport to set aside the conviction, but merely express the President's own evaluation of this case.
(3) A letter to Congress and the Mudd family noting the pardon granted by President Johnson and reaffirming the declarations contained therein regarding doubt as to Dr. Mudd's guilt.
(4) No action.

With reward to each of these, the following should be considered:

(1) Authority of the President to Act. There is a question of whether the President could act to set aside the instant conviction. Citing Executive Department opinions related to this question, the Justice Department memorandum states that the President is without such authority. There is no case law in point and, in the absence of such, it is arguable that the Presisdent, as Commander-in-Chief, can set aside a conviction handed down by a military tribunal established by his predecessor. There would seem to be no reason to question his authority to take a position on Dr. Mudd's innocence under options (2) or (3).
(2) Precedent Setting Effects of the President's Action. It is fairly important to determine the precedent which options (1) and (2) will set. Should the President decide to act favorable, it will also be important to set forth, for the record, the uniqueness of the Mudd case to avoid an onslaught of similar requests in the future.
(3) Separation of Powers. If the Mudd case involved adjudications and determinations made purely by the Executive Branch of government, I would see no problem regarding the separation of powers doctrine. The fact that the district court (an Article III court) decided to deny Dr. Mudd's petition for habeas corpus raises questions. Avoiding a problem may require that the President act in a manner that does not affect or modify issues adjucated by the district court. This might involve overturning the conviction only on the basis of reconsideration of the evidence and a conclusion that it was insufficient for a finding of guilty. There could be a problem if the President's Action purported to modify the district court's determination that the trial by a Military Commission was illegal.

I would strongly recommend asking OCL for an opinion on these points should we decide to recommend options (1) or (2) to the President.

Footnotes
1. The Fifth and Sixth Amendments, while guaranteeing the continuance of certain incidents of trial left unmentioned by Section 2, did not expand the right to jury trial as it had been established by that article. Ex parte Quirin, 317 U.S. 1(1942).
2. Art. 1, Sec. 8 of the Constitution empowers Congress to raise, support and govern armies; Art 2, Sec. 2 designates the President as Commander-in-Chief of the Army and Navy.
3. A concurring minority of four justices concluded that Congress, pursuan to its war powers, could constitutionally establish martial law jurisdiction but had not in fact done so. See discussion infra.
4. Ex parte Mudd. 17 F.R. 954 (1868)
5. General Lee surrendered his army to General Grant at Appomattox, Virginia on April 9, 1865. The last significant Confederate Army surrender occurred at Durham, North Carolina on April 26.
6. The President may act in situations "justifying or excusing peril...in times of insurrection or invasion, or of civil or foreign war, within districts or localities where ordinary law no longer adequately secures public safety or public rights," Ex parte Milligan, supra at 145.

Source: Memo, Subject: Conviction of Dr. Samuel Mudd 5/24/1978 Records of the White House Office of Counsel to the President Archival Research Catalog (ARC) ID: 139959

See Articles: Booth, John Wilkes; Federal Rules of Criminal Procedure; Lincoln, Abraham (Administration of).

1980 PRIMARY DOCUMENT

Memorandum to President Jimmy Carter Regarding Love Canal

The neighborhood of Love Canal in Niagara Falls, New York, became synonymous with the dangers of toxic waste after a state of emergency was declared in 1978. In the 1950s, schools had knowingly been built on the site of a toxic waste dump; two decades later, reports of birth defects, miscarriages, and leukemia were rampant. The government relocated more than 800 families, and Congress passed the Superfund Act, holding polluters accountable for their damage.

May 20, 1980

Memorandum for the President
From: Jack Watson
Subject: Love Canal

As I reported to you on Saturday, we are faced with a volatile situation in Niagara Falls, New York, as a result of the public disclosure of a chromosomal study conducted in the course of the federal against Hooker Chemical Company.

As a result of several meetings in the last three days with all the relevant federal agencies, I am now prepared to recommend to you that, if the Governor requests it, we declare Love Canal eligible for emergency assistance (under the authority of FEMA) to permit the temporary relocation of approximately 750 families in the immediate Love Canal area. The principal reasons for this recommendation, in which Justice EPA, HHS, FEMA, SBA, HUD, OMB, and DPS concur, are as follows:

The chromosomal study, whatever its ultimate significance is one in a long list of pilot studies that have been done on the health and environmental effects of the Love Canal waste site during the last two years. For example, New York State has preliminary studies substantiating adverse reproductive effects; one doctor's studies showing high incidence of miscarriage and birth defects; and another health professional's research indicating peripheral nerve damage. Although all of these studies require further empirical and scientific verification, the adverse psychological effects on the people who live around Love Canal of this endless barrage of "expert" speculations about how they have been, and are being, damaged, are hard to overstate.

In addition to the health studies, environmental studies conducted by EPA indicate that the quantity of hazard chemicals present at the site represents the largest volume of hazardous wastes to which any population is known to be exposed. In addition, the range of hazardous chemicals at Love Canal is the widest that has been encountered in any one site anywhere in the country.

The FEMA statute gives us the flexible authority we need to respond to the situation and makes New York state take the lead responsibility for the temporary relocation. The State will share the costs of the temporary relocation and will work closely with FEMA in actually relocating the families.

As you know, you declared Love Canal eligible for emergency assistance in 1978. As a result of that first declaration, 239 families were relocated; we are now recommending relocation of the additional 750 families who reside within a well defined area and who have been the subjects of the recent studies. Although the Governor may include in his request for emergency assistance a request for federal assistance in both the temporary and permanent relocation of the affected families, we have made absolutely clear to the Governor in telephone conversations this afternoon that the Federal government has no authority to buy the peoples' homes or otherwise permanently relocate them. We have told the Governor that if you were to approve any further federal emergency assistance, it would cover only temporary relocation along the lines outlined above.

The understandable concern and anxiety which have been precipitated by this most recent study require, in our judgment, an immediate response. If you approve this recommendation to give the families emergency relocation assistance, we will work with the State tonight to draft a request from the Governor to you. We would announce jointly with the State tomorrow that:

We are both amending our lawsuits against Hooker Chemical Company to add these additional costs of temporary relocation to the amounts already being claimed against Hooker in the pending litigation;

We are immediately undertaking further scientific studies to assess the nature and extent of the health damage and risks as precisely as possible; and,

In the meantime, we are responding prudently and immediately to the human need which is so evident at Love Canal.

Source: ARC Identifier 593309
Item from Collection JC-1056: Records of the Office of the Staff Secretary, 1976–1981

See Articles: Carter, Jimmy (Administration of); Environmental Crimes; New York.

1981 to 2000

INTRODUCTION

The 1980s and 1990s were a time of dramatic change in the American criminal justice system. Although victimization statistics reveal that violent crime rates remained essentially level in the 1980s, from the early 1990s they began a precipitous fall. Property crime rates also fell during this period. The reasons for this post-1994 decline are still debated by scholars. At the same time, however, incarceration rates sharply increased throughout the 1980s and 1990s, while racial disparities in incarceration rates persisted. A growing national focus on illegal drug use drove the adoption of important related legislation. This era also saw the emergence of correctional innovations, such as private prisons and military-style boot camps for civilian offenders. Hate crimes and domestic violence received greater attention during this period, while new technologies and approaches significantly impacted policing strategies. Although the 1980s were marked by a general decrease in enthusiasm for offender rehabilitation programs, by the late 1990s, many scholars and practitioners expressed renewed faith in various "evidence-based" prevention and rehabilitation initiatives.

The causes and consequences of many of the policy changes that took place during this period can only be fully understood by examining the social, political, and economic contexts in which they occurred. Trends as diverse as increased concern about illegal drug use and decreased availability of manufacturing jobs impacted crime and criminal justice policies in the 1980s and 1990s. Since the impacts of many of these policies continue to be felt today, it is essential to understand how and why these policy changes were made.

Crime in the 1980s and Early 1990s

Two sources offer comprehensive national data about crime trends during this period: the annual Uniform Crime Report (UCR) issued by the Federal Bureau of Investigation (FBI), and the National Crime Victimization Survey (NCVS) overseen by the U.S. Department of Justice's Bureau of Justice Statistics (BJS). The UCR, which was originally devised in 1929, is based upon local police reports and thus only captures crimes that are known to the police. UCR data are released each year in a report, *Crime in the United States*, which also includes data on law enforcement personnel, crimes cleared, and individuals arrested.

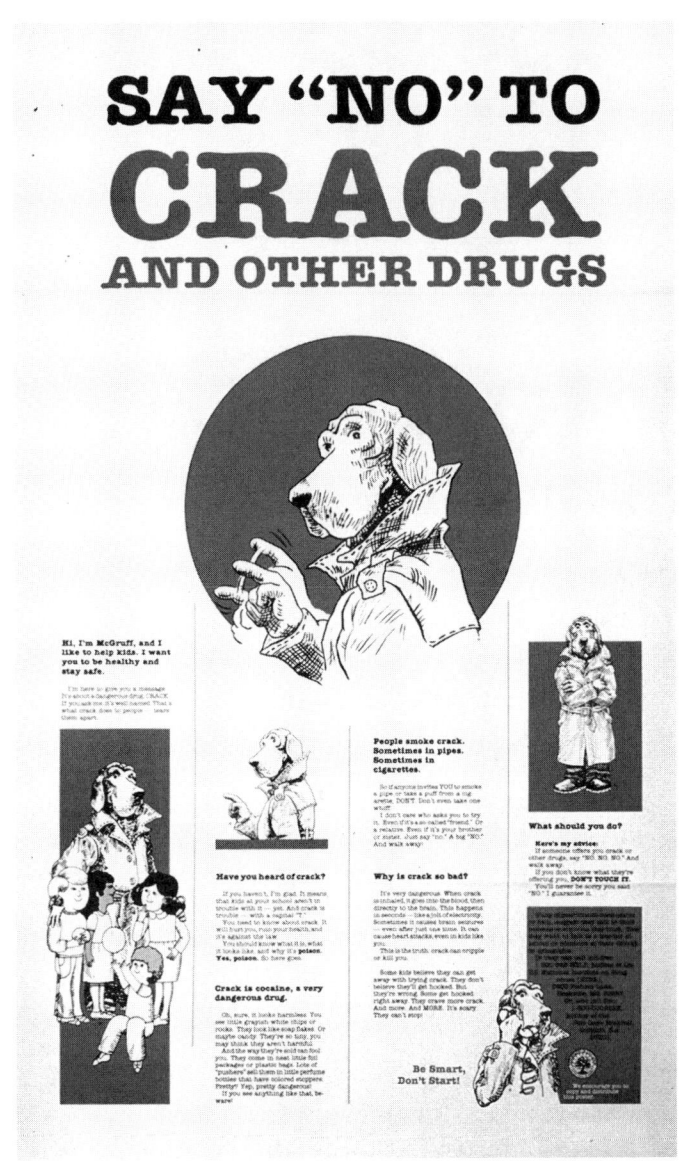

The epidemic of crack-cocaine use in the 1980s led federal agencies, including the Department of Education, to get involved in prevention. The epithet just say no, popularized by First Lady Nancy Reagan, is echoed in this 1980s poster featuring McGruff the Crime Dog.

In contrast, the NCVS is based on a survey of Americans age 12 and over from 40,000 households about their experiences of victimization. In addition to presenting data on the amount and types of victimizations experienced, the NCVS also records the characteristics of the crime (such as where and when it occurred) and, if known and applicable, of the offender (such as age and sex). Crucially, in contrast to the UCR, the NCVS does not only consider crimes reported to the police. This difference is important because many crimes go unrecorded; NCVS data suggest that during the 1980s and early 1990s, only about half of violent victimizations were reported to the police.

UCR data show that, with some fluctuations, both property and violent crime rates increased from the mid-1980s onward, reaching a peak during the early 1990s. In 1991, violent crime reached its highest rate since the UCR began more than 60 years earlier—more than 750 incidents per 100,000 people. Currently, violent crimes in the UCR include homicide, forcible rape of a female, robbery, and aggravated assault. The property crime rate similarly reached a local peak of 5,140 incidents per 100,000 people in 1991. Property crimes include burglary, larceny/theft, and motor vehicle theft.

Many observers, however, have questioned whether these increases in recorded crime reflect true increases in crime rates or merely improved detection of crimes. During the 1980s and early 1990s, police departments throughout the country adopted key reforms and innovations. These reforms may have improved crime detection, thereby increasing the number of crimes recorded by the police. This thesis is supported by NCVS data, which suggest that the violent victimization rate remained relatively consistent throughout the 1980s. According to the NCVS definition, violent victimizations include personal robbery, rape of a male or female, sexual assault, aggravated assault, and simple assault. This definition differs from that in the UCR, which includes homicide, but does not include rape of a male or simple assault. According to the NCVS—and in sharp contrast to the UCR data—the property victimization rate regularly declined throughout the 1980s and early 1990s. Property victimization includes theft and burglary only against households; unlike the UCR, businesses are not taken into account. NCVS data also reveal that both during this decade and the following decade, blacks and Hispanics were more likely to be victims of crimes than whites. The disparity was greater for violent crimes than property crimes. Discrepancies in states' reported crime rates can be detected in UCR data, although it is critical to acknowledge the limitations of such data and abide by the FBI's caution that the data should not be used to rank the effectiveness of law enforcement agencies. Keeping these limitations in mind, UCR data reveal, for example, that Texas had the highest state homicide rate in 1985—a rate 13 times higher than that of North Dakota, the state with the lowest 1985 homicide rate. This discrepancy reveals that within national crime statistics, significant state and local nuances existed.

It is important to contextualize 1980s crime data by referring to one of the most significant social developments of this era: the crack-cocaine epidemic. Crack cocaine is powder cocaine heated and combined with water and baking soda. Since crack cocaine is typically much cheaper than powder cocaine, can be smoked, is highly addictive, and enables a nearly instantaneous high, its use became increasingly popular in a number of U.S. cities—including Los Angeles, New York, Philadelphia, and New Orleans—in the mid- to late 1980s. According to figures released by the Substance Abuse and Mental Health Services Association, there were more than 28,000 cocaine-related emergency room visits in the United States in 1985. This figure rose to over 50,000 in 1986 and increased again to more than 90,000 in 1987, more than tripling during this two-year period. Some scholars, such as criminologist Alfred Blumstein, have linked some of the rising levels of reported crime seen in 1980s UCR data to the crack-cocaine epidemic. The epidemic particularly affected poorer urban communities and, according to these scholars, could also partly explain why the homicide rate among black males between the ages of 14 and 24 approximately doubled in the 10 years after 1984.

White-collar crimes (abuses of trust, but not physical threats or violence to achieve personal or professional goals) are not regular features of either the NCVS or UCR, making historical trends difficult to determine. However, the UCR includes data on arrests for three key white-collar offenses: fraud, forgery/counterfeiting, and embezzlement. Arrests for fraud and embezzlement increased substantially during the late 1980s and 1990s, even as arrests for other kinds of crimes—such as burglary and motor vehicle theft—fell. These increases in arrests may not necessarily indicate rising levels of these crimes. Instead, such increases could indicate increased detection and enforcement efforts.

Crime in the Mid- to Late 1990s

Although UCR and NCVS data offer divergent perspectives on the 1980s and early 1990s, both sources agree that in the mid- to late 1990s, both violent crime and property crime rates spectacularly decreased. Specifically, UCR data indicate that the violent crime rate fell by more than 30 percent between 1991 and 1999, while the homicide rate fell by more than 40 percent. The property crime rate also fell by more than a quarter during the same period. NCVS data mirror these findings; the violent victimization rate fell by about half between 1994 and 2000, while the property victimization rate fell by more than a third between 1991 and 2000. These statistics indicate that in addition to New York City's well-known sharp decline in crime rates during the late 1990s, less dramatic decreases in crime rates also occurred in many other areas of the country during this period.

Scholars have offered different explanations for these declines in crime. The first such explanation is economic. Between 1991 and 2001, the United States experienced a prolonged economic expansion, with unemployment falling by more than a third between 1992 and 1999. The greater availability of jobs may have reduced the incentive to commit crime.

The second explanation concerns incapacitation. Incarceration rates rose substantially in the 1980s and 1990s. Some experts have therefore argued that incapacitation was responsible for the 1990s crime rate declines; more potential offenders were incarcerated during this period and could not commit crimes.

A third explanation is the fading of the crack-cocaine epidemic that had devastated many poor urban areas during the 1980s and is linked by some scholars to higher reported crime rates during the 1980s. By the early 1990s, crack-cocaine use had begun to wane, perhaps in part because a new generation of young people had witnessed the devastation the drug had brought to their communities and therefore shunned its use.

A fourth explanation involves the legalization of abortion. Economist Steven Levitt has controversially argued that following the U.S. Supreme Court's 1973 decision in *Roe v. Wade*, which overturned state bans on abortion, the increased availability of abortion meant that many children who were at high risk of becoming offenders were never born and thus could not commit crimes as teenagers and young adults in the 1990s.

One final explanation centers on reduced lead exposure. Beginning in the 1970s, lead was increasingly removed from gasoline and banned from the paint used to decorate new homes. As a result, between 1975 and 1991, the average level of lead in Americans' blood has been calculated to have declined by 80 percent. Since exposure to lead in childhood can lead to reduced impulse control and increased aggression, both risk factors for later criminal activity. Economist Jessica Wolpaw Reyes has argued that reduced lead exposure may have contributed to the crime declines of the 1990s.

While this wide range of explanations is far from exhaustive, they illustrate that the debate still rages among scholars about which factor—or combination of factors—was most responsible for the 1990s decline in crime rates.

Concerns About Specific Types of Crimes

During the 1980s and 1990s, specific kinds of crimes received increased attention from lawmakers and increased exposure in the media. Hate crimes, which are crimes motivated by prejudice regarding a victim's race, gender, religion, disability, sexual orientation, or other characteristic, were one such category. Two brutal 1998 hate crimes received significant media attention: the murder of a black man named James Byrd in Jasper, Texas, and the murder of a gay man named Matthew Shepard in Laramie, Wyoming. In 1978, California was the first state to adopt a hate crime law, and during the 1980s and 1990s, numerous other states passed legislation specifically targeting various kinds of hate crimes. Congress requested that the FBI collect data on hate crimes in 1990, although state and local participation in the data collection effort was not mandatory.

School shootings also received significant national attention during the 1990s. Although overall rates of violent crime in schools generally declined during the decade, a spate of mass shootings caused significant public concern. In particular, the Columbine High School massacre in 1999—in which 12 students and one teacher were murdered by two fellow students in Colorado—prompted a frenzied national media debate about gun control and violence. Other shootings also took place in Olivehurst, California, in 1992; Moses Lake, Washington, in 1996; Pearl, Mississippi, in 1997; Jonesboro, Arkansas, in 1998; and other American communities.

However, while this specific form of violence perpetrated by juveniles remained at the forefront of national consciousness, and arrests of juveniles sharply increased in the early 1990s, statistics reveal that the overwhelming majority of juvenile arrests in that decade were not for serious violent crimes. For example, UCR figures for 1997 reveal that more than 80 percent of juvenile arrests were for the following crimes: larceny/theft, simple assault, drug offenses, and disorderly conduct. Only 6 percent of juvenile arrests in that year were for the serious violent crimes of murder, rape, robbery, and aggravated assault.

Political Contexts

The political environment of the country during the 1980s and 1990s is important in understanding the criminal justice policy changes enacted during this period. Several key political transformations occurred in these years, directly influencing criminal justice policies. After the stagflation and oil crises of the 1970s, Ronald Reagan won a landslide victory in the 1980 presidential election. During his campaign, he promised smaller government, lower taxes, and increased military strength. By the time Reagan was reelected in 1984, once again by a large margin, American society had moved in a more conservative direction. Reagan's vice president, George H. W. Bush, won the 1988 presidential election and was similarly committed to a conservative policy agenda.

During these years, many of the social welfare tenets of the Great Society initiated in the 1960s during Lyndon Johnson's presidential term were called into question. In

Drug arrests nearly doubled in the 1980s, and by the 1990s, there were approximately 1 million U.S. drug arrests annually. The provisions of the Anti-Drug Abuse Act of 1986 have been criticized for increased black incarceration rates because of the far stiffer penalties for possessing (cheaper) crack cocaine than powder cocaine. Between 1980 and 2003, drug arrests of black Americans in major cities increased three times faster than that of whites.

the 1970s, a scholarly team led by sociologist Robert Martinson undertook a review of numerous evaluations of correctional rehabilitation programs. The review questioned the effectiveness of many of these programs and reinforced the popular belief that "nothing worked" when it came to offender rehabilitation. Gradually, such approaches were deemphasized in favor of crime control and tough punishment.

One area that received significant attention from national politicians during the 1980s was illegal drug use. As early as 1971, President Richard Nixon had declared illegal drugs "public enemy number one." The growing crack-cocaine epidemic began to dominate newspaper headlines during the 1980s, and illegal drug use and the resulting War on Drugs rose to the forefront of the national agenda. In 1988, the Office of National Drug Control Policy (ONDCP) was established to reduce illegal drug use and its negative effects on society. Arrests for drug offenses rose dramatically during the decade and contributed to the increase in incarceration rates.

Another key development of the 1980s was increased political attention to the needs of crime victims. Several prominent advocacy groups, such as Mothers Against Drunk Driving (MADD), were founded in the early 1980s. In 1984, the Victims of Crime Act (VOCA) established a fund to compensate victims of crime, was passed by Congress. A 1988 amendment to VOCA established the Office of Victims of Crime within the U.S. Department of Justice. In 1982, California became the first state to pass a law allowing crime victims and their family members to deliver statements during sentencing and early-release court proceedings. A 1991 U.S. Supreme Court decision upheld the constitutionality of victim impact statements and, by 1997, 44 states authorized their use. Another important state-level development was the adoption of state constitutional amendments upholding certain rights for crime victims, such as the right to be present at relevant criminal justice proceedings and to receive restitution from the offender. The first such constitutional amendment was adopted by California in 1982, and by the end of the 1990s, more than 30 states had adopted similar amendments.

Bill Clinton, a Democrat, was elected president in 1992; he was subsequently reelected with a higher percentage of the popular vote in 1996. Clinton portrayed himself as a moderate Democrat, loyal to New Deal ideas, but "tough on crime." During his 1992 campaign, Clinton returned to his home state of Arkansas where he was governor to ensure that the execution of a double murderer would be carried out. At the time, many commentators argued that this gesture was meant to symbolize Clinton's support of capital punishment and his "tough-on-crime" attitude. In the 1994 elections, for the first time in 40 years, Republicans took control of the U.S. House of Representatives and retained this control throughout the rest of Clinton's term, once again ushering in an era of divided government.

The federal government's interest in crime and criminal justice matters expanded during Clinton's presidential term, and numerous important pieces of criminal justice legislation were adopted at the national level. Key examples include the Brady Handgun Violence Prevention Act of 1993, which mandated background checks for individuals wishing to purchases firearms; and the Violence Against Women Act (VAWA) of 1994, which provided more than $1.5 billion to improve the response to violent crimes against women and was part of the larger 1994 Violent Crime Control Act.

A series of brutal abductions, rapes, and murder of children aroused concern about sex offenders, particularly repeat offenders. States passed legislation mandating registration, restriction of residence, and virtually lifetime surveillance of convicted and released sex offenders. Although most sex offenses occurred within the family or among people who knew each other, a "moral panic" about predators led to federal legislation enacted in 1994 and again in 1996. Hate crime laws, violence against women laws, and sex offender laws represented heightened public awareness of crimes that previously had been either ignored or unpoliced.

Economic Contexts

Economic trends also affected crime rates and criminal justice policies during this period. One particularly influential trend was the decline in domestic production and manufacturing sectors and employment growth in the retail and service sectors. For example, in the 1980s, employment in the retail sector grew by more than a quarter, while employment in the manufacturing sector fell by 7 percent. Between 1980 and 2005, the nation lost more than 4 million manufacturing jobs, and although this decline slowed in the 1990s relative to the 1980s, it increased once more in the early years of the next century.

Economists have advanced a number of explanations for this transformation, including the application of technology and improved productivity in the manufacturing sector (which meant that fewer workers could produce the same number of goods), and increasing globalization. The period was marked by the removal of trade barriers. For example, on January 1, 1994, President Clinton signed into law the North American Free Trade Agreement (NAFTA), designed to eliminate trade and investment barriers among Canada, Mexico, and the United States. Regardless of causation, such dramatic economic change could have affected crime rates as well-paid, low-skilled manufacturing jobs in urban areas were lost and people became more likely to commit crime for economic survival.

In addition to change in economic sectors, it is also crucial to examine change in income inequality and the effects of economic growth overall. During the 1980s, the share of income received by the poorest quintile of families fell slightly, while that received by the wealthiest quintile rose; economists have suggested that the introduction of new technologies increased the wages of highly skilled workers, while the weakening of unions may have slowed down wage growth for blue-collar workers. In the late 1990s, however, an economic boom resulted in workers' wages rising faster than inflation, although wages of the wealthiest workers tended to rise the fastest. Understanding trends in income inequality is important because some research has shown a correlation between income inequality and crime rates, although it is not clear whether this correlation holds true under all conditions. After the 1982 recession, the economy grew during the remainder of the decade. Unemployment fell from a high of around 10 percent in 1982 to under 6 percent in 1989. A second period of dramatic growth occurred in the late 1990s, when enthusiasm for new Internet companies led to a dramatic stock market boom; the speculative "dot com" bubble began to burst in early 2000. Growth is another economic trend that can affect crime rates, and some scholars have argued that the late 1990s boom contributed to the declines in crime rates during this period.

Social Contexts

The 1980s and 1990s witnessed several important social changes. In particular, a growing focus on racial, gender, religious and other forms of equality was reflected in the diffusion of hate crime laws. At the same time, awareness of, and concern about, domestic crimes began to increase. Physical, sexual, and psychological child abuse received more attention during this period, as did the abusive neglect of children. The scope of both these problems was large. For example, according to the National Committee to Prevent Child Abuse in 1995, protection agencies nationwide received more than three million reports about children being abused, neglected, or otherwise harmed. One million reports were substantiated; therefore, there were 14 substantiated reports for every 1,000 Americans under the age of 19. In 1983, growing recognition of these problems spurred the designation of April as Child Abuse Prevention Month. In 1985, the first Child Advocacy Center was founded, designed to coordinate law enforcement, criminal justice, child protection, and other personnel in child abuse investigation cases. This model later spread to many states.

Similarly, beginning in the 1970s, the women's movement helped highlight the problem of domestic violence or spousal abuse. In 1981, Duluth, Minnesota, instituted a community-wide initiative to prevent domestic violence that subsequently influenced prevention policies elsewhere. At the national level, the 1984 Victims of Crime Act was amended in 1988 to encourage compensation for victims of domestic violence. In 1994, the Violence Against Women Act was adopted as part of the Violent Crime Control Act, funding rape and domestic violence victims' services and establishing the federal right of gender-based violence victims to sue their attackers. The 1990s also saw greater research into domestic violence, with scholars paying increased attention to its different causes and cultural contexts.

Increasing technological progress also influenced criminal justice policy. The increasing attainability of personal computers during the 1980s and the availability of the Internet and e-mail in the 1990s transformed the daily lives of many Americans. New technologies also improved crime detection and investigation capabilities. The diffusion of enhanced computing technologies in the 1990s enabled authorities to better analyze and act upon crime patterns. Perhaps the most well-known application of technology to criminal justice in this period was the use of deoxyribonucleic acid, or DNA, to aid crime investigations. Present in biological evidence, DNA can be linked to the profile of an offender via national, state, and local databases. These databases, initiated in the 1980s, were unified as the Combined DNA Index System (CODIS). During the 1980s and early 1990s, states increased the number of DNA profiles present in CODIS by adopting legislation requiring offenders convicted of certain crimes to offer DNA samples. By 2000, when the popular crime drama *CSI* premiered, enthusiasm for new crime-solving technologies was established in the public domain.

Awareness and concern about domestic violence increased at the end of the 20th century. Child abuse garnered more attention as well; in 1995, there were 14 substantiated reports for every 1,000 Americans under the age of 19.

Changes in Criminal Justice Policy

Due to the federalized governmental structure of the United States, important criminal justice policy decisions were taken at both national and state levels during the 1980s and 1990s. In this period, many of the most important changes in national criminal justice policy were contained in five key pieces of legislation: the Comprehensive Crime Control Act of 1984; the Anti-Drug Abuse Act of 1986; the Anti-Drug Abuse Act of 1988; the Crime Control Act of 1990; and the Violent Crime Control and Law Enforcement Act of 1994. Although these acts were adopted at the federal level, they frequently impacted state and local policies through grants and other means.

The Comprehensive Crime Control Act of 1984 led to the establishment of the Sentencing Commission to issue federal sentencing guidelines. These guidelines were intended to reduce disparities in federal sentences and establish a more determinate sentencing approach in the federal system. Determinate sentencing strategies minimize the discretionary power of judges and other officials in the criminal justice process to craft or alter sentences. The guidelines issued by the Sentencing Commission were subsequently adopted in 1987 and overhauled sentencing in the federal system. Other important contributions of the Comprehensive Crime Control Act of 1984 included the creation of the Office of Justice Programs within the Department of Justice to handle certain grant-making responsibilities, as well as a number of other key changes in the federal justice system, such as the elimination of federal parole.

The passage of the Anti-Drug Abuse Act of 1986 was prompted by the shocking death of leading college basketball player Len Bias from a cocaine overdose, an event that further drew media attention to the dangers of drug use. The act was passed at the peak point of the crack-cocaine epidemic in America's inner cities. The legislation allocated $97 million for prison construction, $200 million for antidrug education efforts, and $241 million for drug treatment programs. The act also imposed mandatory minimum sentences for drug-related offenses, such as a minimum federal prison term of five years for those convicted of distributing five grams of crack cocaine or 500 grams of powder cocaine. These provisions have been criticized by some commentators for contributing to increased incarceration rates of black Americans because the acts set far stiffer penalties for possessing crack cocaine than powder cocaine, even though crack cocaine is simply powder cocaine that has been heated and combined with water and baking soda. In the 1980s, the majority of powder cocaine users were white, while most crack-cocaine users were black. Before the 1986 act, however, black Americans on average received 11 percent longer federal drug sentences than whites; by the early 1990s, black Americans received on average nearly 50 percent longer federal drug sentences than whites.

Two years after this legislation was passed, the Anti-Drug Abuse Act of 1988 was adopted. This act created the Office of National Drug Control Policy, an organization tasked with coordinating national antidrug education efforts. The organization was overseen by the "drug czar," a member of the president's cabinet. The fact that the organization's leader was given cabinet-level status indicates the continued prominence of drug-control issues on the federal agenda.

The Crime Control Act of 1990 provided $900 million to states' criminal justice systems. The legislation also enshrined into federal law the Crime Victims' Bill of Rights. Finally, the Violent Crime Control and Law Enforcement Act of 1994 allocated more than $30 billion for various criminal justice and crime-related programs. Some $9 billion of this allocation was earmarked to fund the recruitment of more police officers, while the Violence Against Women Act, contained within the broader 1994 bill, was allocated $1.6 billion in funding. The act also initiated many important policy changes in criminal justice, such as allowing juveniles age 13 and over to be tried as adults for certain federal crimes involving violence or a firearm. For a decade after its enactment, the act also outlawed the manufacture of semi-automatic assault weapons for civilian use, a provision that expired in 2004. The range of federal crimes eligible for the death penalty was widened in the 1994 act, and a "three strikes" federal sentencing provision was introduced to prescribe a sentence of life imprisonment for violent offenders facing a third federal conviction.

Although white-collar crimes did not receive as much attention as violent or drug crimes during this period, a small number of significant pieces of legislation were also adopted in this area. Most significantly, in both 1984 and 1988, Congress passed new legislation targeting insider trading.

Many additional influential policy changes were also made at the state level during this period. Washington state adopted a three-strikes law in 1993, and California's 1994 adoption of a similar policy received significant national attention. These three strikes laws, local precursors to the federal policy, imposed mandatory minimum sentences of life imprisonment for felony offenders convicted of a third offense. Although the specifics of these laws differed by state, similar policies were adopted by many other states during the 1990s. This increasing enthusiasm for determinate sentences can also be seen in the decisions of more than a dozen states to abolish parole between the late 1970s and the late 1990s, further reducing discretion in their criminal justice systems.

"Truth-in-sentencing" laws also spread to numerous states during the early 1990s. These laws mandated that offenders remain incarcerated for a certain percentage of their sentence. As part of the Violent Crime Control and Law Enforcement Act of 1994, the federal government offered states $11 billion for prison construction and expansion, provided that states met certain criteria. One criterion was that the state must have a "truth-in-sentencing" law or legislation mandating that certain violent offenders serve at least 85 percent of their sentences. Prior to this funding incentive, only 4 states had passed such legislation; by 1998, that number had increased to 27.

New correctional policies were also instituted at the state and local levels during this period. Private prisons, or correctional facilities managed by private organizations fulfilling government contracts, became increasingly prevalent as states sought to expand the number of available prison cells. In 1984, the first contract for a private prison was awarded; and by 2000, more than 150 private correctional facilities had opened throughout the country. Supporters of private prisons argued that they would be run more efficiently than public prisons; detractors argued that private prisons would not be as safe as public facilities.

The second correctional policy that spread dramatically during the 1980s and 1990s was the boot-camp prison. These programs exposed civilian offenders to military-style drills, physical exercise, and rigid discipline. Georgia and Oklahoma first instituted these programs in the early 1980s; by the mid 1990s, they had spread to a majority of states. In 1990, a correctional boot camp program was also added to the federal prison system. As with "three-strikes" policies, the diffusion of boot camps was encouraged by the 1994 Violent Crime Control and Law Enforcement Act, which provided funding for some of these programs.

Since many boot camps specifically targeted drug offenders, this approach to correction offers yet another example of how antidrug efforts gained headway during this period. Advocates of boot camps argued that their strict discipline and rigid, military-inspired structure would encourage offenders to change their behavior. Skeptics doubted the programs' rehabilitation potential and feared that the correctional officer–offender power dynamics present in some boot camps might lead to abuse. Although some boot camps produced positive effects, most evaluations showed that boot camps had little or no impact on recidivism.

Some states also made important changes to their juvenile justice systems during this period. In the three years following 1978, nearly half of all states adopted harsher policies for dealing with serious or repeat juvenile delinquents, such as forbidding certain offenses from being tried in juvenile court. Amid rising public concern about juvenile offending during the 1980s, at least 17 states changed the purpose of their juvenile justice systems to focus on protecting the public by incarcerating, rather than rehabilitating delinquents. In the early 1990s, the general trend toward tougher penalties and treatment for juvenile delinquents largely continued as the number of juveniles eligible for trial in the adult, rather than juvenile, system expanded. By the end of the 1990s, more than half of all states had adopted policies specifying that juveniles who met certain criteria could be automatically transferred to the adult justice system.

On the issue of capital punishment, the U.S. Supreme Court's 1976 decision in *Gregg v. Georgia* meant that state executions could be resumed. Eleven executions were carried out between 1977 and the end of 1983. More than 130 executions were carried out between 1984 and the end of 1990. Lethal injection became an increasingly common method of execution during this period, since first being implemented in Texas in 1982.

In the 1986 case *Ford v. Wainwright*, the Supreme Court ruled that offenders judged insane could not be executed. In the 1998 case *Thompson v. Oklahoma*, the Supreme Court ruled that offenders who were under the age of 16 when they committed their crimes could not be executed, a decision reaffirmed in the court's 1989 *Stanford v. Kentucky* ruling. Massachusetts and Rhode Island both abolished the death penalty in 1984, raising to 12 the number of states that did not have the death penalty during this period. Despite these restrictions, nationwide between 1990 and 1999, an average of 48 executions were carried out each year. Although capital punishment remained a contentious issue in American society, during this period opinion polls consistently revealed that a majority of the public supported the death penalty in cases of murder. However, the exact percentage in favor fluctuated over time and reached a peak of 80 percent support in 1994.

Changes in Policing

During this period, spending on policing throughout the United States increased at rates far above that of inflation. In the 1980s, average direct expenditures on

Mayor Marion Barry speaking in Washington, D.C., in the 1980s. In 1990, he was arrested by the FBI on drug charges after being videotaped smoking crack cocaine. In 1992, however, he was elected to city council.

police across federal, state, and local levels skyrocketed by more than 400 percent. Nationwide, the number of police officers relative to the total population rose more than 7 percent between 1990 (when there were 227 police officers per 100,000 U.S. residents) to 2000 (when there were 243 officers per 100,000 residents).

As with sentencing and incarceration policies, new policing approaches also spread during this period. For instance, problem-oriented policing—an approach emphasizing detailed analysis of crime to develop wider prevention strategies—was advocated by Herman Goldstein in a 1979 article and, in greater detail, in a landmark 1990 book. Goldstein's arguments were influential; during the 1990s, many police departments adopted aspects of this approach, and the nonprofit Center for Problem Oriented Policing began to publish related research from 2001.

Community policing—a related approach to problem-orientated policing—also received increased attention during this period. Community policing initiatives seek to build partnerships between law enforcement and stakeholders in local communities to reduce crime and disorder. Community policing is a broad concept that encompasses a variety of different, and more specific, techniques such as encouraging officers to become more familiar with the communities they patrol and holding community meetings for police officers to respond to citizen concerns. The origins of community policing trace back to the ideas of Sir Robert Peel, who founded London's Metropolitan Police Force in 1829. The famous axiom "The police are the public and the public are the police," attributed to Peel, encompasses his belief that the police were meant to work with and serve local citizens. This idea of partnership was revived in the late 20th century in the United States a number of police departments. For example, as early as the 1970s, the San Diego Police Department encouraged officers to become familiar with the characteristics and needs of the communities they patrolled and to tailor patrols to address those needs. The popularity of the general community-based philosophy is evidenced by the federal government's creation of the Office of Community Oriented Policing Services (COPS) as part of the 1994 Violent Crime Control and Law Enforcement Act.

A very different policing style also received notable attention during the 1990s: "zero-tolerance" policing. This approach encourages police to take swift

Ronald Reagan, who won two landslide elections in 1980 and 1984, espoused a tough-on-crime approach that was continued by his vice president, George H. W. Bush, after Bush won the 1988 presidential election.

action against even minor offenses to show that crime and disorder will not be tolerated. The theoretical underpinnings of this approach are frequently traced to the "broken-windows" theory proposed by George Kelling and James Q. Wilson in 1982. Kelling and Wilson argued that if minor crimes and instances of disorder are not addressed, social apathy and lawlessness can set in, resulting in more serious crimes. Rudolph Giuliani, mayor of New York City from 1994 to 2001, was a proponent of the zero-tolerance approach, and his Chief of Police Bill Bratton ensured that more attention was paid to low-level offenses.

Another policing innovation widely adopted in the 1990s was crime-mapping technology. Technological advances meant that by the early to mid-1990s, police were better able to track and analyze crime patterns. Most famously, geographic information system (GIS) technology was employed by New York City's Police Department as part of its CompStat strategy. During regular meetings with their superiors, local precinct commanders were encouraged to develop improved plans to deal with crime patterns and other problems in their local areas. Although some critics have expressed concern that this increased emphasis on crime statistics could encourage some officers to manipulate data, the introduction of crime-mapping technologies is often identified as a significant contributing factor to the large declines in crime experienced in that city during the latter part of the decade.

"Hot spots" policing was a second and related innovation adopted by some police departments during the 1990s. This strategy involves analyzing information about where crimes and incidents of disorder are most likely to take place before actively targeting police resources toward those areas. Research by David Weisburd and other scholars has shown that this strategy can often be effective in reducing crime in the targeted area without "displacing" crime to other nearby areas. However, more research is still needed into whether the strategy delivers long-term reductions in crime. Related strategies have been tried in cities as diverse as Jersey City, Houston, and Minneapolis.

Police departments sometimes showed willingness to experiment, implementing a range of new policing techniques at the same time. For example, Operation Ceasefire was a program designed to combat youth gun violence (and in particular, gang-related gun crimes) that was first implemented in Boston in 1996. The program drew upon both the "hot spots" approach (by focusing on areas with a high likelihood of crime) and problem-oriented policing ideas (by developing a larger, community-involved prevention strategy). Youths were discouraged from carrying guns through both interventions and threats of stiff penalties—a combination that researchers and the National Institute of Justice have referred to as "lever pulling." Operation Ceasefire produced promising early results and was also trialed in Los Angeles, Chicago, and other cities.

The issues of police racism and excessive force received national attention in 1991 when, after being pulled over for speeding, black motorist Rodney King was beaten by officers from the Los Angeles Police Department. Both the beating and the failure of other officers to intervene were caught on video and disseminated widely in the news media. Although the officers were acquitted of using excessive force in a California court—an action that fuelled the 1992 Los Angeles riots—the Justice Department later brought civil rights charges against four of them. Two were convicted and sentenced to 30 months in prison. The torture of Abner Louima in a station house in 1997 and the the shooting of unarmed West African immigrant Amadou Diallo in 1999 by New York police officers—and the protests it prompted—illustrated that, at the end of the decade, controversies about the use of excessive force by the police had not disappeared.

For many minority communities, Rodney King's beating, Amadou Diallo's death, and other high-profile incidents reinforced an already existing sense of police bias and racism. The issue of racial profiling by some police departments received increased attention during this period. In 1984, the Drug Enforcement Administration (DEA) initiated Operation Pipeline, which offered training to 25,000 state and local police officers to help combat drug trafficking. The training encouraged officers to consider the race of a suspect when identifying motorists to stop and question. During the 1990s, as civil rights groups raised legal challenges, more American police departments began to collect statistics on traffic stops by race to better identify and prevent racial profiling. This trend continued into the 21st century, with President George W. Bush declaring his opposition to racial profiling in a February 2001 address to the U.S. Congress.

One final trend from this period was the sharp increase in arrests for drug offenses, which more than doubled in the 1980s. By the early 1990s, there were approximately 1 million drug arrests each year in the United States, about a quarter of which were for marijuana possession. Racial disparities in drug arrests persisted during this period and between 1980 and 2003; drug arrests of black Americans in major cities rose three times faster than drug arrests of white Americans. The increases in arrests for drug offenses sharply contrasted with trends in arrests for other kinds of crimes. In the 1980s and 1990s, the nationwide arrest rate for murder remained relatively constant, with an average of nine arrests for murder for every 100,000 residents. The arrest rate for murder reached a peak in 1991, but between 1991 and 2000, it fell by more than 50 percent, mirroring the decline in the murder rate that took place during the same period. The arrest rate for robbery also fell by a third between 1996 and 1999. The arrest rate for burglary fell by about half between 1980 and 2000. The motor vehicle theft arrest rate increased more than 80 percent between 1983 and 1989 before dramatically declining throughout much of the 1990s.

Increasing Reliance on Incarceration

The 1980s and 1990s both witnessed massive growth in state and federal prison populations. Within the five-year period beginning in 1979, more than 100 new state correctional facilities were opened; in the 11 years between 1984 and 1995, nearly 150 more state correctional facilities were opened. As with policing expenditure, both local and national spending on incarceration sharply outpaced inflation during this period. Through the 1980s, for example, average direct spending on federal, state, and local correctional systems rose by 990 percent. In the 1990s, an average of almost $2 billion was spent each year on the construction of new state prisons. By 2000, approximately $40 billion was spent on prison construction and operations combined.

These numerous new prisons were needed to meet America's ever-escalating incarceration rate. Between the 1940s and the mid-1970s, the overall incarceration rate remained at around 100 inmates per 100,000 U.S. residents. During the late 1970s, the rate began to rise; by 1985, it had reached over 200 inmates per 100,000 U.S. residents, increasing to more than 300 by 1991. By 1995, the rate was in excess of 400, and by 2000, the rate had increased yet again to over 470, reflecting an incredible 343 percent rise over the 1980 rate.

Much of this growth can be attributed to the increased focus on drug offenses; simply put, more arrests and prison sentences for drug offending contributed to a greater number of prisoners. The political focus on drug offending thus had important criminal justice effects. In 1980, only 6 percent of state prison inmates were serving sentences for drug offenses; by 1999, however, this share rose to about 20 percent. Between 1980 and 1999, the incarceration rate for drug offenders skyrocketed by 1,000 percent. Meanwhile, the average duration of prison sentences imposed for drug offenses rose from 13 months to 30 months between 1985 and 1994.

Drug offenses were not only the only type of crime that contributed to the increased incarceration rates during this period, however; sentences for violent crimes also increased. For example, between 1975 and 1989, the average prison sentence for a violent crime tripled. A further factor that played an important role was the emphasis on longer sentences encouraged by the adoption of truth-in-sentencing and three-strikes policies by many states. Truth-in-sentencing policies typically required offenders to serve at least 85 percent of their sentences, while three-strikes policies mandated increased punishment for serious repeat offenders. Since both of these policies diffused widely during this period, their impact on the prison population was substantial.

Incarceration rates did not increase equally everywhere, as a comparison of the nation's two most populous states—Texas and California—reveals. During the 1980s, for example, the incarceration rate rose by 14 percent in Texas, but increased by a staggering 192 percent in California. In the 1990s, however, the incarceration growth in Texas accelerated, and the state maintained the highest average annual increase in the incarceration rate during that decade. California's incarceration rate also continued to grow during the 1990s; by the end of the decade, it was estimated that almost one in six state employees worked in the state's correctional system. More broadly, southern states such as Texas and Louisiana typically had higher incarceration rates during this period than New England states such as Maine and states in the northern midwest such as North Dakota and Minnesota. For example, in 1980, North Carolina had the highest state incarceration

Correctional innovations such as private prisons and military-style boot camps achieved greater prominence during this era. The Wyoming Honor Conservation Camp and Wyoming Boot Camp in Newcastle, which opened in 1990, is a highly structured program for first-time male offenders under the age of 25. The Youthful Offender Program provides an opportunity for a reduced sentence and an alternative to long-term incarceration.

rate, which was more than eight times higher than the lowest state incarceration rate of North Dakota. In 1985, 1990, and 1995, North Dakota retained the lowest state incarceration rate, but the highest rate could be found in Nevada in 1985, South Carolina in 1990, and Texas in 1995. By 2000, the lowest rate could be found in Minnesota (ahead of Maine and then North Dakota), and the highest rate could be found in Louisiana. In 2000, Louisiana's rate was just over six times higher than Minnesota's—a smaller disparity than that between North Carolina and North Dakota in 1980.

Race and class disparities in imprisonment rates persisted throughout this period. During the 1970s and 1990s, the chance that a black man without a high school education would be imprisoned by age 35 more than tripled, while the chance that a black man with some college education would be imprisoned by age 35 actually fell. The chance that a white man without a high school education would be imprisoned by age 35 more than doubled, while the chance that a white man with some college education would be imprisoned by age 35 fell slightly. In the decade following 1985, the number of black Americans sentenced to state prisons for drug offenses shot up by 700 percent. Racial disparities in drug-related incarceration cannot purely be explained by differing rates of drug use, as surveys have revealed that white Americans are as likely, if not more likely, to use illegal drugs as black Americans.

Although lower in absolute terms, the number of women in federal and state correctional facilities increased faster than the number of men during much of the late 1990s. The female incarceration rate more than quintupled between 1980 and 1999. In 1985, there were approximately 40,500 women serving sentences in U.S. jails or prisons. By 1992, this number had increased to approximately 75,000; by 1995, it had increased yet again to about 113,000. Much of this upward trend was due to nonviolent and drug offenses, rather than violent crimes. For example, in 1996, only 28 percent of females in state prisons had been incarcerated for violent crimes, in contrast to 50 percent of females in state prisons in 1979.

In addition to this dramatic increase in incarceration, the 1980s and 1990s also saw the implementation of a range of new "intermediate sanctions," or punishments that do not involve incarceration. One such sanction was electronic monitoring, or surveillance via electronic devices of offenders who must remain within a certain area, such as house arrest. Electronic monitoring was first trialed in Palm Beach County, Florida, in 1984 and by 1988 had spread to more than 30 states. A related alternative sanction was Intensive Supervision Probation (ISP), a more involved form of probation in which offenders were typically required to meet with their probation officer multiple times per week and follow stringent regulations regarding curfews and random drug tests. The concept of reducing probation officer caseloads and offering more individualized attention to

Atypical of the crime statistics at the time of her death, Deanna Cremin's 1995 murder is still unsolved. The nationwide arrest rate for murder remained relatively constant until between 1991 and 2000, when the arrest rate fell by more than 50 percent.

each offender on probation was trialed in some U.S. communities as early as the 1950s. By 1995, at least 40 states had adopted some form of ISP. For offenders with substance abuse issues, day reporting centers (DRCs) were another innovation that received increased attention during this period. A DRC is a nonresidential location where offenders undergo a comprehensive schedule of treatment and skill-building services. Offenders are typically required to report to DRCs multiple times per week. Massachusetts became the first state to operate a DRC in 1986, and over the next nine years, DRCs spread to more than 20 states.

The 1980s witnessed a general turn away from rehabilitation and toward crime control and tough punishment. The popular belief that "nothing worked" in offender rehabilitation was reinforced by Martinson's influential 1970s review of numerous programs. However, by the late 1990s, interest in crime offender rehabilitation programs and services for at-risk young people began to gain strength once again. One such example of a prevention/rehabilitation program introduced during this period was multisystemic therapy (MST), formulated by Scott Henggeler and colleagues to improve outcomes for adolescents with antisocial behavioral patterns. MST aims to take into account the way in which family, school, and neighborhood environments interact to influence adolescents' attitudes. The therapeutic model draws on research about and then targets the risk factors for antisocial behavior, such as inconsistent discipline by parents and a lack of commitment to education by the adolescents. This approach gained increasing prominence during the 1980s and 1990s, and was implemented in a wider range of jurisdictions to treat at-risk juveniles.

Another example of a research-based rehabilitative program that gained greater currency in various areas of the country during this period was Communities That Care (CTC), a program designed by David Hawkins and Richard Catalano. The goal of the program is to reduce antisocial outcomes among at-risk juveniles through a community-wide prevention approach, and CTC is now affiliated with the U.S. federal government's Center for Substance Abuse Prevention (CSAP) within the Substance Abuse and Mental Health Services Administration (SAMHSA).

A third program that also received increased attention during this period was the Nurse-Family Partnership program. In this program, nurses visit the homes of new, economically disadvantaged mothers and their children, offering help and advice. Randomized, controlled trials of the program's effectiveness were conducted in 1977 in Elmira, New York; in 1988 in Memphis, Tennessee; and in 1994 in Denver, Colorado. The results of these trials revealed benefits to both mothers and their young children, including a nearly 50 percent long-term reduction in official rates of child abuse or neglect. By the beginning of 2012, NFP programs were operated in more than 30 states.

Although on the surface, MST, CTC, NFP, and other similar programs implemented during this period may not seem directly related to criminal justice, they caught the attention of developmental criminologists. Developmental criminology focuses on the pathways into crime, or aims to understand why some children and adolescents become involved in criminal activities when they grow up. Many developmental criminologists believe that by identifying and reducing risk factors for criminal involvement among children and adolescents (such as school failure) and by identifying and promoting protective factors (such as impulse control), later offending can be reduced. Developmental criminology's focus on the long-term pathways into crime continues to appeal to many academics and practitioners.

The more general resurgence of interest in research-based rehabilitation and crime prevention that took place during this period can be seen in the 1997 publication of

Preventing Crime: What Works, What Doesn't, What's Promising. This research-intensive, comprehensive report was submitted to Congress by criminologists Lawrence W. Sherman, Denise C. Gottfredson, Doris L. MacKenzie, John Eck, Peter Reuter, and Shawn D. Bushway. The report reviewed research into the effectiveness of numerous crime prevention programs, including community-based, family-based, school-based, place-based, and policing-based initiatives. Similarly, during this period, some criminologists and other scholars championed the use of increasingly rigorous methods for compiling evaluations and literature reviews. Such scholars were eager to follow the example of medicine, where the international organization the Cochrane Collaboration disseminates systematic reviews, which are literature reviews that endeavor to locate absolutely all of the studies in a particular area, and meta-analyses of medical interventions, a statistical technique that allows researchers to combine the effects of multiple studies. In 2000, following the example of the Cochrane Collaboration, the Campbell Collaboration was founded to promote rigorous research into the effectiveness of social programs, including criminal justice interventions.

Conclusion
Every era in U.S. history has witnessed some changes in criminal justice policies, as national, state, and local policymakers have sought to address prevailing contemporary concerns. For example, the 1920s witnessed the development of a national system for compiling crime statistics, which led to the FBI's UCR, and the years immediately following the Omnibus Crime Control and Safe Streets Act of 1968 were marked by increased emphasis on coordinating different policing, criminal justice, and social welfare agencies to prevent crime. However, the changes that occurred in the 1980s and 1990s were especially dramatic; in particular, the unprecedented increases in incarceration rates and the expansion of efforts to control drugs and punish drug offending were significant historical developments. Although the most prominent police-recorded crime statistics and crime victimization survey results tell divergent stories about crime in the 1980s and early 1990s, the two sources agree that both violent crime and property crime declined dramatically in the mid- to late 1990s—an important social trend for which experts have advanced a variety of different explanations. Other less significant but still important developments included the introduction of new technologies to aid crime solving and the wider application of innovative policing strategies such as problem-oriented policing and hot-spots policing, which represented a distinct break from traditional methods. The era also saw the emergence of correctional innovations such as private prisons and military-style boot camps for civilian offenders, while hate crimes, child abuse, and domestic violence received greater attention during this period than in any previous era of U.S. history.

The 1980s and 1990s are also important decades in U.S. criminal justice history because the impacts of many of the trends and policies adopted during this period continue to be felt today. New technologies for solving crimes continue to diffuse, and interest in implementing improved policing practices persists. Racial disparities in incarceration rates and drug arrest rates remain a concern in the 21st century. The Anti-Drug Abuse Act of 1986—enacted during the height of the crack cocaine epidemic in America's inner cities—imposed mandatory minimum sentences for drug-related offenses. These minimums included a 100:1 federal sentencing disparity for crack cocaine relative to powder cocaine. This sentencing disparity has been criticized by some commentators for contributing to racial disparities in incarceration levels, as in the 1980s, the majority of powder cocaine users were white and the majority of crack-cocaine users were black. Concerns about this particular sentencing disparity were voiced by Republican President

George W. Bush during his administration, and by Democratic President Barack Obama, who took office in 2009. Nearly 25 years after this policy was introduced, Congress passed and Obama signed the Fair Sentencing Act (2010), which reduced the federal sentencing disparity from 100:1 to 18:1.

In addition to racial disparities, a second lingering consequence of the policy changes made during this period is a continued upward trend in incarceration rates. Partly as a result of the increased focus on drug offending during the 1980s and 1990s, the United States by 2012 had the highest incarceration rate in the world. According to figures compiled by the International Centre for Prison Studies at King's College London, the 2011 incarceration rate (or number of people incarcerated per 100,000 population) in the United States was 743, compared to 253 in Brazil, 200 in Mexico, 156 in England and Wales, 117 in Canada, 73 in Norway, and 58 in Japan. Housing such a large prison population continues to pose difficulties for certain U.S. states such as California, where prison overcrowding has become so acute that in 2011 the U.S. Supreme Court ordered the state to reduce its prison population by more than 30,000 inmates over the next two years. In California's case, a factor directly contributing to the state's prison overcrowding was the tough three-strikes sentencing law that the state adopted in 1994.

The Reagans and Michael Jackson launch the Campaign Against Drunk Driving at a White House Ceremony on May 14, 1984. There was increased political attention to the needs of crime victims during the 1980s, which included victims of drunk drivers. Reagan credited much of the public attention on the problem to Mothers Against Drunk Driving (MADD), which was founded in the early 1980s.

Although the death penalty remains in use in certain states, as well as in the federal system, the trend toward increasing restrictions on the application of the death penalty has continued into the 21st century. In 2002, the U.S. Supreme Court ruled in *Atkins v. Virginia* that the execution of "mentally retarded" offenders violated the mandate prohibiting "cruel and unusual punishment" in the Eighth Amendment of the U.S. Constitution. In 2005, the U.S. Supreme Court ruled in *Roper v. Simmons* that the execution of offenders who were under the age of 18 at the point when they committed their crimes also violated the Eighth Amendment. At the same time, in line with changing popular opinion, more states also got rid of the death penalty, with New Jersey, New Mexico, and Illinois all abolishing capital punishment between 2007 and 2011. Yet, although a 2011 poll registered the lowest level of U.S. public support for the death penalty since the 1970s, at just over 60 percent, support for the death penalty remains much higher in certain areas of the country.

In summary, the 1980s and 1990s ushered in dramatic policy changes in the American criminal justice system, and the political, economic, and social contexts of these decades shaped those changes. Political conservatism, economic globalization, and changing social reactions to hate crimes and domestic violence are just three of the many political, economic, and social developments that influenced criminal justice policymaking during this period. Probing the wider historical climate of this period affords a deeper understanding of how criminal justice policies—many of which continue to affect American society today—originally came into being.

Tiffany Bergin
University of Cambridge

1981 PRIMARY DOCUMENT

White House Press Briefing on the Reagan Assassination Attempt

On March 30, 1981, John Hinckley Jr. shot President Reagan and three others in an attempt to emulate the end of the film Taxi Driver in order to attract the attention of its co-star, Jodie Foster, with whom he was obsessed. He was found not guilty by reason of insanity and institutionalized. One of those shot, James Brady, became a gun control advocate. Secretary of State Alexander Haig has been criticized for declaring to the press that he was "in control here," despite being fourth in line to the presidency.

The White House
Office of The Secretary
Press Briefing
By Larry Speakers
April 3, 1981
12:13 P.M. Est

MR. SPEAKER: Good Afternoon. First of all I want to let you know that I spoke with Sarah Brady this morning from the hospital. Sarah, is of course, very encouraged by the reports Jim. She specifically wanted to say that she had numerous calls from Jim's friends in the media and that she wanted you to know that she deeply appreciates these telephone calls. She has, of course, not been able to get back to anyone at the present time. But she hopes to soon. She just specifically wanted to call and let you know that she appreciates it.

I transmitted to her that your feelings were that most of these calls were certainly not for news but from friends of Jim who wanted to know about his situation and express your feelings for Jim through Sarah.

I just talked to Dr. Ruge at the hospital. The President has just awakened from a nap and the situation is as we announced it in the medical statement this morning. We anticipate having another medical statement this afternoon, probably around 2:30. These statements, as you know, follow the doctors' rounds in visiting the President and that explains the fluid time as to when they release him.

Q: What do you mean the doctors' rounds?

MR. SPEAKER: When the doctor visits the patient.

Q: You mean Ruge or others?

MR. SPEAKER: Others and Ruge. We are now handing out the personnel announcements, presidential appointments—Kieran O'Doherty to be Commission of the Postal Rate Commission and the President plans to designate him as Chairman, Warren T. Lindquist to be a member of the Board of Directors of the New Community Development Corporation, and, once the appointment is effective, he will become General Manager and Chief Executive Officer: Fred J. Villella to be Deputy Director of the Federal Emergency Management Agency; William M. Gianelli to be Assistant Secretary of the Army for Civil Works; Lawrence J. Korb to be Assistant Secretary of Defense, Manpower Reserve and Reserve Affairs and Logistics; Shelby T. Brewer to be Assistant Secretary of Energy, Nuclear Energy. These had been earlier signed by the President. These are not the ones he signed today which are now going through our normal paperwork procedure. And I don't anticipate having them today. The President—

Q: Larry, how many is he signing today. Do you know?

MR. SPEAKER: No, I'll have to check that figure.

Q: Could we take a look at his signature?

MR. SPEAKER: Yes, we'll let you do that.

Q: This was right before he was shot?

MR. SPEAKER: Yes.

Q: Last week, in other words, late last week?

Q: The Executive Order as well?

MR. SPEAKER: They will come in today. The President, today, this morning, about 7:15 signed an Executive Order amending the generalized system of preferences. And the paper's coming out on that. This is a matter of trade and it will—questions should be directed to the Trade Representative's Office, 395-3406, who can answer them better than we can. Pool assignments for tomorrow: Newsweek writer, Time photographer, Sheridan radio correspondent, Detroit News, ABC, AP and UPI writer. The Vice President's schedule, which you've seen, luncheon with Director Casey at noon. At 2:00, National Security Council Meeting in the Cabinet Room, 5:00 meeting with Dr. Garrett Fitzgerald and at 6:30 a reception, and at 8:00 a performance at the National Theatre.

Q: Were all of these the President's appointments?

MR. SPEAKER: No, Only the National Security Council Meeting was.

Q: Apart from signing the Executive Order and the personnel appointments and the legislation yesterday, what other Presidential business has he been able to conduct?

MR. SPEAKER: Why don't you—I'll come back to that, Bill, if you'll let me tick through a few things here and remind me that you have a question pending.

Q: Okay.

MR. SPEAKER: Tomorrow, the Vice President's schedule, and this is only part of it, and we'll have a detailed one, of course, later, it includes a 1:00 Cabinet meeting, a 2:30 meeting with the Deputy Prime Minister of Poland, a 3:00 meeting with GOP members of the House, Ways and Means Committee. Of that number, the Cabinet meeting and the GOP House members were Presidential meetings that were scheduled. Now some details—

Q: The meeting with the Deputy Prime Minister was not a Presidential—

MR. SPEAKER: Was not a Presidential— He had planned to see the Vice President. Okay, the President—then this is details on the hospital and it's in excrutiating detail.

Q: Good.

MR. SPEAKER: A private room at the hospital measures 11 feet by 4 inches by 15 feet by 7 inches. The cost is—

Q: How high to the ceiling?

MR. SPEAKER: High enough for a man to stand up. The cost is $234.

Q: Who pays for that?

MR. SPEAKER: Wait a minute.

Q: He pays his own bill?

MR. SPEAKER: The President has insurance. It is not the government insurance but I think it's a previous policy he owned from California. Also it's my understanding that he is insured in the military as Commander-in-Chief.

Q: Okay. But what is his California insurance? Is it Blue Cross Blue Shield?

Q: Is it private?

MR. SPEAKER: It could be left over—it could be part of his duties as Governor.

Q: So, you don't know whether it's a private policy or some other public—

MR. SPEAKER: I can check. I hope not.

Q: And he is paying all of the hospital bills, personally?

MR. SPEAKER: I would assume his insurance will. I don't know.

Q: Well, which policy? His private policy or the military insurance? Which will pay?

Q: Why do you assume that?

MR. SPEAKER: I just assume that—

Q: My assumption is that as President and Commander-in-Chief he gets free medical service and all of that.

Q: Do you have a breakdown of the other costs? The cost of the operation? Anesthesia? Emergency room treatment?

MR. SPEAKER: No.

Q: Question?

MR. SPEAKER: Repeat it, son.

Q: Do you have a breakdown of the other costs? The cost of the operation, the emergency room procedure?

MR. SPEAKER: Let me get—

Q: The voice trailed off at that point.

MR. SPEAKER: No. The answer was no.

Q: Can we get it?

MR. SPEAKER: We'll see.

Q: But you say his personal policy is paying it all?

MR. SPEAKER: I thought I had excruciating details. (Laughter)

Q: Just tell me what details you have.

MR. SPEAKER: That's what I'm trying to do.

Q: But we do want to find out if he's going to pick up his own tab over there.

MR. SPEAKER: Okay, good.

Q: Also, Larry, isn't he eligible for Medicare?

MR. SPEAKER: I assume he is eligible. Okay, color of the walls: Beige. There are two blue easy chairs in the room. One rust couch.

Q: Hold on.

MR. SPEAKER: Okay. I'm sorry.

Q: Two blue chairs.

MR. SPEAKER: Easy chairs.

Q: Is this the Presidential Suite?

MR. SPEAKER: This is a standard small hospital room.

Q: Beige walls and blue chairs? (Laughter)

MR. SPEAKER: One rust couch.

Q: That's worse.

MR. SPEAKER: A tv mounted on the wall. It is a standard hospital room. There is a small floral arrangement which was sent from the White House florist. It is not a—not from an outsider. I will have more detail on the flowers. Okay. There is an intercom off the President's room which measures 10 feet by eight inches by nine feet even. It has a small couch and a red leather chair.

Q: What color is the couch?

MR. SPEAKER: I didn't get the color.

Q: Is it a daybed? Does it open up so someone could sleep there?

MR. SPEAKER: I don't know. I'll send Mr. Weinberg out and check it again. (Laughter) It has a bed and it has a White House phone.

Q: What's the room number? What floor is it on, all that?

MR. SPEAKER: Yes, Okay. This morning at 7:15, this is a little bit about what he's done today.

Q: Can you give us the suite number or the room number?

MR. SPEAKER: No.

Q: What floor it's on?

MR. SPEAKER: No.

Q: Why is that?

MR. SPEAKER: Well, I just don't want to. The White House—

Q: Well, that's perfectly unacceptable. (Laughter)

MR. SPEAKER: No, for obvious reasons. Okay. The White House—the floor contains, directly across from the President, an office for the White House Staff. It's mainly where David Fisher and Helene Von Dame are working from. It's also, on the same corridor, in a military—an office for the military aide. Dr. Roge has a room—sleeping room there.

Q: Right there?

MR. SPEAKER: That's right. There is a sitting room for Mrs. Reagan and a staff office that is at the end of the hall.

Q: For whom?

Q: Who's there?

MR. SPEAKER: For workers of the White House staff. I think there's a secretary from the Advance Office there and there are advance people there.

Q: Are any other patients on the wing?

Q: We thought they had a whole corridor. Is that roughly right, Larry?

MR. SPEAKER: Where is Weinberg? I think it is roughly a whole corridor.

Q: Is the government being charged for these additional rooms?

MR. SPEAKER: Possibly. I don't know.

Q: Does the Secret Service have a staff room there?

MR. SPEAKER: They are there.

Q: Do they have a whole operation there?

MR. SPEAKER: Yes. It is virtually a whole corridor.

Q: Was there a photo scheduled this morning and did you people decide to have the White House photographer take a picture?

MR. SPEAKER: There has not been a photo scheduled. We will not do one today but anticipate doing one in the next day or so.

Q: Was there consideration of one today and you decided against it?

Q: You anticipate what, Larry?

MR. SPEAKER: I anticipate doing one in the next day or so. There was a demand from the press, and we considered it and decided, "Let's wait 'til tomorrow."

Q: Why?

MR. SPEAKER: That was our decision. There's no reason. There's no medical reason. There's—

Q: He doesn't look good?

MR. SPEAKER: He looks very good.

Q: Is there a photogenic—

MR. SPEAKER: There is not a photogenic concern.

Q: But does he look good? I mean why would—

MR. SPEAKER: He looks good.

Source: White House Press Briefing Following Assassination Attempt on Ronald Reagan, 4/1/1981. Collection RR-SMOF: White House Staff and Office Collections.

See Articles: Famous Trials; History of Crime and Punishment in America: 1970–Present; Reagan, Ronald (Administration of).

1982 PRIMARY DOCUMENT

White House Directive on Managing Terrorist Incidents

Terrorism was a growing concern in the United States throughout the 1970s. The social unrest of the late 1960s gave way to the violence of Irish Republican Army bombings in England, radical groups in the United States, turmoil in the Middle East, and a widely publicized increase in aircraft hijackings (about 40 per year). Especially vivid in public memory were the holding of American hostages in Iran for over a year and the still-unsolved 1974 bombing of TWA flight 841.

The White House
Washington
National Security Decision
Directive Number 30

The United States is committed, as a matter of national policy, to oppose terrorism domestically and internationally. Efficient and effective management of terrorist incidents is crucial to this commitment. Successful management of terrorist incidents requires a rapid, effective response, immediate access to institutional expertise, and extensive prior planning. Because of these requirements, the management of terrorist incidents of duration will be handled in the following manner:

(1) Responsibilities. If the gravity of a terrorist incident situation warrants, the Assistant to the President for National Security Affairs, at the direction of the Vice President, will convene the Special Situation Group (SSG) to advise the President with respect to decision options on appropriate policies and actions.

(2) The Lead Agency. The coordination of federal response to terrorist incidents will normally be the responsibility of the Lead Agency. The Lead Agency will be that agency with the most direct operational role in dealing with the particular terrorist incident at hand. It will coordinate all operational aspects of the incident, including press and intelligence. The Lead Agency will normally be:

- The State Department, for international terrorist incidents that take place outside of US territory.
- The Department of Justice for terrorist incidents which take place within US territory. Unless otherwise specified by the Attorney General, the FBI will be the Lead Agency within the Department of Justice for operational response to such incidents.
- The FAA for highjackings within the special jurisdiction of the United States.

The Federal Emergency Management Agency will be responsible for planning and managing the public health aspects of a terrorist incident and recovery from the consequences of such incidents.

The Assistant to the President for National Security Affairs will resolve any uncertainty on the designation of the Lead Agency or on agency responsibilities.

(3) The Terrorist Incident Working Group. To support the Special Situation Group, a Terrorist Incident Working Group,

(TIWG) will be established. This group will consist of representatives from State, the DCI, DOD, FBI, FEMA and the NSC staff, with augmentation from other agencies, as required. The TIWG will be activated by the Assistant to the President for National Security Affairs. It will be chaired by a senior representative from the NSC staff.

The purpose of the TIWG is to provide the SSG with direct operational support, to ensure interagency coordination, and to provide advice and recommendations during an incident. The Lead Agency will continue to manage the incident under the direction and coordination of the TIWG and the SSG.

(4) The Interdepartmental Group on Terrorism. The Interdepartmental Group on Terrorism (IG/T), chaired by the Department of State, will be responsible for the development of overall US policy on terrorism, including, inter alia, policy directives, organizational issues, legislative initiatives, and interagency training programs.

(5) White House Operations Group. The White House Operations Group, chaired by the Director of the White House Military Office, will have responsibility for issued relating to threats or acts of terrorism directed against the President or the Vice President or senior US officials and protectees as directed by the President. The NSC staff will effect liaison between this group and the IG/T and TIWG.

(6) Planning and Exercises. In order to ensure effective management of terrorism incidents, prior planning exercise activity are essential. The Interdepartmental Group on Terrorism will be the primary mechanism within the US Government for planning and policy recommendations. To ensure the development of an effective, coordinated interagency exercise program, the Chairman of the IG/T will appoint an Exercise Committee which will coordinate the development of a multi-year exercise program and review all multiple agency counterterrorism exercises. This committee will assure that the government's counterterrorism capabilities are maintained in a high state of readiness and that duplication of exercises is avoided. No multiple agency exercise at the national level may be held without the recommendation of the IG/T and the approval of the Assistant to the President for National Security Affairs.

This National Security Decision Directive supersedes all previous inconsistent directives and instructions on managing terrorism incidents.

Managing Terrorist Incidents, 4/10/1982. Collection RR-NSC: Numbered National Security Policy Papers Archival Research Catalog (ARC) ID: 198191.

See Articles: Federal Bureau of Investigation; Federal Policing; Homeland Security; Justice, Department of; Terrorism.

1985 PRIMARY DOCUMENT

National Security Decision Directive 179

Reagan credited some of his success in the 1980 election to the perception that incumbent President Carter had not strongly defended U.S. interests abroad, especially during the Iran hostage crisis. Terrorism was a central concern of his foreign policy in both terms of office. Vice President Bush, former Central Intelligence Agency chief, chaired the counterterrorism task force described here. It recommended a consolidated intelligence database (which Bush had proposed in 1981), among other directives.

The White House
Washington

July 20, 1985
National Security
Decision Directive 179

International terrorism poses an increasing threat to US citizens and our interests. Terrorists are waging a war against, not only the United States, but all civilized society in which innocent civilians are intentional victims and our servicemen are specific targets.

The United States Government has an obligation to protect its citizens and interests against terrorists who have so little regard for human life and the values we cherish. To the extent we can, we should undertake action in concert with other nations which share our democratic institutions to combat the menace of terrorism. We must, however, be prepared to act unilaterally when necessary. It is, therefore, imperative that we develop a sustained program for combating terrorism.

To ensure that all appropriate resources of the United States Government are dedicated to this task, the Vice President is appointed to convene a government-wide task force on combating terrorism.

The Vice President's task force will:

- review and evaluate the effectiveness of current U.S. policy and programs on combating terrorism, to include:
  - an assessment of national priorities currently assigned to effectively combat terrorism, especially earlier recommendations regarding organization in NSDD-30 and adequacy of intelligence responsibilities in MSDD-138 and Presidential Executive Order 12333;
  - the assignment of responsibilities and accountability for ensuring interagency cooperation and coordination before, during, and after a terrorist incident;
  - a review and evaluation of present laws and law enforcement programs dealing with terrorism;
  - the adequacy of public awareness and support;
  - provisions for funding and personnel; and
  - an evaluation of current levels of programs of international cooperation and coordination.
- make recommendations as appropriate to the President by the end of 1985.

The task force on combating terrorism, chaired by the Vice President, will include the Secretaries of State, Treasury, Defense, and Transportation; the Attorney General, the Director of the Federal Bureau of Investigation; the Director of Central Intelligence; the Director of the Office of Management and Budget; the Assistant to the President for National Security Affairs; the Chairman of the Joint Chiefs of Staff; the Chief of Staff to the President; the Chief of Staff to the Vice President; the Assistant to the Vice President for National Security Affairs; the Executive Director of the Task Force; and others as appropriated.

The Vice President will appoint a senior Executive Director for the task force who will work under the direct supervision of the Vice President. The Executive Director may task any government department or agency, individual or organization to contribute to the work of the task force. To support the work of the task force, a working group will be established for which members may be drawn from departments/agencies represented on the Interdepartmental Group on Combating Terrorism, the Interagency Intelligence Committee on Terrorism, and others as appropriate. The working group will prepare substantive recommendations to the task force for consideration.

The task force will select a group of consultants which will provide advice to the task force as necessary. A Secretarial Staff for the task force may be established as appropriate.

Ronald Reagan

Source: Task force of Combating Terrorism, 7/20/1985, Numbered National Security Policy Papers Archival Research Catalog (ARC) ID: 198299

See Articles: Federal Bureau of Investigation; Federal Policing; Homeland Security; Justice, Department of; Terrorism.

1990 PRIMARY DOCUMENT

Marla Hanson's Testimony to the Senate Judiciary Committee

Model Marla Hanson rejected the sexual advances of her landlord, who retaliated by hiring friends to attack her, permanently scarring her face and ending her modeling career at 24 years old. In court, her character was attacked and the judge scolded her for her comments to the press. Four years later, she and other women testified during the Senate's hearings on the United State's unusually high crime rate against women. The Violence Against Women Act was passed in 1994.

Statement of Marla Hanson

Ms. HANSON. Four years ago when I became a victim of an assault, what puzzled and distressed me most about the whole ordeal was when I realized I was suffering more from the stigma of victimization than from the actual violation. I am not trying to minimize the attack; it was as horrible as you might imagine.

My landlord masterminded a razor attack to my face to end my modeling career. I met him when I moved out of my apartment, I asked for my rent deposit back. He refused to give it back, and when I pressed him he finally said he would, I met him after a modeling assignment rather late one night, around midnight, in a restaurant that occupied the bottom floor of my building.

He said he had the money for me in cash, but he didn't want to give that much cash to me in the bar because it might look wrong, so he asked me if I would step outside. So I did, thinking that I would step outside, get the money, go into my building and up to my apartment. Instead, he had two men waiting for me who grabbed me and began to cut my face.

I was lucky. I got away, ran back to the restaurant. The police were there within 2 minutes. They caught the men at the same time and I was able to identify them the same night. They were convicted and sentenced to the maximum, along with my landlord, or 5 to 35 years.

But in the scope of things, those cuts to my face that night became almost insignificant, except as a reference point. They healed, of course, leaving scars, but it wasn't the scars that hindered the continuance of my modeling career so much as what they represented-violence.

And it was not so much the trauma of the attack that night that has haunted me in the end, but, as I said, it is the stigma of victimization. From the moment the press seized upon my story to the trials of my attackers, I felt as though I was caught in a Kafkaesque world beyond any grasp of reason.

It had never occurred to me to feel ashamed at being attacked. I was, I think, at first embarrassed at not being able to control my situation, but it never occurred to me to blame myself for my own attack; that is, until the courts, the press, and society began to insinuate and to question if I were the architect of my own suffering.

The term "victim" implies innocence, but it seems in this society the term "innocence" implies some sort of guilt, and nowhere is that attitude more apparent than in our current judicial system where it has become a common practice for defense lawyers to blame victims for their own assault and suffering, or at least destroy a victim's credibility and dignity before the trial process is over.

Not only do I find this kind of attitude disgraceful and cruel, but also incredibly ignorant because I feel that by blaming the innocent victims for their own suffering, we are, in fact, excusing the crimes, and thus inviting more crime.

….[T]he first day in the hospital I stated getting hundreds of phone calls from strangers, phone calls like people would call me up and say, well, what were you doing at the bar at 12 at night in the first place? Well, didn't you know that guy was weird? Why are you renting an apartment from a guy that you obviously knew was weird?

That said to me that I was to blame because I was at a bar at 12 at night. I mean, that was subtle, but that continued on. Every press article—they tore across the countryside digging up details about my life, printing them in the paper. Almost every article ended with a question mark. What did she do to deserve this, as if anything I did would merit this kind of attack to my face.

I found that disturbing, but what was most disturbing was the investigation and the court proceedings that followed. The investigation, to me, was like an interrogation. [Police officers] had done research on me. They confronted me with facts about my life and said, true or false. They demanded to know intimate details about my sex life, about everything about my life. They wanted skeletons, they said, out of the closet. And thinking that the prosecutor was my lawyer and that this was privileged information, I shared everything I could think of, only to find out later that the prosecutor was not my lawyer and that this information was not privileged. It was turned over to defense lawyers; that is required by law. And then it was turned over to the press, and you can imagine how violated I felt at that.

That was only the beginning. During the trial process, and especially in the second trial, a lawyer named Alton Maddox, whom I think some of you are familiar with—runs with Al Sharpton—started his opening statement by saying let me tell you about a woman who preyed on every man in this city, who preyed on men and their relationships with women; let me tell you about a girl named Marla Hanson, a girl out of Texas with a lot of racial hang-ups; let me tell you about—he said something about a 45-hour rule, that the police, the prosecutor, myself, and the entire New York City Police Department were involved in a massive coverup.

And then at the end of the trial, he went to the press and said before the end of the trial, I will have Marla Hanson behind bars. Those were his exact words. I mean, that is obviously blame. He went on throughout the trial to humiliate me time after time and insinuate that I was some sort of prostitute and a woman of loose morals.

He made fun of the fact I thought I was about to be raped, made it into a racial issue because the two men were black. But he forgot that my landlord was white and already convicted of master-minding the attack.

Then we spent at least 20 minutes in the trial on the fact that I was wearing a miniskirt, and he opened the question by saying is it true that on that night you were barely dressed, and, well, isn't it true that you hardly had anything on; well, you were wearing a miniskirt, weren't you, as if that in itself was inviting the crime.

And then at one point in the trial he stood up and said this here is a circus and I am the ringmaster and all I need is a whip to bring this "lying bitch" to order. At that point in the trial, I think that was the first time I cried throughout the whole proceeding. It seemed that everywhere I turned I was being blamed for being the architect of my own suffering...

I think the main impact is that I couldn't model again, although I tried.

...[I]t wasn't even the scars that hindered my modeling career. It was what they represented, which was violence. All my big accounts canceled me.

You know, the scars don't show up in pictures, but when people see me, my face represents violent crime and people don't want to see that; they don't want to deal with that. So I couldn't model after that, and it wasn't really the crime; it was the press and everything surrounding it that caused the most suffering to me.

I have flashback sometimes. I think it has changed the way I look at the world forever. It is not a safe place any more, and I think that I have gained a lot of perspective on it in the last four years. But it is one of those things that you never get over. It is always there, and you never know when something is going to trigger a memory and cause you to be, I guess, paralyzed.

Source: Hearing Before the Committee on the Judiciary, U.S. Senate, 101st Congress, Second Session, Part 1 (June 20, 1990).

See Articles: New York City; Sexual Harassment; Victim Rights and Restitution; Violence Against Women Act of 1994; Violent Crimes.

1991 PRIMARY DOCUMENT

Excerpt From *U.S. v. Exxon*

The 1989 oil spill caused by the Exxon Valdez *running aground was one of the worst manmade environmental disasters in history, and was the largest oil spill in U.S. waters until 2010. The accident was caused by multiple instances of negligence. The government fined Exxon and sued it for natural resource damages. Further, a jury awarded $5 billion (one year's profit) in punitive damages in a class action suit, which was reduced to $500 million by the Supreme Court in 2008.*

UNITED STATES DISTRICT COURT
DISTRICT OF ALASKA

United States of America,
Plaintiff,
v.
Exxon Corporation, Exxon Shipping Company, and Exxon Pipeline Company, in personam, and the *T/V Exxon Valdez,* in rem,
Defendants.

Civil Action No A91-082 CIV

State of Alaska,
Plaintiff,
v.
*Exxon Corporation,
and Exxon Shipping Company,*
Defendants.

Civil Action No. A91-083 CIV
AGREEMENT AND
CONSENT DECREE

This Agreement and Consent Decree (the "Agreement") is made and entered into by the United States of America and the State of Alaska ("State") (collectively referred to as the "Governments"), Exxon Corporation and Exxon Shipping Company ("Exxon Shipping") (collectively referred to, together with the T/V EXXON VALDEZ, as "Exxon"), and Exxon Pipeline Company ("Exxon Pipeline").

Introduction
On the night of March 23-24, 1989, the T/V EXXON VALDEZ, owned by Exxon Shipping, went aground on Bligh Reef in Prince William Sound, Alaska. As a result of the grounding, several of the vessel's cargo tanks ruptured and approximately 11 million gallons of crude oil owned by Exxon Corporation spilled into Prince William Sound (the "Oil Spill").

The State has filed an action in the Superior Court for the State of Alaska, Third Judicial District, arising from the Oil Spill, identified as *State of Alaska v. Exxon Corporation*, et al., Civil No. 3AN-89-6852 ("State Court Action"), and Exxon has asserted counterclaims against the State in that action.

On March 13, 1991 and March 15, 1991, respectively, the United States and the State each filed a complaint in this Court against Exxon and Exxon Pipeline, asserting civil claims relating to or arising from the Oil Spill ("Federal Court Complaints"). Exxon and Exxon Pipeline have asserted counterclaims against the United States and the State in their responses to the Federal Court Complaints.

The United States and the State represent that it is their legal position that only officials of the United States designated by the President and state officials designated by the Governors of the respective states are entitled to act on behalf of the public as trustees of Natural Resources to recover damages for injury to Natural Resources arising from the Oil Spill under Section 311 (f) of the Clean Water Act, 33 U.S.C. 1321(f).

Exxon represents that, during the period from the Oil Spill through August, 1991, it expended in excess of $2.1 billion for clean-up activities and reimbursements to the federal, State, and local governments for their expenses of response to the Oil Spill.

The Parties recognize that the payments called for in this Agreement are in addition to those described above, are compensatory and remedial in nature, and are made to the Governments in response to their pending or potential civil claims for damages or other civil relief against Exxon and Exxon Pipeline arising from the Oil Spill.

NOW, THEREFORE, the Parties agree, and it is hereby ORDERED, ADJUDGED, AND DECREED as follows:

Jurisdiction

1. The Court has jurisdiction over the subject matter of the claims set forth in the Federal Court Complaints and over the parties to this Agreement pursuant to, among other authorities …

Source: http://www.fakr.noaa.gov/oil/caA91-082.pdf

See Articles: Alaska; Environmental Crimes; Victim Rights and Restitution.

1993 PRIMARY DOCUMENT

Parchman State Penitentiary Lonely Heart Scam

Instead of preying on their victims' greed, as do many con games, the lonely heart scam is a common confidence trick that preys on emotions, especially their victims' desire for love, affection, or sex. That emotional investment also makes the victim less likely to file a complaint once they realize they've been scammed, due to the embarrassment and perhaps even residual feelings. Typically, such scams occur through correspondence such as the mail, which inmates in Mississippi's Parchman Prison used to clean out thousands of dollars from lonely "pen pals" through a phony money order scheme. The scam was halted by postal inspectors in 1992.

7 F.3d 1155

United States of America,
Plaintiff-Appellee,
v.
Jackie V. Brown,
Defendant-Appellant.

No. 92-7707.
United States Court of Appeals,
Fifth Circuit.

Nov. 10, 1993.

Defendant-appellant Jackie Brown (Brown) participated in a money order scam operating out of Parchman State Penitentiary in Mississippi. A jury found him guilty of conspiracy to alter and pass altered postal money orders and aiding and abetting mail fraud. The district court imposed concurrent sentences of 15 months' imprisonment and 3 years' supervised release on each count, and ordered Brown to pay $1,092 in restitution. Brown appeals the district court's application of the Sentencing Guidelines and certain evidentiary rulings. We affirm.

Facts and Proceedings Below

In January 1992, Evelyn Lomoriello (Lomoriello), a sixty-five-year-old Florida retiree, began corresponding through a "lonely hearts pen-pal club" with Richard Sims (Sims), an inmate at Parchman State Penitentiary in Mississippi. In April 1992, Lomoriello began accepting collect calls from Sims. In their conversations, Sims informed her that he planned to receive several money orders from Johnny Clark, whom he represented as his case worker. Telling Lomoriello that he needed the money to pay his fines, Sims asked her to deposit the money orders in her bank account and to send $5,000 of the money to a man identified as Jackie Brown in Cleveland, Mississippi.

On April 3, 1992, Lomoriello received 8 $700 money orders, totalling $5,600. Pursuant to Sims's instructions, she deposited them in her account, sent $5,000 to Brown in Cleveland by wire transfer, paid $200 to Western Union, and kept $400 for herself to pay for the collect calls. When Lomoriello's bank discovered the money orders had been altered to reflect $700 instead of their true $1 face values, the bank charged the $5,600 back to her account. Two weeks later, Lomoriello received a second set of altered money orders from Clark. By this time, however, police had warned her of the scam, and she turned the altered money orders over to postal authorities.

On April 6, 1992, Brown, a contract food manager at Parchman, received three Western Union drafts (one in the amount of $1,000 and two $2,000 drafts), and attempted to cash them the following day. The Western Union agent cashed only the $1,000 draft and then called the police to inform them that Brown, using Parchman prison identification, had received the money from a woman in Florida. After learning from Lomoriello that she had been corresponding with a Parchman inmate, Detective Serio of the Cleveland Police Department attempted to contact Brown. On April 8, 1992, Brown came to the police station and turned over the two uncashed $2,000 drafts and $500 of the draft that he had cashed. The following day, Brown voluntarily returned to the police station and gave Inspector Collins a handwritten statement admitting that he had picked up the money orders at the direction of Parchman inmate Ronnie Franklin. At trial, Brown admitted he was to receive $500 for smuggling the money into Parchman.

Source: http://law.justia.com/cases/federal/appellate-courts/F3/7/1155/479263

See Articles: Confidence Games and Frauds; Mississippi; Robbery, Contemporary; Victim Rights and Restitution.

1997 PRIMARY DOCUMENT

Excerpt From Monica Lewinsky and Linda Tripp's Telephone Conversations

Monica Lewinsky was a White House intern who had a secret sexual relationship with President Clinton. She discussed the relationship with her friend and coworker Linda Tripp, who recorded the conversations and handed them to Kenneth Starr, the independent counsel investigating Clinton. Starr's original mandate had been an investigation of real estate investments, but it expanded to include allegations of misconduct including unfair firings, mishandling of files, Paula Jones's sexual harassment suit, and Clinton's perjury in that suit when he denied a relationship with Lewinsky.

November 20, 1997

TRIPP: … This navy blue dress. Now all I would say to you is: I know how you feel today and I know why you feel the way you do today, but you have a very long life ahead of you … I would rather you had that in your possession if you need it years from now. That's all I'm gonna say.

LEWINSKY: You think that I can hold onto a dress for 10, 15 years with (REDACTED) from—

TRIPP: Hey, listen. My cousin is a genetic whatchamacalit.

LEWINSKY: Uh.

TRIPP: And during O. J. Simpson, I questioned all the DNA and do you know what he told me?

LEWINSKY: Huh?

TRIPP: … He said that on a rape victim now … if she has preserved a pinprick size of crusted semen, 10 years from that time, if she takes a wet Q-Tip and blobs it on there… they can match the DNA with absolutely with certainty.

LEWINSKY: So why I (sic) can't I scratch that … off and put it in a plastic bag?

TRIPP: You can't scratch it off. You would have to use a Q-Tip. And I feel like this is what I would tell my own daughter ...

LEWINSKY: Well, I'll think about it ...

TRIPP: ... It could be your only insurance policy down the road. Or it could never be needed and you can throw it away.

But I—I never, ever want to read about your going off the deep end because someone comes out and calls you a stalker or something and you have and he confirms it ... Maybe I'm being paranoid ...

Source: http://www.pbs.org/wgbh/americanexperience/features/primary-resources/lewinsky-tripp

See Articles: Adultery; Clinton, William (Administration of); Forensic Science; Morality; Witness Testimony.

1998 PRIMARY DOCUMENT

President Clinton's Statement Following Grand Jury Testimony

The Office of the Independent Counsel was established in 1978 to avoid (or be better prepared for) a repeat of the Watergate scandal; a prosecutor is appointed by a panel of the D.C. court of appeals in order to investigate, with unlimited resources, allegations of misconduct by people in high positions in federal government or presidential campaign organizations. Clinton was impeached by Congress and acquitted by the Senate. He gave this White House address on August 17.

Good evening. This afternoon in this room, from this chair, I testified before the Office of Independent Counsel and the grand jury. I answered their questions truthfully, including questions about my private life, questions no American citizen would ever want to answer. Still, I must take complete responsibility for all my actions, both public and private. And that is why I am speaking to you tonight.

As you know, in a deposition in January, I was asked questions about my relationship with Monica Lewinsky. While my answers were legally accurate, I did not volunteer information. Indeed, I did have a relationship with Miss Lewinsky that was not appropriate. In fact, it was wrong. It constituted a critical lapse in judgment and a personal failure on my part for which I am solely and completely responsible.

But I told the grand jury today and I say to you now that at no time did I ask anyone to lie, to hide or destroy evidence, or to take any other unlawful action. I know that my public comments and my silence about this matter gave a false impression. I misled people, including even my wife. I deeply regret that.

I can only tell you I was motivated by many factors. First, by a desire to protect myself from the embarrassment of my own conduct. I was also very concerned about protecting my family. The fact that these questions were being asked in a politically inspired lawsuit, which has since been dismissed, was a consideration too.

In addition, I had real and serious concerns about an independent counsel investigation that began with private business dealings twenty years ago, dealings, I might add, about which an independent federal agency found no evidence of any wrongdoing by me or my wife over two years ago. The independent counsel investigation moved on to my staff and friends, then into my private life. And now the investigation itself is under investigation.

This has gone on too long, cost too much, and hurt too many innocent people. Now, this matter is between me, the two people I love most-my wife and our daughter-and our God. I must put it right, and I am prepared to do whatever it takes to do so. Nothing is more important to me personally. But it is private, and I intend to reclaim my family life for my family. It's nobody's business but ours. Even presidents have private lives.

It is time to stop the pursuit of personal destruction and the prying into private lives and get on with our national life. Our country has been distracted by this matter for too long, and I take my responsibility for my part in all of this. That is all I can do. Now it is time-in fact, it is past time-to move on. We have important work to do-real opportunities to seize, real problems to solve, real security matters to face.

And so tonight, I ask you to turn away from the spectacle of the past seven months, to repair the fabric of our national discourse, and to return our attention to all the challenges and all the promise of the next American century.

Thank you for watching. And good night.

Source: http://law2.umkc.edu/faculty/projects/ftrials/clinton/clintonstatements.html

See Articles: Adultery; Clinton, William (Administration of); Forensic Science; Morality.

1999
PRIMARY DOCUMENT

FBI Report on Columbine High School Shooting

School shootings were not a new phenomenon in 1999 and had been on the rise throughout the decade: While 71 people were killed by gunfire at school from 1986 to 1990, 1992 alone saw 44 such homicides. The massacre at Columbine on April 20 was the fourth-deadliest school massacre in American history, leading to 13 deaths and 24 injured before the two shooters committed suicide. The long public struggle to find a rationale blamed schools' social climate, bullying, and even video games.

Federal Bureau of Investigation
Precedence: Immediate
Date: 4/21/1999
To: OID
From: Denver
Case Id #: 4-Dn-57405
Title: Eric Harris;
Dylan Klebold;
Unsubs;
Columbine High School
Littleton, Colorado
Firearms Act—Homicide

ARMED AND DANGEROUS

Synopsis: To update FBI Headquarters regarding captioned mass murder case.

Details: At approximately 11:30 a.m. on 04/20/1999, the two referenced subjects entered the Columbine High School Littleton, Colorado, and thereafter began shooting students and staff, and also utilizing explosive devices. It was subsequently determined that prior to entering the school, the two subjects planted explosive devices in and around the school parking lot, and killed two students outside the school building.

Through further investigation, it was determined that the two subjects probably committed suicide after murdering 13 individuals, students and staff. In addition to the homicide victims, there were a total of 23 other victims wounded by gunshots and bomb shrapnel. As of today, 16 of these individuals remain hospitalized with 5 being in critical condition.

To date, the FBI's sole responsibility in this investigation is to assist Jefferson County, Colorado, authorities, as requested. This includes providing two Evidence Response Teams (ERT), the Denver bomb technicians, the SWAT team and a number of Agents used for interviewing purposes. The FBI continues liaison with the Bureau of Alcohol, Tobacco, and Firearms and the U. S. Attorney's Office for Colorado.

On 4/20/1999, the Denver SWAT team assisted with the securing of a perimeter of the Columbine High School and evacuating students. Subsequently, the Denver ERT has been conducting crime scene investigations, including the crime scene investigation regarding the two fatalities outside of the school building, the area outside the school, and vehicles in the school parking lot. The Denver bomb technicians have been assisting EOD personnel in searching for numerous explosive devices at the school, in vehicles, and at residences.

Denver Agents have interviewed an associate of the subjects, which has produced a lead regarding an individual who may have produced a lead regarding an individual who may have sold at least one weapon to the subjects. The cooperating witness has volunteered to take a polygraph to verify his information. This alleged our seller is identified as Philip Joseph Duran, W. M. DOB.

A total of approximately 400 law enforcement officers from 24 agencies have been involved in the investigation.

Denver has requested assistance from the Critical Incident Response Team/EAP to assist Denver employees who were at the crime scene and who had students in this school.

The Denver Command Post number is (303) 626-2721.

Source: FBI FOIA Office. http://vault.fbi.gov/Columbine%20High%20School%20/Columbine%20High%20School%20Part%201%20of%204/view

See Articles: Colorado; History of Crime and Punishment in America: 1970–Present; Juvenile Offenders, Prevention and Education; Juvenile Offenders in Adult Courts; Murder, Contemporary; School Shootings; Serial and Mass Killers.

2000 PRIMARY DOCUMENT

Amnesty International's Plea to President Clinton on Behalf of Juan Garza

Despite Amnesty International's plea, on June 19, 2001, Juan Garza became the first inmate since 1963 to be executed for a federal crime. A Texas drug dealer, Garza had been convicted in 1993 of three murders. One of his appeals was made on the basis of the claim that the jury had not been told that they could sentence him to life. President Clinton responded to this letter with a six-month reprieve so that the Justice Department could investigate allegations of racial bias in the death penalty.

UNITED STATES OF AMERICA
An open letter to President Bill Clinton as the first federal execution looms

14 November 2000

Dear Mr. President

On 12 December 2000, Juan Raul Garza is scheduled to become the first federal prisoner to be executed in the United States of America since 1963. In the name of human rights, justice and decency, Amnesty International urges you to intervene and prevent this backward step.

Juan Raul Garza's life is in your hands. But so too is the international human rights reputation of your country, a reputation that is rapidly eroding as US executions accelerate. Your decision will determine whether the United States diverges yet further from the growing global consensus against the death penalty, or takes a historic step into line with the human rights aspirations of the international community of nations.

In the 37 years since the last federal execution, the world has made remarkable strides towards full protection of this most fundamental of all human rights. In 1963, just 10 countries had abolished the death penalty. Today, 108 countries have abandoned judicial killing in law or practice—a clear majority of the nations of the world. Earlier this year, you said that the USA has become a world leader for human rights under your presidency. The planned resumption of federal executions provides you with a unique opportunity to demonstrate this claim of leadership to the world.

This year has seen a turning point in the death penalty in the United States. Since Governor Ryan announced in January that he was suspending executions in Illinois because of his deep disquiet about the fairness and reliability of that state's capital justice system, national concern about the death penalty has reached unprecedented levels. Governor Ryan's courageous move has paved the way for other political leaders to join calls for a moratorium on executions elsewhere in the USA, in light of the overwhelming evidence that capital justice across the country is indelibly marked by discrimination, arbitrariness and error.

It was in the midst of this growing national concern that the US Justice Department revealed the findings of its review into the federal capital justice system on 12 September. The review confirmed the presence of widespread racial and geographic disparities in the application of the federal death penalty, despite the Department's best efforts to ensure consistency in capital sentencing. Attorney General Reno admitted to being "sorely troubled" by the findings. You, too, expressed concern over the results of the study.

Your administration has told Amnesty International that it is "unalterably opposed" to any unfair or discriminatory application of the death penalty. We believe that you cannot, in good conscience, allow any federal execution to proceed in light of the Justice Department's findings, which indicate that prosecutorial discretion has resulted in an unacceptable arbitrariness in federal capital sentencing. Even supporters of the death penalty must concede that it is surely intolerable to countenance the ultimate punishment if its imposition may have been influenced by where the crime was committed or the colour of the defendant's skin.

In the past eight years almost 500 men and women have been executed in 29 US states, some 70 percent of the country's total judicial death toll since 1977. Amnesty International has determined that many of these executions were carried out in violation of international human rights safeguards, including the execution of child offenders, the mentally impaired, foreign nationals denied their consular rights, and scores of people denied the quality of defence representation demanded under international legal standards. We deeply regret that the federal government has consistently sought to wash its hands of this human rights scandal.

The US Government cannot seek to escape full responsibility for the fate of Juan Raul Garza and the other individuals under federal sentence of death. We therefore urge you to grant clemency to Juan Garza and to declare a moratorium on all federal executions.

Amnesty International believes that you can and should go further, as the organization outlined in its memorandum sent to you last week. We believe, for example, that you should exercise your constitutional authority by commuting the sentences of all prisoners on federal death row. We submit that this act of human rights leadership would be entirely consistent with the findings of the Justice Department report. It is now clear that even the stringent procedural safeguards in federal death penalty procedures have failed to prevent unacceptable arbitrariness in its application.

Just three weeks ago, you issued a Proclamation reaffirming the commitment of the United States to the United Nations, and celebrating the fact that for the past 55 years the UN has led the world in "promoting human rights and human dignity." One of the central goals of the United Nations is the progressive elimination of the death penalty and its eventual worldwide abolition, as an essential measure for the enhancement of human dignity and the development of human rights. At this crucial moment, you are in a position to make a lasting contribution to the promotion and protection of fundamental human rights, by acknowledging that the federal death penalty is inconsistent with the United States' commitment to those universal aspirations. Amnesty International urges you to grasp this historic opportunity.

The world awaits your decision.

Yours sincerely
Pierre Sané
Secretary General
International Secretariat, 1 Easton Street, London Wc1x 0Dw, United Kingdom

Source: http://sobek.colorado.edu/~mciverj/2481_DP_AMR511642000.html

See Articles: Clinton, William (Administration of); Death Row; Executions; Federal Prisons.

2001 to 2012

INTRODUCTION

The September 11, 2001, terrorist attacks and the financial crisis of 2008 are two key events that shaped American society from 2001 to 2012 and influenced the country's criminal justice system. The 9/11 terrorist attacks resulted in law enforcement's increased use of electronic surveillance and a re-examination of citizens' civil rights, especially the right to privacy. The resulting War on Terrorism led to a decade-long struggle over the proper treatment, detention, and trial of enemy combatants. Concerns about border security and domestic terrorism influenced the passage of controversial anti-immigration legislation in Arizona and Alabama. In contrast, the 2008 financial crisis resulted in state budget shortfalls, forcing states to re-examine their incarceration and post-release supervision of offenders in light of burgeoning prison populations and high recidivism rates. As a result, many states are now focusing on rehabilitation of offenders and coordinated reentry strategies, as well as the use of alternatives to imprisonment, such as substance abuse treatment, transitional housing, problem-solving courts, and restorative justice programs. New developments in scientific knowledge, technology, and evidence-based practices were also major influences on criminal justice policy and practice during this decade. The rise of cyber crime and more sophisticated methods of crime investigation, such as the use of global positioning system (GPS) tracking devices, presented a variety of new challenges for both law enforcement and the legal system. New scientific knowledge concerning the results of methamphetamine ("meth") abuse on the brain aided in addressing the meth addiction epidemic, while the proliferation of simple, homemade meth labs throughout American communities created new problems for law enforcement. The use of new DNA evidence to exonerate hundreds of prisoners on death row resulted in a serious re-examination of the death penalty by many states. Supervision of offenders were increasingly grounded in solid, evidence-based practices, which also informed the treatment of juvenile offenders. In addition, police agencies were urged to adopt evidence-based practices in their policing work.

The War Against Terrorism and Military Justice

On October 26, 2001, in response to the 9/11 terrorist attacks, President George W. Bush signed the USA PATRIOT Act into law. The short title of this act stands for "Uniting (and)

Along with retired New York City firefighter Bob Beckwith, President George W. Bush rallies firefighters and rescue workers at the site of the collapsed World Trade Center in New York City, on September 14, 2001. As a response to the attacks, Bush signed the USA PATRIOT Act into law on October 26, 2001. The act broadened law enforcement reach in several areas, including federal intelligence-gathering ability and infinite detainment of terrorist suspects.

Strengthening America (by) Providing Appropriate Tools Required (to) Intercept (and) Obstruct Terrorism." Among other provisions, it broadened the ability of law enforcement to gather intelligence within the United States and expanded access to business records, including library and financial records. The act also allowed law enforcement and immigration officials to indefinitely detain and deport immigrants suspected of terrorism, and expanded the definition of terrorism to include domestic terrorism.

The PATRIOT Act also expanded the use of National Security Letters to allow the Federal Bureau of Investigation (FBI) to search telephone, e-mail, and financial records without a court order. A National Security Letter (NSL) is an administrative subpoena issued by the FBI requesting documents and/or data and does not require probable cause or judicial oversight. Federal courts found this provision unconstitutional because the act does not provide any process through which a telephone or Internet company can oppose an NSL in court, thus violating the First and Fourth Amendments of the U.S. Constitution. In contrast, in 2010, the U.S. Supreme Court in *Holder v. Humanitarian Law Project* upheld a controversial provision of the PATRIOT Act that outlaws the provision of material support to terrorist groups.

The PATRIOT Act provided a sunset date of December 31, 2005, for the majority of its provisions; however, in early 2006, Congress reauthorized most of these provisions. On May 26, 2011, President Barack Obama signed a four-year extension of three provisions of the act: roving wiretaps, the library records provision, and surveillance of "lone wolves," individuals acting alone outside of a terrorist group and suspected of terrorist activities. On December 31, 2011, President Obama signed the National

Defense Authorization Act for Fiscal Year 2012, which included a provision authorizing the indefinite detention of terrorism suspects.

The development of increasingly sophisticated and intrusive surveillance tools used by law enforcement during the last decade presented important privacy questions for the American legal system. In *U.S. v. Jones*, issued on January 23, 2012, the U.S. Supreme Court provided important guidance on the appropriate use of GPS tracking devices by law enforcement. The majority opinion, authored by Justice Antonin Scalia, found that the warrantless attachment of a GPS tracking device to an individual's vehicle by FBI and local law enforcement officers, and the use of that device to gather information about the individual's movements, constituted an unconstitutional search under the Fourth Amendment to the U.S. Constitution. The Fourth Amendment protects individuals' rights to be "secure in their persons, houses, papers and effects" from unreasonable searches and seizures. The majority opinion found that the placement of the GPS tracking device on the car was equivalent to a physical intrusion on an individual's "effect," and therefore such an intrusion could not be used to gather information without a warrant.

While the majority opinion bypassed the question of whether the individual had an expectation of privacy in his movements while operating the car, a concurring opinion by Justice Sonia Sotomayor stated that individuals do have a reasonable expectation of privacy in the totality of their movements, even when in public. The Supreme Court's decision in *U.S. v. Jones* prompted the FBI to turn off approximately 3,000 GPS tracking devices that were in use and, develop new guidelines for the future use of such devices, as well as to address the other individual privacy implications raised by Justice Sotomayor's concurring opinion.

The 2003 invasion of Iraq by the United States led to some controversial problems in the military justice system. In 2004, a military inquiry conducted by Major General Antonio Taguba into the conditions at Abu Ghraib prison in Baghdad, Iraq, revealed numerous incidents of egregious criminal abuse of detainees by military guards. Eleven military personnel were subsequently convicted in military court-martials of violations arising from the criminal abuses committed at Abu Ghraib. Other questions have arisen about the indefinite detention of enemy combatants at Guantánamo Bay; a practice condemned in 2006 by the United Nations (UN) Committee Against Torture, which stated that indefinite detention constitutes a violation of the UN Convention Against Torture.

Since 9/11 and the resulting War on Terror, the United States has struggled to clarify when and how military tribunals can be used to try enemy combatants for alleged war crimes. Military tribunals, which assert jurisdiction over nonmilitary personnel accused of misconduct during war, are distinct from court-martials, which assert jurisdiction over members of the military. On April 13, 2001, President George W. Bush issued a military order for the detention and trial of certain noncitizens accused of terrorism, directing the U.S. Secretary of Defense to establish military commissions to try detainees for violation of the laws of war and other applicable laws. This order provides that, due to the threat to the safety of the country by international terrorism, it is not practicable to apply the principles of law and the rules of evidence used in trials in the U.S. criminal justice system to noncitizen detainees, including basic due process rights and the right to appeal resulting verdicts.

In June 2006, the U.S. Supreme Court invalidated the system of military commissions established by the president's November 2001 military order in *Hamdan v. Rumsfield*. The court found that the president's authority to establish such tribunals is circumscribed by Article 26 of the Uniform Code of Military Justice, which requires that military commissions use the same rules and procedures applicable to court-martials of military personnel, unless a compelling reason exists. The court also found that this military commission system violated Common Article 3 of the Geneva Conventions, requiring trial by just procedures recognized by civilized peoples. In response to this ruling, Congress passed the 2006 Military Commissions Act, which provided the accused the right to be tried by a qualified military judge and a panel of commission members, the right to see all evidence admitted against him or her, the right to be present at all proceedings (unless removed for safety reasons or for being too disruptive), the right to obtain evidence and witnesses on his or her behalf, and the right to appeal. The act also limited the right of detainees to counsel and to seek habeas corpus relief and did not prohibit the use of statements obtained by coercion.

In January 2009, President Obama ordered a stay of military commission proceedings until a comprehensive review of their operations could be completed. In May 2009, the Secretary of Defense issued amendments to the *Manual for Military Commissions*, providing additional rights to counsel and eliminating the use of statements obtained through cruel, inhuman, or degrading treatment. Congress passed the Military Commission Act of 2009, clarifying the role of military commissions and establishing a convening authority appointed by the Secretary of Defense to convene military commissions to try individuals for unlawful conduct associated with war. This act established procedures governing the use of military commissions to try individuals charged under the Uniform Code of Military Justice, including the presumption of innocence until proven guilty beyond a reasonable doubt. Because of the reality of battlefield situations, rules of evidence in military tribunals differ from those in criminal courts. Evidence may not be excluded because it was seized without a search warrant, and statements by accused individuals may not be disallowed because they were not read their Miranda rights. However, statements that are found to be the result of coercion or torture are disallowed.

Charges against nonmilitary personnel are initially referred to the convening authority to make a determination whether there is probable cause to proceed. If the convening authority decides to proceed, a military commission is created to hear the case. Each military commission consists of a military judge and at least five military officers. If an accused individual faces the death penalty, a minimum of 12 commission members must reach unanimous consent on a verdict. The professed mission of military commissions is to balance the public's interest in a fair and transparent process to try enemy combatants with the need to protect national security. To that end, the U.S. military has established a Military Commissions Website, which provides information about the military commission process, upcoming hearings, locations where these hearings can be viewed via video conferencing, and background information on the history of military tribunals.

In addition to enemy combatants, the U.S. military has faced the problem of addressing criminal conduct by its personnel. On November 5, 2009, a single gunman, U.S. Army Major Nidal Malik Hasan, shot and killed 13 people and wounded 29 others at the Fort Hood military base near Killeen, Texas. Hasan was shot by civilian army officers and paralyzed from the waist down. He was charged with 13 counts of murder and 32 counts of attempted murder in court-marital proceedings under the Uniform Code of Military Justice (UCMJ). He could face the death penalty if convicted during his military trial, which was scheduled to start in June 2012 at Fort Hood. On February 23, 2012, Private First Class Bradley Manning, accused of providing hundreds of thousands of classified documents to WikiLeaks, was charged with 22 counts under the UCMJ, including aiding the enemy, which is a capital offense. However, military prosecutors in his case elected not to seek the death penalty.

Illegal Immigrants

Debate over illegal immigrants has also shaped criminal justice policies during the first decade of the 2000s. The Immigration Reform and Control Act of 1986 made it illegal to hire or recruit illegal immigrants. Since 9/11, Americans have become increasingly concerned about border security and domestic terrorism, while also relying heavily on the labor provided by immigrants. In 2006, both houses of Congress passed immigration reform bills, but were unable to reconcile them.

In 2010, due to growing frustration with the federal government's perceived inability to regulate illegal immigration, Arizona enacted the Support Our Law Enforcement and Safe Neighborhoods Act (Senate Bill 1070 or SB 1070). Under federal law, all aliens over the age of 14 who remain in the United States for longer than 30 days must register with the U.S. government and carry required documentation. SB 1070 made it a state misdemeanor for an alien to be in the state without this required documentation and required state law enforcement officers to stop and detain individuals when there is a reasonable suspicion that an individual is an illegal immigrant. One week after this bill was signed by Arizona Governor Jan Brewer, the Arizona legislature amended it to provide that prosecutors would not investigate complaints based on race, color, or national origin; and limited a law enforcement officer's investigation of an individual's immigrant status to situations involving a lawful stop, detention, or arrest.

Arizona's professed goal was to reduce the number of illegal immigrants in the state via attrition by enforcement of its new law. Following the passage of SB 1070, the U.S. Department of Justice promptly filed suit to enjoin Arizona from implementing the law,

First responders at the Fort Hood military base in Killeen, Texas, use a table as a stretcher to transport a wounded soldier to an awaiting ambulance after a shooting on November 5, 2009. During the rampage, the lone gunman, U.S. Army Major Nidal Malik Hasan, shot and killed 13 people and wounded 29 others. His military trial was scheduled to begin in June 2012 at Fort Hood. If convicted, he could face the death penalty.

arguing that federal authority over immigration preempted the state from regulating illegal immigrants within its borders. A preliminary injunction was imposed by the federal court pending resolution of this lawsuit. Arizona was also the subject of numerous protests and boycotts, resulting in the loss of millions of dollars of revenue from business, sporting events, concerts, and other tourist activities. However, public opinion polls indicated that Arizona's law seemed to have the support of the majority of Americans.

On June 9, 2011, Alabama Governor Robert Bentley signed into law the Hammon–Beason Alabama Taxpayer and Citizen Protection Act, the toughest anti-immigration law in the United States. This act requires that if during a legal stop, detention, or arrest a police officer has a reasonable suspicion that an individual is an illegal immigrant, the officer must make a reasonable attempt to ascertain the individual's immigrant status. Under the act, illegal immigrants are prohibited from receiving state or local benefits and are prohibited from attending public colleges and universities within the state. While children who lack the necessary documentation of legal status are allowed to attend public elementary, middle, and high schools, school officials are required to check each student's immigration status and provide totals of suspected illegal immigrants in reports to education officials.

Alabama's Hammon–Beason Alabama Taxpayer and Citizen Protection Act also severely restricts the ability of illegal immigrants to participate in the life of the community in which they live and targets citizens who assist them. Landlords cannot rent

A U.S. Border Patrol Tactical (BORTAC) unit, which is a law enforcement organization within the Department of Homeland Security, conducts a training mission. According to Border Patrol Chief Mike Fisher, the Border Patrol has increased agents, detection capabilities, and infrastructure, including miles of fence and roads that provide increased access. The Border Patrol guards the U.S. northern and southern borders from a number of threats.

to illegal immigrants, employers cannot hire them, and citizens cannot offer them transportation assistance. Illegal immigrants are prohibited from applying for work, and the production of false identification documents is a crime. Proof of citizenship must be presented before voting. Contracts knowingly entered into with an illegal immigrant are null and void.

As in Arizona, the U.S. Department of Justice has sued to enjoin the implementation of the Hammon–Beason Alabama Taxpayer and Citizen Protection Act. While this lawsuit was still working its way through federal court, a federal appellate court granted the U.S. government's request for a preliminary injunction, temporarily blocking implementation of a number of the act's key provisions.

Cyber Crime

Cyber crime involves computers as both the targets and the tools of criminal activities. Crimes that target computers include computer virus attacks, the introduction of malware or malicious software into computer systems, and denial of service attacks, in which an attacker attempts to prevent legitimate users from accessing information or services such as e-mail, Websites, or online bank accounts. The most common denial of service attack occurs when a server is overloaded with repeated requests for information, rendering it inoperable and thus "denying" requested service. In a distributed denial of service attack, an attacker takes control of an individual's computer and uses it to attack another computer. Crimes using computers as tools include identity theft, fraud, cyber stalking, cyber bullying, and phishing, which are attempts to obtain private usernames, passwords, or credit card information via e-mail requests disguised as legitimate communications from trustworthy sources. The U.S. Department of Justice's Computer Crime and Intellectual Property Section promotes "cyber ethics," a code of safe and responsible behavior applicable to the community of Internet users.

Cyber crime has been a growing concern for law enforcement agencies throughout the world. In 1996, Congress passed the National Information Infrastructure Protection Act in response to a perceived increase in incidences of computer hacking and other cyber crimes. The act addressed the unique problems faced by law enforcement officers in combating cyber crime and strengthened definitions of criminal acts involving computers. Since this act was passed, the digital storage of crucial public and private information, including sensitive financial, health, and national security information, has increased exponentially, along with the use of computers in criminal activities around the world. Criminal engagement in cyber crime across national boundaries, or engaging in cyber warfare, may now be prosecuted in the International Criminal Court.

After the 9/11 terrorist attacks, the Department of Homeland Security created the Computer Emergency Readiness Team (US-CERT) as an operational arm of its National Cyber Security Division. Its mission is to pursue the department's national strategy to secure cyberspace and protect public and private computers that provide crucial infrastructure for the sectors of agriculture, food, water, public health, emergency services, government, defense industries, information and telecommunications, energy, transportation, banking and finance, chemicals and hazardous materials, and shipping. It provides public information about preventing cyber attacks and improving computer security, and maintains a national cyber alert system.

The Methamphetamine Epidemic

Another influence on criminal justice policy during this decade was the rise of methamphetamine manufacture and use. Methamphetamine, also known as "meth," is a white crystalline powder that is easily dissolved in liquid and can be snorted, injected, smoked, or taken orally. A stimulant similar to amphetamine, it is legally available only through a nonrefillable doctor's prescription because of its great potential for abuse. The majority of illegal meth is manufactured in foreign or domestic super labs; however, it is increasingly "cooked" by individuals in smaller labs or homes.

Meth labs are highly combustible and toxic and represent a grave public safety risk. Low-cost ingredients and a simple recipe allow anyone to manufacture this drug in a motel room, RV, vehicle, or residence. In addition to the potential for causing intense fires, cooking meth creates toxic substances that can infiltrate drywall, carpet, or other parts of a structure. Exposure to these substances can result in severe reactions and even death, presenting extra dangers for police officers investigating these labs. Because of the public health and environmental risks involved, many states have passed legislation regulating the cleanup of meth labs.

Methamphetamine rapidly increases the neurotransmitter dopamine in the brain, which produces an initial intense euphoria. It is highly addictive and has devastating consequences for the physical and mental health of its users. Chronic abuse of meth reduces motor skills, impairs verbal learning, and causes emotional and cognitive problems. Long-term meth use can result in drastic weight loss, loss of teeth, insomnia, mood disorders, and even psychosis, including visual and auditory hallucinations. Chemical and molecular changes in the brain caused by using meth create addictive behavior that can persist long after the use has ceased. After more than one year of abstinence, reversal and repair of this damage can occur. Treatment of meth addiction is especially challenging because of the long-lasting and sometimes irreversible brain chemistry alterations caused by this insidious drug; relapses are common, and a commitment to long-term recovery is the only real hope to overcome addiction.

The ready availability and low cost of meth and the proliferation of small labs cooking this drug has created challenges for law enforcement. Meth addiction often results in the commission of crimes to fund this addiction, including theft, burglary, and forgery. The reluctance of the federal government to regulate the raw materials from which meth is produced led to an explosion of this drug during the first half of the decade, especially across the western and midwestern states. Recent public information campaigns, including highway billboards graphically illustrating the harmful effects of meth use, have been funded by a number of states. The Substance Abuse and Mental Health Services Admininstration's 2010 National Survey on Drug Use and Health reports that in the second part of the decade, the number of methamphetamine users was cut in half, from 731,000 in 2006 to 353,000 in 2010.

The Private Prison Industry
Since the first private prison contract was awarded to the Correctional Corporation of America (CCA) in 1984, the use of private prisons has expanded to more than 30 states. During the past decade, the number of private prison inmates increased by one-third; more than 90,000 offenders are now housed in private prisons. Recent reforms of correctional supervision of offenders have caused prison populations to level off or even decrease in many states. However, Arizona, Florida, and Ohio were considering expansions of private prison operations in 2012.

While private prisons are promoted as necessary cost-saving measures in many states, research suggests that private prisons may not be able to operate less expensively than public prisons. Private prisons usually do not accept prisoners with major health or mobility issues in an attempt to reduce their costs; nevertheless, 2010 data from the Arizona Department of Corrections reflects that housing an inmate in a private prison can cost as much as $1,600 more per year than housing an inmate in a public prison.

In 2010, a notorious escape from a private prison in Arizona focused attention on security issues surrounding the use of private prisons. On July 30, 2010, three violent offenders—Tracy Province, Daniel Renwick, and John McCuskey—escaped from the Kingman Arizona State Prison, a private prison owned and operated by the Management Training Corporation (MTC). Before Tracy Province, the last escapee, could be apprehended weeks later with his accomplice Casslyn Welch, they murdered a retired couple vacationing in New Mexico during a carjacking. Province and Welch pled guilty to the murders in January 2012. Surviving relatives of the murdered couple are suing MTC for their deaths. A subsequent investigation of the Kingman Arizona State Prison revealed major security problems, and hundreds of violent offenders were transferred out of this prison to more secure facilities.

Addressing the Expanding Prison Population

The United States imprisons almost half of all incarcerated individuals worldwide and has the highest prison population rate of all countries reporting such figures. In 2008, the Pew Center on the States reported that one in 100 adults in the United States was incarcerated, and in 2009, Pew reported that one in 31 adults in the country was under some kind of correctional supervision, including probation, jail, prison, or parole. These statistics reveal that almost every U.S. citizen knows someone who is or has been to prison, and almost every family in the nation has been somehow affected by the criminal justice system.

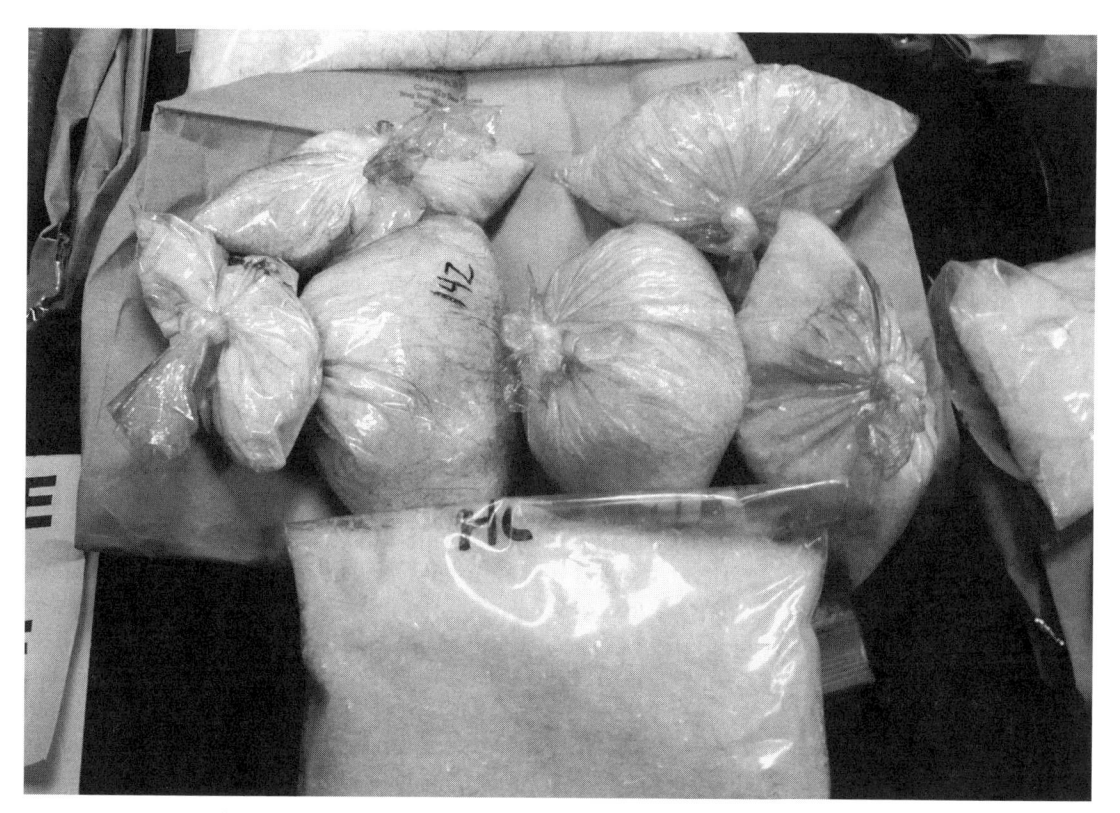

Over 1,200 pounds of methamphetamine were captured on June 9, 2010, during a 22-month-long, multiagency law enforcement investigation in 16 U.S. states. The sting led to the seizure of $154 million and 74.1 tons of drugs, as well as over 2,000 narcotics-related arrests, including a high-priority target. The low cost and ease of cooking meth has led to a proliferation of small meth labs across the country, which has created challenges for law enforcement.

Mirroring the expanding prison population, documentary series such as MSNBC's *Lock-Up* and National Geographic Channel's *American Hardest Prisons*, and dramatic series such as Fox's *Alcatraz* and HBO's *Oz*, proliferated during this decade. These shows, along with the increasing publication of writings by prisoners, propelled the harsh realities of prison life into the heart of American popular culture.

In 2001, Human Rights Watch released a report authored by Joanne Mariner titled "No Escape: Male Rape in U.S. Prisons," which included case studies of brutal incidents of rape suffered by male prisoners and the apparent indifference or inability of correctional officials to protect, or provide redress, for these assaults. As a result, in 2003, the U.S. Congress passed the Prison Rape Elimination Act, which created the National Prison Rape Elimination Commission (NPREC) to gather information on, and report findings, concerning prison rape. The act also requires the U.S. Department of Justice to make the prevention of prison rape a top priority and conduct hearings on prison rape. Federal grants were made available to state agencies to develop programs to further the goals of the act, and the National Institute of Corrections (NIC) was tasked with providing training and technical assistance for programs focusing on rape prevention in correctional facilities. While the original Prison Rape Elimination Act was only in effect for three years, a two-year extension was passed in 2007.

While the U.S. prison population has steadily increased, rates of violent and property crimes have been steadily declining since their peak in the early 1990s. While national crime rates have dropped, some scholars have posited that such reductions may be due to community policing efforts, rather than the increased numbers of incarcerated criminals. Further, the U.S. prison population is disproportionately made up of inhabitants of poorer neighborhoods of color. Critical race theorists such as Michelle Alexander argue that the country's prison system is an extension of the Jim Crow segregation laws of the past and that this system is creating an underclass of citizens permanently disadvantaged because of their incarceration. Former inmates have trouble getting work and find it easier, and more lucrative, to return to more familiar criminal activities, resulting in a return to prison.

At least 95 percent of offenders will eventually be released back into their communities. In 2010, 700,000 individuals were released from state and federal prisons, which represented a 20 percent increase in released prisoners from 2000. On average, over 40 percent of offenders return to prison within three years of being released. Offenders suffer from a number of serious problems that make their reentry into their communities very difficult. Seventy-five percent of offenders suffer from substance abuse disorders. The rate of serious mental illness is two to four times higher among prisoners than among the general public; 70 percent of these mentally ill offenders also have a dual diagnosis of substance abuse. Two out of five offenders do not have a high school diploma or its equivalent, and many offenders face homelessness upon their release.

In addition to the extra challenges faced by offenders returning to their communities, their incarceration and potential return to prison take a toll on their families. Approximately 2 million children have parents who are incarcerated; approximately 10 million children have a parent who has been under the supervision of the criminal justice system at some point. To address these serious social issues, Congress passed the Second Chance Act, which was signed into law in 2008. The act attempted to improve success rates for offenders released from prisons and jails and returning to their communities by providing $165 million in federal grants to government agencies and nonprofit organizations to provide employment assistance, substance abuse treatment, housing, mentoring, and other services in an attempt to reduce recidivism and ease offenders' transition from prison to their communities. The act also created the National Reentry Resource Center, a national clearinghouse to gather and disseminate best reentry practices and provide training.

The country's burgeoning prison population also places tremendous burdens on state budgets that are already strapped because of the fallout from the 2008 financial crisis. State spending on corrections has increased faster than any other budget item, other than health care. An extreme example is California, which has been unable to afford to build the extra prison space it needs. In *Brown v. Plata* (2011), the U.S. Supreme Court found that the extreme overcrowding in California's prisons resulted in packing inmates into open gymnasiums on bunk beds and denying minimal care to prisoners with serious medical and mental health issues, causing these prisoners suffering and even death. The court further found that prison suicide rates were 80 percent higher in California than the national average. The court ordered California to reduce its prison population by more than 30,000 inmates within two years. As a result, the California legislature passed a "public safety realignment" plan, which included sending offenders convicted of nonserious, nonviolent, or non-sex-related crimes to county jails. This legislative plan requires California to invest in community corrections programs and evidence-based practices that have proven track records in reducing recidivism rates in other states.

Nationally, more than 40 percent of offenders return to prison within three years of being released—the common measure of recidivism rates. However, several states have found successful ways to stabilize, and even reverse, burgeoning prison populations. Between 2008 and 2011, Mississippi reduced its prison population by 22 percent and lowered its crime rate by permitting inmates to earn time off their sentences by completing educational and reentry programs. Texas stabilized its growing prison population and achieved a lower crime rate by establishing parolee treatment programs and allowing inmates to earn time off their sentences.

Across the United States, cash-strapped state governments spent part of the decade searching for ways to better manage their offender populations, turning to studies by social scientists to guide their reform efforts. Evidence-based practice, which employs quantitative research data about which practices are effective in a specific context in order to drive policy and strategy decisions, is increasingly regarded and implemented as the new standard for correctional systems. In 2009, the Tides Center released an influential report examining the evidence-based strategies that various states were employing to address their burgeoning prison populations and recidivism rates. Three states—Missouri, Michigan, and Oregon—were discussed as exemplary models.

Facing a budget shortfall in 2002, Missouri examined its growing prison population and discovered that the main reason for this growth was a sharp increase in offenders returned to prison for technical violations while they were on probation or parole. In 2004, Missouri returned over 40 percent of its formerly incarcerated offenders to prison for parole or probation violations. To address its increasing prison population and recidivism rates, Missouri created a work group tasked with reviewing cases involving parole and probation revocations. An interagency team subsequently created a revised, evidence-based supervision program utilizing a new analytical tool to assess offenders' needs and risks of reoffending.

Under the new supervision system, offenders who violate parole or probation rules are subject to a range of disciplinary measures, including verbal reprimands, electronic monitoring, or time in jail. Offenders may also be sent to drug treatment programs. In 2004, Missouri had the second-highest recidivism rate in the country—54.4 percent. As a result of its reform of correctional supervision of offenders released from prison, Missouri's recidivism rate dropped to 36.4 percent in 2009.

During the decade, Michigan implemented the Michigan Prisoner Reentry Initiative (MPRI). Through this initiative, the state achieved a 12 percent reduction in its prison population, closed more than 20 correctional facilities, and improved its recidivism rate. MPRI focused its efforts on giving offenders the tools they needed to succeed after being released from prison and returning to their communities. The process begins with the offender's entry into prison with evaluation of the offender's risks, needs, and strengths. This information is then used to customize educational programming for each offender. Prior to leaving prison on parole, each offender is transitioned to a reentry facility. Customized transition plans are collaboratively created for offenders with the assistance of service providers in the community. After leaving the reentry facility and going on parole, offenders breaking the rules governing parole are subjected to progressive disciplinary procedures, including a short return to the reentry facility if needed, thus reducing the numbers of parolees returned to prison for technical violations.

A recent study revealed that the recidivism rate of parolees released through MPRI is 33 percent lower than the rate for similar offenders who do not participate in the program. As a result of this successful reduction, the Michigan parole board increased its approval of parole applications, approving 3,000 more parolees in 2009 than in 2006.

A similar comprehensive program designed to help offenders reintegrate into their communities and avoid reoffending was implemented in Oregon at the beginning of the decade. Like MPRI, the program involves administering risk and needs assessments of offenders upon their arrival in prison and planning for their transitions to the community six months before they leave. Probation officers across the state use a uniform grid to impose swift, consistent sanctions for rule violations. These progressive sanctions, which can include up to a short stay in jail, have greatly reduced the return of offenders to prison for technical violations. To further bolster reform in Oregon, in 2003, the state legislature passed a bill requiring that all state-funded correctional programs be designed and delivered in conformity with evidence-based practices.

These successful state efforts to reduce prison populations and recidivism rates and strengthen offender reintegration into communities can serve as helpful models for other states seeking to reform their correctional policies and practices. Evidence-based decision making (EBD) and evidence-based practices (EBP) have been actively promoted by the National Institute of Corrections (NIC), a division of the U.S. Department of Justice, through the awarding of grants for developing such collaborative, evidence-based processes in local criminal justice systems.

Community and Evidence-Based Policing (EBP)

The decade witnessed an increase in community and problem-oriented policing. Community policing is grounded in collaborative partnerships between police and the communities they serve and the engagement of these partnerships in proactive, problem-solving efforts such as identifying and prioritizing problems affecting the community, researching and analyzing these problems, and developing potential solutions. Community policing emphasizes thoughtfully considered efforts to provide safer environments and prevent crimes, rather than reacting to crimes as they occur in an incident-specific, 911-response paradigm. The community-policing model also stresses the development of productive relationships between law enforcement and community stakeholders.

Community policing changes the culture of law enforcement agencies to value the systematic examination of problems to collaboratively develop effective responses with community partners. It also enlists community members as active partners invested in the safety and security of their neighborhoods, rendering police officers less isolated in their law enforcement work. Strong neighborhood watch programs, in which neighbors are encouraged and motivated to watch out for each other and report suspicious behavior to the police, have been found to effectively reduce crime.

Similar to the adoption of evidence-based practices in correctional agencies, some scholars and policy analysts advocate the adoption of an evidence-based approach to policing. This approach encourages police agencies to identify and codify policing techniques and strategies that are supported by scientific studies. Evidence-based policing encourages a partnership between social scientists and law enforcement agencies to utilize evidence gleaned from scientific research in police practice, incorporating the scientific method into policing work. Following the establishment of preferred methods and strategies arising from basic scientific research studies, these "best practices" are utilized by police officers. Measurable outcomes from these practices are identified and the results are tracked to provide an ongoing, systematic testing of hypotheses in action.

The focus on using scientific evidence and the ongoing evaluation of measurable outcomes is arguably missing from existing models, including incident-specific, community-oriented, and problem-oriented policing. Incident-specific policing focuses on dealing with specific crimes and calls for assistance as they occur, while community-oriented and problem-oriented policing place more emphasis on a problem-solving process than

New York City mounted police interact with the community in August 2007. The period experienced increased activity in community-based and problem-solving policing, which is based on collaboration between the police and the community they serve. This approach, which has been found to reduce crime, is designed to create active partnerships with officers and their community and encourage neighbors to look out for one another.

measurable outcomes. Evidence-based policing encourages researchers and police agencies to work collaboratively to evaluate the effectiveness of evidence-based practices that have been implemented, providing a continuous feedback loop with helpful information for police agencies, social scientists, and criminologists about what is and what is not working.

Re-Examination of the Death Penalty

The increased utility of scientific evidence in criminal justice work can also be seen in the shift in public opinion concerning the death penalty. The use of new DNA evidence to exonerate hundreds of prisoners on death row has resulted in a serious re-examination by many states of their administration of the ultimate sanction of capital punishment. The U.S. Supreme Court has also cited scientific studies in reconsidering whether the death penalty is appropriate for juveniles convicted of murder.

The Innocence Project is a national litigation and public policy organization that uses DNA testing to exonerate wrongfully convicted individuals and works to reform the criminal justice system. Since 1992, The Innocence Project has focused all of its pro bono litigation efforts on cases in which DNA testing exonerates a defendant. This work has resulted in 289 post-conviction exonerations; 222 of these achieved since 2000. More than half, or 180, of these exonerated individuals are African Americans; 17 of these individuals spent time on death row.

The leading cause of these erroneous convictions was misidentification by eyewitnesses, which was a factor in 75 percent of the 289 post-conviction exonerations. At least 40 percent of these cases were based on cross-racial identification; studies indicate that witnesses are less able to identify the face of someone whose race differs from their own. Forensic science errors (including hair microscopy, bite mark comparisons, firearm tool mark analysis, shoe print comparisons, and blood typing) were a factor in roughly half of the erroneous convictions. Other documented causes include false or coerced confessions or admissions, forensic science and/or government misconduct, informants with incentives to falsify their testimony, and incompetent legal representation.

As a result of the growing number of these exonerations and the systemic flaws they reveal, many states have re-examined their death penalty policies, and several have either imposed moratoriums on the death penalty or abolished the practice completely. On March 9, 2000, Illinois Governor George Ryan declared a moratorium on state executions and appointed a Commission on Capital Punishment to determine what reforms, if any, would ensure that the Illinois capital punishment system is fair, just, and accurate.

After two years of research and deliberation, the Illinois Commission on Capital Punishment issued its report in April 2002. The commission's recommendations included videotaping all interrogations of capital crime suspects, revising suspect lineup and identification procedures, narrowing the list of crimes for which the death penalty may be imposed, creating a commission to review all local state's attorneys' decisions to seek the death penalty, providing for Illinois Supreme Court review of all death penalty sentences, and allowing a trial judge to overrule a jury's recommendation for the death penalty and, alternatively, impose a life sentence. The commission also recommended that the death penalty be unavailable when a conviction is based on the testimony of a single witness, in-custody informant, or uncorroborated accomplice, or when the defendant is mentally retarded. The Illinois legislature ultimately abolished the death penalty in January 2011.

A similar state commission on capital punishment created in Maryland issued its final report to the Maryland General Assembly in December 2008, following months of expert and public evidence collected via public hearings and meetings. By a 13–9 vote, the Commission on Capital Punishment in Maryland recommended abolition of the death penalty because of demonstrated problems of racial and geographic disparity, high costs, risk of innocence, impact on the families of murder victims, and the absence of a deterrent effect. In 2009, the Maryland General Assembly passed the most restrictive death penalty legislation in the United States, limiting the imposition of capital punishment to murder cases with biological or DNA evidence of guilt, a videotaped confession, or a videotape connecting the defendant to a homicide.

Following the lead set by Illinois, the American Bar Association (ABA) created the Death Penalty Moratorium Implementation Project in 2001 to pursue its goal of a nationwide moratorium on capital punishment. In 2007, the ABA called for a national moratorium on executions following a study of the administration of capital punishment in eight sample states: Alabama, Georgia, Indiana, Ohio, Tennessee, Arizona, Florida, and Pennsylvania. Common problems identified by the ABA included racial disparity, inadequate indigent defense, and irregular clemency review processes. The ABA encouraged states to impose moratoriums on executions until they could complete a comprehensive review of capital punishment legislation and administration and correct existing flaws and weaknesses. ABA-sponsored assessments of state capital punishment systems have been conducted in Alabama, Florida, Georgia, Indiana, Kentucky, Ohio, Pennsylvania, and Missouri.

After the peak of executions in 1999 with a total of 98, the annual total has declined; in 2011, 43 defendants were executed. Currently, 34 states still have death penalty statutes, although bills to abolish the death penalty have been proposed in Connecticut (which passed in May 2012), Florida, Georgia, Kansas, Maryland, Missouri, Nebraska, Ohio, and Washington. States abolishing the death penalty between 2000 and 2012 include Illinois, New Jersey, New Mexico, and New York. In November 2011, Oregon Governor John Kitzhaber imposed a moratorium on executions as long as he remains in office, declaring that Oregon's death penalty system fails basic standards of justice.

U.S. Supreme Court decisions also affected some state death penalty laws during this decade. In 2002, the Supreme Court declared in *Ring v. Arizona* that a defendant has the right to have a jury decide whether an aggravating factor exists that would render the defendant eligible for the death penalty. The court held that a death sentence, based on a judge's determination that aggravating factors exist, violates a defendant's constitutional right to a jury trial. This decision prompted a number of states to amend their death penalty legislation to

Lawyers Barry Scheck and Peter J. Neufeld of the Innocence Project, a nonprofit legal clinic that uses post-conviction DNA evidence testing to yield proof of innocence. Created in 1992, the project has totaled 289 exonerations; 222 of these since 2000.

Virginia Tech students attend a memorial service for the 32 students and faculty that were killed during the April 16, 2007, school shooting. The lone shooter committed the deadliest mass shooting in modern U.S. history.

provide for jury determinations of aggravating factors.

In *Atkins v. Virginia* (2002), the Supreme Court held that the execution of a mentally handicapped individual was unconstitutional, finding that a national consensus had developed against it. In light of what it saw as evolving standards of decency, such executions were found excessive and therefore constituted cruel and unusual punishment under the Eighth Amendment to the U.S. Constitution. The court explained that mentally handicapped criminals are not exempt from criminal sanctions, but because they have diminished personal culpability, they face a special risk of wrongful execution. The court found the percentage of states that had eliminated the death penalty for mentally handicapped individuals persuasive. While not dispositive of the issue, the court also considered evidence of the opposition to such executions by a variety of religious and professional organizations as well as the world community to be supportive, along with polling results reflecting that a similar consensus existed among the American public. This 2002 decision overruled the court's prior decision in *Penry v. Lynaugh* (1989), which upheld the execution of mentally handicapped individuals, noting that a national consensus against such executions had not been demonstrated.

In 2005, the U.S. Supreme Court ruled in *Roper v. Simmons* that imposing the death sentence for crimes committed when a defendant was younger than 18 years of age constituted cruel and unusual punishment in violation of the Eighth Amendment of the U.S. Constitution. Prior to this ruling, 71 offenders were on death row for murders committed as juveniles. Two-thirds of these individuals were offenders of color, and more than two-thirds of their victims were white. Texas had the largest percentage of juvenile offenders—40 percent—on death row. In *Roper v. Simmons*, the Supreme Court overruled its prior decision in *Stanford v. Kentucky* (1989), which upheld the death penalty for crimes committed at or about the age of 16. In doing so, the Court again utilized the "evolving standard of decency" test and cited research establishing that juveniles lack the maturity and sense of responsibility of adults.

The complexity of the national debate about the death penalty and the underlying racial fault lines were brought into sharp relief on September 22, 2011. On that day, Georgia executed Troy Davis, an African American man accused of shooting white off-duty police officer Mark McPhail; and Texas executed Lawrence Brewer, a self-professed white racist who was involved with two friends in an attack on an African

American man, James Byrd Jr., who was chained to the back of a pickup truck and dragged to his death. The latter crime led to new state and federal hate crime legislation.

Davis professed his innocence up to the moment before his execution and, after several key witnesses recanted their testimony, his case prompted outraged protests around the world, including from prominent individuals such as former President Jimmy Carter and the Reverend Al Sharpton, and from groups such as the American Bar Association and Amnesty International. Lawrence Brewer also protested his innocence, admitting his participation in the attack on James Byrd, but insisting that he did not kill him.

Gallup polling reveals that the average American's level of support for the imposition of the death penalty in cases of murder held roughly steady throughout the decade at 64 percent of the population. Similarly, for most of this decade, Americans have been split almost equally on this question of whether death or life imprisonment without the possibility of parole were better sanctions for murder.

School Shootings and Juvenile Crime
Dealing with juvenile crime continued to provide challenges for law enforcement and criminal justice officials during the last decade. In the wake of the 1999 Columbine High School massacre, the U.S. Secret Service conducted a review of 37 school shootings in the United States, examining local investigative files involving the attacks and interviewing 10 attackers. In May 2002, the resulting federal *Safe School Initiative* report concluded that not only were most school shootings planned, others also knew about these plans in advance. While no common profile of school shooters emerged, the majority of shooters exhibited warning signs, had been bullied or harassed, had suffered a recent loss or failure, and had access to weapons prior to the attacks. Therefore, school and law enforcement officials were advised to remain vigilant for such early warning signs and take them very seriously. Many schools have instituted "zero tolerance" policies, severely disciplining students who make threats or bring anything to school remotely resembling a weapon; however, some experts warn that such zero tolerance policies may be counterproductive to the goal of encouraging students to come forward if they hear or see anything worrisome or suspicious.

The Columbine massacre prompted changes across the nation in police responses to situations involving an active school shooter. Instead of surrounding the building and containing the situation, police are now trained to take a more active approach to find and "neutralize" the shooter as quickly as possible. This new "active shooter protocol" involves a small team of ideally four officers in a diamond pattern moving toward the sound of gunfire and ignoring any victims they may pass in an attempt to prevent further injury and loss of life.

On April 16, 2007, the deadliest shooting in American history involving a single gunman occurred on the campus of Virginia Polytechnic Institute and State University (Virginia Tech) in Blacksburg, Virginia. Mentally disturbed student Seung-Hui Cho opened fire in two separate locations on the campus, killing five faculty members and 27 students, and wounding 17 others, before committing suicide. Cho suffered from a severe anxiety disorder and had been adjudicated as mentally ill following a stalking incident on campus in 2005. However, Virginia Tech officials were unaware of Cho's mental condition due to federal privacy laws. As a result of these attacks, changes in state law were adopted to make it easier to detect individuals who were adjudicated as mentally ill and to prevent them from buying handguns via the National Instant Criminal Background Check System (NCIS). On January 5, 2008, President George W. Bush signed a federal gun control law strengthening the NCIS.

During the 1990s, a rise in juvenile crime prompted many states to pass laws to create a stronger deterrent to such crime by automatically routing juvenile offenders to the adult criminal justice system for more serious crimes with aggravating circumstances. Subsequent studies indicate that diversion of juveniles from rehabilitative juvenile programs to punitive adult correctional facilities teaches juveniles to become violent, habitual criminals and renders them vulnerable to physical and sexual abuse. Juveniles held in adult correctional institutions are five times more likely to be sexually assaulted than those in juvenile facilities. Thus, many have argued that the deterrent effect of trying juveniles as adults appears to be minimal or nonexistent and actually may contribute to higher recidivism rates. Youth who have been transferred to the adult corrections system recidivate at a higher rate than those managed in the juvenile justice system, and such incarceration increases the difficulty of achieving attitudinal and behavioral changes in juvenile offenders. An open question remains as to what age juveniles attain adult mental capacity, making a determination about the appropriate treatment of juvenile offenders even more challenging. The practice of incarcerating juveniles in adult prisons has also been criticized as having an unfair impact on African American youth.

Violent street gangs represented a growing threat to public safety during the decade. In 2009, 28,100 gangs and 731,000 gang members were identified in 3,500 jurisdictions across the country, representing a 20 percent increase in the growth of gangs since 2002. As gang members move from prison out to communities and back to prison, the boundaries between prison and street gangs blur. In 2007, in an effort to deter and reduce violent gang crime, Congress passed the Gang Deterrence and Community Protection Act, imposing mandatory sentences for specific violent crimes and providing for the forfeiture of property used in the furtherance of, or acquired as a result of, violent gang crime.

Alternatives to incarceration of juveniles include rehabilitation programs that provide vocational skills training, substance abuse treatment, and education about responsibility to victims through restorative justice processes. Some communities employ special problem-solving courts focusing on specific issues such as drug abuse, gun possession, and mental health problems. Nonviolent crimes may be prosecuted in teen courts, where juveniles are judged by a jury of their peers. In cities such as Los Angeles, juveniles committing hate crimes—offenses motivated by hatred of a victim due to race, ethnicity, national origin, handicap, religion, or sexual orientation—are placed in programs like Juvenile Offenders Learning Tolerance to educate and rehabilitate them.

Problem-Solving Courts and Restorative Justice

The decade saw significant growth in the establishment of various problem-solving courts and restorative justice programs throughout the country. Restorative or reparative justice programs operate from the philosophy that crime is an offense not against the state but against victims and their communities. Therefore, restorative justice programs encourage offenders to accept responsibility for their crimes and the resulting harm to their victims and their communities, and to repair that harm through apology, restitution, and/or community service. Restorative justice programs can serve as alternatives to a traditional criminal justice system and are sometimes supplemental, voluntary programs available to incarcerated individuals and their victims. These programs have been especially useful in diverting juveniles from entering the formal criminal justice system. Some states have passed statutes requiring the use of restorative justice programs as alternatives to traditional criminal justice methods of sanctioning crimes.

Community courts are neighborhood-based courts that address local criminal offenses via a problem-solving partnership with community stakeholders, such as schools, churches, and local merchants. Community courts currently exist in 13 states and the District of Columbia; most were established within the last decade. Typically, these courts deal with minor criminal offenses; in sanctioning offenders, alternatives to jail sentences, such as service to the community harmed by the offender's criminal conduct, are utilized. Sometimes, these courts take proactive steps to address crime prevention in their communities, using a collaborative, problem-solving model that strengthens relationships between criminal justice institutions and the communities they serve.

Problem-solving courts focus on finding alternatives to incarceration in dealing with specific social problems such as drug abuse, domestic violence, child neglect, youthful offenders, mentally ill offenders, offenders struggling with reentry to the community after serving a prison term, and veterans charged with crimes. In drug courts, for example, offenders are ordered into treatment programs; in mental health courts, offenders are ordered to take their medications regularly and are provided support services. These courts look beyond the individual offenders and attempt to implement solutions that will benefit both the offender and the community as a whole.

A related program is community prosecution, which involves prosecutors working with community stakeholders to develop strategies to address issues of pubic safety and crime, often working out of offices located within affected communities. This prosecutorial approach, related to community policing, has been found to strengthen community members' investment in solutions to local crime and safety issues and improve their confidence in the criminal justice system. The job performances of prosecutors are not evaluated based on the number of convictions they obtain or the number of offenders

Sandia National Laboratories researcher Dave Hannum demonstrates the Hound system. In south Texas, a variety of law enforcement organizations use the handheld sniffer to detect narcotics shipments in vehicles at checkpoints; locate nitro, heroin, cocaine, and marijuana in schools; seize drug money going into Mexico; and even save lives. The development of new technology has had a profound impact on criminal justice during this period.

they send to prison, but rather on their collaborative relationship with the community in which they work and the productive solutions they succeed in crafting.

Scientific studies on the effectiveness of these various alternative justice programs to improve public safety are needed. While there seems to be consensus that these programs improve relations between the criminal justice system and the surrounding community, and provide cost savings in diverting offenders from serving expensive jail or prison time, the few studies that have investigated effects on recidivism and crime rates have yielded mixed results.

Conclusion

The development of new technology and scientific techniques, as well as collaborative community models such as problem-solving courts, are transforming the U.S. criminal justice system in many ways. As the county's economy improves, it is yet to be seen whether the budget-conscious reforms of state correctional systems will continue. As more studies of the effectiveness of new evidence-based practices and collaborative community models are conducted, it will become evident whether these innovations yield the hoped-for results.

Susan J. Tyburski
Women's College of the University of Denver

Excerpt From Department of Justice Report on Anthrax Attacks

Only a week after the 9/11 attacks, letters were sent to major media outlets proclaiming "DEATH TO AMERICA, DEATH TO ISRAEL, ALLAH IS GREAT" and containing a coarse brown powder of anthrax spores. More letters followed three weeks later, to Democratic Senators Tom Daschle and Patrick Leahy, containing the same message and a more highly refined anthrax powder. At least 22 people developed anthrax infections, and five died; none of those infected were the intended recipients of the letters. When decoded, the letters included yielded a message in the three-letter sequences "FNY" (believed to mean "f--- New York") and PAT (a colleague of Bruce Ivins, the suspect eventually prosecuted). Ivins, who neither confessed to the crime nor explicitly denied being connected, committed suicide the same month that he was informed of the investigation. The findings of the report have been challenged, particularly the handling of the scientific evidence, and Government Accountability Office and the National Academy of Science have both said that criticisms of the investigation raised by technical articles should be addressed.

The United States Department of Justice

Amerithrax Investigative Summary
Released Pursuant to the Freedom of Information Act

Friday, February 19, 2010

This Investigative Summary sets forth much of the evidence that was developed in the Amerithrax investigation.[1] In the fall of 2001, the anthrax letter attacks killed five people and sickened 17 others. Upon the death of the first victim of that attack, agents from the Federal Bureau of Investigation ("FBI") and the United States Postal Inspection Service ("USPIS") immediately formed a Task Force and spent seven years investigating the crime.

The Amerithrax investigation is described below. In its early stages, despite the enormous amount of evidence gathered through traditional law enforcement techniques, limitations on scientific methods prevented law enforcement from determining who was responsible for the attacks. Eventually, traditional law enforcement techniques were combined with groundbreaking scientific analysis that was developed specifically for the case to trace the anthrax used in the attacks to a particular flask of material. By 2007, investigators conclusively determined that a single spore-batch created and maintained by Dr. Bruce E. Ivins at the United States Army Medical Research Institute of Infectious Diseases ("USAMRIID") was the parent material for the letter spores. An intensive investigation of individuals with access to that material ensued. Evidence developed from that investigation established that Dr. Ivins, alone, mailed the anthrax letters.

By the summer of 2008, the United States Attorney's Office for the District of Columbia was preparing to seek authorization to ask a federal grand jury to return an indictment charging Dr. Ivins with Use of a Weapon of Mass Destruction, in violation of Title 18, United States Code, Section 2332a, and related charges. However, before that process was completed, he committed suicide. Aware of the FBI investigation and the prospect of being indicted, Dr. Ivins took an overdose of over-the-counter medications on or about July 26, 2008, and died on July 29, 2008. Administrative and investigative steps taken in the past year toward closure of the investigation confirm the conclusion that Dr. Ivins perpetrated the anthrax letter attacks.

I. THE ANTHRAX LETTER ATTACKS

In September and October 2001, at least five envelopes containing significant quantities of *Bacillus anthracis* (also referred to as "*Ba*") were mailed to United States Senators Patrick

Leahy and Thomas Daschle in the District of Columbia, and to media organizations located in New York City and Boca Raton, Florida. Each of the envelopes contained a photocopy of the following handwritten note:

[not included in public document]

Letters to "Tom Brokaw NBC TV" and "Editor New York Post"

09-11-01

THIS IS NEXT TAKE PENACILIN NOW

DEATH TO AMERICA DEATH TO ISRAEL

ALLAH IS GREAT

Letters to "Senator Leahy" and "Senator Daschle"

09-11-01

YOU CAN NOT STOP US. WE HAVE THIS ANTHRAX. YOU DIE NOW. ARE YOU AFRAID?

DEATH TO AMERICA. DEATH TO ISRAEL. ALLAH IS GREAT.

(*See* Attachments A and B.)

The two letters addressed to Senators Leahy and Daschle had the same, later determined to be fictitious, return address: "4TH GRADE, GREENDALE SCHOOL, FRANKLIN PARK NJ 08852." *See* Attachment C. The letters addressed to the New York Post and Tom Brokaw contained no return address. *See* Attachment D. It appears that at least one more envelope was sent to the American Media, Inc. ("AMI") building, located in Boca Raton, Florida. A contemporaneous anthrax outbreak occurred in that facility, as well as contamination at the postal facilities serving AMI; however, no envelope was ever recovered from AMI.

At least 22 victims contracted anthrax as a result of the mailings. Eleven individuals contracted inhalational anthrax by inhaling *Bacillus anthracis* spores and another 11 suffered cutaneous anthrax by absorbing it through the skin. Five of the inhalational victims died from their infections: (1) Robert Stevens, 63, photo editor, AMI, Boca Raton, Florida, died on October 5, 2001; (2) Thomas L. Morris, Jr., 55, postal worker, Brentwood Post Office, Washington, D.C., died on October 21, 2001; (3) Joseph P. Curseen, Jr., 47, postal worker, Brentwood Post Office, Washington, D.C., died on October 22, 2001; (4) Kathy T. Nguyen, 61, hospital employee, New York City, died on October 31, 2001; and (5) Ottilie Lundgren, 94, Oxford, Connecticut, died on November 21, 2001. Another 31 people tested positive for exposure to anthrax spores. Ten thousand more people, deemed "at risk" from possible exposure, underwent antibiotic prophylaxis.

Thirty-five postal facilities and commercial mailrooms were contaminated. The presence of *Bacillus anthracis* was detected in seven of 26 buildings tested on Capitol Hill. From October through December 2001, the Laboratory Response Network tested more than 120,000 clinical and environmental samples for the presence of *Bacillus anthracis*. The U.S. Postal Service closed two heavily contaminated processing and distribution centers ("P&DC"): Trenton P&DC, located in Hamilton, New Jersey; and Brentwood P&DC, located in Washington, D.C. The Brentwood facility, closed on October 21, 2001, did not become operational again until December 22, 2003. The Trenton facility, which was closed on October 18, 2001, reopened on March 14, 2005. More than 1.8 million letters, packages, magazines, catalogs, and other mailed items were quarantined at these two facilities. The Environmental Protection Agency used $27 million from its Superfund program to pay 27 contractors and three federal and state agencies for the cleanup of the Capitol Hill facilities.

All of these infections and exposures that occurred in fall 2001 resulted from the anthrax mailings described above. All of the anthrax was mailed over a short period of time to locations where all infected individuals were likely exposed. Many of the victims shared places of employment, and the bodies of the five deceased victims all contained the same strain of anthrax. This strain, known as "Ames," was isolated in Texas in 1981, and then shipped to USAMRIID, where it was maintained thereafter. Another natural outbreak of Ames has never again been recorded.

The evidence (as outlined in the time line below) supports the conclusion that the mail attacks occurred on two separate occasions. The two letters used in the first attack were postmarked on September 18, 2001, and were sent to Tom Brokaw at NBC News and to the New York Post, both located in New York City. Three weeks later, two letters postmarked October 9, 2001 were mailed to Senators Daschle and Leahy at their Washington, D.C. offices. Hard evidence of the attacks surfaced on October 3, 2001, when Robert Stevens, the AMI employee who worked in Boca Raton, Florida, was diagnosed as having contracted inhalational anthrax, an infection from which he later died.

Time Line of Offense

9/17-18/01 Letters to New York Post and Brokaw mailed sometime between 5 p.m. on 9/17 and noon the following day.

9/18/01 Letters to New York Post and Brokaw postmarked in Trenton, NJ.

10/3/01 Robert Stevens (AMI employee in Boca Raton, FL) diagnosed with pneumonia; rod-shaped bacteria consistent with anthrax noted in medical report.

10/4/01 Announcement made that Stevens had contracted anthrax.

10/5/01 Stevens died from inhalational anthrax in Boca Raton, FL.

10/6-9/01 Letters to Senators Daschle and Leahy mailed sometime between 3 p.m. on 10/6 and noon three days later.

10/9/01 Letters to Senators Daschle and Leahy postmarked in Trenton, NJ.

10/12/01 Letter to Brokaw recovered by FBI.

10/15/01 Letter to Senator Daschle opened in Hart Senate Office Building.

10/19/01 Letter to New York Post discovered and recovered.

10/21/01 Thomas Morris died (Brentwood Postal Facility employee in Washington, D.C.).

10/22/01 Joseph Curseen, Jr. died (Brentwood Postal Facility employee in Washington, D.C.).

10/31/01 Kathy Nguyen died (New York City, NY).

11/16/01 Letter to Senator Leahy discovered and recovered.

11/21/01 Ottilie Lundgren died in Connecticut (believed to be the result of cross-contaminated mail).

II. EXECUTIVE SUMMARY

A. Overview of the Amerithrax Investigation

Once the first victim, Robert Stevens, was identified, and the letters were recovered from the New York and Washington crime scenes, the FBI began its investigation through its Miami, New York, Newark, New Haven, Baltimore and Washington, D.C. field offices. The Washington Field Office ("WFO") became the lead office, and the "Amerithrax Task Force" was established, comprised of FBI Special Agents and United States Postal Inspectors, as well as various other law enforcement officers. The ensuing criminal investigation was extraordinarily complex, given the possible breadth and scope of this bioterrorism attack. In the seven years following the attack, the Amerithrax Task Force expended over 600,000 investigator work hours, involving in excess of 10,000 witness interviews conducted on six continents, the execution of 80 searches, and the recovery of over 6,000 items of potential evidence. The case involved the issuance of over 5,750 federal grand jury subpoenas and the collection of 5,730 environmental samples from 60 site locations. Several overseas site locations also were examined for relevant evidence with the cooperation of the respective host governments.

During its tenure, the Task Force generally was staffed by 25 to 30 full-time investigators from the FBI and the USPIS, as well as prosecutors from the United States Attorney's Office for the District of Columbia. The investigators scrutinized more than 1,000 individuals as possible suspects, located both at home and abroad. The investigation benefitted significantly from the assistance and cooperation of 29 government, university, and commercial laboratories, which augmented FBI Laboratory efforts to develop the physical, chemical, genetic, and forensic profiles of the anthrax spores, letters and envelopes used in the attacks.

In the early years of the investigation, the Task Force did not know whether the letters were a state-sponsored act of terrorism, the work of an international terrorist organization or a domestic-based group, or were isolated acts. Much of the early efforts focused on attempting to classify genetically the spores used in the mailings and to track the envelopes and the letters used to their source. These investigative initiatives took considerable time, as genetic laboratory tests needed to be developed and validated, and traditional forensic means of examination of the letters were significantly hampered by the fact that these items were contaminated by anthrax spores.

At the same time, investigators were culling through lists of possible suspects, based on likely profiles including: scientific ability, laboratory access to the Ames strain of *Bacillus anthracis*, proximity and other links to Princeton, NJ (from which the letters were mailed), suspicious behavior, tips from the public and the scientific community, and possible motivation or incentive to commit such a crime. Task Force agents conducted interviews, and examined business records and publicly available corporate information, such as Securities and Exchange Commission filings, to identify any business that may have been motivated to commit the anthrax attacks for financial gain. The Task Force also launched initiatives to examine industries—such as the bio-pharmaceutical, bio-pesticide and agricultural/veterinary industries—for possible suspects, given their areas of expertise and the equipment they utilized. After thorough investigation using traditional law enforcement techniques, virtually all of the identified individuals were eventually ruled out.

In 2007, after several years of scientific developments and advanced genetic testing coordinated by the FBI Laboratory, the Task Force determined that the spores in the letters were derived from a single spore-batch of Ames strain anthrax called "RMR-1029." RMR-1029 had been created and maintained by Dr. Bruce E. Ivins at USAMRIID. This was a groundbreaking development in the investigation. It allowed the investigators to reduce drastically the number of possible suspects, because only a very limited number of individuals had ever had access to this specific spore preparation that was housed at USAMRIID. The Task Force then began applying traditional law enforcement techniques to a very limited universe.

B. The Elimination of Dr. Steven J. Hatfill as a Suspect

In August 2002, it became widely known that Dr. Steven J. Hatfill was a person of interest to the Task Force. Early in the investigation, numerous individuals who suspected that he might be involved in the letter attacks contacted the FBI. While working as a researcher at USAMRIID from 1997 to 1999, Dr. Hatfill had virtually unrestricted access to the Ames strain of anthrax, the same strain used in the 2001 mailings. Dr. Hatfill also appeared to know the intricacies of conducting a successful anthrax dissemination by mail, although it was not uncommon for those in the biodefense community to develop such scenarios for training exercises. In addition, he had filled multiple prescriptions for the antibiotic Cipro®

in 2001, which was the only drug approved by the Food and Drug Administration for the treatment of inhalational anthrax; however, its use also was consistent with treatment for a persistent infection from which Dr. Hatfill was suffering at the time.

Ultimately, the FBI's genetic analysis of the organism used in the attacks led investigators to exclude him conclusively as a suspect. Early in the investigation, it was assumed that isolates of the Ames strain were accessible to any individual at USAMRIID with access to the biocontainment labs. Later in the investigation, when scientific breakthroughs led investigators to conclude that RMR-1029 was the parent material to the anthrax powder used in the mailings, it was determined that Dr. Hatfill could not have been the mailer because he never had access to the particular bio-containment suites at USAMRIID that held the RMR-1029. In other words, although Dr. Hatfill had access to Ames strain anthrax while at USAMRIID, he never had access to the particular spore-batch used in the mailings.

C. Summary of the Investigation of Dr. Bruce E. Ivins

Armed with new evidence from the scientific breakthroughs, the Task Force focused its investigation on those researchers who had access to the lab at USAMRIID where RMR-1029 was being stored between September 11 and 18, 2001, and again between October 1 and 8, 2001—the windows of opportunity to have processed and mailed the anthrax used to commit the crime. All of these individuals were interviewed and, when appropriate, polygraphed. The Task Force checked out alibis and examined laboratory notebooks and other records. For each of these individuals, an assessment was made of whether each possessed the requisite skill to produce and dry such concentrated, pure *anthracis* spores. The Task Force conducted searches of home and work computers and examined e-mails. Evidence obtained from these and several other investigative efforts helped rule out all of the other persons with access to RMR-1029, and demonstrated that Dr. Bruce Ivins committed the crime[2].

Investigators learned that Dr. Ivins was alone late at night and on the weekend in the lab where RMR-1029 was stored in the days immediately preceding the dates on which the anthrax could have been mailed. Before the anthrax mailings, Dr. Ivins had never exhibited that pattern of working alone in the lab extensively during non-business hours, and he never did so after the anthrax attacks. When confronted, he was unable to give a legitimate explanation for keeping these unusual and, in the context of the investigation, suspicious hours.

As investigators reviewed Dr. Ivins's voluminous e-mails, including e-mails during the time frame of the anthrax attacks, it became clear that he was suffering from significant psychological problems, which not only further concerned the investigators, but also contributed to their increasing scrutiny and monitoring of him. Investigators obtained authorization to place pen registers[3] on Dr. Ivins's home and work telephones and e-mail accounts, and obtained consent to analyze his home computer hard drives. The Task Force examined his Internet searches and postings and reviewed his e-mail communications from both his personal and USAMRIID computer (with the approval of the Commander at USAMRIID). A GPS device was installed on his car, interviews with his associates were conducted, his trash was regularly searched, and confidential sources were used to gather further information.

By the fall of 2007, agents and prosecutors concluded that they had exhausted the results that could be obtained from using covert investigative tools. Increasingly persuaded that Dr. Ivins was involved in the anthrax attacks, agents obtained search warrants for his residence in Frederick, Maryland, his cars, and his office at USAMRIID, mindful that this would confirm for Dr. Ivins that he was a subject of the investigation. On November 1, 2007, the Task Force executed these search warrants, which resulted in the recovery of numerous items of interest, including a large collection of letters that Dr. Ivins had sent to members of Congress and the news media over the previous 20 years—including one sent to NBC News in 1987 at the same address for NBC used on the Brokaw letter. They also recovered three handguns, two stun guns, a taser, an electronic detection device, computer snooping software, and evidence that portions of the basement were being used as a firing range.

The link between the intended recipients of the seized letters and the recipients of the anthrax attack letters—members of Congress and the news media—was further evidence implicating Dr. Ivins in the anthrax attacks. Searches of his trash and e-mail accounts in the spring of 2008 produced additional evidence linking Dr. Ivins to the anthrax letters. Task Force agents and prosecutors also conducted three interviews with Dr. Ivins with his lawyers present: the first two were "on-the-record" interviews that took place in January and February 2008, and the last was an "off-the-record" debriefing that occurred in June 2008. On July 12, 2008, Task Force agents again searched the Ivins residence, based on new evidence that he had made specific threats in a group therapy session on July 9, 2008. During the search of his residence they recovered a bullet-proof vest, together with a homemade reinforced body armor plate, hundreds of rounds of ammunition, and smokeless handgun powder. Agents also interviewed counselors who had treated Dr. Ivins, including the two therapists present during the group therapy session, in an effort to assess the seriousness of his threats to harm individuals involved in the investigation.

In the months that followed the suicide of Dr. Ivins, investigators continued their review of thousands of e-mails going back ten years, and examined additional evidence that developed in the aftermath of his death. In addition, investigators sought and obtained court orders authorizing access to his mental health records, and interviews of various mental health providers who had treated Dr. Ivins in the past.[4]

[1] Information derived from sources such as the federal grand jury investigation, sealed court orders, and an "off-the-record" interview of Dr. Bruce E. Ivins, while contributing to the overall investigation, is omitted from this Investigative Summary.

[2] Dr. Ivins had transferred small quantities of live, virulent RMR-1029 to two other domestic labs between the time of its creation in October 1997 and the 2001 mailings. Any individual with potential access to those samples during that time also was thoroughly investigated and ruled out using these same methods.

[3] A pen-register, along with a trap-and-trace, allows law enforcement to monitor which phone numbers are being dialed by a particular phone line, as well as which numbers are calling into that phone line. For e-mail accounts, it provides the e-mail accounts that are in communication with the target e-mail account.

[4] The results of that record collection and follow-up interviews remain under seal at this time.

Source: http://www.justice.gov/amerithrax

See Articles: Bush, George W. (Administration of); Kaczynski, Ted; McVeigh, Timothy; Murder, Contemporary; Terrorism.

2002 PRIMARY DOCUMENT

Human Rights Watch Letter to President Bush Regarding Torture

In a December 25, 2002, Washington Post article, anonymous Central Intelligence Agency sources confirmed the use of "stress and duress" techniques during the interrogation of detainees during the ongoing War on Terror. The story of torture inflicted by American agents in the various events and conflicts following 9/11 has continued to unfold. Degrading treatment of prisoners has been alleged or confirmed in Abu Ghraib, Guantanamo Bay, and the Bagram Collection Point, with little evidence of any gains to intelligence.

December 26, 2002
President George W. Bush
The White House
1600 Pennsylvania Avenue, NW
Washington, DC 20500

Dear President Bush:
Human Rights watch is deeply concerned by allegations of torture and other mistreatment of suspected al-Qaeda detainees described in the Washington Post ("U.S. Decries Abuse but Defends Interrogations") on December 26. The allegations, if true, would place the United States in violation of some of the most fundamental prohibitions of international human rights law. Any U.S. government official who is directly involved or complicit in the torture or mistreatment of detainees, including any official who knowingly acquiesces in the commission of such acts, would be subject to prosecution worldwide.

Human Rights Watch urges you to take immediate steps to clarify that the use of torture is not U.S. policy, investigate the Washington Post's allegations, adopt all necessary measures to end any ongoing violations of international law, stop the rendition of detainees to countries where they are likely to be tortured, and prosecute those implicated in such abuse.

I. Prohibitions Against Torture

The Washington Post reports that persons held in the CIA interrogation centers at Bagram air base in Afghanistan are subject to "stress and duress" techniques including "standing or kneeling for hours" and being "held in awkward, painful positions." The Post notes that the detention facilities at Bagram and elsewhere, such as at Diego Garcia, are not monitored by the International Committee Red Cross, which has monitored the U.S. treatment of detainees at Guantanamo Bay, Cuba.

The absolute prohibition against torture is a fundamental and well-established precept of customary and conventional international law. Torture is never permissible against anyone, whether in times of peace or of war.

The prohibition against torture is firmly established under international human rights law. It is prohibited by various treaties to which the United States is a party, including the International Covenant on Civil and Political Rights (ICCPR), which the United States ratified in 1992, and the Convention against Torture and Other Cruel, Inhuman or Degrading Treatment or Punishment, which the United States ratified in 1994. Article 7 of the ICCPR states that "No one shall be subjected to torture or to cruel, inhuman or degrading treatment or punishment." The right to be protected from torture is non-derogable, meaning that it applies at all times, including during public emergencies or wartime.

International humanitarian law (the laws of war), which applies during armed conflict, prohibits the torture or other mistreatment of captured combatants and others in captivity, regardless of their legal status. Regarding prisoners-of-war, article 17 of the Third Geneva Convention of 1949 states: "No physical or mental torture, nor any other form of coercion, may be inflicted on prisoners of war to secure from them information of any kind whatever. Prisoners of war who refuse to answer may not be threatened, insulted, or exposed to any unpleasant or disadvantageous treatment of any kind." Detained civilians are similarly protected by article 32 of the Fourth Geneva Convention. The United States has been a party to the 1949 Geneva Conventions since 1955.

The United States does not recognize captured al-Qaeda members as being protected by the 1949 Geneva Conventions, although Bush administration officials have insisted that detainees will be treated humanely and in a manner consistent with Geneva principles. However, at minimum, all detainees in wartime, regardless of their legal status, are protected by customary international humanitarian law. Article 75 ("Fundamental Guarantees") of the First Additional Protocol to the Geneva Conventions, which is recognized as restating customary international law, provides that "torture of all kinds, whether physical or mental" against "persons who are in the power of a Party to the conflict and who do not benefit from more favorable treatment under the (Geneva) Conventions," shall "remain prohibited at any time and in any place whatsoever, whether committed by civilian or military agents." "(C) ruel treatment and torture" of detainees is also prohibited under common article 3 to the 1949 Geneva Conventions, which is considered indicative of customary international law.

II. Possible U.S. Complicity in Torture

It is a violation of international law not only to use torture directly, but also to be complicit in torture committed by other governments. The Post being told by U.S. officials that "(t)housands have been arrested and held with U.S. assistance in countries known for brutal treatment of prisoners." The Convention against Torture provides in article 4 that all acts of torture, including "an act by any person which constitutes complicity or participation in torture," is an offense "punishable by appropriate penalties which take into account their grave nature."

The Post article describes the rendition of captured al-Qaeda suspects from U.S. custody to other countries where they are tortured or otherwise mistreated. This might also be a violation of the Convention against Torture, which in article 3 states: "No State Party shall expel, return ('refouler') or extradite a person to another State where there are substantial grounds for believing that he would be in danger of being subjected to torture....For the purpose of determining whether there are such grounds, the competent authorities shall take into account all relevant considerations including, where applicable, the existence in the State concerned of a consistent pattern of gross, flagrant or mass violations of human rights."

The U.S. Department of State annual report on human rights practices has frequently criticized torture in countries where detainees may have been sent. These include Uzbekistan, Pakistan, Egypt, Jordan and Morocco. The United States thus could not plausibly claim that it was unaware of the problem of torture in these countries.

III. International Prosecutions for Torture and Command Responsibility

Direct involvement or complicity in torture, as well as the failure to prevent torture, may subject U.S. officials to prosecution under international law.

The willful torture or inhuman treatment of prisoners-of-war or other detainees, including "willfully causing great suffering or serious injury to body or health," are "grave breaches" of the 1949 Geneva Conventions, commonly known as war crimes. Grave breaches are subject to universal jurisdiction, meaning that they can be prosecuted in any national criminal court and as well as any international tribunal with appropriate jurisdiction.

The Convention against Torture obligates States Parties to prosecute persons within their jurisdiction who are implicated or complicit in acts of torture. This obligation includes the prosecution of persons within their territory who committed acts of torture elsewhere and have not been extradited under procedures provided in the convention.

Should senior U.S. officials become aware of acts of torture by their subordinates and fail to take immediate and effective steps to end such practices, they too could be found criminally liable under international law. The responsibility of superior officers for atrocities by their subordinates is commonly known as command responsibility. Although the concept originated in military law, it now is increasingly accepted to include the responsibility of civil authorities for abuses committed by persons under their direct authority. The doctrine of command responsibility has been upheld in recent decisions by the international criminal tribunals for the former Yugoslavia and for Rwanda.

There are two forms of command responsibility: direct responsibility for orders that are unlawful and imputed responsibility, when a superior knows or should have known of crimes committed by a subordinate acting on his own initiative and fails to prevent or punish them. All states are obliged to bring such people to justice.

* * * * *

The allegations made by the Washington Post are extraordinarily serious. They have put the United States on notice that acts of torture may be taking place with U.S. participation or complicity. That creates a heightened duty to respond preventively. As an immediate step, we urge that you issue a presidential statement clarifying that it is contrary to U.S.

policy to use or facilitate torture. The Post's allegations should be investigated and the findings made public.

Should there be evidence of U.S. civilian or military officials being directly involved or complicit in torture, or in the rendition of persons to places where they are likely to be tortured, you should take immediate steps to prevent the commission of such acts and to prosecute the individuals who have ordered, organized, condoned, or carried them out. The United States also has a duty to refrain from sending persons to other countries with a history of torture without explicit and verifiable guarantees that no torture or mistreatment will occur.

Thank you for your attention to these concerns.

Sincerely,
Kenneth Roth
Executive Director

Cc: Colin Powell, Secretary of State
Donald Rumsfeld. Secretary of Defense
Condoleeza Rice, National Security Advisor

Source: National Security Archive

See Articles: Bush, George W. (Administration of); Cruel and Unusual Punishment; Federal Prisons; Terrorism; Torture.

2004 PRIMARY DOCUMENT

Department of Justice Press Release on the Charges Against Kenneth Lay

The Enron accounting scandal detailed in this press release was one of the largest in history and led to the company's bankruptcy in December 2001, the largest corporate bankruptcy until the fall of WorldCom. Multiple executives were indicted, and accounting firm Arthur Andersen LLP was found guilty of obstruction of justice. The Sarbanes–Oxley Act was passed to increase auditing accountability. In 2006, Kenneth Lay was found guilty of 10 counts; he died of a heart attack before his sentencing.

FORMER ENRON CHAIRMAN AND CHIEF EXECUTIVE OFFICER KENNETH L. LAY CHARGED WITH CONSPIRACY, FRAUD, FALSE STATEMENTS

Money Laundering Charges Added Against Former Cao Richard Causey

WASHINGTON, D.C.—Deputy Attorney General James B. Comey, Assistant Attorney General Christopher A. Wray of the Criminal Division, FBI Director Robert Mueller, and Enron Task Force Director Andrew Weissmann announced today that a federal grand jury in Houston has indicted former Enron Corp. Chairman and Chief Executive Officer Kenneth L. Lay on charges of conspiracy, securities fraud, wire fraud, bank fraud and making false statements.

A superseding indictment returned by the grand jury in Houston Wednesday, and unsealed today, charges Lay, 62, of Houston, with conspiracy to commit securities fraud, four counts of securities fraud and two counts of wire fraud, one count of bank fraud and three counts of making false statements to a bank. The superseding indictment joins Lay as a defendant in a case pending against former Enron CEO Jeffrey K. Skilling and former Enron Chief Accounting Officer Richard Causey.

Causey was originally indicted in January 2004, and Skilling was added to the case in February 2004.

The new indictment also adds a money laundering conspiracy count and four counts of money laundering against Causey in connection with fraudulent hedging vehicles, and expands certain factual allegations against Causey in connection with the securities fraud conspiracy. The case is pending before U.S. District Judge Sim Lake in Houston, Texas.

Lay surrendered this morning to FBI agents in Houston and the indictment was unsealed. Lay had an initial appearance this morning before Magistrate Judge Mary Milloy.

"The indictment charges that Lay, Skilling, Causey and others oversaw a massive conspiracy to cook the books at Enron and to create the illusion that it was a robust, growing company with limitless potential when, in fact, Enron was an increasingly troubled business kept afloat only by a series of deceptions," said Deputy Attorney General James B. Comey, who heads the President's Corporate Fraud Task Force. "These charges demonstrate the Department's commitment to the rule of law, its commitment to the principle that no one is above the law, and its commitment to unravel even the most complex of fraudulent schemes."

"This indictment alleges that every member of Enron's senior management participated in a criminal conspiracy to commit one of the largest corporate frauds in American history," said Assistant Attorney General Wray. "Kenneth Lay is charged with abusing his powerful position as Chairman of the Board and CEO and repeatedly lying in an effort to cover up the financial collapse that caused devastating harm to millions of Americans. The progress of this investigation shows that the Department of Justice will work tirelessly to hold corporate America to the high standards imposed by federal law."

"The collapse of Enron was devastating to tens of thousands of people and shook the public's confidence in corporate America," said FBI Director Mueller. "The FBI and our partners on the President's Corporate Fraud Task Force responded with a concerted effort to uncover the truth and to bring those responsible to justice. The charges against Ken Lay, Jeffrey Skilling and Richard Causey take us one step closer to restoring the public confidence in our financial markets." The indictment alleges that at various times between at least 1999 and 2001, Lay, Skilling, Causey and other Enron executives engaged in a wide-ranging scheme to deceive the investing public, the U.S. Securities and Exchange Commission and others about the true performance of Enron's businesses. The alleged scheme was designed to make it appear that Enron was growing at a healthy and predictable rate, consistent with analysts' published expectations, that Enron did not have significant write-offs or debt and was worthy of investment-grade credit rating, that Enron was comprised of a number of successful business units, and that the company had an appropriate cash flow. It had the effect of inflating artificially Enron's stock price, which increased from approximately $30 per share in early 1998 to over $80 per share in January 2001, and artificially stemming the decline of the stock during the first three quarters of 2001.

The indictment alleges that Lay had a significant profit motive for participating in the scheme. As stated in the indictment, between 1998 and 2001, Lay received approximately $300 million from the sale of Enron stock options and restricted stock, netting over $217 million in profit, and was paid more than $19 million in salary and bonuses. During 2001 alone, Lay received a salary of over $1 million, a bonus of $7 million and $3.6 million in long term incentive payments. Additionally, during the period of August 21 through Oct. 26, 2001, Lay sold 918,104 shares of Enron stock to repay advances totaling $26,025,000 he had received from a line of credit extended to Lay by Enron.

As a part of the alleged scheme, unrealistic and unattainable earnings goals were set for Enron, based on analysts' expectations rather than on actual or reasonably achievable business results. When, as expected within the company, Enron consistently fell short of those goals, Lay, Skilling, Causey and others allegedly orchestrated a series of accounting gimmicks designed to make up the shortfall between actual and predicted results. Enron then announced publicly that it had met or exceeded analysts' expectations when, as Lay, Skilling and Causey allegedly knew, it made its numbers only by engaging in fraud. The indictment also alleges that Lay, Skilling and Causey made false and misleading representations about Enron's finances and business operations to analysts, at press conferences, in SEC filings and elsewhere. Lay is principally charged for his conduct during the third quarter of 2001. As the indictment alleges, upon Skilling's abrupt departure from Enron in August 2001, Lay resumed his position as CEO of the company, intensified his oversight of Enron's day-to-day operations, and took control as leader of the conspiracy. Starting in August, according to the indictment, Lay was briefed extensively about mounting and undisclosed financial and operational problems, including overvaluation of Enron's assets and business units by several billion dollars. As a result of these and other issues confronting Enron, Lay privately considered a range of potential solutions, including mergers, restructurings, and even divestiture of Enron's pipelines, assets that Lay considered to be the crown jewels of the company. However, the indictment alleges he failed to disclose Enron's problems to the investing public and affirmatively misled the investing public about Enron's financial condition, while falsely claiming that he was disclosing everything that he had learned.

For example, the indictment states that during August 2001, Lay participated in Management Committee meetings at which reports were presented showing earnings shortfalls in virtually every Enron business unit, totaling approximately $1 billion. During early September 2001, Lay attended a Management Committee retreat in the Woodlands, Texas, at which the serious problems besetting Enron, including underperforming business units and troubled assets, were further discussed. Among other things, executives discussed the need to take in the third quarter of 2001 at least a $1 billion charge and that Enron had committed an accounting error in the amount of $1.2 billion.

The indictment alleges that throughout the remainder of September 2001, Lay engaged in a series of high-level meetings to discuss the growing financial crisis at Enron and the likely impact on Enron's credit rating. Among other things, Lay knew that the total amount of losses embedded in Enron's assets and business units was, at a minimum, $7 billion. Lay also knew that Enron's auditors had changed their position concerning the accounting treatment of four off-balance sheet vehicles called the Raptors, which required Enron to determine in short order whether an acceptable alternative methodology existed or whether, instead, Enron would have to restate its earnings and admit the error.

Despite knowing these negative facts, on Sept. 26, 2001, in an online forum with thousands of Enron employees, many of whom were investors in Enron stock, Lay allegedly stated that Enron was going to "hit [its] numbers." Lay allegedly created the false impression that his confidence in Enron's stock was such that he had increased his personal ownership of Enron stock in the past two months as a sign of his belief in what he was espousing. As the indictment alleges, during the prior two months, Lay actually purchased $4 million in Enron stock while also selling $24 million in Enron stock through nonpublic transactions.

The indictment states that in the weeks leading up to Enron's third quarter earnings release on Oct. 16, 2001, Lay determined that Enron could not publicly report a loss in excess of $1 billion without triggering negative action by Enron's credit rating agencies. Lay thus artificially capped Enron's losses to that amount. Also during this time, Lay learned that changes to the accounting rules governing goodwill (i.e., the difference between what Enron paid for an entity and the book value of that entity's net assets) would require Enron to disclose impairments to certain of its assets, including its interest in Wessex Water, a business located in Bath, England. In order to hide the impact of asset impairment, Lay allegedly claimed, falsely, that Enron was committed to engaging in a "water growth strategy," which would have required Enron to expend between $1 billion and $28 billion in capital investments in the water industry. Lay allegedly knew that Enron had no intention of pursuing such a strategy and did not have the capital to support it.

According to the indictment, on Oct.16, 2001, when Enron announced losses of approximately $1 billion, Lay allegedly sought to minimize the import of the reported losses by falsely describing the losses as "nonrecurring," that is, a one-time or unusual earnings event. Enron also disclosed the same day an approximate $1.2 billion reduction in shareholder equity, which Lay again sought to minimize by falsely attributing it to the unwind of the Raptor vehicles, rather than to an accounting error.

According to the indictment, on October 12, Lay misled a representative of a national credit rating agency about the need to take additional writedowns and the extent of Enron's goodwill problems. On both October 16 and 23, Lay told the investing public that Enron had determined that its goodwill impairment was up to $200 million. However, he failed to disclose the impact on Enron of an additional goodwill impairment of up to $700 million in connection with Wessex. Also on October 23, Lay allegedly espoused faith in Elektro, a Brazilian power plant which Enron carried on its books as worth in excess of $2 billion. In fact, as Lay allegedly knew, Elektro was overvalued by up to $1 billion. Lay also allegedly distributed materials at the road shows that misleadingly described the value of the international portfolio as $6.5 billion. In reality, as Lay knew, this vastly overstated the true value of the international assets by billions of dollars.

These and other schemes alleged in the indictment quickly unraveled, and on Dec. 2, 2001, Enron filed for bankruptcy, making its stock, which less than a year earlier had been trading at over $80 per share, virtually worthless.

Lay was also charged in four counts with bank fraud and making false statements to three banks arising out of his obtaining and using four personal lines of credit worth over $60 million. Lay allegedly promised the banks that the loans would not be used to purchase stock. As a result of these false representations, the banks extended far greater loans to Lay than they otherwise would. The indictment alleges that in spite of his promises, Lay repeatedly used the lines of credit to buy the stock. The lines of credit were collateralized mainly by artificially inflated shares of Enron stock and were repaid with the same.

If convicted of all the charges in the indictment, Lay faces a maximum sentence of 175 years in prison and millions of dollars in fines.

Criminal indictments are only charges and not evidence of guilt. A defendant is presumed to be innocent unless and until proven guilty.

The investigation into Enron's collapse is being conducted by the Enron Task Force, a team of federal prosecutors supervised by the Justice Department's Criminal Division and agents from the FBI and the IRS Criminal Investigations Division. The Task Force also has coordinated with and received considerable assistance from the Securities and Exchange Commission. The Enron Task Force is part of President Bush's Corporate Fraud Task Force, created in July 2002 to investigate allegations of fraud and corruption at U.S. corporations.

Thirty-one defendants have been charged to date, including 21 former Enron executives. Eleven defendants have been convicted to date, including former CFO Andrew Fastow and former Treasurer Ben Glisan. To date, the Enron Task Force has restrained more than $161 million in proceeds derived from criminal activity. The Task Force investigation is continuing.

Source: http://www.justice.gov/enron/index.html

See Articles: Enron; Justice, Department of; White-Collar Crime, Contemporary; White-Collar Crime, History of; White-Collar Crime, Sociology of.

2005 PRIMARY DOCUMENT

Report From the National Institute of Justice on La Cosa Nostra

The names La Cosa Nostra *and* Mafia *both refer to a type of crime syndicate originating in Sicily: an association of criminal organizations styled as families, each of which typically had control of a specific physical territory. Ties between families were more cultural than formal, and ties between the American and Sicilian Mafia groups were looser still. This overview of Mafia activities in the United States was drafted by the National Institute of Justice, a research agency within the Justice Department.*

Organizational Structure

La Cosa Nostra or LCN—also known as the Mafia, the mob, the outfit, the office—is a collection of Italian American organized crime "families" that has been operating in the United States since the 1920s. For nearly three quarters of a century, beginning during the time of Prohibition and extending into the 1990s, the LCN was clearly the most prominent criminal organization in the U.S. Indeed, it was synonymous with organized crime. In recent years, the LCN has been severely crippled by law enforcement, and over the past decade has been challenged in a number of its criminal markets by other organized crime groups. Nevertheless, with respect to those criteria that best define the harm capacity of criminal organizations, it is still pre-eminent. The LCN has greater capacity to gain monopoly control over criminal markets, to use or threaten violence to maintain that control, and to corrupt law enforcement and the political system than does any of its competitors. As one eminent scholar has also pointed out, "no other criminal organization [in the United States] has controlled labor unions, organized employer cartels, operated as a rationalizing force in major industries, and functioned as a bridge between the upperworld and the underworld" (Jacobs, 1999:128). It is this capacity that distinguishes the LCN from all other criminal organizations in the U.S.

Each of the so-called families that make up the LCN has roughly the same organizational structure. There is a boss who controls the family and makes executive decisions. There is an underboss who is second in command. There is a senior advisor or consigliere. And then there are a number of "capos" (caporegimes) who supervise crews made up of "soldiers," who are "made members" of Cosa Nostra. The capos and those above them receive shares of the proceeds from crimes committed by the soldiers and associates.

Made members, sometimes called good fellows or wise guys, are all male and all of Italian descent. The estimated made membership of the LCN is 1100 nationwide, with roughly eighty percent of the members operating in the New York metropolitan area. There are five crime families that make up the LCN in New York City: the Bonanno, the Colombo, the Genovese, the Gambino, and the Lucchese families. There is also LCN operational activity in Boston, Chicago, Philadelphia, and the Miami\South Florida area, but much less so than in New York. In other previous strongholds such as Cleveland, Detroit, Kansas City, Las Vegas, Los Angeles, New Orleans, and Pittsburgh, the LCN is now weak or non-existent. In addition to the made members, there are approximately 10,000 associate members who work for the families. Until the recent demise of much of its leadership, there was a Commission of the bosses of New York's five LCN families that coordinated control of labor unions, construction, trucking and garbage hauling companies, and that resolved disputes between families.

La Cosa Nostra does not enjoy general social acceptance and support. With the exception of a few ethnic Italian neighborhoods where certain of the more brazen exploits and some of the community "good deeds" of bosses are admired, Italian organized crime reinforces a stigma that most Italian Americans want to get rid of. Along with the effectiveness of law enforcement, the absence of support for the LCN means that recruitment has become difficult. Some families have disappeared, and others are only 50 percent to as little as 10 percent of their size 30 years ago. At the same time however, as with all organized crime, it is the community's desire for illicit goods and services that continues to help fuel the survival of the LCN.

Becoming a made member of LCN requires serving an apprenticeship and then being proposed by a Boss. This is followed by gaining approval for membership from all the other families. Once approved, there is a secret, ritualized induction ceremony. Made membership means both honor and increased income. It also, however, entails responsibilities—in particular taking an oath of omerta. Omerta demands silence to the outside world about the criminal affairs of the family, never betraying anyone in the family, and never revealing to law enforcement anything that might incriminate anyone in organized crime. The penalty for violating this oath is death. Any wise guy who takes a plea without authorization by the family runs the risk of the death penalty. That death is indeed used to enforce internal discipline is evidenced by the execution in 1998 of a capo in the Genovese crime family for pocketing money that should have been passed on to his superiors. An underworld source said about this missing capo: "The people they're looking to send a message to is not the general public. It's the mob itself, which totally understands that the guy is gone." At the same time, the fact that there are over a hundred members in the Federal witness protection program suggests that omerta is not nearly as effective as it once was.

Violence

La Cosa Nostra, over many years, established its reputation for the ruthless use of violence. This violence has occurred mostly in the form of beatings and killings. Personal violence, and to a lesser degree violence against property, e.g., bombings, arson, explosions, is the typical pattern of the systematic use of violence as a tool of doing business. Violence, and subsequently just the threat of violence, was the means by which the LCN gained monopoly control over its various criminal enterprises. It discouraged and eliminated competitors, and it reinforced the reputation and credibility of the LCN. Violence was and is also used for internal discipline. Law enforcement experts indicate that the threat of violence is at the core of LCN activities. Murder, or conspiracy to commit murder, has often appeared as one of the predicate offenses in RICO (Racketeer-Influenced and Corrupt Organizations) prosecutions.

That violence continues to be an LCN tool is evidenced in several cases within the past three years. The first two incidents were carried out at the behest of the former head of the Gambino crime family in New York, John Gotti. In a 1997 trial, a member of the Gambino family testified about a torture killing that had been ordered by Gotti. The victim had apparently fired a shot at Gotti. He was tortured with lighted cigarettes and a knife, shot in the buttocks, carried in the trunk of a car, and ultimately killed with five shots to the head. In the second example, the same John Gotti, from his federal prison cell, contracted with two members of the white supremacist group the Aryan Brotherhood to kill the former consigliere of the Gambino crime family who had threatened to kill him.

In a 1997 case that demonstrates the approach of the LCN with respect to the use of violence for retribution and intimidation, there was an LCN plot (not acted upon) to assassinate the federal judge who had presided over some of New York City's biggest mob trials. Finally, in 1999, a member of the Lucchese crime family (also based in New York) and others were charged with conducting a 15-year reign of terror against competitors in the private sanitation business. The charges included setting fire to trucks and buildings of rival carters, damaging businesses that dared to hire carters outside the LCN cartel, and killing a salesman for a rival carting company.

The history of violence and the LCN demonstrates the importance of reputation in this respect. Jacobs and Gouldin (1999) cite criminologist Peter Reuter's point that when there is sufficient credible evidence of the willingness to use violence, actually violence is rarely necessary. This is especially true when the targets are not professional criminals. La Cosa Nostra personifies this principle.

Economic Resources

Jacobs (1999) believes that one of the LCN's major assets is its general business acumen. They are best described, he says, as being entrepreneurial, opportunistic, and adaptable. They find ways to exploit market vulnerabilities, while at the same time maintaining the necessary stability and predictability that business requires to be profitable. One of the ways they do this is by taking over only a piece of a legitimate business—and providing a service in return—rather than taking over the whole business. The latter would, of course, require a management responsibility that they do not want and possibly could not handle, and that would in addition likely upset the business climate necessary for success.

La Cosa Nostra's illegal activities cover a wide range. Gambling and drugs have traditionally been their biggest money makers. Loan sharking is often linked with the gambling and drugs, and is an area that exemplifies the role played by the credible use of violence. The same is true of extortion. The other more traditional crimes also include hijacking, air cargo theft, and of course murder.

Then there a set of crimes that have become specialties of the LCN, and are unique to them in the United States. Although some of these criminal activities have had national effects, they have been carried out almost exclusively by the five crime families in New York City since LCN penetration of the legitimate economy elsewhere in the U.S. is minimal. The specialties of the New York families include labor racketeering, various kinds of business racketeering, bid-rigging, business frauds, and industry cartels. It is in these areas that the LCN demonstrates its most aggressive and effective penetration of the legitimate economy. Labor racketeering involves organized crime control of labor unions. With this control, gained by the threat and use of violence, vast sums of money are siphoned from union pension funds, businesses are extorted in return for labor peace and an absence of strikes, and bribes are solicited for sweetheart contracts. Another speciality, business racketeering, has occurred in New York City in the construction, music, and garbage industries. The LCN controls unions, bars, strip joints, restaurants, and trucking firms. The five families have also controlled at various times the Fulton Fish Market, the Javits Convention Center, the New York Coliseum, and air cargo operations at JFK International Airport, among other targets. Again the principal tools of control are extortion and the use of violence.

One of the best examples of an LCN cartel was their monopoly of the waste hauling industry in New York City for almost 50 years. La Cosa Nostra used its control of local unions to set up a cartel (Jacobs & Hortis, 1998). The cartel monopolized the industry by threatening business disruption, labor problems, and personal violence. As a result of its monopoly control, the LCN forced participants and consumers to pay inflated prices for waste hauling—a practice known as a "mob tax." Over the years this mob tax cost the industry hundreds of millions of dollars.

In part in reaction to effective law enforcement actions in many of the areas mentioned above, La Cosa Nostra has diversified its activities and extended its penetration in legal markets by switching to white-collar crimes in recent years (Raab, 1997). They have carried out multimillion dollar frauds in three areas in particular: health insurance, prepaid telephone cards, and through victimizing small Wall Street brokerage houses. Professional know-how is demonstrated in each of these scams. In an example of their health insurance frauds, mobsters set up Tri-Con Associates, a New Jersey company that arranged medical, dental and optical care for more than one million patients throughout the country. They used non-mob employees of Tri-Con as managers, and intimidated health insurance administrators into approving excessive payments to the company. With the prepaid telephone cards, the Gambino family set up a calling card company that stole more than $50 million from callers and phone companies by means of fraudulent sales. In the case of the stock market, LCN members and associates offer loans to stockbrokers who are in debt or need capital to expand their businesses. The mobsters then force the brokers to sell them most of the low-priced shares in a company before its stock is available to investors through initial public offerings. They then quickly inflate the value of the shares and sell out with huge profits before the overvalued stocks plunge.

La Cosa Nostra's monopoly control over various illegal markets, and its diversification into legal markets, has so far not been matched by any other criminal organization in the United States. This is so despite its having been substantially weakened over the last decade.

Political Resources
As has already been indicated, La Cosa Nostra is today much less powerful and pervasive than it was in the past. A loss of political influence has accompanied its general decline. In its heyday, the LCN exercised its political influence mostly at the local level, through its connections with the political machines that operated in certain U.S. cities such as New York, New Orleans, Chicago, Kansas City, and Philadelphia. With the demise of those machines, and with the advent of political reforms stressing open and ethical government, many of the avenues for corrupt influence were substantially closed. Today, the LCN exercises political influence in certain selected areas and with respect to certain selected issues. For example, it has attempted to influence the passage of legislation regulating legalized gambling in states such as Louisiana.

With respect to police and judicial corruption, again there is much more evidence of this in the past than there is today. In the past three years, there have been a handful of corruption cases involving law enforcement and one or two involving judges that are linked to La Cosa Nostra families. In Chicago, for example, a federal investigation of corruption in the courts (and city government more generally), led to 26 individuals—including judges, politicians, police officers, and lawyers—pleading guilty or being convicted at trial in 1997.

In one of the most notorious cases in recent years, in Boston a former FBI supervisor admitted (under a grant of immunity) to accepting $7,000 in payoffs from two FBI mob informants. The two mobsters were major figures in the New England Cosa Nostra. A second FBI agent was subsequently convicted in the case in 1999. The two FBI agents were charged with alerting the informants to investigations in which they were targets, and with protecting them from prosecution.

There has never been any evidence that La Cosa Nostra has had direct representation in the Congress of the United States, nor in the U.S. executive or diplomatic service. Neither is there any evidence that it has ever been allied with such armed opposition groups as terrorists, guerrillas, or death squads. In this respect, the LCN exemplifies one of the traditional defining characteristics of organized crime in that its goal is an economic rather than a political one. Where there has been political involvement, it has been for the purposes of furthering economic objectives.

Responses of Law Enforcement Agencies to Organized Crime
Law enforcement, and particularly federal law enforcement, has been tremendously successful in combating La Cosa Nostra over the past 10 years. Crime families have been infiltrated by informants and undercover agents, and special investigating grand juries have been employed in state and local jurisdictions. Especially effective use has been made of investigative and prosecutorial techniques that were designed specifically for use against organized crime, and in particular against La Cosa Nostra. These latter techniques include electronic surveillance, the witness protection program, and the Racketeer-Influenced and Corrupt Organizations Act (RICO). The RICO statute has clearly been the single most powerful tool against the LCN. There are now state RICO statutes as well as the federal one. RICO enables law enforcement to attack the organizational structure of organized crime and to levy severe criminal and civil penalties, including forfeitures. It is the threat of these penalties that has convinced many made members of the LCN to become informants and/or to seek immunity from prosecution in return for becoming a cooperating witness. They are then placed in the witness protection program. Civil remedies have included the court-appointment of monitors and trustees to administer businesses and unions that had been taken over by the LCN, to insure that these enterprises remain cleansed of corrupt influences.

Two of the latest weapons against La Cosa Nostra penetration of sectors of the legitimate economy are regulatory initiatives. As such, they are not law enforcement approaches per se, but rather administrative remedies designed to expand a local government's ability to control public services such as waste hauling and school construction. The first instance involves the creation of a regulatory commission. New York City, for example, created the Trade Waste Commission (TWC) that ended the LCN cartel in the waste hauling industry in that city through a process of licensing, investigation, competitive bidding, rate setting, and monitoring (Jacobs & Hortis, 1998). Other jurisdictions are now following suit.

The second example is the creation of a private inspector general. These inspector generals are hired in industries that have historically been controlled by organized crime, and in this case the LCN. An example is the school construction industry in New York City for which a School Construction Authority had already been created. This SCA then utilized a private inspector general to monitor its contractors, to establish corruption controls, and to report back to them on contractor conduct. Jacobs calls this "one of the great contemporary innovations in organized-crime control" (Jacobs, 1999).

La Cosa Nostra is a high priority for the FBI and for law enforcement in New York City. Elsewhere, however, it is a low priority, with attention being characterized by experts as "hit and miss" because of a belief that "things are under control." The FBI pays the most attention to transnational organized crime, with state/local law enforcement paying very little attention. Because La Cosa Nostra is mainly a domestic operation, there is little international cooperation in its investigation and prosecution.

by James O. Finckenauer, Ph.D.
International Center National Institute of Justice

Source: Report from the National Institute of Justice
https://www.ncjrs.gov/pdffiles1/nij/218555.pdf

See Articles: Italian Americans; Murder, Contemporary; New York City; Organized Crime, Contemporary; Organized Crime, Sociology of; Violent Crimes.

2008 PRIMARY DOCUMENT

Official Charges Against Casey Anthony

Casey Anthony was 22 years old when her 2-year-old daughter, Caylee Marie, was reported missing by Casey's mother, Cindy, in July 2008. The initial investigation resulted in Casey being charged with neglect, as listed here. Further investigation and the discovery of Caylee's remains in a trash bag near the home resulted in charges of first-degree murder. After a six-week trial in 2011, the jury acquitted Casey of murder, finding her guilty only of a false report to the police.

IN THE CIRCUIT COURT OF ORANGE COUNTY, STATE OF FLORIDA

The State of Florida
v.
Casey Marie Anthony

INFORMATION # 48-2008-CF-010925-O
DIVISION—16

1. NEGLECT OF A CHILD (F3-L6)
2. FALSE REPORT TO LAW ENFORCEMENT AUTHORITIES (M1)

IN THE NAME AND BY THE AUTHORITY OF THE STATE OF FLORIDA:

LAWSON LAMAR, State Attorney of the Ninth Judicial Circuit prosecuting for the State of Florida in Orange County, OR LAWSON LAMAR, State Attorney of the Ninth Judicial Circuit prosecuting for the State of Florida in Orange County, by and through the undersigned Designated Assistant State Attorney, under oath, CHARGES that CASEY MARIE ANTHONY, between the 15th day of June, 2008 and the 15th day of July, 2008, in said County and State, did willfully or by culpable negligence, in violation of Florida Statutes 827.03(3)(c) and 827.03(3)(a), while a caregiver to XXXXX, a child under 18 years of age, fail or omit to provide XXXXX, with the care, supervision and services necessary to maintain XXXXX'S physical and mental health, or fail to make a reasonable effort to protect XXXXX from abuse, neglect or exploitation by another person.

COUNT TWO

LAWSON LAMAR, State Attorney of the Ninth Judicial Circuit prosecuting for the State of Florida in Orange County, OR LAWSON LAMAR, State Attorney of the Ninth Judicial Circuit prosecuting for the State of Florida in Orange County, by and through the undersigned Designated Assistant State Attorney, under oath, CHARGES that CASEY MARIE ANTHONY, on the 16th day of July, 2008, in said County and State, did, in violation of Florida Statute 837.05(1), knowingly give false information to Detective Yuri Melich, a law enforcement officer for the Orange County Sheriff, concerning the alleged Commission of a crime of Interference with Custody of a Child, said false information being: the date and location where the defendant alleged that she last saw the child XXXXX.

This information encompasses the transaction and all charges listed on Complaint Number 48-2008-CF-010925-O and the bond thereon is hereby superseded. The Orange County Sheriff's Office and the Orange County Corrections Department shall substitute the charge(s) and bond indicated on the information for those on the above cited complaint.

STATE OF FLORIDA
COUNTY OF ORANGE

Personally appeared before me Linda Drane Burdick, Assistant State Attorney of the Ninth Judicial Circuit of Florida, who being first duly sworn, says that he/she has received testimony under oath from the material witness or witnesses, which if true, would constitute the offense herein, and that he/she institutes the prosecution in good faith. The foregoing instrument was acknowledged before me this _____ day of _____, 20 ____ by the aforementioned Assistant State Attorney who is personally known to me and who did take said oath. _____

LAWSON LAMAR, State Attorney
Ninth Judicial Circuit of Florida
By _____
Linda Drane Burdick
Designated Assistant State Attorney
Florida Bar No. 826928

Source: http://investigation.discovery.com/blogs/criminal-report/casey_anthony_full_coverage/files/caylee_anthony_files.html

See Articles: Child Abuse, Contemporary; Famous Trials; Murders, Unsolved; Smith, Susan.

2010 PRIMARY DOCUMENT

State of Utah v. Warren Steed Jeffs

Warren Jeffs was the president of the Fundamentalist Church of Jesus Christ of Latter-Day Saints, the largest polygamy-practicing Latter-Day Saints church (about 10,000 members). He was accused of numerous sexual crimes, some committed in the course of his church leadership. While this Utah Supreme Court decision reversed one conviction, and an Arizona case was dismissed, in 2011 he was convicted on multiple charges of sexual assault on a child and sentenced to life in prison.

IN THE SUPREME COURT OF THE
STATE OF UTAH

State of Utah,
Plaintiff and Appellee,
v.
Warren Steed Jeffs,
Defendant and Appellant.

No. 20080408
FILED July 27, 2010

Fifth District, St. George
The Honorable James L. Shumate
No. 061500526

Attorneys: Mark L. Shurtleff, Att'y Gen., Laura Dupaix, Craig L. Barlow, Asst. Att'ys Gen., Salt Lake City, Brock R. Belnap, Ryan J. Shaum, St. George, for plaintiff
Walter F. Bugden, Jr., Tara L. Isaacson, Salt Lake City, Richard A. Wright, Las Vegas, NV, for defendant

PARRISH, Justice:

INTRODUCTION

1. Defendant Warren Jeffs was convicted of two counts of rape as an accomplice for his role in the compelled marriage of fourteen-year-old Elissa Wall to her nineteen-year-old first cousin, Allen Steed, and the resulting sexual intercourse between them. Jeffs appeals his convictions, arguing a variety of errors in the proceedings before the trial court. While we are unconvinced by the majority of Jeffs' arguments, we conclude that there were serious errors in the instructions given to the jury that deprived Jeffs of the fair trial to which all are entitled under our laws. We therefore reverse the convictions and remand for a new trial.

2. Recognizing the highly publicized nature of this case, we remind the parties, the trial court, and observers, that the presumption of innocence guaranteed to all by our Constitution demands great care from the courts and those who prosecute on behalf of the people. As this state's court of last resort, we are not at liberty to accept less, nor could we, consistent with our oaths to support, obey, and defend the constitutions of this state and country.

BACKGROUND

3. "On appeal, we review the record facts in a light most favorable to the jury's verdict." State v. Holgate, 2000 UT 74, ¶ 2, 10 P.3d 346 (internal quotation marks omitted). Conflicting evidence is presented "only as necessary to understand issues raised on appeal." Id. We recite the facts of this case accordingly.

4. Elissa Wall was raised as a member of the Fundamentalist Church of Jesus Christ of Latter-day Saints ("FLDS Church"). As a follower of that religion, she was extensively exposed to the teachings of the defendant, Warren Jeffs ("Jeffs"), who is the son of, and the former first counselor to, then-FLDS leader Rulon Jeffs ("Rulon"). From the first through the sixth grade, Wall attended school at Alta Academy, a private FLDS school where Jeffs acted as a teacher and as the principal. Outside of school, Wall was further exposed to Jeffs' teachings through Sunday meetings, church literature, and recordings that were broadcast through her home on a speaker system and that she listened to on a personal cassette player.

5. Proper relationships between the sexes figured prominently in Jeffs' teachings. He taught that, prior to marriage, boys and girls were to treat each other as "snakes," avoiding all intermingling or social contact. Girls were to relax this standard only with their husbands after marriage. However, most FLDS girls, including Wall, received no instruction about anatomy or reproduction. Jeffs taught that girls would be trained in these matters by their husbands.

6. Jeffs' teachings also focused extensively on the importance of obedience. As "God on earth," the FLDS prophet and his counselors were to be obeyed completely and willingly. Failure to do so would result in forfeiture of spiritual salvation, loss of family and friends, denial of marriage, and removal from the FLDS

community. In addition to obeying their church leaders, Jeffs taught that women should obey their husbands, who were their individual "priesthood heads."

7. Wall witnessed the consequences of failing to follow these teachings firsthand in 1999 when her father was deemed disobedient to FLDS leaders and had his family "stripped from him." Wall, her mother, and her siblings were removed from her father's home in Salt Lake City and sent to live with Fred Jessop, Rulon's then second counselor, in Hildale, Utah. Jeffs subsequently performed a ceremony marrying Wall's mother to Jessop as one of his plural wives.

8. The doctrine that God will reveal to the FLDS prophet which of his followers should be joined in marriage relationships is fundamental to the FLDS faith. Wall, therefore, expected that church leaders would arrange her marriage. But she was shocked when, in 2001, Jessop told her that the prophet had a "place of marriage" for her and that she was to prepare herself for that place. Wall, who was then only fourteen years old, objected because of her age, but Jessop again told her that she needed to prepare herself. When Wall asked who she was to marry, Jessop told her that it would be "revealed" to her later. A few days before the wedding, Jessop told her she would marry Allen Steed, her nineteen-year-old first cousin. Wall told Jessop she would not marry Steed, but Jessop told her she would have to discuss the matter with the prophet, Rulon, since it was he who had arranged the marriage.

9. Rulon had recently suffered a debilitating stroke and Jeffs was managing his affairs. Wall called Jeffs and arranged a meeting with Rulon. Jeffs was present when Wall spoke with Rulon. She told Rulon that she did not wish to be disobedient, but asked him to let her wait until she was at least sixteen to be married and to place her with someone other than her cousin. Rulon told Wall, "Follow your heart, sweetie. Follow your heart." Wall understood this to mean that she would not have to marry Steed. Jeffs, however, told her afterwards, "The prophet wanted me to remind you that this is the right thing to do. And you will go forward with this." Later that day, Jessop, despite Wall's pleading, confirmed that her wedding to Steed would still take place.

10. Two of Wall's older sisters, both of whom were married to Rulon, tried to intervene on Wall's behalf. Jeffs was present during their conversation with Rulon. Rulon expressed concern over the arrangements, but Jeffs said that Jessop was "insisting that this happen because of who he is" and "[w]e would like to honor his request."

11. Knowing that she would no longer be welcome in Jessop's home and that she would have to give up her relationships with her mother and her siblings if she did not marry Steed, Wall felt she had no option but to go through with the marriage. In April 2001, Wall was taken to Caliente, Nevada, for the wedding. Jeffs performed the ceremony, throughout which Wall cried tears of despair and fear. When Jeffs asked her if she took Steed to be No. 20080408 4 her husband, she hung her head and said nothing. Jeffs repeated the question, and again Wall did not answer. After a long silence, Jeffs asked Wall's mother to stand by Wall and hold her hand. Jeffs repeated the question a third time, and Wall's mother squeezed her hand. Finally, Wall answered, "Okay, I do." Jeffs told Steed he could kiss the bride, but Wall hung her head and shook it. Jeffs commanded, "Lisi, kiss Allen." Wall gave Steed "a peck on the lips," then dropped his hand. Jeffs rejoined Wall's and Steed's hands and pronounced, "Now go forth and multiply and replenish the earth with good priesthood children." Wall then ran from the room and locked herself in a bathroom. Although no marriage license had been obtained, Wall considered herself married to Steed, which made him her leader and "priesthood head."

12. During the honeymoon trip that followed, Steed began touching Wall sexually. Still ignorant of sex, Wall did not understand why he was touching her and was "terrified" and "horrified." She repeatedly asked Steed to stop, telling him that she hated him and did not want him to touch her. Two to three weeks after the wedding, Steed exposed his genitals to Wall at a park. She ran away from him crying and hid in her mother's room. She stayed in her mother's room until the early hours of the morning, hoping that Steed would go to sleep. When she returned to her own room, however, she found Steed sitting on the bed. Over Wall's extensive protests, Steed began to undress her. She broke away and fled back to her mother's room, where she stayed for several days. When Wall eventually returned to her own room, Steed told her, "It is time for you to be a wife and do your duty." Although Wall cried and begged him not to, Steed then had sexual intercourse with Wall. The first of the State's two charges against Jeffs is based on this act of intercourse.

13. In the late spring of 2001, Wall had another meeting with Jeffs. She told Jeffs that Steed was touching her and doing things that she "was not comfortable with and didn't fully understand." She begged Jeffs for a "release" from the marriage, the FLDS equivalent of a divorce. In response, Jeffs told Wall that she needed to "repent" and that she was not being "obedient . . . [and] submissive." Instead of releasing her from the marriage, Jeffs told her that she "needed to go home and give [her]self to [Steed], who was [her] priesthood head and husband, mind, body, and soul and obey without any question." Within days of this meeting, Steed again had sexual intercourse with Wall. The second of the State's two charges against Jeffs is based on this act of intercourse. The relationship between Wall and Steed continued through September 2003, with sex sometimes occurring without Wall's consent and sometimes with her consent.

14. The State charged Jeffs with two counts of rape as an accomplice, a first degree felony, under Utah Code sections 76-2-202 and 76-5-402 (2008). Following a preliminary hearing, Jeffs was bound over for trial. A jury convicted him as charged. Jeffs moved to arrest judgment, alleging that the evidence was insufficient to support his convictions. The trial court denied the motion and sentenced Jeffs to two consecutive prison terms of five years to life. Jeffs moved for a new trial, arguing that the court had erred in seating an alternate juror after deliberations had begun. The court denied this motion on the basis of invited error. This appeal followed. We have jurisdiction pursuant to Utah Code section 78A-3-102(3)(I) (2008).

ANALYSIS

15. Jeffs raises seven issues that he claims invalidate either the jury verdict or the resulting sentences. Jeffs argues that: (1) the accomplice liability and consent instructions given to the jury were erroneous, (2) the trial court erred by failing to instruct the jury that it must reach a unanimous decision on whichever of the prosecution's theories supported its finding that the victim did not consent, (3) there was insufficient evidence to sustain Jeffs' convictions, (4) there was insufficient evidence that Jeffs enticed Wall into a sexual relationship with Steed, (5) the "enticement" language of Utah Code section 76-5-406(11) is unconstitutionally vague, (6) the trial court erred in denying Jeffs' motion for a new trial because the court reconstituted the jury after deliberations had begun, and (7) the trial court erred in imposing consecutive sentences. We agree with Jeffs that the consent instructions given to the jury were erroneous and warrant a reversal of his convictions. Accordingly, we need not reach the remainder of his claims. We do address, however, Jeffs' argument with respect to the correctness of the jury instruction on accomplice liability to give guidance to the trial court on remand.

I. THE JURY INSTRUCTIONS ON CONSENT AND ACCOMPLICE LIABILITY WERE ERRONEOUS

16. Jeffs contends that instructions given to the jury on the issues of consent and accomplice liability were erroneous. Specifically, Jeffs argues that the instruction on consent erroneously focused the jury on Jeffs' relationship with Wall rather than on Steed's relationship with Wall. With respect to the accomplice liability instruction, Jeffs argues that the trial court erred by refusing to instruct the jury that Jeffs could not be found guilty as an accomplice to rape unless Jeffs intended that Steed engage in nonconsensual sexual intercourse with Wall.

Source: http://www.utcourts.gov/media/hpcases/index.cgi?mode=selectcategory&category_id=334

See Articles: Child Abuse, Contemporary; Child Abuse, History of; Child Abuse, Sociology of; Juries; Rape, Contemporary; Rape, Sociology of;Religion and Crime, Contemporary; Religion and Crime, History of; Religion and Crime, Sociology of; Supreme Court, U.S; Utah.

2011 PRIMARY DOCUMENT

Excerpt From the BP Deepwater Horizon Natural Resource Damage Assessment

The explosion of the BP-operated Deepwater Horizon mobile offshore drilling unit resulted in the largest marine oil spill in history. The explosion killed 11 men and caused the undersea wellhead to gush oil unabated for three months, from April to July 2010, at an estimated rate of 53,000 barrels per day. Environmental damage to the Gulf of Mexico was extensive and long-lasting. In March 2012, BP agreed to a settlement in the lawsuits against it for approximately $8 billion.

National Commission on the BP Deepwater Horizon Oil Spill and Offshore Drilling

Natural Resource Damage Assessment: Evolution, Current Practice, and Preliminary Findings Related to the Deepwater Horizon Oil Spill

Staff Working Paper No. 17

Staff Working Papers are written by the staff of the BP Deepwater Horizon Oil Spill Commission for the use of the members of the Commission. They do not necessarily reflect the views of the Commission as a whole or any of its members. In addition, they may be based in part on confidential interviews with government and non-government personnel.

Six months after the oil has stopped flowing from BP's damaged Macondo well, the amount of environmental harm caused by the spill is uncertain, as is the adequacy of existing legal, regulatory, and policy mechanisms to ensure that restoration needed to redress the damage will be fully implemented by government and paid for by responsible parties. This background paper describes the process that was established under the Oil Pollution Act of 1990 for assessing natural resource damages caused by the spill and restoring damaged resources to their pre-spill condition. Known as Natural Resource Damage Assessment (NRDA), this process is still in the early phases of being applied to the BP spill and conclusions about its efficacy or success in this instance will be impossible to draw for a number of years, possibly decades. This background paper describes the history and purpose of the NRDA, reviews the main steps in the NRDA process, and reports on the status of current damage assessment efforts in the Gulf.

Natural Resource Damage Assessment: History and Purpose

In the wake of the *Exxon Valdez* disaster in 1989, Congress passed legislation specifically aimed at responding to and addressing environmental and economic damages from oil spills. As part of the Oil Pollution Act of 1990 (OPA), 33 U.S.C. §§ 2701 et seq., "responsible parties"[1] were made liable for the removal costs and damages resulting from discharges of oil from vessels or facilities. Among other things, this liability extends to:

> Damages for injury to, destruction of, loss of, or loss of use of, natural resources, including the reasonable costs of assessing the damage, which shall be recoverable by a United States trustee, a State trustee, an Indian tribe trustee, or a foreign trustee.[2]

The measure of damages under OPA is:

(A) The cost of restoring, rehabilitating, replacing or acquiring the equivalent of, the damaged natural resources;
(B) The diminution in value of those natural resources pending restoration; plus
(C) The reasonable cost of assessing those damages.[3]

Under OPA, responsibility for promulgating regulations to guide the assessment of natural resource damages fell to the National Atmospheric and Oceanic Administration (NOAA).[4] NOAA completed this task in 1996 and NRDA regulations became effective on February 5, 1996.[5]

Prior to 1990, natural resource damage assessments and the associated cost recovery for oil spills were governed by the Comprehensive Environmental Response, Compensation and Liability Act of 1980, or CERCLA, which imposes liability for damages resulting from releases of "hazardous substances" as defined by the statute.[6] CERCLA regulations provided the model for the natural resource damage assessment authority set forth in OPA and continued to govern damage assessments for oil spills between 1990 and 1996, when NOAA was developing new regulations under OPA.

In its OPA regulations, NOAA seeks to promote cooperation between the trustees and the responsible party in carrying out the natural resource damage assessment. This process, referred to as a cooperative assessment, is being used in the Deepwater Horizon case, where BP (a "responsible party"[7]) is working with government agencies (i.e., the "trustees") to identify and quantify damages.[8] NOAA guidance documents set forth the specifics of the cooperative process, including level of participation, dispute resolution, agreement on scientific methods, sharing of equipment and experts, and funding.[9] As the guidance suggests, these issues are generally laid out in a memorandum of agreement between the trustees and the responsible party. While past attempts to use the cooperative assessment process did not measurably shorten the time or administrative costs incurred between the event and final settlement, trustees are quick to point out that the cooperative assessment process provides other advantages. In particular, states that do not have dedicated natural resource damage assessment programs maintain that they would not have the budget or resources to carry out damage assessments if not for the cooperative agreement that allows for periodic funding and the sharing of equipment and experts. Further, one trustee also pointed out that the more recent emphasis on data collection—as opposed to making assumptions based on past spills or existing scientific knowledge—to quantify damages and reach settlement has lengthened the time to settlement but strengthened the process and its outcome.

[1] In the case of offshore facilities, "responsible party" is defined as the "lessee or permittee of the area in which the facility is located or the holder of the right of use and easement granted under applicable State law or the Outer Continental Shelf Lands Act for the area in which the facility is located (if the holder is a different person than the lessee or permittee) . . ."). 33 U.S.C. § 2701(32).

[2] 33 U.S.C. § 2702(b)(2)(A). Trustees act "on behalf of the public" as trustees for natural resources. Federal trustees are designated by the President. State trustees are designated by their Governors. Affected Tribal and foreign nations can also claim trustee authority. 33 U.S.C. § 2706(b).

[3] 33 U.S.C. § 2706 (d)(1).

[4] Ibid. at § 2706(d).

[5] 15 C.F.R. part 990.

[6] 42 U.S.C. §§ 9601 et seq. CERCLA, in turn, built on provisions in the Clean Water Act Amendments of 1977, which first codified federal authority to recover damages for natural resources. Specifically, CERCLA provided additional direction concerning the measure of damages, the use and effect of natural resource damage assessments, and the designation of trustees.

[7] BP is a responsible party, but other companies involved may be named also once liability issues are established. For the time being, BP has entered into a funding agreement with the Natural Resource Damage Trustees, and is currently reimbursing their costs. If, ultimately, other responsible parties are named, the Trustees must find them jointly and severally liable under the law.

[8] Under CERCLA, by contrast, damage assessments were carried out, for the most part, in a noncooperative and adversarial manner. Since the trustees could essentially dictate how damages would be determined, responsible parties typically opted to conduct their own assessment in preparation for a court defense should the case end up in litigation. CERCLA regulations (and OPA itself) impose a "rebuttable presumption" in favor of the trustee's damage assessment: If the responsible party disagrees with the trustee's assessment, it bears the burden of proving that the assessment was wrong. This regulatory arrangement often set the stage for parallel and dueling assessments, as emerged in the aftermath of the *Exxon Valdez* incident.

[9] NOAA, Preassessment Phase: Guidance Document for Natural Resource Damage Assessment Under the Oil Pollution Act of 1990 (August 1996), http://www.darrp.noaa.gov/library/pdf/PPD_COV.PDF.

Source: http://www.oilspillcommission.gov/sites/default/files/documents/Natural%20Resource%20Damage%20Assessment_Evolution%2C%20Current%20Practice%2C%20and%20Preliminary%20Findings%20Related%20to%20the%20Deepwater%20Horizon%20Oil%20Spill_0.pdf

See Articles: Environmental Crimes; Louisiana; Victim Rights and Restitution.

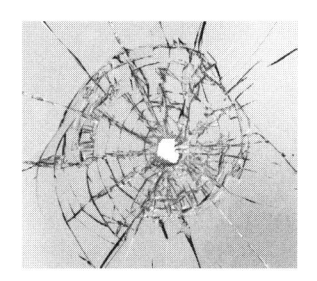

Glossary

Ableman v. Booth: An 1859 case dealing with the Fugitive Slave Act that determined the federal judiciary was the final authority, superior to state courts, on matters concerning the Constitution and laws of the United States. This ruling prevents state courts from annulling federal judgments or holding them unconstitutional, even if they contradict the state's constitution.

Abrams v. United States: A 1917 U.S. Supreme Court decision that upheld the conviction of five individuals charged with distributing pamphlets criticizing U.S. involvement in World War I. The decision is notable for the dissenting opinion written by Oliver Wendell Holmes defending the right of the five defendants to freedom of speech, except in cases when such speech posed a "clear and present danger" to the government or military.

Accessory: One who assists in the commission of a crime but neither takes part in the criminal offense nor (unlike an accomplice) is present at the commission of the crime, such as someone with knowledge of the crime who allows it to occur.

Accomplice: One who participates in the commission of a crime without taking part in the criminal offense, such as a co-conspirator or getaway driver.

Actus reus: "Guilty act," the legal term for the physical act constituting a crime.

Adair v. United States: A 1908 decision of the U.S. Supreme Court that struck down part of the 1898 Erdman Act and upheld the right of employers to prohibit employees from joining labor unions.

Adultery: Infidelity by a married person, classified as a crime in English common law and some jurisdictions. The related term, *alienation of affections*, is the crime committed by the third party, the party with which the adulterer has been unfaithful; this remains a crime in only seven states today.

Adversarial justice: A system of justice in which individuals with a dispute can take their cases before an impartial jury or judge. Each side's point of view is argued by a lawyer or other advocate, who presents his client's side in the best possible light.

Alcatraz: An island in San Francisco Bay that was the site of a military fort and military prison before serving as a high-security federal prison from 1934 to 1963. The federal prison at Alcatraz became a model for other maximum security prisons, and it is believed that there were no successful prisoner escapes from it, due in part to the distance from the mainland.

Alien and Sedition Acts: Four acts passed by the U.S. Congress in 1898 intended to suppres Democratic-Republican opposition to the Federalist Party. Provisions included increasing the period of residence in the United States (to 14 years) necessary for an immigrant to obtain citizenship, permitting the president to deport non-citizens deemed dangerous to the nation, and criminalizing the publication of writings criticizing the government or government officials.

American Law Institute: A nonprofit organization founded in 1923 to clarify and improve American law. Among its accomplishments are the development and monitoring of the Uniform Commercial Code, the Federal Judicial Code Revision, and the Model Code of Evidence.

Americans With Disabilities Act of 1990: A federal law prohibiting discrimination based on disability in employment, public accommodation, public transportation, and telecommunications.

Antitrust law: The body of law regulating anticompetitive practices by businesses, in order to prevent monopolies and maintain a healthy market.

APIS: The Advance Passenger Information System, an international database of security information about airline passengers.

Appellate court: Also called a court of appeals, any court that can review and overturn decisions from lower courts.

Arpaio, Joe: Sheriff of Maricopa County, Arizona, since 1992 and a leading proponent of tougher measures to discourage and punish illegal immigration.

Arraignment: A formal appearance by a defendant before a judge, in two stages. The initial arraignment, which must take place within 48 hours of arrest (72 if arrested on the weekend), informs the defendant of the pending charges against him and determines bail. At the post-indictment arraignment, the defendant enters a plea.

Ashurst-Sumners Act: A U.S. federal law, passed in 1935, that ended the industrial prison era by outlawing interstate commerce in goods manufactured in prison.

Attica Correctional Facility: A maximum-security prison in New York State that in 1971 was the site of a highly publicized riot that highlighted racial and religious tensions within the prison.

Auburn System: A method of penal rehabilitation developed at the Auburn Prison in New York State in the 1820s in which the rule of silence was enforced, prisoners were assigned to work during the day, and they were kept in solitary confinement at night.

Aviation and Transportation Security Act of 2011: A law passed in November 2011 by the U.S. Congress in response to the terrorist attacks of September 11, 2011. This law created the Federal Transportation Security Administration (TSA) and created many changes in how airline passengers and luggage were screened, prohibited or limited some carry-on items, and required increased security measures including reinforced cockpit doors within aircraft.

Bail: A procedure by which persons accused of a crime, but not yet tried, can be released until their hearing if they post a sum of money or other property as assurance that they will appear for their trial. If they do not appear, they will forfeit the money or property.

Bail bondsman: A person who pledges a sum of money to ensure that a defendant released on bail will appear in court.

Ballistics: The study of how a projectile, such as a bullet, travels in flight.

Bertillon System: An identification method developed by Alphonse Bertillon, working for the police department in Paris, using anthropometrics (precise anatomical measurements) to identify prisoners. Bertillon was also instrumental in developing a systematic method of crime scene photography and in standardizing criminal mug shots into front and profile views.

"Billy the Kid": A nickname for William Henry McCarty, an outlaw working primarily in New Mexico who was killed at age 21 and achieved a large role in American folklore due to coverage in newspapers.

"Black Bart": Nickname of Charles E. Boles, a British-born robber known for holding up stagecoaches in the United States. He is famous for operating alone and on foot rather than horseback and for commemorating his robberies with poems. Boles was arrested and convicted of robbery in 1883, serving about four years in San Quentin prison before release.

Black Codes: A series of laws passed in some states after the conclusion of the Civil War that restricted the rights and civil liberties of African Americans.

Black Panther Party: An African American organization founded in Oakland, California, in 1966 by Bobby Seale and Huey Newton. The Black Panthers advocated Black Nationalism and economic and social empowerment of the African American community.

Blood sports: Entertainments or sports, such as dog fighting and cock fighting, which involve violence toward or among animals and may involve the death of one or more animals. Although outlawed in many locales today, blood sports were once popular in Europe: historic examples of blood sports include bear baiting, bull baiting, and eel pulling. Some animal activists include traditional hunting in the category of blood sport as well.

Blue laws: Laws which prohibit certain activities, such as shopping or sale of alcoholic beverages, based on religious traditions or customs. For instance in the United States, some activities have traditionally been prohibited or restricted on Sundays because that day is designated by Christianity as a day of rest.

Bond: The promise by a third party (a commercial bondsman) to meet a defendant's bail obligation; the bondsman typically charges the defendant a fee based on a percentage of the bail amount.

Bonnie and Clyde: The bank robbers Bonnie Parker and Clyde Barrow, who committed numerous robberies in the early years of the Great Depression and became famous in the press due in part to their own self-promotion. They were ambushed and killed by a posse of police officers from Texas and Louisiana in 1934.

Book of the General Laws and Libertyes: The first law code printed in colonial America, the book was published in 1648 in the Massachusetts Bay Colony. It codified rights, duties and criminal penalties and established fundamental principals that served as the basis for later legal codes. The book was a revision of the *Body of Liberties*, published in 1641, a list of 100 provisions about rights and privileges, crimes and punishments, and the roles of ecclesial and civil governance.

Booth, Sherman: Wisconsin abolitionist who, in 1854, helped free fugitive slave Joshua Glover from a Milwaukee jail. Booth was arrested and convicted in a U.S. District Court for violating the Fugitive Slave Act but appealed to the Wisconsin Supreme Court, which held the Fugitive Slave Act unconstitutional. In 1859, the U.S. Supreme Court determined that state courts could not contradict the U.S. Constitution or federal law regarding it, and Booth was returned to jail until pardoned by President James Buchanan in 1861.

Bootlegging: Illegal production, transport, and sale of alcohol and by extension of other prohibited substances, from firearms to illegally copied tapes and DVDs.

Boynton v. Virginia: A 1960 decision by the U.S. Supreme Court that overturned the trespassing conviction of an African American man for being in a "whites only" bus terminal and established that the Interstate Commerce Act banned segregated interstate transportation facilities.

Broken windows hypothesis: A theory introduced in a 1982 article by James Q. Wilson and George L. Kelling that the appearance of disorder and neglect, for instance the presence of broken windows in a building, was associated with increased vandalism and other criminal activity.

Brown v. Board of Education: A 1954 decision by the U.S. Supreme Court declaring that the "separate but equal" standard for schools was insufficient and that states and localities must integrate their schools "with all deliberate speed."

Burglary: A crime defined by the Federal Bureau of Investigation's (FBI's) Uniform Crime Reporting program as involving unlawful entry into a structure to commit a theft or felony; the use of force is not required.

Capital punishment: Execution of an individual convicted of a crime. Hence, crimes that can result in the death penalty are known as "capital crimes."

Clayton Anti-Trust Act of 1914: A federal law that created the Federal Trade Commission and strengthened the Sherman Anti-Trust Act of 1890.

Clemency: Forgiveness for a crime or removal of the penalty for committing it.

Code of Silence: The unofficial rule, also known as the "thin blue line," that criminal justice officials will not report wrongdoing by another in the same profession or testify against them.

Codification: The collection of laws into a legal code. When common law is codified, the process may include restatements and clarifications in order to iron out inconsistencies.

COINTELPRO: A counter-intelligence program run by the FBI targeting domestic organizations considered "subversive," including many involved with the civil rights movement and opposing the Vietnam War. COINTELPRO began in 1956 and continued until 1971, when the program was exposed to the news media.

Common law: Law developed through the judicial branch, rather than the legislative branch, by the decisions of courts. The United States traces its legal heritage to English common law, much of which was formed by decisions of judges forced to rule on matters that the codified laws did not explicitly address. Today, court decisions are informed both by legal code and by common law —which informs not only by the establishment of precedent (a case that is fundamentally distinct from previous cases and bears on the current case), but by the interpretation of the written law as articulated in the court's decisions.

Community policing: A decentralized approach to policing in which officers work with the community to identify and solve problems and improve quality of life.

Comstock Law: A federal law passed in 1873 that prohibited the importation, mailing, or interstate transportation of information about contraception and abortion. It served as a model for many state laws banning dissemination of such information.

Confidence game: Fraudulent activities in which deception is used to deprive a person of items of value by exploiting that person's confidence or trust. Con games are generally assumed to exploit the dishonesty or greed of the victim as well, for instance, by promising to let in on a scheme that will reward them with a large sum of (unearned) money.

Congress of Racial Equality (CORE): A civil rights organization founded in 1941, which pioneered tactics such as sit-ins and the freedom rides to combat segregation.

Consecutive sentences: Sentences served in sequence, as opposed to sentences served concurrently (at the same time).

Convict lease system: A system of renting out the labor of prisoners to private parties, especially associated with the south after the Civil War. The convict lease system, like prison industries, is a way for states to offset the cost of incarceration.

Cooper v. Pate: A 1964 decision of the U.S. Supreme Court ruled that prison inmates may sue for grievances under the Civil Rights Act of 1871. The specific issue at stake was the right of a Black Muslim prisoner in Illinois to buy religious publications, wear distinctive clothing related to his religion, and enjoy similar privileges granted inmates who embraced other religions.

Corporal punishment: Punishment administered to the body (corpus), that is, physical punishment. As a criminal sentence, corporal punishment was once common throughout the world, because it did not require the expense, maintenance, or professional staff associated with incarceration; flogging, whipping, and caning have all been used in the past, as have forms of public humiliation such as the stocks and the pillory. In the modern United States, corporal punishment is generally rejected as cruel and unusual.

Cyber stalking: Use of electronic means, including e-mail and the Internet, to harass an individual or organization.

Daubert v. Merrell Dow Pharmaceuticals: A 1993 decision by the U.S. Supreme Court establishing that the Federal Rules of Evidence superseded the standards of the Frye standard established in *Frye v. United States* (1923). *Daubert* established a new standard for the admission of expert testimony in court: It must be grounded in scientific knowledge, assist the trier of fact in understanding the evidence, and allow the judge to make the threshold determination regarding admissibility.

Deterrence: The use of punishment to prevent criminal offenses. This encompasses the use of the general public's knowledge of criminal sentences as a threat to prevent them from committing crimes; the punishment of a criminal offender to prevent recidivism; and the incapacitation of a criminal offender, for instance by incarceration, in order to prevent his further criminal activity.

DHS: The Department of Homeland Security, a cabinet-level department of the federal government, created in 2002 in response to the September 11, 2001, terrorist attacks. Its goal is to prevent and respond to domestic emergencies, including terrorism.

DOS attack: Denial of service attack, a type of cybercrime in which a concerted attempt is made to make a computer resource, such as a bank or credit card Website, unavailable to its usual users, often by flooding the site with communication requests.

Dred Scott v. Sandford: An 1857 ruling by the U.S. Supreme Court determining that persons who had been brought to the United States as slaves could not be U.S. citizens, nor could their dependents. It also established that, because slaves were not citizens, they could not seek relief in the court system.

Due process: The requirement that the state respect the legal rights of the individual. Though it originated in the Magna Carta, due process has largely developed in American law, where it is central, while it is no longer a part of British law.

Duress: The condition of performing an act under pressure from another party, such as the threat of violence. Duress is a potential legal defense when it is the condition under which the duressed committed a crime. It also has relevance in laws governing rape and sexual assault, because it negates a participant's consent to sexual acts.

Erdman Act: An 1898 federal law that prohibited railroad companies from requiring, as a condition of employment, that the employee not join a union. Parts of the Erdman Act were declared unconstitutional in 1908 by the U.S. Supreme Court in the 1908 decision *Adair v. United States*.

Espionage Act: A federal law passed in 1917 that prohibited various acts that might hamper the U.S. war effort, including interference with military recruitment, lending support to U.S. enemies, or attempting to promote insubordination in the military.

Exclusionary rule: A principle in U.S. law that evidence obtained illegally, for instance objects seized from a person's home without a search warrant, may not be used in criminal prosecution.

Fair Housing Act: A common name for the Civil Rights Act of 1968, which prohibited discrimination in the sale, rental, and financing of housing on the basis of race, religion, or national origin. Gender, disability, and families with children were later added as protected categories.

Fraud: A crime committed in the form of a deliberate deception for the sake of personal gain or damage against another. Fraud is distinguished from negligence, of which a person may be guilty when such damage results from a falsehood of which they are unaware.

Frye v. United States: A 1923 U.S. Supreme Court decision that established rules concerning the admissibility of expert opinion in the court, ruling that such opinions are admissible only if they are based on generally accepted scientific techniques. The Frye standard has generally been superseded by the Federal Rules of Evidence, as determined in *Daubert v. Merrell Dow Pharmaceuticals* (1993).

Fugitive Slave Act: An act passed by Congress as part of the Compromise of 1850, which required federal marshals to assist in the recovery of escaped slaves in free states (those that had abolished slavery) and established commissioners who had concurrent jurisdiction with U.S. district courts in enforcing the law. The Fugitive Slave Act also established rewards for those who assisted in apprehending runaway slaves, fines for federal marshals who refused to assist in the return of escaped slaves, and stated that a claimant's sworn testimony was sufficient to establish fugitive status and that those suspected of being runaways could not testify on their own behalf or request a jury trial.

Gideon v. Wainwright: A 1963 case in which the U.S. Supreme Court ruled that states and localities must provide legal counsel to defendants who cannot afford to hire their own attorney.

Habeas corpus, writ of: A legal action through which a prisoner is released from detention for which there is insufficient cause.

Habeas Corpus Act: A 1659 British law establishing that a person arrested must be brought before a judge within a certain number of days, and released on bail (if the offense is bailable) within a certain number of days, thus protecting the accused against prolonged imprisonment without cause.

Hate crime: A crime committed against a victim chosen because of characteristics such as race, sexual orientation, or political affiliation.

Heart of Atlanta Motel v. United States: A 1964 decision of the U.S. Supreme Court ruling that motel operators did not have the right to refuse accommodation to African American guests because the lack of adequate accommodations for African Americans resulted in unlawful restriction of interstate commerce.

Honor killing: Killing of a member of a social group or family by other members of the same group or family, as punishment for bringing dishonor onto the group or family. The victims of honor killings are most often women and girls accused of sexual improprieties or related behaviors, such as refusing an arranged marriage or being perceived as insufficiently modest.

Hope v. Pelzer: A 2002 decision of the U.S. Supreme Court determining that "qualified immunity" (a rule that government employees may not be sued for actions conducted as part of their jobs) did not apply to the case of an inmate subjected to cruel and unusual punishment in an Alabama prison. The plaintiff was disciplined by being handcuffed to a "hitching post" that held him immobile and exposed him to sunburn and dehydration, a punishment that the court determined violated the Eighth Amendment, thus nullifying the guards' claims of qualified immunity.

Immigration Reform and Control Act of 1986: A federal law that made it illegal for an employer to knowingly hire illegal immigrants and required employers to ascertain the legal status of new employees by making them present identification. The act also provided amnesty to illegal immigrants who had lived in the U.S. continuously since January 1, 1982.

Indian Removal Act: An 1830 law that resulted in the migration (theoretically voluntary but in fact often coerced) of Native Americans from the southeastern United States along the Trail of Tears to a region in what is now Oklahoma.

INTERPOL: The International Criminal Police Organization, established in 1923 to promote cooperation between the police forces of different countries, including sharing of data and assisting in extraditions.

Irene Morgan v. Commonwealth of Virginia: A 1946 U.S. Supreme Court decision that outlawed segregation in interstate transportation. This ruling was expanded in *Boynton v. Virginia* in 1960, also requiring bus terminals used on interstate lines to be desegregated, over-ruling any local laws requiring segregation.

Jim Crow laws: A series of laws enacted in some states and localities following the Civil War that mandated racial segregation in public facilities, including schools, restaurants, public restrooms, and means of transportation, such as buses and trains.

Jurisdiction: The authority of a legal entity to make pronouncements on legal matters and administer justice within a specifically defined sphere of responsibility. Courts hear only cases over which they have jurisdiction, which may be defined both geographically (a court assigned to a particular area) and by category of legal matter.

Jury: A body of citizens convened by the court to render an impartial verdict on a matter submitted to them. The United States uses juries not only in criminal and civil trials, but also in the form of grand juries, which are convened to determine whether there is enough evidence for a criminal trial to go forward.

Juvenile Justice and Delinquency Prevention Act: A 1974 law that called for the deinstitutionalization of juvenile offenders and led to a number of community-based corrections programs aimed at rehabilitation, rather than incarceration.

Kefauver Committee: The U.S. Special Committee to Investigate Crime in Interstate Commerce—a committee chaired by Senator Estes Kefauver that was appointed in 1950 to study police corruption and organized crime in the United States.

Kinsey reports: Two volumes published by Dr. Alfred Kinsey and colleagues, *Sexual Behavior in the Human Male* (1948) and *Sexual Behavior in the Human Female* (1953), are collectively known as the Kinsey reports. These books, based on surveys and interviews with a broad cross-section of Americans, were groundbreaking in their day for their discovery of the discrepancies between actual sexual behavior and that prescribed by conventional morality: For instance, adultery and homosexual behavior were found to be far more common among American adults than was generally thought.

Larceny: The crime of taking possession of the personal property of another person.

Lex talionis: The law of retribution, sometimes expressed as "an eye for an eye."

Lynching: An execution carried out without the authority of a court, especially one intended to intimidate or otherwise influence a population represented by the lynching victim.

Mala in se: Acts that are considered wrong (for instance, murder) in and of themselves, without regard to whether they are prohibited by law or not.

Mala prohibita: Acts that are considered wrong only because there is a law against them (a matter of opinion, but many would consider, for instance, prostitution or gambling to be *mala prohibita* but not *mala in se*).

Malware: A broad category of malicious software used to gather information, disrupt operations, or otherwise exploit weaknesses in computer systems.

Matthew Shepard and James Byrd, Jr. Hate Crimes Prevention Act: An act of Congress in 2009 that expands federal hate crime legislation to include perceived or actual gender or sexual orientation or identity, and disability. It provides funding to investigate and prosecute hate crimes and requires the FBI to report on hate crimes motivated by the victim's gender or sexual identity. The act is named for a gay man tortured and murdered in Wyoming (Matthew Shepard) and an African American man dragged from a truck until he died in Texas (James Byrd, Jr.).

Mens rea: "Guilty mind," the legal term for the mental element of a crime: the intention to commit a wrongful or reckless act. Not every crime requires specific intent.

Miranda v. Arizona: A decision by the U.S. Supreme Court in 1963 establishing that persons held in police custody must be informed of their rights to legal counsel and to refrain from making statements ("the right to remain silent") that might incriminate them.

Moonshine: Illegally produced, distilled alcohol. Though often used to refer to unaged ("white") whiskey, and recently applied to a number of legal products, moonshine properly refers to any spirit produced by an unlicensed still.

Morrill Anti-Bigamy Act: a U.S. federal law passed in 1862 that prohibits bigamy.

Narcotic: A certain class of drugs with overlapping but significantly different meanings in medicine and law. In medicine, a narcotic is a psychoactive compound that induces sleep, especially an opioid, which includes both legal prescription drugs (hydrocodone) and illegal recreational ones (heroin). In law, a narcotic is any illegal drug (including prescription drugs used illegally), including stimulants and hallucinogens.

NCVS: The National Crime Victimization Survey, a method of measuring the incidence of crime using sampling and surveys of crime victims, begun in 1972 to address perceived shortcomings of the Uniform Crime Report.

New York House of Refuge: An early attempt at creating a separate criminal justice system for juveniles. Founded in 1824, the House of Refuge housed only juveniles, and had the goal of rehabilitating and diverting them away from the adult correctional system.

Nolo contendere: "I do not wish to contend" (Latin), a plea made as an alternative to "guilty" or "not guilty." Also known as a plea of no contest. State laws governing *nolo contendere* pleas vary.

Parchman Farm: A Mississippi state prison, established in 1903, which was ordered in the 1972 U.S. Fifth Circuit Court of Appeals decision *Gates v. Collier* (1972) to stop using certain forms of physical punishment and to stop using the trusty system to control inmates.

Parens patriae: A legal doctrine specifying that the courts should act as parental figures toward juvenile offenders and choose correctional treatment judged in the best interest of the child.

Pari-mutuel betting: A type of betting common at racetracks in which the payoff is determined after the pool is closed, generally when the event begins, so the odds are not known at the time a bet is placed. In pari-mutuel betting, the bets are placed in a pool, the house percentage is removed, and the payoff odds are then calculated based on the remaining pool and the number of winning bets.

Parole: An early release from prison, based on an inmate's behavior, followed by a period of supervision by a parole officer.

Peremptory challenge: In the U.S. court system, the right of a lawyer to challenge potential jurors (i.e., have them removed from the jury pool) without having to give a reason for the challenge.

Plea: The defendant's answer to the charges against him or her, typically "guilty" or "not guilty."

Plessy v. Ferguson: An 1896 decision of the U.S. Supreme Court that established the principle of "separate but equal," thus confirming that racial segregation was legal. The specific case referred to segregation in railway transport, but the principle was applied widely in some states to schools, hotels, restaurants, public beaches, and other facilities.

Prigg v. Pennsylvania: An 1842 decision of the U.S. Supreme Court that confirmed the federal Fugitive Slave Act of 1793, prohibiting assisting escaped slaves in any state, overruling any state laws to the contrary.

Prison industries: Revenue-generating activities conducted in correctional facilities in which prisoners serve as laborers. The profits of prison industries, including simple handcrafts and farming, can help offset the cost of incarceration. In some cases, prison industries may serve as a source of cheap labor for the state's other needs, such as the manufacture of license plates or road signage.

Prohibition: A ban on the production, sale, and transportation of alcoholic beverages in the United States from 1920 to 1933, as established in the Eighteenth Amendment to the U.S. Constitution. Prohibition was repealed by passage of the Twenty-First Amendment to the Constitution.

Recidivism: The recurrence of criminal behavior. Various approaches to crime and criminal offenders are weighed in terms of their impact on the offenders' recidivism.

Reconstruction amendments: A term sometimes applied to the Thirteenth, Fourteenth, and Fifteenth amendments to the U.S. Constitution, which were adopted after the conclusion of the Civil War. These amendments abolished slavery (Thirteenth), established citizenship and equal protection under the law without regard to race (Fourteenth), and granted voting rights regardless of race or previous servitude (Fifteenth).

Rehabilitation: The modification of an offender's behavior and habits in order to curb criminal activity and impulses. In practice, proponents of rehabilitation often find themselves opposed by proponents of retribution, though in theory, punishments could serve both points of view.

Restitution: Compensation to the victim of a crime, paid by the criminal offender. Restitutive approaches to criminal justice focus on the needs of the victims.

Retribution: The theory of retributive justice proposes proportionate punishment as a morally appropriate response to crime, not because of any deterrent effects the punishment may have, but because of the satisfaction it will provide to victims and the public. Retribution is typically the motive behind arguments favoring the death penalty.

Robbery: A crime of theft by force, threat of force, or by putting the victim in fear.

Roe v. Wade: A 1973 ruling by the U.S. Supreme court that struck down a Texas law restricting abortions and established that the "right to privacy" included the right of a woman to seek an abortion. *Roe v. Wade* largely overturned state restrictions to a woman's access to abortion during the first trimester of a pregnancy, but allowed more restrictions after that time.

RU-486: A drug, also known as Mifeprisone, which can be used to induce miscarriage, thus providing an abortion alternative to women who do not live near clinics or hospitals offering the procedure (about 80 percent of U.S. counties do not have an abortion provider).

Scopes Monkey Trial: A trial held in Dayton, Tennessee, in 1925 that challenged the Butler Act, making it a crime to teach evolution in the schools. The Scopes Trial was widely publicized (it was the first trial broadcast nationally on the radio) due in part to the participation of high-profile lawyers Clarence Darrow (for the defense) and William Jennings Bryan (for the prosecution). The defendant, high school biology teacher John Scopes, was found guilty of violating the Butler Act. When the verdict was appealed to the Tennessee Supreme Court, the Butler Act was found constitutional, but Scopes's conviction was set aside on a technicality.

Scottsboro Boys: Nine African American teenagers convicted in 1931 of raping two white women. Eight were originally convicted and sentenced to death while the trial of one, a 12 year old, resulted in a hung jury. In 1932, the U.S. Supreme Court reversed their convictions, ruling that they had not been granted effective legal counsel. Tried and convicted a second time, their convictions were again overturned by the U.S. Supreme Court in the decision *Norris v. Alabama* because African Americans had been excluded from the jury pool.

Selective Service System: A system established in 1917 that required men age 21 to 30 to register for military service. The purpose of the system was to create a database of information about young men available for the military draft, and the age limits have changed over the years according to military need: For instance, in 1918 the upper age limit was increased to 45, and in 1940 the younger age limit was reduced to 18.

Sherman Anti-Trust Act: A federal statute, passed in 1890, which was the first U.S. legislation to limit the power of monopolies and cartels.

Son of Sam law: A general term for laws that prohibit criminals from profiting from their crimes, for instance by the sale of books or television rights to their story. The original Son of Sam law was passed in New York State in response to reports that David Berkowitz, the Son of Sam killer, was offered large sums of money for his story.

Stack v. Boyle: A 1951 decision of the U.S. Supreme Court establishing that bail should not be set at a higher level than required to make it reasonably likely that a defendant would appear in court.

Stono Rebellion: The largest slave rebellion in the American colonies prior to the Revolutionary War. It took place in South Carolina in 1739, led by a slave sometimes referred to as "Cato" (hence an alternative name is Cato's Rebellion), and prompted South Carolina to pass the Negro Act of 1740 that restricted the rights of slaves to assemble, move about, or become educated, and imposed a moratorium on the importation of African slaves.

Subpoena: A writ issued by a court or government entity compelling a witness to provide testimony or physical evidence.

Team policing: An approach to policing instituted in some cities in the 1960s and 1970s, in which the patrol force was organized into teams that were assigned permanently to particular neighborhoods. This approach was unsuccessful and was largely abandoned by the 1980s.

Thalidomide: A prescription drug prescribed for morning sickness that often resulted in severe birth defects.

Thoughts on Government: A treatise on government written by John Adams in 1776 that suggests a system of executive, judicial, and legislative branches of government, the latter including two legislative bodies, and a system of checks and balances to prevent any one branch from becoming too powerful.

Three strikes law: A statute enacted by some state governments that requires a greater sentence (typically, a life sentence) for the third instance of a serious criminal offense.

Tort: A civil wrong. A tort may be a criminal act, but need not be; tort law deals with all situations in which the defendant's behavior has unfairly resulted in the plaintiff's loss. Tort law is more restitutive in its aims than criminal law.

Trusty system: A method of maintaining control within a prison by designating certain inmates as empowered to control and punish other inmates. The trusty system, as implemented in the state prison in Parchman, Mississippi, was outlawed in the U.S. Fifth Circuit Court of Appeals decision *Gates v. Collier* (1972), which also placed restrictions on the types of physical punishment that could be used on prisoners. Other states were also required to end their trusty systems as a result of the *Gates v. Collier* decision.

TSA: The Transportation Security Administration, a federal program created in November 2001 and given responsibility for monitoring air and sea transportation security, including hiring and training airport screeners.

UCR: The Uniform Crime Report, a reporting system for crimes, created in the United States in 1930. Local law enforcement agencies provide data to the FBI, which then aggregates it and publishes the results. The reports are used to track the incidence of crime in different locations.

United States Code: The codification of federal statutes, divided into 51 subject-based titles. Federal law is also codified into slip laws and session laws, which are organized chronologically instead of by topic, and which are issued as acts of Congress passed into law.

United States v. One Book Called Ulysses: A 1933 case in the U.S. District for the Southern District of New York, in which Judge John Woolsey ruled that James Joyce's novel *Ulysses* was not obscene, but entitled to constitutional protection as literature. This case established the principle that in evaluating charges of obscenity, the entire work should be considered, rather than isolated excerpts.

USA PATRIOT Act: A law passed in October 2001 that reduced restrictions on the ability of law enforcement officials to search telephone and e-mail communications, and medical and financial records; broadened government abilities to detain and deport individuals; and broadened the definition of terrorism. The bill was a response to the terrorist attacks of September 11. It was intended in part to encourage law enforcement agencies to share information, as well as expand their abilities to obtain information previously considered confidential. Initially, the provisions of the act were to end on December 31, 2005, but in March 2006, the law was reauthorized.

Victimology: A subfield of criminology that studies the characteristics of victims and the victimization process.

Volstead Act: Also known as the National Prohibition Act, passed in 1919. The Volstead Act was the enforcement arm of the Eighteenth Amendment to the U.S. Constitution, which outlawed the sale, production, and transport of intoxicating liquor.

Walnut Street Jail: A Philadelphia jail, named for its location, which was the first U.S. prison to house prisoners in individual cells and to assign them to work details.

Warrant: A writ issued by a judge or government entity authorizing an action; for instance, an arrest warrant authorizes the detainment and arrest of a criminal suspect.

Warwickshire Quarter Sessions: One of the first attempts to deal with juvenile offenders separate from adults, this practice began in England in the 1820s. Juvenile offenders were sentenced to a single day in prison, followed by release to their parents or another responsible adult.

Whitney v. California: A 1927 decision of the U.S. Supreme Court ruling that speech that constituted clear and present danger to society was not protected under the Fourteenth Amendment. The defendant was an organizer for the Communist Labor Party accused of advocating the overthrow of the U.S. government.

Wolf v. Colorado: A 1949 decision of the U.S. Supreme Court establishing that the Fourth Amendment's prohibition against unreasonable search and seizure also applied to state courts. The case involved a physician, Julius Wolf, who was thought to provide abortions illegally and was convicted based on evidence gained by following up on names in his appointment book.

Writ: A common law term for a formal written order issued by a body with judicial or administrative jurisdiction over the matter with which the order is concerned. Warrants and subpoenas are familiar examples.

Yellow-dog contract: A contract that prohibits an employee from joining or maintaining membership in a labor union. The name likens those who would sign such a contract to the lowest breed of mongrel dog.

Sarah Boslaugh
Kennesaw State University

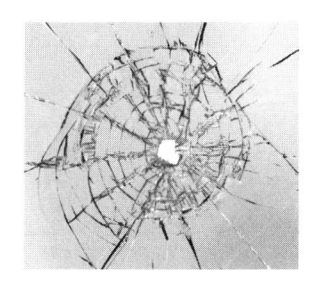

Resource Guide

Books

Acker, Caroline Jean. *Creating the American Junkie: Addiction Research in the Classic Era of Narcotic Control.* Baltimore: Johns Hopkins University Press, 2002.

Acker, James R. *Scottsboro and Its Legacy: The Cases That Challenged American Legal and Social Justice.* Westport, CT: Praeger, 2007.

Agnew, Robert. *Pressured Into Crime: An Overview of General Strain Theory.* Cary, NC: Roxbury Publishing, 2006.

Albini, Joseph L. *The American Mafia: Genesis of a Legend.* New York: Appleton-Century-Crofts, 1971.

Allen, Oliver E. *The Tiger: The Rise and Fall of Tammany Hall.* New York: Addison-Wesley, 1993.

Alotta, Robert L. *Civil War Justice: Union Army Executions Under Lincoln.* Shippensburg, PA: White Man Publishing, 1989.

Amar, Akhil Reed. *The Bill of Rights: Creation and Reconstruction.* New Haven, CT: Yale University Press, 1998.

Arlacchi, Pino. *Mafia Business: The Mafia Ethic and the Spirit of Capitalism.* New York: Oxford University Press, 1988.

Asbury, Herbert. *Gem of the Prairie: An Informal History of the Chicago Underworld.* New York: Alfred A. Knopf, 1940.

Aronson, Jay D. *Genetic Witness: Science, Law, and Controversy in the Making of DNA Profiling.* New Brunswick, NJ: Rutgers University Press, 2007.

Ayers, Edward L. *Vengeance and Justice: Crime and Punishment in the 19th-Century American South.* New York: Oxford University Press, 1984.

Ayers, William. *A Kind and Just Parent: The Children of Juvenile Court.* Boston: Beacon Press, 1997.

Banner, Stuart. *The Death Penalty: An American History.* Cambridge, MA: Harvard University Press, 2002.

Banton, M. *West African City: A Study of Tribal Life in Freetown.* London: Oxford University Press, 1957.

Bartollas, C. and K. Stuart van Wormer. *Women and the Criminal Justice System.* Upper Saddle River, NJ: Prentice Hall, 2011.

Bayley, David. *Police for the Future.* New York: Oxford University Press, 1994.

Bazemore, Gordon and Mara Schiff. *Juvenile Justice Reform and Restorative Justice: Building Theory and Policy From Practice*, Oxford: Willan Publishing, 2005.

Beavan, Colin. *Fingerprints: The Origins of Crime Detection and the Murder Case That Launched Forensic Science.* New York: Hyperion, 2001.

Becker, Howard S. *Outsiders: Studies in the Sociology of Deviance.* New York: Free Press, 1963.

Bechtel, H. Kenneth. *State Police in the United States: A Socio-Historical Analysis.* Westport: CT: Greenwood Press, 1995.

Bedau, Hugo Adam, ed. *The Death Penalty in America: Current Controversies.* New York: Oxford University Press, 1997.

Beecher-Monas, Erica. *Evaluating Scientific Evidence: An Interdisciplinary Framework for Intellectual Due Process.* New York: Cambridge University Press, 2007.

Beeghley, Leonard. *Homicide: A Sociological Explanation.* Lanham, MD: Rowman & Littlefield, 2003

Beisel, Nocola. *Imperiled Innocents: Anthony Comstock and Family Reproduction in Victorian America.* Princeton, NJ: Princeton University Press, 1997.

Bell, Malcolm, *Turkey Shoot: Tracking The Attica Cover-Up.* New York: Grove, 1985.

Belknap, Joanne. *The Invisible Woman: Gender, Crime, and Justice.* Belmont, CA: Thomson Wadsworth, 2007.

Bentham, Jeremy. *An Introduction to the Principles of Morals and Legislation.* London: T. Payne, 1789.

Benton, L. *A Search for Sovereignty: Law and Geography in European Empires, 1400–1900.* New York: Cambridge University Press, 2009.

Bernstein, Iver. *The New York City Draft Riots: Their Significance for American Society and Politics in the Age of the Civil War.* New York: Oxford University Press, 1990.

Bonger, Willem. *Criminality and Economic Conditions.* Boston: Little, Brown and Company, 1905.

Bonnie, Richard J., et al. *A Case Study in the Insanity Defense: The Trial of John W. Hinckley, Jr.* 3rd ed. Mineola, NY: Foundation Press, 2008.

Brown, Charles E., George L. Kelling, Tony Pate, and Duane Dieckman. *The Kansas City Preventive Patrol Experiment: A Technical Report.* Washington, DC: Police Foundation, 1974.

Burgess, Ernest W., Robert E. Park, and Roderick D. McKenzie, eds. *The City: Suggestions for Investigation of Human Behavior in the Urban Environment.* Chicago: University of Chicago Press, 1925.

Burns, James. *Packing the Court: The Rise of Judicial Power and the Coming Crisis of the Supreme Court.* New York: Penguin, 2009.

Burrough, Bryan. *Public Enemies: America's Greatest Crime Wave and the Birth of the FBI, 1933–1934.* New York: Penguin, 2004.

Buss, D. M. *The Evolution of Desire.* New York: Basic Books, 1994.

Byers, Michele and Val Marie Johnson, eds. *The CSI Effect: Television, Crime, and Governance.* Lanham, MD: Lexington Books, 2009.

Callow, Alexander B., Jr. *The Tweed Ring.* New York: Oxford University Press, 1966.

Chalmers, David. *Hooded Americanism: The History of the Ku Klux Klan.* Durham, NC: Duke University Press, 1987.

Cheeseman, Kelly, Del Carmen, Rolando V., Scott Vollum, Durant Frantzen, and Claudia San Miguel. *The Death Penalty: Constitutional Issues, Commentaries, and Case Briefs.* New York: Lexis-Nexis, 2005.

Chermak, Steven and Frankie Y. Bailey. *Crimes and Trials of the Century.* Westport, CT: Greenwood Press, 2007.

Clear, Todd. *Harm in American Penology: Offenders, Victims, and Their Communities.* Albany: State University of New York Press, 1994.

Coffey, Thomas M. *The Long Thirst: Prohibition in America, 1920–1933.* New York: W. W. Norton, 1975.

Coffin, Frank M. *On Appeal: Courts, Lawyering, and Judging.* New York: W. W. Norton, 1994.

Cohen, Albert. *Delinquent Boys: The Culture of the Gang.* Glencoe, IL: Free Press, 1955.

Cohen, D. A. *Pillars of Salt, Monuments of Grace: New England Crime Literature and the Origins of American Popular Culture, 1674–1860.* New York: Oxford University Press, 1993.

Collins, James J., Jr. *Drinking and Crime: Perspectives on the Relationships Between Alcohol Consumption and Criminal Behavior.* New York: Guilford Press, 1981.

Courtwright, David T. *Violent Land: Single Men and Social Disorder From the Frontier to the Inner City*. Cambridge, MA: Harvard University Press, 1996

Cressey, Donald R. *Other People's Money: A Study in the Social Psychology of Embezzlement*. New York: The Free Press, 1953.

Cresswell, Stephen. *Mormons and Cowboys, Moonshiners and Klansmen: Federal Law Enforcement in the South and the West, 1870–1893*. Tuscaloosa: University of Alabama Press, 1991.

Cross, Frank B. *Decision Making in the U.S. Courts of Appeals*. Palo Alto, CA: Stanford University Press, 2007.

Dahrendorf, Ralf. *Class and Class Conflict in Industrial Society*. Palo Alto, CA: Stanford University Press, 1959.

Davis, Carol Anna. *Children Who Kill: Profiles of Preteen and Teenage Killers*. London: Allison & Busby, 2008.

Davis, Nanette. *Prostitution: An International Handbook on Trends, Problems, and Policies*. Westport, CT: Greenwood Press, 1993.

Del Carmen, Rolando V., Scott Vollum, Kelly Cheeseman, Durant Frantzen, and Claudia San Miguel. *The Death Penalty: Constitutional Issues, Commentaries, and Case Briefs*. New York: Lexis-Nexis, 2005.

Denham, David, Lorraine Wolhuter, and Neil Olley. *Victimology: Victimisation and Victims' Rights*. New York: Routledge-Cavendish, 2008.

Dershowitz, Alan M. *America on Trial: Inside the Legal Battles That Transformed Our Nation*. New York: Warner Books, 2004.

Dingwall, Gavin. *Alcohol and Crime*. Portland, OR: Willan Publishing, 2006.

Dodge, L. Mara. *"Whores and Thieves of the Worst Kind": A Study of Women, Crime, and Prisons, 1835–2000*. DeKalb: Northern Illinois University Press, 2002.

Dworkin, Ronald. *Philosophy of Law: Oxford Readings in Philosophy*. New York: Oxford University Press, 1977.

Dugdale, Robert. *"The Jukes": A Study in Crime, Pauperism, Disease and Heredity; Also Further Studies of Criminals*. New York: G. P. Putnam's Sons, 1877.

Elrod, Preston, and Scott R. Ryder. *Juvenile Justice: A Social, Historical and Legal Perspective*. Salsbury, MA: Jacob & Bartlett Publishers, 2011.

English, T. J. *Paddy Whacked: The Untold Story of the Irish American Gangster*. New York: Regan Books. 2005.

Eysenck, Hans. *Dimensions of Personality*. London: Kegan Paul, Trench, Trübner & Co., 1947.

Faigman, David L. et al. *Modern Scientific Evidence: The Law and Science of Expert Testimony*. Vols. 1–4. Eagan, MN: Thomson Reuters/West, 2009.

Farabee, David. *Rethinking Rehabilitation: Why Can't We Reform Our Criminals?* Washington, DC: AEI Press, 2005.

Fidell, Eugene and Dwight Sullivan, eds. *Evolving Military Justice*. Annapolis, MD: U.S. Naval Institute Press, 2002.

Fischer, John F. and Joe Nickell. *Crime Science: Methods of Forensic Detection*. Lexington: University Press of Kentucky, 1999.

Fisher, Louis. *Military Tribunals and Presidential Power: American Revolution to the War on Terrorism*. Kansas City: University Press of Kansas, 2005.

Frederick, David C. *Rugged Justice: The Ninth Circuit Court of Appeals and the American West, 1891–1941*. Berkeley: University of California Press, 1994.

Friedman, Lawrence. *Crime and Punishment in American History*. New York: BasicBooks, 1993.

Garland, David. *Cultures of Control: Crime and Social Order in Contemporary Society*. Chicago: University of Chicago Press, 2001.

Garland, Robert. *Peculiar Institution: America's Death Penalty in an Age of Abolition*. Cambridge, MA: Belknap, 2010.

Geis, Gilbert and Leigh B. Bienen. *Crimes of the Century: From Leopold and Loeb to O.J. Simpson*. Lebanon, NH: Northeastern University Press, 2000.

Gibson, Dirk C. *Serial Murder and Media Circuses*. Westport, CT: Praeger, 2006.

Ginsburg, Faye D. *Contested Lives: Abortion Debate in an American Community*. Berkeley: University of California Press, 1989.

Goldstein, Leslie Friedman. *The Constitutional Rights of Women*, Rev. ed. Madison: University of Wisconsin Press, 1989.

Goring, Charles. *The English Convict: A Statistical Study*. London: H.M.S, 1913.

Gottfredson, Michael. *Control Theories of Crime and Delinquency*. New Brunswick, NJ: Transaction Books, 2003.

Gottschalk, Marie. *The Prison and the Gallows: The Politics of Mass Incarceration in America*. New York: Cambridge University Press, 2006.

Greenfeld, Lawrence A. *Alcohol and Crime: An Analysis of National Data on the Prevalence of Alcohol Involvement in Crime*. Washington, DC: Bureau of Justice Statistics, 1998.

Greenhouse, Linda and Reva B. Siegel. *Before Roe v. Wade: Voices That Shaped the Abortion Debate Before the Supreme Court's Ruling*. New York: Kaplan Publishing, 2010.

Haag, Lucien C. *Shooting Incident Reconstruction*. Amsterdam: Academic Press, 2006.

Hagan, John and Fiona Kay. *Gender in Practice: A Study of Lawyers' Lives*. New York: Oxford University Press, 1995.

Hall, Kermit and James Ely. *The Oxford Guide to United States Supreme Court Decisions*. New York: Oxford University Press, 2009.

Halttunen, Karen. *Confidence Men and Painted Women: A Study of Middle-Class Culture in America, 1830–1870*. New Haven, CT: Yale University Press, 1982.

Hariman, Robert, ed. *Popular Trials: Rhetoric, Mass Media, and the Law*. Tuscaloosa: University of Alabama Press, 1990

Harring, Sidney L. *Policing a Class Society: The Experience of American Cities, 1865–1915*. New Brunswick, NJ: Rutgers University Press, 1983.

Hirschi, Travis. *Causes of Delinquency*. Berkeley: University of California Press, 1969.

Hollon, Eugene. *Frontier Violence: Another Look*. New York: Oxford University Press, 1974.

Hornstein, Alan D. *Appellate Advocacy in a Nutshell*. St. Paul: Thomson West, 1998.

Irons, Peter and Stephanie Guitton. *May It Please the Court*. New York: New Press, 1993.

Jacoby, Joan. *The American Prosecutor: A Search for Identity*. Lexington, MA: Lexington Press Books, 1980.

James, Nathan and Logan Rishard Council. *How Crime in the United States is Measured*. Washington, DC: Congressional Research Service, 2008.

Jeffers, H. Paul. *Commissioner Roosevelt: The Story of Theodore Roosevelt and the New York City Police, 1895–1897*. New York: John Wiley & Sons, 1994.

Johnson, David R. *American Law Enforcement: A History*. Wheeling, IL: Forum Press, 1981.

Joyce, Jaime. *Bullet Proof! The Evidence That Guns Leave Behind*. New York: Scholastic, 2007.

Kahan, Paul. *Seminary of Virtue: The Ideology and Practice of Inmate Reform at Eastern State Penitentiary, 1829–1971*. New York: Peter Lang Publishing, 2012.

Kaufman-Osborn, Timothy V. *From Noose to Needle: Capital Punishment and the Late Liberal State*. Ann Arbor: University of Michigan, 2002.

Kavieff, Paul R. *The Purple Gang: Organized Crime in Detroit 1910–1945*. Fort Lee, NJ: Barricade Books, 2005.

Klein, David E. *Making Law in the United States Courts of Appeals*. New York: Cambridge University Press, 2002.

Klockars, Carl and Steven Mastrofski. *The Police and Serious Crime*. New York: McGraw-Hill, 1990.

Knappman, Edward W. *Great American Trials*. Detroit, MI: Visible Ink Press, 1994

Laband, David N. *Blue Laws: The History, Economics, and Politics of Sunday-Closing Laws*. Lexington, MA: D. C. Heath and Company, 1987.

Langum, David. *Crossing Over the Line: Legislating Morality and the Mann Act*. Chicago: University of Chicago Press, 1994.

Lerner, Michael. *Dry Manhattan: Prohibition in New York City*. Cambridge, MA: Harvard University Press, 2007.

Lurie, Jonathan. *Military Justice in America: The U.S. Court of Appeals for the Armed Forces, 1775–1980*. Lawrence: University Press of Kansas, 2001.

Lynch, James P. and Lynn A. Addington, eds. *Understanding Crime Statistics: Revisiting the Divergence of the NCVS and UCR.* New York: Cambridge University Press, 2007.

Manza, Jeff and Christopher Uggen. *Locked Out: Felon Disenfranchisement and American Democracy.* New York: Oxford University Press, 2006.

Maltz, E. M. *Slavery and the Supreme Court, 1825–1861.* Lawrence: University Press of Kansas, 2009.

Merton, Robert King. *Social Theory and Social Structure.* New York: Free Press, 1949.

Miller, Wilbur R. *Cops and Bobbies: Police Authority in New York and London, 1830–1870.* Chicago: University of Chicago Press, 1973.

Monkkonen, Eric. *Police in Urban America, 1860–1920.* New York: Cambridge University Press, 1981.

Morn, Frank. *"The Eye That Never Sleeps": A History of the Pinkerton National Detective Agency.* Bloomington: Indiana University Press, 1982.

Mosher, Clayton J., Terance D. Miethe, and Dretha M. Phillips. *The Mismeasure of Crime.* Thousand Oaks, CA: Sage, 2002.

Mullings, Leith, ed. *Cities of the United States: Studies in Urban Anthropology.* New York: Columbia University Press, 1987.

Neely, Richard. *Take Back Your Neighborhood.* New York: Donald I. Fine, 1990.

Oswald, Russell, *Attica: My Story.* New York: Doubleday, 1972.

Lane, Roger. *Murder in America: A History.* Columbus: Ohio State University Press, 1997.

Lott, M. Ray. *Police on Screen: Hollywood Cops, Detectives, Marshals, and Rangers.* London: McFarland & Co., 2006.

McGrath, Roger. *Gunfighters, Highwaymen, and Vigilantes: Violence on the Frontier.* Berkeley: University of California Press, 1984.

McShane, Marilyn D. and P. Frank Williams, III, eds. *Youth Violence and Delinquency: Monsters and Myths.* Westport, CT: Praeger Publishers, 2007.

Nelli, Humbert S. *The Business of Crime: Italians and Syndicate Crime in the United States.* Chicago: University of Chicago Press, 1976.

Paternoster, Raymond, Robert Brame, and Sarah Bacon. *The Death Penalty: America's Experience With Capital Punishment.* New York: Oxford University Press, 2008.

Peerenboom, Randall, ed. *Asian Discourses of Rule of Law: Theories and Implementation of Rule of Law.* London: Routledge, 2004.

Pernanen, Kai. *Alcoholism in Human Violence.* New York: Guilford Press, 1991.

Platt, Anthony M. *The Child Savers: The Invention of Delinquency.* Chicago: University of Chicago Press, 1969.

Posner, Richard. *Law, Pragmatism, Democracy,* Boston: Harvard University Press, 2005.

Potter, Claire Bond. *War on Crime: Bandits, G-men, and the Politics of Mass Culture.* New Brunswick, NJ: Rutgers University Press, 1998.

Prassel, Frank R. *The Western Peace Officer: A Legacy of Law and Order.* Norman: University of Oklahoma Press, 1981.

Quinney, Richard. *Bearing Witness to Crime and Social Justice.* Albany: State University of New York Press, 2000.

Radbill, Samuel, X. *The Battered Child.* Chicago: University of Chicago Press, 1968.

Reagan, Leslie J. *When Abortion Was a Crime: Women, Medicine and Law in the United States, 1867–1973.* Berkeley: University of California Press, 1997.

Reamer, Frederic G. *Heinous Crime: Cases, Causes, and Consequences.* New York: Columbia University Press, 2005.

Reaves, Brian A. *Census of State and Local Law Enforcement Agencies, 2008.* NCJ 233982. Washington, DC: U.S. Department of Justice, 2011.

Richards, David A. J. *The Sodomy Cases:* Bowers v. Hardwick *and* Lawrence v. Texas. Lawrence: University Press of Kansas, 2009.

Ringdal, Nils J. *Love For Sale: A World History of Prostitution.* New York: Grove Press, 2004.

Roberts, Marie Mulvey. *Writing for Their Lives: Death Row U.S.A.* Champaign: University of Illinois Press, 2007.

Rosen, Ruth. *The Lost Sisterhood: Prostitution in America 1900–1918.* Baltimore, MD: Johns Hopkins University Press, 1982.

Rosenberg, Mark L. and Mary Ann Fenley, eds. *Violence in America: A Public Health*

Approach. New York: Oxford University Press, 1991.

Roth, Mitchel P. *Crime and Punishment: A History of the Criminal Justice System*. Belmont, CA: Wadsworth, 2011.

Rumbarger, John. *Profits, Power and Prohibition: Alcohol Reform and the Industrializing of America, 1800–1930*. Albany: State University of New York Press, 1989.

Saunders, Kevin. *Degradation: What the History of Obscenity Tells Us About Hate Speech*. New York: New York University Press, 2011.

Schueter, David. *Military Criminal Justice: Practice and Procedure*. New York: Lexis-Nexis, 2008.

Seiter, Richard P. *Corrections: An Introduction*. Upper Saddle River, NJ: Pearson Prentice Hall, 2011.

Siegal, Larry and Clemens Bartollas. *Corrections Today*. Belmont, CA: Cengage, 2011.

Simon, Jonathan. *Governing Through Crime: How the War on Crime Transformed American Democracy and Created a Culture of Fear*. New York: Oxford University Press, 2007.

Skotnicki, Andrew. *Religion and the Development of the American Penal System*. Lanham, MD: University Press of America, 2000.

Stolberg, Mary. *Fighting Organized Crime: Politics, Justice and the Legacy of Thomas E. Dewey*. Lebanon, NH: Northeastern University Press, 1995.

Struckhoff, David R. *The American Sheriff*. Joliet, IL: SL Publishing/JRI, 1994.

Stuntz, William J. *The Collapse of American Criminal Justice*. Cambridge, MA: Harvard University Press, 2011.

Surette, R. *Media, Crime and Criminal Justice: Images and Realities*. Pacific Grove, CA: Brooks/Cole, 1992.

Tannenhaus, David. *Juvenile Justice in the Making*. New York: Oxford University Press, 2004.

Toobin, Jeffrey. *The Nine: Inside the Secret World of the Supreme Court*. New York: Random House, 2007.

Turk, Austin. *Criminality and Legal Order*. Chicago: Rand McNally, 1969.

Unger, Roberto. *Law in Modern Society: Towards a Criticism of Social Theory*. New Yark: Free Press, 1976.

Urey, W. Patrick. *Handgun Wounding Factors and Effectiveness*. Quantico, VA: FBI Academy, 1989.

U.S. Department of Justice. *Blueprint for the Future of the Uniform Crime Reporing Program*. Washington, DC: United States Department of Justice, 1985.

Wade, Wyn Craig. *The Fiery Cross: The Ku Klux Klan in America*. New York: Simon & Schuster, 1987.

Wadman, Robert C. and William T Allison. *To Protect and Serve*. Upper Saddle River, NJ: Pearson Prentice Hall, 2004.

Waldrep, Christopher and Michael Bellesiles, eds. *Documenting American Violence: A Sourcebook*. New York: Oxford University Press, 2006.

Walker, Ida. *The Death Penalty: Essential Viewpoints*. Edina, MN: ABDO Publishing, 2008.

Walters, Ronald. *American Reformers, 1815–1860*. New York: Hill and Wang, 1978.

Watson, Katherine D. *Forensic Medicine in Western Society: A History*. New York: Routledge, 2011.

Whiteacre, Kevin. *Drug Court Justice: Experiences in a Juvenile Drug Court*. New York: Peter Lang Publishing, 2008

Wicker, Tom, *Attica: A Time to Die*. New York: Quadrangle/New York Times Books, 1975.

Wilf, S. *Law's Imagined Republic: Popular Politics and Criminal Justice in Revolutionary America*. New York: Cambridge University Press, 2010.

Williamson, Joel. *The Crucible of Race: Black-White Relations in the American South Since Emancipation*. New York: Oxford University Press, 1984.

Wilson, James Q. *Thinking About Crime*. New York: Basic Books, 1975.

Wilson, Theodore B. *The Black Codes of the South*. Tuscaloosa: University of Alabama Press, 1987.

Wolcott, David B. and Tom Head. *Crime and Punishment in America*. New York: Facts on File, 2010.

Woodward, Bob and Scott Armstrong. *The Brethren: Inside the Supreme Court*. New York: Simon & Schuster, 1979.
Wright, James D., et al. *Under the Gun: Weapons, Crime, and Violence in America*. New York: Aldine, 1983.
Yochelson, Samuel and Stanton Samenow. *The Criminal Personality, Volume I: A Profile for Change*. New York: Jason Aronson, 1977.
Zeiten, Miriam Koktvedgaard. *Polygamy: A Cross-Cultural Analysis*. Oxford: Berg Publishers, 2008.
Zimring, Franklin. *The Contradictions of American Capital Punishment*. New York: Oxford University Press, 2003.

Journals
Aggression and Violent Behavior
American Journal of Legal History
American Journal of Sociology
Behavioral Sciences and the Law
Bulletin of the American Academy of Psychiatry and the Law
Crime, Law and Social Change
Crime and Delinquency
Crime and Justice
Criminal Justice and Behavior
Criminal Justice History
Criminology
Criminology & Criminal Justice
Critical Criminology
Federal Sentencing Reporter
Forensic Science, Medicine, and Pathology
Harvard Law Review
Journal of American Ethnic History
Journal of American Studies
Journal of Behavioral Profiling
Journal of Contemporary History
Journal of Criminal Justice
Journal of Criminal Law and Criminology
Journal of Experimental Criminology
Journal of Family Violence
Journal of Interpersonal Violence
Journal of Police and Criminal Psychology
Journal of Popular Culture
Journal of Quantitative Criminology
Journal of Research in Crime and Delinquency
Journal of Social History
Journal of the Southwest
Journal of Urban History
Justice Quarterly
Law and Critique
Law and History Review
Law and Human Behavior
Law and Society Review
Public Interest
Punishment and Society
Trends in Organized Crime

Internet
After Prison: Roadblocks to Reentry
http://www.lac.org/roadblocks-to-reentry/index.php
American Bar Association—Criminal Justice Section
http://www.americanbar.org/groups/criminal_justice.html
American National Archives
http://www.archives.gov
American Probation and Parole Association
http://www.appa-net.org/eweb
Association of State Correctional Administrators
http://www.asca.net
Bureau of Justice Statistics
http://bjs.ojp.usdoj.gov
Center for Law and Social Policy (CLASP)
http://www.clasp.org
Central Intelligence Agency World Fact Book
https://www.cia.gov/library/publications/the-world-factbook
Council of State Governments—Justice Center
http://www.justicecenter.csg.org
Crime in America.Net
http://www.crimeinamerica.net
Crime Spider—Criminal Justice Directory
http://www.crimespider.com
CrimeReports
http://www.crimereports.com
Criminal Justice Direct
http://cj-direct.com
Criminal Justice Information Services (FBI)
http://www.fbi.gov/about-us/cjis
Criminal Justice Policy Foundation
http://www.cjpf.org
Criminon International
http://www.criminon.org
Famous Trials
http://law2.umkc.edu/faculty/projects/ftrials/ftrials.htm

Federal Bureau of Investigation (FBI): Homepage
http://www.fbi.gov

Federal Bureau of Investigation (FBI): Uniform Crime Reports
http://www.fbi.gov/about-us/cjis/ucr/ucr

Federal Bureau of Investigation (FBI): "The Vault" (Records)
http://vault.fbi.gov

Federal Rules of Criminal Procedure
http://www.uscourts.gov/RulesAndPolicies/FederalRulemaking/Overview/CriminalRules.aspx

The Fingerprint Sourcebook (National Institute of Justice)
http://www.nij.gov/pubs-sum/225320.htm

Homicide Trends in the United States (BJS)
http://bjs.ojp.usdoj.gov/index.cfm?ty=pbdetail&iid=2221

International Center for the Prevention of Crime
http://www.crime-prevention-intl.org

Justice Policy Institute
http://www.justicepolicy.org/index.html

Legal Action Center
http://www.lac.org

National Conference of State Legislatures—Civil and Criminal Justice
http://www.ncsl.org/issues-research.aspx

National Criminal Justice Reference Service (Office of Justice Programs)
https://www.ncjrs.gov

National Public Service Council to Abolish Private Prisons
http://npsctapp.blogspot.com

Nolo Criminal Justice FAQs and Forms
http://www.nolo.com/legal-encyclopedia/criminal-law

Office of Justice Programs' Crime Solutions
http://www.crimesolutions.gov

Officer Down Memorial Page
http://www.odmp.org

President's Task Force on Identity Theft
http://www.idtheft.gov

Prison Reform Movement blog
http://prisonreformmovement.com

Prison Scholar Fund
http://www.prisonscholarfund.org

Right to Vote
http://www.righttovote.org

Sentencing Project
http://www.sentencingproject.org/template/index.cfm

Sourcebook of Criminal Justice Statistics (University at Albany)
http://www.albany.edu/sourcebook

Stanford Criminal Justice Center
http://www.law.stanford.edu/program/centers/scjc

United States Crime Rates 1960–2010 (Disaster Center)
http://www.disastercenter.com/crime/uscrime.htm

Index

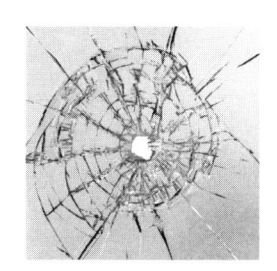

Index note: Volume numbers are in **boldface**. Article titles and their page numbers are in **boldface**. Page references to photo captions are in *italic*.

A

A Is for Alibi (Grafton), **2**:702, **3**:1031
a prima facie, **2**:512
a priori, **1**:390
AA (Alcoholics Anonymous), **2**:787
Aardsma, Betsy, **3**:1167
AAUW (American Association of University Women), **4**:1654–1655
Abbott, Karen, **2**:567
Abdulmutallab, Umar, **2**:802
Abington School District v. Schempp, **4**:1735
***Ableman v. Booth*, 1:xli, 1:1–2**
    Fugitive Slave Act and, **1**:1–2
    significance, **1**:2
abortion, 1:xlvi–xlviii, 1:2–8. See also ***Roe v. Wade***
    after *Roe v. Wade*, **1**:5–7
    Alabama ban, **1**:31–32
    American Law Institute statute, **1**:xliv, **1**:4–5
    in California, **1**:xlvi, **1**:4–5
    in Connecticut, **1**:xl
    during criminalization, **1**:4
    1801 to 1850, **5**:2067, **5**:2069
    gag rule, **1**:6
    information transport, **1**:xli
    laws, **1**:xliv
    legality quest, **1**:4–5
    lifesaving, **1**:4
    Medicaid and, **1**:xlvii, **1**:6
    ongoing debate, **1**:7
    overview, **1**:2–4
    pills, **1**:7
    protesters, **1**:xlviii
    public support for, **1**:xlv
    rates, **1**:7
    state laws, **1**:2
    waiting period, **1**:xlvii
Abraham, **1**:120
Abramoff, Jack, **4**:1925
Abrams, Jacob, **1**:8, **1**:9
***Abrams v. United States*, 1:8–9, 5:2178**
    clear and present danger, **1**:8–9
    Espionage Act of 1917 and, **1**:8
    Oliver Wendell Holmes and, **2**:798
ABSCAM, **1**:349
Abu Ghraib prison, **1**:190, **2**:577
Accardo, Tony, **2**:868
Accomplice, **3**:1026
Ace Books, **2**:467
ACFE (Association of Certified Fraud Examiners), **2**:648
ACLU. See **American Civil Liberties Union**
Acquitted, **2**:623
acts. See laws and acts
actus reus, **2**:463, **2**:902, **4**:1543

Adair v. United States, 1:xlii, 1:9–11
    significance, 1:10–11
    yellow dog contracts, 1:9–10
Adam-12, 4:1766
Adams, Charles, 2:526
Adams, John (administration of), 1:11–12, 1:38, 1:45, 1:346, 2:891
    federalist view, 2:586, 3:1438
    sedition prosecutions, 2:587, 3:1212
    shaping crime and punishment, 1:11
Adams, John Quincy (administration of), 1:12–14
    political career, 1:13–14
    youth and education, 1:12–13
Adamson v. California, 2:712
ADEA (Age Discrimination in Employment Act), 1:266
Adelphia, 4:1923
ADHD (attention deficit hyperactivity disorder), 2:750
Adkins v. Virginia, 1:208
Adler, Freda, 1:412, 4:1967
Administration of Justice Act of 1774, 1:45
Adonis, Joe, 2:783
adultery, 1:14–17
    condemnation, 1:15
    in cyberspace and workplace, 1:16
    defined, 1:14
    history of punishment, 1:14–16
    reasons for, 1:16
Adultery (DeSalvo), 1:16
Advance Passenger Information System (APIS), 1:89
Adventure, 2:467
adversarial justice, 1:17–20
    criticism, 1:20
    English common law and, 1:18
    history, 1:18–19
    modern system, 1:19–20
    theological, political, inquisitorial systems of justice, 1:17–18
AEDPA (Antiterrorism and Effective Death Penalty Act of 1996), 2:728, 3:1421
AFA (Airport Federalization Act), 1:xlviii, 1:88
affirmative action, 2:715–716
AFL (American Federation of Labor), 1:331, 2:807
Africa, John, 3:1140–1141
African Americans, 1:20–30. *See also* slavery
    Black Codes, 1:24–26, 1:263
    on chain gangs and prison labor, 1:214
    children, 1:164–165
    citizenship, 1:24
    civil rights laws and, 1:263

    civil rights movement, 1:27
    civil unrest, 3:1367
    Civil War and, 1:24–25
    death penalty and, 1:xlvi, 1:xlvii
    disenfranchisement, 2:538
    drug use, 1:xlix
    early history, 1:20–21
    early legal status, 1:21–23
    early to mid-20th century, 1:26–27
    Great Migration, 1:199
    in history of crime and punishment in America: 1783–1850, 2:765–766
    interstate commerce and, 1:xlv
    Jim Crow era, 1:25–26
    juries and, 1:xliv
    in law, 1:27–29
    legal complications, 1:23–24
    lynching, 1:26
    Nat Turner's Rebellion, 1:24, 4:1552
    National Black Police Association, 1:28
    Negro Question, 1:26
    police history, 3:1365–1366
    Prosser's Rebellion, 1:24
    rape and, 1:26
    servitude of, 1:xxxix
    Stono's Rebellion, 1:24
    in 21st century, 1:29
    voting and, 1:xlv, 1:24–25
    in World War II, 1:27
Age Discrimination in Employment Act (ADEA), 1:266
Agee, Philip, 2:559
aggressive behavior, 2:494–496
Agnew, Robert, 1:411
Agnew, Spiro, 1:271
Agyrrhius, 2:533
Aid to Families with Dependent Children, 1:5
AIDS/HIV, 1:7, 1:238, 1:342, 2:498, 3:1411, 4:1874
AILTO (American Institute for Law Training within the Office), 1:43
AIM (American Indian Movement), 2:971, 3:1204
Airport Federalization Act (AFA), 1:xlviii, 1:88
Akerman, Amos T., 1:25
Akers, Ronald, 1:380
Akron v. Akron Center for Reproductive Health, 1:6
Al Qaeda, 1:xlviii, 1:188, 2:528, 2:803, 3:1218, 3:1240–1241, 3:1380, 3:1385, 4:1781
    American intelligence agencies and, 4:1853
    CIA and, 2:854

Alabama, 1:30–34. *See also* **Birmingham, Alabama**
  abortion ban, **1:**31–32
  Birmingham Civil Rights Institute, **1:**32
  Bus Boycott (1955-1956), **1:**27
  crime, **1:**31–32
  Dixie Mafia, **1:**31
  Hammon-Beason Alabama Taxpayer and Citizen Protection Act, **5:**2448
  Ku Klux Klan, **1:**30
  police, **1:**30–31
  punishment, **1:**32–33
  16th street Baptist church bombing, **1:**31
  three-strikes laws, **1:**33
  Wetumpka State Penitentiary, **1:**30
  white supremacy, **1:**30
Al-Anon, **2:**480
Alaska, 1:34–36
  crime, **1:**34
  police, **1:**34–35
  punishment, **1:**35
Albany Regency, **1:**176
Albatross, **2:**467
Alberts v. California, **4:**1583
Alcala, Rodney, **1:**xlix
Alcatraz Island Prison, 1:xlii–xliv, **1:**36–37
  criminals, **1:**36
  "Devil's Island," **1:**36
  escape attempts, **1:**37
  Escape From Alcatraz, **2:**614, **2:**624
  "The Rock," **1:**36
  single-occupancy cells, **1:**36
Alcohol and Tobacco Tax Division (ATTD), **1:**174–175
alcohol consumption, **4:**1960–1961
Alcoholics Anonymous (AA), **2:**787
Alden v. Maine, **1:**249
ALDF (Animal Legal Defense Fund), **1:**420
Alexander, Michelle, **5:**2452
Alexander, Myrl, **2:**594
ALF (Animal Liberation Front), **4:**1780
ALI. *See* **American Law Institute**
Alien and Sedition Acts of 1798, 1:xl, **1:**11–12, **1:**37–38
  denouement, **1:**38
  deportation and, **1:**447
  enactment, **1:**38, **1:**346
  parts, **1:**38
  residency requirement, **5:**2035–2036
Alien Registration Act. *See* **Smith Act**
Alito, Samuel, **1:**191
Alix, Ernest Kahlar, **2:**955
Allan, Trevor, **4:**1589

Allen, Arthur Leigh, **4:**1989
Allerfeldt, Kristofer, **2:**536
Allgeyer v. Louisiana, **2:**510
Altgeld, John Peter, **1:**428
Always Running (Rodriguez), **1:**85
AMA (American Medical Association), **1:**2–3, **2:**503
Amalgamated Association of Iron and Steel Workers, **1:**xlii, **2:**771
Amazing Stories, **2:**467
Amazingly Graced (Lane), **3:**1095
American Association of University Women (AAUW), **4:**1654–1655
American Bar Association, 1:39–40, **1:**216, **2:**471
  criminal justice section, **1:**39
  Death Penalty Moratorium Implementation Project, **5:**2457
  mission and activities, **1:**39
American Civil Liberties Union, 1:xlii, **1:**40–42, **1:**156–157
  Bill of Rights and, **1:**40
  founding and history, **1:**40
  Griswold v. Connecticut and, **2:**714
  hanging and, **2:**737
  landmark cases, **1:**41–42
  members, **1:**40
  racial justice, **4:**1516
  sodomy laws and, **2:**812–813
American Colonization Society, **3:**1072
American dream, **1:**380, **2:**678
American Federation of Labor (AFL), **1:**331, **2:**807
American Gangster, **2:**614
American Indian Movement (AIM), **2:**971, **3:**1204
American Institute for Law Training within the Office (AILTO), **1:**43
American Journal of Police Science, **2:**640
American Journal of Radiology, **1:**230
American Law Institute, 1:xliii, **1:**42–44, **1:**285, **4:**1573
  abortion statute, **1:**xliv, **1:**4–5
  creation, **1:**42
  educational opportunities, **1:**43
  Model Penal Code, **2:**840
  publications, **1:**43
  resources, **1:**43
  statutory projects, **1:**43
  structure and function, **1:**42–43
American legal system, **1:**284–285
American Medical Association (AMA), **1:**2–3, **2:**503
American Party, **2:**611–612. *See also* Know-Nothing Party
American Protective League, **4:**1882

American Psychiatric Association, **1:**437, **2:**498
American Psychology/Law Society (AP/LS),
    4:1951–1952
American Public Health Association, **1:**4
American Rattlers, **2:**672
American Revolution and criminal justice, 1:21,
    1:44–46, **4:**1530, **5:**1996
    change from war, **1:**44–45
    counterfeiting and, **1:**355
American Society for Prevention of Cruelty to
    Animals (ASPCA), **1:**420
American Society of Crime Laboratory Directors,
    1:401
American Telephone and Telegraph (AT&T), **1:**267
American Temperance Union, **2:**491
American Tobacco Company, **1:**267
An American Tragedy, **1:**xliii, **1:**46–47, **3:**1274.
    See also Dreiser, Theodore
    based in reality, **1:**47
    plot of, **1:**46–47
    on working poor, **1:**47
American Trial Lawyers Association (ATLA), **3:**995
Americans with Disabilities Act of 1990, **1:**xlvii,
    1:266
America's Most Wanted, **3:**1245, **4:**1766
America's Toughest Sheriff, **1:**65. *See also* **Arpaio,**
    Joseph M.
Ames, Aldrich, **2:**559, **3:**1378
Amistad, **1:**176–177
amnesty
    clemency and, **1:**268–269
    tax, **4:**1750
Amsterdam House of Corrections, **2:**914
Anabaptists, **1:**120–121, **2:**759
Anarchism and Other Essays (Goldman, E.), **1:**49
anarchists, 1:47, **1:**47–51
    arguments, **1:**47–48
    August Spies, **1:**49
    early history, **1:**48–49
    emphasis, **1:**47
    Haymarket bombing, **1:**49–50
    IWMA, **1:**48–49
    modern, **1:**50–51
    personal action, **1:**47
    Propaganda by Deed, **1:**50
anarcho-communism, **1:**48
anarcho-syndicalism, **1:**48
anarchy
    classical, **1:**47
    contemporary, **1:**47
    statutes, **5:**2177

Anaya, Toney, **1:**272
Anderson, Archibald, **1:**198
Anderson, Elijah, **2:**678–679
Anderson, Nels, **4:**1849
Andersonville Prison, **5:**2100
Andre, John, **5:**2035
Andros, Edmund, **1:**294
Andy Griffith Show, **4:**1763
Angela Davis: An Autobiography (Davis), **1:**83
Angiulo, Jerry, **4:**1549
Anglin, Frank, **1:**37
Anglin, John, **1:**37
Animal Legal Defense Fund (ALDF), **1:**420
Animal Liberation (Singer), **1:**420
Animal Liberation Front (ALF), **4:**1780
anomic theory, **3:**1387
anomie theory, **1:**55, **1:**380
Anonymous, **1:**310
Anselmi, Albert, **1:**211
Anslinger, Henry, **2:**778
Anthony, Casey, **4:**1893
Anthony, Caylee, **4:**1893
Anthony, Susan B., **3:**114–115
Anti-Arson Act, **1:**175
Anti-Coolie Act, **1:**194
antidiscrimination
    Strauder v. West Virginia, **4:**1721
    white-collar crime and, **4:**1931
Anti-Draft Riots, **4:**1553
Anti-Drug Abuse Acts of 1986, **1:**28, **1:**187
anti-Federalist Papers, 1:51–52
    constitutional critiques, **1:**51–52
    organization, **1:**52
anti-Federalists, **1:**123, **2:**599–600
Anti-Pinkerton Act, **3:**1423
Anti-Rent War, **4:**1553
antisocial personality disorder (ASPD), **2:**750
Antiterrorism and Effective Death Penalty Act of
    1996 (AEDPA), **2:**728, **3:**1421
antitrust law, 1:52–55. *See also* **Clayton Anti-Trust**
    Act of 1914; Sherman Antitrust Act
    current, **1:**53–54
    history, **1:**52–53
    prosecutions, **1:**54
    violations, **4:**1927–1928
antiwar movements, **2:**785–786
apartment scandal, **1:**321
APIS (Advance Passenger Information System), **1:**89
AP/LS (American Psychology/Law Society),
    4:1951–1952
Apodaca v. Oregon, **2:**899

Apostolic United Bretheren, **1:**122
appeals, 1:55–58. *See also* **courts**
   appellate court proceedings, **1:**57
   attorneys' roles, **1:**56–57
   two-tiered appellate process, **1:**55–56
   verdicts and, **1:**57–58
appellate courts, 1:58–61
   American system, **1:**59–61
   attorneys in, **1:**60
   overview, **1:**58–59
   proceedings, **1:**57
   two-tiered process, **1:**55–56
Applewhite, Marshall, **4:**1642
Appo, George, **1:**85, **3:**1350
Arab American Chalean Council, **2:**482
Arabian Nights, **1:**314
Arbuckle, Roscoe ("Fatty"), **2:**575, **5:***2209,* **5:***2219*
Archaeological Resources Protection Act (ARPA), **2:**546
Archainbaud, George, **2:**623
Archer-Gilligan, Amy, **4:**1963
Argensinger v. Hamlin, **1:**364, **1:**442, **3:**1002
Ariès, Philippe, **4:**1671
Aristophanes, **1:**314
Aristotle, **2:**838, **4:**1587, **4:**1680
Arizona, 1:61–63
   contemporary challenges, **1:**62–63
   statehood, **1:**62
   Support Our Law Enforcement and Safe Neighborhoods Act, **1:**xlix
   territorial era, **1:**61–62
Arizona v. Gant, **1:**364
Arizona v. Roberson, **3:**1000
Arkansas, 1:63–65
   crime, **1:**63–64
   police, **1:**64
   punishment, **1:**64–65
Armed and Dangerous (Gallo), **3:**1092
Armed Career Criminal Act of 1986, **2:**720
armed forces integration, **1:**xliv, **1:**27, **1:**264
Arming America (Bellesiles), **2:**718
Arms Export Control Act, **1:**175
Arnold, Benedict, **5:***2035*
Aronson, Harvey, **1:**99
ARPA (Archaeological Resources Protection Act), **2:**546
Arpaio, Joseph M., 1:63, **1:**65–67, **3:**1402
   America's Toughest Sheriff, **1:**65
   lawsuits, **1:**67
   reforms, **1:**66

arraignment, 1:67–68
   plea bargaining, **1:**68
   process, **1:**67–68
Arridy, Joe, **1:**296
arsenal of democracy, **4:**1579
The Art of War (Sun Tzu), **2:**556
Artaxerxes II, **1:**118
Arthur, Chester (administration of), 1:68–71, **1:**121, **2:**682
   court system and, **1:**69
   cowboys and Indians, **1:**69–70
   polygamy and, **1:**70
Arthur Anderson LLP, **2:**540–541
Articles of Confederation, 1:46, **1:**51–52, **1:**71–72
   criminal law and, **5:**2036–2037
   drafting, **1:**71
   loosely binding, **1:**72
   provisions, **1:**71–72
Arvozo, Gavin, **2:**575
Ashcraft v. Tennessee, **4:**1739, **5:**2268
Ashoka, **4:**1590
Asiatic Barred Zone, **1:**245
ASPCA (American Society for Prevention of Cruelty to Animals), **1:**420
ASPD (antisocial personality disorder), **2:**750
assassinations
   Abraham Lincoln, **1:**xli, **1:**143, **2:**575, **3:**1012, **4:**1887, **5:**2102
   CIA plots, **1:**349, **2:**521
   Garfield, **1:**xli, **2:**682, **2:**716, **3:**1329, **5:**2109
   John F. Kennedy, **1:**xlv, **1:**103, **2:**720, **2:**946, **3:**1312–1313, **4:**1907
   Robert F. Kennedy, **1:**xlvi, **1:**223, **2:**720, **2:**949
   Martin Luther King, Jr., **1:**xlvi, **1:**106, **1:**223, **2:**720, **2:**960, **3:***1384,* **4:**1505–1506, **4:**1554
   Malcolm X, **3:**1063
   McKinley, **1:**xlii, **1:**426, **1:**451, **2:**526, **2:**767, **3:**1088, **5:**2109, **5:**2165
   Obama attempt, **1:**xlix
   Reagan attempt, **1:**xlvii, **2:**575, **2:**840, **4:**1829
Assimilative Crimes Act of 1825, **3:**1465
Assize of Clarendon, **1:**67
Association of Certified Fraud Examiners (ACFE), **2:**648
AT&T (American Telephone and Telegraph), **1:**267
ATF. *See* **Bureau of Alcohol, Tobacco, Firearms and Explosives**
Atkins v. Virginia, **1:**341, **1:**418, **1:**437, **3:**1421, **4:**1895, **5:**2458

ATLA (American Trial Lawyers Association), 3:995
Atlanta, Georgia, 1:72–75
    Atlanta Olympic Games bombing, 2:585
    Atlanta Police Department, 1:72–74
    Leo Frank and, 1:74
    1996 Olympics bombing, 1:74–75
    1906 race riot, 1:74
    youth murders, 1:74
Atlas Shrugged (Rand), 3:1006
ATMs (automatic teller machines), 1:179
ATTD (Alcohol and Tobacco Tax Division), 1:174–175
attention deficit hyperactivity disorder (ADHD), 2:750
Attica, 1:75–77
    aftermath, 1:77
    over time, 1:75
    riot, 1:xlvi, 1:75–77
attorneys. *See also* **district attorney; United States attorneys**
    in appellate courts, 1:60
    role in appeals, 1:56–57
Atzerodt, George, 1:143
Auburn State Prison, 1:77–79, 1:120, 1:278, 3:1332
    Black Solidarity Day, 1:79
    building silent system, 1:77–78, 1:337
    current population, 1:79
    overcrowding, 1:79
    penal reform, 1:78–79
Audubon Society, 2:630
August Spies, 1:49
Augustine of Hippo, 4:1670
Augustus, John, 1:xl, **1:79–81,** 1:338, 3:1432
    probation system and, 1:79–80
    Washington Total Abstinence Society and, 1:79
AUMF (Authorization to Use Military Force), 1:189, 2:802
Austrian General Civil Code, 1:284
Authorization to Use Military Force (AUMF), 1:189, 2:802
auto theft, 1:513
autobiographies, criminals', 1:81–85
    contemporary accounts, 1:84–85
    early, 1:81–82
    political prisoners, 1:83–84
    20th century, 1:82–83
The Autobiography of America's Master Swindler (Weil), 1:82
Autobiography of an L.A. Gang Member (Shakur), 1:85
automatic teller machines (ATMs), 1:179

automobile and the police, 1:xlii, **1:85–88**
    Dodge Police Package, 1:87
    early use, 1:85–86
    Ford LTD Crown Victoria, 1:86
    motorized versus walking patrol, 1:87–88
    paddy wagons, 1:85
    patrol cars, 1:85
    popular models and equipment, 1:86–87
    prowl cars, 1:85
    squad cars, 1:85
Aviation and Transportation Security Act of 2001, 1:xlviii, **1:88–90**
    acceptance and controversy, 1:90
    hand searches, 1:89
    for screening, 1:88–89

B
Babcock Orville E., 2:704
Bacon, Nathaniel, 1:21, 5:*1993*
Bacon's Rebellion (1676), 1:21, 2:757, 5:*1993*
Bad Lieutenant: Port of Call New Orleans, 2:619
Baerwaldt, Wayne, 2:662
Baez, Joan, 4:1749
bail and bond, 1:xxxix, 1:xlv, 1:xlvii, **1:91–95**
    in America, 1:92–94
    bail agents, 1:95
    bail agents and bounty hunters, 1:95
    Eighth Amendment excessive bail clause, 1:95, 1:96, 1:123, 1:287, 1:326
    history, 1:91–92
    purpose, 1:91
    reform, 1:94–95
Bail Reform Act, 1:xlv, 1:xlvii, 1:94, **1:96–98**
    1984 act, 1:97
    1966 act, 1:97
Bailey, Carl, 1:64
Bailey, F. Lee, 1:98–99, 1:449
    controversy, 1:99
    education, 1:98
    notable cases, 1:98
    writings, 1:99
Bailey, Harvey, 2:957
Baird, William, Jr., 2:523
bait-and-switch swindle, 1:320–321
Baker, Frank, 1:127
Baker, Joseph E., 5:*2003*
Baker, Newton, 3:1406
Bakker, Jim, 1:100–101
    conviction and imprisonment, 1:101
    Covenant House, 1:101

700 Club television debut, **1:**100
    sexual encounters, **1:**100–101
Bakker, Lori Graham, **1:**101
Bakker, Tammy Faye, **1:**100–101
Bakley, Bonnie Lee, **2:**575
Bakunin, Mikhail, **1:**48
Baldus Study, **1:**208
Baldwin, Adam, **2:**662
Baldwin, Roger, **1:**xlii, **1:**40
Ballantine Books, **2:**467
Ballard, Donald, **4:**1840–1841
Ballard, Edna, **4:**1840–1841
ballistics, 1:xl, **1:101–105**
    as evidence, **1:**103
    external, **1:**104
    FBI lab, **1:**102–103
    history, **1:**101–103
    investigations, **1:**104
    science of, **1:**103–104
Baltimore, Maryland, 1:105–108
    Baltimore Police Department, **1:**107–108
    Bodymore, Murdaland, **1:**107
    contemporary era, **1:**106–107
    Great Railway Strike of 1877, **1:**106
    heroin epidemic, **1:**106
    historical background, **1:**105–106
    Mob City, **1:**105–106
    politics, **1:**108
    television series, **1:**108
banishment, **4:**1659–1660, **5:**1997
bank robbery, **4:**1560–1561, **5:**2073, **5:**2105.
    See also **Bonnie and Clyde; James, Jesse;**
    train robbery
Banks, Dennis, **2:**971
Banner, Stuart, **2:**571
Barbara, Joseph, **2:**689
Barbour, Haley, **3:**1118
Baretta, **4:**1769
Barfield, Velma, **1:**xlvii
Barker, Bernard, **4:**1916
Barnes, George Kelly ("Machine Gun Kelly"), **1:**xliii
Barney Miller, **4:**1763
Barred Zone Act, **4:**1981
Barreiro Laborda, Oldemar C., **2:**535
Barristi, Frank, **2:**951
***Barron v. Mayor of Baltimore,* 1:**xl, **1:108–109,**
    1:123, **2:**900
    Bill of Rights and, **1:**108–109
    John Marshall conclusion, **1:**109
Barrow, Clyde. *See* **Bonnie and Clyde**
Barry, Marion, **5:***2417*

Barrymore, John, **2:**567
Bartelme, Mary, **2:***921*
Baruch, Bernard, **2:**521
Basile, Joseph, **3:***1176*
Bass, Sam, **2:**938
Bates, Edward, **3:**1011, **3:**1012
Bathory, Elizabeth, **4:**1636
Batson v. Kentucky, **1:**256
The Battered Woman Syndrome (Walker), **2:**481
The Battle With the Slum (Riis), **5:**2162
BAU (Behavioral Analysis Unit), **4:**1643
Bauerdorf, Georgette, **3:**1166
Baugh, Howard, **1:**73
Baumont, Gustave de, 1:xl, **1:110–111**
    American penitentiary investigation, **1:**110–111
    de Tocqueville and, **1:**110–111
Baxley, Bill, **1:**31
Bayley, David, **1:**87
Baze v. Rees, **1:**209, **3:**1421, **4:**1736
Beadle & Adams, **2:**465–466
Beal v. Doe, **1:**5
Bean, Roy, **5:**2105
bear baiting, **1:**134
beats, **4:**1600–1601
Beccaria, Cesare, **1:**xl, **1:**378–379, **1:**407, **2:**569,
    4:1632
    defining crime, **5:**2044
    imprisonment and, **2:**824
    influence, **2:**761
    mandatory minimum sentencing and, **4:**1628
    punishment and, **1:**456, **4:**1514
    vision of, **1:**455–456
Beck, Martin, **3:**1025
Becker, Howard S., **1:**411
Beckwith, Bob, **5:***2444*
Bedard, Henry, **3:**1167
Bedford Hills Correctional Facility, 1:111–113
    decline, **1:**112–113
    initial success, **1:**111–112
    Laboratory of Social Hygiene, **1:**112
    new penology, **1:**112
    today, **1:**113
Beecher, Henry Ward, **1:***15*
Beesmyer, Gilbert H., **2:**534
Beets, Betty Lou, **4:**1963
Behan, Johnny, **1:**162, **2:**515–516
Behavioral Analysis Unit (BAU), **4:**1643
Beirne, P., **3:**1386
Belknap, William W., **2:**704
Bell, Tom, **4:**1562
Bell v. Cone, **3:**1004

Bell v. Wolfish, **1:**364, **4:**1741
Bellesiles, Michael A., **2:**718, **5:**2075
Belloti v. Baird, **1:**6
Belluardo, Josh, **1:**234
Bennett, James, **1:**172, **2:**594, **3:**1249
Bennett, William, **1:**187
Bentham, Jeremy, **1:**378–379, **1:**407, **1:**456, **4:**1628
Benton v. Maryland, **1:**440
Berger, Peter, **4:**1673
Bergh, Henry, **1:**419
Berghuis v. Thompkins, **1:**364, **4:**1736
Berkeley, William, **5:**1993
Berkman, Alexander, **1:**48, **1:**49
Berkowitz, David, **1:**xlvii, **1:**103, **1:**113–115, **2:**576, **4:**1891
Bernstein, Carl, **1:**349
Bertillon, Alphonse, **1:**115, **1:**453, **2:**638, **5:**2162
Bertillon System, **1:**xli, **1:**115–117, **1:**433, **5:**2162
    development, **1:**115
    fingerprinting replacing, **1:**117
    inherent difficulties, **1:**117
    measurement and classification, **1:**116–117
Bethea, Rainey, **2:**569
Better Business Bureau, **2:**814
Betts v. Brady, **2:**697, **3:**1002
Beverly Hills Cop, **2:**617
Beverly's Case, **3:**1124
B'hoys of New York (Buntline), **1:**173
Bianchi, Kenneth, **1:**xlvii
Bible, **1:**117–120, **1:**204
    Brass Buckle of Bible Belt, **2:**939
    crime and punishment in Hebrew Scriptures, **1:**118–119
    crime and punishment in New Testament, **1:**118
    in early American correctional experience, **1:**119–120
    sodomy defined, **4:**1695
    spying in, **2:**556
    Ten Commandments, **4:**1670
Biblical Patriarchal Christian Fellowship of God's Free Men and Women, **1:**121
Biddle, Francis, **4:**1580
Biden, Joseph, **4:**1854
B.I.G., **3:**1169
Big Business, **1:**272
The Big House, **2:**621
Big L. Harlem, **3:**1169
The Big Sleep (Chandler), **3:**1018, **3:**1029–1030

bigamy/polygamy, **1:**70, **1:**120–122
    illegality, **1:**121
    among Mormons, **1:**121–122, **1:**406
    secret practice, **1:**121
Biggers, Earl Dean, **3:**1022
Bill of Rights, **1:**xl, **1:**19, **1:**46, **1:**51, **1:**122–125
    adoption, **1:**37
    American Civil Liberties Union and, **1:**40
    applying, **1:**24, **1:**60
    Barron v. Mayor of Baltimore and, **1:**108–109
    Constitution and, **1:**109, **1:**326–327
    crafting, **5:**2037
    derivation, **1:**122–123
    early version, **1:**442
    effect on criminal justice, **1:**123–124
    incorporation, **1:**124–125
    intention, **1:**167
    Supreme Court on, **1:**xl
    uniform standard, **1:**124–125
Billy the Kid, **1:**125–127, **2:**938
    beginnings, **1:**125–126
    death of, **1:**127
    outlaw, **1:**126–127
bin Laden, Osama, **1:**189, **3:**1380, **3:**1407
biological theories of crime, **4:**1800–1801
Birger, Charlie, **2:**818
Birmingham, Alabama, **1:**127–129
    Birmingham Civil Rights Institute, **1:**32
    as Bombingham, **1:**128
    Children's Crusade, **1:**128
    crime, **1:**129
    Letter From a Birmingham Jail, **1:**128
    police, **1:**128–129
    segregation and civil rights, **1:**127–128
birth control, **1:**5, **1:**7, **1:**313, **2:**523, **3:**1014, **5:**2110. *See also* **abortion**
Birth of a Nation, **1:**244, **2:**835, **2:**906, **2:**968, **3:**1182
BJS (Bureau of Justice Statistics), **1:**341, **1:**382, **1:**396, **2:**494
Black, Hugo, **2:**714, **2:**943, **4:**1841, **4:**1985
Black, Jeremiah S., **1:**168
Black Bart. *See* **Boles, Charles**
Black Chamber, **2:**558
Black Codes, **1:**24–26, **1:**263
    Jackson, Mississippi, **2:**871
    repeal of, **2:**551
Black Hand gang, **5:**2166, **5:**2167, **5:**2173
Black Hawk, **2:**832
Black in Blue, **1:**28
The Black Marble (Wambaugh), **4:**1904
Black Mask, **2:**467, **3:**1029

Black Muslims, 1:75, 3:1061–1062
Black Panthers, 1:xlv, 1:75–76, 1:83, 1:129–131, 1:222
   dissolution, 1:131
   founding, 1:129, 3:1468
   J. Edgar Hoover targeting, 1:130–131
   platform, 1:129–130
   protests and outreach, 1:130–131
   schism, 1:131
The Black Robe, 4:1762
The Blackest Bird (Rose), 2:748
blacklisting, 1:10, 2:734
blackmail, 4:1878
Blackmon, Douglas, 1:330
Blackmun, Harry A., 4:1574–1575
Blackstone, William, 1:xl, 1:131–134, 1:298, 5:*2031*
   Commentaries on the Laws of England, 1:132–133, 1:371, 1:438, 1:441
   education, 1:132
   Enlightenment writings, 5:2042
   legal expertise, 1:132
Blagojevic, Rod, 1:xlix
Blaine, James G., 2:682
Blair, John, 1:248
Blake, Robert, 1:99, 2:575
Blakely v. Washington, 4:1630, 4:1634
blameworthiness, 4:1543–1544
Blanton, Thomas, 1:31
Blauensteiner Elfriede ("Sugar"), 4:1963
Blaylock, Ronda, 3:1169
Blaze v. Rees, 1:418
The Blessing Way (Hillerman), 2:752, 3:1024
blood sports, 1:xlviii, 1:134–136
   bear baiting, 1:134
   cock fighting, 1:134–135
   dog fighting, 1:135
   eel pulling, 1:134
   gander pulling, 1:134
   rat catching, 1:134
   reduction efforts, 1:134–135
Blood Tubs, 2:672
Bloody Barrows gang, 1:140
Blow, 2:614
The Blue Knight (Wambaugh), 4:1904
Blue Laws. *See also* State Blue Laws.
Blue Streak, 2:618
Board of Education v. Earls, 3:1178
Bobbies, 1:450
Bobbit, Lorena, 2:576
Boccaccio, Giovanni, 1:314
Bochco, Steven, 4:1766, 4:1770

Bodie of Liberties, 1:136–137, 5:*2003*
   capital laws, 1:137
   as progressive, 1:136
   promoting religious orthodoxy, 1:137
   Puritans and, 1:136
Bodine, Polly, 1:137–138, 2:684–685, 3:1166
   charges dropped, 1:138
   trials, 1:137–138
   Witch of Staten Island, 1:137
The Body in the Library (Christie), 3:1028–1029
Body of Proof, 4:1762
Bodymore, Murdaland, 1:107
Bogart, Humphrey, 2:613
Boles, Charles, 1:138–139
   apprehension and conviction, 1:139
   modus operandi, 1:138
Bolger v. Youngs Drug Products Corp., 1:314
Bolsheviks, 1:49, 4:1595, 4:1605
Bombingham, 1:128
bombings. *See also* **Birmingham, Alabama; Oklahoma City bombing**
   Atlanta Olympic Games, 2:585
   Haymarket bombing, 1:xli, 1:49–50, 1:220
   Miami, Florida, 3:1100
   1996 Olympics bombing, 1:74–75
   16th Street Baptist Church bombing, 1:xlv, 1:31
   Wall Street bombing of 1920, 1:50
   World Trade Center, 1993, 1:xli, 2:585, 3:1385
Bonanno, Joseph, 1:84
Bonanza, 4:1884
Bonaparte, Charles J., 2:776
Bonaparte, Napoleon, 1:283–284, 2:880
The Bond Street Burlesque (Paul), 1:423
Bones, 4:1762
Bonger, Willem, 1:408
Bonney, William H. *See* **Billy the Kid**
Bonnie and Clyde, 1:139–140, 2:464, 2:707, 3:1157
   Bloody Barrows gang, 1:140
   Bonnie and Clyde (film), 1:xliii, 2:614
   media frenzy, 2:583
   trapping and deaths, 1:140
Booher, G Donald, 3:1324
Book of Life, 4:1671
Book of the General Lawes and Libertyes, 1:141–142
Bookchin, Murray, 1:51
Boomer generation, 1:398, 5:2243
Boomerang, 1:421
boomtowns, 2:653
Boone, David Shelton, 3:1378
Boone, Levi, 1:218, 5:2071

Booth, John Wilkes, 1:xli, 1:142–143, 2:575
    Abraham Lincoln assassination, 1:143, 5:2102
    capture and death of, 1:143
    kidnapping plot, 1:143
Booth, Sherman, 1:1–2, 5:2097
bootlegging, 1:143–145, 2:818
    Al Capone and, 2:818
    crime and, 1:145
    defined, 1:143
    height of activity, 1:144–145
    KKK and, 2:818
    moonlighters and, 1:144
    Prohibition and, 1:144, 3:1448–1449
    Arnold Rothstein and, 4:1585
Borden, Lizzie, 1:145–147, 4:1963
    acquittal, 1:147
    beginning of mystery, 1:145–146
    investigation, 1:146
    trial, 1:146–147
The Border, 2:619
border patrol, 1:147–150
    activities, 1:150
    EPIC, 1:149
    establishment, 1:147–148
    Green Machine training, 1:148–149
    homeland security, 1:148
    nonmilitary security, 1:149–150
border security, 2:822–823
Boren, David, 2:849
Bork, Robert, 4:1916
born criminal, 2:749, 4:1966
Bose, Subhash Chandra, 1:258
Bosket, Willie, 2:921
boss system, 3:1364–1365
    Cincinnati, Ohio, 1:251, 1:253
    mob system, 2:818
Boston, Massachusetts, 1:150–154
    Boston Massacre, 1:45, 5:2006
    Boston Police Department (BPD), 1:150–153
    Boston Port Act of 1774, 1:45
    Boston Tea Party, 4:1552, 4:1749, 5:1996
    crime and criminals, 1:151–152
    criticism and innovation, 1:153–154
    CWACU, 1:152
    law enforcement capabilities, 1:150
    Operation Ceasefire, 2:725–726
Boswell, John, 1:236
Bough Breaks (Kellerman), 3:1024
Boumediene v. Bush, 2:728, 2:731
Bounds v. Smith, 2:889

bounty hunters, 1:95, 1:154–156
    evolution, 1:155
    job skills, 1:156
    modern regulation, 1:155
bourgeoisie, 1:381
Bours v. United States, 1:314
Bow Street Runners, 1:450, 5:1992
Bowers, Michael, 1:157
Bowers v. Hardwick, 1:156–158, 1:178, 4:1697
    aftermath, 1:158
    background, 1:156–157
    protests, 1:157
    right to privacy, 1:157–158, 3:992
Bowery B'houys, 2:674, 2:767–768
boycotts
    Bus Boycott (1955-1956), 1:27
    vigilantism, 4:1883
Boyd, Belle, 2:557
Boyd, Kenneth Lee, 2:571
Boynton v. Virginia, 1:xliv, 1:264, 2:970
BPD (Boston Police Department), 1:150–153
Brace, Charles Loring, 1:236
Bracero Program, 4:1486
Bradford, William, 2:904, 3:1082, 4:1514
Bradley v. State, 2:483
Bradwell v. Illinois, 3:1115
Brady, James, 1:xlvii, 4:1829
Brady Handgun Violence Prevention Act, 2:721, 2:725, 5:2412
Brady v. United States, 3:1355
Bram v. United States, 1:316
Branch Davidians, 1:175, 1:277, 2:577
Branch v. Texas, 2:659
Brandeis, Louis, 2:487, 2:714
Brandenburg, Clarence, 1:158
Brandenburg v. Ohio, 1:158–160, 1:195, 1:446
    Brandenburg test, 1:158–159
    case details, 1:158–159
    decisions overturned, 1:159
    lasting impact, 1:160
    obscenity laws, 3:1280
    per curimam decision, 1:159
branding, 4:1243, 5:2006
Brantingham, Patricia, 1:391
Brantingham, Paul, 1:391
Bratton, William, 1:153
The Brave One, 4:1884
Brawley, Tawanna, 1:28
Brayley, Frederick Augustus, 5:2174
breaker boys, 1:228
Breathalyzer test, 4:1740

Breckenridge, William, **1**:162
Breckinridge, John, **2**:904
Brennan, William J., Jr., 1:160–161, **1**:206, **4**:1583
 Eisenhower nomination, **1**:160
 tenure and cases, **1**:161
Brennen, John O., **2**:*803*
Bretherton, Howard, **2**:623
Brewer, Lawrence, **5**:2458
Brewster, Benjamin, **2**:905
Breyer, Stephen, **1**:212
Brinkerhoff, John, **2**:849
Brisman, Julissa, **4**:1892
Bristow, Benjamin H., **1**:25, **1**:347, **2**:905
Britton, Nan, **2**:740
Brocius, William, 1:161–163, **2**:515–516
 Clanton-McLowery gang member, **1**:162
 death of, **1**:162
 lawman trouble, **1**:162
 outlaw, **1**:161–162
Brockway, William, **1**:357
Brockway, Zebulon, 1:163–164, **1**:339, **2**:518
 Declaration of Principles, **5**:*2111*
 Elmira Prison, **1**:163, **4**:1515
 Irish system and, **3**:1324, **4**:1519
 lecture circuit, **1**:164
 lumpenproletariat, **1**:163
 National Congress on Penitentiary and
  Reformatory Discipline and, **3**:1186–1188
 reform and rehabilitation, **1**:163–164, **5**:*2111*
 self-promotion, **1**:163
Brody, Baruch, **3**:1007
Broken Blossoms, **1**:244
broken windows theory, **1**:xlvii, **1**:392–393
Brooklyn's Finest, **2**:619
Brooks, Charles, **1**:xlvii
Brooks, Jack, **2**:849
Browder v. Gayle, **1**:27
Brown, C. J., **2**:463
Brown, Ed, **1**:166, **1**:315–316
Brown, Elaine, **1**:83
Brown, Frank J., **2**:842
Brown, Gerry, **1**:196
Brown, Grace, **1**:xliii, **1**:47
Brown, Harold, **5**:2112
Brown, John, **1**:24, **1**:169, **2**:569, **2**:577, **2**:771,
 5:*2098–2099*. See also Harper's Ferry
Brown, Linda, **1**:164
Brown, Nicole, **1**:xlviii
Brown, Oliver, **1**:164–165
Brown, William Wells, **1**:23
Brown v. Allen, **3**:1419

Brown v. Board of Education, **1**:xliv, **1**:27,
 1:164–166, **2**:959, **5**:*2277*
 accumulated evidence, **2**:573
 case history, **1**:164–166
 decision, **1**:166, **1**:264
 NAACP and, **1**:165–166
 principle-establishing, **2**:578
 separate but equal ended, **4**:1485, **4**:1554,
  4:1622
 Earl Warren and, **1**:166, **1**:264
Brown v. Mississippi, **1:166–167**, **1**:315–316
 police violence and torture, **1**:167, **4**:1739
 self-incrimination and, **1**:167
Brown v. Topeka, **2**:522
Bryan, William Jennings, **1**:429, **4**:1826
Bryant, Kobe, **2**:575
Buchalter, Louis ("Lepke"), **1**:462, **5**:*2213*
Buchanan, James (administration of), 1:2, 1:167–169,
 2:490, **2**:*611*
 criticisms, **1**:169
 Homestead Act of 1862 veto, **2**:804
 key issues, **1**:169
 save the Union attempts, **1**:168–169
 slave-free discussion, **1**:169
Bucholzer, H., **5**:*2066*
Buck, Carrie, **1**:169–170
Buck, Emma, **1**:170
Buck v. Bell, **1:169–170**, **2**:713
 eugenic rhetoric, **1**:169
 evidence in, **1**:170
 public welfare versus individual rights, **1**:170
Buckley v. Valeo, **4**:1735
Buel, J. W., **5**:*2104*
Buenoano, Judi, **4**:1963
Buffalo Bill, the King of the Border (Buntline), **1**:173
Bulger, James ("Whitey"), **2**:863
Buller, Francis, **2**:480
Bullion, Laura, **2**:685
Bullitt, **2**:619
Bundy, Ted, 1:170–172, **2**:576, **4**:1891
 execution, **1**:172
 serial killing, **1**:170–172
Buntline, Ned, 1:172–174
 Buffalo Bill promotion, **1**:173–174
 dime novels, **1**:172–173
Buono, Angelo, Jr., **1**:xlvii
Burdell, Harvey, **1**:422–423
**Bureau of Alcohol, Tobacco, Firearms and
 Explosives, 1**:103, **1:174–176**, **2**:589
 within DOJ, **1**:174
 evolution, **1**:174–175

modern, 1:175
Waco siege and, 4:1899–1900
Bureau of Forensic Ballistics, 1:xliii
Bureau of Indian Affairs, 1:369
Bureau of Internal Revenue, 1:174
Bureau of Investigation, 1:xliii, 5:2164–2165
   founding, 1:xlii
   J. Edgar Hoover as head, 1:451
   paving way for FBI, 1:451
Bureau of Justice Statistics (BJS), 1:341, 1:382, 1:396, 2:494
Buren, Martin Van (administration of), 1:176–177, 2:829
   Albany Regency and, 1:176
   Amistad and, 1:176–177
   fame as lawyer, 1:176
   social mobility, 1:176
   supporting Andrew Jackson, 1:176
Burge, Jon, 1:223
Burger, Margaret Elizabeth, 1:177
Burger, Wade Allen, 1:177
Burger, Warren, 1:39, 1:161, 1:177–179, 2:523, 4:1570
   Burger court, 1:178
   death and burial, 1:178
   Nixon nomination, 1:178
   political activism, 1:177
   State of the Judiciary speech, 1:178
   Supreme Court Historical Society founder, 1:178
   Supreme Court under, 4:1735
   Watergate tapes and, 4:1845
Burgess, Ernest, 1:380, 4:1849
burglary, contemporary, 1:179–181
   burglary rings, 1:181
   defined, 1:180
   MO, 1:180
   statistics, 1:179–180
   summary findings, 1:180
burglary, history of, 1:181–184
   breaking and entering, 1:183
   burglary definition, 1:184
   evolution of statutes, 1:182
   intent, 1:183–184
   Watergate case history, 1:182
burglary, sociology of, 1:185–186
   burglars, 1:185
   expertise and specialization, 1:185
   risk and, 1:186
   victims, 1:185–186
Burlington Industries Inc. v. Ellerth, 4:1656
Burns, Anthony, 1:22

Burns, Robert E., 1:215
Burns, William J., 2:739
Burr, Aaron, 2:732–733, 2:880
Burr, Dale, 2:860
Burr, Raymond, 3:*1424*
Burris, John, 1:64
Burroughs, George, 1:*19*
Burroughs, Stephen, 1:81
Burton, A. M., 3:1144
Bus Boycott (1955–1956), 1:27
Bush, George H. W. (administration of), 1:28, 1:186–188, 1:271, 1:350
   achievements, 1:187–188
   election, 5:2411–2412
   Nicaragua contras, 2:566
   re-election loss, 1:188
   war on drugs, 1:187
Bush, George W. (administration of), 1:188–191, 1:350, 2:800
   assault weapons ban, 2:725
   federal courts and, 1:190–191
   Homeland Security Act, 1:175
   presidential proclamations, 3:1407
   President's Task Force on Identity Theft, 2:815
   September 11, 2001, terrorist attacks and, 1:188–190
   TSP, 2:528
   USA PATRIOT Act signed, 4:1854
   war on terror and, 1:188–190, 2:802
Bush v. Gore, 4:1736
Buss, David, 1:14
Butch Cassidy and the Sundance Kid, 2:614
Butler Act, 1:429, 2:577, 4:1611–1612
Byrd, James, Jr., 3:1182, 4:1792, 5:2458
Byrnes, Thomas, 1:191–192, 1:452

C

CAA (Clean Air Act), 2:545
Cabot, John, 1:*288*
Cabrini Green, 3:1164
Caged, 2:623
Caged Heat, 2:624
Cagney, James, 2:613
Cagney and Lacey, 4:1771
Cahill, Frank ("Windy"), 1:125
Cain, James M., 2:468
Calderon, Mary, 1:4
Caldwell, Harry, 5:2173
California, 1:193–197. *See also* **Compton, California; Los Angeles, California; Oakland, California; San Francisco, California**

abortion legalized in, **1:**xlvi, **1:**4–5
crime, **1:**195
drivers' licenses, **1:**xlii
drug laws, **1:**196
early history, **1:**193–194
Medical Marijuana Identification Card, **1:**196
police, **1:**194–195
political protest and free speech, **1:**195–196
three strikes law, **1:**196
California v. Greenwood, **1:**327
California v. Stewart, **1:**317
Californians, **4:**1884
Calley, William, **2:**577
Calvin, John, **3:**1471
Calvinism, **4:**1672, **4:**1964
Cambell, Helen, **1:**193
Camden, New Jersey, 1:197–201
 crime, **1:**199–200
 economy and industry, **1:**197–198
 punishment, **1:**199–200
 railroads, **1:**198
 revitalization, **1:**200–201
 society and politics, **1:**198–199
 Urban Enterprise Zones, **1:***200*
Caminetti v. United States, **1:**201–202, **2:**774, **5:**2177
 case details, **1:**201–202
 Mann Act and, **3:**1066
 McKenna dissenting opinion, **1:**202
Camp David Peace Accords, **1:**212
Campbell, Joseph, **1:**198
Campbell Soup Corporation, **1:**198
Campbell v. Wood, **2:**738
Candide (Voltaire), **1:**314
Canfield, Richard, **4:**1584
Cannabis Withdrawal, **2:**498
Cannibal Corpse, **3:**1170
cannibalism, **1:**428, **2:**578
Cannon, Esther Marie, **2:**534
canon law, **4:**1529–1530
Canterbury Tales (Chaucer), **1:**314
capital punishment, 1:xlvi, **1:**202–210, **2:**621, **5:**1999.
 See also death penalty; **death row;** electric chair,
 history of; gas chamber; **hanging;** lethal injection
 corrections and, **1:**341
 current status, **1:**209–210
 declining support, **1:**202
 historical background, **1:**203–204
 in history of crime and punishment in America:
  1783–1850, **2:**761–762
 in history of crime and punishment in America:
  1950–1970, **2:**788

 in history of crime and punishment in America:
  1970–present, **2:**795
 Kansas, **2:**940
 McCleskey v. Kemp and, **2:**795
 NAACP and, **1:**206
 19th and 20th centuries, **1:**204–206
 Pennsylvania, **1:**xl
 Supreme Court and, **1:**206–209
 Texas, **4:**1790–1791
 Washington, **4:**1907–1908
capital sentencing, **4:**1630–1631
Capone, Al, 1:xliii, **1:**36, **1:**145, **1:**210–212, **2:**620
 at Alcatraz, **2:**776
 arrest, **1:**211–212
 bootlegging, **2:**818
 Chicago Outfit, **1:**31, **1:**210–211, **2:**842, **2:**867
 crime syndicate, **2:**705
 death of, **1:**212
 income sources, **2:**868
 Ness tracking, **3:**1209–1210
 1921 to 1940, **5:**2205–2206
 Frank Nitti as enforcer, **3:**1260
 tax evasion, **2:**843
 turf wars, **3:**1157
Capone, Louis, **3:***1003*, **3:***1303*
Capone, Ralph, **1:**211
Capote, Truman, **2:**571, **2:**940
carceral punishment, **4:**1627
Carey, Hugh, **1:**77, **2:**971
Carey v. Population Services International, **2:**523
Carlson v. Landon, **1:**94
Carmichael, Stokely, **1:**131
Carnegie Steel Company, **1:**xli–xlii, **2:**771
CARNIVORE, **2:**560
carpetbaggers, **1:**xli
Carr, Caleb, **1:**117
Carr, John Dickson, **3:**1016–1017
Carr v. State, **1:**430
Carrasco, Ricardo S., **2:**535
Carson, Rachel, **2:**488, **2:**543
Carter, G. W., **3:**1187
Carter, Jimmy (administration of), 1:212–213, **1:**271, **1:**344
 Camp David Peace Accords, **1:**212
 Ethics in Government Act of 1978, **2:**565
 FEMA creation, **2:**849
 Nobel Peace Prize, **1:**212
 public works, **1:**213
 restoring trust, **1:**213
Carter, John, **1:**64
Carver, Allen, **1:**286

The Case of the Velvet Claws (Gardner), 2:680
"Cases of Conscience," 1:360
Cash, Herman, 1:31
Cash, Johnny, 3:*1262*
Caspary, Vera, 3:1026
Cassady, Neal, 4:1600
Cassat, Alexander, 2:529
Castor, John, 1:21
Castro, Fidel
    plots to kill, 2:521
    takeover, 2:845
The Catcher in the Rye (Salinger), 1:218
Catholic Church, 1:5, 3:1471, 4:1529–1530, 4:1671–1672
    Catholic Council on Civil Liberties, 2:714
    Inquisition, 1:17–18
Cato Institute, 3:1006
Catron, John, 2:490
Cauffman, Elizabeth, 1:233
caveat emptor, 1:292
caveat venditor, 1:292
Caverly, John, 3:1005
CBT (cognitive behavior therapy), 2:827
CCA (Corrections Corporation of America), 3:1411
CD (conduct disorder), 2:750
censorship, 3:1275–1276
Central Intelligence Agency (CIA), 1:271
    assassination plots, 1:349, 2:521
    espionage, 2:559
    formation, 2:558
    interrogation practices, 2:854
    Al Qaeda and, 2:854
    Richard Nixon and, 5:2357
    surveillance, 3:1377
    torture, 4:1813
CERCLA (Comprehensive Environmental Response, Compensation, and Liability Act), 2:545–546
CFR (Code of Federal Regulations), 1:370
CGT (criminal geographic targeting), 1:455
Chabas, Paul, 3:1274
Chae Chan Ping v. United States, 1:247
Chaffe, Zachariah, 1:8
chain gangs and prison labor, 1:214–216.
    See also **convict lease system**
    African Americans and, 1:214
    criticism, 1:214–216
    I am a Fugitive From a Chain Gang, 2:621
    racism and, 1:214
    shotgun guards, 1:214
Challenger, 3:1377, 3:1385

Chamberlain, Abiram, 1:323
Chambers, Whittaker, 2:577
Chambliss, Robert, 1:31
Champagne for One (Stout), 3:1019
Chandler, Raymond, 2:468, 3:1016, 3:1018, 3:1029–1030, 3:1425
***Chandler v. Florida*, 1:216–217**
    television cameras and, 1:216–217
    unanimous decision, 1:216
Chapman, Duane ("The Dog"), 1:156
Chapman, Mark David, 1:217–218, 2:575
Charles I, 1:91, 3:1472
Charles II, 1:141, 1:293, 2:729
Charles River Bridge v. Warren, 4:1734
Charlie's Angels, 4:1766
Chase, Salmon P., 3:1011–1012, 3:1120–1121, 4:1734
Chase, Samuel, 2:880
chattel slavery, 1:21
Chaucer, Geoffrey, 1:314
Chauncey, George, 3:993
Cheaters, 4:1765
Cheney, Dick, 1:190
Cherokee, 2:832–833, 2:848, 2:870
Cherokee Bill, 1:63
Cherokee Nation v. Georgia, 2:833, 2:870
Cherry, Bobby, 1:31
Chesnutt, Charles, 1:26
Chesterton, G. K., 3:1032
Chicago, Illinois, 1:xlviii, 1:28, 1:191, 1:218–223
    Chicago Gang Congregation Ordinance, 1:28
    Chicago Outfit, 1:31, 1:210–211, 2:842, 2:867
    City of Chicago v. Morales, 1:xlviii, 1:28
    corruption, 1:348–349
    early crime, 1:220–221
    early law enforcement, 1:218–220
    early punishment, 1:220–221
    1801 to 1850, 5:2071–2072
    Italian Americans, 2:867–868
    juvenile justice law, 1:xlii
    Lager Beer Riot, 1:218
    Prohibition, 1:221
    prostitution, 1:219
    race relations, 1:221–222
    vice commission, 4:1861–1863, 4:1865–1866
    O. W. Wilson in, 4:1944
Chicago School, 4:1849
Chicago Seven/Democratic National Convention of 1968, 1:223–224, 1:349
    Kunstler and, 2:970
    police riot, 1:224
    Vietnam War, 1:223

Chicago Tribune, 1:222
Chief (Gates, D.), 3:1093
Chief Justices. *See also* **Burger, Warren; Supreme Court, U.S.; Warren, Earl**
    John Marshall as, 3:1070–1071
    Taft as, 4:176
child abuse, contemporary, 1:224–227
    burn injuries, 1:225
    physical abuse, 1:225
    sexual abuse, 1:225–226
child abuse, history of, 1:227–229
    breaker boys, 1:228
    Civil War and, 1:228
    colonization and, 1:227–228
    Industrial Revolution, 1:228
    modern society, 1:229
    prevention, 1:228–229
child abuse, sociology of, 1:230–232
    abuse effects, 1:231–232
    Child Abuse and Prevention and Treatment Act, 1:230
    national incidence study results, 1:230–231
    prevention programs, 1:232
child murderers, history of, 1:232–235
    classifications, 1:234–235
    risk factors, 1:233–234
    treatment, 1:235
child pornography, 3:1399–1400
child saving movement, 2:929–930
Childhelp, 1:225
children. *See also* **Convention on the Rights of the Child; juvenile corrections, contemporary; juvenile corrections, history of; juvenile corrections, sociology of; juvenile courts, contemporary; juvenile courts, history of; juvenile delinquency, history of; juvenile delinquency, sociology of; juvenile justice, history of; juvenile offenders in adult courts**
    African American, 1:164–165
    Aid to Families with Dependent Children, 1:5
    Children's Aid Society, 1:236
    Children's Bureau, 1:239
    Children's Crusade, 1:128
    molestation of, 1:xlvii–xlviii, 1:226
    of slaves, 1:xxxix
children, abandoned, 1:235–238
    historical context, 1:236
    modern era, 1:237–238
    reduction approaches, 1:238
children's rights, 1:239–241, 2:783. *See also* **Convention on the Rights of the Child**
    early social reforms, 1:239

Chillicothe Correctional Institution, 1:241–242
Chinese Americans, 1:242–246
    Asiatic Barred Zone, 1:245
    Chinese Triads, 1:244
    citizenship rights, 1:244–245
    early immigration, 1:242–244
    model minority, 1:245–246
    race-based crimes against, 4:1485–1486
    Wyoming, 4:1978
Chinese Exclusion Act, 1:xli, 1:194, 1:243–245, 1:246–248
    deportation and, 1:447
    immigration and, 1:246, 2:822
    resistance, 1:247
    restrictions of, 1:246–247, 4:1981
    unfairness of, 1:247
Chin, Vincent, 1:245
Chisholm, Alexander, 1:248
Chisholm v. Georgia, 1:59, 1:248–249
    case study, 1:248–249
    eleventh amendment and, 1:249
Chomsky, Noam, 1:51, 3:1392, 4:1749
Chou, Neil, 2:815
Christianity, 3:1471, 4:1670
Christie, Agatha, 1:249–251, 2:467, 4:1892
    The Detection Club president, 1:250
    psychological profiling, 1:251
    Queen of Crime, 1:249
    rules of fair play, 1:250
    works, 1:250, 3:1015–1016, 3:1022, 3:1028–1030
Christopher Commission, 3:1371
Church Committee, 1:349, 2:559–560
Church of Jesus Christ of Latter-day Saints, 1:121–122, 4:1546
CIA. *See* Central Intelligence Agency (CIA)
Cincinnati, Ohio, 1:251–255
    boss system, 1:251, 1:253
    corruption, 1:253
    cronyism, 1:253
    Great Migration, 1:252
    police, 1:251–252
    Porkolpolis, 1:252
    racial tensions, 1:252–253
    urban renewal, 1:253–255
circle hooks, 2:630
Circuit Court Act of 1802, 1:363
The Circular Staircase (Rinehart), 3:1020
Cirofici, Frank, 5:*2164*
CITAC (Computer Investigations and Infrastructure Threat Assessment Center), 2:585

citizen participation on juries, 1:255–257
    exclusion, 1:256
    jury instruction, 1:257
    jury qualification, 1:255–257
    women and, 1:256
Citizens United v. Federal Election Commission, 4:1736
citizenship, 1:xl
    African Americans, 1:24, 2:550–551
    Chinese Americans' rights, 1:244–245
    Dred Scott v. Sandford and, 1:488, 2:550–551, 2:658
    Japanese Americans, 2:875–876
    Minor v. Happersett and, 3:1115
    Native Americans, 3:1201
City of Eros (Gilfoyle), 5:2064
civil disobedience, 1:257–260
    modern, 1:260
    nonviolent versus violent, 1:258–259
    Thoreau and, 1:259–260
Civil Disobedience (Thoreau), 1:259
civil law legal tradition, 1:297–298
civil rights, 1:xlv
    antiwar movements and, 2:785–786
    Birmingham, Alabama, 1:127–128
    civil rights movement, 1:27
    CRC, 2:734
    Eisenhower and, 2:522
    Ulysses S. Grant and, 2:704, 3:1212–1213
    Jewish Americans, 2:881–882
    Martin Luther King, Jr. and, 1:265, 2:959
    NAACP and, 3:1181–1182
    riots, 4:1554
    Harry Truman and, 4:1831–18322
    Earl Warren legislation, 4:1906
    women, 4:1495–1496
Civil Rights Act of 1866, 1:xlv, 1:260–261, 1:263–264
    enactment, 1:260
    passage against veto, 2:551
    prosecution, 1:260
Civil Rights Act of 1871, 2:787
Civil Rights Act of 1875, 1:25, 1:262–263, 1:263–264
    Fourteenth Amendment and, 1:262–263
    Supreme Court challenge, 1:262–263
    Thirteenth Amendment and, 1:262–263
Civil Rights Act of 1957, 1:264
Civil Rights Act of 1964, 1:xlv, 1:27, 1:128, 1:264–266, 2:552, 4:1485
Civil Rights Act of 1965, 1:266

Civil Rights Cases, 1:263
Civil Rights Congress (CRC), 2:734
civil rights laws, 1:263–267
    African Americans and, 1:263
    disenfranchised groups, 1:266–267
    early, 1:263–264
    modern, 1:264–266
    presidential action, 1:264
civil unrest, 3:1367
Civil War, 5:2098–2101
    Abraham Lincoln during, 3:1011
    African Americans and, 1:24–25
    child abuse and, 1:228
    counterfeiting and, 1:357
    Dred Scott v. Sandford and, 5:2097–2098
    vigilantism, 4:1881–1882
Clanton, Billy, 2:515
Clanton, Nathan Haynes, 1:162
Clanton-McLowery gang, 1:162
Clarendon Code, 3:1474
Clark, Benjamin C., 3:1432
Clark, Joseph B., 2:714
Clark, Marcia, 3:1095
Clark, Mark, 1:222
Clark, Tom, 2:564–565
Clarke, Ronald, 1:391, 1:394
Clarkson, Lana, 2:575
class-conflict theories, 1:381
classical anarchy, 1:47
classical criminology theory, 1:407–408
Classification Act, 2:819
Clay, Henry, 1:13, 5:2076
Clayton, Henry, 1:267
Clayton Anti-Trust Act of 1914, 1:53, 1:267, 1:267–268
    FTC created, 1:267–268
    trust-busting, 1:268
CLE Journal, 1:43
Clean Air Act (CAA), 2:545
Clean Water Act (CWA), 2:545
Cleared for the Approach (Bailey, F. L., Greenya), 1:99
Cleaver, Eldridge, 1:131
Cleland, John, 3:1275
clemency, 1:268–272
    amnesty and, 1:268–269
    commutation, remission, reprieves, 1:269
    considerations, 1:270
    examples, 1:270–272
    Nixon and, 1:270–271
    pardons, 1:269–270

Presidential Clemency Program, 2:636–637
    Vietnam War and, 1:271
Cleveland, Grover (administration of), 1:191, 1:272–273
    Big Business and, 1:272
    Pullman Strike of 1894, 1:272–273
    respect for law, 1:272
Cleveland, Ohio, 1:273–276
    crime, 1:275
    demographics, 1:273–274
    Hough Riots, 1:275
    Mayfield Road Mob, 3:1210
    Eliot Ness in, 3:1210–1211
    police, 1:274–275
    race relations, 1:275
    Torso Murders, 1:274, 3:1210
Cleveland v. United States, 1:121
Cline, Edward, 2:621
Clinton, DeWitt, 1:78, 2:519
Clinton, George, 2:880
Clinton, Hillary, 1:350
Clinton, William (administration of), 1:74, 1:188, 1:276–278
    Brady Handgun Violence Protection Act, 2:721, 2:725
    crime prevention efforts, 1:276–277
    DADT, 1:266
    Defense of Marriage Act of 1996, 1:267
    election, 5:2412
    FALN and, 1:271
    gag rule and, 1:6
    impeachment, 2:566, 2:574, 2:577
    land fraud accusation, 1:350
    mifepristone testing, 1:7
    presidential proclamations, 3:1406
    terrorism and federal authority, 1:277
    Violent Crime Control and Law Enforcement Act of 1994, 1:276, 1:340
Clinton Correctional Facility, 1:xliii, 1:278–279
    courts program, 1:279
    effectiveness, 1:279
    Merle Cooper program, 1:279
    mine working, 1:278
    rehabilitation and reform, 1:278–279
Clinton v. Jones, 2:566
Closing Circle (Commoner), 2:543
Clothes Line Project, 2:481
Cloward, Richard, 1:380, 2:678
Clubine, Brenda, 2:477, 2:481
Coast Guard, U.S., 2:590–591, 2:780
cocaine, 3:1177

Cochrane Collaboration, 5:2423
cock fighting, 1:134–135
Code Duello, 2:733
Code of Canon Law, 1:284
Code of Federal Regulations (CFR), 1:370
Code of Hammurabi, 1:282, 4:1528, 4:1958
code of silence, 1:279–281
    justifications, 1:281
    thin blue line, 1:280
    validity, 1:281
Code of the Street (Anderson, E.), 2:678–679
codeine, 3:1175
Code-wide Crew, 1:181
codification of laws, 1:281–285
    American legal system, 1:284–285
    ancient codes, 1:282–283
    Austrian General Civil Code, 1:284
    Code of Canon Law, 1:284
    Code of Hammurabi, 1:282
    common law, 1:283
    Dutch Civil Code, 1:284
    General National Law for the Prussian States, 1:283
    Georgia Code, 1:284
    German Civil Code, 1:284
    Law Code of Vishnu, 1:282
    Law of the Twelve Tablets, 1:283
    Mosaic Code, 1:282, 1:291
    Napoleonic Code, 1:283–284, 1:298
    Roman-Byzantine Law, 1:283
    Spanish Civil Code, 1:284
    Sumerian Code of Ur-Nammu Lipit-Ishtar, 1:282
    Swiss Civil Code, 1:284
    U.S.C., 1:284
Cody, William (Buffalo Bill), 1:173–174, 2:938
cognitive behavior therapy (CBT), 2:827
Cohen, Albert, 1:380, 1:411, 2:677–678
Cohen, Lawrence, 1:380, 1:391
Cohen, Selig, 5:2178
Cohens v. Virginia, 1:xl, 1:285–286, 3:1071, 3:1073
COINTELPRO, 1:xliv, 1:349, 2:520–521
    espionage, 2:559, 2:785
    institution, 2:584
Coke, Edmund, 2:507
Coker, Ehrlich Anthony, 1:286
Coker v. Georgia, 1:207, 1:286–287, 1:418, 4:1544, 4:1735
Cold Case, 4:1767
cold war
    Eisenhower and, 2:520–521
    electronic surveillance, 2:528

espionage, 2:558–559
FBI in, 2:584
geopolitics, 1:245
surveillance, 3:1377
Colfax, Schuyler, 2:704
collective action, 1:48
colonial charters and grants, 1:287–290
decline, 1:289–290
early, 1:287–288
settling North America, 1:288–289
colonial courts, 1:290–294
appeals, 1:292–293
procedures, 1:291
punishments, 1:291–292
regional variations, 1:290–291
special purposes, 1:293–294
colonial judges and magistrates, 2:890
colonial sentencing, 4:1628
colonization, 1:227–228
Colorado, 1:294–296
criminal justice system, 1:295–296
early conflicts, 1:295
Japanese internment camps, 1:296
Ludlow Massacre, 1:295
United Mine Workers strike, 1:295
Colosimo, Big Jim, 1:210, 1:220, 2:818, 2:867
Colson, Charles, 4:1531
Columbian burglary ring, 1:181
Columbo, 4:1769
Columbus, Christopher, 1:288
Combat Zone, 4:1889
Comer, Braxton Bragg, 1:127
Commentaries on the Laws of England (Blackstone), 1:xl, 1:132–133, 1:371, 1:438, 1:441
Commissioner (Murphy, P. V.), 3:1093
Committee of Fourteen, 4:1865
Committee on the Establishment of a Permanent Organization, 1:42
Committee to Re-Elect the President (CREEP), 4:1916
common law origins of criminal law, 1:182–183, 1:283, 1:296–300
civil law legal tradition, 1:297–298
historical, 1:300
legal tradition, 1:298–299
religious law legal tradition, 1:296–297
socialist law legal tradition, 1:297
in U.S., 1:299–300
Commoner, Barry, 2:543
Communism, 1:297, 5:2341–2345
Communist Party, 1:445, 2:844

Community Oriented Policing Services (COPS), 1:276, 1:302, 4:1511–1512, 5:2418
community ownership, 1:48
community policing and relations, 1:300–304
early, 1:300–301
elements of, 1:303–304
modern, 1:302–303
19th and 20th century, 1:301–302
ongoing challenges, 1:304
September 11, 2001, terrorist attacks and, 1:304
community service, 1:305–307
history, 1:305
Law Enforcement Assistance Administration, 1:305
outcomes, 1:305–307
research, 1:306–307
sentencing, 4:1627
Vera Institute service program, 1:306
Vermont Reparative Probationers, 1:306
community-based corrections, 1:337–340, 2:788, 2:911–912
commutation, 1:269
Comprehensive Crime Control Act of 1984, 5:2415
Comprehensive Drug Abuse Prevention and Control Act of 1970, 3:1177, 5:2354
Comprehensive Environmental Response, Compensation, and Liability Act (CERCLA), 2:545–546
Compromise of 1850, 1:xli, 1:1
Compton, California, 1:307–308
All American City, 1952, 1:307
crime, 1:308
demographics, 1:307
gangs, 1:307–308
police, 1:308
Compulsion (Levin), 1:83
computer crime, 1:308–313, 4:1563. *See also* cybercrime
cybercrime opportunities, 1:311
cybercrime targets, 1:309–310
cybercrime tools, 1:310–311
FBI on, 1:309
hacking, 1:310
identity theft, 1:311
response to, 1:312
September 11, 2001, terrorist attacks and, 1:312
terrorism and, 1:389–390
Trojan horses, 1:310
vandalism and defacement, 1:310
viruses, 1:310

Computer Investigations and Infrastructure Threat Assessment Center (CITAC), **2**:585
Comstock, Anthony, **1**:3, **1**:313, **1**:460, **5**:2111
    Comstockery coining, **4**:1865
    as vice reformer, **4**:1864–1865
Comstock Law, 1:xli, **1**:3, **1**:313–314, **3**:1274, **5**:2111
    background, **1**:313
    enforcement, **1**:313–314
    postal service and, **1**:313–314
Comstockery, **4**:1865
Comte, Auguste, **1**:407, **1**:408
concentric zone, **1**:380, **4**:1849
concurrent jurisdiction, **2**:902
Condemned Women, **2**:623
conduct disorder (CD), **2**:750
confession, 1:314–319
    custodial interrogation, **1**:317
    due process clause and, **1**:315–316
    Fifth Amendment self-incrimination clause, **1**:316–317
    Miranda v. Arizona and, **1**:316–319
    Sixth Amendment right to counsel standard, **1**:319
Confessions (Rousseau), **1**:314
Confessions of a Missouri Guerrilla (Younger), **1**:82
confidence games and frauds, 1:319–323
    apartment scandal, **1**:321
    bait-and-switch, **1**:320–321
    code of, **1**:322
    cooling off mark, **1**:321–322
    glasses drop, **1**:320
    large scale, **1**:320–321
    life of con, **1**:322–323
    marks, **1**:320
    Nigerian 419, **1**:321, **1**:389
    pigeon drop, **1**:320
    requirements, **1**:319–320
    small-scale, **1**:320
    three card monte, **1**:320–321
The Confidential Agent (Greene), **3**:1028
conflict perspective
    of murder, **3**:1161–1163
    of rape, **4**:1502–1504
Conflict Tactic Scale (CTS), **2**:485
conflict theory, **2**:504, **4**:1532
    criminology, **1**:411–412
    pluralistic, **4**:1503
conformists, **4**:1502
Confucius, **4**:1528
Conger, Everton, **1**:143

Connecticut, **1**:323–325
    abortion in, **1**:xl
    crime, **1**:323
    Newgate prison, **1**:325
    police, **1**:323–324
    punishment, **1**:324–325
Connecticut Dept. of Public Safety v. Doe, **4**:1646–1647
Connolly, John, **1**:151
Conrad, Joseph, **3**:1015
constables, **5**:2071
Constantine, **4**:1529
Constitution of the United States of America, 1:46, **1**:325–328. *See also specific amendments*
    Article 3, **1**:363
    Article 4, Section 2, **1**:21
    Bill of Rights and, **1**:109, **1**:326–327
    criminal law and, **5**:2037–2039
    drafting, **1**:93
    enactment, **1**:19
    Supremacy Clause, **1**:2
    Supreme Court as final authority, **1**:xli, **1**:327–328
    Three Fifths Compromise, **1**:21, **1**:24
Consumer Sentinel Network (CSN), **2**:814
contemporary anarchy, **1**:47
Continental Army, **1**:21
Continental Congress, **1**:71
contraception, **1**:xli, **1**:15, **1**:236, **3**:992. *See also* abortion
Controlled Substances Act, **1**:xlvi
Convention on International Trade in Endangered Species of Wild Fauna and Flora, **2**:630
Convention on the Rights of the Child, 1:328–330
    implementation, **1**:329–330
    provisions, **1**:329
    weaknesses, **1**:330
Convict 13, **2**:621
convict lease system, 1:330–332
    decline, **1**:332
    as racial slavery, **1**:330
    rules and regulations, **1**:331
Convicted Women Against Abuse (CWAA), **2**:477
Convictions (Kroger), **3**:1095
Convict's Parole, **2**:621
Conway, James, **1**:64
Cook, Ransom, **1**:278
Cook, Rufus R., **3**:1432
Cooke, T. Dickerson, **5**:2175
Cool Hand Luke (Pearce), **1**:215

Coolidge, Calvin (administration of), 1:152, 1:332–333, 1:348
    assuming presidency, 1:333
    political life, 1:332
Coonan, James, 2:863
Cooper, Samuel, 1:197
Cooper v. Pate, 1:xlv, 2:787, 3:1419
cop killer bullets, 2:720
Cop Land, 2:619
Cop Rock, 4:1766
Coppage v. Kansas, 1:xlii, 1:10
Coppel, Alec, 3:1026
Copperheads, 3:1011
Coppolino, Carl A., 1:98
COPS (Community Oriented Policing Services), 1:276, 1:302, 4:1511–1512
Corbett, Boston, 1:143
Corliss, John, 2:529
Cornell, David, 4:1832
Cornell, Dewey, 1:234
Cornish, Derek, 1:391
Cornwell, Patricia, 3:1024
corporal punishment, 1:333–336. *See also* capital punishment
    flogging, 1:333–335
    resistance to, 1:335
    sentencing, 4:1627
    whipping, 1:335
corporate kleptocracy, 3:983
corporate social responsibility (CSR), 1:344–345
Corpus Juris Civilis, 1:298
corrections, 1:336–342. *See also* **Bedford Hills Correctional Facility**; jails; juvenile corrections, contemporary; juvenile corrections, history of; juvenile corrections, sociology of; prisons; punishment
    Auburn system, 1:337
    capital punishment, 1:341
    community-based, 1:337–340, 2:788, 2:911–912
    early history, 1:336–337
    goals of, 1:337–338
    halfway houses, 1:340
    Industrial era, 1:337
    institutional, 1:340–341
    intermediate sanctions, 1:340
    Just Deserts era, 1:337–38
    Mass Prison era, 1:337
    parole, 1:338–39
    penal colonies, 1:339
    Penitentiary era, 1:337
    Pennsylvania system, 1:337, 1:339
    probation, 1:338
    Punitive era, 1:337
    re-entry programs, 1:340–341
    special needs offenders, 1:341–342
    Treatment era, 1:337
    Warehousing era, 1:337
    Wisconsin, 4:1947
    women criminals and, 4:1968–1969
Corrections Corporation of America (CCA), 3:1411
corruption, contemporary, 1:343–345
    cash-based industries, 1:343
    computer-mediated, 1:345
    CSR, 1:344–345
    financial industries, 1:343
    Louisiana, 3:1042–1043
    military-industrial complex, 1:343–344
    police, 1:344, 3:1250–1252
    George Walling and, 4:1901
corruption, history of, 1:xlix, 1:345–351
    ABSCAM, 1:349
    Chicago, Illinois, 1:348–349
    CIA assassination plots, 1:349
    COINTELPRO, 1:349
    Credit Mobilier scandal, 1:347
    crime and, 1:345–346, 1:351
    cronyism, 1:346
    in early America, 1:346–348
    Ulysses S. Grant and, 1:347–348, 1:352, 4:1927
    Harding administration, 2:738–739
    Housing and Urban Development scandal, 1:350
    Iran-Contra Scandal, 1:271, 1:349–350, 1:353, 2:566
    IRS and, 1:348
    Knapp Commission reductions, 2:964–965
    LAPD, 1:xliv
    malfeasance, 1:346
    modern, 1:349–351
    nepotism, 1:346
    19th century, 1:348–349
    police, 2:783–785
    in police films, 2:618–619
    Theodore Roosevelt exposure, 5:2111
    savings and loan scandal, 1:350
    Seabury investigation, 1:351
    Tammany Hall, 1:347
    Teapot Dome Scandal, 1:348
    Watergate scandal, 1:349
    Whiskey Ring scandal, 1:347
corruption, sociology of, 1:351–354
    conflicts of interest, 1:354
    gangs, 1:352

Hollywood and, **1**:354
International Teamsters Union, **1**:352
limiting corruption, **1**:353
political corruption, **1**:352–353
Prohibition and, **1**:353
small-scale corruption, **1**:353–354
Cory, Giles, **5**:2002
Costello, Frank, **2**:688–689, **2**:783–784, **2**:863
    bootlegging, **3**:1048
    mob boss, **2**:986
Cotton, John, **1**:141
Coughlin, John ("Bathhouse"), **1**:219, **2**:818
Coulthurst, John Henry ("The Lizard"), **1**:180
counseling, **2**:909–909
counterespionage, **2**:555
counterfeiting, 1:354–358
    American Revolution and, **1**:355
    bills of credit in colonies, **1**:355
    Civil War and, **1**:357
    in Great Depression, **1**:357–358
    greenbacks, **1**:357–358
    history, **1**:355–357
    modern, **1**:358
    Secret Service and, **1**:356–357, **4**:1614
County of Riverside v. McLaughlin, **1**:67
Court of Common Pleas, 1:358–359
    Delaware, **1**:358
    Ohio, **1**:358–359
    Pennsylvania, **1**:359
    South Carolina, **1**:359
Court of Oyer and Terminer, 1:359–360
    demise, **1**:360
    purpose, **1**:359
    Salem Witch Trials, **1**:359–360
Court of Quarter Sessions, 1:360–361
    county government and, **1**:360
    jurisdiction, **1**:360–361
    uses, **1**:360
Courtroom Television Network (Tru-TV), **1**:217
courtroom workgroup, **1**:366
courts, 1:217, 1:361–369. *See also* appeals; appellate courts; attorneys; colonial courts; juries; juvenile courts, contemporary; juvenile courts, history of; juvenile offenders in adult courts; military courts; petty courts; Supreme Court
    adversarial process, **1**:367–368
    civil versus criminal, **1**:361–362
    courtroom workgroup, **1**:366
    crime control model, **1**:366–367
    due process model, **1**:366–367
    history of federal system, **1**:363–364

    history of state system, **1**:364–365
    Kansas City, Missouri, **2**:940–941
    Martin Luther King, Jr. and, **2**:959
    organization of federal, **1**:362–363
    organization of state system, **1**:364
    problem-solving, **5**:2460–2462
    sentencing structures, **1**:368
    specialized, **1**:365–366
Courts of Indian Offenses, 1:369–370
    based on Anglo-American system, **1**:369
    Bureau of Indian Affairs, **1**:369
    CFR courts, **1**:370
Couzens, James M., **1**:459
Covenant House, **1**:101
coverture, doctrine of, 1:370–373
    property rights for women, **1**:371
    removal of, **1**:372
    women as chattel, **1**:371
Cowboys, **2**:515
Cox, Archibald, **2**:565, **4**:1844, **4**:1916
Cox, George B., **1**:253
CPB. *See* Customs and Border Protection (CPB)
CPTED (crime prevention through environmental design), **1**:391, **1**:393–394
CQ Press, **1**:308
Crabtree, Ervin, **1**:373
Crabtree v. State, **1**:373–374
Craig v. Boren, **2**:655
Cramer, Charles F., **2**:739
Crane, Bob, **3**:1167
Crawford v. Marion County Election Board, **4**:1736
CRC (Civil Rights Congress), **2**:734
Creasy, John, **3**:1025
Credit Mobilier scandal, **1**:347, **2**:704
CREEP (Committee to Re-Elect the President), **4**:1916
Cremin, Deanna, **3**:1169, **5**:2422
crime, **1**:xl, **2**:684–685. *See also* cybercrime; **history of crime and punishment in America: colonial; history of crime and punishment in America: 1783–1850; history of crime and punishment in America: 1850–1900; history of crime and punishment in America: 1900–1950; history of crime and punishment in America: 1950–1970; history of crime and punishment in America: 1970–present; livestock and cattle crimes; news media, crime in; organized crime, contemporary; organized crime, history of; organized crime, sociology of; political crimes, contemporary; political crimes, history of; political crimes, sociology of; prisons; tax crimes; television, crime in; Uniform Crime Reporting**

Program; violent crimes; white-collar crime, contemporary; white-collar crime, history of; white-collar crime, sociology of; *specific crimes*
  Alabama, 1:31–32
  Alaska, 1:34
  Arkansas, 1:63–64
  in Bible, 1:118–119
  Birmingham, Alabama, 1:129
  bootlegging and, 1:145
  Boston, Massachusetts, 1:151–152
  California, 1:195
  Camden, New Jersey, 1:199–200
  Chicago, Illinois, 1:220–221
  Cleveland, Ohio, 1:275
  in colonial America, 2:757–758
  Compton, California, 1:308
  computer, 1:308–313
  Connecticut, 1:323
  cost and measurement, 4:1939–1940
  crime-mapping, 1:454
  dark figure of, 1:376, 1:396, 2:926
  Delaware, 1:443–444
  Detroit, Michigan, 1:459
  drinking and, 2:490–497
  drug, 1:386–388
  due process, 1:510–511
  1801 to 1850, 5:2063–2067
  environmental, 2:543–550, 4:1930–1931
  fear of, 2:579–582
  federal common law of, 2:586–587
  in film, 2:612–616
  financial, 2:843
  Florida, 2:634
  gambling as, 2:663–665
  Georgia, 2:689–690
  Great Depression, 2:707–708
  hate, 1:187, 1:188, 1:386–388, 3:1182, 5:2410–2411
  Hawai'i, 2:745
  hereditary, 2:748–751
  in history of corruption, 1:345–346, 1:351
  Idaho, 2:812
  Indiana, 2:836
  Internet-based crime, 2:815
  Iowa, 2:860
  Italian Americans, 2:868
  Jackson, Mississippi, 2:872
  John Adams shaping, 1:11
  Kansas City, Missouri, 2:942
  Kentucky, 2:952
  libertarianism and, 3:1008–1009
  in literature and theater, 3:1014–1020
  livestock and cattle crimes, 3:1032–1034
  Louisiana, 3:1041–1042
  Maine, 3:1060
  Maryland, 3:1075
  Massachusetts, 3:1077–1078
  Memphis, Tennessee, 3:1097
  Michigan, 3:1102
  Minnesota, 3:1112–1113
  Mississippi, 3:1119–1120
  Missouri, 3:1122–1123
  Montana, 3:1130–1131
  NCVS, 1:xlvi
  Nebraska, 3:1205–1206
  New Jersey, 3:1218–1220
  Newark, New Jersey, 3:1240–1241
  news, 5:2216–2217
  1981 to 2000, 5:2407–2410
  1901 to 1920, 5:2161–2169
  North Carolina, 3:1263–1264
  North Dakota, 3:1266
  Ohio, 3:1281–1282
  Oklahoma, 3:1284–1285
  Oregon, 3:1293
  Pennsylvania, 3:1335–1336
  Puritans and, 3:1474
  religion and, 2:758–759
  Rhode Island, 4:1549–1550
  San Francisco, California, 4:1600–1601
  sex, 1:386–388, 2:575, 2:685
  soft on crime, 2:476
  South Carolina, 4:1698–1699
  South Dakota, 4:1701
  St. Louis, 4:1703–1704
  Tennessee, 4:1778–1779
  Texas, 4:1792–1793
  traffic crimes, 4:1815–1819
  Utah, 4:1854–1856
  Vermont, 4:1860–1861
  victimless, 1:388–389, 4:1874–1878
  Virginia, 4:1895
  Washington, D.C., 4:1910
  West Virginia, 4:1921
  Wyoming, 4:1977–1978
Crime, Its Cause and Treatment (Darrow), 1:429
crime and arrest statistics analysis, 1:374–378
  arrests, 1:374–375, 1:374–376
  dark figure of crime, 1:376, 1:396
  offending self-report surveys, 1:376–377
  victimization surveys, 1:377

Crime and Human Nature (Wilson, J., Hernstein), 2:749
Crime and Punishment (Dostoevsky), 2:733, 3:1015
Crime Control Act of 1990, 1:187, 2:720
Crime Control and Safe Streets Act of 1968, 1:318
crime in America, causes, 1:378–382
    American criminology, 1:379–380
    nature versus nurture debate, 1:378
    1950s and 1960s, 1:380–381
    recent developments, 1:381
    research, 1:380
    sociological explanations, 1:378–379
    theoretical integration and general theories, 1:381
crime in America, distribution, 1:382–385
    crime patterns, 1:382–383
    in Great Depression, 1:383
    patterns across place, 1:384
    patterns across social groups, 1:384–385
    patterns across time, 1:383–384
    patterns by type, 1:383
crime in America, types, 1:386–390
    computer crime and terrorism, 1:389–390
    felonies and misdemeanors, 1:386
    organized, 1:389
    victimless, 1:388–389
    violent, sex, property, hate, drug, 1:386–388
    white-collar, 1:389
crime pattern theory, 1:392–393
crime prevention, 1:390–395
    broken windows theory, 1:392–393
    CPTED, 1:391, 1:393–394
    crime pattern theory, 1:392–393
    rational choice theory, 1:391–392
    routine activity theory, 1:391
    situational, 1:394–395
crime prevention through environmental design (CPTED), 1:391, 1:393–394
crime rates, 1:395–399
    Boomer generation, 1:398
    Great Depression, 1:397–398
    measuring, 1:395–397
    official data, 1:395–396
    Roe v. Wade and, 1:398–399
    self-report data, 1:396
    theories, 1:398–399
    trends, 1:397–398
    victim data, 1:396–397
crime scene investigation, 1:399–403, 1:402
    backlogged cases, 1:403
    basic procedure, 1:399–400
    courtroom applications, 1:401–402
    DNA analysis, 1:400–401
    fingerprint analysis, 1:400
    media portrayal, 1:402–403
    scientific advances, 1:400, 1:400–401
Crime Victims' Bill of Rights, 1:187
The Criminal and His Allies (Kavanaugh), 4:1966–1967
criminal correction versus criminal deterrence, 5:2338–2341
criminal geographic targeting (CGT), 1:455
Criminal Investigation (Gross), 1:453
criminal justice. *See also* **American Revolution and criminal justice**
    American Bar Association section, 1:39
    Bill of Rights' effect, 1:123–124
    Colorado, 1:295–296
    Criminal Justice and Forensic Science Reform Act, 2:642
    libertarianism and, 3:1008–1009
    National Commission on Law Observance and Enforcement examination, 3:1184
    Nevada, 3:1214
    policy changes, 5:2414–2418
    politics of, 2:790–792
    pre-American Revolution, 5:2029–2030
    retributivism, 4:1542
    Schenck v. United States in, 1:446
The Criminal Man (Lombrosa), 1:409
The Criminal Mind (Lombroso), 2:749
Criminal Minds, 4:1765
Criminal Sentences (Frankel), 4:1633
Criminality and Economic Conditions (Bonger), 1:408
The Criminality of Women (Pollak), 4:1967
criminalization and decriminalization, 1:403–407
    euthanasia and prostitution, 1:405
    marijuana, 1:406
    marriage laws, 1:406
    process, 1:404–405
    Prohibition and, 1:403–404
    women's rights, 1:405
criminology, 1:407–413
    biological theories, 1:408–410
    biosocial theories, 1:409–410
    classical and neoclassical theory, 1:407–408
    conflict theory, 1:411–412
    demonological theory, 1:407
    DLC, 1:411
    ecological theory, 1:408
    economic theory, 1:408
    feminist theory, 1:412–413
    labeling theories, 1:411

new biological theories, 1:409–410
psychological theories, 1:410
radical Marxist perspectives, 1:413
sociological mainstream theories, 1:410–411
Criminology (Sutherland), 4:1742–1743
The Crisis of Imprisonment (McLennan), 5:2069
critical legal studies movement, 1:413–415
continuing debate, 1:415
development, 1:414
related theories, 1:414–415
critical race theory (CRT), 1:414
criticism
adversarial justice, 1:20
in Anti-Federalist Papers, 1:51–52
Boston, Massachusetts, 1:153–154
chain gangs and prison labor, 1:214–216
Thomas E. Dewey, 1:462
equality, 2:552–554
forensic science, 2:642
James Buchanan, 1:169
Law Enforcement Assistance Administration, 3:991
mandatory minimum sentencing, 3:1064
Miranda v. Arizona, 1:318
Omnibus Crime Control and Safe Streets Act of 1968, 3:1291
William Parker, 3:1322
plea, 3:1357
prison privatization, 3:1412–1413
Prohibition, 3:1447–1448
Roe v. Wade, 4:1575–1576
rule of law, 4:1590
victim rights and restitution, 4:1872–1873
Crocker, Richard, 1:460
Crofton, Walter, 1:339, 3:1187, 3:1423
Croker, Richard, 1:461
Cromwell, John, 2:623
cronyism, 1:253, 1:346
Crooker v. California, 3:998
Crouch, Jan, 1:100
Crouch, Paul, 1:100
Crow, Robert, 3:1005
CRT (critical race theory), 1:414
cruel and unusual punishment, 1:208, 1:415–418
application, 1:416–417
Eighth Amendment, 1:123, 1:196, 1:328, 2:570
Furman v. Georgia, 1:416–418, 2:659
history, 1:416
cruelty to animals, 1:419–420
animal advocacy, 1:420
animals as property philosophy, 1:419

Crump, Edward ("Boss Crump"), 3:1096
Crump, Raymond, 3:1167
Cruz, Indian Charlie, 2:516
CSI: Crime Scene Investigation, 4:1762, 4:1772
CSN (Consumer Sentinel Network), 2:814
CSR (corporate social responsibility), 1:344–345
CTS (Conflict Tactic Scale), 2:485
Cuba, 1:169, 2:521, 2:845
Cullen, Countee, 3:1180
Cummings, Homer, 1:421–422
attorney general, 1:421–422
Democratic National Committee, 1:421
Illinois state attorney, 1:421
Cummins v. County Board of Education, 3:1088
Cumminskey, Edward ("Eddie the Butcher"), 2:863
Cunningham, Emma, 1:422–423
fakery and disgrace, 1:423
sensational trial, 1:422–423
Cunningham, George, 1:422
Cunningham, Tom, 1:139
Cunningham v. California, 4:1630, 4:1634
Currie, Elliot, 4:1672
cursing, 5:1999
Curtiz, Michael, 2:622
Cushing, William, 1:248
Cushman, Pauline, 2:557
custodial interrogation, 1:317
Customs and Border Protection (CPB), 1:148, 1:424–425, 2:590
customs service as police, 1:423–425
agents, 1:425
homeland security, 1:424–425
national interests, 1:424
CWA (Clean Water Act), 2:545
CWAA (Convicted Women Against Abuse), 2:477
cybercrime, 2:646–647, 5:2449
cyber stalking, 1:310
cyber-bullying, 1:xlviii
opportunities, 1:311
targets, 1:309–310
tools, 1:310–311
cyberspace, 1:16
Czolgosz, Leon, 1:xlii, 1:49, 1:426, 2:526, 2:621, 3:1088, 5:2165

D

DADT (Don't Ask Don't Tell), 1:266
Dahmer, Jeffrey, 1:427–428, 2:576, 4:1891
cannibalism, 1:428
serial killer, 1:427–428

Dahrendorf, Ralph, **1:**411
The Dain Curse (Hammett), **2:**733, **3:**1018
Daley, Richard J., **1:**222, **1:**223, **1:**349
Dalitz, Moe, **3:**986
Dalton, James, **1:**81
Daniel, Peter V., **2:**490
Dannay, Frederic, **3:**1017
Dante, **3:**1027
Darden, Christopher, **3:**1095
Daring Dick, the Brooklyn Detective, **3:**1026
dark figure of crime, **1:**376, **1:**396, **2:**926
Darkness and Daylight (Byrnes, Campbell, Knox), **1:**193
Darrow, Clarence, **1:**82, **1:**428–430, **2:**576, **4:**1826
    books, **1:**430
    death penalty opposed by, **1:**429
    defense cases, **1:**428–429, **2:**956
    Leopold and Loeb defense, **3:**1005, **5:**2211
    retirement, **1:**429–430
    Scopes monkey trial, **1:**429
Darwin, Charles, **1:**410, **2:**748–749, **4:**1611, **4:**1878
Darwinism, **4:**1878
The Dating Game, **1:**xlix
Daubert v. Merrill Dow Pharmaceutical, **2:**628, **2:**640, **4:**1828
Daugherty, Harry, **2:**739
David Copperfield (Dickens), **1:**236, **3:**1015
Davis, Angela, **1:**83
Davis, David, **3:**1011
Davis, Debra, **1:**151
Davis, Edwin F., **2:**526
Davis, Katherine Bement, **1:**112–113
Davis, Owen, **3:**1020
Davis, Richard Allen, **2:**576
Davis, Troy Anthony, **1:**344, **5:**2458
Davis v. State, **1:**430–431, **2:**852, **4:**1741
    reversal, **1:**430
    Second Amendment and, **1:**430–431
Day, William, **1:**202
Dayton, Ohio, **1:**431–433
    Bertillon system, **1:**433
    19th century, **1:**431–432
    20th century and beyond, **1:**432–433
    Wright Brothers, **1:**431
de facto segregation, **4:**1619, **4:**1622
de Graff, Robert, **2:**467
de jure segregation, **4:**1620, **4:**1622
De Vianne, Elise, **2:**734
DEA. *See* **Drug Enforcement Administration (DEA)**
Dead Man Walking, **2:**571
Dead Rabbits, **2:**674, **2:**767–768

Dean, John, **1:**349
Dear Mr. Gacy, **2:**662
Death on the Nile (Christie), **1:**250
death penalty, **1:**xl, **1:**206
    African Americans and, **1:**xlvi, **1:**xlvii
    Darrow opposing, **1:**429
    Death Penalty Moratorium Implementation Project, **5:**2457
    Eighteenth Amendment and, **1:**341, **1:**437
    Fourteenth Amendment, **2:**570
    Furman v. Georgia, **1:**445, **2:**570, **2:**659, **2:**738, **2:**795, **3:**1079, **3:**1420, **4:**1735
    Georgia, **2:**692
    Gregg v. Georgia upholding, **1:**207, **1:**341, **1:**445, **2:**660, **2:**692, **2:**710, **2:**795, **3:**1421, **4:**1630, **4:**1735, **5:**2417
    People v. Superior Court of Santa Clara County and, **3:**1340
    prisoner's rights, **3:**1420–1421
    Roper v. Simmons, **1:**437, **3:**1421, **4:**1544, **5:**2458
    Rush opposition, **2:**571
    Supreme Court on, **1:**xlvi, **1:**xlvii
    Thomas Jefferson opposition, **2:**571, **2:**878
    2001 to 2012 re-examination, **5:**2456–2459
death row, **1:**433–437
    DNA exonerations, **1:**434
    execution process, **1:**434
    inhumanity, **1:**434
    inmates, **1:**436–437
    phenomenon, **1:**434–436
    San Quentin State Prison, **4:**1602
debauchery, **1:**202
Debs, Eugene V., **1:**272–273, **1:**428, **2:**739
Debs v. United States, **5:**2178
Decameron (Boccaccio), **1:**314
Declaration of Independence, **1:**11, **1:**437–439
    Enlightenment and, **1:**438
    influence, **1:**439
    principles, **1:**438–439
    ratification, **1:**438
    Thomas Jefferson drafting, **2:**878
    women and, **2:**550
decriminalization. *See* **criminalization and decriminalization**
Deep Blue Good-by (MacDonald), **3:**1031
Deep Throat, **4:**1916
Deepwater Horizon oil spill, **2:**546
defendant's rights, **1:**439–443
    Fifth Amendment and, **1:**439–440
    gag rule, **1:**440–441
    Sixth Amendment and, **1:**440–442

The Defenders, **4:**1762
The Defense Never Rests (Bailey, F. L., Aronson), **1:**99
Defense of Marriage Act of 1996, **1:**267
defensible space, **1:**391
Defensible Space (Newman, O.), **1:**393
Defoe, Daniel, **1:**314
DeForrest, Henry P., **2:**626
DeGelleke, Patrick, **1:**234
Delaware, 1:443–445
 Court of Common Pleas, **1:**358
 crime, **1:**443–444
 Exposure of the Delaware Whipping Post, **2:**621
 punishment, **1:**444–445
 same-sex couples, **1:**xlix
Delinquency and Opportunity (Cloward, Ohlin), **2:**678
Delinquent Boys: The Culture of the Gang (Cohen), **1:**411, **2:**677–678
DeMasi, Donna, **1:**114
Demme, Jonathan, **2:**624
Democratic Party. *See also* **Chicago Seven/Democratic National Convention of 1968**
 Cuba annexation issue, **1:**169
 Democratic National Committee, **1:**182, **1:**421
 Democratic National Convention, 1976, **1:**157
Democratic Republicans, **1:**12, **1:**38, **1:**346, **2:**891
demographics
 Cleveland, Ohio, **1:**273–274
 Compton, California, **1:**307
 guns and violent crime, **2:**723–724
demonological criminology theory, **1:**407–408
Denaro, Carl, **1:**114
Dennehy, Brian, **2:**662
Denning, Michael, **1:**173
Dennis, Eugene, **1:**445–446
Dennis v. United States, **1:**445–446, **2:**487
 historical importance, **1:**446
 Smith Act and, **1:**445–446
Dennis v. U.S., **4:**1690
Department of Defense (DOD), **1:**309, **2:**785
Department of Homeland Security (DHS), **1:**90
 budget, **2:**801
 creation, **2:**800
 federal policing, **2:**589–591
Department of Transportation (DoT), **2:**495
deportation, 1:xl, **1:**446–449
 Alien and Sedition Acts of 1798 and, **1:**447
 Chinese Exclusion Act and, **1:**447
 colonial poor laws, **1:**446–447
 nativism and, **1:**447
 political and economic refugees, **1:**447–448
 second line of defense, **1:**446–449
 terrorists and, **1:**448
DeSalvo, Albert, 1:98, **1:**151, **1:**449–450
 Boston Strangler, **1:**449
 death of, **1:**450
DeSalvo, Louise, **1:**16
DeShields v. State, **2:**738
detection and detectives, 1:450–455
 Bow Street Runners, **1:**450
 CGT, **1:**455
 crime-mapping, **1:**454
 future, **1:**454–455
 G-Man, **1:**452
 past foundations, **1:**450–451
 present-day analysis, **1:**453–454
 private detectives, **1:**452–453
 in the United States, **1:**451–452
The Detection Club, **1:**250
determinant sentencing, **2:**824–825, **4:**1627–1628
deterrence, theory of, 1:455–458, **4:**1625
 tenets, **1:**456–457
 today and tomorrow, **1:**457
 types, **1:**457
Detroit, Michigan, 1:458–460
 crime, **1:**459
 Great Migration, **1:**458–459
 police, **1:**458
 STRESS, **1:**459
developmental and life course (DLC), **1:**411
Devery, William, 1:221, **1:**460–461
 Baltimore Orioles purchase, **1:**461
 death of, **1:**461
 informal policing, **1:**461
 retirement, **1:**460–461
 Tammany Hall and, **1:**460
 trial and acquittal, **1:**460
deviant behavior, **1:**380, **4:**1567
The Devil in the White City (Larson), **2:**576
"Devil's Island," **1:**36
Dew, Rosemary, **3:**1092–1093
Dewey, Thomas E., 1:461–462, **2:**695, **3:**976, **3:**1048
 criticism, **1:**462
 organized crime fighter, **1:**461–462
 writings, **3:**1094
Dewitt, John, **2:**876
Dexter, **4:**1774, **4:**1884
Dexter, Colin, **3:**1025
DHS. *See* Department of Homeland Security (DHS)
Diagnostic and Statistical Manual of Mental Disorders, **1:**437

Diallo, Amadou, **1**:28
Diamond, Jack ("Legs"), **4**:1867
Díaz Lanz, Pedro Luis, **2**:*845*
Dicey, Albert Vann, **4**:1588
Dickens, Charles, **1**:236, **2**:764, **3**:1015, **3**:1027, **4**:1878
Dickenson, John, **1**:71
Dickerson v. United States, **1**:319
Dickinson, Angie, **4**:1771
Die Hard, **2**:613
Diel, John, **1**:114
Dietrichson, Phyllis, **2**:615
differential opportunity theory, **1**:380
Digesta, **4**:1529
Digital Millennium Copyright Act (DMCA), **1**:311
Dillard, James T., **2**:463
Dillard v. Georgia, **2**:463
Dillinger, John, **1**:433, **2**:463–465, **2**:835, **3**:1157
    crime rampage, **2**:464
    prison escape, **3**:1208
    Public Enemy Number One, **2**:464
dime novels, pulps, thrillers, **2**:465–469
    Beadle & Adams, **2**:465–466
    Buntline and, **1**:172–173
    Dime Detective, **2**:467
    lasting influence, **2**:468–469
    origins, **2**:465–467
    themes and subject matter, **2**:467–468
    whodunits, **2**:468
Dinkins, David, **4**:1889
Dirty Harry, **2**:619, **4**:1884
Discipline and Punishment (Foucault), **4**:1616
The Discovery of the Asylum (Rothman), **5**:2046
discretionary decision making, **2**:469–472
    background, **2**:470
    18th and 19th centuries, **2**:470
    overview, **2**:469
    Progressive Era, **2**:471
    recent developments, **2**:471–472
    20th century, **2**:470–471
discrimination. *See also* antidiscrimination
    age, **1**:266
    antidiscrimination, **4**:1721
    antidiscrimination violations, **4**:1931
    banned in defense industry, **1**:xliv
    gender, **1**:266
    Lyndon Johnson and, **1**:xlv
district attorney, **2**:472–476
    case screening and plea bargaining, **2**:474–475
    origins, **2**:473–474
    proactive approach, **2**:475–476

District Attorney's Office for Third Judicial Dist. v. Osborne, **1**:434–435
District of Columbia v. Heller, **1**:191, **2**:726, **4**:1736
Divine Comedy (Dante), **3**:1027
divorce, **1**:15, **3**:1014, **3**:1275, **3**:1423
Dixie Mafia, **1**:31
Dixon, Franklin W., **3**:1019
DLC (developmental and life course), **1**:411
DMCA (Digital Millennium Copyright Act), **1**:311
DNA analysis, **1**:400–401, **1**:434, **1**:453, **2**:640
    evidence, **4**:1502
    exonerations, **5**:2456
    interrogation practices and, **2**:853–854
    police technology, **4**:1758
    Zodiac Killer, **4**:1989
doctrine of discovery, **3**:1199–1200
doctrine of executive privilege, **4**:1845
Doctrine of Incorporation, **2**:810
DOD (Department of Defense), **1**:309
Dodd, Westley Allan, **2**:737
Dodge Police Package, **1**:87
Doe v. Bolton, **1**:xlvi, **1**:5, **4**:1575
Doe v. Commonwealth's Attorney, **1**:156
dog fighting, **1**:xlviii, **1**:135
Doherty, Brian, **3**:1006
DOJ. *See* **Justice, Department of**
Dolan, James, **1**:127
Dolan, Josephine, **2**:734
Dole, Robert, **4**:1572
Dolezal, Frank, **1**:275
Dombrowski v. Pfister, **3**:995
domestic surveillance, **3**:1383–1385
domestic violence, contemporary, **2**:476–479
    challenges and outlook, **2**:478
    gender bias and, **2**:687
    Internet and, **2**:478
    media coverage, **2**:476–477
domestic violence, history of, **2**:479–482
    contemporary issues, **2**:481
    early history, **2**:479–480
    increasing awareness, **2**:481–482
    media coverage, **2**:482
    women's movements, **2**:480–481
domestic violence, sociology of, **2**:482–486
    debates and solutions, **2**:485–486
    etiology, **2**:484–485
    historical and social context, **2**:482–483
    scope, **2**:483–484
Domestic Violence Act of 1978, **2**:481
Don't Ask Don't Tell (DADT), **1**:266
Doremus v. United States, **2**:743

Dorr, Thomas Wilson, **4:**1782, **4:**1834
Dorr's Rebellion, **4:**1782, **4:**1834
Dos Passos, John, **1:**314
Doss, Nancy, **4:**1963
Dostoevsky, Fyodor, **2:**733, **3:**1015
DoT (Department of Transportation), **2:**495
Double Indemnity, **2:**615
double jeopardy, **1:**123
Double Jeopardy, **4:**1884
Dougherty, George S., **5:**2169
Douglas, William O., 1:38, **1:**206–207, **1:487–488, 2:**521
    environmentalism and individualism, **2:**487
    formative years, **1:**487
    Griswold v. Connecticut and, **2:**714
    Securities and Exchange Commission and, **2:**487
    Supreme Court appointment, **1:**487–488
    teaching at Yale Law School, **1:**487
    Yates v. United States and, **4:**1985
Douglas v. California, **3:**1002
Douglass, Frederick, **1:**23, **2:**657, **2:**659, **4:***1686*
Dowd, Michael, **3:**1127
Doyle, Arthur Conan, **1:**117, **1:**250, **2:**467, **3:**1015–1016, **3:**1022
Dragnet, **4:**1762, **4:**1766, **4:**1768–1769
***Dred Scott v. Sandford,* 1:**xli, **1:**22, **1:**168, **1:488–490, 2:**489
    background, **1:**489
    citizenship for slaves, **1:**488, **2:**550–551, **2:**658
    Civil War and, **5:**2097–2098
    free blacks and, **2:**959
    most cited, **1:**490, **4:**1686
    overturn, **1:**261
    pivotal decision, **1:**489–490
Dreiser, Theodore, **1:**xliii, **1:**46–47, **2:**567, **3:**1274
drinking and crime, 2:490–497
    aggressive behavior and, **2:**494–496
    alcoholism and criminality, **2:**494
    alcohol-specific crime, **2:**493
    causal relationship, **2:**496
    drunkenness, **2:**493
    historical survey, **2:**491–493
    impaired driving, **2:**493
    non-alcohol specific crimes, **2:**493–494
    Prohibition, **2:**491–492
    research, **2:**493–494
    women criminals and, **4:**1960–19601
Driscoll, Danny, **2:**862
driving under the influence (DUI), **4:**1817
driving while intoxicated (DWI), **4:**1817

drug abuse and addiction, contemporary, 2:497–499
    marijuana, **2:**497–498
    sentencing trends and drug treatment, **2:**498
    statistics, **2:**497–498
drug abuse and addiction, history of, 2:499–502
    LSD, **2:**501
    mobilization of bias, **2:**500
    morphine, **2:**499–500
    opium dens, **2:**501
    regulation, **2:**500–501
drug abuse and addiction, sociology of, 2:502–504
    arrest and treatment, **2:**504
    conflict theory, **2:**504
    drug policy, **2:**502–503
    medicalization, **2:**503
    social learning theory, **2:**503
    strain theory, **2:**503–504
Drug Enforcement Administration (DEA), 2:505–507
    arrests, **1:**507
    evolution, **1:**506–507
    history, **2:**505–506
    Nixon creating, **1:**xlvi, **1:**505, **2:**589
DRUGFIRE, **1:**103
drugs, **3:**1008, **3:**1177. *See also* **narcotics laws;** war on drugs
    African American use, **1:**xlix
    California drug laws, **1:**196
    cocaine, **3:**1177
    codeine, **3:**1175
    crime, **1:**386–388
    DEA, **1:**xlvi
    Harrison Narcotics Drug Act, **2:**778
    heroin epidemic, **1:**106
    illegal prescription drugs, **4:**1922–1923
    morphine, **3:**1175
    Narcotic Drugs Import and Export Act, **1:**xlii–xliii
    Nixon policies, **3:**1262
    Office of National Drug Control Policy (ONDCP), **5:**2412
    opiates, **3:**1175
    opium, **3:**1175
    Opium Exclusion Act, **1:**xlii, **2:**778
    Opium War, **1:**243
    possession of, **1:**xlvi
    Rockefeller Drug Laws, **1:**xlvi, **2:**498
    victimless crime and, **4:**1876–1877
    women in prison, **4:**1972–1973
Drummond, Edward, **4:**1829
drunkenness, **2:**493, **5:**1999
Du Bois, W. E. B., **1:**24, **1:**26–27, **3:**1179–1180
DuBoc, Claude, **1:**99

due process, 1:109, 1:507–511
	American crime and punishment, 1:510–511
	confession and, 1:315–316
	development of substantive, 1:509–510
	Due Process Revolution, 1:123–124
	entrapment and, 2:542–543
	Fifth Amendment, 1:10, 1:123, 1:508, 2:655
	Fourteenth Amendment, 1:167, 1:315–316, 1:507–508, 2:523, 2:551, 2:697, 2:712, 2:796
	Fourth Amendment, 1:123
	historical perspective, 1:507–509
	juvenile courts, 2:920–921
	in Magna Carta, 1:439
	model, 1:366–367
	principles, 1:509
Duffy, Clinton, 4:1603
Dugdale, Richard, 1:409, 5:2109
DUI (driving under the influence), 4:1817
Dukakis, Michael, 1:187
Duke lacrosse team case, 1:28
Duncan v. Louisiana, 1:440, 2:899
Duren, Billy, 2:512
Duren v. Missouri, 1:256, 1:511–512
Durham v. United States, 2:840
Durkheim, Emile, 1:380, 4:1502, 4:1672, 4:1965
Duro v. Reina, 2:831
Dutch Civil Code, 1:284
Dutch courage, 2:494
Dutch West India Company, 1:44, 1:197
Dvorkin, Ronald, 4:1589
DWI (driving while intoxicated), 4:1817
Dwight, Theodore, 4:1536, 5:2111
Dyer, Mary, 3:1473
Dyer Act, 1:xlii, 1:512–514, 2:777. *See also* National Motor Vehicle Theft Act
	FBI auto theft authority, 1:513
	punishment under, 1:514
	response to changing times, 1:513–514
	stolen defined, 1:514

E

E. F. Hutton, 4:1617
Earle, Wilton, 1:84
Early Alert System, 1:90
Earp, Morgan, 1:162, 2:515
Earp, Virgil, 1:162, 2:515, 2:938
Earp, Wyatt, 1:162, 2:515–516, 2:938, 5:2105
	death of, 2:516
	frontier crime and, 2:653–654
	Hollywood film consultant, 2:516
	lawman, 2:515
	Ordinance #9 enacted, 2:719
	portrayals, 1:516
	shootouts, 2:515–516
Eastern State Penitentiary, 1:24, 2:516–519, 2:764–765
	closure, 2:518–519
	1961 riot, 2:518
	overcrowding, 2:518
	Pennsylvania system, 2:516–517
	radial plan construction, 2:517
Eastman, Crystal, 1:xlii, 1:40
Eastwood, Clint, 2:651, 4:1880, 4:1884
Eaves, Reginald, 1:73
ECHELON, 2:560–561
Eck, John, 5:2423
Eckel, John, 1:422–423
Eco, Umberto, 2:733
ecological criminology theory, 1:408
economic criminology theory, 1:408
economics, 1:408
	Newark, New Jersey, 3:1238
	Nixon policies, 3:1006
	refugees, 1:447–448
	William McKinley, 3:1087–1089
Eddy, A. J., 1:102
Eddy, Thomas, 2:519–520
	mental institutions and, 2:520
	penal reform, 2:519–520
	resignation, 2:520
Eden, William, 4:1536
Edison, Thomas, 2:524–525, 3:1238
Edmunds Act, 1:70, 1:121, 5:2110
education. *See also* ***Brown v. Board of Education; juvenile offenders, prevention and education; rehabilitation; training police***
	American Law Institute, 1:43
	contemporary juvenile corrections, 2:909–909
Edward VI, 3:1471
Edwards v. Arizona, 2:852, 3:999–1000, 4:1740
eel pulling, 1:134
Eel Uprising, 1:134
Eglash, Albert, 1:305
1851 to 1900
	birth of organized crime, 5:2105–2106
	Civil War, 5:2098–2101
	Old West, 5:2103–2105
	police force rise, 5:2106–2109
	Reconstruction, 5:2101–2103
	Victorian Reformation Movement, 5:2109–2112

1801 to 1850
    antebellum frontier, 5:2075
    carceral institutions, 5:2068–2071
    Chicago, Illinois, 5:2071–2072
    Andrew Jackson and Native Americans, 5:2072–2075
    laws and crime, 5:2063–2067
    police, 5:2067–2068
    south and slavery, 5:2075–2076

Eighteenth Amendment, 1:144
    death penalty and, 1:341, 1:437
    enforcing, 2:589
    Prohibition, 1:174, 2:491
    Volstead Act and, 4:1866, 4:1897

Eighth Amendment, 1:91, 1:154, 5:2038
    conflicts, 1:207
    cruel and unusual punishment, 1:123, 1:196, 1:328, 2:570
    excessive bail clause, 1:95, 1:96, 1:123, 1:287, 1:326
    Holt v. Sarver and, 2:799–800
    prison standards, 4:1537
    rights, 2:779
    Roper v. Simmons and, 5:2425
    standard of decency, 2:788

Einstein, Albert, 2:695

Eisenhower, Dwight D. (administration of), 2:520–522, 2:844
    Brennan nomination, 1:160
    Civil Rights Act of 1957, 1:264
    civil rights and, 2:522
    cold war and, 2:520–521
    immigration and, 2:522
    juvenile delinquency and, 2:521
    organized crime and, 2:520–521
    pardons, 4:1831

Eisenstadt, Thomas, 2:523

Eisenstadt v. Baird, 2:523–524, 2:714
    foundation laid, 4:1575
    right to privacy, 3:992

El Paso Intelligence Center (EPIC), 1:149

Eldred v. Ashcroft, 4:1736

electric chair, history of, 1:xli, 1:xliii, 1:205, 2:524–526
    first execution, 2:526
    Gruesome Gertie, 2:525
    lethal injection replacing, 2:526
    Ruth Snyder, 3:1244
    Westinghouse Dynamo, 2:524–525
    Yellow Mama, 1:32

Electrical Execution Act, 2:737

electronic surveillance, 2:526–529
    during cold war, 2:528
    Supreme Court and, 2:528
    telegraph, 2:527
    terrorism and, 2:528
    wiretapping, 2:527–528

The Elementary Forms of Religious Life (Durkheim), 4:1672

Eleventh Amendment, 1:59, 1:249

ELF (Environmental Liberation Front), 4:1780–1781

Elizabeth I, 3:1471

Elkins Act of 1903, 2:529–530
    enactment, 2:529
    Interstate Commerce Commission and, 2:530
    versions, 2:529

Elkins v. United States, 4:1737

Ellington, Arthur, 1:166

Ellington, Yank, 1:316

Ellsworth, Oliver, 1:59

Elmira Prison, 1:163, 1:339, 2:518, 2:530–532
    Zebulon Brockway and, 1:163, 4:1515
    marks system, 2:531
    reformatory period, 2:530–531, 5:2112

Emancipation Proclamation, 3:1012

embezzlement, 2:532–535
    Beesmyer, 2:534
    Cannon, 2:534
    Carrasco, 2:535
    evolution of law, 2:533
    famous embezzlers, 2:533–534
    fraud, 2:532
    Melissa King, 2:535
    Lloyd Benjamin Lewis, 2:534–535
    Mangum, 2:534
    Harold Rossfields Smith, 2:534–535
    white-collar crime, 2:532

Emergency Quota Act of 1921, 2:536–537

Emergency War Labor Board, 1:177

Emerson, John, 2:489

Emerson, Thomas I., 2:714

Emmitt, Thomas Addis, 2:696

empiricism, 4:1878

End Demand laws, 4:1482

Endangered Species Act (ESA), 2:545–546

Enforcement Acts of 1870–71, 2:537–539
    KKK and, 2:537
    protecting right to vote, 2:537–538
    resource demands, 2:538

Engel, George, 1:xli, 1:49

Engel v. Vitale, 4:1735

England, 2:539
   Commentaries on the Laws of England
      (Blackstone), 1:xl, 1:132–133, 1:371,
      1:438, 1:441
   early felony law, 2:601–602
   English common law, 1:123
   habeas corpus, 1:xxxix
   Parliament's Petition of Right, 1:xxxix
   policing 1600 to 1776, 5:1991–1995
   Puritans in, 3:1471–1472
   Statute of Westminster, 1:xxxix, 1:91–92
English Charter of Liberties 1100, 2:539
The English Convict (Goring), 1:409
Enlightenment, 1:204, 1:236, 1:334
   Blackstone writings, 5:2042
   Declaration of Independence and, 1:438
   1777 to 1800, 5:2042–2043
Enmund v. Florida, 1:208, 1:418
Enquiry Concerning Political Justice and Its Influence on Modern Morals and Manners (Godwin),
   1:xl, 1:48
Enron, 2:539–542, 4:1617, 4:1923
   background, 2:540
   scandal and downfall, 2:540–541
   stock plunge, 2:541
entrapment, 2:542–543
   tests and due process, 2:542–543
environmental crimes, 2:543–550
   criminal prosecutions, 2:548–549
   DOJ and, 2:544–549
   enforcement, 2:546–549
   Environmental Quality Council, 2:544
   EPA and, 2:544–549
   respondeat superior doctrine, 2:549
   rule of lenity, 2:549
   SEPs, 2:548
   statutes and regulations, 2:545–546
   white-collar crime, 4:1930–1931
Environmental Liberation Front (ELF), 4:1780–1781
Environmental Protection Agency (EPA)
   environmental crime and, 2:544–549
   establishment, 2:544
   Office of Enforcement and Compliance Assurance (OECA), 2:548
EPB (evidence-based policing), 5:2454–2456
EPIC (El Paso Intelligence Center), 1:149
equal protection, 1:262, 1:372, 2:551, 2:573
equality, concept of, 2:550–554
   Civil Rights Act of 1964 and, 2:552
   critiques of, 2:552–554
   laws toward, 2:551–552

   unequal before the law, 2:550–551
   Voting Rights Act of 1965 and, 2:552
Erdman Act, 1:xlii, 1:10
Erie Canal, 2:519
Erikson, Kai, 4:1672
Erskine, Thomas, 2:838
Ervin, Sam, 4:1916
ESA (Endangered Species Act), 2:545–546
Esau, Alexander, 1:114
Escape From Alcatraz, 2:614, 2:624
Escobedo v. Illinois, 1:41, 1:161, 4:1740, 5:2347
espionage, 2:554–562. *See also* treason
   Black Chamber, 2:558
   CARNIVORE, 2:560
   CIA, 2:559
   classifications of targets, 2:555–556
   COINTELPRO, 2:559, 2:785
   cold war, 2:558–559
   counterespionage, 2:555
   defined, 2:554
   early American, 2:557–558
   ECHELON, 2:560–561
   FBI, 2:584
   FISA, 2:559
   history of, 2:556–557
   HUMINT, 2:555
   IMINT, 2:556
   J. Edgar Hoover obsession, 2:808–809
   modern American, 2:559–560
   NSA, 2:558, 2:561
   problems, 2:561
   sabotage, 5:2267
   SIGINT, 2:555–556
   spy identification, 2:556
   21st century, 2:560–561
   U-2 incident, 2:559
   USA PATRIOT Act, 2:561
   World War II, 2:558–559
   Zimmerman Telegram, 2:558
Espionage Act of 1917, 1:xlii, 1:8, 2:558, 2:562–563, 2:778
   creation, 2:562
   disuse, 2:563
   provisions and application, 2:562–563
Esquire, 1:83
An Essay on Crimes and Punishment (Beccaria), 2:569
Estes, Billie Sol, 1:216, 2:564
Estes v. Texas, 1:216–217, 2:563–565
   Fourteenth Amendment and, 2:563–564
   media coverage and jury bias, 2:564–565

Ethics in Government Act of 1978, 1:349, 2:565–567
    authority, 2:565–566
    Carter signing, 2:565
    lapse of, 2:566
eugenic rhetoric, 1:169
European Court of Human Rights, 1:435
euthanasia, 1:405
The Evaluation of Forensic DNA Evidence, 1:401
Evans, H. W., 5:2206
e-verify, 1:xlix, 2:823
Everleigh sisters, 2:567–568
Evers, Medgar, 2:872
evidence-based policing (EBP), 5:2454–2456
evidence-based sentencing, 4:1630
Evolution of Desire (Buss), 1:14
Ewing v. California, 1:33, 1:416
Ex parte Merryman, 1:106, 2:730–731, 3:1011, 5:2098
Ex parte Milligan, 3:1106–1107, 5:2098
Ex parte Quirin, 3:1107
ex post facto, 1:386, 1:390
The Ex-Convict, 2:621
exclusionary rule
    Fourth Amendment, 1:124, 1:364, 4:1953
    Mallory v. United States, 5:2347
    Mapp v. Ohio, 5:2347
    suspect's rights, 4:1737–1739
    Weeks v. United States, 1:364
Execution of Czolgosz, 2:526, 2:621
The Executioner's Song (Mailer), 2:571
executions, 2:526, 2:568–572, 2:621, 5:2007.
  See also **death row; electric chair, history of; hanging**
    Ted Bundy, 1:172
    contemporary views, 2:569–571
    death row process, 1:434
    Timothy McVeigh, 3:1090
    media portrayals, 2:570
    Herman Mudgett, 3:1143
    private, 2:569–570
    public, 2:568–569
    Quakers, 3:1473
    Sacco and Vanzetti, 4:1596
    San Quentin State Prison, 4:1603–1604
    Ruth Snyder, 3:1244
existentialism, 3:1138–1139
expert testimony, 1:xliii
Exposure of the Delaware Whipping Post, 2:621
external ballistics, 1:104
extraterritorial jurisdiction, 2:902
Eyes on the Prize, 3:1250

Eyewitness Identification Procedures, 4:1951–1952
Eysenck, Hans, 1:410

F

Facebook, 2:477, 2:828, 4:1757
Fair Employment Practices Commission, 1:xliv, 1:264
Fair Sentencing Act, 1:xlviii–xlix, 1:28
Faith Assembly, 4:1533
Falkner, William, 1:314
Fall, Albert, 1:348, 2:740
fallen woman, 4:1965
Falwell, Jerry, 1:101
famous trials, 2:573–579
    celebrity, 2:575–576
    Lindbergh Kidnapping, 2:574
    notorious, 2:576
    Nuremberg War Crimes, 2:574
    political, 2:576–577
    principle-establishing, 2:578–579
Faraday, David, 4:1988
Fargo, 2:615
Farquhar, Robert, 1:248
Farrell, Frank J., 1:460, 1:461
Farwell, My Lovely (Chandler), 3:1018
Fass, Paula, 2:956
Fastown, Andrew, 2:540
Faulds, Henry, 2:626, 2:638
Fawcett, Anthony, 1:218
Fay v. Noia, 2:728
FBI. *See* **Federal Bureau of Investigation**
FDA. *See* Food and Drug Administration (FDA)
fear of crime, 2:579–582
    defining and measuring, 2:579–580
    explaining, 2:580–581
    NCVS measurement, 2:580
    policy implications, 2:581
Featherstone, Mickey, 2:863
Federal Bureau of Investigation, 1:xliii, 2:582–586.
  See also **Uniform Crime Reporting Program**
    ABSCAM, 1:349
    agents, 1:451
    analysts, 2:585
    ballistics lab, 1:102–103
    Branch Davidians and, 1:175, 1:277, 2:577
    CITAC, 2:585
    COINTELPRO, 1:xliv, 1:131, 1:349, 2:520–521, 2:559, 2:584, 2:785
    in cold war, 2:584
    on computer crime, 1:309
    Dyer Act auto theft authority, 1:513
    early history, 2:582–583

espionage, 2:584
establishment, 1:452
founding, 2:639
fraud reported FBI, 2:645–646
G-men, 5:2216–2217
illegal surveillance, 3:1377
J. Edgar Hoover era, 2:583–584
KKK investigation, 2:582
modernization, 2:584–585
NIBRS, 1:375–376, 1:382, 1:396
1921 to 1940, 5:2213–2215
NIPC, 2:585
robbery statistics, 4:1559
SWAT teams, 2:584
Ten Most Wanted Fugitives list, 1:xliv, 2:863
Theodore Roosevelt and, 2:906
Federal Bureau of Prisons, 1:xliii, 1:xlix
federal common law of crime, 2:586–587
early republic, 2:586–587
modern, 2:587
Federal Communications Act, 2:527
Federal Corrupt Practices Act of 1925, 1:348
Federal Election Campaign Act of 1971, 1:349
Federal Emergency Management Agency (FEMA), 2:*803*
Carter creation, 2:849
internment and, 2:849–850
Federal Employees Loyalty Program, 1:446
Federal Firearms Act of 1938, 2:719
Federal Insecticide, Fungicide, and Rodenticide Act (FIFRA), 2:545
Federal Intelligence Surveillance Act (FISA), 1:190, 1:213, 2:559
Federal Intelligence Surveillance Court (FISC), 1:213
Federal Kidnapping Act. *See* **Lindbergh Law**
Federal Law Enforcement Training Center (FLETC), 1:148–149
federal policing, 2:587–591
Coast Guard, 2:590–591
CPB, 2:590
decentralized, 2:588
defined, 2:588
DHS, 2:589–591
DOJ, 2:589
federal forces, 2:591
ICE, 2:590
Secret Service, 2:590, 5:2172
TSA, 2:590
federal prisons, 2:591–596
beginning imprisonment, 2:591–592
first rapid expansion, 2:594

McNeil Island Prison, 2:592–594
medical model, 2:595
meeting need, 2:593–594
Franklin Roosevelt and, 2:594–595
second rapid expansion, 2:595–596
treatment in, 2:594–595
Federal Register, 1:284
Federal Rules of Criminal Procedure, 2:596–599
drafting and development, 2:597
history, 2:596
organization, 2:598
results, 2:597–598
simplification, 2:596–597
updates and modifications, 2:598–599
Federal Security Service (FSB), 1:149
Federal Tort Claim Act, 1:249
Federal Trade Commission (FTC), 1:53–54
Clayton Anti-Trust Act of 1914 creating, 1:267–268
identity theft and, 2:813–815
Franklin Roosevelt and, 1:268
Federal Trade Commission Act of 1914, 1:53
Federalism, 1:207
Federalist Papers, 1:285, 2:599–601, 2:731
colonial PR, 2:600
Federalist Party, 1:12, 1:37–38, 1:346, 2:599–600
Feinberg, Joel, 4:1625
Feiner v. New York, 4:1830
Fellig, Arthur ("Weegee the Famous"), 3:1244–1245
felonies, 1:386, 2:601–609
characteristics of felons, 2:605–606
classifications, 2:603–604
collateral consequences, 2:608–609
early English law, 2:601–602
extent, 2:605–606
felonious larceny, 3:979
ISP, 2:608
murder, 2:604–605
processing, 2:607
punishment, 2:607–608
treason, 2:602, 5:1998
type and degree, 2:604–605
U.S. law, 2:602–603
Felson, Marcus, 1:380, 1:391
FEMA. *See* Federal Emergency Management Agency
The Female Offender (Lombroso), 1:409, 3:1192, 4:1966
The Feminine Mystique (Friedan), 3:1188
feminist criminology theory, 1:412–413
feminists, 1:5, 1:50

Ferguson, Colin, 2:609–610
    Long Island Railroad murder, 2:609–610
    trial and conviction, 2:610
Ferlinghetti, Lawrence, 4:1600
Ferrero, William, 4:1966
Ferri, Enrico, 1:409
feuds, 2:770–771
Field, David Dudley, 1:284
Field, Marshal, Jr., 2:567
Field, Stephen J., 1:59, 3:1148
Fielden, Samuel, 1:xli, 1:49
Fielding, Henry, 1:81, 1:450
FIFRA (Federal Insecticide, Fungicide, and Rodenticide), 2:545
Fifteenth Amendment, 1:24, 1:74, 2:550
    passage, 4:1480
    ratification, 2:537
    right to vote, 2:551
Fifth Amendment
    defendant's rights and, 1:439–440
    double jeopardy, 1:123
    due process clause, 1:10, 1:123, 1:508, 2:655
    grand jury indictment, 1:123, 5:2038
    Interstate Commerce Clause, 1:10
    Miranda v. Arizona and, 1:364, 2:787, 3:999
    self-incrimination, 1:123, 1:316–317, 1:327, 1:364, 2:712, 2:786
Fifth Circuit Court of Appeals, 1:xlvi
Fifty Years of Prison Service (Brockway), 1:164
file swapping, 4:1922–1923
Fillmore, Millard (administration of), 2:610–612, 4:1752
    American Party candidate, 2:611–612
    Fugitive Slave Acts and, 2:611–612
film, crime in, 2:612–616
    comedic crime and heists, 2:615
    dramatic crime films, 2:613–614
    film noir, 2:613
    psychological thrillers, 2:614–615
film, police in, 2:616–620
    comedies, 2:616–617
    comedy interpretations, 2:617
    comedy partnerships, 2:617–618
    corruption dramas, 2:618–619
    heroism dramas, 2:619
    Keystone Kops, 2:616
    realism dramas, 2:619–620
film, punishment in, 2:620–624
    early and pre-code movies, 2:621
    post-1950s prison film, 2:623–624

    production code era, 2:621–623
    women in, 2:623
film noir, 2:613
Final Truth (Gaskins), 1:84
financial crimes, 2:843
financial industries, 1:343
Finch, Stanley W., 2:582
fingerprinting, 1:xlii, 1:117, 1:400, 2:624–628, 2:777, 5:2174
    collection and comparison, 2:626–627
    comparisons, 2:627
    flaws and mistakes, 2:627–628
    Galton ridges, 2:626
    Malpighi layer, 2:626
    origin and history, 2:624–626
Fingerprints (Galton), 2:626
Finkbine, Sherri, 1:xlv, 1:4
fire-eaters, 4:1752
First Amendment, 1:8–9, 1:12
    Brandenburg test, 1:158–160
    Establishment Clause, 2:831
    freedom of press, 2:563
    freedoms, 2:844
    Procunier v. Martinez and, 3:1439
    Schenck v. United States applicability, 4:1606
    violations, 1:38
First International, 1:xli
FISA (Federal Intelligence Surveillance Act), 1:190, 2:528, 2:559, 3:1384
FISC (Federal Intelligence Surveillance Court), 1:213
fish and game laws, 2:628–630
    circle hooks, 2:630
    international regulation, 2:630
    J hooks, 2:630
    national regulation, 2:629
    NGOs and, 2:630
    state regulation, 2:629–630
Fisher, Adolph, 1:xli, 1:49
Fisher, John H., 1:102
Fisk, James, 2:704
Fiske, Robert, 2:566
Fitzgerald, F. Scott, 1:314
Five Joaquins, 1:194
Five Points, 2:861–862, 5:2166
Five Red Herrings (Sayers), 3:1017
flag burning, 1:188
Flegenheimer, Arthur. *See* **Schultz, "Dutch"**
Flemmi, Steve, 1:151, 2:863
Flemming, Ian, 2:554
FLETC (Federal Law Enforcement Training Center), 1:148–149

Fletcher, John Wesley, 1:101
Fletcher v. Peck, 2:630–632
    background, 2:630–631
    case of complicated ownership, 2:631
    Yazoo lands, 2:631
Flickr, 2:477
flogging, 1:333–335, 5:2005
Florence v. Board of Chosen Freeholders of the County of Burlington, 4:1741
Florida, 2:632–634. *See also* **Miami, Florida**
    crime, 2:634
    early statehood, 2:632–633
    20th century, 2:633–634
Flory, Robert, 2:623
Floyd, Charles Arthur ("Pretty Boy"), 2:635–636, 3:1157
Floyd, John Buchanan, 1:168
Flying Aces, 2:467
Flynn, Kevin, 3:1094
focal concern theory, 1:380
Focht, Mark, 3:983
Focus, 4:1674
Food, Drug and Cosmetics Act, 2:778, 3:1470
Food and Drug Administration (FDA), 1:4, 3:1470
For the Defense (Bailey, F. L.), 1:99
Foraker, Joseph B., 1:253
Foran Act, 1:70
Forbes, Charles, 2:739
Forbush v. Wallace, 1:372
Ford, Gerald (administration of), 2:636–637, 4:1572
    courteous and polite politician, 2:636
    Nixon pardon, 1:270–271, 1:349, 2:636
    Presidential Clemency Program, 2:636–637
    presidential proclamations, 3:1407
Ford, Henry, 2:464
Ford, John, 2:651
Ford LTD Crown Victoria, 1:86
Ford Motor Company custom police car, 1:xliv
Ford v. Ford, 1:23, 4:1684
Ford v. Wainwright, 1:208, 1:437, 3:1421, 5:2417
Foreign Corrupt Practices Act of 1977, 1:353–353
Foreign Intelligence Surveillance Act (FISA), 2:528, 3:1384
forensic journalism, 3:1250
forensic science, 2:637–642, 5:2175
    criticisms, 2:642
    DNA fingerprinting, 2:640
    evolution of modern, 2:640–642

    history, 2:638–640
    overview, 2:637–638
fornication laws, 2:643–644
    Fourteenth Amendment and, 2:644
    Lawrence v. Texas and, 2:643
    Martin v. Ziherl and, 2:643–644
Forsythe, William, 2:662
Fortier, Michael, 3:1091
Foster, Jodie, 2:575, 2:840, 4:1884
Foster Bill, 2:742
Foucault, Michael, 3:1400, 4:1616
Fountainhead (Rand), 3:1006
Fourteenth Amendment, 1:xli, 1:10, 1:24, 1:60, 2:550
    civil rights, 1:123
    Civil Rights Act of 1875 and, 1:262–263
    death penalty, 2:570
    due process clause, 1:167, 1:315–316, 1:507–508, 2:523, 2:551, 2:697, 2:712, 2:796
    equal protection clause, 1:262, 1:372, 2:551, 2:573
    Estes v. Texas and, 2:563–564
    fornication laws and, 2:644
    Gideon v. Wainwright and, 2:697
    Grutter v. Bollinger and, 2:715
    passage, 4:1480
    People v. Pinnell and, 3:1339
    Plessy v. Ferguson and, 1:263
    procedural fairness, 4:1832
    protections, 1:164, 1:266
    ratification, 2:537
    self-incrimination clause, 1:167
Fourth Amendment, 1:60
    due process clause, 1:123
    exclusionary rule, 1:124, 1:364, 4:1953
    Katz v. United States and, 2:943
    majority opinion, 4:1953
    protections, 5:2445
    reasonable suspicion, 1:373
    search and seizure, 1:123, 4:1736
    unreasonable searches and, 1:326, 2:786, 5:2038
    Weeks v. United States and, 4:1919
    Wolf v. Colorado and, 4: 1830–1831, 1952–1953
Fox, Richard, 3:1192
Fox News Network, 1:344
Fraley, Oscar, 3:1211
Francis v. Resweber, 1:364
Frank, Leo, 1:74, 2:577
Frankel, Marvin, 4:1628, 4:1633
Frankfurter, Felix, 4:1953
Franklin, Benjamin, 2:516, 4:1514
Franks, Bobby, 1:82–83, 2:576, 3:1004–1005, 3:1156

fraud, 2:532, 2:644–650, 4:1926–1927
    ACFE, 2:648
    common frauds reported to FBI, 2:645–646
    cybercrime and telecommunications, 2:646–647
    government targeted, 2:647–648
    historical examples, 2:648–649
    IC3, 2:647
    medical, 4:1929–1930
    NFIC, 2:647
    Nigerian 419, 2:645
    occupational, 2:648
    Ponzi Scheme, 1:343, 1:389, 2:646
Frazier v. Cupp, 1:281
Frederick the Great, 1:283
free blacks, 1:xl, 1:23
freedom, 1:10
    First Amendment, 2:844
    of press, 2:563, 4:1661–1662
    of speech, 4:1661–1662
    Thirteenth Amendment, 1:261
Freedom of Information Act of 1966, 2:650–651
    amendments and impact, 2:650–651
    landmark legislation, 2:650
Freedom Rides, 1:27, 1:264, 2:970, 5:2344
Freeh, Louis I., 3:1093
free-rider concept, 4:1545
Freikorps, 2:768
Fremont, John Charles, 1:167–168, 2:*611*
The French Connection, 2:619
French Revolution, 1:38
The French Untouchables, 2:620
Freud, Sigmund, 1:16, 1:410, 4:1648, 4:*1649*
Freund, Christine, 1:114
Frick, Henry Clay, 1:49
Fried, Barbara, 3:1008
Friedan, Betty, 1:5, 3:1188
Friedman, Lawrence, 1:15
Friedman, Milton, 3:1006
frontier crime, 2:651–654
    boomtowns, 2:653
    Wyatt Earp and, 2:653–654
    favorable conditions for, 2:652–653
    Doc Holliday and, 2:653–654
    Old West, 2:653–654
    overview, 2:651–652
Frontiero, Sharon, 2:655
Frontiero v. Richardson, 2:655–656
Fry, Elizabeth, 3:1476, 4:1968
Frye v. United States, 1:xliii, 2:640, 4:1828
FSB (Federal Security Service), 1:149
FTC. *See* Federal Trade Commission (FTC)

Fuchs, Klaus, 2:559
Fugate, W. Craig, 2:*803*
Fugitive Slave Act of 1793, 1:xl, 1:xli, 1:1–2, 1:168, 2:656–657
    Prigg v. Pennsylvania and, 2:657
    as slave recovery mechanism, 1:21–22
    George Washington and, 2:656
Fugitive Slave Act of 1850, 2:657–659, 4:1686, 5:2074
    Fillmore and, 2:611–612
    kidnaps, 2:658
    targets, 2:658
Fuller, Melville, 4:1734
Fullers, Lon, 4:1589
Fulton, Robert, 2:696
functionalist perspective
    of murder, 3:1161
    of rape, 4:1502
Furman, William Henry, 2:659
Furman v. Georgia, 1:xlvi, 1:31, 1:161, 1:178, 2:659–660
    cruel and unusual punishment, 1:416–418, 2:659
    death penalty and, 1:445, 2:570, 2:659, 2:738, 2:795, 3:1079, 3:1420, 4:1735
    groundwork, 1:206–207
    impact, 2:820
    principle-setting, 2:578
    rape and, 1:287

G
Gacy, John Wayne, 2:576, 2:661–663
    crime spree, 2:661–662
    ongoing controversy, 2:662
    punishment, 2:662
gag rule, 1:440–441
Gagan, Thomas, 2:*473*
Gagnon v. Scarpelli, 3:1001, 3:1435
Galleani, Luigi, 1:49–50
Galleanists, 1:50
Gallegos v. Colorado, 1:167
Gallo, Gina, 3:1092
Gallucio, Frank, 1:210
Galton, Francis, 2:626, 2:749
Galvani, Luigi, 2:524
Gam Saan, 1:247
Gambino Crime Family, 2:700
gambling, 1:xliii, 2:663–667, 5:1999
    ban, 1:xxxix
    as crime, 2:663–665
    defined, 2:663
    Nevada, 1:xliii, 3:1213–1214

New Jersey, **1:**xlvii
  rise of public-interest, **2:**665–667
  victimless crime, **4:**1876
gander pulling, **1:**134
Gandhi, Mohandas, **1:**259
The Gang (Thrasher), **2:**675–676
Gang of 14, **1:**191
gangs, contemporary, 1:xlviii, **2:**667–671
  Chicago Gang Congregation Ordinance, **1:**28
  Compton, California, **1:**307–308
  corruption and, **1:**352
  impact, **2:**670–671
  increasing fear, **2:**668–669
  National Gang Threat Assessment, **2:**669
  NYGS, **2:**668
  overview, **2:**667–668
  race and gender in, **2:**670
  reasons for activity, **2:**669–670
  St. Louis, **4:**1703–1704
gangs, history of, 2:671–675
  activities, **2:**672–674
  civic wars, **2:**671–672
  in history of crime and punishment in America: 1850–1900, **2:**767–769
  prehistory and context, **2:**671
  recent, **2:**674
  urban gangs, **2:**674
  Winter Hill Gang, **2:**863–864
gangs, sociology of, 2:675–679
  Code of the Street (Anderson, E.), **2:**678–679
  Delinquent Boys: The Culture of the Gang (Cohen), **2:**677–678
  The Gang (Thrasher), **2:**675–676
  People and Folks (Hagedorn), **2:**678
  Street Corner Society (Whyte), **2:**676–677
gansta rap, **1:**308
Garcetti v. Ceballos, **4:**1736
Gardner, Erle Stanley, 2:468, **2:**679–681, **3:**1018
  pseudonyms, **2:**680
  pulp magazines, **2:**680
  writing career, **2:**680
Garfield, James (administration of), 1:68, **2:**681–682, **2:**747
  assassination, **1:**xli, **2:**682, **2:**716, **3:**1329, **5:**2109
  election win, **2:**682
  log cabin president, **2:**681
  Pendleton Act of 1883 and, **3:**1329
Gargantua and Pantagruel (Rabelais), **1:**314
Garner, Tyron, **3:**991
Garofalo, Raffaele, **1:**409, **2:**749
Garrett, Pat, **1:**126–127, **2:**938, **3:**1402

Garrison, Oswald, **3:**1179
Garrison, William Lloyd, **2:**569, **4:***1686*
gas chamber, **1:**205, **1:***209*, **1:**295
Gaskins, Donald ("Pee Wee"), **1:**84
Gasko, Charlie, **1:**151
Gates, Darryl, **3:**1093, **3:**1384
Gates v. Collier, **1:**xlvi, **2:**682–684
  impact, **2:**683
  inmate rights and, **2:**683
  Parchman Farm, **2:**683
Gaudy Nights (Sayers), **3:**1017
gay marriage, **1:**406
GBMI (guilty but mentally ill), **2:**840
Geary Act, **1:**247, **1:**447
Gedney, Bartholomew, **1:**359
Gein, Ed, **1:**428, **4:**1948
Gelbart, Larry, **3:**1020
Gelbspan, Ross, **2:**849
Gelles, Richard, **2:**485
gender
  in contemporary gangs, **2:**670
  contemporary murder and, **3:**1151
  discrimination, **1:**266
gender and criminal law, 2:684–688
  evolution of, **2:**686–687
  gender bias in law, **2:**687–688
  research, **2:**687
  women and crime, **2:**684–685
General National Law for the Prussian States, **1:**283
general social survey (GSS), **2:**579
A General Theory of Crime (Gottfredson, Hirschi), **1:**381, **1:**411
Genovese, Vito, 2:688–689, **3:**1048
  insider revelations, **2:**689
  La Cosa Nostra summit, **2:**689
  organized crime and, **2:**688–689
George III, **1:**438, **4:**1782
Georgia, 2:689–692. *See also* **Atlanta, Georgia**
  Cherokee claims of sovereignty, **2:**832–833
  crime, **2:**689–690
  death penalty, **2:**692
  police, **2:**690–692
  punishment, **2:**690–692
  slave codes, **1:**23
Georgia Code, **1:**284
Georgia v. Allison, **2:**692
Georgia v. Wilson, **2:**692
German Americans, 2:693–695
  early, **2:**693–694
  intellectual migration, **2:**695
  during Prohibition, **2:**694–695

during World War I, 2:695
during World War II, 2:695
German Civil Code, 1:284
German measles (rubella), 1:xlv, 1:4
Gerry, Elbridge, 2:525
Gerry Report, 2:525
Get Christie Love!, 4:1771
get tough movement, 3:1226–1227
Geyser, George, 2:760
G'hals of New York (Buntline), 1:173
Giancana, Sam, 2:868
Gibbard, Allan, 3:1007
Gibbons, Thomas, 2:696
Gibbons v. Ogden, 2:695–697, 2:944, 3:1071
    commerce and, 4:1842
    national versus state authority, 2:696
    unresolved issues, 2:696
Gibbs, Janie, 4:1963
Gibson, Mel, 2:476–477
Gideon, Clarence Earl, 2:578, 2:697
Gideon v. Wainwright, 1:xlv, 1:30, 1:60, 1:327–328, 2:634, 2:697–698
    Fourteenth Amendment and, 2:697
    indigent defendants, 1:442, 2:552, 2:697, 2:786, 3:998
    principle-setting, 2:578
Giffords, Gabrielle, 1:xlix
Gigante, Vincent ("The Chin"), 5:2269
Gilbert, Cass, 4:1746
Gilded Age, 1:273, 5:2108–2110
Gilfoyle, Timothy J., 1:85, 5:2064
Gillette, Chester, 1:xliii, 1:47
Gillette, William, 3:1032
Gilmore, Gary, 2:571, 2:795
gin joints, 3:1133
Ginsberg, Allen, 2:501, 3:1275, 4:1600
Ginsburg, Ruth Bader, 1:7, 1:212, 2:512, 2:655, 2:952
Girls of the Big House, 2:623
Giuffrida, Louis O., 2:849
Giuliani, Rudolph, 2:698–699, 4:1889
    political career, 2:698
    political commentator, 2:699
    during September 11 terrorist attacks, 2:699
Givens, Robin, 2:482
The Glass Key (Hammett), 2:733, 3:1018
glasses drop, 1:320
Glidewell v. State, 2:699–700
GLM (good lives model), 4:1523
global positioning system (GPS), 4:1759–1760
Glorious Revolution, 1:123, 1:289, 1:292

Glover, Joshua, 1:1, 1:22
Glueck, Eleanor, 2:749
Glueck, Sheldon, 2:749
G-men, 5:2215–2216
Goddard, Calvin H., 1:102, 2:639–640
Goddard, Henry, 1:xl, 1:102, 1:409
The Godfather, 1:84, 2:613
Godwin, William, 1:xl, 1:48
Goering, Hermann, 2:574
Goetz, Bernhard, 2:577, 4:1882
Golay, Helen, 4:1963
gold rush, 4:1599–1600, 5:2109–2110
Gold Standard, 1:272
Goldberg v. Kelly, 3:995
Goldman, Emma, 1:49, 3:1008, 5:2178
Goldman, Ronald, 1:xlviii, 1:98, 2:482, 2:575
Goldman v. United States, 5:2178
Goldwater, Barry, 4:1757
Gonzales v. Carhart, 1:7
Gonzalez, Virgilio, 4:1916
good lives model (GLM), 4:1523
Goodfellas, 2:613
Goodman, Paul, 1:51
Google Earth, 4:1760
Gordon, George, 2:968
Gore, Al, 4:1758
Goring, Charles, 1:409, 2:749
Gottfredson, Denise C., 5:2423
Gottfredson, Michael, 1:381, 1:411
Gotti, John, 2:700–702
    Gambino Crime Family, 2:700
    life imprisonment sentence, 2:701
    Teflon Don, 2:701
Gould, Jay, 1:193, 2:704
GPS (global positioning system), 4:1759–1760
Gracy, John Wayne, 4:1891–1892
Grafton, Sue, 2:468, 2:702–703, 3:1017, 3:1019, 3:1031
    alphabet series, 2:702
    awards, 2:702–703
grand juries, 1:123, 2:896, 5:2038
Grant, Hugh, 2:574
Grant, Ulysses S. (administration of), 1:25, 1:313–314, 2:682, 2:703–705
    bankruptcy, 2:704
    civil rights and, 2:704, 3:1212–1213
    corruption and, 1:347–348, 1:352, 4:1927
    KKK suppression, 2:731, 3:1405
    presidential proclamations, 3:1405
    scandal, 2:704
The Grapes of Wrath (Steinbeck), 2:635

Grasmick, Harold, 4:1534
Gravelle, Philip O., 1:102
Graves, Bibb, 1:31
Gray, Kevin, 3:983–984
Grayson, William, 2:894
great chain of being, 4:1680
Great Depression, 1:4, 1:10, 1:79, 1:145, 2:705–709
   counterfeiting in, 1:357–358
   crime and criminals, 2:707–708
   crime control, 2:707
   crime distribution in, 1:383
   crime rates, 1:397–398
   growth of KKK, 2:708
   Herbert Hoover and, 2:805–806, 4:1898
   Prohibition and, 2:705–706
   tensions during, 2:708
Great Expectations (Dickens), 3:1027
Great Law, 3:1475
Great Migration, 1:199, 2:835, 3:1157
   Cincinnati, Ohio, 1:252
   Detroit, Michigan, 1:458–459
   first, 4:1484
Great Railroad Strike of 1877, 1:106, 1:220, 2:747
Great Railway Strike of 1922, 2:739
Great Society, 2:887, 5:2345
Great Train Robbery, 2:613
Green, Anna K., 2:709–710
Green, Anna Katharine, 3:1015
Green Berets, 2:558
Green Machine, 1:148–149
green movement, 1:50
greenbacks, 1:357–358
Greene, Graham, 3:1027–1028
Greene, William, 1:48
Greenya, John, 1:99
Grefory, Ovid, 3:1365
Gregg, Troy Leon, 2:578, 2:711
Gregg v. Georgia, 1:xlvi, 1:32, 1:161, 1:178, 2:710–711
   background, 1:445, 2:660, 2:692, 2:710, 2:711
   death penalty upheld, 1:207, 2:795, 3:1421, 4:1630, 4:1735, 5:2417
   principle-setting, 2:578
Gregory VII, 4:1530, 4:1531
Grieg, Catherine, 1:151
Grier, Robert C., 2:490
Griffin, Edward Dean, 2:711
Griffin, Michael F., 1:xlvii
Griffin v. California, 1:327–328, 2:711–713, 3:1435
   background, 2:711–712
   concurrence and dissent, 2:712–713
   history, 2:712
   ruling, 2:712
Griffin v. Illinois, 3:1002
Griffith, D. W., 1:244, 2:621, 2:968, 3:1182
Grisso, Thomas, 1:233
Griswold v. Connecticut, 1:xlv, 1:5, 1:15, 1:157, 2:488, **2:713–715**
   American Civil Liberties Union and, 2:714
   background, 2:713–714
   Comstock Law and, 2:713
   majority opinion, 2:714
   right to privacy, 3:992, 4:1575, 4:1735
   Roe v. Wade expanding, 2:714
   significance, 2:714
   William O. Douglas and, 2:714
   zone of privacy, 2:523
Gross, Charles, 1:433
Gross, Hans, 1:453, 2:638
Grossburg, Michael, 1:239–240
Grunebaum, James, 3:1007
Grutter, Barbara, 2:715
***Grutter v. Bollinger,* 2:715–716**
   affirmative action interpretation, 2:715–716
   Fourteenth Amendment and, 2:715
   O'Connor in, 2:716
GSS (general social survey), 2:579
Guandique, Ingmar, 1:xlix
Guantanomo Bay prison, 2:731, 2:802, 2:850, 3:1272
Guerry, André-Michel, 1:374, 1:408
guilty but mentally ill (GBMI), 2:840
Guinn v. United States, 3:1182, 4:1622
Guiteau, Charles, 1:xli, 1:68, 2:682, 2:716–717, 3:1329
   hanging, 2:717
   M'Naghten rule applied, 2:717
   preaching, 2:717
gun control, 2:718–723
   Armed Career Criminal Act of 1986, 2:720
   Brady Handgun Violence Prevention Act, 2:721
   cop killer bullets, 2:720
   Crime Control Act of 1990, 2:720
   early history, 2:719
   Federal Firearms Act of 1938, 2:719
   Gun Control Act of 1968, 2:719–720
   Gun Control act of 1968, 2:719–720
   gun rights campaigns, 2:721–722
   Gun Show Loophole Closing Act, 2:721
   National Firearms Act of 1934, 2:719
   NCIS, 2:720–721
   Ordinance #9 enacted, 2:719

Second Amendment and, 2:718–719
21st century, 2:720–721
Gun Show Loophole Closing Act, 2:721
gun violence, 4:1889–1890
Gun-Free School Zones Act, 1:188
Gunfight at O.K. Corral, 2:516, 2:653
Gunn, David, 1:xlvii, 1:7
Gunness, Belle Sorrenson, 4:1963, 5:2168
gun-related homicide, 3:1152
guns and violent crime, 2:723–726
Boston Operation Ceasefire, 2:725–726
demographics, 2:723–724
extent in U.S., 2:723
Kansas City Gun Experiment, 2:725
Los Angeles Operation Ceasefire, 2:726
policy responses, 2:725–726
self-defense, 2:725
Supreme Court on, 2:726
variations, 2:724–725
Guthrie, Woody, 2:635
Guzik, Jake, 1:211

H

habeas corpus, writ of, 2:727–729, 2:849, 3:1419, 5:1994
appellate review, 1:56
applying for, 2:728
in England, 1:xxxix
Abraham Lincoln and, 2:730
Supreme Court restrictions, 2:728
Habeas Corpus Act of 1679, 1:92, 2:729–730
Habeas Corpus Act of 1863, 2:730–731
Habitual Felony Offender Law, 1:33
hacking, 1:310
Hadfield, James, 2:838
Hagan, John, 1:412
Hagedorn, John, 2:678
Hagerman, Amber, 3:1169
Hahn, Jessica, 1:100, 4:1963
Halderman, Robert, 3:984
Hale, Matthew, 2:838, 5:2042
Hale, Nathan, 2:557
Haley, Alex, 1:83
halfway houses, 1:340
Hall, Gary, 4:1533
Hall, Margaret, 4:1533
Haller, Mark, 2:688
Halsey, Harlan Page, 3:1020
Hamdan v. Rumsfeld, 2:731, 2:802, 2:850, 3:1107
Hamdi v. Rumsfeld, 1:190, 2:728

Hamilton, Alexander, 1:51, 2:731–733, 3:1212
Burr duel, 2:732–733
Federalist, 2:599–600
political career, 2:731–732
Whiskey Rebellion and, 2:732
Hamilton, Patrick, 3:1020
Hamilton, Raymond, 1:140
Hamilton v. Alabama, 1:67–68, 3:1001
Hamlet, 4:1884
Hamlin, Louis, 1:234
Hamm, William, Jr., 2:957
Hammett, Dashiell, 2:468, 2:733–734, 3:1016, 3:1018, 3:1029
blacklisting, 2:734
CRC and, 2:734
personal life, 2:734
Pinkerton Agency agent, 2:734
political controversy, 2:734
private eye stereotype, 3:1425
writing career, 2:733
Hammon-Beason Alabama Taxpayer and Citizen Protection Act, 5:2448
Hampton, Fred, 1:75, 1:131, 1:222
Hang 'em High, 4:1880, 4:1884
hanging, 1:205, 2:734–738, 5:2007
American Civil Liberties Union and, 2:737
days of, 2:736–737
Guiteau, 2:717
history, 2:735–736
move to other forms of execution, 2:737–738
private, 2:737–738
procedure, 2:735
Hannum, Dave, 5:2461
Hans v. Louisiana, 1:249
Hansberry v. Lee, 3:995
Hanselman, Mary Jane, 3:1167
Hanssen, Robert, 2:560, 3:1380
Happersett, Reese, 3:1115
hard labor, 3:1135
Hardin, John Wesley, 1:82, 2:938
Harding, Warren G. (administration of), 1:145, 1:333, 1:348, 1:352, 2:738–740
corruption, 2:738–739
scandals, 2:739–740
Hardwick, Michael, 1:156–157
Hardy, Oliver, 2:621
Hargitay, Mariska, 2:477
Harlan, John Marshall, 1:262, 2:810, 2:943, 4:1707
Harlem Riot of 1935, 1:26
Harlem Riot of 1964, 3:1158, 5:2340
Harlot's Progress, 4:1959

Harmelin v. Michigan, 1:364, 1:416, 2:578
Harper's Ferry, 1:24, 1:169, 2:577, 2:771
Harrington, Penny, 3:1371
Harris, Eric. *See* Klebold, Dylan and Eric Harris
Harris, Jean, 1:84
Harris, Kevin, 2:577
Harris v. Forklift Systems, Inc., 4:1656
Harris v. McRae, 1:xlvii, 1:5
Harris v. New York, 1:178
Harrison, Benjamin (administration of), 2:740–741
    Homestead Strike, 2:741
    Sherman Antitrust Act, 2:741
    Sherman Silver Purchase Act, 2:741
    taking office, 2:740
Harrison, Carter, Jr., 2:567
Harrison, Francis Burton, 2:742
Harrison Act of 1914, 1:xlii, 2:500, 2:522, 2:742–743
    passage, 2:743, 3:1177
    specifications, 2:742
Harrison Narcotics Drug Act, 2:778
Hart to Hart, 4:1766
Hartnell, Bryan, 4:1988
Hart-Scott Rodino Anti-Trust Improvements Act of 1976, 1:268
Harvard, Beverly J., 1:73
Hasan, Midal Malik, 5:2447
Haslett, William, 1:162
Hastie, William, 1:28
hate crimes, 1:386–388
    Hate Crime Statistics Act, 1:187, 1:188
    Hate Crimes Prevention Act, 3:1182
    1981 to 2000, 5:2410–2411
Hatfield–McCoy feud, 2:770–771
Hauptman, Bruno, 1:216, 2:743–744, 2:776, 3:1218. *See also* Lindbergh Kidnapping
    electrocution, 2:744
    evidence against, 2:744
    Trial of the Century, 2:743
Haven House, 2:480
Haviland, John, 2:764
Hawai'i, 2:744–745
    annexation, 2:744
    crime, 2:745
    same-sex couples, 1:xlix
Hawaii Five-0, 4:1769
Hawkins, A. E., 4:1613
Hawthorne, Julian, 1:193
Hawthorne, Nathaniel, 2:758
Hay, John, 1:248
Hayden, Tom, 1:224

Hayek, Friedrich, 3:1006
Hayes, Brian, 2:812
Hayes, Rutherford B. (administration of), 1:314, 2:682, 2:746–747
    domestic acts, 2:746
    foreign affairs, 2:746
    as governor, 3:1187
    one-term president, 2:746
Haymarket bombing, 1:xli, 1:49–50, 1:220
Hays, Jacob, 2:747–748
    arrests, 2:748
    Old Hays, 2:748
    personal life, 2:748
    record-keeping, 2:747
Haywood, William, 1:428
Hazardous and Solid Waste Amendments (HSWA), 2:546
healthcare fraud, 4:1923–1925
Hearst, Patty, 1:98, 2:575, 2:957–958
Heart of Atlanta Motel v. United States, 1:xlv, 2:944
Heat, 2:620
Heaven's Gate, 4:1642
Heirens, William, 1:232
Hellman, Lillian, 2:734
Hell's Kitchen, 2:863
Helter Skelter, 2:576
Hemingway, Ernest, 1:314, 3:1029
Henfield, Gideon, 2:586, 3:1212
Henley, J. Smith, 1:64
Hennessey, David, 2:741
Henry, Edward, 1:453
Henry, Patrick, 1:51, 4:1704
Henry: Portrait of a Serial Killer, 2:614
Henry, William, 1:22
Henry II, 1:182, 1:299, 1:358, 2:601
Henry VIII, 3:1471, 5:1992
Hepburn Act of 1906, 2:530, 2:856
hereditary crime, 2:748–751
    ADHD, 2:750
    ASPD, 2:750
    CD, 2:750
    Darwinism and, 2:748–749
    family and twins studies, 2:749–750
    MBD, 2:750
    ODD, 2:750
Hernstein, Richard, 2:749
heroin epidemic, 1:106
Herrera v. Collins, 1:208
Herschel, William, 1:453, 2:626
Hess, Rudolf, 2:574

Heywood, Ezra, 1:48
Hickock, Richard, 2:940
Hickok, Wild Bill, 2:938–939, 3:1122, 3:*1123*, 5:2104–2105
Hill, Anita, 4:1885
Hill, George, 2:621
Hill, Herbert, 3:*1180*
Hill, John, 2:971
Hill, Reginald, 3:*1025*
Hill, Timothy, 1:74
Hill Street Blues, 4:1763, 4:1770–1771
Hillerman, Tony, 2:751–752, 3:1023–1024
    awards, 2:752
    Native American culture and, 2:751–752
    novels, 2:752
Hillside Strangler, 1:xlvii
Himes, Chester, 1:83
Hinckley, John, Jr., 1:xlvii, 2:575, 2:830–840
Hindman, Thomas, 3:1166
Hine, Lewis, 2:914
Hines, Jimmy, 1:462
Hinkley, John, Jr., 4:1829
hippies, 4:1600–1601
Hirabayashi v. United States, 2:876
Hirsch, Adam J., 5:2068
Hirschi, Travis, 1:381, 1:411
Hispanic Americans, 2:752–756
    criminal immigrants, 2:753–754
    Latino Paradox, 2:754–756
    Mariel Cubans, 2:753–754
    race-based crimes against, 4:1485–1486
    research, 2:754–756
    Zoot Suit Riots, 2:753
Hiss, Alger, 2:577, 2:845
history of crime and punishment in America: colonial, 2:756–760
    crime, 2:757–758
    18th century, 2:759–760
    piracy, 2:757
    punishment, 2:758
    religion and crime, 2:758–759
    social and political unrest, 2:757
history of crime and punishment in America: 1783–1850, 2:760–767
    African Americans, 2:765–766
    capital punishment, 2:761–762
    continued debate, 2:766
    jails, 2:762–763
    prison and penitentiary development, 2:763–765

history of crime and punishment in America: 1850–1900, 2:767–773
    gang and vigilante crime and violence, 2:767–769
    KKK, 2:769–770
    management-labor violence, 2:771
    personal violence, 2:770–771
    post-reconstruction crime and violence, 2:772–773
    racial violence and feuding, 2:769–770
    reformatory movement, 2:771–772
    Wild West, 2:769
history of crime and punishment in America: 1900–1950, 2:774–781
    correctional system, 2:779–781
    crime, 2:775–776
    law enforcement professionalization, 2:776–777
    legislation, 2:774–775
    new takes on old crimes, 2:778–779
    prostitution, 2:778
    regulatory laws, 2:777–778
history of crime and punishment in America: 1950–1970, 2:781–788
    capital punishment, 2:788
    civil rights and antiwar movements, 2:785–786
    community-based corrections, 2:788
    courts, 2:786–787
    crime and social movements, 2:782–783
    imprisonment, 2:787–788
    nature of crime, 2:781–782
    police and corruption, 2:783–785
history of crime and punishment in America: 1970–present, 2:788–795
    capital punishment, 2:795
    changing patterns, 2:789–790
    diversity and innovation, 2:792–793
    mass incarceration, 2:793–795
    polarization, 2:790
    politics of criminal justice, 2:790–792
The History of Prostitution (Sanger), 4:1966
Hitchcock, Alfred, 1:428
Hitchman Coal & Coke Co. v. Mitchell, 1:10
HIV/AIDS, 1:7, 1:238, 1:342, 2:498, 3:1411, 4:1874
Hobbes, Thomas, 1:381
The Hobo (Anderson), 4:1849
Hodgson v. Minnesota, 1:6
Hodson, Mae, 2:711
Hoffa, James R., 5:2272
Hoffman, Abbie, 1:224
Hogan, George, 2:863
Hogarth, William, 4:1959
Hoke v. United States, 1:201

Holden v. Hardy, 2:795–797
   background, 2:795–796
   rulings, 2:796–797
Holiday, Billie, 4:1865
Holliday, Doc, 2:515, 2:653–654, 2:769, 2:938
Hollis, Herman, 2:635
Hollywood, 1:354, 2:516. *See also* film, crime in; film, police in; film, punishment in
Holmes, H. H., 2:576
Holmes, Oliver Wendell, Jr., 1:8–9, 1:170, 2:779, 2:797–799, 5:2174
   Abrams v. United States and, 2:798
   education, 2:797
   jurist and scholar, 2:797
   Supreme Court appointment, 2:798–799
Holmes, Rupert, 3:1026, 3:1032
Holt v. Sarver, 1:64, 2:799–800, 4:1537
   background, 2:799
   Eighth Amendment and, 2:799–800
   inmate safety, 2:800
Holton, Mark, 2:662
homeland security, 2:800–803
   failed attacks, 2:802
   future of, 2:803
   Homeland Security Act of 2002, 1:148
   institutionalizing, 2:800–801
   legislation and government policies, 2:802–803
Homer, 2:838
Homestead Act of 1862, 2:804–805
   Buchanan veto, 2:804
   passage, 2:804
   public land disposal, 2:804–805
Homestead Strike, 2:741
Homicide: Life on the Street, 1:108
Homolka, Karla, 4:1957
homosexuality, 4:1696, 4:1736, 4:1876
Hoover, Herbert (administration of), 1:339, 2:775, 2:805–807
   presidential proclamations, 3:1406
   Prohibition and Great Depression, 2:805–806, 4:1898
   racism and, 2:807
   Wickersham Commission, 2:705, 2:806–807
Hoover, J. Edgar, 1:xliii, 1:433, 2:528, 2:807–809, 5:2343
   anticommunist crusade, 2:520–521
   appointment, 2:739
   Black Panthers targeted, 1:130–131
   Bureau of Investigation head, 1:451
   espionage obsession, 2:808–809

   FBI era, 2:583–584, 4:1837, 5:2213–2214
   recognition, 2:809
   ultimate G-man, 2:808
Horan, Ellen, 1:423
Horn v. State, 1:31
Horowitz, Helen Lefkowitz, 5:2066
Horror Stories, 2:467
Horsley, Albert, 2:812
Horton, William, 1:187
hot spots policing, 5:2419
Hough Riots, 1:275
Houlihan, Gerald, 1:77
House of Refuge, New York City, 2:914
House Un-American Activities Committee, 1:445–446
Housing and Urban Development scandal, 1:350
Housman, Ann Eliza, 1:137
Housman, Emeline Van Pelt, 1:137
Housman, George W., 1:137
Howard, John, 2:762, 3:1476, 4:1536
Howell, Clark, 1:74
Howl and Other Poems, 3:1275
Hoyt v. Florida, 2:634
HRW (Human Rights Watch), 4:1538
HSWA (Hazardous and Solid Waste Amendments), 2:546
Hudson, Jennifer, 2:575
Hudson v. McMillan, 1:188, 4:1537
Hughes, Charles, 4:1734
Hughes, Francine, 2:481
Hughes, Langston, 3:1180
human intelligence (HUMINT), 2:555
Human Rights Watch (HRW), 4:1538
"The Human Sacrifice," 2:569
human trafficking, 1:xlii
Hume, James, 1:139
HUMINT (human intelligence), 2:555
Hunt, E. Howard, Jr., 4:1916
Hunthausen, Raymond, 4:1749–1750
Hurricane Katrina, 2:803, 3:1407
Hurtado v. California, 1:124, 2:809–810
   arguments, 2:810
   background, 2:809–810
   Doctrine of Incorporation, 2:810
Hussein, Saddam, 1:189
Huston, Tillinghast, 1:461
Hutchinson, Anne, 2:759, 5:1997
Hutchinson, Thomas, 5:2045
Hutto v. Finney, 3:1419
Hutton, Bobby, 1:131

Huxley, Aldous, **2**:501
Hyde Amendment, **1**:xlvii, **1**:5–6

I

I Am a Fugitive From a Georgia Chain Gang! (Burns, R. E.), **1**:215
I Am movement, **4**:1840–1841
"I Have a Dream" speech, **5**:2344
IACP. *See* **International Association of Chiefs of Police**
IADL (International Association of Democratic Lawyers), **3**:995
IC3 (Internet Crime Complaint Center), **1**:309, **2**:647, **2**:814
ICE. *See* Immigration and Customs Enforcement (ICE)
Ice-T, **3**:1170
Idaho, 2:811–813
    crime, **2**:812
    police and punishment, **2**:811–812
    sodomy, **2**:812
Idaho v. Hayes, **2**:812
Idaho v. Limberhand, **2**:812
idealism
    nonreligious, **3**:1136–1137
    religious, **3**:1134–1136
identity theft, 1:311, 2:813–816
    CSN and, **2**:814
    federal efforts against, **2**:814–815
    FTC and, **2**:813–815
    Identity Theft and Assumption Deterrence Act, **2**:647
    Internet-based crime, **2**:815
    ITAC for, **2**:815–816
    methods, **2**:813–814
    NFIC and, **2**:814
    research, **2**:815
    victim advocacy, **2**:815–816
Identity Theft Assistance Center (ITAC), **2**:815–816
idleness, **5**:1999
If Christ Came to Chicago (Stead), **1**:220, **2**:567
IGRA (Indian Gaming Regulatory Act), **3**:1204
illegal immigrants, **5**:2447–2449
Illinois, 2:816–820. *See also* **Chicago, Illinois**
    Illinois State Penitentiary, **4**:1492
    law enforcement, **2**:816–818
    Navou, **2**:8167–818
    punishment, **2**:818–820
    state penitentiary, **1**:xli
Illinois v. Patane, **4**:1740
Illinois v. Perkins, **1**:281

image intelligence (IMINT), **2**:556
immigration
    Chinese Americans, **1**:242–244
    Chinese Exclusion Act and, **1**:246, **2**:822
    Eisenhower and, **2**:522
    ICE, **1**:148, **1**:425
    illegal immigrants, **5**:2447–2449
    Immigration Reform and Control Act of 1986, **1**:xlvii, **1**:147
    Japanese Americans, **2**:874–875
    Jewish Americans, **2**:881–882
Immigration and Customs Enforcement (ICE), **1**:148, **1**:425, **2**:590
Immigration and Naturalization Service (INS)
    formation of, **1**:xliii
    functions, **1**:148
    Operation Wetback, **1**:522
immigration crimes, 2:820–824
    border security, **2**:822–823
    DOJ and, **2**:821
    enforcement, **2**:821–822
    e-verify and, **2**:823
    historical perspective, **2**:822
    workplace enforcement, **2**:823
impaired driving, **2**:493
impeachment
    Andrew Johnson, **5**:2103
    William Clinton, **2**:566, **2**:574, **2**:577
In Cold Blood (Capote), **2**:571, **2**:940
In Contempt (Darden), **3**:1095
In re Gault, **1**:240, **2**:578, **2**:921, **2**:923–924, **5**:2347
In re Medley, **3**:1418
In re Neagle, **1**:59
In re Winship, **2**:578
incapacitation, theory of, 2:824–826, 4:1625
    determinant sentencing, **2**:824–825
    rehabilitative model, **2**:824
    selective incapacitation, **2**:825–826
incarceration rates
    in history of crime and punishment in America: 1970–present, **2**:793–795
    in juvenile corrections, **2**:909
    racism and, **4**:1489
incest, 2:826–827
    effects if sexual abuse, **2**:827
    sibling, **2**:826–827
Inches, James W., **1**:459
indecent exposure, 2:827–829
    role of media, **2**:828
Indemnity Only (Paretsky), **3**:1031
Independence Institute, **3**:1006

Independent Counsel Act, 2:566
Independent Treasury Act, 2:829–831
    new federal system, 2:830
    passage, 2:829
Indian Bill of Rights, 3:1203
Indian Citizenship Act, 3:1201
Indian Civil Rights Act, 2:831–832
    enforcement, 2:831–832
    passage, 2:831
Indian Gaming Regulatory Act (IGRA), 3:1204
Indian Removal Act, 1:xl, 2:832–834
    Cherokee claims of sovereignty, 2:832–833
    Andrew Jackson and, 2:833
    Thomas Jefferson and, 2:832
    political support, 2:833
    Trail of Tears, 2:833–834
Indian Reorganization Act, 3:1201
Indian Territory, 1:xl, 1:70
Indiana, 2:834–836
    crime, 2:836
    KKK, 2:835–836
    police and punishment, 2:834–835
Indianapolis v. Edmond, 1:42
indigent defendants, 1:xlv, 1:442, 2:552, 2:697, 2:786
individuals, situations, opportunities, organizations, resource adequacy (ISOR), 3:1389
Industrial era of corrections, 1:337
Industrial Revolution, 1:228, 2:771
Industrial Workers of the World (IWW), 1:259, 2:779
industry
    Camden, New Jersey, 1:197–198
    defense, 1:xliv
    Las Vegas, Nevada, 3:987–988
    music, 3:1172
    Newark, New Jersey, 3:1238
    private prison, 5:2450–2451
infanticide, 2:836–837
    proving, 2:837
    punishment, 2:837
    underreported, 2:836
Ingraham v. Wright, 1:335
inmate safety, 2:800
Inquisition, 1:17–18
INS. *See* Immigration and Naturalization Service (INS)
insanity defense, 2:838–841
    GBMI, 2:840
    historic evolution, 2:838–840
    Insanity Defense Reform Act, 2:840
    John Hinkley defense, 2:840–841
    M'Naghten rule, 2:839–840
    NGRI, 2:841
    wooden cage punishment, 2:839
Inside American Jail, 4:1776
Inside the Company (Agee), 2:559
Integrated Ballistics Information Network Program (NIBIN), 1:103
integration. *See also* segregation
    Supreme Court on school, 1:xliv
    in U.S. armed forces, 1:xliv, 1:27, 1:264
intellectual migration, 2:695
intellectual property rights, 3:1008
Intensive Supervision Probation (ISP), 2:608, 5:2422
Interdepartmental Committee on Narcotics, 2:522
Internal Revenue Service, 2:841–843
    background, 2:841–842
    corruption and, 1:348
    tax crimes and, 4:1750
    tax evasion and, 2:842–843
    terrorism and financial crimes and, 2:843
Internal Security Act of 1950, 2:844–845. *See also* McCarran Internal Security Act of 1950
    background, 2:844
    current effects, 2:845
International Association of Chiefs of Police, 1:374, 2:845–847
    achievements, 2:846–847
    structure, 2:847
International Association of Democratic Lawyers (IADL), 3:995
International Game Fish Association, 2:630
International Ladies Garment Workers Union, 4:1723
International Teamsters Union, 1:352
International Union on Conservation of Nature (IUCN), 3:1341
International Working Man's Association (IWMA), 1:xli. *See also* First International
    anarchists, 1:48–49
    Russian Revolution of 1917 and, 1:49
Internet
    domestic violence and, 2:478
    Internet Crime Complaint Center (IC3), 1:309, 2:647, 2:814
    Internet-based crime, 2:815
    vigilantism, 4:1883–1884
internment, 2:847–850
    Cherokee, 2:848
    contemporary issues, 2:850
    FEMA and, 2:849–850
    Japanese during World War II, 2:848–849
    Operation Garden Plot, 2:849–850

interrogation practices, 2:851–855
    CIA enhanced, 2:854
    court decisions, 2:852–853
    DNA evidence, 2:853–854
    Miranda v. Arizona and, 2:851–853, 4:1739
    Barack Obama and, 2:855
    suspect rights, 2:851–852
    suspect's rights, 4:1739–1740
    terrorism and, 2:854–855
    torture, 4:1813
Interstate Commerce Act of 1887, 1:xli, 2:855–857
    Interstate Commerce Commission, 2:530, 2:856
    national regulation, 2:856
intimate partner violence, 2:486
Intolerable Acts of 1774, 2:857–858
Iowa, 2:858–860
    crime, 2:860
    police and punishment, 2:859–860
    Prohibition, 2:859
IRA (Irish Republican Army), 4:1781
Iran-Contra scandal, 1:271, 1:349–350, 1:353, 2:566
Iraq invasion, 5:2445
Iredell, James, 1:248
Ireland: Social, Political, and Religious (de Beaumont), 1:110
Irey, Elmer L., 2:842
Irish Americans, 2:860–864
    early struggles, 2:861
    organized crime, 2:862–863, 3:1300–1301
    Tammany Hall and Five Points, 2:861–862
    Winter Hill Gang, 2:863–864
Irish Republican Army (IRA), 4:1781
Irish system, 3:1324, 4:1519
iron gag, 2:764
Ironside, 3:1425, 4:1769
IRS. *See* Internal Revenue Service
Irvin, v. Dowd, 2:564
ISOR (individuals, situations, opportunities, organizations, resource adequacy), 3:1389
ISP (Intensive Supervision Probation), 2:608, 5:2422
Israel, Harold, 1:421–422
ITAC (Identity Theft Assistance Center), 2:815–816
Italian Americans, 2:864–868
    Chicago, Illinois, 2:867–868
    crime, 2:868
    immigrating, 2:866–867
    life in *mezzogiorno*, 2:864–866
    Mafia and, 2:865–866
    in New York, 2:867–868
    organized crime, 3:1302–1304
The Italian Job, 2:615
IUCN (International Union on Conservation of Nature), 3:1341
IWMA. *See* International Working Man's Association (IWMA)
IWW (Industrial Workers of the World), 1:259, 2:779

J

J hooks, 2:630
Jackson, Andrew (administration of), 1:xl, 1:13, 2:869–870
    Indian Removal Act and, 2:833
    Jacksonian democracy, 2:870
    National Bank and, 2:830, 2:869
    Native Americans and, 5:2072–2075
    Van Buren supporting, 1:176
Jackson, Ed, 2:835
Jackson, George, 1:75, 1:258, 4:1603
Jackson, Maynard, 1:73
Jackson, Michael, 1:xlix, 2:575, 5:2425
Jackson, Mississippi, 2:870–872
    Black Codes, 2:871
    crime, 2:872
    prisons, 2:872
Jackson, Robert, 4:1841
Jackson, Vickie Dawn, 4:1963
Jackson v. Georgia, 2:659
The Jack-Roller (Shaw, C.), 4:1849
Jacobs, Harriet, 1:23
Jacobson v. Massachusetts, 1:170
jails. *See also* **penitentiaries**; **prisons**
    in history of crime and punishment in America: 1783–1850, 2:762–763
    Letter From a Birmingham Jail, 1:128
    Quakers in, 2:762
    Walnut Street Jail, 2:763, 3:1330–1331, 4:1902–1904, 5:2045, 5:2046
James, Frank, 1:82, 2:769
James, Jesse, 1:xli, 1:82, 2:769, 2:872–874
    life of an outlaw, 2:872–874
    robberies, 4:1560–1661
James, William, 3:1137
James I, 1:288
James II, 1:123, 1:141, 1:289
Jamestown, Virginia, 1:xxxix
James-Younger Gang, 1:82, 3:1122
Japanese Americans, 1:246, 2:874–877
    citizenship, 2:875–876
    criminalization of, 2:877

immigration, 2:874–875
internment camps, 1:xliv, 1:296, 2:848–849, 2:876–877, 4:1905–1906
picture brides, 2:875
Jaworski, Leon, 4:1916
Jay, John, 2:600, 2:731
jaywalking, 4:1877
The Jazz Singer, 5:2219
Jefferson, Thomas, 1:11–12, 1:37–38, 1:51, 1:346, 2:877–879
Anti-Federalist, 2:599–600
death penalty opposition, 2:571, 2:878
Declaration of Independence drafting, 2:878
Indian Removal Act and, 2:832
legal codes and, 5:2044
Monticello building, 2:877–878
reformer, 4:1514
Jefferson, Thomas (administration of), 2:879–880
background to presidency, 2:879
terms of presidency, 2:880
Jeffrey, C. Ray, 1:391, 1:393
Jeffries, Jim, 5:2165
Jehovah's Witnesses, 1:60, 4:1753
Jenckes, Thomas, 2:905
Jenkins, Phillip, 2:827
Jensen, Betty Lou, 4:1988
Jerry Springer, 4:1765
"Jersey Shore Thrill Killer," 3:1218
Jeserich, Paul, 1:102
Jewell, Richard, 1:74
Jewett, Helen, 4:1243–1244, 5:2065
Jewish Americans, 2:881–883
civil rights movement, 2:881–882
immigration, 2:881–882
Mafia and, 2:881–882
mainstream identity, 2:883
organized crime, 3:1302
radical politics, 2:881
Jim Crow laws, 1:25–26, 2:551, 2:790, 4:1619–1622, 5:2452
Joey the Hitman: The Autobiography of a Mafia Killer (Joey the Hitman), 1:84
John Lennon: One Day at a Time (Fawcett), 1:218
John of Leyden, 1:120
Johns, Kathleen, 4:1989
Johnson, Andrew (administration of), 1:263, 1:271, 2:883–886
impeachment, 5:2103
Mississippi v. Johnson and, 3:1120–1121
presidency, 2:884–886
rise to power, 2:884

Johnson, Anthony, 1:21
Johnson, Gregory Lee, 2:970
Johnson, Jack, 2:567, 2:774, 5:2165
Johnson, James Weldon, 3:1180
Johnson, Leon, 2:779
Johnson, Lyndon B. (administration of), 1:xlv, 2:886–888. *See also* war on poverty
Civil Rights Act of 1964, 1:264–265
Civil Rights Act of 1965, 1:266
crime control, 2:886–887
discrimination and, 1:xlv
federal assistance to states, 2:887
Great Society, 2:887, 5:2345
mixed legacy, 2:888
Voting Rights Act of 1965, 1:xlv, 1:265–266
Johnson, Stephen, 3:1011
Johnson v. Avery, 2:888–889
Johnson-O'Malley Act, 3:1201
Jones, Mike, 3:1254
Jones, Paula, 2:566
Jones, Thomas, 1:72
Jones-Miller Act, 2:778, 3:1177. *See also* Narcotic Drugs Import and Export Act
Journal of the American Medical Association, 2:526
Jowers, Loyd, 4:1506
Joyce, James, 1:314, 3:1275, 4:1846
Joyner, John, 1:140
Joyner v. Joyner, 1:371, 2:483
Judaism, 1:118, 4:1670
Judd, Ashley, 4:1884
Judge Joe Brown, 4:1765
Judge Judy, 4:1765
Judge Mathis, 4:1765
judges and magistrates, 2:889–893
colonial, 2:890
federal courts, 2:892
federal judiciary origins, 2:890–892
Midnight Judges Act, 1:12, 2:891
state courts, 2:892–893
judicial lawlessness, 4:1628
Judiciary Act, 2:586
Judiciary Act of 1789, 1:xl, 1:59, 1:93–94, 2:893–894
court system objective, 2:893–894
effects, 2:894
Office of Attorney General established, 2:894
U.S. attorneys created, 4:1839
Judiciary Act of 1793, 1:59
Judiciary Act of 1801, 1:12, 1:363
Juergensmeyer, Mark, 4:1535
The Jungle (Sinclair), 1:46, 3:1469

juries, 2:895–900. *See also* citizen participation on juries
   African Americans and, 1:xliv
   composition, size, selection, 2:896–897
   deliberation and nullification, 2:899–900
   grand jury, 1:123, 2:896, 5:2038
   role and behavior, 2:897–899
   types, 2:895–896
   unanimous verdicts, 2:899
jurisdiction, 2:900–903
   actus reus, 2:902
   concurrent and special, 2:902
   extraterritorial, 2:902
   history, 2:900–901
   personal, 2:901–902
   subject-matter, 2:901
   territorial, 2:902
just deserts, 1:337–38, 4:1625
Justice, Department of, 1:xliii, 1:xlvi, 1:53–54, 2:903–907
   ATF within, 1:174
   burglars and, 1:185
   early challenges, 2:905–906
   environmental crime and, 2:544–549
   evolution, 2:906–907
   federal policing, 2:589
   headquarters, 2:904
   immigration crimes and, 2:821
   KKK and, 2:905–906
   mission, 2:903
   origin, 2:904–905
   Qui Pro Domina Justitia Sequitur, 2:903
   services and operations, 2:906–907
Justice League of America, 4:1764
juvenile corrections, contemporary, 2:907–909
   decreased incarceration, 2:909
   rehabilitation, education, counseling, 2:909–909
   U.S. system, 2:907–908
juvenile corrections, history of, 2:909–913
   community-based corrections, 2:911–912
   parens patriae doctrine, 2:911–912
   secure facilities, 2:912–913
   Warwickshire Quarter Sessions, 2:910
juvenile corrections, sociology of, 2:913–916
   Amsterdam House of Corrections, 2:914
   children seen as adults, 2:913
   females and, 2:914–915
   House of Refuge, New York City, 2:914
   minorities and, 2:915

juvenile courts, contemporary, 2:916–918
   characteristics, 2:917–918
   drug courts, 2:916–917
   gun courts, 2:917
   mental health, 2:917
   racial justice, 4:1516–1517
   reform movements in justice, 4:1515–1516
   teen, 2:917
juvenile courts, history of, 2:918–922
   due process, 2:920–921
   juveniles in criminal courts, 2:921–922
   parens patriae doctrine, 2:918–920
   probation and reform, 2:920
juvenile delinquency, history of, 2:922–925
   National Conference on Prevention and Control of Juvenile Delinquency, 5:2264
   parens patriae doctrine, 2:922
   refuge houses, 2:922
   rehabilitation, 2:922
juvenile delinquency, sociology of, 2:521, 2:925–929
   dark figure of crime, 2:926
   nature and extent, 2:926–927
   social construction, 2:925–926
   social groupings, 2:927–928
   theories of crime, 2:927
   urbanization and, 4:1849–1851
juvenile justice, history of, 2:929–932
   child saving movement, 2:929–930
   juvenile court system, 2:931
   Lindsey as advocate, 3:1013–1014
   loco parentis doctrine, 2:930
   racism and, 4:1489–1490
   superpredators, 2:931
juvenile offenders, prevention and education, 2:932–934
   evolution of programs, 2:932–933
   programs by age and gender, 2:933–934
juvenile offenders in adult courts, 2:934–936
   arguments for and against waivers, 2:935–936
   methods of transfer, 2:935
Juvenile Psychopathic Institute, 1:239

K
K-9, 2:617
Kaczynski, Theodore, 1:xlviii, 1:277, 2:937–938, 4:1785, 1804
Kanka, Megan, 1:xlvii–xlvii
Kansas, 2:938–940
   Brass Buckle of Bible Belt, 2:939
   capital punishment, 2:940
   law enforcement, 2:938–939

Kansas City, Missouri, 2:940–942
    courts, 2:940–941
    crime, 2:942
    Kansas City Gun Experiment, 2:725
    Kansas City Preventative Patrol Experiment, 1:xlvi
    police, 2:941
Kansas-Nebraska Act, 1:168
Kant, Immanuel, 4:1625
Karmen, Andrew, 2:783
Katcher, Gary, 3:983
Katz, Charles, 2:578
Katz v. United States, 2:578, 2:942–943
    arguments, 2:943
    Fourth Amendment and, 2:943
Katzenbach, Nicholas, 3:986, 3:1408
Katzenbach v. McClung, 2:944–945
Katzman, Frederick G., 4:1596
Kavanaugh, Marcus, 4:1966–1967
Kazan, Elia, 1:421
Keating, Charles, 1:350
Keating Five, 1:350
Keaton, Buster, 2:621
Keenan, Rosemary, 1:114
Keene, Carolyn, 3:1019
Kefauver, Estes, 2:783, 5:2268–2269
Kefauver Commission, 1:xliv, 1:462, 2:783–784
Keighley, William, 2:623
Keitel, Wilhelm, 2:574
Kellerman, Jonathan, 3:1024
Kelling, George, 1:xlvi, 1:xlvii, 1:87, 1:392–393
Kellor, Frances, 4:1968
Kelly, George ("Machine Gun"), 1:36, 1:129, 2:776, 2:957
Kelly, John, 4:1584
Kelly, Raymond, 3:1127
Kelo v. City of New London, 4:1736
Kemmler, William, 1:xli, 2:737
Kendall, George, 2:568
Kenna, Michael ("Hinky Dink"), 1:219–220, 2:818
Kennedy, Anthony, 3:992
Kennedy, Brenda, 1:33
Kennedy, John F. (administration of), 2:945–947, 5:2343
    assassination, 1:xlv, 1:103, 2:720, 2:946, 3:1312–1313, 4:1907
    Boynton v. Virginia and, 1:264
    election, 1:349
    pardons, 4:1831–1832
    speeches, 2:946

Kennedy, Robert F., 1:75, 2:947–949, 3:986, 4:*1516*
    assassination, 1:xlvi, 1:223, 2:720, 2:949
    Attorney General, 2:948
    early life, 2:947–948
    organized crime and, 2:689, 5:2343
    racial equality, 4:1516
    U.S. Senator, 2:948–949
Kennedy v. Louisiana, 1:207, 1:418, 4:1736
Kent State Massacre, 2:949–951, 3:1376
    aftermath, 2:950–951
    background and events, 2:949–950
    Scranton Commission, 2:949–950
Kent v. United States, 2:921, 2:934, 5:2355
Kentucky, 2:951–953
    crime, 2:952
    Louisville, 4:1863
    Louisville vice commission, 4:1863
    police, 2:951–952
    punishment, 2:952
Kerlilowske, Gil, 1:*444*
Kerner Report, 5:2350
Kerouac, Jack, 2:501, 4:1600
Kertbeny, Karoly, 4:1696
Kevorkian, Jack, 2:576, 2:953–954
Key, Phillip Barton, 4:1829
Keystone Cops, 2:616, 5:2219
kidnapping, 2:954–958. *See also* Lindbergh Law
    Booth plot, 1:143
    Fugitive Slave Act of 1850 and, 2:658
    increases, 2:957–958
    by Leopold and Loeb, 3:1004
    Lindbergh, 2:574, 2:583, 2:743, 2:776, 2:957, 5:2218–2219
    ransom, 2:955–958
    research, 2:955–956
    slavery and, 2:954–955
Kindergarten Cop, 2:617
The Kindness of Strangers (Boswell), 1:236
King, Hollis D., 2:952
King, Martin Luther, Jr., 1:75, 1:258, 2:958–960
    assassination, 1:xlvi, 1:106, 1:223, 2:720, 2:960, 3:1384, 4:1505–1506, 4:1554
    Civil Rights Act of 1964, 1:264–265
    civil rights and, 1:265, 2:959
    courts and, 2:959
    "I Have a Dream" speech, 5:2344
    Letter From a Birmingham Jail, 1:128, 2:960
    marches, 5:2344
    nonviolent tactics, 2:959–960
    political dissident, 3:1391–1392
    Satyagraha and, 2:959

King, Melissa, 2:535
King, Rodney, 1:28, 2:577, 2:792, 2:960–961
    Christopher Commission investigation, 3:1371
    LAPD assault, 2:960, 3:1246, 3:1378, 5:2419
    Los Angeles riots, 3:1039–1040, 4:1555–1556
    public outcry, 2:961
Kinkel, Kip, 4:1608
Kinsey Reports, 1:14
Kirby v. Illinois, 3:999
Kissinger, C. Clark, 4:*1728*
KKK. *See* Ku Klux Klan
Klaas, Polly, 1:276, 2:576
Klaus, Olivia, 2:477
Klebold, Dylan, and Eric Harris, 1:xlviii, 2:576, 2:962–963
    aftermath, 2:962–963
    Columbine High School massacre, 1:xlviii, 2:962
Klockars, Carl, 1:87
Knapp Commission, 1:281, 1:351, 2:963–965
    corruption reduction, 2:964–965
    findings, 2:964
    formation, 2:964
    Mollen Commission and, 3:1127
    Serpico harassment, 2:964, 3:1127
Knots Untied (McWatters), 3:1092
Knott, Frederick, 3:1020
Know-Nothing Party, 1:167, 1:172, 2:612, 4:1882, 4:1883
Knox, Thomas W., 1:193
Kojak, 4:1769
Korean War, 2:558
Korematsu, Fred, 2:967
Korematsu v. United States, 2:876, 2:965–967, 4:1580, 4:1734, 5:2265
    background, 2:965
    practical principle, 2:967
Koresh, David, 3:1379, 4:1899
Kroger, John, 3:1095
Ku Klux Klan (KKK), 1:260, 2:967–969, 5:2344–2345
    Alabama, 1:30
    attacks, 1:27
    bootlegging and, 2:818
    call for renewed, 1:74
    cross burnings, 1:159
    defense of, 1:40
    DOJ and, 2:905–906
    Enforcement Acts of 1870-71 and, 2:537
    FBI investigating, 2:582
    first incarnation, 2:967–968
    founding in Tennessee, 1:xli, 4:1778
    Great Depression growth, 2:708
    in history of crime and punishment in America: 1850–1900, 2:770
    Indiana, 2:835–836
    militants, 1:25
    rallies, 1:158–159
    second incarnation, 2:968–969
    terrorism, 4:1783
    third incarnation, 2:969
    Ulysses S. Grant suppression, 2:731, 3:1405
    United Klans of America, 1:31
    vigilantism, 4:1881
    violent crimes, 4:1887
Kuby, Ronald, 2:971
Kunstler, William, 1:224, 2:969–971
    Chicago Seven and, 2:970
    defenses, 2:970–971
    Freedom Riders and, 2:970
    Wounded Knee incident and, 2:971

L

L.A. Confidential, 2:619
La Cosa Nostra, 1:389, 2:689
La Guardia, Fiorello, 2:*924*, 3:975–977
    Charlie Luciano and, 3:976–977
    New York City mayor, 3:976–977
    political career, 3:975–976
L.A. Law, 4:1762, 4:1766
labeling criminology theories, 1:411, 2:927
labor exploitation, 4:1931
Laboratories of Virtue (Meranze), 5:2064
Ladies They Talk About, 2:623
Lady Chatterley's Lover (Lawrence, D. H.), 3:1274
Lady Gangster, 2:623
LaFollette, Robert, 3:1083–1084
Lager Beer Riot, 1:218
laissez-faire capitalism, 1:273
Lake, Stuart, 2:516
land pirates, 4:1881
Landers, Lew, 2:623
Landrum-Griffin Act of 1959, 3:977–978
    amendments, 3:97
    origin and passage, 3:977–978
Lane, Rose Wilder, 3:1006
Lane, Wes, 3:1095
Lansky, Meyer, 1:462, 2:*881*, 2:882, 3:1048
LAPD. *See* Los Angeles Police Department (LAPD)
larceny, 3:978–984
    art objects, 3:983
    corporate kleptocracy, 3:983
    determining, 3:978

federal level, 3:979–980
felonious, 3:979
historical aspects, 3:980–981
New York City, 3:980–981
1960s and beyond, 3:982
notorious cases, 3:982–984
Larson, Erik, 2:576
Larsson, Steig, 3:1026
Las Vegas, Nevada, 3:984–989
criminals and casinos, 3:986–987
El Rancho Vegas, 3:985–986
growth of legitimate industry, 3:987–988
Latham, James Douglas, 2:940
Latimer Massacre, 3:1402
Latino Paradox, 2:754–756
Lauf v. F. G. Shiner & Co., 1:10
Laughlin, Harry, 1:169
Laura, 3:1026
Laurel, Stan, 2:621
Lauria, Donna, 1:114
Law and Order, 4:1776–1777
Law and Order: Criminal Intent, 4:1765, 4:1772
Law and Order: SVU, 2:477, 4:1763
Law Code of Vishnu, 1:282
law enforcement. *See also* police
Boston, Massachusetts, 1:150
Chicago, Illinois, 1:218–220
FLETC, 1:148–149
Franklin Roosevelt, 4:1578–1579
Illinois, 2:816–818
Kansas, 2:938–939
Maine, 3:1059–1060
New Mexico, 3:1221
1901 to 1920, 5:2169–2176
Philadelphia, Pennsylvania, 3:1347
professionalization, 2:776–777
Ruby Ridge standoff as disaster, 4:1585–1587
Support Our Law Enforcement and Safe Neighborhoods Act, 1:xlix
Violent Crime Control and Law Enforcement Act of 1994, 1:276, 1:340
Washington, 4:1907
Law Enforcement Administration Agency (LEAA), 5:2349
Law Enforcement Assistance Act, 3:989–990
Law Enforcement Assistance Administration, 1:305, 3:990–991
criticisms, 3:991
effects of, 3:990–991
OAA established, 3:990
Law of the Twelve Tablets, 1:283

Lawes, Lewis, 4:1676
Lawrence, D. H., 1:314, 3:1274
Lawrence, John, 3:991
***Lawrence v. Texas,* 1:15, 1:158, 1:267, 2:509, 3:991–993**
court opinion, 3:991–992
fornication laws and, 2:643
private sexual conduct and, 3:991, 4:1736
problematic reasoning, 3:993
Laws, John, 4:1589
laws and acts. *See also* **Bodie of Liberties;** *Book of the General Lawes and Libertyes;* **Chinese Exclusion Act; Clayton Anti-Trust Act of 1914; codification of laws; Comstock Law; coverture, doctrine of; Espionage Act of 1917; Fugitive Slave Act of 1793; Fugitive Slave Act of 1850; Mann Act; Omnibus Crime Control and Safe Streets Act of 1968; Pendleton Act of 1883; sex offender laws; slavery, law of**
abortion state laws, 1:2
ADEA, 1:266
Administration of Justice Act of 1774, 1:45
AFA, 1:xlviii, 1:88
African Americans in, 1:27–29
Alien and Sedition Acts of 1798, 1:xl, 1:11–12, 1:37–38
American Law Institute statute, 1:xliv, 1:4–5
Americans with Disabilities Act of 1990, 1:xlvii, 1:266
anarchy statute, 5:2177
Anti-Arson Act, 1:175
Anti-Coolie Act, 1:194
Anti-Drug Abuse Acts of 1986, 1:28, 1:187
Anti-Pinkerton Act, 3:1423
Antiterrorism and Effective Death Penalty Act of 1996, 2:728
Anti-Terrorism Effective Death Penalty Act (AEDPA), 2:728, 3:1421
antitrust, 1:52–55
Armed Career Criminal Act of 1986, 2:720
Arms Export Control Act, 1:175
ARPA, 2:546
Assimilative Crimes Act of 1825, 3:1465
Aviation and Transportation Security Act of 2001, 1:xlviii, 1:88–90
Bail Reform Act, 1:xlv, 1:xlvii, 1:94, 1:96–98
Barred Zone Act, 4:1981
Boston Port Act of 1774, 1:45
Brady Handgun Violence Prevention Act, 2:721, 2:725, 5:2412
Butler Act, 1:429, 2:577, 4:1611–1612

CAA, 2:545
California drug laws, 1:196
CERCLA, 2:545–546
Chicago Gang Congregation Ordinance, 1:28
Child Abuse and Prevention and Treatment Act, 1:230
Circuit Court Act of 1802, 1:363
Civil Rights Act of 1866, 1:xlv, 1:260–261, 1:263–264, 2:551
Civil Rights Act of 1871, 1:xlv
Civil Rights Act of 1875, 1:25, 1:262–264
Civil Rights Act of 1957, 1:264
Civil Rights Act of 1964, 1:xlv, 1:27, 1:128, 1:264–266, 2:552, 4:1485
Civil Rights Act of 1965, 1:266
Classification Act, 2:819
colonial poor laws, 1:446–447
common law origins of criminal law, 1:182–183, 1:283, 1:296–300
Comprehensive Crime Control Act of 1984, 5:2415
Comprehensive Drug Abuse Prevention and Control Act of 1970, 3:1178, 5:2354
Controlled Substances Act, 1:xlvi
Crime Control Act of 1990, 1:187, 2:720
Crime Control and Safe Streets Act of 1968, 1:318
Criminal Justice and Forensic Science Reform Act, 2:642
CWA, 2:545
Defense of Marriage Act of 1996, 1:267
DMCA, 1:311
Domestic Violence Act of 1978, 2:481
Dyer Act, 1:xlii
early English law, 2:601–602
Edmunds Act, 1:70, 1:121, 5:2110
1801 to 1850, 5:2063–2067
Electrical Execution Act, 2:737
Elkins Act of 1903, 2:529–530
embezzlement, 2:533
Emergency Quota Act of 1921, 2:536–537
End Demand laws, 4:1482
Enforcement Acts of 1870-71, 2:537–539
English common law, 1:18, 1:123
environmental crimes, 2:545–546
Erdman Act, 1:xlii, 1:10
ESA, 2:545–546
Ethics in Government Act of 1978, 1:349, 2:565–567
evolution of burglary statutes, 1:182
Fair Sentencing Act, 1:xlviii–xlix, 1:28
Family Law Act, 1:15

federal common law of crime, 2:586–587
Federal Communications Act, 2:527
Federal Corrupt Practices Act of 1925, 1:348
Federal Election Campaign Act of 1971, 1:349
Federal Firearms Act of 1938, 2:719
Federal Tort Claim Act, 1:249
Federal Trade Commission Act of 1914, 1:53
FIFRA, 2:545
FISA, 1:190, 1:213, 2:528, 2:559
fish and game laws, 2:628–630
Food, Drug and Cosmetics Act, 2:778
Foran Act, 1:70
Foreign Corrupt Practices Act of 1977, 1:353–354
fornication laws, 2:643–644
Foster Bill, 2:742
Freedom of Information Act of 1966, 2:650–651
Geary Act, 1:247, 1:447
Gun Control act of 1968, 2:719–720
Gun Show Loophole Closing Act, 2:721
Gun-Free School Zones Act, 1:188
Habeas Corpus Act of 1679, 1:92, 2:729–730
Habitual Felony Offender Law, 1:33
Hammon-Beason Alabama Taxpayer and Citizen Protection Act, 5:2448
Harrison Act of 1914, 1:xlii, 2:500, 2:522, 2:742–743, 3:1177
Harrison Narcotics Drug Act, 2:778
Hart-Scott Rodino Anti-Trust Improvements Act of 1976, 1:268
Hate Crime Statistics Act, 1:187, 1:188
Hate Crimes Prevention Act, 3:1182, 3:1272
Hepburn Act of 1906, 2:530, 2:856
Homeland Security Act of 2002, 1:148
Identity Theft and Assumption Deterrence Act, 2:647
IGRA, 3:1204
Immigration Reform and Control Act of 1986, 1:xlvii, 1:147
Independent Counsel Act, 2:566
Indian Citizenship Act, 3:1201
Indian Removal Act, 1:xl
Indian Reorganization Act, 3:1201
Insanity Defense Reform Act, 2:840
Internal Security Act of 1950, 2:844–845
Interstate Commerce Act, 1:xli
Intolerable Acts of 1774, 2:857–858
Jim Crow laws, 1:25–26, 2:551, 2:790, 4:1619–1622, 5:2452
Johnson-O'Malley Act, 3:1201
Jones-Miller Act, 2:778, 3:1177
Judiciary Act of 1789, 1:xl, 1:59, 1:93–94, 4:1839

Judiciary Act of 1793, 1:59
Judiciary Act of 1801, 1:12, 1:363
Kansas-Nebraska Act, 1:168
Landrum-Griffin Act of 1959, 3:977–978
Lindbergh Law, 1:xliii, 3:1012–1013
Lloyd-La-Follette Act of 1912, 1:353
Magnuson Act, 1:xli, 1:245, 4:1981
marriage, 1:406
Married Women's Property Act of 1869, 1:371
Maryland Toleration Act of 1649, 3:1076–1077
Massachusetts Government Act of 1774, 1:45
McCarran Internal Security Act of 1950, 2:844–845
McCarran-Walter Act, 1:447
Midnight Judges Act, 1:12, 2:891
Military Commission Act, 1:190, 2:802
Morrill Anti-Bigamy Act, 1:xli, 1:70, 1:406, 5:2110
Mother's Pension Law, 3:1014
Narcotic Addict Rehabilitation Act (NARA), 4:1520
Narcotic Drugs Import and Export Act, 1:xlii–xliii, 2:778
narcotics laws, 3:1175–1179
National Emergency Centers Establishment Act, 2:850
National Firearms Act of 1934, 1:174, 2:719
National Information Infrastructure Protection Act, 1:312
National Motor Vehicle Theft Act, 2:777
National Prohibition Act, 2:774
National Security Act of 1947, 2:558
Nationality Act of 1952, 4:1881
Native Americans, 3:1200–1201
Navigation Acts, 1:293
Negro Act, 1:xxxix–xl
Norris-La Guardia Act, 1:xliii, 1:10
obscenity laws, 3:1277–1280
Ohio Criminal Syndicalism statute, 1:158
OPA, 2:546
Opium Exclusion Act, 1:xlii, 2:778
Organized Crime Control Act, 5:2351–2353
Page Act, 1:247
Pain-Capable Unborn Child Protection Act, 1:32
Poison Act, 2:778
Posse Comitatus Act, 1:70, 3:1400, 3:1405
Prison Litigation Reform Act (PLRA), 3:1421
Professional and Amateur Sports Protection Act, 1:xlvii, 2:666
Public Health Service Act, 1:6
Punishment of Crimes Act, 1790, 3:1464–1466

Pure Food and Drug Act of 1906, 2:777, 3:1469–1471
Quartering Act of 1774, 1:45
Quebec Act of 1774, 1:45
RCRA, 2:545–546
regulatory, 2:777–778
Robinson Patman Act, 1:268
Rockefeller Drug Laws, 1:xlvi, 2:498
Sarbanes-Oxley Act of 2002, 1:353
SDWA, 2:545
Second Chance Act, 4:1521, 5:2452
Securities and Exchange Act, 1:54, 2:777
Sedition Act of 1918, 4:1618–1619
segregation laws, 4:1619–1623
Selective Service Act of 1967, 4:1623–1624
Sharia law, 1:17
Sherman Antitrust Act, 1:52–53, 1:267–268, 2:741
Sherman Silver Purchase Act, 2:741
Smith Act, 1:445–446, 4:1689–1690
Stamp Act of 1765, 1:45, 2:760, 4:1704–1705
state abortion, 1:2
Statute of Westminster, 1:xxxix, 1:91–92
Support Our Law Enforcement and Safe Neighborhoods Act, 1:xlix
Tea Act of 1773, 1:45, 4:1754–1755
Telemarketing Fraud Prevention Act, 4:1615
three strikes, 1:33, 1:196, 4:1629, 4:1805–1806
Tillman Act of 1907, 1:348
Townshend Acts of 1767, 4:1814–1815
TSCA, 2:545
USA PATRIOT Act, 1:189–190
Violence Against Women Act of 1994, 2:477–478, 2:481, 3:1190, 4:1885–1886
Violence Prevention and Services Act, 2:478
Violent Crime Control and Law Enforcement Act of 1994, 1:276, 1:340, 1:388, 5:2416
Volstead Act, 1:174, 1:348, 2:492, 2:589, 2:775, 4:1866
Voting Rights Act of 1965, 1:xlv, 1:27, 1:265–266, 2:552, 4:1485
War Revenue Act of 1919, 2:719
Welfare Reform Act, 4:1974
WHBA, 2:546
Wheelbarrow Law, 1:xl, 2:762
White Slave Traffic Act, 1:xlii, 1:201, 3:1064, 4:1582
Wilderness Act of 1964, 2:546–547
Witness Protection Act, 4:1870
Laws and Liberties of Massachusetts, 3:993–994

Lawyers Guild, 3:994–996
    history, 3:995
    membership and structure, 3:994–995
Lay, Kenneth, 2:540
LEAA (Law Enforcement Administration Agency), 5:2349
Leache, Richard, 3:1042
The League of Men (Stout), 3:1018
Leahy, Patrick, 2:642
The Leavenworth Case (Green), 3:1015
Leavenworth Federal Penitentiary, 3:996–997
Leblan, Maurice, 1:117
Lee, Charles, 2:904
Lee, George W., 2:584
Lee, Harper, 3:1052, 4:1806–1807
Lee, Manfred Bennington, 3:1017
Lee, Richard Henry, 2:894
Lee, Robert E., 3:1197
left libertarianism, 3:1007–1008
Legal Aid Society, 1:57
legal counsel, 3:997–1004
    appointment of, 3:1002–1003
    ineffectual, 3:1003–1004
    right to, 3:999–1001
    roles and types, 3:998
    Sixth Amendment and, 3:1001–1002
legal lynching, 5:2355
legislation. *See also* laws and acts
    criminal law 1901 to 1920, 5:2176–2179
    Earl Warren, 4:1906
    Freedom of Information Act of 1966 as landmark, 2:650
    in history of crime and punishment in America: 1900–1950, 2:774–775
    homeland security, 2:802–803
    medical experimentation, 3:1420
    New Deal, 4:1731
    rape, 4:1496–1497
    Ronald Reagan, 4:1507–1508
    sex offender, 4:1644–1646
    strikes, 4:1725
    xenophobia, 4:1981–1982
Lem Moon Sing v. United States, 1:247
Lennon, John, 1:217–218, 2:575
Leopold and Loeb, 1:82–83, 1:429, 2:576, 2:956, 3:1004–1005
    Darrow defending, 3:1005, 5:2211
    kidnapping by, 3:1004
    1921 to 1940, 5:2210–2211
    prison sentence, 3:1005
    thrill killing, 3:1156, 5:2211

LeRoy, Mervyn, 2:621
Lethal Imagination (Bellesiles), 5:2075
lethal injection, 1:xlvii, 1:209, 3:1341
    replacing electric chair, 2:526
    Supreme Court on, 1:xlviii
Lethal Weapon, 2:617
Letter From a Birmingham Jail, 1:128, 2:960
Letterman, David, 3:984
Leuci, Robert, 3:1093
Levin, Ira, 3:1020, 3:1026, 3:1032
Levin, Meyer, 1:83
Levison, Stanley, 2:882
Levitt, Steven, 1:398
Levy, Chandra, 1:xlix
Lewinsky, Monica, 2:566
Lewis, Lloyd Benjamin, 2:534–535
Lewis, Sam, 4:1524
Lewis v. Casey, 2:889
Lewis William H., 1:28
lex talionis, 1:408
Libby, Scooter, 1:271
libertarianism, 3:1005–1009
    crime and criminal justice, 3:1008–1009
    intellectual property rights, 3:1008
    left, 3:1007–1008
    right, 3:1006–1007
    socialist, 3:1008
Liberty Party, 1:22
Liddy, G. Gordon, 4:1916
Life in a Western Penitentiary, 2:621
life in prison without parole (LWOP), 2:571
The Life of David Gale, 2:571
The Life of John Wesley Hardin as Written by Himself (Hardin), 1:82
Life of Washington (Marshall, J.), 3:1072
Life on the Mississippi (Twain), 2:626
Life Plus Ninety Nine Years (Leopold), 1:83
Lilburne, John, 1:439
Lincoln, Abraham (administration of), 3:1009–1012, 4:1783
    assassination, 1:xli, 1:143, 2:575, 3:1012, 4:1887, 5:2102
    call for troops, 1:105
    during Civil War, 3:1011
    early life, 3:1010
    Emancipation Proclamation, 3:1012
    Lincoln-Douglas debates, 1:169
    lucrative law practice, 3:1010–1011
    Morrill Anti-Bigamy Act signing, 1:xli
    presidential proclamations, 3:1404–1405
    writ of habeas corpus and, 2:730

Lincoln, Levi, Jr., 2:904
Lincoln, Mary Todd, 1:143
Lincoln County War, 1:127
Lindbergh, Anne, 1:216, 2:575
Lindbergh, Charles, 1:xliii, 1:216, 2:575, 2:744, 2:776
    exile, 5:*2210*
    Lucky Lindy, 3:1012
    testimony, 3:1218
Lindbergh kidnapping, 2:574, 2:583, 2:743, 2:776, 2:957, 5:2217–2218
Lindbergh Law, 1:xliii, 3:1012–1013
    background, 3:1012
    kidnapping response, 3:1013
Linder v. United States, 4:1918
Lindsey, Ben, 2:919, 3:1013–1014
    juvenile justice advocate, 3:1013–1014
    laws passed, 3:1014
    writings, 3:1014
Lingg, Louis, 1:xli, 1:49
literature and theater, crime in, 3:1014–1020
    golden age, 3:1016–1018
    growth in popularity, 3:1015–1016
    origins, 3:1015
    pulps and hard-boiled genre, 3:1018–1019
    theater, 3:1020
literature and theater, police in, 3:1021–1026
    American procedurals, 3:1023–1025
    background, 3:1021–1022
    early appearances, 3:1021–1022
    international procedurals, 3:1025–1026
    police procedurals, 3:1022–1023
    theater, 3:1026
literature and theater, punishment in, 3:1027–1032
    changing conception of punishment, 3:1027–1028
    social consciousness, 3:1030–1031
    theater, 3:1031–1032
    traditional and hard-boiled fiction, 3:1028–1030
livestock and cattle crimes, 3:1032–1034
    18th and 19th centuries, 3:1033–1034
    20th and 21st centuries, 3:1034
Livingston, Edward, 3:1034–1036
Lloyd, Frank, 2:621
Lloyd-La-Follette Act of 1912, 1:353
Locard, Edmond, 1:453, 2:627
Locascio, Frank, 2:701
Locher, Ralph, 1:275
Lochner v. New York, 2:510, 3:1036–1037
Locke, John, 1:438, 2:879
Lockup, 4:1776
loco parentis doctrine, 2:930

Loeb, Richard. *See* **Leopold and Loeb**
Logan, James A., 2:529
Lohman, Ann Trow (Madame Restell), 5:2066, 5:*2069*
loitering, 1:xlviii
Lolita (Nabokov), 3:1276
Lombrosa, Cesare, 1:408–409, 2:492, 3:1192
    on "born criminal," 2:749, 4:1966
    criminal characteristics, 5:2109
Lomino, Joanne, 1:114
The Long Goodbye (Chandler), 3:1018
Long Island Railroad murder, 2:609–610
Longabaugh, Larry ("Sundance Kid"), 1:453
Longnecker, Mary, 1:433
looting, 4:1563
Lord, Jack, 4:1769
Los Angeles, California, 3:1037–1041
    Los Angeles Operation Ceasefire, 2:726
    Los Angeles Riots of 1992, 1:28
    1950s and 1960s, 3:1039
    1900–1950, 3:1038–1039
    Rodney King riots, 3:1039–1040
Los Angeles Police Department (LAPD)
    corruption, 1:xliv
    Rodney King and, 2:792, 2:960, 3:1246, 3:1378, 5:2419
    William Parker and, 3:1321
    police academy, 3:1362
    professional conduct, 2:784
    O. J. Simpson and, 3:1252
    August Volmer and, 4:1896
The Lost New Year's Dinner, 2:622
lottery, 1:xlv
Loughner, Jared Lee, 1:xlix
Louima, Abner, 1:28
Louis XIV, 1:14
Louisiana, 3:1041–1046. *See also* **New Orleans, Louisiana**
    corruption, 3:1042–1043
    crime, 3:1041–1042
    police, 3:1043
    prisons, 3:1045–1046
    punishment, 3:1043–1045
Loving v. Virginia, 3:1046–1047
Loy, Myrna, 2:734
LSD, 2:501
Luciano, "Lucky," 1:64, 1:145, 1:462, 2:688, 3:1047–1048
    bootlegging, 2:705
    deportation, 3:1048
    father of organized crime, 3:*1306*

La Guardia and, 3:976–977
power broker, 3:1048
testimony, 2:783
Lucky Lindy, 3:1012
Ludlow Massacre, 1:295
lumpenproletariat, 1:163
Lunn, Bryan, 3:1365
Lupo, Salvatore, 1:114
Luster, Andrew, 1:156
Luther, Martin, 4:1672
Luther v. Borden, 4:1783
LWOP (life in prison without parole), 2:571
Lynch, Mona, 4:1523
lynchings, 1:74, 3:1049–1052
African Americans, 1:26
legal action, 3:1051
legal lynching, 5:2355
media depictions, 3:1052
post-Civil War era, 3:1049
studies, 2:818
20th century, 3:1049–1051
in vigilantism, 4:1880
Lyon, Patrick, 2:762, 4:1560
Lyons, Danny, 2:862
Lyons, Ernest, 1:73
Lysistrata (Aristophanes), 1:314

M
MacDonald, John D., 3:1031
Macdonald, Ross, 2:468, 2:702, 3:1019, 3:1030, 3:1053–1054
awards, 3:1054
education and early life, 3:1053
Kenneth Millar pen name, 3:1053
works and characters, 3:1053–1054
MacDonald v. Chicago, 1:191
Machiavelli, Niccolo, 2:556
MacKenzie, Doris L., 5:2423
Maconochie, Alexander, 1:339, 3:1423
MacVeagh, Wayne, 2:905
MADD (Mothers Against Drunk Driving), 5:2412
Madden, Owen Vincent ("Owney"), 2:863
Madison, James (administration of), 1:13, 1:123, 1:442, 2:600, 3:1054–1056
foreign engagements, 3:1056
Supreme Court and, 3:1054–1055
Madoff, Bernard, 1:343, 1:389, 3:1056–1057
contemporary white-collar crime, 4:1925
philanthropy, 3:1057
Ponzi scheme, 3:1056, 4:1617
suspicion, 3:1057

Mafia, 1:280, 2:521, 2:783–784
growth of, 2:689
Italian Americans and, 2:865–866
Jewish Americans and, 2:881–882
Mafia Affair, 2:741
New Orleans, Louisiana, 3:1224–1225
1921 to 1940, 5:2206–2207
Magna Carta, 1:67, 1:123, 1:326, 1:328, 1:416, 3:1057–1059
due process, 1:439
influence, 3:1059
provisions, 3:1058
right to change in, 1:438
right to speedy trial, 1:440
viewing, 4:1588
Magnuson Act, 1:xli, 1:245, 4:1981
Maher v. Roe, 1:5
Mahew, Susan, 1:232
Mailer, Norman, 2:571
Maine, 3:1059–1060
crime, 3:1060
law enforcement, 3:1059–1060
mala in se, 1:389, 2:603
mala prohibita, 1:389, 2:603
Malcolm X, 1:xlv, 1:75, 1:83–84, 1:129, 1:258, 3:1061–1063
assassination, 3:1063
Black Muslim involvement, 3:1061–1062
charismatic speaker, 3:1062
delinquency, 3:1061
split with Nation of Islam, 3:1062–1063
Malcom, John, 2:760
Maleaska, the Indian Wife of the White Hunter (Stephen), 2:465
malfeasance, 1:346
Mallory v. United States, 5:2347
Malloy v. Hogan, 2:712–713
Malpighi, Marcello, 2:626
The Maltese Falcon (Hammett), 2:733, 3:1018
Malvo, Lee Boyd, 2:576
A Man of Honor (Bonanno), 1:84
The Man Who Shot Liberty Valence, 4:1884
mandatory minimum sentencing, 3:1063–1064, 4:1628–1629. *See also* **sentencing; sentencing: indeterminate versus fixed**
Beccaria and, 4:1628
Bentham and, 4:1628
criticisms, 3:1064
research findings, 3:1064
Mangum, Minnie, 2:534
Mann, Horace, 1:80

Mann, James Robert, 3:1064
Mann, Thomas, 2:695
Mann Act, 1:xlii, **1:**201, **2:**774, **3:1064–1066.**
 See also **White Slave Traffic Act**
   Caminetti v. United States and, 3:1066
   clarifications and amendments, 3:1065–1066
   passage, 3:1064
   prosecutions under, 3:1066
Manson, Charles, 2:576, **2:**782, **3:1066–1067,** **4:**1892
   conviction, 3:1067
   family, 3:1066–1067
   Helter Skelter, 3:1067
Manson, Marilyn, 3:1170, 3:*1171*
Manzi, Warren, 3:1020
Mapp, Dollree, 2:786, 3:1068
Mapp v. Ohio, **1:**xliv, **1:**41, **1:**124, **1:**161, **1:**364, **3:1067–1069**
   appeals, 3:1068–1069
   exclusionary rule, 5:2347
   illegal searches, 2:552, 2:786, 4:1511
   precedents, 3:1067–1068
   silver-platter doctrine eliminated, 4:1737
Maranzano, Salvatore, 2:867
Marbury v. Madison, **1:**59, **1:**286, **2:**891, **3:1054–1055, 3:1069–1070**
   John Marshall judicial opinion, 3:1069–1071, 4:1732–1733
   Supreme Court legitimacy, 3:1070
Marie; or, Slavery in the United States (de Beaumont), 1:110
Mariel Cubans, 2:753–754
marijuana
   Cannabis Withdrawal, 2:498
   criminalization and decriminalization, 1:406
   drug abuse and addiction, 2:497–498
   Medical Marijuana Identification Card, 1:196
Marionization, 4:1538
marriage. *See also* **bigamy/polygamy;** divorce
   Defense of Marriage Act of 1996, 1:267
   gay marriage, 1:406
   laws, 1:406
   Married Women's Property Act of 1869, 1:371
The Marrow of Tradition (Chesnutt), 1:26
Marsh, Ngaio, 3:1022
Marshall, Frank, 1:193
Marshall, John, 1:12, **1:**285–286, **2:**696, **2:**880, **3:1070–1072**
   American Colonization Society, 3:1072
   Barron v. Mayor of Baltimore conclusion, 1:109
   chief justice, 3:1070–1071

   life outside court, 3:1072
   Marbury v. Madison judicial opinion, 3:1069–1072, 4:1732–1733
   significant rulings, 3:1071–1072
   Supreme Court under, 4:1732–1733
Marshall, Thurgood, 1:28, 1:207, 3:*1180*
Marshall v. United States, 4:1520
martial law, 2:849, 3:1404–1405
Martin v. Hunter's Lessee, **3:1072–1073**
   decision, 3:1073
   ramifications, 3:1073
Martin v. Ziherl, 2:643–644
Martinez, Bob, 1:187
Martinez, Eugenio, 4:1916
Martinez, Ramiro, Jr., 2:754–755
Martinson, Robert, 4:1520–1521, 4:1625, 4:1628, 5:2358
Marvel Tales, 2:467
Marx, Karl, 1:48, 1:381, 1:408, 3:1388–1389
Marxism, 1:297
Maryland, 3:1073–1076. *See also* **Baltimore, Maryland**
   crime, 3:1075
   police, 3:1074
   punishment, 3:1074–1075
Maryland Toleration Act of 1649, 3:1076–1077
Maryland v. Craig, 1:441
Maryland v. Shatzer, 1:364
Mason, George, 5:2042
mass incarceration, 2:793–795, 4:1517
mass media oligopoly, 3:1255–1256
Mass Prison era of corrections, 1:337
Massachusetts, 3:1077–1079. *See also* **Boston, Massachusetts; Salem witch trials**
   crime, 3:1077–1078
   gambling ban, 1:xxxix
   Massachusetts Government Act of 1774, 1:45
   police, 3:1078
   prisons, 1:xxxix
   probation system, 1:xli
   punishment, 3:1078–1079
   Salem witch trials, 1:xxxix
Masters of Deceit (Hoover, J. E.), 2:584
Masterson, Bat, 2:938
Masur, Louis, 2:569
Mater, Cotton, 1:360
Mater, Increase, 1:360
Matlock, 4:1762
Matteawan State Hospital, 3:1079–1081
   evolution of system, 3:1081
   housing criminally insane, 3:1079–1081

Mattei, Ugo, 4:1590
Matthews, Rod, 1:232
Matthews, Stanley, 2:810
Maury, 4:1765
Max Factor cosmetics, 1:156
Mayfield, Brandon, 2:628
Mayfield Road Mob, 3:1210
Mayflower Compact, 3:1081–1083
    need for, 3:1082
    nonspecificity, 3:1082
MBD (minimal brain dysfunction), 2:750
MCA (Military Commission Act), 1:190, 2:802, 3:1107
McAdoo, William, 2:*891*
McBain, Ed, 3:1023–1024
McCain, John, 1:350
McCarran, Patrick, 2:844
McCarran Internal Security Act of 1950, 2:844–845
McCarran-Walter Act, 1:447
McCarthy, Joseph, 1:445, 2:559, 3:1083–1084
    LaFollette defeat, 3:1083–1084
        McCarthy hearings, 2:845, 3:1084, 4:1784
        McCarthyism, 2:559, 3:1084
McCarty, William Henry. *See* **Billy the Kid**
McClatchy, V. S., 2:875
McClaughry, Robert W., 1:xli, 1:117
McClean, James, 2:863
McClellan, George, 2:557
McCleskey v. Kemp, 1:xlvii, 1:208–209, 1:437, 3:1084–1086
    background, 3:1084–1085
    capital punishment and, 2:795
    court's opinion, 3:1085
    statistical evidence, 2:552
McCloskey, J. J., 3:1020, 3:1026
McCloskey, William, 1:127
McCord, James W., Jr., 4:1916
McCorkle, William, 1:99
McCorvey, Norma, 4:1573
McCulloch v. Maryland, 1:286, 3:1071, 3:1086–1087
    principles established, 3:1087
    taxes and, 3:1086–1087
McDonald, Douglas, 1:306
McDonald, Michael Cassius ("King Mike"), 2:863
McDonald, Mike, 1:219
McGovern, George, 1:224
McGrath, Eddie, 2:863
McGurn, Jack ("Machine Gun"), 1:211
McIntosh v. Johnson, 3:1199
McKay, Henry, 4:1743, 4:1849–1850

McKay Commission, 1:75–76
McKeiver v. Pennsylvania, 5:2355
McKenna, Joseph, 1:202
McKie, Shirley, 2:628
McKinley, William (administration of), 3:1087–1089
    assassination, 1:xlii, 1:426, 1:451, 2:526, 2:767, 3:1088, 5:2109, 5:2165
    economic and military measures, 3:1087–1089
    mine strikes and, 3:1088
McLaughlin, James, 3:1197
McLaury, Frank, 2:515
McLaury, Tom, 2:515
McLean, John, 2:490
McLennan, Rebecca, 5:2069
McNabb v. United States, 3:1089–1090
    appeal, 3:1090
    untaxed whiskey and, 3:1089–1090
McNamara, James, 1:428–428
McNamara, John, 1:428–428
McNeil Island Prison, 2:592–594
McParland, James, 2:812
McPhail, Mark, 5:2458
McVeigh, Timothy, 1:277, 2:577, 3:1090–1091, 3:1380
    execution, 3:1090
    Oklahoma City bombing, 3:1090–1091, 3:1286
McWatters, George S., 3:1092
MDC (Metropolitan Detention Center), 2:850
Means, Russell, 2:971
Medellín cartel, 2:506
media coverage. *See also* **news media, crime in; news media, police in; news media, punishment in**
    crime scene investigation, 1:402–403
    domestic violence, 2:476–477, 2:482
    execution portrayal, 2:570
    role in indecent exposure, 2:828
    vigilantism, 4:1884
Medicaid, 1:xlvii, 1:6
medical fraud, 4:1929–1930
Medical Marijuana Identification Card, 1:196
medical model of rehabilitation, 2:595, 4:1519–1520
Medical Students for Choice, 1:7
Meese, Edwin, III, 3:1385
Meese Commission, 3:1398
Megan's Law, 1:xlvii–xlvii
Megreya, A. M., 3:1144
Meier, Megan, 1:xlviii
Meiji Restoration, 1:284
Melcher, Terry, 4:1892
Melville, Herman, 2:569

memoirs, police and prosecutors, 3:1092–1095
    administrators, 3:1093
    female officers, 3:1092–1093
    movie adaptations, 3:1093–1094
    prosecutors, 3:1094–1095
    subgenres, 3:1094
Memoirs of a Woman of Pleasure (Cleland), 3:1275
Memoirs of Stephen Burroughs (Burroughs, S.), 1:81
Memoirs v. Massachusetts, 3:1397
Memorandum of Agreement (MOA), 2:821
Memorial Day Massacre, 1:*280*
Mempa v. Rhay, 3:1002
Memphis, Tennessee, 3:1095–1097
    Crump machine, 3:1096
    police, 3:1096–1097
    punishment and crime, 3:1097
Mencken, H. L., 4:1611
Menendez, Lyle and Erik, 1:xlviii, 2:576, 3:1097–1098
    burglary and murder, 3:1098
    conviction and imprisonment, 3:1098
mens rea, 2:532, 2:841, 4:1543
mental health
    contemporary juvenile courts, 2:917
    women in prison, 4:1972–1973
Meranze, Michael, 5:2064, 5:2069
Meredith, James, 1:264, 2:*871*
Merritor Savings Bank v. Vinson, 4:1655
Merryman, John, 1:106, 2:730–731, 3:1011
Merton, Robert King, 1:410–411, 4:1502
Messerschmidt, J., 3:1386
methamphetamine epidemic, 5:2449–2450
method of operation (MO), 1:180, 1:226, 4:1559
Methvin, Henry, 1:140
Methvin, Ivy, 1:140
Metropolitan Detention Center (MDC), 2:850
Meyer, Mary, 3:1167
mezzogiorno, 2:864–866
Miami, Florida, 3:1099–1101
    bombings, 3:1100
    continuing tensions, 3:1100–1101
    post–World War II, 3:1099–1100
    riots, 3:1101
Miami Vice, 4:1770–1771
Miami-Erie Canal, 1:252
Michigan, 3:1101–1104. *See also* Detroit, Michigan
    crime, 3:1102
    future, 3:1104
    Michigan Prisoner Reentry Initiative, 5:2454
    Native Americans, 3:1101
    police, 3:1102–1103
    punishment, 3:1103–1104

Michigan v. Moseley, 2:852
Micke, William, 2:659
Midnight Judges Act, 1:12, 2:891
mifepristone, 1:7
Military Commission Act, 1:190, 2:802
military courts, 3:1105–1108
    courts-martial, 3:1105
    military tribunals, 3:1105–1107
    modern tribunals, 3:1107–1108
    Nazi Saboteur Case, 3:1107
military police, 3:1108–1111
    modern, 3:1111
    in Vietnam War, 3:1110–1111
    in world wars, 3:1109–1110
military tribunals, 3:1105–1107
military-industrial complex, 1:343–344
Milk, Harvey, 4:1829
Millar, Kenneth. *See* Macdonald, Ross
Miller, Henry, 3:1274
Miller, James, 1:431–432
Miller, Jonathan, 1:234
Miller, Samuel Freeman, 3:1011
Miller, Walter, 1:380
Miller v. California, 1:314, 3:1397
Miller v. Overholser, 3:1419
Miller v. United States, 3:1278
Milligan, Lambdin P., 3:1405
Milne, A. A., 3:1020, 3:1032
Milwaukee Free Democrat, 1:1
Minersville School District v. Gobitis, 4:1753
minimal brain dysfunction (MBD), 2:750
Minkins, Shadrack, 1:22
Minnesota, 3:1111–1114
    crime, 3:1112–1113
    police, 3:1113
    punishment, 3:1113–1114
Minnick v. Mississippi, 4:1741
Minor, Virginia Louise, 3:114–115
Minor v. Happersett, 3:1114–1116
    arguments, 3:1115
    background, 3:1114–1115
    exclusionary voting practices and, 3:1115
    unequal citizenship endorsement, 3:1115
Minuteman Project, 4:1882
Miranda, Ernesto, 1:317, 2:578
Miranda rights, 1:39, 4:1735, 4:1739
Miranda v. Arizona, 1:xlv, 1:42, 1:60, 1:124, 1:161, 1:167, 3:1116–1117
    background, 2:786–787
    case, 3:1116
    challenges, 1:318–319

confession and, 1:316–319
criticisms, 1:318
Fifth Amendment and, 1:364, 2:787, 3:999
interrogation practices and, 2:851–853, 4:1739
outcome, 3:1116–1117
principle-establishing, 2:578
public safety exception, 4:1740
regulations, 3:1117
right to counsel, 3:998–999, 4:1511
scope, 4:1736
Earl Warren and, 1:317–318, 2:552
Miranda Warnings, 1:xlv, 1:60, 4:1740. *See also* **Miranda v. Arizona**
misdemeanors, 1:386
Mississippi, 3:1117–1120. *See also* **Jackson, Mississippi**
crime, 3:1119–1120
police and punishment, 3:1117–1119
Mississippi v. Johnson, 3:1120–1121
Missouri, 3:1121–1123. *See also* **Kansas City, Missouri; St. Louis, Missouri**
crime, 3:1122–1123
James-Younger Gang, 3:1122
police and punishment, 3:1121–1122
Mitchell, Brian David, 1:xlix
Mitchell, Clarence M., Jr., 3:1181
Mitchell, John, 4:1916
Mitchell, William, 2:527
Mitchell v. Clark, 2:731
M'Naghten, Daniel, 2:717, 3:1124–1125, 4:1829
M'Naghten test, 2:717, 2:837, 3:1123–1126
creation, 3:1124–1125
definition, 3:1125–1126
early cases, 3:1124
example, 3:1126
insanity defense, 2:839–840
MO (method of operation), 1:180, 1:226, 4:1559
MOA (Memorandum of Agreement), 2:821
mob boss, 2:862
Mob City, 1:105–106
mobsters, 5:2341–2345
The Mod Squad, 4:1762, 4:1769
Model Penal Code, 2:603, 2:840, 4:1516
Moll Flanders (Defoe), 1:314
Mollen Commission, 1:351, 3:1126–1128
final report, 3:1127–1128
Knapp Commission and, 3:1127
Monell v. Department of Social Services, 3:995
Monkkonen, Eric, 5:2170
The Monogamy Myth (Vaughan), 1:14

Monroe, James (administration of), 1:13, 3:1128–1129
era of good feelings, 3:1128–1129
foreign affairs, 3:1129
slavery and, 3:1129
Monroe Doctrine, 2:747
Monster, 2:615
Montana, 3:1129–1131
crime, 3:1130–1131
police and punishment, 3:1130
Montesquieu, Baron, 5:2042–2043
Montgomery, Olen, 4:1613
Moon, Henry L., 3:*1180*
Mooney-Billings case, 4:1941
moonlighters, 1:144
moonshine, 2:775, 3:1131–1133
in new millennium, 3:1133
Prohibition, 3:1132–1133
speakeasies and gin joints, 3:1133
Whiskey Rebellion, 3:1131–1132
Moore, Alvin, 1:317
Moore, Blanche, 4:1963
Moore, Fred H., 4:1595
Moore, Michael, 3:1390, 3:1392
Moral Majority, 1:101, 4:1674
morality, 3:1133–1140
existentialism, 3:1138–1139
meaning of, 3:1134
nonreligious idealism, 3:1136–1137
positivism, 3:1137
postmodernism, 3:1139
pragmatism, 3:1137–1138
religious idealism, 3:1134–1136
social contract theory, 3:1139
utilitarianism, 3:1136
Moran, George ("Bugsy"), 1:211
Morello, Giuseppe, 5:2166
Morgan, Margaret, 1:22
Morissey, John, 2:862
Mormons, 1:70, 1:121–122, 1:406, 4:1531
morphine, 2:499–500, 3:1175
Morrill Anti-Bigamy Act, 1:xli, 1:70, 1:406, 5:2110
Morris, Frank, 1:37
Morris, Herbert, 4:1545
Morrissey, John J., 3:1324
Morrissey v. Brewer, 3:1324, 3:1435
Morse, Harry, 1:139
Morse Patrol and Detective Agency, 1:139
Morse v. Frederick, 4:1736
Morton, Bill, 1:127
Mosaic Code, 1:282, 1:291

Moscowitz, Henry, 3:1179
Moselye, Walter, 3:1019
Moses, 1:59, 2:556, 4:1670
Moskowitz, Stacy, 1:114
Moss, Frank, 1:460
Moss, Jason, 2:662
Mothers Against Drunk Driving (MADD), 5:2412
Mother's Pension Law, 3:1014
Motion Picture Producers and Distributors of America (MPPDA), 2:622
The Mousetrap (Christie), 3:1016
MOVE, 3:1140–1141
    John Africa's commune, 3:1140–1141
    public scrutiny, 3:1141
The Moving Target (Macdonald), 2:702, 3:1030
MPPDA (Motion Picture Producers and Distributors of America), 2:622
muckrakers, 1:220
Mudd, Samuel, 1:143
Mudgett, Herman, 3:1141–1143
    conviction and execution, 3:1143
    first U.S. serial killer, 3:1141, 4:1636
    Murder Castle, 3:1142–1143
mug shots, 1:115, 3:1143–1146
    eyewitness accuracy, 3:1144–1145
    problems, 3:1145
    research, 3:1144
mugging, 4:1562
Muhammad, John Allen, 2:576, 3:1147, 4:1760, 4:1891
mulattos, 1:xxxix
Mullen, James, 1:140
Muller, Gallus, 1:117
Muller, Marcia, 2:468, 3:1017, 3:1019
Muller v. Oregon, 3:1147–1148
Munchausen syndrome, 4:1957
Munn v. Illinois, 2:856, 3:1148–1149
Munsey, Frank, 2:466
murder, contemporary, 1:250, 1:462, 2:467, 3:1149–1152
    age and, 3:1151
    Atlanta youth murders, 1:74
    Cleveland Torso Murderer, 1:274
    felonies, 2:604–605
    gender and, 3:1151
    gun-related homicide, 3:1152
    homicide measurement, 3:1149–1150
    Long Island Railroad, 2:610–611
    race and, 3:1150
    victim–offender relationship, 3:1151–1152

murder, history of, 3:1152–1160
    colonial America, 3:1153–1154
    19th century, 3:1154–1156
    20th century, 3:1156–1159
murder, sociology of, 3:1160–1165
    conflict perspective, 3:1161–1163
    functionalist perspective, 3:1161
    social disorganization perspective, 3:1163–1164
    symbolic interactionist perspective, 3:1164–1165
Murder at the Vicarage (Christie), 1:250
Murder Castle, 3:1142–1143
Murder Inc., 1:462
Murder Must Advertise (Sayers), 3:1017
The Murder of Roger Ackroyd (Christie), 1:250, 3:1016
Murder on the Orient Express (Christie), 1:250, 3:1030, 4:1892
murders, unsolved, 3:1165–1169
    early 20th century, 3:1166–1167
    early America, 3:1165–1166
    mid and late 20th century, 3:1167–1169
    21st century, 3:1169
"The Murders on the Rue Morgue," 2:467, 3:1015, 3:1360
Murphy, Frank, 4:1841
Murphy, Jack ("The Smurph"), 1:180
Murphy, Michael, 1:460
Murphy, Patrick V., 3:1093
Murray, Conrad, 1:xlix
Murrieta, Joaquin, 1:194
music and crime, 3:1170–1173
    criminal activity in music, 3:1171–1172
    music as cause of crime, 3:1170–1171
    organized crime, 3:1172
    piracy, 3:1172–1173
Mutual Welfare League (MWL), 1:79
My Darling Clementine, 2:516
My FBI (Freeh), 3:1093
Myers, Wade, 1:235
MySpace, 2:477
Mysteries and Miseries of New York (Buntline), 1:173
The Mysterious Affair at Styles (Christie), 1:250, 3:1016, 3:1022
The Mystery of Edwin Drood (Dickens), 3:1015
"The Mystery of Marie Roget," 3:1360

N

NAACP. *See* **National Association for the Advancement of Colored People**
Nabokov, Vladimir, 3:1276
Nader, Laura, 4:1590

NAFTA (North American Free Trade Agreement), 5:2413
The Naked Gun, 2:616–617
NAMBLA (North American Man/Boy Love Association), 1:40
The Name of the Rose (Eco), 2:733
Napoleon III, 1:111
Napoleonic Code, 1:283–284, 1:298
Napolitano, Janet, 2:*803*
Narcotic Addict Rehabilitation Act (NARA), 4:1520
Narcotic Drugs Import and Export Act, 1:xlii–xliii, 2:778
narcotics laws, 3:1175–1179
    Comprehensive Drug Abuse Prevention and Control Act of 1970, 3:1178
    drug testing, 3:1178–1179
    early U.S., 3:1176–1177
    in modern era, 3:1177–1178
    racism and, 3:1176
narcotics sales, 1:xliii
Narrative (Douglass, F.), 2:659
NASDAQ, 4:1616–1617
Nassar, George, 1:449
Nation, Lee M., 2:512
National Abortion and Reproductive Rights Action League, 1:5
National American Woman Suffrage Association (NAWSA), 1:259–260
National Association for the Advancement of Colored People, 2:807, 3:1179–1184
    Brown v. Board of Education and, 1:165–166
    capital punishment and, 1:206
    civil rights era, 3:1181–1182
    contemporary issues, 3:1182–1184
    early advocacy efforts, 3:1181
    formation, 3:1179–1181
    investigations, 1:458–459
    racial justice, 4:1516
    Stamp out Mississippi-ism!, 3:1180
National Bank, 2:830, 2:869
National Black Police Association, 1:28
National Center for the Analysis of Violent Crime (NCAVC), 4:1642–1643
National Center for Women and Policing (NCWP), 3:1371
National Coalition against Domestic Violence, 2:481
National Commission on Law Observance and Enforcement, 3:1184–1186, 4:1938
    criminal justice examination, 3:1184
    findings, 3:1185
    members, 3:1184

National Conference of Commissioners on State Laws, 1:42–43
National Conference on Prevention and Control of Juvenile Delinquency, 5:*2264*
National Congress on Penitentiary and Reformatory Discipline, 3:1186–1188
    methods of investigation, 3:1187
    principles of, 3:1187–1188
    reformers congregate, 3:1186–1187
    Zebulon Brockway and, 3:1186–1188
National Crime Victimization Survey (NCVS), 1:xlvi, 1:180
    administration of, 1:377
    crime reflection, 1:397
    fear of crime measurement, 2:580
    implementation, 1:396
    random, 1:378
    release of data, 4:1954
National Emergency Centers Establishment Act, 2:850
National Firearms Act of 1934, 1:174, 2:719
National Fraud Information Center (NFIC), 2:647, 2:814
National Gang Threat Assessment, 2:669
National Gay Task Force (NGTF), 1:156
National Gay Task Force v. Board of Education of Oklahoma City, 1:156
National Guard, 1:xlv
National Highway Traffic Safety Administration, 2:493
National Incident-Based Reporting System (NIBRS), 1:375–376, 1:382, 1:396
    collections, 2:606
    data presentation, 4:1838
National Information Infrastructure Protection Act, 1:312
National Infrastructure Protection Center (NIPC), 2:585
National Instant Check System (NCIS), 2:720–721
National Institute of Justice (NIJ), 3:991, 4:1496
National Institute on Alcohol Abuse and Alcoholism, 2:493
National Integrated Ballistic Information Network, 1:175
National Liberal League, 1:314
National Marine Fisheries Service, 2:630
National Motor Vehicle Theft Act, 2:512, 2:777
National Organization for Victim Assistance (NOVA), 4:1869

National Organization for Women, 1:5, 3:1188–1190
    formation and early years, 3:1188–1189
    recent activism, 3:1189–1190
    Violence Against Women Act, 3:1190
National Organization for Women v. Scheidler,
    1:xlviii, 1:6
National Park Service, 1:xliv
National Police Gazette, 1:xl, 3:1190–1192
    criminology influence, 3:1192
    cultural influence, 3:1191
    favoring crime-fighting activities, 3:1249
    regular columns, 3:1191
National Prison Association, 3:1192–1194
    accreditation granting, 3:1194
    declaration of principles, 3:1192–1193
    founding, 3:1192
    structure and function, 3:1193–1194
National Prison Rape Elimination Commission
    (NPREC), 4:1539–1540
National Prohibition Act, 2:774
National Prohibition Party, 2:491–492
National Research Council, 1:401
National Rifle Association (NRA), 2:722
national security, 4:1579–1580
National Security Act of 1947, 2:558, 3:1194–1195
National Security Agency (NSA), 2:558, 2:561
National Survey of Child and Adolescent Well-Being
    (NSCAW), 1:231
National Survey on Drug Use and Health (NSDUH),
    1:376
National Treasury Employees Union v. Von Raab,
    3:1178
national versus state authority, 2:696
National Violence Against Women Survey, 4:1496
National White-Collar Crime Center, 1:309
National Women's Party, 1:372
National Youth Gang Survey (NYGS), 2:668
National Youth Survey (NYS), 2:926
National Youth Survey Family Study (NYSFS), 1:376
Nationality Act of 1952, 4:1881
Native American Tribal Police, 3:1195–1198
    modern tribal police, 3:1197–1198
    policing Indian country, 3:1196–1197
Native Americans, 3:1198–1205. *See also* Peltier,
    Leonard
    boarding schools, 3:1201–1202
    citizenship, 3:1201
    clashes with federal government, 3:1203–1204
    contemporary, 3:1204–1205
    culture, 2:751–752
    doctrine of discovery, 3:1199–1200

    Indian Bill of Rights, 3:1203
    Indians term versus, 3:1198
    Andrew Jackson and, 5:2072–2075
    Michigan, 3:1101
    migration, 1:xl
    Nez Perce War, 2:747
    rights and laws, 3:1200–1201
    sovereignty, 3:1202–1203
Native Son (Wright, R.), 2:570
nativism, 1:167
    deportation and, 1:447
    rise of, 4:1596
nature versus nurture debate, 1:378
Navigation Acts, 1:293
NAWSA (National American Woman Suffrage
    Association), 1:259–260
Nazis, 1:170, 1:297
    Nazi Saboteur Case, 3:1107
    radical movements, 4:1579
NCAVC (National Center for the Analysis of Violent
    Crime), 4:1642–1643
NCIS (National Instant Check System), 2:720–721
NCVS. *See* National Crime Victimization Survey
    (NCVS)
NCWP (National Center for Women and Policing),
    3:1371
Neagle, David, 1:59
Nebbia v. New York, 2:510
Nebraska, 3:1205–1207
    agriculture, 3:1205
    crime, 3:1205–1206
    Kansas-Nebraska Act, 1:168
    punishment, 3:1206–1207
Neebe, Oscar, 1:xli, 1:49
Negro Act, 1:xxxix–xl
Negro Plot, 3:1235
Negro Question, 1:26
Nelles, Walter, 1:xlii, 1:40
Nelson, "Baby Face," 3:1207–1209
    robbery and murder, 3:1207–1208
    shooting death of, 3:1208
Nelson, Knute, 2:529
Nelson, Samuel, 2:490
Nelson, William Edward, 1:15
neoclassical criminology theory, 1:407–408
nepotism, 1:346, 1:352
Ness, Eliot, 3:1209–1211
    in Cleveland, Ohio, 3:1210–1211
    memoirs, 3:1211
    tracking Al Capone, 3:1209–1210
Neufeld, Peter, 2:640, 5:2457

Neumar, Betty, 4:1963
neutrality enforcement in 1793-1794, 3:1211–1213
    challenges, 3:1212
    controversy over, 3:1212–1213
Nevada, 3:1213–1215. *See also* **Las Vegas, Nevada**
    criminal justice, 3:1214
    gambling, 1:xliii
    prostitution and gambling, 3:1213–1214
    sports betting, 1:xlvii
Neville, John, 4:1915
The New Centurions (Wambaugh), 3:1024, 4:1904
New Deal, 2:901, 4:1731
"The New Departure," 3:114–115
New England Association of Farmers, Mechanics and Other Workingmen, 1:239
New England Company, 1:289
New Hampshire, 3:1215–1217
    lottery, 1:xlv
    police, 3:1215
    punishment, 3:1215–1217
New Jersey, 3:1217–1220. *See also* **Camden, New Jersey; Newark, New Jersey**
    Al Qaeda, 3:1218
    casino gambling, 1:xlvii
    crime and punishment, 3:1218–1219
    "Jersey Shore Thrill Killer," 3:1218
    lottery, 1:xlv
    Megan's Law, 1:xlvii–xlvii
    Native Americans in, 3:1217
    Newark riots, 3:1219
    prisons, 3:1218–1219
    Quarkers in, 3:1217
    The Sopranos, 3:1218
    trends, 3:1219
New Mexico, 3:1220–1222
    law enforcement, 3:1221
    penitentiary riots, 3:1221
New Orleans, Louisiana, 3:1222–1225
    American ascendancy, 3:1223–1224
    early history, 3:1222–1223
    Mafia, 3:1224–1225
    police, 3:1225
    political violence, 3:1224
    Storyville, 3:1224
"new punitiveness," 3:1225–1229
    confinement and parole changes, 3:1227–1228
    get tough movement, 3:1226–1227
    increased prison populations, 3:1228–1229
New Right, 1:5

New York, 3:1229–1234
    drunk driving, 1:xliii
    female prisons, 3:1233
    lottery, 1:xlv
    prison history, 3:1230–1233
    punishment and police, 3:1229–1230
    state prison system, 1:xlii
New York City, 3:1234–1238. *See also* **September 11, 2001, terrorist attacks**
    House of Refuge, 2:914
    hub of trade, 3:1234–1236
    Italian Americans, 2:867–868
    La Guardia as mayor, 3:976–977
    larceny, 3:980–981
    parallel growth, 3:1236–1238
New York Daily News, 1:xliii, 3:1244
New York Herald, 3:1243, 3:1249
New York Police Department (NYPD), 1:451, 2:785
    anarchy statute and, 5:2177
    creation, 3:1230
    mounted police, 5:2455
New York Times, 1:107
New York v. Ferber, 3:1278–1280
New York v. Quarles, 4:1739
Newark, New Jersey, 3:1238–1242
    Al Qaeda, 3:1240–1241
    crime and punishment, 3:1240–1241
    economics and industry, 3:1238
    renaissance, 3:1241
    riots, 3:1219
    society and politics, 3:1240
    Thomas Edison, 3:1238
    trends, 3:1240
Newgate prison, 1:325
Newman, Oscar, 1:391, 1:393
news media, crime in, 3:1242–1248
    America's Most Wanted, 3:1245
    corrections, 3:1247
    crime suspects, 3:1245
    crime victims, 3:1245–1246
    early crime news, 3:1242–1243
    Arthur Fellig ("Weegee the Famous"), 3:1244–1245
    Helen Jewett, 4:1243–1244
    Rodney King, 3:1246
    moral panics, 3:1247
    New York Daily News, 1:xliii, 3:1244
    New York Herald, 3:1243
    19th-century crime news, 3:1243
    Pennsylvania Gazette, 3:1243
    police, 3:1246–1247

Mary Rogers, 4:1243–1244
San Francisco Examiner, 3:1244
school shootings, 3:1247
Ruth Snyder execution, 3:1244
The Sun, 3:1243–1244
trial coverage, 3:1247
20th-century crime news, 3:1244–1244
John Walsh, 3:1245
news media, police in, 3:1248–1254
    forensic journalism, 3:1250
    good cops in, 3:1252–1254
    historical context, 3:1248–1249
    image and image management, 3:1249–1250
    police corruption and violence, 3:1250–1252
news media, punishment in, 3:1254–1260
    learning about crime and punishment, 3:1254–1255
    mass media oligopoly, 3:1255–1256
    media shifts, 3:1255
    representation of crime and punishment, 3:1257–1259
    social constructionist perspective, 3:1256–1257
Newton, Huey, 1:xlv, 1:129, 3:1468
Newton, Joe, 1:82
Newton, Tem Demetrius, 1:33
The Newton Boys (Newton, J.), 1:82
Nez Perce War, 2:747
NFIC (National Fraud Information Center), 2:647, 2:814
NGOs. *See* nongovernmental organizations (NGOs)
NGRI (not guilty by reason of insanity), 2:841
NGTF (National Gay Task Force), 1:156
NIBIN (Integrated Ballistics Information Network Program), 1:103
NIBRS. *See* National Incident-Based Reporting System (NIBRS)
Nicholas, Marsy, 4:*1872*
Nichols, Terry, 3:1090–1091, 3:1380
Nickel Mines attack, 3:1253
Nicolls v. Ingersoll, 1:95
Nielsen, Leslie, 2:617
Nietzsche, Frederich, 1:82, 5:2211
Nigerian 419, 1:321, 1:389, 2:645
Night Court, 4:1763
NIJ (National Institute of Justice), 3:991, 4:1496
Nine Taylors (Sayers), 3:1017
1901 to 1920
    crime and criminal behavior, 5:2161–2169
    criminal law and legislation, 5:2176–2179
    law enforcement, 5:2169–2176
    trial and punishment, 5:2179–2180

1921 to 1940, 5:2201–2203
    Al Capone, 5:2205–2206
    crime news, 5:2216–2217
    FBI, 5:2213–2215
    G-men, 5:2215–2216
    Leopold and Loeb, 5:2210–2211
    Lindbergh kidnapping, 5:2217–2218
    Mafia, 5:2206–2207
    Marion Parker case, 5:2217
    public enemy era, 5:2212–2213
    Sacco and Vanzetti, 5:2208–2210
    Scottsboro Boys, 5:2211–2212
    urbanization and organized crime, 5:2203–2205
    xenophobia, 5:2207–2208
1941 to 1960, 5:2263–2278
    civil rights movement, 5:2277–2278
    criminal espionage, 5:2265–2266
    gangs, 5:2271–2273
    Japanese internment camps, 5:2265–2266
    Mafia, 5:2263, 5:2269
    McCarthyism, 5:2269–2271
    postwar organized crime, 5:2268–2269
    prison riots, 5:2275–2277
    professionalization of police force, 5:2273–2275
    Puerto Rican nationalism, 5:2269–2271
    racial tensions, 5:2263–2264
    Red Scare, 5:2269–2271
    serial killers, 5:2275–2277
    war crimes trials, 5:2267–2268
    wartime films, 5:2267–2268
    Zoot Suit riots, 5:2263–2264
1961 to 1980, 5:2337–2338
    communists, mobsters, klansmen, 5:2341–2345
    criminal correction versus criminal deterrence, 5:2338–2341
    law and order and deterrence, 5:2351–2356
    war on poverty, 5:2345–2351
    Watergate, 5:2356–2358
    "What Works?", 5:2358
1981 to 2000
    crime, 5:2407–2410
    criminal justice policy changes, 5:2414–2417
    economic contexts, 5:2412–2413
    hate crimes and school shootings, 5:2410–2411
    incarceration resilience, 5:2420–2424
    policing changes, 5:2417–2420
    political contexts, 5:2411–2412
    social contexts, 5:2413–2414
1996 Olympics bombing, 1:74–75
Nineteenth Amendment, 3:1115
Ninth Amendment, 2:523

NIPC (National Infrastructure Protection Center), 2:585
Nishimura Ekiu v. United States, 1:247
Nitti, Frank, 1:211, 2:868, **3:1260–1261**
    Al Capone enforcer, 3:1260
    shakedown scheme, 3:1261
    suicide, 3:1261
Nixle, 4:1758
Nixon, Richard (administration of), 1:97, 1:353, 2:522, **3:1261–1263**. *See also United States v. Nixon;* Watergate
    Burger nomination, 1:178
    CIA and, 5:2357
    clemency example, 1:270–271
    DEA created by, 1:xlvi, 1:505, 2:589
    drug policies, 3:1262
    economic policies, 3:1006
    Environmental Quality Council, 2:544
    Ford pardon, 1:270–271, 1:349, 2:636
    organized crime and, 3:1262–1263
    presidential proclamations, 3:1406
    resignation, 1:213, 1:349, 1:350, 2:565, 4:1572, 4:1917
    Scranton Commission, 2:949–950
    war on drugs, 3:1177
No Backup (Dew), 3:1092–1093
no punishment without law, 4:1843–1844
Noble Experiment, 2:492
Nolan, Joseph, 2:523
nolo contendere, 1:68
nongovernmental organizations (NGOs), 2:630
nonreligious idealism, 3:1136–1137
nonviolent crimes, 3:1376
Norhup, Solomon, 2:657
Norris, Clarence, 4:1613
Norris v. Alabama, 1:xliv, 1:26
Norris-La Guardia Act, 1:xliii, 1:10
North, Oliver, 2:566, 2:849
North American Free Trade Agreement (NAFTA), 5:2413
North American Man/Boy Love Association (NAMBLA), 1:40
North Carolina, **3:1263–1265**
    crime, 3:1263–1264
    punishment, 3:1264–1265
    riots of 1898, 1:26
    sit-ins (1960), 1:27
North Dakota, **3:1265–1267**
    crime, 3:1266
    punishment, 3:1266–1267
North Side Gang, 1:211

Northern Securities Co. v. United States, 4:1842
Northrup, Solomon, 1:22, 1:23
Northwest Ordinance of 1787, 3:1267–1268
not guilty by reason of insanity (NGRI), 2:841
NOVA (National Organization for Victim Assistance), 4:1869
Novello, Antonia, 2:481
NPREC (National Prison Rape Elimination Commission), 4:1539–1540
NRA (National Rifle Association), 2:722
NSA (National Security Agency), 2:558, 2:561
NSCAW (National Survey of Child and Adolescent Well-Being), 1:231
NSDUH (National Survey on Drug Use and Health), 1:376
nullum crimen, null poena sine praevia lege poenali, 4:1844
Numbered Men, 2:621
Nuremberg War Crimes, 2:574
N.W.A. rap group, 1:308, 3:1170
Nye, Ivan F., 1:376
NYGS (National Youth Gang Survey), 2:668
NYPD. *See* New York Police Department
NYPD Blue, 4:1766, 4:1770, 4:1771
NYS (National Youth Survey), 2:926
NYSFS (National Youth Survey Family Study), 1:376

O

OAA (Office of Academic Assistance), 3:990
Oakland, California, 3:1269–1271
    current, 3:1269–1271
    20th century, 3:1269–1271
OAM (Office of Air and Marine), 1:148
Obama, Barack (administration of), 1:189–190, 2:803, **3:1271–1273**, 4:1632
    assassination attempt, 1:xlix
    closing Guantanamo Bay prison, 3:1272
    drug laws, 3:1272–1273
    Fair Sentencing Act, 1:xlviii–xlix
    Hate Crimes Prevention Act, 3:1272
    interrogation practices and, 2:855
    presidential proclamations, 3:1406
    Uniform Code of Military Justice, 5:2446
    Violence Prevention and Services Act, 2:478
O'Banion, Dean, 1:211, 2:863
obscenity, 3:1273–1277
    availability, 3:1276–1277
    censorship in 20th century, 3:1275–1276
    early laws, 3:1274

obscenity laws, 3:1277–1280
　Brandenburg v. Ohio, 3:1280
　Miller v. United States, 3:1278
　New York v. Ferber, 3:1278–1280
　Roth v. United States, 3:1277–1278, 4:1583
occupational fraud, 2:648–649
Occupational Safety and Health Administration (OSHA), 3:1378
Occupy Wall Street protests, 3:1251
Ocean's 11, 2:614
O'Connor Sandra Day, 1:191, 2:716
ODD (oppositional defiant disorder), 2:750
OECA (Office of Enforcement and Compliance Assurance), 2:548
Of Crime and Punishment (Beccaria), 1:407, 4:1632
Of Plymouth Plantation (Bradford), 3:1082
Office of Academic Assistance (OAA), 3:990
Office of Air and Marine (OAM), 1:148
Office of Attorney General, 2:894
Office of Enforcement and Compliance Assurance (OECA), 2:548
Office of Juvenile Justice and Delinquency Prevention (OJJDP), 2:667–668
Office of National Drug Control Policy (ONDCP), 5:2412
Office of Strategic Services (OSS), 2:558
Office of Terrorist Financing and Financial Crimes (OTFFC), 2:843
Ohio, 3:1281–1283. *See also* **Cincinnati, Ohio; Cleveland, Ohio**
　　Court of Common Pleas, 1:358–359
　　crime, 3:1281–1282
　　Ohio Criminal Syndicalism statute, 1:158
　　police, 3:1282
　　punishment, 3:1282–1283
Ohio Gang, 2:739
Ohio v. Akron Center for Reproductive Health, 1:6
Ohlin, Lloyd, 1:380, 2:678
Oil Pollution Act (OPA), 2:546
oil spills, 2:546
OJJDP (Office of Juvenile Justice and Delinquency Prevention), 2:667–668
Oklahoma, 3:1283–1285
　　crime, 3:1284–1285
　　Indian Territory, 1:xl
Oklahoma City bombing, 1:277, 2:585, 3:1090–1091, **3:1285–1288,** 3:1380, 3:1385
　　McVeigh investigation, 3:1286
　　political rhetoric and violence, 3:1287
　　trial, 3:1286–1287
Old Hays, 2:748

Old Sleuth, 2:467–468
Oliver, Peter, 5:2045
Oliver Twist (Dickens), 1:236
Olmstead v. United States, 2:527, 2:943, **3:1288–1289**
Omi, Michael, 4:1486
Omnibus Crime Control and Safe Streets Act of 1968, 3:991, **3:1289–1291,** 4:1885
　　criticism, 3:1291
　　titles, 3:1289–1291
On Crimes and Punishment (Beccaria), 1:xl, 1:204, 1:455–456, 2:761
On the Penitentiary System in the United States and Its Application in France (de Beaumont, de Tocqueville), 1:110–111
ONDCP (Office of National Drug Control Policy), 5:2412
one pot meth cooking, 2:860
O'Neill, Catherine, 3:*1144*
O'Neill, Eugene, 1:314
The Onion Field (Wambaugh), 4:1904
Ono, Yoko, 1:218
OPA (Oil Pollution Act), 2:546
Operation Garden Plot, 2:849–850
Operation Grouper, 2:506
Operation Rescue, 1:7
Operation Wetback, 1:522
opium, 1:xli, 2:501, 3:1175
　　Opium Exclusion Act, 1:xlii, 2:778
　　Opium War, 1:243, 1:247
oppositional defiant disorder (ODD), 2:750
Oregon, 3:1291–1293
　　crime, 3:1293
　　police and punishment, 3:1291–1293
Oregon v. Mathiason, 1:281
organized crime, contemporary, 1:xliv, **3:1294–1298.** *See also* **La Cosa Nostra; Mafia**
　　Chinese Triads, 1:244
　　code of silence, 1:280
　　in courtroom, 2:564
　　Dewey fighting, 1:461–462
　　Eisenhower and, 2:520–521
　　forms of modern, 3:1295–1297
　　Gambino Crime Family, 2:700
　　Genovese and, 2:688–689
　　historical development, 3:1294
　　Irish Americans and, 2:862–863
　　Robert Kennedy and, 2:689, 5:2343
　　in music industry, 3:1172
　　Nixon and, 3:1262–1263
　　pornography and, 3:1399

Prohibition and, 1:353
today, 3:1294–1295
organized crime, history of, 3:1298–1305, 5:2105–2106
    Irish American in New York City, 3:1300–1301
    Irish American in other cities, 3:1301–1302
    Italian, 3:1302–1304
    Jewish American, 3:1302
    modern, 3:1304–1305
    1921 to 1940, 5:2203–2205
    pirates, 3:1298–1300
organized crime, sociology of, 3:1305–1311
    causes, 3:1310
    formal structure, 3:1305–1307
    hierarchy, 3:1308
    longevity, 3:1308–1310
    organization size, 3:1307–1308
Organized Crime Control Act, 5:2351–2353
Oriental Stories, 2:467
Origin of the Species (Darwin), 2:748–749, 4:1611
Ortega-Hernandez, Oscar, 1:xlix
Orthwood, Anne, 1:292
Orwell, George, 1:258, 3:1008
Osborne, Thomas Mott, 1:79, 2:518, 4:1676
OSHA (Occupational Safety and Health Administration), 3:1378
Oshinsky, David, 1:330
OSS (Office of Strategic Services), 2:558
Oswald, Lee Harvey, 1:xlv, 1:103, 2:946, 3:1311–1313
    Kennedy assassination, 3:1312–1313, 4:1907
    military service, 3:1311–1312
Oswald, Russell, 1:76
OTFFC (Office of Terrorist Financing and Financial Crimes), 2:843
Otis, James, 5:2045
Otsuka, Michael, 3:1007
Our American Cousin, 1:143
Our Penal Machinery and Its Victims (Altgeld), 1:428
The Outlaw Josey Wales, 4:1884
outlaws
    Billy the Kid, 1:126–127
    William Brocius, 1:161–162
    Jesse James, 2:872–874
Ovington, Mary White, 3:1179
Oxford, Edward, 2:838
Oxford Union, 1:258
Oz, 4:1776–1777
Ozawa v. United Stated, 2:875–875
Ozbourne, Ozzy, 3:1170

P

paddy wagons, 1:85
Padilla, Jose, 3:1315
Padilla v. Kentucky, 3:1315–1316
Page Act, 1:247, 4:1981
Pain-Capable Unborn Child Protection Act, 1:32
Paine, Thomas, 3:1316–1318
    call for revolution, 3:1318
    political writing, 3:1317–1318
Palko v. Connecticut, 1:60
Palmer, A. Mitchell, 4:1595
Palmer, George A., 2:582
Palmer Raids, 1:447
Parchman Farm, 2:683
pardons
    clemency, 1:269–270
    Eisenhower and, 4:1831
    John Kennedy and, 4:1832
    Nixon, 1:270–271, 1:349, 2:636
    Harry Truman and, 4:1831–18322
parens patriae doctrine, 2:911–912, 2:918–920, 2:922
Parenthood of Southeastern Pennsylvania v. Casey, 1:xlvii
Paretsky, Sara, 2:468, 3:1017, 3:1019, 3:1031, 3:1318–1319
    crime and detective fiction, 3:1318
    popularity and awards, 3:1319
Park, Robert, 4:1849
Parker, Bonnie. *See* **Bonnie and Clyde**
Parker, Isaac, 3:1319–1320
    early career, 3:1319
    hanging judge, 3:1319
    reputation, 3:1320
Parker, Isaac C., 5:2105
Parker, John, 2:807
Parker, Marion, 5:2217
Parker, Robert ("Butch Cassidy"), 1:453, 4:1561
Parker, Robert B., 2:468
Parker, Theodore, 1:80, 2:569
Parker, William, 1:xliv, 2:784, 3:1321–1322, 5:2275
    criticism, 3:1322
    LAPD, 3:1321
    during World War II, 3:1321
Parkhurst, Charles, 1:460
Parnell, Sean, 1:35
parole, 1:338–339, 3:1227–1228, 3:1322–1326
    challenges, 3:1324–1325
    development, 3:1322–1323

process, 3:1325–1326
reform movements in justice, 4:1515–1516
in U.S., 3:1324
Wickersham Commission, 4:1940
Parsons, Albert, 1:xli
partus sequitur ventrem, 1:xxxix, 1:21
Pataki, George, 1:77
Patriarca, Raymond, Jr., 4:1549
patrol cars, 1:85
patroons, 1:44
Patterson, Haywood, 4:1613
Patterson, Isabel, 3:1006
Paul, Raymond, 1:423
Paul, Saint, 1:59, 1:119
Paul Blart: Mall Cop, 2:617
Paul the Apostle, 4:1670
PCB, 2:544
Pearce, Donn, 1:215
Pearl Harbor, 1:xliv
Peck, Gregory, 3:1052
pedophile, 1:226
Peel, Robert, 1:450, 2:717
peine forte et dure, 5:1993, 5:2002
Peltier, Leonard, 3:1326–1328
  incarceration, 3:1328
  Pine Ridge Reservation, 3:1326–1327
  Wounded Knee incident and, 3:1327–1328
penal colonies, 1:339
Pendleton Act of 1883, 1:69, 2:717, 3:1328–1330
  Garfield and, 3:1329
  merit appointments, 5:2111
  passage, 3:1328–1329
penitentiaries, 2:621, 3:1136, 3:1330–1332. *See also* **Eastern State Penitentiary;** jails; **National Congress on Penitentiary and Reformatory Discipline;** prisons
  Auburn State Prison, 3:1332
  Baumont investigation, 1:110–111
  Eastern State Penitentiary, 3:1331
  era in corrections, 1:337
  Illinois, 1:xli
  Illinois State Penitentiary, 4:1492
  Leavenworth Federal Penitentiary, 3:996–997
  New Mexico riots, 3:1221
  reformatory movement, 3:1332
  transition to in New Republic, 5:2046–2049
  Wetumpka State Penitentiary, 1:30
Penitentiary Study Commission, 3:1332–1333
Penn, Arthur, 1:xliii
Penn, William, 3:1334–1335, 3:*1476,* 4:1514

Pennsylvania, 3:1335–1337. *See also* Philadelphia, Pennsylvania; Pittsburgh, Pennsylvania
  capital punishment, 1:xl
  Court of Common Pleas, 1:359
  crime, 3:1335–1336
  police, 3:1336
  punishment, 3:1336
Pennsylvania Department of Corrections v. Yeskey, 3:1321
Pennsylvania Gazette, 3:1243
Pennsylvania system of reform, 1:337, 1:*339,* 3:1337–1338
Pennsylvania v. Muniz, 3:1321
Penry v. Lynaugh, 1:418, 5:2458
Pentagon, 1:xlviii, 3:1379
People and Folks (Hagedorn), 2:678
People for the Ethical Treatment of Animals (PETA), 1:420
People of Darkness (Hillerman), 2:752
People v. Jennings, 4:1828
The People v. John Doe, 2:621
***People v. Pinnell,* 3:1338–1340**
  background, 3:1338–1339
  Fourteenth Amendment and, 3:1339
  jury selection, 3:1339
***People v. Superior Court of Santa Clara County,* 3:1340–1341**
  death penalty and, 3:1340
  rationale, 3:1340–1341
People's Court, 4:1765
People's History of the United States (Zinn), 2:882
Pequot War, 1:136
per curiam decision, 1:159
Percival, Robert V., 3:1341–1343
  research, 3:1341
  writings, 3:1341
perjury, 1:351
permanent bondage, 1:xxxix
Perry, Rick, 1:*189*
personal jurisdiction, 2:901–902
Perverted Justice, 4:1883
PETA (People for the Ethical Treatment of Animals), 1:420
Peters v. Kiff, 2:512
Peterson, Scott, 2:576, 3:1343–1344
Petition of Right, 1:xxxix
petty courts, 3:1344–1346
  cases, 3:1344–1345
  procedures, 3:1346
  sanctions, 3:1345–1346
Pfauhl, Russell, 1:433

PFFA (Planned Parenthood Federation of America), 1:xliv, 1:4, 1:6, 2:523, 2:714
Pfohl, Stephen, 4:1671
Philadelphia, Pennsylvania, 3:1347–1348
    law enforcement, 3:1347
    prison reform, 3:1348
The Philadelphia Negro (Du Bois), 1:24
Philadelphia Society for Alleviating the Miseries of Public Prisons (PSAMPP), 2:516–517
Phillips, Watts, 3:1022
Phillips, Wendell, 1:80, 2:569
Phipps, William, 1:359–360
PhoneBusters, 2:814
A Pickpocket's Tale (Gilfoyle), 1:85
pickpockets, 3:1348–1351
    American, 3:1349
    George Appo, 3:1350
    defined, 3:1348
picture brides, 2:875
Pierce, Charles Sander, 3:1137
Pierce, Franklin (administration of), 1:168, 3:1351–1352
    domestic and foreign policy, 3:1352
    slavery and, 3:1351–1352
Pierce, Samuel, Jr., 1:350
Pieter Bruegel the Elder, 4:*1671*
pigeon drop, 1:320
Pinckney, Charles, 2:880
Pine Ridge Reservation, 3:1326–1327
The Pink Panther, 2:615
Pinkerton, Allan, 1:193, 1:452–453, 3:*1423*, 3:1429
Pinkerton agents, 1:xlii, 1:139, 2:734, 2:769, 2:812
    Anti-Pinkerton Act, 3:1423
    Pinkerton's Protective Patrol, 3:1429
    private detectives, 3:1422–1423, 4:1561, 5:2172
Pinkney, William, 2:904
Pippin, Roddy Dean, 3:892
piracy, 2:757, 3:1172–1173
pirates, 3:1298–1300
Pistone, Joseph D., 3:1093
Pittman, Frank, 1:16
Pittsburgh, Pennsylvania, 3:1352–1354
    early history, 3:1352–1353
    19th century, 3:1353–1354
    20th century, 3:1354
Place, Martha, 5:2112
Placido, Judy, 1:114
Plaine, William, 4:1696
Plame, Valerie, 1:271
Planet Stories, 2:467

Planned Parenthood Federation of America (PFFA), 1:xliv, 1:4, 1:6, 2:523, 2:714
Planned Parenthood of Central Missouri v. Danforth, 1:xlvii, 1:6
Planned Parenthood of Kansas City v. Ashcroft, 1:6
Planned Parenthood of Southeastern Pennsylvania v. Casey, 1:6
Planned Parenthood v. Casey, 4:1736
Plata v. Schwarzenegger, 3:1321, 4:1537
Plato, 3:1587
plea, 3:1354–1358
    benefits to justice system, 3:1357
    criticisms, 3:1357
    defined, 3:1354
    plea bargaining, 3:1355–1356
    rules, 3:1356–1357
plea bargaining, 1:68, 2:474–475, 3:1355–1356, 4:1824
Pledge of Allegiance, 4:1753
Plessy v. Ferguson, 1:xlii, 1:25, 1:164, 1:166, 1:262, 3:1358–1359
    background, 3:1358–1359
    Fourteenth Amendment and, 1:263
    furthering segregation, 3:1359
    separate but equal, 3:1088
    state laws and, 1:263–264
PLRA (Prison Litigation Reform Act), 3:1421
Plug Uglies, 2:672
pluralistic conflict theory, 4:1503
Plymouth Company, 1:288–289
Poe, Edgar Allan, 2:467, 2:639, 3:1015, 3:1028, 3:1359–1360
    gothic tradition, 3:1359
    publications, 3:1359–1360
Poelker v. Doe, 1:5
Poindexter, John, 2:566
Poison Act, 2:778
Polanski, Roman, 2:575
police, contemporary, 1:xlii, 3:1361–1363.
    See also automobile and the police; code of silence; community policing and relations; customs service as police; film, police in; literature and theater, police in; news media, police in; rural police; sheriffs; state police; technology, police; television, police in
    Alabama, 1:30–31
    Alaska, 1:34–35
    anti-Chinese violence, 4:1978
    Arkansas, 1:64
    Atlanta Police Department, 1:72–74
    Baltimore Police Department, 1:107–108

battling crime, 3:1361–1362
Birmingham, Alabama, 1:128–129
BPD, 1:150–153
California, 1:194–195
Cincinnati, Ohio, 1:251–252
Cleveland, Ohio, 1:274–275
Compton, California, 1:308
Connecticut, 1:323–324
COPS, 1:276
corruption, 1:344, 2:783–785, 3:1250–1252
custom police car, 1:xliv
Dayton, Ohio, 1:432
Detroit, Michigan, 1:458
environment, 3:1362–1363
Georgia, 2:690–692
Idaho, 2:811–812
Indiana, 2:834–835
Iowa, 2:859–860
Kansas City, Missouri, 2:941
Kentucky, 2:951–952
LAPD, 1:xliv, 3:1246
Louisiana, 3:1043
Maryland, 3:1074
Memphis, Tennessee, 3:1096–1097
Michigan, 3:1102–1103
Minnesota, 3:1113
Mississippi, 3:1117–1119
Missouri, 3:1121–1122
Montana, 3:1130
Native American Tribal Police, 3:1195–1198
New Hampshire, 3:1215
New Orleans, Louisiana, 3:1225
New York, 3:1229–1230
North Carolina, 3:1264
NYPD, 1:451
Ohio, 3:1282
Oregon, 3:1291–1293
Pennsylvania, 3:1336
Rhode Island, 4:1547–1549
South Carolina, 4:1697–1698
South Dakota, 4:1700
Tennessee, 4:1778
torture, 4:1812–1813
Utah, 4:1856
Vermont, 4:1859–1860
violence, 1:167, 3:1250–1252
Virginia, 4:1894–1895
West Virginia, 4:1920–1921
Wyoming, 4:1977–1978

police, history of, 3:1363–1367
  African American police, 3:1365–1366
  boss system, 3:1364–1365
  civil unrest, 3:1367
  community interaction, 3:1366
  1801 to 1850, 5:2067–2068
  formal systems development, 3:1363–1364
  frontier police, 3:1365
  migration, 3:1365
police, sociology of, 3:1367–1368
  police role and functions, 3:1367–1368
  studies, 3:1368
police, women as, 3:1368–1372
  officers, 3:1370–1371
  police matrons, 3:1369–1370
  police officers, 3:1370–1371
  policewomen, 3:1370
police abuse, 3:1372–1375
  factors in, 3:1374–1375
  history of, 3:1373
  overview, 3:1372–1373
  types of, 3:1373–1374
Police Academy, 2:616–617
The Police Chief, 2:847
Police Story, 4:1763, 4:1770
Police Woman, 4:1771
policing. *See also* Community Oriented Policing Services (COPS); **community policing and relations; federal policing; political policing**
  American colonies, 1600 to 1776, 5:2000–2001
  COPS, 5:2418
  William Devery and, 1:461
  England, 1600 to 1776, 5:1991–1995
  evidence-based policing (EBP), 5:2454–2456
  hot spots, 5:2419
  Native American Tribal Police, 3:1196–1197
  NCWP, 3:1371
  1981 to 2000 changes, 5:2417–2420
  POP, 4:1512–1513
  robbery, 4:1564–1565
  Wickersham Commission, 4:1940–1941
  zero-tolerance, 1:393
political crimes, contemporary, 3:1376–1381
  1960s, 3:1376
  1970s, 3:1376–1377
  1980s, 3:1377–1378
  1990s, 3:1378–1380
  2000s, 3:1380

political crimes, history of, 3:1381–1385
    domestic surveillance, 3:1383–1385
    foundling period, 3:1381–1382
    interwar period, 3:1382–1383
    1950s, 3:1383
    1960s to present, 3:1383
    19th century, 3:1382
    World War I, 3:1382
    World War II, 3:1383
political crimes, sociology of, 3:1386–1389
    anomic theory, 3:1387
    interpretation, 3:1387–1389
    predisposing conditions, 3:1387
    structural conflict theory, 3:1387
    structural dysfunctionalism, 3:1387
    theories, 3:1387–1388
political dissidents, 3:1389–1393
    Noam Chomsky, 3:1392
    contemporary, 3:1391–1392
    Martin Luther King, Jr., 3:1391–1392
    Michael Moore, 3:1392
    prominent, 3:1390–1391
    risks, 3:1390
political policing, 3:1393–1395
    governmental justification, 3:1394–1395
    historical context, 3:1393–1394
political prisoners, 1:83–84
political violence, 3:1224
politics
    Baltimore, Maryland, 1:108
    Camden, New Jersey, 1:198–199
    of criminal justice, 2:790–792
    Jewish Americans, 2:881
    Newark, New Jersey, 3:1240
    political corruption, 1:352–353
Polk, James K. (administration of), 3:1395–1396
    law practice, 3:1396
    Texas annexation, 3:1396
Pollak, Otto, 4:1967
Pollard, Jonathan, 2:559
polygamy. See bigamy/polygamy
polygraph testing, 1:xliii
Ponzi, Charles, 2:646
Ponzi scheme, 1:343, 1:389, 2:646, 3:1056, 4:1617
poolroom trust, 1:460
Poor Bear, Myrtle, 3:1328
POP (problem-oriented policing), 4:1512–1513
Popish Plot of 1678, 2:729
Popular Library, 2:467
Populist Party, 1:331, 2:741
Porkolpolis, 1:252

pornography, 3:1397–1400
    child, 3:1399–1400
    organized crime and, 3:1399
    overview, 3:1397–1399
Porter, Edwin, 2:621
Porterfield, Austin, 1:396
positivism, 3:1137
Posner, Richard, 3:1140
posse coitatus, 2:817, 3:1405
posses, 3:1400–1403
    legal basis, 3:1400
    in Old West, 3:1400–1402
    Posse Comitatus Act, 1:70, 3:1400, 3:1405
    Regulators, 3:1401
postmodernism, 3:1139
Postmortem (Cornwell), 3:1024
posttraumatic stress disorder (PTSD), 2:486, 4:1957
Potter, Robert D., 1:101
Pound, Roscoe, 3:1184
poverty
    robbery and, 4:1565–1566
    Victorian Compromise and, 4:1879
    war on poverty, 5:2345–2351
Powell, James, 4:*1555*
Powell, Lewis, 1:143, 2:523, 4:1570
Powell, Ozie, 4:1613
Powell, William, 2:734
Powell v. Alabama, 1:26, 1:30, 1:327–328, 1:442
Powell v. State, 1:158
Powers, Gary Francis, 2:559
Practical Lawyer, 1:43
Practical Litigator, 1:43
pragmatism, 3:1137–1138
Pratt, Henry, 3:1201
predisposing conditions, 3:1387
Presidential Crime Commission, 2:471
presidential proclamations, 3:1403–1407
    George W. Bush, 3:1407
    William Clinton, 3:1406
    18th century, 3:1403–1404
    Gerald Ford, 3:1407
    Ulysses S. Grant, 3:1405
    Herbert Hoover, 3:1406
    Abraham Lincoln, 3:1404–1405
    martial law, 3:1404–1405
    Richard Nixon, 3:1406
    Barack Obama, 3:1406
    oversight, 3:1406–1407
    powers and limits, 3:1403
    Franklin Roosevelt, 3:1406
    Harry Truman, 3:1406

George Washington, 3:1403–1404
Woodrow Wilson, 3:1405–1406
World War I, 3:1405–1406
President's Commission on Law Enforcement and the Administration of Justice, 3:1407–1410
    challenge in free society, 3:1408–1409
    convening, 3:1407–1408
The President's Daughter (Nan), 2:740
"Pretty Boy Floyd," 2:635
Prevent Child Abuse America, 1:232
Price, Cecil, 2:577
Priest, Judas, 3:1170
Prigg v. Pennsylvania, 1:22, 2:657
The Prince (Machiavelli), 2:556
Prince v. Massachusetts, 1:240
Printz v. United States, 2:721
Prison Break, 4:1776–1777
Prison Litigation Reform Act (PLRA), 3:1421
Prison Memoirs of an Anarchist (Berkman), 1:48, 1:49
prison privatization, 3:1410–1414, 5:2450–2451
    corporations, 3:1411–1412
    criticisms, 3:1412–1413
    history of, 3:1410–1411
    modern facilities, 3:1413–1414
prison riots, 3:1414–1418
    causes, 3:1416–1417
    early, 3:1414–1415
    Eastern State Penitentiary 1961, 2:518
    New Mexico penitentiary, 3:1221
    rage, 3:1416
prisoner's rights, 3:1418–1422
    death penalty litigation, 3:1420–1421
    early Republic, 3:1418–1419
    expanding, 3:1419
    medical experimentation legislation, 3:1420
    welfare reform, 3:1421–1422
prisons, 1:xl. *See also* **Alcatraz Island Prison; Attica; Auburn State Prison; Bedford Hills Correctional Facility; Clinton Correctional Facility; Elmira Prison; federal prisons;** jails; **National Prison Association;** penitentiaries; **Pennsylvania system of reform; reports on prison conditions; San Quentin State Prison**
    Abu Ghraib, 1:190, 2:577
    Andersonville Prison, 5:2100
    Chillicothe Correctional Institution, 1:241–242
    early American correctional experience, 1:119–120
    Federal Bureau of Prisons, 1:xliii, 1:xlix
    Guantanomo Bay prison, 2:731, 2:802, 2:850
    in history of crime and punishment in America: 1783–1850, 2:763–765
    increased populations, 3:1228–1229
    inmate safety, 2:800
    Jackson, Mississippi, 2:872
    Louisiana, 3:1045–1046
    Massachusetts, 1:xxxix
    New Jersey, 3:1218–1219
    New York, 1:xlii
    New York female, 3:1233
    New York history, 3:1230–1233
    Newgate prison, 1:325
    overcrowding, 4:1540–1541
    Parchman Farm, 2:683
    Philadelphia reform, 3:1348
    political prisoners, 1:83–84
    post 1950s prison film, 2:623–624
    Quaker reforms, 3:1136
    rehabilitation programs, 1:xliii
    Sing Sing Correctional Facility, 4:1675–1677
    strikes, 4:1726–1727
    2001 to 2012 expanding populations, 5:2451–2454
    WIP, 2:623
private detectives, 3:1422–1426
    impact of technology, 3:1424
    nature of work, 3:1423–1424
    Pinkerton agents, 3:1422–1423, 4:1561
    in popular culture, 3:1424–1425
    society and, 3:1425
private police, 3:1426–1427
    issues, 3:1426–1427
    public sector and, 3:1427
private security services, 3:1427–1431
    origin, 3:1428–1429
    services provided, 3:1430–1431
    war and, 3:1429–1430
probable cause, 4:1736
probation, 1:xl, 1:338, 3:1431–1437
    administration, 3:1435–1436
    defined, 3:1431
    early, 3:1432–1433
    Intensive Supervision Probation (ISP), 2:608, 5:2422
    John Augustus and, 1:79–80
    juvenile courts, 2:920
    in Massachusetts, 1:xli
    mechanics, 3:1434–1435
    reasons for, 3:1432
    reform movements in justice, 4:1515–1516
    Wickersham Commission, 4:1940
problem-oriented policing (POP), 4:1512–1513
problem-solving courts, 5:2460–2462

Proclamation for Suppressing Rebellion and Sedition of 1775, 3:1437–1438
   bluntness, 3:1438
   Olive Branched Petition, 3:1438
Procter, Maurice, 3:1022
Procter and Gamble, 1:252
Procunier v. Martinez, 3:1438–1440
   First Amendment and, 3:1439
   mail censorship, 3:1438
Professional and Amateur Sports Protection Act, 1:xlvii, 2:666
Professional Criminals in America (Byrnes), 1:193, 1:451
professionalization of police, 3:1440–1444
   consequences, 3:1442
   current status, 3:1442–1444
   development, 3:1440–1441
   future, 3:1444
   proponents, 3:1441–1442
   tenets, 3:1440
Proffit v. Florida, 3:1340, 4:1630
Progressive Era, 2:471
Prohibition, 3:1445–1449
   bootlegging and, 1:144, 3:1448–1449
   Chicago, Illinois, 1:221
   criminalization and decriminalization, 1:403–404
   criticisms, 3:1447–1448
   drinking and crime, 2:491–492
   Eighteenth Amendment, 1:174, 2:491
   enforcement, 3:1445
   evasion, 3:1446–1447
   German Americans during, 2:694–695
   Great Depression and, 2:705–706
   Herbert Hoover and, 2:805–806, 4:1898
   Iowa, 2:859
   moonshine, 3:1132–1133
   Noble Experiment, 2:492
   organized crime and, 1:353
   repeal arguments, 3:1449
   vice reformers and, 4:1866–1867
   Volstead Act and, 4:1897–1898
   Wickersham Commission and, 4:1939
   Woodrow Wilson and, 4:1946
Prohibition Mania (Darrow), 1:429
Project Innocence, 1:20
pro-life movement, 1:5
Propaganda by Deed, 1:50
property crime, 1:386–388
proportionality, 1:207–208
Prosser's Rebellion, 1:24

prostitution, contemporary, 2:868, 3:1450–1456, 4:1959
   characteristics and risk factors, 3:1450–1452
   Chicago, Illinois, 1:219
   clients, 3:1451–1452
   in contemporary corruption, 1:343
   contemporary views, 3:1453–1454
   criminalization and decriminalization, 1:405
   Everleigh sisters, 2:567
   explanations, 3:1452–1453
   facilitators, 3:1452
   in history of crime and punishment in America: 1900–1950, 2:778
   The History of Prostitution (Sanger), 4:1966
   media and, 3:1453
   Nevada, 3:1213–1214
   new approaches, 3:1455–1456
   responses to, 3:1454–1455
   victimless crime, 4:1874–1875
prostitution, history of, 3:1456–1460
   early history, 3:1456–1457
   modern laws, 3:1459–1460
   19th century, 3:1458–1459
prostitution, sociology of, 3:1460–1464
   conflict perspective, 3:1462–1463
   functionalist perspective, 3:1461–1462
Protestantism, 2:556, 3:1471, 4:1672
Proudhon, Pierre-Joseph, 1:48
prowl cars, 1:85
PSAMPP (Philadelphia Society for Alleviating the Miseries of Public Prisons), 2:516–517
Psycho, 1:428, 2:614, 4:1947–1948
psychological theories of crime, 4:1800–1801
PTSD (posttraumatic stress disorder), 2:486, 4:1957
public enemies, 2:464, 2:613, 5:2212–2213
The Public Enemy, 2:613
Public Enemy Number One, 2:464
Public Health Service Act, 1:6
public humiliation, 4:1658–1659
public labor, 1:xl
Pullman, George, 1:273
Pullman Strike of 1894, 1:220, 1:272–273
pulps, 3:1018–1019
Punch, John, 1:xxxix
punishment. *See also* **cruel and unusual punishment;** death penalty; **history of crime and punishment in America: colonial;** history of crime and punishment in America: 1783–1850; history of crime and punishment in America: 1850–1900; history of crime and punishment in America: 1900–1950; history of crime and punishment in America:

1950–1970; history of crime and punishment in America: 1970–present; news media, punishment in; television, punishment in
  John Adams, **1:**11
  Alabama, **1:**32–33
  Alaska, **1:**35
  alternatives, 1777 to 1800, **5:**2041–2042
  Arkansas, **1:**64–65
  Beccaria and, **1:**456, **4:**1514
  in Bible, **1:**118–119
  Camden, New Jersey, **1:**199–200
  carceral, **4:**1627
  Chicago, Illinois, **1:**220–221
  in colonial America, **2:**758
  colonial courts, **1:**291–292
  in colonies, 1600 to 1776, **5:**2004–2007
  Connecticut, **1:**324–325
  corporal, **1:**333–336
  Delaware, **1:**444–445
  due process, **1:**510–511
  under Dyer Act, **1:**514
  failure of traditional, 1777 to 1800, **5:**2039–2041
  felonies, **2:**607–608
  in film, **2:**620–624
  flogging, **5:**2005
  Gacy, **2:**662
  Georgia, **2:**690–692
  Idaho, **2:**811–812
  Illinois, **2:**818–820
  Indiana, **2:**834–835
  infanticide, **2:**837
  Iowa, **2:**859–860
  Kentucky, **2:**952
  in literature and theater, **3:**1027–1032
  Louisiana, **3:**1043–1045
  Maryland, **3:**1074–1075
  Memphis, Tennessee, **3:**1097
  Michigan, **3:**1103–1104
  Minnesota, **3:**1113–1114
  Mississippi, **3:**1117–1119
  Missouri, **3:**1121–1122
  Montana, **3:**1130
  Nebraska, **3:**1206–1207
  New Hampshire, **3:**1215–1217
  New Jersey, **3:**1218–1219
  New York, **3:**1229–1230
  Newark, New Jersey, **3:**1240–1241
  1901 to 1920, **5:**2179–2180
  North Carolina, **3:**1264–1265
  North Dakota, **3:**1266–1267
  Ohio, **3:**1282–1283
  Oregon, **3:**1291–1293
  Pennsylvania, **3:**1336
  pre-Revolutionary, **5:**2031–2033
  Puritans, **3:**1474
  Rhode Island, **4:**1547–1549
  shaming and shunning, **4:**1657–1660
  in slavery, **1:**23
  South Carolina, **4:**1697–1698
  South Dakota, **4:**1700
  stocks, **5:**2005
  Tennessee, **4:**1779
  Utah, **4:**1856
  Vermont, **4:**1859–1860
  Virginia, **4:**1894–1895
  West Virginia, **4:**1920–1921
  Wyoming, **4:**1977–1978
Punishment of Crimes Act, 1790, 3:1464–1466
  background, **3:**1464–1465
  writing and provisions, **3:**1465
punishment within prison, 3:1466–1469
  contemporary, **3:**1468–1469
  19th century, **3:**1466–1467
  the paddle, **3:**1467
  20th century, **3:**1468
Punitive era of corrections, **1:**337
Purdy, Ann Maria, **5:**2067
Pure Food and Drug Act of 1906, 2:777, 3:1469–1471
  background, **3:**1469–1470
  FDA founding, **3:**1470
  passage, **3:**1470
  revisions and amendments, **3:**1470–1471
Puritans, 1:135, 1:141, 3:1471–1474, 4:1672
  in America, **3:**1472–1473
  Calvinist ideas, **4:**1964
  Clarendon Code, **3:**1474
  crime and punishment, **3:**1474
  decline, **3:**1474
  in England, **3:**1471–1472
  influence of teachings, **3:**1134
  orthodoxy, **1:**291
  religious persecution, **3:**1473–1474
  Separatists, **3:**1472
Purkinji, John Evangelist, **2:**626
"The Purloined Letter," **3:**1360
Purvis, Melvin, **2:**635

Q

Al Qaeda, **1:**xlviii, **1:**188, **2:**528, **2:**803, **3:**1218, **3:**1240–1241, **3:**1380, **3:**1385, **4:**1781
  American intelligence agencies and, **4:**1853
  CIA and, **2:**854

Qin Code, 4:1590
Quakers, 1:77, **1:**119–120, **2:**519–520, **2:**759, **3:**1475–1477
   emergence, 3:1475
   executions, 3:1473
   Great Law, 3:1475
   influence of teachings, 3:1134, 3:1477–1477
   jailing, 2:762
   prison reforms, 3:1136
The Quality of Hurt (Himes), 1:83
Quantrill's Raiders, 1:82
Quartering Act of 1774, 1:45
Quebec Act of 1774, 1:45
Queen, Ellery, 2:467, 3:1016
Queen, William, 3:1094
Queen of Crime, 1:249
Quetelet, Lambert Adolpe Jacques, 1:408
Qui Pro Domina Justitia Sequitur, 2:903
Quinney, Richard, 1:411, 4:1503

R
Rabelais, François, 1:314
race, class, and criminal law, 4:1479–1483
   contemporary, 4:1481–1482
   in contemporary gangs, 2:670
   controversial practices, 4:1482–1483
   critical race theory (CRT), 1:414
   in history of crime and punishment in America: 1850–1900, 2:769–770
   1906 Atlanta race riot, 1:74
   suicide, 1:3
   in U.S. history, 4:1479–1481
   witness testimony and, 4:1950–1951
race relations
   Chicago, Illinois, 1:221–222
   Cleveland, Ohio, 1:275
race-based crimes, 4:1483–1486
   against Chinese and Mexican Americans, 4:1485–1486
   contemporary murder and, 3:1150
   early America, 4:1483–1484
   post World War II, 4:1484–1485
Racial Formation in the United States (Winant, Omi), 4:1486
racial stereotypes, 1:385
racism, 4:1486–1490
   in chain gangs and prison labor, 1:214
   Hoover administration and, 2:807
   incarceration rates and, 4:1489
   juvenile justice system and, 4:1489–1490
   narcotics laws and, 3:1176
   overview, 4:1486–1487
   police surveillance and, 4:1487–1488
   racial identities, 4:1486
   sentencing and, 4:1488–1489
   torture, 4:1812
Racketeer Influenced Corrupt Organizations Act (RICCO), 5:2353
Rader, Dennis, 1:xlviii, **2:**576, **4:**1490–1491
radical conflict theory, 3:1388–1389
Ragen, Joseph, 4:1492–1493
Ragonese, Paul, 3:1094
railroads. *See also* train robbery
   Camden, New Jersey, 1:198
   Great Railroad Strike of 1877, 1:220
Rainbow Retreat, 2:480
Rainer, Elizabeth, 2:571
Ramirez, Richard, 4:1493–1494
Ramsey, Jon-Benet, 2:576
Rand, Ayn, 3:1006
Randolph, A. Philip, 1:264
Randolph, Edmund, 1:248, 2:904
Randolph, Edward, 1:293–294
rape, contemporary, **1:**207, **1:**286–287, **2:**782, **4:**1494–1497. *See also* **victim rights and restitution**
   African Americans and, 1:26
   Coker v. Georgia and, 4:1735
   legislation, 4:1496–1497
   mistaken notions, 4:1494–1495
   reports on prison conditions, 4:1539–1540
   research, 4:1496
   slavery and, 1:23
   statistics, 4:1496
   violent crimes, 4:1888
   women's civil rights and, 4:1495–1496
rape, history of, 4:1497–1501
   context, 4:1497–1499
   debates and solutions, 4:1500–1501
   slavery and, 1:23
   social definitions and legal responses, 4:1499–1500
rape, sociology of, 4:1501–1505
   conflict perspective, 4:1502–1504
   functionalist perspective, 4:1502
   symbolic interactionist perspective, 4:1504–1505
Rappe, Virginia, 2:575
Rasul v. Bush, 1:190, 2:728
rat catching, 1:134
Rathbone, Henry, 1:143
Rather, Dan, 1:224
rational choice theory, 1:391–392
rationalism, 5:2043–2044
Rawhide, 4:1884

Rawle, William, 3:1212
Rawls, John, 3:1139
Ray, James Earl, 1:xlvi, **4:1505–1507**
    Martin Luther King, Jr. assassination, 4:1505–1506
    London capture, 4:1506
Raz, Joseph, 4:1589
RCA, 1:199
RCRA (Resource Conservation and Recovery Act), 2:545–546
Reagan, Ronald (administration of), 1:28, **1:**212, **4:1507–1509**
    abortion bill signed, 1:5
    assassination attempt, 1:xlvii, 2:575, 2:840
    elections, 5:*2418*
    Family Law Act, 1:15
    Iran-Contra scandal, 1:271, 1:349–350, 1:353, 2:566
    law and order theme, 2:790, 4:1507
    legislation, 4:1507–1508
    war on crime, 4:1508–1509
realpolitik, 2:556
Reason Foundation, 3:1006
reasonable suspicion, 1:373, 4:1736
reckless driving, 4:1817–1818
Recollections of a New York City Chief of Police (Walling, G.), 4:1901
Reconstruction, 4:1887, 5:2101–2103
Red Harvest (Hammett), 2:733
Red Scare, 1:8, 1:445, 2:849, 2:882
Redding, Kent, 3:1007
Reed, Stanley, 4:1841
Reed v. Reed, 2:655, 4:1575
Reefer Madness, 2:501
Reeves, Jeremiah, 1:32
reform, police and enforcement, 4:1509–1513
    court rulings, 4:1511
    discretion and, 4:1513
    1960s to present, 4:1511–1513
    police professionalization, 4:1509–1510
    technology and, 4:1510–1511
reform movements in justice, 4:1514–1518
    correctional institutions, 4:1517
    early reforms, 4:1514–1515
    mass incarceration, 4:1517
    Model Penal Code, 4:1516
    parole, probation, indeterminate sentencing, juvenile court, 4:1515–1516
    restorative justice, 4:1517–1518
Reformation, 3:1471
reformatory movement, 2:530–531, 2:771–772, 3:1332

Regents of the University of California v. Bakke, 4:1735
Regina v. Benjamin Hicklin, 3:1397
Regina v. Dudley and Stephens, 2:578
Regina v. Hicklin, 3:1274
Regina v. Oxford, 2:838
regulation
    bounty hunters, 1:155
    CFR, 1:370
    convict lease system, 1:331
    drug abuse and addiction, 2:500–501
Regulators, 3:1401
rehabilitation, 4:1518–1525
    Clinton Correctional Facility, 1:278–279
    contemporary juvenile corrections, 2:909–909
    decline in popularity, 4:1520–1521
    early history, 4:1519
    generic, 4:1524
    juvenile delinquency, 2:922
    medical model, 4:1519–1520
    medical model of, 2:595
    modern theory, 4:1523–1524
    Narcotic Addict Rehabilitation Act (NARA), 4:1520
    prisons, 1:xliii
    rehabilitative model, 2:824
    research, 4:1520–1521
    revival, 4:1521–1523
    sentencing, 4:1625
    Zebulon Brockway and, 1:163–164
Rehnquist, William, 1:161, 1:191, 2:523, 4:1570, 4:1575, 4:1735–1736
Reid, Rober, 5:*1996*
Relentless Pursuit (Flynn), 3:1094
religion. *See also specific religions*
    Reformation, 3:1471
    religious idealism, 3:1134–1136
    religious law legal tradition, 1:296–297
    religious persecution, 3:1473–1474
religion and crime, contemporary, 2:758–759, **4:1525–1528**
    effect on behavior, 4:1525–1527
    religiosity, 4:1527
religion and crime, history of, 4:1528–1532
    American context, 4:1530–1531
    canon law and secularization, 4:1529–1530
    early experience, 4:1528–1529
religion and crime, sociology of, 4:1532–1536. *See also* **sin**
    frameworks, 4:1532–1533
    issues, 4:1533–1535

September 11, 2001, terrorist attacks, 4:1535
typology, 4:1535–1536
remission, 1:269
Reno, Janet, 1:276, 2:566
Reno Brothers Gang, 4:1560
rent strikes, 4:1726
rent-seeking, 1:352
Report on the Prisons and Reformatories of the United States and Canada (Wines, Dwight), 4:1536
reports on prison conditions, 4:1536–1541
    constitutionally adequate conditions, 4:1537–1538
    early reports, 4:1536–1537
    prison overcrowding, 4:1540–1541
    rape and sexual abuse, 4:1539–1540
    in supermax facilities, 4:1538–1539
reprieves, 1:269
Republican Party, 1:5, 1:25
Rescue 911, 4:1763
research. *See also* **crime and arrest statistics analysis; crime scene investigation; critical legal studies movement; reports on prison conditions**
    community service, 1:306–307
    crime causes, 1:380
    DOD, 2:785
    drinking and crime, 2:493–494
    family and twins studies, 2:749–750
    gender and criminal law, 2:687
    Hispanic Americans, 2:754–756
    identity theft, 2:815
    indecent exposure, 2:828
    kidnapping, 2:955–956
    lynching, 2:818
    mandatory minimum sentencing, 3:1064
    mug shots, 3:1144
    National Research Council, 1:401
    Penitentiary Study Commission, 3:1332–1333
    Percival, 3:1341
    police sociology, 3:1368
    rape, 4:1496
    rehabilitation, 4:1520–1521
    riots, 4:1556–1557
    rural police, 4:1593
    sexual harassment, 4:1654–1655
    urbanization, 4:1849–1851
    Washington, D.C., 4:1912
    white-collar crime, 4:1934–1935
Reservoir Dogs, 2:615
Resource Conservation and Recovery Act (RCRA), 2:545–546
respondeat superior doctrine, 2:549
Restell, Madame, 1:2

restorative justice, 5:2460–2462
retributivism, 4:1541–1546
    blameworthiness, 4:1543–1544
    as criminal justice theory, 4:1542
    deserved punishment, 4:1544–1545
    limit on punishment, 4:1545
    proportionality, 4:1544
    sentencing, 4:1625
Reuter, Peter, 5:2423
revenoors, 1:174
Revolutionary Communist Youth Brigade, 2:970
Revolutionary Suicide (Newton), 3:1468
Rex v. Arnold, 3:1124
Rex v. Bazeley, 2:533
Rex v. Hadfield, 2:838
***Reynolds v. United States*, 1:121, 4:1546–1547, 5:2110**
Rhode Island, 4:1547–1550
    crime, 4:1549–1550
    police and punishment, 4:1547–1549
    slavery in, 1:xxxix
Rhode Island v. Innis, 4:1739
Rhodes, James, 2:949, 2:951
Rhodes v Chapman, 3:1420
Ribicoff, Abraham, 1:224
Ricca, Paul, 2:868
***Ricci v. DeStefano*, 4:1550–1551**
    decision, 4:1551
    facts, 4:1550–1551
RICCO (Racketeer Influenced Corrupt Organizations Act), 5:2353
Rice, Thomas, 4:1619
Rich, Marvin, 2:882
Rideau v. Louisiana, 2:564
Ridge, Tom, 2:800
Ridgway, Gary Leon, 4:1891
riding the circuits, 2:894
right libertarianism, 3:1006–1007
rights. *See also* affirmative action; Bill of Rights; **children's rights;** civil rights; **Civil Rights Act of 1866; Civil Rights Act of 1875;** Civil Rights Act of 1964; **Convention on the Rights of the Child; defendant's rights**
    Chinese Americans citizenship, 1:244–245
    to counsel standard, 1:319, 1:327, 1:364, 3:998–1001, 4:1511
    Eighth Amendment, 2:779
    European Court of Human Rights, 1:435
    to fair trial, 1:326, 1:440, 2:563, 5:2038
    gun rights campaigns, 2:721–722

intellectual property, 3:1008
to marital privacy, 1:xlv
Miranda rights, 1:39
National Abortion and Reproductive Rights Action League, 1:5
National Abortion Rights Action League, 1:5
Native Americans, 3:1200–1201
1906 Atlanta race riot, 1:74
Parliament's Petition of Right, 1:xxxix
prisoner's, 3:1418–1420
to privacy, 3:992, 4:1575, 4:1735
Sixth Amendment defendant's rights, 1:440–442, 2:552
suspect's, 2:851–852, 4:1737–1742
victim rights and restitution, 4:1867–1873
victims, 2:783
Voting Rights Act of 1965, 1:xlv, 1:27, 1:265–266, 2:552, 4:1485
women, 1:405
women's property, 1:371

Rihanna, 2:477
Riis, Jacob, 5:2162–2163
Riley, Sidney, 2:554
Rineheart, Mary Roberts, 3:1015, 3:1020
Ring v. Arizona, 1:445, 4:1630, 5:2457
Ringo, Johnny, 1:162
riots, 4:1551–1557. *See also* **Kent State Massacre; prison riots**
    Anti-Draft Riots, 4:1553
    Anti-Rent War, 4:1553
    Attica Correctional Facility, 1:xlvi, 1:75–77
    Chicago Seven/Democratic National Convention of 1968, 1:224
    civil rights, 4:1554
    early 20th century, 4:1555–1556
    early American, 4:1552–1554
    Harlem Riot of 1935, 1:26
    Harlem Riot of 1964, 3:1158, 5:2340
    Haymarket bombing, 1:xli, 1:49–50
    Hough Riots, 1:275
    Rodney King, 3:1039–1040, 4:1555–1556
    Lager Beer Riot, 1:218
    Los Angeles Riots of 1992, 1:28
    Miami, Florida, 3:1101
    Newark riots, 3:1219
    North Carolina Riots of 1898, 1:26
    research, 4:1556–1557
    Sing Sing Correctional Facility, 4:1676
    Stamp Act Protests, 4:1552
    Tenderloin police riot, 1:460
    University of California, Berkeley, 1:xlv
    Watts, 1965, 1:xlv, 1:28, 2:785, 4:1554
    Zoot Suit Riots, 2:753, 5:2263–2264
Rip Raps, 2:672
The Rise of the Penitentiary (Hirsch), 5:2068
Ritter, Bill, 1:296
Rizzo, Frank, 3:1384
Roache, Mickey, 1:153
robbery, contemporary, 4:1557–1560
    FBI statistics, 4:1559
    investigation methods, 4:1559–1560
    motivation and violence factor, 4:1558–1559
    patterns, 4:1557–1558
robbery, history of, 4:1560–1565
    bank, 4:1560–1561
    computer crime, 4:1563
    looting, 4:1563
    mugging, 4:1562
    perpetrators and victims, 4:1563–1564
    policing, 4:1564–1565
    shoplifting, 4:1562–1563
    train, 4:1561–1562
robbery, sociology of, 4:1565–1568
    deviant behavior, 4:1567
    poverty and, 4:1565–1566
    state and, 4:1565
    striking against the state, 4:1568
    workplace, 4:1567–1568
Robbins, Tim, 2:571
Roberson, Willie, 4:1613
Roberts, Florian, 2:623
Roberts John, 1:190–191, 4:1736
Roberts v. Louisiana, 1:287, **4:1568–1570**
    dissent, 4:1570
    majority opinion, 4:1570
Robertson v. Delaware, 1:445
Robinson, Gwen, 4:1523
Robinson, H. R., 5:2070
Robinson Patman Act, 1:268
Robinson v. California, 3:1419, 4:1543
RoboCop, 2:619
Rochin v. California, 1:61
"The Rock," 1:36
Rock, John Swett, 1:27
Rockefeller, John D., 1:53, 1:76, 2:567
Rockefeller, John D., Jr., 1:112
Rockefeller, Nelson, 1:xlvi, 1:76, 4:1570–1573, 5:2354
    early life and career, 4:1570–1571
    government service, 4:1571
    governor, 4:1571–1572
    presidential run, 4:1572

Rockefeller Drug Laws, 1:xlvi, 2:498
Rockford Files, 3:1425
Rodney, Caesar, 2:904
Rodriguez, Luis J., 1:84–85
Roe v. Wade, 1:xlvi, 1:178, 1:266, 1:405, 4:1573–1576
    abortion after decision, 1:5–7
    Blackmun majority opinion, 4:1574–1575
    case, 4:1573–1574
    controversial ruling, 4:1735
    crime rates and, 1:398–399
    criticisms, 4:1575–1576
    expanding *Griswold v. Connecticut,* 2:714
    principle-establishing, 2:578
    right to privacy, 3:992
    zone of privacy, 2:523
Rogers, Mary, 1:3, 4:1243–1244
Roman-Byzantine Law, 1:283
Romer v. Evans, 1:158, 4:1576–1577
Roosevelt, Eleanor, 2:521
Roosevelt, Franklin D. (administration of), 1:267, 1:421, 2:528, 4:1577–1581
    Executive Order 8802, 1:xliv
    Executive Order 9066, 1:296
    Fair Employment Practices Commission, 1:xliv, 1:264
    federal law enforcement, 4:1578–1579
    federal prisons and, 2:594–595
    FTC and, 1:268
    immediate action, 4:1577–1578
    international relations, 4:1579
    Thurgood Marshall appointment, 1:28
    national security versus individual rights, 4:1579–1580
    presidential proclamations, 3:1406
    during World War II, 4:1580
Roosevelt, Rhinebeck, 4:1578
Roosevelt, Theodore (administration of), 1:3, 1:193, 1:460, 2:529, 2:776, 4:1581–1583
    achievements, 4:1582–1583
    corruption exposure, 5:2111
    FBI and, 2:906
    meatpacking investigation, 3:1469
    monopolies and, 5:2175
    political ascendancy, 4:1582
Root, Elihu, 1:42, 1:43
Roper v. Simmons, 1:208, 1:235, 1:341, 1:364
    death penalty and, 1:437, 3:1421, 4:1544, 5:2458
    Eighth Amendment and, 5:2425
Rose, Joel, 2:748

Rosenberg, Ethel, 1:xliv, 2:882, 5:2270
Rosenberg, Julius, 1:xliv, 2:882, 5:2270
Roth v. United States, 3:1275, 3:1277–1278, 4:1583–1584
    decision, 4:1583–1584
    obscenity and, 3:1277–1278, 4:1583
    shortcomings, 4:1584
Rothbard, Murray, 3:1006, 3:1009
Rothblatt, Henry, 1:99
Rothman, David, 3:1324, 5:2046
Rothstein, Arnold, 4:1584–1585
    bootlegging, 4:1585
    Chicago White Sox and, 4:1585
rouges gallery, 1:191–192
Rousey, Dennis, 3:1043
Rousseau, Jean-Jacques, 1:314, 1:438
routine activity theory, 1:391
Rubin, Jerry, 1:224
Ruby Ridge standoff, 2:577, 4:1585–1587
    law enforcement disaster, 4:1585–1587
    siege and outcome, 4:1586–1587
    warrant issued, 4:1586
Rudolph, Eric, 1:74–75
Rudolph v. Alabama, 1:206
Ruffin v. Commonwealth of Virginia, 2:787
Ruggles, David, 2:657
rule of law, 4:1587–1590
    background, 4:1587–1588
    contemporary, 4:1588–1589
    criticism, 4:1590
    formal and substantive, 4:1589–1590
    non-Western ancient conceptualization, 4:1590
    Qin Code, 4:1590
rule of lenity, 2:549
Ruppert, Jacob, 1:461
rural police, 4:1591–1593
    history, 4:1592–1593
    informal control, 4:1593
    office of sheriff, 4:1592
Rush, Benjamin, 2:499, 2:516, 2:571, 4:1514, 5:2068
Rush, Richard, 2:904
Rush Hour, 2:617
Russian Revolution of 1917, 1:49
Rust v. Sullivan, 1:6
Rutledge, Wiley, 4:1841
Rutterschmidt, Olga, 4:1963
Ryan, Dennis, 1:233
Ryan, George, 1:223, 1:272, 2:820
Ryder, Winona, 2:574, 3:984

Rynders, Isaiah, 2:862
Rynerson, William, 1:126

S

sabotage, 1:129, 2:554, 2:585, 2:782, 2:849, 5:2267
    Nazi, 3:*1106*
    nonviolent crimes, 3:1376
    political crimes, 3:1381
Sacco and Vanzetti, 2:577, 2:640, **4:1595–1596,**
    4:1784
    charges, 4:1595
    execution, 1:xliii, 4:1596
    Galleanists, 1:50
    1921 to 1940, 5:2208–2210
    trial, 4:1595–1596
The Sacred Canopy (Berger), 4:1673
Safe Drinking Water Act (SDWA), 2:545
Salem witch trials, 1:xxxix, 1:359–360, **4:1596–1599,**
    4:1959–1960
    background, 4:1596–1597
    executions, 5:1997
    mass hysteria, 4:1597–1599
    paralleling Europe, 4:1671
Salinger, J. D., 1:218
Saltsonstall, Nathaniel, 1:359
Samenow, Stanton, 1:410
same-sex couples, 1:xlix, 1:267, 1:406
    conduct, 3:992
    legalizing, 2:859
    violence, 2:485–486
Sampson, Robert J., 4:1812, 4:1850
San Francisco, California, 4:1599–1602
    beats and hippies, 4:1600–1601
    Chinatown, San Francisco, 1:*243*
    City Lights Bookstore, 4:1600
    crime, 4:1600–1601
    gold rush and vigilantes, 4:1599–1600
    opium dens, 1:xli
    renaissance, 4:1600
San Francisco Examiner, 3:1244
San Quentin State Prison, 4:1602–1604
    death row, 4:1602
    executions, 4:1603–1604
    reform, 4:1603
Sanders, Mary S., 2:463
Sanders, William H., 2:463
Sandford, John F. A., 2:489
Sanger, William, 4:1966
Santa Clara Pueblo v. Martinez, 2:831
Santobello v. New York, 3:1355, **4:1604–1605**
Sarbanes-Oxley Act of 2002, 1:353

Satrom, Leroy, 2:949
Saturday Night Massacre, 1:349
Satyagraha, 2:959
Savage, James, 1:234
Saving Grace, 4:1771
savings and loan scandal, 1:350
Savio, Mario, 1:195
Sawyer, Grant, 3:986
Saxton, Anthony D., 4:1760
Sayers, Dorothy, 1:250, 3:1016–1017
SBS (shaken baby syndrome), 1:225
Scalise, Jon, 1:211
scandals
    apartment scandal, 1:321
    Credit Mobilier, 1:347, 2:704
    Enron, 2:540–541
    Ulysses S. Grant, 2:704
    Harding administration, 2:739–740
    Housing and Urban Development, 1:350
    Iran-Contra, 1:271, 1:349–350, 1:353, 2:566
    savings and loan, 1:350
    Teapot Dome, 1:348, 2:739–740
    Whiskey Ring, 1:347, 2:704
    Whitewater, 2:566
Scared Straight, 4:1775
The Scarlet Letter (Hawthorne), 2:758
Schaefer, William Donald, 1:106
Schall v. Martin, 1:97
Scheck, Barry, 5:*2457*
Schenck v. United States, 2:779, 2:798, **4:1605–1606,**
    4:1690, 5:*2178*
    in criminal justice, 1:446
    First Amendment applicability, 4:1606
    World War I opposition, 4:1605
Schmoke, Kurt L., 1:106
school shootings, 4:1606–1609, 5:*2410–2411,*
    5:*2458. See also* **Klebold, Dylan, and Eric Harris**
    Columbine High School massacre, 1:xlviii, 2:962,
        3:1253, 4:1608
    school factors, 4:1608–1609
    shooter characteristics, 4:1606–1608
    social reaction, 4:1609
    2001 to 2012, 5:2459–2460
Schultz, "Dutch," 1:462, 2:694, 3:1048, **4:1610–1611**
    gunning down, 4:1610–1611
    numbers racket, 4:1867
    organized crime and, 4:1610
Schwab, Michael, 1:xli, 1:49
Schwarz, Robert, 1:233
Scooby-Doo, 4:1764
Scopes, John T., 1:429, 2:574, 2:577, **4:1611–1612**

Scopes monkey trial, 4:1611–1612
    background, 4:1611
    Clarence Darrow and, 1:429
    coining, 4:1611
    impact, 4:1612
    indictment, 4:1611
The Score, 2:615
Scott, Joel, 3:1410
Scott, Winfield, 3:1011
Scottsboro Boys cases, 1:xliv, 1:26, 2:577, 2:807, 4:1613–1614
    arrests, 4:1613
    1921 to 1940, 5:2211–2212
    Powell v. Alabama, 1:442
    trials and convictions, 4:1613
Scranton Commission, 2:949–950
SDWA (Safe Drinking Water Act), 2:545
Seabury investigation, 1:351
Seale, Bobby, 1:xlv, 1:129, 1:224
search and seizure, 1:364, 4:1736
    Fourth Amendment and, 1:123, 4:1736, 5:2038
    Weeks v. United States and, 4:1919–1920
search warrants, 1:xlii, 1:xliv, 1:123, 1:178, 1:326
The Searchers, 4:1880, 4:1884
Sears, Leah Ward, 1:28
SEC. *See* Securities and Exchange Commission
Second Amendment, 1:191
    Davis v. State and, 1:430–431
    gun control and, 2:718–719
Second Chance Act, 4:1521, 5:2452
Second Great Awakening, 4:1530
The Secret Agent (Conrad), 3:1015
Secret Service, 1:xlii, 2:780, 4:1614–1616
    budgeting and agents, 4:1615
    counterfeiting and, 1:356–357, 4:1614
    establishment, 4:1614, 5:2109
    evolution, 4:1614–1615
    federal policing, 2:590, 5:2172
    personnel, 5:2167
secularization, 4:1529–1530
Securities and Exchange Act, 1:54, 2:777
Securities and Exchange Commission, 2:487, 4:1616–1618
    function, 4:1617
    SRO, 4:1616
    structure and organization, 4:1616–1617
Sedition Act of 1918, 4:1618–1619. *See also* Alien and Sedition Acts of 1798
segregation
    Birmingham, Alabama, 1:127–128
    de facto, 4:1619, 4:1622

de jure, 4:1620, 4:1622
    Plessy v. Ferguson furthering, 3:1359
    in public transportation facilities, 1:xliv
    Supreme Court on, 1:xlii
segregation laws, 4:1619–1623
    in north, 4:1620
    in south, 4:1620–1621, 4:1620–1622
Seigel, Don, 2:624
Selective Service Act of 1967, 4:1623–1624
self-incrimination
    Brown v. Mississippi and, 1:167
    Fifth Amendment, 1:123, 1:316–317, 1:327, 1:364, 2:712, 2:786
    Fourteenth Amendment, 1:167
self-regulatory organizations (SROs), 4:1616
Sellers, Sean, 1:233
Sellin, Thorsten, 1:411
Seminole Tribe v. Florida, 4:1735
sentencing, 4:1624–1631. *See also* mandatory minimum sentencing
    capital, 4:1630–1631
    carceral punishment, 4:1627
    colonial, 4:1628
    community supervision, 4:1627
    corporal punishment, 4:1627
    determinant, 2:824–825
    determinant versus intermediate, 4:1627–1628
    deterrence, 4:1625
    disparity, 4:1628
    evidence-based, 4:1630
    Fair Sentencing Act, 1:xlviii–xlix, 1:28
    goals, 4:1624–1625
    guidelines, 4:1629–1630
    incapacitation, 4:1625
    mandatory minimum, 4:1628–1629
    racism and, 4:1488–1489
    reform movements in justice, 4:1515–1516
    rehabilitation, 4:1625
    retribution, 4:1625
    servitude, 5:2040
    structures, 1:368
    three strikes laws, 4:1629
    trends and drug treatment, 2:498
    trials, 4:1829–1830
    types, 4:1625–1627
sentencing: indeterminate versus fixed, 4:1631–1635
    debates and directions, 4:1634–1635
    fixed, 4:1633–1634
    indeterminate, 4:1631–1632

separate but equal, **1**:xlii, **1**:xliv, **4**:1734
    Brown v. Board of Education ending, **4**:1485, **4**:1554, **4**:1622
    in *Cummins v. County Board of Education*, **3**:1088
    in *Plessy v. Ferguson*, **3**:1088
SEPs (Supplemental Environmental Projects), **2**:548
September 11, 2001, terrorist attacks, **1**:xlviii, **1**:148, **1**:175, **2**:561, **2**:800, **4**:1781
    George W. Bush and, **1**:188–190
    community policing and relations, **1**:304
    computer crime and, **1**:312
    enemy combatant tribunal, **3**:1107
    espionage and, **2**:561
    Giuliani during, **2**:699
    religion and crime, **4**:1535
    rescue workers, **5**:*2444*
Sergeant, Peter, **1**:359
serial and mass killers, 1:xlv–xlviii, 4:1635–1643
    beyond race, gender, and nationality, **4**:1637–1638
    Ted Bundy, **1**:170–172
    characteristics, **4**:1638–1640
    history, **4**:1635–1636
    Herman Mudgett, **3**:1141, **4**:1636
    responses to, **4**:1642–1643
    typologies, **4**:1639–1642
    Wisconsin, **4**:1947–1948
Serpico, **2**:619
Serpico, Frank, **1**:281, **1**:351, **2**:964, **3**:1127
Seung-Hui Cho, **1**:xlviii
700 Club, **1**:100
1777 to 1800
    Articles of Confederation, **5**:2036–2037
    demographic changes, **5**:2033–2034
    Enlightenment during, **5**:2042–2043
    failure of traditional punishment, **5**:2039–2041
    north versus south, **5**:2044–2046
    post-Revolutionary America, **5**:2033
    post-Revolutionary priorities, **5**:2034–2036
    pre-Revolutionary criminal justice, **5**:2029–2030
    pre-Revolutionary punishment, **5**:2031–2033
    pre-Revolutionary sexuality and immorality crimes, **5**:2030–2031
    punishment alternatives, **5**:2041–2042
    rationalism and utilitarianism, **5**:2043–2044
    transition to penitentiaries in New Republic, **5**:2046–2049
    U.S. Constitution and criminal law, **5**:2037–2039
77 Sunset Strip, **4**:1766

Sewall, Samuel, **1**:359
Seward, William, **1**:143
sex crimes, **1**:386–388, **2**:575, **2**:685
sex offender laws, 1:xlviii, 4:1643–1647
    constitutional challenges, **4**:1646–1647
    legislation, **4**:1644–1646
    origin, **4**:1644
Sex Offender Management Assistance (SOMA), **4**:1646
sex offenders, 4:1647–1652
    characteristics, **4**:1648–1650
    history, **4**:1648–1649
    predisposing factors, **4**:1650–1651
    tests, **4**:1651
    triggering and inhibiting factors, **4**:1651
sexual abuse
    incest and, **2**:827
    reports on prison conditions, **4**:1539–1540
Sexual Behavior in the Human Female, **1**:14
Sexual Behavior in the Human Male, **1**:14
sexual harassment, 4:1652–1657
    complaints, **4**:1654
    court cases, **4**:1655–1657
    defined, **4**:1652
    male victims, **4**:1655
    research, **4**:1654–1655
    types, **4**:1652–1654
Shaffer, Anthony, **3**:1032
shaken baby syndrome (SBS), **1**:225
Shakespeare, William, **3**:1031, **4**:1884
Shakur, Sanyika, **1**:85
Shakur, Tupac, **3**:1169, **3**:1170
shaming and shunning, 4:1657–1660
    banishment, **4**:1659–1660
    public exposure penalties, **4**:1657–1658
    public humiliation, **4**:1658–1659
Shanley, Mary A., **1**:*452*
Shapiro, Gurrah, **1**:462, **3**:1048
Shapiro, Robert, **1**:99
Sharia law, **1**:17
Sharpton, Al, **4**:*1484*
Shaw, Clifford, **4**:1743, **4**:1849–1850
The Shawshank Redemption, **2**:614
Sheck, Barry, **2**:640
Sheen, Charlie, **2**:476
Sheldon, William, **2**:749
Sheldon v. Sill, **4**:1733–1734
Shelley v. Kraemer, **4**:1831
Shepard, Mathew, **3**:1182, **5**:2410
Shephard, Cecilia, **4**:1988
Sheppard, Marilyn, **3**:1167

Sheppard, Sam, **1:**98–99, **2:**576, **4:**1660–1661
Sheppard v. Maxwell, **2:**564, **4:**1661–1662
    facts, **4:**1661
    freedom of speech and press, **4:**1661–1662
    holding, **4:**1662
Sherbert v. Verner, **4:**1753
sheriffs, 4:1592, **4:**1662–1666
    American west, **4:**1663–1664
    current, **4:**1664–1666
    English, **4:**1662–1663
Sherman, John, **2:**682
Sherman, Lawrence W., **5:**2423
Sherman, William Tecumseh, **2:**682
Sherman Antitrust Act of 1890, 1:52–53, **1:**267–268, **2:**741, **4:**1666–1668, **4:**1927
    challenges and implications, **4:**1667–1668
    Rule of Reason, **4:**1667
    trustees, **4:**1667
    United States v. E. C. Knight Company and, **4:**1842–1843
Sherman Silver Purchase Act, **2:**741
Shields, Henry, **1:**166, **1:**316
Shimin, Symeon, **4:***1644*
Shocks-the-Conscience rule, **1:**61
Shohara, Jimmie, **2:***876*
The Shootist, **4:**1884
shoplifting, **4:**1562–1563
Short, Elizabeth, **3:**1166, **3:***1168*
Short, James F., **1:**376
sibling incest, **2:**826–827
Sickles, Daniel Edgar, **4:**1829
Siegel, Bugsy, **2:**881, **2:**882, **3:**986, **3:**1048
Sierra Club, **2:**488, **2:**630
Sierra Club v. Morton, **2:**488
signal intelligence (SIGINT), **2:**555–556
The Silence of the Lambs, **2:**614
Silent Spring (Carson), **2:**488, **2:**543
Silent Witness Project, **2:**481
silver-platter doctrine, **4:**1737–1738
Simmel, Georg, **1:**411
Simon & Schuster, **2:**467
Simpson, Nicole Brown, **1:**98, **2:**482, **2:**575, **4:**1892–1893
Simpson, O. J., 1:217, **2:**482, **2:**574, **4:**1668–1670
    acquittal, **1:**xlviii
    F. Lee Bailey and, **1:**98–99
    guilty verdict, **2:**575–576
    imprisonment, **4:**1669
    LAPD and, **3:**1252
    trial, **4:**1668–1669
Sims, Lee, **1:**64

Sims, Thomas, **1:**22
sin, 4:1670–1675
    in America, **4:**1673
    defined, **4:**1670–1671
    reemergence, **4:**1673–1674
    sociology of, **4:**1671–1673
Sin by Silence, **2:**477
Sin in the Second City (Abbott), **2:**567
Sinclair, Upton, **1:**46, **3:**1469
Sing Sing Correctional Facility, 2:518, **2:**765, **4:**1675–1677
    brutality history, **4:**1676
    reform attempts, **4:**1676
    riots, **4:**1676
    20,000 Years in Sing Sing, **2:**622
Singer, Peter, **1:**420
Sirhan, Sirhan, 1:xlvi, **2:**949, **4:**1677–1678
Sister Carrie (Dreiser), **1:**46
sit-ins (1960), **1:**27
Sitting Bull, **3:**1197
situational crime prevention, **1:**394–395
1600 to 1776
    criminal procedures and policing in England, **5:**1991–1995
    criminal procedures in colonies, **5:**2001–2004
    policing in colonies, **5:**2000–2001
    punishment in colonies, **5:**2004–2007
    substantive criminal law in colonies, **5:**1995–2000
16th Street Baptist Church bombing, **1:**xlv, **1:**31
Sixth Amendment, **1:**30, **1:**58
    criminal prosecution, **1:**123
    defendant's rights and, **1:**440–442, **2:**552
    defense lawyer, **1:**123
    right to counsel standard, **1:**319, **1:**327, **1:**364, **3:**1001–1002
    right to fair trial, **1:**326, **2:**563, **5:**2038
Sizemore, Tom, **2:**574
Skilling, Jeffrey, **2:**540–541
Skinner, Gurrhus Frederic, **1:**410
Skinner v. Oklahoma, **2:**487, **2:**713
Skinner v. Railway Labor Executives Association, **3:**1178
Skinwalkers (Hillerman), **2:**752
SLA (Symbionese Liberation Army), **2:**575
Slaughter, Bradley, **1:**72
Slaughterhouse Cases, **2:**509, **3:**1115, **3:**1148, **4:**1621, **4:**1686, **5:**2102
slave patrols, 1:xl, **4:**1678–1680
    justification, **4:**1678–1679
    organization, **4:**1679

slavery, 4:1680–1683. *See also* **Dred Scott v. Sandford**
- *Amistad*, 1:176–177
- chattel, 1:21
- children, 1:xxxix
- criminal brutality, 1:23
- *Dred Scott v. Sandford* and, 2:550–551
- early history, 4:1680–1681
- 1801 to 1850, 5:2075–2076
- escaped slaves, 1:xli
- Jamestown, Virginia, 1:xxxix
- kidnapping and, 2:954–955
- literacy and, 1:xl
- James Monroe and, 3:1129
- Franklin Pierce and, 3:1351–1352
- prohibition of, 1:xli
- punishment in, 1:23
- rape and, 1:23
- restraint instruments, 1:22
- in Rhode Island, 1:xxxix
- sanctioning, 1:10
- slave-free discussion, 1:169
- Thirteenth Amendment abolishing, 1:123, 2:551, 4:1682–1683
- torture, 4:1812
- types, 4:1683
- in U.S., 4:1681–1682

slavery, law of, 4:1684–1687, 5:1999–2000. *See also* **Fugitive Slave Act of 1793; Fugitive Slave Act of 1850; state slave codes**
- federal laws, 4:1685–1687
- property and criminal laws, 4:1685
- Slave Codes, 4:1684–1685

SLCC. *See* Southern Christian Leadership Conference (SLCC)
Sleight of Hand, 3:1026, 3:1032
Slesers, Anna, 1:449
Sleuth, 3:1032
Slidell, John, 4:1882
Smart, Elizabeth, 1:xlix
Smith, Anthony David, 1:103
Smith, Edward, 1:74
Smith, Harold Rossfields, 2:534–535
Smith, Hoke, 1:74
Smith, Jess W., 2:739
Smith, Joseph, 1:121, 2:817, 2:818
Smith, Lamar, 2:584
Smith, Ormond G., 2:467
Smith, Perry, 2:940
Smith, Susan, 2:477, **4:1687–1689**, 4:1957
- conviction, 4:1688–1689
- trial, 4:1688

Smith, William Kennedy, 1:217
Smith Act, 1:445–446, **4:1689–1690**
Smith v. Allwright, 4:1622
Smith v. Doe, 4:1646
Smithsonian Institution, 1:178
smuggling, **4:1690–1694**
- history, 4:1691–1693
- human, 4:1693
- points of entry, 4:1691
- technological advances, 4:1693

Snapped, 4:1765
SNCC (Student Nonviolent Coordinating Committee), 1:131, 2:882
Snyder, Gary, 4:1600
Snyder, Ruth, 1:xliii, 3:1244, **4:1694–1695**
social constructionist perspective, 3:1256–1257
social contract theory, 1:381, 3:1139
social control and environmental theories, 4:1801–1802
Social Darwinism, 1:170, 1:409, 4:1967, 5:2162
social disorganization theory, 1:380, 2:927, 3:1163–1164, 4:1850
social learning theory, 2:503
social process theories, 2:927
Social Reality of Crime (Quinney), 4:1503
socialism, 1:297
socialist law legal tradition, 1:297
socialist libertarianism, 3:1008
Socialist Worker's Party, 2:785
society
- Camden, New Jersey, 1:198–199
- Legal Aid Society, 1:57
- Newark, New Jersey, 3:1240
- private detectives and, 3:1425
- Supreme Court Historical Society, 1:178
- Washington Total Abstinence Society, 1:79

sociology
- of burglary, 1:185–186
- of child abuse, 1:230–232
- of corruption, 1:351–354
- of domestic violence, 2:482–486
- of drug abuse and addiction, 2:502–504
- of gangs, 2:675–679
- of juvenile corrections, 2:913–916
- of juvenile delinquency, 2:925–929
- of murder, 3:1160–1165
- of organized crime, 3:1305–1311
- of police, 3:1367–1368
- of political crimes, 3:1386–1389
- of prostitution, 3:1460–1464
- or rape, 4:1501–1505

of religion and crime, 4:1532–1536
of robbery, 4:1565–1568
of sin, 4:1671–1673
of white-collar crime, 4:1931–1936
of women criminals, 4:1964–1970
sodomy, 1:157–158, **4:1695–1697,** 5:1999
ACLU and, 2:812–813
American laws and, 4:1695–1697
Biblical definition, 4:1695
English Common Law and, 4:1695
greater tolerance, 4:1697
Idaho, 2:812
Soering, Jens, 1:435
soft on crime, 2:476
Soledad Brother (Jackson, G.), 4:1603
Solem v. Helm, 1:416
Solitary Confinement, 3:1032
Solomon, 1:120
SOMA (Sex Offender Management Assistance), 4:1646
Sooners, 1:70
The Sopranos, 3:1218, 4:1765
Sotomayer, Sonia, 1:362
The Soul of a Cop (Ragonese), 3:1094
Souter, David, 1:188, 1:249
South Carolina, 4:1697–1699
Court of Common Pleas, 1:359
crime, 4:1698–1699
Negro Act, 1:xxxix–xl
police and punishment, 4:1697–1698
South Dakota, 4:1699–1701
crime, 4:1701
police, 4:1700
punishment, 4:1700
Wounded Knee incident, 4:1701
South Dakota State Penitentiary, 4:1701
Southern Christian Leadership Conference (SLCC), 1:128
Southland, 4:1774
Southwick, Alfred Porter, 2:524
Spanish Civil Code, 1:284
Spano v. New York, 1:161
Sparf v. United States, 2:900
speakeasies, 3:1133
special needs offenders, 1:341–342
Special Weapons and Tactics (SWAT), 2:584
Speck, Richard, 1:xlv–xlvi, 2:576, 2:749, 2:782
Spector, Phil, 2:575
Speed, 2:619
Speed, James, 3:1012
Spellbound, 1:99

Spence, Gerry, 4:1586
Spicy Detective, 2:467
Spies, August, 1:xli
Spillane, Mickey, 2:468, **4:1702–1703**
awards, 4:1702
early life, 4:1702
publications, 4:1702–1703
sports betting, 1:xlvii
Spotswood, Alexander, 1:294
Springer, William, 2:905
Springville City v. Thomas, 2:899
spy identification, 2:556
squad cars, 1:85
SROs (self-regulatory organizations), 4:1616
St. Clair, Arthur, 1:251
St. Louis, Missouri, 4:1703–1704
crime, 4:1703–1704
gangs, 4:1704
Mafia, 4:1703–1704
St. Valentine's Day massacre, 1:211, 2:863, 3:1156
Stack v. Boyle, 1:94, 1:96, 1:364, 4:1830
Stamp Act of 1765, 1:45, 2:760, **4:1704–1705**
Stamp Act Protests, 4:1552
Stanberry, Henry, 3:1120
***Standard Oil Co. of New Jersey v. United States,*
4:1706–1707**
background, 4:1706
ruling, 4:1706–1707
Standard Oil Trust, 1:267
Stanford v. Kentucky, 1:416, 1:418, 5:2458
Stanton, M., 5:2103
stare decisis, 1:283, 2:959, 4:1844
Starr, Belle, 2:938, 3:1192
Starr, Henry, 1:63–64
Starr Report, 2:566
Starskey and Hutch, 4:1766, 4:1770
Startling Stories, 2:467
Stassen, Harold, 1:177
State Blue Laws, 4:1707–1711
colonial, 4:1708–1709
current repeal, 4:1711
evolution, 4:1709–1711
historical context, 4:1708
State Line Mob, 1:31
The State of the Prisons (Howard), 2:762, 3:1476, 4:1536
state police, 4:1711–1715
future, 4:1715
jurisdiction, 4:1713–1714
primary agencies, 4:1712–1713
State Prison of New York (Eddy, T.), 2:520

state slave codes, 4:1684–1685, **4:1715–1718**
    influential, 4:1717–1718
    revisions, 4:1718
    themes, 4:1715–1717
State v. Baker, 2:486
State v. Burris, 2:738
State v. Butchek, 2:738
State v. Ciskie, 2:486
State v. Heitman, 4:1718–1719
State v. Maner, 1:24
State v. Mann, 1:22, 4:1684
State v. Oliver, 2:483
State v. Searles, 4:1828
State v. Wanrow, 2:481
Statute of Westminster, 1:xxxix, 1:91–92
Stauder v. West Virginia, 1:255
Stead, William T., 1:220, 2:567
Stearns, Junius Brutus, 5:2000
Steenburgh, Sam, 4:1720
Steinauer, Jody, 1:7
Steinbeck, John, 1:314, 2:635
Steinberg, Laurence, 1:233
Steiner, Hillel, 3:1007
Stenberg v. Carhart, 1:6
Stephen, Ann S., 2:465
Stephenson, D. C., 2:835–836
Steve Wilkos, 4:1765
Stevens, John Paul, 2:488
Stevens, Thaddeus, 2:885
Stewart, John, 5:*2040*
Stewart, Martha, 2:575, 4:1617, 4:1923–1925
Stewart, Potter, 1:207, 2:488, 2:713, 2:714
Stewart, Raymond, 1:315
Stillwell, Frank, 2:515–516
Stinney, George Junius, Jr., 1:341
stock market manipulation, 4:1928
stocks, 5:2005
Stokes, Carl, 1:275
Stone, Harlan Fiske, 5:2213
Stono's Rebellion, 1:24
Stop the Robberies, Enjoy Safe Streets (STRESS), 1:459
Storer, Horatio, 1:3
Storey, Moorfield, 3:1180
The Story of My Life (Darrow), 1:429
Stout, Rex, 3:1016, 3:1018–1019
Stover, Leroy, 1:128
strain theory, 2:503–504, 2:927, 4:1502
Stranger in Two Worlds (Harris, J.), 1:84
Strauder v. West Virginia, 4:1721–1722
    antidiscrimination, 4:1721
    jury makeup, 4:1721

Strayer, Frank, 2:623
Street Corner Society (Whyte), 2:676–677
STRESS (Stop the Robberies, Enjoy Safe Streets), 1:459
Strickland v. Washington, 1:442
strikes, 1:xli–xlii, 3:1088, **4:1722–1727**
    Colorado United Mine Workers, 1:295
    Great Railroad Strike of 1877, 1:106, 1:220, 2:747
    Great Railway Strike of 1922, 2:739
    Homestead Strike, 2:741
    labor, 4:1722–1724
    legislation, 4:1725
    prisons, 4:1726–1727
    Pullman Strike of 1894, 1:220, 1:272–273
    rent, 4:1726
    strikebreaking and rats, 4:1724–1725
    student, 4:1727
    syndicalism, 4:1725–1726
strip searching, 4:1741
Stromberg, Elvera, 1:177
Strong Poison (Sayers), 3:1017
Stroud, Robert ("Birdman of Alcatraz"), 1:xliii, 2:776
Stroughton, William, 1:359
structural conflict theory, 3:1387
structural dysfunctionalism, 3:1387
Stuart, Carol, 1:152
Stuart, Charles, 1:152
Stuart, John, 4:1878
Stuart, W. M., 4:1837
Student Nonviolent Coordinating Committee (SNCC), 1:131, 2:882
student strikes, 4:1727
Students for Democratic Society and the Weathermen, 2:785, **4:1727–1729**
    founding, 4:1728
Sturgis, Frank, 4:1916
subculture theories, 1:380
subject-matter jurisdiction, 2:901
Subway Vigilante, 2:577
Successful Techniques for Criminal Trials (Bailey, F. L., Rothblatt), 1:99
Sue, Eugene, 1:173
sui generis, 4:1672
Sullivan, Timothy Daniel ("Big Tim"), 2:862
Sumerian Code of Ur-Nammu Lipit-Ishtar, 1:282
Summers, Robert, 4:1589
The Sun, 3:1243–1244
Sun Tzu, 2:556
supermales, 2:749

supermax prisons, 1:277, 4:1538–1539, **4:1729–1731**
  automated institutions, 4:1729
    challenges to, 4:1730–1731
    development, 4:1730
superpredators, 2:931
Supplemental Environmental Projects (SEPs), 2:548
Support Our Law Enforcement and Safe Neighborhoods Act, 1:xlix
Supremacy Clause, 1:2
Supreme Court, U.S., 1:xlvi–xlviii, **4:1731–1737.**
  See also specific cases
    on Bill of Rights, 1:xl
    Burger court, 4:1735
    capital punishment and, 1:206–209
    Civil Rights Act of 1875 challenge, 1:262–263
    court of last resort, 1:363
    on death penalty, 1:xlvi, 1:xlvii
    William O. Douglas appointment, 1:487–488
    electronic surveillance and, 2:528
    on expert testimony, 1:xliii
    final authority on Constitution, 1:xli, 1:327–328
    function and procedures, 4:1731–1732
    on guns and violent crime, 2:726
    habeas corpus restrictions, 2:728
    on indigent defendants, 1:xlv
    James Madison and, 3:1054–1055
    judicial review, 1:285–286
    legitimacy in *Marbury v. Madison,* 3:1070
    on lethal injection, 1:xlviii
    on loitering, 1:xlviii
    Marshall court, 4:1732–1733
    power over state courts, 1:xl
    Rehnquist court, 4:1735–1736
    on right to marital privacy, 1:xlv
    Roberts court, 4:1736
    on school integration, 1:xliv
    on search warrants, 1:xlii, 1:xliv
    on segregation, 1:xlii
    on self-recrimination, 1:xlv
    Supreme Court Historical Society, 1:178
    from Taney to Vinson, 4:1733–1734
    Warren court, 4:1734–1735, 4:1953
    writ of certiorari, 1:55
Suriani, Valentina, 1:114
Surrat, Mary, 1:143
surveillance. *See also* **electronic surveillance**
  Central Intelligence Agency (CIA), 3:1377
  cold war, 3:1377
  domestic, 3:1383–1385
  FBI illegal, 3:1377
  Federal Intelligence Surveillance Act (FISA), 1:190, 1:213, 2:559
  Federal Intelligence Surveillance Court (FISC), 1:213
  Foreign Intelligence Surveillance Act (FISA), 2:528, 3:1384
    racism and, 4:1487–1488
  Terrorist Surveillance Program (TSP), 1:190, 2:528, 2:802
suspect's rights, 2:851–852, **4:1737–1742**
  assistance of counsel, 4:1740–1741
  exclusionary rule, 4:1737–1739
  interrogation, 4:1739–1740
  strip searching, 4:1741
Sutherland, Edward Hardin, 4:1921–1922
Sutherland, Edwin, **4:1742–1743**
  influence on criminology, 4:1742–1743
  sociological criminologist, 4:1742–1743
Swango, Joseph Michael, 1:xlviii
SWAT (Special Weapons and Tactics), 2:584
Swayne, Noah Haynes, 3:1011
Sweet, Osian, 1:429, 1:458–459
Swinney, Everette, 2:538
Swiss Civil Code, 1:284
Symbionese Liberation Army (SLA), 2:575
symbolic interactionist perspective
  of murder, 3:1164–1165
  of rape, 4:1504–1505
Symmes, John Cleves, 1:251
syndicalism, 4:1725–1726
Szent-Gyorgi, Albert, 4:1749

T

Tactical Infrastructure Program (TIP), 1:150
Taft, William Howard (administration of), 1:42, 1:43, 1:201, 1:267, 2:943, **4:1745–1746**
  as Chief Justice, 4:176
  political choices, 4:1745–1746
Tahash, Ralph, 3:1221
Taiping Rebellion, 1:243
Takao Ozawa, 2:875
Take Back the Night, 2:481
Talbert, Martin, 2:634
A Tale of Two Cities (Dickens), 3:1015
Talley v. Stephens, 1:335, 3:1419
Talton v. Mayes, 3:1203
Tammany Hall
  corruption, 1:347
  Devery and, 1:460
  Irish Americans and, 2:861–862
  leaders, 1:462

Taney, Roger B., 2:488–490, 3:1011, 4:1686, 4:1733–1734
Tarbell, Ida M., 4:*1707*, 5:2168
Tarnower, Herman, 1:84
A Taste of Power (Brown, E.), 1:83
Tate, Lionel, 1:233
Tate, Sharon, 2:*576*, 3:1067
Taussig, Helen Brooke, 1:4
tax crimes, 4:1746–1751
    Internal Revenue Service and, 4:1750
    in popular culture, 4:1750
    tax amnesty, 4:1750
    tax evasion, 2:842–843, 4:1747
    tax protesters, 4:1748–1750
    transfer pricing and corporate crime, 4:1747–1748
Taxpayer Compliance Measurement Program (TCMP), 4:1747
Taylor, Tom, 3:1022, 3:1031–1032
Taylor, Zachary (administration of), 2:611, **4:1751–1752**
    death of, 4:1752
    moderation and compromise, 4:1751–1752
    Whig Party, 4:1751–1752
Taylor v. Louisiana, 2:512
***Taylor v. State*, 4:1752–1754**
Taylor v. Taintor, 1:95
TCMP (Taxpayer Compliance Measurement Program), 4:1747
Tea Act of 1773, 1:45, **4:1754–1755**
Tea Parties, 3:1007, 3:1009, 4:1882
Teach, Edward, 5:1998
Teapot Dome Scandal, 1:348, 2:739–740
technology, police, 4:1755–1761
    community policing era, 4:1757–1758
    databases, 4:1760
    DNA analysis, 4:1758
    Google Earth, 4:1760
    GPS, 4:1759–1760
    laser cameras, 4:1760
    overview, 4:1755–1756
    private detectives and, 3:1424
    professional model era, 4:1756–1757
    reform and enforcement, 4:1510–1511
    smuggling, 4:1691
    at trials, 4:1828–1829
    21st-century innovations, 4:1760–1761
    video cameras, 4:1760
    x-ray devices, 4:1760
Teflon Don, 2:701
telecommunications fraud, 2:646–647
telegraph, 2:527
Telemarketing Fraud Prevention Act, 4:1615
television, crime in, 4:1761–1767
    police procedurals, 4:1762–1763
    representation of criminal justice system, 4:1761–1762
    representation of criminals, 4:1763–1766
    representation of victims, 4:1766
    various genres, 4:1763–1764
    violent and victimless, 4:1763–1764
television, police in, 4:1767–1774
    early shows, 4:1768–1769
    1970s, 4:1769–1770
    2000s, 4:1773–1774
television, punishment in, 4:1774–1778
    Law & Order, Oz, and *Prison Break*, 4:1776–1777
    Lockup and *Inside American Jail*, 4:1776
    Scared Straight, 4:1775
Temperance League, 1:403
Ten Commandments, 4:1670
Ten Most Wanted Fugitives list, 1:xliv, 2:863
Tenderloin police riot, 1:460
Tennessee, 4:1778–1779. See also **Memphis, Tennessee**
    crime, 4:1778–1779
    KKK founded, 1:xli, 4:1778
    police, 4:1778
    punishment, 4:1779
Tennessee v. Garner, 3:1362, 4:1511
Tenth Amendment, 1:12, 1:201
Terminiello v. Chicago, 2:487
Terrell, Robert H., 1:27
territorial jurisdiction, 2:902
terrorism, 1:90, **4:1780–1788.** See also **bin Laden, Osama; bombings; McVeigh, Timothy; Oklahoma City bombing; Al Qaeda; riots; September 11, 2001, terrorist attacks; strikes**
    Antiterrorism and Effective Death Penalty Act of 1996, 2:728
    William Clinton and, 1:277
    computer crime and, 1:389–390
    defined, 4:1780
    deportation and, 1:448
    early in America, 4:1782–1784
    electronic surveillance and, 2:528
    individual action, 4:1785–1786
    interrogation practices, 2:854–855
    IRS and, 2:843
    KKK, 4:1783
    McCarthy hearings, 4:1784

methods, 4:1781–1782
1996 Olympics bombing, 1:74–75
OTFFC, 2:843
purposes, 4:1780–1781
TIA, 1:90
as tool, 4:1782
TSP, 1:190
20th-century America, 4:1784–1785
21st-century America, 4:1786–1787
war on terror, 1:188–190, 2:728, 2:802, 5:2443–2446
Terrorist Information Awareness (TIA), 1:90
Terrorist Surveillance Program (TSP), 1:190, 2:528, 2:802
Terry, David S., 1:59
Terry, Randall, 1:7
Terry v. Ohio, 4:1788–1789
    case, 4:1788
    ruling, 4:1788–1789
Texas, 4:1789–1793
    annexation, 3:1396, 4:1834
    cameras in courtroom, 4:1792
    capital punishment, 4:1790–1791
    crime, 4:1792–1793
    James Byrd, Jr., 4:1792
    reproductive rights and sexual behavior, 4:1791–1792
Texas A&M shooting, 1966, 3:1253
Texas Justice, 4:1765
Texas Rangers, 4:1793–1795
    duties, 4:1794–1795
    history, 4:1793–1794
Texas v. Johnson, 1:188, 2:970
Texas v. Ohio, 1:364
Texas v. White, 4:1795–1796
Thalidomide, 1:xlv, 1:4
Thatcher, Peter Oxenbridge, 3:1432
Thaw, Harry K., 4:1796–1797, 4:1826
theater. *See* literature and theater, crime in; literature and theater, police in; literature and theater, punishment in
Thelma and Louise, 2:615
theories of crime, 4:1797–1803
    biological and psychological, 4:1800–1801
    modern trends, 4:1802–1803
    pre-modern, 4:1798–1800
    social-psychological, 4:1801–1802
Thimm, James, 1:233
The Thin Blue Line, 2:620
The Thin Man (Hammett), 2:733
third degree, 1:193

Thirteenth Amendment, 1:xli, 2:550
    abolishing slavery, 1:123, 2:551, 4:1682–1683
    Civil Rights Act of 1875 and, 1:262–263
    freedoms, 1:261
    passage, 4:1480
31 Bond Street (Horan), 1:423
Thomas, Clarence, 1:28, 1:188, 4:1885
Thomas, Philip Francis, 1:168
Thomas, W. I., 4:1966
Thomas and Wife v. Winchester, 1:371
Thompson, Gilbert, 2:626
Thompson, Jacob, 1:168
Thompson, William Hale, 1:221
Thompson v. McNeil, 1:435
Thompson v. Oklahoma, 1:418
Thoreau, Henry David, 1:259, 4:1749, 4:1784, 4:1803–1804
    comments, 4:1804
    radicalism, 4:1804
Thornburgh v. American College of Obstetricians and Gynecologists, 1:178
Thoughts on Government, 1:11
Thrasher, Frederick, 2:675–676
three card monte, 1:320–321
Three Fifths Compromise, 1:21, 1:24
three strikes law, 1:33, 1:196, 4:1629, 4:1805–1806
Three Years After (Buntline), 1:173
thrill killing, 3:1156, 5:2211
Thrilling Wonder Stories, 2:467
Throop, George, 1:278
TIA (Terrorist Information Awareness), 1:90
TIA (Total Information Awareness), 2:560
Tideman, Nicolaus, 3:1007
Till, Emmett, 1:xliv, 2:584
Tillman Act of 1907, 1:348
Time magazine, 1:83
TIP (Tactical Infrastructure Program), 1:150
Tisdale, E., 4:1887
Tison v. Arizona, 1:208
To Catch a Killer, 2:662
To Kill a Mockingbird, 3:1052, 4:1806–1807
Tocqueville, Alexis de, 1:xl, 1:110–111, 2:764, 4:1807–1808
Tom Jones (Fielding), 1:81
Tombstone, 2:516, 2:653
Tonight Show With Johnny Carson, 1:99
Tonry, Michael, 1:28
Torah, 4:1670
Torrio, John, 1:210, 2:867, 4:1808–1809
Torso Murders, 1:274, 3:1210

torture, 4:1809–1814
    CIA interrogations, 4:1813
    colonial, 4:1811–1812
    defined, 4:1810–1811
    justifications, 4:1811
    methods, 4:1811
    military interrogations, 4:1813
    police and third degree, 4:1812–1813
    slavery and racism, 4:1812
Total Information Awareness (TIA), 2:560
Townshend Acts of 1767, 4:1814–1815
Toxic Substances Control Act (TSCA), 2:545
traffic crimes, 4:1815–1819
    cell phones and, 4:1818
    common offenses, 4:1816–1817
    DUI, 4:1817
    DWI, 4:1817
    in popular culture, 4:1818–1819
    reckless driving, 4:1817–1818
Trail of Tears, 2:833–834, 2:848
train robbery, 2:1122, 2:1284, 4:1561–1563, 4:1977
Training Day, 2:619
training police, 4:1819–1824
    methods, 4:1821–1822
    reasons for, 4:1820–1821
    scope and delivery, 4:1822–1823
Transportation Security Administration (TSA), 2:590
treason, 2:602, 5:1998. *See also* sabotage
Treasury Enforcement Services, 2:780
Treat, Lawrence, 3:1023
Treatise on Man and the Development of His Faculties (Quetelet), 1:408
treatment era of corrections, 1:337
Treaty of Ghent, 1:13
trials, 4:1824–1830
    evolution, 4:1824–1825
    insanity, 4:1829
    jury, 4:1827
    1901 to 1920, 5:2179–2180
    plea bargains, 4:1824
    presentation of evidence, 4:1827–1828
    pretrial proceedings, 4:1827
    public interest, 4:1825–1827
    sentencing, 4:1829–1830
    technology and evidence, 4:1828–1829
Trojan horses, 1:310
Trop v. Dulles, 1:206, 1:416, 2:788
Tropic of Cancer (Miller, H.), 3:1274
Trotsky, Leon, 1:258

Truman, Harry S. (administration of), 1:348, 2:844, 4:1830–1832, 5:2264
    armed forces integration, 1:xliv, 1:27, 1:264
    civil rights and pardons, 4:1831–1832
    Executive Order 9981, 1:xliv
    Federal Employees Loyalty Program, 1:446
    influence in law, 4:1830–18321
    presidential proclamations, 3:1406
trust-busting, 1:268
trusty system, 1:xlvi
Tru-TV (Courtroom Television Network), 1:217
TSA (Transportation Security Administration), 2:590
TSCA (Toxic Substances Control Act), 2:545
TSP (Terrorist Surveillance Program), 1:190, 2:528, 2:802
Tucker Telephone, 1:64
Tufts, John Q., 3:1196
Tugee Cult, 4:1636
Tunstall, John, 1:127
turf wars, 3:1157
Turk, Austin, 1:411
Turner, Nat, 1:24
Turner & Hooch, 2:617
Tuthill, Richard, 2:919
Tutt, David, 3:1123
Tutu, Desmond, 1:344
Twain, Mark, 2:626, 2:704, 5:2174
Twenty Against the Underworld (Dewey, T. E.), 3:1094
20,000 Years in Sing Sing, 2:622
Twenty-first Amendment, 2:492
Twenty-sixth Amendment, 2:523
Twining Albert, 4:1832
Twining v. New Jersey, 1:124, 2:712, 4:1832–1833
Twitter, 2:477, 2:828, 4:1757
2001 to 2012
    evidence-based policing (EBP), 5:2454–2456
    expanding prison populations, 5:2451–2454
    illegal immigrants, 5:2447–2449
    methamphetamine epidemic, 5:2449–2450
    private prison industry, 5:2450–2451
    problem-solving courts and restorative justice, 5:2460–2462
    re-examination of death penalty, 5:2456–2459
    school shootings, 5:2459–2460
    war against terrorism, 5:2443–2446
two-tiered appellate process, 1:55–56
Tyco, 4:1923
Tydings, Joseph, 2:523

Tyler, John (administration of), 4:1833–1835
    ascending to presidency, 4:1833
    Dorr's Rebellion and, 4:1834
    political career, 4:1833–1834
    Texas annexation and, 4:1834
Tyson, Mike, 2:482, 2:575

U

U-2 incident, 2:559
UCC (Uniform Commercial Code), 1:43, 1:285
UCR. *See* Uniform Crime Reporting Program
Uelmen, Gerald, 2:573–574
Ulysses (Joyce), 1:314, 3:1275, 4:1846. *See also United States v. One Book Called* Ulysses
The Unadjusted Girl (Thomas, W. I.), 4:1966
Under and Alone (Queen, W.), 3:1094
Unger, Roberto, 4:1590
UNICEF (United Nations Children's Fund), 1:329
Uniform Code of Military Justice, 5:2446
Uniform Commercial Code (UCC), 1:43, 1:285
Uniform Crime Reporting Program, 1:xliii, 1:179–180, 1:374–375, 4:1835–1838
    categories in, 1:388
    collection, 1:382
    creation, 2:776
    crime statistics interpretation, 4:1837–1838
    data accuracy, 4:1836–1837
    data collection, 1:395–396, 4:1836
    incident-based measures, 4:1838
    as model, 5:2214
    participation, 1:383
    reports, 4:1835
    shortcomings, 2:606
    types of data, 4:1836
Union Pacific Railroad, 2:704
unions, 1:48. *See also specific unions*
    rallies, 1:xli
    strikes, 1:xli–xlii
    sympathizers, 1:xli
    yellow-dog contracts, 1:xlii, 1:xliii, 1:9–10
United Klans of America, 1:31
United Mine Workers, 1:127, 1:295
United Nations Children's Fund (UNICEF), 1:329
United States attorneys, 4:1838–1840
    changes, 4:1840
    evolution, 4:1839–1840
    history, 4:1839

    Judiciary Act of 1789 creating, 4:1839
    overview, 4:1838–1839
United States Code (USC), 1:284, 2:588
United States v. Ballard, 4:1840–1842
    decision and convictions, 4:1841
    I Am movement and, 4:1840–1841
United States v. Booker, 4:1482, 4:1634
United States v. Byrd, 1:58
United States v. Clapox, 1:370
United States v. Classic, 1:261
United States v. Cronic, 3:1004
United States v. Cruikshank, 4:1621
United States v. Doremus, 4:1918
United States v. E. C. Knight Company, 2:696, 4:1707, 4:1842–1843
    majority opinion, 4:1842
    Sherman Antitrust Act and, 4:1842–1843
United States v. Forty Barrels and Twenty Kegs of Coca-Cola, 3:1471
United States v. Hudson and Goodwin, 4:1843–1844
    effect on common law, 4:1844
    no punishment without law, 4:1843–1844
United States v. Jose Santiago, 1:103
United States v. Ju Toy, 1:247
United States v. Lee, 4:1754
United States v. Leon, 1:161
United States v. Lopez, 4:1735
United States v. Michael J. O'Driscoll, 1:103
United States v. Miller, 2:719
United States v. Mottolo, 2:549
United States v. Moylan, 2:900
United States v. Nixon, 4:1844–1846, 4:1917
    doctrine of executive privilege, 4:1845
    unanimous decision, 4:1845
    Watergate tapes and, 4:1844–1845
United States v. One Book Called Ulysses, 4:1846–1847
United States v. One Package, 1:314
United States v. Rabinowitz, 4:1830
United States v. Richard Hicks, 1:103
United States v. Salerno et al., 1:94, 1:97
United States v. Sullivan, 2:842–843
United States v. 31 Photographs, 3:1398
United States v. U.S. District Court, 1:178
United States v. Vuitch, 1:xlvi, 1:5, 4:1573
United States v. Won Kim Ark, 1:247
Universal Declaration of Human Rights, 1:43
University of California, Berkeley
    court cases, 4:1735
    riots, 1:xlv

Unknown, 2:467
Unnatural Death (Sayers), 3:1017
unreasonable searches, 1:326, 2:786
The Untouchables, 1:145, 3:1211
Urban Enterprise Zones, 1:200
urbanization, 4:1847–1852
    characteristics of urban areas, 4:1847–1848
    criminological issues, 4:1848–1849
    environmental issues, 4:1851
    future directions, 4:1852
    juvenile delinquency, 4:1849–1851
    1921 to 1940, 5:2203–2205
    research, 4:1849–1851
    trends, 4:1851–1852
Urschel, Charles F., 2:957
U.S. News and World Report, 1:245
USA PATRIOT Act of 2001, 1:189–190, 2:561, 3:1380, 4:1852–1854
    amending National Information Infrastructure Protection Act, 1:312
    George W. Bush signing, 4:1854
    espionage, 2:561
    increased penalties, 4:1854
    information gathering, 2:792
    information sharing, 4:1853
    passage, 2:802, 5:2443–2444
    restricted persons identified, 4:1853
    search warrants, 4:1853–1854
USA Today, 1:107
USC (United States Code), 1:284, 2:588
Utah, 4:1854–1856
    crime, 4:1854–1856
    police and punishment, 4:1856
utilitarianism, 3:1136, 4:1878, 5:2043–2044

V

V Is for Vengeance (Grafton), 2:702
vagrancy, 4:1857–1859
    application of laws, 4:1858–1859
    defined, 4:1857
    English origins, 4:1857–1858
Valachi, Joseph, 2:689
Valenti, Jody, 1:114
Vallentyne, Peter, 3:1007
Van Dine, S. S., 3:1017
Van Parijs, Philippe, 3:1007
Van Wyck, Robert, 1:460
Vanderbilt, Cornelius, 1:193
Vanzetti, Bartolomeo. *See* **Sacco and Vanzetti**
Vaughan, Peggy, 1:14
Vera Institute service program, 1:306

verdicts
    appeals and, 1:57–58
    O. J. Simpson, 2:575–576
    unanimous, 2:899
Vermont, 4:1859–1861
    crime, 4:1860–1861
    police and punishment, 4:1859–1860
    Vermont Reparative Probationers, 1:306
Vernonia School District v. Acton, 3:1178
vi et armis, 2:489
ViCAP (Violent Criminal Apprehension Program), 4:1643
vice commission, 4:1861–1864
    Chicago, 4:1861–1863
    Louisville, 4:1863
vice reformers, 4:1864–1867
    activities, 4:1864
    Anthony Comstock as, 4:1864–1865
    Chicago commission, 4:1865–1866
    Committee of Fourteen, 4:1865
    Prohibition and, 4:1866–1867
    WCTU as, 4:1865
Vick, Michael, 1:xlviii, 1:135, 1:420
victim rights and restitution, 4:1867–1873
    criticisms, 4:1872–1873
    traditional and punitive, 4:1870–1872
    for women, 4:1868–1870
victimless crime, 1:388–389, 4:1874–1878
    drugs and, 4:1876–1877
    gambling, 4:1876
    homosexuality and, 4:1876
    jaywalking, 4:1877
    prostitution, 4:1874–1875
    state and, 4:1877
victim–offender relationship, 3:1151–1152
victims, 1:428
    burglary, 1:185–186
    crime rate data, 1:396–397
    Crime Victims' Bill of Rights, 1:187
    identity theft advocacy, 2:815–816
    rights, 2:783
    robbery, 4:1563–1564
    victimization surveys, 1:377
    white-collar crime, 4:1935
Victor Metta Fuller, 3:1015
Victoria, Queen, 2:838, 4:1879
Victorian Compromise, 4:1878–1879
    blackmail and, 4:1878
    contradictions, 4:1879
    Darwinism and, 4:1878
    empiricism and, 4:1878

poverty and, 4:1879
vice and, 4:1878–1879
Vietnam War, 2:624
Chicago Seven/Democratic National Convention of 1968, 1:223
clemency and, 1:271
leftists, 3:1006
military police in, 3:1110–1111
vigilantism, 4:1879–1885
American Protective League, 4:1882
boycotts, 4:1883
Civil War era, 4:1881–1882
current quasi activities and impulses, 4:1882–1883
in drama and media, 4:1884
early American, 4:1880–1881
in history of crime and punishment in America: 1850–1900, 2:767–769
Internet, 4:1883–1884
KKK, 4:1881
land pirates, 4:1881
lynchings in, 4:1880
Minuteman Project, 4:1882
overview, 4:1879–1880
Perverted Justice, 4:1883
San Francisco, 4:1599–1600
Subway Vigilante, 2:577
Tea Parties and, 4:1882
World War I, 4:1882
Vignera v. New York, 1:317
Vinson, Fred, 4:1734
Violante, Robert, 1:114
violence, 2:477–478, 3:1190. *See also* **domestic violence, contemporary; domestic violence, history of; domestic violence, sociology of**
Brady Handgun Violence Prevention Act, 2:721, 2:725
factor in robbery, 4:1558–1559
gun, 4:1889–1890
intimate partner, 2:486
management-labor, 2:771
National Coalition against Domestic Violence, 2:481
New Orleans, Louisiana, 3:1224
Oklahoma City bombing, 3:1287
personal, 2:770–771
police, 1:167, 3:1250–1252
political, 3:1224
racial, 2:769–770
against Republican Party, 1:25
youth, 4:1890–1891

Violence Against Women Act of 1994, 2:477–478, 2:481, 3:1190, 4:1885–1886
funding, 5:2412
Omnibus Crime Bill and, 4:1885
passage, 4:1885
restitution clause, 4:1885
Violence Prevention and Services Act, 2:478
Violent Crime Control and Law Enforcement Act of 1994, 1:276, 1:340, 1:388, 5:2416
violent crimes, 1:386–388, 4:1886–1893
gun violence, 4:1889–1890
increase in, 4:1887–1889
KKK, 4:1887
notorious, 4:1891–1893
pre-20th century, 4:1886–1887
rape, 4:1888
Washington, 4:1909
youth, 4:1890–1891
Violent Criminal Apprehension Program (ViCAP), 4:1643
Virginia, 1:xl, 4:1893–1895
children of slaves in, 1:xxxix
crime, 4:1895
Jamestown slavery, 1:xxxix
permanent bondage in, 1:xxxix
police and punishment, 4:1894–1895
Virginia Company, 1:289
Virginia Plan, 1:248
Virginia tech shootings, 1:xlviii
Virginia v. Black, 1:160
Virginia v. Hicks, 1:42
Viterna, Jocelyn S., 3:1007
Vold, Georg, 1:411
Vollmer, August, 2:639, 3:1441, 4:1510, 4:1895–1897
LAPD and, 4:1896
lasting influence, 4:1896
professionalism, 5:2173
service career, 4:1896
O. W. Wilson as protégé, 4:1896
Volstead Act, 1:174, 1:348, 2:492, 2:775, 4:1897–1898
Eighteenth Amendment and, 4:1866, 4:1897
enforcing, 2:589
Prohibition and, 4:1897–1898
repeal efforts, 4:1898
Voltaire, 1:314
von Bulow, Claus, 1:99
von Mises, Ludwig, 3:1006
von Ribbentrop, Joachim, 2:574
Voskerichian, Virginia, 1:114

voting
    African Americans and, **1**:xlv, **1**:24–25
    Fifteenth Amendment and, **2**:551
    Voting Rights Act of 1965, **1**:xlv, **1**:27, **1**:265–266, **2**:552, **4**:1485

W

Wabash, St. Louis & Pacific Railway Company v. Illinois, **1**:xli
Waco siege, 4:1899–1900
Wade, Henry, **4**:1574
Wagner, Mark, **1**:170
Waite, Charles E., **1**:102
Waite, George, **1**:137
Waite, Morrison, **3**:1148, **4**:1734
Walden (Thoreau), **4**:1803–1804
Walker, John Anthony, **2**:559
Walker, Lenore, **2**:481
Walker, Robert J., **1**:168
Walker Report, **1**:224
Wall Street bombing of 1920, **1**:50
Wallace, Edgar, **2**:467
Wallace, George, **1**:128, **4**:1613
Wallace, Henry, **4**:1580
Wallace, Irving, **2**:568
Wallace, Mike, **1**:224
Walling, George, 4:1900–1901
    corruption and, **4**:1901
    public safety and memoir, **4**:1901
Walling, William English, **3**:1179
Walnut Street Jail, 2:763, **3**:1330–1331, **4**:1902–1904, **5**:*2045*, **5**:2046
    model for future, **4**:1903
    opening, **4**:1902–1903
    overcrowding and disruptions, **4**:1903
    reform, **5**:2068–2069
Walsh, John, **3**:1245
Walsh, Lawrence, **2**:566
Walsh, Thomas ("Fatty"), **1**:421, **2**:863
Wambaugh, Joseph, 3:1023–1024, **4**:1904–1905
    awards, **4**:1905
    novels, **4**:1904–1905
    screenplays, **4**:1905
war on drugs, **2**:522, **2**:589, **3**:1008
    George H. W. Bush and, **1**:187
    Richard Nixon and, **3**:1177
    women criminals and, **4**:1961–1962
war on poverty, **5**:2345–2351
war on terror, **1**:188–190, **2**:728, **2**:802, **5**:2443–2446
War Revenue Act of 1919, **2**:719
Ward, Nathaniel, **1**:136, **1**:141

Warden v. Hayden, **1**:161
Warehousing era of corrections, **1**:337
Warren, Earl, 1:109, **1**:124, **1**:161, **2**:488, **4**:1905–1907
    Brown v. Board of Education and, **1**:166, **1**:264
    civil rights legislation, **4**:1906
    fairness and interpretation of law, **4**:1906–1907
    Japanese internment camps and, **4**:1905–1906
    Miranda v. Arizona and, **1**:317–318, **2**:552
    Supreme Court under, **4**:1734–1735, **4**:1953
    on voiding convictions, **2**:786
Warren, Josiah, **1**:48, **4**:1784
Warren Commission, **1**:xlv, **2**:946, **4**:1907
Warwickshire Quarter Sessions, **2**:910
Washington, 4:1907–1909
    capital punishment, **4**:1907–1908
    law enforcement, **4**:1907
    violent crimes, **4**:1909
Washington, D.C., 4:1909–1914
    background of crime, **4**:1910
    culture, **4**:1913
    mapping crime, **4**:1910–1912
    migration and, **4**:1912–1913
    research, **4**:1912
Washington, George (administration of), 1:12, **1**:38, **3**:1212, **4**:1914–1915, **5**:*2000*
    federalist view, **2**:586
    Fugitive Slave Act of 1793, **2**:656
    military service, **4**:1914–1915
    presidential proclamations, **3**:1403–1404
    spies employed, **2**:557
    Whiskey Rebellion and, **4**:1915, **5**:*2039*
Washington, Raymond, **3**:1169
Washington Post, **1**:187, **1**:349
Washington Total Abstinence Society, **1**:79
watchmen, **5**:2071
Watergate, 2:559, **2**:624, **4**:1915–1917, **5**:2356–2358
    arrest and investigation, **4**:1915–1916
    break in, **1**:182, **2**:565
    case study, **1**:182
    corruption example, **1**:349
    CREEP and, **4**:1916
    Deep Throat, **4**:1916
    espionage, **2**:559
    Richard Nixon resignation, **4**:1917
    White House tapes, **4**:1916–1917
Watkins, James K., **1**:459
Watts riots, 1965, **1**:xlv, **1**:28, **2**:785, **4**:1554
Watts v. Indiana, **1**:167
Watts v. United States, **1**:38
Waugh, Hillary, **3**:1025

Wayne, James M., **2:**490
Wayne, John, **2:**651, **4:**1880, **4:**1884
Wayward Puritans (Erikson), **4:**1672
WCTU (Woman's Christian Temperance Union), **2:**491–492, **4:**1865
We Can Prevent Crime (Cummings), **1:**421
Weathermen, The. *See* Students for a Democratic Society and the Weathermen
Weaver, Randy, **1:**175, **2:**577, **3:**1378, **4:**1585–1586
Webb, Jack, **4:**1766, **4:**1768–1769
***Webb v. United States*, 2:743, 2:778, 4:1917–1918**
    arguments, **4:**1918
    case details, **4:**1918
Weber, Max, **4:**1672
Weber Lois, **2:**621
Webster v. Reproductive Health Services, **1:**6
Weeks, Kevin, **1:**151, **2:**863
***Weeks v. United States*, 3:1067, 4:1511, 4:1734, 4:1737, 4:1919–1920**
    background, **4:**1919
    exclusionary rule, **1:**364
    Fourth Amendment and, **4:**1919
    unlawful search and seizure, **1:**xliv, **4:**1919–1920
Weems, Charlie, **4:**1613
Weems v. United States, **1:**416
Weil, Joseph ("Yellow Kid"), **1:**82
Weinberg, Jack, **1:**195
Weinberger, Casper, **1:**350
Weird Tales, **2:**467
Weiss, Emanuel ("Mendy"), **3:***1003*, **3:***1303*
Welfare Reform Act, **4:**1974
Wells, Alice Stebbins, **3:**1370
Wells, Ida B., **2:**818
Welsh v. Wisconsin, **1:**161
Wen Ho Lee, **1:**246, **2:**560
West, Mae, **3:**1274
West, Rosemary, **4:**1957
West Coast Hotel v. Parrish, **2:**510, **4:**1734
West Side Story, **4:**1890
West Virginia, 4:1920–1921
    crime, **4:**1921
    police and punishment, **4:**1920–1921
West Virginia State Board of Education v. Barnette, **1:**60, **4:**1753
Western Federation of Mines, **2:**812
Westinghouse, George, **2:**524–525
Westover v. United States, **1:**317
Wetumpka State Penitentiary, **1:**30
"What Gay Studies Taught the Court," **3:**993
"What Works?", **5:**2358

WHBA (Wild Free-Roaming Horse and Burro Act), **2:**546
Wheatley, Phillis, **1:**21
Wheelbarrow Law, **1:**xl, **2:**762
When the Husband Is the Suspect (Bailey, F. L.), **1:**99
Whig Party, **1:**167, **2:**830, **4:**1751–1752
whipping, **1:**335
Whiskey Rebellion, **4:**1748, **5:**2038
    Alexander Hamilton and, **2:**732
    moonshine, **3:**1131–1132
    George Washington and, **4:**1915, **5:***2039*
Whiskey Ring scandal, **1:**347, **2:**704
White, Byron, **1:**157–158, **1:**207, **2:**713, **4:**1570, **4:**1575
White, Fred, **1:**162
White, William, **2:**516
white extremism, **2:**538
White Hand Gang, **1:**210, **5:**2173
White Slave Traffic Act, **1:**xlii, **1:**201, **3:**1064, **4:**1582
white supremacy, **1:**30
white-collar crime, contemporary, 1:389, 2:532, 4:1921–1926
    Jack Abramoff, **4:**1925
    coining, **4:**1921–1922
    Enron, Worldcom, Tyco, Adelphia, **4:**1923
    fraud and Martha Stewart, **4:**1923–1925
    illegal prescription drugs and file swapping, **4:**1922–1923
    Bernie Madoff, **4:**1925
white-collar crime, history of, 4:1926–1931, 5:2416
    antidiscrimination violations, **4:**1931
    antitrust violation, **4:**1927–1928
    environmental crime, **4:**1930–1931
    fraud, **4:**1926–1927
    labor exploitation, **4:**1931
    medical fraud, **4:**1929–1930
    Sherman Antitrust Act of 1890, **4:**1927
    stock market manipulation, **4:**1928
white-collar crime, sociology of, 4:1931–1936
    defined, **4:**1932
    research, **4:**1934–1935
    theories, **4:**1935–1936
    types, **4:**1932–1934
    victims, **4:**1935
Whitewater scandal, **2:**566
Whitman, Walt, **5:**2110
Whitney, Anita, **1:**195
***Whitney v. California*, 1:159, 1:160, 4:1936–1937**
Whittier, John Greenleaf, **2:**569
whore/Madonna duality, **4:**1966
Whyos, **2:**862

Whyte, William, 2:676–677
Wickard v. Filburn, 2:944
Wickersham, George, 2:582, 4:1707, 4:1937–1939, **4:1937–1939**
   early life, 4:1937
   National Commission on Law Observance and Enforcement, 4:1938
   political life, 4:1938
Wickersham Commission, 2:705, 2:775, 2:806–807, 4:1510, **4:1939–1941**
   cost and measurement of crime, 4:1939–1940
   delinquency and, 4:1940
   immigration and foreign born, 4:1940
   impact, 4:1941
   Mooney-Billings case, 4:1941
   penal institutions, probation, parole, 4:1940
   policing, 4:1940–1941
   Prohibition and, 4:1939
   prosecution and courts, 4:1940
Wide Awakes, 2:767
wife abuse, 2:484
wife battering, 2:484
WikiLeaks, 1:310
Wild West
   1851 to 1900, 5:2103–2105
   frontier crime, 2:653–654
   history of crime and punishment in America: 1850–1900, 2:769
   posses, 3:1400–1402
   sheriffs, 4:1663–1664
Wilde, Kathy, 1:157
Wilde, Oscar, 1:314
Wilderness Act of 1964, 2:546–547
Wild Free-Roaming Horse and Burro Act (WHBA), 2:546
Wilkes, George, 3:1191
Wilkie, John, 5:2167
Wilkins, Roy, 3:*1180*
William III, 1:289, 1:294
Williams, Eugene, 4:1613
Williams, Roger, 2:759, 3:1473
Williams, Wayne, 1:74
Williams, William E., 1:423
Williams v. Florida, 2:897
Wilson, Colin, 1:84
Wilson, Floyd, 1:63
Wilson, Francis, 1:23
Wilson, James Q., 1:xlvii, 1:87–88, 1:248, 2:749, **4:1941–1943**
   broken windows theory, 4:1942
   crime causes, 4:1942

   reformer, 4:1514
   theories in action, 4:1942–1943
Wilson, John, 2:733
Wilson, O. W., 1:222, 3:1367, 3:1441, 4:1510, **4:1943–1944**
   in Chicago, 4:1944
   influence and writing, 4:1944
   military and academic service, 4:1943–1944
   as Vollmer protégé, 4:1896
Wilson, Woodrow (administration of), 1:267, 2:562, **4:1945–1946**
   narcotics law, 2:742
   presidential proclamations, 3:1405–1406
   Prohibition and, 4:1946
   during World War I, 4:1945–1946
Wilson v. State, 1:430
Winant, Howard, 4:1486
Wines, Enoch Cobb, 3:1186, 4:1536, 5:2111
Winter, Howie, 2:863
Winter Hill Gang, 1:151, 2:863–864
Winthrop, John, 3:1472, 4:1696
Winthrop, Wait Still, 1:359
The Wire, 1:108, 4:1770, 4:1773–1774
wiretapping, 2:527–528
Wirt, William, 2:696, 2:904
Wirth, Louis, 4:1848
Wirz, Henry, 1:*205*, 5:2100
Wisconsin, **4:1946–1948**
   corrections, 4:1947
   serial killers, 4:1947–1948
   Supreme Court, 1:2
Wisconsin v. Yoder, 4:1754
witch hunts, 2:559
Witch of Staten Island, 1:137
Witherspoon v. Illinois, 5:2355
Within the Law, 2:621
Without a Doubt (Clark, M.), 3:1095
Without a Trace, 4:1762, 4:1767
Without Sanctuary, 3:1052
Witness for the Prosecution (Christie), 3:1030
Witness Protection Act, 4:1870
witness testimony, **4:1948–1952**
   accuracy, 4:1949
   factors affecting, 4:1949–1950
   overview, 4:1948–1949
   race and memory, 4:1950–1951
   wrongful convictions, 4:1951–1952
Witz, Henry, 1:*205*
Wolf, Dick, 4:1766

Wolf v. Colorado, 3:1067–1068, 4:1738, 4:1830–1831, **4:1952–1953**
    Fourth Amendment and, 4:1952–1953
    majority opinion, 4:1953
Wolff v. McDonnell, 2:889
Wolfgang, Marvin, 2:492, 2:825
Woman's Christian Temperance Union (WCTU), 2:491–492, 4:1865
women, 1:xlviii, 1:6, 1:121, 2:684–685. *See also* **abortion; Bedford Hills Correctional Facility; police, women as**
    as chattel, **1:**371
    citizen participation on juries, **1:**256
    civil rights, **4:**1495–1496
    CWAA, **2:**477
    Declaration of Independence and, **2:**550
    juvenile corrections and, **2:**914–915
    Married Women's Property Act of 1869, **1:**371
    National Organization for Women, **1:**5
    National Violence Against Women Survey, **4:**1496
    National Women's Party, **1:**372
    NAWSA, **1:**259–260
    New York prisons, **3:**1233
    prisoners, **1:**111–112
    property rights, **1:**371
    in punishment film, **2:**623
    rights, **1:**405
    victim rights and restitution, **4:**1868–1870
    Violence Against Women Act, **2:**477–478, **2:**481
    wife abuse, **2:**484
    wife battering, **2:**484
    WIP, **2:**623
    womanhood, **2:**463
    women's movements, **2:**480–481, **2:**782
women criminals, contemporary, 4:1954–1957
    activity and justice response patterns, 4:1955
    crimes of, 4:1955–1956
    debates and solutions, 4:1956–1957
    historical context, 4:1954
women criminals, history of, 4:1957–1964.
  See also **Borden, Lizzie; Wuornos, Aileen; Yates, Andrea**
    drinking and, 4:1960–19601
    early crimes, 4:1958–1959
    early traditions, 4:1958
    gender-specific crimes, 4:1962–1964
    war on drugs and, 4:1961–1962
    witch hunts, 4:1959–1960
women criminals, sociology of, 4:1964–1970
    colonial theories, 4:1964–1965
    contemporary theories, 4:1969
    corrections and women, 4:1968–1969
    19th century theories, 4:1965–1966
    Social Darwinism, 4:1967
    20th century theories, 4:1966–1968
women in prison, 2:623, 4:1970–1976
    contemporary picture, 4:1971–1972
    drugs/trauma/mental health, 4:1972–1973
    experiences, 4:1972–1973
    history, 4:1970–1971
    mothers, 4:1973
    prisoner reentry and collateral consequences, 4:1973–1975
Women Without Names, 2:623
Women's Advocates, 2:480
Won Kim Ark v. United States, 1:244
Wonders of the Invisible World (Mather, I.), 1:360
Wong, Barbara Uphouse, 2:745
Wong Sun v. United States, 4:1738
Wood, William, 1:357, 4:1614
Woodson v. North Carolina, 1:207, 1:287, 1:416
Woodward, Bob, 1:349
Woolsey, John, 4:1846
Worcester v. Georgia, 2:833
Wordcom, 4:1923
Work, Monroe, 1:25–26
workplace robbery, 4:1567–1568
World Health Organization, 2:503
World Trade Center, 1:175, 1:277, 2:585, 3:1385
World War I
    German Americans during, 2:695
    political crimes, 3:1382
    presidential proclamations, 3:1405–1406
    Red Scare, 1:8
    Schenck v. United States, 4:1605
    vigilantism, 4:1882
    Woodrow Wilson during, 4:1945–1946
World War II, 1:4, 2:558–559
    African Americans in, 1:27
    espionage, 2:558–559
    Franklin Roosevelt during, 4:1580
    German Americans during, 2:695
    political crimes, 3:1383
    race-based crimes, 4:1484–1485
    William Parker in, 3:1321
Wounded Knee incident, 2:971, 3:1204, 3:1327–1328, 4:1701
Wright, Andy, 4:1613
Wright, Jonathan J., 1:27
Wright, Louis T., 3:1180
Wright, Richard, 2:570
Wright, Roy, 4:1613

Wright Brothers, 1:431
writ of certiorari, 1:55
Write Me a Murder, 3:1026
Wuornos, Aileen, 1:xlviii, 2:615, 2:576, 4:1963, 4:1976–1977
    arrest, 4:1976
    execution, 4:1976
Wyatt Earp, 2:516
Wynn, A. A., 2:467
Wyoming, 4:1977–1978
    anti-Chinese violence, 4:1978
    crime, police, punishment, 4:1977–1978
    Wyoming Honor Conservation Camp and Boot Camp, 5:2421
Wyrick v. Fields, 3:1000

X

xenophobia, 4:1979–1982
    actions, 4:1982
    Irish and Chinese immigrants, 4:1980–1981
    legislation, 4:1981–1982
    1921 to 1940, 5:2207–2208
Xerxes, 2:556
xy males, 2:749
XYZ Affair, 5:2035–2036

Y

Yale, Frankie, 1:210
Yates, Andrea, 2:477, 4:1893, 4:1957, 4:1983–1984
    appeal, 4:1984
    crime and trial, 4:1983–1984
    reaction to, 4:1984

Yates v. United States, **4:1690, 4:1984–1985**
    advocate interpretation, 4:1985
    conviction overturned, 4:1985
Yellow Mama, 1:32
yellow press, 2:772
yellow-dog contracts, 1:xlii, 1:xliii, 1:9–10
Yippies, 1:224
Yochelson, Samuel, 1:410
Yoo, John, 1:188
York, Ronald, 2:940
Young, S. Glen, 2:818
Young Lords, 1:76
Younger, Cole, 1:xli, 1:82
Youngstown Sheet & Tube v. Sawyer, 3:1406
Yousef, Ramzi, 1:277
youth violence, 4:1890–1891
YouTube, 2:828, 4:1758

Z

Zangara, Joseph, 4:1577
Zeisel, Hans, 4:1987–1988
zero-tolerance policing, 1:393
Zerzan, John, 1:51
Zimbalist, Efrem, Jr., 4:1762
Zimmerman Telegram, 2:558
Zimring, Franklin, 1:233, 1:398, 2:720
Zinn, Howard, 2:882
Zodiac Killer, 1:xlvi, 4:1988–1989
    DNA analysis, 4:1989
    letters, 4:1989
Zoot Suit Riots, 2:753
Zouaves, Ellsworth, 1:191
Zuiker, Anthony E., 4:1767

Photo Credits

VOLUME 1: Library of Congress: 3, 9, 13, 15, 19, 22, 25, 28, 32, 36, 43, 45, 48, 53, 60, 65, 69, 80, 83, 112, 115, 116, 119, 121, 130, 133, 135, 139, 142, 144, 146, 153, 157, 159, 160, 168, 184, 192, 205, 213, 219, 228, 237, 240, 243, 247, 252, 254, 256, 259, 271, 280, 295, 331, 334, 339, 347, 350, 356, 367, 369, 372, 379, 404, 409, 412, 419, 417, 429, 441, 452, 458; U.S. Customs: 89, 149, 317, 423, 448; Wikimedia Commons: 50, 56, 66, 78, 86, 106, 110, 126, 173, 265, 277, 288, 362, 402, 461; White House Photo: 76; U.S. Army: 102; FEMA: 189; U.S. Marines: 194; U.S. Department of State: 211; National Archives and Records: 124, 198, 397; FBI: 451; U.S. Air Force: 226, 309, 312, 401; U.S. Coast Guard: 387; USAID: 231; Flickr: 6, 41, 62, 73, 93, 96, 100, 107, 165, 171, 177, 180, 200, 209, 222, 250, 274, 282, 293, 298, 303, 306, 315, 321, 324, 327, 342, 375, 383, 392, 432, 435, 436, 444.

VOLUME 2: Library of Congress: 473, 480, 487, 489, 492, 495, 501, 505, 508, 513, 518, 521, 527, 538, 551, 557, 564, 568, 599, 611, 615, 618, 622, 636, 652, 656, 658, 664, 666, 677, 681, 685, 691, 698, 703, 706, 710, 723, 732, 735, 736, 739, 741, 742, 746, 750, 754, 758, 762, 764, 768, 770, 772, 775, 780, 786, 798, 801, 806, 812, 817, 819, 823, 829, 832, 835, 839, 842, 845, 848, 857, 861, 865, 873, 876, 878, 881, 885, 887, 891, 896, 898, 904, 910, 914, 919, 921, 923, 924, 929, 939, 944, 947, 956, 959, 968; U.S. Customs: 608, 821, 852; National Archives and Records: 553, 592, 595, 966; U.S. Marines: 950; U.S. Air Force: 484; U.S. Army: 477, 560, 718, 854; NOAA: 544; FBI: 583, 585, 625, 639, 641, 777; SCG photo by Colin White: 547; FEMA: 806; National Library of Medicine: 602; U.S. Coast Guard: 588, 633; U.S. Fish & Wildlife Services: 629; Wikimedia Commons: 468, 499, 517, 525, 574, 576, 613, 673, 688, 722, 724 (Shane McCoy), 784, 871, 953, 970; Flickr: 465, 466, 530 (Monica Palmer), 534, 541 (Jay Lee), 580, 606, 644, 669, 686, 715, 791, 794, 825, 908, 933, 941, 963.

VOLUME 3: Library of Congress: 976, 981, 985, 988, 996, 1003, 1010, 1014, 1020, 1024, 1029, 1033, 1035, 1036, 1044, 1055, 1061, 1062, 1065, 1071, 1074, 1077, 1080, 1083, 1086, 1106, 1109, 1129, 1132, 1135, 1138, 1144, 1147, 1155, 1158, 1180, 1183, 1166, 1188, 1199, 1206, 1210, 1216, 1223, 1232, 1237, 1274, 1300, 1303, 1331, 1369, 1419, 1423, 1438, 1446; U.S. Customs: 1103; Kay Chernush for U.S. Department of State: 1461; U.S. Immigration Services: 129; Department of Interior: 1196; FEMA: 1091, 1287; FBI: 1097, 1208; U.S. Army: 1394; U.S. Air Force: 1379; U.S. Navy: 1100; White House Photo: 1272; The Cleveland Press Collection, Michael Schwartz Library, Cleveland State University: 1068; Flickr: 1000, 1007; ThinkStock: 1246; Division of Probation and Parole: 1433; Photos.com: 1226, 1231, 1240, 1243 (both), 1256, 1258, 1279, 1343, 1349, 1355, 1415, 1451; Wikimedia Commons: 983, 922, 1017, 1040, 1050, 1118, 1123, 1124, 1142, 1150, 1168, 1171, 1191, 1213, 1220, 1235, 1239, 1251 (Dave Shankbone), 1253, 1262, 1267, 1270, 1275, 1282, 1284, 1290, 1292, 1299, 1306, 1309, 1312, 1317, 1320, 1323, 1327, 1329, 1334, 1337, 1341, 1347, 1362, 1373, 1384, 1398, 1401, 1404, 1408, 1410, 1424, 1428, 1443, 1457, 1467, 1470, 1473, 1476; Kentucky State Police: 1167; Leland Police Department, South Carolina: 1264; National Archives and Records: 1058, 1094, 1112, 1115, 1162, 1176, 1202; National Library of Medicine: 1157; Bergen Country Sheriff: 1193; Morguefile: 1353.

VOLUME 4: Library of Congress: 1480, 1516, 1537, 1553, 1555, 1581, 1588, 1591, 1598, 1621, 1675, 1689, 1682, 1692, 1705, 1710, 1716, 1720, 1723, 1783, 1808, 1826, 1847, 1862, 1866, 1887, 1914, 1981; U.S. Senate: 512, 1540; White House Photo: 1632, 1853; Cañon City Local History Center: 1515; Wikimedia Commons: 1483, 1484, 1490, 1492, 1498, 1503, 1508, 1510, 1512, 1519, 1526, 1529, 1531, 1534, 1546, 1548, 1564, 1571, 1574, 1584, 1596, 1601, 1607, 1610, 1612, 1617, 1623, 1626, 1629, 1636, 1638, 1641, 1644, 1647, 1649, 1653, 1659, 1665, 1671, 1677, 1680, 1683, 1686, 1694, 1696, 1698, 1701 (Jake DeGroot), 1707, 1713, 1728, 1738, 1746, 1759, 1764, 1769, 1772, 1778, 1791, 1794, 1803, 1810, 1831, 1837, 1841, 1855, 1858, 1864, 1869, 1872 (Jeff Granbery), 1875, 1878, 1880, 1883, 1905, 1908 (Joe Mable), 1911, 1916, 1920, 1924, 1929, 1930, 1945, 1959, 1963 (both), 1971, 1989; Photos.com: 1487, 1495, 1522, 1543, 1550, 1558, 1569, 1730, 1733, 1740, 1749, 1753, 1775, 1799, 1876, 1892, 1902, 1933, 1934, 1949, 1956, 1965; U.S. Army: 1656, 1669; Kansas Historical Society: 1561; ThinkStock: 1566; NASA: 1603, 1850; National Archives and Records: 1578, 1615, 1619, 1726, 1845; Department of Defense: 1756; StockXchange: 1815, 1821; Flickr: 1786 (Wally Gobetz).

VOLUME 5: Library of Congress: 1996, 2000, 2003, 2032, 2035, 2036, 2040, 2045, 2065, 2066, 2070, 2073, 2074, 2099, 2100, 2104, 2107, 2108, 2111, 2163, 2164, 2167, 2168, 2171 (both), 2172, 2175, 2178, 2203, 2206, 2209, 2210, 2213, 2216, 2267 (right), 2269, 2270, 2272, 2349, 2417; Wikimedia Commons: 1999, 2031, 2039, 2069, 2340, 2422, 2455; Sandia National Archives and Records: 2274, 2276; National Laboratory: 2461; White House Photo: 2458 (Eric Draper); U.S. Drug Enforcement Agency: 2451; National Library of Medicine: 2352, 2357, 2408, 2457; Department of Defense: 2447, 2448; Photos.com: 2411, 2414; National Park Service: 1993; Wyoming State: 2421; National Archives: 2006; 2264; 2267 (left); 2339, 2343, 2346, 2418, 2425, 2444.